Marketing Management
Knowledge and Skills

Text   Analysis   Cases   Plans

Marketing Management
Knowledge and Skills

Text   Analysis   Cases   Plans

J. Paul Peter
James R. McManus–Bascom Professor in Marketing
University of Wisconsin–Madison

James H. Donnelly, Jr.
Turner Professor of Marketing
University of Kentucky

Second Edition 1989

BPI
IRWIN

Homewood, IL 60430
Boston, MA 02116

Sponsoring editor: Elizabeth J. Schilling
Project editor: Karen Smith
Production manager: Bette Ittersagen
Cover design: Keith McPherson
Compositor: Better Graphics, Inc.
Typeface: 10/12 Century Schoolbook
Printer: R. R. Donnelley & Sons Company

LIBRARY OF CONGRESS
Library of Congress Cataloging-in-Publication Data

Peter, J. Paul.
Marketing management : knowledge and skills : text, analysis, cases, plans / J. Paul Peter, James H. Donnelly, Jr.—2nd ed.
p. cm.
Bibliography: p.
Includes indexes.
ISBN 0-256-06668-X
1. Marketing—Management. 2. Marketing—Management—Case studies.
I. Donnelly, James H. II. Title.
HF5415.13.P387 1989
658.8—dc19 88-18572
CIP

Printed in the United States of America
2 3 4 5 6 7 8 9 0 DO 6 5 4 3 2 1 0 9

Preface

Our goal in the first edition of this text was to develop a complete student resource for marketing management education. This goal has not changed in the second edition. We continue to focus our efforts on enhancing student *knowledge* of marketing management and on developing their *skills* in using this knowledge to develop and maintain successful marketing strategies.

The structure of the first edition of our book developed over many years as we experimented successfully and unsuccessfully with various approaches to teaching marketing management and as our individual teaching philosophies developed. In this second edition the structure remains the same, although there are important refinements in the content of Sections 4 and 5. These were made because both adopters and nonadopters of the book suggested a need for a greater number and a greater variety of cases.

Thus, our five-stage learning approach has been revised to include (1) learning basic marketing principles; (2) learning approaches and tools for marketing problem analysis; (3) analyzing marketing management cases; (4) analyzing strategic marketing cases; and (5) developing original marketing plans. These five stages are the focus of the seven sections in this book and have as their objective both *knowledge enhancement* and *skill development*. The framework for our book is presented in the following diagram, which will be used throughout the text to integrate the various sections.

STAGE 1: LEARNING OF BASIC MARKETING PRINCIPLES

It is clearly necessary for students to learn and understand basic definitions, concepts, and logic before they can apply them in the analysis of marketing problems or attempts to develop marketing

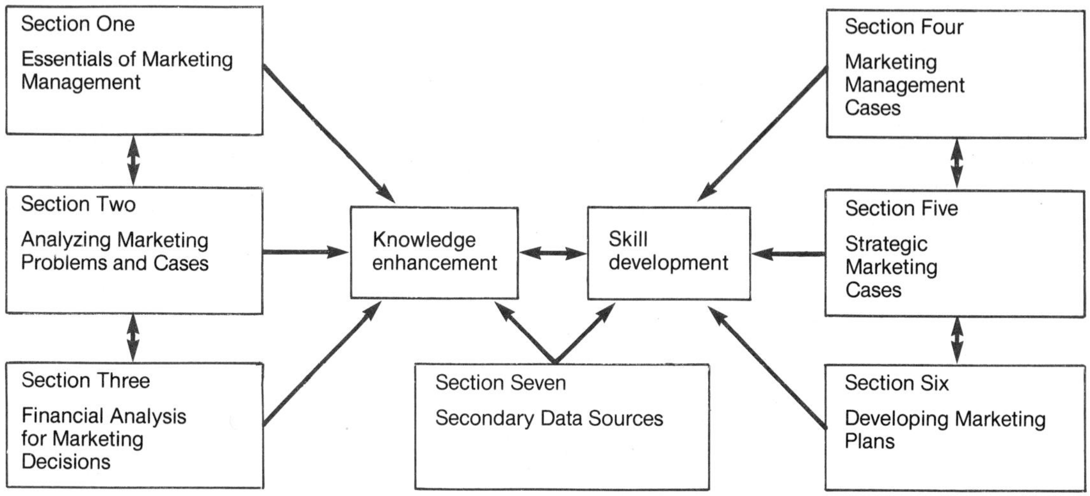

plans. Section 1 of the book contains 14 chapters which we believe present the essentials of marketing management. One problem we continually face in more advanced case-oriented marketing management courses is that most students have long ago discarded or sold their basic texts. Consequently, when they are faced with case problems to analyze they have nothing to rely on but their memories. We believe this seriously detracts from the usefulness of case analysis. Thus, we include this section as a reference source for key marketing concepts. Our objective in this section is to focus on material that is most relevant for analyzing marketing problems.

STAGE 2: LEARNING APPROACHES AND TOOLS FOR PROBLEM ANALYSIS

The second stage in our approach involves offering students basic tools and approaches for solving marketing problems. Sections 2 and 3 present these tools in addition to a framework which students can adapt when analyzing marketing problems. Section 7 of the book, an annotated bibliography of important secondary sources of marketing information, will aid students in researching a particular industry or firm and can greatly improve their depth of analysis. Eight classifications of secondary sources are presented: (1) selected periodicals; (2) general marketing information sources; (3) selected marketing information services; (4) selected retail trade publications; (5) financial information sources; (6) basic U.S. statistical sources; (7) general business and industry sources; and (8) indexes and abstracts.

STAGE 3: ANALYZING MARKETING MANAGEMENT CASES

It has been our experience that few students have the confidence and experience necessary to analyze complex strategic marketing cases in their first exposure to this type of learning. We believe it is far better for them to apply their skills at analyzing cases for which traditional marketing principles can be applied somewhat directly before they attempt more challenging problems. Accordingly, Section 4 of the book has been expanded to include 31 marketing management cases, organized into six groups: market opportunity analysis, product strategy, promotion strategy, distribution strategy, pricing strategy, and selected issues in marketing management. Within each group, cases are sequenced so that later cases contain more information and typically require higher levels of marketing management skills than earlier ones.

STAGE 4: ANALYZING STRATEGIC MARKETING CASES

Once students have developed sufficient skills to provide thoughtful analyses of marketing management cases, we believe they are prepared to tackle strategic marketing cases. These cases go beyond traditional marketing principles and focus on the role of marketing in the development of business or organizational strategies. Eleven such cases are included in Section 5 of our book. They are sequenced so that the later cases contain more information and require higher levels of management skill to analyze them properly.

STAGE 5: DEVELOPING MARKETING PLANS

The final stage in our approach involves the development of an original marketing plan. We believe that after a two-course sequence in marketing management, students should be able to do one thing very well and should know that they can do it well: Students should be able to construct a quality marketing plan for any product or service. Section 6 provides a framework for developing such a plan. Instructors can consult the *Instructor's Manual* which accompanies this book for alternative ways to incorporate this stage into their course if they should desire to do so.

We have found that this five-stage process is very flexible and can easily be adapted to the needs of the students and the objectives of the instructor. For example, if the course is the first formal learning experience in marketing, then emphasis could be placed on the first three stages. If students progess well through these stages, then marketing management cases can be assigned on an individual or a group basis.

If the course is for students with one or more previous courses in marketing, or is the capstone marketing management course, then major attention should shift to stages two through five. In this instance, Section 1 becomes a resource for review and reference, and the focus of the course can be more fully on skill development.

Finally, the text can be used for a two-course sequence in marketing management. The first course can emphasize stages one through three and the second concentrate on stages four and five.

We are indebted to those individuals who contributed cases to our book. Our case search was a long and difficult one. We wanted cases from a variety of time periods, in a variety of industries, and concerning well-recognized organizations. We wanted them to cover a variety of different types and sizes of both profit and nonprofit organizations as well as deal with both products and services. We also wanted cases which included problems at all levels of marketing management. The results of our search yielded what we believe is an outstanding collection, and we would like to express our heartfelt thanks to each contributor. This volume would not be possible without their contributions.

Finally, we acknowledge Dean James Hickman of the School of Business at the University of Wisconsin and Dean Richard Furst of the College of Business and Economics, University of Kentucky, who have supported our efforts, as well as Vern Dougherty and Judy Haywood for their skilled typing and production efforts.

J. PAUL PETER
JAMES H. DONNELLY, JR.

Contents

Section 1
Essentials of Marketing Management 1

Part A
Introduction 3

1 Strategic Planning and the Market Management Process 5

The Marketing Concept, ***5*** What is Marketing? ***7*** What is Strategic Planning? ***7*** *Strategic Planning and Marketing Management. The Strategic Planning Process. Organizational Mission. Organizational Objectives. Organizational Strategies. Organizational Portfolio Plan. The Complete Strategic Plan.* The Marketing Management Process, ***20*** *Organizational Mission and Objectives. Situation Analysis. Marketing Planning. Implementation and Control of the Marketing Plan. Marketing Information Systems and Marketing Research.* The Relationship Between the Strategic Plan and the Marketing Plan, ***26*** Conclusion, ***28*** Appendix: Portfolio Models, ***29***

Part B
Marketing Information, Research, and Understanding the Target Market 35

2 Marketing Decision Support Systems and Marketing Research 37

Marketing Decision Support Systems. ***38*** *The Marketing Information Center. Marketing Decision Making.* Marketing Research. ***42*** *The Research Process. Problems in the Research Process.* Conclusion, ***53***

3 *Consumer Behavior* 55
The Buying Process, ***55*** *Felt Need. Alternative Search. Alternative Evaluation. Purchase Decision. Postpurchase Feelings.* Group Influences on Consumer Behavior, ***65*** *Cultural and Subcultural Influences. Social Class. Reference Groups.* Product Class Influences, ***72*** Situational Influences, ***72*** Conclusion, ***74*** Appendix: Selected Consumer Behavior Data Sources, ***75***

4 *Industrial Buyer Behavior* 76
Product Influences on Industrial Buying, ***76*** Organizational Influences on Industrial Buying, ***79*** *Multiple Buying Influence or Joint Decision Making. Diffusion of Buying Authority. Company-Specific Factors.* Behavioral Influences on Industrial Buying, ***81*** *Nonpersonal Motivations. Personal Motivations. Role Perception.* Stages in the Buying Process, ***85*** *Problem Recognition. Assignment of Buying Authority. Search Procedures.* Conclusion, ***88***

5 *Market Segmentation* 89
Delineate the Firm's Current Situation. Determine Consumer Needs and Wants. Divide Markets on Relevant Dimensions. Develop Product Positioning. Decide Segmentation Strategy. Design Marketing Mix Strategy. Conclusion. ***104***

Part C
The Marketing Mix 107

6 *Product Strategy* 109
Basic Issues in Product Management. Product Definition. Product Classification. Product Mix and Product Line. Packaging and Branding. Produce Life Cycle. ***117*** The Product Audit. ***121*** *Deletions. Product Improvement.* Organizing for Product Management. ***122*** Conclusion. ***125***

7 *New Product Planning and Development* 127
New Product Policy. ***128*** New Product Planning and Development Process. ***131*** *Idea Generation. Idea Screening. Project Planning. Product Development. Test Marketing. Commercialization.* Causes of New Product Failure. ***135*** *Need for Research.* Conclusion. ***137***

8 *Promotion Strategy: Advertising and Sales Promotion* 138
The Promotion Mix. ***138*** Advertising: Planning and Strategy. ***140*** *Objectives of Advertising. Specific Tasks of Advertising.* Advertising Decisions. ***144*** *The Expenditure Question. The Allocation Question.* Sales Promotion. ***153*** Conclusion. ***155*** Appendix: Major Federal Agencies Involved in Control of Advertising ***156***

9 *Promotion Strategy: Personal Selling* 158
Importance of Personal Selling. ***158*** The Sales Process. ***160*** *Selling Fundamentals. Managing the Sales Process. The Sales Management Task. Controlling the Sales Force.* Conclusion. ***175***

10 *Distribution Strategy* 176
The Need for Marketing Intermediaries. ***176*** Classification of Marketing Intermediaries and Functions. ***177*** Channel of Distribution. ***179*** Selecting Channels of Distribution. ***1*** *General Considerations. Specific Considerations.* Managing a Channel of Distribution. ***185*** *A Channel Leader.* Conclusion. ***189***

11 *Pricing Strategy* 191
Demand Influences on Pricing Decisions. ***191*** *Demographic Factors. Psychological Factors. Price Elasticity.* Supply Influences on Pricing Decisions. ***194*** *Pricing Objectives. Cost Considerations in Pricing. Product Considerations in Pricing.* Environmental Influences on Pricing Decisions. ***198*** *Competition. Government Regulations* A General Pricing Decision Model. ***201*** *Conclusion.* ***202***

Part D
Marketing in Special Fields 205

12 *The Marketing of Services* 207
Important Characteristics of Services. ***208*** *Intangibility. Inseparability. Perishability and Fluctuating Demand. Highly Differentiated Marketing Systems. Client Relationship.* Roadblocks to Innovation in Service Marketing. ***212*** *Limited View of Marketing. Limited Competition. Noncreative Management. No Obsolescene.* Innovations in the Distribution of Services. ***214*** *Marketing Intermediaries in the Distribution of Services. Implications for Service Marketers.* Conclusion. ***218***

13 *International Marketing* 220
Organizing for International Marketing. **221** *Problem Conditions: External. Problem Conditions: Internal.* Programming for International Marketing. **224** *International Marketing Research. Product Planning for International Markets. International Distribution Systems. Pricing for International Marketing. International Advertising.* Strategies for International Marketing. **230** *Strategy One: Same Product, Same Message Worldwide. Strategy Two: Same Product, Different Communications. Strategy Three: Different Product, Same Communications. Strategy Four: Different Product, Different Communications. Strategy Five: Product Invention.* Conclusion. **232**

Part E
Marketing Response to a Changing Society 235

14 *Marketing and Society* 237
Marketing's Social Responsibility. **237** *Societal Concept. Marketing Ethics. Consumerism. Recent Efforts.* Broadening the Concept of Marketing. **243** Conclusion. **246**

Section 2
Analyzing Marketing Problems and Cases 247

Section 3
Financial Analysis for Marketing Decisions 265

Section 4
Marketing Management Cases 279

Case Group A
Market Opportunity Analysis 281

1 *Timex Corp.* 281
J. Paul Peter, *University of Wisconsin-Madison*

2 *Wyler's Unsweetened Soft Drink Mixes* 284
Don E. Schultz, *Northwestern University*

3 *Texas Blues* 292
JoAnn K. L. Schwinghammer, *Mankato State University;*

Gopala Krishnan Ganesh, *North Texas State University;* and William C. Green, *Loyola Marymount University*

4 *TenderCare Disposable Diapers* 303
James E. Nelson, *University of Colorado*

5 *The Adirondack Manor* 314
Lawrence M. Lamont, *Washington and Lee University*

Case Group B
Product Strategy 339

6 *The Seven-Up Company* 339
J. Paul Peter, *University of Wisconsin–Madison*

7 *Mead Products: The Trapper Keeper* 342
Peter S. Carusone, *Wright State University*

8 *MidAmerica BancSystem, Inc.* 357
James E. Nelson, *University of Colorado*

9 *VideoShop—Mark-Tele, Inc. (II)* 367
Michael P. Mokwa and Karl Gustafson, *Arizona State University*

10 *The Gillette Company* 386
Charles M. Kummel and Jay E. Klompmaker, *University of North Carolina*

Case Group C
Promotion Strategy 409

11 *General Foods* 409
Jerry C. Olson, *Penn State University*

12 *Outdoor Sporting Products, Inc.* 412
Zarrel V. Lambert, *Auburn University;* and Fred W. Kniffen, *University of Connecticut*

13 *Computing Systems, Ltd.* 420
Adrian B. Ryans, *University of Western Ontario*

14 *Hanover-Bates Chemical Corporation* 429
Robert E. Witt, *University of Texas–Austin*

15 *S. C. Johnson—The Agree Line* 436
Stephen B. Ash and Sandra Safran, *University of Western Ontario*

Case Group D
Distribution Strategy 461

16 *Tupperware* 461
J. Paul Peter, *University of Wisconsin–Madison*

17 *Cub Foods* 463
J. Paul Peter, *University of Wisconsin–Madison*

18 *Thompson Respiration Products, Inc.* 465
James E. Nelson and William R. Woolridge, *University of Colorado*

19 *Apple Computer Inc.* 479
Charles Hinkle and Esther L. Stineman, *University of Colorado*

20 *K Mart Stores: Where America Shops and Saves* 498
John L. Little, *University of North Carolina–Greensboro;* and Larry D. Alexander, *Virginia Polytechnic Institute and State University*

Case Group E
Pricing Strategy 523

21 *Delta Airlines* 523
Margaret L. Friedman, *University of Wisconsin–Whitewater*

22 *Young Attitudes—Pricing a New Product Line* 527
Jon M. Hawes, *University of Akron*

23 *Rockwood Manor* 530
William R. Wynd, *Eastern Washington University*

24 *S. C. Johnson and Son, Limited (R)* 540
Carolyn Vose, *University of Western Ontario*

25 *Island Shores* 556
Cynthia J. Frey, *Boston College*

Case Group F
Selected Issues in Marketing Management 573

26 *Tylenol* 573
Margaret L. Friedman, *University of Wisconsin–Whitewater*

27 *Denver Art Museum* 577
Patricia Stocker, *University of Maryland*

28 *The Deep South Civic Center* 583
Jeffrey D. Schaffer, *University of New Orleans*

29 *The Arthritis Foundation* 598
P. A. Papka III and Jon M. Hawes, *University of Akron*

30 *Rogers, Nagel, Langhart (RNL PC), Architects and Planners* 607
H. Michael Hayes, *University of Colorado–Denver*

31 *Babcock Swine, Inc.* 625
Lester Neidell and Floy Schrage, *University of Tulsa*

Section 5
Strategic Marketing Cases 647

1 *Maytag Company* 649
Lester Neidell, *University of Tulsa*

2 *TSR Hobbies, Inc.—"Dungeons and Dragons"* 652
Margaret L. Friedman, *Univeristy of Wisconsin in Whitewater*

3 *Caterpillar Tractor Company* 660
Donald W. Eckrich, *Ithaca College*

4 *Hershey Foods* 673
Richard T. Hise, *Texas A & M University*

5 *Comshare, Inc. (A)—Strategic Actions in the Computer Services Industry* 701
Donald W. Scotton, Allan D. Waren, and Bernard C. Reimann, *Cleveland State University*

6 *Comshare, Inc. (B)—Strategic Marketing of System W* 719
Donald W. Scotton, Allan D. Waren, and Bernard C. Reimann, *Cleveland State University*

7 *The American Express Company* 732
James R. Lang, *University of Kentucky*

8 *Coke Tries to Counter the Pepsi Challenge* 756
Dhruv Grewal, *Virginia Polytechnic Institute and State University*

9 *Campbell Soup Company* 781
Arthur A. Thompson and Sharon Henson, *University of Alabama*

10 Mary Kay Cosmetics 806
Arthur A. Thompson and Robin Romblad, *University of Alabama*

11 MeraBank 853
Michael P. Mokwa, John A. Grant, and Richard E. White, *Arizona State University*

Section 6
Developing Marketing Plans 891

Section 7
Secondary Data Sources 907

Indexes

Case Index 920

Name Index 921

Subject Index 925

Section 1

Essentials of Marketing Management

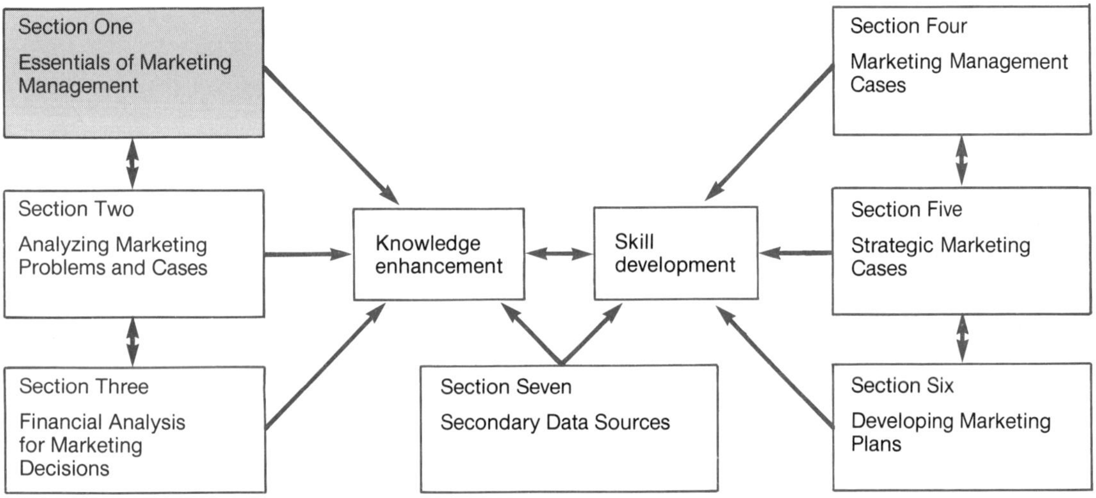

Marketing Management: Knowledge and Skills

NOTE TO THE STUDENT

This section contains 14 chapters concerned with basic issues in marketing management. For students who have taken previous courses in marketing, these chapters are designed to provide a useful review. For students who have not taken previous courses in marketing, these chapters should serve as a foundation of basic marketing knowledge. In either case, they provide a resource of marketing logic and information to be used in solving marketing problems and cases and developing marketing plans.

Part A

Introduction

CHAPTER 1
Strategic Planning and the Marketing Management Process

Chapter 1

Strategic Planning and the Marketing Management Process

The purpose of this introductory chapter is to present the marketing management process and outline what marketing managers must "manage" if they are to be effective. In doing so, it will also present a framework around which the remaining chapters are organized. Our first task is to review the organizational philosophy known as the marketing concept, since it underlies much of the thinking presented in this book. The remainder of this chapter will focus on the process of strategic planning and its relationship to the process of marketing planning.

THE MARKETING CONCEPT

Simply stated, the marketing concept means that *an organization should seek to make a profit by serving the needs of customer groups*. It is very straightforward and has a great deal of commonsense validity. Perhaps this is why it is often misunderstood, forgotten, or overlooked.

The purpose of the marketing concept is to rivet the attention of marketing managers on serving broad classes of customer needs (customer orientation), rather than on the firm's current products (production orientation) or on devising methods to attract customers to current products (selling orientation). Thus, effective marketing starts with the recognition of customer needs and then works backward to devise products and services to satisfy these needs. In this way, mar-

HIGHLIGHT 1-1
Basic Elements of the Marketing Concept

1. Companywide managerial awareness and appreciation of the consumer's role as it is related to the firm's existence, growth, and stability. As Drucker has noted, business enterprise is an organ of society; thus, its basic purpose lies outside the business itself. And the valid definition of business purpose is the creation of customers.
2. Active companywide managerial awareness of, and concern with, interdepartmental implications of decisions and actions of an individual department. That is, the firm is viewed as a network of forces focused on meeting defined customer needs, and comprising a system within which actions taken in one department or area frequently result in significant repercussions in other areas of the firm. Also, it is recognized that such actions may affect the company's equilibrium with its external environment, for example, its customers, its competitors.
3. Active companywide managerial concern with innovation of products and services designed to solve selected consumer problems.
4. General managerial concern with the effect of new products and service introduction on the firm's profit position, both present and future, and recognition of the potential rewards which may accrue from new product planning, including profits and profit stability.
5. General managerial appreciation of the role of marketing intelligence and other fact-finding and reporting units within, and adjacent to the firm, in translating the general statements presented above into detailed statements of profitable market potentials, targets, and action. Implicit in this statement is not only an expansion of the traditional function and scope of formal marketing research, but also assimilation of other sources of marketing data, such as the firm's distribution system and its advertising agency counsel, into a potential marketing intelligence service.
6. Companywide managerial effort, based upon participation and interaction of company officers, in establishing corporate and departmental objectives, which are understood by and acceptable to these officers, and which are consistent with enhancement of the firm's profit position.

Source: Robert L. King, "The Marketing Concept: Fact or Intelligent Platitude," *The Marketing Concept in Action*, Proceedings of the 47th National Conference (Chicago: American Marketing Association, 1964), p. 657. For an up-to-date discussion of the marketing concept, see Franklin S. Houston, "The Marketing Concept: What It Is and What It Is Not," *Journal of Marketing*, April 1986, pp. 81–87.

keting managers can satisfy customers more efficiently in the present and anticipate changes in customer needs more accurately in the future. It is hoped that the end result is a more efficient market in which the customer is better satisfied and the firm is more profitable.

The principal task of the marketing function operating under the marketing concept is not to manipulate customers to do what suits the interests of the firm, but rather to find effective and efficient means of making the business do what suits the interests of customers. This is not to say that firms practice marketing in this way. Clearly, many firms still emphasize only production and sales. However, effective marketing, as defined in this text, requires that consumer needs come first in organizational decision making.

One qualification to this statement deals with the question of a conflict between consumer wants and societal needs and wants. For example, if society deems clean air and water as necessary for survival, then this need may well take precedence over a consumer's want for goods and services that pollute the environment.

WHAT IS MARKETING?

One of the most persistent conceptual problems in marketing is its definition.[1] The American Marketing Association has recently defined marketing as "the process of planning and executing conception, pricing, promotion, and distribution of ideas, goods, and services to create exchanges that satisfy individual and organizational objectives."[2] Although this broad definition allows the inclusion of nonbusiness exchange processes (i.e., persons, places, organizations, ideas) as part of marketing, the primary emphasis in this text is on marketing in the business environment. However, this emphasis is not meant to imply that marketing concepts, principles, and techniques cannot be fruitfully employed in other areas of exchange. In fact, some discussions of nonbusiness marketing take place later in the text.

WHAT IS STRATEGIC PLANNING?

Before a production manager, marketing manager, and personnel manager can develop plans for their individual departments, hopefully, some larger plan or blueprint for the *entire* organization has been

---

[1] See Reinhard Angelmar and Christian Pinson, "The Meaning of Marketing," *Philosophy of Science*, June 1975, pp. 208–14.

[2] Board of Directors, American Marketing Association, 1985.

HIGHLIGHT 1-2
Ten Key Principles for Marketing Success

Principle 1. Create Customer Want Satisfaction.
Principle 2. Know Your Buyer Characteristics.
Principle 3. Divide the Market into Segments.
Principle 4. Strive for High Market Share.
Principle 5. Develop Deep and Wide Product Lines.
Principle 6. Price Position Products and Upgrade Markets.
Principle 7. Treat Channels as Intermediate Buyers.
Principle 8. Coordinate Elements of Physical Distribution.
Principle 9. Promote Performance Features.
Principle 10. Use Information to Improve Decisions.

Source: Fred C. Allvine, *Marketing: Principles and Practices* (New York: Harcourt Brace Jovanovich, 1987), p. viii.

developed. Otherwise, on what would the individual departmental plans be based?

In other words, there is a larger context for planning activities. Let us assume that we are dealing with a large business organization which has several business divisions and several product lines within each division (e.g., General Electric, Philip Morris). Before any marketing planning can be done by individual divisions or departments, a plan has to be developed for the *entire* organization.[3] Then objectives and strategies established at the top level provide the context for planning in each of the divisions and departments by divisional and departmental managers. These lower-level managers develop their plans within the constraints developed at the higher levels.[4]

Strategic Planning and Marketing Management

Many of this country's most successful business organizations are here today because many years ago they offered the right product at the right time to a rapidly growing market. The same can also be said for nonprofit and governmental organizations. Many of the critical deci-

---

[3] John H. Grant and William R. King, *The Logic of Strategic Planning* (Boston: Little, Brown, 1982), chap. 1. This section is based on J. H. Donnelly, Jr., J. L. Gibson, and J. M. Ivancevich, *Fundamentals of Management*, 6th ed. (Plano, Tex.: Business Publications, 1987), chap. 5.

[4] L. Rosenberg and C. D. Schewe, "Strategic Planning: Fulfilling the Promise," *Business Horizons*, July-August 1985, pp. 54-63.

FIGURE 1-1 The Strategic Planning Process

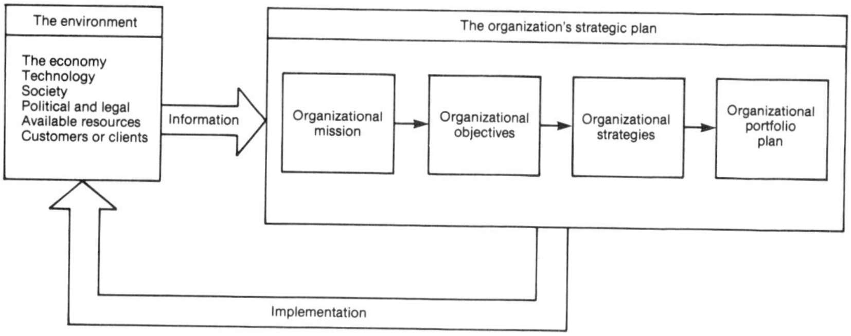

sions of the past were made without the benefit of strategic thinking or planning. Whether these decisions were based on wisdom or were just luck is not important. They resulted in a momentum which has carried these organizations to where they are today. However, present-day managers are increasingly recognizing that wisdom and intuition alone are no longer sufficient to guide the destinies of their large organizations in today's ever-changing environment. These managers are turning to strategic planning.[5]

Strategic planning includes all of the activities that lead to the development of a clear organizational mission, organizational objectives, and appropriate strategies to achieve the objectives for the entire organization. Figure 1-1 presents the process of strategic planning. It indicates that the organization gathers information about the changing elements of its environment. This information is useful in aiding the organization to adapt better to these changes through the process of strategic planning.[6] The strategic plan(s)[7] and supporting plan are

---

[5] C. Anderson and C. P. Zeithaml, "Stage of the Product Life Cycle, Business Strategy, and Business Performance," *Academy of Management Journal,* March 1984, pp. 5-24.

[6] The process depicted in Figure 1-1 is a generally agreed upon model of the strategic planning process, although some may include or exclude a particular element. For example, see A. A. Thompson and A. J. Strickland III, *Strategic Management: Concepts and Cases,* 4th ed. (Plano, Texas: Business Publications, Inc., 1987), and Philip Kotler, *Marketing Management: Analysis, Planning, and Control,* 5th ed. (Englewood Cliffs, N.J.: Prentice-Hall 1984).

[7] The process may differ depending on the type of organization or management approach, or both. For certain types of organizations, one strategic plan will be sufficient. Some manufacturers with similar product lines or limited product lines will develop only one strategic plan. However, organizations with widely diversified product lines and widely diversified markets may develop strategic plans for units or divisions. These plans usually are combined into a master strategic plan.

for answering them must be with top management.[8] In developing a statement of mission, management must take into account three key elements:[9]

1. *The organization's history.* Every organization—large or small, profit or nonprofit—has a history of objectives, accomplishments, mistakes, and policies. In formulating a mission the critical characteristics and events of the past must be considered.
2. *The organization's distinctive competences.* While there are many things an organization may be able to do, it should seek to do what it can do best. Distinctive competences are things that an organization does well; so well, in fact, they give it an advantage over similar organizations. Procter & Gamble could probably enter the synthetic fuel business but such a decision would certainly not take advantage of its major distinctive competence: knowledge of the market for low-priced, repetitively purchased consumer products. No matter how appealing an opportunity may be, the organization must have the competences to capitalize on it.[10]
3. *The organization's environment.* The organization's environment dictates the opportunities, constraints, and threats which must be identified before a mission statement is developed. Technological developments in the communications field may have a negative impact on travel and should certainly be considered in the mission statement of a large motel chain.[11]

However, it is extremely difficult to write a useful and effective mission statement. It is not uncommon for an organization to spend one or two years developing a useful mission statement. When completed, an effective mission statement will be: *focused on markets rather than products, achievable, motivating, and specific.*[12]

---

[8] Lewis W. Walker, "The CEO and Corporate Strategy in the Eighties: Back to Basics," *Interfaces,* January-February 1984, pp. 3–9; Peter Drucker, *Management: Tasks, Responsibilities, Practices* (New York: Harper & Row, 1974), chap. 7.

[9] Kotler, *Marketing Management,* chap. 2.

[10] For a study of the relationship between corporate distinctive competencies and performance in 185 firms, see M. A. Hitt and R. D. Ireland, "Corporate Distinctive Competence, Strategy and Performance," *Strategic Management Journal,* July-September 1985, pp. 273–93.

[11] See C. Smart and I. Vertinsky, "Strategy and the Environment: A Study of Corporate Responses to Crises," *Strategic Management Journal,* April-June 1984, pp. 199–214. This study of the largest U.S. and Canadian companies examines the relationship between a firm's external environment and its repertoire of strategic responses to cope with crisis.

[12] Drucker, *Management,* pp. 77–89; Kotler, *Marketing Management,* chap. 2.

Focused on Markets Rather Than Products. The customers or clients of an organization are critical in determining its mission. Traditionally, many organizations defined their business in terms of what they made, "our business is glass," and in many cases they named the organization for the product or service (e.g., National Cash Register, Harbor View Savings and Loan Association). Many of these organizations have found that, when products and technologies become obsolete, their mission is no longer relevant and the name of the organization may no longer describe what it does. Thus, a more enduring way of defining the mission is needed. In recent years, therefore, a key feature of mission statements has been an *external* rather than *internal* focus. In other words, the mission statement should focus on the broad class of needs that the organization is seeking to satisfy (external focus), *not* on the physical product or service that the organization is offering at present (internal focus). This has been clearly stated by Peter Drucker. He argues:

> A business is not defined by the company's name, statutes, or articles of incorporation. It is defined by the want the customer satisfies when he buys a product or service. To satisfy the customer is the mission and purpose of every business. The question "What is our business?" can, therefore, be answered only by looking at the business from the outside, from the point of view of customer and market.[13]

While Drucker was referring to business organization, the same necessity exists for both nonprofit and governmental organizations.[14] That necessity is to state the mission in terms of serving a particular group of clients or customers and meeting a particular class of need.

Achievable. While the mission statement should "stretch" the organization toward more effective performance, it should, at the same time, be realistic and achievable. In other words, it should open a vision of new opportunities but should not lead the organization into unrealistic ventures far beyond its competences.

Motivational. One of the side (but very important) benefits of a well-defined mission is the guidance it provides employees and managers working in geographically dispersed units and working on independent tasks. It provides a shared sense of purpose outside the various

---

13 Drucker, *Management,* p. 79.

14 Paul C. Nutt, "A Strategic Planning Network for Nonprofit Organizations" *Strategic Management Journal,* January-March 1984, pp. 57–76; Peter Smith Ring and James L. Perry, "Strategic Management in Public and Private Organizations: Implications of Distinctive Contexts and Constraints," *Academy of Management Review,* April 1985, pp. 276–86.

HIGHLIGHT 1-3
Some Actual Mission Statements

Organization	*Mission*
1. Office equipment manufacturer	We are in the business of problem solving. Our business is to help solve administrative, scientific, and human problems.
2. Credit union	To produce a selected range of quality services to organizations and individuals to fulfill their continuing financial needs.
3. Large conglomerate	Translating new technologies into commercially salable products.
4. Consumer products paper company	The development and marketing of inedible food store products.
5. State department of health	Administering all provisions of law relating to public health laws and regulations of the State Board of Health, supervising and assisting county and regional boards and departments of health, and doing all other things reasonably necessary to protect and improve the health of the people.
6. Appliance manufacturer	A willingness to invest in any area of suitable profit and growth potential in which the organization has or can acquire the capabilities.

activities taking place within the organization. Therefore, such end results as sales, patients cared for, and reduction in violent crimes can then be viewed as the result of careful pursuit and accomplishment of the mission and not as the mission itself.[15]

Specific. As we mentioned earlier, public relations should not be the primary purpose of a statement of mission. It must be specific to provide direction and guidelines to management when they are choosing between alternative courses of action.[16] In other words, "to produce the highest quality products at the lowest possible cost" sounds very good, but it does not provide direction for management.

---

[15] "Who's Excellent Now," *Business Week,* November 5, 1984, pp. 76–88.

[16] Drucker, *Management,* p. 87.

Organizational Objectives

Organizational objectives are the end points of an organization's mission and are what it seeks through the ongoing, long-run operations of the organization. The organizational mission is defined into a finer set of specific and achievable organizational objectives. These objectives must be *specific, measurable, action commitments* by which the mission of the organization is to be achieved.

As with the statement of mission, organizational objectives are more than good intentions. In fact, if formulated properly, they will accomplish the following:

1. They can be converted into specific actions.
2. They will provide direction. That is, they can serve as a starting point for more specific and detailed objectives at lower levels in the organization. Each manager will then know how his or her objectives relate to those at higher levels.
3. They can establish long-run priorities for the organization.
4. They can facilitate management control because they serve as standards against which overall organizational performance can be evaluated.

Organizational objectives are necessary in any and all areas which may influence the performance and long-run survival of the organization. Peter Drucker believes that objectives should be established in at least eight areas of organizational performance. These are market standing, innovations, productivity, physical and financial resources, profitability, manager performance and responsibility, worker performance and attitude, and social responsibility.[17]

The above objectives are by no means exhaustive. An organization may very well have additional ones. The important point is that management must translate the organizational mission into specific objectives that will support the realization of the mission. The objectives may flow directly from the mission or be considered subordinate necessities for carrying out the mission of the organization. Table 1–1 presents some examples of organizational objectives. Note that they are broad statements which serve as guides and that they are of a continuing nature. They specify the end points of an organization's mission and the results that it seeks in the long run both externally and internally. Most important, however, the objectives in Table 1–1

[17] Peter Drucker, *The Practice of Management* (New York: Harper & Row, 1954); and re-emphasized in Drucker's *Management*.

TABLE 1-1 Sample Organizational Objectives (manufacturing firm)

Area of Performance	*Possible Objective*
1. Market standing	To make our brands number one in their field in terms of market share.
2. Innovations	To be a leader in introducing new products by spending no less than 7 percent of sales for research and development.
3. Productivity	To manufacture all products efficiently as measured by the productivity of the work force.
4. Physical and financial resources	To protect and maintain all resources—equipment, buildings, inventory, and funds.
5. Profitability	To achieve an annual rate of return on investment of at least 15 percent.
6. Manager performance and responsibility	To identify critical areas of management depth and succession.
7. Worker performance and attitude	Maintain levels of employee satisfaction consistent with our own and similar industries.
8. Social responsibility	To respond appropriately whenever possible to societal expectations and environmental needs.

are *specific, measurable, action commitments* on the part of the organization.

Organizational Strategies

Hopefully, when an organization has formulated its mission and developed its objectives, it knows where it wants to go. The next managerial task is to develop a "grand design" to get there. This grand design constitutes the organizational strategies. The role of strategy in strategic planning is to identify the general approaches that the organization will utilize to achieve its organizational objectives. It involves the choice of major directions the organization will take in pursuing its objectives.

Achieving organizational objectives comes about in two ways. It is accomplished by better managing what the organization is presently doing and/or finding new things to do. In choosing either or both of

FIGURE 1-2 Product/Market Matrix

Products / *Markets*	*Present Products*	*New Products*
Present customers	Market penetration	Product development
New customers	Market development	Diversification

these paths, the organization then must decide whether to concentrate on present customers or to seek new ones, or both. Figure 1-2 presents the available strategic choices. It is known as a product/market matrix and indicates the strategic alternatives available to an organization for achieving its objectives. It indicates that an organization can grow in a variety of ways by concentrating on present or new products and on present or new customers.[18]

Market Penetration Strategies. These organizational strategies focus on improving the position of the organization's present products with its present customers. For example:

A dairy concentrates on getting its present customers to purchase more of its products.

A charity seeks ways to increase contributions from present contributors.

A bank concentrates on getting present depositors to use additional services.

Such a strategy may involve devising a marketing plan to encourage present customers to purchase more of the product or a production plan to produce more efficiently what is being produced at present. In other words, it concentrates on improving the efficiency of various functional areas in the organization.

Market Development Strategies. Following this strategy, an organization would seek to find new customers for its present products. For example:

---

[18] Originally discussed in the classic H. Igor Ansoff, *Corporate Strategy* (New York: McGraw-Hill, 1965).

A manufacturer of industrial products may decide to develop products for entrance into consumer market.

A governmental social service agency may seek individuals and families who have never utilized the agency's services.

A manufacturer of children's hair care products decides to enter the adult market because of the declining birth rate.

Product Development Strategies. In choosing either of the remaining two strategies, the organization, in effect, seeks new things to do. With this particular strategy, the new products developed would be directed to present customers. For example:

A candy manufacturer may decide to offer a low-calorie candy.

A social service agency may offer additional services to present client families.

A college or university may develop programs for senior citizens.

Diversification. An organization diversifies when it seeks new products for customers it is not serving at present. For example:

A discount store purchases a savings and loan association.

A cigarette manufacturer diversifies into real estate development.

A college or university establishes a corporation to find commercial uses for the results of faculty research efforts.

On what basis does an organization choose one (or all) strategies? The answer lies in the organization's mission and its distinctive competences. This underscores the critical role the mission statement plays in the direction(s) the organization takes. Management should select those strategies which capitalize on the organization's distinctive competences and are consistent with its mission.[19]

Organizational Portfolio Plan

The final phase of the strategic planning process is the formulation of the organizational portfolio plan. In reality, most organizations at a particular time are a portfolio of businesses, that is, product lines, divisions, schools. To illustrate, an appliance manufacturer may have

---

[19] N. Venkatramen and J. C. Camillus, "Exploring the Concept of 'Fit' in Strategic Management," *Academy of Management Review*, July 1984, pp. 513–25; H. Mintzberg and J. A. Waters, "Of Strategies, Deliberate and Emergent," *Strategic Management Journal*, July-September 1985, pp. 257–72.

several product lines (e.g., televisions, washers and dryers, refrigerators, stereos) as well as two divisions, consumer appliances and industrial appliances. A college or university will have numerous schools (e.g., education, business, law, architecture) and several programs within each school. Some widely diversified organizations, such as Philip Morris, are in numerous unrelated businesses, such as cigarettes, land development, industrial paper products, and a brewery.

Managing such groups of businesses is made a little easier if resources are plentiful, cash is plentiful, and each is experiencing growth and profits. Unfortunately, providing larger and larger budgets each year to all businesses is seldom feasible. Many are not experiencing growth, and profits and resources (financial and nonfinancial) are becoming more and more scarce. In such a situation, choices must be made and some method is necessary to help management make the

HIGHLIGHT 1-4
Some Commonly Used Performance Standards

Effectiveness Standards

A. Sales Criteria.

1. Total sales.
2. Sales by product or product line.
3. Sales by geographic region.
4. Sales by salesperson.
5. Sales by customer type.
6. Sales by market segment.
7. Sales by size of order.
8. Sales by sales territory.
9. Sales by intermediary.
10. Market share.
11. Percentage change in sales.

B. Customer Satisfaction.

1. Quantity purchased.
2. Degree of brand loyalty.
3. Repeat purchase rates.
4. Perceived product quality.
5. Brand image.
6. Number of letters of complaint.

HIGHLIGHT 1-4 ***(concluded)***

Efficiency Standards

C. Costs.

1. Total costs.
2. Costs by product or product line.
3. Costs by geographic region.
4. Costs by salesperson.
5. Costs by customer type.
6. Costs by market segment.
7. Costs by size of order.
8. Costs by sales territory.
9. Costs by intermediary.
10. Percentage change in costs.

Effectiveness-Efficiency Standards

D. Profits.

1. Total profits.
2. Profits by product or product line.
3. Profits by geographic region.
4. Profits by salesperson.
5. Profits by customer type.
6. Profits by market segment.
7. Profits by size of order.
8. Profits by sales territory.
9. Profits by intermediary.

Source: Charles D. Schewe, *Marketing: Principles and Strategies* (New York: Random House, 1987), p. 593.

choices. Management must decide which businesses to build, maintain, or eliminate, or which new businesses to add.[20]

Obviously, the first step in this approach is to identify the various

[20] There are several portfolio models; each has its detractors and supporters. The interested reader should consult Richard G. Hamermesh and Roderick E. White, "Manage Beyond Portfolio Analysis," *Harvard Business Review,* January–February 1984, pp. 103–9, and J. A. Seeger, "Revising the Images of BCG's Growth/Share Matrix," *Strategic Management Journal,* January–March 1984, pp. 93–97.

division's product lines and so on that can be considered a "business." When identified, these are referred to as *strategic business units* (SBUs) and have the following characteristics:

They have a distinct mission.

They have their own competitors.

They are a single business or collection of related businesses.

They can be planned independently of the other businesses of the total organization.

Thus, depending on the type of organization, an SBU could be a single product, product line, division; a department of business administration; or a state mental health agency. Once the organization has identified and classified all of the SBUs, some method is then necessary to determine how resources should be allocated among the various SBUs. These methods are known as *portfolio models*. For those readers interested, Appendix A of this chapter presents two of the most popular portfolio models, the Boston Consulting Group model and the General Electric model.

The Complete Strategic Plan

Figure 1-1 indicates that at this point the strategic planning process is complete and the organization has a time-phased blueprint that outlines its mission, objectives, and strategies. Completion of the strategic plan facilitates the development of marketing plans for each product, product line, or division of the organization. Given a completed strategic plan, each area knows exactly where the organization wishes to go and can then develop objectives, strategies, and programs that are consistent with the strategic plan.[21] This important relationship between strategic planning and marketing planning is the subject of the final section of this chapter.

THE MARKETING MANAGEMENT PROCESS

Marketing management can be defined as "the analysis, planning, implementation, and control of programs designed to bring about desired exchanges with target markets for the purpose of achieving organizational objectives. It relies heavily on designing the organiza-

---

[21] R. A. Linneman and H. E. Klein, "Using Scenarios in Strategic Decision Making," *Business Horizons*, January–February 1985, pp. 64–74.

FIGURE 1–3 Strategic Planning and Marketing Planning

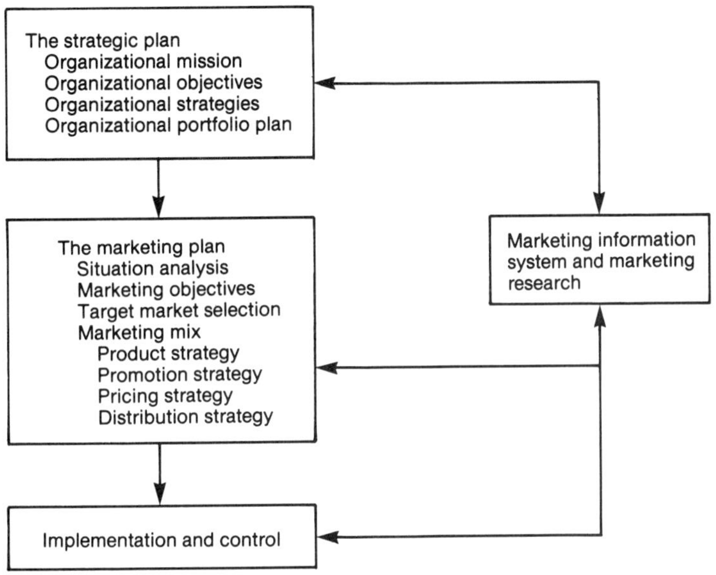

tion's offering in terms of the target market's needs and desires and on using effective pricing, communication, and distribution to inform, motivate, and service the market."[22] It should be noted that this definition is entirely consistent with the marketing concept, since it emphasizes the serving of target market needs as the key to achieving organizational objectives. The remainder of this section will be devoted to a discussion of the marketing management process in terms of the model in Figure 1–3.

Organizational Mission and Objectives

Marketing activities should start with a clear understanding of the organization's mission and objectives. These factors provide marketing management direction by specifying the industry, the desired role of the firm in the industry (such as research-oriented innovator, custom-batch specialist, or mass producer), and, hopefully, a precise statement of what the firm is trying to accomplish. However, since written mis-

[22] Kotler, *Marketing Management,* p. 14.

sion statements and objectives are often ambiguous or ill-defined, the marketing manager may have to consult with other members of top management to determine precisely what the firm is trying to accomplish, both overall and during a specific planning period. For example, a commonly stated organizational objective is "growth." Obviously, this objective is so general that it is practically useless. On the other hand, a statement such as "sustained growth of 14 percent in profits before taxes" provides a quantitative goal which the marketing manager can use for determining desired sales levels and the marketing strategies to achieve them. In addition, the marketing manager must monitor any changes in mission or objectives and adapt marketing strategies to meet them.

Situation Analysis

With a clear understanding of organizational objectives and mission, the marketing manager must then analyze and monitor the position of the firm and, specifically, the marketing department, in terms of its past, present, and future situation. Of course, the future situation is of primary concern. However, an analysis of past trends and current situation are most useful for predicting the future situation.

The situation analysis can be divided into six major areas of concern: (1) the cooperative environment, (2) the competitive environment, (3) the economic environment, (4) the social environment, (5) the political environment, and (6) the legal environment. In analyzing each of these environments, the marketing executive must search both for opportunities and for constraints or threats to achieving objectives. Opportunities for profitable marketing often arise from changes in these environments that bring about new sets of needs to be satisfied. Constraints on marketing activities, such as limited supplies of scarce resources, also arise from these environments.

The Cooperative Environment. The cooperative environment includes all firms and individuals who have a vested interest in the firm's accomplishing its objectives. Parties of primary interest to the marketing executive in this environment are (1) suppliers, ((2) resellers, (3) other departments in the firm, and (4) subdepartments and employees of the marketing department. Opportunities in this environment are primarily related to methods of increasing efficiency, while constraints consist of such things as unresolved conflicts and shortages of materials.

The Competitive Environment. The competitive environment includes primarily other firms in the industry that rival the organization for both resources and sales. Opportunities in this environment include such things as (1) acquiring competing firms, (2) offering demonstrably better value to consumers and attracting them away from competitors, and (3) in some cases, driving competitors out of the industry. The primary constraints in this environment are the demand stimulation activities of competing firms and the number of consumers who cannot be lured away from competition.

The Economic Environment. The state of the macroeconomy and changes in it also bring about marketing opportunities and constraints. For example, such factors as high inflation and unemployment levels can limit the size of the market that can afford to purchase a firm's top-of-the-line product. At the same time, these factors may offer a profitable opportunity to develop rental services for such products or to develop less expensive models of the product. In addition, changes in technology can provide significant threats and opportunities. For example, in the communication industry, technology has developed to a level where, in the not too distant future, it may be possible to have totally wireless communication anywhere in the

HIGHLIGHT 1–5
Some Important Federal Regulatory Agencies

Agencies	*Responsibilities*
Federal Trade Commission (FTC)	Enforces laws and develops guidelines regarding unfair business practices.
Food and Drug Administration (FDA)	Enforces laws and develops regulations to prevent distribution and sale of adulterated or misbranded foods, drugs, cosmetics, and hazardous consumer products.
Consumer Product Safety Commission (CPSC)	Enforces the Consumer Product Safety Act—which covers any consumer product not assigned to other regulatory agencies.
Interstate Commerce Commission (ICC)	Regulates interstate rail, bus, truck, and water carriers.
Federal Communications Commission (FCC)	Regulates interstate wire, radio, and television.
Environmental Protection Agency (EPA)	Develops and enforces environmental protection standards.
Office of Consumer Affairs (OCA)	Responds to consumers' complaints.

world. Obviously, such a system poses a severe threat to the existence of telephone and telegraph industries as they are today.

The Social Environment. This environment includes general cultural and social traditions, norms, and attitudes. While these values change slowly, such changes often bring about the need for new products and services. For example, a change in values concerning the desirability of large families brought about an opportunity to market better methods of birth control. On the other hand, cultural and social values also place constraints on marketing activities. As a rule, business practices that are contrary to social values become political issues, which are often resolved by legal constraints.

The Political Environment. The political environment includes the attitudes and reactions of the general public, social and business critics, and other organizations, such as the Better Business Bureau. Dissatisfaction with such business and marketing practices as unsafe products, products that waste resources, and unethical sales procedures can have adverse effects on corporation image and customer loyalty. However, adapting business and marketing practices to these attitudes can be an opportunity. For example, these attitudes have brought about markets for such products as unbreakable children's toys, high-efficiency air conditioners, and more economical automobiles.

The Legal Environment. This environment includes a host of federal, state, and local legislation directed at protecting both business competition and consumer rights. In past years legislation reflected social and political attitudes and has been primarily directed at constraining business practices. Such legislation usually acts as a constraint on business behavior, but again can be viewed as providing opportunities for marketing safer and more efficient products. In recent years there has been less emphasis on creating new laws for constraining business practices, i.e., deregulation has been more common.

Marketing Planning

In the previous sections it was emphasized that (1) marketing activities must be aligned with organizational objectives and (2) marketing opportunities are often found by systematically analyzing situational environments. Once an opportunity is recognized, the marketing executive must then plan an appropriate strategy for taking advantage of the opportunity. This process can be viewed in terms of three interrelated tasks: (1) establishing marketing objectives, (2) selecting the target markets, and (3) developing the marketing mix.

Establishing Objectives. Marketing objectives usually are derived from organizational objectives; in some cases where the firm is totally marketing-oriented, the two are identical. In either case objectives must be specified and performance in achieving them should be measurable. Marketing objectives are usually stated as standards of performance (e.g., a certain percentage of market share or sales volume) or as tasks to be achieved by given dates. While such objectives are useful, the marketing concept emphasizes that profits rather than sales should be the overriding objective of the firm and marketing department. In any case, these objectives provide the framework for the marketing plan.

Selecting the Target Markets. The success of any marketing plan hinges on how well it can identify consumer needs and organize its resources to satisfy them profitably. Thus, a crucial element of the marketing plan is selecting the group or segments of potential consumers the firm is going to serve with each of its products. Four important questions must be answered:

1. What do consumers need?
2. What must be done to satisfy these needs?
3. What is the size of the market?
4. What is its growth profile?

Present target markets and potential target markets are then ranked according to *(a)* profitability, *(b)* present and future sales volume, and *(c)* the match between what it takes to appeal successfully to the segment and the organization's capabilities. Those that appear to offer the greatest potential are selected. Chapters 3, 4, and 5 are devoted to discussing consumer behavior, industrial buyers, and market segmentation.

Developing the Marketing Mix. The marketing mix is the set of controllable variables that must be managed to satisfy the target market and achieve organizational objectives. These controllable variables are usually classified according to four major decision areas: product, price, promotion, and place (or channels of distribution). The importance of these decision areas cannot be overstated and, in fact, the major portion of this text is devoted to analyzing them. Chapters 6 and 7 are devoted to product and new product strategies; Chapters 8 and 9 to promotion strategies in terms of both nonpersonal and personal selling; Chapter 10 to distribution strategies and Chapter 11 to pricing strategies. In addition, marketing mix variables are the focus of analysis in two chapters on marketing in special fields, that is, the marketing of services (Chapter 12) and international marketing (Chapter 13). Thus, it should be clear to the reader that the marketing mix is the core of the marketing management process.

The output of the foregoing process is the marketing plan. It is a formal statement of decisions that have been made on marketing activities; it is a blueprint of the objectives, strategies, and tasks to be performed.

Implementation and Control of the Marketing Plan

Implementing the market plan involves putting the plan into action and performing marketing tasks according to the predefined schedule. Even the most carefully developed plans often cannot be executed with perfect timing. Thus, the marketing executive must closely monitor and coordinate implementation of the plan. In some cases, adjustments may have to be made in the basic plan because of changes in any of the situational environments. For example, competitors may introduce a new product, which may make it desirable to speed up or delay implementation of the plan. In almost all cases, some minor adjustments or "fine tuning" will be necessary in implementation.

Controlling the marketing plan involves three basic steps. First, the results of the implemented marketing plan are measured. Second, these results are compared with objectives. Third, decisions are made on whether the plan is achieving objectives. If serious deviations exist between actual and planned results, then adjustments may have to be made to redirect the plan toward achieving objectives.

Marketing Information Systems and Marketing Research

Throughout the marketing management process current, reliable, and valid information is needed to make effective marketing decisions. Providing this information is the task of the marketing decision support systems (MDSS) and marketing research. These topics are discussed in detail in Chapter 2.

THE RELATIONSHIP BETWEEN THE STRATEGIC PLAN AND THE MARKETING PLAN

Strategic planning is clearly a top-management responsibility. However, marketing managers and mid-level managers in the organization are indirectly involved in the process in two important ways: (1) they

HIGHLIGHT 1-6

Key Elements in the Marketing Plan

People	— What is the target market for the firm's product(s)? What is its size and growth potential?
Profit	— What is the expected profit from implementing the marketing plan? What are the other objectives of the marketing plan and how will their achievement be evaluated?
Personnel	— What personnel will be involved in implementing the marketing plan? Will only intrafirm personnel be involved or will other firms, such as advertising agencies or marketing research firms, also be employed?
Product	— What product(s) will be offered? What variations in the product will be offered in terms of style, features, quality, branding, packaging, and terms of sale and service? How should products be positioned in the market?
Price	— What price or prices will products be sold for?
Promotion	— How will information about the firm's offerings be communicated to the target market?
Place	— How, when, and where will the firm's offerings be delivered for sale to the target market?
Policy	— What is the overall marketing policy for dealing with anticipated problems in the marketing plan? How will unanticipated problems be handled?
Period	— For how long a time is the marketing plan to be in effect? When should the plan be implemented and what is the schedule for executing and evaluating marketing activities?

often influence the strategic planning process by providing inputs in the form of information and suggestions relating to their particular products, product lines, and areas of responsibility; and (2) they must be aware of what the process of strategic planning involves as well as the results because everything they do, the marketing objectives and strategies they develop, must be derived from the strategic plan. There is rarely a strategic planning question or decision that does not have marketing implications.

Thus, if strategic planning is done properly, it will result in a clearly defined blueprint for managerial action at all levels in the organization. Figure 1-4 illustrates the hierarchy of objectives and strategies using one possible objective and two strategies from the strategic plan (above the dotted line) and illustrating how these relate to elements of the marketing plan (below the dotted line). Many others could have

FIGURE 1–4 Relating the Marketing Plan to the Strategic Plan

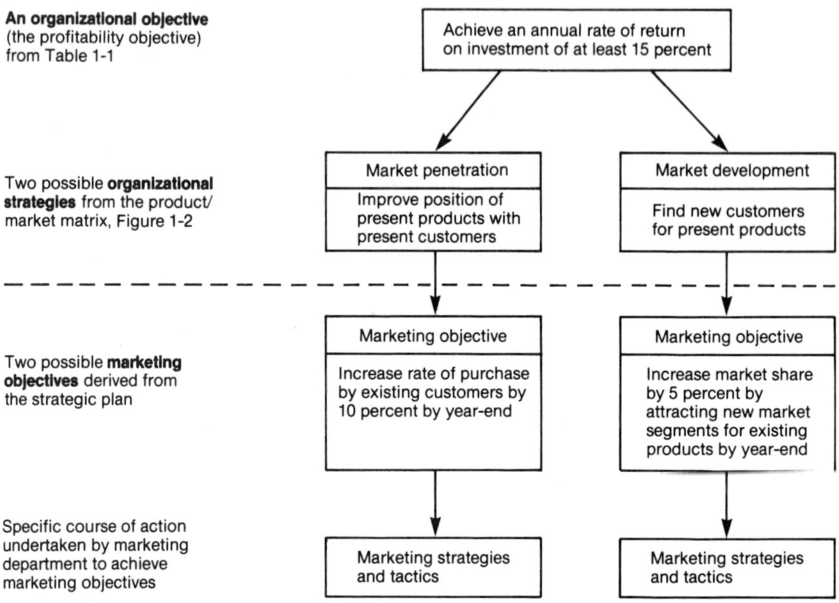
An organizational objective
(the profitability objective)
from Table 1-1
Achieve an annual rate of return on investment of at least 15 percent
Two possible **organizational strategies** from the product/market matrix, Figure 1-2
Market penetration
Improve position of present products with present customers
Market development
Find new customers for present products
Two possible **marketing objectives** derived from the strategic plan
Marketing objective
Increase rate of purchase by existing customers by 10 percent by year-end
Marketing objective
Increase market share by 5 percent by attracting new market segments for existing products by year-end
Specific course of action undertaken by marketing department to achieve marketing objectives
Marketing strategies and tactics
Marketing strategies and tactics

been developed, but our purpose is to illustrate how the marketing plan must be derived from and contribute to the achievement of the strategic plan.

CONCLUSION

This chapter has described the marketing management process and provided an outline for many of the remaining chapters in this text. At this point it would be useful for the reader to review Figure 1–3 as well as the Table of Contents. This will enable you to relate the content and progression of material to the marketing management process.

Appendix Portfolio Models

Portfolio models have become a valuable aid to marketing managers in their efforts to develop effective marketing plans. The use of these models has become widespread as marketing managers face a situation that can best be described as "more products, less time, and less money." More specifically, (1) as the number of products a firm produces expands, the time available for developing marketing plans for each product decreases; (2) at a strategic level, management must make resource allocation decisions across lines of products and, in diversified organizations, across different lines of business; and (3) when resources are limited (which they usually are), the process of deciding which strategic business units (SBUs) to emphasize becomes very complex. In such situations, portfolio models can be very useful.

Portfolio analysis is not a new idea. Banks manage loan portfolios seeking to balance risks and yields. Individuals who are serious investors usually have a portfolio of various kinds of investments (common stocks, preferred stocks, bank accounts, and the like), each with different characteristics of risk, growth, and rate of return. The investor seeks to manage the portfolio to maximize whatever objectives he or she might have. Applying this same idea, most organizations have a wide range of products, product lines, and businesses, each with different growth rates and returns. Similar to the investor, managers should seek a desirable balance among alternative SBUs. Specifically, management should seek to develop a business portfolio that will assure long-run profits and cash flow.

Portfolio models can be used to classify SBUs to determine the future cash contributions that can be expected from each SBU as well as the future resource requirements that each will require. Remember, depending on the organization, an SBU could be a single product, product line, division, or distinct business. While there are many different types of portfolio models, they generally examine the competitive position of the SBU and the chances for improving the SBU's contribution to profitability and cash flow.

There are several portfolio analysis techniques. Two of the most widely used are discussed in this Appendix. To truly appreciate the concept of portfolio analysis, however, we must briefly review the development of portfolio theory.

A Review Portfolio Theory

The interest in developing aids for managers in the selection of strategy was spurred by an organization known as the Boston Consulting Group over 25 years ago. Its ideas, which will be discussed shortly, and many of those that followed were based on the concept of experience curves.

Experience curves are similar in concept to learning curves. Learning curves were developed to express the idea that the number of labor hours it takes to produce one unit of a particular product declines in a predictable

FIGURE 1A-1 Experience Curve and Resulting Profit Curve

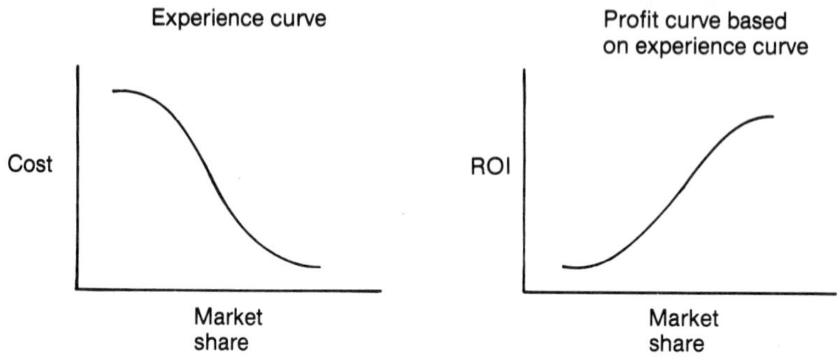

manner as the number of units produced increases. Hence, an accurate estimation of how long it takes to produce the hundredth unit is possible if the production time for the 1st and 10th unit are known.

The concept of experience curves was derived from the concept of learning curves. Experience curves were first widely discussed in the ongoing Profit Impact of Marketing Strategies (PIMS) study conducted by the Strategic Planning Institute. The PIMS project studies 150 firms with more than 1,000 individual business units. Its major focus is on determining which environmental and internal firm variables influence the firm's return on investment (ROI) and cash flow. The researchers have concluded that seven categories of variables appear to influence the return on investment: (1) competitive position, (2) industry/market environment, (3) budget allocation, (4) capital structure, (5) production processes, (6) company characteristics, and (7) "change action" factors.[23]

The experience curve includes all costs associated with a product and implies that the per unit cost of a product should fall, due to cumulative experience, as production volume increases. In a given industry, therefore, the producer with the largest volume and corresponding market share should have the lowest marginal cost. This leader in market share should be able to underprice competitors, discourage entry into the market by potential competitors, and, as a result, achieve an acceptable return on investment. The linkage of experience to cost to price to market share to ROI is exhibited in Figure 1A-1. The Boston Consulting Group's view of the experience curve led the members to develop what has become known as the BCG Portfolio Model.

[23] George S. Day and David B. Montgomery, "Diagnosing the Experience Curve," *Journal of Marketing*, Spring 1983, pp. 44-58.

FIGURE 1A-2 The Boston Consulting Group Portfolio Model

		Relative Market Share	
		High	*Low*
Market Growth Rate	*High*	Stars	Question marks
	Low	Cash cows	Dogs

The BCG Model

The BCG model is based on the assumption that profitability and cash flow will be closely related to sales volume. Thus, in this model, SBUs are classified in terms of their relative market share and the growth rate of the market the SBU is in. Using these dimensions, products are either classified as stars, cash cows, dogs, or question marks. The BCG model is presented in Figure 1A-2.

- *Stars* are SBUs with a high share of a high-growth market. Because high-growth markets attract competition, such SBUs are usually cash users because they are growing and because the firm needs to protect their market share position.
- *Cash cows* are often market leaders but the market they are in is not growing rapidly. Because these SBUs have a high share of a low-growth market, they are cash generators for the firm.
- *Dogs* are SBUs that have a low share of a low-growth market. If the SBU has a very loyal group of customers, it may be a source of profits and cash. Usually, dogs are not large sources of cash.
- *Question marks* are SBUs with a low share of a high-growth market. They have great potential but require great resources if the firm is to successfully build market share.

As you can see, a firm with 10 SBUs will usually have a portfolio that includes some of each of the above. Having developed this analysis, management must determine what role each SBU should assume. Four basic objectives are possible:

1. *Build share.* This objective sacrifices immediate earnings to improve market share. It is appropriate for promising question marks whose share has to grow if they are ever to become stars.
2. *Hold share.* This objective seeks to preserve the SBU's market share. It is very appropriate for strong cash cows to ensure that they can continue to yield a large cash flow.
3. *Harvest.* Here, the objective seeks to increase the product's short-term cash flow without concern for the long-run impact. It allows market share to decline in order to maximize earnings and cash flow. It is an appropriate objective for weak cash cows, weak question marks, and dogs.
4. *Divest.* This objective involves selling or divesting the SBU because better investment opportunities exist elsewhere. It is very appropriate for dogs and those question marks the firm cannot afford to finance for growth.

The General Electric Model

Although the BCG model can be useful, it does assume that market share is the sole determinant of an SBU's profitability. Also, in projecting market growth rates, a manager should carefully analyze the factors that influence sales and any opportunities for influencing industry sales.

Some firms have developed alternative portfolio models to incorporate more information about market opportunities and competitive positions. The GE model is one of these. The GE model emphasizes all the potential sources of strength, not just market share, and all of the factors that influence the long-term attractiveness of a market, not just its growth rate. As Figure 1A–3

FIGURE 1A–3 The General Electric Portfolio Model

		Business Strength		
		Strong	*Average*	*Weak*
Industry Attractiveness	*High*	A	A	B
	Medium	A	B	C
	Low	B	C	C

FIGURE 1A–4 Components of Industry Attractiveness and Business Strength at GE

Industry Attractiveness	*Business Strength*
	Market position:
Market size	Domestic market share.
Market growth	World market share.
Profitability	Share growth.
Cyclicality	Share compared with leading competitor.
Ability to recover from inflation	Competitive strengths:
World scope	Quality leadership.
	Technology.
	Marketing.
	Relative profitability.

indicates, all SBUs are classified in terms of *business strength and industry attractiveness*. Figure 1A–4 presents a list of items that can be used to position SBUs in the matrix.

Industry attractiveness is a composite index made up of such factors as those listed in Figure 1A–4. For example: *market size*—the larger the market the more attractive it would be; *market growth*—high-growth markets are more attractive than low-growth markets; *profitability*—high-profit-margin markets are more attractive than low-profit-margin industries.

Business strength is a composite index made up of such factors as those listed in Figure 1A–4. For example: *market share*—the higher the SBU's share of market, the greater its business strength; *quality leadership*—the higher the SBU's quality compared to competitors, the greater its business strength; *share compared with leading competitor*—the closer the SBU's share to the market leader, the greater its business strength.

Once the SBU's are classified, they are placed on the grid (Figure 1A–3). Priority "A" SBUs (often called "the green zone") are those in the three cells at the upper left, indicating that these are SBUs high in both industry attractiveness and business strength, and that the firm should "build share." Priority "B" SBUs (often called "the yellow zone") are those medium in both industry attractiveness and business strength. The firm will usually decide to "hold share" on these SBUs. Priority "C" SBUs are those in the three cells at the lower right (often called "the red zone"). These SBUs are low in both industry attractiveness and business strength. The firm will usually decide to "harvest" or "divest" these SBUs.

Whether the BCG, the GE model, or a variation of these models is used, some analysis must be made of the firm's current portfolio of SBUs as part of any strategic planning effort. Marketing must get its direction from the organization's strategic plan.

Part B

Marketing Information, Research, and Understanding the Target Market

CHAPTER 2
Marketing Decision Support Systems and Marketing Research
CHAPTER 3
Consumer Behavior
CHAPTER 4
Industrial Buyer Behavior
CHAPTER 5
Market Segmentation

Chapter 2

Marketing Decision Support Systems and Marketing Research

It is obvious that the American business system has been capable of producing a vast quantity of goods and services. However, in the past two decades the American business system has also become extremely capable of producing massive amounts of information and data. In fact, the last decade has often been referred to as the "Information Era" and the "Age of Information."

This situation is a complete reverse from what previously existed. In the past, marketing executives did not have to deal with an oversupply of information for decision-making purposes. In most cases they gathered what little data they could and hoped that their decisions would be reasonably good. In fact, it was for this reason that marketing research came to be recognized as an extremely valuable staff function in the 1930s and 1940s. It provided marketing management with information where previously there had been little or none and, thereby, alleviated to a great extent the paucity of information for marketing decision making. However, marketing management in many companies has failed to store marketing information, and much valuable marketing information is lost when marketing personnel change jobs or companies.

Today, marketing managers often feel buried by the deluge of information and data that comes across their desks. How can it be, then, that so many marketing managers complain that they have insufficient or inappropriate information on which to base their everyday operating decisions? Specifically, most of these complaints fall into the following categories:

1. There is too much marketing information of the wrong kind and not enough of the right kind.
2. Marketing information is so dispersed throughout the company that great effort is usually needed to locate simple facts.
3. Vital information is sometimes suppressed by other executives or subordinates for personal reasons.
4. Vital information often arrives too late to be useful.
5. Information often arrives in a form that provides no idea of its accuracy, and there is no one to turn to for confirmation.

Marketing management requires current, reliable information before it can function efficiently. Because of this need, and the information explosion of the past decade, many large corporations have banked their total marketing knowledge in computers. Well-designed marketing decision support systems (MDSS) can eliminate corporate losses of millions of dollars from lost information and lost opportunities.

This chapter is concerned with marketing decision support systems and marketing research. Since the two concepts are easily confused, it is important initially to distinguish one from the other. In general terms, a marketing decision support system is concerned with the continuous gathering, processing, and utilization of pertinent information for decision-making purposes. The primary objective of a MDSS is to ensure that the right information is available to the right decision maker at the right time. Marketing research, on the other hand, usually focuses on a specific marketing problem with the objective of providing information for a particular decision. As such, marketing research is an integral part of the overall marketing decision support system but usually is project-oriented rather than a continuous process.

MARKETING DECISION SUPPORT SYSTEMS

A marketing decision support system is a new type of marketing information system. This type of information system is designed to support all phases of marketing decision making—from problem identification to choosing the relevant data to work with, picking the approach to be used in making the decision, and evaluating alternative courses of action. This type of information system can be defined as:

> a coordinated collection of data, systems, tools, and techniques with supporting software and hardware by which an organization gathers and interprets relevant information from business and environment and turns it into a basis for marketing action.[1]

---

[1] John D. C. Little, "Decision Support Systems for Marketing Managers," *Journal of Marketing*, Summer 1979, p. 22.

FIGURE 2–1 The Marketing Decision Support System

Figure 2–1 illustrates the concept of a MDSS. There are two main changes depicted in this figure: (1) the conversion of data to information and (2) the conversion of information to action. The first conversion is the task of the marketing information center, while the second is the major purpose of marketing decision making.

The Marketing Information Center

Although the growth of the concept of a marketing decision support system has been fairly recent, most experts agree that a single, separate marketing information center must exist to centralize responsibility for marketing information within the firm. This is necessary because both the users and suppliers of such information are widely scattered throughout the organization and some unit is needed to oversee the entire operation.

The general purpose of this organizational unit is to maintain, as well as to improve and upgrade, the accuracy, completeness, and timeliness of information for marketing management decisions. Operationally, this means that the information center must gather raw data from various environments and markets and process them so they can be obtained and analyzed by marketing executives. Data must be gathered from both internal and external sources. Internally, such data as sales, costs, and profits, as well as other company reports, need

> **HIGHLIGHT 2-1**
> **AMP's MIS Was Not a MDSS**
>
> In 1980, AMP, Inc., ran a sales contest. Unfortunately, the firm's executives could not name a winner. The reason: They did not have the information. Although the firm's headquarter's regularly received sales reports, it did not have the breakdown by product line to find the best salesperson.
>
> *Source:* "Helping Decision Makers Get at Data," *Business Week,* September 13, 1982, pp. 118–19.

to be converted to information and stored in the computer. Externally, data from trade journals, magazines, newspapers, government publications, and other sources of pertinent information used by marketing executives for decision making also must be converted and stored.

A critical point here is that the MDSS converts raw data into information that marketing management can actually use for making intelligent decisions. A MDSS must produce information in a form marketing executives can understand, when it is needed, and have it under the manager's control. In other words, a key distinction that separates a MDSS from other types of marketing information systems is that a MDSS has the direct and primary objective of supporting marketing management decision making.[2] Figure 2–2 provides examples of two firms with conventional MISs and two firms with MDSSs to illustrate this important difference.

Marketing Decision Making

Earlier we stated that the main purpose of marketing executives is to convert information to actions through the process of decision making. Note that, in Figure 2–1, two up-and-down arrows connect marketing decision making with the marketing information center. These arrows represent an important aspect of the MDSS (i.e., it is an *interactive system* in which marketing executives sit at computer terminals and actively analyze information and convert it to actions).

In previous types of marketing information systems, the information center often attempted to prepare reports to meet the individual needs of different marketing executives at different levels in the organization. More often than not, such attempts provide too much information

[2] See Gilbert A. Churchill, Jr., *Marketing Research: Methodological Foundations* (Hinsdale, Ill.: Dryden Press, 1987), chap. 18.

FIGURE 2–2 Examples of MISs and MDSSs

A Marketing Information System (MIS) at Savin Corporation

Savin Corporation has installed a computer terminal in each of its warehouses to keep track of every item in its inventory. The system identifies the quantity on hand, the location and movement of stock, and the status of all orders. The system is used to plan shipments, locate single items in inventory, and locate customer records.

A Marketing Information System (MIS) at United Services Automobile Association

The United Services Automobile Association, the nation's eighth largest insurer of passenger cars, purchased a $4 million system that now contains virtually all of the company's written records. When a customer reports an accident, an adjustor can call up the customer's file, check the coverage, and keep track of all the paperwork through the final settlement of the claim. The company figures that it used to take five people a day and a half to perform tasks that one person now handles in 20 minutes.

A Marketing Decision Support System (MDSS) at Crocker National Bank

The Crocker National Bank in San Francisco has purchased desk-top terminals for most of its top-level executives. Each terminal is tapped into the huge computers that record all bank transactions. The executives are able to make comparisons, analyze problems, and prepare charts and tables in response to simple commands. For example, they can analyze emerging trends in deposits and loans and monitor the influence of various interest rates and loan maturities on the bank.

A Marketing Decision Support System (MDSS) at Gould, Inc.

Gould, Inc., has developed a decision support system to help managers retrieve, manipulate, and display information needed for making decisions. The system combines a large visual display and video terminals with a computerized information system. The system is designed solely to assist managers to make comparisons and analyze problems for decision-making purposes. The MDSS instantly prepares tables and color charts in response to simple commands.

---

of the wrong kind and not enough information of the right kind. However, in addition to the flexibility, timeliness, and detail provided by a MDSS, such problems do not occur because marketing executives themselves retrieve and manipulate the information.

Many experts believe that, in a few years, most marketing executives will be sharing their desk space with a personal computer. Personal computers have the capability of increasing both the productivity of marketing managers and the quality of their decisions. First, the capacity of the computers to extract, process, and analyze data swiftly and accurately is awesome. Second, computers have gotten smaller, faster, and smarter in a shorter time than any other technological innovation in history. A desktop personal computer can solve ordinary arithmetic problems 18 times faster than the world's first large-scale computer built less than 50 years ago (weighing 30 tons). Finally, computers have become extremely inexpensive in comparison to earlier models. Just 30 years ago a medium-sized computer cost a quarter of a million dollars. A firm can now buy a desk-top computer with three times the memory capacity for less than $2,000. While it may take some time for marketing executives to learn to use the equipment, the potential for better, more profitable decision making may outweigh the brief inconvenience.

MARKETING RESEARCH

Marketing research should be an integral part of a marketing decision support system. In essence, marketing research combines insights and intuition with the research process to provide information for making marketing decisions. In general, marketing research can be defined as:

> the function which links the consumer and the customer to the organization through information—information used to identify and define marketing problems; generate, refine, and evaluate marketing actions; monitor marketing performance; and improve our understanding of marketing as a process.[3]

Today's marketing managers should understand the role of research in decision making. It cannot be overstated that *marketing research is an aid to decision making and not a substitute for it.* In other words, marketing research does not make decisions but it can substantially increase the probability that the best decision will be made. Unfortunately, too often marketing managers view marketing research reports as the final answer to their problems. Instead, marketing managers should recognize that (1) even the most carefully controlled research projects can be fraught with pitfalls and (2) decisions should be made in the light of their own knowledge and experience and other factors that are not explicitly considered in the research project. The introduction and subsequent failure of the Edsel automobile is a classic

---

[3] Gilbert A. Churchill, Jr., *Basic Marketing Research* (Hinsdale, Ill.: Dryden Press, 1988).

HIGHLIGHT 2-2
Marketing Research that Influenced Marketing Strategies

Marketing research can be a useful aid in decision making. Below are several examples of marketing research that helped firms develop their marketing strategies.

Eastman Kodak Company

The Eastman Kodak Company was faced with flat sales and needed to devise a strategy to improve sales performance. The company knew that amateur photographers goof on more than 2 billion pictures a year and had its technical researchers look at 10,000 photos to see what kinds of things users were doing wrong. The study led to a number of design ideas for the Kodak disc camera that helped eliminate almost one half of the out-of-focus and underexposed shots. The disc camera has been one of the most successful products in Kodak history.

M&M/Mars Candy Company

In an attempt to determine the proper weight for its candy bars, M&M/Mars Candy Company conducted a 12-month test in 150 stores. For the test it altered the size of its products across the stores but kept the prices constant. It found that, in those stores where the dimensions were increased, sales went up 20 to 30 percent. As a result of this research, the company decided to change almost its entire product line.

American Express

American Express was disappointed with its inability to attract female cardholders. A group of American Express executives listened in on a market research panel of women discussing credit cards. The panel members indicated that they were very familiar with American Express and thought highly of it, but few saw it as a card for them. It seemed that the prestige image promoted for years using various celebrities appealed more to men than to women. Based on this research, the company developed a new ad campaign that did away with celebrities and emphasized that American Express is "part of a lot of interesting lives."

Mercedes Benz

When Mercedes Benz made its initial foray into the U.S. market, it conducted consumer surveys. The research showed that people wanted a no-nonsense car with distinct quality, engineering, design, and performance. This research served as the basis for selecting models to be introduced in the United States and also influenced print ads to emphasize facts, rather than gimmickry.

Source: Adapted from Gilbert A. Churchill, Jr., *Marketing Research: Methodological Foundations,* 4th ed. (Hinsdale, Ill.: Dryden Press, 1987), pp. 3-4.

example of the use of marketing research findings that were not properly tempered with sound executive judgment.[4]

Although marketing research does not make decisions, it is a direct means of reducing risks associated with managing the marketing mix and long-term marketing planning. In fact, a company's return on investment from marketing research is a function of the extent to which research output reduces the risk inherent in decison making. For example, marketing research can play an important role in reducing new product failure costs by evaluating consumer acceptance of a product prior to full-scale introduction.

In a highly competitive economy a firm's survival depends on the marketing manager's ability to make sound decisions, to outguess competitors, to anticipate consumer needs, to forecast business conditions, and to plan for company growth. Marketing research is one tool to help accomplish these tasks. Research is also vital for managerial control, because without appropriate data, the validity of past decisions on the performance of certain elements in the marketing system (e.g., the performance of the sales force or advertising) cannot be evaluated reliably.

Although many of the technical aspects of marketing research, such as sampling design or statistical analysis, can be delegated to experts, the process of marketing research begins and ends with the marketing manager. In the beginning of a research project it is the marketing manager's responsibility to work with researchers to define the problem carefully. When the research project is completed, the application of the results in terms of decision alternatives rests primarily with the marketing manager.[5] For these reasons, and since the marketing manager must be able to communicate with researchers throughout the course of the project, it is vital for managers to understand the research process from the researcher's point of view.

The Research Process

Marketing research can be viewed as a systematic process for obtaining information to aid in decision making. Although there are many different types of marketing research, the framework illustrated in Figure 2–3 represents a general approach to defining the research process. Each element of this process will be briefly discussed.

---

[4] For an excellent discussion of this classic failure, see Robert J. Hartley, "The Edsel: Marketing Planning and Research Gone Awry," in *Marketing Mistakes,* 2nd ed. (Columbus, Ohio: Grid, 1981), pp. 115–27.

[5] For a discussion of the use of research findings in marketing decision making, see Rohit Deshpande, "The Organizational Context of Market Research Use," *Journal of Marketing,* Fall 1982, pp. 91–101.

FIGURE 2-3 The Five Ps of the Research Process

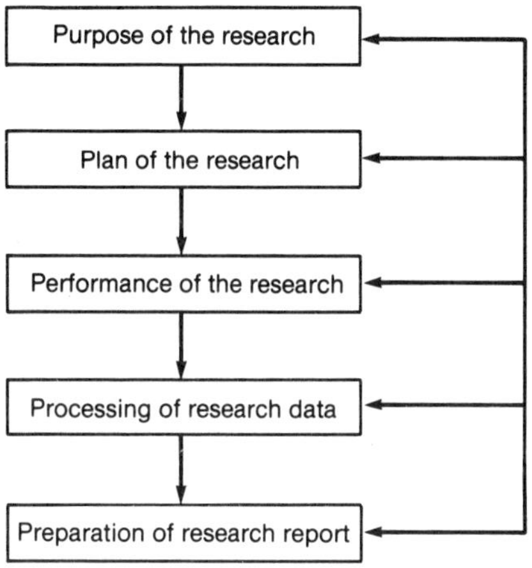

Purpose of the Research. The first step in the research process is to determine explicitly the purpose of the research. This may well be much more difficult than it sounds. Quite often a situation or problem is recognized as needing research, yet the nature of the problem is not clear or well defined. Thus, an investigation is required to clarify the problem or situation. This investigation includes such things as interviewing corporate executives, reviewing records, and studying existing information related to the problem. At the end of this stage the researcher should know (1) the current situation, (2) the nature of the problem, and (3) the specific question or questions the research is to find answers to—that is, why the research is being conducted.

Plan of the Research. The first step in the research plan is to formalize the specific purpose of the study. Once this is accomplished, the sequencing of tasks and responsibilities for accomplishing the research are spelled out in detail. This stage is critical since decisions are made that determine the who, what, when, where, and how of the research study.

An initial decision in this stage of the process is the type of data that will be required. The two major types of data are primary and secondary. Primary data is data that must be collected from original sources for the purposes of the study. Secondary data is information which has been previously collected for some other purpose but can be used for the purposes of the study.

If the research project requires primary data, decisions have to be made on:

then implemented in the environment. The results of this implementation are fed back as new information so that continuous adaptation can take place.

The Strategic Planning Process

The output of the strategic planning process is the development of a strategic plan. Figure 1-1 indicates there are four components of a strategic plan: mission, objectives, strategies, and portfolio plan. Let us carefully examine each one.

Organizational Mission

Every organization's environment supplies the resources that sustain the organization, whether it is a business organization, a college or university, or a governmental agency. In exchange for these resources, the organization must supply the environment with goods and services at an acceptable price and quality. In other words, every organization exists to accomplish something in the larger environment, and that purpose or mission is usually clear at the start. However, as time passes and the organization expands, the environment changes, and managerial personnel change, one or more things are likely to occur. First, the original purpose may become irrelevant as the organization expands into new products, new markets, and even new industries. Second, the original mission remains relevant but some managers begin to lose interest in it. Finally, changes in the environment may make the original mission inappropriate. The result of any or all of these three conditions is a "drifting" organization, without a clear mission or purpose to guide critical decisions. When this occurs, management must search for a purpose or restate the original purpose.

The mission statement of an organization should be a long-run vision of what the organization is trying to become: the unique aim that differentiates the organization from similar ones. Note that the need is not a stated purpose, such as "to fulfill the educational needs of college students," that will enable stockholders and managers to feel good or to use for good public relations. The need is for a stated mission that will provide direction and significance to all members of the organization regardless of their level in the organization.

The basic questions that must be answered when an organization decides to examine and restate its mission are: "What is our business?" "What should it be?" While such questions may appear simple, they are in fact such difficult and critical ones that the major responsibility

HIGHLIGHT 2–3
A Comparison of Five Methods of Marketing Research

	Definition	*Advantages*	*Disadvantages*
Observation	Systematic description of behavior.	Documents the variety of ongoing behavior. Unobtrusive observation captures what happens naturally, when no experimenter is present.	Time consuming. Requires careful training of observers. Observer may interfere with behavior and alter what is happening.
Case study	In-depth description of a single person, family, or organization.	Focuses on the complexity and uniqueness of the individual.	May lack generalizability. Data may reflect the interests and perspective of the investigator.
Survey research	Asking questions to a comparatively large number of people about their opinions, attitudes, or behavior.	Permits data collection from large numbers of subjects.	The way questions are asked can influence the answers. Survey response may not be directly related to behavior.
Experimentation	An analysis of cause-effect relations by manipulating some conditions and holding others constant.	Permits statements about causality. Permits control and isolation of specific variables.	Laboratory findings may not be applicable to other settings.
Correlational research	Assessing the strength of relationship among variables.	Determines whether information on variable A can be used to predict variable B.	Difficult to infer causality. Cannot detect nonlinear relationships.

Source: Adapted from P. R. Newman and B. M. Newman, *Principles of Psychology* (Chicago, Ill.: Dorsey Press, 1983), p. 28.

1. How will the data be collected? Personal interviews? Mail questionnaires? Telephone interviews?
2. How much data is needed?
3. What measures will be used and how will they be checked for reliability and validity?[6]
4. Who will design the measures and collect the data?
5. Where will the data be collected? Nationally? Regionally? Locally? At home? At work?
6. When and for how long will data be collected?

If secondary data will suffice for the research question(s), similar decisions have to be made. However, since the data are already in existence, the task is much simpler (and cheaper). For example, most of the sources of secondary data listed in Section 7 of this text are available in a public or university library.

In addition to determining data requirements, the research plan also specifies the method of data analysis, procedures for processing and interpreting the data, and the structure of the final report. In other words, the entire research project is sequenced, and responsibility for

[6] For sources of information and discussion of reliability and validity issues, see J. Paul Peter and Gilbert A. Churchill, Jr., "The Relationships among Research Design Choices and Psychometric Properties of Rating Scales: A Meta-Analysis," *Journal of Marketing Research,* February 1986, pp. 1–10.

HIGHLIGHT 2–4
Examples of Information That Marketing Research Can Obtain

1. Population in geographical areas and population trends.
2. Income obtained by the market and income trends.
3. Estimates of market potentials (total number of units of a product that could be purchased by a given market).
4. Sales volume forecasts (how many units of a product an individual firm expects to sell).
5. Which kinds of purchasers account for the largest percentage of total units sold.
6. Who are the purchasers who consistently buy a specific brand.
7. Who makes the actual decision to buy.
8. Which segments of the market are profitable and which segments are unprofitable.
9. How the product is actually used by the market.

Source: R. T. Hise, P. L. Gillett, J. K. Ryans, Jr., *Marketing: Concepts, Decisions, Strategies* (Cambridge, Mass.: Winthrop Publishers, 1984), p. 20.

the various tasks is assigned. Thus, the research plan provides the framework for the coordination and control of the entire project.

When the research plan is fully specified, the time and money costs of the project are estimated. If management views the benefits of the research as worth the costs, the project proceeds to the next phase. A sample research plan is presented in Figure 2-4.

FIGURE 2-4 Sample Research Plan

I. *Tentative projective title.*

II. *Statement of the problem.*

One or two sentences to outline or to describe the general problem under consideration.

III. *Define and delimit the problem.*

Here the writer states the purpose(s) and scope of the problem. *Purpose* refers to goals or objectives. Closely related to this is *justification.* Sometimes this is a separate step, depending on the urgency of the task. *Scope* refers to the actual limitations of the research effort; in other words, what is *not* going to be investigated. Here is the point where the writer spells out the various hypotheses to be investigated or the questions to be answered.

IV. *Outline.*

Generally, this is a tentative framework for the entire project by topics. It should be flexible enough to accommodate unforeseen difficulties. Statistical tables should be shown in outline form and also show graphs planned. Tables should reflect the hypotheses.

V. *Method and data sources.*

The types of data to be sought (primary, secondary) are briefly identified. A brief explanation of how the necessary information or data will be gathered (e.g., surveys, experiments, library sources) is given. *Sources* refer to the actual depositories for the information, whether from government publications, company records, actual people, and so forth. If measurements are involved, such as consumers' attitudes, the techniques for making such measurements are stated. All of the techniques (statistical and nonstatistical) should be mentioned and discussed about their relevance for the task at hand. The nature of the problem will probably indicate the types of techniques to be employed, such as factor analysis, depth interviews, or focus groups.

VI. *Sample design.*

This provides the limits of the universe or population to be studied and how it will be listed (or prepared). The writer specifies the population, states the sample size, whether sample stratification will be employed, and how. If a nonrandom sample is to be used, the justification and the type of sampling strategy to be employed, such as convenience sample, are stated.

FIGURE 2–4 *(concluded)*

VII. *Data collection forms.*

The forms to be employed in gathering the data should be discussed and, if possible, included in the plan. For surveys, this will involve either a questionnaire or an interview schedule. For other types of methods, the forms could include IBM cards, inventory forms, psychological tests, and so forth. The plan should state how these instruments have been or will be validated, and the reader should be given some indication of their reliability and validity.

VIII. *Personnel requirements.*

This provides a complete list of all personnel who will be required, indicating exact jobs, time duration, and expected rate of pay. Assignments should be made indicating each person's responsibility and authority.

IX. *Phases of the study with a time schedule.*

This is a detailed outline of the plan to complete the study. The entire study should be broken into workable pieces. Then, considering the person who will be employed in each phase, their qualifications and experience, and so forth, the time in months for the job is estimated. Some jobs may overlap. This will help in estimating the work months required. The overall time for the project should allow for time overlaps on some jobs.

Illustration:

1. Preliminary investigation—two months.
2. Final test of questionnaire—one month.
3. Sample selection—one month.
4. Mail questionnaires, field follow-up, and so forth—four months
5. Additional phases. . . .

X. *Tabulation plans.*

This is a discussion of editing and proof of questionnaires, data preparation, and the type of computer analysis. An outline of some of the major tables required is very important.

XI. *Cost estimate for doing the study.*

Personnel requirements are combined with time on different phases to estimate total personnel costs. Estimates on travel, materials, supplies, drafting, computer charges, and printing and mailing costs must also be included. If an overhead charge is required by the administration, it should be calculated and added to the subtotal of the above items.

Performance of the Research. *Performance* is used here in the narrow sense of preparing for data collection and actually collecting the data. It is at this point that the research plan is put into action.

The preparations obviously depend on the type of data desired and method of data collection. For primary research, questions and questionnaire items must be pretested and validated. In addition, preparations for mail surveys include such things as sample selection, questionnaire printing, and envelope and postage considerations. For telephone or personal interviews, such things as interviewer scoring forms, instructions, and scheduling must be taken care of. For secondary data, such things as data recording procedures and instructions need attention.

In terms of actual data collection, a cardinal rule is to obtain and record the maximal amount of useful information, subject to the constraints of time, money, and interviewee privacy. Failure to obtain and record data clearly can obviously lead to a poor research study, while failure to consider the rights of subjects or interviewees raises both ethical and practical questions. Thus, both the objectives and constraints of data collection must be closely monitored.[7]

Processing Research Data. Processing research data includes the preparation of data for analysis and the actual analysis of the data. Preparations include such things as editing and structuring the data, and perhaps coding and preparing it for computer analysis. Data sets should be clearly labeled to ensure that they are not misinterpreted or misplaced. The data are then analyzed according to the procedure specified in the research plan and are interpreted according to standard norms of the analysis.

Preparation of Research Report. The research report is a complete statement of everything accomplished relative to the research project and includes a writeup of each of the previous stages. Figure 2–5 illustrates the types of questions the researcher should ask prior to submitting the report to the appropriate decision maker.

The importance of clear and unambiguous report writing cannot be overstressed, since the research is meaningless if it cannot be communicated. Often the researcher must trade off the apparent precision of scientific jargon for everyday language that the decision maker can understand. It should always be remembered that research is an aid for decision making and not a substitute for it.

---

[7] For excellent discussions of some innovative methods of data collection and analysis, see Fern Schumer, "The New Magicians of Market Research," *Fortune*, July 25, 1983, pp. 72–74; and Joseph Poindexter, "Shaping the Consumer," *Psychology Today*, May 1983, pp. 65–68.

FIGURE 2–5 Six Criteria for Evaluating Marketing Research Reports

1. Under what conditions was the study made? The report should provide:
   a. Full statement of the problems to be investigated by the study.
   b. Source of financing for the study.
   c. Names of organizations participating in the study, together with their qualifications and vested interests.
   d. Exact time period covered in data collection.
   e. Definitions of terms employed.
   f. Copies of data collection instruments.
   g. Source of collateral data.
   h. Complete statement of method.
2. Has the questionnaire been well designed?
3. Has the interviewing been adequately and reliably done?
4. Has the best sampling plan been followed or has the best experimental design been used?
5. Was there adequate supervision and control over the editing, coding, and tabulating?
6. Have the conclusions been drawn in a logical and forthright manner?

Problems in the Research Process

Although the foregoing discussion presented the research process in a simplified framework, this does not mean that conducting research is a simple task. There are many problems and difficulties that must be overcome if a research study is to be of value. For example, consider the difficulties in one type of marketing research, *test marketing.*

The major goal of most test marketing is to measure new product sales on a limited basis where competitive retaliation and other factors are allowed to operate freely. In this way, future sales potential can be estimated. Test market research is a vital element in new product marketing. Listed below are a number of problem areas that can invalidate test market study results.[8]

1. Representative test areas are improperly selected from the standpoint of size, geographical location, population characteristics, and promotional facilities.
2. Sample size and design are incorrectly formulated because of ignorance, budget constraints, or an improper understanding of the test problem.

[8] For a discussion of some general problems in marketing research, see Alan G. Sawyer and J. Paul Peter, "The Significance of Statistical Significance Testing in Marketing Research," *Journal of Marketing Research,* May 1983, pp. 122–33

3. Pretest measurements of competitive brand's sales are not made, which means that the researcher has no realistic base to use for comparison purposes.
4. Attempts are not made to control the cooperation and support of test stores. Consequently, certain package sizes might not be carried or pricing policies might not be adhered to.
5. Test market products are overadvertised or overpromoted during the test.
6. The full effect of such sales-influencing factors as sales force, season, weather conditions, competitive retaliation, shelf space, and so forth are not fully evaluated.
7. Market test periods are too short to determine whether the product is fully accepted by consumers or only tried on a limited basis.

HIGHLIGHT 2-5
Techniques of Collecting Survey Data

Personal Interview	*Mail*	*Telephone*
Advantages		
Most flexible means of obtaining data. Identity of respondent known. Nonresponse generally very low. Distribution of sample controllable in all respects.	Wider and more representative distribution of sample possible. No field staff. Cost per questionnaire relatively low. People may be more frank on certain issues (e.g., sex). No interviewer bias; answers in respondent's own words. Respondent can answer at his or her leisure, has time to "think things over." Certain segments of population more easily approachable.	Representative and wider distribution of sample possible. No field staff. Cost per response relatively low. Control over interviewer bias easier; supervisor present essentially at interview. Quick way of obtaining information. Nonresponse generally very low. Callbacks simple and economical.

HIGHLIGHT 2–5 (*concluded*)

Personal Interview	*Mail*	*Telephone*
Disadvantages		
Likely to be most expensive of all. Headaches of interviewer supervision and control. Dangers of interviewer bias and cheating.	Bias due to nonresponse often indeterminate. Control over questionnaire may be lost. Interpretation of omissions difficult. Cost per return may be high if nonresponse very large. Certain questions, such as extensive probes, cannot be asked. Only those interested in the subject may reply. Not always clear who replies. Certain segments of population not approachable (e.g., illiterates). Likely to be slowest of all.	Interview period not likely to exceed five minutes. Questions must be short and to the point; probes difficult to handle. Certain types of questions cannot be used. Nontelephone owners as well as those without listed numbers cannot be reached.

Similar problems could be listed for almost any type of marketing research. However, the important point to be recognized is that careful planning, coordination, and control are imperative if the research study is to accomplish its objective.

CONCLUSION

This chapter has been concerned with marketing decision support systems and with marketing research. In terms of marketing decision support systems, one of the major reasons for increased interest has been the rapid growth in information-handling technology. However, as we have seen in this chapter, the study of MDSSs is not the study of computers. The study of MDSSs is part of a much larger task: the study of more efficient methods for marketing management decision making.

In terms of marketing research, this chapter has emphasized the importance of research as an aid for marketing decision making. Just as planning is integral for marketing management, the research plan is critical for marketing research. A research plan not only formalizes the objectives of the study but also details the tasks and responsibilities of the research team as well as cost estimates. Conducting research is a matter of following the research plan and reporting the events of each stage clearly and unambiguously. Finally, emphasis was placed on the extreme care that must be taken to avoid research difficulties and pitfalls.

Additional Readings

Boyd, Harper W., Jr.; Ralph Westfall; and Stanley F. Stasch. *Marketing Research: Text and Cases*. 7th ed. Homewood, Ill.: Richard D. Irwin, 1989.

Churchill, Gilbert A., Jr. *Marketing Research: Methodological Foundations*. 4th ed. Hinsdale, Ill.: Dryden Press, 1987.

________. *Basic Marketing Research*. Hinsdale, Ill.: Dryden Press, 1988.

Kinnear, T. C., and J. R. Taylor. *Marketing Research: An Applied Approach*. 2nd ed. New York: McGraw-Hill, 1983.

Lehmann, Donald R. *Marketing Research and Analysis*. 3rd ed. Homewood, Ill.: Richard D. Irwin, 1989.

Tull, Donald S., and Del I. Hawkins. *Marketing Research: Measurement and Method*. 3rd ed. New York: Macmillan, 1987.

Chapter 3

Consumer Behavior

The marketing concept emphasizes that profitable marketing begins with the discovery and understanding of consumer needs and then develops a marketing mix to satisfy these needs. Thus, an understanding of consumers and their needs and purchasing behavior is integral to successful marketing.

Unfortunately, there is no single theory of consumer behavior that can totally explain why consumers behave as they do. Instead, there are numerous theories, models, and concepts making up the field. In addition, the majority of these notions have been borrowed from a variety of other disciplines, such as sociology, psychology, social psychology, and economics, and must be integrated to understand consumer behavior.

In this chapter some of the many influences on consumer behavior will be examined in terms of the buying process. The reader may wish to examine Figure 3–1 closely, since it provides the basis for this discussion.

The chapter will proceed by first examining the buying process and then discussing the group, product class, and situational influences on this process.

THE BUYING PROCESS

The buying process can be viewed as a series of five stages: felt need, alternative search, alternative evaluation, purchase decision, and postpurchase feelings. In this section, each of these stages will be discussed. It should be noted at the outset that this is a general model for depicting a logical sequence of buying behavior. Clearly, individuals will vary from this model because of personal differences in such

FIGURE 3-1 An Overview of the Buying Process

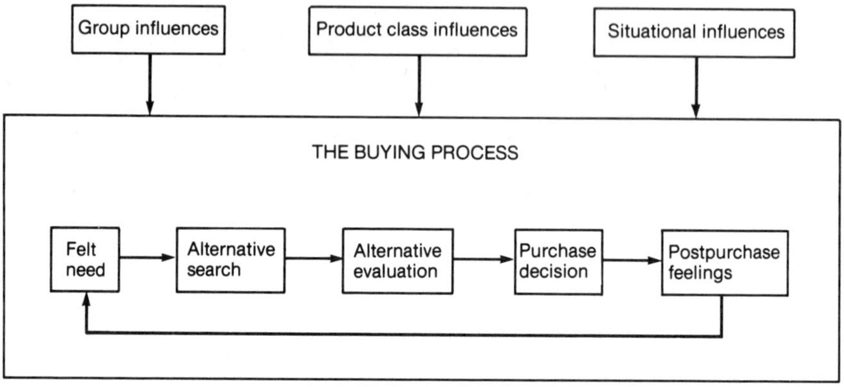

things as personality, self-concept, subjective perceptions of information, the product, and the purchasing situation. However, the model provides a useful framework for organizing our discussion of consumer behavior.

Felt Need

The starting point for most behavior is the recognition of an unsatisfied need. It is no different for consumer behavior, since the purchase and use of products and services are one means of satisfying needs. A need can be activated either internally (e.g., a person feels hungry) or externally (as when a person sees a McDonald's sign and then feels hungry).

It is the task of marketing management to discover the needs that operate in a particular market or the needs that a particular product can satisfy. This includes not only being aware of currently operating needs (i.e., what buyers are really seeking when they purchase a particular product) but also identifying insufficiently developed or unsatisfied needs (i.e., what needs consumers have that current market offerings are not fully satisfying). Thus, an understanding of basic human needs is important for adapting marketing strategies to the consumer.

A widely adopted classification of needs was developed some years ago by A. H. Maslow.[1] The basic tenets of this framework are that:

[1] A. H. Maslow, *Motivation and Personality* (New York: Harper & Row, 1954). This book is one of the most cited references in the entire psychological literature.

HIGHLIGHT 3-1
How Much Do American Consumers Consume?

It may be difficult for many people to appreciate how much Americans purchase and consume. For example, in an average day, Americans . . .

- Eat 5.8 million pounds of chocolate candy.
- Use 550,000 pounds of toothpaste and gargle 69,000 gallons of mouthwash.
- Buy 190,000 watches, about half of which are for gifts.
- Eat 228,000 bushels of onions.
- Buy 120,000 new radios and 50,000 new television sets.
- Eat 47 million hot dogs.
- Buy almost 5 million books.
- Spend $200,000 to buy roller skates.
- Spend $40 million for automobile repairs and replacements caused by rust.
- Wear more than 3 million pounds of rubber off their tires, enough to make 250,000 new tires.
- Buy 38,000 Ken and Barbie dolls.
- Buy about 35 million paper clips and 4 million eraser-tipped wooden pencils.
- Buy 12,000 new refrigerators and 10,000 new kitchen ranges.
- And last, but not least, snap up 82,000 mousetraps.

Source: Excerpted from Tom Parker, *In One Day* (Boston: Houghton Mifflin, 1984).

1. Human beings are wanting animals whose needs depend on what they already have. Only needs not yet satisfied can influence behavior; a satisfied need is not a motivator.
2. Human needs are arranged in a hierarchy of importance. Once one need is satisfied, another higher level need emerges and demands satisfaction.

Maslow hypothesized five classes of needs. In the order of their importance, these are: (1) physiological, (2) safety, (3) belongingness, (4) esteem, (5) self-actualization. He placed them in a formal framework, referred to as the *hierarchy of needs,* because of the different levels of importance indicated. This framework is presented in Figure 3–2. Less described, and hence, not as well known are the cognitive and aesthetic needs hypothesized by Maslow. Cognitive needs relate to the need to know or to understand, and aesthetic needs are satisfied by moving from ugliness to beauty. Maslow did not include them in the formal hierarchy framework.

Maslow states that, if all a person's needs are unsatisfied at a

FIGURE 3-2 Hierarchy of Needs

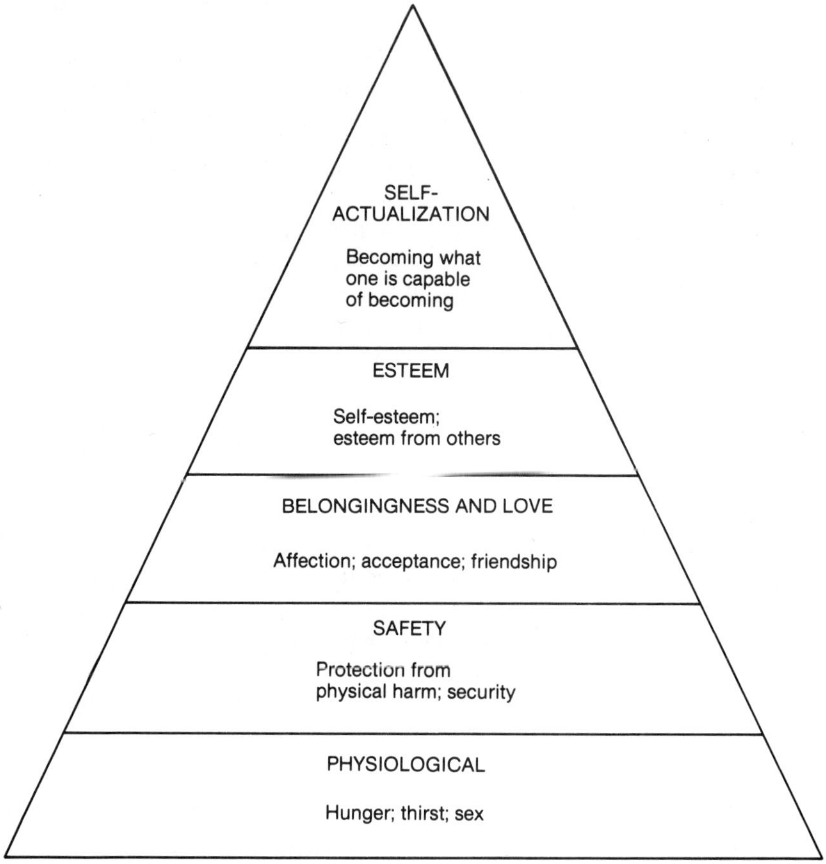

particular time, satisfaction of the most prepotent needs will be more pressing than the others. Those that come first must be satisfied before a higher-level need comes into play, and only when they are satisfied are the next ones in line significant. Each level will now be briefly examined.

Physiological Needs. This category consists of the primary needs of the human body, such as food, water, and sex. Physiological needs will dominate when all needs are unsatisfied. In such a case, none of the other needs will serve as a basis for motivation.

Safety Needs. With the physiological needs met, the next higher level assumes importance. Safety needs consist of such things as protection from physical harm, ill health, economic disaster, and avoidance of the unexpected.

Belongingness and Love Needs. These needs are related to the social and gregarious nature of humans and the need for companionship. This level in the hierarchy is the point of departure from the physical or quasiphysical needs of the two previous levels. Nonsatisfaction of this level of need may affect the mental health of the individual.

Esteem Needs. These needs consist of both the need for the self-awareness of importance to others (self-esteem) and actual esteem from others. Satisfaction of these needs leads to a feeling of self-confidence and prestige.

Self-Actualization Needs. Maslow defines this need as the "desire to become more and more what one is, to become everything one is capable of becoming."[2] This means that the individual will fully realize the potentialities of given talents and capabilities. Maslow assumes that satisfaction of these needs is only possible after the satisfaction of all the needs lower in the hierarchy.

While the hierarchy arrangement of Maslow presents a convenient explanation, it is probably more realistic to assume that the various need categories overlap. Thus, in affluent societies, many products may satisfy more than one of these needs. For example, gourmet foods may satisfy both the basic physiological need of hunger as well as esteem and status needs for those who serve gourmet foods to their guests.

Alternative Search

Once a need is recognized, the individual then searches for alternatives for satisfying the need.[3] There are five basic sources from which the individual can collect information for a particular purchase decision.

---

[2] Ibid., p. 92.

[3] For further discussion of the search process, see William L. Moore and Donald R. Lehmann, "Individual Differences in Search Behavior for a Nondurable," *Journal of Consumer Research,* December 1980, pp. 296–307; Geoffrey C. Kiel and Roger A. Layton, "Dimensions of Consumer Information Seeking Behavior," *Journal of Marketing Research,* May 1981, pp. 233–39; Howard Beales, Michael B. Mazis, Steven C. Salop, and Richard Staelin, "Consumer Search and Public Policy," *Journal of Consumer Research,* June 1981, pp. 11–22; Calvin P. Duncan and Richard W. Olshavsky, "External Search: The Role of Consumer Beliefs," *Journal of Marketing Research,* February 1982, pp. 32–43; John A. Carlson and Robert J. Gieseke, "Price Search in a Product Market," *Journal of Consumer Research,* March 1983, pp. 357–65.

1. *Internal sources*. In most cases the individual has had some previous experience in dealing with a particular need. Thus, the individual will usually "search" through whatever stored information and experience is in his or her mind for dealing with the need. If a previously acceptable product for satisfying the need is remembered, the individual may purchase with little or no additional information search or evaluation. This is quite common for routine or habitual purchases.
2. *Group sources*. A common source of information for purchase decisions comes from communication with other people, such as family, friends, neighbors, and acquaintances. Generally, some of these (i.e., relevant others) are selected which the individual views as having particular expertise for the purchase decision. Although it may be quite difficult for the marketing manager to determine the exact nature of this source of information, group sources of information often are considered to be the most powerful influence on purchase decisions.
3. *Marketing sources*. Marketing sources of information include such factors as advertising, salespeople, dealers, packaging, and displays. Generally, this is the primary source of information about a particular product. These sources of information will be discussed in detail in the promotion chapters of this text.
4. *Public sources*. Public sources of information include publicity, such as a newspaper article about the product, and independent ratings of the product, such as *Consumer Reports*. Here product quality is a highly important marketing management consideration, since such articles and reports often discuss such features as dependability and service requirements.
5. *Experiential sources*. Experiential sources refer to handling, examining, and perhaps trying the product while shopping. This usually requires an actual shopping trip by the individual and may be the final source consulted before purchase.

Information collected from these sources is then processed by the consumer. However, the exact nature of how individuals process information to form evaluations of products is not fully understood. In general, information processing is viewed as a four-step process in which the individual is (1) exposed to information, (2) becomes attentive to the information, (3) understands the information, and (4) retains the information.[4]

---

[4] For further discussion of information processing, see J. Paul Peter and Jerry C. Olson, *Consumer Behavior: Marketing Strategy Perspectives* (Homewood, Ill.: Richard D. Irwin, 1987), chap. 3.

HIGHLIGHT 3–2
Determinants of the Extent of Information Search

Market environment:
—Number of alternatives.
—Complexity of alternatives.
—Marketing mix of alternatives.
—Stability of alternatives on the market (new alternatives).
—Information availability.

Situational variables:
—Time pressure.
—Social pressure (family, peer, boss).
—Financial pressure.
—Organizational procedures.
—Physical and mental condition.
—Ease of access to information sources.

Potential payoff/product importance:
—Price.
—Social visibility.
—Perceived risk.
—Difference among alternatives.
—Number of crucial attributes.
—Status of decision-making activity (in the family, organization, society).

Knowledge and experience:
—Stored knowledge.
—Usage rate of product.
—Previous information.
—Previous choices (number and identity).
—Satisfaction.

Individual differences:
—Ability.
—Training.
—Approach to problem solving (compulsiveness, open-mindedness, preplanning, innovativeness).
—Approach to search (enjoyment of shopping, sources of information, etc.).
—Involvement.
—Demographics (age, income, education, marital status, household size, social class, occupation).
—Personality/life style variables (self-confidence, etc.).

Conflict and conflict-resolution strategies

Source: William L. Moore and Donald R. Lehmann, "Individual Differences in Search Behavior for a Nondurable," *Journal of Consumer Research,* December 1980, p. 298.

Alternative Evaluation

During the process of collecting information or, in some cases, after information is acquired, the consumer then evaluates alternatives based on what has been learned. One approach to describing the evaluation process can be found in the logic of attitude modeling.[5] The basic logic can be described as follows:

1. The consumer has information about a number of brands in a product class.
2. The consumer perceives that at least some of the brands in a product class are viable alternatives for satisfying a felt need.
3. Each of these brands has a set of attributes (color, quality, size, and so forth).
4. A set of these attributes are relevant to the consumer, and the consumer perceives that different brands vary in terms of how much of each attribute they possess.
5. The brand that is perceived as offering the greatest number of desired attributes in the desired amounts and desired order will be the brand the consumer will like best.
6. The brand the consumer likes best is the brand the consumer will intend to purchase.

Purchase Decision

If no other factors intervene after the consumer has decided on the brand that is intended for purchase, the actual purchase is a common result of search and evaluation. Actually, a purchase involves many decisions, which include product type, brand, model, dealer selection, and method of payment, among other factors. In addition, rather than purchasing, the consumer may make a decision to modify, postpone, or avoid purchase based on an inhibitor to purchase, or a perceived risk.

Traditional risk theorists believe that consumers tend to make risk-minimizing decisions based on their *perceived* definition of the particular purchase. The perception of risk is based upon the possible consequences and uncertainties involved. Consequences may range from

---

[5] For further discussion of attitude modeling, see Richard J. Lutz, "Lessons Learned from a Decade of Multiattribute Attitude Research," in *Proceedings of the 11th Paul D. Converse Symposium,* ed. David M. Gardner and Frederick W. Winters (Chicago: American Marketing Association, 1982), pp. 107–23; Michael J. Ryan, "Behavioral Intention Formation: The Interdependency of Attitudinal and Social Influence Variables," *Journal of Consumer Research,* December 1982, pp. 263–78.

economic loss, to embarrassment if a new food product does not turn out well, to actual physical harm. Perceived risk may be either functional (related to financial and performance considerations) or psychosocial (related to whether the product will further one's self- or reference group image). The amount of risk a consumer perceives in a particular product depends on such things as the price of the product and whether other people will see the individual using the product.

The perceived risk literature emphasizes that consumers generally try to reduce risk in their decision making.[6] This can be done by either reducing the possible consequences or by reducing the uncertainty. The possible consequences of a purchase might be minimized by purchasing in small quantities or by lowering the individual's aspiration level to expect less in the way of results from the product. However, this cannot always be done. Thus, reducing risk by attempting to increase the certainty of the purchase outcome is the more widely used strategy. This can be done by seeking additional information regarding the proposed purchase. In general, the more information the consumer collects prior to purchase, the less likely postpurchase dissonance is to occur.

Postpurchase Feelings

In a general behavioral sense, if the individual finds that a certain response achieves a desired goal or satisfies a need, the success of this cue-response pattern will be remembered. The probability of responding in a like manner to the same or similar situation in the future is positively reinforced. In other words, the response has a higher probability of being repeated when the need and cue appear together again, and thus it can be said that learning has taken place. Frequent reinforcement increases the habit potential of the particular response. Likewise, if a response does not satisfy the need adequately, the probability that the same response will be repeated is reduced.

For some marketers this means that, if an individual finds a particular product fulfills the need for which it was purchased, then the probability is high that the product will be repurchased the next time the need arises. The firm's promotional efforts often act as the cue. If an individual repeatedly purchases a product with favorable results,

---

[6] Richard H. Evans, "Measuring Perceived Risk: A Replication and an Application of Equity Theory," in *Advances in Consumer Research,* vol. 9, ed. Andrew Mitchell (Chicago: Association for Consumer Research, 1982), pp. 550–55; Terence A. Shimp and William O. Bearden, "Warranty and Other Extrinsic Cue Effects on Consumers' Risk Perceptions," *Journal of Consumer Research,* June 1982, pp. 38–46.

then loyalty may result toward the particular product or brand. This loyalty can result in habitual purchases, and such habits are often extremely difficult for competing firms to alter.

Although many studies in the area of buyer behavior center around the buyer's attitudes, motives, and behavior before and during the purchase decision, emphasis has also been given to study of behavior after the purchase. Specifically, studies have been undertaken to investigate postpurchase dissonance, as well as postpurchase satisfaction.[7]

The occurrence of postdecision dissonance is related to the concept of cognitive dissonance. This theory states that there is often a lack of consistency or harmony among an individual's various cognitions, or attitudes and beliefs, after a decision has been made—that is, the individual has doubts and second thoughts about the choice made. Further, it is more likely that the intensity of the anxiety will be greater when any of the following conditions exist:

1. The decision is an important one psychologically or financially, or both.
2. There are a number of forgone alternatives.
3. The forgone alternatives have many favorable features.

These factors can relate to many buying decisions. For example, postpurchase dissonance might be expected to be present among many purchasers of such products as automobiles, major appliances, and homes. In these cases, the decision to purchase is usually an important one both financially and psychologically, and there are usually a number of favorable alternatives available.

When dissonance occurs after a decision has been made, the individual may attempt to reduce it by one or more of the following methods:

1. By seeking information that supports the wisdom of the decision.
2. By perceiving information in a way to support the decision.
3. By changing attitudes to a less favorable view of the forgone alternatives.
4. By avoiding the importance of the negative aspects of the decision and enhancing the positive elements.

Dissonance could, of course, be reduced by admitting that a mistake had been made. However, most individuals are reluctant to admit that

---

[7] For further discussion of consumer satisfaction, see Gilbert A. Churchill, Jr., and Carol Suprenant, "An Investigation into the Determinants of Consumer Satisfaction," *Journal of Marketing Research,* November 1982, pp. 491–504; William O. Bearden and Jesse E. Teel, "Selected Determinants of Consumer Satisfaction and Complaint Reports," *Journal of Marketing Research,* February 1983, pp. 21–28.

a wrong decision has been made. Thus, it is more likely that a person will seek out supportive information to reduce dissonance.

These findings have much relevance for the marketer. In a buying situation, when a purchaser becomes dissonant it is reasonable to predict such a person would be highly receptive to advertising and sales promotion that supports the purchase decision. Such communication presents favorable aspects of the product and can be useful in reinforcing the buyer's wish to believe that a wise purchase decision was made. For example, purchasers of major appliances or automobiles might be given a phone call or sent a letter reassuring them that they have made a wise purchase.[8]

GROUP INFLUENCES ON CONSUMER BEHAVIOR

Behavioral scientists have become increasingly aware of the powerful effects of the social environment and personal interactions on human behavior. In terms of consumer behavior, culture, social class, and reference group, influences have been related to purchase and consumption decisions. It should be noted that these influences can have both direct and indirect effects on the buying process. By direct effects we mean direct communication between the individual and other members of society concerning a particular purchase decision. By indirect effects we mean the influence of society on an individual's basic values and attitudes as well as the important role that groups play in structuring an individual's personality.

Cultural and Subcultural Influences

Culture is one of the most basic influences on an individual's needs, wants, and behavior, since all facets of life are carried out against the background of the society in which an individual lives. Cultural antecedents affect everyday behavior, and there is empirical support for the notion that culture is a determinant of certain aspects of consumer behavior.[9]

Cultural values are transmitted through three basic organizations: the family, religious organizations, and educational institutions, and,

---

[8] For additional discussion of postpurchase feelings and behavior, see Mary C. Gilly and Betsy D. Gelb, "Post-Purchase Consumer Processes and the Complaining Consumer," *Journal of Consumer Research,* December 1982, pp. 323–28.

[9] For a discussion of some major cultural changes, see John Naisbitt, *Megatrends: Ten New Directions Transforming Our Lives* (New York: Warner Books, 1984).

HIGHLIGHT 3–3
A Summary of American Cultural Values

Value	*General Features*	*Relevance to Consumer Behavior and Marketing Management*
1. Achievement and success	Hard work is good; success flows from hard work.	Acts as a justification for acquisition of goods ("You deserve it").
2. Activity	Keeping busy is healthy and natural.	Stimulates interest in products that are time-savers and enhance leisure-time activities.
3. Efficiency and practicality	Admiration of things that solve problems (e.g., save time and effort).	Stimulates purchase of products that function well and save time.
4. Progress	People can improve themselves; tomorrow should be better.	Stimulates desire for new products that fulfill unsatisfied needs; acceptance of products that claim to be "new" or "improved."
5. Material comfort	"The good life."	Fosters acceptance of convenience and luxury products that make life more enjoyable.
6. Individualism	Being one's self (e.g., self-reliance, self-interest, and self-esteem.	Stimulates acceptance of customized or unique products that enable a person to "express his or her own personality."
7. Freedom	Freedom of choice.	Fosters interest in wide product lines and differentiated products.
8. External conformity	Uniformity of observable behavior; desire to be accepted.	Stimulates interest in products that are used or owned by others in the same social group.

HIGHLIGHT 3–3 ***(concluded)***

Value	*General Features*	*Relevance to Consumer Behavior and Marketing Management*
9. Humanitarianism	Caring for others, particularly the underdog.	Stimulates patronage of firms that compete with market leaders.
10. Youthfulness	A state of mind that stresses being young at heart or appearing young.	Stimulates acceptance of products that provide the illusion of maintaining or fostering youth.
11. Fitness and health	Caring about one's body, including the desire to be physically fit and healthy	Stimulates acceptance of food products, activities, and equipment perceived to maintain or increase physical fitness.

Source: Leon G. Schiffman and Leslie Kanuck, *Consumer Behavior,* 2nd ed. (Englewood Cliffs, N.J.: Prentice-Hall, 1987), p. 506.

in today's society, educational institutions are playing an increasingly greater role in this regard. Marketing managers should adapt the marketing mix to cultural values and constantly monitor value changes and differences in both domestic and international markets. To illustrate, one of the changing values in America is the increasing emphasis on achievement and career success. This change in values has been recognized by many business firms that have expanded their emphasis on time-saving, convenience-oriented products.

In a nation as large as the United States the population is bound to lose a significant amount of its homogeneity, and thus subcultures arise. In other words, there are subcultures in the American culture where people have more frequent interactions than with the population at large and thus tend to think and act alike in some respects. Subcultures are based on such things as geographic areas, religions, nationalities, ethnic groups, and age. Many subcultural barriers are decreasing because of mass communication, mass transit, and a decline in the influence of religious values. However, age groups, such as the teen market, baby boomers, and the mature market, have become increasingly important for marketing strategy. For example, since baby boomers (those born between 1946 and 1962) make up about a third of the U.S. population and soon will account for about half of discretionary spending, many marketers are repositioning products to serve them. Snickers candy bars, for instance, used to be promoted to children as a treat but are now promoted to adults as a wholesome, between-meals snack.

Social Class

While one likes to think of America as a land of equality, a class structure does exist. Social classes develop on the basis of such things as wealth, skill, and power. The single best indicator of social class is occupation. However, interest at this point is in the influence of social class on the individual's behavior. What is important here is that different social classes tend to have different attitudinal configurations and values, which influence the behavior of individual members. Figure 3–3 presents a social class hierarchy developed specifically for marketing analysis and describes some of these important differences in attitudes and values.

For the marketing manager, social class offers some insights into consumer behavior and is potentially useful as a market segmentation variable. However, there is considerable controversy whether social class is superior to income for the purpose of market segmentation.[10]

Reference Groups

Groups that an individual looks to (uses as a reference) when forming attitudes and opinions are described as reference groups.[11] Primary reference groups include family and close friends, while secondary reference groups include fraternal organizations and professional associations. A buyer may also consult a single individual about various

---

[10] See Charles M. Schaninger, "Social Class versus Income Revisited: An Empirical Investigation," *Journal of Marketing Research,* May 1981, pp. 192–208.

[11] See William O. Bearden and Michael J. Etzel, "Reference Group Influence on Product and Brand Purchase Decisions," *Journal of Consumer Research,* September 1982, pp. 183–94; Peter H. Reingen, Brian L. Foster, Jacqueline Johnson Brown, and Stephen B. Seidman, "Brand Congruence in Interpersonal Relations: A Social Network Analysis," *Journal of Consumer Research,* December 1984, pp. 771–83.

FIGURE 3–3 Social Class Groups for Marketing Analysis

Upper Americans (14 percent of population). This group consists of the upper-upper, lower-upper, and upper-middle classes. They have common goals and are differentiated mainly by income. This group has many different lifestyles, which might be labeled postpreppy, conventional, intellectual, and political, among others. The class remains the segment of our society in which quality merchandise is most prized, special attention is paid to prestige brands, and the self-image ideal is "spending with good taste." Self-expression is more prized than in previous generations, and neighborhood remains important. Depending on income and priorities, theater, books, investment in art, European travel, household help, club memberships for tennis, golf, and swimming, and prestige schooling for children remain high consumption priorities.

Middle-class (32 percent of population). These consumers definitely want to "do the right thing" and buy "what's popular." They have always been concerned with fashion and following recommendations of "experts" in print media. Increased earnings result in better living, which means a "nicer neighborhood on the better side of town with good schools." It also means spending more on "worthwhile experiences" for children, including winter ski trips, college educations, and shopping for better brands of clothes at more expensive stores. Appearance of home is important, because guests may visit and pass judgment. This group emulates upper Americans, which distinguishes it from the working class. It also enjoys trips to Las Vegas and physical activity. Deferred gratification may still be an ideal, but it is not often practiced.

Working-class (38 percent of population). Working-class Americans are "family folk" depending heavily on relatives for economic and emotional support (e.g., tips on job opportunities, advice on purchases, help in times of trouble). The emphasis on family ties is only one sign of how much more limited and different working-class horizons are socially, psychologically, and geographically compared to those of the middle class. In almost every respect, a parochial view characterizes this blue-collar world. This group has changed little in values and behaviors in spite of rising incomes in some cases. For them, "keeping up with the times" focuses on the mechanical and recreational, and thus, ease of labor and leisure is what they continue to pursue.

Lower Americans (16 percent of population). The men and women of lower America are no exception to the rule that diversities and uniformities in values and consumption goals are to be found at each social level. Some members of this world, as has been publicized, are prone to every form of instant gratification known to humankind when the money is available. But others are dedicated to resisting worldly temptations as they struggle toward what some believe will be a "heavenly reward" for their earthly sacrifices.

Source: Excerpted from Richard P. Coleman, "The Continuing Significance of Social Class to Marketing," *Journal of Consumer Research,* December 1983, pp. 265–80.

decisions and this individual would be considered a reference individual.

A person normally has several reference groups or reference individuals for various subjects or different decisions. For example, a woman may have one reference group when she is purchasing a car and a different reference group for lingerie. In other words, the nature of the product and the role the individual is playing during the purchasing process influences which reference group will be consulted. Reference group influence is generally considered to be stronger for products that are "public" or conspicuous—that is, products that other people see the individual using such as clothes or automobiles.

As noted, the family is generally recognized to be an important reference group, and it has been suggested that the household, rather than the individual, is the relevant unit for studying consumer behavior.[12] This is because within a household the purchaser of goods and services is not always the user of these goods and services. Thus, it is important for marketing managers to determine not only who makes the actual purchase but also who makes the decision to purchase. In addition, it has been recognized that the needs, income, assets, debts, and expenditure patterns change over the course of what is called the *family life cycle*. Basic stages in the family life cycle include:

1. Bachelor stage: young single people not living at home.
2. Newly married couples: young, no children.
3. Full nest I: young married couples with youngest child under six.
4. Full nest II: young married couples with youngest child six or over.
5. Full nest III: older married couples with dependent children.
6. Empty nest I: older married couples, no children living with them, household head(s) in labor force.
7. Empty nest II: older married couples, no children living at home, household(s) retired.
8. Solitary survivor in labor force.
9. Solitary survivor, retired.

Because the life cycle combines trends in earning power with demands placed on income, it is a useful way of classifying and segmenting individuals and families.[13]

---

[12] See Rosann L. Spiro, "Persuasion in Family Decision Making," *Journal of Consumer Research,* March 1983, pp. 393–402.

[13] See Janet Wagner and Sherman Hanna, "The Effectiveness of Family Life Cycle Variables in Consumer Expenditure Research," *Journal of Consumer Research,* December 1983, pp. 281–91.

HIGHLIGHT 3–4
Some Common Verbal Tools Used By Reference Groups

Below are a number of verbal tools used by reference groups to influence consumer behavior. If the statements listed below were made to you by a close friend or someone you admired or respected, do you think that they might change your behavior?

Tools	*Definitions*	*Examples*
Reporting	Talking about preferences and behaviors.	"All of us drink Budweiser."
Recommendations	Suggesting appropriate behaviors.	"You should get a Schwinn High Sierra."
Invitations	Asking for participation in events.	"Do you want to go to the Lionel Richie concert with us?"
Requests	Asking for behavior performance.	"Would you run down to the corner and get me a newspaper?"
Prompts	Suggesting desired behaviors.	"It sure would be nice if someone would buy us a pizza!"
Commands	Telling someone what to do.	"Get me some Kleenex, and be quick about it!"
Promises	Offering a reward for performing a behavior.	"If you'll go to Penney's with me, I'll take you to lunch later."
Coercion	Threatening to punish for inappropriate behavior.	"If you don't shut up, I'm going to stuff a sock in your mouth!"
Criticism	Saying something negative about a behavior.	"Quit hassling the salesclerk. You're acting like a jerk."
Compliments	Saying something positive about a behavior.	"You really know how to shop. I bet you got every bargain in the store!"
Teasing	Good-natured bantering about behavior or appearance.	"Man, that shirt makes you look like Bozo the clown!"

Source: J. Paul Peter and Jerry C. Olson, *Consumer Behavior: Marketing Strategy Perspectives* (Homewood, Ill.: Richard D. Irwin, 1987), p. 440.

PRODUCT CLASS INFLUENCES

The nature of the product class selected by the consumer to satisfy an aroused need plays an important role in the decision-making process. Basically, the nature of the product class and the brands within it determine (1) the amount of information the consumer will require before making a decision and consequently (2) the time it takes to move through the buying process. In general, product classes in which there are many alternatives that are expensive, complex, or new will require the consumer to collect more information and take longer to make a purchase decision. As illustration, buying an automobile is probably one of the most difficult purchase decisions most consumers make. An automobile is expensive, complex, and there are many new styles and models to choose from. Such a decision will usually require extensive information search and time before a decision is made.

A second possibility is referred to as limited decision making. For these purchases a lesser amount of information is collected and less time is devoted to shopping. For example, in purchasing a new pair of jeans the consumer may already have considerable experience, and price and complexity are somewhat limited. However, since there are many alternative styles and brands, some information processing and decision making is generally needed.

Finally, some product classes require what is called "routinized decision making." For these product classes, such as candy bars or other food products, the consumer has faced the decision many times before and has found an acceptable alternative. Thus, little or no information is collected and the consumer purchases in a habitual, automatic manner.

SITUATIONAL INFLUENCES

Situational influences can be defined as "all those factors particular to a time and place of observation which do not follow from a knowledge of personal and stimulus attributes and which have a demonstrable and systematic effect on current behavior."[14] In terms of purchasing

[14] Russell W. Belk, "An Exploratory Assessment of Situational Effects in Buyer Behavior," *Journal of Marketing Research,* May 1974, pp. 156–63. Also see Joseph A. Cote, Jr., "Situational Variables in Consumer Research: A Review," working paper (Washington State University, 1985).

situations, five groups of situational influences have been identified.[15] These influences may be perceived either consciously or subconsciously and may have considerable effect on product and brand choice.

1. *Physical surroundings* are the most readily apparent features of a situation. These features include geographical and institutional location, decor, sounds, aromas, lighting, weather, and visible configurations of merchandise or other material surrounding the stimulas object.
2. *Social surroundings* provide additional depth to a description of a situation. Other persons present, their characteristics, their apparent roles, and interpersonal interactions are potentially relevant examples.
3. *Temporal perspective* is a dimension of situations that may be specified in units ranging from time of day to season of the year. Time also may be measured relative to some past or future event for the situational participant. This allows such conceptions as time since last purchase, time since or until meals or paydays, and time constraints imposed by prior or standing commitments.
4. *Task definition* features of a situation include an intent or requirement to select, shop for, or obtain information about a general or specific purchase. In addition, task may reflect different buyer and user roles anticipated by the individual. For instance, a person shopping for a small appliance as a wedding gift for a friend is in a different situation than when shopping for a small appliance for personal use.
5. *Antecedent states* make up a final feature that characterizes a situation. These are momentary moods (such as acute anxiety, pleasantness, hostility, and excitation) or momentary conditions (such as cash on hand, fatigue, and illness) rather than chronic individual traits. These conditions are further stipulated to be immediately antecedent to the current situation to distinguish the states the individual brings to the situation from states of the individual resulting from the situation. For instance, people may select a certain motion picture because they feel depressed (an antecedent state and a part of the choice situation), but the fact that the movie causes them to feel happier is a response to the consumption situation. This altered state then may become antecedent for behavior in

---

[15] Russell W. Belk, "Situational Variables and Consumer Behavior," *Journal of Consumer Research,* December 1975, pp. 156–64. Also see Jacob Hornik, "Situational Effects on the Consumption of Time," *Journal of Marketing,* Fall 1982, pp. 44–55.

the next choice situation encountered, such as passing a street vendor on the way out of the theater.

CONCLUSION

The purpose of this chapter was to present an overview of consumer behavior in terms of an analysis of the buying process. The buying process is viewed as a series of five stages: felt need, alternative search, alternative evaluation, purchase decision, and postpurchase feelings. This process is influenced by group, product class, and situational factors. Clearly, the marketing manager must understand the buying process to formulate effective marketing strategies.

Appendix Selected Consumer Behavior Data Sources

1. **Demographic information:**
   U.S. Census of Population.
   Marketing Information Guide.
   A Guide to Consumer Markets.
   State and city governments.
   Media (newspapers, magazines, television, and radio stations) make demographic data about their readers or audiences available.
2. **Consumer Research Findings:**
   Journal of Consumer Research
   Journal of Advertising Research
   Journal of Marketing
   Journal of Consumer Marketing
   Journal of Marketing Research
   Journal of Applied Psychology
   Journal of Advertising
   Advances in Consumer Research
3. **Marketing Applications:**
   Advertising Age
   Nation's Business
   Marketing Communications
   Fortune
   Sales Management
   Forbes
   Business Week
   Industry and trade magazines

Additional Readings

Assael, Henry. *Consumer Behavior and Marketing Action.* 3rd ed. Boston: Kent Publishing, 1987.

Engel, James F.; Roger D. Blackwell; and Paul W. Miniard. *Consumer Behavior.* 5th ed. Hinsdale, Ill.: Dryden Press, 1986.

Hawkins, Del; Kenneth A. Coney; and Roger Best, Jr. *Consumer Behavior: Implications for Marketing Strategy.* 3rd ed. Plano, Tex.: Business Publications, 1986.

Mohen, John C. *Consumer Behavior.* New York: Macmillan Publishing Co., 1987.

Peter, J. Paul and Jerry C. Olson. *Consumer Behavior: Marketing Strategy Perspectives.* Homewood, Ill.: Richard D. Irwin, 1987.

Robertson, Thomas S.; Joan Zielinski; and Scott Ward. *Consumer Behavior.* Glenview, Ill.: Scott Foresman, 1984.

Schiffman, Leon G., and Leslie Kanuck. *Consumer Behavior.* 3rd ed. Englewood Cliffs, N.J.: Prentice-Hall, 1987.

Wilkie, William L. *Consumer Behavior.* New York: John Wiley & Sons, 1986.

Chapter 4

Industrial Buyer Behavior

In recent years the individuals who purchase goods and services for organizations and institutions, industrial buyers, have been examined from a behavioral science perspective. Traditionally, the industrial buying situation was usually described as more "rational" or economic in nature than consumer buying. The implicit assumption was that the psychosocial factors operating in consumer buying situations were not present or at least did not significantly influence the industrial buyer. This viewpoint has changed over the years as marketers have come to realize that, while industrial and institutional markets are composed of organizations of many types, sales are not made to organizations, sales are made to individuals (or groups of individuals) within organizations. Thus, in addition to economic factors, behavior influences have been recognized as important influences on industrial purchasing.

The purpose of this chapter is to examine the industrial buying process and the factors which influence it. Figure 4-1 provides the framework for the discussion in this chapter. It presents a model of the industrial buying process.

PRODUCT INFLUENCES ON INDUSTRIAL BUYING

A major consideration that affects the industrial buying process is the nature of the product itself. Such factors as the price, riskiness, and technical complexity of the product affect the process in three ways. First, they affect how long it will take for the firm to make a purchasing decision. Second, they have an effect on how many individuals will be involved in the purchasing process. Last, these factors may affect whether organizational or behavioral influences play the major role in the purchasing process.

FIGURE 4–1 A Simplified Model of the Industrial Buying Process

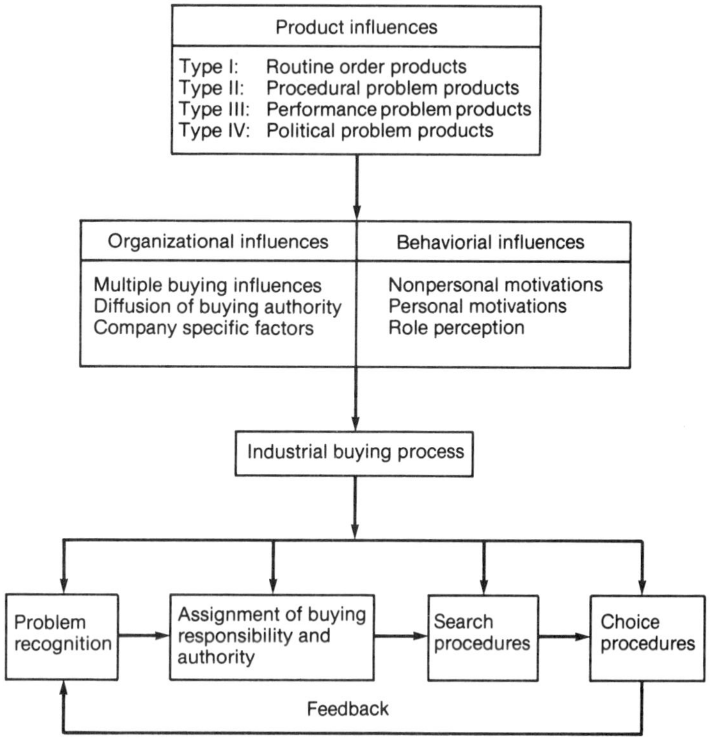

A useful classification for examining product influences was developed by Professors Lehmann and O'Shaughnessy.[1] In their approach, products are classified on the basis of problems inherent in their adoption. They identify four basic types:

Type 1: Routine order products. A Type I product is frequently ordered and used. There is no problem in learning how to use such products, nor is there any question about whether the product will do the job. In short, this type of product is expected to cause no significant problems in use.

[1] Donald R. Lehmann and John O'Shaughnessy, "Difference in Attribute Importance for Different Industrial Products," *Journal of Marketing,* April 1974, pp. 36–42. The reader should also see Thomas T. Semon, "A Cautionary Note on 'Differences in Attribute Importance for Different Industrial Products,'" *Journal of Marketing,* January 1975, p. 79; John O'Shaughnessy and Donald R. Lehmann, "A Reply to 'A Cautionary Note on Difference in Attribute Importance for Different Industrial Products,'" *Journal of Marketing,* January 1975, p. 80.

Type II: Procedural problem products. For Type II products, the buyer is also confident the product will do the job. However, problems are likely because personnel must be taught how to use the product. A buyer intent on minimizing problems associated with such a product will favor the supplier whose total offering is perceived as likely to reduce to a minimum the time and difficulty required to learn the product's operation.

Type III: Performance problem products. With Type III products, there is doubt whether the product will perform satisfactorily in the application for which it is being considered. Here the problem concerns the technical outcomes of using the product. There is likely to be no firm buying commitment until this problem has been resolved. It is argued that the buyer will favor the supplier who can offer appropriate technical service, providing a free trial period, and who appears flexible enough to adjust to the demands of the buyer's company.

Type IV: Political problem products. Type IV products give rise to "political" problems, because there is likely to be difficulty in reaching agreement among those affected if the product is adopted. "Political" problems occur when products necessitate large capital outlays, since there are always allocational rivals for funds. More frequently, political problems arise when the product is an input to several departments whose requirements may not be congruent.

There are two important implications of this classification for industrial marketers. First, in a study of purchasing agents in both the United States and Great Britain, it was found that different product attributes were rated as relatively more important, depending on the type of product. For example, the most important attributes for Type I products were the reliability of delivery and price; for Type II products, the most important attributes were technical service offered, ease of operation or use, and training offered by supplier; for Type III products, the technical service offered, flexibility of supplier, and product reliability were rated as most important; for Type IV products, the price, reputation of supplier, data on product reliability, reliability of delivery, and flexibility of supplier were rated as most important. Thus, marketing strategy for industrial products should be adapted to variations in buyer perceptions of problems in selection, introduction, and performance.

Second, the type of product may influence whether organizational or behavioral factors are relatively more important in the industrial purchasing process. For example, behavioral influences may decrease from Type I to Type IV products while organizational influences may increase. A routine order product is most probably the sole responsibility of the purchasing agent. Here organizational influences, such as joint decision making, are minimal, and the purchasing agent may well be more strongly influenced by behavioral influences, such as a personal friendship with the supplier. On the other hand, Type IV product decisions may require considerable joint decision making—

HIGHLIGHT 4-1
Typical Differences in Three Industrial Buying Situations

Buying Situations	*Consideration of New Alternatives*	*Frequency of Occurrence*	*Degree of Search*	*Total of Time*
1. Straight rebuy	None.	Most common.	Minimal.	Low.
2. Modified rebuy	Limited.	Occasional.	Moderate.	Medium.
3. New task	Maximum.	Least frequent.	Maximum.	High.

Source: Based on Rowland T. Moriarty, *Industrial Buyer Behavior: Concepts, Issues, and Applications* (Cambridge, Mass.: Marketing Science Institute, 1983), p. 19.

such as a purchasing committee—and thus be more influenced by organizational factors.

ORGANIZATIONAL INFLUENCES ON INDUSTRIAL BUYING

As was noted previously, sales are not made to organizations but to individuals within organizations. Thus, to gain an understanding of industrial buyers it is necessary to examine the environment in which they exist. Since they must function within an organizational setting, organizationally determined factors will influence their buying behavior.

Multiple Buying Influence or Joint Decision Making

This refers to situations where more than one person influences the purchase of a particular product. Such a situation is common in industrial buying. The problem for the seller is to determine which individuals hold the decisive influence for purchasing the product. Obviously, where several persons influence the decision, the marketer may need to use a variety of means to reach each individual or group, since each must be convinced of the product's worth before a buying decision is reached. Fortunately, it is often easy to find executives involved in purchasing in industrial companies because many such companies provide this type of information to their suppliers. They do this because it makes the suppliers more knowledgeable about their purchasing practices, and this saves time and effort by the company's purchasing people.

HIGHLIGHT 4–2

Major Differences between Organizational Buyers and Final Consumers

Differences in Purchases

1. Organizational buyers acquire for further production, use in operations, or resale to other consumers. Final consumers acquire only for personal, family, or household use.
2. Organizational buyers commonly purchase installations, raw materials, and semifinished materials. Final consumers rarely purchase these goods.
3. Organizational buyers purchase on the basis of specifications and technical data. Final consumers frequently purchase on the basis of description, fashion, and style.
4. Organizational buyers utilize multiple-buying and team-based decisions more often than final consumers.
5. Organizational buyers are more likely to apply value and vendor analysis.
6. Organizational buyers more commonly lease equipment.
7. Organizational buyers more frequently employ competitive bidding and negotiation.

Differences in the Market

1. The demand of organizational buyers is derived from the demand of final consumers.
2. The demand of organizational buyers is more subject to cyclical fluctuations than final-consumer demand.
3. Organizational buyers are fewer in number and more geographically concentrated than final consumers.
4. Organizational buyers often employ buying specialists.
5. The distribution channel for organizational buyers is shorter than for final consumers.
6. Organizational buyers may require special services.
7. Organizational buyers are more likely than final consumers to be able to make goods and services as alternatives to purchasing them.

Source: Adapted from Joel R. Evans and Barry Berman, *Marketing,* 3rd ed. (New York: Macmillan, 1987), p. 165.

Diffusion of Buying Authority

Placing the actual order is usually the responsibility of a purchasing agent, regardless of who influences the decision. Also, the purchasing department usually has the authority on standardized, established products that involve no great technical or commercial uncertainty.

However, because of the factor of multiple buying influence, more and more industrial marketers appear to be centering attention on the buying function, rather than on the specific individual who places the order. Apparently, they realize the functional responsibilities and job titles are not always perfectly matched and that buying responsibility is diffused throughout the firm. Thus, it is important to study how the buying function is discharged, rather than investigating the specific responsibilities of the purchasing agent or buyer. In some cases, the seller may be misled into thinking that the firm's purchasing power lies in one individual or department, when in reality the purchasing agent may be only one of a group of people who influence the purchasing decisions or may only be carrying out someone else's purchasing decision.

Company-Specific Factors

There are three primary organization-specific factors that influence the industrial purchasing process: company orientation, company size, and degree of centralization. First, if the company is technology oriented, it is likely to be dominated by the engineering people and the buying decisions will, in essence, be made by them. Similarly, if the company is production oriented, the buying decision will be made by the production personnel. Second, if the company is a large corporation, decision making will tend to be joint. Finally, the greater the degree of centralization, the less likely it is that the decisions will be joint. Thus, a privately owned small company with technology or production orientation will tend toward autonomous decision making, and a large-scale public corporation with considerable decentralization will tend to have greater joint decision making.[2]

BEHAVIORAL INFLUENCES ON INDUSTRIAL BUYING

Much has been written on the rationality of industrial buying decisions, and most psychologists agree that human behavior is "goal directed." That is, individuals establish behavior patterns to achieve some previously established goal. Therefore, to avoid making value judgments on the rationality or irrationality of an individual's behav-

---

[2] Jagdish N. Sheth, "A Model of Industrial Buyer Behavior," *Journal of Marketing,* October 1973, pp. 50–56. Also see Paul F. Anderson and Terry M. Chambers, "A Reward/Measurement Model of Organizational Buying Behavior," *Journal of Marketing,* Spring 1985, pp. 7–23.

ior, a two-way classification of motivations influencing the industrial buyer will be examined: nonpersonal motivations and personal motivations.

Nonpersonal Motivations

Traditionally, industrial purchases have been viewed from a normative standpoint as methodical, objective, preplanned undertakings. Thus, industrial buyers are viewed as basing purchase decisions on such factors as quality of product, cost of product, delivery reliability, technical ability and reliability of the supplier, information and market services provided by suppliers, general reputation of suppliers, geographical location of suppliers, and the suppliers' technical innovativeness. By considering these factors, industrial buyers are assumed to make their decisions in a way to maximize the profit obtained through their purchases.

Personal Motivations

Industrial buyers are, of course, subject to the same personal motives or motivational forces as other individuals. Although it is hoped that industrial buyers emphasize nonpersonal motives in their buying activities, it has been found that industrial buyers often are influenced by such personal factors as friendship, professional pride, fear and uncertainty (risk), and personal ambitions in their buying activities.

For example, professional pride often expresses itself through efforts to attain status in the firm. One way to achieve this might be to initiate or influence the purchase of goods that will demonstrate their value to the company. If new materials, equipment, or components result in cost savings or increased profits, the individuals initiating the changes have demonstrated their value to the company at the same time. Fear and uncertainty are strong motivational forces on industrial buyers, and reduction of risk is often important to them. This can have a strong influence on purchase behavior. Industrial marketers should understand the relative strength of personal gain versus risk-reducing motives and emphasize the more important motives when dealing with buyers.[3]

Thus, in examining industrial buyer motivations, it is necessary to

---

[3] See Christopher P. Puto, Wesley E. Patton III, and Ronald H. King, "Risk Handling Strategies in Industrial Vendor Selection Decisions," *Journal of Marketing,* Winter 1985, pp. 89–98.

HIGHLIGHT 4-3
An Operational View of the Industrial Buying Process

Although there is no single format dictating how industrial companies actually purchase goods and services, there is a relatively standard process that is followed in most cases. This process is as follows:

1. A department discovers or anticipates a problem in its operation that it believes can be overcome with the addition of a certain product or service.
2. The department head then draws up a requisition form describing the desired specifications he feels the product or service must have to solve his problem.
3. The requisition form is then sent by the department head to the firm's purchasing department.
4. Based on the specifications required, the purchasing department then conducts a search for qualified sources of supply.
5. Once sources have been located, proposals based on the specifications are solicited, received, and analyzed for price, delivery, service, and so on.
6. Proposals are then compared with the cost of producing the product in-house in a make or buy decision: if it is decided that the buying firm can produce the product more economically, the buying process for the product in question is terminated; however, if the inverse is true, the process continues.
7. A source or sources of supply is selected from those who have submitted proposals.
8. The order is placed, and copies of the purchase order are sent to the originating department, accounting, credit, and any other interested departments within the company.
9. After the product is shipped, received, and used, a follow-up with the originating department is conducted to determine that department's level of satisfaction or dissatisfaction with the purchased product in terms of the problem faced for which the product was purchased.

Although there are many variations of this process in actual operation, this is typical of the process by which industrial goods and services are purchased. It must be understood that in actual practice these are not separate steps, but, in fact, are often combined. Nevertheless, the process described in the preceding section is probably a good illustration of the operation of the industrial purchasing process.

Source: Robert W. Haas, *Industrial Marketing Management,* 2nd ed. (Boston: Kent Publishing, 1982), pp. 84–85.

HIGHLIGHT 4-4
The Industrial Buyer

The typical buyer is a man past middle-life, wrinkled, intelligent, cold, passive, noncommittal with eyes like a codfish, polite in contact, but at the same time, unresponsive, cool, calm, and damnably composed as a concrete post or a plaster of Paris cat; a human petrification with a heart of feldspar and without charm; or the friendly germ, minus bowels, passions, or a sense of humor. Happily they never reproduce, and all of them finally go to Hell.

Source: Louis E. Boone and Robert E. Stevens, "Emotional Motives in the Purchase of Industrial Goods: Historically Considered," *Purchasing,* August 1970, p. 48.

consider both personal and nonpersonal motivational forces and to recognize that the relative importance of each is not a fixed quantity. It will vary with the nature of the product, the climate within the organization, and the relative strength of the two forces in the particular buyer.

Role Perception

A final factor that influences industrial buyers is their own perception of their role. The manner in which individuals perform their roles depends on their perception of it, their commitment to what they believe is expected of their role, the "maturity" of the role type, and the extent to which the institution is committed to the role type.

Different industrial buyers will have different degrees of commitment to their buying role which will cause variations in role behavior from one buyer to the next. By commitment we mean willingness to perform their job according to the manner in which the organization expects them to perform. For example, some buyers seek to take charge in their role as buyer and have little commitment to company expectations. The implication for the industrial marketer is that such buyers expect, even demand, that they be kept constantly advised of all new developments to enable them to more effectively shape their own role. On the other hand, other buyers may have no interest in prescribing their role activities and accept their role as given to them. Such a buyer is most concerned with merely implementing prescribed company activities and buying policies with sanctioned products. Thus, some buyers will be highly committed to play the role as the firm dictates it (i.e., the formal organization's perception of their role) while others might be extremely innovative and uncommitted to the expected role performance. Obviously, roles may be heavily influenced by the organizational climate existing in the particular organization.

Organizations can be divided into three groups based on differences in degree of commitment. These groups include innovative, adaptive, and lethargic firms. In *innovative* firms, individuals approach their occupational roles with a weak commitment to expected norms of behavior. In an *adaptive* organization, there is a moderate commitment, while in a *lethargic* organization, individuals express a strong commitment to traditionally accepted behavior and behave accordingly. Thus, a buyer in a lethargic firm would probably be less innovative to maintain acceptance and status within the organization and would keep conflict within the firm to a minimum.

Buyers' perception of their role may differ from the perception of their role held by others in the organization. This can result in variance in perception of the proper and the actual purchase responsibility to be held by the buyer. One study involving purchasing agents revealed that in every firm included in the study, the purchasing agents believed they had more responsibility and control over certain decisions than the other influential purchase decision makers in the firm perceived them as having. The decisions were (1) design of the product, (2) cost of the product, (3) performance life, (4) naming of the specific supplier, (5) assessing the amount of engineering help available from the supplier, and (6) reduction of rejects. This variance in role perception held true regardless of the size of the firm or the significance of the item purchased to the overall success of the firm. It is important, therefore, that the marketer be aware such perceptual differences may exist and to determine as accurately as possible the amount of control and responsibility over purchasing decisions held by each purchase decision influencer in the firm.

STAGES IN THE BUYING PROCESS

As with consumer buying, most industrial purchases are made in response to a particular need or problem faced by the firm. Recognition of the need, however, is only the first step in the industrial buying process. The following four stages represent one model of the industrial buying process:

1. Problem recognition.
2. Organizational assignment of buying responsibility and authority.
3. Search procedures for identifying product offerings and for establishing selection criteria.
4. Choice procedures for evaluating and selecting among alternatives.

Problem Recognition

As mentioned previously, most industrial purchases are made in response to a particular need or problem. The product purchased is hopefully the means to solve the particular problem. Industrial buyers must be concerned with budgets and profits since the firm cannot put forth a great amount of financial resources if it does not have sufficient funds, regardless of the benefits that might be derived from the purchase. However, as was mentioned, there is more "subjective" buying and "persuasion" in the industrial buying process than some earlier writers have indicated.

Assignment of Buying Authority

The influence of individuals on the buying decision will be determined in part by their responsibility as defined by the formal organization. An individual's responsibility in a given buying situation will be a function of (1) the technical complexity of the product, (2) the importance of the product to the firm either in dollar terms or in terms of its relationship with the process or system that will use the product, (3) the product-specific technical knowledge that the individual has, (4) the individual's centrality in the process or system that will use the product.

In some organizations the responsibility for the purchasing decision is assigned to a centralized purchasing unit. When centralization of the buying function occurs, it is usually based on the assumption that knowledge of the market and not knowledge of the physical product itself is the major consideration in the buying decision. Therefore, the purchasing agent will concentrate on such market variables as price, delivery, and seller performance, rather than on the technical aspects of the product.

Search Procedures

This stage involves the search procedures for identifying product offerings and for establishing selection criteria.[4] Basically, industrial buyers perform two key tasks related to the collection and analysis of information. First, the criteria against which to evaluate potential sellers have to be developed. These are usually based on a judgment about what is needed compared to what is available. Second, alter-

---

[4] See Rowland T. Moriarty and Robert E. Spekman, *Sources of Information Utilized During the Industrial Buying Process: An Empirical Overview,* Report No. 83-101 (Cambridge, Mass.: Marketing Science Institute, 1983).

HIGHLIGHT 4-5
Industrial Buyer Information Sources

Information Source	*Description*
Salespeople	Sales personnel representing manufacturers or distributors of the product in question.
Technical sources	Engineering personnel internal or external to the subject's firm.
Personnel in buyer's firm	Peer group references (e.g., other purchasing agents in the subject's firm).
Purchasing agents in other companies	Peer group references external to the buyer's firm.
Trade association	Cooperatives voluntarily joined by business competitors designed to assist its members and industry in dealing with mutual problems (e.g., National Association of Purchasing Management).
Advertising in trade journals	Commercial messages placed by the manufacturer or distributor of the product in question.
Articles in trade journals	Messages relating to the product in question but not under the control of the manufacturer or distributor.
Vendor files	Information pertaining to the values of various sources of supply as developed and maintained by the buyer's firm.
Trade registers	Buyer guides providing listings of suppliers and other marketing information (e.g., *Thomas' Register*).
Product literature	Specific product and vendor information supplied by the manufacturing or distributing firm.

Source: Adapted from H. Lee Matthews, James Robeson, and Peter J. Banbic, "Achieving Seller Acceptability in Industrial Markets: Development of the Communication Mix," in *Consumer and Industrial Buying Behavior,* ed. Arch Woodside, Jagdish N. Sheth, and Peter D. Bennett (New York: Elsevier North-Holland Publishing, 1977), p. 223.

native product candidates must be located in the market. The important point here is that buyers seek sellers just as sellers seek buyers.

Choice Procedures

The final stage in the industrial buying process involves establishing choice procedures for evaluating and selecting among alternatives. Once alternative products and alternative suppliers have been identified, the buyer must choose from among the alternatives. The choice process is guided by the use of decision rules and specific criteria for evaluating the product offering. These decision rules evolve from objectives, policies, and procedures established for buying actions by management. Often some type of rating scheme or value index is used.

The above stages in the industrial buying process have particular significance for industrial marketers in their method of approach to potential buyers. This is not to say that these stages are the only activities industrial buyers go through before making a purchase, or that they are even aware that they are going through them. The stages are presented here only as a convenient way to examine the industrial buying process and the importance of certain activities during particular stages.

CONCLUSION

The industrial sector has long been regarded as the stepchild of marketing in terms of the amount of research effort devoted to its problems. However, considerable recent research has been conducted and in this chapter an overview of the industrial buying process has been presented. Basically, the model viewed industrial buying as a process of problem recognition, assignment of buying authority, search procedures, and choice procedures. Product, organizational, and behavioral influences were recognized as playing important roles in terms of the speed and complexity of this process.

Additional Readings

Anderson, Paul F., and Terry M. Chambers. "A Reward/Measurement Model of Organizational Buying Behavior." *Journal of Marketing,* Spring 1985, pp. 7–23.

Assael, Henry. *Consumer Behavior and Marketing Action.* 3rd ed. Boston: Kent Publishing, 1987, chap. 23.

Fern, Edward F., and James R. Brown. "The Industrial/Consumer Marketing Dichotomy: A Case of Insufficient Justification." *Journal of Marketing,* Spring 1984, pp. 68–77.

Krapfel, Robert E., Jr. "An Advocacy Behavior Model of Organizational Buyers' Vendor Choice." *Journal of Marketing,* Fall 1985, pp. 51–59.

Puto, Christopher P.; Wesley E. Patton III; and Ronald H. King. "Risk Handling Strategies in Industrial Vendor Selection Decisions." *Journal of Marketing,* Winter 1985, pp.89–98.

Vyas, Niren, and Arch G. Woodside. "An Inductive Model of Industrial Supplier Choice Processes." *Journal of Marketing,* Winter 1984, pp. 30–45.

Chapter 5

Market Segmentation

Market segmentation is one of the most important concepts in the marketing literature. In fact, a primary reason for studying consumer and industrial buyer behavior is to provide bases for effective segmentation, and a large portion of marketing research is concerned with segmentation. From a marketing management point of view, selection of the appropriate target market is paramount to developing successful marketing programs.

The logic of market segmentation is quite simple and is based on the idea that a single product item can seldom meet the needs and wants of *all* consumers. Typically, consumers vary as to their needs, wants, and preferences for products and services, and successful marketers adapt their marketing programs to fulfill these preference patterns. For example, even a simple product like chewing gum has multiple flavors, package sizes, sugar contents, calories, consistencies (e.g., liquid centers), and colors to meet the preferences of various consumers. While a single product item cannot meet the needs of all consumers, it can almost always serve more than one consumer. Thus, there are usually *groups of consumers* who can be served well by a single item. If a particular group can be served *profitably* by a firm, then it is a viable market segment. In other words, the firm should develop a marketing mix to serve the group or market segment.

In this chapter we consider the process of market segmentation. We define *market segmentation* as the process of dividing a market into groups of similar consumers and selecting the most appropriate group(s) for the firm to serve. We break down the process of market segmentation into six steps, as shown in Figure 5–1. While we recognize that the order of these steps may vary, depending on the firm and situation, there are few if any times when market segmentation analysis can be ignored. In fact, even if the final decision is to "mass market"

FIGURE 5-1 A Model of the Market Segmentation Process

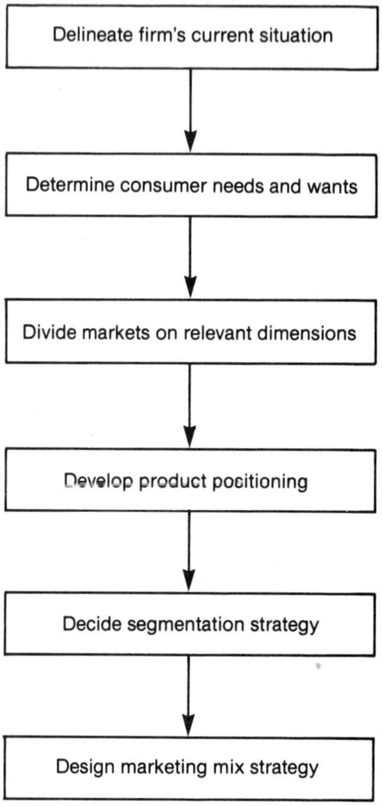

and not segment at all, this decision should be reached only *after* a market segmentation analysis has been conducted. Thus, market segmentation analysis is a cornerstone of sound marketing planning and decison making.

Delineate the Firm's Current Situation

As emphasized in Chapter 1, a firm must do a complete situational analysis when embarking on a new or modified marketing program. At the marketing planning level, such an analysis aids in determining objectives, opportunities, and constraints to be considered when selecting target markets and developing marketing mixes. In addition, marketing managers must have a clear idea of the amount of financial and other resources that will be available for developing and executing a marketing plan. Thus, the inclusion of this first step in the market segmentation process is intended to be a reminder of tasks to be performed prior to marketing planning.

Determine Consumer Needs and Wants

As emphasized throughout this text, successful marketing strategies depend on discovering and satisfying consumer needs and wants. In some cases, this idea is quite operational. To illustrate, suppose a firm has a good deal of venture capital and is seeking to diversify its interest into new markets. A firm in this situation may seek to discover a broad variety of unsatisfied needs. However, in most situations, the industry in which the firm operates specifies the boundaries of a firm's need satisfaction activities. For example, a firm in the communication industry may seek more efficient methods for serving consumers' long-distance telephone needs.

As a practical matter, new technology often brings an investigation of consumer needs and wants for new or modified products and services. In these situations, the firm is seeking the group of consumers whose needs could best be satisfied by the new or modified product. Further, at a strategic level, consumer needs and wants usually are translated into more operational concepts. For instance, consumer attitudes, preferences, and benefits sought, which are determined through marketing research, are commonly used for segmentation purposes.

Divide Markets on Relevant Dimensions

In a narrow sense, this step is often considered to be the whole of market segmentation (i.e., consumers are grouped on the basis of one or more similarities and treated as a homogeneous segment of a heterogeneous total market). There are three important questions to be considered here:

1. Should the segmentation be a priori or post hoc?
2. How does one determine the relevant dimensions or bases to use for segmentation?
3. What are some bases for segmenting consumer and industrial buyer markets?

A Priori versus Post Hoc Segmentation. Real-world segmentation has followed one of two general patterns.[1] An *a priori segmentation* ap-

[1] Yoram Wind, "Issues and Advances in Segmentation Research," *Journal of Marketing Research,* August 1978, pp. 317–37.

proach is one in which the marketing manager has decided on the appropriate basis for segmentation in advance of doing any research on a market. For example, a manager may decide that a market should be divided on the basis of whether people are nonusers, light users, or heavy users of a particular product. Segmentation research is then conducted to determine the size of each of these groups and their demographic or psychographic profiles.

Post hoc segmentation is an approach in which people are grouped into segments on the basis of research findings. For example, people interviewed concerning their attitudes or benefits sought in a particular product category are grouped according to their responses. The size of each of these groups and their demographic and psychographic profiles are then determined.

Both of these approaches are valuable, and the question of which to use depends in part on how well the firm knows the market for a particular product class. If through previous research and experience a marketing manager has successfully isolated a number of key market dimensions, then an a priori approach based on them may provide more useful information. In the case of segmentation for entirely new products, a post hoc approach may be useful for determining key market dimensions. However, even when using a post hoc approach, some consideration must be given to the variables to be included in the research design. Thus, some consideration must be given to the relevant segmentation dimensions regardless of which approach is used.

Relevance of Segmentation Dimensions. Unfortunately, there is no simple solution for determining the relevant dimensions for segmenting markets. Certainly, managerial expertise and experience are needed for selecting the appropriate dimensions or bases on which to segment particular markets. In most cases, however, at least some initial dimensions can be determined from previous research, purchase trends, and managerial judgment. For instance, suppose we wish to segment the market for all-terrain vehicles. Clearly, several dimensions come to mind for initial consideration including sex (male), age (18 to 35 years), lifestyle (outdoorsman), and income level (perhaps $15,000 to $25,000). At a minimum, these variables should be included in subsequent segmentation research. Of course, the most market-oriented approach to segmentation is on the basis of what benefits the potential consumer is seeking. Thus, consideration and research of sought benefits is a strongly recommended approach in the marketing literature. This approach will be considered in some detail in the following section.

Bases for Segmentation. A number of useful bases for segmenting consumer and industrial markets are presented in Figure 5–2. This is

FIGURE 5-2 Useful Segmentation Bases for Consumer and Industrial Markets

Consumer Markets

Segmentation Base	*Base Categories*
Geographic:	
Region	Pacific, Mountain, West North Central, West South Central, East North Central, East South Central, South Atlantic, Middle Atlantic, New England.
City, county, or SMSA size	Under 5,000; 5,000–19,999; 20,000–49,999; 50,000–99,000; 100,000–249,999; 250,000–499,999; 500,000–999,999; 1,000,000–3,999,999; 4,000,000 or over.
Population density	Urban, suburban, rural.
Climate	Warm, cold.
Demographic:	
Age	Under 6; 6–12; 13–19, 20–29; 30–39, 40–49; 50–59; 60+.
Sex	Male, female.
Family size	1–2; 3–4, 5+.
Family life cycle	Young, single; young, married, no children; young, married, youngest child under 6; young, married, youngest child 6 or over; older, married, with children; older, married, no children under 18; older, single; other.
Income	Under $5,000; $5,000–$7,999; $8,000–$9,999; $10,000–$14,999; $15,000–$24,999; $25,000–$34,999; $35,000 or over.
Occupation	Professional and technical; managers, officials, and proprietors; clerical, sales; craftsmen, foremen; operatives; farmers; retired; students; housewives, unemployed.
Education	Grade school or less; some high school; graduated high school; some college; graduated college; some graduate work; graduate degree.
Religion	Catholic, Protestant, Jewish, other.
Race	White, black, oriental, other.
Nationality	American, British, French, German, Italian, Japanese, and so on.
Psychographic:	
Social class	Lower-lower, upper-lower, lower-middle, upper-middle, lower-upper, upper-upper.
Lifestyle	Traditionalist, sophisticate, swinger.
Personality	Compliant, aggressive, detached.

FIGURE 5-2 *(concluded)*

Consumer Markets

Segmentation Base	*Base Categories*
Cognitive and behavioral:	
Attitudes	Positive, neutral, negative.
Benefits sought	Convenience, economy, prestige.
Readiness stage	Unaware, aware, informed, interested, desirous, intention to purchase.
Perceived risk	High, moderate, low.
Innovativeness	Innovator, early adopter, early majority, late majority, laggard.
Involvement	Low, high.
Loyalty status	None, some, total.
Usage rate	None, light, medium, heavy.
User status	Nonuser, ex-user, potential user, current user.

Industrial Buyer Markets

Segmentation Base	*Base Categories*
Source loyalty	Purchase from one, two, three, four, or more suppliers.
Size of company	Small, medium, large relative to industry.
Average size of purchase	Small, medium, large.
Usage rate	Light, medium, heavy.
Product application	Maintenance, production, final product component, administration.
Type of business	Manufacturer, wholesaler, retailer; SIC categories.
Location	North, East, South, West; sales territories.
Purchase status	New customer, occasional purchaser, frequent purchaser, nonpurchaser.
Attribute importance	Reliability of supply, price, service, durability, convenience, reputation of supplier.

by no means a complete list of possible segmentation variables but represents some useful bases and categories. Two commonly used approaches for segmenting markets include benefit segmentation and psychographic segmentation. We will discuss these two in some detail.

Benefit Segmentation. The belief underlying this segmentation approach is that the benefits people are seeking in consuming a given product are the basic reasons for the existence of true market seg-

HIGHLIGHT 5-1
Market Segmentation at Campbell Soup Company

There is probably no more durable symbol of American mass marketing than the Campbell Soup can. The familiar red-and-white label is a machine-age symbol of standardization, volume production, and national brand identity. For most of this century, it has stood for a line of products made the same way and marketed the same way all across the country.

Yet Campbell's recently cooked up its own version of market segmentation, which it calls "regionalization." Basically, the company divided the United States into 22 regions, each with its own marketing and sales force. Each regional staff studies marketing strategies and media buying and has its own ad and trade-promotion budget. Eventually, up to 50 percent of Campbell's ad budget may be the responsibility of the regional groups, rather than corporate headquarters.

Regional staffs have come up with a number of innovative methods to sell Campbell's products, including:

- In Texas and California, where consumers like their food with a bit of a kick, Campbell's nacho cheese soup is spicier than in other parts of the country.
- In New York, when the Giants were bound for the Super Bowl, a local sales manager used part of her ad budget to arrange a football-related radio promotion for Swanson Frozen dinners.
- In Nevada, Campbell treats skiers at Ski Incline resort to hot samples of its soup of the day.
- In the South, Campbell has experimented with a Creole soup and a red-bean soup for the Hispanic market.

While the company is still ironing out logistical problems, regionalization is a way to deal with the end of the American mass market and perhaps to serve consumers better. Other consumer goods companies are bound to study Campbell's recipe.

Source: "Marketing's New Look," *Business Week,* January 26, 1987, pp. 64–69.

ments.[2] Thus, this approach attempts to measure consumer value systems and consumer perceptions of various brands in a product class. To illustrate, the classic example of a benefit segmentation was provided by Russell Haley and concerned the toothpaste market. Haley

---

[2] Russell I. Haley, "Benefit Segmentation: A Decision-Oriented Research Tool," *Journal of Marketing,* July 1968, pp. 30–35; Russell I. Haley, "Benefit Segmentation—20 Years Later," *Journal of Consumer Marketing,* no. 2 (1983), pp. 5–13; Russell I. Haley, "Benefit Segments: Backwards and Forwards," *Journal of Advertising Research,* February-March 1984, pp. 19–25.

FIGURE 5–3 Toothpaste Market Benefit Segments

	Sensory Segment	*Sociable Segment*	*Worrier Segment*	*Independent Segment*
Principal benefit sought	Flavor and product appearance.	Brightness of teeth.	Decay prevention.	Price.
Demographic strengths	Children.	Teens, young people.	Large families.	Men.
Special behavioral characteristics	Users of spearmint-flavored toothpaste.	Smokers.	Heavy users.	Heavy users.
Brands disproportionately favored	Colgate.	Macleans, Ultra Brite.	Crest.	Cheapest brand.
Lifestyle characteristics	Hedonistic.	Active.	Conservative.	Value-oriented.

Source: Adapted from Russell I. Haley, "Benefit Segmentation: A Decision-Oriented Research Tool," *Journal of Marketing,* July 1968, pp. 30–35.

identified five basic segments, which are presented in Figure 5–3. Haley argued that this segmentation could be very useful for selecting advertising copy, media, commercial length, packaging, and new product design. For example, colorful packages might be appropriate for the Sensory Segment, perhaps aqua (to indicate fluoride) for the Worrier Group, and gleaming white for the Social Segment because of this segment's interest in white teeth.

Calantone and Sawyer also used a benefit segmentation approach to segment the market for bank services.[3] Their research was concerned with the question of whether benefit segments remain stable across time. While they found some stability in segments, there were some differences in attribute importance, size, and demographics at different times. Thus, they argue for ongoing benefit segmentation research to keep track of any changes in a market which might affect marketing strategy.

Benefit segmentation is clearly a market-oriented approach to segmentation that seeks to identify consumer needs and wants and to satisfy them by providing products and services with the desired benefits. It is clearly very consistent with the approach to marketing suggested by the marketing concept.

---

[3] Roger J. Calantone and Alan G. Sawyer, "The Stability of Benefit Segments," *Journal of Marketing Research,* August 1978, pp. 395–404; also see James R. Merrill and William A. Weeks, "Predicting and Identifying Benefit Segments in the Elderly Market," in *AMA Educator's Proceedings,* ed. Patrick Murphy et al. (Chicago: American Marketing Association, 1983), pp. 399–403.

Psychographic Segmentation. Whereas benefit segmentation focuses on the benefits sought by the consumer, psychographic segmentation focuses on the personal attributes of the consumer. The psychographic or lifestyle approach typically follows a post hoc model of segmentation. Generally, a large number of questions are asked concerning consumer's activities, interests, and opinions, and then consumers are grouped together empirically based on their responses. Although questions have been raised about the validity of this segmentation approach, it provides much useful information about markets.[4] For example, a well-known psychographic segmentation is called VALs, which stands for values and lifestyles.[5] This approach divides consumers into four basic groups. *Need-driven consumers* purchase primarily to satisfy basic, subsistance-level needs. *Outer-directed consumers* are influenced by a desire to impress other people. *Inner-directed consumers* are motivated by a desire for self-awareness. *Combined outer- and inner-directed consumers* integrate both social and self orientations. These groups are then refined into the nine psychographic segments shown in Figure 5–4.

Research has found differences in purchase behavior consistent with these lifestyles. For example, Achievers tend to buy luxury cars; the Societally Conscious tend to buy economy cars; Emulators and Experientials tend to buy muscle cars; Inner-directed consumers are far more likely to buy foreign cars than are Belongers. Clearly, psychographic segmentation is used to get a tremendous amount of information about consumers and is based on the idea that, if marketers know and understand more about consumers, better marketing strategies can be developed.

Develop Product Positioning

By this time the firm should have a good idea of the basic segments of the market that could potentially be satisfied with its product. The current step is concerned with positioning the product in the minds of consumers relative to competing products. Undoubtedly, the classic example of positioning is the 7UP "Uncola" campaign. Prior to this campaign, 7UP had difficulty convincing consumers that the product could be enjoyed as a soft drink and not just as a mixer. Consumers

---

[4] John L. Lastovicka, "On Validation of Lifestyle Traits: A Review and Illustration," *Journal of Marketing Research,* February 1982, pp. 126–38; also see Jack A. Lesser and Marie Adele Hughes, "The Generalizability of Psychographic Market Segments Across Geographic Locations," *Journal of Marketing,* January 1986, pp. 18–27.

[5] Arnold Mitchell, *The Nine American Lifestyles: Who We Are and Where We're Going* (New York: Macmillan, 1983); also see James Atlas, "Beyond Demographics," *Atlantic Monthly,* October 1984, pp. 49–58.

FIGURE 5-4 VALs Nine American Lifestyles

Need-Driven Consumers

Survivors (4 percent of the U.S. adult population). These consumers are elderly and intensely poor. They are often widowed and living only on Social Security income. Some have been born into poverty and never escape it; others have slipped to this lifestyle because of bad luck, lack of enterprise, or the onslaughts of old age. Entertainment consists of watching television; basic staples are purchased with an emphasis on low price.

Sustainers (7 percent of the U.S. adult population). These consumers are angry, distrustful, anxious, combative, and live on the edge of poverty. Unlike Survivors, the Sustainers have not given up hope; they try for a better life. They are careful shoppers and cautious buyers for their large families.

Outer-Directed Consumers

Belongers (38 percent of the U.S. adult population). These consumers typify what is generally regarded as middle-class America. Traditional, conservative, and old-fashioned, these consumers prefer the status quo or the ways of the past and do not like change. These consumers want to fit in rather than stand out, and they follow the rules of society. They value their home and family and seek security.

Emulators (10 percent of the U.S. adult population). These consumers are intensely striving people, seeking to be like those they consider richer and more successful. They are more influenced by others than any other lifestyle group and are ambitious, competitive, and ostentatious. Many have attended technical school; few have college degrees. Emulators are in a turbulent transition stage; most of them will not make it to Achiever status. They are conspicuous consumers.

Achievers (20 percent of the U.S. adult population). These consumers are the driving and driven people who have built "the system" and are now at the helm. They are effective corporate executives, skilled professionals, such as doctors, lawyers, and scientists, adroit politicians, money-oriented athletes and entertainers, and successful artists. They live comfortable, affluent lives and in so doing they have set the standard for much of the nation. They are major consumers of luxury and top-of-the-line products.

Inner-Directed Consumers

I-Am-Me (3 percent of the U.S. adult population). These consumers are young and in a transition period from an outer-directed to an inner-directed way of life. Many have come from Achiever parents, and the transition to new values is full of turmoil and confusion of personal identity. Most are students in their 20s and have very energetic, active lives. Clothes and other purchases may be made to differentiate these consumers from their parents and Establishment values.

FIGURE 5–4 *(concluded)*

Experientials (5 percent of the U.S. adult population). Many of these consumers passed through the I-Am-Me stage a few years earlier. They tend to be artistic, liberal, and to seek vivid, direct experiences with other persons, things, and events. They are highly educated, very energetic, and engage in social activities ranging from outdoor sports to wine tasting. Most are in their late 20s and prefer natural products.

Societally Conscious (11 percent of the U.S. adult population). These consumers are well-educated, prosperous, politically liberal, and deeply concerned with social issues. They are approaching 40 years of age and are the leaders of movements for improving consumer rights, reducing environmental pollution, and protecting wildlife. Many ride a bike or drive an economy car, insulate their home or install solar heating, and eat only foods grown without pesticides and prepared without additives.

Combined Outer- and Inner-Directed Group

Integrateds (2 percent of the U.S. adult population). These consumers are psychologically mature and find both outer-direction and inner-direction good, powerful, and useful. They have an unusual ability to weigh consequences and to solve difficult problems. They tend to be open, self-assured, self-expressive, keenly aware of nuance, and command respect and admiration. They tend to be middle-aged or older.

Source: J. Paul Peter and Jerry C. Olson, *Consumer Behavior: Marketing Strategy Perspectives* (Homewood, Ill.: Richard D. Irwin, 1987), pp. 482–83.

believed that colas were soft drinks but apparently did not perceive 7UP in this way. However, by positioning 7UP as the "Uncola" the company was capable of positioning the product (1) as a soft drink that could be consumed in the same situations as colas and (2) as an alternative to colas. This positioning was very successful.

In determining the appropriate positioning of the product, the firm must consider its offering relative to competition. Some experts argue that different positioning strategies should be used, depending on whether the firm is the market leader or a follower, and that followers usually should not attempt positioning directly against the industry leader.[6] While there are many sophisticated research tools available for investigating positioning, they are beyond the scope of this text. The main point here is that, in segmenting markets, some segments otherwise appearing to be approachable might be forgone, since competitive products may already dominate that segment in sales and in

[6] See Al Ries and Jack Trout, *Positioning: The Battle for Your Mind* (New York: Warner Books, 1981); Al Ries and Jack Trout, *Marketing Warfare* (New York: McGraw-Hill, 1986).

HIGHLIGHT 5-2

An Operational Approach to Person-Situation Benefit Segmentation

Peter Dickson argues that market segmentation has focused too narrowly on customer characteristics and needs to include the usage situation in segmentation research. Not only do different types of people purchase different types of products but they also purchase them for use in different situations. For example, different types of camping gear are needed for cold weather versus hot weather versus mountain-climbing situations. Below is an operational approach for segmenting markets on the basis of both person and situational factors.

Step 1: Use observational studies, focus group discussions and secondary data to discover whether different usage situations exist and whether they are determinant, in the sense that they appear to affect the importance of various product characteristics.

Step 2: If *step 1* produces promising results, undertake a benefit, product perception, and reported market behavior segmentation survey of consumers. Measure benefits and perceptions by usage situation as well as by individual difference characteristics. Assess situation usage frequency by recall estimates or by usage situation diaries.

Step 3: Construct a person-situation segmentation matrix. The rows are the major usage situations; the columns are groups of users identified by a single chracteristic or a combination of characteristics.

Step 4: Rank the cells in the matrix in terms of their submarket sales volume. The situation-person combination that results in the greatest consumption of the generic product would be ranked first.

Step 5: State the major benefits sought, the important product dimensions, and the unique market behavior for each nonempty cell of the matrix (some person types will never consume the product in certain usage situations).

Step 6: Position your competitors' offerings within the matrix. The person-situation segments they currently serve can be determined by the product feature they promote and their marketing strategy.

Step 7: Position your offering within the matrix on the same criteria.

Step 8: Assess how well your current offering and marketing strategy meet the needs of the submarkets, compared to the competition.

Step 9: Identify market opportunities based on submarket size, needs, and competitive advantage.

Source: Peter R. Dickson, "Person-Situation: Segmentation's Missing Link," *Journal of Marketing,* Fall 1982, p. 61.

HIGHLIGHT 5-3
Typical Items Used on Psychographic Segmentation Research

1. I often watch the newspaper advertisements for announcements of department store sales.
2. I like to watch or listen to baseball or football games.
3. I often try new stores before my friends and neighbors do.
4. I like to work on community projects.
5. My children are the most important thing in my life.
6. I will probably have more money to spend next year than I have now.
7. I often seek out the advice of my friends regarding which store to buy from.
8. I think I have more self-confidence than most people.
9. I enjoy going to symphony concerts.
10. It is good to have charge accounts.

(These items are scored on a "agree strongly" to "disagree strongly" scale.)

the minds of consumers. Product positioning studies also are useful for giving the marketing manager a clearer idea of consumer perceptions of market offerings.

Decide Segmentation Strategy

The firm is now ready to select its segmentation strategy. There are four basic alternatives. First, the firm may decide not to enter the market. For example, analysis to this stage may reveal there is no viable market niche for the firm's offering. Second, the firm may decide not to segment but to be a mass marketer. There are at least three situations when this may be the appropriate decision for the firm:

1. The market is so small that marketing to a portion of it is not profitable.
2. Heavy users make up such a large proportion of the sales volume that they are the only relevant target.
3. The brand is the dominant brand in the market, and targeting to a few segments would not benefit sales and profits.[7]

Third, the firm may decide to market to one segment. And fourth, the firm may decide to market to more than one segment and design a separate marketing mix for each. In any case, the firm must have some

---

[7] Shirley Young, Leland Ott, and Barbara Feigin, "Some Practical Considerations in Market Segmentation," *Journal of Marketing Research,* August 1978, p. 405.

HIGHLIGHT 5-4
Positioning Your Product

A variety of positioning strategies is available to the advertiser. An object can be positioned:

1. By attributes—Crest is a cavity fighter.
2. By price/quality—Sears is a "value" store.
3. By competitor—Avis positions itself with Hertz.
4. By application—Gatorade is for flu attacks.
5. By product user—Miller is for the blue-collar, heavy beer drinker.
6. By product class—Carnation Instant Breakfast is a breakfast food.

The selection of a positioning strategy involves identifying competitors, relevant attributes, competitor positions, and market segments. Research-based approaches can help in each of these steps by providing conceptualization even if the subjective judgments of managers are used to provide the actual input information to the positioning decision.

Source: David A. Aaker and J. Gary Shansby, "Positioning Your Product," *Business Horizons,* May–June 1982, p. 62.

criteria on which to base its segmentation strategy decisions. Three important criteria on which to base such decisions are that a viable segment must be (1) measurable, (2) meaningful, and (3) marketable.

1. *Measurable.* For a segment to be selected, the firm must be capable of measuring its size and characteristics. For instance, one of the difficulties with segmenting on the basis of social class is that the concept and its divisions are not clearly defined and measured. Alternatively, income is a much easier concept to measure.
2. *Meaningful.* A meaningful segment is one that is large enough to have sufficient sales potential and growth potential to offer long-run profits for the firm.
3. *Marketable.* A marketable segment is one that can be reached and served by the firm in an efficient manner.

Segments that meet these criteria are viable markets for the firm's offering. The firm must now give further attention to completing its marketing mix offering.

Design Marketing Mix Strategy

The firm is now in a position to complete its marketing plan by finalizing the marketing mix or mixes to be used for each segment. Clearly, selection of the target market and designing the marketing mix go hand in hand, and thus many marketing mix decisions should

HIGHLIGHT 5-5
Segmentation Bases for Particular Marketing Decision Areas

For general understanding of the market:

—Benfits sought.
—Product purchase and usage patterns.
—Needs.
—Brand loyalty and switching patterns.
—A hybrid of the variables above.

For positioning studies:

—Product usage.
—Product preference.
—Benefits sought.
—A hybrid of the variables above.

For new product concepts (and new product introduction):

—Reaction to new concepts (intention to buy, preference over current brand, and so on).
—Benefits sought.

For pricing decisions:

—Price sensitivity.
—Deal proneness.
—Price sensitivity by purchase/usage patterns.

For advertising decisions:

—Benefits sought.
—Media usage.
—Psychographic/lifestyle.
—A hybrid (of the variables above or purchase/usage pattern, or both).

For distribution decisions:

—Store loyalty and patronage.
—Benefits sought in store selection.

Source: Yoram Wind, "Issues and Advances in Segmentation Research," *Journal of Marketing Research,* August 1978, p. 320.

have already been carefully considered. To illustrate, the target market selected may be price-sensitive, so some consideration has already been given to price levels, and clearly product positioning has many implications for promotion and channel decisions. Thus, while we place marketing mix design at the end of the model, many of these decisions are clearly made in *conjunction* with target market selection. In the

HIGHLIGHT 5-6
Differences in Marketing Strategy for Three Segmentation Alternatives

Strategy Elements	*Mass Marketing*	*Single Market Segmentation*	*Multiple Market Segmentation*
Market definition	Broad range of consumers.	One well-defined consumer group.	Two or more well-defined consumer groups.
Product strategy	Limited number of products under one brand for many types of consumers.	One brand tailored to one consumer group.	Distinct brand for each consumer group.
Pricing strategy	One "popular" price range.	One price range tailored to the consumer group.	Distinct price range for each consumer group.
Distribution strategy	All possible outlets.	All suitable outlets.	All suitable outlets—differs by segment.
Promotion strategy	Mass media.	All suitable media.	All suitable media—differs by segment.
Strategy emphasis	Appeal to various types of consumers through a uniform broad-based marketing program.	Appeal to one specific consumer group through a highly specialized, but uniform, marketing program.	Appeal to two or more distinct market segments through different marketing plans catering to each segment.

Source: Adapted from Joel R. Evans and Barry Berman, *Marketing*, 3rd ed. (New York: Macmillan, 1987), p. 191.

next six chapters of this text, marketing mix decisions will be discussed in detail.

CONCLUSION

The purpose of this chapter was to provide an overview of market segmentation. Market segmentation was defined as the process of dividing a market into groups of similar consumers and selecting the most appropriate group(s) for the firm to serve. Market segmentation was analyzed as a six-stage process: (1) delineate the firm's current situation, (2) determine consumer needs and wants, (3) divide the market on relevant dimensions, (4) develop product positioning, (5) decide segmentation strategy, and (6) design marketing mix strategy.

Additional Readings

Bonoma, Thomas V., and Benson R. Shapiro. *Segmenting the Industrial Market.* Lexington, Mass.: Lexington Books, 1983.

Cosmas, Stephen C. "Life Styles and Consumption Patterns." *Journal of Consumer Research,* March 1982, pp. 453–55.

Doyle, Peter, and John Saunders. "Market Segmentation and Positioning in Specialized Industrial Markets." *Journal of Marketing,* Spring 1985, pp. 24–32.

Kahle, Lynn R. "The Nine Nations of North America and the Value Basis of Geographic Segmentation." *Journal of Marketing,* April 1986, pp. 37–47.

Zeithaml, Valarie A. "The New Demographics and Market Fragmentation." *Journal of Marketing,* Summer 1985, pp. 64–75.

Part C

The Marketing Mix

CHAPTER 6
Product Strategy
CHAPTER 7
New Product Planning and Development
CHAPTER 8
Promotion Strategy: Advertising and Sales Promotion
CHAPTER 9
Promotion Strategy: Personal Selling
CHAPTER 10
Distribution Strategy
CHAPTER 11
Pricing Strategy

Chapter 6

Product Strategy

Product strategy is a critical element of marketing and business strategy, since it is through the sale of products and services by which companies survive and grow. This chapter discusses four important areas of concern in developing product strategies. First, some basic issues are discussed including product definition, product classification, product mix and product line, and packaging and branding. Second, the product life cycle and its implications for product strategy are explained. Third, the product audit is reviewed, and finally, five ways to organize for product management are overviewed. These include the marketing manager system, product (brand) manager system, product planning committee, new-product manager system, and venture team approaches.

Basic Issues in Product Management

Successful marketing depends on understanding the nature of products and basic decision areas in product management. In this section, we discuss the definition and classification of products and the nature of a product mix and product lines. Also considered is the role of packaging and branding.

Product Definition

The way in which the product variable is defined can have important implications for the survival, profitability, and long-run growth of the firm. For example, the same product can be viewed at least three different ways. First, it can be viewed in terms of the tangible prod-

HIGHLIGHT 6–1
Elements of Product Strategy

1. *An audit of the firm's actual and potential resources.*
   a. Financial strength.
   b. Access to raw materials.
   c. Plant and equipment.
   d. Operating personnel.
   e. Management.
   f. Engineering and technical skill.
   g. Patents and licenses.
2. *Approaches to current markets.*
   a. More of the same products.
   b. Variations of present products in terms of grades, sizes, and packages.
   c. New products to replace or supplement current lines.
   d. Product deletions.
3. *Approaches to new or potential markets.*
   a. Geographical expansion of domestic sales.
   b. New socioeconomic or ethnic groups.
   c. Overseas markets.
   d. New uses of present products.
   e. Complementary goods.
   f. Mergers and acquisitions.
4. *State of competition.*
   a. New entries into the industry.
   b. Product imitation.
   c. Competitive mergers or acquisitions.

uct—the physical entity or service that is offered to the buyer. Second, it can be viewed in terms of the extended product—the tangible product along with the whole cluster of services that accompany it. Third, it can be viewed in terms of the generic product—the essential benefits the buyer expects to receive from the product.

From the standpoint of the marketing manager, to define the product solely in terms of the tangible product is to fall into the error of "marketing myopia." Executives who are guilty of committing this error define their company's product too narrowly, since overemphasis is placed on the physical object itself. The classic example of this mistake can be found in railroad passenger service. Although no amount of product improvement could have staved off its decline, if the industry had defined itself as being in the transportation business, rather than the railroad business, it might still be profitable today. On the positive side, toothpaste manufacturers have been willing to exercise flexibility in defining their product. For years toothpaste was an oral hygiene product where emphasis was placed solely on fighting tooth decay and bad breath (e.g., Crest with fluoride). More recently, many manufacturers have recognized the need to market toothpaste as a cosmetic item—to clean teeth of stains. As a result, special-purpose brands have been designed to serve these particular needs, such as Macleans, Ultra Brite, and Close-Up.

In line with the marketing concept philosophy, a reasonable definition of product is *the sum of the physical, psychological, and sociological satisfactions that the buyer derives from purchase, ownership, and consumption.* From this standpoint, products are consumer-satisfying objects that include such things as accessories, packaging, and service.

Product Classification

A product classification scheme can be useful to the marketing manager as an analytical device to assist in planning marketing strategy and programs. A basic assumption underlying such classifications is that products with common attributes can be marketed in a similar fashion. In general, products are classed according to two basic criteria: (1) end use or market and (2) degree of processing or physical transformation.

1. *Agricultural products and raw materials.* These are goods grown or extracted from the land or sea, such as iron ore, wheat, and sand. In general these products are fairly homogeneous, sold in large volume, and have low value per unit or bulk weight.
2. *Industrial goods.* Such products are purchased by business firms for the purpose of producing other goods or for running the business. This category includes the following:
   a. Raw materials and semifinished goods.
   b. Major and minor equipment, such as basic machinery, tools, and other processing facilities.
   c. Parts or components, which become an integral element of some other finished good.
   d. Supplies or items used to operate the business but that do not become part of the final product.
3. *Consumer goods.* Consumer goods can be divided into three classes:
   a. Convenience goods, such as food, which are purchased frequently with minimum effort. Impulse goods would also fall into this category.
   b. Shopping goods, such as appliances, which are purchased after some time and energy are spent comparing the various offerings.
   c. Specialty goods, which are unique in some way so the consumer will make a special effort to obtain them.

HIGHLIGHT 6–2

A. Characteristics of Classes of Consumer Goods and Some Marketing Considerations

Characteristics and Considerations	*Type of Consumer Good*		
	Convenience	*Shopping*	*Specialty*
Characteristics:			
1. Time and effort devoted by consumer to shopping	Very little.	Considerable.	Cannot generalize; consumer may go to nearby store and buy with minimum effort or may have to go to distant store and spend much time and effort.
2. Time spent planning the purchase	Very little.	Considerable.	Considerable.
3. How soon want is satisfied after it arises	Immediately.	Relatively long time.	Relatively long time.
4. Are price and quality compared?	No.	Yes.	No.
5. Price	Low.	High.	High.
6. Frequency of purchase	Usually frequent.	Infrequent.	Infrequent.
7. Importance	Unimportant.	Often very important.	Cannot generalize.
Marketing considerations:			
1. Length of channel	Long.	Short.	Short to very short.
2. Importance of retailer	Any single store is relatively unimportant.	Important.	Very important.
3. Number of outlets	As many as possible.	Few.	Few; often only one in a market.
4. Stock turnover	High.	Lower.	Lower.
5. Gross margin	Low.	High.	High.
6. Responsibility for advertising	Manufacturer's.	Retailer's	Joint responsibility.
7. Importance of point-of-purchase display	Very important.	Less important.	Less important.
8. Advertising used	Manufacturer's.	Retailer's	Both.
9. Brand or store name important	Brand name.	Store name.	Both.
10. Importance of packaging	Very important.	Less important.	Less important.

B. Classes of Industrial Products—Some Characteristics and Marketing Considerations

Characteristics and Marketing Considerations	*Type of Industrial Good*				
	Raw Materials	*Fabricating Parts and Materials*	*Installations*	*Accessory Equipment*	*Operating Supplies*
Example:	Iron ore	Engine blocks	Blast furnaces	Storage racks	Paper clips
Characteristics:					
1. Unit Price	Very low.	Low.	Very high.	Medium.	Low.
2. Length of life	Very short.	Depends on final product.	Very long.	Long.	Short.
3. Quantities purchased	Large.	Large.	Very small.	Small.	Small.
4. Frequency of purchase	Frequent delivery; long-term purchase contract.	Infrequent purchase, but frequent delivery.	Very infrequent.	Medium frequency.	Frequent.
5. Standardization of competitive products	Very much; grading is important.	Very much.	Very little; custom-made.	Little.	Much.
6. Limits on supply	Limited; supply can be increased slowly or not at all.	Usually no problem.	No problem.	Usually no problem.	Usually no problem.
Marketing considerations:					
1. Nature of channel	Short; no middlemen.	Short; middlemen only for small buyers.	Short; no middlemen.	Middlemen used.	Middlemen used.
2. Negotiation period	Hard to generalize.	Medium.	Long.	Medium.	Short.
3. Price competition	Important.	Important.	Not important.	Not main factor.	Important.
4. Presale/postsale service	Not important.	Important.	Very important.	Important.	Very little.
5. Demand stimulation	Very little.	Moderate.	Sales people very important.	Important.	Not too important.
6. Brand preference	None.	Generally low.	High.	High.	Low.
7. Advance buying contract	Important; long-term contracts used.	Important; long-term contracts used.	Not usually used.	Not usually used.	Not usually used.

Source: William J. Stanton and Charles Futrell, *Fundamentals of Marketing,* 8th ed. (New York: McGraw-Hill, 1987), pp. 195, 198.

In general, the buying motive, buying habits, and character of the market are different for industrial goods vis-à-vis consumer goods. A primary purchasing motive for industrial goods is, of course, profit. As mentioned in a previous chapter, industrial goods are usually purchased as means to an end, and not as an end in themselves. This is another way of saying that the demand for industrial goods is a derived demand. Industrial goods are often purchased directly from the original source with few middlemen, because many of these goods can be bought in large quantities; they have high unit value; technical advice on installation and use is required; and the product is ordered according to the user's specifications. Many industrial goods are subject to multiple-purchase influence and a long period of negotiation is often required.

The market for industrial goods has certain attributes that distinguish it from the consumer goods market. Much of the market is concentrated geographically, as in the case of steel, auto, or shoe manufacturing. For certain products there are a limited number of buyers; this is known as a *vertical market,* which means that *(a)* it is narrow, because customers are restricted to a few industries, and *(b)* it is deep, in that a large percentage of the producers in the market use the product. Some products, such as office supplies, have a *horizontal market,* which means that the goods are purchased by all types of firms in many different industries. In general, buyers of industrial goods are reasonably well informed. As noted previously, heavy reliance is often placed on price, quality control, and reliability of supply source.

In terms of consumer products, many market scholars have found the convenience, shopping, and specialty classification inadequate and have attempted to either refine it or to derive an entirely new typology. None of these attempts appear to have met with complete success.[1] Perhaps there is no "best" way to deal with this problem. From the standpoint of the marketing manager, product classification is useful to the extent that it assists in providing guidelines for developing an appropriate marketing mix. For example, convenience goods generally require broadcast promotion and long channels of distribution as opposed to shopping goods, which generally require more targeted promotion and somewhat shorter channels of distribution.

Product Mix and Product Line

The *product mix* is the composite of products offered for sale by the firm; *product line* refers to a group of products that are closely related,

---

[1] For a review and suggestions for product classification, see Patrick E. Murphy and Ben M. Enis, "Classifying Products Strategically," *Journal of Marketing,* July 1986, pp. 24–42.

either because they satisfy a class of need, are used together, are sold to the same consumer groups, are marketed through the same types of outlets, or fall within given price ranges. There are three primary dimensions of a firm's product mix: (1) width of the product mix, which refers to the number of product lines the firm handles; (2) depth of the product mix, which refers to the average numbers of products in each line; (3) consistency of the product mix, which refers to the similarity of product lines. Thus, McDonald's hamburgers represent a product item in its line of sandwiches; whereas hot cakes or Egg McMuffins represent items in a different line, namely, breakfast foods.

Development of a plan for the existing product line has been called the most critical element of a company's product planning activity.[2] In designing such plans, management needs accurate information on the current and anticipated performance of its products, which should encompass:

1. Consumer evaluation of the company's products, particularly their strengths and weaknesses vis-à-vis competition (i.e., product positioning by market segment information).
2. Objective information on actual and anticipated product performance on relevant criteria, such as sales, profits, and market share.[3]

Packaging and Branding

Distinctive or unique packaging is one method of differentiating a relatively homogeneous product. To illustrate, boil-a-pak dinners, pump rather than aerosol deodorant and hair spray containers, and different sizes and designs of tissue packages are attempts to differentiate a product through packaging and to satisfy consumer needs at the same time.

In making packaging decisions, the marketing manager must again consider both the consumer and costs. On one hand, the package must be capable of protecting the product through the channel of distribution to the consumer. In addition, it is desirable for packages to be of convenient size and easy to open for the consumer. Hopefully, the package is also attractive and capable of being used as an in-store promotional tool. However, maximizing these objectives may increase the cost of the product to such an extent that consumers are no longer willing to purchase it. Thus, the marketing manager must determine the optimal protection, convenience, and promotional strengths of packages, subject to cost constraints.

---

[2] Yoram Wind and Henry J. Claycamp, "Planning Product Line Strategy: A Matrix Approach," *Journal of Marketing,* January 1976, p. 2.

[3] Ibid.

As a product strategy, many firms produce and market their own products under a so-called private label. For example, A&P uses the Ann Page label, among others, and Sears uses the Kenmore label, among others. Such a strategy is highly important in industries where the middleman has gained control over distribution to the consumer. The advent of large chain stores, such as K mart, has accelerated the growth of private brands. If a manufacturer refuses to supply certain middlemen with private branded merchandise, then the alternative is for these middlemen to go into the manufacturing business, as in the case of Kroger.

As a general rule, private brands are lower priced than national brands because there are some cost savings involved, and this has been the strongest appeal of private brand merchandisers. If a manufac-

HIGHLIGHT 6-3
Advantages and Disadvantages of Full versus Limited Product Lines

Marketing managers must decide whether the firm will be better off by having a full or limited line of products. Below is a list of the advantages and disadvantges of these alternatives.

Full Line

Advantages:

1. Customers may prefer to deal with one supplier, simplifying their buying.
2. More items carried should mean more opportunities to make sales.
3. Shipping many items from one source may lower total transportation costs.
4. A full line may permit coordination of product offerings—(e.g., stove and refrigerator).
5. A supplier's image may be enhanced by being a source of a full line of merchandise.

Disadvantages:

1. Manufacturing costs are greater as production must be adjusted to produce disparate items.
2. Handling and transportation costs per unit should be greater than for standardized products.
3. Inventory costs may be higher as different items must be held for different customers.
4. Competitors practicing limited-line strategies may gain advantages related to specialization and economies of scale.
5. Sales force and other resources must be spread over a wider range of offerings.

HIGHLIGHT 6–3 (*concluded*)

Limited Line

Advantages:

1. If line is limited to products sold in high volume, economies of scale in production and distribution should result.
2. Supplier's image may be enhanced if perceived as a "specialist."
3. Line can be limited to include only high-profit items.
4. A limited product offering may be more closely related to specific target markets or segments.
5. Buyers may prefer limited-line suppliers as a more certain source of supply or in the belief that savings due to specializing are passed on to buyers.

Disadvantages:

1. Some sales lost due to lack of full line.
2. Channel members may prefer dealing with full-line supplier and resist dealing with limited-line dealers.
3. If customers buy in small lots, increased transportation costs could result because of small shipments.
4. There is no opportunity to offer a coordinated line of merchandise such as apparel items or appliances.
5. Consumer recognition problems could result. Due to advertising of many products, Kellogg's is a better known name than Maltex.

Source: William Zikmund and Michael D'Amico, *Marketing,* 2nd ed. (New York: John Wiley & Sons, 1986), p. 265.

turer is selling its national branded products to middlemen under a private label, then the Robinson-Patman Act requires that any price differential reflect *(a)* genuine differences in grade and quality or *(b)* cost savings in manufacturing or distribution. One of the reasons why manufacturers will supply resellers with private branded merchandise is to utilize their production capacity more fully. Similarly, generic brands use excess capacity and offer manufacturers an alternative for selling their products.

PRODUCT LIFE CYCLE

A firm's product strategy must take into account the fact that products have a life cycle. Figure 6–1 illustrates this life-cycle concept. Products

FIGURE 6–1

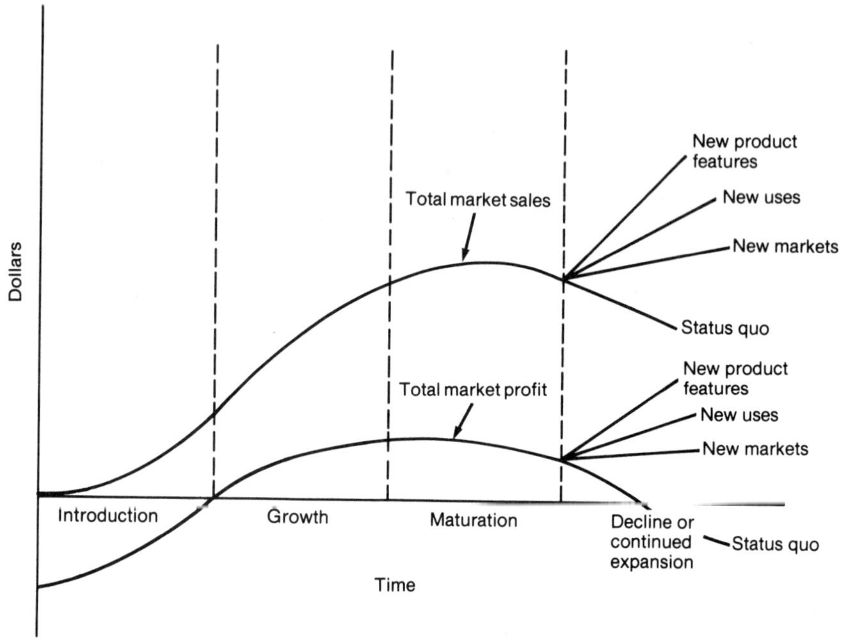

are introduced, grow, mature, and decline. This cycle varies according to industry, product, technology, and market. Marketing executives need to be aware of the life-cycle concept because it can be a valuable aid in developing marketing strategies.

During the introduction phase of the cycle, there are usually high production and marketing costs and, since sales are only beginning to materialize, profits are low or nonexistent. Profits increase and are positively correlated with sales during the growth stage as the market begins trying and adopting the product. As the product matures, profits for the initiating firm do not keep pace with sales because of competition. Here the seller may be forced to "remarket" the product, which may involve making price concessions, increasing product quality, or expanding outlays on advertising and sales promotion just to maintain market share. At some time sales decline, and the seller must decide whether to *(a)* drop the product, *(b)* alter the product, *(c)* seek new uses for the product, *(d)* seek new markets, or *(e)* continue with more of the same.[4]

[4] Note that the labeling of the new product features, new uses, and new markets curves is arbitrary. In other words, any of the three may result in the highest sales and profits depending on the product and situation.

HIGHLIGHT 6–4
Why Branding Is Advantageous to Marketers

There are five basic reasons why it is useful for marketers to brand their merchandise:

1. Encourages repeat buying	A good brand speeds up shopping for the customer and thus reduces the marketer's selling time and effort. When a customer finds it convenient to repeat purchases by brand, promotion costs are reduced and sales volume is increased.
2. Customer franchise	Whether the brander is a manufacturer, wholesaler, or retailer, brand loyalty provides protection from competition because the brander, in effect, is given a customer franchise.
3. Market segmentation	A brander can use various brands to segment markets and meet the needs of various intermediate consumers.
4. Profitability	By offering customers what amounts to a "guarantee" of quality, branders may be able to obtain a price that is higher than the cost of giving this guarantee.
5. Corporate image	Good brands can enhance the company's name, simplifying the introduction of additional products.

Source: Adapted from E. Jerome McCarthy and William D. Perreault, Jr., *Basic Marketing: A Managerial Approach,* 8th ed. (Homewood, Ill.: Richard D. Irwin, 1984), p. 310.

The usefulness of the product life-cycle concept is primarily that it forces management to take a long-range view of marketing planning. In doing so, it should become clear that shifts in phases of the life cycle correspond to changes in the market situation, competition, and demand. Thus, the astute marketing manager should recognize the necessity of altering the marketing mix to meet these changing conditions. When applied with sound judgment, the life-cycle concept

[5] For an overview of issues concerning the product life cycle, see George Day, "The Product Life Cycle: Analysis and Application Issues," *Journal of Marketing,* Fall 1981, pp. 60–67. This is the introductory article to a special section dealing with the product life cycle.

HIGHLIGHT 6–5

Marketing Strategy Implications of the Product Life Cycle

	Stages of the Product Life Cycle			
Effects and Responses	*Introduction*	*Growth*	*Maturity*	*Decline*
Competition	None of importance.	Some emulators.	Many rivals competing for a small piece of the pie.	Few in number, with a rapid shakeout of weak members.
Overall strategy	Market establishment; persuade early adopters to try the product.	Market penetration; persuade mass market to prefer the brand.	Defense of brand position; check the inroads of competition.	Preparations for removal; milk the brand dry of all possible benefits.
Profits	Negligible because of high production and marketing costs.	Reach peak levels as a result of high prices and growing demand.	Increasing competition cuts into profit margins and ultimately into total profits.	Declining volume pushes costs up to levels that eliminate profits entirely.
Retail prices	High, to recover some of the excessive costs of launching.	High, to take advantage of heavy consumer demand.	What the traffic will bear; need to avoid price wars.	Low enough to permit quick liquidation of inventory.
Distribution	Selective, as distribution is slowly built up.	Intensive; employ small trade discounts since dealers are eager to store.	Intensive; heavy trade allowances to retain shelf space.	Selective; unprofitable outlets slowly phased out.
Advertising strategy	Aim at the needs of early adopters.	Make the mass market aware of brand benefits.	Use advertising as a vehicle for differentiation among otherwise similar brands.	Emphasize low price to reduce stock.
Advertising emphasis	High, to generate awareness and interest among early adopters and persuade dealers to stock the brand.	Moderate, to let sales rise on the sheer momentum of word-of-mouth recommendations.	Moderate, since most buyers are aware of brand characteristics.	Minimum expenditures required to phase out the product.
Consumer sales and promotion expenditures	Heavy, to entice target groups, with samples, coupons, and other inducements to try the brand.	Moderate, to create brand preference (advertising is better suited to do this job).	Heavy, to encourage brand switching, hoping to convert some buyers into loyal users.	Minimal, to let the brand coast by itself.

Source: William Zikmund and Michael D'Amico, *Marketing,* 2nd ed. (New York: John Wiley & Sons, 1986), p. 255.

can aid in forecasting, pricing, advertising, product planning, and other aspects of marketing management.[5] However, the marketing manager must also recognize that the length and slope of the product life cycle varies across products. Thus, while the product life cycle is useful for recognizing the stages a product will go through, it is difficult to forecast the exact time periods for these stages.

THE PRODUCT AUDIT

The product audit is a marketing management technique whereby the company's current product offerings are reviewed to ascertain whether each product should be continued as is, improved, or modified, or be deleted. The audit is a task that should be carried out at regular intervals as a matter of policy. Product audits are the responsibility of the product manager unless specifically delegated to someone else.

Deletions

It can be argued that the major purpose of the product audit is to detect "sick" products and then bury them. Criteria must be developed for deciding whether a product is a candidate for deletion. Some of the more obvious factors to be considered are:

- *Sales trends.* How have sales moved over time? What has happened to market share? Why have sales declined? What changes in sales have occurred in competitive products both in our line and in those of other manufacturers?
- *Profit contribution.* What has been the profit contribution of this product to the company? If profits have declined, how are these tied to price? Have selling, promotion, and distribution costs risen out of proportion to sales? Does the product require excessive management time and effort?
- *Product life cycle.* Has the product reached a level of maturity and saturation in the market? Are there more effective substitutes on the market? Has the product outgrown its usefulness? Can the resources used on this product be put to better use?

The above factors should be used as guidelines for making the final decision to delete a product. Deletion decisions are very difficult to make because of their potential impact on customers and the firm. For example, eliminating a product may force a company to lay off some employees. There are other factors to consider, such as keeping consumers supplied with replacement parts and repair service and maintaining the good will of distributors who have an inventory of the product. The deletion plan should provide for the clearing out of stock in question.[6]

Product Improvement

One of the other important objectives of the audit is to ascertain whether to alter the product in some way or to leave things as they are. Altering the product means changing one or more of the product's attributes or marketing dimensions. Attributes refer mainly to product features, design, package, and so forth. Marketing dimensions refer to such things as price, promotion strategy, and channels of distribution.

It is possible to look at the product audit as a management device for controlling the product strategy. Here, control means feedback on product performance and corrective action in the form of product improvement. Product improvement is a top-level management decision, but the information needed to make the improvement decision may come from the consumer or the middlemen. Suggestions are often made by advertising agencies or consultants. Reports by the sales force should be structured in a way to provide management with certain types of product information; in fact, these reports can be the firm's most valuable improvement tool. Implementing a product improvement decision will often require the coordinated efforts of several specialists, plus some research. For example, product design improvement decisions involve engineering, manufacturing, accounting, and marketing. When a firm becomes aware that a product's design can be improved, it is not always clear as to how consumers will react to the various alterations. Consequently, it is advisable to conduct some market tests.

ORGANIZING FOR PRODUCT MANAGEMENT

A firm can organize for managing its products in a variety of ways.[7] Figure 6-2 describes five methods and the types of companies for which they are most useful. Under a *marketing-manager system,* all the functional areas of marketing report to one manager. These in-

---

[6] For further discussion of product deletion decisions, see George J. Avlonitis, "Product Elimination Decision Making: Does Formality Matter?" *Journal of Marketing,* Winter 1985, pp. 41–52.

[7] This section is based on Joel R. Evans and Barry Berman, *Marketing,* 3d ed. (New York: Macmillan, 1987), pp. 248–49.

FIGURE 6–2 Five Methods of Organizing for Product Management

	Characteristics		
Organization	*Staffing*	*Ideal Use*	*Permanency*
Marketing-manager system	All functional areas of marketing report to one manager.	A company makes one product line or has a dominant line.	The system is ongoing.
Product (brand) manager system	A middle manager focuses on a single product or group of products.	A company makes many distinct products, each requiring expertise.	The system is ongoing.
Product-planning committee	Executives from various functional areas participate.	The committee should supplement another product organization.	The committee meets irregularly.
New-product manager system	Separate managers direct new products and existing products.	A company makes several existing products and substantial time, resources, and expertise are needed for new products.	The system is ongoing, but new products are shifted to product managers after production.
Venture team	An independent group of specialists guides all phases of a new product's development.	A company wants to create vastly different products than those currently made, and it needs an autonomous structure to aid development.	The team disbands after a new product is introduced, turning responsibility over to a product manager.

Source: Joel R. Evans and Barry Berman, *Marketing*, 3rd ed. (New York: Macmillan, 1987), p. 249.

clude sales, advertising, sales promotion, and product planning. Such companies as PepsiCo, Purex, Eastman Kodak, and Levi Strauss use some form of the marketing-manager system.

With the *product (brand) manager system* there is a middle manager in the organization who focuses on a single product or a small group of new or existing products. Typically, this manager is responsible for everything from marketing research to package design to advertising. This method of organizing is sometimes criticized because product managers often do not have authority commensurate with their responsibilities. However, such companies as General Mills, Pillsbury, and Proctor & Gamble (until recently) have successfully used this method.

HIGHLIGHT 6–6

A 10-Point Vitality Test for Older Products, or How to Get That Sales Curve to Slope Upward Again

1. Does the product have new or extended uses? Sales of Arm & Hammer baking soda increased considerably after the product was promoted as a refrigerator deodorant.
2. Is the product a generic item that can be branded? Sunkist puts its name on oranges and lemons, thus giving a brand identity to a formerly generic item.
3. Is the product category "underadvertised?" Tampons were in this category until International Playtex and Johnson & Johnson started spending large advertising appropriations, particularly on television ads.
4. Is there a broader target market? Procter & Gamble increased the sales if Ivory soap by promoting it for adults, instead of just for babies.
5. Can you turn disadvantages into advantages? The manufacturer of Smucker's jams and jellies advertised: "With a name like Smucker's, it has to be good."
6. Can you build volume and profit by cutting the price? Sales of Tylenol increased considerably after Johnson & Johnson cut Tylenol's price to meet the lower price set by Bristol-Myers' Datril brand.
7. Can you market unused by-products? Lumber companies market sawdust as a form of kitty litter.
8. Can you sell the product in a more compelling way? Procter & Gamble's Pampers disposable diapers were only a moderate success in the market when they were sold as a convenience item for mothers. Sales increased, however, after the advertising theme was changed to say that Pampers kept babies dry and happy.
9. Is there a social trend to exploit? Dannon increased its sales of yogurt tremendously by linking this product to consumers' interest in health foods.
10. Can you expand distribution channels? Hanes Hosiery Company increased its sales of L'eggs panty hose by distributing this product through supermarkets.

Source: William J. Stanton and Charles Futrell, *Fundamentals of Marketing,* 8th ed. (New York: McGraw-Hill, 1987), p. 224.

A *product-planning committee* is staffed by executives from functional areas, including marketing, production, engineering, finance, and R&D. The committee handles product approval, evaluation, and development on a part-time basis and typically disbands after a product is introduced. The product then becomes the responsibility of a product manager.

A *new-product manager system* uses separate managers for new and existing products. After a new product is introduced, the new-product manager turns it over to a product manager. This system can be expensive and can cause discontinuity when the product is introduced. However, such firms as General Foods, NCR, and General Electric have used this system successfully.

A *venture team* is a small, independent department consisting of a broad range of specialists who manage a new product's entire development process. The team disbands when the product is introduced. While it can be an expensive method, Xerox, IBM, and Westinghouse use a venture team approach.

Which method to use depends on the diversity of a firm's offerings, the number of new products introduced, the level of innovation, company resources, and management expertise. A combination of product management methods also can be used and many firms find this desirable.

CONCLUSION

This chapter has been concerned with a central element of marketing management—product strategy. The first part of the chapter discussed some basic issues in product strategy, including product definition and classification, product mix and product lines, and packaging and branding. The product life cycle was discussed as well as the product audit. Finally, five methods of organizing for product management were presented. Although product considerations are extremely important, remember that the product is only one element of the marketing mix. Focusing on product decisions alone, without consideration of the other marketing mix variables would be an ineffective approach to marketing strategy.

Additional Readings

Gupta, Ashok K.; S. P. Raj; and David Wilemon. "A Model for Studying R&D—Marketing Interface in the Product Innovation Process." *Journal of Marketing,* April 1986, pp. 7–17.

McEnally, Martha R., and Jon M. Hawes. "The Market for Generic Brand Grocery Products: A Review and Extension." *Journal of Marketing,* Winter 1984, pp. 75–83.

Park, C. Whan; Bernard J. Jaworski; and Deborah J. Macinnis. "Strategic Brand Concept-Image Management." *Journal of Marketing,* October 1986, pp. 135–45.

Pessemier, Edgar E. *Product Management.* 2nd ed. New York: John Wiley & Sons, 1981.

Varadarajan, P. Rajan. "Product Diversity and Firm Performance: An Empirical Investigation." *Journal of Marketing,* July 1986, pp. 43–57.

Wind, Yoram. *Product Policy: Concepts, Methods, and Strategy.* Reading, Mass.: Addison-Wesley Publishing, 1982.

Chapter 7

New Product Planning and Development

New products are a vital part of a firm's competitive growth strategy. Booz Allen & Hamilton, a leading management consultant firm whose experience with over 4,000 firms dates back to 1914, made an early study of the problem of new product management and development. Some of the important conclusions of their research can be briefly summarized:

1. Most manufacturers cannot live without new products. It is commonplace for major companies to have 50 percent or more of current sales in products new in the past 10 years.
2. Many new products are failures. Estimates of new product failure range from 33 percent to 90 percent.
3. Companies vary widely in the effectiveness of their new product programs.
4. Common elements tend to appear in the management practices that generally distinguish the relative degree of efficiency and success between companies.
5. About four out of five hours devoted by scientists and engineers to technical development of new products are spent on projects that do not reach commercial success.[1]

In one recent year, almost 10,000 supermarket items were introduced into the market. Less than 20 percent met sales goals. A single

---

[1] Also see *New Products Management for the 1980s: Phase I* (Chicago: Booz Allen & Hamilton, 1981).

HIGHLIGHT 7-1
Some Important New Product Decisions

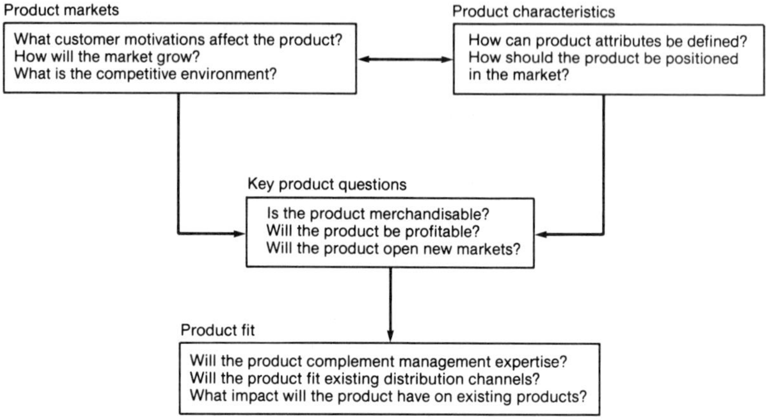
Product markets
What customer motivations affect the product?
How will the market grow?
What is the competitive environment?
Product characteristics
How can product attributes be defined?
How should the product be positioned in the market?
Key product questions
Is the product merchandisable?
Will the product be profitable?
Will the product open new markets?
Product fit
Will the product complement management expertise?
Will the product fit existing distribution channels?
What impact will the product have on existing products?

product failure can cost from $75,000 in a test market to $20 million for a national introduction. In addition to the outlay cost of new product failures, there are also opportunity costs. These opportunity costs refer not only to the alternative uses of funds spent on product failures but also to the time spent in unprofitable product development. Product development can take many years. For example, Hills Brothers spent 22 years in developing its instant coffee, while it took General Foods 10 years to develop Maxim, its concentrated instant coffee.

Good management with heavy emphasis on planning (and organization) seems to be a key factor contributing to a firm's success in launching new products. However, if the causes of new product failure are analyzed, faulty marketing management does not show up as a primary cause. Instead, the secondary causes are revealed, which can be traced back to poor decision making and inadequate marketing planning.

NEW PRODUCT POLICY

In developing new product policies, the first question a marketing manager must ask is: "In how many ways can a product be new?" There are at least nine different ways:

1. A product performing an entirely *new function,* such as television, which for the first time permitted the transmission of audiovisual signals.

2. A product that offers *improved performance of an existing function,* such as a wristwatch whose balance wheel has been replaced by a tuning fork.
3. A product that is a *new application of an existing product.* For example, the aerosol bomb, which was first developed for insecticides, was later applied in paints.
4. A product that offers *additional functions.* The hands-free telephone, for instance, does what the earlier telephone did, plus more.
5. An existing product offered to a *new market.* This may be done, for example, by repositioning or by taking a regional brand into other regions.
6. A product that through *lower cost* is able to reach more buyers. Hand calculators are an example.
7. An upgraded product defined as an *existing product integrated into another existing product.* The clock-radio is an example.
8. A *downgraded product.* For example, a manufacturer switches from buying a component to producing a cheaper component in-house and marketing it.
9. A *restyled product.* Annual auto and clothing changes are examples.[2]

Another approach to the "new" product question has been developed by H. Igor Ansoff in the form of "growth vectors."[3] This is the matrix that first appeared in Chapter One that indicates the direction in which the organization is moving with respect to its current products and markets. It is shown again in Figure 7–1.

Market penetration denotes a growth direction through the increase in market share for present product-markets. *Market development* refers to finding new customers for present products. *Product development* refers to creating new products to replace existing ones. *Diversification* refers to developing new products and cultivating new markets.

In Figure 7–1, market penetration and market development are product line strategies where the focus is upon altering the breadth and depth of the firm's existing product offerings. Product development and diversification can be characterized as product mix strategies. New products, as defined in the growth vector matrix, usually require the firm to make significant investments in research and development and may require major changes in its organizational structure.

It has already been stated that new products are the lifeblood of

---

[2] C. Merle Crawford, *New Product Management,* 2nd ed. (Homewood, Ill.: Richard D. Irwin, 1987), p. 18.

[3] H. Igor Ansoff, *Corporate Strategy* (New York: McGraw-Hill, 1965), pp. 109–10.

FIGURE 7-1 Growth Vector Components

Markets	*Products*	
	Present	*New*
Present	Market penetration	Product development
New	Market development	Diversification

successful business firms. Thus, the critical product policy question is not whether to develop new products but in what direction to move. One way of dealing with this problem is to formulate standards or norms that new products must meet if they are to be considered candidates for launching. In other words, as part of its new product policy, management must ask itself the basic question: "What is the potential contribution of each anticipated new product to the company?"

Each company must answer this question in accordance with its long-run goals, corporate mission, resources, and so forth. Unfortunately, some of the reasons commonly given to justify the launching of new products are so general that they become meaningless. Phrases such as "additional profits" or "increased growth" or "cyclical stability" must be translated into more specific objectives. For example, one objective may be to reduce manufacturing overhead costs by utilizing plant capacity better. This may be accomplished by using the new product as an off-season filler. Naturally, the new product proposal would also have to include production and accounting data to back up this cost argument.

HIGHLIGHT 7-2
Ten Steps in the Development of a New Product Policy

1. Prepare a long-range industry forecast for existing product lines.
2. Prepare a long-range profit plan for the company, using existing product lines.
3. Review the long-range profit plan.
4. Determine what role new products will play in the company's future.
5. Prepare an inventory of company capabilities.
6. Determine market areas for new products.
7. Prepare a statement of new product objectives.
8. Prepare a long-range profit plan, incorporating new products.
9. Assign new product responsibility.
10. Provide for evaluation of new product performance.

HIGHLIGHT 7-3
Some Sources of New Product Ideas

1. *Sales force.*
   a. Knowledge of customers' needs.
   b. Inquiries from customers or prospects.
   c. Knowledge of the industry and competition.
2. *Research and engineering.*
   a. Application of basic research.
   b. Original or creative thinking.
   c. Testing existing products and performance records.
   d. Accidental discoveries.
3. *Other company sources.*
   a. Suggestions from employees.
   b. Utilization of by-products or scrap.
   c. Specific market surveys.
4. *Outside sources.*
   a. Inventors.
   b. Stockholders.
   c. Suppliers or vendors.
   d. Middlemen.
   e. Ad agencies.
   f. Customer suggestions.

In every new product proposal some attention must be given to the ultimate economic contribution of each new product candidate. If the argument is that a certain type of product is needed to "keep up with competition" or "to establish leadership in the market," then it is fair to ask, "Why?" To put the question another way, top management can ask: "What will be the effect on the firm's long-run profit picture if we do not develop and launch this or that new product?" Policymaking criteria on new products should specify *(a)* a working definition of the profit concept acceptable to top management, *(b)* a minimum level or floor of profits, and *(c)* the availability and cost of capital to develop a new product.

NEW PRODUCT PLANNING AND DEVELOPMENT PROCESS

Ideally, products that generate a maximum dollar profit with a minimum amount of risk should be developed and marketed. However, it is very difficult for planners to implement this idea because of the number and nature of the variables involved. What is needed is a systematic, formalized process for new product planning. Although such a process does not provide management with any magic answers, it can increase the probability of new product success. Initially, the firm must establish some new product policy guidelines that include: the product fields of primary interest, organizational responsibilities for managing the various stages in new product development, and criteria for making go-ahead decisions. After these guidelines are established, a process such as the one shown in Figure 7-2 should be useful in new product development.

Idea Generation

Every product starts as an idea. But all new product ideas do not have equal merit or potential for economic or commercial success. Some estimates indicate that as many as 60 or 70 ideas are necessary to yield one successful product. This is an average figure, but it serves to illustrate the fact that new product ideas have a high mortality rate. In

FIGURE 7-2 The New Product Development Process

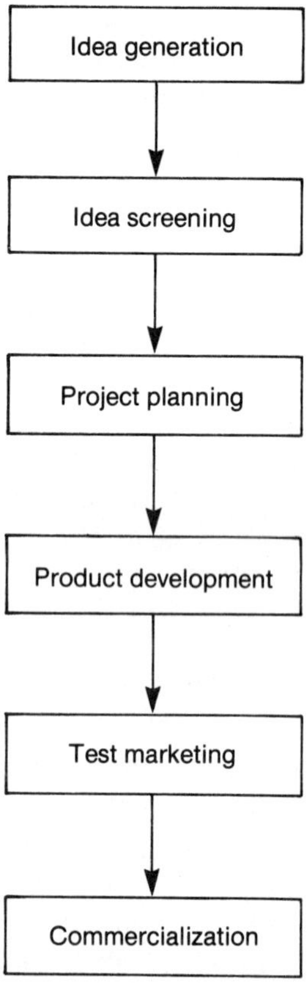

terms of money, of all the dollars of new product expense, almost three fourths go to unsuccessful products.

The problem at this stage is to ensure that all new product ideas available to the company at least have a chance to be heard and evaluated. This includes recognizing available sources of new product ideas and funneling these ideas to appropriate decision makers for screening.

Idea Screening

The primary function of the screening stage is twofold: first, to eliminate ideas for new products that could not be profitably marketed by the firm and, second, to expand viable ideas into a full product concept. New product ideas may be eliminated either because they are outside the fields of the firm's interest or because the firm does not have the necessary resources or technology to produce the product at a profit. However, other ideas are accepted for further study because they appear to have adequate profit potential and offer the firm a competitive advantage in the market.

Project Planning

This stage of the process involves several steps. It is here that the product proposal is evaluated further and responsibility for the project is assigned to a project team. The proposal is analyzed in terms of production, marketing, financial, and competitive factors. A development budget is established, and some preliminary marketing and technical research is undertaken. The product is actually designed in a rough form. Alternative product features and component specifications are outlined. Finally, a project plan is written up, which includes estimates of future development, production, and marketing costs along with capital requirements and manpower needs. A schedule or timetable is also included. Finally, the project proposal is given to top management for a go or no-go decision.

Product Development

At this juncture the product idea has been evaluated from the standpoint of engineering, manufacturing, finance, and marketing. If it has met all expectations, it is considered a candidate for further research and testing. In the laboratory, the product is converted into a finished good and tested. A development report to management is prepared that spells out in fine detail: *(a)* the results of the studies by the engineering

HIGHLIGHT 7-4
Screening Criteria Used by Major Companies

Product Criteria	*Market Criteria*	*Financial Criteria*
Newness	Market size, share	Overall profit contribution
Fit with existing facilities and skills	Market growth	Return on investment
Proprietary position	Market positioning	Investment requirement
Servicing requirements	Effect on existing product line	Profit-risk ratio
Technical feasibility (development and production)	Competitive status	Effect on cash flow
Legal considerations	Distribution characteristics	Accessory income possibilities
Organizational support		

Source: Thomas C. Kinnear and Kenneth L. Bernhardt, *Principles of Marketing*, 2nd ed. (Glenview, Ill.: Scott Foresman, 1986), p. 307.

department, *(b)* required plant design, *(c)* production facilities design, *(d)* tooling requirements, *(e)* marketing test plan, *(f)* financial program survey, and *(g)* an estimated release date.

Test Marketing

Up until now the product has been a company secret. Now management goes outside the company and submits the product candidate for customer approval. Test marketing programs are conducted in line with plans for launching the product. At this stage, primary attention is given to the general marketing strategy to be used and the appropriate marketing mix. Test findings are analyzed, the product design is frozen into production, and a marketing plan is finalized.

Commercialization

This is the launching step. During this stage, heavy emphasis is on the organization structure and management talent needed to implement the marketing strategy. Emphasis is also given to following up such things as bugs in the design, production costs, quality control, and inventory requirements. Procedures and responsibility for evaluating the success of the new product by comparison with projections are also finalized.

> **HIGHLIGHT 7-5**
> **Six Ss for New Product Success**
>
> Below is a list of product attributes that have been found to have a significant effect on new product purchase and acceptance by consumers:
>
> 1. *Superiority*. The degree to which the new product has a clear differential or relative advantage over previous products.
> 2. *Sociability*. The degree to which the new product is compatible or consistent with consumers' existing beliefs, values, and lifestyles.
> 3. *Satisfaction*. The degree to which the new product satisfies consumers' felt needs.
> 4. *Simplicity*. The degree to which the new product is easy for consumers to understand and use and for marketers to promote and make available.
> 5. *Separability*. The degree to which the new product can be tested on a trial basis with limited investment by consumers.
> 6. *Speed*. The degree to which the benefits of the products are experienced immediately, rather than at a later time.

CAUSES OF NEW PRODUCT FAILURE

Many new products with satisfactory potential have failed to make the grade. Many of the reasons for new product failure relate to execution and control problems. Below is a brief list of some of the more important causes of new product failures after they have been carefully screened, developed, and marketed.

1. Faulty estimates of market potential.
2. Unexpected reactions from competitors.
3. Poor timing in the introduction of the product.
4. Rapid change in the market (economy) after the product was approved.
5. Inadequate quality control.
6. Faulty estimates in production costs.
7. Inadequate expenditures on initial promotion.
8. Faulty test marketing.
9. Improper channel of distribution.

Some of thc above problems are beyond the control of management; but it is clear that successful new product planning requires large amounts of reliable information in diverse areas. Each department assigned functional responsibility for product development automatically becomes an input to the information system needed by the new product decision maker. For example, when a firm is developing a new product, it is wise for both engineers and marketers to consider both the kind of market to be entered (e.g., consumer, industrial, defense, or export) and specific target segments. These decisions will influence the design and cost of the finished good, which will, of course, directly influence price, sales, and profits.

Need for Research

In many respects it can be argued that the keystone activity of any new product planning system is research—not just marketing research but technical research as well. Regardless of the way in which the new product planning function is organized in the company, new product development decisions by top management require data that provide a base for making more intelligent choices. New product project reports ought to be more than a collection of "expert" opinions. Top management has a responsibility to ask certain questions, and the new product planning team has an obligation to generate answers to these questions based on research that provides marketing, economic, engineering, and production information. This need will be more clearly understood if some of the specific questions common raised in evaluating product ideas are examined:

1. What is the anticipated market demand over time? Are the potential applications for the product restricted?
2. Can the item be patented? Are there any antitrust problems?
3. Can the product be sold through present channels and sales force? What will be the number of new salespersons needed? What additional sales training will be required?
4. At different volume levels, what will be the unit manufacturing costs?
5. What is the most appropriate package to use in terms of color, material, design, and so forth?
6. What is the estimated return on investment?
7. What is the appropriate pricing strategy?

While this list is not intended to be exhaustive, it serves to illustrate the serious need for reliable information. Note, also, that some of the essential facts required to answer these questions can only be obtained through time-consuming and expensive marketing research studies. Other data can be generated in the engineering laboratories or pulled from accounting records. Certain types of information must be based on assumptions, which may or may not hold true, and on expectations about what will happen in the future, as in the case of "anticipated competitive reaction" or the projected level of sales.

Another complication is that many different types of information must be gathered and formulated into a meaningful program for decision making. To illustrate, in trying to answer questions about return on investment of a particular project, the analyst must know something about (1) the pricing strategy to be used and (2) the investment outlay. Regardless of the formula used to measure the investment worth of a new product, different types of information are required. Using one of the simplest approaches—the payback method (the ratio of investment outlay to annual cash flow)—one needs to estimate the magnitude of the product investment outlay and the annual cash flow. The investment outlay requires estimates of such things as production equipment, R&D costs, and nonrecurring introductory marketing expenditures; the annual cash flow requires a forecast of unit demand and price. These data must be collected or generated from many different departments and processed into a form that will be meaningful to the decision maker.

CONCLUSION

This chapter has focused on the nature of new product planning and development. Attention has been given to the management process required to have an effective program for new product development. It should be obvious to the reader that this is one of the most important and difficult aspects of marketing management. The problem is so complex that, unless management develops a plan for dealing with the problem, it is likely to operate at a severe competitive disadvantage in the marketplace.

Additional Readings

Crawford, C. Merle. *New Products Management.* 2nd ed. Homewood, Ill.: Richard D. Irwin, 1987.

Hopkins, David. *New Product Winners and Losers.* New York: The Conference Board, 1980.

Narasimhan, Chakravarthi, and Subrata K. Sen. "New Product Models for Test Market Data." *Journal of Marketing,* Winter 1983, pp. 11–24.

Robertson, Thomas S., and Hubert Gatignon. "Competitive Effects on Technology Diffusion." *Journal of Marketing,* July 1986, pp. 1–12.

Urban, Glen L., and John R. Hauser. *Design and Marketing of New Products.* Englewood Cliffs, N.J.: Prentice-Hall, 1980.

von Hippel, Eric. "Get New Products from Customers." *Harvard Business Review,* March–April 1982, pp. 117–22.

Chapter 8

Promotion Strategy: Advertising and Sales Promotion

To simplify the discussion of the general subject of promotion, the topic has been divided into two basic categories, personal selling and nonpersonal selling. Personal selling will be discussed in detail in the next chapter and this chapter will be devoted to nonpersonal selling.

Nonpersonal selling includes all demand creation and demand maintenance activities of the firm, other than personal selling. It is mass selling. In more specific terms, nonpersonal selling includes *(a)* advertising, *(b)* sales promotion, and *(c)* publicity. For purposes of this text, primary emphasis will be placed on advertising and sales promotion. Publicity is a special form of promotion that amounts to "free advertising," such as a writeup about the firm's products in a newspaper article. It will not be dealt with in detail in this text.

THE PROMOTION MIX

The promotion mix concept refers to *the combination and types of promotional effort the firm puts forth during a specified time period.* Most business concerns make use of more than one form of promotion, but some firms rely on a single technique. An example of a company using only one promotional device would be a manufacturer of novelties who markets its products exclusively by means of mail order.

In devising its promotion mix the firm should take into account three basic factors: (1) the role of promotion in the overall marketing

HIGHLIGHT 8–1
Some Advantages and Disadvantages of Major Promotion Methods

Advertising

Advantages

Can reach many consumers simultaneously.

Relatively low cost per exposure.

Excellent for creating brand images.

High degree of flexibility and variety of media to choose from; can accomplish many different types of promotion objectives.

Disadvantages

Many consumers reached are not potential buyers (waste of promotion dollars).

High visibility makes advertising a major target of marketing critics.

Advertisement exposure time is usually brief.

Advertisements are often quickly and easily screened out by consumers.

Personal Selling

Advantages

Can be the most persuasive promotion tool; salespeople can directly influence purchase behaviors.

Allows two-way communication.

Often necessary for technically complex products.

Alows direct one-on-one targeting of promotional effort.

Disadvantages

High cost per contact.

Sales training and motivation can be expensive and difficult.

Personal selling often has a poor image, making salesforce recruitment difficult.

Poorly done sales presentations can hurt sales as well as company, product, and brand-images.

Sales Promotion

Advantages

Excellent approach for short-term price reductions for stimulating demand.

A large variety of sales promotion tools to choose from.

Can be effective for changing a variety of consumer behaviors.

Can be easily tied in with other promotion tools.

Disadvantages

May influence primarily brand-loyal customers to stock up at lower price but attract few new customers.

May have only short-term impact.

Overuse of price-related sales promotion tools may hurt brand image and profits.

Effective sales promotions are easily copied by competitors.

Source: J. Paul Peter and Jerry C. Olson, *Consumer Behavior* (Homewood, Ill.: Richard D. Irwin, 1987), p. 536.

mix, (2) the nature of the product, and (3) the nature of the market. Also, it must be recognized that a firm's promotion mix is likely to change over time to reflect changes in the market, competition, the product's life cycle, and the adoption of new strategies. The following example illustrates how one firm developed its promotion mix along these lines.

When IBM began to market its magnetic character sensing equipment for banks, the company defined the 500 largest banks as its likeliest market and a research firm was commissioned to study the marketing problems. They selected a representative sample of 185 banks and interviewed the officer designated by each bank as the person who would be most influential in deciding whether or not to purchase the equipment. Researchers sought to establish which of the following stages each banker had reached in the sales process: (1) *awareness* of the new product; (2) *comprehension* of what it offered; (3) *conviction* that it would be a good investment; or (4) the *ordering* stage. They also tried to isolate the promotional factors that had brought the bankers to each stage. IBM's promotional mix consisted of personal selling, advertising, education (IBM schools and in-bank seminars), and publicity (through news releases). Figure 8–1 illustrates the process.

The findings were a revelation to IBM. In the marketing of such equipment IBM had consistently taken the position that advertising had a very minor role to play; that nothing could replace the sales call. IBM found it could cut back on personal selling in the early stages of the selling process, thereby freeing salespeople to concentrate on the vital phase of the process—the actual closing of the sale. While these results may not hold true for all products, they are an excellent example of the concept of the promotion mix and the effectiveness of different combinations of promotion tools for achieving various objectives.

ADVERTISING: PLANNING AND STRATEGY

Advertising seeks to promote the seller's product by means of printed and electronic media. This is justified on the grounds that messages can reach large numbers of people and inform, persuade, and remind them about the firm's offerings. The traditional way of defining advertising is as follows: It is any paid form of nonpersonal presentation of ideas, goods, or services by an identified sponsor.[1]

---

[1] Committee on Definitions of the American Marketing Association, *Marketing Definitions: A Glossary of Marketing Terms* (Chicago: American Marketing Association, 1960).

FIGURE 8–1 An Example of the Role of Various Promotion Tools in the Selling Process

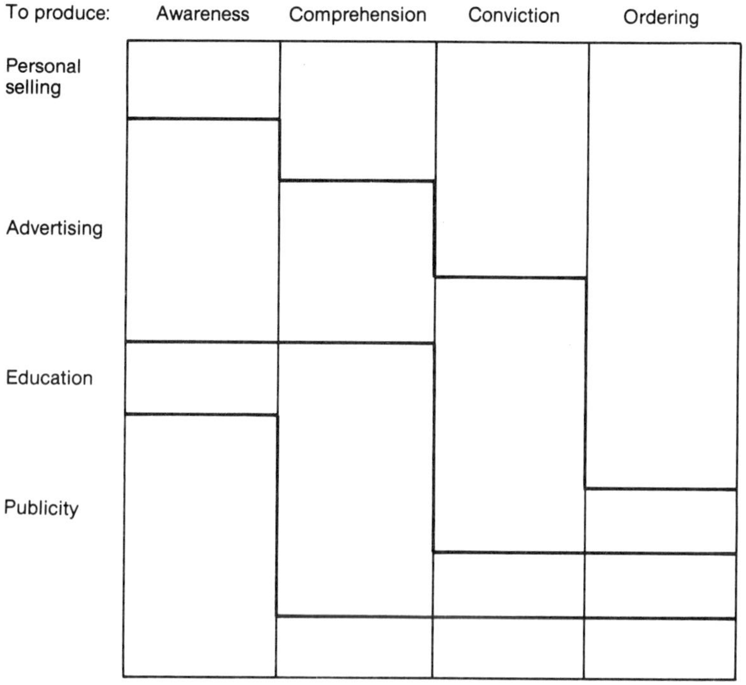

From a management viewpoint, advertising is a strategic device for gaining or maintaining a competitive advantage in the marketplace. For manufacturers and resellers alike, advertising budgets represent a large and growing element in the cost of marketing goods and services. For example, by 1990 advertising expenditures could reach $100 billion, more than four times the amount spent in 1980.[2] As part of the seller's promotion mix, advertising dollars must be appropriated and budgeted according to a marketing plan that takes into account such factors as:

1. Nature of the product, including life cycle.
2. Competition.
3. Government regulations.
4. Nature and scope of the market.

[2] *Advertising Age,* May 6, 1985.

5. Channels of distribution.
6. Pricing strategy.
7. Availability of media.
8. Availability of funds.
9. Outlays for other forms of promotion.

Objectives of Advertising

In the long run, and often in the short run, advertising is justified on the basis of the revenues it produces. Revenues in this case may refer either to sales or profits. Economic theory assumes that firms are profit maximizers, and that advertising outlays should be increased in every market and medium up to the point where the additional cost of getting more business just equals the incremental profits. Since most business firms do not have the data required to use the marginal analysis of economic theory, they usually employ a less sophisticated decision-making model. There is also evidence to show that many executives advertise to maximize sales on the assumption that higher sales mean more profits (which may or may not be true).

The point to be made here is that the ultimate goal of the business advertiser is sales and profits. To achieve this goal an approach to advertising is needed that provides guidelines for intelligent decision making. This approach must recognize the need for measuring the results of advertising, and these measurements must be as valid and reliable as possible. Marketing managers must also be aware of the fact that advertising not only complements other forms of selling but is subject to the law of diminishing returns. This means that for any advertised product it can be assumed a point is eventually reached at which additional adertising produces little or no additional sales.

Specific Tasks of Advertising

In attempting to evaluate the contribution of advertising to the economic health of the firm, there are at least three different viewpoints on the subject. The generalist viewpoint is primarily concerned with sales, profits, return on investment, and so forth. At the other extreme, the specialist viewpoint is represented by advertising experts who are primarily concerned with measuring the effects of specific ads or campaigns; here primary attention is given to such matters as the Nielsen Index, Starch Reports (Starch Advertising Readership Service), copy appeal, and so forth. A middle view, one that might be classified as more of a marketing management approach, understands and appreciates the other two viewpoints but, in addition, views advertising as a competitive weapon. Emphasis in this approach is given to the strategic aspects of the advertising problem. Following are some of the marketing tasks generally assigned to the advertising function as part of the overall marketing mix:

1. Maintaining dealer cooperation.
2. Familiarizing the consumer with the use of the product.
3. Emphasizing a trademark or brand.
4. Obtaining a list of prospects.
5. Creating goodwill for the product, brand, or company.
6. Stressing unique features of the product.
7. Introducing new products.
8. Generating store traffic.
9. Informing customers of sales prices.
10. Building customer or brand loyalty.
11. Establishing a relationship between the producer and distributor.

The above list is representative but not exhaustive, and it should be noted that some of the points pertain more to middlemen than to producers. For example, the first point is a "channel task," where advertising and other forms of sales promotion are employed to facilitate the flow of the producer's goods through distributors to the ulti-

HIGHLIGHT 8–2
Preparing the Advertising Campaign: The Eight-M Formula

Effective advertising should follow a plan. There is no one best way to go about planning an advertising campaign, but, in general, marketers should have good answers to the following eight questions:

1. *The management question:* Who will manage the advertising program?
2. *The money question:* How much should be spent on advertising as opposed to other forms of selling?
3. *The market question:* To whom should the advertising be directed?
4. *The message question:* What should the ads say about the product?
5. *The media question:* What types and combinations of media should be used?
6. *The macro-scheduling question:* How long should the advertising campaign be in effect before changing ads or themes?
7. *The micro-scheduling question:* At what times and dates would it be best for ads to appear during the course of the campaign?
8. *The measurement question:* How will the effectiveness of the advertising campaign be measured and how will the campaign be evaluated and controlled?

mate consumer; "cooperative advertising" programs are specifically designed to meet this objective. This is where a channel member, such as a retailer, will receive a certain percentage of gross sales as an advertising allowance. Some manufacturers also provide advertising copy, illustrations, and so forth.

ADVERTISING DECISIONS

In line with what has just been said, the marketing manager must make two key decisions. The first decision deals with determining the size of the advertising budget, and the second deals with how the advertising budget should be allocated. Although these decisions are highly interrelated, we deal with them separately to achieve a better understanding of the problems involved.

The Expenditure Question

Most firms determine how much to spend on advertising by one of the following methods:

Percent of Sales. This is one of the most popular rule-of-thumb methods and its appeal is found in its simplicity. The firm simply takes a percentage figure and applies it to either past or future sales. For example, if next year's sales are estimated to be $1 million, then using a 2 percent of sales criterion, the ad budget would be $20,000. This approach is usually justified by its advocates in terms of the following argument: *(a)* advertising is needed to generate sales; *(b)* a number of cents, that is, the percentage used, out of each dollar of sales should be devoted to advertising in order to generate needed sales; and *(c)* the percentage is easily adjusted and can be readily understood by other executives. The percent of sales approach is popular in retailing.

Per Unit Expenditure. Closely related to the above technique is one in which a fixed monetary amount is spent on advertising for each unit of the product expected to be sold. This method is popular with higher-priced merchandise, such as automobiles or appliances. For instance, if a company is marketing color televisions priced at $500, then it may decide that it should spend $30 per set on advertising. Since this $30 is a fixed amount for each unit, this method amounts to the same thing as the percent of sales method. The big difference is in the rationale used to justify each of the methods. The per unit expenditure method attempts to determine the retail price by using production costs as a base. Here the seller realizes that a reasonably competitive price must

HIGHLIGHT 8-3
An Advertising Process Model

Consumer Psychosocial State	*Marketing Situation*
1. Ignorance	Consumer has no knowledge of the product.
2. Indifference	Consumer is conscious of product's existence by means of advertising.
3. Awareness	Advertising messages generate an awareness of a need for the product or reinforce a need once generated.
4. Interest	Consumer begins seeking more product-brand information by paying closer attention to various ads.
5. Comprehension	Consumer knows main features of product and various brands after intense ad exposure.
6. Conviction	Consumer is receptive to purchase and ready to act.
7. Action	Consumer shops for the product often as a result of the "act now" advertisements or special sales.

be established for the product in question and attempts to cost out the gross margin. All this means is that, if the suggested retail price is to be $500 and manufacturing costs are $250, then there is a gross margin of $250 available to cover certain expenses, such as transportation, personal selling, advertising, dealer profit, and so forth. Some of these expense items are flexible, such as advertising, while others are nearly fixed, as in the case of transportation. The basic problem with this method and the percentage of sales method is that they view advertising as a function of sales, rather than sales as a function of advertising.

All You Can Afford. Here the advertising budget is established as a predetermined share of profits or financial resources. The availability of current revenues sets the upper limit of the ad budget. The only advantage to this approach is that it sets reasonable limits on the expenditures for advertising. However, from the standpoint of sound marketing practice, this method is undesirable because there is no necessary connection between liquidity and advertising opportunity. Any firm that limits its advertising outlays to the amount of available funds will probably miss opportunities for increasing sales and profits.

Competitive Parity. This approach is often used in conjunction with other approaches, such as the percent of sales method. The basic philosophy underlying this approach is that advertising is defensive. Advertising budgets are based on those of competitors or other members of the industry. From a strategy standpoint, this is a "followership" technique and assumes that the other firms in the industry know what they are doing and have similar goals. Competitive parity is not a preferred method, although some executives feel it is a "safe" approach. This may or may not be true depending in part on the relative market share of competing firms and their growth objectives.

The Research Approach. Here the advertising budget is argued for and presented on the basis of research findings. Advertising media are studied in terms of their productivity by the use of media reports (such as the Starch Reports) and research studies. Costs are also estimated and compared with study results. A typical experiment is one in which three or more test markets are selected. The first test market is used as a control, either with no advertising or with normal levels of advertising. Advertising with various levels of intensity are used in the other markets, and comparisons are made to see what effect different levels of intensity have. The advertising manager then evaluates the costs and benefits of the different approaches and intensity levels to determine the overall budget. Although the research approach is generally more expensive than some other models, it is a more rational approach to the expenditure decision.

The Task Approach. Well-planned advertising programs usually make use of the task approach, which initially formulates the advertising goals and defines the tasks to accomplish these goals. Once this is done, management determines how much it will cost to accomplish each task and adds up the total. This approach is often used in conjunction with the research approach. A variation of the task approach is referred to as the *marketing-program approach*. Here all promotional or selling programs are budgeted in relation to each other, and, given a set of objectives, the goal is to find the optimum promotional mix. It should be clear that, in the task or marketing-program approach, the expenditure and allocation decision are inseparable.

The Allocation Question

This question deals with the problem of deciding on the most effective way of spending advertising dollars. A general answer to the question is that management's choice of strategies and objectives determines the media and appeals to be used. In other words, the firm's or product division's overall marketing plan will function as a general guideline for answering the allocation question.

From a practical standpoint, however, the allocation question can be framed in terms of message and media decisions. A successful ad campaign has two related tasks: (1) say the right things in the ads themselves and (2) use the appropriate media in the right amounts at the right time to reach the target market.

Message Strategy. The advertising process involves creating messages with words, ideas, sounds, and other forms of audiovisual stimuli that are designed to affect consumer (or distributor) behavior. It follows that much of advertising is a communication process. To be effective, the advertising message should meet two general criteria: (1) it should take into account the basic principles of communication and (2) it should be predicated upon a good theory of consumer motivation and behavior.[3]

The basic communication process involves three elements: (1) the sender or source of the communication, (2) the communication or message, and (3) the receiver or audience. Advertising agencies are considered experts in the communications field and are employed by most large firms to create meaningful messages and assist in their dissemination. Translating the product idea or marketing message into an effective ad is termed *encoding*. In advertising, the goal of encoding is to generate ads that are understood by the audience. For this to occur, the audience must be able to decode the message in the ad so that the perceived content of the message is the same as the intended content of the message. From a practical standpoint, all this means is that advertising messages must be sent to consumers in an understandable and meaningful way.

Advertising messages, of course, must be transmitted and carried by particular communication channels commonly known as advertising media. These media or channels vary in efficiency, selectivity, and cost. Some channels are preferred to others because they have less "noise," and thus messages are more easily received and understood. For example, a particular newspaper ad must compete with other ads, pictures, or stories on the same page. In the case of radio or TV, while only one firm's message is usually broadcast at a time, there are other distractions (noise) that can hamper clear communications, such as driving while listening to the radio.

---

[3] For a full discussion of message strategy, see James F. Engel, Martin R. Warshaw, and Thomas C. Kinnear, *Promotional Strategy*, 6th ed. (Homewood, Ill.: Richard D. Irwin, 1987).

The relationship between advertising and consumer behavior is quite obvious. For many products and services, advertising is an influence that may affect the consumer's decision to purchase a particular product or brand. It is clear that consumers are subjected to many selling influences, and the question arises about how important advertising is or can be. Here is where the advertising expert must operate on some theory of consumer behavior. The reader will recall from the discussion of consumer behavior that the buyer was viewed as progressing through various stages from an unsatisfied need through and beyond a purchase decision. The relevance of this discussion is illustrated in Figure 8–2, which compares the role of advertising in various stages of the buying process.

The planning of an advertising campaign and the creation of persuasive messages requires a mixture of marketing skill and creative know-how. Relative to the dimension of marketing skills, there are some important pieces of marketing information needed before launching an ad campaign. Most of this information must be generated by the firm and kept up to date. Listed below are some of the critical types of information an advertiser should have:

1. *Who* the firms' customers and potential customers are; their demographic, economic, and psychological characteristics; and any other factors affecting their likelihood of buying.

FIGURE 8–2 Advertising and the Buying Process

Stage in the Buying Process	*Possible Advertising Objective*	*Examples*
1. Unsatisfied need.	Awareness.	"The reciprocating engine is inefficient." "Dishwashing roughens hands."
2. Alternative search and evaluation.	Comprehension.	"The Wankel engine is efficient." "Palmolive is mild."
3. Purchase decision.	Conviction-ordering.	"Come in and see for yourself." "Buy some today."
4. Postpurchase feelings.	Reassurance.	"Thousands of satisfied owners." "Compare with any other brand."

Source: Adapted for the purposes of this text from Ben M. Enis, *Marketing Principles: The Management Process* (Santa Monica, Calif.: Goodyear Publishing, 1980), p. 466.

2. *How many* such customers there are.
3. *How much* of the firm's type and brand of product they are currently buying and can reasonably be expected to buy in the short-term and long-term future.
4. *What* individuals, other than customers, and potential customers, *influence* purchasing decisions.
5. *Where* they *buy* the firm's brand of product.
6. *When* they buy, and frequency of purchase.
7. *What* competitive brands they buy and frequency of purchase.
8. *How* they *use* the product.
9. *Why* they buy particular *types* and *brands* of products.

Media Mix. Media selection is no easy task. To start with, there are numerous types and combinations of media to choose from. Below is a general outline of some of the more common advertising media.

A. **Printed media.**
   1. National.
      a. Magazines.
      b. Newspapers.
      c. Direct mail.
   2. Local.
      a. Newspapers.
      b. Magazines.
      c. Direct mail.
      d. Handbills or flyers.
      e. Yellow Pages.

B. **Electronic media.**
   1. National (network).
      a. Radio.
      b. Television.
   2. Local.
      a. Radio (AM—FM).
      b. Television.

C. **Other.**
   1. Outdoor (example: billboards).
   2. Transit.
   3. Specialty (giveaways).
   4. Point-of-purchase.
   5. Telemarketing (telephone selling).

Of course, each of the above media categories can be further refined. For example, magazines can be broken down into more detailed classes, such as mass monthlies *(Reader's Digest),* news weeklies *(Time),* men's magazines *(Playboy),* women's fashion magazines *(Vogue),* sports magazines *(Sports Illustrated),* business magazines

(Forbes), and so forth. Clearly, one dimension of this advertising management problem involves having an overabundance of media to select from. With only four media to choose from there are 16 possible go or no-go decisions. With 10 media, there would be approximately 1,000 combinations.

Although the number of media and media combinations available for advertising is overwhelming at first glance, four interrelated factors limit the number of practical alternatives. First, *the nature of the product* limits the number of practical and efficient alternatives. For instance, a radically new and highly complex product could not be properly promoted using billboard advertisements. Second, *the nature and size of the target market* also limits appropriate advertising media. For example, it is generally inefficient to advertise industrial goods in mass media publications. Third, *the advertising budget* may restrict the use of expensive media, such as television. And fourth, *the availability* of some media may be limited in particular geographic areas. Although these factors reduce media alternatives to a more manageable number, specific media must still be selected. A primary consideration at this point is media effectiveness or efficiency.

In the advertising industry a common measure of efficiency or productivity of media is "cost per thousand." This figure generally refers to the dollar cost of reaching 1,000 prospects, and its chief advantage is in making media comparisons. Generally, such measures as circulation, audience size, and sets in use per commercial minute are used in the calculation. Of course, different relative rankings of media can occur, depending on the measure used. Another problem deals with what is meant by "reaching" the prospect, and at least five levels of reaching are possible:

1. *Distribution*. This level refers to circulation or physical distribution of the vehicle into households or other decision-making units. In only some of these households or decision-making units are there genuine prospects for the product.
2. *Exposure*. This level refers to actual exposure of prospects to the message. If the TV set is on, distribution is taking place; but only if the program is being watched can exposure occur.
3. *Awareness*. This level refers to the prospect becoming alert to the message in the sense of being conscious of the ad. Actual information processing starts at this point.
4. *Communication*. This level goes one step beyond awareness—to the point where the prospect becomes affected by the message. Here the effect is to generate some sort of change in the prospect's knowledge, attitude, or desire concerning the product.
5. *Response*. This level represents the overt action that results because of the ad. Response can mean many things, such as a simple telephone or mail inquiry, a shopping trip, or a purchase.

HIGHLIGHT 8–4
Some Relative Merits of Major Advertising Media

Newspapers

Advantages

1. Flexible and timely.
2. Intense coverage of local markets.
3. Broad acceptance and use.
4. High believability of printed word.

Disadvantages

1. Short life.
2. Read hastily.
3. Small "pass-along" audience.

Television

Advantages

1. Combination of sight, sound, and motion.
2. Appeals to senses.
3. Mass audience coverage.
4. Psychology of attention.

Disadvantages

1. Nonselectivity of audience.
2. Fleeting impressions.
3. Short life.
4. Expensive.

Radio

Advantages

1. Mass use (over 25 million radios sold annually).
2. Audience selectivity via station format.
3. Low cost (per unit of time.)
4. Geographic flexibility.

Disadvantages

1. Audio presentation only.
2. Less attention than TV.
3. Chaotic buying (nonstandardized rate structures).
4. Short life.

Magazines

Advantages

1. High geographic and demographic selectivity.
2. Psychology of attention.
3. Quality of reproduction.
4. Pass-along readership.

Disadvantages

1. Long closing periods (6 to 8 weeks prior to publication).
2. Some waste circulation.
3. No guarantee of position (unless premium is paid).

Outdoor

Advantages

1. Flexible.
2. Relative absence of competing advertisements.
3. Repeat exposure.
4. Relatively inexpensive.

Disadvantages

1. Creative limitations.
2. Many distractions for viewer.
3. Public attack (ecological implications).
4. No selectivity of audience.

Direct Mail

Advantages

1. Audience selectivity.
2. Flexible.
3. No competition from competing advertisements.
4. Personalized.

Disadvantages

1. Relatively high cost.
2. Consumers often pay little attention and throw it away.

The advertiser has to decide at what level to evaluate the performance of a medium, and this is a particularly difficult problem. Ideally, the advertiser would like to know exactly how many dollars of sales are generated by ads in a particular medium. However, this is very difficult to measure since so many other factors are simultaneously at work that could be producing sales. On the other hand, the distribution of a medium is much easier to measure but distribu-

HIGHLIGHT 8-5
Procedures for Evaluating Advertising Programs, and Some Services Using the Procedures

Procedures for evaluating specific advertisements

1. *Recognition tests:* Estimate the percentage of people claiming to have read a magazine who recognize the ad when it is shown to them (e.g., Starch Message Report Service).
2. *Recall tests:* Estimate the percentage of people claiming to have read a magazine who can (unaided) recall the ad and its contents (e.g., Gallup and Robinson Impact Service; various services for TV ads as well).
3. *Opinion tests:* Potential audience members are asked to rank alternative advertisements as most interesting, most believable, best liked.
4. *Theater tests:* Theater audience is asked for brand preferences before and after an ad is shown in context of a TV show (e.g., Schwerin TV Testing Service).

Procedures for evaluating specific advertising objectives

1. *Awareness:* Potential buyers are asked to indicate brands that come to mind in a product category. A message used in an ad campaign is given and buyers are asked to identify the brand that was advertised using that message.
2. *Attitude:* Potential buyers are asked to rate competing or individual brands on determinant attributes, benefits, characterizations using rating scales.

Procedures for evaluating motivational impact

1. *Intention to buy:* Potential buyers are asked to indicate the likelihood they will buy a brand (on a scale from "definitely will not" to "definitely will").
2. *Market test:* Sales changes in different markets are monitored to compare the effects of different messages, budget levels.

Source: Joseph Guiltinan and Gordon Paul, *Marketing Management* (New York: McGraw-Hill, 1985), p. 263.

tion figures are much less meaningful. For example, a newspaper may have a distribution (circulation) of 100,000 people, yet none of these people may be prospects for the particular product being advertised. Thus, if this media were evaluated in terms of distribution, it might be viewed as quite effective even though it may be totally ineffective in terms of producing sales. This problem further illustrates the importance of insuring that the media selected are those used by the target market.

From what has been said so far, it should be clear that advertising decisions involve a great deal of complexity and a myriad of variables. Not surprising, therefore, is that application of quantitative techniques have become quite popular in the area. Linear programming, dynamic programming, heuristic programming, and simulation have been applied to the problem of selecting media schedules, and more comprehensive models of advertising decisions have also been developed. Although these models can be extremely useful as an aid in advertising decision making, they must be viewed as tools and not as replacement for sound managerial decisions and judgment.

SALES PROMOTION

In marketing, the word *promotion* is used in many ways. For instance, it is sometimes used to refer to a specific activity, such as advertising or publicity. In the general sense, promotion has been defined as "any identifiable effort on the part of the seller to persuade buyers to accept the seller's information and store it in retrievable form." However, the term *sales promotion* has a more restricted and technical meaning and has been defined by the American Marketing Association as follows:

> those marketing activities, other than personal selling, advertising and publicity, that stimulate consumer purchasing and dealer effectiveness, such as display, shows, and exhibitions, demonstrations, and various non-recurrent selling efforts not in the ordinary routine.[4]

This definition illustrates that the term *sales promotion* is used for categorizing selling activities that cannot be conveniently classified as one of the other types of promotion. Listed below are some of the more common forms of sales promotion activities.[5]

---

[4] Ralph S. Alexander et al., *Marketing Definitions: A Glossary of Marketing Terms* (Chicago: American Marketing Association, 1960), p. 20.

[5] For discussions of some recent trends in methods of sales promotion, see John A. Quelch and Kristina Cannon-Bonaventre, "Better Marketing at the Point-of-Purchase," *Harvard Business Review,* November–December 1983, pp. 162–69; and "Special Report on Sales Promotion," *Advertising Age,* February 6, 1986, pp. 13–14.

Catalogs	Fixtures
Contests	Games
Conventions	Missionary salespeople
Coupons	Point-of-purchase displays
Deals—merchandise, price	Premiums
Films	Salesperson's aids
Free Samples	Trading stamps
Rebates	Trade exhibits

In examining this list, it should be noted that, in some cases, it is not possible to distinguish between certain types of sales promotion activities and advertising. To illustrate, point-of-purchase displays are sometimes classified as advertising. Likewise, coupon offers and contests are frequently considered part of an advertising campaign. However, regardless of this ambiguity, sales promotion activities are

HIGHLIGHT 8-6
Tools for Reaching Sales Promotion Objective

Objective	*Tool*
Increase trial	Sampling Couponing Price packs Bonus packs On-pack, in-pack, or near-pack premiums Refund packs Free mail-in premium
Increase consumer inventory	Bonus pack "Two-for" packs Price packs Prepriced packs Multiple-proof premiums or refunds
Encourage repurchase	Price packs Bonus packs Contests, sweepstakes On-pack, in-pack, or near-pack premiums Refund packs Self-liquidating items On-pack couponing good on next purchase Multiple-proof free premiums or refunds

Source: Marketing and Sales Promotion (New York: Sales and Marketing Management, 1979), p. 13. Copyright 1979 by *Sales and Marketing Management* magazine.

generally thought of as complementary activities that facilitate advertising and personal selling.

Because sales promotion involves so many diverse activities, it is difficult to make meaningful generalizations. For example, some sales promotion tools, such as special price deals or coupon offers, may be easy to justify on the basis of measured responses; however, other activities are more difficult to evaluate in terms of sales response or goodwill. Two common justifications for sales promotion in the latter case are (1) it is customary in the trade (as in the case of giving free drug samples to doctors) or (2) it is necessary because competition does it (as in the case of trading stamps).

Finally, note that some sales promotion activities can be classified as semiprice competition rather than as nonprice competition. For example, trading stamps, special deals, or merchandise offers have the effect of giving the buyer a lower price. Another dimension to the problem is that, with these types of promotion, competitors can easily retaliate and, in some cases, cancel out the benefits to all sellers. For example, one reason for the decline in the use of trading stamps in grocery stores is that, once all major competitors offered them, this form of sales promotion no longer gave the individual stores or chains a differential advantage.

CONCLUSION

This chapter has been concerned with nonpersonal selling. Remember that advertising and sales promotion are only two of the ways by which sellers can affect the demand for their products. Advertising and sales promotion are only part of the firm's promotion mix and, in turn, the promotion mix is only part of the overall marketing mix. Thus, advertising begins with the market plan and not with the advertising plan. Ignoring this point can produce ineffective promotional programs because of a lack of coordination with other elements of the marketing mix.

Appendix Major Federal Agencies Involved in Control of Advertising

Agency	*Function*
Federal Trade Commission	Regulates commerce between states; controls unfair business practices; takes action on false and deceptive advertising; most important agency in regulation of advertising and promotion.
Food and Drug Administration	Regulatory division of the Department of Health, Education, and Welfare; controls marketing of food, drugs, cosmetics, medical devices, and potentially hazardous consumer products.
Federal Communications Commission	Regulates advertising indirectly, primarily through the power to grant or withdraw broadcasting licenses.
Postal Service	Regulates material that goes through the mails, primarily in areas of obscenity, lottery, and fraud.
Alcohol and Tobacco Tax Division	Part of the Treasury Department; has broad powers to regulate deceptive and misleading advertising of liquor and tobacco.
Grain Division	Unit of the Department of Agriculture responsible for policing seed advertising.
Securities and Exchange Commission	Regulates advertising of securities.

Information Source	*Description*
Patent Office	Regulates registration of trademarks.
Library of Congress	Controls protection of copyrights.
Department of Justice	Enforces all federal laws through prosecuting cases referred to it by other government agencies.

Additional Readings

Aaker, David A., and Donald E. Bruzzone. "Causes of Irritation in Advertising." *Journal of Marketing,* Spring 1985, pp. 47–57.

Bovēe, Courtland L., and William F. Arens. *Contemporary Advertising,* 2nd ed. Homewood, Ill.: Richard D. Irwin, 1987.

Healy, John S., and Harold H. Kassarjian. "Advertising Substantiation and Advertiser Response: A Content Analysis of Magazine Advertisements." *Journal of Marketing,* Winter 1983, pp. 107–17.

Heath, Robert L., and Richard A. Nelson. "Image and Issue Advertising: A Corporate and Public Policy Perspective." *Journal of Marketing,* Spring 1985, pp. 58–68.

Pollay, Richard W. "The Subsiding Sizzle: A Descriptive History of Print Advertising, 1900–1980." *Journal of Marketing,* Summer 1985, pp. 24–37.

Pollay, Richard W. "The Distorted Mirror: Reflections on the Unintended Consequences of Advertising." *Journal of Marketing,* April 1986, pp. 18–36.

Rothschild, Michael L. *Advertising.* Lexington, Mass.: D. C. Heath, 1987.

Sandage, C. H.; V. Fryburger; and K. R. Rotzell. *Advertising Theory and Practice.* 11th ed. Homewood, Ill.: Richard D. Irwin, 1983.

Sewall, M. A., and D. Sarel. "Characteristics of Radio Commercials and Their Recall Effectiveness." *Journal of Marketing,* January 1986, pp. 52–60.

Chapter 9

Promotion Strategy: Personal Selling

Personal selling, unlike advertising or sales promotion, involves direct face-to-face relationships between the seller and the prospect or customer. The behavioral scientist would probably characterize personal selling as a type of personal influence. Operationally, it is a complex communication process, one not completely understood by marketing scholars.

IMPORTANCE OF PERSONAL SELLING

Most business firms find it impossible to market their products without some form of personal selling. To illustrate, some years ago vending machines became quite popular. The question may be raised about whether or not these machines replaced the salesperson. The answer is both yes and no. In a narrow sense of the word, the vending machine has replaced some retail sales clerks who, for most convenience goods, merely dispensed the product and collected money. On the other hand, vending machines and their contents must be "sold" to the vending machine operators, and personal selling effort must be exerted to secure profitable locations for the machines.

The policies of self-service and self-selection have done much to eliminate the need for personal selling in some types of retail stores. However, the successful deployment of these policies have required manufacturers to do two things: *(a)* presell the consumer by means of larger advertising and sales promotion outlays and *(b)* design packages for their products that would "sell" themselves, so to speak.

The importance of the personal selling function depends partially on the nature of the product. As a general rule, goods that are new, technically complex, and/or expensive require more personal selling effort. The salesperson plays a key role in providing the consumer with information about such products to reduce the risks involved in purchase and use. Insurance, for example, is a complex and technical product that often needs significant amounts of personal selling. In addition, many industrial goods cannot be presold, and the salesperson (or sales team) has a key role to play in finalizing the sale. However, most national branded convenience goods are purchased by the consumer without any significant assistance from store clerks.

The importance of personal selling also is determined to a large extent by the needs of the consumer. In the case of pure competition (a large number of small buyers with complete market knowledge of a homogeneous product), there is little need for personal selling. A close

HIGHLIGHT 9-1

America's Best Sales Forces, as Rated by Sales Managers, in 11 Industries

Company	*Industry*	*Rating Criteria, in Order of Importance*
DuPont	Chemicals	1. Reputation among customers
IBM	Computers and office equipment	2. Holding old accounts
Marriott	Diversified services	3. Quality of management
Motorola	Electronics	4. Ability to keep top sales people
Pepsi-Cola USA	Food and beverages	5. Opening new accounts
Georgia-Pacific	Forest products	6. Product/technical knowledge
Textron	Industrial and farm equipment	7. Meeting sales targets
Chromalloy American	Metal products	8. Quality of training
Johnson & Johnson	Pharmaceuticals	9. Innovativeness
Eastman Kodak	Precision instruments	10. Frequency of calls/territory coverage
Blue Bell	Textiles and apparel	

Source: Sales and Marketing Management, December 3, 1984, pp. 19–24.

approximation to this situation is found at auctions for agricultural products, such as tobacco or wheat. At the other extreme, when a product is highly differentiated, such as housing, and marketed to consumers with imperfect knowledge of product offerings, then personal selling becomes a key factor in the promotion mix. In fact, in some cases, the consumer may not even be seeking the product; for instance, life insurance is often categorized as an unsought good. Finally, sellers who differentiate their products at the point of sale will usually make heavy use of personal selling in their promotion mix. For example, automobile buyers are given the opportunity to purchase various extras or options at the time of purchase.

THE SALES PROCESS

Personal selling is as much an art as it is a science. The word *art* is used to describe that portion of the selling process that is highly creative in nature and difficult to explain. This does not mean there is little control over the personal selling element in the promotion mix. It does imply that, all other things equal, the trained salesperson can outsell the untrained one.

Before management selects and trains salespeople, it should have an understanding of the sales process. Obviously, the sales process will differ according to the size of the company, the nature of the product, the market, and so forth, but there are some elements common to almost all selling situations that should be understood. For the purposes of this text, the term *sales process* refers to two basic factors: (1) the sequence of stages or steps the salesperson should follow in trying to sell goods and services and (2) a set of basic principles that, if adhered to, will increase the likelihood of a sale being made.

The traditional approach to personal selling involves a formula or step-by-step procedure. It is known as the AIDAS formula and has five steps: (1) get the prospect's *attention;* (2) arouse the prospect's *interest;* (3) stimulate the prospect's *desire* for the product; (4) get buying *action;* and (5) build *satisfaction* into the transaction. This approach to selling implies two things. First, the prospect or potential buyer goes through these five steps. Second, the salesperson can influence the behavior of the prospect if this process is managed skillfully. Although this model represents a logical approach to explaining the sales process, it emphasizes a how-to-approach to selling, rather than attempting to explain why sales are made or, conversely, why purchases are made.

An explanation of the selling process in terms of why individuals purchase would require a full understanding of consumer behavior. Obviously, as we saw in Chapter 3, this is a difficult task, because so many variables are difficult to measure or control. However, a useful

FIGURE 9–1 A Model of the Selling Process

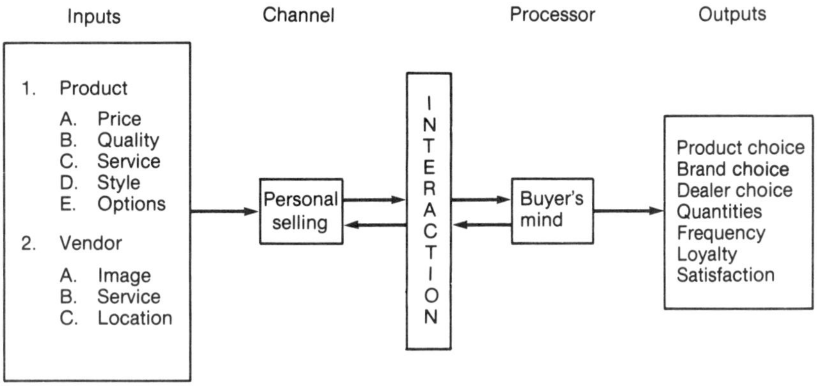

framework for a better understanding of the selling process is illustrated in Figure 9–1.

This approach views the selling process as an input-output system: the inputs are marketing stimuli, such as price, quality, service, style, and so forth. Personal selling is viewed as one of the channels by which knowledge about these marketing stimuli are transmitted to the buyer. In this model, the buyer's mind is a processor of the various stimuli, and, since the workings of the mind are only partially understood, it can be considered a "black box." The explanation of what goes on in this black box depends on which approach or theory of behavior is employed.[1] The outputs for the model represent purchasing responses, such as brand choice, dealer choice, and the like. Here the sales process is viewed as a social situation involving two persons. The interaction of the two persons depends on the economic, social, physical, and personality characteristics of both the seller and the buyer.[2] A successful sale is situationally determined by these factors and can be considered social behavior as well as individual behavior. The prospect's perception of the salesperson is a key factor in determining the salesperson's effectiveness and role expectations.[3] The salesperson's confidence and

---

[1] For a review, see J. Paul Peter and Jerry C. Olson, *Consumer Behavior: Marketing Strategy Perspectives*, Homewood, Ill.: Richard D. Irwin, 1987.

[2] Kaylene C. Williams and Rosann L. Spiro, "Communication Style in the Salesperson-Customer Dyad," *Journal of Marketing Research*, November 1985, pp. 434–43.

[3] Barton A. Weitz, Harish Sujen, and Mita Sujen, "Knowledge, Motivation, and Adaptive Behavior: A Framework for Improving Selling Effectiveness," *Journal of Marketing*, October 1986, pp. 174–91.

HIGHLIGHT 9–2

Qualities Most Valued, Disliked, and Hated in Salespersons by Purchasing Agents

Most Valued	
Reliability/credibility	98.6%
Professionalism/integrity	93.7
Product knowledge	90.7
Innovativeness in problem solving	80.5
Presentation/preparation	69.7

And in the purchasing agents' own words:

Qualities Liked

"Honesty"
"Lose a sale graciously"
"Admits mistakes"
"Problem-solving capabilities"
"Friendly but professional"
"Dependable"
"Adaptability"
"Knows my business"
"Well prepared"
"Patience"

Qualities Disliked

"No follow-up"
"Walking in without an appointment"
"Begins call by talking sports"
"Puts down competitor's products"
"Poor listening skills"
"Too many phone calls"
"Lousy presentation"
"Fails to ask about needs"
"Lacks product knowledge"
"Wastes my time"

Qualities Hated

"Wise-ass attitude"
"Calls me 'dear' or 'sweetheart' (I am female)"
"Gets personal"
"Doesn't give purchasing people credit for any brains"
"Whiners"
"Bullshooters"
"Wines and dines me"
"Plays one company against another"
"Pushy"
"Smokes in my office"

Source: "PAs Examine the People Who Sell to Them," *Sales and Marketing Management* (November 11, 1985), p. 39.

ability to "play the role" of a salesperson is crucial in determining behavior and is influenced by personality, knowledge, training, and previous experience.[4]

Selling Fundamentals

From what has been said so far, the only reasonable conclusion that can be drawn is that there is no one clear-cut theory of personal selling nor one single technique that can be applied universally. Most sales training programs attempt to provide the trainee with the fundamentals of selling, placing emphasis on the "how" and "what" and leaving the "why" questions to the theorists.

A primary objective of any sales training program is to impart knowledge and techniques to the participants. An analysis of numerous training manuals reveals subjects or topics common to many programs. Following are brief descriptions of fundamentals well-trained salespeople should know.

1. They should have thorough knowledge of the company they represent, including its past history. This includes the philosophy of management as well as the firm's basic operating policies.
2. They should have thorough technical and commercial knowledge of their products or product lines. This is particularly true when selling industrial goods. When selling very technical products, many firms require their salespeople to have training as engineers.
3. They should have good working knowledge of competitors' products. This is a vital requirement because the successful salesperson will have to know the strengths and weaknesses of those products that are in competition for market share.
4. They should have in-depth knowledge of the market for their merchandise. The market here refers not only to a particular sales territory but also to the general market, including the economic factors that affect the demand for their goods.
5. They should have accurate knowledge of the buyer or the prospect (the decision-making unit) to whom they are selling. Under the marketing concept, knowledge of the customer is a vital requirement; also, effective selling requires salespeople to understand the unique characteristics of each account.
6. They should have some basic knowledge of sales tactics, which will permit them to overcome obstacles encountered in the field. Tactics here refer to such matters as how to handle objections or how to close a sale.

---

[4] Alan J. Dubinsky, Roy D. Howell, Thomas N. Ingram, and Danny N. Bellinger, "Salesforce Socialization," *Journal of Marketing,* October 1986, pp. 192–207.

HIGHLIGHT 9–3

A Comparison of Order Takers, Order Generators, and Sales Support Personnel

	Order Takers	*Order Generators*	*Sales Support Personnel*
Typical position	Retail sales clerk	IBM mainframe computer salesperson	Pharmaceutical detailer
Purpose	Process routine orders or reorders	Identify new sales opportunities	Promote new products or services
Type of sales transaction	Simple rebuy	New product sales or a modified rebuy situation	Stimulate interest in either a routine rebuy or a new product opportunity
Product line	Well-known, simple products	Complex or customized products	Typically responsible for both simple and complex product lines
Training	Minimum and limited to order processing	Technical skills in addition to extensive skills training	Technical skills and interpersonal communication skills
Compensation	Primarily salary	Either straight commission or combination of salary and a commission	Primarily salary
Source of sales	Existing customers	New customers	Both existing customers and targeted new customers

Source: J. Barry Mason and Hazel F. Ezell, *Marketing: Principles and Strategy* (Plano, Texas: Business Publications, 1987), p. 635.

There are no magic secrets of successful selling. The difference between good salespeople and mediocre ones is often the result of training plus experience. Training is no substitute for experience; the two complement each other. The difficulty with trying to discuss the selling job in terms of basic principles is that experienced, successful salespeople will always be able to find exceptions to these principles. Often successful selling seems to defy logic and, sometimes, common sense. Trying to program salespeople to follow definite rules or principles in every situation can stifle their originality and creativity.[5]

Managing the Sales Process

Every personal sale can be divided into two parts: the part done by the salespeople and the part done for the salespeople by the company. For example, from the standpoint of the product, the company should provide the salesperson with a product skillfully designed, thoroughly tested, attractively packaged, adequately advertised, and priced to compare favorably with competitive products. Salespeople have the responsibility of being thoroughly acquainted with the product, its selling features, points of superiority, and a sincere belief in the value of the product. From a sales management standpoint, the company's part of the sale involves the following:

1. Efficient and effective sales tools, including continuous sales training, promotional literature, samples, trade shows, product information, and adequate advertising.
2. An efficient delivery and reorder system to ensure that customers will receive the merchandise as promised.
3. An equitable compensation plan that rewards performance, motivates the salesperson, and promotes company loyalty. It should also reimburse the salesperson for all reasonable expenses incurred while doing the job.
4. Adequate supervision and evaluation of performance as a means of helping salespeople do a better job, not only for the company but for themselves as well.

The Sales Management Task

Since the advent of the marketing concept, a clear-cut distinction has been made between marketing management and sales management. Marketing management refers to all activities in the firm that have to

---

[5] For a review of research findings regarding factors that are predictive of salespeople's performance, see Gilbert A. Churchill, Jr., Neil M. Ford, Steven W. Hartley, and Orville C. Walker, Jr., "The Determinants of Salesperson Performance: A Meta-Analysis," *Journal of Marketing Research,* May 1985, pp. 87–93.

do with satisfying demand. Sales management is a narrower concept dealing with those functions directly related to personal selling. Generally speaking, sales managers are in middle management and report directly to the vice president of marketing. Their basic responsibilities can be broken down into at least seven major areas: (1) developing an effective sales organization for the company; (2) formulating short-range and long-range sales programs; (3) recruiting, training, and supervising the sales force; (4) formulating sales budgets and controlling selling expenses; (5) coordinating the personal selling effort with other forms of promotional activities; (6) maintaining lines of communication between the sales force, customers, and other relevant parts of the business, such as advertising, production, and logistics; and in some firms, (7) developing sales forecasts and other types of relevant marketing studies to be used in sales planning and control.

Sales managers are line officers whose primary responsibility is establishing and maintaining an active sales organization. In terms of authority, they usually have equivalent rank to that of other marketing executives who manage aspects of the marketing program, such as advertising, product planning, or physical distribution. The sales organization may have separate departments and department heads to perform specialized tasks, such as training, personnel, promotion, and forecasting. Figure 9–2 is an example of such sales organization.

In other cases, a general marketing manager may have product managers, or directors, reporting to them. This is common in cases where the firm sells numerous products and each product or product line is handled by a separate manager. Another common arrangement is to have sales managers assigned to specific geographic regions or customer groups. This type of specialization enables the sales force to operate more efficiently by avoiding overlaps. Regardless of the method used, the sales force should be structured to meet the unique needs of the consumer, the company, and its management.

FIGURE 9–2 An Example of a Sales Organization

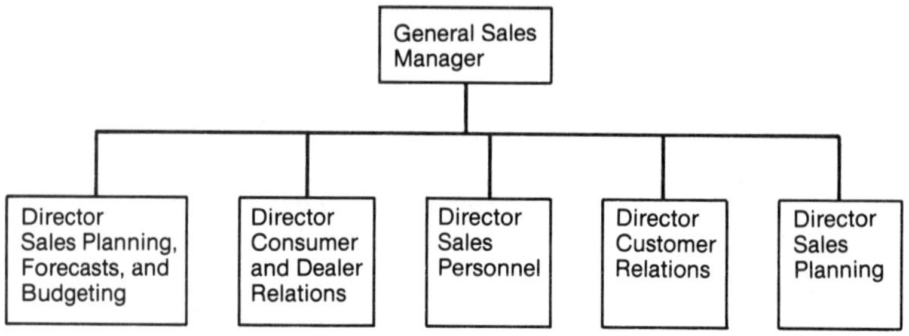

Controlling the Sales Force

There are two obvious reasons why it is critical that the sales force be properly controlled. First, personal selling can be the largest marketing expense component in the final price of the product. Second, unless the sales force is somehow directed, motivated, and audited on a continual basis, it is likely to be less efficient than it is capable of being. Controlling the sales force involves four key functions: (1) forecasting sales; (2) establishing sales territories and quotas; (3) analyzing expenses; and (4) motivating and compensating performance.

Forecasting Sales. Sales planning begins with a forecast of sales for some future period or periods. From a practical standpoint, these forecasts are made on a short-term basis of a year or less, although long-range forecasts of one to five years are made for purposes other than managing the sales force, such as financing, production, and development. Generally speaking, forecasting is the marketing manager's responsibility. In large firms, because of the complexity of the task, it is usually delegated to a specialized unit, such as the marketing research department. Forecast data should be integrated into the firm's marketing decision support system for use by sales managers and other corporate executives. For many companies the sales forecast is the key instrument in the planning and control of operations.[6]

The sales forecast is an estimate of how much of the company's output, either in dollars or in units, can be sold during a specified future period under a proposed marketing plan and under an assumed set of economic conditions. A sales forecast has several important uses: (1) it is used to establish sales quotas; (2) it is used to plan personal selling efforts as well as other types of promotional activities in the marketing mix; (3) it is used to budget selling expenses; and (4) it is used to plan and coordinate production, physical distribution, inventories, personnel, and so forth.

Sales forecasting has become very sophisticated in recent years, especially with the increased availability of computer hardware and software. It should be mentioned, however, that a forecast is never a substitute for sound business judgment. At the present time there is no single method of sales forecasting known that gives uniformly accu-

---

[6] For additional discussion on the use of technological systems in sales management, see "Selling Meets the Technological Age," *Sales and Marketing Management* (special section on the "Computer in Marketing"), December 6, 1982, pp. 45–54; and Brad Hamman, "Rebirth of a Salesman: Willy Loman Goes Electronic," *Business Week,* February 27, 1984, p. 103.

rate results with infallible precision. Outlined below are some commonly used sales forecasting methods.[7]

1. *Jury of executive opinion method.* This combines and averages the views of top management representing marketing, production, finance, purchasing, and administration.
2. *Sales force composite method.* This is similar to the first method in that it obtains the combined views of the sales force about the future outlook for sales. In some companies all salespeople, or district managers, submit estimates of the future sales in their territory or district.
3. *Customer expectations method.* This approach involves asking customers or product users about the quantity they expect to purchase.
4. *Time series analyses.* This approach involves analyzing past sales data and the impact of factors that influence sales (long-term growth trends, cyclical fluctuations, seasonal variations).
5. *Correlation analysis.* This involves measuring the relationship between the dependent variable, sales, and one or more independent variables that can explain increases or decreases in sales volumes.
6. *Other quantitative techniques.* Numerous statistical and mathematical techniques can be used to predict or estimate future sales. Two of the more important techniques are *(a)* growth functions, which are mathematical expressions specifying the relationship between demand and time; *(b)* simulation models, where a statistical model of the industry is developed and programmed to develop values for the key parameters.

Establishing Sales Territories and Quotas. The establishment of sales territories and sales quotas represents management's need to match personal selling effort with sales potential (or opportunity). Sales territories are usually specified geographic areas assigned to individual salespeople. These areas represent an attempt to make the selling task more efficient.[8] The underlying rationale is that the control of sales operations will be facilitated by breaking down the total market into smaller and more manageable units. Implied here is the notion that there are some distinct economic advantages to dividing the total market into smaller segments. These segments should represent clusters of customers, or prospects, within some degree of physical proximity. Of course, there are criteria other than geography for

---

[7] Based on a survey by the National Industrial Conference Board: "Forecasting Sales," *Studies in Business Policy,* No. 106.

[8] For a complete discussion of establishing territories and quotas, see William J. Stanton and Richard H. Buskirk, *Management of the Sales Force,* 7th ed. (Homewood, Ill.: Richard D. Irwin, 1987).

establishing territories. One important criterion is that of product specialization. In this case, salespeople are specialists relative to particular product or customer situations.

From a marketing management point of view, there are many advantages to establishing sales territories. First, it facilitates the process of sales planning by making it easier to coordinate personal selling, transportation, storage, and other forms of promotion. Second, it promotes better customer relations because salespeople will be more familiar with the accounts they service. Third, it is an effective way of making sure that each market is well covered. Fourth, it aids management in the evaluation and control of selling costs. And fifth, it helps in the evaluation of performance.[9]

The question of managing sales territories cannot be discussed meaningfully without saying something about quotas. *Sales quotas* represent specific sales goals assigned to each territory or sales unit over a designated time period. Quotas are primarily a planning and control device, because they provide management with measurable, quantitative standards of performance. The most common method of establishing quotas for territories is to relate sales to forecasted sales potential. For example, if the Ajax Drug Company's territory M has an estimated industry sales potential for a particular product of $400,000 for the year, then the quota might be set at 25 percent of that potential, or $100,000. The 25 percent figure represents the market share Ajax estimates to be a reasonable target. This $100,000 quota may represent an increase of $20,000 in sales over last year (assuming constant prices) that is expected from new business.

In establishing sales quotas for its individual territories or sales personnel, management needs to take into account three key factors. First, all territories will not have equal potential and, therefore, compensation must be adjusted accordingly. Second, all salespeople will not have equal ability, and assignments may have to be made accordingly. Third, the sales task in each territory may differ from time period to time period. For instance, the nature of some territories may require that salespeople spend more time seeking new accounts, rather than servicing established accounts, especially in the case of so-called new territories. The point to be made here is that quotas can vary, not only by territory but also by assigned tasks. The effective sales manager should assign quotas not only for dollar sales but also for each major selling function. Figure 9–3 is an example of how this is done for the Ajax Drug Company, where each activity is assigned a quota and a weight reflecting its relative importance.

---

[9] For additional discussion, consult Andris Zoltners and P. Sinha, "Sales Territory Alignment: A Review and Model," *Management Science*, November 1983, pp. 1237–56.

FIGURE 9–3 Ajax Drug Company Sales Activity Evaluation

Territory: M
Salesperson: Smith

Functions	*(1) Quota*	*(2) Actual*	*(3) Percent (2 ÷ 1)*	*(4) Weight*	*(5) Score (3 × 4)*
Sales volume:					
A. Old business	$380,000	$300,000	79	0.7	55.7
B. New business	$ 20,000	$ 20,000	100	0.5	50.0
Calls on prospects:					
A. Doctors	20	15	75	0.2	15.0
B. Druggists	80	60	75	0.2	15.0
C. Wholesalers	15	15	100	0.2	20.0
D. Hospitals	10	10	100	0.2	20.0
				2.0	175.7

Performance Index = 175.7

Analyzing expenses. Sales forecasts should include a sales expense budget. In some companies sales expense budgets are developed from the bottom up. Each territorial or district manager submits estimates of expenses and forecasted sales quotas. These estimates are usually prepared for a period of a year and then broken down into quarters and months. The chief sales executive then reviews the budget requests from the field offices and from staff departments. Expenses may be classified as fixed, semivariable or variable, and direct or indirect. Certain items, such as rent or administrative salaries, are fixed. In field offices, employee compensation is the principal expense and it may be fixed or semivariable, depending on the plan. Other items, such as travel, samples, or other promotional material, are variable in nature. Some expenses are directly traceable to the sale of specific products, such as samples or displays, while other expenses are indirect, as in the case of administrative salaries and rent. Sales commissions and shipping expenses tend to vary in direct proportion to sales, while travel expense and entertainment may not be tied to sales volume in any direct proportion.

It should be understood that selling costs are budgeted much in the same way as manufacturing costs. Selling costs are usually broken down by product lines, sales region, customers, salespersons, or some other unit. Proper budgeting requires a reasonable cost accounting system. From a budgeting stand point, the firm should use its accounting system to analyze marketing costs as a means of control.

HIGHLIGHT 9–4
Effort- and Results-Oriented Measures for Evaluating Salespersons

Effort-Oriented Measures	*Results-Oriented Measures*
1. Number of sales calls made.	1. Sales volume (total or by product or model).
2. Number of complaints handled.	2. Sales volume as a percentage of quota.
3. Number of checks on reseller stocks.	3. Sales profitability (dollar gross margin or contribution).
4. Uncontrollable lost job time.	4. Number of new accounts.
5. Number of inquiries followed up.	5. Number of stockouts.
6. Number of demonstrations completed.	6. Number of distributors participating in programs.
	7. Number of lost accounts.
	8. Percentage volume increase in key accounts.
	9. Number of customer complaints.
	10. Distributor sales-inventory ratios.

Source: Joseph P. Guiltinan and Gordon Paul, *Marketing Management* (New York: McGraw-Hill, 1985), p. 341.

Motivating and Compensating Performance. The sales manager's personnel function includes more than motivating and compensating the sales force; but from the vantage point of sales force productivity, these two tasks are of paramount importance. Operationally, it means that the sales manager has the responsibility of keeping the morale and efforts of the sales force at high levels through supervision and motivation.

These closely related tasks are accomplished through interaction with the sales force (1) by contacts with supervisors, managers, or sales executives individually or in group meetings; (2) through communication by letters or telephone; and (3) through incentive schemes by which greater opportunity for earnings (as in sales contests) or job promotion may bc achieved.

Compensation is a principal method by which firms motivate and retain their sales forces. Devising a compensation plan for a company is a technical matter, but there are some general guidelines in formulating such a plan. First, a firm should be mindful of any modifications necessary to meet its particular needs when adopting another company's compensation plan. Second, the plan should make sense (i.e., should have a logical rationale) to both management and sales force. Third, the plan should not be so overly complex that it cannot be understood by the average salesperson. Fourth, as suggested in the section on quotas, the plan should be fair and equitable to avoid penalizing the sales force because of factors beyond their control; conversely, the plan should ensure reward for performance in proportion to results. Fifth, the plan should allow the sales force to earn salaries that permit them to maintain an acceptable standard of living. Finally, the plan should attempt to minimize attrition by giving the sales force some incentive, such as a vested retirement plan, for staying with the company.

There are two basic types of compensation: salary and commission. Salary usually refers to a specific amount of monetary compensation at an agreed rate for definite time periods. Commission is usually monetary compensation provided for each unit of sales and expressed as a percentage of sales. The base on which commissions are computed may be: volume of sales in units of product, gross sales in dollars, net sales after returns, sales volume in excess of a quota, and net profits. Very often, several compensation approaches are combined. For example, a salesperson might be paid a base salary, a commission on sales exceeding a volume figure, and a percentage share of the company's profits for that year.

Some other important elements of sales compensation plans are:

1. *Drawing account.* Periodic money advances at an agreed rate. Repayment is deducted from total earnings computed on a commission or other basis, or is repaid from other assets of the salesperson if earnings are insufficient to cover the advance (except in the case of a guaranteed drawing account).
2. *Special payments for sales operations.* Payments in the nature of piece rates on operations, rather than commissions on results. Flat payments per call or payments per new customer secured can be included in this category. To the extent that these payments are estimated by size of customers' purchases, they resemble commissions and are sometimes so labeled. Other bases for special payments are demonstrations, putting up counter or window displays, and special promotional work.
3. *Bonus payments.* Usually, these are lump-sum payments, over and above contractual earnings, for extra effort or merit or for results beyond normal expectation.
4. *Special prizes.* Monetary amounts or valuable merchandise to reward the winners of sales contests and other competetions. Practices vary from firms that never use this device to firms where there is continuous use and almost every member of the sales force ex-

HIGHLIGHT 9–5
Characteristics Related to Sales Performances in Different Types of Sales Jobs

Type of Sales Job	*Characteristics That Are Relatively Important*	*Characteristics That Are Relatively Less Important*
Trade selling	Age, maturity, empathy, knowledge of customer needs and business methods.	Aggressiveness, technical ability, product knowledge, persuasiveness.
Missionary selling	Youth, high energy and stamina, verbal skill, persuasiveness.	Empathy, knowledge of customers, maturity, previous sales experience.
Technical selling	Education, product and customer knowledge—usually gained through training, intelligence.	Empathy, persuasiveness, aggressiveness, age.
New business selling	Experience, age and maturity, aggressiveness, persuasiveness, persistence.	Customer knowledge, product knowledge, education, empathy.

Source: Gilbert A. Churchill, Jr.; Neil M. Ford; and Orville C. Walker, *Sales Force Management: Planning Implementation and Control* (Homewood, Ill.: Richard D. Irwin, 1985), p. 290.

pects to get some compensation from this source during the year, in which case prizes amount to a form of incentive payment.

5. *Profit sharing.* A share of the profits of the business as a whole, figured on the basis of earnings, retail sales, profits in an area, or other factors. Sometimes profit sharing is intended to build up a retirement fund.
6. *Expense allowances.* Provision for travel and other business expenses, which becomes an important part of any compensation plan. No agreement for outside sales work is complete without an understanding about whether the company or the salesperson is to pay travel and other business expenses incurred in connection with work; and, if the company is responsible, just what the arrangements should be. Automobile, hotel, entertainment, and many other items of expense may be included in the agreement.
7. *Maximum earnings or cutoff point.* A limitation on earnings. This figure may be employed for limiting maximum earnings when it is

HIGHLIGHT 9–6
The Most Widely Used Sales-Force Compensation Methods

Method	*How Often Used*	*Most Useful*	*Advantages*	*Disadvantages*
Straight salary	30.3	When compensating new salespersons; when firm moves into new sales territories that require developmental work; when salespersons need to perform many nonselling activities.	Provides salesperson with maximum amount of security; gives sales manager large amount of control over salespersons; easy to administer; yields more predictable selling expenses.	Provides no incentive; necessitates closer supervision of salespersons' activities; during sales declines, selling expenses remain at same level.
Straight commission	20.8	When highly aggressive selling is required; when nonselling tasks are minimized; when company cannot closely control salesforce activities.	Provides maximum amount of incentive; by increasing commission rate, sales managers can encourage salespersons to sell certain items; selling expenses relate directly to sales resources.	Salespersons have little financial security; sales manager has minimum control over sales force; may cause salespeople to provide inadequate service to smaller accounts; selling costs less predictable.
Combination	48.9	When sales territories have relatively similar sales potentials; when firm wishes to provide incentive but still control sales-force activities.	Provides certain level of financial security; provides some incentive; selling expenses fluctuate with sales revenue.	Selling expenses less predictable; may be difficult to administer.

Source: Adapted from John P. Steinbrink, "How to Pay Your Sales Force," *Harvard Business Review,* July–August 1978, p. 113.

impossible to predict the range of earnings under commission or other types of incentive plans.

8. *Fringe benefits*. Pensions, group insurance, health insurance, and so forth. These are commonly given to sales forces as a matter of policy and become a definite part of the compensation plan.[10]

CONCLUSION

This chapter has attempted to outline and explain the personal selling aspect of the promotion mix. Before ending the discussion, a brief comment might be made concerning the overall value of personal selling. Personal selling in a growing economy must always play an important part in the marketing of goods and services. As long as production continues to expand through the development of new and highly technical products, personal selling will occupy a key role in our marketing system.

Additional Readings

Busch, Paul. "The Sales Manager's Bases of Social Power and Influence upon the Sales Force." *Journal of Marketing,* Summer 1980, pp. 91–101.

Cron, William L. "Industrial Salesperson Development: A Career Stages Perspective." *Journal of Marketing,* Fall 1984, pp. 41–52.

Dubinsky, Alan J.; Charles H. Fay; Thomas N. Ingram; and Marc J. Wallace. "Market Bonuses: How Attractive Are They?" *Business Horizons,* May–June 1983, pp. 11–14.

Dubinsky, Alan J., and Thomas N. Ingram. "Salespeople View Buyer Behavior." *Journal of Personnel Selling and Sales Management,* Fall 1982, pp. 6–11.

Futrell, Charles M., and A. Parasuramen. "The Relationship of Satisfaction and Performance to Salesforce Turnover." *Journal of Marketing,* Fall 1984, pp. 33–40.

Ingram, Thomas N., and Danny N. Bellenger. "Personal and Organizational Variables: Their Relative Effect on Reward Valences of Industrial Salespeople." *Journal of Marketing Research,* May 1983, pp. 198–205.

Skinner, Steven J.; Alan J. Dubinsky; and James H. Donnelly, Jr. "The Use of Social Bases of Power in Retail Sales." *Journal of Personnel Selling and Sales Management,* November 1984, pp. 48–56.

---

[10] For an excellent review of recruiting, selecting, and motivating sales personnel, see James M. Comer and Alan J. Dubinsky, *Managing the Successful Sales Force* (Lexington, Mass.: D. C. Heath, 1985).

Chapter 10

Distribution Strategy

Channel of distribution decisions involve numerous interrelated variables that must be integrated into the total marketing mix. Because of the time and money required to set up an efficient channel, and since channels are often hard to change once they are set up, these decisions are critical to the success of the firm.

This chapter is concerned with the development and management of channels of distribution and the process of goods distribution in an extremely complex, highly productive, and specialized economy. It should be noted at the outset that channels of distribution provide the ultimate consumer or industrial user with time, place, and possession utility. Thus, an efficient channel is one that delivers the product when and where it is wanted at a minimum total cost.

THE NEED FOR MARKETING INTERMEDIARIES

A channel of distribution is the combination of institutions through which a seller markets products to the user or ultimate consumer. The need for other institutions or intermediaries in the delivery of goods is sometimes questioned, particularly since the profits they make are viewed as adding to the cost of the product. However, this reasoning is generally fallacious, since producers use marketing intermediaries because the intermediary can perform functions *more cheaply and more efficiently* than the producer can. This notion of efficiency is critical when the characteristics of our economy are considered.

For example, our economy is characterized by heterogeneity in terms of both supply and demand. In terms of numbers alone, there are over 5 million establishments comprising the supply segment of our economy, and there are over 60 million households making up the demand side. Clearly, if each of these units had to deal on a one-to-one

HIGHLIGHT 10-1
What Intermediaries Add to the Cost of a Record Album

Vinyl and pressing	$ .48		
Record jacket	1.02		
American Federation of Musicians dues	.09		
Songwriter's royalties	.25		
Recording artist's royalties	.82		
Freight to wholesaler	.07		
Manufacturer's advertising and selling expenses	.70		
Manufacturer's administrative expenses	.69		
Manufacturer's cost	$4.12		
Manufacturer's profit	.62		
Manufacturer's price to wholesaler		4.74	
Freight to retailer		.03	
Wholesaler's advertising, selling, and administrative expense		.15	
Wholesaler's cost		4.92	
Wholesaler's profit		.30	
Wholesaler's price to retailer			$5.22 (intermediaries)
Retailer's advertising, selling, and administrative expenses			.84
Retailer's profit			2.33
Retailer's price to consumer			$8.39

Source: Thomas C. Kinnear and Kenneth L. Bernhardt, *Principles of Marketing* (Glenview, Ill.: Scott, Foresman, 1986), p. 333.

basis to obtain needed goods and services, and there were no intermediaries to collect and disperse assortments of goods, the system would be totally inefficient. Thus, the primary role of intermediaries is to bring supply and demand together in an efficient and orderly fashion.

CLASSIFICATION OF MARKETING INTERMEDIARIES AND FUNCTIONS

There are a great many types of marketing intermediaries, many of which are so specialized by function and industry that they need not be discussed here. Figure 10-1 presents the major types of marketing

FIGURE 10-1 Major Types of Marketing Intermediaries

Middleman—any intermediary between manufacturer and end-user markets; synonymous with *reseller.*

Agent—any middleman with legal authority to act on behalf of the manufacturer.

Manufacturer's representative—a middleman who sells the product but usually does not take legal title to or physical possession of the merchandise.

Wholesaler—a middleman who sells to other middlemen, usually to retailers. This term usually applies to consumer markets.

Retailer—a middleman who sells to consumers.

Broker—a middleman who performs limited selling functions, usually only writing orders to be turned over to the manufacturer for delivery, and usually specializing in sales to a particular kind of customer, such as grocery stores.

Sales agent—a middleman who agrees to sell all of the output of a manufacturer, at a stated commission rate or for a stated fee, but who usually does not take physical possession of or legal title to the merchandise.

Distributor—an imprecise term, usually used to describe a middleman who performs a variety of distribution functions, including selling, maintaining inventories, extending credit, and so on. It is a more common term in industrial markets but may also be used to refer to wholesalers.

Dealer—an even more imprecise term that can mean the same as distributor, retailer, wholesaler, and so forth. It is virtually synonymous with *middleman.*

Jobber—usually used in an industrial marketing context to refer to distributors, or in certain fields, such as paper and hardware, to refer to wholesalers characterized by broad lines and reasonably complete service offerings.

Source: Frederick E. Webster, Jr., *Marketing for Managers* (New York: Harper & Row, 1974), p. 191. Copyright © 1974 by Frederick E. Webster, Jr. Reprinted by permission of Harper & Row, Inc.

intermediaries common to many industries. Although there is some overlap in this classification, these categories are based on the marketing functions performed. That is, various intermediaries perform different marketing functions and to different degrees. Figure 10-2 is a listing of the more common marketing functions performed in the channel.

It should be remembered that whether or not a manufacturer utilizes intermediaries to perform these functions, the functions have to be performed by someone. In other words, the managerial question is not whether to perform the functions but who will perform them and to what degree.

FIGURE 10–2 Marketing Function Performed in Channels of Distribution

Selling—promoting the product to potential customers.
Buying—purchasing a variety of products from various sellers, usually for resale.
Assorting—providing an assortment of items (often interrelated) for potential customers.
Financing—offering credit to potential customers to facilitate the transaction; also, providing funds to sellers to help them finance their affairs.
Storage—protecting the product and maintaining inventories to offer better customer service.
Sorting—buying a quantity and breaking bulk items into amounts desired by customers.
Grading—judging products and labeling them as to quality.
Transportation—physically moving the product between manufacturer and end user.
Market information—information needed by manufacturers about market conditions, including expected sales volume, fashion trends, and pricing conditions.
Risk-taking—absorbing business risks, especially risks of maintaining inventories, product obsolescence, and the like.

Source: Frederick E. Webster, Jr., *Marketing for Managers* (New York: Harper & Row, 1974), p. 191.

CHANNEL OF DISTRIBUTION

As previously noted, a channel of distribution is the sequence of firms comprised of all intermediaries involved in moving goods, and the title to them, from the producer to the consumer. Some of these links assume the risks of ownership, others do not. Some perform marketing functions while others perform nonmarketing or facilitating functions, such as transportation. The typical channel of distribution patterns for consumer goods markets are shown in Figure 10–3.

Some manufacturers use a direct channel, selling directly to the ultimate consumer (e.g., Avon Cosmetics). In other cases, one or more intermediaries may be used. For example, a manufacturer of paper cartons may sell to retailers, or a manufacturer of small appliances may sell to retailers under a private brand. The most common channel in the consumer market is the one in which the manufacturer sells through wholesalers to retailers. For instancc, a cold remedy manufacturer may sell to drug wholesalers who, in turn, sell a vast array of drug products to various retail outlets. Small manufacturers may also use agents, since they do not have sufficient capital for their own sales

FIGURE 10–3 Typical Channels of Distribution for Consumer Goods

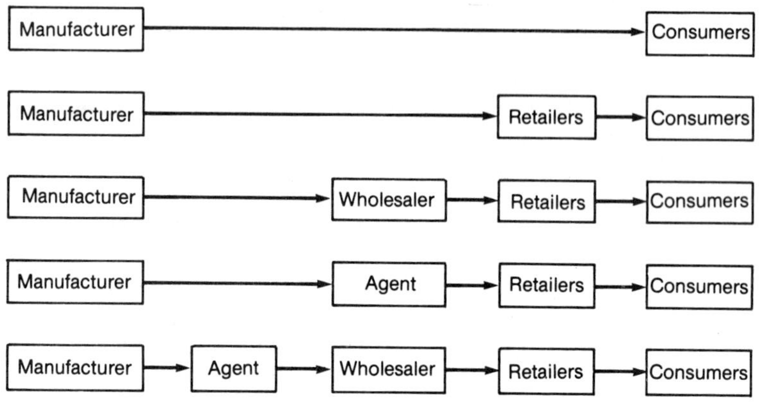

forces. Agents are commonly used intermediaries in the jewelry industry. The final channel in Figure 10–3 is used primarily when small wholesalers and retailers are involved. Channels with one or more intermediaries are referred to as indirect channels.

In contrast to consumer products, the direct channel is often used in the distribution of industrial goods. The reason for this stems from the structure of most industrial markets, which often have relatively few but extremely large customers. Also, many industrial products, such as computers, need a great deal of presale and postsale service. Distributors are used in industrial markets when the number of buyers is large and the size of the buying firm is small. As in the consumer market, agents are used in industrial markets in cases where manufacturers do not wish to have their own sales forces. Such an arrangement may be used by small manufacturers or when the market is geographically dispersed. The final channel arrangement in Figure 10–4 may also be used by a small manufacturer or when the market consists of many small customers. Under such conditions, it may not be economical for sellers to have their own sales organization.

SELECTING CHANNELS OF DISTRIBUTION

General Considerations

Given the numerous types of channel middlemen and functions that must be performed, the task of selecting and designing a channel of distribution may at first appear to be overwhelming. However, in

FIGURE 10-4 Typical Channels of Distribution for Industrial Goods

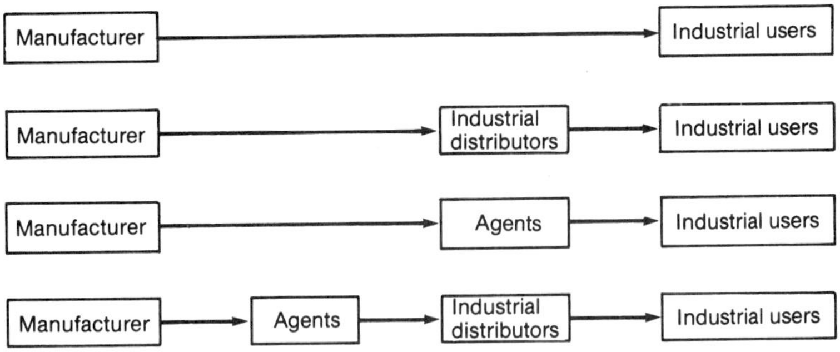

many industries, channels of distribution have developed over many years and have become somewhat traditional. In such cases, the producer may be limited to this type of channel to operate in the industry. This is not to say that a traditional channel is always the most efficient

HIGHLIGHT 10-2
"Are Channels of Distribution What the Textbooks Say?"

The middleman is not a hired link in a chain forged by manufacturer, but rather an independent market, the focus of a large group of customers for whom he buys. Subsequent to some market analysis of his own, he selects products and suppliers, thereby setting at least one link in the channel.

After some experimentation, he settles upon a method of operation, performing those functions he deems inescapable in the light of his own objectives, forming policies for himself whenever he has freedom to do so. Perhaps these methods and policies conform closely to those of a Census category of middleman, but perhaps they do not.

It is true that his choices are in many instances tentative prosposals. He is subject to much influence from competitors, from aggressive suppliers, from inadequate finances and faulty information, as well as from habit. Nonetheless, many of his choices are independent.

As he grows and builds a following, he may find that his prestige in his market is greater than that of the suppliers whose goods he sells. In some instances his local strength is so great that a manufacturer is virtually unable to tap that market, except through him. In such a case the manufacturer can have no channel policy with respect to that market.

Source: Phillip McVey, "Are Channels of Distribution What the Textbooks Say?" *Journal of Marketing,* January 1960, pp. 61–65. This article can be considered a classic in the field of marketing.

FIGURE 10-5 Considerations in Channel Planning

1. *Customer characteristics.*
   a. Number.
   b. Geographical dispersion.
   c. Purchasing patterns.
   d. Susceptibilities to different selling methods.
2. *Product characteristics.*
   a. Perishability.
   b. Bulkiness.
   c. Degree of standardization.
   d. Installation and maintenance services required.
   e. Unit value.
3. *Middleman characteristics.*
   a. Availability.
   b. Willingness to accept product or product line.
   c. Strengths.
   d. Weaknesses.
4. *Competitive characteristics.*
   a. Geographic proximity.
   b. Proximity in outlet.
5. *Company characteristics.*
   a. Financial strength.
   b. Product mix.
   c. Past channel experience.
   d. Present company marketing policies.
6. *Environmental characteristics.*
   a. Economic conditions.
   b. Legal regulations and restrictions.

and that there are no opportunities for innovation, but the fact that such a channel is widely accepted in the industry suggests it is highly efficient. A primary constraint in these cases and in cases where no traditional channel exists is that of *availability* of the various types of middlemen. All too often in the early stages of channel design, executives map out elaborate channel networks only to find out later that no such independent middlemen exist for the firm's product in selected geographic areas. Even if they do exist, they may not be willing to accept the seller's products. In general, there are six basic considerations in the initial development of channel strategy. These are outlined in Figure 10-5.[1]

[1] This figure was formulated from Philip Kotler, *Marketing Management: Analysis, Planning, and Control,* 5th ed. (Englewood Cliffs, N.J.: Prentice-Hall, 1984), pp. 538–60.

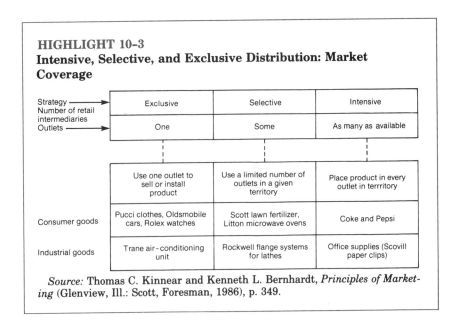

HIGHLIGHT 10-3
Intensive, Selective, and Exclusive Distribution: Market Coverage

Strategy →	Exclusive	Selective	Intensive
Number of retail intermediaries Outlets →	One	Some	As many as available
	Use one outlet to sell or install product	Use a limited number of outlets in a given territory	Place product in every outlet in terrritory
Consumer goods	Pucci clothes, Oldsmobile cars, Rolex watches	Scott lawn fertilizer, Litton microwave ovens	Coke and Pepsi
Industrial goods	Trane air-conditioning unit	Rockwell flange systems for lathes	Office supplies (Scovill paper clips)

Source: Thomas C. Kinnear and Kenneth L. Bernhardt, *Principles of Marketing* (Glenview, Ill.: Scott, Foresman, 1986), p. 349.

It should be noted that for a particular product any one of these characteristics may greatly influence choice of channels. To illustrate, highly perishable products generally require direct channels, or a firm with little financial strength may require middlemen to perform almost all of the marketing functions.

Specific Considerations

The above characteristics play an important part in framing the channel selection decision. Based on them, the choice of channels can be further refined in terms of (1) distribution coverage required, (2) degree of control desired, (3) total distribution cost, and (4) channel flexibility.

Distribution Coverage Required. Because of the characteristics of the product, the environment needed to sell the product, and the needs and expectations of the potential buyer, products will vary in the intensity of distribution coverage they require. Distribution coverage can be viewed along a continuum ranging from intensive to selective to exclusive distribution.

Intensive Distribution. Here the manufacturer attempts to gain exposure through as many wholesalers and retailers as possible. Most convenience goods require intensive distribution based on the characteristics of the product (low unit value) and the needs and expectations of the buyer (high frequency of purchase and convenience).

Selective Distribution. Here the manufacturer limits the use of middlemen to the ones believed to be the best available. This may be based on the service organization available, the sales organization, or the reputation of the middleman. Thus, appliances, home furnishings, and better clothing are usually distributed selectively. For appliances, the middleman's service organization could be a key factor, while for better clothing and home furnishings, the middleman's reputation would be an important consideration.

Exclusive Distribution. Here the manufacturer severely limits distribution, and middlemen are provided exclusive rights within a particular territory. The characteristics of the product are a determining factor here. Where the product requires certain specialized selling effort and/or investment in unique facilities or large inventories, this arrangement is usually selected. Retail paint stores are an example of such a distribution arrangement.

Degree of Control Desired. In selecting channels of distribution, the seller must make decisions concerning the degree of control desired over the marketing of the firm's products. Some manufacturers prefer to keep as much control over the policies surrounding their product as possible. Ordinarily, the degree of control achieved by the seller is proportionate to the directness of the channel. One Eastern brewery, for instance, owns its own fleet of trucks and operates a wholly owned delivery system direct to grocery and liquor stores. Its market is very concentrated geographically, with many small buyers, so such a system is economically feasible. However, all other brewers in the area sell through wholesalers or distributors.

When more indirect channels are used, the manufacturer must surrender some control over the marketing of the firm's product. However, attempts are commonly made to maintain a degree of control through some other indirect means, such as sharing promotional expenditures, providing sales training, or other operational aids, such as accounting systems, inventory systems, or marketing research data on the dealer's trading area.[2]

Total Distribution Cost. The total distribution cost concept has developed out of the more general topic of systems theory. The concept suggests that a channel of distribution should be viewed as a total

---

[2] For further discussion, see John Gaski, "The Theory of Power and Conflict in Channels of Distribution," *Journal of Marketing,* Summer 1984, pp. 9–29.

system composed of interdependent subsystems, and that the objective of the system (channel) manager should be to optimize total system performance. In terms of distribution costs, it generally is assumed that the total system should be designed to minimize costs, other things being equal. The following is a representative list of the major distribution costs to be minimized.

1. Transportation.
2. Order processing.
3. Cost of lost business (an "opportunity" cost due to inability to meet customer demand).
4. Inventory carrying costs, including:
   a. Storage-space charges.
   b. Cost of capital invested.
   c. Taxes.
   d. Insurance.
   e. Obsolescence and deterioration.
5. Packaging.
6. Materials handling.

The important qualification to the total cost concept is the statement "other things being equal." The purpose of the total cost concept is to emphasize total system performance to avoid suboptimization. However, other important factors must be considered, not the least of which are level of customer service, sales, profits, and interface with the total marketing mix.

Channel Flexibility. A final consideration relates to the ability of the manufacturer to adapt to changing conditions. To illustrate, in recent years much of the population has moved from inner cities to suburbs and thus make most of their purchases in shopping centers and malls. If a manufacturer had long-term, exclusive dealership with retailers in the inner city, the ability to adapt to this population shift could have been severely limited. In general, the less certain the future seems to be, the less favorable are channel alternatives involving long commitments.

MANAGING A CHANNEL OF DISTRIBUTION

Once the seller has decided on the type of channel structure to use and selected the individual members, the entire coalition should operate as a total system. From a behavioral perspective, the system can be viewed as a social system since each member interacts with the others, each member plays a role vis-à-vis the others, and each has certain

HIGHLIGHT 10-4
Franchising: An Alternative to Traditional Channels of Distribution

A franchise is a means by which a producer of products or services achieves a direct channel of distribution without wholly owning or managing the physical facilities in the market. In effect, the franchisor provides the franchisee with the franchisor's knowledge, manufacturing, and marketing techniques for a financial return.

Ingredients of a Franchised Business

Six key ingredients should be included within a well-balanced franchise offered to a franchisee. These are given in order of importance:

- *Technical knowledge* in its practical form is supplied through an intensive course of study.
- *Managerial techniques* based on proven and time-tested programs are imparted to the franchisee on a continuing basis, even after the business has been started or taken over by the franchisee.
- *Commercial knowledge* involving prescribed methods of buying and selling is explained and codified. Most products to be obtained, processed, and sold to the franchisee are supplied by the franchisor.
- *Financial instruction* on managing funds and accounts is given to the franchisee during the indoctrination period.
- *Accounting controls* are set up by the franchisor for the franchisee.
- *Protective safeguards* are included in the intensive training of the franchisee for his employees and customers, including the quality of his product, as well as the safeguards for his assets through adequate insurance controls.

Elements of an Ideal Franchise Program

- **High gross margin.** In order for the franchisee to be able to afford a high franchise fee (which the franchisor needs), it is necessary to operate on a high gross margin percentage. This explains the widespread application of franchising in the food and service industries.
- **In-store value added.** Franchising works best in those product categories where the product is at least partially processed in the store. Such environments require constant on-site supervision—a chronic problem for company-owned stores using a hired manager. Owners simply are willing to work harder over longer hours.
- **Secret processes.** Concepts, formulas, or products that the franchisee can't duplicate without joining the franchise program.
- **Real estate profits.** The franchisor uses income from ownership of property as a significant revenue source.
- **Simplicity.** The most successful franchises have been those that operate on automatic pilot: All the key decisions have been thought through, and the owner merely implements the decisions.

Source: Partially adapted from Philip D. White and Albert D. Bates, "Franchising Will Remain Retailing Fixture, but Its Salad Days Have Long Since Gone," *Marketing News,* February 17, 1984, p. 14.

HIGHLIGHT 10-5
Manufacturers and Middlemen: A Perfect Working Relationship

The Perfect Middleman

1. Has access to the market that the manufacturer wants to reach.
2. Carries adequate stocks of the manufacturer's products and a satisfactory assortment of other products.
3. Has an effective promotional program—advertising, personal selling, and product displays. Promotional demands placed on the manufacturer are in line with what the manufacturer intends to do.
4. Provides services to customers—credit, delivery, installation, and product repair—and honors the product warranty conditions.
5. Pays its bills on time and has capable management.

The Perfect Manufacturer

1. Provides a desirable assortment of products—well designed, properly priced, attractively packaged, and delivered on time and in adequate quantities.
2. Builds product demand for these products by advertising them.
3. Furnishes promotional assistance to its middlemen.
4. Provides managerial assistance for its middlemen.
5. Honors product warranties and provides repair and installation service.

The Perfect Combination

1. Probably doesn't exist.

Source: William J. Stanton and Charles Futrell, *Fundamentals of Marketing,* 8th ed. (New York: McGraw-Hill, 1987), p. 380.

expectations of the other.[3] Thus, the behavioral perspective views a channel of distribution as more than a series of markets or participants extending from production to consumption.

[3] F. Robert Dwyer and M. Ann Welsh, "Environmental Relationships of the Internal Political Economy of Marketing Channels," *Journal of Marketing Research,* November 1985, pp. 397–414; and John F. Gaski and John R. Nevin, "The Differential Effects of Exercised and Unexercised Power Sources in a Marketing Channel, *Journal of Marketing Research,* May 1985, pp. 130–42.

HIGHLIGHT 10-6
Pushing or Pulling through the Channel System

A producer has a special challenge with respect to channel systems: How to ensure that the product reaches the end of the channel. Middlemen—especially retailers—don't have this problem, since they already control that end of the channel.

The two basic methods of recruiting middlemen are *pushing* and *pulling*.

Pushing a product through the channels means using normal promotion effort—personal selling and advertising—to help sell the whole marketing mix to possible channel members. This method is common—since these sales transactions are usually between rational, presumably profit-oriented buyers and sellers. The approach emphasizes the importance of building a channel—and securing the wholehearted cooperation of channel members. The producer—in effect—tries to develop a team that will work well together to get the product to the user.

By contrast, pulling means getting consumers to ask middlemen for the product. This usually involves highly aggressive promotion to final consumers or users—perhaps using coupons or samples—and temporary bypassing of middlemen. If the promotion works, the middlemen are forced to carry the product—to satisfy their customers.

Source: E. Jerome McCarthy and William D. Perreault, Jr., *Basic Marketing: A Managerial Approach,* 9th ed. (Homewood, Ill.: Richard D. Irwin, 1987), pp. 292–93.

A Channel Leader

If a channel of distribution is viewed as a social system comprised of interacting firms with a common set of objectives, then integration among them seems desirable. This is because the channel, as a system, can be conceived as a competitive unit in and of itself; in other words, any success that the product has is determined largely by the effectiveness and efficiency with which human, material, and monetary resources have been mobilized throughout the entire interfirm network.

If the above view is taken, the question arises about who should exert primary leadership in the channel—that is, becomes the "channel captain" or "channel commander." There is little agreement about the answer. Some marketers believe the manufacturer or the owner of the brand name should be the channel captain. The argument here is that the manufacturer or brand name owner (1) has the most to lose if the system malfunctions or fails, (2) has the most technical expertise, and (3) in many cases has greater resources than other channel members. Others believe the retailer should be the channel captain, since the retailer is the closest link to the consumer and, therefore, can judge better the consumer needs and wants. Still others argue the wholesaler should seek to gain channel control, or that the locus of control should be at the level where competition is greatest.

In some channels of distribution, one member may be large and powerful with respect to other members. It may be a manufacturer, wholesaler, or large retailer. Consider the power Sears Roebuck & Co. has over a small supply manufacturing firm, since 90 percent of Sears products are under its own label. In such cases, the powerful member may assume leadership.

While the issue is certainly not clear, the tendency appears to lean toward channels controlled by the manufacturer, with a few notable exceptions. For example, for their own brands, Sears Roebuck and K mart likely play the primary leadership role, while the manufacturer plays a subordinate role. In some cases where wholesalers have their own brands, the manufacturer and retailer probably assume a subordinate role. However, in many cases, manufacturers have absorbed functions previously performed by middlemen and, thereby, obtained even greater channel control.

CONCLUSION

The purpose of this chapter has been to introduce the reader to the process of distribution of goods in an extremely complex, highly productive, and highly specialized economy. It is important that the reader understand the vital need for marketing intermediaries in such an economy to bring about exchanges between buyers and sellers in a reasonably efficient manner. If the reader appreciates this concept, then the major objective of this chapter has been achieved. The chapter also examined the typical channels of distribution for both consumer goods and industrial goods, and the various types of marketing intermediaries available to a seller. Finally, two important aspects of channels of distribution were discussed: the selection and management of channels of distribution.

Additional Readings

Frazier, Gary L. "Interorganizational Exchange Behavior in Marketing Channels: A Broadened Perspective." *Journal of Marketing,* Fall 1983, pp. 68–73.

Frazier, Gary L., and Jagdish N. Sheth. "An Attitude-Behavior Framework for Distribution Channel Management." *Journal of Marketing,* Summer 1985, pp. 38–48.

Hunt, Shelby D., and Lawrence B. Chonko. "Marketing and Machiavellianism." *Journal of Marketing,* Summer 1984, pp. 30–42.

Ingene, Charles A. "Labor Productivity in Retailing: What Do We Know and How Do We Know It?" *Journal of Marketing,* Fall 1985, pp. 99–106.

John, George. "An Empirical Investigation of Some Antecedents of Opportunism in a Marketing Channel." *Journal of Marketing Research,* August 1984, pp. 278–89.

Schul, Patricia L.; William M. Pride; and Taylor Little. "The Impact of Channel Leadership Behavior on Interchannel Conflict." *Journal of Marketing,* Summer 1984, pp. 21–34.

Stern, Louis W., and Adel I. El-Ansary. *Marketing Channels.* Englewood Cliffs, N.J.: Prentice-Hall, 1982.

Chapter 11

Pricing Strategy

One of the most important and complex decisions a firm has to make relates to pricing its products. In America, the price system is generally an "administered" one, in contrast to a system where prices are determined solely by the interaction of supply and demand.[1] This does not mean that market forces are not important considerations in determining prices. What it does mean is that executive decisions are juxtaposed between demand and supply forces. Thus, it is executive decisions that determine not only the initial price of new products but also changes in price after products have been on the market for some time.

This chapter discusses demand, supply, and environmental influences that affect pricing decisions and emphasizes that all three must be considered for effective pricing. However, as will be discussed in the chapter, many firms price their products without explicitly considering all of these influences.

DEMAND INFLUENCES ON PRICING DECISIONS

Demand influences on pricing decisions concern primarily the nature of the target market and expected reactions of consumers to a given price or change in price. There are three primary considerations here: demographic factors, psychological factors, and price elasticity.

[1] Much of economic price theory is based on the latter assumption and thus is not completely useful for this treatment of pricing strategy.

HIGHLIGHT 11-1
The Meaning of Price

Alternative Terms	*What Is Given in Return*
Price	Most physical merchandise.
Tuition	College courses, education.
Rent	A place to live or the use of equipment for a specific time period.
Interest	Use of money.
Fee	Professional services: for lawyers, doctors, consultants.
Fare	Transportation: air, taxi, bus.
Toll	Use of road or bridge, or long-distance phone rate.
Salary	Work of managers.
Wage	Work of hourly workers.
Bribe	Illegal actions.
Commission	Sales effort.

Source: Thomas C. Kinnear and Kenneth L. Bernhardt, *Principles of Marketing* (Glenview, Ill.: Scott, Foresman, 1986), p. 546.

Demographic Factors

In the initial selection of the target market that a firm intends to serve, a number of demographic factors are usually considered. Demographic factors that are particularly important for pricing decisions include the following:

1. Number of potential buyers.
2. Location of potential buyers.
3. Position of potential buyers (resellers or final consumers).
4. Expected consumption rates of potential buyers.
5. Economic strength of potential buyers.

These factors help determine market potential and are useful for estimating expected sales at various price levels.

Psychological Factors

Psychological factors related to pricing concern primarily how consumers will perceive various prices or price changes. For example, marketing managers should be concerned with such questions as:

1. Will potential buyers use price as an indicator of product quality?
2. Will potential buyers be favorably attracted by odd pricing?

3. Will potential buyers perceive the price as too high relative to the service the product gives them?
4. Are potential buyers prestige-oriented and therefore willing to pay higher prices to fulfill this need?
5. How much will potential buyers be willing to pay for the product?

While psychological factors have a significant effect on the success of a pricing strategy and ultimately on marketing strategy, answers to the above questions may require considerable marketing research. In fact, a review of buyers' subjective perceptions of price concluded that very little is known about how price affects buyers' perceptions of alternative purchase offers and how these perceptions affect purchase response.[2] However, some tentative generalizations about how buyers perceive price have been formulated. For example, research has found that persons who choose high-priced items usually perceive large quality variations within product categories and see the consequences of a poor choice as being undesirable. They believe that quality is related to price and see themselves as good judges of product quality. In general, the reverse is true for persons who select low-priced items in the same product categories. Thus, although information on psychological factors involved in purchasing may be difficult to obtain, marketing managers must at least consider the effects of such factors on their desired target market and marketing strategy.[3]

Price Elasticity

Both demographic and psychological factors affect price elasticity. Price elasticity is a measure of consumers' price sensitivity, which is estimated by dividing relative changes in the quantity sold by the relative changes in price:

$$e = \frac{\Delta Q/Q}{\Delta P/P}$$

Although difficult to measure, there are two basic methods commonly used to estimate price elasticity. First, price elasticity can be estimated from historical data or from price/quantity data across different sales

---

[2] Kent B. Monroe, "Buyers' Subjective Perceptions of Price," *Journal of Marketing Research,* February 1973, pp. 70–80.

[3] See Zarrel V. Lambert, "Price and Choice Behavior," *Journal of Marketing Research,* February 1972, p. 40; James R. Bettman, "Perceived Price, and Product Perceptual Variables," *Journal of Marketing Research,* February 1973, pp. 100–102; and Eitan Gerstner, "Do Higher Prices Signal Higher Quality?" *Journal of Marketing Research,* May 1985, pp. 209–14.

districts. Second, price elasticity can be estimated by sampling a group of subjects from the target market and polling them concerning various price/quantity relationships. While both of these approaches provide estimates of price elasticity, the former approach is limited to the consideration of price changes, while the latter approach is often expensive and there is some question as to the validity of subjects' responses.[4] However, even a crude estimate of price elasticity is a useful input to pricing decisions.

SUPPLY INFLUENCES ON PRICING DECISIONS

For the purpose of this text, supply influences on pricing decisions can be discussed in terms of three basic factors. These factors relate to the objectives, costs, and nature of the product.

Pricing Objectives

Pricing objectives should be derived from overall marketing objectives, which in turn should be derived from corporate objectives. Since it is traditionally assumed that business firms operate to maximize profits in the long run, it is often thought that the basic pricing objective is solely concerned with long-run profits. However, the profit maximization norm does not provide the operating marketing manager with a single, unequivocal guideline for selecting prices. In addition, the marketing manager does not have perfect cost, revenue, and market information to be able to evaluate whether or not this objective is being reached. In practice, then, many other objectives are employed as guidelines for pricing decisions. In some cases, these objectives may be considered as operational approaches to achieve long-run profit maximization.

Research has found that the most common pricing objectives are (1) pricing to achieve a target return on investment, (2) stabilization of price and margin, (3) pricing to achieve a target market share, and (4) pricing to meet or prevent competition.

---

[4] For additional discussion of price elasticity, see Philip Kotler, *Marketing Management: Analysis, Planning and Control*, 5th ed. (Englewood Cliffs, N.J.: Prentice-Hall, 1984), pp. 508–12.

HIGHLIGHT 11-2
Some Potential Pricing Objectives

1. Target return on investment.
2. Target market share.
3. Maximum long-run profits.
4. Maximum short-run profits.
5. Growth.
6. Stabilize market.
7. Desensitize customers to price.
8. Maintain price-leadership arrangement.
9. Discourage entrants.
10. Speed exit of marginal firms.
11. Avoid government investigation and control.
12. Maintain loyalty of middlemen and get their sales support.
13. Avoid demands for "more" from suppliers—labor in particular.
14. Enhance image of firm and its offerings.
15. Be regarded as "fair" by customers (ultimate).
16. Create interest and excitement about the item.
17. Be considered trustworthy and reliable by rivals.
18. Help in the sale of weak items in the line.
19. Discourage others from cutting prices.
20. Make a product "visible."
21. "Spoil market" to obtain high price for sale of business.
22. Build traffic.
23. Maximum profits on product line.
24. Recover investment quickly.

Source: Adapted from Alfred R. Oxenfeldt, "A Decision-Making Structure for Price Decisions," *Journal of Marketing,* January 1973, p. 50.

Cost Considerations in Pricing

The price of a product usually must cover costs of production, promotion, and distribution, plus a profit for the offering to be of value to the firm. In addition, when products are priced on the basis of costs plus a "fair" profit, there is an implicit assumption that this sum represents the economic value of the product in the marketplace.

Cost-oriented pricing is the most common approach in practice, and there are at least three basic variations: *markup pricing, cost-plus pricing,* and *rate-of-return pricing.* Markup pricing is commonly used in retailing, where a percentage is added to the retailer's invoice price to determine the final selling price. Closely related to markup pricing is cost-plus pricing, where the costs of producing a product or completing a project are totalled and a profit amount or percentage is added on. Cost-plus pricing is most often used to describe the pricing of jobs that are nonroutine and difficult to "cost" in advance, such as construction and military weapon development.[5]

Rate-of-return or target pricing is commonly used by manufacturers. In this method, price is determined by adding a desired rate of return on investment to total costs. Generally, a break-even analysis is performed for expected production and sales levels and a rate of return is added on. For example, suppose a firm estimated production and sales to be 75,000 units at a total cost of $300,000. If the firm desired a before-tax return of 20 percent, then the selling price would be $(300{,}000 + 0.20 \times 300{,}000) \div 75{,}000 = \$4.80$.

Cost-oriented approaches to pricing have the advantage of simplicity, and many practitioners believe that they generally yield a good price decision. However, such approaches have been criticized for two basic reasons. First, cost approaches give little or no consideration to demand factors. For example, the price determined by markup or cost-plus methods has no necessary relationship to what people will be willing to pay for the product. In the case of rate-of-return pricing, little emphasis is placed on estimating sales volume. Even if it were, rate-of-return pricing involves circular reasoning, since unit cost depends on sales volume but sales volume depends on selling price. Second, cost approaches fail to reflect competition adequately. Only in industries where all firms use this approach and have similar costs and markups can this approach yield similar prices and minimize price competition. Thus, in many industries, cost-oriented pricing could lead to severe price competition, which could eliminate smaller firms. Therefore, although costs are a highly important consideration in price decisions, numerous other factors need to be examined.[6]

Product Consideration in Pricing

Although numerous product characteristics can affect pricing, three of the most important are (1) perishability, (2) distinctiveness, and (3) stage in the product life cycle.

---

[5] Kotler, *Marketing Management,* pp. 516–17.

[6] For an excellent discussion of problems and alternatives to cost-oriented pricing, see Joseph P. Guiltinan, "Risk Aversive Pricing Policies: Problems and Alternatives," *Journal of Marketing,* January 1976, pp. 10–15.

Perishability. Goods that are very perishable in a physical sense must be priced to promote sales without costly delays. Foodstuffs and certain types of raw materials tend to be in this category. Products can be considered perishable in two other senses. High fashion, fad, and seasonal products are perishable not in the sense that the product deteriorates but in the sense that demand for the product is confined to a specific time period. Perishability also relates to consumption rate, which means that some products are consumed very slowly, as in the case of consumer durables. Two important pricing considerations here are that (1) such goods tend to be expensive because large amounts of service are purchased at one time and (2) the consumer has a certain amount of discretionary time available in making replacement purchase decisions.

Distinctiveness. Products can be classified in terms of how distinctive they are. Homogeneous goods are perfect substitutes for each other, as in the case of bulk wheat or whole milk, while most manufactured goods can be differentiated on the basis of certain features, such as package, trademark, engineering design, and chemical features. Thus, few consumer goods are perfectly homogeneous, and one of the primary

HIGHLIGHT 11-3
Basic Break-Even Formulas

The following formulas are used to calculate break-even points in units and in dollars:

$$BEP_{(\text{in units})} = \frac{FC}{(SP - VC)}$$

$$BEP_{(\text{in dollars})} = \frac{FC}{1 - (VC/SP)}$$

where

FC = Fixed cost
VC = Variable cost
SP = Selling price

If, as is generally the case, a firm wants to know how many units or sales dollars are necessary to generate a given amount of profit, profit *(P)* is simply added to fixed costs in the above formulas. In addition, if the firm has estimates of expected sales and fixed and variable costs, the selling price can be solved for. (A more detailed discussion of break-even analysis is provided in Section 3 of this book.)

marketing objectives of any firm is to make its product distinctive in the minds of buyers. Large sums of money are often invested to accomplish this task, and one of the payoffs for such investments is the seller's ability to charge higher prices for distinctive products.

Life Cycle. The stage of the life cycle that a product is in can have important pricing implications.[7] With regard to the life cycle, two approaches to pricing are skimming and penetration price policies. A *skimming* policy is one in which the seller charges a relatively high price on a new product. Generally, this policy is used when the firm has a temporary monopoly and in cases where demand for the product is price inelastic. In later stages of the life cycle, as competition moves in and other market factors change, the price may then be lowered. Digital watches and calculators are examples of this. A *penetration* policy is one in which the seller charges a relatively low price on a new product. Generally, this policy is used when the firm expects competition to move in rapidly and where demand for the product is, at least in the short run, price elastic. This policy is also used to obtain large economies of scale and as a major instrument for rapid creation of a mass market. A low price and profit margin may also discourage competition. In later stages of the life cycle, the price may have to be altered to meet changes in the market.

ENVIRONMENTAL INFLUENCES ON PRICING DECISIONS

Environmental influences on pricing decisions include variables that are uncontrollable by the marketing manager. Two of the most important of these are competition and government regulation.

Competition

In setting or changing prices, the firm must consider its competition and how competition will react to the price of the product. Initially, consideration must be given to such factors as:

1. Number of competitors.
2. Size of competitors.
3. Location of competitors.
4. Conditions of entry into the industry.

---

[7] See Hermann Simon, "Dynamics of Price Elasticity and Brand Life Cycles: An Empirical Study," *Journal of Marketing Research,* November 1979, pp. 439–52.

HIGHLIGHT 11-4

Market Share Price Strategies

Option	*When to Use It*	*Pricing Strategy*	*Financial Implications*
1. Significantly increase market share	Growth market. Have or can get equal or superior competitive strength. No. 1 in market or good position to take it.	Pricing at or below market, depending on competitive strength.	Low profit now. High profit later. Low cash flow now.
2. Hold share	No. 1 in market. Nongrowth market. Very strong competition.	Maintain or increase price.	Profits/cash flow now.
3. Divest share	Dying market. Inordinately high competitors' strength.	High price premium.	Maximum profit/cash flow in near term.

Source: C. Davis Fogg and Kent H. Kohnken, "Price-Cost Planning," *Journal of Marketing,* April 1978, p. 104.

5. Degree of vertical integration of competitors.
6. Number of products sold by competitors.
7. Cost structure of competitors.
8. Historical reaction of competitors to price changes.

These factors help determine whether the firm's selling price should be at, below, or above competition. Pricing a product at competition (i.e., the average price charged by the industry) is called "going rate pricing" and is popular for homogeneous products, since this approach represents the collective wisdom of the industry and is not disruptive of industry harmony.[8] An example of pricing below competition can be found in sealed-bid pricing, where the firm is bidding directly against competition for project contracts. Although cost and profits are initially calculated, the firm attempts to bid below competitors to obtain the job contract. A firm may price above competition because it has a superior product or because the firm is the price leader in the industry.

Government Regulations

Prices of certain goods and services are regulated by state and federal governments. Public utilities are examples of state regulation of prices. However, for most marketing managers, federal laws that make certain pricing practices illegal are of primary consideration in pricing decisions. The list below is a summary of some of the more important legal constraints on pricing. Of course, since most marketing managers are not trained as lawyers, they usually seek legal counsel when developing pricing strategies to ensure conformity to state and federal legislation.

1. Price-fixing is illegal per se. Sellers must not make any agreements with *(a)* competitors or *(b)* distributors concerning the final price of the goods. The Sherman Antitrust Act is the primary device used to outlaw horizontal price fixing. Section 5 of the Federal Trade Commission has been used to outlaw price fixing as an "unfair" business practice.
2. Deceptive pricing practices are outlawed under Section 5 of the Federal Trade Commission Act. An example of deceptive pricing would be to mark merchandise with an exceptionally high price and then claim that the lower selling price actually used represents a legitimate price reduction.
3. Price discrimination that lessens competition or is deemed injurious to it is outlawed by the Robinson-Patman Act (which amends Sec-

[8] Kotler, *Marketing Management,* p. 519.

tion 2 of the Clayton Act). Price discrimination is not illegal per se, but sellers cannnot charge competing buyers different prices for essentially the same products if the effect of such sales is injurious to competition. Price differentials can be legally justified on certain grounds, especially if the price differences reflect cost differences. This is particularly true of quantity discounts.

4. Promotional pricing, such as cooperative advertising, and price deals are not illegal per se; but if a seller grants advertising allowances, merchandising service, free goods, or special promotional discounts to customers, it must do so on proportionately equal terms. Sections 2(d) and 2(e) of the Robinson-Patman Act are designed to regulate such practices so that price reductions cannot be granted to some customers under the guise of promotional allowances.

A GENERAL PRICING DECISION MODEL

From what has been discussed thus far, it should be clear that effective pricing decisions involve the consideration of many factors and, depending on the situation, any of these factors can be the primary consideration in setting price. In addition, it is difficult to formulate an exact sequencing of when each factor should be considered. However, several general pricing decision models have been advanced with the clearly stated warning that all pricing decisions will not fit the framework.[9] Below is one such model, which views pricing decisions as a nine-step sequence.

1. *Define market targets.* All marketing decision making should begin with a definition of segmentation strategy and the identification of potential customers.
2. *Estimate market potential.* The maximum size of the available market determines what is possible and helps define competitive opportunities.
3. *Develop product positioning.* The brand image and the desired niche in the competitive marketplace provide important constraints on the pricing decision as the firm attempts to obtain a unique competitive advantage by differentiating its product offering from that of competitors.
4. *Design the marketing mix.* Design of the marketing mix defines the

---

[9] For an excellent discussion of pricing decisions, see Kent B. Monroe and Albert J. Della Bitta, "Models for Pricing Decisions," *Journal of Marketing Research,* August 1978, pp. 413–28.

role to be played by pricing in relation to and in support of other marketing variables, especially distribution and promotional policies.
5. *Estimate price elasticity of demand.* The sensitivity of the level of demand to differences in price can be estimated either from past experience or through market tests.
6. *Estimate all relevant costs.* While straight cost-plus pricing is to be avoided because it is insensitive to demand, pricing decisions must take into account necessary plant investment, investment in R&D, and investment in market development, as well as variable costs of production and marketing.
7. *Analyze environmental factors.* Pricing decisions are further constrained by industry practices, likely competitive response to alternative pricing strategies, and legal requirements.
8. *Set pricing objectives.* Pricing decisions must be guided by a clear statement of objectives that recognizes environmental constraints and defines the role of pricing in the marketing strategy while at the same time relating pricing to the firm's financial objectives.
9. *Develop the price structure.* The price structure for a given product can now be determined and will define selling prices for the product (perhaps in a variety of styles and sizes) and the discounts from list price to be offered to various kinds of middlemen and various types of buyers.[10]

While all pricing decisions cannot be made strictly on the basis of this model, such an approach has three advantages for the marketing manager. First, it breaks the pricing decision into nine manageable steps. Second, it recognizes that pricing decisions must be fully integrated into overall marketing strategy. Third, it aids the decision maker by recognizing the importance of both qualitative and quantitative factors in pricing decisions.

CONCLUSION

Pricing decisions that integrate the firm's costs with marketing strategy, business conditions, competition, consumer demand, product variables, channels of distribution, and general resources can determine the success or failure of a business. This places a very heavy burden on the price maker. Modern-day marketing managers cannot ignore the complexity or the importance of price management. Pricing

[10] Frederick E. Webster, *Marketing for Managers* (New York: Harper & Row, 1974), pp. 178–79.

policies must be continually reviewed and must take into account the fact that the firm is a dynamic entity operating in a very competitive environment. There are many ways for money to flow out of a firm in the form of costs, but often there is only one way to bring revenues in and that is by the price-product mechanism.

Additional Readings

Aaker, David A., and Gary Ford. "Unit Pricing Ten Years Later: A Replication." *Journal of Marketing,* Winter 1983, pp. 118–22.

Berkowitz, Eric N., and John R. Walton. "Contextual Influences on Consumer Price Responses: An Experimental Analysis." *Journal of Marketing Research,* August 1980, pp. 349–58.

Burt, David N., and Joseph E. Boyett, Jr. "Reduction in Selling Price After the Introduction of Competition." *Journal of Marketing Research,* May 1979, pp. 275–79.

Curry, David J. "Measuring Price and Quality Competition." *Journal of Marketing,* Spring 1985, pp. 106–17.

Monroe, Kent B. *Pricing: Making Profitable Decisions.* New York: McGraw-Hill, 1979.

Sheffet, Mary Jane, and Debra L. Scammon. "Resale Price Maintenance: Is It Safe to Suggest Retail Prices." *Journal of Marketing,* Fall 1985, pp. 82–91.

Part D

Marketing in Special Fields

CHAPTER 12
The Marketing of Services
CHAPTER 13
International Marketing

Chapter 12

The Marketing of Services

For many years, the fastest growing segment of the American economy has not been the production of tangibles but the performance of services. Spending on services has increased to such an extent that today it captures about 50 cents of the consumer's dollar. However, for the most part, the entire area of service marketing remains ill-defined.[1]

Unfortunately, many marketing textbooks also devote little, if any, attention to program development for the marketing of services. This omission is usually based on the assumption that the marketing of goods and the marketing of services are the same, and, therefore, the techniques discussed under goods apply as well to the marketing of services. Basically, this assumption is true. Whether selling products or services, the marketer must be concerned with developing a marketing strategy centered around the four controllable decision variables that comprise the marketing mix: the product (or service), the price, the distribution system, and promotion. In addition, the use of marketing research is as valuable to the marketer of services as it is to the marketer of goods.

However, because services possess certain distinguishing characteristics, the task of determining the marketing mix ingredients for a service marketing strategy may present different and more difficult problems than might appear at first glance. The purpose of this chapter is to acquaint the reader with the special problems of service marketing so the material in the other chapters of the book can be integrated into a better understanding of the marketing of services.

---

[1] Valerie A. Zeithaml, A. Parasuraman, and L. L. Berry, "Problems and Strategies in Services Marketing," *Journal of Marketing,* Spring 1985, pp. 33–46.

Before proceeding, some attention must be given to what the authors refer to when using the term *services*. Probably the most frustrating aspect of the available literature on services is that the definition of what constitutes a service remains unclear. The fact is that no common definition and boundaries have been developed to delimit the field of services. The American Marketing Association has defined services as "activities, benefits, or satisfaction which are offered for sale, or are provided in connection with the sale of goods."[2] This definition lacks the precision needed for the purposes of this chapter, since it does not separate those services that are separate and identifiable activities from those services that exist only in connection with the sale of a product or another service. Such a delineation is needed for this chapter.

Therefore, "services" will be defined here as "separately identifiable, intangible activities that provide want satisfaction, and that are not necessarily tied to the sale of a product or another service."[3] This definition includes such services as insurance, entertainment, airlines, and banking, but does not include such services as wrapping and delivery, because these services exist only in connection with the sale of a product or another service. This is not to suggest, however, that marketers of goods are not also marketers of services.

IMPORTANT CHARACTERISTICS OF SERVICES

Services possess several unique characteristics that often have a significant impact on marketing program development. These special features of services may cause unique problems and often result in marketing mix decisions that are substantially different from those found in connection with the marketing of goods. Some of the more important of these characteristics are intangibility, inseparability, perishability and fluctuating demand, highly differentiated marketing systems, and a client relationship.

Intangibility

The obvious basic difference between goods and services is the intangibility of services, and many of the problems encountered in the marketing of services are due to this intangible nature. These problems are unique to service marketing.

---

[2] Committee on Definitions, *Marketing Definitions: A Glossary of Marketing Terms* (Chicago: American Marketing Association, 1960), p. 21.

[3] William J. Stanton and Charles Futrell, *Fundamentals of Marketing*, 8th ed. (New York: McGraw-Hill, 1987), p. 496.

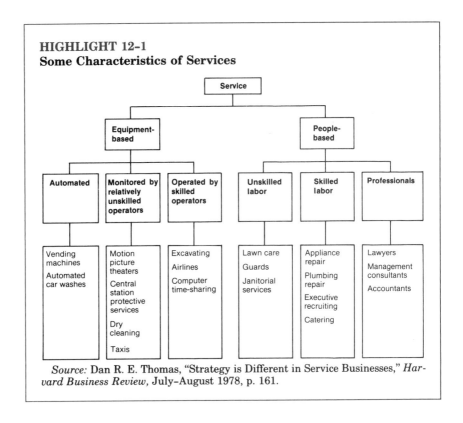

HIGHLIGHT 12-1
Some Characteristics of Services

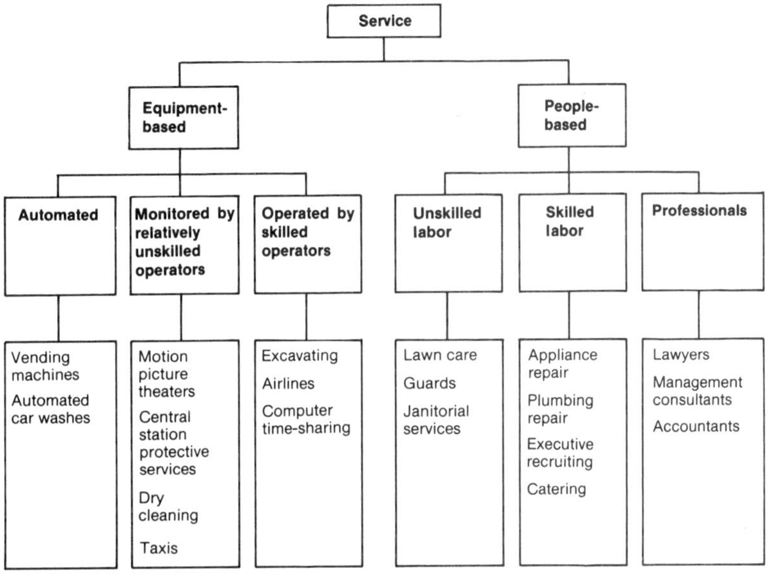

Source: Dan R. E. Thomas, "Strategy is Different in Service Businesses," *Harvard Business Review,* July–August 1978, p. 161.

The fact that many services cannot appeal to a buyer's sense of touch, taste, smell, sight, or hearing before purchase places a burden on the marketing organization. Obviously, it is most heavily felt in a firm's promotional program; but, as will be discussed later, it may affect other areas. Depending on the type of service, the intangibility factor may dictate direct channels of distribution because of the need for personal contact between the buyer and seller. Since a service firm is actually selling an idea, not a product, it must tell the buyer what the service will do, since it is often unable to illustrate, demonstrate, or display the service in use. Such a situation obviously makes promotion difficult.

Inseparability

In many cases, a service cannot be separated from the person of the seller. In other words, the service must often be created and marketed simultaneously. Because of the simultaneous production and marketing of most services, the main concern of the marketer is usually the creation of time and place utility. For example, the barber produces the service of a haircut and markets it at the same time. Many services, therefore, are "tailored" and non-mass-produced.

The implications of inseparability for the selection of channels of distribution are important. Inseparable services cannot be inventoried, and thus direct sale is the only feasible channel of distribution. In fact, until recently, most service firms did not differentiate between the production and marketing of services and, in many cases, viewed the two as equivalent.

Some industries have been able to modify the inseparability characteristics. In such industries, there may be a tangible representation of the service, such as a contract, by someone other than the producer. In other words, if tangible representations of the service are transferable, various middlemen, like agents, can be utilized. The reader is probably most famliar with this in the marketing of insurance. The service itself remains inseparable from the seller, but the buyer has a tangible representation of the service in the form of a policy. This enables the use of middlemen in the marketing of insurance. Another example would be service contracts on such equipment as computers or typewriters. However, these often are product-related, in that they are sometimes tied to the actual sale of the tangible product. More will be said about the distribution of services later in the chapter.

Perishability and Fluctuating Demand

Services are perishable, and the markets for most services fluctuate by seasons and, for many, even by day or week. Unused telephone capacity, electrical power, vacant seats on trains, buses, planes, and in stadiums represent business that is lost forever. (Standby plans in air travel are an attempt at solving this type of problem.)

The combination of perishability and fluctuating demand has created many problems for marketers of services. Specifically in the area of distribution, channels must be found to have the service available for peak periods, and new channels must be developed to make use of the service during slack periods. Many firms are currently attempting to cope with the latter problem, and several innovations in the distribution of services have occurred in recent years. These will be discussed later in the chapter.

Highly Differentiated Marketing Systems

Although the marketer of a tangible product is not compelled to use an established marketing system, such systems often are available and may be the most efficient. If an established system is not available, the marketer can at least obtain guidelines from the systems used for similar products. In the case of services, however, there may be little

HIGHLIGHT 12-2
Intangibility and Marketing Strategy

If marketers of services are to deal effectively with the fact that services are intangible, they must fully understand the concept. The concept of intangibility has two meanings:

1. That which cannot be touched: impalpable.
2. That which cannot be easily defined, formulated, or grasped mentally.

Unfortunately, most services are both of these, or doubly intangible. Overcoming intangibility, therefore, really involves dealing with two problems. Each must be attacked separately, in different ways, and with different elements of the marketing mix. For example:

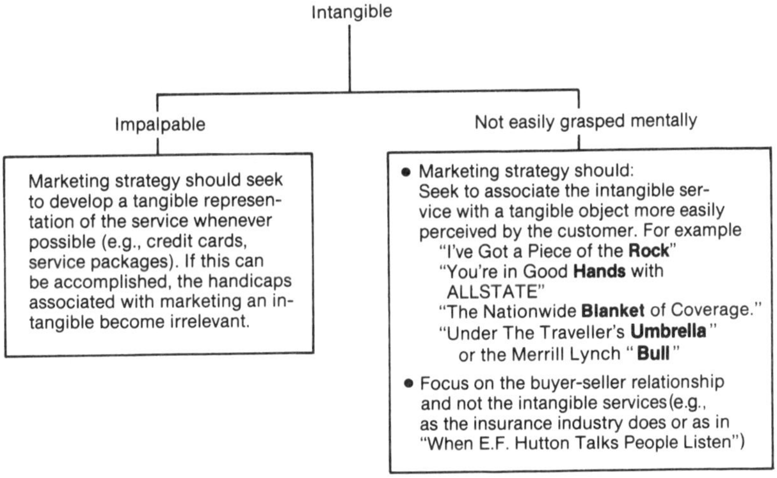

Source: James H. Donnelly, Jr., "Intangibility and Marketing Strategy for Retail Bank Services," *Journal of Retail Banking,* June 1980, pp. 39–43.

similarity between the marketing system needed and those used for other services. To illustrate, the marketing of banking and other financial services bears little resemblance to the marketing of computer services or labor services. The entire area of service marketing, therefore, demands greater creativity and ingenuity on the part of marketing management.

Client Relationship

In the marketing of a great many services, a client relationship exists between the buyer and seller as opposed to a customer relationship. Examples of this type of relationship would be the physician-patient and financial institution-investor relationship. The buyer abides by the suggestions or advice provided by the seller, and these relationships may be of an ongoing nature. Also, since many service firms are client-serving organizations, they may approach the marketing function in a more professional manner, as seen in health care, financial, legal, governmental, and educational services.

ROADBLOCKS TO INNOVATION IN SERVICE MARKETING

The factors of intangibility and inseparability make total comprehension of service marketing extremely difficult. However, in view of the size and importance of services in our economy, considerable innovation and ingenuity are needed to make these services available at convenient locations for consumers as well as businesspeople. In fact, the area of services probably offers more opportunities for imagination and creative innovation about distribution than do goods.

Unfortunately, in the past most service firms have lagged in the area of creative marketing. Even those service firms that have done a relatively good marketing job have been extremely slow in recognizing opportunities for innovation in all aspects of their marketing programs. Four reasons have been given for this lack of innovative marketing on the part of service industries: (1) a limited view of marketing, (2) a lack of competition, (3) a lack of creative management, and (4) no obsolescence.

Limited View of Marketing

Because of the nature of their service, many service firms depend to a great extent on population growth to expand sales. A popular example here is the telephone company, which did not establish a marketing department until 1955. It was then that the company realized it had to be concerned not only with population growth but also with meeting the needs of a growing population. Increases in educational levels and rises in the standards of living also bring about the need for new and diversified services.

Service firms must meet these changing needs by developing new services, developing new channels, and altering existing channels to meet the changing needs of the population. For many service industries, growth potential is limited unless new channels of distribution are found.

In terms of specific differences between manufacturing and service firms in handling marketing functions, one early study found that service firms appear to be (1) generally less likely to have marketing mix activities carried out in the marketing department, (2) less likely to perform industry analysis, (3) more likely to handle their advertising internally rather than go to outside agencies, (4) less likely to have an overall sales plan, (5) less likely to develop sales training programs, (6) less likely to use marketing research firms and marketing consultants, and (7) less likely to spend as much on marketing when expressed as a percentage of gross sales.[4] These results clearly suggest that marketing activities are more limited and less well understood in the service sector.

Limited Competition

A second major cause of the lack of innovative marketing in many service industries is the lack of competition that exists in many of these industries. Many service industries, like banking, railroads, and public utilities, have, throughout their histories, faced very little competition; some have even been regulated monopolies. Obviously, in an environment characterized by little competition, there is not likely to be a great deal of innovative marketing. However, some service industries have developed innovative marketing programs. Primary among those industries have been insurance companies and some financial institutions as deregulation in recent years has revolutionized the financial services industry. Each of these industries has been actively seeking new and better ways to market its services. Many of these innovations will be discussed later in the chapter.

Noncreative Management

For many years, the managements of service industries have been criticized for not being progressive and creative. Railroad management, for example, was criticized for being slow to innovate. More recently, however, railroads have become leading innovators in the field of freight transportation—introducing such innovations as piggyback service and containerization. Some other service industries, however, have been slow to develop new services or to innovate in the marketing of their existing services.

---

[4] William R. George and Hiram Barksdale, "Marketing Activities in the Service Industry," *Journal of Marketing,* October 1974, pp. 65–70.

No Obsolescence

A great advantage for many service industries is the fact that many services, because of their intangibility, are less subject to obsolescence than goods. While this is an obvious advantage, it also has led some service firms to be sluggish in their approach to marketing. Manufacturers of goods may continually change their marketing plans and seek new and more efficient ways to distribute their product. Since service firms are often not faced with obsolescence, they often have failed to recognize the necessity for formal marketing planning. However, one area in which there is considerable evidence of innovation in service marketing is distribution.

INNOVATIONS IN THE DISTRIBUTION OF SERVICES

As discussed in Chapter 10, the channel of distribution is viewed as the sequence of firms involved in moving a product from the producer to the user. The channel may be direct, as in the case where the manufacturer sells directly to the ultimate consumer, or it may contain one or more institutional middlemen. Some of the middlemen assume risks of ownership, some perform various marketing functions, such as advertising, while others may perform nonmarketing or facilitating functions, such as transporting and warehousing.[5]

Apparently using this concept as a frame of reference, most marketing writers generalize that, because of the intangible and inseparable nature of services, direct sale is the only possible channel for distributing most services. The only traditional indirect channel used involves one-agent middlemen. This channel is used in the distribution of such services as securities, housing, entertainment, insurance, and labor. In some cases, individuals are trained in the production of the service and franchised to sell it, as in the case of dance studios and employment agencies. They note that, because they are intangible, services cannot be stored, transported, or inventoried; and since they cannot be separated from the person of the seller, they must be created and distributed simultaneously. Finally, because there is no physical product, traditional wholesalers and other intermediaries can rarely operate in such markets and retailing cannot be an independent activity. For

[5] This section of the chapter draws from James H. Donnelly, Jr., "Marketing Intermediaries in Channels of Distribution for Services," *Journal of Marketing,* January 1976, pp. 55–77; and James H. Donnelly, Jr., and Joseph P. Guiltinan, "Selecting Channels of Distribution for Services," in *Handbook of Modern Marketing,* ed. Victor P. Buell (New York: McGraw-Hill, 1986), chap. 24.

these reasons, it is generally concluded that the geographic area in which most service marketers can operate is restricted.

All of these generalizations are certainly true, using the concept of "channels of distribution" developed for goods. However, the practice of viewing the distribution of services using the framework developed for goods has severely limited thinking. It has focused attention away from understanding the problem and identifying the means to overcome the handicaps of intangibility and inseparability. Most important, however, it has led to a failure to distinguish conceptually between the production and distribution of services; hence, it supports the idea that services must be created and distributed simultaneously. This had resulted in a lack of attention to channel decisions for producers of services.

Marketing Intermediaries in the Distribution of Services

Despite traditional thinking concerning the distribution of services, channels of distribution have evolved in many service industries that use separate organizational entities as intermediaries between the producer and user of the service. These intermediaries play a variety of roles in making services available to prospective users. Some examples from various service industries illustrate this point.

Financial. The retailer who extends a bank's credit to its customers is an intermediary in the distribution of credit. In the marketing of credit card plans, banks rely heavily on the retail merchant to assist in encouraging customers to apply for and use the cards. In fact, many banks have actually compensated merchants for various kinds of incentive credit card promotions. Thus, when retailers become part of a credit card plan they are, in effect, becoming intermediaries in the channel of distribution for credit.

In recent years, the banking industry has been very active in developing new retail banking services, particularly those using the technology of more sophisticated hardware and data processing systems. One of these, "direct pay deposit," permits employees to have their pay deposited directly into their checking account. By authorizing employers to deposit their pay, employees save a trip to the bank and avoid forgetting to make a deposit. They get a receipt from the employer and deposits are shown on their monthly bank statement. Bankers benefit by the reduced paperwork involved in the processing of checks. In the marketing of such plans, banks obviously must rely heavily on employers to encourage employees to apply for the service. Thus, when an organization agrees to become part of such a plan, it becomes an intermediary in the distribution of a bank's service.

Health Care. The distribution of health care services is of vital concern. In health care delivery, the inseparability characteristic presents more of a handicap than in other service industries because users (patients) literally place themselves in the hands of the seller. However, although direct personal contact between producer and user is often necessary, new and more efficient channels of distribution appear to be evolving.

While medical care is traditionally associated with the solopractice, fee-for-service system, several alternative delivery systems have been developed. One method is the health maintenance organization (HMO) concept. This type of delivery system stresses the creation of group health care clinics using teams of salaried health practitioners (physicians, pharmacists, technicians, and so forth) that serve a specific enrolled membership on a prepaid basis.

The HMO performs an intermediary role between practitioner and patient. It increases availability and convenience by providing a central location and "one-stop shopping." For example, a member can visit a general practitioner for a particular ailment and undergo treatment by the appropriate specialist in the same visit. The HMO also assumes responsibility for arranging for or providing hospital care, emergency care, and preventive services. In addition, the prepaid nature of the program encourages more frequent preventive visits, while the traditional philosophy of medical care is primarily remedial. HMO programs have inspired similiar innovations in other phases of health care, such as dentistry.

Insurance. The vending machines found in airports for aircraft accident insurance have been finding their way into other areas, such as travel accident insurance, which is now available in many motel chains. Group insurance written through employers and labor unions also has been extremely successful. In each instance, the insurance industry has used intermediaries to distribute its services.

Communication. Firms in the communication industry have sought ways to increase the availability and convenience of their services. One means has been the walk-up telephone. Companies or organizations that provide space for a walk-up phone serve as intermediaries for the telephone communication.

In each of the examples cited here, means of distribution were used that consisted of separate organizational entities between the producer of the service and the user for the purpose of making the service available. These intermediaries were not the traditional institutional middlemen that comprise the channel of distribution for goods. While the goods-based concept of channel of distribution does not provide for

HIGHLIGHT 12-3
Types of Questions That Need To Be Answered in Developing the Services Marketing Plan

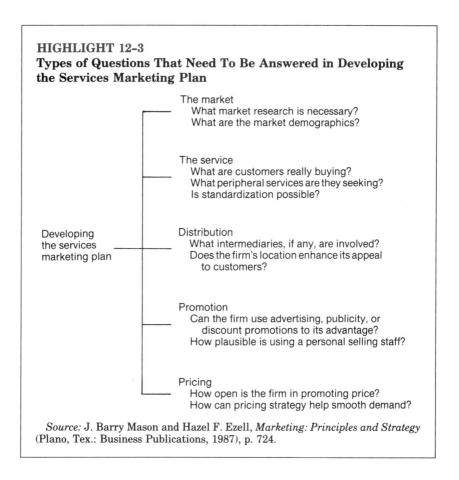

Developing the services marketing plan

- The market
  - What market research is necessary?
  - What are the market demographics?
- The service
  - What are customers really buying?
  - What peripheral services are they seeking?
  - Is standardization possible?
- Distribution
  - What intermediaries, if any, are involved?
  - Does the firm's location enhance its appeal to customers?
- Promotion
  - Can the firm use advertising, publicity, or discount promotions to its advantage?
  - How plausible is using a personal selling staff?
- Pricing
  - How open is the firm in promoting price?
  - How can pricing strategy help smooth demand?

Source: J. Barry Mason and Hazel F. Ezell, *Marketing: Principles and Strategy* (Plano, Tex.: Business Publications, 1987), p. 724.

this, the concept itself is not inadequate. Rather, the concept of "marketing intermediary" must be defined in the context of services. We propose that any extra-corporate entity between the producer of a service and prospective users that is utilized to make the service available and more convenient is a marketing intermediary for that service.

Implications for Service Marketers

Services must be made available to prospective users, and this implies distribution in the marketing sense of the word. The revised concept of the distribution of services appears to have at least two important implications for service marketers.

First, service marketers can and must distinguish conceptually between the production and distribution of services. The problem of making services more efficiently and widely available must not be ignored in favor of other elements of the marketing mix that are easier to deal with. For example, many service industries have been criticized for an overdependence on advertising. The problem of overdependence on one or two elements of the marketing mix is one that service marketers cannot afford. The sum total of the marketing mix elements represents the total impact of the firm's marketing strategy. The slack created by severely restricting one element cannot be compensated by heavier emphasis on another, since each element in the marketing mix is designed to address specific problems and achieve specific objectives.

Second, this discussion points out the critical role of "product" development in the distribution of services. It indicates that making services available is often a product development as well as a distribution problem. In several of the examples described, indirect distribution of the service was made possible because "products" were developed that included a tangible representation of the service. This facilitates the use of intermediaries, because the service can now be separated from the producer.

Of course, the process might be reversed: intermediaries could be located and appropriate "products" developed. For example, the bank credit card is a tangible representation of the service of credit, though it is not the service itself. As such, it has enabled banks to overcome the inseparability problem and to use the retail merchant as an intermediary in the distribution of credit. The credit card also has made it possible for banks to expand their geographic markets by maintaining credit customers far outside their immediate trading areas, since it enables subscribers to maintain an "inventory" of the bank's credit for use at their convenience. The same is true for the HMO membership card. Members can be treated or hospitalized while away from home and still be covered by their HMO membership.

CONCLUSION

This chapter has dealt with the complex topic of service marketing. While the marketing of services has much in common with the marketing of products, unique problems in the area require highly creative marketing management skills. Many of the problems in the service area can be traced to the intangible and inseparable nature of services. However, considerable progress has been made in understanding and reacting to these difficult problems, particularly in the area of distribution. In view of the major role services play in our economy, it is important for marketing practitioners to better understand and appreciate the unique problems of service marketing.

Additional Readings

Berry, L. L. "Services Marketing Is Different." *Business,* June 1980, pp. 24–29.

————. "Big Ideas in Services Marketing." *Journal of Consumer Marketing,* Spring 1986, pp. 47–51.

Donnelly, J. H., and W. R. George, eds. *Marketing of Services.* Chicago: American Marketing Association, 1981.

Donnelly, J. H.; L. L. Berry; and T. W. Thompson. *Marketing Financial Services.* Homewood, Ill.: Dow Jones-Irwin, 1985.

Kotler, P. *Marketing for Nonprofit Organizations.* 2nd ed. Englewood Cliffs, N.J.: Prentice-Hall, 1982.

Lovelock, C. H. "Classifying Services to Gain Strategic Marketing Insights." *Journal of Marketing,* Summer 1983, pp. 9–20.

————. *Services Marketing.* Englewood Cliffs, N.J.: Prentice-Hall, 1984.

Lovelock, C. H., and C. B. Weinberg. *Marketing for Public and Nonprofit Managers.* New York: John Wiley & Sons, 1984.

Parasuraman, A.; V. A. Zeithaml; and L. L. Berry. "A Conceptual Model of Service Quality and Its Implications for Future Research." *Journal of Marketing,* Fall 1985, pp. 41–50.

Chapter 13

International Marketing

A growing number of U.S. corporations have traversed geographical boundaries and have become truly multinational in character. These firms are increasing their investments of private capital in overseas divisions, branches, and subsidiaries at a rate of about 10 percent per year.

These multinational firms have invested in foreign countries for the same basic reasons they invested capital in the domestic United States. These reasons vary from firm to firm, but most fall under the interrelated goals of (1) increasing long-term growth and profit prospects, (2) maximizing total sales revenue, and (3) improving overall market position. As some domestic markets approach saturation, American firms look to foreign markets as outlets for surplus productive capacity and as potential sources of larger profit margins and returns on investments.

Basically, marketing abroad is the same as marketing at home. Regardless of which part of the world the firm sells in, the marketing program must still be built around a sound product or service that is properly priced, promoted, and distributed to a target market that has been carefully analyzed. In other words, the marketing manager has the same controllable decision variables in both domestic and nondomestic markets.

Although the development of a marketing program may be the same in either domestic or nondomestic markets, special problems may be involved in the implementation of marketing programs in nondomestic markets. These problems often arise because of the environmental differences that exist among various countries that marketing managers may be unfamiliar with.

In this chapter, marketing management in an international context

HIGHLIGHT 13-1
Reasons to Go International

Eleven reasons why American firms are likely to become more export-minded:

1. To escape from recessions in the domestic market.
2. To counter adverse demographic changes (like declining birth rates).
3. To export technology to less developed nations.
4. To increase their political influence.
5. To keep up with or to escape competition.
6. To enjoy economies of scale in production.
7. To extend a product's life cycle.
8. To dispose of inventories.
9. To enjoy tax advantages.
10. To create research opportunities (by testing products in foreign markets).
11. To establish a progressive image.

Source: Douglas G. Norvell and Sion Raveed, "Eleven Reasons for Firms to Go International," *Marketing News,* October 17, 1980, pp. 1–2.

will be examined and several potential marketing strategies for a multinational firm will be discussed. In examining each of these areas, the reader will find that a common thread—knowledge of the local cultural environment—appears to be a major prerequisite for success in each area.

ORGANIZING FOR INTERNATIONAL MARKETING

When compared with the tasks it faces at home, a firm attempting to establish an international marketing organization faces a much higher degree of risk and uncertainty. In a foreign market, management is often less familiar with the cultural, political, and economic situation, the institutional structure of the distribution network, potential competitors and their actions, and the reliability and validity of media and market data. Many of these problems are the result of conditions external to the firm, while others arise as the result of internal management situations.[1]

---

[1] Philip R. Cateora, *International Marketing,* 6th ed. (Homewood, Ill.: Richard D. Irwin, 1987).

Problem Conditions: External

While numerous problems could be cited, attention here will focus on the ones U.S. firms most often face when entering foreign markets.

Cultural Misunderstanding. Differences in the cultural environment of foreign countries may be misunderstood or not even recognized because of the tendency for marketing managers to use their own cultural values as a frame of reference. This tendency to rely on one's own cultural values has been called the major cause of many international marketing problems.

Political Uncertainty. Governments are unstable in many countries, and social unrest and even armed conflict must sometimes be reckoned with. Other nations are newly emerging and anxious to exert their independence. These and similar problems can greatly hinder a firm seeking to establish its position in a foreign market.

Import Restrictions. Tariffs, import quotas, and other types of import restrictions hinder international business. These are usually established to promote national self-sufficiency and can be a huge roadblock for the multinational firm.

Exchange Controls. Often a nation will establish limits on the amount of earned and invested funds that can be withdrawn from that nation. These exchange controls are usually established by nations that are experiencing balance-of-payment problems. Nevertheless, these and other types of currency regulations are important considerations in the decision to expand into a foreign market.

Ownership and Personnel Restrictions. In many nations, governments have a requirement that the majority ownership of a company operating in that nation be held by nationals of the country. Other nations require that the majority of the personnel of a foreign firm be local citizens. Each of these restrictions can act as obstacles to foreign expansion.

Problem Conditions: Internal

Given the types of external problems just discussed, the reader can see that the external roadblocks to success in a foreign market are substantial. Unfortunately, several major internal management problems also may arise.

HIGHLIGHT 13-2
Characteristics of Domestic and International Operations

Domestic	*International*
One primary language and nationality.	Multilingual, multinational, and multicultural.
Relatively homogeneous market.	Fragmented and diverse markets.
Data available, usually accurate, and easy to collect.	Data collection formidable task, requiring significantly higher budgets and personnel allocation.
Political factors relatively unimportant.	Political factors frequently vital.
Relative freedom from government interference.	National economic plans, government influences on business decisions common.
Individual corporation has little effect on environment.	"Gravitational" distortion by large companies.
Relatively stable business environment.	Multiple environments, many highly unstable (but potentially very profitable).
Uniform financial climate.	Variety of financial climates, ranging from very conservative to wildly inflationary.
One currency.	Currencies differing in stability and real value.
Business rules mature and understood.	Rules diverse, changeable, and unclear.
Management generally accustomed to sharing responsibilities and using financial controls.	Management frequently autonomous and unfamiliar with budgets and controls.

Source: William C. Cain, "International Planning: Mission Impossible?" *Columbia Journal of World Business,* July–August 1970, p. 58. Although almost 20 years old, these ideas still have validity today.

Coordination. Some firms have problems in getting management to view the firm as a single integrated unit, rather than viewing it in terms of a domestic organization with a separate international division. This is a problem in the orientation of top executives.

Organization. As a result of the first problem, organizational difficulties arise when the international division is established as a separate unit. This occurs because the international operation tends to become isolated and to be treated as a stepchild.

Control. Problems with organization and coordination ultimately will result in problems with control. Controlling the multinational firm has probably received more attention than any other management problem in international business. This is because it encompasses (or is the result of) all of the other management problems. The question is: Should managerial control be *centralized* at corporate headquarters or should it be vested in *decentralized* foreign locations?

The important management question has been explored from many viewpoints. For example, one viewpoint states that local personnel employed by a multinational firm may prefer authoritarian control, because of their cultural background and environment. For this reason it is suggested that the firm centralize its overseas activities as much as possible.

Others have suggested that marketing operations must be decentralized. The common rationale appears to be that the need for specific knowledge of local customs, buying habits, traditions, and mores, and the general need to adapt to a variety of foreign cultures and market environments, make decentralized control of advertising and marketing decisions necessary. Overall, then, whether a firm should centralize its international operations depends on the nature of the company and its products, and in how different the foreign culture is from the domestic market.

PROGRAMMING FOR INTERNATIONAL MARKETING

In this section of the chapter, the major areas in developing an international marketing program will be examined. As was mentioned at the outset, marketing managers must organize the same controllable decision variables that exist in domestic markets. However, many firms that have been extremely successful in marketing in the United States have not been able to duplicate their success in foreign markets.

International Marketing Research

Because the risks and uncertainties are so high, marketing research is equally important (and probably more so) in foreign markets than in domestic markets.[2] In attempting to analyze foreign consumers and

---

[2] S. Tamer Cavusgil, "Guidelines for Export Market Research," *Business Horizons*, November–December 1985, pp. 27–33.

HIGHLIGHT 13-3
Product Categories Most Suited for Global Marketing

1. Computer hardware.
2. Airlines.
3. Photography equipment.
4. Heavy equipment.
5. Machine tools.
6. Consumer electronics/computer software (tied for 6th).
7. Automobiles.
8. Major appliances.
9. Hardware/wines and spirits (tied for 10th).
10. Nonalcoholic beverages.
11. Tobacco.
12. Paper products.
13. Cosmetics.
14. Beer.
15. Household cleaners.
16. Toiletries/food (tied for 17th).
17. Confections/clothing (tied for 18th).

Source: "Global Marketing: How Executives Really Feel," *Ad Forum,* April 1985, p. 30.

industrial markets, at least three important dimensions must be considered.

Population Characteristics. Obviously, population is one of the major components of a market, and significant differences exist between and within foreign countries. The marketing manager should be familiar with the total population and with the regional, urban, rural, and interurban distribution. Other demographic variables, such as the number and size of the families, education, occupation, and religion, are also important. In many markets, these variables can have a significant impact on the success of a firm's marketing program. For example, in the United States, a cosmetics firm can be reasonably sure of the desire to use cosmetics being almost universal among women of all income classes. However, in Latin America the same firm may be forced to segment its market by upper-, middle-, and lower-income groups, as well as by urban and rural areas. This is because upper-income women want high-quality cosmetics promoted in prestige media and sold through exclusive outlets. In some rural and less prosperous areas, the cosmetics must be inexpensive, while in other rural areas women do not accept cosmetics. Even in markets that are small in geographical area, consumers may differ in many of the variables mentioned. Any one or set of such differences may have a strong bearing on consumers' ability and willingness to buy.

Ability to Buy. To assess the ability of consumers in a foreign market to buy, four broad measures should be examined: (1) gross national product or per capita national income, (2) distribution of income, (3) rate of growth in buying power, and (4) extent of available financing. Since each of these vary in different areas of the world, the marketing opportunities available must be examined closely.

Willingness to Buy. The cultural framework of consumer motives and behavior is integral to the understanding of the foreign consumer. Cultural values and attitudes toward the material culture, social organizations, the supernatural, aesthetics, and language should be analyzed for their possible influence on each of the elements in the firm's marketing program. It is easy to see that such factors as the group's values concerning acquisition of material goods, the role of the family,

HIGHLIGHT 13-4
The Difficulties of Transcultural Variables

Many firms have found serious problems in international new product marketing:

A firm introduced refrigerators into several Middle Eastern countries and included a photo of a well-stocked refrigerator interior—with a large ham on a central shelf!

Cambell's condensed soups didn't sell well in England because the Campbell's cans appeared small, relative to noncondensed English competitors.

Lever Brothers promised white teeth from its toothpaste, but made the promise to Southeast Asians who held discolored teeth to be a mark of prestige.

Chevrolet introduced its Nova automobile into South America without realizing that "no va" in Spanish means something like "won't go."

Baby food was introduced into several African nations, with baby pictures on the labels. Potential consumers thought the jars contained ground-up babies.

Translators converted:

"Body by Fisher" into "Corpse by Fisher."

"Come Alive with Pepsi" into "Come Alive out of the Grave."

"Car Wash" into "Car Enema."

Source: C. Merle Crawford, *New Products Management,* 2nd ed. (Homewood, Ill.: Richard D. Irwin, 1987), p. 44.

the positions of men and women in society, as well as the various age groups and social classes will all have an effect on marketing, because each influences consumer behavior, values, and the overall pattern of life.

In some areas there appears to be a convergence of tastes and habits, with different cultures becoming more and more integrated into one homogeneous culture, although still separated by national boundaries. This appears to be the case in Western Europe, where consumers are developing into a mass market. This obviously will simplify the task for a marketer in this region. However, cultural differences still prevail among most areas of the world and strongly influence consumer behavior.

Product Planning for International Markets

Before a firm can market a product, there must be something to sell—a product or a service. From this standpoint, product planning is the starting point for the entire marketing program. Once this is accomplished, management can then determine whether there is an adequate market for the product and can decide how the product should be marketed. Most firms would not think of entering a domestic market without extensive product planning. Unfortunately, this is often not the case with foreign markets. Often, firms will enter foreign markets with the same product sold in the United States, or at best, one with only minor changes. In many cases, these firms have encountered serious problems. An example of such a problem occurred when American manufacturers began to export refrigerators to Europe. The firms exported essentially the same models sold in the United States. However, the refrigerators were the wrong size, shape, and temperature range for some areas and had weak appeal in others—thus failing miserably. Although adaptation of the product to local conditions may have eliminated this failure, this adaptation is easier said than done. For example, even in the domestic market, over proliferation of product varieties and options can dilute economies of scale. This dilution results in higher production costs, which may make the price of serving each market segment with an "adapted" product prohibitive. The solution to this problem is not easy. In some cases, changes can be made rather inexpensively, while in others the sales potential of the particular market may not warrant extensive product changes. In any case, management must examine these problems carefully to avoid foreign marketing failures.[3]

---

[3] See Theodore Levitt, "The Globalization of Markets," *Harvard Business Review*, May–June 1983, pp. 92–102, for an excellent discussion of the extent to which a company can market the same product in different countries.

International Distribution Systems

The role of the distribution network in facilitating the transfer of goods and titles and in the demand stimulation process is as important in foreign markets as it is at home. Figure 13–1 illustrates some of the most common channel arrangements in international marketing. The continuum ranges from no control to almost complete control of the distribution system by manufacturers.

The channel arrangement where manufacturers have the least control is shown at the left of Figure 13–1. These are the most indirect channels of distribution. Here manufacturers sell to resident buyers, export agents, or export merchants located in the United States. In reality, these are similar to domestic sales, since all of the marketing functions are assumed by the middlemen.[4]

Manufacturers become more directly involved and, hence, have greater control over distribution when agents and distributors located in foreign markets are selected. Both perform similar functions, except that agents do not assume title to the manufacturers' products, while distributors do. If manufacturers should assume the functions of foreign agents or distributors and establish their own foreign branch,

FIGURE 13–1 Common Distribution Channels for International Marketing

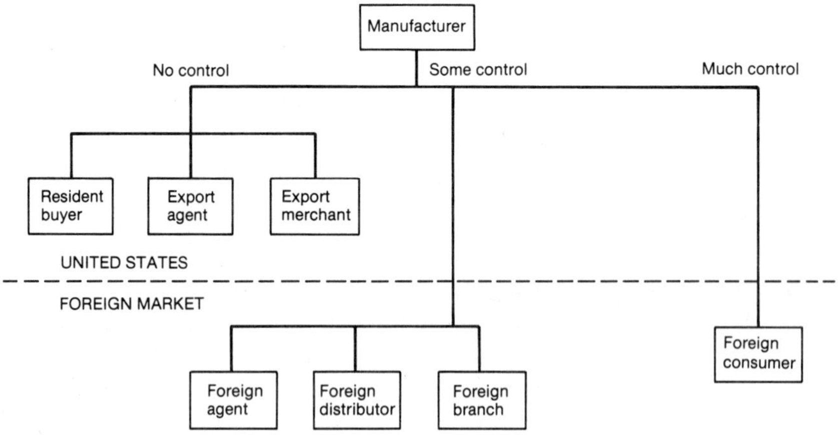

4 The manufacturer does have slightly more control over the export agent than the resident buyer or export merchant, since the export agent does not take title to the goods.

they greatly increase control over their international distribution system. Manufacturers' effectiveness will then depend on their own administrative organization, rather than on independent intermediaries. If the foreign branch sells to other intermediaries, such as wholesalers and retailers, as is the case with most consumer goods, manufacturers again relinquish some control. However, since the manufacturers are located in the market area, they have greater potential to influence these intermediaries.

The channel arrangement that enables manufacturers to exercise a great deal of control is shown at the right of Figure 13-1. Here, manufacturers sell directly to industrial users or ultimate consumers. This arrangement is most common in the sale of industrial goods.

Pricing for International Marketing

In domestic markets, pricing is a complex task. The basic approaches used in price determination in foreign markets are the same as those discussed earlier in the chapter on pricing. However, the pricing task is often more complicated in foreign markets, because of additional problems with tariffs, taxes, and currency conversion.

Import duties are probably the major constraint for foreign marketers and are encountered in many markets. Management must decide whether import duties will be paid by the firm, by the foreign consumer, or shared by both. This and similar constraints may force the firm to abandon an otherwise desirable pricing strategy or may force the firm out of a market altogether.

Another pricing problem arises because of the rigidity in price structures found in many foreign markets. Many foreign middlemen are not aggressive in their pricing policies. They often prefer to maintain high unit margins at the expense of low sales volume, rather than develop large sales volume by means of lower prices and smaller margins per unit. Many times this rigidity is encouraged by legislation that prevents retailers from cutting prices substantially at their own discretion. These are only a few of the pricing problems encountered by foreign marketers. Clearly, the marketer must be aware of such constraints prior to entering the market area.

International Advertising

When expanding their operations into the world marketplace, most firms are aware of the language barriers that exist and realize the importance of translating their messages into the proper idiom. However, there are numerous other issues that must be resolved, such as selecting appropriate media and advertising agencies in foreign markets.

There are many problems in selecting media in foreign markets. Often the media that are traditionally used in the domestic market are not available in foreign markets. If they are available, they may be so on a limited basis only or they may not reach the potential buyers. (For example, one firm was forced to use sound trucks or roving movie vans to reach potential buyers in the sub-Sahara area of Africa.) In addition to the problem of availability, other difficulties arise from the lack of accurate media information. There is no rate and data service or media directory that covers all the media available throughout the world. Where data are available, the accuracy is often questionable.

Another important promotion decision that must be made is the type of agency used to prepare and place the firm's advertisements. There are two major approaches. The first is to use a local agency in each area where the advertisement is to appear. The rationale for this approach is that a local agency employing local nationals can better adapt the firm's message to the local culture. The other approach is to use a U.S.-based international agency with overseas branches in the general area where the advertisement is to appear. Much discussion has developed over which approach is best, and it appears that both approaches can be used successfully by particular firms.

STRATEGIES FOR INTERNATIONAL MARKETING

Although the task of international marketing is similar to that at home, there are areas where significant differences arise that can have an important influence on the outcome of a marketing program. These differences must be considered when developing alternative marketing strategies for foreign markets. One approach to this problem involves five alternative strategies for marketing abroad.[5] Each of these strategies is based on the idea of adapting either the product or the communications appeal, or both, to the particular market.

Strategy One: Same Product, Same Message Worldwide

This approach involves a uniform strategy for each market, offering the same product and same advertising appeals. Obviously, this approach has numerous advantages: It is simple, demands on manage-

---

[5] This section is based on Warren J. Keegan, "Five Strategies for Multinational Marketing," *European Business,* January 1970, pp. 35–40. Also see Warren J. Keegan, "Multinational Product Planning: Strategic Alternatives," *Journal of Marketing,* January 1969, pp. 58–62.

ment time are minimal, and it requires no original analysis or data generation. The product is unchanged, so there are opportunities for economies of scale in production as well as marketing. In sum, it is the lowest-cost strategy.

Unfortunately, the uniform strategy does not work for all products, although some firms, such as Pepsi-Cola and Coca-Cola, have been successful using this strategy. Other firms, such as Chrysler and some food product manufacturers, have not been successful with the uniform approach. These firms have been forced to adapt their marketing mix.

Strategy Two: Same Product, Different Communications

This strategy becomes necessary when the product fills a different need or is used differently but under conditions similar to those in the domestic market. Thus, the only adjustment necessary is in marketing communications. Examples of products where this strategy can be used are bicycles and motorcycles. In the United States, they fill a recreation need, while in many parts of the world they serve as basic transportation.

Since the product remains unchanged, this strategy is also a relatively low-cost alternative. Additional costs would be incurred in identifying different product functions and reformulating the advertising and other communications.

Strategy Three: Different Product, Same Communications

This strategy involves a uniform approach to communications with the product being adapted to local conditions. This strategy assumes that the product will serve the same function in the foreign market but under different use conditions.

Strategy Four: Different Product, Different Communications

This strategy involves adapting both the product and the communications to local conditions. This is necessary because of different market conditions or because the product serves different functions.

Nescafe was forced to use this strategy when its instant coffee, which sold well in Europe, did poorly in England. Thus, a special blend was developed for England. When marketing the new blend, it was found that coffee was viewed as a nontraditional drink, since tea was the traditional drink. The firm was forced to develop special advertisements emphasizing that coffee was for the young person looking for something different.

Strategy Five: Product Invention

When customer needs and conditions under which the product is used are in no way similar to the domestic market, then this strategy may be necessary. This involves the invention or development of an entirely new product, designed to satisfy specific customer needs at a price within reach of the consumer. This strategy may be necessary in the less developed areas of the world. While it is often costly to pursue this strategy, it may be a rewarding one for mass markets in less developed nations of the world. Figure 13–2 summarizes the five strategies.

The choice of a particular strategy, of course, depends on the specific product-market-company mix. Depending on the area of the world under consideration and the particular product, different degrees of adaptation of the product and communications may be necessary. Some markets may require little change if similar to the home market. Others may require some adaptation of both product or communications, or both, while still others may require a specially made product. Whatever the case, each decision should be based on a complete product-market analysis.

CONCLUSION

Many people see the day when there will be truly a "world market." While this day may be far into the future, the trends all appear to aim in that direction. This is why American firms are becoming more internationally minded and are in agreement that many marketing opportunities and challenges of the future lie in international marketing.

FIGURE 13–2 Multinational Product-Communication Mix: Strategic Alternatives

Product Strategy	*Communications Strategy*	*Product Examples*	*Product Function or Need Satisfied*	*Conditions of Product Use*
1. Same	Same.	Soft drinks, automobiles.	Same.	Same.
2. Same	Different.	Bicycles, recreation, transportation.	Different.	Same.
3. Different	Same.	Gasoline, detergents.	Same.	Different.
4. Different	Different.	Clothing, greeting cards.	Different.	Different.
5. Invention	Develop new communications.	Hand-powered washing machine.	Same.	Different.

Additional Readings

Bello, Daniel C., and N. C. Williamson. "The American Export Trading Company: Designing a New International Marketing Institution." *Journal of Marketing,* Fall 1985, pp. 60–69.

Berlew, Kingston. "The Joint Venture—A Way into Foreign Markets." *Harvard Business Review,* July-August 1984, pp. 48–55.

Green, Robert, and Arthur Allaway. "Identification of Export Opportunities: A Shift Share Approach." *Journal of Marketing,* Winter 1985, pp. 83–88.

Hulbert, James M.; William K. Brandt; and Raimer Richers. "Marketing Planning in the Multinational Subsidiary." *Journal of Marketing,* Summer 1980, pp. 7–15.

Kaikati, Jack G., and Wayne A. Label. "American Bribery Legislation: An Obstacle to International Marketing." *Journal of Marketing,* Fall 1980, pp. 38–43.

Kale, Sudhir H. "Dealer Perceptions of Manufacturer Power and Influence Strategies in a Developing Country." *Journal of Marketing Research,* November 1980, pp. 387–93.

Lazer, William; Shoji Murata; and Hiroshi Kosaki. "Japanese Marketing: Towards a Better Understanding." *Journal of Marketing,* Spring 1985, pp. 69–81.

Lodge, George Cabot, and William Glass. "U.S. Trade Policy Needs One Voice." *Harvard Business Review,* May–June 1983, pp. 72–81.

Part E

Marketing Response to a Changing Society

CHAPTER 14
Marketing and Society

Chapter 14

Marketing and Society

The primary concern of this chapter is the role of marketing in society. Basically, two issues are involved. The first issue deals with the responsibility marketing and marketers have to society. In examining this issue, three subtopics will be discussed: (1) the societal concept of marketing, (2) marketing ethics, and (3) consumerism. The second issue deals with the boundaries of marketing and is concerned with the extent to which marketing is involved in our society.

MARKETING'S SOCIAL RESPONSIBILITY

Because business is essentially a social activity, marketing has a very critical social responsibility. Fulfilling this responsibility is both an ethical and practical matter. As an ethical matter, business and marketing have a responsibility to abide by society's laws, whether written or unwritten. As a practical matter, attracting and keeping a profitable customer franchise is a difficult task, and failure to fulfill social responsibilities can result in the loss of corporate image as well as customers. Of all the business functions, marketing is most often criticized for failing to fulfill social responsibilities.[1]

The turbulent decade of the 1960s witnessed an articulate generation of young people attacking the so-called establishment. A large share of this attack was directed at big business. These criticisms cut across an entire spectrum of issues—economic, social, political, and

[1] For an insightful discussion of the source of much of this criticism of marketing, see Robert L. Steiner, "The Prejudice against Marketing," *Journal of Marketing,* July 1976, pp. 2–9.

ethical. Neil Jacoby has studied the problem and provided a meaningful summary of the criticisms leveled at big business in America.[2]

Thesis 1. Big business corporations exercise concentrated economic power, contrary to the public interest.
Thesis 2. Big business corporations exercise concentrated political power, contrary to the public interest.
Thesis 3. Big businesses are controlled by a self-perpetuating, irresponsible power-elite.
Thesis 4. Big corporate businesses exploit and dehumanize workers and customers.
Thesis 5. Big corporate businesses degrade the environment and the quality of life.

A careful review of the above five propositions will reveal that their scope is very broad and societal in nature; also, no one thesis is exclusively an attack on marketing practices. Nevertheless, each thesis, if analyzed carefully, can be said to have some marketing dimension to it, either directly or indirectly. Thus, it is not so much the issue about whether big business and marketing are being maligned by critics; the critical issue is what should marketers do to get their "house in order" as a means of better serving not only individual consumers but society as a whole.

Societal Concept

Like the marketing concept, the societal concept of marketing recognizes profit as a major business motive.[3] It counsels the firm to market goods and services that will satisfy consumers under circumstances that are fair to consumers and enable them to make intelligent purchase decisions. It counsels firms to avoid marketing practices that have negative consequences for society. Many business firms may resist the societal marketing concept because it requires changes in business conduct and marketing strategies that involve costs without yielding visible incremental profits.

It should be mentioned that the societal concept of marketing is, to some extent, at odds with the so-called laissez-faire business ethic, which is still the guiding philosophy of many business executives.

---

[2] Neil Jacoby, *Corporate Power and Social Responsibility* (New York: Macmillan, 1973), chap. 1.

[3] See Philip Kotler, *Marketing Management,* 5th ed. (Englewood Cliffs, N.J.: Prentice-Hall, 1984), pp. 28–30.

Unfortunately, these executives have not recognized that our "free enterprise system" can no longer be equated with laissez-faire capitalism. Instead, large and small corporations alike must manage their affairs in a politico-economic environment that is not only subject to the pressures of competition but is also highly constrained by antitrust laws, trade regulations, governmental agencies, consumer groups, and so forth. One might describe this situation as "managed capitalism."

The societal concept of marketing is closely related to another concept, namely "social marketing." This term in the present context has at least two meanings. It can be defined as "that branch of marketing concerned with the uses of marketing knowledge, concepts, and techniques to enhance social ends as well as the social consequences of marketing policies, decisions, and actions." The term *social marketing* is also used in another and closely related sense, where the focus is on the marketing of social goods, ideas, or causes. For example, "Social marketing is the design, implementation, and control of programs calculated to influence the acceptability of social ideas and involving consideration of product planning, pricing, communication, distribution, and marketing research."[4] Although there is clearly some ambiguity in these definitions, the point to be made is that marketing is now viewed as something more than a business activity. As such, it is considered to have more involvement with and greater responsibility to society.

Marketing Ethics

There are many definitions of ethics and there are many viewpoints of what constitutes ethical behavior. In an organizational framework, it is reasonable to define ethics as a discipline of standards and practical judgment and questions relative to those standards. Marketing managers are confronted with a set of ethical standards imposed on them by society through legislation. They are also constrained by policies established by top-level planners in their own organizations. Aside from these two major constraints, however, marketing managers have a good deal of freedom to operate according to a wide range of ethical codes. Behavior in most cases is guided by so-called situation ethics, where moral decisions are made in the context of a particular set of

---

[4] Philip Kotler and Gerald Zaltman, "Social Marketing: An Approach to Planned Social Change," *Journal of Marketing,* July 1971, pp. 5–12. A representative work is Philip Kotler and Alan Andreasen, *Strategic Marketing for Nonprofit Organizations,* 3rd ed. (Englewood Cliffs, N.J.: Prentice-Hall, 1987).

facts. In other words, marketing managers apply their own ethical principles or rules to each particular situation.[5]

This general discussion of ethical viewpoints is not intended to provide the reader with solutions. If anything, the objective is to raise questions that must be faced by marketers. Perhaps if the reader understands the questions, then the problem is well on its way to being resolved. With this in mind, a few key questions that all marketing managers have to face are listed below.

1. What are the goals of the marketing program, and do they conflict with the goals of society?
2. What is the morality of a product strategy, such as planned obsolescence?
3. What is the morality of using deceptive advertising techniques to manipulate consumer groups, such as children or the uneducated poor?
4. Should ethical criteria be established for salespeople and then pressure be exerted to tempt salespeople to violate these standards?
5. Should the company's ethical standards for its product be no higher than the law requires, even though this legal minimum does not eliminate all the known dangers connected with product use?

Consumerism

One result of the perceived social irresponsibility of corporations is consumerism. Although no one definition will suffice, it is important to first clarify the concept in the form of a working definition. The following is offered: Consumerism is a political, economic, and social movement aimed at promoting and protecting the rights of buyers and the consuming public.

This definition implies several things. First, that the consumerism movement is not merely an economic or marketing issue. Second, that buyers and the consuming public have some basic rights, which originate in various laws, systems of ethics, and the American tradition. Finally, it implies that sellers or producers have significant market power along with obligations to use that power wisely. The power referred to here includes many things. For example:

---

[5] Gene R. Laczniak, Robert F. Lusch, and Patrick E. Murphy, "Social Marketing: Its Ethical Dimensions," *Journal of Marketing,* Spring 1979, pp. 29–36; and O. C. Ferrell and L. G. Gresham, "A Contingency Framework for Understanding Ethical Decision Making in Marketing," *Journal of Marketing,* Summer 1985, pp. 87–96.

HIGHLIGHT 14-1
Code of Ethics of the American Marketing Association

As a member of the American Marketing Association, I recognize the significance of my professional conduct and my responsibilities to society and to the other members of my profession:

1. By acknowledging my accountability to society as a whole as well as to the organization for which I work.
2. By pledging my efforts to assure that all presentations of goods, services, and concepts be made honestly and clearly.
3. By striving to improve marketing knowledge and practice in order to better serve society.
4. By supporting free consumer choice in circumstances that are legal and are consistent with generally accepted community standards.
5. By pledging to use the highest professional standards in my work and in my competitive activity.
6. By acknowledging the right of the American Marketing Association, through established procedure, to withdraw my membership if I am found to be in violation of ethical standards of professional conduct.

Source: The American Marketing Association, Chicago.

1. Sellers have the right to introduce any product in any size, style, or color, so long as it meets minimum requirements of health and safety.
2. Sellers have the right to price the product as they please as long as they avoid discriminations that are harmful to competition.
3. Sellers have the right to promote the product using any amount of resources, media, or message so long as no deception or fraud is involved.
4. Sellers have the right to introduce any buying incentive schemes they wish so long as they are not discriminatory.
5. Sellers have the right to alter the product offerings at any time.
6. Sellers have the right to distribute the product in any reasonable manner.
7. Sellers have the right to limit the product guarantee or postsale services.[6]

---

[6] Philip Kotler, "What Consumerism Means for Marketers," *Harvard Business Review,* May–June 1972, pp. 48–57. Also see Paul N. Bloom and Stephen A. Greyser, "The Maturing of Consumerism," *Harvard Business Review,* November-December 1981, pp. 130–39.

HIGHLIGHT 14-2
The Consumer Bill of Rights

The right—to safety
to be informed
to choose
to be heard

Source: President John F. Kennedy, *The Consumer Bill of Rights,* 1962.

The above list is not exhaustive, but it serves to illustrate the relatively greater power of sellers and the need to balance the rights and power of buyers and sellers. Consumerism in this context can be understood best if it is thought of as consumer actions reflecting dissatisfaction on the buyer's side of the marketing equation.

The broad scope of consumerism is evidenced by the Consumer Advisory Council's list of the 10 major fields of interest to consumers. The 10 original fields are:

1. Consumer standards, grades, and labels.
2. Two-way flow of information and opinion between government and the consumer.
3. Effective consumer representation in government.
4. To study the consumer credit situation and improve it if necessary.
5. To improve the administration, enforcement, and scope of programs in federal agencies.
6. To accelerate economic growth.
7. Improvement of levels of consumption of low-income groups.
8. Antitrust action and prevention of price-fixing.
9. Provision of adequate housing for the nation's families.
10. Adequate medical care for all citizens.

From all of the above, it is clear that the scope of consumerism is quite broad. However, there is a high probability that consumerism will eventually become part of two other areas of social concern: distortions and inequalities in the economic environment and the declining quality of the physical environment. Concern over the economic environment has manifested itself in antitrust laws and other forms of public policy regulations. In addition, the establishment of such government agencies as the Small Business Administration and the Minority Enterprise Small Business Investment Company are further indications of public concern with inequalities in the economic environment.

Consumerism has also been identified with the widespread concern of the physical environment—pollution in particular. For example, manufacturers of soap products have in some cases altered the chemical composition of their laundry products to avoid pollution, and auto manufacturers are still working on better devices to eliminate certain unwanted gas emissions from car engines.

Recent Efforts

The social responsibility of corporations is a key issue today, and it is slowly being resolved. A study of the National Industrial Conference Board covering over 1,000 companies clearly showed that the vast majority of chief executives feel that public affairs is a primary concern of top management. There is little question that most managers recognize that society takes a serious interest in their affairs and expects them to act in a socially responsible manner. Citizen organizations, such as The Project on Corporate Responsibility, have attacked such giants as GM to force acceptance of the basic principle that "the corporation should undertake no activity which is inconsistent with the public interest." Both federal and state governments have enacted laws and established agencies to protect consumers as well as the environment.

One of the most forceful and articulate statements on this issue can be found in the Council of Economic Development's statement, *Social Responsibilities of Business Corporations*. CED's policy statement starts with the basic proposition that business functions by public consent, and that the basic purpose of it is to serve constructively the needs of society, to the satisfaction of society. Years ago the idea that business is party to a contract with society would have provoked an indignant snort from many businesspeople. The real impact of the CED's report is that it represents the thinking of top-management persons who have arrived at a concerted opinion of the corporate stake in a good society. Indeed, this policy report is a useful benchmark as to what some of the Fortune 500 top corporations think about business and marketing's social responsibility.

BROADENING THE CONCEPT OF MARKETING

Up to this point, the focus of this text primarily has been on marketing in the business firm. Basically, the text has taken a microview of marketing management dealing with planning and decision making, primarily in the business firms and exchanges between business firms and consumers or industrial users. However, in recent years, market-

FIGURE 14-1 Some Organizations and Their Products and Customer Groups

Organization	*Product*	*Customer group*
Museum	Cultural appreciation.	General public.
National Safety Council	Safer driving.	Driving public.
Political candidate	Honest government.	Voting public.
Family Planning Foundation	Birth control.	Fertile public.
Police department	Safety.	General public.
Church	Religious experience.	Church members.
University	Education.	Students.

ing scholars have increasingly emphasized an expanded concept of what marketing entails.

A broadened or generic concept of marketing views marketing as consisting of much more than simply business transactions.[7] In this broadened context, marketing is defined as "human activity directed at satisfying needs and wants through exchange processes,"[8] and a product is defined as "something that is viewed as capable of satisfying a want."[9] Thus, the arena for marketing activities and application of marketing principles has been expanded to include nonbusiness areas in society, including the marketing of persons, places, organizations, and ideas. Figure 14-1 illustrates some examples.[10]

A distinction between many of these types of organizations and the business firm is that these organizations generally are not profit oriented. However, the basic goal of survival, which requires income, is common to both these types of organizations and business firms, and both must perform marketing functions to accomplish this goal. In fact, nonprofit organizations have three primary marketing tasks: resource attraction, resource allocation, and persuasion; and the concept of the marketing mix—communication, distribution, pricing, and product—is indeed applicable to these organizations.

---

[7] For important works dealing with this topic, see Philip Kotler and Sidney J. Levy, "Broadening the Concept of Marketing," *Journal of Marketing,* January 1969, pp. 10–15; Philip Kotler, "A Generic Concept of Marketing," *Journal of Marketing,* April 1972, pp. 46–54; Richard P. Bagozzi, "Marketing as an Organized Behavioral System of Exchange," *Journal of Marketing,* October 1974, pp. 77–81; Richard P. Bagozzi, "Marketing as Exchange," *Journal of Marketing,* October 1975, pp. 32–39.

[8] Kotler, *Marketing Management,* p. 14.

[9] Ibid.

[10] From Kotler, "A Generic Concept of Marketing," p. 47. Also see Karen F. A. Fox and Philip Kotler, "The Marketing of Social Causes: The First 10 Years," *Journal of Marketing,* Fall 1980, pp. 24–33.

HIGHLIGHT 14-3
Environmental Trends That Are Likely to Continue over the Next Three to Five Years

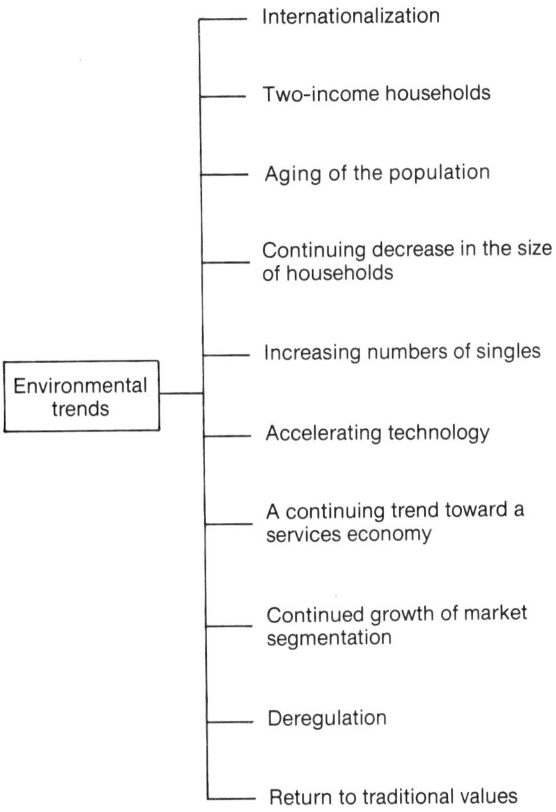

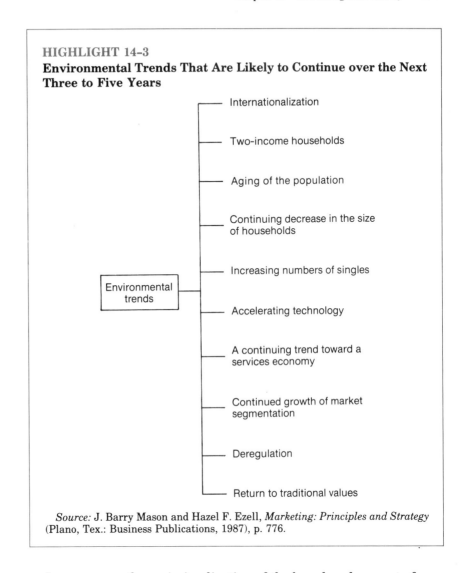

Source: J. Barry Mason and Hazel F. Ezell, *Marketing: Principles and Strategy* (Plano, Tex.: Business Publications, 1987), p. 776.

In summary, the main implication of the broadened concept of marketing is that marketing planning can enable nonbusiness organizations to improve their operations. However, it will be some time before the exact boundaries of marketing will be agreed upon by all marketers.[11]

---

11 For discussion, see David J. Luck, "Broadening the Concept of Marketing—Too Far," *Journal of Marketing,* July 1969, pp. 53–55; Ben M. Enis, "Deepening the Concept of Marketing," *Journal of Marketing,* October 1973, pp. 57–62; F. Kelly Shuptrine and Frank A. Osmanski, "Marketing's Changing Role: Expanding or Contracting?" *Journal of Marketing,* April 1975, pp. 53–66.

CONCLUSION

This chapter was concerned with the role of marketing in society. The two basic issues discussed were social responsibility and the boundaries of the marketing discipline. It was suggested that marketing managers should pay close attention to the needs of society and that marketing principles can be useful for bringing about nonbusiness exchanges.

Additional Readings

Bloom, Paul N., ed. *Consumerism and Beyond: Research Perspectives on the Future Social Environment.* Cambridge, Mass.: Marketing Science Institute, 1982.

Boddewyn, J. J. "Advertising Regulation: Fiddling with the FTC While the World Burns." *Business Horizons,* May–June 1985, pp. 32–40.

Chonko, L. B., and Shelby D. Hunt. "Ethics and Marketing Management: An Empirical Examination." *Journal of Business Research,* August 1985, pp. 339–59.

Davis, Keith, and William C. Fredrick. *Business and Society.* 5th ed. New York: McGraw-Hill, 1984.

Fornell, C., and R. A. Westbrook. "The Vicious Circle of Consumer Complaints." *Journal of Marketing,* Summer 1984, pp. 68–78.

Gaski, John F. "Dangerous Territory: The Societal Marketing Concept Revisited." *Business Horizons,* July–August 1985, pp. 42–47.

Holak, Susan L., and S. K. Reddy. "Effects of a Television and Radio Advertising Ban: A Study of the Cigarette Industry." *Journal of Marketing,* October 1986, pp. 219–27.

Laczniak, Gene R. and Patrick E. Murphy, eds. *Marketing Ethics: Guidelines for Managers.* Lexington, Mass.: Lexington Books, 1986.

Rothschild, M. L. "Marketing Communications in Nonbusiness Situations or Why It's So Hard to Sell Brotherhood Like Soap." *Journal of Marketing,* Spring 1979, pp. 11–20.

Sturdivant, Frederick D. *Business and Society: A Managerial Approach.* 3rd ed. Homewood, Ill.: Richard D. Irwin, 1985.

Section 2

Analyzing Marketing Problems and Cases

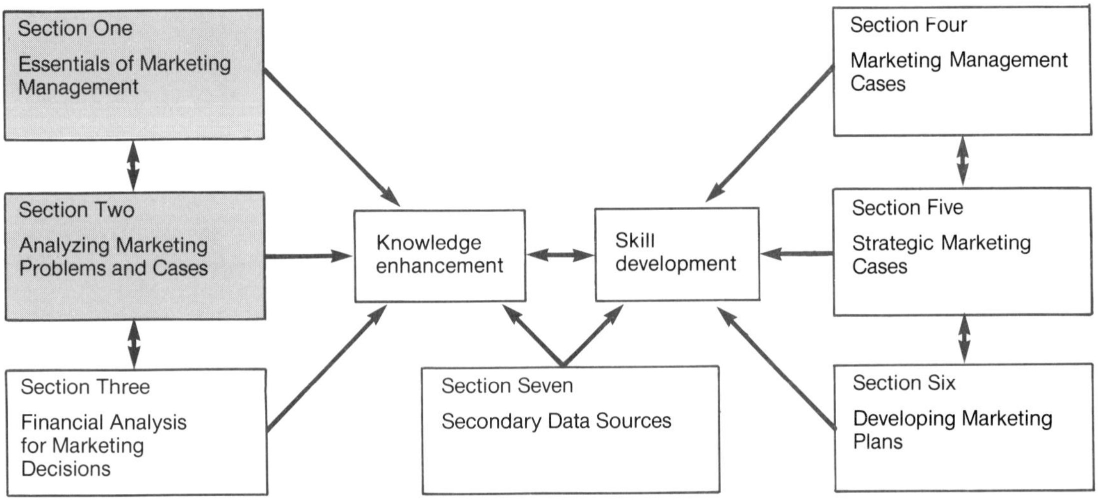

Marketing Management: Knowledge and Skills

NOTE TO THE STUDENT

This section contains a detailed approach to analyzing marketing problems and cases. While the approach is designed primarily for the analysis of comprehensive marketing cases, the logic involved is also applicable to more limited cases. While no approach to marketing problem and case analysis can be expected to fit every situation, we believe that following this approach will direct appropriate analysis and problem recognition for the majority of situations.

HIGHLIGHT 1
A Case for Case Analysis

Cases assist in bridging the gap between classroom learning and the so-called real world of marketing management. They provide us with an opportunity to develop, sharpen, and test our analytical skills at:

- Assessing situations.
- Sorting out and organizing key information.
- Asking the right questions.
- Defining opportunities and problems.
- Identifying and evaluating alternative courses of action.
- Interpreting data.
- Evaluating the results of past strategies.
- Developing and defending new strategies.
- Interacting with other managers.
- Making decisions under conditions of uncertainty.
- Critically evaluating the work of others.
- Responding to criticism.

Source: David W. Cravens and Charles W. Lamb, Jr., *Strategic Marketing: Cases and Applications,* 2nd ed. (Homewood, Ill.: Richard D. Irwin, 1986), p. 55.

The use of business cases was developed by faculty members of the Harvard Graduate School of Business Administration in the 1920s. Case studies have been widely accepted as one effective way of exposing students to the decision-making process.

Basically, cases represent detailed descriptions or reports of business problems. They are usually written by a trained observer who actually had been involved in the firm or organization and had some dealings with the problems under consideration. Cases generally entail both qualitative and quantitative data which the student must analyze to determine appropriate alternatives and solutions.

The primary purpose of the case method is to introduce a measure of realism into management education. Rather than emphasizing the teaching of concepts, the case method focuses on application of concepts and sound logic to real-world business problems. In this way the student learns to bridge the gap between abstraction and application and to appreciate the value of both.

The primary purpose of this section is to offer a logical format for the analysis of case problems. Although there is no one format that can be successfully applied to all cases, the following framework is intended to be a logical sequence from which to develop sound analyses. This framework is presented for analysis of comprehensive marketing cases; however, the process should also be useful for shorter marketing cases, incidents, and problems.

HIGHLIGHT 2
What Does Case "Analysis" Mean?

A common criticism of prepared cases goes something like this: "You repeated an awful lot of case material but you really didn't analyze the case." Yet, at the same time, it is difficult to verbalize exactly what "analysis" means—that is, "I can't explain exactly what it is but I know it when I see it!"

This is a common problem since the term *analysis* has many definitions and means different things in different contexts. In terms of case analysis, one thing that is clear is that analysis means going beyond simply describing the case information. It includes determining the implications of the case information for developing strategy. This may involve careful mathematical analysis of sales and profit data or thoughtful interpretation of the text of the case.

One way of thinking about analysis involves a series of three steps: synthesis, generalizations, and implications. Below is a brief example of this process.

The high growth rate of frozen pizza sales has attracted a number of large food processors, including Pillsbury (Totino's), Quaker Oats (Celeste), American Home Products (Chef Boy-ar-dee), Nestle (Stouffer's), General Mills (Saluto), and H. J. Heinz (La Pizzeria). The major independents are Jeno's, Tony's, and John's. Jeno's and Totino's are the market leaders, with market shares of about 19 percent each. Celeste and Tony's have about 8 to 9 percent each, and the others have about 5 percent or less.	Case Material ↓
The frozen pizza market is a highly competitive and highly fragmented market.	Synthesis ↓
In markets such as this, attempts to gain market share through lower consumer prices or heavy advertising are likely to be quickly copied by competitors and thus not be very effective.	Generalizations ↓
Lowering consumer prices or spending more on advertising are likely to be poor strategies. Perhaps increasing freezer space in retail outlets could be effective (this might be obtained through trade discounts). A superor product, e.g., better-tasting pizza, microwave pizza, or increasing geographic coverage of the market, may be better strategies for obtaining market share.	Implications

Note that none of the three analysis steps includes any repetition of the case material. Rather, they involve abstracting a meaning of the information and, by pairing it with marketing principles, coming up with the strategic implications of the information.

A CASE ANALYSIS FRAMEWORK

A basic approach to case analyses involves a four-step process. First, the problem is defined. Second, alternative courses of action are formulated to solve the problem. Third, the alternatives are analyzed in terms of their strengths and weaknesses. And fourth, an alternative is accepted and a course of action is recommended. This basic approach is quite useful for the student well versed in case analysis, particularly for shorter cases or incidents. However, for the newcomer this framework may well be inadequate and oversimplified. Thus, the following expanded framework and checklists are intended to aid the student in becoming proficient at case and problem analysis.

1. Analyze and Record the Current Situation

Whether the analysis of a firm's problems is done by a manager, student, or paid business consultant, the first step is to analyze the current situation. This does not mean writing up a history of the firm but entails the type of analysis described below. This approach is useful not only for getting a better grip on the situation but also for discovering both real and potential problems—the central concern of any case analysis.

Phase 1: The Environment. The first phase in analyzing a marketing problem or case is to consider the environment in which the firm is operating. The economic environment can have a decided effect on an industry, firm, and marketing program. For example, a depressed economy with high unemployment may not be an ideal situation for implementing a larger price increase. The social and cultural environment also can have considerable effect on both multinational and domestic firms. To illustrate, the advent of men's hairstyling could be considered an appropriate reaction to longer hairstyles, whereas a price reduction to stimulate demand for haircuts could well be inappropriate.

Phase 2: The Industry. The second phase involves analysis of the industry in which the firm operates. This phase can be critical, particularly in terms of how the firm's product is defined. A too-narrow definition of the industry and competitive environment can be disastrous not only for the firm but also for the individual analyzing the case. In appraising the industry, it is useful to first categorize it by the

Class	*Possible Implications*
1. A few giants (oligopolistic). *Examples:* Aluminum producers. Cigarette manufacturers.	Price cutting is fruitless. Antitrust action is a hazard. Concerned action leads to a monopolistic situation facing the customers. Very high capital costs to enter the industry.
2. A few giants and a relatively small number of "independents." *Examples:* Auto industry. Oil industry. Tire industry. Meat processors.	Price cutting by smaller companies may bring strong retaliation by giants. Follow-the-leader pricing. Antitrust action against the giants is a hazard. Monopolistic prices. Squeeze on the independents. High capital costs to enter the industry.
3. Many small independent firms. *Examples:* Food brokers. Sales reps. Auto supply parts. Kitchen cabinet manufacturers. Real estate firms. Tanneries.	Cost of entry is low. Special services. Usual local market. Threat of regional or national linking into a major competitor. Sophisticated business practices often lacking.
4. Professional service firms. *Examples:* CPA firms. Management consultants. Marketing research firms. Advertising agencies.	Confusion of standards. Easy entry (and exit). Secretive pricing, often based on what the traffic will bear.
5. Government regulated to a degree. *Examples:* Banking. Stock brokerages. Rail industry.	Entry is usually difficult. Government provides a semi-monopoly that may lead to high profits or inability to survive in a changing world.

Standard Industrial Classification (SIC) and in terms of the accompanying list.[1]

[1] Murdick, Robert G., Richard H. Eckhouse, R. Carl Moore, Thomas W. Zimmer, *Business Policy: A Framework for Analysis,* 4th ed. (Columbus, Ohio: Grid, 1984), p. 296.

After initial definition and classification, attention should be paid to such factors as:

1. *Technology.*
   a. Level.
   b. Rate of change.
   c. Technological threats to the industry.
2. *Political-legal-social influences.*
   a. Trends in government controls.
   b. Specific regulations.
   c. Social responsibility pressure.
   d. Consumer perceptions of industry.
3. *Industrial guidelines and trends.*
   a. Pricing policies.
   b. Promotion.
   c. Product lines.
   d. Channels of distribution.
   e. Geographic concentration.
   f. Increases or declines in firms or profitability.
4. *Financial indicators.*
   a. Financial ratios.
   b. Working capital required.
   c. Capital structure.
   d. Sources and uses of funds.
   e. Sales.
   f. Profitability.[2]

Sources of information and analysis of financial ratios are contained in Section 3 of this book, and sources for the other types of information are contained in Section 7.

Phase 3: The Firm. The third phase involves analysis of the firm itself not only in comparison with the industry and industry averages but also internally in terms of both quantitative and qualitative data. Key areas of concern at this stage are such factors as objectives, constraints, management philosophy, strengths, weaknesses, and structure of the firm.

Phase 4: The Marketing Program. Although there may be internal personnel or structural problems in the marketing department itself that need examination, typically an analysis of the current marketing strategy is the next phase. In this phase the objectives of the marketing department are analyzed in comparison with those of the firm in

---

[2] This list is based on Murdick et al., *Business Policy,* p. 299.

terms of agreement, soundness, and attainability. Each element of the marketing mix as well as other areas, like marketing research and decision support systems, is analyzed in terms of whether it is internally consistent and synchronized with the goals of the department and firm. Although cases often are labeled in terms of their primary emphasis, such as "Pricing" or "Advertising," it is important to analyze the marketing strategy and entire marketing mix, since a change in one element will usually affect the entire marketing program.

In performing the analysis of the current situation, the data should be analyzed carefully to extract the relevant from the superfluous. Many cases contain information that is not relevant to the problem; it is the analyst's job to discard this information to get a clearer picture of the current situation. As the analysis proceeds, a watchful eye must be kept on each phase to determine (1) symptoms of problems, (2) current problems, and (3) potential problems. Symptoms of problems are indicators of a problem but are not problems in and of themselves. For example, a symptom of a problem may be a decline in sales in a particular sales territory. However, the problem is the root cause of the decline in sales—perhaps the field representative quit making sales calls and is relying on phone orders only.

The following is a checklist of the types of questions that should be asked when performing the analysis of the current situation.

Checklist for Analyzing the Current Situation

Phase 1: The environment.

1. Are there any trends in the environment that could have an effect on the industry, firm, or marketing program?
2. What is the state of the economy? Inflation? Depression?
3. What is the cultural, social, and political atmosphere?
4. Are there trends or changes in the environment that could be advantageous or disadvantageous to the industry, firm, or marketing program? Can the marketing program be restructured to take advantage of these trends or changes?

Phase 2: The industry.

1. What industry is the firm in? What class of industry? Are there other industries the firm is competing with?
2. What is the size of the firm relative to the industry?
3. How does the firm compare in terms of market share, sales, and profitability with the rest of the industry?

4. How does the firm compare with other firms in the industry in terms of a financial ratio analysis?
5. What is the firm's major competition?
6. Are there any trends in terms of government control, political, or public atmosphere that could affect the industry?

Phase 3: The firm.

1. What are the objectives of the firm? Are they clearly stated? Attainable?
2. What are the strengths of the firm? Managerial expertise? Financial? Copyrights or patents?
3. What are the constraints and weaknesses of the firm?
4. Are there any real or potential sources of dysfunctional conflict in the structure of the firm?
5. How is the marketing department structured in the firm?

Phase 4: The marketing program.

1. What are the objectives of the marketing program? Are they clearly stated? Are they consistent with the objectives of the firm? Is the entire marketing mix structured to meet these objectives?
2. What marketing concepts are at issue in the program? Is the marketing program well planned and laid out? Is the program consistent with sound marketing principles? If the program takes exception to marketing principles, is there a good reason for it?
3. To what target market is the program directed? Is it well defined? Is the market large enough to be profitably served? Does the market have long-run potential?
4. What competitive advantage does the marketing program offer? If none, what can be done to gain a competitive advantage in the market place?
5. What products are being sold? What is the width, depth, and consistency of the firm's product lines? Does the firm need new products to fill out its product line? Should any product be deleted? What is the profitability of the various products?
6. What promotion mix is being used? Is promotion consistent with the products and product images? What could be done to improve the promotion mix?
7. What channels of distribution are being used? Do they deliver the product at the right time and right place to meet consumer needs? Are the channels

typical of those used in the industry? Could channels be made more efficient?
8. What pricing strategies are being used? How do prices compare with similar products of other firms? How are prices determined?
9. Are marketing research and information systematically integrated into the marketing program? Is the overall marketing program internally consistent?

The relevant information from this preliminary analysis is now formalized and recorded. At this point the analyst must be mindful of the difference between facts and opinions. Facts are objective statements, such as financial data, whereas opinions are subjective interpretations of facts or situations. The analyst must make certain not to place too much emphasis on opinions and to carefully consider any variables that may bias such opinions.

Regardless of how much information is contained in the case or how much additional information is collected, the analyst usually finds that it is impossible to specify a complete framework for the current situation. At this point, assumptions must be made. Clearly, since each analyst may make different assumptions, it is critical that assumptions be explicitly stated. When presenting a case, the analyst may wish to distribute copies of the assumption list to all class members. In this way, confusion is avoided in terms of how the analyst perceives the current situation, and others can evaluate the reasonableness and necessity of the assumptions.

2. Analyze and Record Problems and Their Core Elements

After careful analysis, problems and their core elements should be explicitly stated and listed in order of importance. Finding and recording problems and their core elements can be difficult. It is not uncommon on reading a case for the first time for the student to view the case as a description of a situation in which there are no problems. However, careful analysis should reveal symptoms, which lead to problem recognition.

Recognizing and recording problems and their core elements is most critical for a meaningful case analysis. Obviously, if the root problems are not explicitly stated and understood, the remainder of the case analysis has little merit, since the true issues are not being dealt with. The following checklist of questions is designed to assist you in performing this step of the analysis.

Checklist for Analyzing Problems and Their Core Elements

1. What is the primary problem in the case? What are the secondary problems?
2. What proof exists that these are the central issues? How much of this proof is based on facts? On opinions? On assumptions?
3. What symptoms are there that suggest these are the real problems in the case?
4. How are the problems, as defined, related? Are they independent or are they the result of a deeper problem?
5. What are the ramifications of these problems in the short run? In the long run?

3. Formulate, Evaluate, and Record Alternative Courses of Action

This step is concerned with the question of what can be done to resolve the problem defined in the previous step. Generally, a number of alternative courses of action are available that could potentially help alleviate the problem condition. Three to seven is usually a reasonable number of alternatives to work with. Another approach is to brainstorm as many alternatives as possible initially and then reduce the list to a workable number.

Sound logic and reasoning are very important in this step. It is critical to avoid alternatives that could potentially alleviate the problem, but that at the same time, create a greater new problem or require greater resources than the firm has at its disposal.

After serious analysis and listing of a number of alternatives, the next task is to evaluate them in terms of their costs and benefits. Costs are any output or effort the firm must exert to implement the alternative. Benefits are any input or value received by the firm. Costs to be considered are time, money, other resources, and opportunity costs, while benefits are such things as sales, profits, goodwill, and customer satisfaction. The following checklist provides questions to be used when performing this phase of the analysis.

Checklist for Formulating and Evaluating Alternative Courses of Action

1. What possible alternatives exist for solving the firm's problems?
2. What limits are there on the possible alternatives? Competence? Resources? Management preference? Social responsibility? Legal restrictions?

3. What major alternatives are now available to the firm? What marketing concepts are involved that affect these alternatives?
4. Are the listed alternatives reasonable given the firm's situation? Are they logical? Are the alternatives consistent with the goals of the marketing program? Are they consistent with the firm's objectives?
5. What are the costs of each alternative? What are the benefits? What are the advantages and disadvantages of each alternative?
6. Which alternative best solves the problem and minimizes the creation of new problems, given the above constraints?

4. Select, Implement, and Record the Chosen Alternative Course of Action

In light of the previous analysis, the alternative is now selected that best solves the problem with a minimum creation of new problems. It is important to record the logic and reasoning that precipitated the selection of a particular alternative. This includes articulating not only why the alternative was selected but also why the other alternatives were not selected.

No analysis is complete without an action-oriented decision and plan for implementing the decision. The accompanying checklist indicates the type of questions that should be answered in this stage of analysis.

Checklist for Selecting and Implementing the Chosen Alternative

1. What must be done to implement the alternative?
2. What personnel will be involved? What are the responsibilities of each?
3. When and where will the alternative be implemented?
4. What will be the probable outcome?
5. How will the success or failure of the alternative be measured?

PITFALLS TO AVOID IN CASE ANALYSIS

Below is a summary of some of the most common errors analysts make when analyzing cases. When evaluating your analysis or those of others, this list provides a useful guide for spotting potential shortcomings.

HIGHLIGHT 3
An Operational Approach to Case and Problem Analysis

1. Read the case quickly to get an overview of the situation.
2. Read the case again thoroughly. Underline relevant information and take notes on potential areas of concern.
3. Review outside sources of information on the environment and the industry. Record relevant information and the source of this information.
4. Perform comparative analysis of the firm with the industry and industry averages.
5. Analyze the firm.
6. Analyze the marketing program.
7. Record the current situation in terms of relevant environmental, industry, firm, and marketing program parameters.
8. Make and record necessary assumptions to complete the situational framework.
9. Determine and record the major issues, problems, and their core elements.
10. Record proof that these are the major issues.
11. Record potential courses of actions.
12. Evaluate each initially to determine constraints that preclude acceptability.
13. Evaluate remaining alternatives in terms of costs and benefits.
14. Record analysis of alternatives.
15. Select an alternative.
16. Record alternative and defense of its selection.
17. Record the who, what, when, where, how, and why of the alternative and its implementation.

1. *Inadequate definition of the problem.* By far the most common error made in case analysis is attempting to recommend a course of action without first adequately defining or understanding the problem. Whether presented orally or in a written report, a case analysis must begin with a focus on the central issues and problems represented in the case situation. Closely related is the error of analyzing symptoms without determining the root problem.
2. *The search for "the answer."* In case analysis, there are no clear-cut solutions. Keep in mind that the objective of case studies is learning through discussion and exploration. There is no one "official" or "correct" answer to a case. Rather, there are usually several reasonable alternative solutions.
3. *Not enough information.* Analysts often complain there is not

enough information in some cases to make a good decision. However, there is justification for not presenting "all" of the information in a case. As in real life, a marketing manager or consultant seldom has all the information necessary to make an optimal decision. Thus, reasonable assumptions have to be made, and the challenge is to find intelligent solutions in spite of the limited information.

4. *Use of generalities.* In analyzing cases, specific recommendations are necessarily not generalities. For example, a suggestion to increase the price is a generality; a suggestion to increase the price by $1.07 is a specific.
5. *A different situation.* Considerable time and effort are sometimes exerted by analysts contending that "If the situation were different, I'd know what course of action to take" or "If the marketing manager hadn't already fouled things up so badly, the firm wouldn't have a problem." Such reasoning ignores the fact that the events in the case have already happened and cannot be changed. Even though analysis or criticism of past events is necessary in diagnosing the problem, in the end, the present situation must be addressed and decisions must be made based on the given situation.
6. *Narrow vision analysis.* Although cases are often labeled as a specific type of case, such as "Pricing," "Product," and so forth, this does not mean that other marketing variables should be ignored. Too often analysts ignore the effects that a change in one marketing element will have on the others.
7. *Realism.* Too often analysts become so focused on solving a particular problem that their solutions become totally unrealistic. For instance, suggesting a $1 million advertising program for a firm with a capital structure of $50,000 is an unrealistic solution.
8. *The marketing research solution.* A quite common but unsatisfactory solution to case problems is marketing research; for example, "The firm should do this or that type of marketing research to find a solution to its problem." Although marketing research may be helpful as an intermediary step in some cases, marketing research does not solve problems or make decisions. In cases where marketing research is recommended, the cost and potential benefits should be fully specified in the case analysis.
9. *Rehashing the case material.* Analysts sometimes spend considerable effort rewriting a two- or three-page history of the firm as presented in the case. This is unnecessary since the instructor and other analysts are already familiar with this information.
10. *Premature conclusions.* Analysts sometimes jump to premature conclusions instead of waiting until their analysis is completed. Too many analysts jump to conclusions upon first reading the case

and then proceed to interpret everything in the case as justifying their conclusions, even factors logically against it.

COMMUNICATING CASE ANALYSES

The final concern in case analysis deals with communicating the results of the analysis. The most comprehensive analysis has little value if it is not communicated effectively. There are two primary media through which case analyses are communicated—the written report and the oral presentation.

The Written Report

Since the structure of the written report will vary by the type of case analyzed, the purpose of this section is not to present a "one and only" way of writing up a case. The purpose of this section is to present some useful generalizations to aid the student in case writeups.

First, a good written report generally starts with an outline. The purpose of the outline is to:

1. Organize the case material in a sequence that makes it easy for the reader to follow.
2. Highlight the major thoughts of the case and show the relationships among subsidiary ideas and major ideas.
3. Reinforce the student's memory of the case ideas and provide the framework for developing these ideas.
4. Serve to refresh the student's memory of the case when it has to be referred to weeks later.[3]

The outline format should avoid too fine a breakdown, and there should be at least two subdivisions for any heading. The following is an example of typical outline headings:

I. Current Situation.
- **A.** *Environment.*
  1. Economic.
  2. Cultural and social.
  3. Political and legal.
- **B.** *Industry.*
  1. Definition.
  2. Classification.
  3. Technology.

[3] Murdick et al., *Business Policy*, p. 307.

4. Political-legal-social factors.
5. Industrial guidelines and trends.
6. Financial indicators.

C. *Firm.*

1. Objectives.
2. Constraints.
3. Management philosophy.
4. Strengths.
5. Weaknesses.
6. Structure.

D. *Marketing program.*

1. Objectives.
2. Constraints.
3. Strengths.
4. Weaknesses.
5. Target market(s).
6. Product considerations.
7. Promotion considerations.
8. Pricing considerations.
9. Channel considerations.
10. Information and research considerations.

II. Problems.

A. *Primary problem(s).*

1. Symptoms.
2. Proof.

B. *Secondary problem(s).*

1. Symptoms.
2. Proof.

III. Alternatives.

A. *Alternative 1.*

1. Strengths and benefits.
2. Weaknesses and costs.

B. *Alternative 2.*

1. Strengths and benefits.
2. Weaknesses and costs.

C. *Alternative 3.*

1. Strengths and benefits.
2. Weaknesses and costs.

IV. Decision and Implementation.

A. *What.*
B. *Who.*
C. *When.*
D. *Where.*
E. *Why.*
F. *How.*

V. Technical Appendix.

Writing the case report now entails filling out the details of the outline in prose form. Clearly, like any other skill, it takes practice to determine the best method for writing a particular case. However, simplicity, clarity, and precision are prime objectives of the report.

The Oral Presentation

Case analyses are often presented by an individual or team. As with the written report, a good outline is critical, and it is usually preferable to hand out the outline to each class member. Although there is no best way to present a case or to divide responsibility between team members, simply reading the written report is unacceptable since it encourages boredom and interferes with all-important class discussion.

The use of visual aids can be quite helpful in presenting class analyses. However, simply presenting financial statements contained in the case is a poor use of visual media. On the other hand, graphs of sales and profit curves can be more easily interpreted and can be quite useful for making specific points.

Oral presentation of cases is particularly helpful to students for learning the skill of speaking to a group. In particular, the ability to handle objections and disagreements without antagonizing others is a skill worth developing.

CONCLUSION

From the discussion it should be obvious that good case analyses require a major commitment of time and effort. Individuals must be highly motivated and willing to get involved in the analysis and discussion if they expect to learn and succeed in a course where cases are utilized. Persons with only passive interest who perform "night before" analyses cheat themselves of valuable learning experiences that can aid them in their careers.

Additional Readings

Bernhardt, Kenneth L., and Thomas C. Kinnear. *Cases in Marketing Management.* 4th ed. Plano, Tex.: Business Publications, 1988.

Cravens, David W., and Charles W. Lamb, Jr. *Strategic Marketing: Cases and Applications.* 2nd ed. Homewood, Ill.: Richard D. Irwin, 1986, chap. 3.

Edge, Alfred G., and Denis R. Coleman. *The Guide to Case Analysis and Reporting.* Honolulu: Systems Logistics, 1978.

O'Dell, William F; Andrew C. Ruppel; Robert H. Trent; and William J. Kehoe. *Marketing Decision Making: Analytic Framework and Cases.* 3rd ed. Cincinnati: South-Western Publishing, 1988.

Section 3

Financial Analysis for Marketing Decision Making

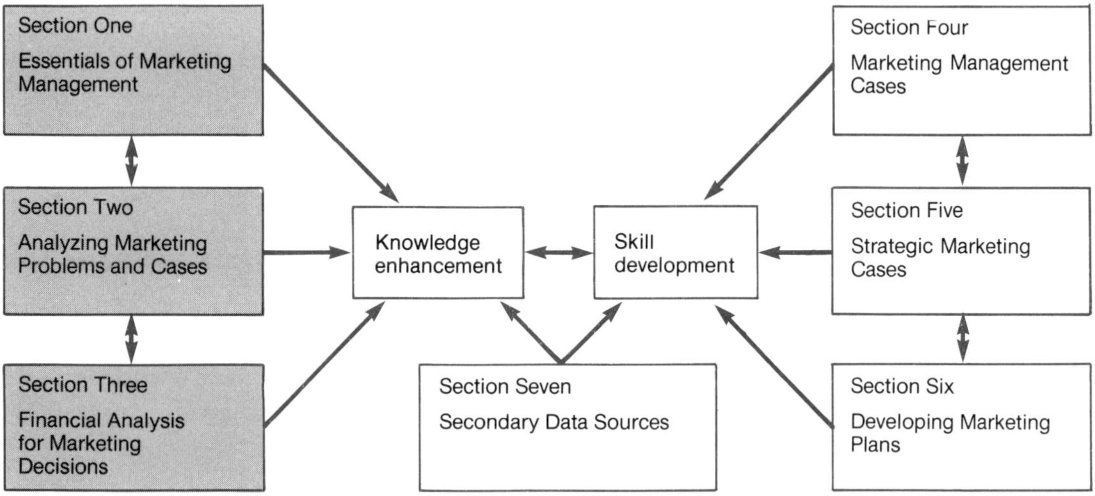

Marketing Management: Knowledge and Skills

NOTE TO THE STUDENT

Financial analysis is an important tool for analyzing marketing problems and cases and is useful for determining problems and defending chosen courses of action. While it is beyond the scope of this text to offer detailed coverage of financial management, we have selected three financial tools which we believe are very useful. These are break-even analysis, net present value analysis, and ratio analysis.

FINANCIAL ANALYSIS

Financial analysis is an important aspect of marketing decision making and planning and should be an integral part of marketing problem and case analysis. In this section we present several financial tools that are useful for analyzing marketing problems and cases. First, we investigate break-even analysis, which is concerned with determining the number of units or dollar sales, or both, necessary to break even on a project or to obtain a given level of profits. Second, we illustrate net present value analysis, which is a somewhat more sophisticated tool for analyzing marketing alternatives. Finally, we investigate ratio analysis, which can be a quite useful tool for determining the financial condition of the firm, including its ability to invest in a new or modified marketing program.

Break-Even Analysis

Break-even analysis is a common tool for investigating the potential profitability of a marketing alternative. The *break-even point* is that level of sales in either units or sales dollars at which a firm covers all of its costs. In other words, it is the level at which total sales revenue just equals the total costs necessary to achieve these sales.

To compute the break-even point, an analyst must have or be able to obtain three values. First, the analyst needs to know the selling price per unit of the product (SP). For example, suppose the Ajax Company plans to sell its new electric car through its own dealerships at a retail price of $5,000. Second, the analyst needs to know the level of fixed costs (FC). Fixed costs are all costs relevant to the project that do not change regardless of how many units are produced or sold. For instance, whether Ajax produces and sells 1 or 100,000 cars, Ajax executives will receive their salaries, land must be purchased for a plant, a plant must be constructed, and machinery must be purchased. Other fixed costs include such things as interest, lease payments, and sinking fund payments. Suppose Ajax has totaled all of its fixed costs and the sum is $1.5 million. Third, the analyst must know the variable costs per unit produced (VC). As the name implies, variable costs are those that vary directly with the number of units produced. For example, for each car Ajax produces, there are costs for raw materials and components to build the car, such as batteries, electric motors, steel bodies, and tires; there are labor costs for operating employees; there are machine costs, such as electricity and welding rods. Suppose these are totaled by Ajax and it is determined that the variable costs for each car produced equal $3,500. With this information, the analyst can now determine the break-even point, which is the number of units that must be sold to just cover the cost of producing the cars. The break-even point is determined by dividing total fixed costs by the *contribution margin*. The contribution margin is simply the difference between the selling price per unit (SP) and variable costs per unit (VC). Algebraically,

$$BEP_{(\text{in units})} = \frac{\text{Total fixed costs}}{\text{Contribution margin}} = \frac{FC}{SP - VC}$$

Substituting the Ajax estimates,

$$BEP_{(\text{in units})} = \frac{1{,}500{,}000}{5{,}000 - 3{,}500} = \frac{1{,}500{,}000}{1{,}500} = 1{,}000 \text{ units}$$

In other words, the Ajax Company must sell 1,000 cars to just break even (i.e., for total sales revenue to cover total costs).

Alternatively, the analyst may want to know the break-even point in terms of dollar sales volume. Of course, if the preceding analysis has been done, one could simply multiply the $\text{BEP}_{(\text{in units})}$ times the selling price to determine the break-even sales volume (i.e., 1,000 units × \$5,000/unit = \$5 million). However, the $\text{BEP}_{(\text{in dollars})}$ can be computed directly, using the formula below:

$$BEP_{(\text{in dollars})} = \frac{FC}{1 - \dfrac{VC}{SP}} = \frac{1{,}500{,}000}{1 - \dfrac{3{,}500}{5{,}000}} = \frac{1{,}500{,}000}{1 - .7} = \$5{,}000{,}000$$

Thus, Ajax must produce and sell 1,000 cars, which equals \$5 million sales, to break even. Of course, firms do not want to just break even but want to make a profit. The logic of break-even analysis can easily be extended to include profits (P). Suppose, Ajax decided that a 20 percent return on fixed costs would make the project worth the investment. Thus, Ajax would need 20% × \$1,500,000 = \$300,000 before-tax profit. To calculate how many units Ajax must sell to achieve this level of profits, the profit figure (P) is added to fixed costs in the above formulas. (We will label the break-even point as BEP′ to show that we are now computing unit and sales levels to obtain a given profit level.) In the Ajax example:

$$
\begin{aligned}
BEP'_{\text{(in units)}} &= \frac{FC + P}{SP - VC} \\
&= \frac{1{,}500{,}000 + 300{,}000}{5{,}000 - 3{,}500} \\
&= \frac{1{,}800{,}000}{1{,}500} \\
&= 1{,}200 \text{ units}
\end{aligned}
$$

In terms of dollars,

$$
\begin{aligned}
BEP'_{\text{(in dollars)}} &= \frac{FC + P}{1 - \dfrac{VC}{SP}} \\
&= \frac{1{,}500{,}000 + 300{,}000}{1 - \dfrac{3{,}500}{5{,}000}} \\
&= \frac{1{,}800{,}000}{1 - .7} \\
&= \$6{,}000{,}000
\end{aligned}
$$

Thus, Ajax must produce and sell 1,200 cars (sales volume of $6 million) to obtain a 20 percent return on fixed costs. Analysis must now be directed at determining whether a given marketing plan can be expected to produce sales of at least this level. If the answer is yes, then the project would appear to be worth investing in. If not, then Ajax should seek other opportunities.

Net Present Value Analysis

The profit-oriented marketing manager must understand that the capital invested in new products has a cost. It is a basic principle in business that whoever wishes to use capital must pay for its use. Dollars invested in new products could be diverted to other uses—to pay off debts, pay out to stockholders, or buy U.S. Treasury bonds—which would yield economic benefits to the corporation. If, on the other hand, all of the dollars used to finance a new product have to be borrowed from lenders outside the corporation, then interest has to be paid on the loan.

One of the best ways to analyze the financial aspects of a marketing alternative is *net present value* analysis. This method employs a "discounted cash flow," which takes into account the time value of money and its price to the borrower. The following example will illustrate this method.

To compute the net present value of an investment proposal, the cost of capital must be estimated. The cost of capital can be defined as the required rate of return on an investment that would leave the owners of the firm as well off as if the project was not undertaken. Thus, it is the minimum percentage return on investment that a project must make to be worth undertaking. There are many methods of estimating the cost of capital. However, since these methods are not the concern of this text, we will simply assume that the cost of capital for the Ajax Corporation has been determined to be 10 percent.[1] Again, it should be noted that once the cost of capital is determined, it becomes the minimum rate of return required for an investment—a type of cutoff point. However, some firms in selecting their new product investments, select a minimum rate of return that is above the cost of capital figure to allow for errors in judgment or measurement.

The Ajax Corporation is considering a proposal to market instant developing movie film. After conducting considerable marketing research, sales were projected to be $1 million per year. In addition, the finance department compiled the following information concerning the projects:

New equipment needed	$700,000
Useful life of equipment	10 years
Depreciation	10 % per year
Salvage value	$100,000
Cost of goods and expenses	$700,000 per year
Cost of capital	10 %
Tax rate	50 %

To compute the net present value of this project, the net cash flow for each year of the project must first be determined. This can be done in four steps:

1. Sales − Cost of goods and expenses = Gross income

or

$1,000,000 − 700,000 = $300,000.

[1] For methods of estimating the cost of capital, see Diana R. Harrington and Brent D. Wilson, *Corporate Financial Analysis,* 2nd ed. (Plano, Tex.: Business Publications, 1986), chap. 5.

2. Gross income − Depreciation = Taxable income

   or

   $$\$300{,}000 - (10\% \times 600{,}000) = \$240{,}000.$$

3. Taxable income − Tax = Net income

   or

   $$\$240{,}000 - (50\% \times 240{,}000) = \$120{,}000.$$

4. Net income + Depreciation = Net cash flow

   or

   $$\$120{,}000 + 60{,}000 = \$180{,}000 \text{ per year.}$$

Since the cost of capital is 10 percent, this figure is used to discount the net cash flows for each year. To illustrate, the $180,000 received at the end of the first year would be discounted by the factor $1/(1 + 0.10)$, which would be $180{,}000 \times 0.9091 = \$163{,}638$; the $180,000 received at the end of the second year would be discounted by the factor $1(1 + 0.10)^2$, which would be $180{,}000 \times 0.8264 = \$148{,}752$, and so on. (Most finance textbooks have present value tables that can be used to simplify the computations). Below are the present value computations for the 10-year project. It should be noted that the net cash flow for year 10 is $280,000 since there is an additional $100,000 inflow from salvage value.

Year	*Net Cash Flow*	*0.10 Discount Factor*	*Present Value*
1	$ 180,000	0.9091	$ 163,638
2	180,000	0.8264	148,752
3	180,000	0.7513	135,234
4	180,000	0.6830	122,940
5	180,000	0.6209	111,762
6	180,000	0.5645	101,610
7	180,000	0.5132	92,376
8	180,000	0.4665	83,970
9	180,000	0.4241	76,338
10	280,000	0.3855	107,940
Total	$1,900,000		$1,144,560

Thus, at a discount rate of 10 percent, the present value of the net cash flow from new product investment is greater than the $700,000 outlay required, and so the decision can be considered profitable by this standard. Here the *net present value* is $444,560, which is the difference between the $700,000 investment outlay and the $1,144,560 discounted cash flow. The present value ratio is nothing more than the present value of the net cash flow divided by the cash investment. If this ratio is one or larger than one, then the project would be profitable for the firm to invest in.

There are many other measures of investment worth, but only one additional method will be discussed. It is the very popular and easily understood "payback method." Payback refers to the amount of time required to pay back the original outlay from the cash flows. Staying with the example, the project is expected to produce a stream of cash proceeds that is constant from year to year, so the payback period can be determined by dividing the investment outlay by this annual cash flow. Dividing $700,000 by $180,000, the payback period is approximately 3.9 years. Firms often set a minimum payback period before a project will be accepted. For example, many firms refuse to take on a project if the payback period exceeds five years.

This example should illustrate the difficulty in evaluating marketing investments from a profitability or economic worth standpoint. The most challenging problem is that of developing accurate cash flow estimates, because there are many possible alternatives, such as price of the product and channels of distribution, and the consequences of each alternative must be forecast in terms of sales volumes, selling costs, and other expenses. In spite of all the problems, management must evaluate the economic worth of new product decisions, not only to reduce some of the guesswork and ambiguity surrounding marketing decision making, but also to reinforce the objective of trying to make profitable decisions.

HIGHLIGHT 1
Selected Present Value Discount Factors

Years	*8%*	*10%*	*12%*	*14%*	*16%*	*18%*
1	.9259	.9091	.8929	.8772	.8621	.8475
2	.8573	.8264	.7972	.7695	.7432	.7182
3	.7938	.7513	.7118	.6750	.6407	.6086
4	.7350	.6830	.6355	.5921	.5523	.5158
5	.6806	.6209	.5674	.5194	.4761	.4371
6	.6302	.5645	.5066	.4556	.4104	.3704
7	.5835	.5132	.4523	.3996	.3538	.3139
8	.5403	.4665	.4039	.3506	.3050	.2660
9	.5002	.4241	.3606	.3075	.2630	.2255
10	.4632	.3855	.3220	.2697	.2267	.1911

Ratio Analysis

Firms' income statements and balance sheets provide a wealth of information that is useful for marketing decision making. Frequently, this information is included in marketing cases, yet analysts often have no convenient way of interpreting the financial position of the firm to make sound marketing decisions. Ratio analysis provides the analyst an easy and efficient method for investigating a firm's financial position by comparing the firm's ratios across time or with ratios of similar firms in the industry or with industry averages.

Ratio analysis involves four basic steps:

1. Choose the appropriate ratios.
2. Compute the ratios.
3. Compare the ratios.
4. Check for problems or opportunities.

1. Choose the Appropriate Ratios. The five basic types of financial ratios are: (1) liquidity ratios, (2) asset management ratios, (3) profitability ratios, (4) debt management ratios, and (5) market value ratios.[2] While calculating ratios of all five types is useful, liquidity, asset management, and profitability ratios provide information that is most directly relevant for marketing decision making. Although many ratios can be calculated in each of these groups, we have selected two of the most commonly used and readily available ratios in each group to illustrate the process.

Liquidity Ratios. One of the first considerations in analyzing a marketing problem is the liquidity of the firm. *Liquidity* refers to the ability of the firm to pay its short-term obligations. If a firm cannot meet its short-term obligations, there is little that can be done until this problem is resolved. Simply stated, recommendations to increase advertising, to do marketing research, or to develop new products are of little value if the firm is about to go bankrupt!

The two most commonly used ratios for investigating liquidity are the *current ratio* and the *quick ratio* (or "acid test"). The current ratio is determined by dividing current assets by current liabilities and is a measure of the overall ability of the firm to meet its current obligations. A common rule of thumb is that the current ratio should be about 2:1.

The quick ratio is determined by subtracting inventory from current assets and dividing the remainder by current liabilities. Since in-

---

[2] See Eugene F. Brigham, *Fundamentals of Financial Management* (Hinsdale, Ill.: Dryden Press, 1986).

ventory is the least liquid current asset, the quick ratio deals with assets that are most readily available for meeting short-term (one-year) obligations. A common rule of thumb is that the quick ratio should be at least 1:1.

Asset Management Ratios. Asset management ratios investigate how well the firm handles its assets. For marketing problems, two of the most useful asset management ratios are concerned with *inventory turnover* and *total asset utilization*. The inventory turnover ratio is determined by dividing sales by inventories.[3] If the firm is not turning its inventory over as rapidly as other firms, it suggests that too many funds are being tied up in unproductive or obsolete inventory. In addition, if the firm's turnover ratio is decreasing over time, it suggests that there may be a problem in the marketing plan, since inventory is not being sold as rapidly as it had been in the past. One problem with this ratio is that, since sales usually are recorded at market prices and inventory usually is recorded at cost, the ratio may overstate turnover. Thus, some analysts prefer to use cost of sales rather than sales in computing turnover. We will use cost of sales in our analysis.

A second useful asset management ratio is total asset utilization. It is calculated by dividing sales by total assets and is a measure of how productively the firm's assets have been used to generate sales. If this ratio is well below industry figures, it suggests that marketing efforts may be relatively less effective than other firms or that some unproductive assets should be disposed of.

Profitability Ratios. Profitability is the goal of marketing and is the real test of the quality of marketing decision making in the firm. Two key profitability ratios are *profit margin on sales* and *return on total assets*. Profit margin on sales is determined by dividing profit before tax by sales. Serious questions about the firm and marketing plan should be raised if profit margin on sales is declining across time or is well below other firms in the industry. Return on total assets is determined by dividing profit before tax by total assets. This ratio is the return on investment for the entire firm.

2. Compute the Ratios. The next step in ratio analysis is to compute the ratios. Table 1 presents the balance sheet and income statement for the Ajax Home Computer Company. The six ratios can be calculated from the Ajax balance sheet and income statement as follows:

---

[3] It is useful to use average inventory rather than a single end-of-year estimate if monthly data are available.

TABLE 1 Balance Sheet and Income Statement for Ajax Home Computer Company

AJAX HOME COMPUTER COMPANY
Balance Sheet
March 31, 1980
(in thousands)

Assets		Liabilities and Stockholders' Equity	
Cash	$ 30	Trade accounts payable	$ 150
Marketable securities	40	Accrued	25
Accounts receivable	200	Notes payable	100
Inventory	430	Accrued income tax	40
Total current assets	700	Total current liabilities	315
Plant and equipment	1,000	Bonds	500
Land	500	Debentures	85
Other investments	200	Stockholders' equity	1,500
Total assets	$2,400	Total liabilities and stockholders' equity	$2,400

AJAX HOME COMPUTER COMPANY
Income Statement
For the 12-Month Period Ending March 31, 1980
(in thousands)

Sales	$3,600
Cost of sales:	
Labor and materials	2,000
Depreciation	200
Selling expenses	500
General and administrative expenses	80
Total cost	2,780
Net operating income	820
Less interest expense:	
Interest on notes	20
Interest on debentures	200
Interest on bonds	300
Total interest	520
Profit before tax	300
Federal income tax (@ 40%)	120
Net profit after tax	$ 180

Liquidity ratios:

$$\text{Current ratio} = \frac{\text{Current assets}}{\text{Current liabilities}} = \frac{700}{315} = 2.2$$

$$\text{Quick ratio} = \frac{\text{Current assets} - \text{Inventory}}{\text{Current liabilities}} = \frac{270}{315} = .86$$

Asset management ratios:

$$\text{Inventory turnover} = \frac{\text{Cost of sales}}{\text{Inventory}} = \frac{2{,}780}{430} = 6.5$$

$$\text{Total asset utilization} = \frac{\text{Sales}}{\text{Total assets}} = \frac{3{,}600}{2{,}400} = 1.5$$

Profitability ratios:

$$\text{Profit margin on sales} = \frac{\text{Profit before tax}}{\text{Sales}} = \frac{300}{3{,}600} = 8.3\%$$

$$\text{Return on total assets} = \frac{\text{Profit before tax}}{\text{Total assets}} = \frac{300}{2{,}400} = 12.5\%$$

3. Compare the Ratios. While rules of thumb are useful for analyzing ratios, it cannot be overstated that comparison of ratios is always the preferred approach. The ratios computed for a firm can be compared in at least three ways. First, they can be compared over time to see if there are any favorable or unfavorable trends in the firm's financial position. Second, they can be compared with the ratios of other firms in the industry of similar size. Third, they can be compared with industry averages to get an overall idea of the firm's relative financial position in the industry.

Table 2 provides a summary of the ratio analysis. The ratios com-

TABLE 2 Ratio Comparison for Ajax Home Computer Company

	Ajax	*Industry Firms with 1–10 Million in Assets*	*Industry Median*
Liquidity ratios:			
Current ratio	2.2	1.8	1.8
Quick ratio	.86	.9	1.0
Asset management ratios:			
Inventory turnover	6.5	3.2	2.8
Total assets utilization	1.5	1.7	1.6
Profitability ratios:			
Profit margin	8.3%	6.7%	8.2%
Return on total assets	12.5%	15.0%	14.7%

HIGHLIGHT 2
Financial Ratios: Where to Find Them

1. *Annual Statement Studies.* Published by Robert Morris Associates, this work includes 11 financial ratios computed annually for over 150 lines of business. Each line of business is divided into four size categories.
2. Dun and Bradstreet provides 14 ratios calculated annually for over 100 lines of business.
3. *The Almanac of Business and Industrial Financial Ratios.* The almanac, published by Prentice-Hall, Inc., lists industry averages for 22 financial ratios. Approximately 170 businesses and industries are listed.
4. *The Quarterly Financial Report for Manufacturing Corporations.* This work, published jointly by the Federal Trade Commission and the Securities and Exchange Commission, contains balance-sheet and income-statement information by industry groupings and by asset-size categories.
5. Trade associations and individual companies often compute ratios for their industries and make them available to analysts.

Source: James C. Van Horne, *Financial Management and Policy* (Englewood Cliffs, N.J.: Prentice-Hall, 1986), pp. 767–68.

puted for Ajax are presented along with the median ratios for firms of similar size in the industry and the industry median. The median is often reported in financial sources, rather than the mean, to avoid the strong effects of outliers.[4]

4. Check for Problems or Opportunities. The ratio comparison in Table 2 suggests that Ajax is in reasonably good shape, financially. The current ratio is above the industry figures, although the quick ratio is slightly below them. However, the high inventory turnover ratio suggests that the slightly low quick ratio should not be a problem, since inventory turns over relatively quickly. Total asset utilization is slightly below industry averages and should be monitored closely. This, coupled with the slightly lower return on total assets, suggests that some unproductive assets should be disposed of. While the problem could be ineffective marketing, the high profit margin on sales suggests that marketing effort is probably not the problem.

[4] For a discussion of ratio analysis and industry ratios for retailing, see Joseph B. Mason and Morris L. Mayer, *Modern Retailing: Theory and Practice,* 2nd ed. (Plano, Tex.: Business Publications, 1984), chap. 10.

CONCLUSION

This section has focused on several aspects of financial analysis that are useful for marketing decision making. The first, break-even analysis, is commonly used in marketing problem and case analysis. The second, net present value analysis, is quite useful for investigating the financial impact of marketing alternatives, such as new product introductions. The third, ratio analysis, is a useful tool sometimes overlooked in marketing problem solving. Performing a ratio analysis as a regular portion of marketing problem and case analysis can increase the understanding of the firm and its problems and opportunities.

Additional Readings

Brigham, Eugene F. *Fundamentals of Financial Management.* 3rd ed. Hinsdale, Ill.: Dryden Press, 1986.

Harrington, Diana R., and Brent D. Wilson. *Corporate Financial Analysis.* 3rd ed. Homewood, Ill.: Business Publications/Irwin, 1989.

Van Horne, James C. *Fundamentals of Financial Management.* Englewood Cliffs, N.J.: Prentice-Hall, 1986.

Weston, J. Fred, and Eugene F. Brigham. *Essentials of Managerial Finance.* 7th ed. Hinsdale, Ill.: Dryden Press, 1985.

Section 4

Marketing Management Cases

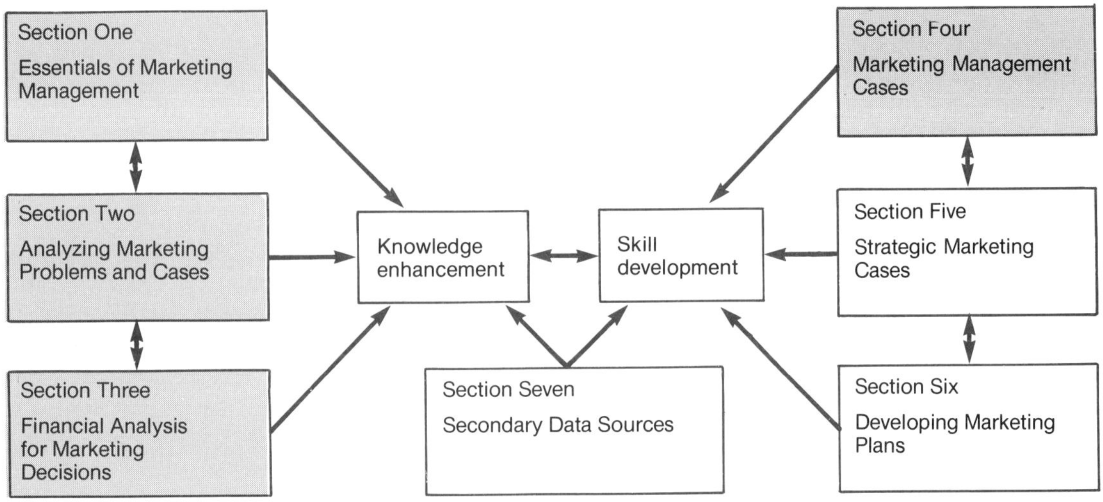

Marketing Management: Knowledge and Skills

NOTE TO THE STUDENT

The primary emphasis of the thirty-one cases in this section is on marketing as a functional business or organizational area. As such, much of the analysis in these cases involves research and selection of appropriate target markets and the development and management of marketing mix variables.

We have divided these cases into six groups to help focus your analysis. These six groups include cases dealing with market opportunity analysis, product strategy, promotion strategy, distribution strategy, pricing strategy, and selected issues in marketing management. However, keep in mind that regardless of how the case is classified, you should not become too focused on a single issue or marketing mix variable and ignore other elements of marketing strategy.

Case Group A

Marketing Opportunity Analysis

Case 1

Timex Corp.

J. Paul Peter
University of Wisconsin–Madison

Timex Corp. was one of the first companies to offer low-cost, durable mechanical watches. These watches were mass produced with hard-alloy bearings which were less costly than jeweled bearings. They were also much longer lasting than nonjeweled watches had been before. Timex attempted to sell these watches in jewelry stores offering a 30 percent markup. However, jewelers commonly received 50 percent markup on merchandise and therefore many refused to stock them. The company then began selling direct to drugstores, hardware stores, and even cigar stands. At one point the company had a distribution system of nearly a quarter of a million outlets. This mass-distribution strategy was coupled with heavy TV advertising demonstrating the

---

Sources: "Timex Takes the Torture Test," *Fortune,* June 27, 1983, pp. 112–20; "Can Timex Take a Licking and Keep on Ticking?" *Business Week,* February 20, 1984, p. 102; "The Swiss Put Glitz in Cheap Quartz Watches," *Fortune,* August 20, 1984, p. 102.

durability of the watches. For example, one of the ads showed a Timex watch being strapped to an outboard motor propellor and continuing to work after the engine had been run for several minutes. Such ads were used to support the contention that Timex watches could "take a licking and keep on ticking." In order to keep dealers and prices firmly in line, Timex limited production to about 85 percent of anticipated demand, making them somewhat scarce.

This strategy was extremely successful. By the late 1960s Timex had 50 percent market share in America and as much as 20 percent of world-wide sales. In 1970, Timex had after-tax profits of $27 million on sales of $200 million.

After a quarter of a century of dominance in the low-price watch market, Timex began to face serious competition by the mid-1970s. One of the major technological advances was the development of electronic watches which Timex executives initially judged to be unimportant. By the time they recognized the importance of this technological change and introduced an electronic watch, competitors had already developed and marketed much improved models. In fact, the Timex electronic watches were so big and clumsy that employees nicknamed them "quarter pounders" and prices ended up 50 percent above competitive, much more attractive watches.

By 1983 Timex's U.S. market share had plummeted to about 17 percent and operating losses approached $100 million. Distribution outlets had declined to 100,000 outlets. Timex ranked fifth in volume behind Japan's Seiko, Citizen, and Casio, and a Swiss combine, ASUAG-SSIH Ltd. Digital and quartz analog watches dominated the market and even the successful Japanese companies faced increased price competition from manufacturers in Hong Kong. In fact, the export price of the average digital watch dropped from $5 in 1981 to less than $2 and many companies were forced out of business with margins of only a few cents per watch.

At this point Timex decided to attempt to rebuild its watch market. (It also decided to make itself less vulnerable by diversifying into home health care products and home computers.) To rebuild its timekeeping business, the company invested over $100 million to retool and redesign its watch and clock lines. Timex's marketing vice president supported this investment by stating that "We were thick, fat, ugly, overpriced, and behind in technology." The strategy then became to produce watches that were just as attractive as higher-priced brands and keep the major portion of the line priced at under $50. Of course, this forced Timex to compete in a world already overloaded with too many inexpensive watch brands. In addition to watches from Japan and Hong Kong, Swiss manufacturers scored a big hit with a trendy timepiece called Swatch which was brightly colored plastic and sold for $30. Sales soared to 100,000 units per month and swatches could not be produced fast enough.

Timex also attempted to compete in the over $100 price range with its superthin quartz analog Elite collection which was sold in department and jewelry stores for up to $120. However, as one competitor summed it up in evaluating the market potential of the Timex Elite collection, "It's got one disadvantage; it's got a $12.95 name on it."

DISCUSSION QUESTIONS

1. What opportunities are available to Timex in the low-priced watch market?
2. Assume that Timex Elite watches have variable costs of $30 apiece while overhead and other fixed costs amount to $18 million. What is the break-even point for this product? How many Elite watches would have to be sold to make a profit of $3.6 million?
3. What problems does Timex face in entering the more expensive watch market?

Case 2

Wyler's Unsweetened Soft Drink Mixes*

Don E. Schultz
Mark Traxler
both of Northwestern University

As Mr. Kenneth Otte sat in his office in Northbrook, Illinois, in early August 1977, he felt a bit like Jack in the children's story "Jack and the Beanstalk." He was facing a major challenge against a dominant foe, General Foods' Kool-Aid powdered soft drink mix, the giant of the unsweetened drink mix category.

The question Mr. Otte was considering was whether to recommend a major national introduction of Wyler's Unsweetened Soft Drink Mix against Kool-Aid in 1978 or to continue testing the product. He knew RJR Foods's Hawaiian Punch was considering a national introduction of an unsweetened soft drink mix, and because of Kool-Aid's dominant position in the market—a 92 percent share and virtually unchallenged in its fifty-year existence—he questioned whether there was room for two additional brands in the market. If he waited another year, it might be too late. If, however, he introduced a new product in 1978 and Hawaiian Punch did too, then perhaps neither product would be successful.

The question was more complex than whether or not to introduce the product nationally. Wyler's Unsweetened Soft Drink Mix was just completing a test market under Mr. Otte's direction. There was certainly time to make changes and adjustments to the program should he decide to continue testing or launch a national introduction. But the question was: What changes should he investigate or recommend prior to a January meeting with the Wyler sales and broker force?

Management had requested a review of the situation and Mr. Otte's recommendations by October 1, 1977. Since a national introduction in 1978 would require substantial marketing expenditures, Mr. Otte had

---

* This case was prepared by Professor Don E. Shultz and Mark Traxler of Northwestern University as a basis for class discussion and is not designed to illustrate appropriate or inappropriate handling of administrative situations. Revised 1982. Reprinted with permission.

several questions facing him. Should he recommend a national program for 1978? If not, what recommendation should he make? Another test market? A fine tuning of his present program? Major changes? What?

As Mr. Otte prepared to develop his recommendation, he reviewed the entire situation of the category, the product, competition, and test market results. Did he have enough ammunition to challenge Kool-Aid?

WYLER FOODS

Wyler Foods is a Chicago-based company that manufactures consumer products. Their line includes instant soups, bouillion powders and cubes, and powdered soft drink mixes, among other products.

The original company was organized in the late 1920s and in 1930 introduced "Cold Kup" soft drink mix, a presweetened mix in a pouch. It was available in four flavors. About the same time, Peskin Company introduced "Kool-Aid," an unsweetened soft drink mix. Peskin was later acquired by General Foods and Wyler was purchased by Borden. Wyler continued to concentrate on the presweetened soft drink mix market. In 1954 a powdered lemonade mix was introduced very successfully. By 1977 the lemonade flavor accounted for approximately 40 percent of all Wyler soft drink mix sales.

Wyler and Kool-Aid continue to do battle in the soft drink mix market, with Wyler dominant in the presweetened market and Kool-Aid in the unsweetened area. In the early 1960s Kool-Aid entered the presweetened market with an artificially sweetened product using cyclamates. This sweetener was banned by the federal government in 1969 and Wyler, with its sugar sweetening, rapidly gained ground in the mix market. As a result of the ban, Wyler moved up to a 20 percent share of the presweetened market. In 1972 Wyler introduced an industry "first" by packaging presweetened soft drink mixes in cannisters equivalent to 10 to 15 quarts. With this innovation, Wyler's share of the presweetened market increased to over 40 percent. Shares have declined slightly from this level as increased competitive pressures have segmented the market. Wyler did not have an unsweetened entry until initiating the market test described in this case.

SOFT DRINK MIX MARKET

The liquid refreshment market, comprised of hot, cold, and alcoholic beverages, is limited in growth by the "share of belly" concept, which suggests that human beings can consume just so much liquid in a given year. All entries in the soft drink mix market are competing with all other potable refreshments for some space in an unexpandable belly. The level of per-capita liquid consumption, under this concept, is tied to the U.S. population growth rate or changing consumer preferences.

The soft drink mix business, the twelfth-largest dry grocery product category, accounts for about 10 percent of all soft drink sales. It has increased in both quart and dollar sales each year since 1970. This growth is due to a greater demand for more product convenience, a wider assortment of flavors, and a more economical cold beverage alternative to carbonated drinks and single-strength canned drinks. In 1977 soft drink mixes are expected to produce sales of 14.5 million Wyler equivalent cases.[1] Mr. Otte noted industry predictions that with a 5 percent volume growth in 1978, soft drink mixes would generate 15.2 million Wyler equivalent cases.

In comparison with other beverage categories, soft drink mixes are inexpensive, with unsweetened drink mixes the least expensive of all. Mixes cost less than half as much as carbonated beverages and single-strength canned drinks. Unsweetened mixes are least expensive due to the economy of adding one's own sugar. The typical cost per four-ounce serving of unsweetened powdered mix is 3 cents, while the cost of presweetened powdered mix is 4.7 cents. By comparison, the cost per four-ounce serving of carbonated soft drinks and of chilled orange juice is 11.7 cents.

The powdered drink mix market divides as follows. In terms of case volume, the market is divided into 52.4 percent presweetened and 47.6 percent unsweetened. In terms of dollar sales, the split is 74.6 percent presweetened and 25.4 percent unsweetened. The major difference is the cost per quart of the sweetened product versus the unsweetened.

Soft drink mix sales are highly seasonal. Sales peak during the summer months (May–August) and drop off almost entirely during the remainder of the year. Many grocers, particularly those in the northern climates, do not stock soft drink mixes during the winter months after the summer inventory is sold. An attempt to overcome this extreme seasonality was initiated in 1976 by Wyler's. Their "second-season" promotion strategy, which promotes to both the consumer and the trade, was designed to encourage year-round product usage.

Soft Drink Mix Buyer

The buyer profile for soft drink mix users shows that about two-thirds of all U.S. households purchase the product. The primary purchaser is the female homemaker between the ages of 18 and 44, with the heavi-

---

[1] One case contains 288 two-quart foil pouches, or the equivalent of 576 quarts of liquid beverage.

est concentration in the 25 to 34 age range. She is unemployed and has a high school education. The husband's occupation is blue-collar, clerk, or salesman. Annual household income lies between $10,000 and $20,000. The family has three or more individuals, including children under age 18. Powdered soft drink mix users and heavy users, who consume at least five glasses per day, are concentrated in the north-central and southern states.

More families purchase presweetened soft drink mixes than unsweetened; however, the buyer of unsweetened soft drink mixes appears to be a much heavier consumer (or purchaser at least). The presweetened mix buyer purchases the product an average of every 56.5 days, compared to the more frequent purchase pattern of the unsweetened mix buyer, who purchases every 46.7 days. Consumer panel data show that purchasers of both unsweetened and presweetened mixes pick up an average of six pouches on each shopping occasion.

Unsweetened Soft Drink Mixes

A comparison of the available and most popular flavors shows that the "red" flavors and grape are by far the fastest selling among unsweetened flavors. The available flavors for Wyler's and, in the case of Kool-Aid, the 6 of 16 flavors that constitute 73 percent of their unsweetened mix volume, are shown in Exhibit 1. The flavors listed for Hawaiian Punch are those that have been offered in the presweetened line.

Industry estimates indicate that Kool-Aid accounts for about 92 percent of the unsweetened soft drink mix segment. Private labels such as A&P's Cheri-Aid and Kroger's Flavor-Aid account for the remainder.

The out-of-store or retail price per pouch of unsweetened drink mixes ranges from 10 cents to 13 cents. The suggested retail price is 12 cents,

EXHIBIT 1 Unsweetened Mix Flavors

Kool-Aid	*Wyler's*	*Hawaiian Punch*
Strawberry	Strawberry	Strawberry
Cherry	Cherry	Cherry
Fruit punch	Fruit punch	Red punch
Grape	Grape	Grape
Orange	Orange	Orange
Lemonade	Lemonade	Lemonade
		Raspberry

and the typical broker price is 9.4 cents per pouch. The 12 cents price provides a 21.7 percent gross profit margin for grocery retailers, which is slightly higher than the grocery retailer storewide gross profit margin. The inventory turnover of soft drink mixes is higher than that of most nonperishable grocery store items during the summer peak season.

Unsweetened as well as presweetened soft drink mixes are sold to retailers through food brokers. Brokers, serving as middlemen between the producer and the retailer, receive a 7 percent commission per case for performing the distribution function.

INTRODUCTION OF WYLER'S UNSWEETENED

Target Market Selection

The target market selected for Wyler's introduction differed slightly from the one selected by Kool-Aid. The notable differences were household head's occupation and market size. Exhibit 2 summarizes the market's demographics. The primary users were children aged 2 through 12, who were thought to have little influence on the purchase decision. The female homemaker bought the products she thought best for her family. Hence, most Wyler advertising was directed at mothers.

Advertising and Promotion

Wyler entered the test market with two main copy themes in advertising: (1) "double economy" stressed that Wyler's as an unsweetened drink for the entire family was economical because users added their own sugar and the entire family enjoyed it and (2) claimed that Wyler's unique flavor boosters (salt and other flavor enhancers) made Wyler's taste better. Both executions emphasized the red flavors and vitamin C

EXHIBIT 2 Selected Demographics of Wyler's and Kool-Aid Buyers

	Wyler's	*Kool-Aid*
Income	$15,000–$19,999	$15,000–$19,999
Household size	3 or more	3 or more
Age of female head	Under 45	Under 45
Age of children	12 and under	Any under 18
Occupation of household head	White-collar	Blue-collar
Market size (population)	500,000–2,500,000	Non-SMSA

content and soft-pedaled lemonade. While the two campaigns were used in the test, they were both considered interim efforts.

The double-economy commercial was tested on two different occasions. One test indicated that the commercial generated high recall among target buyers and particularly among female homemakers between the ages of 25 and 34. However, the other test, while identifying strong awareness of the Wyler brand name, indicated that the specific recall of Wyler's unsweetened mix was low. On the basis of these tests, a different campaign based even more strongly on flavors was being considered. This approach involved the use of Roy Clark, the television personality, who would stress the good taste of Wyler's, as spokesperson.

Kool-Aid's advertising came in three varieties with separate messages for general brand awareness, economy of use, and appeal to children. The general brand-awareness execution, a nostalgia appeal to mothers, said, "You loved it as a kid. You trust it as a mother." The economy-of-use execution showed children's preferences for Kool-Aid's flavor over single-strength beverages and the economy of adding one's own sugar. The execution with child appeal showed the Kool-Aid "smiling pitcher" saving the day by thwarting some dastardly deeds. Most advertising was placed in television: 70 percent network and 30 percent spot evenly divided between day and night.[2] It was anticipated that Hawaiian Punch would take advantage of their character, "Punchy," to introduce the new unsweetened mix, since he has been used extensively before.

For the 1977 test, Wyler had divided the media budget into a peak and second-season push. A total of $10.1 million was invested in spot television in the 33 broker areas that made up the test. From mid-April to mid-August, Wyler had purchased spot TV in prime, day, and early-fringe time. For the second season, the schedule was to be composed of day, early-, and late-fringe time from September until Christmas and from late January into late March. Mr. Otte had already received a suggestion from the agency and his assistant that should the test be continued in 1978, staggered media tests should probably be undertaken since a level spending pattern had been used in the 1977 test markets.

Compared to Wyler's test program, Kool-Aid's program was spending approximately $18 million nationally in measured media in 1977. Six million dollars was being spent for presweetened, $6 million for unsweetened, and $6 million for the Kool-Aid brand. Two-thirds of the network budget was being used for weekdays and was directed toward

---

[2] Network television provides simultaneous coverage of a nationwide market; spot television involves selecting individual stations to reach specific markets.

women. The remainder was being spent on a Saturday/Sunday rotation directed at children. Spot TV funds were being allocated almost evenly between day (36 percent), night/late night (34 percent), and early fringe (30 percent). During the peak season, Kool-Aid planned on spending $13.405 million divided into $6.58 million in the second quarter and $6.825 million in the third quarter. The second-season expenditure was $4.59 million, divided into $2.57 million in the first quarter and $2.025 million in the fourth quarter. It was expected that Kool-Aid would spend about $20 million in 1978 for consumer advertising in measured media.

Mr. Otte anticipated that Hawaiian Punch, if they introduced nationally, would spend $4.7 million for television in a 1978 introduction. Two-thirds would probably be used in network (33.5 percent each for day and prime) and 33 percent for spot. Advance information indicated that this budget would break down to $3.2 million for network ($1.6 million in prime and daytime) and $1.5 million for spot television.

In addition to the consumer advertising, Wyler's spent $827,670 for consumer promotions during the tests. Expenditures included the cost of samples and coupons. Several print media, such as Sunday supplements and best-food-day newspaper sections, were being used to deliver both coupons and samples. It was still too early to determine the results of these promotions for this year.

Trade promotions during the market tests were budgeted at $292,330. Trade promotions consisted of case allowances to encourage retailers to stock Wyler's unsweetened mix. No matter how much money Wyler's spent on consumer advertising and promotion, it appeared from the tests that grocery retailers would not stock another soft drink mix without sizable case allowances since most of the soft drink mix inventory traditionally had been sold to retailers using case allowances. Mr. Otte felt that to achieve successful distribution, whether entering additional testing or going national in 1978, a case allowance of $3.60 between the end of February and the end of April would be needed. Given the seasonal nature of the market, approximately 60 percent of annual volume would be shipped during this period. This case allowance would be the highest ever offered in the unsweetened drink mix category, since typical case allowances were $2.88 for Kool-Aid. Industry sources indicated that Hawaiian Punch would offer a case allowance of $1.44.

Preliminary Test Market Results and Options

Wyler's unsweetened mix was introduced into 33 broker areas representing 28 percent of the U.S. population and 40 percent of total unsweetened soft drink mix category sales. Only 25 of the 33 areas had achieved adequate distribution by mid-1977. The 25 successful areas comprised 17.2 percent of the U.S. population and 33.7 percent of total unsweetened mix category volume. Wyler's sold 116,000 cases in the test cities.

As Mr. Otte began to draft his recommendations for the October 1 meeting, he pondered a number of issues. First, if he decided to continue the test market in 1978, Mr. Otte was advised that he would need a minimum expenditure of $4 million for Wyler's unsweetened mix. The plan would involve $2.2 million in media advertising and $1.8 million in consumer promotions, plus the case allowances. If he decided to introduce nationally, he would of course need a substantially larger budget. The expenditure level would be part of his presentation whether or not he recommended a national introduction. Second, the amount of the case allowance was an issue needing attention. He was operating with a $25.20 case price and a 50 percent gross profit margin (excluding case allowances) in the test market at the 9.4 cent price to retailers. If the $3.60 case allowance was adopted, would this trade promotion secure increased distribution coverage and could he afford it? Third, the advertising question loomed. Should another test market or a national introduction include the revised message and claims rather than the "double economy" approach. Also, would the advertising schedule be more potent if it were staggered in a manner similar to Kool-Aid?

What to do? Should he risk another test and perhaps lose the opportunity to go national as Hawaiian Punch was contemplating, or should he develop a plan to invade Kool-Aid's territory in 1978 on a national basis? The risks and the rewards were great either way.

Case 3

Texas Blues*

JoAnn K. L. Schwinghammer
Mankato State University

Gopala Krishnan Ganesh
North Texas State University

William C. Green
Loyola Marymount University

"When we left our meeting two weeks ago, Larry, I thought it would be relatively easy to gather information about our growers," Brent was explaining. As President of the Texas Blueberry Growers Association (TBGA), Brent Ramage had volunteered to come up with some facts to describe the operations of blueberry growers in east Texas, where he lived. Two weeks ago he had been in Austin, meeting with Larry Strange, a Texas Department of Agriculture (TDA) official, to review the potential of the Texas blueberry industry. Larry's TDA responsibilities included identifying and analyzing special high-growth potential agricultural projects for the Department, and Brent was anxious to secure his help. As President of the Association, Brent was interested in good relations with the TDA, and as the owner of a sizeable blueberry farm near Hooks, Texas, he was enthusiastic about the rapid increase in blueberry plantings in the state.

"Can we get a handle on the current stage of production in the state, overall?" Larry asked.

"Well, that's harder to estimate than I thought it would be. We know from our TBGA membership lists generally who owns blueberry farms, but estimating acreage is another thing. There's so much variation. On the one hand you've got a few growers like Don at Fincastle, with a highly developed operation, and on the other hand, some folks have just put plants in the ground. In the middle are quite a few small operators, just trying to do things right.

---

* This case was written by JoAnn K. L. Schwinghammer, Associate Professor of Marketing, Mankato State University (Minnesota); Gopala Krishnan Ganesh, Assistant Professor of Marketing, North Texas State University; and William C. Green, Assistant Professor of Marketing, Loyola Marymount University (California). Reprinted with permission.

"I have to agree with you about the information problem. My experience has been similar. I think we've got some pretty good information from the horticultural researchers about growing conditions. And coming up with production and shipment figures wasn't all that difficult. It remains to be seen how much of it will be useable."

As his part of the plan to investigate Texas blueberry potential, Larry had drawn upon his information sources at TDA and his keen investigative skills to ascertain characteristics of blueberry production in east Texas and blueberry production levels in the rest of the nation. The two men intended to pool their information today, April 12, 1985, to determine the current state of blueberry production in Texas, and to define the steps necessary for understanding and planning the future of "Texas Blues."

"Let's start with the growing conditions," Larry went on. "Take a look at what I've found."

Horticultural Factors

By consulting horticultural researchers in the Texas Agricultural Experiment Station system, it had been learned that blueberry production in the United States consists of three varieties that vary by the type of berry and the growing region (hence, length of growing season): highbush, lowbush, and rabbiteye. Each of these three varieties has some distinguishing characteristics.

Highbush berries are predominantly grown in the east coast areas of North Carolina to New Jersey, westward to Michigan, currently the nation's largest producer, and south to northern Arkansas. While these berries are grown in other areas of the country, acreage is limited. Highbush berries are perhaps more susceptible to disease, injury, and frost than other varieties. They are most usually processed or frozen and appear in such products as baked goods, ice cream, and prepared baking mixes. Increasing emphasis has been placed on the fresh market, particularly by Michigan growers.

Lowbush berries are grown only in the very northern regions of Maine and parts of Canada. They are a smaller berry not appropriate for the fresh market, but they grow wild, and therefore require little or no care for a prolific crop. The disadvantage of this variety is that the bushes are short-lived, hence to increase production over a period of time, extensive fertilizers are needed. Because this is costly, growers have found that it is cheaper and easier to burn the bushes off every three years. This ensures a fresh crop of productive plants, but requires a time lag while the plants are reaching maturity. Production of these berries is believed to vastly affect the processor market. In fact, it is believed that there is a glut of processed berries currently on the market.

Berries of the rabbiteye variety (so named because in the immature, red stage, they resemble rabbit eyes) are those grown predominantly in Georgia, Florida, Mississippi, Louisiana, Alabama, South Carolina, and Texas. Arkansas and Oklahoma have recently experimented with growing rabbiteye berries, as well. These berries are larger and have thicker skins, which means they are more resistant to damage. They also have a smaller stem scar when picked, which means that they are less susceptible to infection and disease. These berries, because of their size, are most suited for the fresh berry market. They are, however, also well suited for a process called puff drying, in which berries are put under a high-heat, pressurized condition causing a mini-explosion which pinholes the berries (ruptures the skin). They are then tunnel-dried to reduce moisture to 8 to 10 percent of their original content. This process, of course, releases the moisture, allowing for reduced weight and bulk (estimates range from 6–10 to one), reducing costs of storage and shipment. This process can be done with rabbiteye berries, but it cannot be done with highbush or lowbush varieties. There are, however, only a limited number of puff driers in the country. These driers are reputed to cost as much as three-quarters of a million dollars, which explains partially why there aren't very many of them. The volume of blueberry production necessary to support the operation of a puff drier is believed to be quite large.

Rabbiteye blueberries can be damaged by extensive frost, though they are resistant to damage by only slight frost, which affects the early flowering and reduces slightly the size of the crop. Rabbiteye berries do not require as much chilling to break dormancy as do the other varieties, which, of course, makes them more suitable to growth in the southern regions. Rabbiteye berries, however, must be irrigated. These berries do not suffer greatly from being harvested mechanically. Where mechanical harvesters are used, there are three markets for the produce: (1) the firm berries go to the fresh market, (2) damaged or overripe berries go to the processed and/or frozen market, while (3) green berries may be used for juice stock. Rabbiteye berries may be grown herbicide- and pesticide-free, if other growing conditions are right. In addition, they can be harvested 4–6 weeks earlier than the highbush or lowbush varieties.

Rabbiteye berry bushes are relatively long-lived; some are known to have reached 60 years old. Typically, a new plant must be started in a nursery and will be ready for field planting at about 18 months. During that first year in the field the plant will produce about one pound of berries. Its growth and production rates follow, roughly, a pattern of producing 3 pounds in the second year, 5–6 pounds in the third year, 6–8 pounds in the fourth year, and on to about 30 pounds in the tenth or twelfth year. Where berries are picked with a mechanical harvester, the plants must be kept smaller, and consequently will produce about 20 to 25 pounds per year, maximum. Reasonable production density averages 600 plants per acre, and 12,000 pounds per acre. It is not uncommon that a first commercial harvest occurs in the fifth to seventh year, possibly the third year, if well cared for up to and during this first harvest. Once the plants are mature, there is little maintenance required: some spraying when necessary, fertilization, irrigation, and weeding. While pruning is occasionally necessary for plants that are hand-picked, where mechanical harvesters are used, pruning is an integral part of plant care. The shelf life of these fresh berries is two to three weeks, if they are cooled immediately after picking. If not cooled, shelf life is about one week.

"And blueberries are a healthy fruit: a good source of Vitamins A and C, potassium, phosphorus and calcium. Most people probably don't know that a half-cup has only 44 calories," Larry explained. "Now, here's what I found out about nationwide production."

National Production

Blueberries are the third most popular noncitrus fruit in the United States. The largest producer of blueberries in the United States is the state of Michigan, which produces about 12,000 acres of berries. (Exhibit 1 presents national acreage and production figures.) Approximately 90 percent of Michigan's blueberries go to the processor market. These are sold for about \$.40 to \$.50 per pound, grower's price. Of the Michigan berries sold to the fresh market (estimates of 12% to 18%), growers get about \$.90 or a little more per pound. Consumers pay \$1.39 to \$2.98 per pound at the supermarket. Alliances of Michigan associations with Southern growers had been reported in years past, perhaps evidence of Michigan growers recognizing the potential competitive advantage gained by the earlier ripening rabbiteye varieties. Also rumored were feelings among Northern producers that there are currently too many frozen blueberries in storage. It is not known what length of time would be necessary for this surplus to be exhausted.

Fresh blueberries grown in New Jersey and North Carolina are shipped nationwide. While these states supply as far west as California with fresh blueberries, in 1984 only 10 truckloads and 1 railcar of blueberries were delivered to Los Angeles grocers. This amounts to about 1,100,000 pounds for the entire Los Angeles market for 1984. California is one western state believed to hold greater potential for blueberry consumption.

Of the southern producers, Georgia is the largest, with Florida in second position. Georgia has the most well-developed fresh and processor market capabilities, producing about 3,000 acres of rabbiteye

EXHIBIT 1 North American Blueberry

	1983 Estimated Acreage by John W. Nelson (acres)				*Production by J. P. Holbein (000 lbs.)*	
	Planted	*Harvested*	*Non-Bearing*		*1983*	*Projected to 1990*
Highbush						
Northwest						
Oregon	800	700	100		5,250	8,250
Washington	900	800	100		6,512	7,500
British Columbia	2,500	2,000	500		12,000	15,000
Midwest						
Michigan	12,000	10,000	2,000		49,148	60,000
Illinois/Indiana/Ohio	1,000	800	200			
Northeast						
Rhode Island/ Connecticut/New Hampshire/Vermont/ Massachusetts	1,300	1,000	300			
New York	600	400	200			
Ontario	300	120	180			
Atlantic						
New Jersey	8,000	7,500	500		23,000	28,000
Maryland	500	400	100			
Virginia	100	25	75			
No. Carolina	4,000	3,100	900		5,100	6,900
So. Carolina	200	200	0			
				All others	10,500	15,000
Central						
Pennsylvania	500	300	200			
Kentucky	100	25	75			
Arkansas/Oklahoma	550	200	350			
Missouri	150	100	50			
Total Highbush	33,500	27,670	5,830			
Rabbiteye						
So. Carolina	500	50	450			
Georgia	3,000	1,500	1,500		1,800	3,800
Florida	1,000	500	500			
Alabama	200	50	150			
Mississippi	400	200	200			
Louisiana	200	50	150			
Texas	250	50	200			
				All others	3,150	9,000
Total Rabbiteye	5,550	2,400	3,150			
Total Highbush	39,050	30,070	8,980		116,460	153,450

EXHIBIT 1 ***(concluded)***

	1983 Estimated Acreage by John W. Nelson (acres)			*Production by J. P. Holbein (000 lbs.)*	
	Planted	*Harvested*	*New Burn*	*1983*	*Projected to 1990*
Lowbush					
Maine	46,000	23,000	23,000	44,653	55,000
Nova Scotia	20,000	10,000	10,000	19,502	25,000
New Brunswick	12,000	6,000	6,000	8,768	10,000
Quebec	20,000	10,000	10,000	7,300	9,000
Newfoundland	3,500	1,750	1,750	1,440	2,500
Prince Edward Island	2,000	1,000	1,000	800	1,200
Total Lowbush	103,500	51,750	51,750	82,463	102,700
Grand total production				198,923	256,150
U-Pick and used locally				10,500	21,000
Total for commercial marketing				188,423	235,150

Note: In the next five years, good yields and increased harvested acreage could produce 235,150,000 lbs. of commercially marketed blueberries, an increase of 25 percent in six years!

berries. Among those states with puff driers, Georgia is the only state to use puff drying for processing blueberries. Georgia also has a well-organized grower's association, relying on a centralized structure for cooling, grading, and sorting berries for commercial purposes. Growers in the state are netting approximately $5,000 per acre.

Although Arkansas blueberry production is quite young, it is somewhat more advanced than production in Texas, and it has similar growing conditions and problems. Arkansas sold about 850,000 to one million pounds of blueberries last year, which didn't meet even the Ozark demand, according to university agricultural researchers. They believe the outlook for sales of their berries to be good where blueberries are not produced: they also sell to California and western parts of the United States, as well as small amounts to Japan. In fact, Arkansas blueberries (as well as some from Georgia and Michigan) had begun appearing in supermarket produce areas in the metropolitan Texas cities in the summer of 1984, selling for as much as $1.89 at the beginning of the season, and closer to $.99 at the end of the season. Arkansas growers are increasingly placing emphasis on the fresh market, although of the fresh blueberries that were sold by Arkansas growers in 1984, only about 15 percent were sold to the fresh market, with 85 percent sold to the frozen market. Of the frozen berries, 70 percent were sold in the United States, 30 percent foreign.

With regard to imports, New Zealand ships blueberries to the United

States, although current figures for the amount of these imports are difficult to track. Blueberries are exported to Japan, where there seems to be an appreciation of the berry, not only for its taste and nutrition, but also because it is blue.

The North American Blueberry Council, located in New Jersey, represents the interests of those blueberry growers who produce a minimum of 250,000 pounds of berries annually. There are, likewise, state growers' associations, some more well organized than others.

Texas Production

"We may have a long way to go to reach international distribution, but you've got to admit we've come a long way since blueberries were first grown for sale in the state in 1968," Brent laughed. "We didn't get agricultural research on blueberries started until 1971. Here's the rest of the state production information I could come up with."

Blueberry farms are scattered throughout east Texas, from Hooks in the north, to Beaumont in the south, encompassing about 250 to 300 sparsely scattered areas. (Exhibit 2 presents Texas blueberry growing areas.) Most of the growers run small operations, many producing berries on under one acre. There are probably under five growers who have up to 35 producing acres. In terms of typical fruit and vegetable retail pallet and shipment sizes, most growers do not produce near pallet size, where one pallet equals 96 flats, and a flat equals 12 one-pint containers, weighing about 10 pounds. A shipment is equal to about 50,000 to 75,000 pounds volume.

Texas blueberries ripen as early as blueberries anywhere else in the country, with very few exceptions. Texas blueberry bushes often produce blueberries ready for picking in early- to mid-June and continue producing through July, a span of six, and sometimes eight, weeks.

Texas berries are of a variety which feasibly could be mechanically harvested (one harvester exists in the state). Mechanical harvesting is ultimately more cost effective than labor for harvesting where crops equal about 50 acres or more.

No blueberry production in Texas is commercial. A small amount of blueberries are sold at farmers' markets and roadside fruit and vegetable stands. The largest share of production is in pick-your-own (PYO) operations. People seem to be willing to drive from metropolitan and other rural areas to berry farms to pick blueberries for their own use. The PYO farms, however, vary in the services they provide to pickers. Some provide containers or plastic bags, at other farms pickers must provide their own containers. Some growers grow and sell other kinds of fruit and vegetables, as well as blueberries. Some growers know they have repeat patrons, but few growers have a very clear under-

EXHIBIT 2 Texas Blueberry Growing Areas

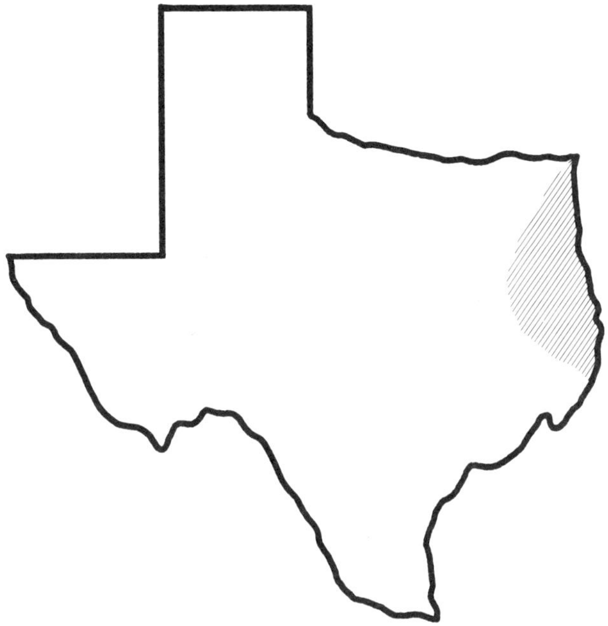

standing of who their customers are, how far they have driven, how long they stay once at the farm, their average size of purchase, why people choose their PYO farm, or even why people choose to pick their own berries. Most PYO operators realize, however, that once people know the blueberries are ready to pick, there are almost never any left on the bushes at the end of the season.

Growers were selling blueberries for $.99 to $.69 per pound, the higher prices earned at the beginning of the season. Growers also varied in whether they sold blueberries in pounds or pints, and frequently the two were used interchangeably.

In trying to assess why there seemed to be an increasing demand for blueberries, some growers felt that people who had grown up in the North but had moved to Texas brought with them the taste for blueberries and the habit of berry picking and eating. Not only is the influx of Northerners expected to continue, but these people have "educated" native Texans about picking and eating blueberries.

Competition for blueberries is felt to be from other berries, such as strawberries, cherries, and other fruits that can be put on cereal and in pies and other baked goods. Some growers felt that blueberries might be more like grapes in terms of the costs and risks of production, although the market would be smaller. But no other berry or fruit seemed to offer a model by which to compare growth or consumption patterns.

Nationally, Americans eat an annual average of about 7 ounces of berries of all kinds. With a Texas population of 15 million people, even a conservative estimate points toward a good-sized market for fresh blueberries.

The Texas Blueberry Growers Association is the official organization of the growers, and their membership numbers about 75 to 85 growers. About 90 percent of Texas blueberry growers are members of the Association. It is the intention of the organization to assist growers with whatever problems might arise, to encourage research, and to work toward controlled growth of blueberry acreage.

"That sounds like a fairly thorough summation of where we stand with production, Brent. In your conversations with other growers this week, what appeared to be their concerns about the future?"

"Well, Larry, most feel that this is a good time for blueberries. The Association has picked up a few new growers each year for the past few years, and we're getting more and more people coming out to pick berries. Some Association members are concerned, though, that we ought to have a better handle on how much demand we have—how many pickers we can support. The blueberry industry is relatively new to Texas, and the Association is just beginning to take an active part.

"We don't regularly collect information from the members," Brent continued, "but it would be helpful if we could try to determine how fast we are growing. We don't have a very good idea of how many acres are planted new each year. Of course, the most important thing we want to guard against is reaching a saturation point."

"You're right about that," Larry responded. "It doesn't appear that demand is slacking off. On the other side of the coin, maybe new areas of demand could be tapped. Now might also be a good time to try to assess the commercial market for blueberries, at least on an in-state basis. Let's talk a little more about these two issues—saturation and commercialization. I've got some other figures here we can take a look at."

Saturation Point

The two men considered the issue of saturation of prime importance to the Texas blueberry growers. At what level of production, in terms of acres planted or pounds of berries produced, would demand be exhausted? Up to this time, growers agreed that they had more pickers than could be accommodated. But they were certain that, with continued rapid growth and assuming present sales methods—PYO operations—would continue as before, there would likely be some point in the future when they would have more berries than could be picked. But how far into the future?

No one, to Larry's knowledge, had studied PYO blueberry farm trade areas, specifically. Researchers at the University of Illinois at Urbana-Champaign's Cooperative Extension Service, investigating Illinois's PYO strawberry operations in the 1970s and early 1980s, used an adaptation of the Huff retail gravitation model to study trade areas. They defined the retail trade area for PYO strawberry farms to consist of primary (75 percent of all customers living closest to the farm), secondary (the next 15 percent of all customers who lived beyond the primary trade area), and tertiary trade areas (all remaining customers, 10 percent). For the primary trade area, the maximum radii averaged about 20.5 miles, and customers drove an average of about 12.5 miles. More simply, one acre of strawberries would support 2,500 people within a 20-mile radius. Such estimates, of course, depended on the proximity of centers of population and advertising, at the least. Researchers in North Carolina estimated that one acre of PYO blueberries would support 2,000 people within a 25-mile radius. These figures would depend on advertising and the familiarity of the population with blueberry consumption.

The Illinois researchers found that strawberry PYO patrons were more likely to be residents in farm populations, small towns, and small cities surrounding the PYO's. The pickers generally had rural or farm backgrounds, lower incomes, larger families, and relied for PYO information on word of mouth, roadside signs, and local newspapers and radio programs. Residents of larger cities who visited the strawberry PYO farms considered the visits a form of recreation. Though the Illinois researchers collected data from 37 PYO strawberry farms and over 13,300 customer sales, they strongly cautioned against applying their estimates to other crops.

Commercialization Potential

The saturation issue could be viewed from another standpoint. With an outlook toward expansion of blueberry operations in Texas, commercialization could be viewed as a viable alternative if production exceeded PYO demand.

Commercialization was estimated to take approximately 3 to 10 years, and would be feasible for an individual farm of at least 50 acres in size. Initial start-up costs would be high, perhaps up to a half million dollars. Return would be negative for the first three, if not the first five years, with break-even occurring in about the fifth year. A problem for the growers, given the high initial costs, is outside funding. Most bankers are unwilling to lend for unproven operations; there is not a realistically similar model for costing or potential of this market. Other considerations for the growers are the possibilities of sharing facilities for cooling, grading, and sorting, similar to the Georgia example. In Texas, however, growers are more widespread, and distances are much farther. It is estimated that three central locations might be required to perform such a function. In addition, opportunities must be sought for use of the cooling facilities in the off-season, thereby offsetting some of the large initial costs.

Potential markets for fresh blueberries that could be examined include farmers' markets, small and local grocery operations, and large chain grocery operations. A major retail grocery chain has expressed potential need for three truckloads per day, for seven weeks in the summer to the three largest Texas markets (Dallas-Fort Worth, Houston, and San Antonio). This demand alone would require the production of 600 acres of blueberries at current production rates. This is, however, an untested estimate of demand. Rumors hold that retailers would pay $16 per flat FOB for the earliest berries to perhaps a low of $10 to $12 per flat at season's end.

Potential for processing might also be examined. Suggestions include bakeries, ice cream makers, cereal makers, or makers of mass-produced frozen desserts, as well as suppliers for such chains as Wendy's and McDonald's. Processors for frozen or fresh, whole or damaged berries could be sought.

The Research Task

"We have quite a bit of information here, Larry."

"You're right, and most of it is from the production side. We know very little about who picks or eats blueberries, why they pick, or even what they do with blueberries once they get them home. If there's one thing I remember from my marketing classes, it's 'find out who your customers are'.

"We're really talking about trying to estimate demand, aren't we? To solve the saturation puzzle, we need to know how much demand exists for the PYO farms. And for the commercialization issue, we need to know what overall consumer demand might be."

"Yes, that's all! Now, what we need to do is sit down and develop a research plan. And it would be even better if we could have it ready for this year's blueberry season."

Case 4

TenderCare Disposable Diapers*

James E. Nelson
University of Colorado

Tom Cagan watched as his secretary poured six ounces of water onto each of two disposable diapers laying on his desk. The diaper on the left was a new, improved Pampers, introduced in the summer of 1985 by Procter & Gamble. The new, improved design was supposed to be drier than the preceding Pampers. It was the most recent development in a sequence of designs that traced back to the original Pampers, introduced to the market in 1965. The diaper on his right was a TenderCare diaper, manufactured by a potential supplier for testing and approval by Cagan's company, Rocky Mountain Medical Corporation (RMM). The outward appearance of both diapers was identical.

Yet the TenderCare diaper was different. Just under its liner (the surface next to the baby's skin) was a wicking fabric that drew moisture from the surface around a soft, waterproof shield to an absorbent reservoir of filler. Pampers and all other disposable diapers on the market kept moisture nearer to the liner and, consequently, the baby's skin. A patent attorney had examined the TenderCare design, concluding that the wicking fabric and shield arrangement should be granted a patent. However, it would be many months before results of the patent application process could be known.

As soon as the empty beakers were placed back on the desk, Cagan and his secretary touched the liners of both diapers. They agreed that there was no noticeable difference, and Cagan noted the time. They repeated their "touch test" after one minute and again noted no difference. However, after two minutes, both thought the TenderCare

---

* This case was written by Professor James E. Nelson, University of Colorado. This case is intended for use as a basis for class discussion rather than to illustrate either effective or ineffective administrative decision making. Some data are disguised.

diaper to be drier. At three minutes, they were certain. By five minutes, the TenderCare diaper surface seemed almost dry to the touch, even when a finger was pressed deep into the diaper. In contrast, the Pampers diaper showed little improvement in dryness from three to five minutes and tended to produce a puddle when pressed.

These results were not unexpected. Over the past three months, Cagan and other RMM executives had compared TenderCare's performance with 10 brands of disposable diapers available in the Denver market. TenderCare diapers had always felt drier within a two- to four-minute interval after wetting. However, these results were considered tentative because all tests had used TenderCare diapers made by RMM personnel by hand. Today's test was the first made with diapers produced by a supplier under mass manufacturing conditions.

ROCKY MOUNTAIN MEDICAL CORPORATION

RMM was incorporated in Denver, Colorado, in late 1982 by Robert Morrison, M.D. Sales had grown from about $400,000 in 1983 to $2.4 million in 1984 and were expected to reach $3.4 million in 1985. The firm would show a small profit for 1985, as it had each previous year.

Management personnel as of September 1985 included six executives. Cagan served as president and director, positions held since joining RMM in April 1984. Prior to that time he had worked for several high-technology companies in the areas of product design and development, production management, sales management, and general management. His undergraduate studies were in engineering and psychology; he took an M.B.A. in 1981. Dr. Morrison currently served as chairman of the board and vice-president for research and development. He had completed his M.D. in 1976 and was board certified to practice pediatrics in the state of Colorado since 1978. John Bosch served as vice president of manufacturing, a position held since joining RMM in late 1983. Lawrence Bennett was vice president of marketing, having primary responsibilities for marketing TenderCare and RMM's two lines of phototherapy products since joining the firm in 1984. Bennett's background included an M.B.A. received in 1981 and three years' experience in groceries product management at General Mills. Two other executives, both also joining RMM in 1984, served as vice-president of personnel and as controller.

Phototherapy Products

RMM's two lines of phototherapy products were used to treat infant jaundice, a condition experienced by some 5 to 10 percent of all newborn babies. One line was marketed to hospitals under the trademark

Alpha-Lite. Bennett felt that the Alpha-Lite phototherapy unit was superior to competing products because it gave the baby 360-degree exposure to the therapeutic light. Competing products gave less complete exposure, with the result that the Alpha-Lite unit treated more severe cases and produced quicker recoveries. Apart from the Alpha-Lite unit itself, the hospital line of phototherapy products included a light meter, a photo-mask that protected the baby's eyes while undergoing treatment, and a "baby bikini" that diapered the baby and yet facilitated exposure to the light.

The home phototherapy line of products was marketed under the trademark Baby-Lite.™ The phototherapy unit was portable, weighing about 40 pounds, and was foldable for easy transport. The unit when assembled was 33 inches long, 20 inches wide, and 24 inches high. The line also included photo-masks, a thermometer, and a short booklet telling parents about home phototherapy. Parents could rent the unit and purchase related products from a local pharmacy or durable medical equipment dealer for about $75 per day. This was considerably less than the cost of hospital treatment. Another company, Acquitron, Inc., had entered the home phototherapy market in early 1985 and was expected to offer stiff competition. A third competitor was rumored to be entering the market in 1986.

Bennett's responsibilities for all phototherapy products included developing marketing plans and making final decisions about product design, promotion, pricing, and distribution. He directly supervised two product managers, one responsible for Alpha-Lite and the other for Baby-Lite. He occasionally made sales calls with the product managers, visiting hospitals, health maintenance organizations, and insurers.

TenderCare Marketing

Right now most of Bennett's time was spent on TenderCare. Bennett recognized that TenderCare would be marketed much differently than the phototherapy products. TenderCare would be sold to wholesalers, who in turn would sell to supermarkets, drugstores, and mass merchandisers. TenderCare would compete either directly or indirectly with two giant consumer goods manufacturers, Procter & Gamble and Kimberly-Clark. TenderCare represented considerable risk to RMM.

Because of the uncertainty surrounding the marketing of TenderCare, Bennett and Cagan had recently sought the advice of several marketing consultants. They reached formal agreement with one, a Los Angeles consultant named Alan Anderson. Anderson had had extensive experience in advertising at J. Walter Thompson. He also had had responsibility for marketing and sales at Mattel and Teledyne, specifically for the marketing of such products as IntelliVision,™

the Shower Massage,(TM) and the Water Pik.(TM) Anderson currently worked as an independent marketing consultant to several firms. His contract with RMM specified that he would devote 25 percent of his time to TenderCare the first year and about 12 percent the following two years. During this time, RMM would hire, train, and place their own marketing personnel. One of these people would be a product manager for TenderCare.

Bennett and Cagan also could employ the services of a local marketing consultant who served on RMM's advisory board. The board consisted of 12 business and medical experts who were available to answer questions and provide direction. The consultant had spent over 25 years in marketing consumer products at several large corporations. His specialty was developing and launching new products, particularly health and beauty aids. He had worked closely with RMM in selecting the name TenderCare,(TM) and had done a great deal of work summarizing market characteristics and analyzing competitors.

MARKET CHARACTERISTICS

The market for babies' disposable diapers could be identified as children, primarily below age three, who use the diapers, and their mothers, primarily between ages 18 and 49, who decide on the brand and usually make the purchase. Bennett estimated there were about 11 million such children in 1985, living in about 9 million households. The average number of disposable diapers consumed in these households was thought to range from 0 to 15 and to average about 7.

The consumption of disposable diapers is tied closely to birth rates and populations. However, two prominent trends also influence consumption. One is the disposable diaper's steadily increasing share of total diaper usage by babies. Bennett estimated that disposable diapers would increase their share of total diaper usage from 75 percent currently to 90 percent by 1990. The other trend is toward the purchase of higher-quality disposable diapers. Bennett thought the average retail price of disposable diapers would rise about twice as fast as the price of materials used in their construction. Total dollar sales of disposable diapers at retail in 1985 were expected to be about $3.0 billion, or about 15 billion units. Growth rates were thought to be about 14 percent per year for dollar sales and about 8 percent for units.

Foreign markets for disposable diapers would add to these figures. Canada, for example, currently consumed about $0.25 billion at retail, with an expected growth rate of 20 percent per year until 1990. The U.K. market was about twice this size and growing at the same rate.

The U.S. market for disposable diapers was clearly quite large and growing. However, Bennett felt that domestic growth rates could not be maintained much longer because fewer and fewer consumers were available to switch from cloth to disposable diapers. In fact, by 1995, growth rates for disposable diapers would begin to approach growth rates for births, and unit sales of disposable diapers would become directly proportional to numbers of infants using diapers. A consequence of this pronounced slowing of growth would be increased competition.

COMPETITION

Competition between manufacturers of disposable diapers was already intense. Two well-managed giants—Procter & Gamble and Kimberly-Clark—accounted for about 80 percent of the market in 1984 and 1985. Bennett had estimated market shares at:

	1984	*1985*
Pampers	32%	28%
Huggies	24	28
Luvs	20	20
Other brands	24	24
	100%	100%

Procter & Gamble was clearly the dominant competitor with its Pampers and Luvs brands. However, Procter & Gamble's market share had been declining, from 70 percent in 1981 to about 50 percent today. The company had introduced its thicker Blue Ribbon™ Pampers recently in an effort to halt the share decline. It had invested over $500 million in new equipment to produce the product. Procter & Gamble spent approximately $40 million to advertise its two brands in 1984. Kimberly-Clark spent about $19 million to advertise Huggies in 1984.

The 24 percent market share held by other brands was up by some 3 percentage points from 1983. Weyerhaeuser and Johnson & Johnson manufactured most of these diapers, supplying private-label brands for Wards, Penneys, Target, K mart, and other retailers. Generic disposable diapers and private brands were also included here, as well as a number of very small, specialized brands that distributed only to local markets. Some of these brands positioned themselves as low-cost alternatives to national brands; others occupied premium ("designer") niches with premium prices. As examples, Universal Converter entered the northern Wisconsin market in 1984 with two brands priced at 78 and 87 percent of Pampers' case price. Riegel Textile Corporation's Cabbage Patch™ diapers illustrated the premium end, with higher prices and attractive print designs. Riegel spent $1 million to introduce Cabbage Patch diapers to the market in late 1984.

Additional evidence of intense competition in the disposable diaper industry was the major change of strategy by Johnson & Johnson in 1981. The company took its own brand off the U.S. market, opting instead to produce private-label diapers for major retailers. The company had held about 8 percent of the national market at the time and decided that this simply was not enough to compete effectively. Johnson & Johnson's disposable diaper was the first to be positioned in the industry as a premium product. Sales at one point totaled about 12 percent of the market but began to fall when Luvs and Huggies (with similar premium features) were introduced. Johnson & Johnson's advertising expenditures for disposable diapers in 1980 were about $8 million. The company still competed with its own brand in the international market.

MARKETING STRATEGIES FOR TENDERCARE

Over the past month, Bennett and his consultants had spent considerable time formulating potential marketing strategies for TenderCare. One strategy that already had been discarded was simply licensing the design to another firm. Under a license arrangement, RMM would receive a negotiated royalty based on the licensee's sales of RMM's diaper. However, this strategy was unattractive on several grounds. RMM would have no control over resources devoted to the marketing of TenderCare: the licensee would decide on levels of sales and advertising support, prices, and distribution. The licensee would control advertising content, packaging, and even the choice of brand name. Licensing also meant that RMM would develop little marketing expertise, no image or even awareness among consumers, and no experience in dealing with packaged-goods channels of distribution. The net result would be that RMM would be hitching its future with respect to TenderCare (and any related products) to that of the licensee. Three other strategies seemed more appropriate.

The "Diaper Rash" Strategy

The first strategy involved positioning the product as an aid in the treatment of diaper rash. Diaper rash is a common ailment, thought to affect most infants at some point in their diapered lives. The affliction usually lasted two to three weeks before being cured. Some infants are more disposed to diaper rash than others; however, the ailment probably affects a majority of babies at some point in their diapered lives. The ailment is caused by "a reaction to prolonged contact with urine and feces, retained soaps and topical preparations, and friction maceration" (Nelson's *Text of Pediatrics,* 1979, p. 1884). Recommended treatment includes careful washing of the affected areas with warm water and without irritating soaps. Treatment also includes the application of protective ointments and powders (sold either by prescription or over the counter).

The diaper rash strategy would target physicians and nurses in either family or general practice and physicians and nurses specializing either in pediatrics or dermatology. Bennett's estimates of the numbers of general or family practitioners in 1985 was approximately 65,000. He thought that about 45,000 pediatricians and dermatologists were practicing in 1985. The numbers of nurses attending all these physicians was estimated at about 290,000. All 400,000 individuals would be the eventual focus of TenderCare marketing efforts. However, the diaper rash strategy would begin (like the other two strategies) where approximately 11 percent of the target market was located—California. Bennett and his consultants agreed that RMM lacked resources sufficient to begin in any larger market. California would provide a good test for TenderCare because the state often set consumption trends for the rest of the U.S. market. California also showed fairly typical levels of competitive activity.

Promotion activities would emphasize either direct mail and free samples or in-office demonstrations to the target market. Mailing lists of most physicians and some nurses in the target market could be purchased at a cost of about $60 per 1,000 names. The cost to print and mail a brochure, cover letter, and return postcard was about $250 per 1,000. To include a single TenderCare disposable diaper would add another $400 per thousand. In-office demonstrations would use registered nurses (employed on a part-time basis) to show TenderCare's superior dryness. The nurses could be quickly trained and compensated on a per-demonstration basis. The typical demonstration would be given to groups of two or three physicians and nurses and would cost RMM about $6. The California market could be used to investigate the relative performance of direct mail versus demonstrations.

RMM would also advertise in trade journals such as the *Journal of Family Practice, Journal of Pediatrics, Pediatrics,* and *Pediatrics Digest.* However, a problem with such advertisements was waste coverage because none of the trade journals published regional editions. A half-page advertisement (one insertion) would cost about $1,000 for each journal. This cost would be reduced to about $700 if RMM placed several advertisements in the same journal during a one-year period. RMM would also promote TenderCare at local and state medical conventions in California. Costs per convention were thought to be about $3,000. The entire promotion budget as well as amounts allocated to direct mail, free samples, advertisements, and medical conventions had yet to be decided.

Prices were planned to produce a retail price per package of 12 TenderCare diapers at around $3.80. This was some 8 to 10 percent higher than the price for a package of 18 Huggies or Luvs. Bennett thought that consumers would pay the premium price because of TenderCare's position: the pennies-per-day differential simply would not matter if a physician prescribed or recommended TenderCare as part of a treatment for diaper rash. "Besides," he noted, "in-store shelf placement of Tender-Care under this strategy would be among diaper rash products, not with standard diapers. This will make price comparisons by consumers even more unlikely." The $3.80 package price for 12 TenderCare diapers would produce a contribution margin for RMM of about 9 cents per diaper. It would give retailers a per-diaper margin some 30 percent higher than that for Huggies or Luvs.

The Special-Occasions Strategy

The second strategy centered around a "special-occasions" position that emphasized TenderCare's use in situations where changing the baby would be difficult. One such situation was whenever diapered infants traveled for any length of time. Another occurred daily at some 10,000 daycare centers that accepted infants wearing diapers. Yet another came every evening in each of the 9 million market households when babies were diapered at bedtime.

The special-occasions strategy would target mothers in these 9 million households. Initially, of course, the target would be only the estimated one million mothers living in California. Promotion would aim particularly at first-time mothers, using such magazines as *American Baby* and *Baby Talk*. Per-issue insertion costs for one full-color, half-page advertisement in such magazines would average about $20,000. However, most baby magazines published regional editions where single insertion costs averaged about half that amount. Black and white advertisements could also be considered; their costs would be about 75 percent of the full-color rates. Inserting several ads per year in the same magazine would allow quantity discounts and reduce the average insertion cost by about one third.

Lately Bennett had begun to wonder if direct mail promotion could be used instead to reach mothers of recently born babies. Mailing lists of some 1–3 million names could be obtained at a cost of around $50 per 1,000. Other costs to produce and mail promotional materials would be the same as those for physicians and nurses. "I suppose the real issue is, just how much more effective is direct mail over advertising? We'd spend at least $250,000 in baby magazines to cover California while the cost of direct mail would probably be between $300,000 and $700,000, depending on whether or not we gave away a diaper." Regardless of Bennett's decision on consumer promotion, he knew RMM would also direct some promotion activities toward physicians and nurses as part of the special-occasions strategy. Budget details were yet to be worked out.

Distribution under the special-occasions strategy would have TenderCare stocked on store shelves along with competing diapers. Still at issue was whether the package should contain 12 or 18 diapers (like Huggies and Luvs) and how much of a premium price TenderCare could command. Bennett considered the packaging and pricing decisions interrelated. A package of 12 TenderCare diapers with per-unit retail prices some 40 percent higher than Huggies or Luvs might work just fine. Such a packaging/pricing strategy would produce a contribution margin to RMM of about 6 cents per diaper. However, the same pricing strategy for a package of 18 diapers probably would not work. "Still," he thought, "good things often come in small packages, and most mothers probably associate higher quality with higher price. One thing is for sure—whichever way we go, we'll need a superior package." Physical dimensions for a TenderCare package of either 12 or 18 diapers could be made similar to the size of the Huggies or Luvs package of 18.

The Head-On Strategy

The third strategy under consideration met major competitors in a direct, frontal attack. The strategy would position TenderCare as a noticeably drier diaper that any mother would prefer to use anytime her baby needed changing. Promotion activities would stress mass advertising to mothers using television and magazines. However, at least two magazines would include a dollar-off coupon to stimulate trial of a package of TenderCare diapers during the product's first three months on the market. Some in-store demonstrations to mothers using "touch tests" might also be employed. Although no budget for California had yet been set, Bennett thought the allocation would be roughly 60:30:10 for television, magazines, and other promotion activities, respectively.

Pricing under this strategy would be competitive with Luvs and Huggies, with the per-diaper price for TenderCare expected to be some 9 percent higher at retail. This differential was needed to cover additional manufacturing costs associated with TenderCare's design. TenderCare's package could contain only 16 diapers and show a lower price than either Huggies or Luvs with their 18-count packages. Alternatively, the package could contain 18 diapers and carry the 9 percent higher price. Bennett wondered if he really wasn't putting too fine a point on the pricing/packaging relationship. "After all," he had said to

Anderson, "we've no assurance that retailers or wholesalers would pass along any price advantage TenderCare might have due to a smaller package. Either one or both might instead price TenderCare near the package price for our competitors and simply pocket the increased margin!" The only thing that was reasonably certain was TenderCare's package price to the wholesaler. That price was planned to produce about a 3 cent contribution margin to RMM per diaper, regardless of package count.

Summary of the Three Strategies

When viewed together, the three strategies seemed so complex and so diverse as to defy analysis. Partly the problem was one of developing criteria against which the strategies could be compared. Risk was obviously one such criterion; so were company fit and competitive reaction. However, Bennett felt that some additional thought on his part would produce more criteria against which the strategies could be compared. He hoped this effort would produce no more strategies; three were plenty.

The other part of the problem was simply uncertainty. Strengths, weaknesses, and implications of each strategy had yet to be given much thought. Moreover, each strategy seemed likely to have associated with it some surprises. An example illustrating the problem was the recent realization that the Food and Drug Administration (FDA) must approve any direct claims RMM might make about TenderCare's efficacy in treating diaper rash. The chance of receiving this federal agency's approval was thought to be reasonably high; yet it was unclear just what sort of testing and what results were needed. The worst-case scenario would have the FDA requiring lengthy consumer tests that eventually would produce inconclusive results. The best case could have the FDA giving permission based on TenderCare's superior dryness and on results of a small-scale field test recently completed by Dr. Morrison. It would be probably a month before the FDA's position could be known.

"The delay was unfortunate—and unnecessary," Bennett thought, "especially if we eventually settle on either of the other two strategies." In fact, FDA approval was not even needed for the diaper rash strategy if RMM simply claimed (1) that TenderCare diapers were drier than competing diapers and (2) that dryness helps treat diaper rash. Still, a single-statement, direct-claim position was thought to be more effective with mothers and more difficult to copy by any other manufacturer. And yet Bennett did want to move quickly on TenderCare. Every month of delay meant deferred revenue and other postponed benefits that would derive from a successful introduction.

Delay also meant the chance that an existing (or other) competitor might develop its own drier diaper and effectively block RMM from reaping the fruits of its development efforts. Speed was of the essence.

FINANCIAL IMPLICATIONS

Bennett recognized that each marketing strategy held immediate as well as long-term financial implications. He was particularly concerned with finance requirements for start-up costs associated with the California entry. Cagan and the other RMM executives had agreed that a stock issue represented the best option to meet these requirements. Accordingly, RMM had begun preparation for a sale of common stock through a brokerage firm that would underwrite and market the issue. Management at the firm felt that RMM could generate between $1 and $3 million, depending on the offering price per share and the number of shares issued.

Proceeds from the sale of stock had to be sufficient to fund the California entry and leave a comfortable margin remaining for contingencies. Proceeds would be used for marketing and other operating expenses as well as for investments in cash, inventory, and accounts receivable assets. It was hoped that TenderCare would generate a profit by the end of the first year in the California market and show a strong contribution to the bottom line thereafter. California profits would contribute to expenses associated with entering additional markets and to the success of any additional stock offerings.

Operating profits and proceeds from the sale of equity would fund additional research and development activities that would extend RMM's diaper technology to other markets. Dr. Morrison and Bennett saw almost immediate application of the technology to the adult incontinent diaper market, currently estimated at about $300 million per year at retail. Underpads for beds constituted at least another $50 million annual market. However, both of these uses were greatly dwarfed by another application, the sanitary napkin market. Finally, the technology could almost certainly be applied to numerous industrial products and processes, many of which promised great potential. All these opportunities made the TenderCare situation that much more crucial to the firm: making a major mistake here would affect the firm for years.

Case 5

The Adirondack Manor*

Lawrence M. Lamont
Washington and Lee University

Burt Gray, Director of Sales for the Adirondack Manor, could feel the pressure as he was preparing to attend the weekly sales meeting. In just a few months, the Manor would be opening a new conference facility designed to enable the resort hotel to better serve the growing meetings and conventions market. Mr. Gray knew he would be asked for a marketing strategy to market the resort to the corporations and professional associations who were potential target customers.

Over the past several months, the Sales Department had been actively recruiting sales personnel and collecting information from trade publications on the meetings and conventions market. Recently, Burt had received a report from a marketing research firm that had been retained to study the buying and decision-making process used by meeting planners for corporations and associations to select locations and facilities for off-premise meetings. He was planning to use the findings from the research study to formulate a marketing strategy. Several questions came to mind as he thought about the marketing issues:

1. Was the resort's present organizational structure satisfactory to enable it to manage its marketing efforts?
2. How should the resort be positioned to best serve the meetings and conventions market?
3. Given the positioning, what marketing strategy would be appropriate to expand the Manor's market?

---

* This case was prepared by Professor Lawrence M. Lamont, Washington and Lee University, Department of Administration. The author acknowledges the research assistance of Steven Daub, Stewart Kerr, and Bennett Ross, all graduates of Washington and Lee University. Assistance in case preparation was provided by Perry Goodbar, also a graduate of Washington and Lee.

Historical Background

The Adirondack Manor traced its beginning to the summer of 1750, when a local doctor noticed that visitors were attracted to the area for the mineral water from a large hot spring. The doctor began advertising that the spring water was recommended for such maladies as gout, rheumatism, paralysis, and spinal irritations. Later, in 1776, the doctor built a private home and operated it as an inn for visitors.

The inn passed from owner to owner until 1890 when the Chief Executive Officer of a major railroad purchased the property. By 1892, several improvements were under way, and the following year the Adirondack Manor opened its doors as a classic resort hotel.

In 1901, the hotel was destroyed by fire. Before the embers had been quenched, management was making plans for a larger and more modern resort. By the spring of 1902, the main section of the new hotel had been rebuilt, and by 1914, new East and West wings had been added. The Manor was becoming very fashionable for vacationing social guests from Boston, New York, Philadelphia, and Washington, D.C.

In 1959, a ski and skating area were added to improve the seasonal appeal of the Manor. Although the winter weather was somewhat unpredictable, this expenditure was looked upon favorably. It was soon a successful reality, with the installation of snow- and ice-making equipment.

The most recent addition to the hotel will be a modern conference facility. It will house additional guest rooms as well as a center capable of accommodating 1,000 people for banquets, conventions, and professional meetings. This addition will enhance the appeal of the Manor to the meetings and conventions market, as well as to the resort's social guests.

Present Facilities

With the completion of the conference facility, the resort's properties will include a luxury hotel with over 500 sleeping rooms, several dining rooms, three swimming pools, and attractive meeting facilities. The 20,000 surrounding acres, also owned by the Manor, contain three championship golf courses, 19 tennis courts, a skeet and trap shooting range, horseback riding and hiking trails, a trout stream, skiing and ice skating facilities, and numerous other recreational amenities.

The Manor directs much of its marketing effort at the social market because its accommodations, dining services, and recreational attractions strongly appeal to the families and individuals in the upper social classes. Most of these customers are destination vacationers who use the resort on a regular basis, while a few are walk-in guests that arrive without reservations. In recent years, the resort has also been somewhat successful marketing to corporations and associations interested in using the facilities for off-premise business meetings and conventions. While these marketing efforts have been modest, the resort has achieved some success in attracting small business meetings and conventions. Management now believed that the addition of the new conference center would enable the resort to substantially improve its competitive position in the market.

Location

Adirondack Manor, one of the largest mountain resorts in the United States, is located in the heart of the Adirondack Mountains[1]. It is surrounded by a small, historic village that has a variety of specialty shops and restaurants that are attractive to visitors and guests. The Manor is located along a two-lane U.S. highway about 20 miles from a major interstate highway.

The Manor is served by nearby McMullen Field which has the capability of handling private and corporate aircraft. The runway is constructed of concrete and is 5,600 feet long, 100 feet wide, and 3,100 feet above sea level, making it the highest air strip East of the Mississippi.

Presently, there are two daily and three weekend flights scheduled into McMullen by an air charter service which operates out of La Guardia in New York. The service takes about 55 minutes and uses Beechcraft 99s with a capacity of 12 passengers. However, four additional planes are available, upon request, when there is a large group needing service. McMullen is located 17 miles from the hotel, but ground transportation is available through the resort.

An alternative method of reaching the resort is to fly into Foxboro Regional Airport, located 60 miles away. Foxboro is served daily with flights by two national carriers using 112-passenger Boeing 737s and a regional airline flying Beechcraft 99s. Again, complete ground transportation to the resort is available at Foxboro.

Climate

While the Manor's location is quite remote, the resort is surrounded by rolling hills and beautiful mountains. The climate is moderate throughout the year with summer temperatures averaging 75–80 de-

[1] The Manor is a privately owned company. Annual sales are approximately $20 million and employment is 700 people.

grees, and winter temperatures 30–35 degrees. The precipitation varies during the year with an inordinate amount of rainfall during March and April. Business is slower at these times, because social guests and meeting attendees don't want to chance the weather and be unable to take advantage of the recreational opportunities.

The resort has skiing and ice skating, although the weather is not always suitable for these activities. Most of the snow falls from December through early March, and averages 60 to 70 inches a year. In some months, the snow fall is inadequate to support the winter activities. However, snow-making equipment augments the natural snow to make these activities possible during the winter season.

Organization and Management of the Adirondack Manor

The Adirondack Manor uses a functional organization to manage its business. The organization chart illustrated in Exhibit 1 shows the functional departments, and elaborates the activities and reporting

EXHIBIT 1 Formal Organization of the Adirondack Manor

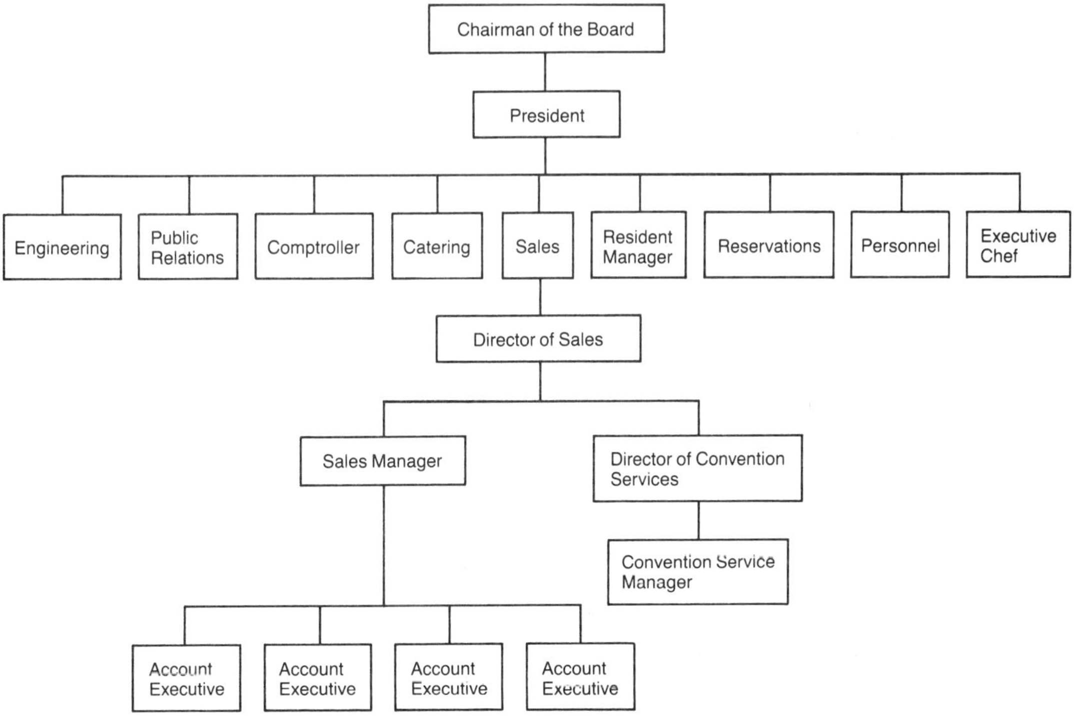

relationships in the sales department. The President, Mr. Wright, is responsible for the daily operations of the resort. Several functional department managers report to Mr. Wright informally during a weekly staff meeting designed to give each manager an opportunity to review the activities of his department and coordinate them with the other managers. In addition, department managers benefit from Mr. Wright's open door policy which creates an informal line of communication and helps to resolve the day-to-day problems that arise.

Although each department is crucial to the successful operation of the Manor, the sales department has the dual responsibility of selling the resort's meeting and convention capabilities and, through the convention services group, assisting planners with meeting arrangements to assure that meetings run smoothly. Thus, the sales department has the dual responsibility of sales and customer service.

Burt Gray, Director of Sales, manages the Manor's sales department. He is knowledgeable about the industry, having had 10 years of sales experience in resort hotels. The Director's duties include representing the department at staff meetings, preparing budgets for the sales department, and developing sales plans specifying the types of meetings and geographic areas where selling efforts will be concentrated.

Reporting to Mr. Gray is a sales manager and a director of convention services. The sales manager directs the daily activities of the account executives and assists with sales calls and training when necessary. Once a sale is made, responsibility for the customer is transferred to the convention services manager and his staff. As mentioned, this group works closely with the corporation or association meeting planner to finalize the meeting arrangements and attend to any problems that might arise during the meeting at the Manor.

THE MEETING AND CONVENTIONS MARKET

According to trade sources, the off-premise meetings and conventions market has grown from $8.7 billion in 1973 to $34.6 billion in 1985. Growing at an annual rate of 12.2 percent, the market has become a vital aspect of the nation's economy and increasingly attractive to resort hotels that have traditionally served the needs of affluent families and individuals. A recent survey, covering most of the market, indicates that corporations and associations sponsored over 903,000 meetings in 1985 with annual meeting expenditures exceeding $31.4 billion dollars. As shown in Exhibit 2, the majority of the off-premise meetings were held by corporations; however, they only accounted for 24 percent of the total annual expenditures. In part, this is explained by the fact that many of the corporate meetings are smaller. Atten-

EXHIBIT 2 Total Off-Premise Meetings and Expenditures, 1985

Off-Premise Meetings Held during Year			*Total Annual Expenditures*	
Corporate meetings	706,100	(78.0%)	$ 7,527,800,000	(24.0%)
Association major conventions	12,240	(1.5%)	12,675,800,000	(40.3%)
Association other meetings	185,400	(20.5%)	11,213,300,000	(35.7%)
Total meetings	903,740	(100.0%)	$31,416,900,000*	(100.0%)

* Based on a survey. When projected to the total meetings market, total expenditures are $34,643,100,000.

Source: *The Meetings Market Study, 1985,* Murdoch Magazines Research Department, New York, N.Y., 1986.

dance at off-premise meetings held by corporations and associations was spread over a variety of different types of meetings. Exhibit 3 shows the attendance by type of meeting in 1985 for both corporations and associations. Regional and national sales meetings accounted for 24 percent of the attendance at corporation meetings, while national conventions were responsible for 43 percent of the attendance at meetings held by associations.

EXHIBIT 3 Attendance at Corporation and Association Off-Premise Meetings

Type of Meeting	*Corporations*	*Associations*
Training seminars	6,868,400 (17%)	
Sales meetings	9,361,000 (24%)	
Management meetings	8,011,300 (20%)	
Professional/technical meetings	3,959,300 (10%)	3,641,000 (11%)
Incentive trips	2,425,300 (6%)	
New product introductions	4,064,600 (10%)	
Stockholder meetings	2,077,300 (5%)	
Educational seminars		6,208,100 (20%)
Board meetings		1,156,000 (3%)
Regional/state/local chapter meetings		4,336,400 (14%)
National conventions		13,537,400 (43%)
Other meetings	3,021,000 (8%)	2,831,200 (9%)
Total	39,788,200 (100%)	31,710,100 (100%)

Source: *The Meetings Market Study, 1985,* Murdoch Magazines Research Department, New York, N.Y., 1986.

Economic Environment

Generally, the economic environment does not affect the number of meetings and conventions held annually because they are viewed as a necessary expense of conducting business. However, adverse economic conditions have caused corporate and association meeting planners to become concerned about expenses and to search for ways of reducing the costs. Items such as transportation, room accommodations, meal functions, and receptions have come under careful scrutiny. Many organizations are reducing transportation costs by using central locations or staying closer to headquarters facilities. The cost of meals and banquets is another area for cutting meeting and convention expenses. Many organizations have eliminated cocktail receptions and moved away from meal plans which include three daily meals.

Economic conditions do have an effect on attendance. For instance, during recessions the number of "no shows" at scheduled meetings and conventions is always a problem. Meeting planners are extremely conscious of attendance because a conference that is not well attended is a waste of time and money. To reduce the number of "no shows," corporations and associations constantly work to improve the programming and marketing of large meetings and conventions. According to meeting planners, resorts can be more attractive than city hotels because they provide facilities for a serious business meeting while offering enough recreation incentives to act as a lure. Further, the self-contained nature of many resort hotels makes those who attend a captive audience.

Competitive Environment

Competition in the meetings and conventions market is intense and, for any type of meeting or budget, meeting planners have a variety of locations and facilities to choose from. As illustrated in Exhibit 4, facilities range from a midtown hotel or motor inn in cities like New York or Chicago to mountain or ocean resorts in New England and the South.

Resort hotels have always been popular for off-premise meetings. Many resorts, in addition to Adirondack Manor, have built special conference facilities to accommodate meetings and conventions. The competition has come from other sources as well. The major hotel chains such as Marriott, Hilton, and Westin, which are not typical resort hotels, have concentrated on marketing their hotels and motor inns as such. By offering a meeting and recreation package, they are able to compete in the market as a resort. Many of their facilities are located in urban and suburban areas, often close to airports.

Teleconferencing has become an alternative to extensive traveling

EXHIBIT 4 Type of Facilities Used for Off-Premise Meetings*

Type of Facilities	*Corporate Planners*	*Association Planners†*
Resort hotel	44%	40%
Suburban hotel or motor inn	45	39
Midtown hotel or motor inn	58	70
Airport hotel or motor inn	27	31
Privately-owned conference center	17	15
Condominium resort	9	4
Suite hotel	9	5
University-owned conference center	5	10
Cruise	5	1

* Totals exceed 100 percent because of multiple response.
† Excludes major conventions, most of which are held at mid-town hotels.

Source: *The Meetings Market Study, 1985,* Murdoch Magazines Research Department, New York, N.Y., 1986.

for meetings. However, at present it is not a serious competitive threat due to the cost and the slow adoption of the technology. As teleconferencing costs decline, it is likely that meeting planners will make greater use of the technology for future meetings.

Faced with unused capacity in the off-season, resorts often offer attractive rates for meetings. Rates are discounted in the so-called shoulder periods (the weeks immediately before and after a peak season) and the low season (December–February), now popularly called the "value" season by many resorts.

Seven luxury resorts, all rated as five-star resort hotels by the Mobil Travel Guide, are in direct competition with the Manor. In Exhibit 5, it can be noted that while the resorts are somewhat comparable in their accommodations, the dining plans vary. Differences are also apparent in the recreational amenities available at each resort. As shown in Exhibit 6 they generally reflect the unique features of each resort's environment and location.

Of greatest importance to meeting planners, however, is the facilities the resort has for the business sessions of the meeting or convention. Exhibit 7 provides a comparison of the meeting facilities of each resort hotel. These facilities, along with the prices of the resort's accommodations, dining service, and recreational amenities gives each resort a somewhat distinctive position in the market. It also makes prices difficult to compare among the competing resorts. Some resorts quoted meeting planners a daily rate that included the room, a meal plan, and use of the resort's meeting and recreation facilities. Others quoted the various services separately and allowed the meeting planner to construct a package that best met the needs of his meeting.

The manor's prices were based on the full American plan where the

EXHIBIT 5 Accommodations and Dining Plans by Resort

	Accommodations				*Dining Plan**			
	Single Occupancy	*Double Occupancy*	*Suites*	*Cottages*	*European*	*Modified American*	*Full American*	*Off-Season Rates*
The Arizona Biltmore	X	X			X			X
The Breakers	X	X	X		X	X	X	X
The Broadmoor	X	X	X		X	X†		X
The Greenbrier	X	X				X		X
The Homestead	X	X	X	X		X	X	X
The Lodge	X	X	X		X	X		
Colonial Williamsburg	X	X	X		X	X‡	X‡	X
Adirondack Manor	X	X	X				X	X

* European Plan (Meals not included in daily room rate)
Modified American Plan (two meals included in daily room rate)
Full American Plan (three meals included in daily room rate)
† Available for groups of 350 or more.
‡ Available by arrangement for special conference packages.

Source: Resorts' promotional materials.

EXHIBIT 6 Recreational Amenities by Resort

Resort Hotel	*Golf*	*Tennis*	*Horseback Riding*	*Swimming*	*Bowling*	*Sailing*	*Trap & Skeet*	*Skiing*	*Skating*	*Fishing*	*Spa*
The Arizona Biltmore	X	X		X							X
The Breakers	X	X		X		X				X	
The Broadmoor	X	X		X		X	X	X	X		
The Greenbrier	X	X	X	X	X		X		X	X	X
The Homestead	X	X	X	X	X		X	X	X	X	X
The Lodge	X	X	X	X						X	X
Colonial Williamsburg	X	X	X	X							
Adirondack Manor	X	X	X	X			X	X	X	X	X

Source: Resorts' promotional material.

EXHIBIT 7 Meeting Facilities by Resort

	Capacity of Largest Function Room			*Number of Meeting Rooms of Various Seating Capacity**					
Resort Hotel	*Theater Style*	*Banquet Style†*	*Total*	*1000+*	*500–999*	*250–499*	*100–249*	*50–99*	*49 below*
The Arizona Biltmore	1,250	940	17	1	2	3	4	3	4
The Breakers	1,200	1,000	20	1	1	—	2	12	4
The Broadmoor	2,600	1,600	34	2	6	4	4	6	12
The Greenbrier	2,000	1,200	25	1	2	4	8	4	6
The Homestead	1,250	1,020	25	1	2	3	4	2	13
The Lodge	600	400	5	—	1	1	1	1	1
Colonial Williamsburg	850	700	21	—	3	3	6	5	4
Adirondack Manor	1,000	815	23	1	2	3	4	2	11

* Based on theater style arrangement (chairs, no tables).
† Banquet style is set for dinner.

Source: Resort's promotional material.

rate included the room and three daily meals. For corporations and associations planning a meeting or convention, the per-person-daily rate also included meeting rooms, audio visual equipment, receptions, and refreshment breaks. Recreational activities such as golf and tennis were usually priced separately, with group rates available for corporations and associations planning large functions. Off-season rates were also available at the Manor to stimulate demand during the low occupancy periods. Discounts of up to 30 percent were applied to the regular season rates for groups using the resort's meeting and convention facilities during these times. Following is a brief description of major competitors offering services similar to those of the Adirondack Manor.

The Arizona Biltmore

The Arizona Biltmore is a luxury resort owned by the Westin chain. It is located in Phoenix, 20 minutes from the Phoenix International Airport, and has over 500 guest rooms and three dining facilities.

The Biltmore's promotional efforts are supported by an extensive advertising campaign designed to build preference for all of the hotels in the Westin Chain. It provides a complete conference facility and competes in the higher price, luxury segment of the meetings and conventions market. Sixty percent of the resort's meeting rooms are designed for groups of 50–500 people.

The Breakers

The Breakers is a glamorous ocean resort located on the Atlantic Ocean 15 minutes from the Palm Beach International Airport. It has 568 rooms and two dining facilities. During the hot summer and fall months (July–October), the Breakers offers special off-season conference rates which are generally below the industry average. With 60 percent of its meeting rooms designed for groups of 50 or less, the Breakers is an ideal site for smaller meetings. The resort emphasizes its prestigious location, elegant facilities, and excellent service in promotion to meeting planners.

The Broadmoor

The Broadmoor is a four-season Colorado resort, although it is more popular in the winter months when skiing is available. It is located 15 minutes from the airport serving Colorado Springs, and has 560 rooms and four dining facilities. The Broadmoor has pursued a pricing strategy which enables the resort to compete in the lower price segment of the luxury hotels. It emphasizes a central location and moderate weather, in order to attract business. The resort has approximately 25 percent of its meeting rooms designed for groups of 500 or more.

The Greenbrier

The Greenbrier is a mountain resort nestled in the Allegheny Mountains in White Sulphur, West Virginia. It is close to a major interstate highway and 15 minutes from the Greenbrier Valley Airport. The resort has 700 rooms, three dining rooms, three golf courses, and many other recreational attractions. The Greenbrier's dining service emphasizes the modified American plan which does not include lunch. This feature is attractive to health-conscious executives and meeting planners interested in reducing costs by eliminating an afternoon meal.

Information concerning The Greenbrier is contained in an impressive promotional brochure which includes a 43-page meeting planner's manual. Advertisements describing the conference facilities of The Greenbrier have appeared in *Sales and Marketing Management, Dun's Business Month,* and *The Wall Street Journal.* To encourage corporations and associations to plan meetings at The Greenbrier, the resort offers special meeting packages that are available from November through March. With 61 percent of its meeting rooms designed for groups from 50 to 500 it is well suited for moderate size meetings and conventions.

The Homestead

The Homestead, only a short drive from the Greenbrier, is a classic mountain resort, located in Hot Springs, Virginia. The location is somewhat remote but it is adequately served by Ingalls Field, a small airport 25 minutes away, and Woodrum Field in Roanoke, Virginia, 75 miles away. The resort provides ground transportation from both airports.

The Homestead is self-contained and provides a complete range of services for guests including specialty shops, a theatre, night clubs, and live entertainment. The resort has 540 sleeping rooms, three dining facilities, three golf courses, skiing and skating, and a variety of other recreational amenities. Promoted as a resort for all seasons and all meetings, it has received the prestigious Mobil 5-Star Award for 21 consecutive years and has been honored with the Gold Key Award from *Meetings and Conventions* Magazine.

The Homestead is also a complete conference facility that operates with both the full and modified American plan. About 65 percent of its meeting rooms are designed for groups from 50 to 500, but it can handle conventions with up to 2,000 people. Special rates are also available from The Homestead for meeting planners who want to plan meetings during the November–March off-season.

The Lodge

The Lodge is a Pebble Beach company resort located in the Del Monte Forest on California's Monterey Peninsula. It is best known for its championship golf courses, Pebble Beach, Spyglass Hill, and Old Del Monte, the first course west of the Mississippi. In addition, The Lodge offers a variety of other recreational, social, and sightseeing activities, benefitting from its proximity to some of the most beautiful scenery and unique tourist attractions on the California coast.

Easily accessible, The Lodge is located just off a U.S. highway and is only eight miles from the Monterey Airport which is served by United Airlines, Air California, and other carriers. Since its beginning, the Pebble Beach Company has tried to develop The Lodge as a resort which provides elegant shopping, fine dining, and excellent recreation facilities to accommodate many types of business meetings. By design, however, it is intended for smaller meetings. The capacity of the largest meeting room at The Lodge is only 600 with banquet facilities for 400. Moreover, the resort offers a selection of only five meeting rooms in which to hold business functions. As a result, the number of conferences and meetings that are suitable for The Lodge is quite limited.

Colonial Williamsburg

Located in historic Williamsburg, Virginia, The Colonial Williamsburg Inn and Conference Center offers professional and business organizations a distinctive and unusual setting for a business conference. The Conference Center is part of a complex which includes The Williamsburg Lodge, The Williamsburg Inn, and the Colonial guest houses. Also, the Williamsburg Motor House and Meeting Center are located just north of The Lodge. In addition to the traditional recreation amenities, Williamsburg has numerous attractions of historical significance to occupy visitors and guests. Guided tours of the Historic Area may be arranged to suit the interests of a conference group.

Colonial Williamsburg is readily accessible by any mode of transportation and this feature makes it attractive to meeting planners. The resort can accommodate groups of nearly 900 with banquet services for over 700 guests. The 21 meeting rooms offer a high degree of flexibility and choice for most group customers. However, with over 70 percent of its meeting rooms designed for groups of less than 250, Colonial Williamsburg seems best suited for smaller scale executive meetings and conferences.

BUYER BEHAVIOR IN THE MEETINGS AND CONVENTIONS MARKET

During the planning for the new conference facility, the Manor retained an independent marketing research firm to study the purchase behavior of the corporations and associations in the meetings and conventions market. Using secondary data and the survey method, the research examined the motives for holding off-premise meetings, the information used by meeting planners to plan meetings, the factors used in selecting a meeting location and facility, and many other important aspects of the purchase decision.[2] An important result of the research was a conceptual model of the buying and decision-making process. This model, shown in Exhibit 8, and discussed in the sections which follow, was expected to be helpful to the Manor in developing the marketing strategy for its meeting and convention services.

The Motivation for an Off-Premise Meeting

Corporate and association meetings are held to communicate the results of operations, to discuss the problems and decisions that arise during the course of business, to train individuals, and reward outstanding performance. While most association meetings are required in their bylaws, the need for many corporate meetings is recognized by the managers of functional areas. For example, an executive may determine that a management meeting is necessary to explain new company policies or introduce a new product.

There are basically two reasons for holding an off-premise meeting. The first is that the organization does not have the capabilities to hold the meeting on its premises. The second is to move the attendees away from the business environment and insure uninterrupted attendance and attention. In addition, off-premise meetings fulfill certain needs of the organization and the individual attendees. Meetings can improve employee motivation, increase productivity, and satisfy the personal

[2] The survey results are based on a nationwide respondent sample of 303 meeting planners: 141 meeting planners for corporations and 162 association meeting planners.

EXHIBIT 8 The Buying and Decision-Making Model

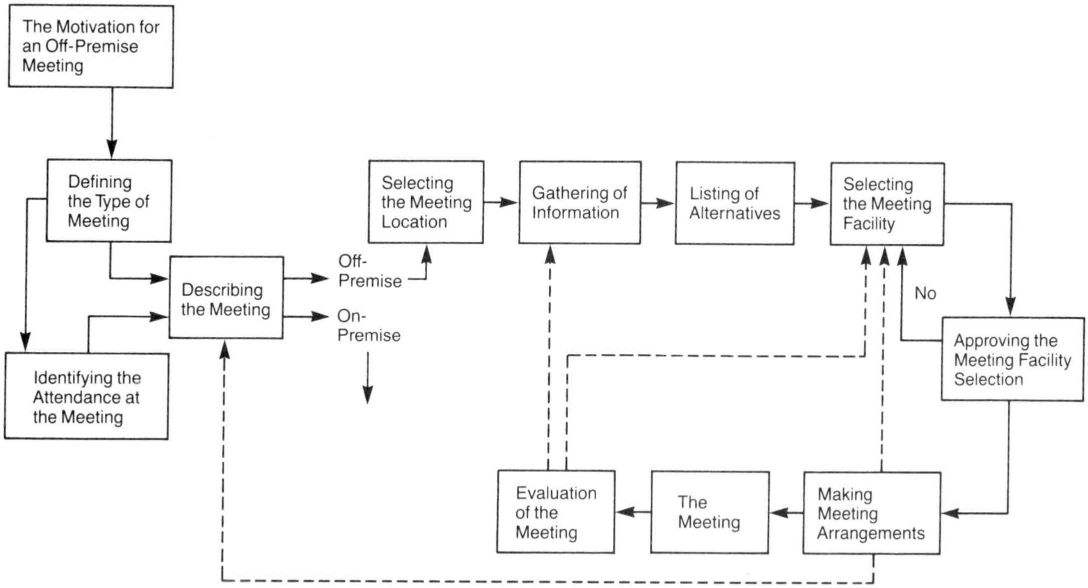

Note: Dotted line indicates information feedback.

Source: Independent Marketing Research Study.

and social needs of those attending. For example, by holding the meeting at a luxury resort, it can satisfy the employees' need for recognition of outstanding personal achievement.

Defining the Meeting

As shown in Exhibit 9, corporations and associations hold a variety of off-premise meetings, each designed to accomplish a specific purpose. Defining the type of meeting to be held is important because it determines who will be responsible for the planning and decision making and the lead time necessary to organize the meeting. Few corporations have employees whose sole responsibility is to plan meetings. The meeting planner's primary job responsibility could be in sales and marketing, public relations, corporate administration, personnel and training, manufacturing and operations, travel, or occasionally meeting planning. The type of meeting to be held usually determines who plans it. For example, 44 percent of the management meetings and 61

EXHIBIT 9 Numbers and Types of Corporate and Association Off-Premise Meetings

	Corporations	*Associations*
Training seminars	163,500 (23%)	—
Sales meetings	157,400 (22%)	—
Management meetings	178,000 (25%)	—
Professional/technical meetings	63,900 (9%)	31,900 (16%)
Incentive trips	27,600 (4%)	—
New product introductions	67,750 (10%)	—
Stockholder meetings	21,900 (3%)	—
Educational seminars	—	63,300 (32%)
Board meetings	—	37,300 (19%)
Regional/state/local chapter meetings	—	31,900 (16%)
National conventions	—	12,240 (6%)
Other meetings	26,050 (4%)	21,000 (11%)
Total	706,100 (100%)	197,640 (100%)

Source: *The Meetings Market Study, 1985,* Murdoch Magazines Research Department, New York, N.Y., 1986.

percent of the sales meetings were planned by individuals in sales and marketing, while 73 percent of the stockholders meetings were planned by corporate administrators and meeting planners. Generally, the decision on a location or facility did not rest entirely with the individual planning the meeting. Many decisions were made in collaboration with department managers or special committees.

The planning of association meetings was often done by an individual whose title might be executive director, meeting planner, administrative assistant, vice president, president, or secretary-treasurer. As with corporate meetings, the type of meeting often indicated who was responsible for planning. Board meetings, educational meetings, and national conventions, for example, are planned primarily by the executive director or the association's meeting planner. Compared to corporate meetings, the individuals planning the association meetings are more likely to have decision-making authority in selecting the meeting location and facility. However, in the case of decisions involving the location of national conventions and board meetings, the associations executive committee may exercise final approval.

Finally, the type of meeting tells the planner the length of time needed for planning and selecting the appropriate facility. The shortest average lead time for off-premise meetings held by corporations is 4.0 months for management meetings, and the longest is 13.1 months for incentive trips (sales award meetings); the overall average for all types of meetings is 7.7 months. The shortest average lead time for associations is 8.1 months for regional or local chapter meetings, and the longest is 38.9 months for National Conventions. Excluding national conventions, the average according to association meeting planners, is about 10.2 months.

Identifying the Attendance at the Meeting

Once the type of meeting to be held is defined, it becomes necessary for the meeting planner to determine who will attend. This is important because the attendance often influences the selection of a meeting location and the choice of a facility. For instance, meetings which involve corporate executives are more likely to be held at a resort with recreation facilities than at an airport motor inn. Also, for association meetings, such as national membership conventions where attendance is not mandatory, the selection of a glamorous or popular facility helps to stimulate attendance.

Another important consideration is the number of individuals expected to attend. In Exhibit 10 it can be seen that, in general, attendance will depend on the type of meeting being planned. The facility requirements, such as the number of sleeping and meeting rooms, are solely a function of the expected attendance. For this reason, when the meeting planner considers specific meeting or convention facilities, a basic criterion in evaluation is the capacity to accommodate the expected group.

The final aspect of identifying the attendance at the meeting in-

EXHIBIT 10 Average Attendance at Corporate and Association Meetings

	Corporations	*Associations*
Training seminars	33	—
Sales meetings	62	—
Management meetings	40	—
Professional/technical meetings	62	166
Incentive trips	103	—
New Product introductions	49	—
Stockholder meetings	85	—
Educational seminars	—	153
Board meetings	—	45
Regional/state/local chapter meetings	—	149
National conventions	—	1,044
Other meetings	97	201

Source: The Meetings Market Study, 1983, *Meetings and Conventions Magazine*.

volves considering the areas in which the attendees are located. Meeting planners are conscious of the travel time and costs associated with off-premise meetings. Corporations will often arrange a meeting in a central location to reduce travel expenses, while associations concerned with attendance levels are less likely to select a facility that requires members to pay large sums of money to reach the meeting location.

Describing the Meeting

Once the meeting has been defined and its attendance specified, the meeting planner begins to develop the program for the meeting. This process begins with an understanding of the work requirements of the meeting and the need for social and recreational activities to complement the working sessions. Corporate management meetings, for example, usually include presentations and discussions with some time for leisure activities. This blend of work and leisure must be defined before a meeting location is selected. Also, the attendance of spouses at a meeting or convention must be considered early in the planning process. A meeting which includes spouses must provide activities in the program for those not involved in the business sessions.

Meeting length is another aspect that must be considered. In general, the length of either a corporate or association meeting depends on the type of meeting and who is expected to attend. For example, corporate stockholder meetings and association board meetings last less than two days on average, while corporate incentive trips to reward outstanding performance typically last longer than five days. Exhibit 11 gives additional information on the average length of corporation and association meetings.

The final aspect of describing the meeting involves a consideration of any financial constraints. Planners must be aware of the budget and organize meetings within the financial limits imposed by the organization. In addition, meeting planners must be careful when arranging a meeting that might impose a financial burden on attendees by requiring them to draw on personal accounts. Association planners, in particular, must give special attention to the total cost of a meeting or convention package if the members must pay their own expenses.

Selecting a Meeting Location

Given a description of the attendance and the work requirements of the meeting, the meeting planner proceeds to select a location. The marketing research identified seven factors that meeting planners

EXHIBIT 11 Average Length (Days) of Corporate and Association Meetings

	Corporations	*Associations*
Training seminars	2.8	—
Sales meetings	2.8	—
Management meetings	2.2	—
Professional/technical meetings	2.3	2.4
Incentive trips	5.5	—
New Product introductions	2.0	—
Stockholder meetings	1.4	—
Educational seminars	—	2.3
Board meetings	—	1.9
Regional/state/local chapter meetings	—	2.6
National conventions	—	N.A.
Other meetings	2.8	3.0
Average	2.6	2.4

Source: *The Meetings Market Study, 1985,* Murdoch Magazines Research Department, New York, N.Y., 1986.

consider in selecting the geographic location: ease of transporting attendees to the location, image of location, environmental setting and climate, transportation costs, recreational activities, sightseeing activities, and distance from attendees. The research also identified the importance that meeting planners attached to the various factors. Exhibit 12 ranks each factor in terms of its importance in location decisions for corporation and association meetings. As can be noted from the table, the most important location factors are similar for both corporations and associations, but some differences do exist, such as the distance of the location from the attendees.

EXHIBIT 12 Importance of Factors in the Selection of a Meeting Location

Location Selection Factors	*Corporate Planner*	*Association Planner*
Ease of transporting attendees to location	1	1
Image of location	2	2
Environmental setting/climate	3	3
Transportation costs	4	5
Recreational activities	5	6
Sightseeing activities	6	7
Distance from attendees	7	4

Source: Independent marketing research study.

Gathering of Information

As the meeting location is being selected, the corporate or association planner is also gathering information on specific meeting facilities. Meeting planners obtain information at different times from as many as nine sources, shown in Exhibit 13. The information gathered from an on-site inspection, is the most important. An inspection gives the meeting planner an opportunity to sample and evaluate the hotel or resort's services before the facility is finally selected. Some meeting planners spend a majority of their time visiting different hotels and resorts inspecting them for future meetings. This is encouraged by the sales people in the hotel or resorts, because it is easier to convince someone to bring a meeting to a particular facility if they can actually experience what it has to offer. The second most important source of information in the selection of a meeting facility is the organization's previous experience with a specific hotel or resort. A productive meeting previously held at a particular hotel or resort will ensure that the facility is considered again as a meeting site. Conversely, an unsatisfactory experience will reduce the likelihood that the hotel or resort will be considered for future meetings.

Although advertising and promotional material ranked low in importance as sources of information used by meeting planners, promotion probably has an indirect effect on the meeting planning process. An effective promotion program can influence a meeting planner's perception of the meeting facility and lead to its consideration as a prospective site.

EXHIBIT 13 Information Sources Used to Select a Meeting Facility

Information Source	*Corporate Planner*	*Association Planner*
On-site inspection	1 (tie)	1
Previous personal experience with hotel or resort	1 (tie)	2
Personal perception of hotel or resort	2	3
Hotel or resort's sales personnel	3	4
Hotel or resort's promotional material	4	6
Meeting planners magazines	5	7
Hotel or resort's advertisements	6	8
Meeting planners with other organizations	7	5
Travel agents	8	9

Source: Independent marketing research study.

Listing of Alternatives

Based on the planner's assessment of the information gathered from various sources, and after considering the appropriateness of the hotels or resorts in the geographic location selected for the meeting, a list of individual facilities is compiled for further consideration.

Selecting a Meeting Facility

In selecting a meeting facility, the meeting planner may evaluate the alternative hotels or resorts on several different factors. The nine most important factors, considering all types of meetings, are ranked for both corporations and associations in Exhibit 14. A decision on a specific hotel or resort to be used for a meeting is made when a facility is judged to be superior on the factors appropriate for the meeting being planned.

Individual factors may vary in importance. The most important factors in the selection of a facility for corporate directors' meetings and association board meetings are the number/quality of sleeping and meeting rooms, the quality of food service, the efficiency of check-in/check-out/billing procedures, and the price/value relationship. The least important are the price of meeting rooms, the price of sleeping rooms, the price of food service, and recreation, shopping, and entertainment. This distinction between quality and price is consistent among all types of corporate meetings and reflects a willingness on the part of many corporations to pay for quality meeting facilities and

EXHIBIT 14 Importance of Factors in the Selection of a Meeting Facility

Facility Selection Factors	*Corporate Planner*	*Association Planner*
Quality of food service	1	2
Number/quality of sleeping rooms	2 (tie)	4
Price/value relationship	2 (tie)	1
Efficiency of check-in/check-out/billing	3	5
Number/quality of meeting rooms	4	3
Price of sleeping rooms	5	7
Price of food service	6	8
Price of meeting rooms	7	6
Recreation/shopping/entertainment	8	9

Source: Independent marketing research study.

accommodations. The same is true for the board meetings of associations and some national conventions. In this instance, the meeting reflects on the association which necessitates quality facilities and accommodations with less concern about price. The other association meetings such as professional/technical, educational, and regional/state/local chapter meetings are more concerned with the prices of meeting and sleeping rooms and the price of food service. The reason is that these meetings are "business oriented" and the attendees have limited expense accounts or are paying their own expenses.

Approving the Meeting Facility Selection

Following the selection of a meeting facility, approval of the choice is the next step in the planning and decision-making process. In corporations, final approval of the meeting facility often rests with the manager of the functional area holding the meeting. A Vice President of Sales, for example, will approve a facility recommended by the meeting planner for a sales meeting.

The association facility approval is often a group decision and many associations have committees for this purpose. Since an association tries to represent the interests of its membership, board meetings and membership conventions are usually moved from region to region. The committee will generally follow the regional members' recommendations for a meeting because they know the facilities in their region that are most suitable.

If a facility is approved, making the meeting arrangements is the next step. However, if facility approval is not obtained, other alternative meeting facilities will be examined, as was shown in Exhibit 8.

Making Meeting Arrangements

Following approval of the facility, the planner, acting as a liaison between the corporation or association and the hotel or resort, makes the arrangements for the meeting. This includes making reservations for the sleeping and meeting rooms and arranging for food and beverage services, audiovisual equipment, and recreational activities. The meeting planner also decides on the registration and check-out procedures, the billing procedure to be followed, the deposit requirement, and the payment procedure. As the details of the meeting are finalized, the meeting planner reviews the program and makes any additions or changes that are necessary. Usually the program is finalized about two weeks prior to the meeting.

As the meeting arrangements are being made, the planner begins to notify the attendees of the time and place for the meeting and appropriate travel arrangements are made. Finally, just prior to the meeting, a package summarizing the program is prepared for all attendees.

The Meeting

During the meeting, the meeting planner or another designated individual acts as a liaison to handle problems that arise and gather information on how those in attendance are enjoying the meeting. This information is useful in evaluating the meeting and deciding whether or not to return to a particular facility. It is also customary for the hotel or resort to designate a member of the marketing staff to serve as a contact person while the meeting is in progress.

Evaluation of the Meeting

At the conclusion of many meetings, the planner may ask the attendees to formally evaluate the meeting. Areas for evaluation are the meeting program and the hotel or resort's performance in such areas as food services, meeting and sleeping rooms, and recreational facilities and activities.

One method of evaluation is to have the planner ask the attendees, on an informal basis, about the meeting. This method is appropriate for the smaller meetings, such as directors' meetings and board meetings, because the executives are treated in a personal manner. The second evaluation technique is having the meeting attendees complete formal questionnaires. Because a large number of responses can be obtained with relative ease, formal questionnaires are suitable for larger meetings such as national membership conventions.

The results of both methods of evaluation will influence the meeting planner's perceptions of a hotel or resort facility. Since personal perceptions are an important source of information in the selection of a facility, a poor evaluation could reduce the likelihood that the facility will be considered or selected for any future meetings.

EVALUATION OF THE ADIRONDACK MANOR

A final aspect of the marketing research asked meeting planners to evaluate Adirondack Manor on several attributes judged to be important in selecting a conference facility. While the meeting planners had not seen the new facility at the time the evaluation was made, many of the planners were familiar with the resort and several had attended

EXHIBIT 15 Ratings of Adirondack Manor by Corporate and Association Meeting Planners*

Aspects of the Manor	*Corporate Planners*	*Association Planners*	*All Planners*
Reputation/image	4.21	4.37	4.30
Recreational facilities	3.95	4.26	4.14
Environmental setting	3.82	4.30	4.10
Overall quality of the resort	3.97	4.12	4.06
Food	3.78	4.12	4.01
Helpfulness/dependability of sales staff	3.67	4.04	3.88
Courtesy/helpfulness of bellhops, waiters, maids, etc.	3.77	4.18	3.86
Sleeping rooms	3.31	3.68	3.53
Price/value	3.08	3.49	3.32
Meeting facilities	2.50	2.59	2.55
Location/accessibility	2.25	2.21	2.23

* Average scores are from a 5-point rating scale where 1 = Unsatisfactory and 5 = Ideal.

Source: Independent marketing research study.

small meetings in the previous facility or had visited the Manor as a social guest.

The ratings, shown in Exhibit 15, indicate that the Manor is viewed favorably on many of the factors important to meeting planners. Association planners, in particular, rated the Manor favorably because a higher percentage had planned and attended meetings there and were simply more familiar with the resort than their corporate counterparts who spent less time planning meetings.

The management of the Manor was encouraged by the evaluations, because a number of the factors that were rated highly could be considered competitive strengths. For instance, both corporate and association meeting planners rated the Manor's reputation/image as being almost ideal, and the recreational facilities, environmental setting, food services, and overall quality were also rated highly. The fact that the environmental setting was viewed as highly favorable seemed to suggest that, although the Manor was difficult to reach, the seclusion of the resort may be worth the extra travel. Management was not especially concerned about the planner's evaluation of the Manor's meeting facilities. The new facility was expected to accommodate the future needs of meeting planners and remedy this competitive weakness.

Case Group B

Product Strategy

Case 6

The Seven-Up Company

J. Paul Peter
University of Wisconsin–Madison

7UP was first introduced in 1929 under the name "Bib-Label Lithiated Lemon-Lime Soda." It was soon renamed "7UP" and handily outsold the more than 600 other lemon-lime drinks on the market. It is still the traditional lemon-lime soft drink and the number one seller in that category. It has been promoted over the years with a number of campaigns including "Nothing does it like 7UP," "Wet and Wild," "The Uncola," "America is turning 7UP," and "Never had it, never will." The last campaign mentioned focused on the fact that 7UP does not have caffeine in it as do most colas. By far, the most successful of these campaigns was "The Uncola" campaign which positioned 7UP as an alternative to colas rather than just a mixer or a medicinal product.

The Seven-Up Company was purchased in 1978 by Philip Morris, a

Sources: "A Slow Rebound for Seven-Up," *Business Week,* October 12, 1981, pp. 107–8; "Seven-Up's Sudden Taste for Cola," *Fortune,* May 17, 1982, pp. 101–3; "Knocked from Third Place, 7UP Is Going Flat," *Fortune,* May 14, 1984, p. 96.

company known for its marketing skills with successful products such as Marlboro cigarettes and Miller Lite beer. However, 7UP has lost money four of the first five years that it has been a Philip Morris company. For example, in 1983, 7UP had an operating loss of $10.8 million on revenues of $650 million.

The soft drink industry is growing about 4 percent per year and is dominated by colas, which account for 62 percent of the $17-billion-a-year U.S. soft drink market. While about 17 percent of adults in the U.S. drink lemon-lime soft drinks, this category accounts for only about 12 percent of total soft drink sales. While 7UP's market share varies, in 1983 it captured 5.6 percent of the soft drink market. While it is traditionally the number three soft drink behind Coke and Pepsi, in 1984 it slid to fourth place behind Diet Coke.

While 7UP faces fierce competition from colas, it also has a variety of competitors in the lemon-line market. In addition to Bubble-Up and Teem, the Coca-Cola company aggressively promotes Sprite, a 7UP equivalent, with the stated goal of converting 7UP users. In 1981, Sprite was mentioned in twice as many ads as 7UP. In 1984, PepsiCo introduced its own lemon-lime drink, Slice, which contains 10 percent real fruit juice, and aggressively promoted it against both 7UP and Sprite.

As mentioned, 7UP promotion in 1984 focused on the fact that 7UP is caffeine free. Research by the company indicated that 66 percent of American adults and 47 percent of teenagers stated they would be interested in buying a soda without caffeine. The Seven-Up Company used the same caffeine-free positioning in 1982 when it introduced its own cola, Like. While the introduction was supported with a $50-million advertising campaign, Like did not capture a large market share. The anticaffeine position was easily neutralized as both Coke and Pepsi introduced caffeine-free versions of most of their colas.

7UP is distributed by 464 bottlers. Of these, 337 also distribute a competing cola such as Coke, Pepsi, or Royal Crown. It has been reported that there may be more conflict between 7UP and its bottlers than between Coke and Pepsi and their bottlers. For one thing, many of the bottlers viewed 7UP's anticaffeine promotion as a threat to them and the soft drink industry. Also, it has been reported that Coke and Pepsi offer more and better discounts to bottlers than does 7UP. Finally, at the retail level, many restaurants prefer to deal with only one bottler who has a full line of soft drinks. For example, McDonald's has elected to standardize beverages in its 6,250 U.S. restaurants and approves only three drinks: Coke, Sprite, and an orange flavor. However, McDonald's managers can still stock Diet 7UP as it is on the company-authorized list of optional beverages.

DISCUSSION QUESTIONS

1. What are the major situational factors affecting 7UP?
2. What is 7UP's competitive differential advantage?
3. What is the target market for 7UP?
4. What should 7UP do to regain market share and profitability?

Case 7

Mead Products: The Trapper Keeper®*

Peter S. Carusone
Wright State University

"You know, this just might be the most fantastic product we've ever launched. I think it's really going to shake up the school supplies market!" The man who spoke was Bryant Crutchfield, Mead Products' New Ventures manager.

Mr. Crutchfield had just concluded a meeting in Wichita, Kansas, with Bob Crandall, the regional sales manager, where the two men reviewed results of an August 1978 market test. The purpose of the test was to measure market acceptance of Trapper® Portfolio and the Trapper Keeper® Notebook.

As he prepared to depart Wichita Airport for Dayton, Ohio, Mr. Crutchfield felt good about the success of the test. A new unique product unlike anything else on the market—and a total sell-through in test market.

But Crutchfield also thought about plans for 1979 and the big question yet to be resolved. "How many can we sell nationally?"

MEAD CORPORATION

Mead's traditional base is in forest products. From a strong base in pulp, paper, and paperboard, Mead has developed a family of related businesses. Lumber operations complement those in pulp. Other divisions convert paper and paperboard into packaging, containers, school supplies, and many more industrial and consumer products; some specialize in their distribution.

Still other Mead businesses provide additional growth opportunities and balance—engineered castings, molded rubber parts, distribution of piping and electrical supplies, and advanced digital systems for

* This case was written by Peter S. Carusone, Professor of Marketing, Wright State University. Copyrighted by Peter S. Carusone. Reprinted with permission.

managing and reproducing vast amounts of information. See Appendix A for a list of the Mead divisions and affiliates.

Innovation at Mead in the 1970s focused on areas beyond but closely related to its traditional businesses. Advanced and sophisticated product developments emerged from expertise and knowledge in printing technology, pollutant management, information handling, and digital technology.

Mead Data Central's LEXIS and NEXIS are the world's most sophisticated services for text research of case law and news materials. Information is channeled into the system from the courts, Congress, news media, and other sources, and flows on demand to thousands of subscriber terminals in the professions, business, government, and education.

Ink-jet printing, which involved the parallel development of hardware and software by Mead Digital Systems, is a new technology that promises to revolutionize the printing industry in many fields. The process results from generating and directing millions of minute drops of ink—precisely and at high speed—to form words, numerals, and images. Ink-jet printing makes it possible to simultaneously compose and imprint personalized materials three times faster than any conventional method.

Mead's CompuChem special chemical analysis service has opened the nation's largest automated laboratory devoted exclusively to the analysis of priority pollutants. Client companies in the petroleum, coal, pulp, paper, rubber, and other industries ship samples to the SuperLab where materials that the Environmental Protection Agency has ruled as potentially hazardous are identified and measured (in parts per trillion).

The Mead Corporation's development philosophy was summarized in the company's 1980 Annual Report:

> Mead's underlying strategic principle is to devote its investment resources to market segments that are growing, that need products and services we are prepared to deliver, and that offer us the opportunity to build or retain a position of cost-effective leadership.

In 1980 Mead sales hit a record $2.7 billion, a 69 percent increase from 1976. The firm employs 25,000 men and women. Its World Headquarters is located in Dayton, Ohio.

MEAD PRODUCTS

A division of Mead Corporation, Mead Products (formerly Westab) is the largest U.S. manufacturer and marketer of school and college supplies, stationery, photo albums, and home/office supplies. Westab was founded in 1927 (as the Western Tablet and Stationery Corp.) and merged with Mead Corporation in 1966.

Since its inception, Mead Products has developed and marketed numerous items which stand as all-time best sellers in the retail school supply and stationery markets. Perhaps it is most famous for its line of *Spiral®* brand wirebound school supplies that uses a unique method of wire-binding large quantities of tablet paper, and revolutionized the design and production of notebooks, theme books, and memo pads.

The Organizer®, a tri-fold pockets and pad binder, introduced in 1972 was the industry's best-selling school supply item for three consecutive years. Other exclusive Mead Products' introductions include *The System®* (in 1973), *The Spiral Organizer®* (in 1974), the Data Center® (in 1975), and *The Pinchless One®* (in 1976). These also have been best sellers.

Other well-known Mead Products include: *The Big Chief®* writing tablet, a best seller for over seven generations; *The Valet®* tablet and envelope stationery line which started a revolution in the 59-cents-per-item market; *Academie™* brand artists pads, books, water colors, and crayons; and *Montag®*, a famous name in quality, boxed stationery. See Appendix B for a list of key Mead Products trademarks.

The company traditionally has been a trendsetter in the industry. In 1966, for example, Mead Products was the first to replace the drab, blue canvas coverings on loose-leaf binders with various fabrics in fashionable colors and designs. More recently, through innovative manufacturing techniques, "photo-graphics" have been applied to the covers of numerous school supply items.

Another industry first was Mead Products' decision 12 years ago to advertise on national network television. During the season the commercials are running (late August, early September), Mead Products becomes one of the largest TV advertisers in the country—of any product.

Today, Mead Products, with its own sales force, markets over 3,000 separate items. National distribution is obtained through wholesalers, distributors, and jobbers, as well as direct to chain discount, drug, variety, food and convenience stores, and department and college stores. The company operates seven plants and 12 sales offices/showrooms in 10 states. See Appendix C for facility locations.

HOW THE TRAPPER® AND THE TRAPPER KEEPER® ORIGINATED

The idea for *The Trapper®* and *The Trapper Keeper®* was identified by extensive informal exploration of the school supplies market and its total environment. "Management requires us to do a complete situation analysis," Mr. Crutchfield points out. "We have to understand what's happening in the marketplace."

A situation analysis at Mead Products entails extensive study of everything that happens from production of products, through the channels of distribution, to their consumption. It includes analysis of educational trends, consumer trends, sales trends, product usage, competition, the trade, and pertinent external factors.

Consumer Definition

People of all ages involved in the learning process are the consumers of school supplies. The range is from the preschooler just learning how to hold a crayon up to and including the adult taking refresher courses to update professional skills.

Consumer Population

The total student population was projected to continue to increase over the next five years but at a lesser rate than in the past. While the number of grade, junior, and senior high school students was declining slightly, the decline would be more than offset by increases in two other consumer segments: (1) preschool kids who in just a few years will become primary customers and (2) college enrollment and adult basic and occupational education. See Exhibit 1 for consumer population/enrollment trends.

Product Usage

Consumer product usage in the growth market segments (except for preschoolers) was basically the same as that of students in grade and high school: wirebounds, filler, binders, and portfolios. And, increasing in popularity were portfolios, wirebound notebooks, and selected binders. These select binders are those having pads and pockets that provide for versatile storage of a variety of materials. The demand for filler paper and ring notebooks was relatively flat. See Exhibit 1 for product usage by consumer group and consumer expenditures by product category.

Educational Trends

Important educational trends were identified, along with implications for future demand of various kinds of school supplies. It was learned, for example, that students were taking more courses, more advanced courses, and more individualized instruction. Also uncovered were increased use of timely, specialized portable materials, more use of shared classrooms, and smaller lockers. The impact of the energy shortage and emergence of a market for left-handed students also were assessed. See Exhibit 1 for detailed analysis of educational trends.

Trade Analysis

As changes in education were affecting the need for, and usage of, school supplies, so changes in retail shopping patterns were affecting the opportunities for effective distribution of school supply products. Combination stores (food and drug) were growing. Independent drugstores were declining while the drug chains were merging. Growing rapidly and becoming very popular were the convenience food stores particularly in certain markets. There were, for example, 864 convenience stores in Houston; 627 in Atlanta. In some cities the number of convenience stores was twice the number of food stores. Another important retail type store beginning to emerge was the minicombo (convenience and drug combination).

Competition

The school supplies market was very fragmented. Competition was mostly regional due to the high cost of freight. Only one or two companies other than Mead Products were selling nationally. Mead was the leader nationally, but this varied by product line and by region.

A NEED UNFULFILLED

The outcome of the situation analysis was that it led Mr. Crutchfield to formulate the following thesis: *There is a need for a notebook to hold and organize the portfolios.*

"We saw that students were taking more courses—some of these a variety of 'mini' courses. We saw an increase in the use of pocket portfolios—growth in excess of 20 percent annually. We knew from research that they were using one portfolio per subject or class. With the increased number of classes and portfolios, a student needs some place to keep them organized. What's more," Mr. Crutchfield points out, "traditional ports with horizontal pockets have a tendency to spill their contents when mistakenly turned upside down. So, the Trapper® Portfolio and the Trapper Keeper® notebook would provide the student with both better portfolios and a place to keep them organized." Exhibit 2 shows a picture of the two products.

EXHIBIT 1

Mead

School Supplies

CONSUMER AND EDUCATIONAL INFORMATION

Consumer Population/Enrollment

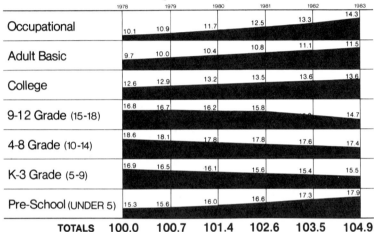

	1978	1979	1980	1981	1982	1983
Occupational	10.1	10.9	11.7	12.5	13.3	14.3
Adult Basic	9.7	10.0	10.4	10.8	11.1	11.5
College	12.6	12.9	13.2	13.5	13.6	13.6
9-12 Grade (15-18)	16.8	16.7	16.2	15.8	[illegible]	14.7
4-8 Grade (10-14)	18.6	18.1	17.8	17.8	17.6	17.4
K-3 Grade (5-9)	16.9	16.5	16.1	15.6	15.4	15.5
Pre-School (UNDER 5)	15.3	15.6	16.0	16.6	17.3	17.9
TOTALS	**100.0**	**100.7**	**101.4**	**102.6**	**103.5**	**104.9**

Product Usage by Consumer Group

	HIGH	MEDIUM	BOUGHT BY
Occupational	Wirebound Notebooks Ring Notebooks Notebook Paper Portfolios/Folders		Adult user—some purchased in regular channels others are provided by employers
Adult	Wirebound Notebooks Ring Notebooks Notebook Paper Portfolios/Folders		Adult user
College	Wirebound Notebooks	Ring Notebooks Notebook Paper Portfolios/Folders	Nearly 100% user
9-12 Grade	Wirebound Notebooks Clipboards Ring Notebooks Lt. Wt. Ring Notebooks Portfolios/Folders	Spiral Organizer* Wirebound Data Center* The System* Data Center* Notebook Paper	89% Student 11% Parent (Parents buy primarily parity products)
4-8 Grade	Ring Notebooks Clipboards Notebook Paper The System* The Organizer* Data Center* Portfolios/Folders	Wirebound Notebooks Classifiler*	75% Student 25% Parent (Parents buy primarily parity products)
K-3 Grade	Pencil Tablets Folders Drawing Paper	Classifiler* The System* The Organizer* Data Center* Ring Notebooks Portfolios/Folders	80-90% Parent 20-10% Student
Pre-School	Drawing Paper Scribble Pads	Pencil Tablets	Parent/child influence

Mead

Courthouse Plaza, Northeast, Dayton, Ohio 45463

EXHIBIT 1 *(concluded)*

EDUCATIONAL TRENDS

MORE COURSES

- Today's students are taking more courses. The average student takes in excess of seven . . . these courses consist of special subjects, like: Black History; Literature; mini-courses in specialized fields; plus, art and hobby and craft courses.
- With this increase in the average number of courses taken, students have increased their usage of lightweight portable supplies (like portfolios and wirebound notebooks). They tend to use one per subject, class or project.

MORE ADVANCED COURSES

- College level courses are being taught more and more in secondary schools—and courses that have traditionally been considered high school courses—languages, mathematics, etc.—are now available at lower levels.
- Students taking these advanced courses have increased their use of college-type products, such as wirebound notebooks with college ruling and, especially, the popular 9½" x 6" products.

MORE INDIVIDUALIZED INSTRUCTION

- Individualized instruction and programmed learning are on the increase and are most frequently coupled with the use of specialized workbooks, multi-media material and computer terminals.
- Loose-leaf filler is on the decline since students tend to use printed workbooks and computer printouts (or readouts), supplemented with bound books (wirebounds, etc.) for notes, and supplies with pockets for filing and organizing handout materials.

INCREASED USE OF TIMELY, SPECIALIZED PORTABLE MATERIALS

- More and more use is being made of Xerography (to produce materials for classrooms, such as handouts), computer retrieval and microfiche.
- Because of the amount of new information, together with the high cost of editing textbooks, pressure on school budgets and the relative decline in copying costs, textbooks are now being updated with Xeroxed handouts. Due to the quantity of handouts, students have shifted to products with pockets (portfolios, wirebounds with pockets, and special ring notebooks) for storing/organizing handout materials.

SHARED CLASSROOMS

- More and more classrooms are shared due to limited specialized teaching materials. Pilferage has increased with this trend.
- Students are forced to carry valuables with them. This creates a need for products capable of housing everything from pencils to calculators.

SMALLER LOCKERS

- New schools are providing smaller lockers for students and this space is often shared. These students are forced to use lightweight portable supplies.
- Portfolios, wirebounds, special notebooks with pockets, and bags are increasing in popularity.

LEFT-HANDED STUDENTS

- 15% to 20% of today's students (estimated) are left-handed.[1] They are becoming vocal about being forced to use products designed for right-handers.
- Top-bound products are increasing in popularity and usage by this group.

ENERGY SHORTAGE

- Energy shortages are changing the traditional school calendars. There is an increase in trimester and year-round schedules with longer breaks during periods when energy use is high.
- These schedule changes mean more promotional opportunities at times other than the normal school opening dates.

CONSUMER EXPENDITURES IN RETAIL DOLLARS[2]

(ESTIMATED)

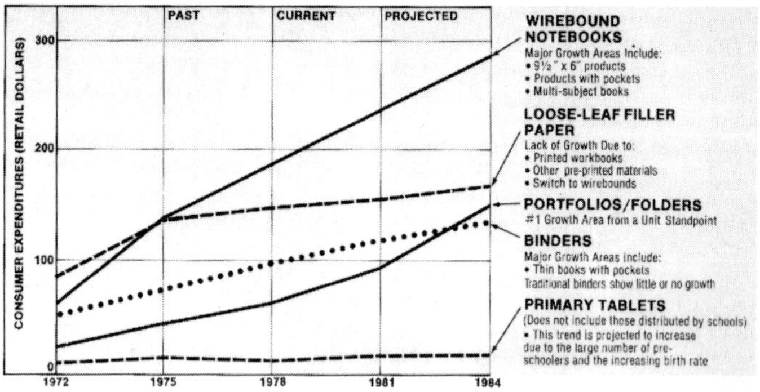

1. Source: International Left-Handers' Society, Milwaukee, Wisc., 1978
2. Sources: Harvard Study, 1971; Burke Study, 1977; A. C. Nielsen Retail Audits, 1978, and S.I.C. Data.

30-79

The best-selling portfolio on the West Coast (Pee-Chee®) has a vertical pocket—but it had never been popular east of the Rockies. It is interesting to note that part of the rationale for the item occurred to Mr. Crutchfield as the result of a conversation at home with his 13-year-old daughter. In retrospect, he describes the experience as one of "creative listening." In asking his daughter about the usage of port-

EXHIBIT 2

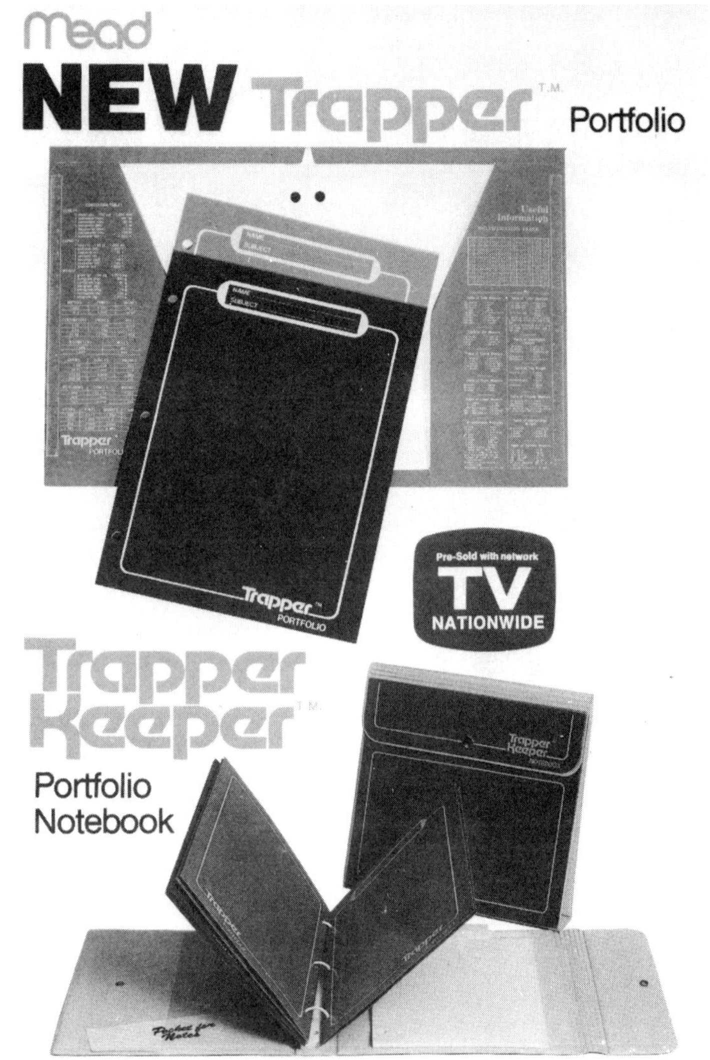

folios in her classes, Mr. Crutchfield thought he heard her relate how the teacher required the students to submit their assignments in portfolios as a time-saving device. The teacher wanted to use the ports both for collecting assignments and for redistributing them, along with handouts, so students could pick up their own portfolios and save classtime. When a Mead researcher was dispatched by Mr. Crutchfield to talk with the teacher, he discovered that the teacher never said that. And when the 13-year-old daughter was questioned further, it was found that she never said that either. But, the results of the research were positive. The teacher thought the "nonexistent procedure" was a good one.

TESTING THE TRAPPER KEEPER®

"We saw this to be a fantastic concept," Mr. Crutchfield recalls. "A portfolio with vertical pockets so that everything is trapped inside when they're closed, and a Trapper Keeper® to keep Trapper® ports organized." Other features added to the inside pockets included a metric ruler, an English ruler, multiplication tables, metric conversion charts, and more. The portfolio (the Trapper®) was punched to fit on rings inside a special portfolio notebook (the Trapper Keeper®) designed to hold the Trapper® ports. The Trapper Keeper® was designed, in turn, with nylon, pinchless rings, three Trapper® ports, a pocket for holding loose materials, and a clip that holds a pad for notes and a place for the pencil. After school or class everything can be snapped together for transporting home—nothing falls out.

Teacher Research

The next step in development of the Trapper® and Trapper Keeper® was to determine if the basic product concept had merit. Before making any product, illustrations of the concept were drawn and used to conduct a focus group session with teachers. Was there truly a need for this product? Would teachers recommend it?

Basically, the results were: teachers said that student organization was their biggest problem, and that they would recommend this or any product that helped students improve their organization.

Market Test

To get some measure of student reaction, a test market was set up in Wichita, Kansas, in August 1978. The primary objectives of the test were to determine:

1. Product salability.
2. Rate of sale compared to The Organizer®, Data Center®, The System®, plus comparable competitive products.

Pricing of the Trapper Keeper® was pegged at the same level as the Data Center® and The Organizer®, ranging from a low of $1.99 (on a weekend sale) to a high of $3.99—the most frequent price being $2.49. The Trapper® ranged from four for 98 cents to 29 cents each—the most frequent price being 29 cents.

The total market (ADI) was monitored from a sell-in and sell-through standpoint. Fifteen representative stores were audited: seven discount, three variety, three drug, and two food. The product was advertised on TV at 180 GRPs, which is equivalent to everyone seeing the commercial 1.8 times. A photoscript of the commercial is presented as Exhibit 3.

The market test results, in audited stores, were as follows:

1. For every 100 Trapper Keeper® notebook purchased by the consumer—77 Trapper® portfolios, 90 Data Center®, 65 The Organizer®, and 39 The System® notebooks were sold.
2. Trapper® portfolios totally sold out in over 90 percent of the stores, so the top potential was not known.
3. There was very little cannibalization of The Organizer®, Data Center®, or The System® notebooks. These items sold at approximately the same level this year as last—in some cases, they were totally sold out.
4. Total unit sales of all items increased 38.5 percent in the monitored stores.

Consumer Post-Test Research

Consumer cards were placed in all the test market products offering a free memo book for filling out and returning a questionnaire card. Over 1,500 cards were returned. Some of the results were:

62 percent of the purchasers were female.

35 percent were between the ages of 9 and 12; 44 percent between 13 and 15; 10 percent between 16 and 18.

81 percent of the portfolio users preferred the Trapper® pocket design over traditional horizontal pockets.

Only 56 percent of the purchasers had used portfolios prior to finding the Trapper®.

Exhibit 4 contains some of the comments of purchasers as to why they purchased Trapper Keeper® rather than other type binders.

Six weeks after the test market, a number of purchasers were inter-

EXHIBIT 3 Photoscript of Trapper Commercial

Teacher Research

Teachers exposed to the product concept in a focus group session concluded the idea was good—it helps solve one of their greatest problems . . . student's organization. The teachers said they would recommend students use Trapper Keeper® notebooks or any school product that helps them organize their school work.

Market Test

The products were tested for salability and rate of sale compared to The Organizer®, Data Center® and comparable competitive products. Trapper Keeper® outsold them all in monitored stores. For every 100 Trapper Keepers®, 90 Data Centers®, 65 Organizers® and 39 The Systems® were sold. Best of all . . . total unit sales (all items) increased 38.5% in the monitored stores. This means plus business for you as new users were created.

Post Use Research

A sample of Trapper Keeper® notebook purchasers/users were interviewed via phone after 2½ months of product use:

- 95% rated the Trapper Keeper® notebook excellent or good.
- 88% said the Trapper Keeper® notebook was better than previous product used.
- 84% intended to repurchase the Trapper Keeper® notebook.
- Trapper Keeper® notebook users tended to be older.

Introduced to educators in early 1979

Educators will be introduced to Trapper® portfolios and Trapper Keeper® notebooks through contacts at the Board of Education level and through teachers' magazines.

Presold on Network TV in August

The following commercial will be shown on network TV in August. Approximately 250 GRP's, which is equivalent to everyone seeing the following ad 2.5 times.

TWO HIGH SCHOOL BOYS AT THEIR LOCKERS, TAKING OUT THEIR TEXT BOOKS FOR THE NEXT CLASS. ONE BOY HAS ONLY A TRAPPER® PORTFOLIO THE OTHER HAS A THICK NOTEBOOK BRIMMING WITH LOOSE PAPERS. (BELL RINGS)

1ST BOY: That's all you're taking to class?

2ND BOY: Everything I need is in my Trapper Portfolio.

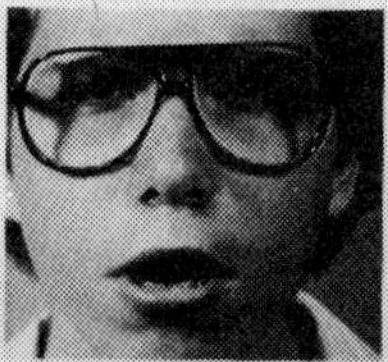

1ST BOY: Trapper?

HE OPENS THE TRAPPER, SLIDES PAPERS IN AND OUT TO DEMONSTRATE.
2ND BOY: It traps in all my papers. The pocket is built this way . . . so . . .

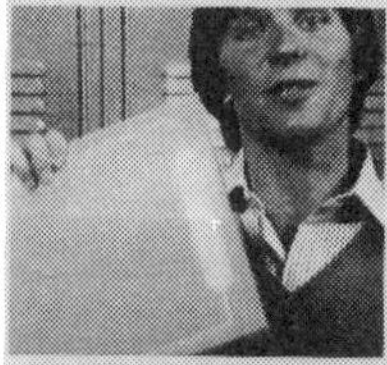

HE CLOSES THE TRAPPER . . . THEN SHAKES IT UP AND DOWN . . . DEMONSTRATING HOW THE PAPERS CAN'T FALL OUT.
2ND BOY: . . . close the Trapper . . . and the papers are trapped in. One Trapper for each class.

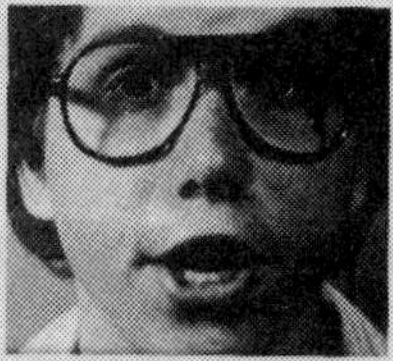

1ST BOY: Where do you keep um?

CUT TO THE TRAPPER KEEPER.
2ND BOY: In the Trapper Keeper . . .

2ND BOY: . . . which also has a note pad and pencil clip.

HE CLOSES THE TRAPPER KEEPER® NOTEBOOK AND SNAPS IT SHUT.
2ND BOY: After school snap everything in my Trapper Keeper and take it home . . . what could be neater.

GIRL APPROACHES
1ST BOY: (GESTURING TOWARD THE GIRL) . . . a date with her.

CUT TO PRODUCT SHOT.
SUPER: "TRAPPER"
"TRAPPER KEEPER" "MEAD"
VO ANNCR: The Trapper and Trapper Keeper, only from Mead.

2ND BOY INTRODUCES GIRL TO 1ST BOY . . . THE COVER OF 1ST BOY'S BINDER FLOPS OPEN, SPILLING THE PAPERS.
2ND BOY: Hi . . .
MEAD SUPER APPEARS.

EXHIBIT 4 Selected Comments from Consumer Cards

- "Because it's new, slender, and the way it's put together."
- "One reason, it had separate folders, but mainly because of the colors."
- "My mother got it by mistake but I'd seen it on TV, so decided to keep it."
- "Because I like neat, and things are easy to find. Thanks."
- "Our teacher made us buy one—but I have been very pleased with it."*
- "I heard it was good. My girlfriend had one."
- "If you trip, all your papers won't go flying all over the place."
- "Because they keep your papers where they belong. They're really great—everybody has got one."
- "I saw ad on TV."
- "Instead of taking the whole thing you can take only one part home."
- "So when the kids in my class throw it, the papers won't fly all over."
- "It was the only one left in the store."

* Several cards with comments like this were received and traced back to a 9th grade teacher (Mrs. Willard) in Wellington, Kansas. Mrs. Willard agreed to endorse the Trapper Keeper® and her comments were used in an ad campaign to other teachers. See ad in Exhibit 5.

viewed and asked to evaluate the products. The key results of this research were as follows:

General Reaction:
95%—believe Trapper Keeper® to be excellent or good
88%—rate Trapper Keeper® better than product used previously

Trapper Keeper® features most liked:
89%—ports inside, paper won't fall out, and one portfolio for each subject.
84%—intended to repurchase the Trapper Keeper®

Trapper® features most liked:
47%—vertical pocket/papers won't fall out
21%—helpful information (metric conversion, etc.)

NATIONAL PLANS

It was decided to introduce the Trapper Keeper® nationally for school opening 1979. The introduction was to be backed by a national, prime-time, network television campaign of 230 to 250 GRPs—approximately 20 spots.

Products were to be presented to teachers and boards of education during the spring for approval and recommendations at school opening in August/September. Teachers' magazines and personal calls were planned to reach the teachers and administrators. Teachers were offered a sample Trapper Keeper® at a special price to cover handling

EXHIBIT 5

Why did Mrs. Willard in Wellington, Kansas advise her students to purchase a Mead Trapper Keeper™ Notebook? For the same reasons you will.
"As a 9th grade teacher, I'm always on the lookout for products that will help my students do a better job in school. Last year, I found the Trapper™ portfolio and Trapper Keeper™ notebook from Mead and recommended them to my class.
Mead developed the products because today's students are taking more courses than ever. They average over seven courses per student. They can't carry seven notebooks, so they are switching to portfolios.
Mead has designed a new portfolio called the Trapper. It traps in all the student's papers so they won't fall out. Mead has also developed a notebook to carry all these portfolios, called the Trapper Keeper.
Most students keep the Trapper Keeper in their locker. Then, they just change Trappers from class to class, taking only one Trapper to each class. With no large notebooks to carry around, they travel light and easy. After school, they take the Trapper Keeper home with all the Trappers inside.
The Trapper and Trapper Keeper have been tested in actual use. Everyone, teachers and students alike, agree that the Trapper and Trapper Keeper make school easier and better."
Special Teacher Offer. Because the Trapper and Trapper Keeper may help you in organizing your classes, Mead wants you to have a sample of the Trapper Keeper (with 3 Trapper portfolios included) for the cost of postage and handling ($2.00). These products will be available to your students the start of school next fall. So, it's a good chance to try it out ahead of your students. You might find you want to recommend it.
Mead
I'd like to try the Trapper and Trapper Keeper. I'm sending along $2.00 (to cover postage and handling). Would you please send me a set of the 3 Trappers and a Trapper Keeper.
Send to: Mead Products, PO Box 148, 11th & Mitchell Avenue, St. Joseph, Missouri 64502.
Name
Address
City
State Zip
Offer expires December 31, 1979

and postage. A copy of the "Mrs. Willard Testimonial" advertisement to teachers is reproduced in Exhibit 5.

The Trapper® portfolio had a suggested retail price of 29 cents each. Three colors—red, blue, and green—were packaged per assortment. The Trapper Keeper® had a suggested retail of $4.85 each. These were available in three solid colors and three designs: soccer, dog and cat, and Oregon coast.

The distribution plan covered all major types of outlets: mass merchandisers, food, drug, combo stores, variety stores, and others. The strategy would be to concentrate on major regional and national chains.

The sales presentation methods were to include use of a "sell brochure," a slide presentation, a TV commercial, a TV storyboard, and a chain survey sheet.

A sales forecast, by region, would be needed by December 1978. The national account contacts would be made in December and January, with regional sell taking place in February through May. Key account activity would be monitored weekly.

Appendix A Mead Corporation

Divisions

- Mead Paper—Chillicothe (OH)
- Mead Fine Paper
- Mead Publishing Paper
- Gilbert Paper
- Specialty Paper
- Mead Paperboard
- Mead Paperboard Products
- Mead Containers
- Mead Packaging
- Mead Pulp Sales, Inc.
- Mead Products
- Mead Merchants
- Gulf Consolidated Services
- Lynchburg Foundry
- Mulga Coal Company
- Murray Rubber
- Mead Data Central
- Mead Digital Systems
- Mead CompuChem
- Mead Office Services
- Mead Reinsurance

Affiliates (50 percent owned)

- Georgia Kraft Company
- Brunswick Pulp & Paper Company
- Northwood Forest Industries Limited
- Schoeller Technical Papers, Inc.

Appendix B Key Mead Products Trademarks

The Spiral®
The Organizer®
Data Center®
The System®
The Home Organizers™
The Classifiler™
Twin Wire®
The Pinchless One®
The Valet®
Campus®
Class Mate®
Montag®
Trapper® Portfolio
Trapper Keeper® Notebook
Flex 3™ Notebook
Flex 3™ Expandable
Envelok™ Folio

Appendix C Mead Products Locations

Headquarters
Mead Products
Mead World Headquarters
Courthouse Plaza, Northeast
Dayton, Ohio 45463

Plants
Garden Grove, California
Atlanta, Georgia
Kalamazoo, Michigan
St. Joseph, Missouri
Salem, Oregon
Alexandria, Pennsylvania
Garland, Texas

Sales Offices/Showrooms
Garden Grove, California
San Jose, California
Atlanta, Georgia
Des Plaines (Chicago), Illinois
Braintree, Massachusetts
Kalamazoo, Michigan
Shawnee Mission (Kansas City), Missouri
Union City, New Jersey
Salem, Oregon
Dallas, Texas

Case 8

MidAmerica BancSystem, Inc.*

James E. Nelson
University of Colorado

Chuck Smith walked briskly across the lobby of the Fairview Heights bank to his office. It was 7:30 A.M., November 2, 1984. He would have at least two hours before the rush of Friday customers would begin. Friday always meant a great deal of "public relations" for Smith in terms of his exchanging greetings and small talk with customers. "Today I could do without it," Smith thought. "I'd much rather work on what the marketing committee discussed yesterday." However, he knew that many customers expected to see his door open and his face break into a smile of recognition whenever they voiced a greeting. Two hours would give him enough time to get some thoughts down on the automated teller machine (ATM) issue. The other topics that he had discussed with the committee would have to wait until the weekend.

MIDAMERICA BANCSYSTEM, INC.

MidAmerica Bank and Trust Company of Fairview Heights was one of six members of MidAmerica BancSystem, Inc., a multibank holding company under the laws of the state of Illinois. Five of the six subsidiaries were located within 25 miles of each other in St. Clair and Madison counties. The sixth, MidAmerica Bank and Trust Company of Carbondale, was almost 80 miles away in Jackson County. St. Clair and Madison counties were due east of St. Louis, Missouri, just across the Mississippi River. Jackson County to the southeast also bordered the Mississippi.

MidAmerica BancSystem, Inc., was formed on August 31, 1982,

* This case was written by Professor James E. Nelson, University of Colorado. This case is intended for use as a basis for class discussion rather than to illustrate either effective or ineffective administrative decision making. Some data are disguised.

about one year after enactment of an Illinois law permitting multibank holding companies. Prior to this date, the six subsidiary banks were considered "affiliated" in the sense that they shared a number of officers and directors. MidAmerica BancSystem, Inc., provided auditing, investment, and accounting services for its subsidiaries. It contracted with an independent organization for computer services and managed the ATM service. In short, the holding company had authority and responsibility for major financial and marketing decisions for all subsidiaries. As an example of financial decision making, senior management of the holding company had decided in late 1983 to sell $14.7 million (par value) of long-term securities at a loss of over $1.2 million. The sale made possible the purchase of higher yielding U.S. government securities with much shortened maturities. Senior management also had charged off about $2.7 million in loans (primarily agricultural) in late 1983, an amount some nine times that for 1982. Together the actions had produced a net loss of $2.9 million for 1983 (see Exhibit 1 for financial data) but promised long-term benefits in terms of liquidity, flexibility, and return.

Senior management had been less decisive in making marketing decisions. However, now that financial matters had been resolved, attention turned to marketing. A marketing committee had been formed at the request of the holding company's new chairman of the board and president, James Watt. Watt had joined the holding company in this capacity in late 1983, replacing David Charles who had served as chairman and president since 1958. Watt's previous experience included positions as senior vice president of Essex County Bank and Trust in Boston, senior vice president of the Bank Marketing Association in Chicago, and vice president of Beverly Bancorporation in Chicago. Watt held an MS in marketing and thus took a keen interest in the marketing issues facing MidAmerica BancSystem, Inc. Chuck Smith chaired the marketing committee.

MARKETING ISSUES

Smith settled into his chair (the office door shut) and reread the four marketing issues he had summarized last night:

1. What should be our response to the Shop and Save proposal to allow installation of MidAmerica ATMs in 20 supermarkets in St. Clair and Madison counties?
2. How can we increase use of our current ATMs?
3. How do we translate corporate financial goals in marketing goals? How do we make marketing goals part of the management process?
4. What should be MidAmerica's marketing strategy over the next five years?

EXHIBIT 1 Financial Data

	1981	*1982*	*1983*	*1984**
Assets	$198,339	$211,067	$202,104	$208,093
Liabilities	183,268	195,415	189,872	194,312
Stockholders' equity	15,071	15,652	12,232	13,781
Interest income	22,687	23,399	20,807	16,871
Interest expense	14,300	15,460	12,871	10,051
Net interest income	8,387	7,939	7,936	6,820
Provision for possible loan losses	285	309	4,140	258
Net interest income after provision for possible loan losses	8,102	7,630	3,796	6,562
Other income	1,676	1,685	711	1,758
Other expenses	7,473	7,924	8,482	6,242
Income (loss) before income taxes and extraordinary item	2,305	1,391	(3,975)	2,078
Income taxes	401	43	(1,080)	803
Income (loss) before extraordinary item	1,904	1,348	(2,895)	1,275
Extraordinary item tax benefit	—	—	—	713
Net income (loss)	1,904	1,348	(2,895)	1,988
Deposit growth (%)	3.9	6.2	−2.0	−1.5
Return on assets (%)	1.0	0.6	−1.4	1.0
Return on equity (%)	12.6	8.6	−23.7	14.4
Capital to assets (%)	7.6	7.4	6.1	6.6

Note: All data are stated in thousands of dollars except data for deposit growth, return on assets, return on equity, and capital to assets.
* As of September 1984.

Smith knew that senior management of the holding company considered all issues to be high-priority items.

The Shop and Save Proposal

Early in October the president of the Fairview Heights bank had paid a call on the manager of a Shop and Save supermarket located in nearby Belleville, Illinois. The purpose of the call was to see if the store had any interest in installing a MidAmerica ATM. The timing could not have been better—the store was soon to begin a remodeling project and could easily accommodate an ATM. The store's policies did not permit check cashing, nor would they allow a customer to write a check for an amount greater than that purchased. Consequently, the store manager was greatly interested in the installation, provided the system could be used by a large number of the store's customers.

This meant that the ATM had to be available to customers of banks that belonged to Magna Group, Inc., a nine-bank holding company serving many of the same market areas as MidAmerica. Contact with the marketing director for Magna had disclosed that Magna had about 60,000 cards and 36 ATMs in use in the two-county area. These figures greatly exceeded MidAmerica's 10,100 cards and 12 ATMs. The marketing director had shown strong interest in sharing ATM facilities currently in operation, as well as any others either holding company might add. Senior management at both organizations viewed ATMs as a highly desirable service. They also felt that a key to successful implementation of the service was convenient and widespread locations.

A letter from the marketing director summarized Magna's interest and its desire for a $1.50 charge for each interchange transaction. That is, each time a MidAmerica cardholder used a Magna ATM, MidAmerica would be billed $1.50. The same amount would be billed to Magna for each of their cardholders' transactions on a MidAmerica ATM. Smith thought that the charge could be negotiated upward or downward by 25 cents.

Smith was not sure just what sharing meant in terms of interchange usage. He estimated that MidAmerica cardholders might use Magna ATMs for between 10,000 and 30,000 transactions per month. On the other hand, Magna cardholders could use MidAmerica ATMs between 10,000 and 60,000 times per month. The most likely outcome was somewhere in between.

Once MidAmerica had obtained agreement with Magna, negotiations with chain management at Shop and Save could proceed. Chain management had become involved with the Belleville store decision and had quickly proposed that MidAmerica place ATMs in all 20 stores in St. Clair and Madison counties. The chain wanted placement in each store because of its check-cashing policies and what it saw as an opportunity for increased revenues. The proposal called for Shop and Save to receive $600 per ATM per month in rent and 10 cents per each transaction beyond 2,500 per ATM per month. The proposal noted that a similar system in its Springfield, Illinois, stores averaged about 10,000 transactions per ATM per month.

Smith thought that MidAmerica would be lucky to average 4,000 transactions per ATM per month initially in these stores and might reach 10,000 per month in three to five years. He thought the ratio of MidAmerica cardholder transactions to Magna cardholder transactions would be about 1:3. Shop and Save figures showed the 20 stores to average about 65,000 customers per month, although one store showed only 41,000. Smith thought that Shop and Save might come down somewhat on their rental and transaction charges; he doubted that they would move from their 2,500 figure.

MidAmerica estimates of the installed cost of each ATM were $40,000. The practical life of an ATM was considered to be about six years. Monthly fixed operating costs totalled about $400 per ATM for the computer telephone line, bookkeeping, maintenance, and the service to supply the machines with cash and to collect deposits. The computer service itself charged 40 cents per transaction.

MidAmerica currently billed each of its cardholders $1.00 per transaction. However, many banks in the St. Louis area charged only 50 cents, and some charged nothing. Smith felt that the marketing committee would soon recommend the MidAmerica charge be reduced to 50 cents, although there was some feeling among members that the charge should simply be eliminated.

"Either action should increase usage," Smith thought as he scanned a table of last month's transaction activity. The table showed that usage of cards at MidAmerica's 12 locations actually had fallen 5 percent from September of a year ago. The drop contrasted only slightly with July and August activity, which had shown no growth over usage for the previous year. The 28,400 transactions for September were based on 10,100 cards outstanding, a number that was 4 percent higher than a year ago. Something would have to be done to improve usage to at least 5,000 transactions per ATM per month. This figure was generally considered an industry standard, representing a break-even point between the cost of an ATM and the teller function for which it substituted.

Marketing Goals

The committee also had spent some time discussing marketing goals at MidAmerica. The members' lack of extensive marketing backgrounds made discussion difficult. Nonetheless, Watt and the committee felt it important that MidAmerica personnel at both the holding company and each subsidiary give marketing goals considerable thought. Marketing goals would encourage aggressive marketing actions and give focus to marketing efforts. Marketing goals would also form a standard against which performance could be measured.

This was the first time that the holding company and subsidiaries had ever set marketing goals. Most officers were familiar with financial goal setting and the holding company's financial goals for 1985; an 8 percent growth in deposits, a 1.2 percent return on assets; a 16 percent return on equity; and a 7 percent capital-to-assets ratio. Each subsidiary's financial goals departed somewhat from these figures, dependent on local market conditions and forecasts.

Neither the holding company nor the subsidiaries had translated financial goals into marketing goals. The committee had discussed some criteria for the translation, concluding that marketing goals should be consistent with financial goals and be stated in specific and measurable terms at realistic levels. The committee had even tried to write some marketing goals:

Obtain 200 Vacation Club accounts by October 1985.

Increase IRA deposits by 15 percent.

Book 150 Equity Plus loans by the end of 1985.

Each member had promised to spend more time thinking about marketing goals after yesterday's meeting. Each was also to produce a more complete list of goals by the end of next week, send it to other committee members, and be ready for a discussion at the next meeting. It would be important to get some marketing goals approved at the holding company level before expecting each subsidiary to write its own.

Also at issue was how to integrate marketing goals into the management process. The committee had touched on this matter, noting that marketing goals would be an idle exercise unless officers actually used them. A way to mandate use would be to include marketing goals and marketing performance in each officer's annual performance evaluation. Both the officer and his or her supervisor would then examine each goal and its associated performance and reach formal agreement on progress. However, one committee member strongly opposed such use because of his and MidAmerica's lack of experience with marketing goals. The other members had agreed—something else should be done.

Marketing Strategy

The last major issue discussed by the marketing committee was MidAmerica's marketing strategy over the next five years. Watt had requested that the committee study this topic and propose two options, each with clearly identified strengths and weaknesses. He had also asked for the committee's choice between the options. The committee had until December 31 to complete his request.

The first strategic option was growth via market development. This strategy would emphasize the marketing of existing financial services to new markets defined in terms of either geographic areas or market segments. Growth via new geographic areas could be done three ways.

The first would be to stay in St. Clair and Madison counties and locate in such cities as Cahokia, Collinsville, and Edwardsville, for example. The second would be to expand eastward and southward to other Illinois counties.The third would be to cross the Mississippi and enter the St. Louis market area, perhaps in the St. Charles area about 20 miles west of Alton. MidAmerica could move into Missouri by means of its directors establishing a Missouri corporation in the banking industry. Alternatively, it could enter Missouri by offering a limited-service bank that would provide all of MidAmerica's services except commercial loans. A limited-service bank escaped federal and state laws prohibiting interstate banking. However, MidAmerica might be able to expand into Missouri with all of its services as soon as 1986 if an existing bill were enacted by the Illinois and Missouri legislatures. Smith thought that chances of the bill becoming law by 1986 were 50-50.

Watt and the directors wanted any new market area chosen to show a deposit growth potential in excess of 8 percent per year; any new facility should show an operating profit within the first five years. Committee members thought that careful selection of new market areas could meet these criteria. However, the consequences of a mistake in their judgment could be substantial.

Less risky was a market development strategy based not on new geographic areas but on new market segments. These new segments would be in the local community where MidAmerica's reputation was strongest. Examples of new segments were professionals, commercial accounts (mostly retailing and light industry), and the military at nearby Scott Air Force Base. Potential here was probably not as great as with geographic expansion.

The second strategic option was growth via service development. This strategy would emphasize the marketing of new financial services to existing markets. New services could be aimed at either existing consumer or commercial accounts with the goal of increasing deposits, loans, or service fees. There were literally hundreds of new services that MidAmerica could add. Some of the more promising ones had been mentioned in yesterday's meeting. In-home banking would allow customers to link their home computers with the bank's system and pay bills, transfer funds, and check on account balances. Optimistic forecasts here called for about 10 percent of U.S. households to use some form of home banking by the early 1990s. Auto leasing would have MidAmerica as lessor to individual customers. Experts forecast a 10–15 percent annual growth rate for the service, reaching a level of about 40 percent of all new car deliveries in the early 1990s. Personal financial planning would use financial advisers at the bank to investigate middle-aged customers' financial objectives and resources and then recommend a financial program. A "prestige" credit card would provide increased services and higher loan limits to upscale customers. The committee recognized the need for careful research before recommending one new service over another.

The committee also recognized that a recommendation to market any new service would subject MidAmerica to the chance of failure. Costs associated with failure depended on the new service. However, in no case did the committee think that a major new service could be introduced for less than $60,000 in training, marketing, and other start-up costs.

Finally, the committees recognized that growth objectives could be met by either strategy and that MidAmerica almost certainly would not pursue one strategy to the exclusion of the other. A mix between the two would be best; the issue really was which of the two strategies should be emphasized. Further, adoption of either strategy would not mean abandonment of existing customer segments. All MidAmerica subsidiaries would be expected to continue to show growth via penetrating existing segments through the offering of present services.

HOLDING COMPANY STRATEGY

Choosing between a market development and a product development strategy was the final decision in formulating the holding company's strategy. Earlier in the year, Watt and the directors had agreed on other strategic components: profitable growth, liquidity, active asset/liability management, financial and marketing control over subsidiaries, capable personnel, and market leadership. All components were tied to a community bank orientation: suburban locations, a high profile in local community affairs, personal relationships with customers, and deposits and loans generated in the local community.

"For the next few years, our strategy could also be described as 'conservative,'" Watt had told the committee. He had gone on to explain that a conservative approach was called for because it would

1. Avoid risk and produce profits (important because of last year's loss).
2. Allow MidAmerica time to train and develop its associates and officers and to improve its management procedures.
3. Minimize the risk of costly mistakes by allowing some important industry trends to emerge.

The net effect of a conservative approach should be intermediate and long-term profitability. However, Watt noted that in the short-term the approach might mean some missed opportunities and some stronger competitors.

Watt and several other officers considered it almost certain that MidAmerica would be sold to a much larger holding company in the next five years. Industry sources predicted hundreds of such sales, beginning shortly after Congress permitted interstate banking. Bank sales and interstate banking were both parts of a broad industry trend called *deregulation* (see next section). The sale of MidAmerica would take place at a premium if MidAmerica could show capable personnel and strong performance. The present strategy should produce both characteristics by 1987.

DEREGULATION

The term *deregulation* was misleading because governments at federal and state levels would never allow banks to operate without regulation. Instead, deregulation meant reducing regulation, giving banks more freedom to pay and to charge interest rates of their choice, to develop and to market new services, and to locate limited service banks in more than one state. Deregulation had begun in the late 1970s and was expected to continue until at least 1990. Congress; federal regulatory agencies (the Federal Reserve Board, the Federal Deposit Insurance Corporation, the Comptroller of the Currency); and state regulatory agencies all expected that the trend would make banking more competitive and, hence, more efficient.

Increased competition and efficiency would cause some banks to disappear. As of October 1984, there were almost 800 banks on the Federal Reserve Board's problem list. Industry sources expected that about 60 of these would fail in the next 12 months. Already the country had seen 65 failures in 1984, making it a strong candidate for the second highest year for failures since 1937. The same sources predicted that about 2,300 or 15 percent of all U.S. banks would close, merge, or be sold over the next five years. The pace could greatly accelerate if Congress were to permit interstate banking.

Deregulation also meant the threat of other firms competing in the financial service industry. Generally these firms had large retail networks and sophisticated data processing systems. The largest was Sears Roebuck & Co. Sears had purchased Coldwell Banker (the nation's largest real estate broker) and Dean Witter (the nation's fifth-largest investment broker) for over $800 million in 1981. The purchased organizations complemented functions performed by Sears' Allstate Insurance (the nation's second-largest casualty insurer). Sears was expected to place Financial Centers at 300 of its 806 stores by the end of 1984. At each center, a Sears customer could trade securities as well as invest in a money market mutual fund and in certificates of deposit. Increased deregulation might mean that Sears could offer the nation a complete line of what used to be exclusively banking services.

Already banks had seen most of their traditional services extended to savings and loan associations, credit unions, and other institutions inside and outside the financial service industry. Consumers now could keep demand and time deposits, obtain mortgage and installment loans, and, in short, satisfy almost all financial needs at institutions other than banks. Consumers had more choices than ever before.

To some consumers, increased choice meant greater sophistication in managing their finances. Smith thought that these people might be kept by MidAmerica's strategy. They would not move a $20,000 certificate of deposit, for example, just because a competitor's interest rate was 20 basis points higher. The $40 annual difference in interest earned (before taxes) would not be worth the reduction in service. Nor would the higher rate move the deposits of unsophisticated consumers. These people placed greater importance on location and on habit than on return. However, in between these groupings were consumers that Smith worried about. These people would move for $40 per year, not caring about the loss of service or the increased inconvenience.

THE MORNING MAIL

Smith's thoughts were broken by his secretary and the morning mail. A headline on the front page of the *St. Louis Business Journal* caught his attention: "Citicorp's St. Louis 'Bank' Bid." The accompanying article explained that Citicorp, a New York bank with over $130 billion in assets, had applied to the comptroller of the currency for permission to open a limited-service bank in St. Louis. Citicorp expected to receive permission. However, it would not seek permission from Missouri regulators because Citicorp felt that the planned operation would technically not be a bank and the matter was, therefore, beyond control of the Missouri commissioner of finance. The commissioner was quoted as willing to bring suit to stop Citicorp. Lawyers for Citicorp responded that any suit would be decided in their favor because federal law superseded Missouri law.

The article also summarized fears of the St. Louis banking community that Citicorp's entry would "trigger a bidding war for consumer deposits and hurt local bank earnings." Not only that, the local bankers thought that if Citicorp entered their market, at least three or four other banks would soon follow. The net effect would be much more aggressive marketing of financial services.

A hearty "Hello!" took Smith away from the article. He looked through his now-opened door to see one of the bank's eldest customers and responded. He thought, "It must be 9:30."

Case 9

VideoShop—Mark-Tele, Inc. (II)*

Michael P. Mokwa
Karl Gustafson
both of Arizona State University

Cable television began to spread rapidly across the United States during the late 1970s. It was promoted to subscribers predominantly as an entertainment media that would provide an expanded choice of high-quality television programming.

Some advertising and marketing experts perceived cable television differently. They saw it as opening a revolution in commercial communications. As telecommunication technology improved, cable television could become a direct threat to conventional shopping systems. Most experts, however, forecasted that significant changes in consumer shopping patterns were at least a decade or two away. Mr. Richard Johnson disagreed. He was the managing director of Mark-Tele, Inc., one of the most innovative and aggressive cable television companies.

During the fall of 1981, Mr. Johnson began to prepare a proposal for presentation to his board of directors. The proposal would suggest that Mark-Tele develop several new television channels. Most cable channels involved either an entertainment, educational, or public information format. The proposed new channels would involve innovative commercial formats using telecommunications technology that would allow organizations to market and sell directly to consumers in their own homes. Mr. Johnson named this concept "VideoShop."

THE NEW VENTURE

Several months earlier, Mr. Johnson had created a new ventures task force to generate and study novel programming formats that could be

* This is an abridged version of a case prepared by Professor Michael P. Mokwa and Karl Gustafson of Arizona State University as a basis for class discussion. It is not intended to illustrate either effective or ineffective handling of a managerial situation.

developed into new cable channels in the near term, and possibly into new networks in the long run. These channels would be used by Mark-Tele to generate additional revenues, to increase its subscription base, and to allocate operating costs more effectively.

The current capacity of the Mark-Tele cable system was 52 channels. But only 31 were in use. When Mark-Tele began operations, they had only 12 channels but had grown steadily. Costs had been relatively constant regardless of the number of channels that Mark-Tele operated. Thus, Mr. Johnson perceived Mark-Tele's cost structure as highly fixed, and he foresaw the development of new channels as a means of distributing these costs. Mr. Johnson expected that new channels would draw new subscribers, that subscription rates could be raised as more channels were added, and that subscription revenue could grow faster than corresponding operating costs.

The new ventures task force included the operations and sales managers from Mark-Tele, two product development specialists from Mark-Tele's parent company, and a consultant from the communications industry. An excerpt of their report is presented in the Appendix. The task force recommended that Mark-Tele develop several new cable channels using the television as the primary medium for shopping.

Mr. Johnson was thrilled with the new venture idea and the task force report. He wanted to develop and implement the new concept quickly. He selected a distinctive name for the venture, identifying it as VideoShop. He met informally with some prospective salespeople, distributors, and retailers from different product and service fields, and sensed strong but very cautious interest and support from prospective suppliers.

Mr. Johnson felt that a number of proposed channels were feasible, but he wanted to focus his efforts on those products and services *(a)* that appeared to be easiest and most profitable to implement in the near term, and *(b)* that appeared to have the strongest interest among the prospective suppliers with whom he had met. He selected five prospects for development:

1. Catalog sales by regional and national retailers.
2. Ticket reservations for concerts, plays, and sporting events, as well as reservations at local restaurants.
3. Airline ticket reservations and vacation planning.
4. A multiple-listing service for real estate companies to display homes and commercial property that were for sale in the area or possibly from areas across the country.
5. Grocery products.

Mr. Johnson expected that he could find outstanding firms from each product or service field to participate in the VideoShop venture under terms that Mark-Tele would set forth.

MARK-TELE'S BACKGROUND

Mark-Tele was founded in 1977, as a wholly owned subsidiary of Intertronics, Inc., a large corporation based in New York City. Intertronics was founded in 1973 as a joint venture among three well-respected, multinational firms. One firm was primarily in the information processing industry. Another was a publishing and broadcasting conglomerate, and the third was a high-technology producer in electronics. The mission of Intertronics was to design, develop, and implement innovative, applied telecommunications systems for domestic consumer markets. Intertronics received financial support and full technological cooperation from its parent companies, but was operated as an autonomous venture. Intertronics managed each of its subsidiaries using the same orientation.

During 1978, Mark-Tele bid to install cable television systems in several large metropolitan areas in the United States. Late that year, Mark-Tele was granted the right to install a cable television system in a large, growing southwestern metropolitan area. The area had more than a sufficient number of households to profitably support a cable television company according to industry standards. More important, the population was growing rapidly. Corporations were locating headquarters or building large manufacturing facilities in the area. Growth was projected to continue for at least the next 15 years, thus representing a very attractive cable market for Mark-Tele.

Intertronics would use Mark-Tele's location as the test site for a new type of cable television technology. The traditional type of cable used in cable television systems was a "one-way" cable—a signal could be directed only from the cable television company *to* the individual households attached to the service. Recently, Intertronics had developed a "two-way" cable that was capable of transmitting and receiving signals both from the cable television company and from individual households connected to the system. The cost of the new two-way cable was nearly four times the cost of one-way cable. Because Mark-Tele was a test site, they and their subscribers received the cable system at a substantially reduced cost.

To implement the two-way cable, Mark-Tele installed an interactive device to the television set of each of its subscribers. The interactive devices were expensive to install, but Intertronics absorbed most of the installation cost. The subscription charge for basic cable services from Mark-Tele was $11 per month. The comparable rate for one-way cable would be $8.50 per month.

Mark-Tele's first year of operations concluded with 5,000 subscribers and a small negative net operating profit. In the following year, Mark-Tele subscriptions increased to 38,000, generating a net profit of almost $1.4 million. In 1980, Mark-Tele continued to aggressively at-

EXHIBIT 1

MARK-TELE, INC.
Income Statement
Fiscal Years Ending
December 31, 1979, and 1980

	*1979**	*1980†*
Revenues:		
Subscription revenue	$4,560,000	$ 6,600,000
Pay service revenue	4,104,000	5,400,000
Total revenue	$8,664,000	$12,000,000
Expenses:		
Operation expense (includes salaries)	$3,852,000	$ 5,248,000
Sales expense	1,913,400	2,610,300
Interest expense	136,200	136,200
Depreciation expense	74,800	74,800
Rent expense	46,000	46,000
Equipment maintenance expense	32,500	34,700
Total expense	$6,054,900	$ 8,150,000
Gross profit	$2,609,100	$ 3,850,000
Taxes @ 47%	$1,226,277	$ 1,848,000
Net profit	$1,382,823	$ 2,002,000

* Based on subscriptions of 38,000 homes with a subscription rate of $10 per month per home, and average home "pay service" of $9 per month per home.
† Based on total subscriptions of 50,000 homes with a subscription rate of $11 per month per home, and average home "pay service" of $9 per month per home.

tract more subscribers, reaching 50,000 total. Net profit increased to exceed $2 million. Financial statements for 1979 and 1980 are presented in Exhibit 1.

Research by Mark-Tele suggested that the potential number of homes for the cable network in their market area exceeded 400,000 over the next five years. In 10 years, the market potential was forecasted to be nearly 750,000 homes. A demographic profile of current subscribers is presented in Exhibit 2.

Mark-Tele offered a wide variety of programming for virtually any type of viewer. Several of the channels were "pay television." For these, a household would pay an additional charge beyond the basic monthly rate. The revenue from pay services nearly matched basic subscription revenue for Mark-Tele in 1980. A schedule for the allocation of Mark-Tele's 52-channel capacity is presented in Exhibit 3. Both current and prospective channels are listed.

EXHIBIT 2 1980 Demographic Analysis of Mark-Tele Subscribers*

Family Size	*Percent*	*Family Income*	*Percent*	*Number of Hours Home Television Active per Week*	*Percent*	*Age of Paying Subscriber*	*Percent*	*Residency*	*Percent*	*Number of Years of Education of Paying Subscribers*	*Percent*
1	17.6%	$ 0 -$ 8K	1.3%	0– 7	2.5%	18–25	22.4%	Homeowners	71.6%	0– 8	1.4%
2	22.8	$ 9K–$18K	15.7	8–14	15.1	26–35	19.2	Renters	28.4	9–11	22.5
3	10.8	$19K–$28K	18.3	15–21	17.2	36–45	19.6			12–	21.8
4	19.3	$29K–$35K	17.5	22–28	40.7	46–55	17.7			13–15	26.3
5	15.1	$36K–$45K	19.6	29–35	20.8	56–65	7.1			16+	28.0
6	5.8	$46K–$59K	12.7	36+	3.7	66–75	8.3				
7+	8.6	$60,000+	14.9			76+	5.7				

* Based on 50,000 subscribers.

EXHIBIT 3 Channel Allocation Schedule

Cable Channel Number	*Designated Programming Service*
1	Mark-Tele Channel Listing*
2	Program Guide*
3	Local Transit Schedule*
4	Classified Ads and Yard Sales*
5	Weather Radar and Time*
6	Dow Jones Cable News*
7	Reserved for future use
8†	Home Box Office*
9†	Showtime*
10†	The Movie Channel*
11†	Golden Oldies Channel*
12	Reserved for future use
13	Reserved for future use
14	Cable News Network*
15	Reserved for future use
16	UPI News Scan*
17	Government Access*
18	Music Television*
19†	Stereo Rock Concert*
20	Educational Access*
21	Educational Access: New York University*
22	Proposed educational access
23	Proposed interactive channel for lease
24	Proposed interactive channel for lease
25	Proposed interactive channel for lease
26	VideoShop: *Retail Sales Channel*
27	VideoShop: *Entertainment Tickets and Restaurants*
28	VideoShop: *Grocery Products*
29	VideoShop: Reserved
30	VideoShop: Reserved
31	USA Network*
32	WTBS, Atlanta, channel 17*
33	WOR, New York, channel 9*
34	K/ / /, local ABC affiliate
35	Christian Broadcasting Network*
36	ESPN (Sports) Network*
37	K/ / /, local station, channel 15*
38	K/ / /, local NBC affiliate, channel 8*
39	K/ / /, local CBS affiliate, channel 11*
40	Proposed channel for lease
41	Concert Connection*
42	WGN, Chicago, channel 9*
43	Public Access: Cultural Bulletin Board*

EXHIBIT 3 *(concluded)*

Cable Channel Number	*Designated Programming Service*
44†	Proposed games channel
45	Public Access: Library information*
46	Proposed public access
47	Public Broadcasting System
48	Reserved for future banking transactions
49	VideoShop: *Airline Tickets and Travel*
50	VideoShop: *Real Estate Showcase*
51	Reserved for future use
52	Reserved for future use

* Active channel.
† Optional pay service.

CABLE TELEVISION TECHNOLOGY

The Mark-Tele cable television system was controlled by a sophisticated configuration of computers with high-speed communications between each processor. Three computers, each used for a different task, insured that viewers would have access to the cable network at all times. The main computer transmitted cable signals to each individual home using the two-way cable lines. The second computer's function was to back up the main computer in the event that a system failure occurred. The second computer would be a vital element of the VideoShop system because it could be used as an update system for suppliers to amend information regarding their products or services. This computer also could be used to transmit the orders or reservations placed by "shopping" subscribers directly to prospective suppliers. The third computer functioned as another backup, if system failures would occur simultaneously to the main computers. A very sophisticated software application integrating the communication network and operating system had been developed to assure 99 percent uptime for the cable system. A diagram sketching the Mark-Tele cable system is presented in Exhibit 4.

The cable system incorporated two different types of store devices. The first type of storage disk (a magnetic disk) was used to store data, such as billing information about a particular subscriber. The second type of disk involved an innovative technology that could be used extensively by the VideoShop suppliers. Images of products and services could be stored on these disks so that subscribers to the cable system could access the images at any time. Only through the use of

EXHIBIT 4 VideoShop—Mark-Tele, Inc.: Mark-Tele Two-Way Cable System

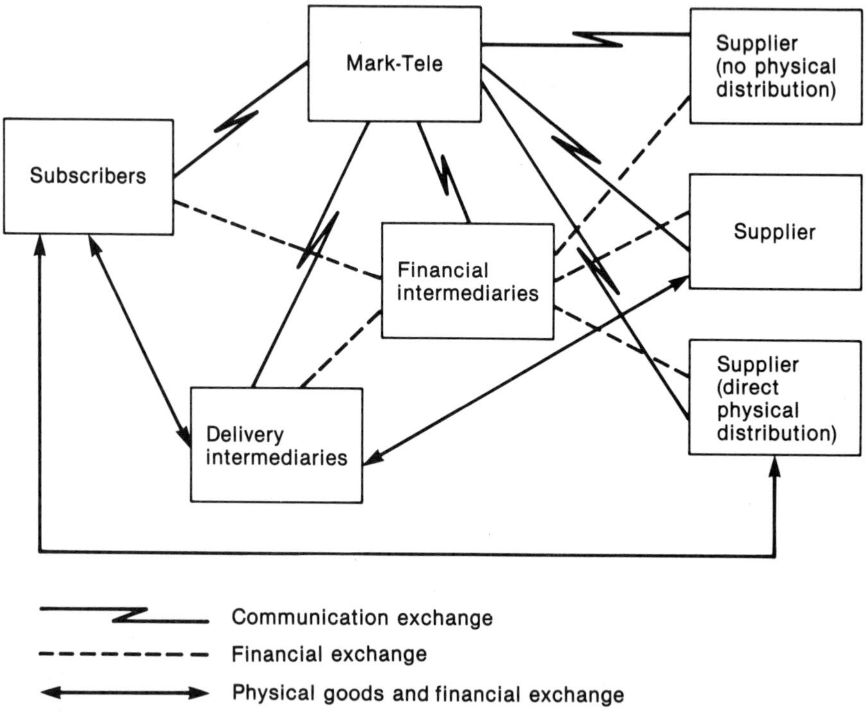

the new two-way cable developed by Intertronics would it be possible to incorporate the video disk units (VDU) into a cable network. The two-way cable allowed signals to travel from the main computer to an individual television, and from the television back to the main computer.

Two-way communication was possible through the use of an interactive indexing device attached to each subscriber's television. This indexing device contained special electronics allowing the device to transmit data back to the main computer. On top of the indexing device were 12 keys, simply called the keypad. An individual subscriber could use the keypad to call up "menus," sort through a menu, and send data back to the main computer. A *menu* is a computer term used to describe listings of general categories from which additional information can be drawn.

Using a prospective VideoShop example, a menu for a channel containing airline information could first indicate to a viewer the different airlines from which to choose. The viewer could then push the key on the keypad that corresponds to the airline that he or she was interested in using. The next menu could show all the different cities to which the chosen airline flies. The viewer then could push the key on the keypad that corresponds to the city to which he or she wishes to travel. The following screen could provide the flight numbers and times during which flights are available. From the information on that screen, the user could make a reservation, which would be transmitted to the airline's computer through the Mark-Tele computer. Finally, the reservation would be logged, confirmed, and ticket(s) mailed to the viewer.

VIDEOSHOP CHANNELS

Mr. Johnson felt that the five shopping channels that he had selected from the list generated by the task force would work well. He prepared a brief description for each of the prospective shopping channels. He would use these to build his presentation for the forthcoming board meeting and to develop a prospectus to sell the VideoShop concept to suppliers.

The Catalog Sales Channel(s)

National and regional retailers could use the VideoShop system to sell and promote their entire merchandise lines including their most current items and prices. Shoppers would have the opportunity to view merchandise on the television screen in their own home, avoiding the inconvenience of a shopping trip or the boredom of thumbing through a catalog book. Information about products and prices could be presented in a format similar to catalog books, or innovative action formats could be developed to simulate a store environment or create some novel context. Retailers would be responsible for developing appropriate video disk units and keeping information current. Mark-Tele could provide a consulting service to help suppliers produce effective video disks. Mark-Tele could also reserve the right to reject any material that was felt to be inappropriate.

A shopper could use the interactive indexing device to direct and control an entire shopping experience. This could involve viewing information about product features and prices from one retailer, and then quickly switching to another retailer's presentation for comparative information. In addition, a shopper desiring more extensive information could access a brief demonstration or informative advertisement about a product. After selecting a product, the interactive device could transmit the order through Mark-Tele's computing system directly to the retailer's processing system. The retailer could present alternative payment programs and specific delivery schedules or instructions. The shopper could charge purchases using national or store credit cards and could pick up the merchandise directly or have it delivered.

Mark-Tele could charge each retailer a service fee based on a fixed percentage of shoppers' invoice values (before taxes). Individual retailers could be billed monthly, and various payment programs could be formulated. The new ventures task force estimated that an average home would purchase a minimum of $300 worth of retail merchandise annually through VideoShop. They proposed a service charge rate of 2 percent. Mark-Tele could also generate revenue by selling video consulting services to the suppliers.

Ticket Sales and Restaurant Reservation Channel

VideoShop could provide detailed information concerning local entertainment alternatives to subscribers. Entertainment organizations could present exciting promotional spots using the video disk technology and sell tickets directly to VideoShop subscribers. Another dimension of this channel could be a restaurant promotion and reservation feature. Restaurant menus and promotional spots could be made accessible for diners. Once diners have chosen a particular restaurant using the memo and spots, they could make a reservation and even select a specific table (if the restaurant developed, as part of its VideoShop system, a seating arrangement routine similar to that of the entertainment organizations).

All VideoShop ticket purchases and reservations could be transmitted directly from the shopper's home through Mark-Tele computers to the restaurant or ticket outlet. Most restaurants and small entertainment organizations would have to purchase or lease a small "intelligence" computing terminal to receive reservations or ticket orders and to keep information updated. Intertronics could supply these.

The task force felt that this channel could generate at least $150,000 revenue per year given the current subscriber base. They recommended a $25 per month minimum charge to restaurants and a 50-cent service fee per ticket reservation. They were unsure of a fee schedule for entertainment organizations that would only promote events and would not be selling tickets directly through VideoShop. However, they thought that rates similar to commercial advertising rates would be appropriate.

Airline Ticket Sales and Travel Accommodations Channel

Discussions with the task force concluded that an airline ticket sales channel could be the easiest for Mark-Tele to implement and operate in the short run, and also could be the most lucrative financially. Projected revenue for the first year of operating this channel was $400,000 based on a very conservative usage rate and an extremely competitive pricing policy. This channel could allow subscribers to make airline reservations, purchase their tickets, and select travel accommodations using the same fundamental interactive shopping procedures as other VideoShop channels.

Perhaps the most important characteristic of this channel could be the potential ease of implementation, once cooperation was secured from the airlines. The format and basic system used within the airlines industry to transmit, display, and process schedules, fares, and ticket information appeared to be compatible with the Mark-Tele system. VideoShop could be used to link shoppers directly with airline ticket reservation systems, bypassing reservationists and travel agents. Subscribers could select itineraries, then secure reservations and pay, using major credit cards. Tickets could be mailed or picked up at airport ticket counters or other service locations.

Mark-Tele could record each ticket purchase and charge the appropriate airline a fixed fee of $4 per ticket. This rate was approximately half of the average rate charged by most travel agents. The task force believed that a minimum average of two tickets would be purchased by each subscribing household per year. Revenue estimates were not made for the travel accommodations feature of this channel.

Multiple-Listing Service Channel

A few local realtors expressed strong interest in the VideoShop concept. Traditional promotional tools used to stimulate buyers' interest and assist them in making decisions about what properties to see in person included classified newspaper ads, newspaper supplements, brochures, "for sale" signs, the multiple-listing catalog, and photographs of properties posted on an agency's wall. Most realtors and buyers found these boring. More important, these simply did not present most properties effectively. A frequent complaint among realtors and buyers was the high cost in time and dollars wasted traveling to and viewing personally properties that were not represented well in a promotion or informational item. VideoShop could provide an exciting and effective method for presenting realty.

A specific issue regarding this channel was whether to limit access to realty agencies and others willing to pay an additional fee for it or to open it for public access. The task force recommended open access and suggested that a minimum of 30 realty agencies would need to participate. Each could be charged a monthly fee of $100 for producing and maintaining high-quality video disks with accurate and updated information. Mark-Tele could provide technical assistance and would monitor this channel carefully.

Grocery Products Channel

One of the most exciting prospects for VideoShop could be a grocery products channel. It was the most interesting but difficult channel for which to design a format.

A VideoShop grocery channel could provide consumers with convenience, comfort, low shopping risks, and potential savings. For suppliers, it could generate increased control over operations and costs, and higher profits. However, this VideoShop channel would directly attack an expensive, firmly established distribution network and basic, traditional patterns of shopping. Strong resistance from many consumers could be anticipated, and suppliers not involved in the venture could be expected to retaliate competitively. Also, there could be critical barriers to providing shoppers a total assortment of grocery products including frozen and "fresh" items and to implementing a cost-effective delivery service or pickup procedure. Undoubtedly, these "bugs" could be worked out.

CONCLUSION—A TIME FOR REFLECTION AND . . . OR ACTION

One more time, Mr. Johnson reviewed the task force report and his brief descriptions of prospective VideoShop channels. He felt excitement, enthusiasm, and some frustration. He and the task force had worked hard and creatively to formulate the idea of VideoShop. They thought that most technological barriers could be overcome, and they projected a very favorable cost structure. Definitely, VideoShop was a concept whose time had arrived! But, Mark-Tele is a small company with only a few people and tight resources. It is a high-investment and high-risk experimental venture receiving considerable financial support and subsidy from Intertronics. Would Intertronics feel that VideoShop is an extension of the Mark-Tele experiment, or a contamination of it?

Appendix New Venture Task Force Report Proposing a Telecommunications Shopping System for Mark-Tele

We recommend that Mark-Tele design and implement a telecommunication shopping (TCS) system immediately. This proposed new venture appears to be a natural extension of Mark-Tele's experimental mission and an excellent application of Mark-Tele's distinctive technological capabilities in the telecommunications field.

A TCS system would allow a Mark-Tele subscriber to become an active shopper and buyer in the privacy of the home using only the television. Facilitated by Mark-Tele's sophisticated communications and computing technologies, a TCS system subscriber would be able to view and buy a large variety of products and services that conventionally would have required the shopper to leave the home and travel to view and purchase. A TCS system would also serve the suppliers of many different products and services with an opportunity to break away from costly traditional market channels and to inexpensively expand their market coverage and increase sales substantially.

For Mark-Tele, a TCS system would increase revenues, diversify its revenue base, and distribute its high fixed costs efficiently. A TCS system could be used as a promotional tool to build and maintain Mark-Tele's local subscription base. Current subscription rates could be raised with the addition of the TCS system, or an additional fee could be charged to subscribers who desire to participate in the TCS system. Suppliers and shopping subscribers would also be charged for services that Mark-Tele would provide in the development and operation of the TCS system. In the longer run, Mark-Tele could potentially develop TCS networks that could be sold to other cable systems. Clearly, early entry into the TCS field would be lucrative financially for Mark-Tele.

THE ENVIRONMENT OF TCS

Economic, technological, legal and regulatory, and social trends are emerging in support of a TCS system. Increased consumer spending is predicted to continue, but gains for retailers will be restricted by inflationary pressures. There will be a slower pace of store expansion during the 1980s. Many of the major metropolitan areas are overbuilt with retail space, and developers often are experiencing difficulty obtaining sites and financing. Retailers similarly are experiencing rising rents. Sales growth at many shopping centers has fallen due to slow growth of suburban communities and shrinking distances that consumers are willing to travel to shop.

Retailers are attempting to boost productivity, consolidate store space, and cut costs to improve returns. Inflation has increased operating costs more rapidly than sales during the last 10 years. Many retailers have been attracted to discount pricing policies. The catalog showroom has become one of the fastest growing segments of discount merchandising, featuring national brand products at discount prices.

Considering sociocultural trends, women are continuing to enter the work force, thus have less time to engage in shopping. Greater emphasis on recreational activities continues, and individuals are reluctant to sacrifice leisure time to shop in stores. Convenience is emerging as a high priority.

Consumers are emphasizing their self-identity. As such, consumers are demanding more individuality in goods and services, often desiring distinctive products that individual stores may not be able to afford to inventory and display. Definitely, there has been more intense consumer preference for specialty items and services difficult to find in the Mark-Tele market area.

An increase in the number of single-parent and single-person households has led to increased in-home shopping. Nonstore innovations such as pay-by-phone, specialty mail-order catalogs, and toll-free phone ordering have become increasingly popular. Catalog shopping currently offers a full line of merchandise together with prices and features that permit a consumer to comparison shop at home without having to spend time inefficiently searching for products in crowded stores, waiting for sales help, or at times being annoyed by overzealous clerks. In addition, the increasing age of the population, proliferation of retirement communities, and declining mobility of individuals in their later years make catalog shopping very attractive.

There are significant technological advances that will influence the TCS system. In the past, alphanumerics and graphics but not still or moving "pictures" could be retrieved from a data bank and displayed on a television screen; however, Intertronics' innovative technologics have advanced moving picture capabilities. This new technology has permitted the consumer to control the timing, sequence, and content of information through the use of the keypad.

Development of videodiscs and videocassettes, which to date have been used by viewers to record television programs, have significant promise for advertising and catalog media. Potential exists for suppliers to mail lower-cost video catalogs on a complimentary basis or in lieu of printed direct-mail offerings.

Consumers are being exposed to, and are accepting, complex, technical items such as videotape recorders, home computers, and debit cards for use with automatic teller machines. Home computers and the development of *videotex,* the generic term for home information-retrieval systems, will provide functions compatible with those of the TCS system.

The political-legal context is confusing. The Federal Communications Commission has decided that cable franchising is mainly the province of local jurisdictions. All cable companies must interact with local governments to obtain and maintain authority to operate. While Mark-Tele has secured exclusive rights in their metropolitan area, changes in federal and local policy must be monitored.

The TCS venture raises questions concerning supplier and financial contractual arrangements. The antitrust implications of arrangements with some large institutions should be studied in more detail on a case-by-case basis. Moreover, movement into the retail sector by Mark-Tele through the TCS system will mean closer scrutiny by federal and local consumer protection agencies such as the Federal Trade Commission and the Consumer Product Safety Commission. Finally, Mark-Tele will need to carefully consider protection of the privacy of personal, financial, and transactional data about subscribers of the TCS system. Controls must be established to prevent unauthorized access to information in the system data banks and to guard against unauthorized purchasing.

THE GENERAL COMPETITIVE CONTEXT

Industry observers clearly are divided when projecting the evolution of electronic shopping and its acceptance by both consumers and the industry. However, all forms of nonstore retailing currently are growing rapidly, and continued growth is forecasted. Major developments in nonstore retailing will be reviewed.

Mail-Order Catalogs

General department store merchandisers, catalog showrooms, and specialty houses periodically mail catalogs to targeted groups of consumers. An average mail-order house distributes from 6 to 20 catalog issues yearly at a cost often approaching $2 each. Circulations range from about 100,000 to over 1 million for each mailing. The results have been outstanding. Over $26 billion was spent by consumers on mail-order items in 1978—an increase of $12 billion in three years. By comparison, in-store retailing sales grew at a rate less than half of the mail-order rate. Specialty-oriented catalogs are accounting for 75 percent of total mail-order sales, and mail-order catalogs currently contribute 15 percent of the total volume of Christmas season sales. Telephone- and mail-generated orders received by traditional store retailers such as Bloomingdales, J.C. Penney, and Sears are increasing three to five times faster than in-store sales. In-flight shopping catalogs used by major airlines are additional evidence of the increasing popularity of nonstore shopping. MasterCard, American Express and Visa have increased their direct-mail offerings to their credit card holders and are expanding their assortments of merchandise.

The Catalog Showrooms

The catalog showroom is one of the fastest growing fields of retailing. Catalogs are used to promote and feature jewelry, housewares, appliances, sporting goods, and toys at discount prices. Customers visit the showroom to inspect merchandise and to make purchases. Sales for 1980 are estimated to be $7.8 billion, an increase of 11 percent from 1979. Forecasts for 1981 suggest a 20 percent gain in sales revenue. The number of showrooms across the country is nearly 2,000.

Noninteractive Shopping Using the Cable

Comp-U-Card, of Stamford, Connecticut, is a seven-year-old telephone merchandising firm. For an annual fee of $18, it offers members a discount on a broad line of durable goods. Members shop around, familiarizing themselves with products and prices. Then, they call Comp-U-Card toll free for specific information about an item's availability and price. If a purchase decision is made, the consumer provides membership and credit card numbers to an operator, and the merchandise is prepared for delivery. An experimental project has been proposed in which Comp-U-Card would use cable systems and satellite transmission to present product and price information to its subscribers. A transmitted schedule would alert subscribers to the time when particular product information would be presented. Subscribers would continue to use the telephone when ordering.

Telephone purchasing systems using cable presentations are currently operating in Europe. In March 1979, the British Post Office, which runs Britain's telephone system, opened a "viewdata" service called Prestel. Viewers are presented listings of games, restaurants, and consumer product evaluations. Products and services can be purchased on credit by phone. France launched a similar service, called Antiope, in 1979.

A few U.S. companies are testing similar systems. Viewdata Corp., a subsidiary of the Knight-Ridder newspaper chain, proposes to install a permanent system in southern Florida by 1983. First Bank System of Minneapolis will be testing a videotex system in North Dakota similar to the Antiope system of France.

Interactive Cable Systems and Videotex

Since December 1977, Warner Communications and American Express have been involved with a $70 million joint venture testing the QUBE two-way system of Warner Amex Cable in Columbus, Ohio. Currently, the system serves 30,000 of the 105,000 homes in its service area. American Express and Warner Communications propose to build other QUBE systems in such metropolitan areas as Houston, Pittsburgh, and Cincinnati. Both Sears and J.C. Penney currently are testing the QUBE system.

In May 1981, American Telephone & Telegraph Co. (AT&T) endorsed a videotex concept in which a home computer terminal must be purchased. AT&T has set out to develop its own system. AT&T would be a formidable opponent to anyone in the market, considering the firm's capabilities and financial strength. Thus, there are a number of legal actions being undertaken to prevent AT&T's direct entry into the videotex market, fearing it could become a monopoly power. However, strong deregulation sentiments may overcome the opposition and facilitate AT&T's entry into the market.

Over $100 million already has been invested by U.S. firms to design and test various TCS systems, and at least 83 experimental projects are being conducted around the world. As a result, Mark-Tele must be prepared to match formidable competition, and we feel confident that Mark-Tele can.

TARGET MARKET CONSIDERATIONS

There are two different markets that must be considered when developing this venture: (1) the suppliers and (2) the shoppers. We propose that the TCS system be "targeted" to the ultimate *user*—the subscribing shopper. A TCS system that is designed well should sell itself to suppliers. Suppliers, therefore, should be considered as a dimension of the total product that will be offered to target shoppers. This approach will allow Mark-Tele to retain maximum control and autonomy in the design and implementation of this venture.

The Target Market—Shoppers

A review of the size and characteristics of the current and potential Mark-Tele subscription base indicates substantial market potential and buying power. However, critical analysis of shopping and buying behavior is necessary to isolate the most lucrative prospective customer segments and to understand their prospective TCS behavior. Three buying factors appear to be very important: (1) risk perceptions, (2) convenience orientations, and (3) buyer satisfaction.

Buying is a complex experience filled with uncertainty and related risks of unfavorable consequences. Fundamentally, consumers confront the uncertainty of achieving their buying goals and risks such as embarrassment or wasting time, money, or effort in a disappointing buying or shopping experience. A consumer must have a satisfying experience each time that the TCS system is used. Otherwise, it is very likely that the consumer will not use TCS again and may discuss the bad experience with other shoppers and discourage their future use of the system.

Supplier Market Implications

After selecting general product and service categories and designing a general format for each TCS channel, Mark-Tele should direct attention to the supplier market. Mark-Tele should evaluate prospective suppliers regarding the relevance of their product or service assortment, their delivery and financial capabilities, and quality of their promotional strategies, and their desire to enter into this unconventional market. We feel that Mark-Tele's technical competence and captive subscription base will provide substantial leverage in all negotiations with suppliers. The actual marketing effort should involve personal selling programs, custom designed for each prospective target supplier.

PROSPECTIVE PRODUCTS AND SERVICES

Preliminary research has uncovered a number of product and service lines that are appropriate for our target market and appear to be financially and technically feasible. As this innovative approach to shopping evolves and consumer acceptance and involvement grows, many other products and services could be incorporated. However, the most feasible products and services currently are:

Standard catalog items.

Grocery items.

Gifts and specialty items.

Appliances, home entertainment, and personal computer equipment.

Toys, electronic games and equipment, basic sporting goods.

Banking and financial services.

Classified ads.

Multiple-listing service of local properties.

Ticket, restaurant, and accommodations reservations.

Educational and recreational classes.

Automobiles.

We cannot stress too strongly that TCS will involve a high degree of risk perceived by consumers. This must be reduced by offering products and services with which consumers are familiar and comfortable and which involves a minimum number of basic shopping decisions for consumers.

The consumer must *learn* to use the TCS system. Mark-Tele must guide this learning experience and make sure that consumers have consistent, positive shopping experiences that become reinforcing. The following services/features should be incorporated into the TCS system to reduce shopping risks and facilitate consumer satisfaction:

Easy-to-use indexing devices.

Top-quality visual and audio representation.

Professional promotions.

Up-to-date information on specials.

Competitive pricing policies and convenient payment methods.

TCS availability 24 hours per day, seven days per week.

Maintenance service availability 24 hours per day, seven days per week.

Accurate order taking and fulfilling.

Prompt delivery or pickup services.

Quick and equitable handling and resolution of customer complaints.

Exceptional reliability.

Eventually, the TCS product and service assortment could be broadened and channel features changed. However, the products and service lines outlined in this report appear to involve minimal consumer risks, high potential for competitive advantage and target consumer satisfaction, and substantial returns for Mark-Tele.

THE COMPETITIVE ADVANTAGE

A competitive advantage over conventional suppliers can be achieved by Mark-Tele if the TCS system is designed to serve the needs and expectations of the identified target market by actively considering their prepurchase deliberations, by guiding their purchase activities, and by reinforcing their postpurchase satisfaction. This must be complemented with accurate and reliable order processing and with prompt, efficient logistical support. Above all, Mark-Tele must communicate and promote its distinctive capabilities. We believe that the following distinctive features of the TCS system should be emphasized:

The extensive variety and depth of product and service assortments.

The vast amount of relevant information that is easily accessible and allows consumers to make better choices.

The excitement, involvement, convenience, and satisfaction of shopping in the privacy of one's home, using space-age technology and the simplicity of the television.

The insignificant, negligible, and indirect costs to consumers, particularly when compared to the opportunities and benefits.

The recommendation of our committee is that Mark-Tele design and implement the proposed new venture concept. We have identified the target customers and viable products and services to satisfy their needs and Mark-Tele's objectives. Development of the supplier market and control over suppliers also has been discussed. We recommend immediate action.

Case 10

The Gillette Company*

Charles M. Kummel
Jay E. Klompmaker
both of University of North Carolina

In July 1978, Mike Edwards, brand manager for TRAC II®,[1] is beginning to prepare his marketing plans for the following year. In preparing for the marketing plan approval process, he has to wrestle with some major funding questions. The most recent sales figures show that TRAC II has continued to maintain its share of the blade and razor market. This has occurred even though the Safety Razor Division (SRD) has introduced a new product to its line, Atra. The company believes that Atra will be the shaving system of the future and, therefore, is devoting increasing amounts of marketing support to this brand. Atra was launched in 1977 with a $7 million advertising campaign and over 50 million $2 rebate coupons. In less than a year, the brand achieved a 7 percent share of the blade market and about one third of the dollar-razor market. Thus, the company will be spending heavily on Atra, possibly at the expense of TRAC II, still the number one shaving system in America.

Edwards is faced with a difficult situation, for he believes that TRAC II still can make substantial profits for the division if the company continues to support it. In preparing for 1979, the division is faced with two major issues:

1. What are TRAC II's and Atra's future potentials?
2. Most important, can SRD afford to heavily support two brands? Even if they can, is it sound marketing policy to do so?

COMPANY BACKGROUND

The Gillette Company was founded in 1903 by King C. Gillette, a 40-year-old inventor, utopian writer, and bottle-cap salesman in Boston,

* This case was written by Charles M. Kummel under the direction of Professor Jay E. Klompmaker, Graduate School of Business Administration, University of North Carolina.

[1] TRAC II® is a registered trademark of The Gillette Company.

Massachusetts. Since marketing its first safety razor and blades, the Gillette Company, the parent of the Safety Razor Division, has been the leader in the shaving industry. The Gillette safety razor was the first system to provide a disposable blade that could be replaced at low cost and that provided a good inexpensive shave. The early ads focused on a shave-yourself theme: "If the time, money, energy, and brain-power which are wasted (shaving) in the barbershops of America were applied in direct effort, the Panama Canal could be dug in four hours."

The Pre-World War Years

With the benefit of a 17-year patent, Gillette was in a very advantageous position. However, it was not until World War I that the safety razor began to gain wide consumer acceptance. One day in 1917 King Gillette came into the office with a visionary idea: to present a Gillette razor to every soldier, sailor, and marine. Other executives modified this idea so that the government would do the presenting. In this way, millions just entering the shaving age would give the nation the self-shaving habit. In World War I, the government bought 4,180,000 Gillette razors as well as smaller quantities of competitive models.

Daily Shaving Development

Although World War I gave impetus to self-shaving, World War II popularized frequent shaving—12 million American servicemen shaved daily. This produced two results: (1) Gillette was able to gain consumer acceptance of personal shaving and (2) the company was able to develop an important market to build for the future.

Postwar Years

After 1948, the company began to diversify through the acquisition of three companies which gave Gillette entry into new markets. In 1948, the acquisition of the Toni Company extended the company into the women's grooming aid market. Paper Mate, a leading maker of writing instruments, was bought in 1954, and the Sterilon Corporation, a manufacturer of disposable supplies for hospitals, was acquired in 1962.

Diversification also occurred through internal product development propelled by a detailed marketing survey conducted in the late 1950s. The survey found that the public associated the company as much or more with personal grooming as with cutlery and related products. Gillette's response was to broaden its personal care line. As a result,

Gillette now markets such well-known brands as Adorn hair spray, Tame cream rinse, Right Guard anti-perspirant, Dry Look hair spray for men, Foamy shaving cream, Earth Borne and Ultra Max shampoos, Cricket lighter, Pro Max hair dryers as well as Paper Mate, Eraser Mate, and Flair pens.

Gillette Today

Gillette is divided into four principal operating groups (North America, International, Braun AG, Diversified Companies) and five product lines. As Exhibit 1 indicates, the importance of blades and razors to company profits is immense. In nearly all the 200 countries in which its blades and razors are sold, Gillette remains the industry leader. In 1977, Gillette reported increased worldwide sales of $1,587.2 million with income after taxes of $79.7 million (see Exhibit 2). Of total sales, $720.9 million were domestic and $866.3 million were international, with profit contributions of $109 million and $105.6 million, respectively. The company employs 31,700 people worldwide with 8,600 employees in the United States.

Statement of Corporate Objectives and Goals

At a recent stockholders' meeting, the chairman of the board outlined the company's strategy for the future:

> The goal of The Gillette Company is sustained growth. To achieve this, the company concentrates on two major objectives: to maintain the strength of existing product lines and to develop at least two new significant businesses or product lines that can make important contributions to the growth of the company in the early 1980s.

EXHIBIT 1 Gillette Sales and Contributions to Profits by Business Segments

	Blades and Razors		*Toiletries and Grooming Aids*		*Writing Instruments*		*Braun Electric Razors*		*Other*	
	Net Sales	*Contributions to Profits*	*Net Sales*	*Contributions to Profits*	*Net Sales*	*Contributions to Profits*	*Net Sales*	*Contributions to Profits*	*Net Sales*	*Contributions to Profits*
1977	31%	75%	26%	13%	8%	6%	23%	13%	12%	(7)%
1976	29	71	28	15	7	6	21	10	15	(2)
1975	30	73	30	15	7	5	20	8	13	(1)
1974	30	69	31	17	7	6	20	5	12	3
1973	31	64	32	20	7	5	22	10	8	1

Source: *Gillette Annual Report for 1977*, p. 28.

EXHIBIT 2 The Gillette Company Annual Income Statements, 1963–1977 (in thousands)

Year	*Net Sales*	*Gross Profit*	*Profit from Operations*	*Income before Taxes*	*Federal and Foreign Income Taxes*	*Net Income*
1977	$1,587,209	$834,786	$202,911	$158,820	$79,100	$79,720
1976	1,491,506	782,510	190,939	149,257	71,700	77,557
1975	1,406,906	737,310	184,368	146,954	67,000	79,954
1974	1,246,422	667,395	171,179	147,295	62,300	84,995
1973	1,064,427	600,805	155,949	154,365	63,300	91,065
1972	870,532	505,297	140,283	134,618	59,600	75,018
1971	729,687	436,756	121,532	110,699	48,300	62,399
1970	672,669	417,575	120,966	117,475	51,400	66,075
1969	609,557	390,858	122,416	119,632	54,100	65,532
1968	553,174	358,322	126,016	124,478	62,200	62,278
1967	428,357	291,916	101,153	103,815	47,200	56,615
1966	396,190	264,674	90,967	91,666	41,800	49,866
1965	339,064	224,995	75,010	75,330	33,000	42,330
1964	298,956	205,884	72,594	75,173	35,500	37,673
1963	295,700	207,552	85,316	85,945	44,400	41,545

In existing product lines, the company broadens its opportunities for growth by utilizing corporate technology to create new products. In other areas, growth is accomplished through either internal development or the acquisition of new businesses.

The company uses a number of guidelines to evaluate growth opportunities. Potential products or services must fulfill a useful function and provide value for the price paid; offer distinct advantages easily perceived by consumers; be based on technology available within, or readily accessible outside the company; meet established quality and safety standards; and offer an acceptable level of profitability and attractive growth potential.

THE SAFETY RAZOR DIVISION

The Safety Razor Division has long been regarded as the leader in shaving technology. Building on King Gillette's principle of using razors as a vehicle for blade sales and of associating the name "Gillette" with premium shaving, the division has been able to maintain its number one position in the U.S. market.

Share of Market

Market share is important in the shaving industry. The standard is that each share point is equivalent to approximately $1 million in pretax profits. Over recent history, Gillette has held approximately 60

EXHIBIT 3 Gillette Percentage of U.S. Blade Sales (estimated market share)

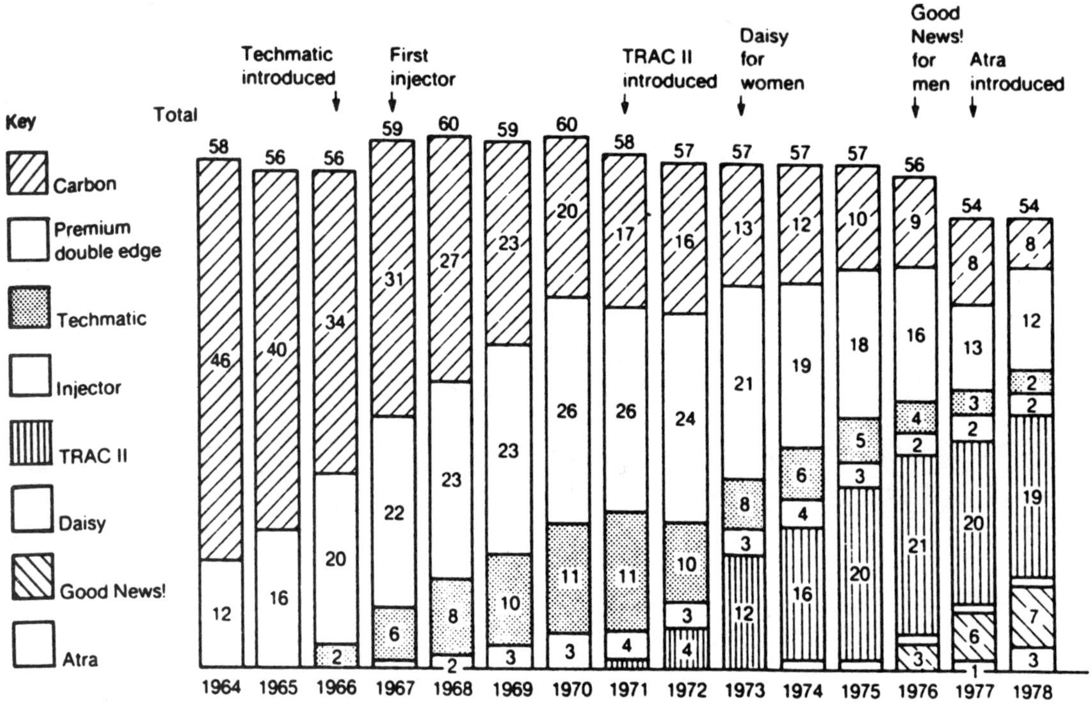

percent of the total dollar market. However, the division has put more emphasis on increasing its share from its static level.

Product Line

During the course of its existence, Gillette has introduced many new blades and razors. In the last 15 years, the shaving market has evolved from a double-edged emphasis to twin-bladed systems (see Exhibit 3). Besides Atra and TRAC II, Gillette markets Good News! disposables, Daisy for women, double-edge, injector, carbon, and Techmatic band systems (see Exhibit 4). Within their individual markets, Gillette sells 65 percent of all premium double-edged blades, 12 percent of injector sales, and almost all of the carbon and band sales.

Marketing Approach and Past Traditions

During 1977, the Gillette Company spent $207.9 million to promote all its products throughout the world, of which $133.1 million was spent for advertising, including couponing and sampling, and $74.8 million

EXHIBIT 4 Safety Razor Division Product Line, June 1978

Product Line	*Package Sizes*	*Manufacturer's Suggested Retail Price*
Blades:		
TRAC II	5,9,14,Adjustable 4	$1.60, 2.80, 3.89, 1.50
Atra	5,10	$1.70, 3.40
Good News!	2	$.60
Daisy	2	$1.00
Techmatic	5,10,15	$1.50, 2.80, 3.50
Double-edged:		
Platinum Plus	5,10,15	$1.40, 2.69, 3.50
Super-Stainless	5,10,15	$1.20, 2.30, 3.10
Carbon:		
Super Blue	10,15	$1.50, 2.15
Regular Blue	5,10	$.70, 1.25
Injector:		
Regular	7,11	$1.95, 2.60
Twin Injector	5,8	$1.40, 2.20
Razors:		
TRAC II	Regular	$3.50
	Lady	$3.50
	Adjustable	$3.50
	Deluxe	$3.95
Atra		
Double-edged:		
Super Adjustable		$3.50
Lady Gillette		$3.50
Super Speed		$1.95
Twin Injector		$2.95
Techmatic	Regular	$3.50
	Deluxe	$3.95
Three-Piece		$4.50
Knack		$1.95
Cricket Lighters	Regular	$1.49
	Super	$1.98
	Keeper	$4.49

for sales promotion. In terms of the domestic operation, the Safety Razor Division uses an eight-cycle promotional schedule whereby every six weeks a new program is initiated. During any one cycle, some but not all the products and their packages are sold on promotion. Usually one of the TRAC II packages is sold on promotion during each of these cycles.

Gillette advertising is designed to provide information to consumers and motivate them to buy the company's products. Sales promotion ensures that these products are readily available, well located, and attractively displayed in retail stores. Special promotion at the point of purchase offers consumers an extra incentive to buy Gillette products.[2]

In the past the company has concentrated its advertising and promotion on its newest shaving product, reducing support for its other established lines. The theory is that growth must come at the expense of other brands. When TRAC II was introduced, for example, the advertising budget for other brands was cut, with the double-edged portion being decreased from 47 percent in 1971 to 11 percent in 1972 and TRAC II receiving 61 percent of the division budget (see Exhibit 5).

A long-standing tradition has been that razors are used as a means for selling blades. Thus, with razors, the emphasis is on inducing the consumer to try the product by offering coupon discounts, mail samples, and heavy informational advertising. Blade strategy has been to emphasize a variety of sales devices—such as discounts, displays, and sweepstakes at pharmacies, convenience stores, and supermarkets—to encourage point-of-purchase sales. In spite of this tradition, razor sales are a very significant portion of division sales and profits.

At the center of this marketing strategy has been the company's identification with sports. The Gillette "Cavalcade of Sports" began with Gillette's radio sponsorship of the 1939 World Series and continues today with sponsorship of the World Series, Super Bowl, professional and NCAA basketball, as well as boxing. During the 1950s and 1960s, Gillette spent 60 percent of its ad dollars on sports programming. Influenced by research showing that prime-time entertainment offered superior audience potential, the company switched to a prime-time emphasis in the early 1970s. However, Gillette has recently returned in the last two years to its sports formula.

Marketing Research

Both product and marketing research have contributed to the success of the company. For example, Gillette was faced in 1917 with the expiration of its basic patents and the eventual flood of competitive models. Six months before the impending expiration, the company came out with new razor models including one for a dollar. As a result, the company made more money than ever before. In fact, throughout the history of shaving, Gillette has introduced most of the improvements in shaving technology. The major exceptions are the injector,

[2] *1977 Gillette Company Annual Report,* p. 14.

EXHIBIT 5 Gillette Advertising Expenditures, 1965–1978 (percentage of total market)

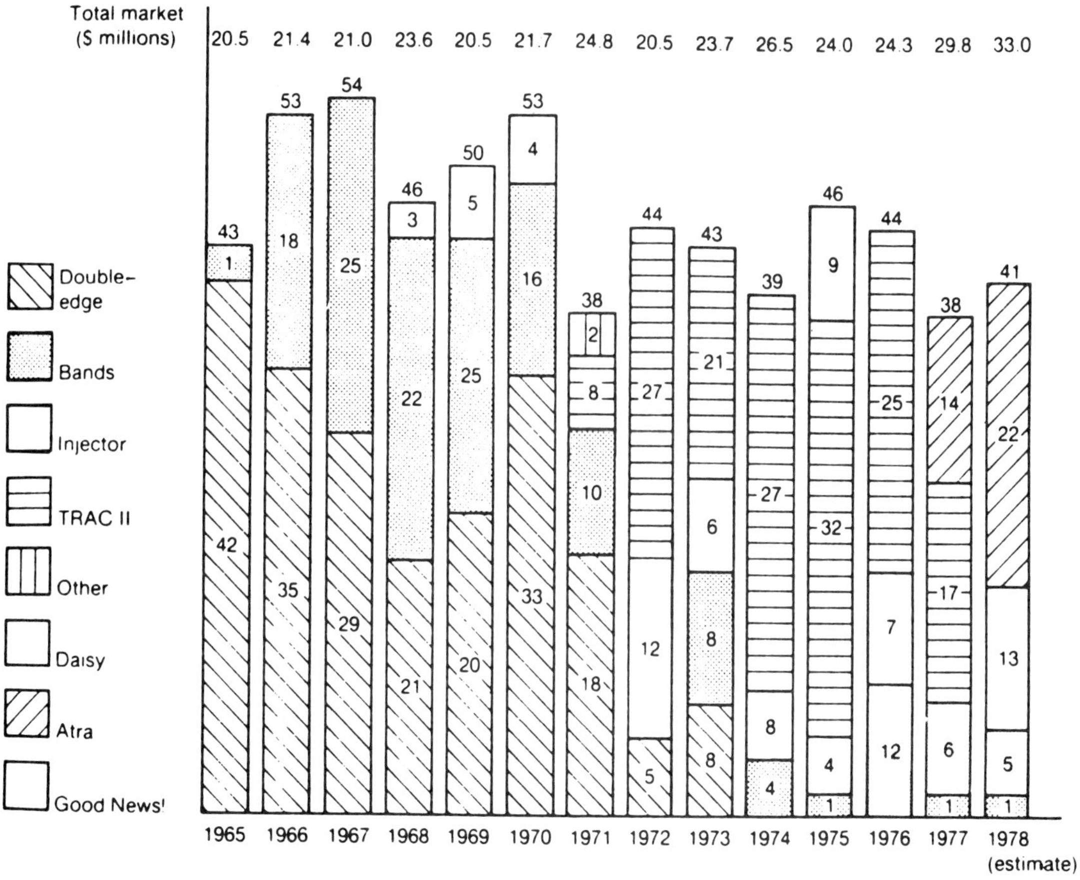

which was introduced by Schick, and the stainless-steel double-edged blade introduced by Wilkinson.

The company spends $37 million annually on research and development for new products, product improvements, and consumer testing. In addition to Atra, a recent development is a new sharpening process called "Microsmooth" which improves the closeness of the shave and the consistency of the blade. This improvement was to be introduced on all of the company's twin blades by early 1979. Mike Edwards believes that this will help to ensure TRAC II's retention of its market.

At the time of Atra's introduction, Gillette research found that users would come from users of TRAC II and nontwin-blade systems. This projected loss was estimated to be 60 percent of TRAC II users. Recent research indicates that with heavy marketing support in 1978, TRAC II's loss will be held to 40 percent.

THE SHAVING MARKET

The shaving market is divided into two segments, wet and electric shavers. Today, the wet shavers account for 75 percent of the market. In the United States alone, 1.9 billion blades and 23 million razors are sold annually. Gillette participates in the electric market through sales of electric razors by its Braun subsidiary.

Market Factors

There are a number of factors at work within the market: (1) the adult shaving population has increased in the past 15 years to 74.6 million men and 68.2 million women, (2) technological improvements have improved the quality of the shave as well as increased the life of the razor blade, and (3) the volume of blades and razors has begun to level off after a period of declining and then increasing sales (see Exhibit 6). Although the shaving market has increased slightly, there are more competitors. Yet Gillette has been able to maintain its share of the market—approximately two thirds of the dollar-razor market and a little over half of the dollar-blade market.

Market Categories

The market is segmented into seven components: new systems, disposables, injector, premium double-edged, carbon double-edged, continuous bands, and single-edged systems. In the early 1900s the shaving market consisted primarily of straight-edges. During the past 70 years, the market has evolved away from its single- and then double-edged emphasis to the present market of 60 percent bonded systems (all systems in which the blade is encased in plastic). Exhibit 7 shows the recent trends within the market categories.

Competitors

Gillette's major competitors are Warner-Lambert's Schick, Colgate-Palmolive's Wilkinson, American Safety Razor's Personna, and BIC. Each has its own strongholds. Schick, which introduced the injector

EXHIBIT 6 Razor and Blade Sales Volume, 1963–1979

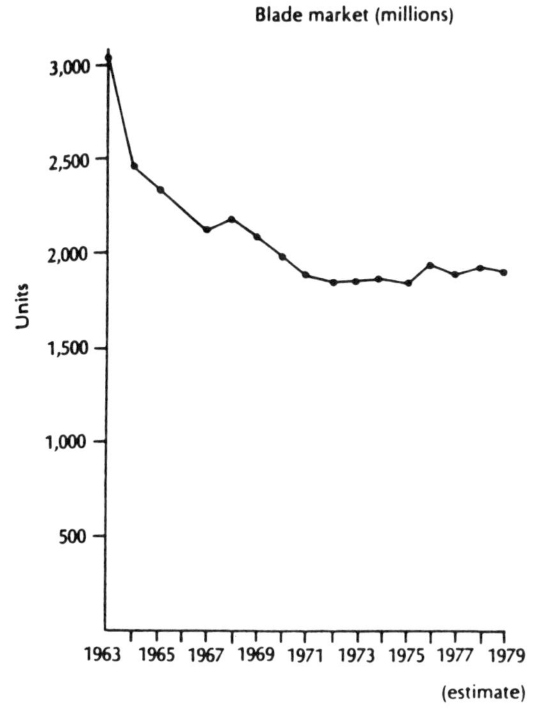

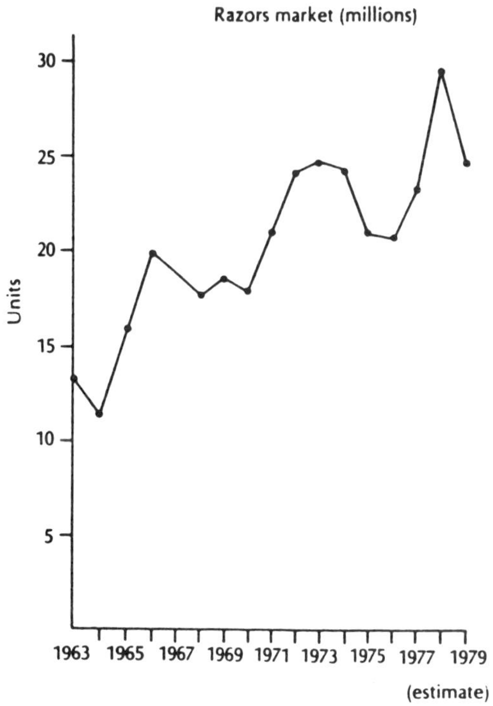

system, now controls 80 percent of that market. ASR's Personna sells almost all of the single-edged blades on the market. Wilkinson's strength is its bonded system which appeals to an older, wealthier market. BIC has developed a strong product in its inexpensive disposable system.

Competitive pricing structure is comparable to Gillette within the different system categories. Although all the companies have similar suggested retail prices, the differences found on the racks in the market are a function of the companies' off-invoice rates to the trade and their promotional allowances. It is not much of a factor at this time; private label covers the range of systems and continues to grow.

Market Segmentation

The success of Gillette's technological innovation can be seen in its effect on the total shaving market. Although there are other factors at

EXHIBIT 7 Recent Share Trends (percent)

Volume	*1972*	*1973*	*1974*	*1975*	*1976*	*1977*	*1978, 1st Half*
Units:							
New systems	8.8%	20.6%	28.8%	36.2%	39.9%	40.8%	43.8%
Injector	20.2	17.6	17.1	16.3	15.7	14.2	12.8
Double-edged:							
Premium	39.4	34.9	30.8	27.4	24.5	21.1	10.0
Carbon	12.0	10.6	9.4	8.1	7.3	7.6	6.6
Bands	13.1	10.3	8.0	6.4	4.7	3.7	2.7
Disposables	—	—	—	—	2.5	6.9	9.7
Single-edged	6.5	6.0	5.9	5.6	5.4	5.7	5.4
Total Market	100.0%	100.0%	100.0%	100.0%	100.0%	100.0%	100.0%
Dollars:							
New systems	11.8%	26.9%	36.9%	46.0%	50.1%	50.1%	52.1%
Injector	21.8	18.6	17.8	16.4	15.0	13.8	12.5
Doubled-edged:							
Premium	41.5	34.2	28.7	24.0	20.8	18.1	16.1
Carbon	6.1	5.4	4.7	4.2	4.0	4.1	3.5
Bands	15.4	11.8	8.7	6.5	4.8	3.6	2.8
Disposables	—	—	—	—	2.8	7.5	10.5
Single-edged	3.4	3.1	3.2	2.9	2.5	2.8	2.5
Total market	100.0%	100.0%	100.0%	100.0%	100.0%	100.0%	100.0%

play in the market, new product introductions have contributed significantly to market expansion as Exhibit 8 indicates.

TWIN-BLADE MARKET

Research played a key role in the development of twin blades. Gillette had two variations—the current type in which the blades are in tandem; the other type in which the blades' edges faced each other and required an up-and-down scrubbing motion. From a marketing standpoint, and because the Atra swivel system had problems in testing development, TRAC II was launched first. The research department played a major role in the positioning of the product when it discovered hysteresis, the phenomenon of whiskers being lifted out and after a time receding into the follicle. Thus, the TRAC II effect was that the second blade cut the whisker before it receded.

Since its introduction in 1971, the twin-blade market has grown to account for almost 60 percent of all blade sales. The twin-blade market

EXHIBIT 8 New Product Introductions and Their Effects on the Market, 1959–1977

Year	*Product Segment*	*Sales Blade/Razor Market ($ millions)*	*Change (percent)*
1959	Carbon	122.4	Base
1960	Super blue	144.1	+ 17.7 over 1959
1963	Stainless	189.3	+ 31.3 over 1960
1965	Super stainless	201.2	+ 6.3 over 1963
1966	Banded system	212.1	+ 5.4 over 1965
1969	Injector	246.8	+ 16.3 over 1966
1972	Twin blades	326.5	+ 32.2 over 1969
1975	Disposable	384.0	+ 17.6 over 1972
1977	Pivoting head	444.9	+ 15.9 over 1975

is defined as all bonded razors and blades (e.g., new systems; Atra and TRAC II; disposables: Good News! and BIC). Exhibit 9 shows the trends in the twin-blade market.

During this period many products have been introduced. These include the Sure Touch in 1971; the Deluxe TRAC II and Schick Super II in 1972; the Lady TRAC II, Personna Double II, and Wilkinson Bonded in 1973; the Personna Flicker, Good News!, and BIC Disposable in 1974; the Personna Lady Double II in 1975; and the Adjustable TRAC II and Schick Super II in 1976.

Advertising

In the race for market share, the role of advertising is extremely important in the shaving industry. Of all the media expenditures,

EXHIBIT 9 The Twin-Blade Market, 1972–1978 (in millions)

	1972	*1973*	*1974*	*1975*	*1976*	*1977*	*1978, Estimate*	*1979, Estimate*
Razors	$ 29.5	$ 32.1	$ 31.4	$ 31.3	$ 31.5	$ 39.7	$ 53.8	
Disposables	—	—	—	—	14.5	41.5	64.9	
Blades	31.6	72.0	105.7	147.5	176.3	183.7	$209.2	
Total twin	61.1	104.1	137.1	176.2	222.3	264.9	327.9	
Total market	$326.5	$332.6	$342.5	$384.0	$422.2	$444.9	$491.0	$500.0

EXHIBIT 10 Estimated Media Expenditures (in thousands)

	1976	*1977, 1st Half*	*1977, 2d Half*	*Total 1977*	*1978, 1st Half*	*Total 1978 Estimate*
Companies:						
Gillette	$10,800	$ 4,800	$ 6,400	$11,200	$ 8,100	$13,800
Schick	7,600	3,700	4,300	8,000	4,300	8,900
Wilkinson	2,700	1,400	2,200	3,600	1,400	2,200
ASR	2,600	700	200	900	200	800
BIC	600*	4,300	1,800	6,100	4,000	7,300
Total market	$24,300	$14,900	$14,900	$29,800	$18,000	$33,000
Brands:						
TRAC II	$ 6,000	$ 3,300	$ 1,700	$ 5,000	$ 2,400	$ 4,000
Atra	—	—	4,000	4,000	4,500	7,500
Good News!	1,900	1,200	600	1,800	700	1,600
Super II	2,600	1,400	2,600	4,000	3,000	4,600

* Product introduction

television is the primary vehicle in the twin-blade market. For Gillette, this means an emphasis on maximum exposure and sponsorship of sports events. The company's policy for the use of television is based on the concept that TV is essentially a family medium and programs should therefore be suitable for family viewing. Gillette tries to avoid programs that unduly emphasize sex or violence.

As the industry leader, TRAC II receives a great deal of competitive pressure in the form of aggressive advertising from competitors and other Gillette twin-blade brands (see Exhibit 10). For example, the theme of recent Schick commercials was the "Schick challenge," and BIC emphasized its lower cost and cleaner shave in relation to those of other twin-blade brands. However, competitive media expenditures are such that their cost per share point is substantially higher than TRAC II's.

Despite competitive pressures, TRAC II is aggressively advertised too. As a premium product, it does not respond directly to competitive challenges or shifts in its own media; rather, the advertising follows a standard principle of emphasizing TRAC II's strengths. As Exhibits 11 and 12 indicate, the TRAC II media plan emphasizes diversity with a heavy emphasis on advertising on prime-time television and on sports programs. In addition, TRAC II is continually promoted to retain its market share.

EXHIBIT 11 Media Plan, 1976, 1977 (in thousands)

	Quarter				
	1	*2*	*3*	*4*	*Total*
1976					
Prime	935	575	1,200	500	3,160
Sports	545	305	450	1,040	2,440
Network total	1,480	880	1,650	1,590	5,650
Other	80	85	70	165	400
Total	1,560	965	1,720	1,755	6,000
1977					
Prime	1,300	900	300	—	2,500
Sports	500	400	400	400	1,700
Network total	1,800	1,300	700	400	4,200
Print	—	—	200	200	400
Black	75	75	75	75	300
Military, miscellaneous	25	25	25	15	100
Total	1,900	1,400	1,000	700	5,000

For 1978, the division budgeted $18 million for advertising, with Atra and TRAC II receiving the major portion of the budget (see Exhibit 13). The traditional Gillette approach is for the newest brand to receive the bulk of the advertising dollars (see Exhibit 5). Therefore, it is certain that Atra will receive a substantial increase in advertising for 1979. Whether the division will increase or decrease TRAC II's budget as well as whether it will increase the total ad budget for 1979 is unknown at this time.

TRAC II

The 1971 introduction of TRAC II was the largest in shaving history. Influenced by the discovery of the hysteresis process, by the development of a clogfree dual-blade cartridge, and by consumer-testing data which showed a nine to one preference for TRAC II over the panelists' current razors, Gillette raced to get the product to market. Because the introduction involved so many people and was so critical to reversing a leveling of corporate profits (see Exhibit 2), the division president

EXHIBIT 12 TRAC II Media Plan, 1978 (in thousands)

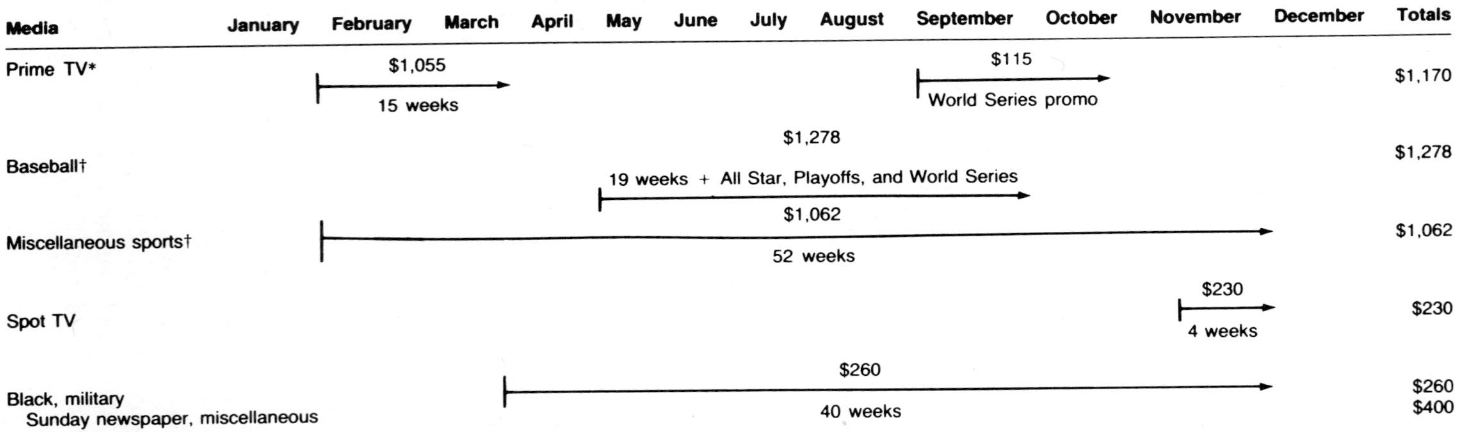
Media
January
February
March
April
May
June
July
August
September
October
November
December
Totals
Prime TV*
$1,055
15 weeks
$115
World Series promo
$1,170
Baseball†
$1,278
19 weeks + All Star, Playoffs, and World Series
$1,278
Miscellaneous sports†
$1,062
52 weeks
$1,062
Spot TV
$230
4 weeks
$230
Black, military
Sunday newspaper, miscellaneous
$260
40 weeks
$260
$400

* Prime-time TV advertising:

KAZ	Love Boat
ABC Friday Movie	Different Strokes
Tuesday Big Event	Real People
ABC Sunday Movie	Duke
Roots Two	Rockford Files

† Sports TV advertising:

Wide World of Sports	NBA Basketball
College Basketball	History of Baseball
NBA All Star Game	Game of the Week Day
International Teen Boxing	This Week Baseball
Wide World of Sports, Sunday.	

EXHIBIT 13 Razor Division Marketing Budget, 1978

	Atra Line	*TRAC II Line*	*Good News!*	*Double-Edged Blades*	*Double-Edged Razors*	*Techmatic Line*	*Daisy*	*Injector Line*	*Twin Injector*	*Total Blade/Razor*
Marketing expenses:										
Promotion*	42.3	69.4	65.2	92.2	75.4	52.7	58.4	77.5	48.3	60.7
Advertising†	55.6	28.8	31.2	4.6	—	—	39.0	—	26.3	36.5
Other	2.1	1.8	3.6	3.2	24.6	47.3	2.6	22.5	25.4	2.8
Total marketing	100.0	100.0	100.0	100.0	100.0	100.0	100.0	100.0	100.0	100.0
Percentage Line/total direct marketing	34.1	38.4	14.9	7.6	.4	.3	3.4	.2	.7	100.0
Percentage Line/total full revenue sales	20.5	41.8	13.4	16.8	1.4	2.1	2.2	.6	1.2	100.0

* Defined as off-invoice allowances, wholesale push money, cooperative advertising, excess cost, premiums, contests, and prizes.
† Defined as media, sampling, couponing, production, and costs.

personally assumed the role of product development manager and lived with the project day and night through its development and introduction.[3]

Launched during the 1971 World Series promotion, TRAC II was the most frequently advertised shaving system in America during its introductory period. Supported by $10 million in advertising and promotion, TRAC II results were impressive: 1.7 million razors and 5 million cartridges were sold in October; and during the first year, the introductory campaign made 2 billion impressions and reached 80 percent of all homes an average of 4.7 times a week. In addition, a multimillion-unit sampling campaign was implemented in 1972 which was the largest of its kind.

For five years TRAC II was clearly the fastest growing product on the market, and it helped to shape the switch to twin blades. Its users are predominantly young, college-educated, metropolitan, suburban, and upper-income men. The brand reached its peak in 1976 when it sold 485 million blades and 7 million razors. In comparison, projected TRAC II sales for 1978 are 433 million blades and 4.2 million razors. During this period, TRAC II brand contribution decreased 10 percent (see Exhibit 14). Competitors' responsive strategies seem to be effective. The growth of Super II during the last two years is attributed to certain advantages it has over TRAC II. Super II has higher trade allowances (20 percent versus 15 percent), improved distribution, an increased media expenditure, and generally lower everyday prices.

In preparing the 1979 marketing plans, the objective for TRAC II was to retain its consumer franchise despite strong competitive challenges through consumer-oriented promotions and to market the brand aggressively year round. Specifically, TRAC II was

1. To obtain a 20 percent share of the cartridge and razor market.
2. To deliver 43 percent of the division's profit.
3. To retain its valuable pegboard space at the checkout counters in convenience, food, and drug stores as well as supermarkets.

In 1978, Mike Edwards launched a new economy-size blade package (14 blades) and a heavy spending campaign to retain TRAC II's market share. He employed strong trade and consumer promotion incentives supported by (1) new improved product claims of a "microsmooth" shave, (2) new graphics, and (3) a revised version of the highly suc-

---

[3] For an excellent account of the TRAC II introduction, by the president of Gillette North America, see William G. Salatich, "Gillette's TRAC II: The Steps to Success," *Market Communications,* January 1972.

EXHIBIT 14 TRAC II Line Income Statement, 1972–1978

	*1972**	*1973*	*1974*	*1975*	*Base 1976*	*1977*	*Estimated 1978*
Full revenue sales (FRS):							
Promotional	28	41	71	100	100	110	112
Nonpromotional	38	91	89	83	100	80	65
Total	32	60	78	93	100	99	95
Direct cost of sales:							
Manufacturing	63	77	93	111	100	88	83
Freight	51	80	91	106	100	82	80
Total	62	77	93	111	100	88	83
Standard profit contribution	26	56	75	89	100	101	97
Marketing expenses							
Promotional expenses:							
Lost revenue	26	39	72	100	100	114	126
Wholesale push money	455	631	572	565	100	562	331
Cooperative advertising	27	36	58	71	100	115	133
Excess cost	25	50	59	83	100	63	92
Premiums	3	29	16	28	100	78	217
Contests and prizes	7	21	110	115	100	215	109
Total	26	40	67	90	100	112	129
Advertising:							
Media	90	83	110	119	100	96	75
Production	96	128	130	104	100	196	162
Couponing and sampling	470	344	177	112	100	166	131
Other	19	120	68	78	100	54	54
Total	124	110	108	117	100	96	78
Other marketing expenses	108	120	847	617	100	242	86
Market research	122	65	47	34	100	134	91
Total assignable marketing expenses	67	69	87	102	100	106	108
Net contribution:	14	53	81	85	100	100	94
Percentage of promotional FRS/total FRS	56	43	58	76	63	70	74
Percentage of promotional expense/promo FRS	15	16	16	15	11	17	20
Percentage of promotional expenses/total FRS	9	7	9	10	11	12	15
Percentage of advertising expenses/total FRS	28	13	10	9	7	7	6
Percentage of media expenses/total FRS	17	8	8	8	6	6	5

* Each year's data are shown as a percentage of 1976's line item. For example, 1972 sales were 32 percent of 1976 sales.

cessful "Sold Out" advertising campaign (see Exhibit 15). Midyear results indicated that TRAC II's performance had exceeded division expectations as it retained 21.6 percent of the blade market and its contribution exceeded the budget by $2 million.

ATRA (AUTOMATIC TRACKING RAZOR ACTION)

Origin

Research for the product began in Gillette's United Kingdom Research and Development Laboratory in 1970. The purpose was to improve the high standards of performance of twin-blade shaving and, specifically, to enhance the TRAC II effect. The company's scientists discovered that a better shave could be produced, if, instead of the shaver moving the hand and face to produce the best shaving angle for the blade, the razor head could pivot in such a way as to maintain the most effective twin-blade shaving angle. Once the pivoting head was shown to produce a better shave, test after test, research continued in the Boston headquarters on product design, redesigning, and consumer testing.

The name "Atra" came from two years of intensive consumer testing of the various names which could be identified with this advanced razor. The choice was based on how easy it was to remember the name, how well it communicated the technology, its uniqueness, and the feeling of the future it conveyed. Atra stands for *Automatic Tracking Razor Action.*

Introduction

Atra was first introduced in mid-1977. The introduction stressed the new shaving system supplemented by heavy advertising coupled with $2 razor rebate coupons to induce trial and 50-cent coupons toward Atra blades to induce brand loyalty. An example of Atra advertising is shown in Exhibit 16. During its first year on the national market, Atra was expected to sell 9 million razors although 85 percent of all sales were sold on a discount basis. Early results showed that Atra sold at a faster level than Gillette's previously most successful product, TRAC II. The Atra razor retails for $4.95. Blades are sold in packages of 5 and 10. TRAC II and Atra blades are not interchangeable. Because of Gillette's excellent distribution system, it has not had much problem gaining valuable pegboard space.

EXHIBIT 15

Gillette TRAC II®
THE GILLETTE COMPANY
SAFETY RAZOR DIVISION
BBDO
"SOLD OUT"
LENGTH: 30 SECONDS
(MICROSMOOTH-GIRL) SUPER II
COMM'L NO.: GSRD 8033
IRVING: Sold out again!???
(SFX: DING!)
CUSTOMER 1: The new improved Gillette TRAC II, please.
IRVING: Er . . . say . . . who needs improved when these twin blades'll do.
CUSTOMER 1: TRAC II has micro-smooth edges . . . makes the blades smoother than ever.
IRVING: Shave better than these?
CUSTOMER 1: Better, safer, smoother . . . and comfortable.
IRVING: Comfort . . . schmomfort . . . you don't have . . . But . . . but . . .b-b . . .
CUSTOMER 2: Do you have the new improved Gillette TRAC II?
IRVING: Improved TRAC II?? (INNOCENTLY) Improved TRAC II?
A better shave.
Gillette TRAC II
microsmooth
ANNCR: The new improved Gillette TRAC II. Micro-smooth edges make it a better shave.

EXHIBIT 16

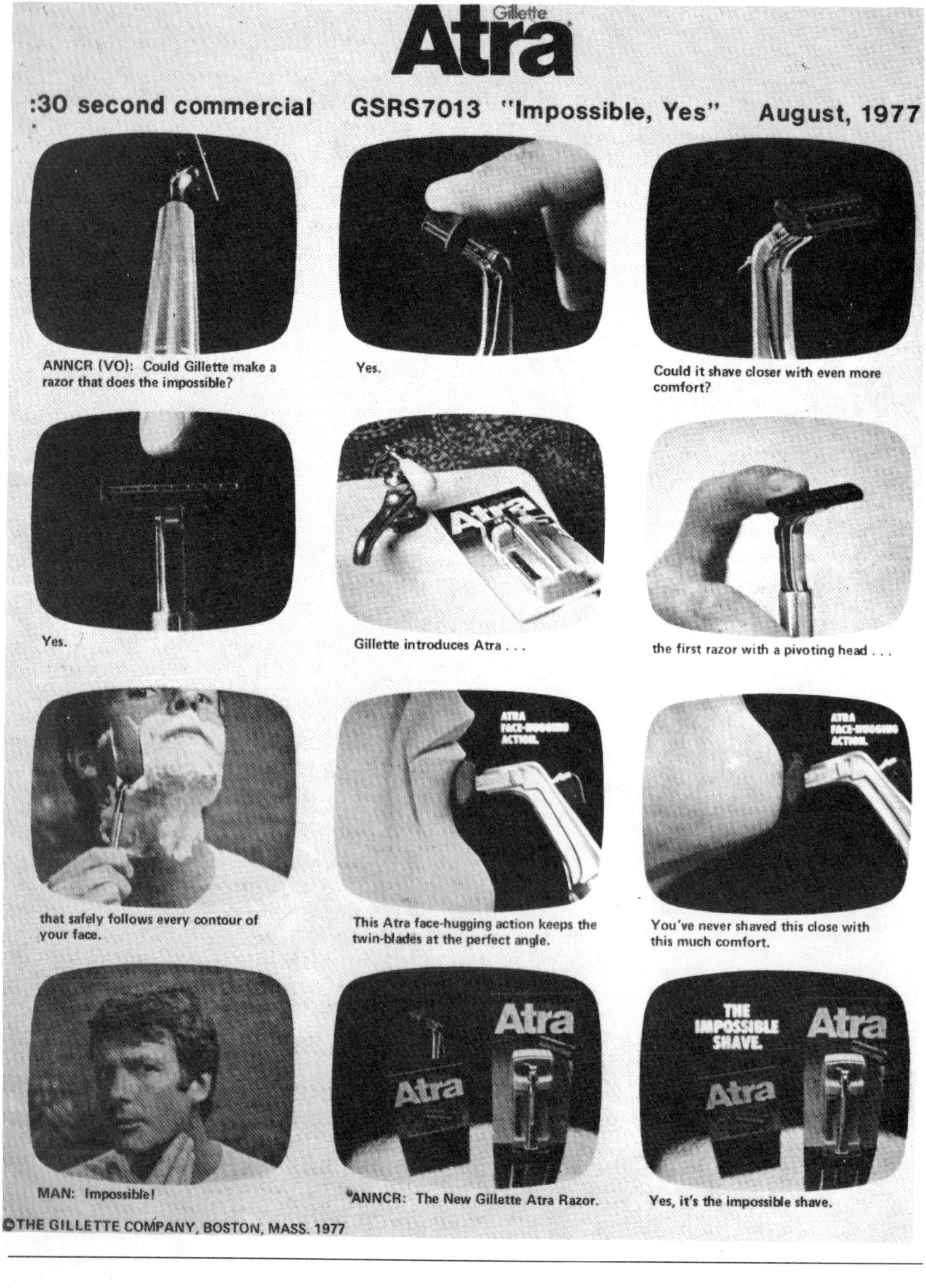
Gillette
Atra
:30 second commercial
GSRS7013 "Impossible, Yes"
August, 1977
ANNCR (VO): Could Gillette make a razor that does the impossible?
Yes.
Could it shave closer with even more comfort?
Yes.
Atra
Gillette introduces Atra . . .
the first razor with a pivoting head . . .
that safely follows every contour of your face.
ATRA FACE-HUGGING ACTION.
This Atra face-hugging action keeps the twin-blades at the perfect angle.
ATRA FACE-HUGGING ACTION.
You've never shaved this close with this much comfort.
MAN: Impossible!
Atra
Atra
ANNCR: The New Gillette Atra Razor.
THE IMPOSSIBLE SHAVE.
Atra
Atra
Yes, it's the impossible shave.
©THE GILLETTE COMPANY, BOSTON, MASS. 1977

CURRENT TRENDS AND COMPETITIVE RESPONSES IN THE TWIN-BLADE MARKET

There was quite a bit of activity in the shaving market during the first half of 1978. Atra has increased the total Gillette share in the razor and blade market. During the June period, Atra razors continued to exceed TRAC II as the leading selling razor whereas Atra blades share was approximately 8 percent, accounting for most of Gillette's 4 percent share growth since June 1977. Thus, the growth of Atra has put more competitive pressure on TRAC II. In addition, the disposable segment due to BIC and Good News! has increased by five share points to a hefty 12 percent dollar share of the blade market. Combined with TRAC II's resiliency in maintaining share, competitive brands have lost share: Schick Super II, ASR, and Wilkinson were all down two points since June 1977.

In response to these recent trends, the TRAC II team expected competition to institute some changes. In an effort to recover its sagging share, Edwards expected the Schick Muscular Dystrophy promotion in October 1977 to help bolster Super II with its special offer. The pressure may already be appearing with Schick's highly successful introduction of Personal Touch for women in this year, currently about 10 percent of the razor market, which has to draw TRAC II female shavers. In addition, it appears inevitable that Schick will bring out an Atra-type razor. This will remove Atra's competitive advantage but increase pressure on TRAC II with the addition of a second pivoting head competitor.

Continuing its recent trends, it appears that the disposable segment of the market will continue to expand. The first sign of this is the BIC ads offering 12 BIC disposables for $1. Good News! received additional advertising support in the latter half of the year as well as the introduction of a new package size. One of Edward's major objectives is to emphasize the importance of TRAC II to upper management. Besides the introduction of the microsmooth concept, a price increase on TRAC II products will be implemented soon. It is unclear whether the price change will have an adverse effect on brand sales.

In preparing the 1979 TRAC II marketing plan, Edwards realized that Atra would be given a larger share of the advertising dollars following a strong year, and the disposable market would continue to grow. TRAC II share remained questionable, depending on the level of marketing support it received. Whether TRAC II will be able to continue its heavy spending program and generate large revenues for the division remains to be seen. These factors, as well as the company's support of Atra, made 1979 a potentially tough year for Mike Edwards and TRAC II.

1979 MARKETING PLAN PREPARATION

Edwards recently received the following memorandum from the vice president of marketing:

> Memo to: Brand Group
>
> From: P. Meyers
>
> Date: July 7, 1978
>
> Subject: 1979 Marketing Plans
>
> In preparation for the marketing plan approval process and in developing the division strategy for 1979, I would like a preliminary plan from each brand group by the end of the month. Please submit statements of objective, corresponding strategy, and levels of dollar support requested for the following:
>
> 1. Overall brand strategy[4]—target market.
> 2. Blade and razor volume and share goals.
> 3. Sales promotion.
> 4. Advertising.
> 5. Couponing and sampling.
> 6. Miscellaneous—new packaging, additional marketing research, marketing cost saving ideas, etc.
>
> See you at the weekly meeting on Wednesday.

In developing the TRAC II marketing plan, Edwards had to wrestle with some strategy decisions. To get significant funding, how should he position TRAC II in relation to Atra and the disposables? Also, how does he convince the vice president that dollars spent for TRAC II are more effective than expenditures on Good news! or Gillette's electric razors?

---

[4] Brand strategy means positioning the brand in such a way that it appeals to a distinguishable target market.

Case Group C

Promotion Strategy

Case 11

General Foods*

Jerry C. Olson
Penn State University

In 1984, General Foods' Post cereal division suffered a drubbing at the hands of Kellogg, the market leader. Kellogg had begun to turn up the competitive heat in the early 1980s by increasing advertising expenditures and introducing a stream of new cereal products. During 1984, Kellogg increased its market share by 2 percent (up to 40 percent), while number-three-ranked GF dropped 2 percent (down to a 14 percent market share). The number two company, General Mills, held on to about a 20 percent market share, which had not changed significantly since 1980. These were not small changes. The ready-to-eat cereal market is a $4 billion market, so each share point was worth about $40 million in sales.

---

* This case was written by Jerry C. Olson, George and Lillian Binder Professor of Marketing, Penn State University. It is adapted from J. Paul Peter and Jerry C. Olson, *Consumer Behavior: Marketing Strategy Perspectives* (Homewood Ill.: Richard D. Irwin, 1987), pp. 657–58. Original source: Excerpted from Pamela Sherrid, "Fighting Back at Breakfast," *Forbes,* October 7, 1985, pp. 126–30.

Post did have one hugely successful product in 1984, Fruit & Fiber, which cleverly satisfied two potentially contradictory desires of adult cereal consumers—a healthful cereal that tastes good. On the negative side was the costly failure of Smurfberry Crunch that fizzled early despite very heavy advertising promotion. The heavy ad expenditures on these two brands had left little for promoting the other Post brands. So, while Kellogg was gearing up for its ad blitz, Post actually reduced ad spending by 24 percent to $44 million. Instead, GF spent additional promotional dollars on cents-off coupons and discounts to grocers. This strategy encouraged one-time sales, but didn't build long-term loyalty the way advertising does. In 1984, the disparity got worse, Kellogg increased its advertising spending by 49 percent to $160 million, while GF's rose only 16 percent to $52 million. At the same time Post's share sank from 15.5 to 14.6 percent.

But a different strategy was being planned at GF. Management decided to increase ad spending to match Kellogg's—but not over all its 14 brands. Instead, it would concentrate its dollars on five core brands—Raisin Bran, Grape Nuts, Fruit & Fiber, Super Golden Crisp, and Pebbles—which together account for 75 percent of Post's cereal sales. They increased ad expenditures by 40 percent in 1984 and again in 1985. But dollars alone don't do the trick in the cereal business. According to David Hurwitt, who runs GF's $500-million Post cereal business, "It costs just as much to run a lousy commercial as a good one." In fact, one of the reasons Post ad spending had decreased in 1983 was because GF (and their ad agencies) couldn't come up with the right advertising strategies and campaigns. Why spend money to show ineffective advertising?

More than most products, cereal is what marketers call "marketing sensitive." Dollars spent on mediocre marketing simply fall into the void—they have no noticeable effect. The same amount of money, however, spent on a well-designed communication strategy can dramatically increase sales. For instance, Post's Grape Nuts campaign—with its tag line "Are you right for Grape Nuts?"—offended many people. However, sales increased about 10 percent, compared to industry growth of only 3 percent.

Post's strategy was illustrated by the new campaign for Raisin Bran, launched in late 1985 at a cost of about $15 million. Hurwitt had changed the product to fit people's tendencies to eat what they think are "natural" foods. He removed the preservatives, increased the fiber, and took the sugar off the raisins. Then he hired singer John Denver—to some people the essence of all that is wholesome—for about $1 million to pitch the new product in a series of TV ads. Late in 1985, GF introduced another new cereal called Horizon, aimed at the active adult segment. The cereal is based on a "trail mix" concept, which means peanuts and grains clumped together, not in flakes.

Will Post's strategies work? The odds aren't good. Of dozens of new product entries, only a few cereals such as General Mill's Honey Nut Cheerios and Post's Fruit & Fiber have earned a sustainable 1 percent share in recent years. It's a big risk, but the potential payoffs are big, too.

Discussion Questions

1. Assume you are the brand manager for Raisin Bran. Present your arguments explaining why it is reasonable to spend $15 million in advertising on your brand even though only small (perhaps only 1 percent) shifts in market share are likely to be created. Make assumptions about the other costs that may be involved.
2. What are the relative advantages and disadvantages of using advertising and sales promotion strategies such as cents-off coupons, price reductions, and prizes and premiums to promote breakfast cereals?

Case 12

Outdoor Sporting Products, Inc.*

Zarrel V. Lambert
Auburn University

Fred W. Kniffen
University of Connecticut

The annual sales volume of Outdoor Sporting Products, Inc., for the past six years had ranged between $6.2 million and $6.8 million. Although profits continued to be satisfactory, Mr. Hudson McDonald, president and chief operating officer, was concerned because sales had not increased appreciably from year to year. Consequently, he asked a consultant in New York City and the officers of the company to submit proposals for improving the salesmen's compensation plan, which he believed was the basic weakness in the firm's marketing operations.

Outdoor's factory and warehouse were located in Albany, New York, where the company manufactured and distributed sporting equipment, clothing, and accessories. Mr. Hudson McDonald, who managed the company, organized it in 1956 when he envisioned a growing market for sporting goods resulting from the predicted increase in leisure time and the rising levels of income in the United States.

Products of the company, numbering approximately 700 items, were grouped into three lines: (1) fishing supplies, (2) hunting supplies, and (3) accessories. The fishing supplies line, which accounted for approximately 40 percent of the company's annual sales, included nearly every item a fisherman would need such as fishing jackets, vests, caps, rods and reels of all types, lines, flies, lures, landing nets, and creels. Thirty percent of annual sales were in the hunting supplies line, which consisted of hunting clothing of all types including insulated and thermal underwear, safety garments, shell holders, whistles, calls, and gun cases. The accessories line, which made up the balance of the company's annual sales volume, included items such as compasses,

---

* Adapted from a case written by Zarrel V. Lambert, Auburn University, and Fred W. Kniffen, University of Connecticut, Stamford. Used with permission.

cooking kits, lanterns, hunting and fishing knives, hand warmers, and novelty gifts.

While the sales of the hunting and fishing lines were very seasonal, they tended to complement one another. The January–April period accounted for the bulk of the company's annual volume in fishing items, and most sales of hunting supplies were made during the months of May through August. Typically, the company's sales of all products reached their lows for the year during the month of December.

Outdoor's sales volume was $6.57 million in the current year with self-manufactured products accounting for 35 percent of this total. Fifty percent of the company's volume consisted of imported products, which came principally from Japan. Items manufactured by other domestic producers and distributed by Outdoor accounted for the remaining 15 percent of total sales.

Mr. McDonald reported that wholesale prices to retailers were established by adding a markup of 50 to 100 percent to Outdoor's cost for the item. This rule was followed on self-manufactured products as well as for items purchased from other manufacturers. The resulting average markup across all products was 70 percent on cost.

Outdoor's market area consisted of the New England states, New York, Pennsylvania, Ohio, Michigan, Wisconsin, Indiana, Illinois, Kentucky, Tennessee, West Virginia, Virginia, Maryland, Delaware, and New Jersey. The area over which Outdoor could effectively compete was limited to some extent by shipping costs, since all orders were shipped from the factory and warehouse in Albany.

Outdoor's salesmen sold to approximately 6,000 retail stores in small- and medium-sized cities in its market area. Analysis of sales records showed that the firm's customer coverage was very poor in the large metropolitan areas. Typically, each account was a one- or two-store operation. Mr. McDonald stated that he knew for a fact that Outdoor's share of the market was very low, perhaps 2 to 3 percent; and for all practical purposes, he felt the company's sales potential was unlimited.

Mr. McDonald believed that with few exceptions. Outdoor's customers had little or no brand preference and in the vast majority of cases they bought hunting and fishing supplies from several suppliers.

It was McDonald's opinion that the pattern of retail distribution for hunting and fishing products had been changing during the past 10 years as a result of the growth of discount stores. He thought that the proportion of retail sales for hunting and fishing supplies made by small- and medium-sized sporting goods outlets had been declining compared to the percent sold by discounters and chain stores. An analysis of company records revealed Outdoor had not developed business among the discounters with the exception of a few small discount stores. Some of Outdoor's executives felt that the lack of business with discounters might have been due in part to the company's pricing policy and in part to the pressures which current customers had exerted on company salesmen to keep them from calling on the discounters.

Outdoor's Sales Force

The company's sales force played the major role in its marketing efforts since Outdoor did not use magazine, newspaper, or radio advertising to reach either the retail trade or consumers. One advertising piece that supplemented the work of the salesmen was Outdoor's merchandise catalog. It contained a complete listing of all the company's products and was mailed to all retailers who were either current accounts or prospective accounts. Typically, store buyers used the catalog for purposes of reordering.

Most accounts were contacted by a salesman two or three times a year. The salesmen planned their activities so that each store would be called upon at the beginning of the fishing season and again prior to the hunting season. Certain key accounts of some salesmen were contacted more often than two or three times a year.

Management believed that product knowledge was the major ingredient of a successful sales call. Consequently, Mr. McDonald had developed a "selling formula," which each salesman was required to learn before he took over a territory. The "formula" contained five parts: (1) the name and catalog number of each item sold by the company; (2) the sizes and colors in which each item was available; (3) the wholesale price of each item; (4) the suggested retail price of each item; and (5) the primary selling features of each item. After a new salesman had mastered the product knowledge specified by this "formula" he began working in his assigned territory and was usually accompanied by Mr. McDonald for several weeks.

Managing the sales force consumed approximately one third of Mr. McDonald's efforts. The remaining two thirds of his time was spent purchasing products for resale and in general administrative duties as the company's chief operating officer.

Mr. McDonald held semiannual sales meetings, had weekly telephone conversations with each salesman, and had mimeographed bulletins containing information on products, prices, and special promotional deals mailed to all salesmen each week. Daily call reports and attendance at the semiannual sales meetings were required of all salesmen. One meeting was held the first week in January to introduce the spring line of fishing supplies. The hunting line was presented at the second meeting, which was scheduled in May. Each of these sales meetings spanned four to five days so the salesmen were able to study the new products being introduced and any changes in sales and company policies. The production manager and comptroller attended these sales meetings to answer questions and to discuss problems which the salesmen might have concerning deliveries and credit.

On a predetermined schedule each salesman telephoned Mr. McDonald every Monday morning to learn of changes in prices, special promotional offers, and delivery schedules of unshipped orders. At this time the salesman's activities for the week were discussed, and sometimes the salesman was asked by Mr. McDonald to collect past due accounts in his territory. In addition, the salesmen submitted daily call reports, which listed the name of each account contacted and the results of the call. Generally, the salesmen planned their own itineraries in terms of the accounts and prospects that were to be contacted and the amount of time to be spent on each call.

Outdoor's sales force during the current year totaled 11 full-time employees. Their ages ranged from 23 to 67 years, and their tenure with the company ranged from 1 to 10 years. Salesmen, territories, and sales volumes for the previous year and the current year are shown in Exhibit 1.

EXHIBIT 1 Salesmen: Age, Years of Service, Territory, and Sales

				Sales	
Salesmen	*Age*	*Years of Service*	*Territory*	*Previous Year*	*Current Year*
Allen	45	2	Illinois and Indiana	$ 330,264	$ 329,216
Campbell	62	10	Pennsylvania	1,192,192	1,380,240
Duvall	23	1	New England	—	414,656
Edwards	39	1	Michigan	—	419,416
Gatewood	63	5	West Virginia	358,528	358,552
Hammond	54	2	Virginia	414,936	414,728
Logan	37	1	Kentucky and Tennessee	—	447,720
Mason	57	2	Delaware and Maryland	645,032	825,088
O'Bryan	59	4	Ohio	343,928	372,392
Samuels	42	3	New York and New Jersey	737,024	824,472
Wates	67	5	Wisconsin	370,712	342,200
Salesmen terminated in previous year				1,828,816	—
House account				257,384	244,480
Total				$6,478,816	$6,374,816

Compensation of Salesmen

The salesmen were paid straight commissions on their dollar sales volume for the calendar year. The commission rate was 5 percent on the first $300,000, 6 percent on the next $200,000 in volume, and 7 percent on all sales over $500,000 for the year. Each week a salesman could draw all or a portion of his accumulated commissions. McDonald encouraged the salesmen to draw commissions as they accumulated since he felt the men were motivated to work harder when they had a very small or zero balance in their commission accounts. These accounts were closed at the end of the year so each salesman began the new year with nothing in his account.

The salesmen provided their own automobiles and paid their traveling expenses, of which all or a portion were reimbursed by per diem. Under the per diem plan, each salesman received $70 per day for Monday through Thursday and $42 for Friday, or a total of $322 for the normal workweek. No per diem was paid for Saturday, but a salesman received an additional $70 if he spent Saturday and Sunday nights in the territory.

In addition to the commission and per diem, a salesman could earn cash awards under two sales incentive plans that were installed two years ago. Under the Annual Sales Increase Awards Plan, a total of $10,400 was paid to the five salesmen having the largest percentage increase in dollar sales volume over the previous year. To be eligible for these awards, a salesman had to show a sales increase over the previous year. These awards were made at the January sales meeting, and the winners were determined by dividing the dollar amount of each salesman's increase by his volume for the previous year with the percentage increases ranked in descending order. The salesmen's earnings under this plan for the current year are shown in Exhibit 2.

Under the second incentive plan, each salesman could win a Weekly Sales Increase Award for each week in which his dollar volume in the current year exceeded his sales for the corresponding week in the previous year. Beginning with an award of $4 for the first week, the amount of the award increased by $4 for each week in which the salesman surpassed his sales for the comparable week in the previous year. If a salesman produced higher sales during each of the 50 weeks in the current year, he received $4 for the 1st week, $8 for the 2nd week, and $200 for the 50th week, or a total of $4,100 for the year. The salesman had to be employed by the company during the previous year to be eligible for these awards. A check for the total amount of the awards accrued during the year was presented to the salesmen at the sales meeting held in January. Earnings of the salesmen under this plan for the current year are shown in Exhibit 2.

The company frequently used "spiffs" to promote the sales of special

EXHIBIT 2 Salesmen's Earnings and Incentive Awards in the Current Year

	Sales		*Annual Sales Increase Awards*			
Salesmen	*Previous Year*	*Current Year*	*Increase in Sales (percent)*	*Award*	*Weekly Sales Increase Awards (total accrued)*	*Earnings**
Allen	$ 330,264	$ 329,216	(0.3%)	—	$1,012	$30,000†
Campbell	1,192,192	1,380,240	15.8	$3,000 (2d)	2,244	88,617
Duvall	—	414,656	—	—	—	30,000†
Edwards	—	419,416	—	—	—	30,000†
Gatewood	358,528	358,552	(0.1)	400 (5th)	1,104	18,513
Hammond	414,936	414,728	—	—	420	30,000†
Logan	—	447,720	—	—	—	30,000†
Mason	645,032	825,088	27.9	4,000 (1st)	3,444	49,756
O'Bryan	343,928	372,392	8.3	1,000 (4th)	1,512	19,344
Samuels	737,024	824,472	11.9	2,000 (3d)	1,300	49,713
Wates	370,712	342,200	(7.7)	—	612	17,532

* Exclusive of incentive awards and per diem.
† Guarantee of $600 per week or $30,000 per year.

items. The salesman was paid a spiff, which usually was $4, for each order he obtained for the designated items in the promotion.

For the past three years in recruiting salesmen, Mr. McDonald had guaranteed the more qualified applicants a weekly income while they learned the business and developed their respective territories. During the current year five salesmen, Allen, Duvall, Edwards, Hammond, and Logan, had a guarantee of $600 a week, which they drew against their commissions. If the year's cumulative commissions for any of these salesmen were less than their cumulative weekly drawing accounts, they received no commissions. The commission and drawing accounts were closed on December 31 so each salesman began the new year with a zero balance in each account.

The company did not have a stated or written policy specifying the maximum length of time a salesman could receive a guarantee if his commissions continued to be less than his draw. Mr. McDonald held the opinion that the five salesmen who currently had guarantees would quit if these guarantees were withdrawn before their commissions reached $30,000 per year.

Mr. McDonald stated that he was convinced the annual earnings of Outdoor's salesmen had fallen behind earnings for comparable selling positions, particularly in the past six years. As a result, he felt that the company's ability to attract and hold high-caliber professional salesmen was being adversely affected. He strongly expressed the opinion that each salesman should be earning $50,000 annually.

Compensation Plan Proposals

In December of the current year, Mr. McDonald met with his comptroller and production manager, who were the only other executives of the company, and solicited their ideas concerning changes in the company's compensation plan for salesmen.

The comptroller pointed out that the salesmen having guarantees were not producing the sales that had been expected from their territories. He was concerned that the annual commissions earned by four of the five salesmen on guarantees were approximately half or less than their drawing accounts.

Furthermore, according to the comptroller, several of the salesmen who did not have guarantees were producing a relatively low volume of sales year after year. For example, annual sales remained at relatively low levels for Gatewood, O'Bryan, and Wates, who had been working four to five years in their respective territories.

The comptroller proposed that guarantees be reduced to $250 per week plus commissions at the regular rate on all sales. The $250 would not be drawn against commissions as was the case under the existing plan but would be in addition to any commissions earned. In the comptroller's opinion, this plan would motivate the salesmen to increase sales rapidly since their incomes would rise directly with their sales. The comptroller presented Exhibit 3, which showed the incomes of the five salesmen having guarantees in the current year as compared with the incomes they would have received under his plan.

From a sample check of recent shipments, the production manager

EXHIBIT 3 Comparison of Earnings in Current Year under Existing Guarantee Plan with Earnings under the Comptroller's Plan*

		Existing Plan			*Comptroller's Plan*		
Salesmen	*Sales*	*Commissions*	*Guarantee*	*Earnings*	*Commissions*	*Guarantee*	*Earnings*
Allen	$329,216	$16,753	$30,000	$30,000	$16,753	$12,500	$29,253
Duvall	414,656	21,879	30,000	30,000	21,879	12,500	34,379
Edwards	419,416	22,165	30,000	30,000	22,165	12,500	34,665
Hammond	358,552	18,513	30,000	30,000	18,513	12,500	31,013
Logan	447,720	23,863	30,000	30,000	23,863	12,500	36,363

* Exclusive of incentive awards and per diem.

had concluded that the salesmen tended to overwork accounts located within a 50-mile radius of their homes. Sales coverage was extremely light in a 60- to 100-mile radius of the salesmen's homes with somewhat better coverage beyond 100 miles. He argued that this pattern of sales coverage seemed to result from a desire by the salesmen to spend most evenings during the week at home with their families.

He proposed that the per diem be increased from $70 to $90 per day for Monday through Thursday, $42 for Friday, and $90 for Sunday if the salesman spent Sunday evening away from his home. He reasoned that the per diem of $90 for Sunday would act as a strong incentive for the salesmen to drive to the perimeters of their territories on Sunday evenings rather than use Monday morning for traveling. Further, he believed that the increase in per diem would encourage the salesmen to spend more evenings away from their homes, which would result in a more uniform coverage of the sales territories and an overall increase in sales volume.

The consultant from New York City recommended that the guarantees and per diem be retained on the present basis and proposed that Outdoor adopt what he called a "Ten Percent Self-Improvement Plan." Under the consultant's plan each salesman would be paid, in addition to the regular commission, a monthly bonus commission of 10 percent on all dollar volume over his sales in the comparable month of the previous year. For example, if a salesman sold $40,000 worth of merchandise in January of the current year and $36,000 in January of the previous year, he would receive a $400 bonus check in February. For salesmen on guarantees, bonuses would be in addition to earnings. The consultant reasoned that the bonus commission would motivate the salesmen, both those with and without guarantees, to increase their sales.

He further recommended the discontinuation of the two sales incentive plans currently in effect. He felt the savings from these plans would nearly cover the costs of his proposal.

Following a discussion of these proposals with the management group, Mr. McDonald was undecided on which proposal to adopt, if any. Further, he wondered if any change in the compensation of salesmen would alleviate all of the present problems.

Case 13

Computing Systems Ltd.*

Adrian B. Ryans
University of Western Ontario

"Bob doesn't appear to be too happy. He isn't making money, because he isn't selling. His own self-image is . . . well, he likes to spend money. He likes nice clothes, a nice car, and a nice house, that kind of thing, but he can't afford to live that way." These thoughts passed through Mike Hagen's mind in February 1980, as he reviewed once again the possible courses of action in dealing with one of his salespeople, Bob Nichols. Mike Hagen was the district manager in Winnipeg, Manitoba, for Computing Systems Ltd., a major full-line computer manufacturer. Mike had become increasingly concerned about Bob's performance in the last year. While the other salespeople in the district were having a very successful year, it had become quite clear to Mike that Bob was not even going to achieve his quota. Bob was thus hindering the district in its drive to meet its goals.

THE COMPANY

Computing Systems Ltd. was the Canadian subsidiary of Computing Systems, Inc., a major multinational manufacturer of a wide range of computers and peripheral equipment. The Computing Systems product lines were in direct competition with some of the computer lines of other major computer manufacturers.

The head office of Computing Systems was located in Toronto. The vice-president of marketing, who was located in the Toronto head office, oversaw all the firm's marketing activities. Reporting were the various marketing staff groups and three regional marketing managers who coordinated the marketing activities in the Western, Central, and Eastern regions. The Winnipeg office was located in the Western Region, and Mike Hagen reported to the Western Region marketing manager in Calgary. A partial organization chart of the Computing Systems marketing organization is shown in Exhibit 1.

EXHIBIT 1 Partial Organization Chart of Computing Systems Marketing Department

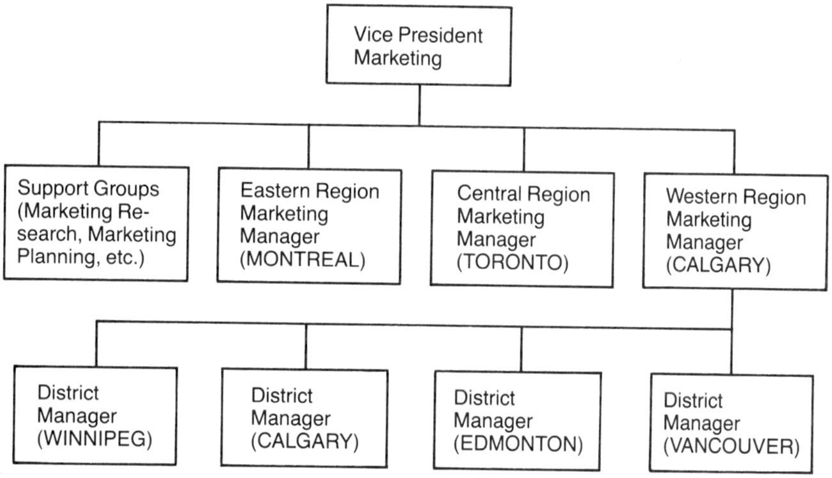

THE WINNIPEG DISTRICT

Mike Hagen had two groups of people reporting to him in the Winnipeg District. Three sales representatives reported directly to him. There were also 10 programmer analysts who reported to him through the district systems manager. A partial organization chart of the Winnipeg Branch is shown in Exhibit 2.

EXHIBIT 2 Organization of the Winnipeg District

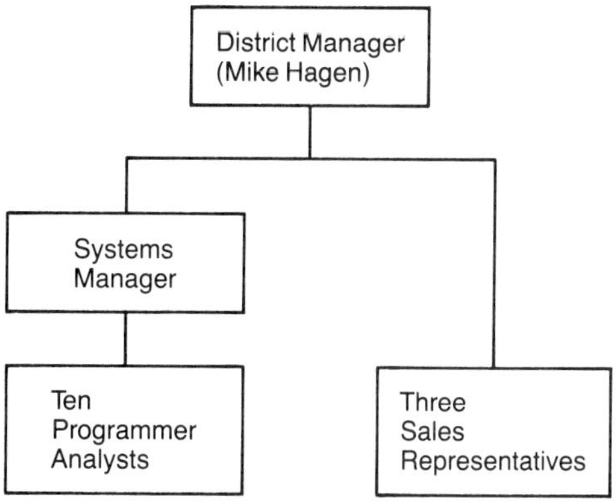

The programmer analysts in each district were responsible for providing systems support to the firm's customers. Many of the programmer analysts worked exclusively with one customer, while the others acted essentially as systems consultants for several of the firm's smaller customers. The programmer analysts were often involved in the presales evaluation of a customer's systems requirements. In this capacity, one or more systems analysts formed a team with one of the district's sales representatives, and together they evaluated the customer's needs and developed a proposed system that they felt would satisfy these needs. Programmer analysts were compensated on a salary basis, with raises dependent on job performance.

SALES ACTIVITIES

When asked to describe and comment on the sales job in the computer business, Mike Hagen said:

> The sales job is broken down into prospecting, qualifying prospects, planning the sales campaign, and all those activities related to closing. Now prospecting, generally speaking, is taken rather lightly by the sales reps, and I think that is a big mistake. It's a very, very difficult activity and it is closely related to qualifying—they dovetail very closely together. We're in the stage of the computer business where there is enough activity out there that you don't have to create demand. We qualify a prospect by asking, "Are you going to make a computer buying decision within the next 6 to 12 months?" If not, we just keep in touch. We don't really have time to say to a prospect, "Well, why don't you think of making this new application or why don't you think of buying that new equipment?" We may go in and try to develop a need if we see an area where a company could computerize, and then make a proposition and try and get their interest. But if they are not immediately interested, we forget it, because we really don't have the time or the resources to do it. So, the key thing in any salesperson's success is to have a big prospect list, because you don't get'em all. And the key thing with the prospect list is how well they are qualified. Will the person buy from us? Are we talking to the right person? Are they going to make the decision in the time frame they say? Timing is particularly important. If you peak out in your sales campaign to a prospect too early, you know your competitor is going to pick up the dice. It is very competitive. So the qualifying aspect is whether you are talking to the right person, will they make the decision, and do they have the guts to be the internal salesperson—the person to carry the ball for you in getting others in the company, the boss and so on, to agree to the purchase. All those questions in any sales campaign are very key because the next steps cost a lot of money in terms of time and resources. So once you get the customers to the point where you can say they are a qualified prospect, you can assume they will make a decision within a reasonable period of time. We have to restrict our dealings to qualified prospects because a person has got to make quota in the 12-month period. That's because, unfortunately, we work on a 12-month planning horizon.

Planning is probably one of the things that most sales-oriented people do worst. They respond to immediate conversations, interactions, and stimuli. The difficult thing is to say, "Well, when are you going to do this? What are you going to do if? What are your contingency plans?" And so on. It's an easy thing really for a manager to get salespeople to put together a plan in terms of putting it down on paper and saying this is what I am going to do. The hard part is to get them to do it, and to discipline themselves to do it when they say they are going to do it. And then to constantly ask the customer for the order, to go through trial closes to get objections. You see, in a sense, the qualifying process in our business never really ends, you never get to that point unless you have the order. So you are constantly asking questions and directing your campaign to further substantiate your qualifications. With one key order we got here in Winnipeg, for example, we didn't qualify until a week before we got the order. We didn't really consider them a prospect until we got very close to the order, because we hadn't been able to get to the top people.

The point at which the systems representative comes in depends on the level of gear. We sell computers anywhere from a $1,000 per month to $100,000 per month. Selling covers such a wide range of activities and such a wide range of customer prospect situations, that you might sell a small computer without ever getting a systems person in. You just go in and you say, "You want to computerize your payroll? No problem, we have just the package for you. It will do a super job for you. Sign here." Generally speaking, customers don't know their own needs well enough to evaluate anything properly anyway, so that after you sell it, anything that you can give them is a hell of a lot better than what they currently have. So if you know a little bit about receivables and payables you don't need a systems person, but you might bring in one or two people to impress the customer. When you get into, say, a large system, you need a host of technical people, not just in systems but in specialized areas of systems, such as data base management, communications, and operations management. With a large system you may have five or six computer operations raising hell, and you've got to coordinate that as a basic management function. When you only have a little main frame, you have a much simpler problem. You have only one person, so it's not really a coordination problem. Thus, the systems support that a salesperson needs varies dramatically from one situation to the next.

Each salesperson in Computing Systems was assigned an annual sales quota. The company used a "top-down" approach in developing sales quotas. Each year the marketing group in Toronto analyzed the anticipated levels of activity in the Canadian economy, the previous years' sales, the trends in the computer industry, etc., to develop a reasonable sales forecast for the following year. This forecast was then broken down into sales quotas for the individual districts, and these quotas were communicated to the district managers. It was then the responsibility of the district managers to develop quotas for the individual salespeople. Mike Hagen felt that this method resulted in salespeople receiving reasonable, attainable quotas. In fact, Mike said that if he asked any of his salespeople what was a reasonable quota for the next year, they usually gave him a figure higher than the quota he would assign them.

Salespeople were compensated largely on a commission basis, receiving a commission on each sale related to the profitability of the sale to the company. Generally, total compensation was highly correlated with quota achievement.

THE GROWTH OF THE WINNIPEG OFFICE

Mike Hagen had joined Computing Systems after graduating with an M.B.A. degree from an eastern university in 1976. Mike had spent his first few months with the company in its sales training course in Toronto. On completion of the course he had become a sales representative in Toronto. After one year with Computing Systems, Mike had been transferred to Winnipeg as a sales representative. Initially, he was the only sales representative in Winnipeg, and he reported to the district manager in the Calgary office. In September 1977, two additional experienced salespeople, Jill Cooper and Nick Johnston, were hired from outside the computer business and joined the Winnipeg office. In 1977, Mike met his sales quota, and in 1978, he was one of the top Computing Systems salespeople in Canada. In June 1978, Winnipeg became a separate district, and a district manager was appointed. The district manager then reported directly to the Western Region marketing manager in Calgary. About six months after moving to Winnipeg, the district manager was promoted and left Winnipeg, and in January 1979, Mike Hagen was promoted to district manager. Mike felt the decision to promote him to district manager had been a difficult one for the company, since he was relatively inexperienced, having only been employed by Computing Systems for two and one-half years. Mike thus felt he had a lot to prove in his new job, and he was anxious to prove that he could do a superior job as district manager.

Shortly before Mike Hagen became District Manager, Bob Nichols was transferred to Winnipeg from Vancouver. Bob Nichols had joined the company directly after graduating from college with a B.Sc. in 1974. Bob spent his initial six months with the company in a training program for systems analysts. After completing the training program in November 1974, Bob became a systems representative in the Vancouver office. He progressed well in the job, and in 1975 he received a President's Award for his outstanding performance as a systems representative. Even though he had spent very little time as a systems representative, Bob's superiors considered him one of the most promising systems people in Canada. The following year Bob requested a move from systems to sales. Bob entered the company's basic sales training program and received part of his training in Toronto, and, in fact, for a couple of months he and Mike worked in the same office in Toronto. Bob's switch into sales was motivated largely by his desire for the higher compensation a successful sales representative could earn. A few of Bob's friends from his undergraduate days, who had been quite successful financially, were also living in Vancouver, and the group of young couples led an active social life. Bob thought that a salesperson's compensation would allow him to lead that type of life.

Within a few months of beginning work as a sales representative, one of Bob's customers purchased a major system, one of the largest systems ever installed by Computing Systems in Canada. The sale of this system was the culmination of a major selling job by Bob and a couple of his superiors in the Vancouver office. Largely as a result of being credited with this sale, Bob won a second President's Award in 1977 for his performance as a sales representative. Bob did not have such a successful year in 1978. In the first nine months of 1978 Bob did not meet his quota, although his performance was considered acceptable. In September 1978, Bob was transferred to Winnipeg because company management felt the change of environment might result in improved sales performance. Although Mike saw very little of Bob and his wife socially after they moved to Winnipeg, he gathered from his conversations with Bob that they were adjusting reasonably well to their new life.

MIKE HAGEN AS DISTRICT MANAGER

When Mike Hagen assumed the job of district manager in January 1979 he had four salespeople reporting to him. His first year in the new job was reasonably successful, and the Winnipeg office made quota at a time when several other districts did not.

The quota achievements for the four salespeople in the Winnipeg District for 1978 and 1979 are shown in Exhibit 3. In late 1979, Tony Webb, whose performance had been satisfactory in 1978 but marginal in 1979, was transferred to the Vancouver office. The performance of Jill Cooper and Nick Johnston both showed a significant improvement between 1978 and 1979. In 1979, they were both among the top Computing Systems salespeople in Canada.

Bob, in his short period in Winnipeg in 1978, had not met his quota, which was not surprising, since it took a few months to develop a list of prospects. However, his performance was again marginal in 1979. As Mike Hagen reviewed Bob's performance record and prospect list in February 1980, it appeared very likely to him that Bob would not make his quota again in 1980. From his previous discussions with Bob

EXHIBIT 3 Sales Performance as a Percent of Quota—Winnipeg District

	Percentage of Achievement Quota	
Salespeople	*1978*	*1979*
Tony Webb	100	81*
Jill Cooper	105	195
Nick Johnston	53	205
Bob Nichols	55*	63

* Quota prorated for the period in Winnipeg.

about his performance, he knew that Bob realized this too, although Bob would probably not openly admit it. Bob seemed uneasy that he, the senior salesperson in the office, was performing much worse than other, less experienced salespeople.

Mike felt that he had developed a good business relationship with Bob in their 18 months together in the Winnipeg office. Shortly after becoming manager Mike had assisted Bob in landing a major order. The order had required a lot of internal selling within Computing Systems, and Mike had spent many hours convincing Computer Systems personnel that the deal he and Bob had worked out with the customer was a good one for Computing Systems. Mike felt that Bob realized that he would not have been able to do the internal selling job himself, and thus, he felt he had gained Bob's respect for his skill and efforts.

THE SITUATION IN FEBRUARY 1980

As he reviewed the situation in February 1980, Mike Hagen felt there were at least four possible courses of action he could take. The first alternative was simply to ask Bob for his resignation. Mike was personally not very happy with this alternative, since he knew there were several other Computing Systems salespeople in other districts performing less satisfactorily than Bob. However, Bob's performance was inconsistent with Mike's goals for the Winnipeg district. He had also broached the subject of Bob's performance with the Western Region marketing manager, and he felt his attitude and the attitude of other people in senior management was that Bob was worth saving.

The second alternative was transferring Bob to another district as a sales representative. This was probably the easiest course of action.

The third alternative was for Mike to spend additional time with Bob trying to improve his sales performance. Mike had spent a large amount of time the previous year accompanying Bob and each of the other salespeople on sales calls and critiquing their selling methods. Mike felt that Bob did an excellent job right up to the point of actually trying to close the sale. In Mike's words, "Bob doesn't have that killer instinct—to go for the throat—the real pressure that you have to exert to get some orders—the real pushing hard, brass-knuckled approach that is sometimes absolutely necessary to get an order." Mike also felt that Bob did not handle risk well, and often seemed to want to "give away" the systems when he got close to the sale. Mike also believed that Bob was not very effective in doing the internal selling that had to be done inside Computing Systems. Since the computer systems packages were often customized to an individual customer's needs, the computer salesperson had to convince Computing Systems management that the deal they were proposing to the customer was also profitable from Computing Systems' viewpoint. Mike felt Bob had a very difficult time handling the two sets of conflicting demands.

Mike also knew that one of Bob's goals was eventually to move into sales management, but in Computing Systems a necessary condition for promotion into sales management was a good selling record. For this reason he felt he should consider making further efforts to develop Bob in the sales area. He wondered, however, where he would be able to find additional time to spend with Bob without neglecting the other salespeople and, even if he did spend the time, whether he would be successful.

The final alternative was to try to change Bob's career path from sales back into systems. Mike had checked with senior management about any suitable openings for Bob in other offices in Canada in a systems capacity, but there were none. Thus, any move would have to be made within the Calgary office. Mike thought he might be able to persuade Bob to accept a position as a senior systems analyst, but he knew that it would be a difficult switch for Bob to accept. The salary as a senior systems analyst would be comparable to Bob's total compensation in 1979. However, had he made quota in 1979, his total compensation as a salesperson would have been about 50 percent higher than the amount he could earn as a systems analyst. The switch also had other potential problems: Mike felt his systems manager would deeply resent having to take on a "loser" from sales. The personalities of Bob and the systems manager were different, and this was also likely to be an area of further conflict. Furthermore, Mike did not feel he could discuss this alternative with the systems manager before making the decision, since he felt the systems manager would attempt to prevent the change. Mike also felt some of the systems staff would resent a salesperson moving into a senior systems position in the office. If it hadn't been for all these potential problems, Mike felt that Bob would probably do an outstanding job as a senior systems analyst.

As he weighed the pros and cons of the different alternatives in his mind, Mike wondered if there were any other alternatives he had overlooked. He was also concerned about how he should reveal his decision to Bob and to what extent he should involve the Western Region marketing manager and other senior company personnel. Mike knew he had to come to a decision quickly, since he was flying to Calgary in three days to see the Western Region marketing manager. He wanted to tell his superior what course of action he planned to follow and to get his approval.

Case 14

Hanover-Bates Chemical Corporation*

Robert E. Witt
University of Texas–Austin

James Sprague, newly appointed northeast district sales manager for the Hanover-Bates Chemical Corporation, leaned back in his chair as the door to his office slammed shut. "Great beginning," he thought. "Three days in my new job and the district's most experienced sales representative is threatening to quit."

On the previous night, James Sprague, Hank Carver (the district's most experienced sales representative), and John Follet, another senior member of the district sales staff, had met for dinner at Jim's suggestion. During dinner Jim had mentioned that one of his top priorities would be to conduct a sales and profit analysis of the district's business in order to identify opportunities to improve the district's profit performance. Jim had stated that he was confident that the analysis would indicate opportunities to reallocate district sales efforts in a manner that would increase profits. As Jim had indicated during the conversation, "My experience in analyzing district sales performance data for the national sales manager has convinced me that any district's allocation of sales effort to products and customer categories can be improved." Both Carver and Follet had nodded as Jim discussed his plans.

Hank Carver was waiting when Jim arrived at the district sales office the next morning. It soon became apparent that Carver was very upset by what he perceived as Jim's criticism of how he and the other district sales representatives were doing their jobs—and, more particularly, how they were allocating their time in terms of customers and products. As he concluded his heated comments, Carver said:

> This company has made it darned clear that 34 years of experience don't count for anything . . . and now someone with not much more than two

* This case was prepared by Professor Robert E. Witt, The University of Texas, Austin, and is intended to serve as a basis for class discussion rather than to illustrate effective or ineffective management.

EXHIBIT 1 Hanover-Bates Chemical Corporation: Summary Income Statements, 1981–1985

	1981	*1982*	*1983*	*1984*	*1985*
Sales	$19,890,000	$21,710,000	$19,060,000	$21,980,000	$23,890,000
Production expenses	11,934,000	13,497,000	12,198,000	13,612,000	14,563,000
Gross profit	7,956,000	8,213,000	6,862,000	8,368,000	9,327,000
Administrative expenses	2,606,000	2,887,000	2,792,000	2,925,000	3,106,000
Selling expenses	2,024,000	2,241,000	2,134,000	2,274,000	2,399,000
Pretax profit	3,326,000	3,085,000	1,936,000	3,169,000	3,822,000
Taxes	1,512,000	1,388,000	790,000	1,426,000	1,718,000
Net profit	$ 1,814,000	$ 1,697,000	$ 1,146,000	$ 1,743,000	$ 2,104,000

years of selling experience and two years of pushing paper for the national sales manager at corporate headquarters tells me I'm not doing my job. . . . Maybe it's time for me to look for a new job . . . and since Trumbull Chemical [Hanover-Bates's major competitor] is hiring, maybe that's where I should start looking . . . and I'm not the only one who feels this way.

As Jim reflected on the scene that had just occurred, he wondered what he should do. It had been made clear to him when he had been promoted to manager of the northeast sales district that one of his top priorities should be improvement of the district's profit performance. As the national sales manager had said, "The northeast sales district may rank third in dollar sales, but it's our worst district in terms of profit performance."

Prior to assuming his new position, Jim had assembled the data presented in Exhibits 1 through 6 to assist him in analyzing district

EXHIBIT 2 District Sales Quota and Gross Profit Quota Performance, 1985

		Sales		*Gross Profit*	
District	*Number of Sales Reps*	*Quota*	*Actual*	*Quota**	*Actual*
1	7	$ 3,880,000	$ 3,906,000	$1,552,000	$1,589,000
2	6	3,750,000	3,740,000	1,500,000	1,529,000
3	6	3,650,000	3,406,000	1,460,000	1,239,000
4	6	3,370,000	3,318,000	1,348,000	1,295,000
5	5	3,300,000	3,210,000	1,320,000	1,186,000
6	5	3,130,000	3,205,000	1,252,000	1,179,000
7	5	2,720,000	3,105,000	1,088,000	1,310,000
		$23,800,000	$23,890,000	$9,520,000	$9,327,000

* District gross profit quotas were developed by the national sales manager in consultation with the district managers and took into account price competition in the respective districts.

EXHIBIT 3 District Selling Expenses, 1985

District	*Sales Rep Salaries**	*Sales Commission*	*Sales Rep Expenses*	*District Office*	*District Manager Salary*	*District Manager Expenses*	*Sales Support*	*Total Selling Expenses*
1	$177,100	$19,426	$56,280	$21,150	$33,500	$11,460	$69,500	$ 388,416
2	143,220	18,700	50,760	21,312	34,000	12,034	71,320	351,346
3	157,380	17,030	54,436	22,123	35,000†	12,382	70,010	368,529
4	150,480	16,590	49,104	22,004	32,500	11,005	66,470	348,153
5	125,950	16,050	42,720	21,115	33,000	11,123	76,600	326,558
6	124,850	16,265	41,520	20,992	33,500	11,428	67,100	315,655
7	114,850	17,530	44,700	22,485	31,500	11,643	58,750	300,258
								$2,398,915

* Includes cost of fringe benefit program, which was 10 percent of base salary.
† Salary of Jim Sprague's predecessor.

sales and profits. The data had been compiled from records maintained in the national sales manager's office. Although he believed the data would provide a sound basis for a preliminary analysis of district sales and profit performance, Jim had recognized that additional data would probably have to be collected when he arrived in the northeast district (District 3).

In response to the national sales manager's comment about the northeast district's poor profit performance, Jim had been particularly interested in how the district had performed on its gross profit quota. He knew that district gross profit quotas were assigned in a manner that took into account variation in price competition. Thus he felt that poor performance in the gross profit quota area reflected misallocated

EXHIBIT 4 District Contribution to Corporate Administrative Expense and Profit, 1985

District	*Sales*	*Gross Profit*	*Selling Expenses*	*Contribution to Administrative Expense and Profit*
1	$ 3,906,000	$1,589,000	$ 388,416	$1,200,544
2	3,740,000	1,529,000	351,346	1,177,654
3	3,406,000	1,239,000	368,529	870,471
4	3,318,000	1,295,000	348,153	946,847
5	3,210,000	1,186,000	326,558	859,442
6	3,205,000	1,179,000	315,376	863,624
7	3,105,000	1,310,000	300,258	1,009,742
	$23,890,000	$9,327,000	$2,398,636	$6,928,324

EXHIBIT 5 Northeast (# 3) and North-Central (#7) District Sales and Gross Profit Performance by Account Category, 1985

District	*(A)*	*(B)*	*(C)*	*Total*
		Sales by Account Category		
Northeast	$915,000	$1,681,000	$810,000	$3,406,000
North-central	751,000	1,702,000	652,000	3,105,000
		Gross Profit by Account Category		
Northeast	$356,000	$ 623,000	$260,000	$1,239,000
North-central	330,000	725,000	255,000	1,310,000

sales efforts either in terms of customers or in the mix of product line items sold. To provide himself with a frame of reference, Jim had also requested data on the north-central sales district (District 7). This district was generally considered to be one of the best, if not the best, in the company. Furthermore, the north-central district sales manager, who was only three years older than Jim, was highly regarded by the national sales manager.

THE COMPANY AND INDUSTRY

The Hanover-Bates Chemical Corporation was a leading producer of processing chemicals for the chemical plating industry. The company's products were produced in four plants located in Los Angeles, Houston, Chicago, and Newark, New Jersey. The company's production process was, in essence, a mixing operation. Chemicals purchased from a broad range of suppliers were mixed according to a variety of user-based formulas. Company sales in 1985 had reached a new high of $23.89 million, up from $21.98 million in 1984. Net pretax profit in 1985 had

EXHIBIT 6 Potential Accounts, Active Accounts, and Account Call Coverage: Northeast and North-Central Districts, 1985

	Potential Accounts			*Active Accounts*			*Account Coverage (total calls)*		
District	*(A)*	*(B)*	*(C)*	*(A)*	*(B)*	*(C)*	*(A)*	*(B)*	*(C)*
Northeast	90	381	635	53	210	313	1,297	3,051	2,118
North-central	60	286	499	42	182	218	1,030	2,618	1,299

been $3.822 million, up from $3.169 million in 1984. Hanover-Bates had a strong balance sheet, and the company enjoyed a favorable price-earnings ratio on its stock, which traded on the OTC market.

Although Hanover-Bates did not produce commodity-type chemicals (e.g., sulfuric acid and others), industry customers tended to perceive minimal quality differences among the products produced by Hanover-Bates and its competitors. Given the lack of variation in product quality and the industrywide practice of limited advertising expenditures, field sales efforts were of major importance in the marketing programs of all firms in the industry.

Hanover-Bates's market consisted of several thousand job-shop and captive (in-house) plating operations. Chemical platers process a wide variety of materials including industrial fasteners (e.g., screws, rivets, bolts, washers, and others), industrial components (e.g., clamps, casings, couplings, and others), and miscellaneous items (e.g., umbrella frames, eyelets, decorative items, and others). The chemical plating process involves the electrolytic application of metallic coatings such as zinc, cadmium, nickel, brass, and so forth. The degree of required plating precision varies substantially, with some work being primarily decorative, some involving relatively loose standards (e.g., 0.0002 zinc, which means that anything over two ten-thousandths of an inch of plate is acceptable) and some involving relatively precise standards (e.g., 0.0003–0.0004 zinc).

Regardless of the degree of plating precision involved, quality control is of critical concern to all chemical platers. Extensive variation in the condition of materials received for plating requires a high level of service from the firms supplying chemicals to platers. This service is normally provided by the sales representatives of the firm(s) supplying the plater with processing chemicals.

Hanover-Bates and the majority of the firms in its industry produced the same line of basic processing chemicals for the chemical plating industry. The line consisted of a trisodium phosphate cleaner (SBX), anesic aldahyde brightening agents for zinc plating (ZBX), cadmium plating (CBX) and nickel plating (NBX), a protective post-plating chromate dip (CHX), and a protective burnishing compound (BUX). The company's product line is detailed as follows:

Product	*Container Size*	*List Price*	*Gross Margin*
SPX	400-lb. drum	$ 80	$28
ZBX	50-lb. drum	76	34
CBX	50-lb. drum	76	34
NBX	50-lb. drum	80	35
CHX	100-lb. drum	220	90
BUX	400-lb. drum	120	44

COMPANY SALES ORGANIZATION

Hanover-Bates's sales organization consisted of 40 sales representatives operating in seven sales districts. Sales representatives' salaries ranged from $14,000 to $24,000 with fringe-benefit costs amounting to an additional 10 percent of salary. In addition to their salaries, Hanover-Bates's sales representatives received commissions of 0.5 percent of their dollar sales volume on all sales up to their sales quotas. The commission on sales in excess of quota was 1 percent.

In 1983 the national sales manager of Hanover-Bates had developed a sales program based on selling the full line of Hanover-Bates products. He believed that if the sales representatives could successfully carry out his program, benefits would accrue to both Hanover-Bates and its customers:

1. Sales volume per account would be greater and selling costs as a percentage of sales would decrease.
2. A Hanover-Bates's sales representative could justify spending more time with such an account, thus becoming more knowledgeable about the account's business and becoming better able to provide technical assistance and identify selling opportunities.
3. Full-line sales would strengthen Hanover-Bates's competitive position by reducing the likelihood of account loss to other plating chemical suppliers (a problem that existed in multiple-supplier situations).

The national sales manager's 1983 sales program had also included the following account call-frequency guidelines:

A accounts (major accounts generating $12,000 or more in yearly sales)—two calls per month.

B accounts (medium-sized accounts generating $6,000–$11,999 in yearly sales)—one call per month.

C accounts (small accounts generating less than $6,000 yearly in sales)—one call every two months.

The account call-frequency guidelines were developed by the national sales manager after discussions with the district managers. The national sales manager had been concerned about the optimum allocation of sales effort to accounts and felt that the guidelines would increase the efficiency of the company's sales force, although not all of the district sales managers agreed with this conclusion.

It was common knowledge in Hanover-Bates's corporate sales office that Jim Sprague's predecessor as northeast district sales manager had not been one of the company's better district sales managers. His attitude toward the sales plans and programs of the national sales manager had been one of reluctant compliance rather than acceptance and support. When the national sales manager succeeded in persuading Jim Sprague's predecessor to take early retirement, he had been faced with the lack of an available qualified replacement.

Hank Carver, who most of the sales representatives had assumed would get the district manager job, had been passed over in part because he would be 65 in three years. The national sales manager had not wanted to face the same replacement problem again in three years and also had wanted someone in the position who would be more likely to be responsive to the company's sales plans and policies. The appointment of Jim Sprague as district manager had caused considerable talk, not only in the district but also at corporate headquarters. In fact, the national sales manager had warned Jim that "a lot of people are expecting you to fall on your face . . . they don't think you have the experience to handle the job, in particular, and to manage and motivate a group of sales representatives, most of whom are considerably older and more experienced than you." The national sales manager had concluded by saying, "I think you can handle the job, Jim. . . . I think you can manage those sales reps and improve the district's profit performance . . . and I'm depending on you to do both.

Case 15

S.C. Johnson—The Agree Line*

Stephen B. Ash
Sandra Safran
both of the University of Western Ontario

As Mel Liston reviewed the latest material received from the firm's advertising agency, he felt very pleased that his recommendations on product positioning had been approved by senior management. These recommendations centered around a new targeting strategy for Agree Shampoo and Agree Creme Rinse and Conditioner that would shift marketing effort away from the "all women, aged 18 to 45" segment toward the "teenage female" segment of the market. As product manager of the Agree line at S.C. Johnson & Son, Ltd., in Brantford, Ontario, his current task was to develop a comprehensive marketing communications program aimed at the new target audience for the fiscal year (FY) 1980–1981. It was May 1980, and he would have to make strategic decisions on advertising, consumer sales promotion, and trade promotion within the next few weeks in order to finalize a plan that could be implemented by July 1, the start of the new fiscal year.

COMPANY BACKGROUND

S.C. Johnson & Son, Ltd., better known as Johnson Wax, was founded in 1886 in Racine, Wisconsin, as a manufacturer of parquet flooring. When customers became concerned with the care and protection of their flooring, Johnson began making and selling a prepared paste wax. The popularity of parquet flooring began to fade, and by 1917 the company was concentrating solely on floor wax and other wood finish-

* This case was prepared by Stephen B. Ash and Sandra Safran, University of Western Ontario, as a basis for class discussion and is not intended to illustrate effective or ineffective handling of administrative situations. Used with permission.

ing products. The Canadian operation was created in 1920, by which time there were also plants in England and Australia.

By 1980, the company had grown into a $2 billion corporation with operations in 41 countries and 110 distribution centers around the world. At that time, 78 percent of the company's sales were derived from the Consumer Products Group which comprised the U.S. Division and the International Division. The Canadian company was part of the latter group, although it had a separate management structure and research facilities. This arrangement ensured a high degree of autonomy in decisions related to marketing, finance, and research and development. Some products were developed in Canada—for example, Glade Flo-Thru Air Freshener and Super Soap—and these were frequently adopted by other subsidiaries. Other products were developed abroad and were later marketed in Canada.

Until the late 1970s, Johnson's primary emphasis was on floor and furniture care products. These were relatively mature markets that, in recent years, had suffered a slow but steady decline. Two reasons accounted for this slowdown: no-wax floors were becoming increasingly popular, and consumers' attitudes toward floor and furniture care were softening with the growth of low-maintenance chrome, glass, and wood veneer products. At this time, Johnson controlled over two thirds of the shrinking floor market. The company responded to these trends by improving and repositioning existing products as well as by adding new products to the line. Although the company believed that these tactics helped it to maintain a market leadership position, management recognized that it would have to look farther afield in order to sustain existing sales and profitability.

NEW MARKET OPPORTUNITY

Personal care products were designated by Johnson as a key growth area at this time, and the firm began to explore the possibility of entering these markets. Market research indicated that after-shampoo products had grown recently by more than 20 percent per year despite the fact that users were apparently dissatisfied with the feel of their hair after using these oily conditioning products. Research findings suggested that consumers wanted control and softness in hair that both looked and felt clean. Owing to its wide-ranging R&D program, Johnson had developed the technology to formulate a unique creme rinse product that was 99 percent oil-free but still conditioned hair.[1]

[1] The 1 percent oil component was included to provide a fragrance base. At that time, a major competing brand, Tame, contained approximately 40 percent oil.

EXHIBIT 1 S.C. Johnson—Agree, Creme Rinse and Conditioner, Market Shares for the 12 Months Ending September/October 1975–1979 (percentages)

Brand	*1975*	*1976*	*1977*	*1978*	*1979*
Tame	23.3	23.5	18.1	13.7	11.2
Clairol (total)*	18.3	16.2	13.2	9.1	10.8
Alberto Culver	9.4	8.0	—	—	—
Breck Clean Rinse	4.0	3.9	—	—	—
Revlon Flex	—	5.2	11.7	11.4	13.3
Wella Balsam	—	—	5.2	6.0	7.8
Agree	—	—	—	13.5	13.8
All others	45.0	41.6	47.0	41.0	40.0

* Includes Herban Essence, Balsam, and Clairol Conditioner.

Source: Company records.

The company had recently hired personnel who were experienced in the production and marketing of hair care products.

Agree Creme Rinse and Conditioner (CRC), was first launched in the United States in 1976. During the fall of that year, marketing research was undertaken in Canada to develop profiles of typical shampoo and/or CRC consumers. Findings from the "Usage and Attitude Study" indicated that 95 percent of all Canadians used a shampoo product, with women accounting for the heaviest usage. The rate of usage varied, however, from once a day to once a week or less. In addition, the study found that 40 percent of all women used CRCs "some of the time."

Agree CRC was then introduced in Canada in June 1977 and became the Canadian CRC market leader by 1979 (see Exhibit 1). Some of its success was due to Johnson's Canadian advertising budget, set at $700,000 in the launch year compared to $868,000 for all other firms in the CRC industry, including $200,000 spent by Gillette on its CRC product, Tame, the market leader prior to Agree's introduction.[2] The Johnson product was also successful because of its superior formulation, which was emphasized in its advertising (see Exhibit 2). Finally, a large-scale sampling promotion contributed to the early success of Agree CRC.[3]

The extraordinary success of Agree CRC prompted Johnson to introduce a second Agree product. Johnson entered the large, highly com-

---

[2] Many of Johnson's figures have been disguised, but basic relationships have not been altered significantly.

[3] During the sampling campaign, 3/4-ounce sachets were distributed in a full national mailing to approximately 3.2 million Canadian households.

EXHIBIT 2 S.C. Johnson—Agree, 1977 Advertisement for Agree Creme Rinse and Conditioner

"I used to get the greasies"
"With Agree I can forget the greasies!"
New Agree Creme Rinse & Conditioner Helps Stop the "Greasies"
The "greasies." That's oily, greasy hair too soon after using some creme rinse and conditioners. But now there's new Agree. New Agree Creme Rinse and Conditioner actually helps stop the greasies.
New Agree is 99% Oil Free
Agree's formula is very different. Some creme rinse and conditioners contain oil up to 40% oil. And oil causes the greasies. Agree's formula is actually 99% oil free. So there's no oil to give you the greasies. Yet, be assured. Agree still gives you beautiful wet combing, great conditioning.
40% OIL
99% OIL FREE
Does Agree Really Work?
Yes. Agree was tested. And retested. People like yourself were asked to use Agree and compare it with the leading creme rinse and conditioner. Agree was preferred. It actually helped solve the problem of the greasies.
Agree's Wet Combing is Proved Effective in Detangling Hair.
More tests were conducted at the Hair Care Laboratories of S. C. Johnson & Son. A laboratory instrument (commonly called an Instron) measured the force required to remove tangles. Agree removed the tangles significantly easier than the leading creme rinse and conditioner.
Agree Actually Conditions Hair
Shown below are actual examples of damaged and healthy looking hair. The conditioners in Agree, used regularly, will reduce fly away, make wet combing easy and add body and shine—all signs of healthy looking hair.
Damaged Hair
Healthy Hair
Agree is pH Balanced
Most hair care experts agree that normal healthy-looking hair is mildly acidic with a pH range from 4.0 to 5.0. Agree has a compatible pH level of 4.0 to 5.0.
The people of the Hair Care Laboratories, Personal Care Division of S.C. Johnson believe that Agree is the finest creme rinse and conditioner available in either salons or retail stores. Try Agree for yourself.
Agree
creme rinse & conditioner

EXHIBIT 3 S.C. Johnson—Agree, Market Shares of Shampoos, Early 1978

Leading Brands	*Share*
Head & Shoulders	16
Johnson & Johnson Baby Shampoo	12
Clairol Herbal Essence	5
Breck Golden	6
Revlon Flex	4
Short & Sassy	3
Earth Born	3
Sales by Formula Type (Percentage)	
Dandruff medicated segment	20
Cosmetic segment (including baby shampoos)	80

Note: The total shampoo category consisted of over 150 brands and more than 700 sizes and types.

Source: Company records.

petitive and fragmented shampoo market early in 1978, almost a year after its Agree CRC introduction (see Exhibit 3). Agree shampoo was formulated to clean hair more thoroughly than most of the shampoos then on the market. The slogan, "Helps stop the greasies between shampoos" combined with the Agree name helped to make the new shampoo number three in the market within six months, close behind Head & Shoulders and Johnson & Johnson (J&J) Baby Shampoo.

By 1979, most other CRCs on the market were reformulated to be oil-free, thus converting Agree's main benefit into a generic one. Management recognized the potential threat posed by this move and began to consider alternative steps that could be taken to prevent any erosion of Agree's market share.

PRODUCT MANAGEMENT

S.C. Johnson employed a product management system to guide the strategic plans and activities of the firm's marketing department. Under this system, the director of marketing delegated responsibility for specific groups of products to group product managers (e.g., personal care products, furniture and floor care), who, in turn, reassigned responsibility for one or more brands within the group to product managers and assistant product managers.

Product managers at Johnson adhered to a well-defined policy governing new product development. Under this policy, a new product was permitted to lose money during its introductory year(s) but was expected to achieve annual corporate profitability goals thereafter. Because the CRC and the shampoo had been introduced at different times, the goal for the full Agree line had been set at 11 percent in FY 1979–1980. A target of 12.5 percent had been set for FY 1980–1981.

From the inception of Agree shampoo in 1978 until late 1979, Agree CRC and shampoo were handled by two separate product managers within Johnson. The rationale for this division of responsibility reflected management's belief that the competitive environments for CRCs and shampoos were quite distinct during that period. This policy resulted in the development of separate advertising and pricing strategies for Agree CRC and shampoo.

During the latter part of 1979, market analysis was undertaken by S.C. Johnson to identify and describe Agree CRC and shampoo users (see Exhibit 4). Management was quite surprised to discover that the user base for Agree was not women aged 18 to 45, but primarily girls in the 12 to 24 age group. This study also showed that there was as high as 65 percent cross-usage between the Agree CRC and shampoo brands, one of the highest nationally, although they were not advertised as being essential to one another. Interestingly, earlier advertising tracking studies had indicated that approximately 24 percent of viewers of any Agree shampoo commercial recalled it as one for Agree CRC and vice versa.

In view of these research results, the product management group for Agree became increasingly convinced that consumers seemed to think about Agree products as a unit. As a result, the separate product manager positions for Agree CRC and shampoo were combined in order to achieve economies of scale and to foster better communications. As part of this integration, management decided that Agree products eventually would share a common pricing strategy together with joint trade and consumer promotions. Since Agree products would now be viewed as a family, advertising would be scheduled to alternate between shampoo and CRC. The combined FY 1979–1980 sales for these products were estimated to total $12 million at retail.

Mel Liston had recently been appointed product manager for both Agree CRC and shampoo products. As a result of the 1979 market research study, he believed that repositioning Agree would strengthen its chances for continued success. In particular, the information pertaining to the current user base for Agree products led Mel Liston to define the primary target market as girls in the 12-to-18 age bracket and the secondary target market as women aged 19 to 24. New advertising copy and media schedules aimed at implementing the revised strategy for Agree were requested from Johnson's advertising agency.

Mel Liston said, "If we're going to be the 'bubble gum' shampoo, we have to gear most of our plans to this new market. We must change our

EXHIBIT 4 S.C. Johnson—Agree, Shampoo/CRC Markets, Importance by Sex and Age Group

Group	*Population (millions)*	*Percentage Who Use*	*Frequency of Use per Year*	*Number of Uses (millions)*	*Adjusting Factors*	*Equivalent Volume Used*	*Percentage of Volume Represented*	*Percentage of Volume of Agree Used*
A. Hair Conditioner Market: Importance by Sex and Age Group								
Females:								
12–18	1.35	80	200	216	1.25	270	23	32
19–24	1.37	93	157	200	1.1	220	19	10
25–34	1.96	84	134	220	1.0	220	19	13
35–54	2.60	87	98	221	0.75	166	15	15
55 +	2.33	85	70	138	0.60	83	7	4
Males:								
13–34	5.2	57	53	157	1.0	157	14	24
35 +	4.8	42	11	22	0.8	18	3	2
B. Shampoo Market: Importance by Sex and Age Group								
Females:								
12–18	1.35	100	260	351	1.25	439	15	23
19–24	1.37	100	239	327	1.1	360	12	8
25–34	1.96	100	208	407	1.0	407	14	11
35–54	2.60	100	175	455	0.75	341	11	12
55 +	2.33	100	95	221	0.6	132	4	3
Males:								
13–34	5.2	99	175	900	1.0	900	30	37
35 +	4.8	97	102	474	0.8	380	14	6

Source: Company records.

thinking in order to fully exploit our knowledge of the consumer base for Agree."

THE AGREE MARKET

By May 1980, both Agree CRC and Agree shampoo were being offered on a continuous basis in three regular sizes and three formulas (see Exhibit 5). A fourth size, 50 ml, was offered each year, although mainly as a back-to-school trial size. This trial size was typically offered in promotional packages containing other personal care products sold by a variety of companies.

At that time, there were at least 150 kinds of shampoos and 80 CRCs on the market. Less than half of them were branded, and of these, only about 10 were supported by an advertising or consumer promotion. The rest were "price brands"—reasonably priced, acceptable products that were low priced to consumers and were promoted heavily to the trade. Two of the more familiar of the price brands were Unicare and Suave.

EXHIBIT 5 S.C. Johnson—Agree, Types, Sizes, and Colors of Agree Products, 1980

CRCs

Formula Name	*Bottle Color*	*Sales Volume (percentage)*
Extra Body with Balsam	Orange	27
Regular Formula	Green	41
For Extra Oily Hair	Yellow	32

Shampoos

Formula Name	*Shampoo Color (bottle is clear plastic)*	*Sales Volume (percentage)*
Extra Gentle	Orange	29
Regular	Green	40
Oily Hair	Yellow	31

Size	*Type*
50 ml	Trial (promotional only)
225 ml	Regular
350 ml	Family
450 ml	Economy (introduced in Feb. 1980)

Source: Company records.

EXHIBIT 6 S.C. Johnson—Agree, Market Shares for Agree Shampoo/CRC

	Share of Dollar Sales		*Share of Volume Sales*	
	*1979–1980 to Date**	*Percentage Change from 1978–1979*	*1979–1980 to Date*	*Percentage Change from 1978–1979*
A. Shampoo				
Total market volume	107,742,000	11	6,725†	1
Total Agree	6.3	32	5.5	37
50 ml	0.1		0.1	
225 ml	1.5		1.1	
350 ml	4.1		3.7	
450 ml	0.7		0.6	
Head & Shoulders	16.5	22	10.8	16
J&J	7.6	2	7.9	(7)
Body on Tap	3.5	66	3.6	64
Revlon Flex	5.8	22	5.6	15
All others	60.3	6	67.4	(5)
B. CRC				
Total market volume	37,455,600	21	2,034.4	12
Total Agree	13.8	19	14.5	15
50 ml	0.3		0.5	
225 ml	2.8		2.4	
350 ml	6.1		6.5	
450 ml	4.6		5.2	
Tame	8.0	(2)	10.9	(11)
Silkience	2.9	N‡	1.2	N‡
Revlon Flex	10.5	43	12.0	29
Condition II	4.0	N	6.1	N
All others	60.8	10	55.3	1

* Based on approximately 10 months of sales. FY 1979–1980 ends on June 30.
† Represents the liquid measure of millions of cases of 12 350-ml bottles.
‡ New; no data for year ago.

Source: Company records.

Market share estimates for the different shampoo and CRC sizes are summarized in Exhibit 6. By May 1980 the total CRC market in Canada had reached almost $37.5 million and was growing at an annual rate of approximately 20 percent. At that time, Agree CRC was the leading brand in the category, with sales of $5.2 million at retail representing almost 13.8 percent of the total CRC market in dollar terms. The total shampoo market had risen to almost $108 million, with a growth rate of about 12 percent per year. Agree was second in terms of market share, with sales amounting to $6.8 million or close to 6.3 percent of the total shampoo market. The 350-ml bottle accounted for the bulk of total Agree sales, both in the CRC and shampoo categories (see Exhibit 6).

THE CONSUMER

Company sales records indicated that by May 1980 consumers were purchasing 75 percent as much Agree CRC as shampoo. Buying habits for these two items were quite different from those associated with Johnson's other products. For example, a 1979 market research study indicated that purchase frequency was relatively high—every few weeks as opposed to every few months. If the product that the consumer wanted was not on the shelf, she would rarely postpone her purchase until the following week. Instead, she normally would switch to another brand.

According to the 1979 study, the consumer typically owned about three brands at a time. Many of the purchasers, principally women, apparently believed that they became sensitized to one particular brand after a while.[4] Consequently, they would try another brand in their "evoked brand set"—those four or five brands that they were prepared to buy at any one time. Since people tended to rotate between brands within their own set, a key objective of management was to encourage users to come back to Agree more often, thereby ensuring its position as the brand with the highest frequency of use in the category. Purchases tended to be made largely on impulse, particularly for conditioners, which generally were considered to be less essential in the household than shampoos.

SALES AND DISTRIBUTION

When Agree CRC was first introduced in 1977, Johnson's distribution system was oriented primarily toward the food trade. However, the launch of Agree, a personal care item, underscored the need for greater dependency on the drug trade in order to obtain widespread distribution for this type of product. Management decided to partially realign its field sales effort in order to place increased emphasis on the drug

---

[4] As a rule, people consider their hair care requirements to be highly unique. After repeated uses of any single brand, many people gradually become concerned that the brand no longer works as effectively as it once did. It is this concern that prompts brand-switching behavior.

EXHIBIT 7 S.C. Johnson—Agree, Sales Percentage by Outlet Type

	Food	*Drug*	*Mass Merchandise*
Industry shampoo sales, 1978	43*	42	15
Industry CRC sales, 1978	36	42	22
Agree shampoo sales, 1979–1980	47.4	38.5	17.0
Agree CRC sales, 1979–1980	35	46.3	18.5

* To be read: "43% of all units sold were purchased in food stores."

Source: Company records.

trade. By 1980 more than 97 percent of the drug stores in Canada were included as part of the Johnson distribution system. Food stores constituted the primary outlets for Agree products, followed by drug and mass merchandising outlets, such as Woolco, Kmart, and Zellers (see Exhibit 7).

Johnson had clear objectives for shelf management. In particular, it sought to have the 18 different bottles arranged at the retail outlet in a "billboard" or "ribbon" effect for maximum eye-catching appeal. Inserts and shelf talkers were frequently included to increase the likelihood of eye contact (see Exhibit 8).[5] Most retail outlets did not, in fact, carry every size and formula of the Agree line, despite aggressive sales force efforts to achieve this stocking pattern.

Johnson maintained its own sales force of approximately 80 people, who were required to sell all of its products, including Agree. By May 1980 additional penetration of distribution channels was no longer a primary objective. However, it was recognized that continued trade support would depend, in part, on the frequency and quality of both consumer and trade promotions. Sales representatives were well trained and were compensated by a salary plus incentives scheme, where the incentives included things like free trips and prizes. Management attempted to provide strong support for the sales force through regular meetings and discussions and by furnishing selling aids. Some of the Johnson products which the sales group sold, for example, "Raid" and "Off," were seasonal. In the case of Agree, however, the variation per season was slight, averaging 3 or 4 percent higher in midsummer and 1 or 2 percent lower in winter.

---

[5] *Case inserts* are written instructions indicating where to stock the brand on the shelf. *Shelf talkers* ae small signs attached to the front of a shelf on which the product is stocked.

EXHIBIT 8 S.C. Johnson—Agree, Case Insert (Top) and Shelf Talker (Bottom)

PRICING

When Agree CRC was first introduced, the retail price was pegged to that of the leading brand, Tame. The regular cost to the retailer initially was $12.86 per case for one dozen 225-ml bottles and $16.94 per case for 350-ml bottles. At that time, retail selling prices ranged from $1.39 to $1.79 for the 225-ml size and from $1.79 to $2.39 for the 350-ml size. By May 1980 trade costs and suggested retail selling prices for Agree CRC were as follows:

Bottle Size	*Trade Cost (per case)*	*Suggested Retail Selling Prices*
225 ml	$14.65	$1.59–$1.79
350 ml	$19.20	$2.09–$2.29
450 ml	$23.50	$2.59–$2.79

The suggested retail selling prices for Agree CRC provided trade margins in the 23–31 percent range.

By May 1980, trade costs and suggested retail selling prices for Agree shampoo were as follows:

Bottle Size	*Trade Cost (per case)*	*Suggested Retail Selling Prices*
225 ml	$16.55	$1.79–$1.99
350 ml	$24.25	$2.59–$2.79
450 ml	$28.00	$2.99–$3.19

Suggested retail selling prices for Agree shampoo typically provided trade margins in the 23–27 percent range.

The initial pricing strategy for Agree CRC was to introduce the product at a consumer price equal to that of Tame, or to Gillette Earth Born if Tame was not stocked in a particular outlet. A similar pricing strategy was pursued for Agree shampoo in that the pricing objective was parity with Johnson & Johnson Baby Shampoo, or with Clairol Herbal Essence if the former was not available. Over the next few years, Agree CRC and shampoo moved to a slight premium price relative to the top selling brands.

ADVERTISING

Mel Liston was about to set a marketing communications budget that would include expenditures for advertising, consumer promotion, and trade promotion. As a starting point, he examined the budgets for the fiscal years 1978–1979 and 1979–1980 (see Exhibit 9). In doing so, however, he recognized that some important factors had changed in the interim. For example, deal and promotional costs had been higher in FY 1978–1979 than in the following year because of the introductory expenses incurred for the launch of Agree shampoo. Although the current year was estimated to be slightly below target, his projected budget for FY 1980–1981 would still have to provide for a pretax profit level of at least 12.5 percent.

Foote, Cone & Belding, Johnson's advertising agency, was requested to prepare scripts that would direct advertising toward the new target audience. The agency created material that it felt would be effective and then made suggestions about how to use the advertising package, for example, the level of frequency required to achieve maximum impact with a particular audience. The agency commission would be included in Mr. Liston's budget as a fixed percent of his expected net revenue (see Exhibit 9).

The primary marketing objective was to maintain or increase current sales levels for Agree. To meet this goal, Mel Liston believed that it would be necessary to achieve a 90 percent awareness level for Agree

EXHIBIT 9 S.C. Johnson—Agree, Mel Liston's P&L Worksheet for His 1980–1981 Budget (CRC and Shampoo Combined)

	1978–1979 ($000)	*Percentage of Net Sales*	*1979–1980* ($000)*	*Percentage of Net Sales*	*1980–1981 ($000)*	*Percentage of Net Sales*
Net sales	8,158	100	9,300	100		100
Cost of goods sold†	2,941	36	3,160	34		33
Gross profit	5,217	64	6,140	66		
Advertising	1,875	23	1,578	17		
Consumer promotion	816	10	553	6		
Deals	1,225	15	1,197	13		
Other‡	890	11	920	10		
Total promotion	4,806	59	4,248	46		
Functional expenses§	900	11	927	10		
Operating profit	489	(6)	965	10		≥12.5

* Projected from mid-May to June 30 year end.
† Includes labor, materials, standard overhead.
‡ Includes external marketing services, sales meetings, agency fees.
§ Overhead allocations and fixed costs.

Source: Company records.

within the new primary target audience of women aged 12 to 18. A secondary target audience was defined as women aged 19 to 24 and he hoped to achieve at least a 60 percent awareness level for this group.

Research undertaken by the advertising agency on Canadian teens' and young women's television viewing habits indicated a national weekly reach of 99 percent for the 12-to-18 age bracket and 98 percent for the 19-to-24-year-old group, with average weekly viewing times of 21.3 and 21.5 hours, respectively. One of the tasks facing Mel Liston was to select specific programs and parts of the day (e.g., 4:00–9:00 P.M.) that achieved optimal viewing levels within the budget that he set. He felt that consumer magazine advertising was important as a support vehicle to television, since magazines provided increased reach against the light television viewer (see Exhibit 10).

The agency proposed a television commercial for each Agree product, scripts for radio advertising, and layouts for print media. Total media costs to run the television commercials on a complete network daily basis were estimated at $1.05 million for 52 weeks if late afternoon time slots were scheduled versus $1.6 million for a prime time insertion schedule. These figures incorporated a discount, which could range from 10 to 15 percent on a full 52-week purchase. In keeping with Agree's younger image, the agency recommended a fast-paced, exciting commercial featuring a strong musical beat, which appeared to be favored by teens.

EXHIBIT 10 S.C. Johnson—Agree, Media Plan Excerpts

A. Quintile Analysis

The quintiles of the 1980–1981 media plan were compared with the quintiles of a television-only campaign, which would run for 52 weeks with a 45 percent weekly reach. The target group was women aged 12–18.

TV Watcher Quintile	*TV Only— % Total Impressions*	*Index*	*TV/Consumer Magazines— % Total Impressions*	*Index*
1 + 2 (light)	15.9	100	25.9	163
3 (medium)	21.5	100	33.6	156
4 + 5 (heavy)	62.6	100	40.6	70

B. Publication Costs (for full-page ads)

Publication	*Cost/Insertion(s)*	*Total Readers Women 12–18 (000)*	*CPM*($)*
Chatelaine (E)	15,078.15	350	43.08
Flare	5,174.80	224	23.10
Homemaker's	14,614.00	176	83.03
Chatelaine (F)	4,996.85	42	118.97
Madame au Foyer	4,199.13	27	155.52
Clin d'Oeil	1,921.50	60	32.01

Note: The above analysis reflects the fact that the inclusion of consumer magazines provides increased reach against the light TV viewer. In addition, the multimedia schedule provides a more even distribution of impressions against the light, medium, and heavy quintiles.

* Cost per thousand impressions.

Source: Foote, Cone and Belding.

The product management group also considered radio advertising, which had been directed mainly at the "teen" segment of the Agree market during the previous two years. In FY 1979–1980, Johnson ran a seven-week radio campaign (see Exhibit 11). For FY 1980–1981, it was estimated by the agency that the media cost for 27 station national radio would amount to approximately $35,000 per week.

Since its introduction, Agree had been promoted regularly in magazines and newspapers. During the launch periods, seven American and three Canadian magazines had carried full-page color advertisements for Agree. In Canada, Johnson had paid for the Canadian material and had received the American magazine spillover, estimated at approximately $200,000 per year, at no cost, although it was recognized that U.S. advertising would still be directed at the historical U.S. target audience, women aged 18 to 45.

EXHIBIT 11 S.C. Johnson—Agree, Agree Radio Plan

Target group: Primary Teens 12–18
Target group: Secondary Women 19–24
Reach objective: 55% weekly
Announcements: 30 seconds
Duration: 7 weeks

Market	*Number of Stations*	*Number of Weekly Announcements for Each Product*
Vancouver	2 CKLG/CFUN	40
Victoria	1 CKDA	20
Calgary	1 CKXL	25
Edmonton	1 CHED	25
Regina	1 CJME	25
Saskatoon	1 CKOM	25
Winnipeg	2 CKRC/CFRW	35
Toronto	3 CHUM-FM/CFTR/CHUM	50
Hamilton	1 CKOC	25
Ottawa	2 CFRA/CFGO	45
Kitchener	1 CHYM-AM	30
London	1 CJBK	25
Montreal		
English	2 CKGM/CHOM-FM	40
French	2 CKLM/CKAC	30
Quebec City	2 CHOI-FM/CFLS	50
Halifax	1 CJCH	20
St. John/Moncton	2 CFBC/CKCW	20
St. John's	1 VOCM	20

Source: Company records.

As Mel Liston began to work on developing a marketing communications program for FY 1980–1981, he tried to imagine a profile of a typical teen girl and the type of advertising she would be most likely to notice. Studies on women 18 years old and over had shown that heavy users of hair products were not necessarily heavy watchers of television. However, he wondered how applicable this result was, given the age disparity with the Agree primary target group. There was even less statistical information on magazine readership in the target age group. Thus, Mel Liston wondered whether or not the reading habits of the typical young female consumer would justify spending a significant part of his budget on print advertising, in either magazines or newspapers. If a decision was reached to run a print campaign, he believed that any print advertising that did appear would have to be young and vibrant like the ads that the agency was proposing for the coming year (see Exhibit 12).

EXHIBIT 12 S.C. Johnson—Agree, 1980–1981 Proposed Print Ad

CONSUMER PROMOTION

Johnson had introduced its Agree products with heavy consumer promotion. The CRC was introduced with a six-month sampling campaign, which consisted of a direct mailing to approximately three million potential users of a 3/4-ounce plastic sachet good for about two uses. This was followed by a second six-month campaign, which included 400,000 3/4-ounce plastic sachets and 15 cent coupons using a cross-promotion with Close-Up toothpaste.[6] Agree shampoo was introduced by using similar sachets to 3.2 million homes, and this campaign included a fact book and another 15 cent coupon. The net effective coverage of these promotional events was approximately 50 percent of Canadian homes.

Another launch promotion for Agree consisted of 3/4-ounce pouches of free shampoo, which were attached to CRC bottles. One million of these pouches were distributed free to stores, in addition to 1.5 million 50-ml samples, which were prepriced at 39 cents each. The unit cost to Johnson was 5 cents per sachet of CRC and 7 cents per sachet of shampoo. Bulk distribution costs were estimated at $30 per thousand. Although sales for each product increased significantly during the trial period, the cost to Johnson of distributing such high quantities of free or virtually free merchandise was very high.

After Agree CRC and shampoo had been launched, other consumer promotion opportunities were considered. Refund campaigns were run twice during FY 1979–1980. Coupons that offered 50 cents off the next purchase were distributed in bulk mailings and in magazines directed toward homemakers. Cash refunds of one dollar were later offered in exchange for two Agree labels. The redemption rates were 3 percent and 2 percent, respectively. This coupon program proved rather disappointing, since there was little, if any, change in sales volume during the promotion period.

In 1979, Agree in the United States had been packaged with a free Warner-Lambert razor, normally sold at $3.69. Although the perceived value of this "gift" was high, the impact on sales duing the promotion period was disappointing. After calculating the total cost of the distributed premiums, this campaign was responsible for a substantial loss incurred by American Agree. A similar promotion was tried in the United States six months later. Free pantyhose were attached to Agree products. During the promotion period, sales remained relatively stable. However, the result of this promotion was less damaging to profits than the free razor campaign, since the cost to Johnson was only 40

---

[6] Cross-promotions are samples, coupons, and the like placed on or inside the package of a noncompeting product usually sharing the same market as the promoted brand.

cents per pair of pantyhose. Despite these results, Mel Liston was unwilling to describe either of the premium campaigns as a failure, since other longer-term objectives such as increases in usage frequency and brand loyalty appeared to have been met. Furthermore, in judging any sales promotion campaign, he realized, as a general rule, that most promotion events did lose money during the deal period.

One promotion being considered by Mel Liston was an "instant win" tag, whereby the purchaser would be notified if she had won a free pair of Jordache jeans. Jordache would be asked to supply the jeans free in exchange for being featured in advertising and in-store promotion. Other costs for this contest would include plastic prize tickets, special labels, backer cards, and labor. Some of these expenses would overlap into the trade promotion category. Total promotional costs for the Jordache Sweepstakes were estimated at $120,000, at least $20,000 of which would include store items such as end aisle displays.

Mel Liston believed that consumer promotions were important merchandising devices, since all customers who learned about such offers could take advantage of them. In contrast, trade promotions, particularly off-invoice allowances, were important to retailers, but the benefits from these deals were not necessarily passed along to consumers in the form of lower prices. The primary objective of a consumer promotion was to induce the consumer to buy Agree more often, perhaps every other time, rather than every fourth or fifth time.

Since the product was in the non-price-sensitive 50 percent of the market where consumers tended to buy on impulse, Mel Liston felt that nonprice promotions might be very effective. Deals such as bonus packs were nondiscretionary in that anyone who bought the product received the bonus. However, Mr. Liston wondered whether bonuses were merely a way to subsidize or reward the already loyal purchaser. In his mind, it was unclear whether or not larger amounts of an untried product would, in fact, induce trial.

As Mel Liston began to think about consumer promotion plans for the coming year, he recognized the importance of establishing a clearly defined personality for Agree CRC and shampoo. One possible promotion event consisted of a contest that would offer as the grand prize a rock group concert at the winner's school or community center. Although somewhat unusual, this type of promotion might reinforce the image he was trying to project for Agree. He said, "We want a commercial image with an underlying message which tells the kids that the music and the special Agree products are mainly for them; they're not something meant to appeal to the whole family." Other consumer promotion possibilities included couponing and redemption ideas. For example, one opportunity under consideration was cross-ruff couponing, perhaps on Pledge or Flo-Thru Air Freshener or one of the company's other home care products.

TRADE PROMOTION

Trade spending was something that companies such as Johnson felt they *had* to do; it was not truly discretionary. As part of each year's budget, a percentage of sales dollars was set aside in order to meet shelf space objectives. The FY 1979–1980 discretionary pool of funds was set at 7.9 percent of projected sales. Without special deals, there might be insufficient reason for stores to try to sell Agree instead of competing brands.

Johnson allocated funds to trade promotion for two main reasons. First, trade deals were viewed as essential simply to get and keep products listed. A variety of trade deals were possible such as off-invoice allowances (e.g., $1.20 off each case ordered during the deal period). During FY 1979–1980, trade spending varied widely both in the CRC and shampoo markets (see Exhibit 13).

The other reason for trade spending was related to cooperative advertising. Contributions to these programs normally were calculated according to a formula that included some percentage of a retailer's previous sales, typically around 2 percent. Advertising "slicks" (see Exhibit 14) were provided to retailers to encourage their active participation in coop advertising campaigns.[7]

To encourage retailers to sell stock at "feature prices" from time to time, S.C. Johnson provided off-invoice allowances (also called *deal money*) to the trade. Deal money was occasionally passed on to consumers as reduced prices but frequently was viewed by the retailer as a means to increase the trade margin. For example, Mel Liston estimated that only 40–50 percent of all stock sold on deal to the trade was actually retailed at the feature price. The balance was sold at the regular price, thereby increasing the retailer's trade margin. It seemed to Mel Liston that a large number of retailers were more concerned about obtaining deal money than about an extensive advertising campaign that the manufacturer might undertake to build a longer-term brand franchise.

Although advertising was sometimes cut if fourth-quarter sales were disappointing, trade deals hardly ever were cut. The risk of suffering a loss in shelf positioning was considered too great to justify a reduction in trade promotion activity. Retailers typically tried to buy and stock up at the end of a deal period to keep annual inventory costs down as much as possible. Retailer expectations regarding trade deals were not expected to change in FY 1980–1981.

---

[7] Advertising "slicks" are reproducible copy and pictures supplied by manufacturers to participating retailers during a cooperative advertising campaign.

EXHIBIT 13 S.C. Johnson—Agree, Selected Promotional Influences for Major Brands, July–August 1979 to March–April 1980 (three periods)

A. Shampoo

	Agree			*Head & Shoulders*			*Johnson & Johnson*			*Body on Tap*			*All Others*		
	1979 July Aug.	*Nov. Dec.*	*1980 Mar Apr.*	*1979 July Aug*	*Nov. Dec.*	*1980 Mar. Apr.*	*1979 July Aug.*	*Nov. Dec.*	*1980 Mar. Apr.*	*1979 July Aug.*	*Nov. Dec.*	*1980 Mar. Apr.*	*1979 July Aug.*	*Nov. Dec.*	*1980 Mar. Apr.*
Sales share	6.4	5.4	5.7	9.5	10.8	10.1	7.3	7.3	8.6	4.0	3.3	3.9	72.7	73.1	71.7
Deal percentage of market*	2.8	1.2	0.4	0.1	0	0	0.5	0.8	0.4	1.5	0.5	1.0	7.5	7.0	6.4
	(43.8)	(22.2)	(7.0)	(1.0)	(0.0)	(0.0)	(6.8)	(10.9)	(4.7)	(37.5)	(15.2)	(25.6)	(10.3)	(9.6)	(8.9)
TV advertising ($000)	12.9	40.8	181.2	157.5	152.8	151.1	186.2	2	169.8	24.6	28.3	115.3	456	283	856
Radio advertising ($000)	139	3.7	0	31.3	7.0	36.2	0	0	10.9	0	0	0	5	2	15
Press advertising ($000)	0	0	17.2	13.7	16.2	7.4	0	0	0	7.1	0	11.0	105	46	220
Total advertising volume ($000)	152	45	198	203	176	195	186	2	181	31.8	28.3	126.3	566	331	1091
Advertising share:†	13.4	4.6	11.1	17.8	31.3	10.9	16.4	0.2	10.1	2.8	5.0	7.1	49.7	58.8	60.9
Coop share:‡															
Food	32	20	31	35	30	34	53	61	59	29	1	10			
Drug	48	44	72	64	64	86	56	57	76	41	20	31			
Mass merchandiser	83	10	59	113	46	95	64	87	102	64	29	55			
Displays share:‡															
Food	9	6	8	16	7	8	6	14	13	3	2	4			
Drug	13	16	21	21	20	19	19	17	19	7	7	15			
Mass merchandiser	34	3	50	25	22	28	28	45	50	9	10	43			

B. CRC

	Agree			Revlon Flex			Silkience			Tame			Condition II			All Others		
	1979 July Aug.	*Nov. Dec.*	*1980 Mar. Apr.*	*1979 July Aug.*	*Nov. Dec.*	*1980 Mar. Apr.*	*1979 July Aug.*	*Nov. Dec.*	*1980 Mar. Apr.*	*1979 July Aug.*	*Nov. Dec.*	*1980 Mar. Apr.*	*1979 July Aug*	*Nov. Dec.*	*1980 Mar. Apr.*	*1989 July Aug.*	*Nov. Dec.*	*1980 Mar. Apr.*
Sales share	15.6	15.1	13.7	14.5	11.1	12.8	2.7	4.5	6.1	9.2	10.3	9.2	7.1	8.1	6.2	50.9	51.8	51.2
Deal percentage of market*	4.6	5.3	2.1	6.0	2.1	1.4	0	0	0	1.3	2.5	1.1	1.5	2.6	0.9	10.5	11.2	9.9
	(29.5)	(35.1)	(15.3)	(41.4)	(18.9)	(10.9)	(0.0)	(0.0)	(0.0)	(14.1)	(24.3)	(11.9)	(21.1)	(32.1)	(14.5)	(20.6)	(21.6)	(19.3)
TV advertising ($000)	33.7	243.8	0	58.9	7.3	0	133.0	100.8	75.7	0	0	85.1	11.8	5.8	8.9	124.6	81.5	41.3
Radio advertising ($000)	47.5	0	0	0	0	0	0	0	0	0	0	0	0	0	0	1.8	0	0
Press advertising ($000)	0	0	0	0	0	0	0	19.0	30.4	0	35.1	5.2	0	10.4	28.0	71.8	7.6	99.8
Total advertising volume ($000)	81.1	243.8	0	58.9	7.3	0	133.0	119.8	106.1	0	35.1	90.3	11.8	16.2	37	198.2	89.1	141.1
Advertising share†	16.8	47.7	0	12.2	1.4	0	27.5	23.4	25.6	0	6.9	21.8	2.4	3.2	8.9	41.0	17.4	43.7
Co-op share:‡																		
Food	19	9	15	19	5	14	7	14	15	13	17	17	1	7	6			
Drug	36	31	43	15	21	29	45	40	46	29	28	26	27	42	32			
Mass merchandiser	53	16	32	40	10	33	29	26	29	44	26	50	31	45	36			
Displays share:§																		
Food	9	4	2	5	5	7	3	8	8	13	7	6	1	4	1			
Drug	20	15	18	17	12	19	13	24	12	22	23	5	10	14	8			
Mass merchandiser	37	22	50	6	16	21	19	13	7	34	6	18	15	35	21			

* The Neilsen Market Survey defines a deal as any package/price configuration that is different from the company's regular market configuration. The figures in the row are the proportion of brand sales that were sold on deal. For example, during July–August 1979 in the shampoo market, approximately 43.8 percent (6.4 ÷ 2.8) of Agree shampoo sales were "on deal," compared to 22.2 percent (5.4 ÷ 1.2) of sales for Agree during November–December 1979.

† Advertising share denotes Agree share of total advertising expenditures on the product category during each period. For example, the calculation for July–August 1979:

$$\frac{12.9 + 139.0}{(12.9 + 139.0) + (157.5 + 31.3 + 13.7) \ldots + (456.0 + 5.0 + 105.0)} = 13.4\% \text{ (rounded)}$$

‡ Co-op share is supplied by A.C. Neilsen. It is a period result defined as the number of stores that did co-op advertising (i.e., newspapers, flyers) weighted by their sales importance to the shampoo category. For example, in July–August 1979, food stores doing 32 percent of shampoo sales in the food trade had coop advertising on Agree.

§ Display share is the unweighted percentage of stores that had display activity when the store was audited by A.C. Neilsen at the end of the bimonthly period. For example, at the end of August 1979, 9 percent of food stores had Agree on display. *Display* is defined by Neilsen as the product being somewhere in the store other than its normal shelf position.

EXHIBIT 14 S.C. Johnson—Agree, Example of an Advertising Slick

SP 183-1515

THE TASK

As Mel Liston began to think about developing a comprehensive marketing communications program for the Agree line in FY 1980–1981, he remembered that the first step in the process was to establish a set of clear and specific objectives against which campaign results could be measured. In addition, he understood that decisions about advertising, consumer promotions, and trade deals were highly interrelated. Thus overall success in implementing the revised positioning strategy for Agree CRC and shampoo would depend on his ability to design a well-integrated communications program. In this type of program, decisions across advertising, consumer, and trade promotion activities would have to be well coordinated with in-store merchandising to achieve a strong reinforcing effect.

Mr. Liston was frequently overheard explaining this philosophy to new people in his department. He told them that exposure was worth more than price—that is, an end aisle display with 10 cents off was more valuable to the company than a one dollar sale sitting on a shelf—but that both types of promotion might be necessary. In addition, he believed that an end aisle display with no cents off or no contest was merely a nice arrangement of stock instead of a sales booster.

The complete marketing communications plan was required by July 1, 1980. The document itself would outline decisions reached in the following areas: total communications budget for FY 1980–1981 and allocation of those funds across advertising, consumer, and trade promotion activities; message strategy; and selection and scheduling of advertising media, consumer promotions, and trade deals. In addition, the plan would outline any steps needed to coordinate the marketing communications activities proposed for FY 1980–1981. Given the importance of these decisions to the future position of Agree CRC and shampoo in the market, Mel Liston planned to consult other members of the Agree product management group before finalizing the plan.

Case Group D

Distribution Strategy

Case 16

Tupperware

J. Paul Peter
University of Wisconsin–Madison

In 1958 Justin Dart purchased Tupperware from former Du Pont chemist Earl Tupper for $10 million. From that time until 1983 Tupperware earned an estimated $1.5 billion pretax and had a phenomenal 25-year record of doubling sales and earnings every 5 years. In 1983, Tupperware sales slipped 7 percent to $827 million and operating profits sank 15 percent to $192 million.

Tupperware is sold by 90,000 part-time sales people and 10,000 full-time managers in the United States. The plastic products are sold at in-house Tupperware parties which consist of a part-time salesperson inviting friends over and displaying the many varieties of plastic products. The party typically includes refreshments, a free sample of Tupperware, casual conversation, and formal offering of Tupperware products. Customers order at the party and pay for the products on delivery by the salesperson.

Sources: "Tupperware's Party Times Are Over," *Fortune,* February 20, 1984, pp. 113–20; "Dart & Kraft Turns Back to its Basic Business—Food," *Business Week,* June 11, 1984, pp. 100–105.

Four explanations have been offered for the decline in Tupperware sales in 1983. First, since the economy was recovering, many of the part-time salespeople quit to take full-time jobs with other companies. This resulted in 7 percent fewer salespeople and 5 percent fewer parties in the first 11 months of the year.

Second, Tupperware commissions to salespeople are somewhat less than other in-home sellers such as Avon and Mary Kay cosmetics. Avon pays commissions of 35 percent to 50 percent depending on sales volume and Mary Kay pays from 40 percent to 50 percent. Tupperware pays a flat 35 percent commission to dealers. Tupperware does offer merchandise bonuses but their value has been decreasing. As one executive put it: "Salespeople aren't stupid. They can see they're being asked to sell more to win goods that have less value. People aren't as motivated to sell as hard, because the thrill of earning those big-ticket gifts isn't what it used to be."

Third, one study found that the average family of four owned 28 pieces of Tupperware. While this might not be a concern given the broad product line, some questions could be raised concerning market saturation.

Fourth, competition increased greatly in the inexpensive plastic bowl market. For example, Eagle Affiliates ran a series of national TV ads pointing out that it was more convenient and less expensive to buy these products in supermarkets rather than purchase them at an in-home party. Rubbermaid also increased its marketing effort to sell an expanded line of plastic bowls in supermarkets.

One approach taken by Tupperware to overcome its dealer recruiting problems and to position the firm for the long run was the development of new products. For example, the company introduced a new line called Modular Mates. These compact, stackable containers were targeted at smaller families with less storage space available. In addition, a line of cookware for microwave ovens was developed. Most analysts agreed that Tupperware would revive but would never again grow at 17 percent compounded annually as it did in the 1970s.

Discussion Questions

1. What accounts for the overall success of Tupperware?
2. Evaluate each of the reasons given for the decrease in sales and operating profits in 1983.
3. In addition to offering new products, what else should Tupperware do to avoid losses in sales and profits?

Case 17

Cub Foods*

J. Paul Peter
University of Wisconsin–Madison

Leslie Wells's recent expedition to the new Cub Foods store in Melrose Park, Illinois, was no ordinary trip to the grocery store. "You go crazy," says Wells, sounding a little shell-shocked. Overwhelmed by Cub's vast selection, tables of samples, and discounts as high as 30 percent, Wells spent $76 on groceries—$36 more than she planned. Wells fell prey to what a Cub executive calls "the wow factor"—a shopping frenzy brought on by low prices and clever marketing. That's the reaction Cub's super warehouse stores strive for—and often get.

Cub Foods has been a leader in shaking up the food industry and forcing many conventional supermarkets to lower prices, increase services, or—in some cases—to go out of business. With Cub and other super warehouse stores springing up across the country, shopping habits are changing, too. Some shoppers drive 50 miles or more to a Cub store instead of going to the nearest neighborhood supermarket. Their payoff is that they find almost everything they need under one roof, and most of it is cheaper than at competing supermarkets. Cub's low prices, smart marketing, and sheer size encourage shoppers to spend far more than they do in the average supermarket.

The difference between Cub and most supermarkets is obvious the minute a shopper walks through Cub's doors. The entry aisle, called by some "power alley," is lined two stories high with specials, such as bean coffee at $2 a pound and half-price apple juice. Above, the ceiling joists and girders are exposed, giving "the subliminal feeling of all the spaciousness up there. It suggests there's massive buying going on that translates in a shopper's mind that there's tremendous savings going on as well," says Paul Suneson, director of marketing research for Cub's parent, Super Valu Stores Inc., the nation's largest food wholesaler.

* This case is taken from J. Paul Peter and Jerry C. Olson, *Consumer Behavior: Marketing Strategy Perspectives* (Homewood, Ill.: Richard D. Irwin, 1987), pp. 655–56. Based on Steve Weiner and Betsy Morris, "Bigger, Shrewder and Cheaper Cub Leads Food Stores into the Future," *The Wall Street Journal,* August 26, 1985, p. 17.

Cub's wider-than-usual shopping carts, which are supposed to suggest expansive buying, fit easily through Cub's wide aisles, which channel shoppers toward high-profit impulse foods. The whole store exudes a seductive, horn-of-plenty feeling. Cub customers typically buy in volume and spend $40 to $50 a trip, four times the supermarket average. The average Cub store has sales of $800,000 to $1 million a week, quadruple the volume of conventional stores.

Cub Foods has a simple approach to grocery retailing: low prices, made possible by rigidly controlled costs and high-volume sales; exceptionally high quality for produce and meats—the items people build shopping trips around; and immense variety. It's all packaged in clean stores that are twice as big as most warehouse outlets and four times bigger than most supermarkets. A Cub store stocks as many as 25,000 items, double the selection of conventional stores, mixing staples with luxury, ethnic, and hard-to-find foods. This leads to overwhelming displays—88 kinds of hot dogs and dinner sausages, 12 brands of Mexican food, and fresh meats and produce by the ton.

The store distributes maps to guide shoppers. But without a map or a specific destination, a shopper is subliminally led around by the arrangement of the aisles. The power alley spills into the produce department. From there the aisles lead to highly profitable perimeter departments—meat, fish, bakery, and frozen food. The deli comes before fresh meat, because Cub wants shoppers to do their impulse buying before their budgets are depleted on essentials.

Overall, Cub's gross margin—the difference between what it pays for its goods and what it sells them for—is 14 percent, six to eight points less than most conventional stores. However, because Cub relies mostly on word of mouth advertising, its ad budgets are 25 percent less than those of other chains.

Discussion Questions

1. List at least five marketing tactics Cub Foods employs in its stores to increase the probability of purchases.
2. What accounts for Cub's success in generating such large sales per customer and per store?
3. Given Cub's lower prices, quality merchandise, excellent location, and superior assortment, what reasons can you offer for why many consumers in its trading areas refuse to shop there?

Case 18

Thompson Respiration Products, Inc.*

James E. Nelson
William R. Woolridge
both of the University of Colorado

Victor Higgins, executive vice president for Thompson Respiration Products, Inc. (TRP), sat thinking at his desk late one Friday in April 1986. "We're making progress," he said to himself. "Getting Metro to sign finally gets us into the Chicago Market . . . and with a good dealer at that." *Metro,* of course, was Metropolitan Medical Products, a large Chicago retailer of medical equipment and supplies for home use. "Now, if we could just do the same in Minneapolis and Atlanta," he continued.

However, getting at least one dealer in each of these cities to sign a TRP Dealer Agreement seemed remote right now. One reason was the sizeable groundwork required—Higgins simply lacked the time to review operations at the well over 100 dealers currently operating in the two cities. Another was TRP's lack of dealer-oriented sales information that went beyond the technical specification sheet for each product and the company's price list. Still another concerned two conditions in the Dealer Agreement itself—prospective dealers sometimes balked at agreeing to sell no products manufactured by TRP's competitors and differed with TRP in interpretations of the "best efforts" clause. (The clause required the dealer to maintain adequate inventories of TRP products, contact four prospective new customers or physicians or respiration therapists per month, respond promptly to sales inquiries, and represent TRP at appropriate conventions where it exhibited.)

---

* This case was written by Professor James E. Nelson and DBA Candidate William R. Woolridge, the University of Colorado. This case illustrates neither effective nor ineffective administrative decision making. Some data are disguised.

"Still," Higgins concluded, "we signed Metro in spite of these reasons, and 21 others across the country. That's about all anyone could expect—after all, we've only been trying to develop a dealer network for a year or so."

THE PORTABLE RESPIRATOR INDUSTRY

The portable respirator industry began in the early 1950s when polio-stricken patients who lacked control of muscles necessary for breathing began to leave treatment centers. They returned home with hospital-style iron lungs or fiber-glass chest shells, both being large chambers that regularly introduced a vacuum about the patient's chest. The vacuum caused the chest to expand and, thus, the lungs to fill with air. However, both devices confined patients to a prone or semiprone position in a bed.

By the late 1950s, TRP had developed a portable turbine blower powered by an electric motor and battery. When connected to a mouthpiece via plastic tubing, the blower would inflate a patient's lungs on demand. Patients could now leave their beds for several hours at a time and realize limited mobility in a wheelchair. By the early 1970s, TRP had developed a line of more sophisticated turbine respirators in terms of monitoring and capability for adjustment to individual patient needs.

At about the same time, applications began to shift from polio patients to victims of other diseases or of spinal cord injuries, the latter group existing primarily as a result of automobile accidents. Better emergency medical service, quicker evacuation to spinal cord injury centers, and more proficient treatment meant that people who formerly would have died now lived and went on to lead meaningful lives. Because of patients' frequently younger ages, they strongly desired wheelchair mobility. Respiration therapists obliged by recommending a Thompson respirator for home use or, if unaware of Thompson, recommending a Puritan-Bennett or other machine.

Instead of a turbine, Puritan-Bennett machines used a bellows design to force air into the patient's lungs. The machines were widely used in hospitals but seemed poorly suited for home use. For one thing, Puritan-Bennett machines used a compressor pump or pressurized air to drive the bellows, much more cumbersome than Thompson's electric motor. Puritan-Bennett machines also cost approximately 50 percent more than a comparable Thompson unit and were relatively large and immobile. On the other hand, Puritan-Bennett machines were viewed by physicians and respiration therapists as industry standards.

By the late 1970s, TRP had developed a piston and cylinder design (similar in principle to the bellows) and placed it on the market. The product lacked the sophisitication of the Puritan-Bennett machines but was reliable, portable, and much simpler to adjust and operate. It also maintained TRP's traditional cost advantage. Another firm, Life Products, began its operations in 1981 by producing a similar design. A third competitor, Lifecare Services, had begun operations somewhat earlier.

Puritan-Bennett

Puritan-Bennett was a large, growing, and financially sound manufacturer of respiration equipment for medical and aviation applications. Its headquarters were located in Kansas City, Missouri. However, the firm staffed over 40 sales, service, and warehouse operations in the United States, Canada, United Kingdom, and France. Sales for 1985 exceeded $100 million while employment was just over 2,000 people. Sales for its Medical Equipment Group (respirators, related equipment, and accessories, service, and parts) likely exceeded $40 million for 1985; however, Higgins could obtain data only for the period 1981–1984 (see Exhibit 1). Puritan-Bennett usually sold its respirators through a system of independent, durable medical equipment dealers. However, its sales offices did sell directly to identified "house accounts" and often competed with dealers by selling slower-moving products to all accounts. According to industry sources, Puritan-Ben-

EXHIBIT 1 Puritan-Bennett Medical Equipment Group Sales

	1981	*1982*	*1983*	*1984*
Domestic sales:				
Model MA-1:				
Units	1,460	875	600	500
Amount ($ millions)	8.5	8.9	3.5	3.1
Model MA-2:				
Units	—	935	900	1,100
Amount ($ millions)	—	6.0	6.1	7.8
Foreign sales:				
Units	250	300	500	565
Amount ($ millions)	1.5	1.8	3.1	3.6
IPPB equipment ($ millions)	6.0	6.5	6.7	7.0
Parts, service, accessories ($ millions)	10.0	11.7	13.1	13.5
Overhaul ($millions)	2.0	3.0	2.5	2.5
Total ($ millions)	28.0	34.0	35.0	37.5

Source: *The Wall Street Transcript.*

nett sales were slightly more than three fourths of all respirator sales to hospitals in 1985.

However, these same sources expected Puritan-Bennett's share to diminish during the late 1980s because of the aggressive marketing efforts of three other manufacturers of hospital-style respirators: Bear Medical Systems, Inc.; J. H. Emerson; and Siemens-Elema. The latter firm was expected to grow the most rapidly, despite its quite recent entry into the U.S. market (its headquarters were in Sweden) and a list price of over $16,000 for its basic model.

Life Products

Life Products directly competed with TRP for the portable respirator market. Life Products had begun operations in 1981 when David Smith, a TRP employee, left to start his own business. Smith had located his plant in Boulder, Colorado, less than a mile from TRP headquarters.

He began almost immediately to set up a dealer network and by early 1986 had secured over 40 independent dealers located in large metropolitan areas. Smith had made a strong effort to sign only large, well-managed durable medical equipment dealers. Dealer representatives were required to complete Life Product's service training school, held each month in Boulder. Life Products sold its products to dealers (in contrast to TRP, which both sold and rented products to consumers and to dealers). Dealers received a 20 to 25 percent discount off suggested retail price on most products.

As of April 1986, Life Products offered two respirator models (the LP3 and LP4) and a limited number of accessories (such as mouthpieces and plastic tubing) to its dealers. Suggested retail prices for the two respirator models were approximately $3,900 and $4,800. Suggested rental rates were approximately $400 and $500 per month. Life Products also allowed Lifecare Services to manufacture a respirator similar to the LP3 under license.

At the end of 1985, Smith was quite pleased with his firm's performance. During Life Products' brief history, it had passed TRP in sales and now ceased to see the firm as a serious threat, at least according to one company executive:

> We really aren't in competition with Thompson. They're after the stagnant market and we're after a growing market. We see new applications and ultimately the hospital market as our niche. I doubt if Thompson will even be around in a few years. As for Lifecare, their prices are much lower than ours but you don't get the service. With them you get the basic product, but nothing else. With us, you get a complete medical care service. That's the big difference.

EXHIBIT 2 Lifecare Services, Inc., Field Offices

Augusta, Ga.	Houston, Tex.
Baltimore, Md.	Los Angeles, Calif.
Boston, Mass.	New York, N.Y.
Chicago, Ill.	Oakland, Calif.
Cleveland, Ohio	Omaha, Nebr.
Denver, Colo.	Phoenix, Ariz.
Detroit, Mich.	Seattle, Wash.
Grand Rapids, Mich.*	St. Paul, Minn.

* Suboffice.

Source: Trade literature.

Lifecare Services, Inc.

In contrast to the preceding firms, Lifecare Services, Inc. earned much less of its revenues from medical equipment manufacturing and much more from medical equipment distributing. The firm primarily resold products purchased from other manufacturers, operating out of its headquarters in Boulder as well as from its 16 field offices (Exhibit 2). All offices were stocked with backup parts and an inventory of respirators. All were staffed with trained service technicians under Lifecare's employ.

Lifecare did manufacture a few accessories not readily available from other manufacturers. These items complemented the purchased products and, in the company's words, served to "give the customer a complete respiratory service." Under a licensing agreement between Lifecare and Life Products, the firm manufactured a respirator similar to the LP3 and marketed it under the Lifecare name. The unit rented for approximately $175 per month. While Lifecare continued to service the few remaining Thompson units it still had in the field, it no longer carried the Thompson line.

Lifecare rented rather than sold its equipment. The firm maintained that this gave patients more flexibility in the event of recovery or death and lowered patients' monthly costs.

THOMPSON RESPIRATION PRODUCTS, INC.

TRP currently employed 13 people, 9 in production and 4 in management. It conducted operations in a modern, attractive building (leased) in an industrial park. The building contained about 6,000 square feet of space, split 75/25 for production/management purposes. Production operations were essentially job shop in nature: skilled technicians assembled each unit by hand on work benches, making frequent quality control tests and subsequent adjustments. Production lots usually ranged from 10 to 75 units per model and probably averaged around 40. Normal production capacity was about 600 units per year.

Product Line

TRP currently sold seven respirator models plus a large number of accessories. All respirator models were portable but differed considerably in terms of style, design, performance specifications, and attendant features (see Exhibit 3). Four models were styled as metal boxes with an impressive array of knobs, dials, indicator lights, and switches. Three were styled as less imposing, "overnighter" suitcases with less prominently displayed controls and indicators. (Exhibit 4 reproduces part of the specification sheet for the M3000, as illustrative of the metal box design.)

Four of the models were designed as *pressure machines,* using a turbine pump that provided a constant, usually positive, pressure. Patients were provided intermittent access to this pressure as breaths per minute. However, one model, the MV Multivent, could provide either a constant positive or a constant negative pressure (i.e., a vacuum, necessary to operate chest shells, iron lungs, and body wraps). No other portable respirator on the market could produce a negative pressure. Three of the models were designed as *volume machines,* using a piston pump that produced intermittent, constant volumes of pressurized air as breaths per minute. Actual volumes were prescribed by each patient's physician based on lung capacity. Pressures depended on the breathing method used (mouthpiece, trach, chest shell, and others) and on the patient's activity level. Breaths per minute also depended on the patient's activity level.

Models came with several features. The newest was an assist feature (currently available on the Minilung M25 but soon to be offered also on the M3000) that allowed the patient alone to "command" additional breaths without having someone change the dialed breath rate. The sigh feature gave patients a sigh, either automatically or on demand. Depending on the model, up to six alarms were available to indicate a patient's call, unacceptable low pressure, unacceptable high pressure, low battery voltage/power failure, failure to cycle, and the need to replace motor brushes. All models but the MV Multivent also offered automatic switchover from alternating current to either an internal or an external battery (or both) in the event of a power failure. Batteries provided for 18 to 40 hours of operation, depending on usage.

EXHIBIT 3 TRP Respirators

*Model**	*Style*	*Design*	*Volume (cc)*	*Pressure (cm. H_2O)*
M3000	Metal box	Volume	300–3,000	+10 to +65
MV Multivent	Metal box	Pressure (positive or negative)	n.a.	−70 to +80
Minilung M15	Suitcase	Volume	200–1,500	+5 to +65
Minilung M25 Assist (also available without the assist feature)	Suitcase	Volume	600–2,500	+5 to +65
Bantam GS	Suitcase	Pressure (positive)	n.a.	+15 to +45
Compact CS	Metal box	Pressure (positive)	n.a.	+15 to +45
Compact C	Metal box	Pressure (positive)	n.a.	+15 to +45

Model	*Breaths per minute*	*Weight (lbs)*	*Size (cubic ft.)*	*Features*
M3000	6 to 30	39	0.85	Sigh, four alarms, automatic switchover from AC to battery
MV Multivent	8 to 24	41	1.05	Positive or negative pressure, four alarms, AC only
Minilung M15	8 to 22	24	0.70	Three alarms, automatic switchover from AC to battery
Minilung M25 Assist (also available without the assist feature)	5 to 20	24	0.70	Assist, sigh, three alarms, automatic switchover from AC to battery
Bantam GS	6 to 24	19	0.75	Sigh, six alarms, automatic switchover from AC to battery
Compact CS	8 to 24	25	0.72	Sigh, six alarms, automatic switchover from AC to battery
Compact C	6 to 24	19	0.50	Sigh, four alarms, automatic switchover from AC to battery

Note: n.a. = not applicable.
* Five other models considered obsolete by TRP could be supplied if necessary.

Source: Company sales specification sheets.

Higgins felt that TRP's respirators were superior to those of Life Products. Most TRP models allowed pressure monitoring in the airway itself rather than in the machine, providing more accurate measurement. TRP's suitcase-style models often were strongly preferred by patients, especially the polio patients who had known no others. TRP's

THOMPSON

M3000 MINILUNG
Portable Volume Ventilator

M3000 MINILUNG

PORTABLE VOLUME VENTILATOR

What it can mean to the User . . .

• The M3000 is a planned performance product designed to meet breathing needs. It is a significant step in the ongoing effort of a company which pioneered the advancement of portable respiratory equipment.

• This portable volume ventilator sets high standards for flexibility of operation and versatility in use. The M3000 has gained its successful reputation as a result of satisfactory usage in hospitals, for transport, in rehabilitation efforts and in home care. This model grew out of expressed needs of users for characteristics which offer performance PLUS. It is engineered to enable the user to have something more than just mechanical breathing.

• Now breathing patterns can be comfortably varied with the use of a SIGH, which can be obtained either automatically or manually.

• Besides being sturdy and reliable, the M3000 can be adjusted readily.

• Remote pressure sensing in the proximal airway provides for more accurate set up of the ventilator pressure alarms.

• This model has the option of a patient-operated call switch.

• AC-DC operation of the M3000 is accomplished with ease because automatic switch-over is provided on AC power failure, first to external battery, then to internal battery.

THOMPSON takes pride in planning ahead.

See reverse for specifications.

Innovators in Respiratory Equipment for Over 25 Years
Thompson Respiration Products, Inc. 1680 Range Street Boulder Colorado 80301 303/443-3350

SPECIFICATIONS:

300 to 3000 ml adjustable volume
10 to 65 cm. water pressure
6 to 30 breaths per minute
Automatic or Manual Sigh
Alarms:
  Patient operated call alarm
  Low Pressure alarm and light
  High Pressure alarm and light
  Low Voltage light with delayed alarm
  Automatic switchover provided on AC power failure, first to external battery, then to internal battery
  Alarm delay switch
Pilot lamps color-coded and labeled
Remote pressure connector
Self-contained battery for 2 hour operation — recharges automatically
Power sources:
  120 volt, 60 hz; 12 volt external battery; and internal battery
Size: 12⅝ W x 11¼ D x 10¼ inches H
Weight: 39 pounds (Shipping weight: 48 pounds)

volume models offered easier volume adjustments and all TRP models offered more alarms. On the other hand, he knew that TRP had recently experienced some product reliability problems of an irritating—not life threatening—nature. Further, he knew that Life Products had beaten TRP to the market with the assist feature (the idea for which had come from a Puritan-Bennett machine).

TRP's line of accessories was more extensive than that of Life Products. TRP offered the following for separate sale: alarms, call switches, battery cables, chest shells, mouthpieces, plastic tubing, pneumobelts and bladders (equipment for still another breathing method that utilized intermittent pressure on a patient's diaphragm), and other items. Lifecare Services offered many similar items.

Distribution

Shortly after joining TRP, Higgins had decided to switch from selling and renting products directly to patients to selling and renting products to dealers. While it meant lower margins, less control, and more infrequent communication with patients, the change had several advantages. It allowed TRP to shift inventory from the factory to the dealer, generating cash more quickly. It provided for local representation in market areas, allowing patients greater feelings of security and TRP more aggressive sales efforts. It shifted burdensome paperwork (required by insurance companies and state and federal agencies to effect payment) from TRP to the dealer. It also reduced other TRP administrative activities in accounting, customer relations, and sales.

TRP derived about half of its 1985 revenue of $3 million directly from patients and about half from the dealer network. By April 1986, the firm had 22 dealers (see Exhibit 5) with 3 accounting for over 60

EXHIBIT 5 TRP Dealer Locations

Bakersfield, Calif.	Salt Lake City, Utah
Baltimore, Md.	San Diego, Calif.
Birmingham, Ala.	San Francisco, Calif.
Chicago, Ill.	Seattle, Wash.
Cleveland, Ohio	Springfield, Ohio
Fort Wayne, Ind.	Tampa, Fla.
Greenville, N.C.	Tucson, Ariz.
Indianapolis, Ind.	Washington, D.C.
Newark, N.J.	Montreal, Canada
Oklahoma City, Okla.	Toronto, Canada
Pittsburgh, Pa.	

Source: Company records.

percent of TRP dealer revenues. Two of the three serviced TRP products as did two of the smaller dealers; the rest preferred to let the factory take care of repairs. TRP conducted occasional training sessions for dealer repair personnel but distances were great and turnover in the position high, making such sessions costly. Most dealers requested air shipment of respirators, in quantities of one or two units.

Price

TRP maintained a comprehensive price list for its entire product line. (Exhibit 6 reproduces part of the current list.) Each respirator model carried both a suggested retail selling price and a suggested retail rental rate. (TRP also applied these rates when it dealt directly with patients.) The list also presented two net purchase prices for each model along with an alternative rental rate that TRP charged to dealers. About 40 percent of the 300 respirator units TRP shipped to dealers in 1985 went out on a rental basis. The comparable figure for the 165 units sent directly to consumers was 90 percent. Net purchase prices allowed an approximate 7 percent discount for orders of three or more units of each model. Higgins had initiated this policy early last year with the aim of encouraging dealers to order in larger quantities. To date one dealer had taken advantage of this discount.

Current policy called for TRP to earn a gross margin of approximately 35 percent on the dealer price for one or two units. All prices included shipping charges by United Parcel Service (UPS); purchasers requesting more expensive transportation service paid the difference between actual costs incurred and the UPS charge. Terms were net 30 days with a 1.5 percent service charge added to past due accounts. Prices were last changed in late 1985.

EXHIBIT 6 Current TRP Respirator Price List

	Suggested Retail			*Dealer Price*	
Model	*Rent/month*	*Price*	*Dealer Rent/month*	*1–2*	*3 or More*
M3000	$380	$6,000	$290	$4,500	$4,185
MV Multivent	270	4,300	210	3,225	3,000
Minilung M15	250	3,950	190	2,960	2,750
Minilung M25	250	3,950	190	2,960	2,750
Bantam GS	230	3,600	175	2,700	2,510
Compact CS	230	3,600	175	2,700	2,510
Compact C	200	3,150	155	2,360	2,195

Source: Company sales specification sheets.

CONSUMERS

Two types of patients used respirators, depending on whether the need followed from disease or from injury. Diseases such as polio, sleep apnea, chronic obstructive pulmonary disease, and muscular dystrophy annually left about 1,900 victims unable to breathe without a respirator. Injury to the spinal cord above the fifth vertebra caused a similar result for about 300 people per year. Except for polio, incidences of the diseases and injury were growing at about 3 percent per year. Most patients kept one respirator at bedside and another mounted on a wheelchair. However, Higgins did know of one individual who kept eight Bantam B models (provided by a local polio foundation, now defunct) in his closet. Except for polio patients, life expectancies were about five years. Higgins estimated the total number of patients using a home respirator in 1981 as follows:

Polio	3,000
Other diseases	6,500
Spinal cord injury	1,000

Almost all patients were under a physician's care as well as that of a more immediate nurse or attendant (frequently a relative). About 95 percent paid for their equipment through insurance benefits or foundation monies. About 90 percent rented their equipment. Almost all patients and their nurses or attendants had received instruction in equipment operation from respiration therapists employed by medical centers or by dealers of durable medical equipment.

The majority of patients were poor. Virtually none were gainfully employed and all had seen their savings and other assets diminished to varying degrees by treatment costs. Some had experienced a divorce. Slightly more patients were male than female. About 75 percent lived in their homes with the rest split between hospitals, nursing homes, and other institutions.

Apart from patients, Higgins thought that hospitals might be considered a logical new market for TRP to enter. Many of the larger and some of the smaller general hospitals might be convinced to purchase one portable respirator (like the M3000) for emergency and other use with injury patients. Such a machine would be much cheaper to purchase than a large Puritan-Bennett and would allow easier patient trips to testing areas, X-ray, surgery, and the like. Even easier to convince should be the 14 regional spinal cord injury centers located across the country (Exhibit 7). Other medical centers that specialized in treatment of pulmonary diseases should also be prime targets. Somewhat less promising but more numerous would be public and private schools that trained physicians and respiration therapists. Higgins estimated the numbers of these institutions at:

EXHIBIT 7 Regional Spinal Cord Injury Centers

Birmingham, Ala.	Houston, Tex.
Boston, Mass.	Miami, Fla.
Chicago, Ill.	New York, N.Y.
Columbia, Mo.	Philadelphia, Pa.
Downey, Calif.	Phoenix, Ariz.
Englewood, Colo.	San Jose, Calif.
Fishersville, Va.	Seattle, Wash.

General hospitals (100 beds or more)	3,800
General hospitals (fewer than 100 beds)	3,200
Spinal cord injury centers	14
Pulmonary disease treatment centers	100
Medical schools	180
Respiration therapy schools	250

DEALERS

Dealers supplying homecare medical products (as distinct from dealers supplying hospitals and medical centers) showed a great deal of diversity. Some were little more than small areas in local drugstores that rented canes, walkers, and wheelchairs in addition to selling supplies like surgical stockings and colostomy bags. Others carried nearly everything needed for home nursing care—renting everything from canes to hospital beds and selling supplies from bed pads to bottled oxygen. Still others specialized in products and supplies for only certain types of patients.

In this latter category, Higgins had identified dealers of oxygen and oxygen-related equipment as the best fit among existing dealers. These dealers serviced victims of emphysema, bronchitis, asthma, and other respiratory ailments, a growing market that Higgins estimated was about 10 times greater than that for respirators. A typical dealer had begun perhaps 10 years ago selling bottled oxygen (obtained from a welding supply wholesaler) and renting rather crude metering equipment to patients at home under the care of a registered nurse. The same dealer today now rented and serviced oxygen concentrators (a recently developed device that extracts oxygen from the air), liquid oxygen equipment and liquid oxygen, and much more sophisticated oxygen equipment and oxygen to patients cared for by themselves or by relatives.

Most dealers maintained a fleet of radio-dispatched trucks to deliver products to their customers. Better dealers promised 24-hour service and kept delivery personnel and a respiration therapist on call 24 hours a day. Dealers usually employed several respiration therapists who would set up equipment, instruct patients and attendants on equipment operation, and provide routine and emergency service. Dealers often expected the therapists to function as a sales force. The therapists would call on physicians and other respiration therapists at hospitals and medical centers, on discharge planners at hospitals, and on organizations such as muscular dystrophy associations, spinal cord injury associations, and visiting nurse associations.

Dealers usually bought their inventories of durable equipment and supplies directly from manufacturers. They usually received a 20 to 25 percent discount off suggested list prices to consumers and hospitals. Only in rare instances might dealers instead lease equipment from a manufacturer. Dealers aimed for a payback of one year or less, meaning that most products began to contribute to profit and overhead after 12 months of rental. Most products lasted physically for upwards of 10 years but technologically for only 5 to 6: every dealer's warehouse contained idle but perfectly suitable equipment that had been superseded by models demanded by patients, their physicians, or their attendants.

Most dealers were independently owned and operated, with annual sales ranging between $5 million and $10 million. However, a number had recently been acquired by one of several parent organizations that were regional or national in scope. Such chains usually consisted of from 10 to 30 retail operations located in separated market areas. However, the largest, Abbey Medical, had begun operations in 1924 and now consisted of over 70 local dealers. Higgins estimated 1985 sales for the chain (which was itself acquired by American Hospital Supply Corporation in April 1981) at over $60 million. In general, chains maintained a low corporate visibility and provided their dealers with working capital, employee benefit programs, operating advice, and some centralized purchasing. Higgins thought that chain organizations might grow more rapidly over the next 10 years.

THE ISSUES

Higgins looked at his watch. It was 5:30 and really time to leave. "Still," he thought, "I should jot down what I see to be the immediate issues before I go—that way I won't be tempted to think about them over the weekend." He took a pen and wrote the following:

1. Should TRP continue to rent respirators to dealers?
2. Should TRP protect each dealer's territory (and how big should a territory be)?

3. Should TRP require dealers to stock no competing equipment?
4. How many dealers should TRP eventually have? Where?
5. What sales information should be assembled in order to attract high-quality dealers?
6. What should be done about the "best efforts" clause?

As he reread the list, Higgins considered that there probably were still other short-term-oriented questions he might have missed. Monday would be soon enough to consider them all.

Until then, he was free to think about broader, more strategic issues. Some reflections on the nature of the target market, a statement of marketing objectives, and TRP's possible entry into the hospital market would occupy the weekend. Decisions on these topics would form a substantial part of TRP's strategic marketing plan, a document Higgins hoped to have for the beginning of the next fiscal year in July. "At least I can rule out one option," Higgins thought as he put on his coat. That was an idea to use independent sales representatives to sell TRP products on commission: a recently completed two-month search for such an organization had come up empty. "Like my stomach," he thought, as he went out the door.

Case 19

Apple Computer Inc.*

Charles Hinkle
Esther L. Stineman
both of the University of Colorado

> HELLO, I'M YOUR INFORMATIVE AND INEXPENSIVE ELECTRONIC COMPANION. LINK YOUR MIND WITH MY MICROPROCESSOR AND LET US MAKE TIMELY DECISIONS TOGETHER.[1]
>
> MAKE BREAD WITH AN APPLE. EVEN IF YOUR COMPANY HAS A BIG COMPUTER SYSTEM, YOU COULD PROBABLY DO YOUR JOB BETTERFASTERSMARTER WITH AN APPLE . . . SITTING ON YOUR DESK.[2]
>
> MY NAME IS REVEREND APPLE. . . . GROOM, WHAT'S YOUR NAME?[3]

Apple Computer Inc. hasn't given its blessing to the computer marriages, but a spokesperson has said, "It's good to have divinity on your side." Reputedly the world's first ordained computer, the Apple II's human co-pastor in a California church used his electronic helper "to get people interested in marriage, the church, and God," offering the programmed ceremony free along with marriage counseling by a warm-blooded being for the lucky couple.

Personal computer-craze cartoons abound. For example, a boy stares incredulously at a book, a gift just handed to him by someone who looks suspiciously like a harried mother, and asks how it can be full of information since it doesn't even have a display screen.[4] Another lists on a house-for-sale sign features that include nine rooms, three baths, and two computer terminals.[5] The third example, a cover cartoon, portrays a psychoanalyst fingering a lap-held keyboard and asking the

---

* Permission to reprint this case granted by Charles Hinkle and Esther Stineman.

[1] Opening conversational gambit on an Apple II.

[2] Excerpt from Fall 1981 Apple Computer Inc. advertisement.

[3] Marilyn Chase, "Do You Take This Input to Be Your Lawfully Wedded Interface?" *The Wall Street Journal,* July 28, 1981, p. 29.

[4] *The Wall Street Journal,* n.d.

[5] *The New Yorker,* July 26, 1982, p. 33.

couch occupant to tell him when the urge first struck to buy a home computer.[6]

CORPORATE BACKGROUND

Widely acknowledged as the leader in the personal computer arena, Apple Computer Inc. was founded in 1976 by 21-year-old Steve Jobs, whose private goal was to make computer capability widely accessible—not unlike Henry Ford's desire to provide automobiles for the masses, and by Steve Wozniak, both college dropout design engineers.

> Basically, Steve Wozniak and I invented the Apple because we wanted a personal computer. Not only couldn't we afford the computers that were on the market, those computers were impractical for us to use. We needed a Volkswagen. . . . After we launched the Apple in 1976, all our friends wanted one.[7]

Jobs likened the Apple offspring's contribution to human efficiency to the IBM Selectric typewriter, the calculator, the Xerox copying machine, and advanced telephone systems.

The youthful entrepreneurs used $1,300 from the sale of a Volkswagen to assemble their first prototype. Both Steves wanted to avoid a threatening name, one smacking of high technology, and Jobs was a fruitarian, so the corporate name "Apple" sounded appropriate. The unspoken corporate motto might well have been, "Don't trust any computer you can't lift."

After meeting in the garage of a mutual friend, Jobs and Wozniak's friendship evolved into the partnership that became Apple Computer Inc. primarily by the happenstance of assembling computers for friends, not realizing that they were on to something that could be a leading-edge effort in making computers available to the masses. Before forming the company, Wozniak worked as a technician at Hewlett-Packard and Jobs was employed developing video games at Atari. Apple II was designed for the most part by fall 1976, using 4K dynamic random access memories (RAMs), which no other firm used at the time. As Jobs put it, "Going out with a product based on dynamic memories was untried; fortunately, we didn't know how risky it was." According to the chairman, Commodore saw the Apple II and immediately made overtures to acquire the fledgling firm, which would have transformed Apple II to Commodore I. The partners wanted reliable manufacturers who could build a total package for them, so they visited familiar haunts. "Atari couldn't get involved because of a heavy

---

[6] *Forbes,* August 2, 1982, front outside cover.

[7] Fall 1981, corporate advertisement.

commitment, quite correctly, to developing their games, and Hewlett-Packard, which was working on the HP-85 at that time, was dubious of our abilities, I'm convinced, because we didn't have electrical engineering or computer science degrees."

ADVENT OF PERSONAL COMPUTING

What is a personal computer (PC)? It is an extension of the microprocessor, a computer on a chip, developed by Intel Corp. in the early 1970s and in those earlier years bought principally by hobbyists. Unlike their predecessors, units of the 1980s became total systems, including input keyboards, video readout monitors, and software found at laboratory benches, in manufacturing plants, on executive side tables, and in schools and private dwellings.

The PC industry grew from nothing in 1975 to an estimated $1.5 billion plus in 1981 and was forecasted by industry specialists to continue an annual growth of from 40 to 50 percent through the mid-1980s. Stock prices of such firms as Apple, Tandy, and Commodore soared. Apple went on the market at $22 a share in 1980, and traded over-the-counter at $25 in August 1981, or roughly 100 times earnings, definitely a glamour stock. In November 1982, prices hovered in the area of $30, having risen from $11 earlier in the year.

Apple's first units, small, simple, and relatively inexpensive, were designed for consumer use not for business and scientific applications, but after add-on small-disk memory was introduced in 1978, many software authors started developing Apple programs for business. One, a general-purpose financial analysis program, is credited with giving Apple a year's lead time over competitors, making it the top banana in the business PC bunch.

According to various sources at the company's Cupertino, California, headquarters, independent software vendors were thought to spend a large proportion, possibly more than half, of their time on Apple software. The April 1982 issue of *BYTE* had no fewer than 11 pages of ads from companies promoting products to boost Apple II's performance. Rather than a hardware race, software technology was seen as the desirable focus to help buyers increase the usefulness of their machines.

As research and development proceeded rapidly, Apple III was announced in May 1980, finally making a full-fledged debut in March 1981. Initially technical problems had led to customer complaints that were covered by a policy of outright exchange. Both software and hardware came in for varied and widespread criticism as users bombarded Apple management with queries and grievances. It was rumored that the new units were about to be replaced by improved hardware and operating systems, but management denied this, predicting a 10-year life span for Apple III.

Operating mostly in leased facilities, manufacturing operations consisted of purchase, assembly, and test of materials and components used in Apple products. Facilities were located in Dallas; Cupertino, San Jose, and Los Angeles, California; County Cork, Ireland; and Singapore.

Purchases of personal computers for home use were at first disappointing; still, leading producers continued to emphasize these markets while consumer analysts warned that sales to these segments would not be sensational until the hardware and software were designed to serve the needs of household users. Home computers can be entertaining and educational and might even prove useful as information and transaction devices. One writer, whose personal computer was an Apple II, described dialing into a central network to view an airline schedule and suggested numerous other potential dimensions of what he called "home computer bulletin boards," speculating that students would have access to information comparable to the complete Library of Congress and that mail would be instantaneous.[8]

As electronic hobbyists' purchases dwindled in the late 1970s and early 1980s, manufacturers started eyeing the 80 million U.S. households, stressing fun and educational aspects. Predictions were that one of every four American homes would have a computer by the late 1980s. Planners spoke of two or three in every home and one atop every businesspersons' desk. Speedups in automation, including PCs, were to affect directly the jobs of some 9 million managers and 14 million professionals in American industry.[9] Small computers were expected to be information processing building blocks in this changing structure.

CULTIVATING EDUCATIONAL MARKETS

In 1979, Apple helped to create the nonprofit Foundation for the Advancement of Computer-Aided Education with the goal of furthering efforts of software authors. In 1980, Atari and Texas Instruments sponsored software writing contests. About this time, Tandy launched collaborative efforts with textbook publishers to enrich educational software. Most microprocessor makers hoped that expanded use in schools would stimulate computer sales in the home market. Educators

---

[8] Neil Shapiro, "Now Your Home Computer Can Call Other Computers on the Telephone," *Popular Mechanics,* February 1981, p. 130.

[9] "The Speedup in Automation," Special Report in *Business Week,* August 3, 1981, pp. 55–67.

claimed that poor software, frustrated users, and attempts at electronic humor in response to users' errors were insulting deterrents to students, although youngsters were said to approach the keyboard enthusiastically and to become comfortable quickly when exposed to computers.

Far below expectations, 1980 shipments of 50,000 microcomputers to schools were predicted by many to rise to some 250,000 units annually over a five-year period. Sales to schools in 1981 were estimated at $150 million. The shrinking cost of computer power was credited with the sudden popularity of school computers. C. Gregory Smith, director of educational marketing at Apple, expressed conviction that not only were schools sold on computers but they also were more likely than business buyers to make repeat purchases. That computer literacy would become a survival skill equal in importance to reading, writing, and arithmetic was not in doubt in the Apple hierarchy.

Engineering and business students at many colleges and universities opted for their own computers—individual units either owned or leased—partly because of the difficulties encountered gaining access to the institution's central devices. Several schools began leasing computers and telephone modems so students could have remote access to the larger processors on campus. Some colleges—for example, Stevens Institute of Technology in Hoboken, New Jersey—required that a student studying science, systems analysis, management, and other computer-intensive courses in 1982 own a microprocessor. Quite apart from relieving demand for the institutions' scarce terminals, schools taking this approach expected it to encourage students to become more familiar with and dependent upon computers, to treat them as an integral part of their intellectual support systems.

Donating an Apple II computer to some 83,000 public elementary and secondary schools in the United States seems a laudable and easily attainable goal, one that could be accomplished simply by management fiat. Not so, however, particularly when the would-be contributor posed a condition: boosting the ceiling on the annual amount of such a donation to 30 percent of its taxable income from 10 percent, the existing maximum. Without success Apple lobbied for a change permitting it to "further the cause of computer literacy in the nation's public schools," an attempt rejected by the House Ways and Means Committee.

New hope came in September 1982, as the House passed part of a temporary tax break giving the proposed program a boost.[10] The legislation (323 for and 62 against) would permit computer manufacturers

---

[10] "Apple Clears Hurdle on Its Plan to Send Computers to Class," *The Wall Street Journal,* September 23, 1982, p. 31.

to donate computers to public schools and to receive the favorable tax treatment reserved for donations of scientific equipment to universities. Congressional tax analysts estimated the tax break to be worth about $36 million in fiscal years 1982 and 1983 for Apple or for any others who wished to make such contributions. The Senate was yet to consider a similar bill. Apple executives thought the bill would stimulate computer education and, in turn, the computer industry; Treasury Department spokespersons opposed the idea on grounds that tax law should not be used to form social policy.

TOP-LEVEL ORGANIZATIONAL CHANGES

In early 1981, Apple Computer Inc. restructured its management team, naming former vice president of marketing, then chairman, A. C. Markkula, Jr., 39 years old, to the post of president and chief executive officer to concentrate on day-to-day operations of the company; Markkula was succeeded in the chairmanship by former Vice Chairman Jobs. Michael Scott, age 38, shifted from the position of president/CEO to the role of vice chairman, in charge of long-range business growth planning, and in 1982 left the company.

Self-taught computer engineer Stephen Wozniak programmed himself out of the Apple family portrait when he decided to seek gratification beyond the corporate agenda. Following an airplane wreck and a five-week loss of memory, he took a leave of absence from the company and enrolled at the University of California-Berkeley, under an assumed name, to take undergraduate computer science courses he had dropped out of for lack of interest 11 years previously.[11] The wizard—"Woz" to his friends—promoted a new-kind-of-unity rock concert at which 200,000 Californians and others showed up to hear music and relate to a philosophy pushing "us" instead of "me." At 32, with an estate thought to be over $50 million, Wozniak was said to be out approximately $3 million unless subsequent film and album revenues would cover his expenditures.[12]

FINANCIAL HIGHLIGHTS

As unemployment hovered around 10.4 percent in October 1982, and many industries were in the doldrums, the microcomputer marketers enjoyed continued increases in sales and profits. "One reason," CEO

---

[11] Paul Ciotti, "California Magazine," in the *Denver Post,* August 1, 1982, p. D-1.

[12] Rom Morganthau, David R. Friendly, and William Cook, "A Wizard called 'Woz'," *Newsweek,* September 20, 1982, p. 69.

EXHIBIT 1 Selected Apple Financial Statistics, Fiscal Years September 30, 1977–1982 (in millions, rounded)

	1977	*1978*	*1979*	*1980*	*1981*	*1982*
Net sales	$0.8	$7.9	$48	$117	$335	$583
R&D expenses	n.a.	0.6	4	7	21	38
Marketing expenses	n.a.	1.3	4	12	46	32
Net income	0.4	0.8	5	12	39	61

n.a. = Not available.

Notes: Net sales increases were not greatly affected by price changes.

Net income in 1981 was increased principally by improved gross margins and higher interest income, partially offset by increased marketing (increased advertising and other promotion costs and expansion of the distribution system) and general and administrative expenses (resulting mainly from foreign exchange losses, which were included in G&A expenses in 1981). Interest income in 1981 of $11.7 million was over 10 times the previous year's, resulting from investment in short-term securities of the proceeds from Apple's common stock offering in December 1980.

Apple paid no cash dividends, choosing to reinvest earnings to finance growth.

During the first quarter, a one-time, after-tax charge of $700,000 was accrued for an extra week's vacation awarded to employees as the company exceeded $100 million in quarterly sales for the first time.

A common stock issue of 2,600,000 shares was subscribed in 1981. Apple's 13 officers and directors own approximately 25 million of the company's almost 58 million common shares outstanding; Jobs has over 7.5 million, Markkula over 7 million, and Wozniak over 4 million, the three totaling almost a third of all shares.

Markkula pointed out, "is that a recession prompts many companies to invest in products that will boost productivity. That perspective has helped our sales not just here but also in Europe and England." Apple estimated that its profits rose 70 percent on sales gains of 80 percent in the fourth quarter ending in September. For its fiscal year, earnings were up more than 50 percent on a revenue increase of almost 75 percent. Exhibit 1 provides a review of selected financial statistics.

Cash flow was consistently healthy at Apple, partly because the company encouraged its 1,400 North American and 1,600 international dealers and distributors to pay in full for shipments within two weeks, while Apple generally took up to six weeks to pay its own suppliers.

Markkula was pleased with the company's financial shape, pointing to return on equity of 28 percent, return on assets of 20 percent, and return on investment of 33 percent. The balance sheet at the end of fiscal 1982 also revealed about $150 million in cash and equivalents and negligible debt, stellar performance from a company in existence only five years. There was talk around the company of breaking into the *Fortune 500* list.

FACING THE COMPETITION

Digital Equipment Corporation

After a winter of discontent that saw IBM storm down the field and a surge by Tandy and Commodore, 1982 was the season for Digital's challenge in the personal computer wars. Months earlier the company had moved into office automation. The acknowledged leader in superminicomputers—machines offering the performance of larger mainframe systems for a mini's price—presumably was counting on a strong position in information processing at major companies to give it a needed competitive edge. Digital bought advertisements in a few trade magazines in early summer and ran announcement-type ads in selected business periodicals. Observers concluded that this campaign was intended to reach the company's existing markets, not to cultivate awareness and interest in the much wider market already penetrated by the microprocessor pioneers and believed that Digital looked to the new line as an aid to sustain its high growth rate. However, insiders expected that the company would concentrate on sales to professionals and small businesses in an attempt to gain a share of the crowded $2.5 billion microcomputer markets. Meanwhile, by 1982 Digital had had three years of experience operating its chain of retail stores, computer shops intended to eliminate computer fear, to communicate benefits information in a friendly atmosphere, and to be flexible in how its sytems were presented to the public. The overall goal was to keep prospects from being intimidated.

Osborne Computer Corporation

Fall 1982 brought an advertising headline "the best holiday offer your career ever had," showing a picture of the unit followed by "The Osborne Personal Business Computer. $1795. dBASE II Data Base Software. Free." Most of the body copy promoted available software packages. The pre-Christmas theme (the free offer was to end December 24) announced "the best buy in a personal computer just got better."

Commodore International

An enviable stock performance record reflected this company's second-generation system's success. Entering the market in 1976 by purchasing MOS Technology to get a supply of calculator chips, CI benefited serendipitously from the acquired firm's research and development in microprocessor technology. The principal result of that development was named PET (personal electronic transactor) and was merchandised primarily in Europe simply because there was less competition there than in the United States. Calling themselves "the American Japanese," Commodore's strategy became that of offering a processor that could emulate those made by others, offering it at a price of $1,000, compared with prices of four times that for competitors' models. The rallying cry from Commodore was "A real computer for the price of a toy," while insisting that this computer went beyond games to teach computing skills to users. "The Commodore 64. Only $595. What nobody else can give you at twice the price," showing a picture of a user's hands, a keyboard, and color graphics, covered one side of a two-page advertisement. The opposite page showed how favorably Commodore 64 compared with Apple II ($1,530), IBM ($1,565), TRS-80 III ($999), and Atari 800 ($899). Commodore was apparently "coming home" to make its mark against entrenched microprocessor makers.

Tandy Corporation

Industry sources estimated that Tandy's 25 percent of the PC market in 1981 had declined to 24 percent in 1982. Tandy distributed through its chain of about 8,000 Radio Shack outlets, 200 of which sold only personal computers. Its TRS-80 and Apple were the most common stand-alone computers used by managers. Tandy widely advertised low prices ranging from $250 for a hand-held computer to a $10,000 system for small businesses. Science and science-fiction author Isaac Asimov was spokesman for Radio Shack's TRS-80, announcing in 1982 a price of $399.95 for the color computer. A 1981 survey reported that businesses typically spent about $9,460 for a computer system, while hobbyists' outlays averaged $1,574.[13] Factors delaying proliferation of executive desk-top computers reportedly included lack of communication software and physical design as well as resistance from entrenched data processing departments in the larger firms.[14]

Texas Instruments

Lessons learned in selling hand-held calculators were apparently being used by Texas Instruments in slashing the price of its entry in the home computer field. The offer was a $100 rebate to customers

---

[13] Small Business Section, *The Wall Street Journal,* July 6, 1981, p. 17.

[14] "Microcomputers Invade the Executive Suite," *Computer Decisions,* February 1981, p. 70.

buying the 99–4A computer. The predecessor 99–4 system came on the market in 1979 at about $1,000, the 4A was introduced in 1981 at $525, and the 1982 list price was pegged at $299.50. Comedian Bill Cosby was spokesman for TI's home computer.

Sinclair and Timex

"Under $200," advertised Sinclair Research Ltd. for its ZX80, describing it as a complete and powerful full-function computer that matched or surpassed other computers costing "many times more." The 1981 brochures proclaimed, "You simply take it out of the box, connect it to your TV, and turn it on. . . . With the manual in your hand, you'll be running programs in an hour. Within a week, you'll be writing complex programs with confidence." The company announced a 30-day moneyback guarantee and a 90-day limited warranty along with its national service-by-mail facility. After Timex acquired the computer maker, Timex Sinclair's 1000 became an update of the ZX series and was called "the first ready-to-go personal computer for under $100" (actually $99.95), aimed at the consumer market. Should the machine become available where Timex watches were distributed, 100,000 retail outlets might display and sell the ZX 1000. Some analysts recommended that the leaders should carefully observe the progress of this efficient and low-priced product, claiming it could well provide a substantial impetus for the personal computers revolution. The assumption was that introducing neophytes to computers with low-priced units could provide a reservoir of demand for trading up to units such as those made by Apple.

IBM

In all its years of successful EDP product introductions, IBM avoided growing slovenly or complacent, even though the giant firm was not always the undisputed leader in new products. With its large war chest of R&D and promotional funds and an eye for where much of the present, and probably a considerable portion of the future, seemed to lie, the company's riposte in microprocessors made its mark in this burgeoning field, eliminating the down-side risk of ignoring the opportunities and sharing in the upside potential after parrying opponents' lunges. IBM personal computers were distributed through 150 ComputerLand stores and at Sears Business Systems Centers, as well as at IBM product centers that sold and serviced the system. October 1982 demand for its systems exceeded supply, as the company announced anticipated output of 15,000 machines each month. While prophets of gloom heralded IBM's entry as a severe blow to competitive hardware precursors, many observers considered it yet another good omen for the booming business of software, an industry based on writing those coded sets of instructions that provide maps for computers to follow in processing data. As with all other entrants, IBM's success in PC markets would depend heavily on availability of software to drive the systems. With an estimated 5,000-plus software producers in the United States alone, competition was strong, and after details of IBM's configuration became available, conversion work in software supply houses became a major priority.

In an amicable mood, an Apple ad campaign in 1981 forthrightly greeted the newcomer: "Welcome, IBM. Seriously. . . . to the most exciting and important marketplace since the computer revolution began 35 years ago. . . . When we invented the first personal computer system, we estimated that over 140 million people worldwide could justify the purchase of one, if only they understood its benefits. Next year alone, we project that well over 1 million will come to that understanding. . . . We look forward to responsible competition in the massive effort to distribute this American technology to the world. . . . what we are doing is increasing social capital by enhancing individual productivity. Welcome to the task."

Using mass media to address the general public about its personal computer, IBM's fall 1982 advertisements pushed such product features as nonglare screen (easy on the eyes), 80 characters a line (with upper- and lower-case letters for a quick and easy read), flexibility of moving components about (the keyboard could be placed on one's lap and the user could rest his or her feet on the desk or elsewhere), and user memory expandable up to 256K, with 40K of permanent memory. Friendliness to users was claimed; BASIC language and high-resolution color graphics on the user's own TV set were mentioned as IBM invited shoppers to look around and compare theirs with others. The action imperative asked readers and viewers to visit an authorized IBM Personal Computer dealer, promising an address, along with other information, at an 800 number. And the competitive price was mentioned: "The quality, power and performance of the IBM Personal Computer are what you'd expect from IBM. The price isn't."[15] One headline announced: "30 years of computer experience: $1,565 and up."

---

[15] Early in 1982, IBM announced standardizing its typewriter line, cutting prices on some models and offering volume discounts for the first time. In late 1982, American Express Company sent a special mailer to cardholders announcing availability of the Selectric III, through American Express, at the going price, equal payments over 20 months, and no interest charges.

On television, IBM employed a "humanizing" approach to hawking its machines by claiming they "are warm and friendly and okay to touch." The Chaplin-like figure attempting to understand a computer's intricacies, and finally emerging triumphant, presumably was meant to persuade the reluctant that microprocessing could be conquered.

Meanwhile, Dick Cavett was acting as spokesman for Apple, and Tandy planned to show some at-home, family sorts of applications for its machines during the 1982 fall broadcasts, but the NFL strike altered those intentions. All three producers pushed utilitarian simplicity.

Hewlett-Packard

HP announced its desk-top model, designed to compete with the IBM Personal Computer and Apple III, in late winter 1982. This producer of precision electronics, with annual sales of over $4 billion, fired promotional salvos headlining HP–87 maximum memory of 544K, analytic software including the CP/M module, and the read-only-memory-based operating system that put built-in BASIC to work for the user. "We're building power, friendliness and reliability . . ." announced the body copy, with the tag line, "It's very good at what you do." HP's program library offered only two games in contrast to the dozens provided by competitive producers. One of HP's advertisements used the headline: "The personal computer comes of age." Perhaps the idea was old or useless by this time, but Apple ran no promotion welcoming Hewlett-Packard to the field of front-runners. Moving rapidly, in late summer, the company unveiled HP–75, its 26-ounce, battery-operated machine set to retail at $995. HP sources indicated the easily portable unit was intended to provide a transition between pocket calculators and desk-top computers.

Xerox

A formidable entry was Xerox, going for a total system configuration by promoting integrated office automation products—including a microcomputer doubling as a low-cost word processor—and threatening to vie for the anticipated largesse ready to be harvested in homes across the land.

Other competitors were expected to emerge, particularly since the capital gains tax, which was cut to 40 percent (from 50 percent) in 1978, favored high-technology entrepreneurs ready, with this added incentive, to start new businesses in the data processing field.

MARKET SHARES AND DISTRIBUTION

Based on several sources, it was estimated in mid-1982 that personal computer sales were shared as follows: Apple and Tandy/Radio Shack combined dominating almost half the market, with market shares of 24 percent each; next came Commodore at 9 percent; Nippon Electric Company with 6 percent; Hewlett-Packard and IBM at 5 percent each; Osborne accounting for 3 percent; and others, including Xerox, Digital Equipment, Texas Instruments, and perhaps 20 smaller producers sharing the remainder.

Estimates varied widely, but it was conjectured that stores were the channel of distribution for about 60 percent of desk-top computers purchased in 1982, while mail order accounted for 15 to 20 percent and direct sales 10 to 15 percent, the remainder being sold by other means.

Except for Tandy and Texas Instruments' units, personal computers were available at computer stores; and Texas Instruments sold through department stores and catalogs. Struggling for display space was a way of life, and marketing became extremely vital to PC sales. Such firms as Sears reportedly planned to carry no more than four brands in 1983, all chosen according to what seems logical for the most customers. The chain's 26 business retail centers stocked IBM, Osbourne, and Vector Graphics systems in 1982. A Sears manager rejected the idea that this limited array hindered customers' choices: "Most suppliers are merely assemblers of components by other firms that provide the same components for many manufacturers, so it is difficult when you look inside the case to tell them all apart." MOS Technology, Zilog, Inc., and Intel Corporation were the leading processor designers.

Apple's retail dealers were asked by the company, in November 1981, to sign an amended dealer contract to prohibit telephone and mail-order sales of its products under penalty of losing dealership status. The rationale was simple: success depends on customer satisfaction, which, in turn, depends on dealers providing support services to users. Although some mail-order firms were discounting prices, Apple management said that this was not the issue, maintaining that its effort to eliminate mail-order sales was legal and in line with the company's philosophy of adequately serving customers' postpurchase needs. Filing a suit to block the company from enforcing the new policy, a group of mail-order distributors accused Apple of bowing to pressure from full-service dealers by attempting to fix prices and restrain trade.

A long-standing central buying agreement with a Minneapolis-based retail chain was renewed for 1983. Team Central, entering its sixth year of association with Apple, is a franchiser of approximately

90 retail stores that sell general consumer products in medium-sized and smaller markets nationwide.[16]

"We're happy the negotiations are complete and look forward to another strong selling year with the Team organization," announced Gene Carter, Apple vice president of sales. "Team provides Apple with an important presence in secondary and tertiary markets."

Gary Thorne, Team executive vice president of sales and marketing, said his company's strategy in 1983 would be to emphasize personal computer sales through its franchisees. "The pervasiveness of personal computers and Team's importance in the markets we serve make the Apple line an exciting part of our sales thrust in the coming year."

Earlier in the year, Apple ended a similar agreement with ComputerLand Corp. to help achieve geographic control of new franchisees.

APPLE'S DIRECT ATTACK

In February 1982 Apple's offensive included this campaign: "NOW THAT YOU'VE SEEN THEIR FIRST GENERATION, TAKE A LOOK AT OUR THIRD," making the comparison shown in Exhibit 2. Highlights of claims for the Apple III are shown in Exhibit 3.

Promoting its third generation, Apple announced: "The only thing we didn't build into the Apple III is obsolescence." The new product was available at over 1,000 dealers in the United States and Canada, all offering technical support.

In contrast to some Apple advertisements that were hard-hitting and directly confrontational, others were somewhat whimsical, appealing to specific market segments. Consider these headlines: "Grow Corn with an Apple," targeted the agribusiness segment, pushing its more than 1,000 full-service dealers as the contact point of farmers desiring to aid their decision making; "E.F. Hutton simplifies life with Apples," attempted to persuade life insurance agents to have an Apple to help ensure their futures; "Make bread with an Apple," was a third-party testimony about Apple's role at Pepperidge Farm; "Baked Apple," described how a fire-damaged Apple, *"mirabile dictu,"* still worked when brought into one of the nearly 1,000 Apple dealers with complete service centers, where everything would be "well done"; and a fourth quarter 1982 ad listed 1,100 Apple compatible computer programs.

> Consumer awareness and brand recognition are prerequisites to long-term success in a marketplace of intensifying competition. Apple has been known for its marketing emphasis, with a resultant identity that we consider

---

[16] Based on corporate press release, August 12, 1982.

EXHIBIT 2 Apple's Comparison of Its Features with Those of Selected Competitors

	Xerox 820	*Hewlett-Packard 125, Model 10*	*IBM Personal Computer*	*Apple III*
Standard memory	64K	64K	64K	128K
Maximum memory when fully configured*	64K	64K	192K	256K
Expandability	No expansion slots	No expansion slots	No extra expansion slots in fully configured* 192K system	4 extra expansion slots in fully configured* 256K system
Diskette storage (per drive)	92K	256K	160K	140K
Mass storage (per drive)	—	1.16 megabyte floppy disk	—	5 megabyte hard disk
Display graphics capability	High resolution, B/W	High resolution, B/W	High resolution, B/W or 4-color (color requires additional card)	High resolution, B/W or 16-color
Software available	Word processing	Word processing	Word processing	Prod processing
	SuperCalc®	VisiCalc® 125	VisiCalc®	VisiCalc® III
	—	Business graphics	—	Business graphics
	—	Data base management	—	Data base management
	Communications	Communications	Communications	Communications
	—	—	—	Apple II software library
	CP/M® library	CP/M® library	CP/M® 86 programs	CP/M® library (Spring 1982)

* "Fully configured" means that the system includes, at a minimum, monitor, printer, two disk drives, and RS-232 communicator.
Note: Based on manufacturer's information available as of December 1981.

memorable and strong. Awareness of Apple, according to market surveys, rose from approximately 10 percent at the beginning of 1981 to nearly 80 percent at year-end.[17]

[17] *1981 Annual Report,* p. 3.

EXHIBIT 3 Claims for Apple III, 1982

Dollar for dollar, the most powerful personal computer.

Up to 256K of usable internal memory.

New software packages exclusively for the Apple III, including VisiCalc III.

Apple Writer III software—professional work processing capability—for less than the price of most word processors.

Apple business graphics—plots, graphs, bars, or pie charts in 16 high-resolution colors or 16 gray scales.

Mail list manager lets you store nearly 1,000 names on one disk.

Access III communications software: access to mainframe computers.

Apple III can run thousands of Apple II programs . . . soon . . . thousands of CP/M programs. More available software than any other personal computer.

ProFile, a new hard-disk option. With this addition, Apple III can store over 1,200 pages of text (5 million bytes of information). Enables you to handle problems once reserved for big computers.

Apple also launched Apple Expo—a dealer trade seminar, trade show, and public exposition—in major U.S. cities and created extensive merchandising aids and dealer training programs.

> [Apple's] marketing emphasis in the past two years has been on the business, professional and managerial segment, which today accounts for approximately 40 percent of revenues. . . . Ultimately, the greatest demand for personal computers will come from a broader spectrum.[18]

Apple supported the advertising campaigns of retail dealers with reimbursements of up to 3 percent of their dollar purchases from the company for actual advertising expenses incurred and provided there was compliance with standards set by Apple. At its own expense, Apple provided demonstration models, brochures, and point-of-sale posters and conducted sales seminars to assist dealers. Corporate expenditures for product advertising accelerated from $573,000 in 1978, to $2 million in 1979, $4.5 million in 1980, $6.4 million in 1981, and an estimated $26 million in 1982. Internal estimates were, as Apple continued fending off those who would challenge its industry leadership, that advertising expenditures would remain in the interval of 4 to 5 percent of sales.

[18] Ibid., p. 3.

SUMMER OF 1982 LEGAL ISSUES[19]

Imitators of good ideas seemed to come out of the woodwork as Apple's executives lost count of look-alikes. In July 1982 the company filed a number of lawsuits overseas, notably in Taiwan, Hong Kong, and New Zealand, in an ongoing effort too stop the manufacture and export of bogus Apple II personal computers. Investigations continued in Japan, Singapore, and Australia.

In Taipei, Taiwan, Apple brought a civil action under Taiwan's copyright laws against Sunrise Computer, maker of the "Apolo II" computer, an Apple copy.[20] As a first step in this action in accordance with Taiwanese law, Apple seized as evidence several Apolo computers during a surprise raid on a Sunrise facility in Taipei. Apple planned to press similar charges against another Taiwanese manufacturer. The government of Taiwan, according to the company, was collaborating with Apple to help prevent export of Apple II copies.

In Hong Kong, Apple filed a civil action under local patent laws against a small manufacturer selling Apple II copies, a number of which were seized as evidence in a surprise raid similar to the one in Taiwan. Sales and purchase records of the company were also seized. Because its patents and copyrights were enforceable in Hong Kong, Apple expected to halt all manufacturing and selling of copies there.

In New Zealand, Apple obtained an injunction against Orbit Electronics, which was passing off "Orange" computers from an unknown Taiwanese manufacturer as Apple II computers.

Apple registered its trademarks and copyrights with U.S. Customs authorities and expected that bogus Apple products would be confiscated by the U.S. government at the port of entry. On August 19, Apple announced that the U.S. Customs Service had begun detaining and seizing imitations of the Apple II personal computer. "All copies seized will be destroyed," a company spokesperson reported. "The imitations originated in Taiwan and Hong Kong. The company will take whatever action is necessary to prevent unlawful reproduction of its products from being imported and sold in the United States and abroad."

On August 16, 1982, Apple reported asking the U.S. District Court of eastern Pennsylvania in Philadelphia to reconsider its denial made on

---

[19] Based primarily on corporate memoranda, July–August 1982.

[20] During a trip to the Orient, the casewriters were made aware of Taiwanese-assembled microprocessors closely resembling Apple II selling at prices below U.S. $300, and in the shadow of a major Hong Kong shopping complex, counterfeit computers very much like Apple II regularly sold at 60 percent less than local retail for the U.S.-made counterpart and could be bargained down on slow days.

August 2 of a preliminary injunction in Apple's lawsuit against Franklin Computer Corporation.

On the same day as the district court denial, the Third Circuit Court of Appeals in Philadelphia issued its opinion in the *Williams Electronics, Inc.* v. *Artic International, Inc.* case involving similar uses. The circuit court, Apple believes, decided some of the key issues that the district judge in the Apple case felt were open questions. Specifically, the circuit court found that U.S. copyright statutes cover object code stored in a computer's read-only memory (ROM) components.

On May 13, Apple sued Franklin for "patent infringement, copyright infringement, unfair competition, and misappropriation," charging Franklin with copying Apple's diskette- and ROM-form computer programs. Apple sought preliminary and permanent injunctions against the manufacture or sale of Franklin products. A company report claimed, "Copying the programs enabled Franklin to produce a computer known as the ACE 100 which can run programs available for the Apple II personal computer."

TOWARD NEW HORIZONS

Chairman Stephen Jobs summarized his view of the corporate mission: "Apple is dedicated to making the personal computer not only indispensable, but understandable." Indications are that the company that invented the personal computer, specializing in nothing else, had just about mastered the delicate balance of technology and customer need in its stated intent to bring "computer power to all the people." Like IBM, Apple has been characterized by restlessness, change, and an absence of complacency, as management spanned the gap between the conflicting aphorisms "haste makes waste" and "those who hesitate are lost."

Speaking with schoolchildren, operating as part of management's information systems, performing as factory servomechanism controllers, translating foreign languages for tourists, playing "Dungeons and Dragons," handling back-at-home and in-home shopping transactions—the list of potential applications seems endless. In the words of Chairman Jobs, "There are 140 million people in the world who could justify buying a personal computer, if they could only see the benefits to be derived from it."

As the year ended, President and Chief Executive Officer Mike Markkula and his staff were grappling with such crucial issues as product distribution, long-term product strategy, dealer relations, software development, pricing and promotional strategies, and a variety of issues that ordinarily confront rapidly growing organizations.

Your Task

1. Address Mike Markkula's concerns:
   a. Product distribution—how is Apple doing so far? As you perceive the future, what alternatives should the management team be considering?
   b. Dealer relations—assess the immediate issues broached by the dealers who accused Apple of wrongdoing. Depending upon how you see the outcome, who stands to lose in this conflict?
   c. What might the company do to enhance dealer relations toward improving effectiveness of channels of distribution?
   d. Assess the company's current activities in software development—from the case and from what you read in external literature.
   e. Compare Apple's pricing strategies, as you infer them, with those of competitors. Given changing competitive circumstances, will present practices be sufficient later on?
   f. Is 4 to 5 percent of sales sufficient for advertising? Explain how you would go about setting the promotional budget. If the advertising manager asked you to suggest a model for him to use in estimating the returns from advertising, how would you respond?
   g. Given the CEO's statements and Chairman Job's expectations about future markets, assess Apple's product strategy.
2. Assuming that the president might like to contemplate additional ideas, advise him and the strategic planning committee.
3. Summarize the company's key strengths and weaknesses.
4. Summarize the significant threats and opportunities facing Apple.
5. Overall, what is your prognosis for the microprocessor business in *(a)* North America, *(b)* Europe, and *(c)* Third World countries?
6. Is dramatic shakeout imminent in this industry?
7. Would you invest in Apple stock?
8. Would you work for the company?

Case 20

K Mart Stores: Where America Shops and Saves*

John L. Little
University of North Carolina–Greensboro

Larry D. Alexander
Virginia Polytechnic Institute and State University

INTRODUCTION

The S.S. Kresge Company opened hundreds of K mart stores throughout the United States after its first store opened for business in the early 1960s. The company maintained a practice of keeping the stores very uniform in layout and appearances throughout most of this period. Each store was a simple box-like building usually located as freestanding away from shopping malls. K mart stores sold low to medium quality merchandise that was priced lower than its competitors. This approach proved to be very successful, especially among price conscious shoppers who left full service department stores to shop at K mart and other discounters. The K mart logo itself became a symbol of low prices in the minds of many shoppers.

In the dynamic 1980s, important changes were taking place in the retail industry. Younger shoppers had become more discriminating than their parents and many had a greater amount of disposable income to spend. These younger shoppers wanted higher quality merchandise and they were willing to pay for it. While K mart stuck with its traditional approach, other retailers had moved in to satisfy this

* This case was written by John L. Little, Assistant Professor of Strategic Management at the University of North Carolina at Greensboro, and Larry D. Alexander, Associate Professor of Strategic Management at Virginia Polytechnic Institute and State University.

new consumer group. In the process, these competitors created a retail environment that had never been more competitive. Furthermore, the successful market penetration of warehouse clubs and specialty stores into the retailing industry meant even more intense competition for discount stores such as K mart.

How K mart should respond to these and other issues remained unclear. One thing did seem certain. Unless K mart made changes to remain aligned with a changing retail environment, its future financial performance would probably decline.

HISTORY

The S.S. Kresge Company was founded in 1899 with the opening of a single store in downtown Detroit, Michigan. Its founder, Sebastian Kresge, who followed a slogan of "Nothing over ten cents," rapidly opened more stores in new locations. He standardized the mix of merchandise, continued to emphasize low prices, and centralized the purchasing function. This latter move greatly increased the bargaining power that Kresge had over suppliers while at the same time reducing administrative overhead. This made the opening of new stores easier by spreading startup costs over a wider base. Kresge soon developed operating procedures that permitted centralized control over a growing number of uniform stores. The lower prices charged by Kresge caused individual store volume to increase and profits to rise which provided the necessary funds to open still more stores. When the company was incorporated in 1912, Kresge's "five and ten" style stores numbered 85 and had a combined annual sales of more than $10 million.

Variety stores, which carried a variety of inexpensive kitchen, stationery, toy, soft good items, and hard goods, grew in popularity throughout the 1920s and 1930s as a more convenient means of shopping than the earlier established specialty stores. A number of variety store chains had been established by 1940, with their limited selection of a wider array of product lines. The greater buying power available to these chain stores allowed them to underprice the specialty stores that concentrated in just one product line. The combination of lower prices and a wider selection of different product categories was a powerful attraction to customers. Furthermore, since more and more shoppers had their own cars, they were willing to travel further from home to save money.

During the 1950s, the introduction of shopping centers and supermarkets began to draw customers away from variety stores. To counter this, some variety retailers began looking for new ways to attract customers. In 1954, for example, Marty Chase converted an old mill in

Cumberland, Rhode Island, into a discount store named Ann and Hope. The store sold ribbon, greeting cards, and women's clothing. As other discount stores opened throughout the 1950s, then Kresge President, Harry Cunningham, began to consider a similar approach. Finally, in 1962, Kresge responded by opening its first K mart discount store in Garden City, Michigan.

K mart discount stores were nothing more than a large scale version of the earlier Kresge retail stores. They still emphasized low prices, a wide selection, and low overhead costs which combined to create profits. The first K mart stores were stocked primarily with Kresge merchandise. A number of licensees, who operated departments within the store, added their merchandise to the selection. Later, licensee merchandise was replaced entirely with K mart's own merchandise. The initial stores were a great success, and by 1966, they numbered 162 with a combined sales of over $1 billion.

The K mart success formula remained relatively unchanged for many years. Many new stores were added each year, sometimes by the hundreds. Almost all of them were uniform, freestanding stores located away from large shopping centers. By erecting simple, freestanding buildings in suburban areas, K mart opened its stores more quickly than competitors, who had to wait for shopping centers to be completed. This also helped to keep overhead costs down since its freestanding stores were not located in expensive shopping malls, where rent was high. Over time, K mart stores became located in almost all major U.S. metropolitan areas. During the 1960s and 1970s, annual sales grew by an average of 20 percent per year, primarily due to the fact that consumers found K mart's blend of low price and wide selection very attractive. The company's smaller Kresge stores, unlike its K mart stores, were not as profitable and many were closed during this period.

By 1976, the Kresge Company had become the second largest general merchandise retailer in the United States, behind only Sears. During the next year, the corporate name was changed from the Kresge Company to the K mart Corporation because K mart stores accounted for 94.5 percent of all corporate sales.

By the late 70s, several problems were impacting on K mart. Good locations for new K mart stores were becoming more difficult to find. Other discount chains were drawing some K mart shoppers away. Industry surveys indicated that the needs of the customers were changing. While other discounters started upgrading their stores and started emphasizing brand name merchandise, K mart continued to sell primarily low-priced K mart private label and generic goods in their same austere-looking stores. Furthermore, during these same years, K mart sales growth started to flatten.

In 1980, Bernard Fauber was named K mart's new chief executive officer. He replaced an unusual arrangement in which three men shared the office of the president. Fauber quickly moved to refurbish its dated K mart stores, and to upgrade the quality of goods which it carried. New display racks, better point of purchase displays, and improved traffic flow through the stores helped to make K mart stores more attractive to customers.

FUNCTIONAL AREA STRATEGIES WITHIN THE K MART STORES

Marketing

Early on, K mart stores emphasized low prices as an important marketing weapon. Its low prices often meant that the product being offered was of a lower quality. For hard goods such as kitchen appliances, this usually meant that just the basic product was carried, without the extra features that competing retailers' higher priced models offered.

K mart focused on satisfying the needs of low- and middle-income families with limited budgets. Customers in this market segment were unwilling to pay higher prices for similar products with extra features. Still, it was estimated in the 1980s that 80 percent of all Americans shopped at K mart at least once during a calendar year.

The sales promotion of K mart's products was accomplished in several ways. First, sales promotion was emphasized by more attractive in-store, point of purchase displays. Second, K mart's well known "blue light specials" were used to promote specific products for short periods of time during the day. Third, its products were promoted in numerous newspaper ads.

K mart relied heavily on newspaper advertising to promote its goods. Newspaper inserts were designed at corporate headquarters and sent to newspapers throughout the country for publication. Advertising copy was sent to store managers in advance so they could prepare for the sales. The company placed approximately 120 million inserts in 1,700 different newspapers each week throughout the United States by the mid-1980s. While the company continued to emphasize newspapers, increased attention was being given to television advertising. This advertising only became relatively economical once K mart had opened thousands of stores across the nation.

With its high level of market penetration, K mart initiated a new effort to get customers to buy more goods per trip. Management felt this would be possible because disposable family income of many K mart customers was rising. This rise in family income was partially the result of a significant increase in the number of two-income families. K mart estimated that 19 percent of its customers were from households with annual incomes of at least $40,000; however, this customer group typically bought only low priced items such as tennis balls, batteries, and shampoo at K mart.

K mart added more national brand merchandise and higher quality private labels, and then displayed them in a more attractive manner. Brand name products such as Casio, Minolta, Nike, MacGregor, Wilson, and General Electric were increasingly found throughout the store. K mart hoped that this action would help attract higher income customers to other product areas and increase their per sale purchases. At the same time, the company hoped to retain its less affluent customers by continuing to offer an assortment of lower priced, lower quality merchandise.

K mart did extremely well in certain departments, but performed weakly in others. It was the leader in housewares and the second largest appliance retailer behind only Sears. Many customers were attracted to its brand name appliances and housewares by K mart's low prices. These same customers, however, were turned off by K mart's cheap clothing, which had a low image among many consumers. Its apparel departments, in fact, had been a major shortcoming for K mart throughout the years. K mart tried to address this problem by upgrading many lines of clothing. Furthermore, the responsibility for ordering apparel was taken away from store managers and given to professional staff buyers at corporate headquarters, who were more knowledgeable about fashion.

K mart had also moved into specialty discount stores through several acquisitions. The first Designer Depot, which was a discount price specialty apparel store, was started in Detroit during 1982. These stores sold quality brand-name merchandise at discounts of 20 percent to 70 percent. Some stores also sold shoes, while others sold bedroom and bathroom soft goods.

The company also acquired several other impressive specialty chains. Waldenbook Company, Inc., another K mart acquisition in 1985, operated 943 stores in all 50 states. Builders Square, Inc., a warehouse type home improvement center chain, was acquired in 1984. By 1985, the company had 25 stores located in eight states. Fredrick Stevens, executive vice president of specialty retailing operations, argued that 400 locations across the country could support the volume requirements of these huge discount builders' supply warehouses. Builders Square was hoping to capture a 25 percent share of that market.[1]

Pay Less Drug Stores Northwest, another K mart acquisition in 1985, was the 10th largest drug chain in the nation. Pay Less was a

---

[1] "K mart: A Look inside the Nation's Largest Discounter," *Mass Market Retailers*, December 16, 1985, p. 42.

discount chain, supported by a very cost efficient operation, and strong management. With sales approaching $1 billion and 176 stores, the chain hoped to penetrate rapidly in its present markets in California, Oregon, Washington, Idaho, and Nevada.

Two final K mart acquisitions were in the restaurant industry. Furr's Cafeterias, acquired earlier in 1980, and Bishop Buffets, acquired in 1983, had a total of 162 units by 1985. Due to slow growth in the cafeteria industry, however, future growth for new cafeterias in this acquisition was expected to be limited to 10 percent per year.

K mart Corporation had limited involvement in overseas markets. It did have, however, a 20 percent interest in G.L. Coles and Coy Limited, a food and general merchandise retailer in Australia. It also had a 44 percent interest in Astra, S.A., which operated a food and general merchandise chain in Mexico.

Store Operations

During the 1980s, K mart was approaching market saturation, with its stores located almost everywhere throughout 48 states. Its 2,332 stores by the end of 1985 were located in 250 of this country's 255 Standard Metropolitan Statistical Areas (SMSA). From a record 271 new stores opening in 1976, only 18 new K mart stores were opened in 1985.

Because of market saturation, K mart switched its emphasis from opening new stores to renovating existing ones. This effort, which started in the early 1980s, was intended to increase productivity as well as to upgrade the store image. Wider and taller display cases carried more merchandise and made better use of cubic space. This allowed for a wider assortment of merchandise to be displayed within the same square footage. It also reduced the need for additional back-room storage. A new store layout was developed around a wide center aisle which let consumers walk through every department without leaving the aisle. As one K mart store manager put it, "We want to encourage people to go into areas where they would not normally go . . . to pass by merchandise they were not planning to buy!"[2]

All K mart stores were designed around the same basic floor plan, as shown in Exhibit 1. As shoppers entered the store, they were no longer confronted with the smell of popcorn and the sight of gumball machines. Instead, they might be greeted by the jewelry department with a wide selection of watches and jewelry of various price ranges. The main aisle down the center of the store separated soft goods from hard goods. Located on the soft goods side of the store were women's apparel, then men's apparel, with infants' wear, and children's clothes nearby.

---

[2] Ibid., p. 20

EXHIBIT 1 Typical K mart Store Floor Layout

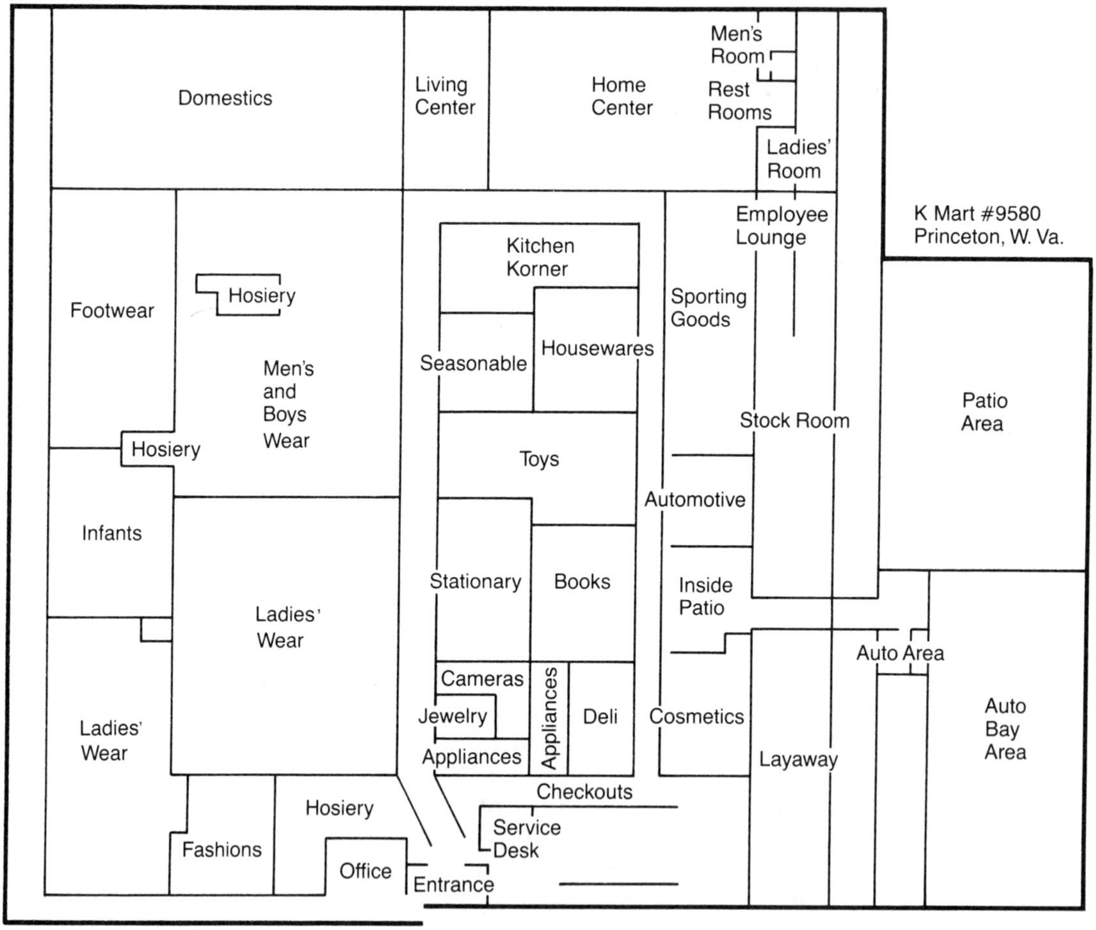

Source: K mart Pamphlet, 1985.

Popular crafts and yarn were also located on this side, where homemakers were most likely to look for them. In the hard goods half of the store, housewares, sporting goods, automotive supplies, and hardware were located at the rear of the store, drawing men and women past the high impulse, high margin merchandise in the greeting cards, jewelry, and toy departments. The health and beauty items and the pharmacies, for the minority of stores that had them, were typically located in the right front section of the store.

Electronic communications systems connected all stores to 10 enormous regional distribution centers. These centers were located in California, Nevada, Texas, Kansas, Minnesota, Michigan, Indiana, Ohio, Pennsylvania, and Georgia, as shown in Exhibit 2. These highly automated distribution centers contained a combined 15 million square feet of warehouse space. Together, they operated a fleet of 250 tractors and 1,000 trailers, which provided weekly delivery to every K mart store requesting it.

Approximately 25 percent of K mart's merchandise was handled by these distribution centers. In contrast, 75 percent of all store purchases were shipped directly from suppliers to the stores in order to minimize shipping cost. The delivery of products from suppliers was usually fast in order to keep such a large account as K mart satisfied. This reduced inventory level requirements at stores to minimum levels. A significant reduction in reorder time had been achieved by installing optical scanners on cash registers at K mart stores. Scanning, coupled with a company-wide computer network, permitted automated replenishment

EXHIBIT 2 Store Distribution Network

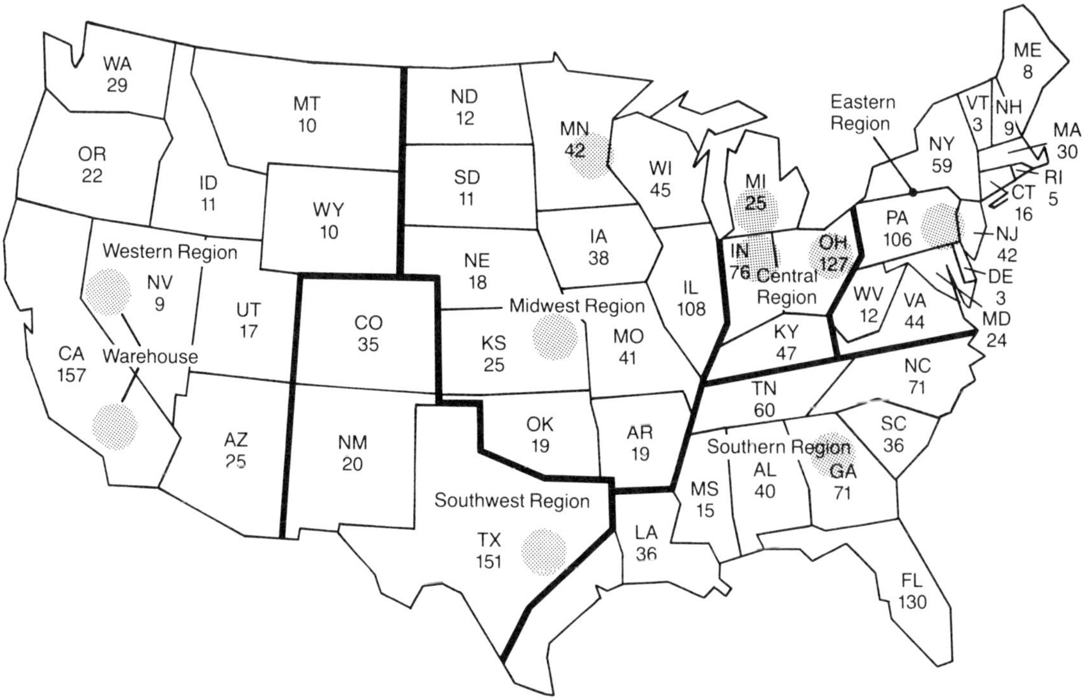

Source: *Mass Market Retailers,* December 16, 1985, p. 42.

of merchandise, and made it possible to differentiate the seasonal needs of each region.

As part of its efforts to upgrade its image, K mart was completing a major remodeling program of store interiors to present a more modern store appearance to shoppers. This new effort, called "The K mart of the Eighties," incorporated a new color scheme on interior walls and floors, broader aisles, and more attractive displays. Low volume lines were dropped or consolidated to achieve a store within a store format. The Kitchen Corner, Home Care Center, and Domestic Center were arranged along the back wall and emphasized fashion and style at discount prices. The early success of the plan was encouraging. Sales per square foot had risen from $139 in 1980 to $168 four years later. While this was superior to the $128 per square foot typical among discounter department stores, it was far behind such discounters as Target and Wal-Mart.

Product categories no longer in demand were eliminated. For example, K mart's 360 automotive service departments in rural stores were closed in 1982. Unprofitable stores were closed altogether, freeing up more than $1 million each in capital for use elsewhere in the corporation.

The more than 2,000 K mart stores were organized into six regions, each of which had from 266 to 422 stores. Each region was comprised of about 20 districts, while each district had from 10 to 20 stores.

K mart stores came in 5 basic sizes. The smallest was the 40,000-square-foot-size store, which was placed in smaller markets. At the other end, the jumbo 120,000-square-foot store was placed in large metropolitan markets. These freestanding stores were located in suburban areas with large parking lots, and were usually leased rather than owned. Buildings usually were erected by local contractors, but a K mart subsidiary built several stores each year to allow the company to remain knowledgeable about building costs and procedures.

K mart's decision to avoid shopping center locations was part of its low overhead philosophy. Leasing costs at shopping centers were very high compared to K mart locations. Shopping centers generally did not want discounters as tenants anyway, due to the negative image associated with them. Also, specialty stores did not want to locate next to a discount store because of the significant price difference between their products and a discounter's. Sometimes, K mart would buy existing buildings in shopping centers or develop properties in good locations and sublease retail space to specialty stores.

FINANCE

Total sales for the K mart Corporation, as shown in its consolidated statement of income in Exhibit 3, were $22.4 billion for fiscal year

EXHIBIT 3

K Mart Corporation
Consolidated Statements of Income
(millions, except per-share data)

	Fiscal Year Ended		
	January 29, 1986	*January 30, 1985*	*January 25, 1984*
Sales	$22,420	$21,096	$18,598
Licensee fees and rental income	225	207	191
Equity in income of affiliated retail companies	76	65	57
Interest income	24	40	38
	22,745	21,408	18,884
Cost of merchandise sold (including buying and occupancy costs)	16,181	15,260	13,447
Selling, general and administrative expenses	4,845	4,428	3,880
Advertising	567	554	425
Interest expense:			
Debt	205	147	84
Capital lease obligations	191	193	189
	21,989	20,582	18,025
Income from continuing retail operations before income taxes	756	826	859
Income taxes	285	327	366
Income from continuing retail operations	471	499	493
Discontinued operations	(250)	—	(1)
Net income for the year	$ 221	$ 499	$ 492
Earnings per common and common equivalent share:			
Continuing retail operations	$3.63	$3.84	$3.81
Discontinued operations	(1.90)	—	(.01)
Net income	$1.73	$3.84	$3.80

Source: K mart Corporation, *1985 Annual Report*, p. 30.

1985, which ended on January 29, 1986. This represented a 6.3 percent increase over the sales for the previous year. Net income after taxes for that same year was $221.0 million. The consolidated balance sheet for fiscal 1985 and 1984 is shown in Exhibit 4. Finally, a comparison of

EXHIBIT 4

K Mart Corporation
Consolidated Balance Sheets
(millions)

	January 29, 1986	*January 30, 1985*
Assets		
Current Assets:		
Cash (includes temporary investments of $352 and $294, respectively)	$ 627	$ 492
Merchandise inventories	4,537	4,588
Accounts receivable and other current assets	363	231
Total current assets	5,527	5,311
Investments in affiliated retail companies	293	188
Property and equipment—net	3,644	3,339
Other assets and deferred charges	527	220
Investments in discontinued operations	—	204
Total assets	$9,991	$9,262
Liabilities and Shareholders' Equity		
Current Liabilities:		
Long-term debt due within one year	$ 15	$ 2
Capital lease obligations due within one year	76	74
Notes payable	127	235
Accounts payable—trade	1,908	1,917
Accrued payrolls and other liabilities	548	362
Taxes other than income taxes	218	200
Income taxes	198	99
Total current liabilities	3,090	2,889
Capital lease obligations	1,713	1,780
Long-term debt	1,456	1,107
Other long-term liabilities	345	163
Deferred income taxes	114	89
Shareholders' equity	3,273	3,234
Total liabilities and shareholders equity	$9,991	$9,262

Source: K mart Corporation, *1985 Annual Report,* p. 31.

sales and various financial data for K mart over a 10-year period are presented in Exhibit 5.

Retail sales at K mart were extremely seasonal with a high proportion of sales and profits coming during the Christmas shopping season. For example, some 33 percent of K mart's 1984 sales and 41 percent of its profits came during the fourth quarter alone.

EXHIBIT 5 K mart Corporation—10-Year Financial Summary

	1984	*1983*	*1982*	*1981*	*1980*	*1979*	*1978*	*1977*	*1976*	*1975*
Summary of operations *(millions)*										
Sales	$21,096	$18,598	$16,772	$16,527	$14,204	$12,731	$11,696	$9,941	$8,382	$6,798
Cost of merchandise sold	$15,260	$13,447	$12,299	$12,360	$10,417	$ 9,283	$ 8,566	$7,299	$6,147	$4,991
Selling, general and administrative expenses	$ 4,982	$ 4,305	$ 4,049	$ 3,810	$ 3,326	$ 2,839	$ 2,503	$2,085	$1,750	$1,409
Interest expense—net	$ 300	$ 235	$ 219	$ 230	$ 200	$ 149	$ 132	$ 116	$ 103	$ 89
Income before income taxes	$ 820	$ 854	$ 419	$ 323	$ 436	$ 625	$ 634	$ 564	$ 484	$ 395
Net income	$ 499	$ 492	$ 262	$ 220	$ 261	$ 358	$ 344	$ 298	$ 262	$ 196
Per-share data *(dollars)*										
Earnings per common and common equivalent share	$ 3.84	$ 3.80	$ 2.06	$ 1.75	$ 2.07	$ 2.84	$ 2.74	$ 2.39	$ 2.11	$ 1.61
Cash dividends declared	$ 1.24	$ 1.08	$ 1.00	$ .96	$ .92	$ .84	$ .72	$ .56	$ .32	$ .24
Book value	$ 25.87	$ 23.35	$ 20.89	$ 19.81	$ 18.99	$ 17.79	$ 15.68	$13.56	$11.62	$ 9.69
Financial data *(millions)*										
Working capital	$ 2,422	$ 2,268	$ 1,827	$ 1,473	$ 1,552	$ 1,403	$ 1,308	$1,231	$1,074	$ 904
Total assets	$ 9,262	$ 8,183	$ 7,344	$ 6,657	$ 6,089	$ 5,635	$ 4,836	$4,489	$3,983	$3,336
Long-term obligations—Debt	$ 1,107	$ 711	$ 596	$ 415	$ 419	$ 209	$ 209	$ 211	$ 211	$ 210
—Capital leases	$ 1,780	$ 1,822	$ 1,824	$ 1,752	$ 1,618	$ 1,422	$ 1,294	$1,266	$1,155	$ 989
Shareholders' equity	$ 3,234	$ 2,940	$ 2,601	$ 2,456	$ 2,343	$ 2,185	$ 1,916	$1,649	$1,409	$1,169
Capital expenditures-owned property	$ 622	$ 368	$ 306	$ 361	$ 302	$ 292	$ 217	$ 162	$ 123	$ 112
Depreciation and amortization-owned property	$ 203	$ 168	$ 157	$ 141	$ 119	$ 93	$ 77	$ 65	$ 56	$ 52
Average shares outstanding	126	125	124	124	123	123	122	122	121	121

Source: K mart Corporation, *1984 Annual Report*, p. 16, 17

K mart did not offer a charge card and did not encourage credit sales. By comparison, approximately 58 percent of arch rival Sears' sales were on credit. MasterCard and VISA credit cards were accepted at K mart and limited in-house credit was provided on appliance sales. Many K mart stores required customers to follow a rigid two-step procedure for writing checks. The customer first had to get approval from the service desk, and then wait at a checkout line to pay for the purchased items.

K mart's policy for granting exchanges or refunds, on merchandise which did not satisfy the customer, was quite liberal. Most items could be returned for cash by customers without a hassle. This policy was inherited from the old Kresge variety stores. Similarly, K mart customers could get a rain check on any advertised item not found in stock at the time of the sale.

INNOVATION

The K mart approach to innovation was to adopt new ideas only after they had been developed and proven successful by someone else. This approach avoided risk and had served K mart well throughout the years. Once a good idea was identified, however, K mart showed its genius in applying and perfecting it. For example, when the discount store idea emerged, Kresge was the first to refine the concept with its K mart stores. K mart pursued rapid expansion while other retailers looked on with amazement. The idea of standardizing the store floor plan and layout was another example of how K mart borrowed a good idea from elsewhere and perfected it.

HUMAN RESOURCES/PERSONNEL

K mart Corporation employed more than 290,000 people in 1985, but tried to encourage a small business feeling within its individual stores. Loyalty among store managers was unusually high; consequently, their turnover rate was low. Many K mart managers had never worked for any other employer, and 25-year-service pins were common. Furthermore, promotion to managerial positions was almost entirely done from within. For those selected, management training consisted of a 16-week program on all phases of a K mart store's operation. After the program, the trainees became assistant managers with responsibility for several departments. Typically, trainees were rotated through various departments and stores for 6 to 10 years before they were ready to manage their own stores.

The opportunity for promotion was strong in the 1970s when new stores were being opened at the rate of several per week. That changed in the 1980s when K mart greatly curtailed its new store openings. This threatened to increase employee turnover as assistant managers became impatient to move up. At the same time, K mart was reducing the number of assistant managers from three to two per store in order to cut administrative costs.

K mart relied heavily on part-time employees to operate its stores. The company goal was to have 60 percent part-time and 40 percent full-time employees within each store. This gave the store manager greater flexibility in matching the work force with the amount of traffic during different periods of the day. Also, the labor costs for part-time employees were considerably lower because they started at minimum wage and were not paid benefits. The great majority of these employees were women who preferred to work part-time because of their family obligations. The company, however, did have an employee savings plan even for part-timers in which K mart contributed 50 cents in K mart stock for every one dollar that the employee contributed.

MANAGEMENT

Harry Cunningham developed the basic K mart strategy and lead the company during its rapid growth from 1962 to 1972. When he stepped down in 1972, he appointed K mart's Robert Dewar, Ervin Wardlow, and Walter Tennga to collectively run the company. Dewar, with 32 years of legal and financial background but no store experience, was named chairman. Wardlow, with strong merchandising experience, was named president. Finally, Tennga, a real estate and financial executive, was named vice chairman. These three executives ran the company for eight years. Although sales tripled during this period, the three could not agree on which direction K mart should take.

In 1980, Bernard Fauber was named the new chief executive officer at the suggestion of Dewar, who felt that K mart needed a store man at the top, rather than a staff man. Since then, K mart has made dramatic changes in its approach to business. As Fauber conceded:

> For 20 years we had been just about the most successful retailer in America, so it was not easy getting our people to admit that some changes were advisable and others were necessary.[3]

In explaining the reasons behind K mart's decision to diversify into other areas, Fauber added:

---

[3] Ibid., p. 54.

> We realized that we must do something else for growth since it was no longer possible to open 100 to 120 K mart stores each year.[4]

Fauber, like all but one previous CEO, was not a college graduate. He first came to work for the company in 1941 as an 18-year-old stockroom boy in a Kresge store. Nine years later, he joined the management training program. Later he gained experience as a store manager and district manager, and in 1968 became vice president of the Western Region. Like nearly all K mart executives, Fauber had never worked for any other company.

K mart's philosophy was to train their store managers as generalists, than allow them wide discretion in running their stores. They had an incentive plan based on store profits to avoid the mistake Sears made in the 1970s when it tied its department managers' incentive plan to sales volume. The Sears incentive system, which has since been changed, caused its managers to focus on low-margin merchandise which boosted sales and their bonuses, but which hurt profits.

Store managers at K mart were encouraged to involve themselves and the store in community activities, such as the United Way. One socially responsible effort K mart undertook was its "Lost Child Program" in 1985. The prime exposure available nationwide at its stores made K mart a good vehicle for the program and enhanced the corporate image.

THE RETAIL INDUSTRY

Market Segments

The retail industry was divided into several general segments which somewhat overlapped one another. There were full-line department stores, discount department stores, discount drug stores, specialty stores, supermarkets, and convenience shops. Exhibit 6 shows the top 15 general merchandise chains for 1985, which includes many of these store types. The trend towards one-stop shopping had blurred the distinctions among these various kinds of stores in recent years. For example, shoppers could find food items in drugstores and discount stores, and clothing and hardware in supermarkets. Within the discount department store category, the emerging warehouse stores were the fastest growing segment along with discount specialty stores.

---

[4] Ibid.

EXHIBIT 6 Top 15 General Merchandise Chains for 1985

Rank and Company	*Net Sales ($000)*	*Net income ($000)*	*Earnings per share*	*Location of Headquarters*
1. Sears Roebuck	$40,715,300	$1,303,300	$3.53	Chicago
2. K mart	22,420,002	221,242	1.73	Troy, Mich.
3. J. C. Penney	13,747,000	397,000	5.31	New York
4. Federated Department Stores	9,978,027	286,626	5.88	Cincinnati
5. Dayton Hudson	8,793,372	283,620	2.92	Minneapolis
6. Wal-Mart Stores	8,580,910	327,473	1.16	Bentonville, Ark.
7. F. W. Woolworth	5,958,000	177,000	5.50	New York
8. BATUS	5,881,408	163,532	—	Louisville
9. Montgomery Ward	5,388,000	(298,000)	—	Chicago
10. May Department Stores	5,079,900	235,400	5.38	St. Louis
11. Melville	4,805,380	210,812	3.90	Harrison, N.Y.
12. Associated Dry Goods	4,385,019	119,696	3.00	New York City
13. R. H. Macy	4,368,386	189,315	3.69	New York City
14. Wickes Companies	4,362,454	76,130	0.47	Santa Monica, Calif.
15. Allied Stores	4,135,027	159,275	3.70	New York City

Source: "The 50 Largest Retailing Companies," *Fortune*, June 9, 1986, pp. 136–37.

External Threats

By the mid-1980s, the retail environment was extremely competitive. Retailers were also being squeezed by two powerful factors. One factor was slower growth in customer demand for general merchandise in recent years. Industry forecasts suggested a continuing trend in this direction with a declining proportion of disposable income being spent on general merchandise in coming years. The other factor was the excess number of stores that existed in the industry. These two realities along with several others were making retail merchants somewhat worried about the future.

The decline in the teenage population had decreased per capita spending on apparel. Apparel chains, which had expanded so rapidly in the 1960s and 1970s to capitalize on the lucrative teenage market, were now facing an older customer base with less interest in fashion. As Americans grew older, their spending patterns were shifting toward health and leisure services and away from general merchandise.

Another source of trouble for retailers was the extremely high level of consumer credit in the mid 1980s. Some industry observers feared this would lead to a decline in consumer spending and increased woes for retailers. Part of this was due to the catch-up spending that people did for consumer durables after the 1981–1983 recession.

Competition

A recent challenge within the retail industry was wholesale clubs and specialty stores. They were at opposite ends of the retailing spectrum. Still, both of these store types were very profitable, and they were making it harder for stores in the middle.

The wholesale club concept was first introduced in 1976 by Sal and Robert E. Price with their first Price Club in San Diego. For a $25 membership fee, small businessmen could buy such diverse goods as food, office supplies, and appliances at wholesale prices. This membership approach meant that the Price Club got an interest-free loan in advance and locked in the customer with switching costs if they decided to move to another such club. By stocking 4,000 high-moving items, as compared to 60,000 items found in typical discount stores, Price Club stores turned over their inventory 15 times a year, compared to just 5 times for a full-line discount store. The Price Club had grown to 25 stores, and the concept was being copied by other retailers.

Specialty stores enjoyed strong growth in the early 1980s. A number of large retailers had established chains of small stores specializing in single product lines like shoes, women's apparel, and books. Woolworth had found success in stationery supplies with Harold's Square, Lucky Stores with its Minnesota Fabrics, and Allied Stores with its Catherine's Stout Shoppes. The attraction of such stores was the greater depth of choice in a specific line for which many consumers were willing to pay extra.

Between the wholesale clubs and the specialty stores were full-line department stores. This was where the primary battle within the retailing industry was taking place. The saturation of the market with these one-stop shopping stores had caused many changes. For example, both Sears and J.C. Penney had curtailed most new store openings. Instead, they both were moving to upgrade their existing stores with higher quality, higher priced merchandise. Both sought to establish a fashion image to differentiate themselves from the discount chains.

Sears

K mart's greatest competition came from Sears Roebuck & Co., the world's largest retailer with its 435 full-line departments stores, 397 medium-sized department stores, and 1,971 catalog sales offices. Sears stores generated sales of $21.5 billion in 1985, which rose to a staggering $40.7 billion when all other Sears strategic business units were included. For its full-line department stores, Sears' breadth in departments was unsurpassed by any competitor.

During the 1970s, Sears first moved to higher priced, more stylish merchandise. This confused many customers who preferred to go to discounters for lower prices and specialty shops for greater product line depth. Under CEO Edward Telling, who took office in 1978, the company made drastic changes. Twenty percent of its work force was cut, 200 stores were closed, and the remaining stores renovated. Many Sears clothing labels were replaced by fashion labels associated with such names as Arnold Palmer, Joe Namath, and Cheryl Tiegs.

With its move into financial services, Sears envisioned the day when a customer could walk into a Sears store and buy a house through its Coldwell Banker realty division, insure it through its Allstate Insurance division, and furnish it before he or she left. Sears' charge card was already held by 58 percent of Americans. Visa cards, on the other hand, were held by only 53 percent of all households. The opportunity existed for Sears to convert its ordinary credit accounts into savings and checking accounts. Furthermore, the deregulated banking environment of the 1980s made it possible to offer multiple financial services in retail stores, an option Sears seemed to be pursuing.

J.C. Penney

While Sears had its strength in hard goods, J.C. Penney Company, Inc., had a well-established reputation for quality in soft goods. The company got its initials J. and C. from G. Johnson and T. Callahan, who founded the firm back in 1902. During the 1960s and 1970s, Penney's tried to move into hard goods to counter Sears' well established strength there. Penney's did this in several key instances by teaming up with well-known suppliers. For example, it formed an alliance with General Electric to sell its washers, dryers, refrigerators, stoves, etc., in its retail stores.

During 1985, when Penney's had total sales of approximately $13.7 billion, it made a retrenchment of sorts. It discontinued its auto accessories department, eliminated children's toys, and even discontinued selling many hard goods such as G.E. appliances. Instead, it renewed its commitment to emphasize soft goods in its 574 metropolitan market stores, 133 metropolitan market soft-line stores, and 696 geographic market stores in nonmetropolitan markets. With this move, the firm refocused its efforts on selling quality clothing to men, women, boys, girls, and infants. In addition to clothing, Penney's continued to emphasize its towels, sheets, etc. for which it was noted.

Discount Chains

In 1985, there were more than 8,700 general merchandise discount stores in the United States. Exhibit 7 gives a comparison of profitability and growth performance of the top discount, variety, and department store chains. The average discount store had 55,792 square feet of selling space, which had been rising in recent years. The average customer transaction was $12.35. The annual sales per square foot, as shown in Exhibit 8, varied from the $603 in the photography department to $132 in men's and boy's wear.

There were a number of regional chains within the discount segment of the retail industry. They included Mervyn's in the West, Target in the Midwest, Caldor in New England, and Richway in the Southeast. For the most part, they had done very well by differentiating themselves from K mart. Some firms had accomplished this by appealing to the high end of the discount market. Other discounters sold department store quality merchandise at discount prices in attractive stores. As a result, they succeeded in attracting many affluent shoppers who would not normally shop at K mart.

One of the most successful retailers in recent years was Wal-Mart, a discount chain headquartered in Bentonville, Arkansas. Much of its success was due to the location of its stores. Its 834 discount stores and 19 Sam's Warehouse Clubs were concentrated in small towns in the South and Midwest. By clustering up to 150 stores within several hours drive of a central warehouse and stocking only name brand merchandise, Wal-Mart consistently led the industry in return on investment.

SUPPLIERS

Retailers dealt with thousands of suppliers to stock the wide range of merchandise they carried. This was due in part to the fact that most retailers did not manufacture the merchandise they carried. The bargaining power of large retail chains in relation to their suppliers was great. Sears, J. C. Penney, K mart, and others, were such large and welcome customers that suppliers often became overly dependent on them.

Each year, many new products were introduced by the major chains, replacing old products which were discontinued. Each supplier knew that their products were expected to generate targeted levels of sales. Those that didn't achieve these goals were dropped with little regard for the supplier. On occasion, suppliers were encouraged to increase production capacity only to find their product dropped a short time later on. Often, orders were cancelled at the last minute, leaving

EXHIBIT 7 General Merchandise Retailers, 1985—*Yardsticks of Management Performance*

		Profitability—Return on Equity					*Growth—Sales*			*Earnings per Share*		
Company	*% in —Segment— Sales/Profits*	*Rank*	*5-Year Average*	*Latest 12 Months*	*Debt as % of Equity*	*Net Profit Margin*	*Rank*	*5-Year Average*	*Latest 12 Months*	*Rank*	*5-Year Average*	*Latest 12 Months*
Department stores:												
R. H. Macy	•/•	1	21.4%	16.3%	14.0%	4.3%	4	14.2%	7.5%	2	21.1%	−15.6%
Lucky Stores	25/13	2	19.2	17.5	61.3	1.1	12	9.5	6.5	12	−0.3	12.8
Dillard Dept. Stores	•/•	3	18.6	19.8	70.4	3.9	1	25.2	49.3	1	40.5	32.0
Mercantile Stores	•/•	4	16.3	15.0	28.0	5.0	7	10.9	6.8	4	17.5	4.2
May Dept. Stores	68/72	5	16.0	17.3	41.2	4.4	10	9.8	10.2	5	14.6	9.3
Federated Dept. Strs	67/89	6	14.6	13.1	27.9	3.3	8	10.8	8.0	10	8.5	11.0
Allied Stores	•/•	7	12.8	15.3	70.9	3.9	5	13.8	5.7	9	9.9	25.5
J. C. Penney	79/NA	8	12.7	10.1	54.7	2.9	13	3.0	2.3	8	13.3	−18.6
Strawbridge	•/•	9	12.5	16.0	125.8	3.7	6	11.5	12.5	3	20.1	16.6
Associated Dry Goods	61/73	10	11.8	12.2	33.8	2.8	2	19.6	9.5	6	13.6	−0.7
Carson Pirie Scott	50/45	11	10.8	13.4	104.2	2.0	3	19.6	23.2	11	4.2	132.5
Sears Roebuck	67/57	12	10.6	10.7	87.4	2.9	9	10.4	4.6	7	13.5	−19.9
Carter Hawley Hale	73/52	13	9.4	7.3	84.6	1.6	11	9.6	−2.0	13	−0.3	−50.0
Equitable of Iowa	41/2	14	7.0	4.3	9.2	2.6	14	2.7	4.9	14	−15.0	−10.2
Alexander's	•/•	15	1.4	7.4	87.0	1.0	15	1.9	0.5		NM	24.7
Medians			12.7	13.4	61.3	2.9		10.8	6.8		13.3	9.3
Discount and variety:												
Wal-Mart Stores	•/•	1	34.9	30.7	49.6	3.9	1	39.9	32.2	1	43.0	24.1
SCOA Industries	84/•	2	24.8	22.6	88.5	2.9	8	10.4	5.1	8	9.3	9.8
Ames Dept. Stores	•/•	3	23.1	19.7	60.6	3.1	2	20.1	30.8	5	23.5	19.4
Stop & Shop Cos	48/73	4	19.2	12.8	52.8	1.3	7	11.2	12.8	2	33.6	−26.9
Dayton-Hudson	71/73	5	16.8	16.1	43.2	3.3	4	19.0	12.2	9	9.1	10.3
Zayre	70/65	6	15.7	19.0	46.5	2.6	5	16.0	19.9	3	28.7	22.1
Rose's Stores	•/•	7	15.6	14.2	16.6	2.1	6	14.0	9.2	4	28.1	−13.9
K mart	•/•	8	13.2	12.4	89.3	1.8	9	10.0	13.4	7	10.5	−23.2
Household Intl.	26/8	9	12.0	13.6	236.0	2.6	10	9.1	5.3	10	4.7	−4.6
Associated Dry Goods	38/26	10	11.8	12.2	33.8	2.8	3	19.6	9.5	6	13.6	−0.7
Heck's	86/DD	11	9.3	def	89.3	def	11	2.0	6.5		NM	P-D
F. W. Woolworth	68/39	12	3.5	14.5	35.4	2.6	13	−5.6	3.2		NM	20.6
Cook United	•/DD	13	def	def	NE	def	12	−2.8	−47.7		NM	D-D
Medians			15.6	14.2	49.6	2.6		11.2	9.5		10.5	−0.7

Source: Industry Survey-Retailing, *Forbes*, January 13, 1986, p. 202.

EXHIBIT 8 Discount Store Sales by Category

Category	*Volume ($ billions)*	*Sales per Store ($ millions)*	*Annual Sales per Sq. Ft.*	*Annual Turns*	*Initial Markup (%)*	*Gross Margin (%)*
Women's apparel	$14.3	$1,763	$176	4.6	48.0%	37.2%
Men's and boys' wear	8.2	1,011	132	3.4	44.6	36.0
Housewares	6.3	777	135	3.2	41.1	30.2
Consumer electronics	5.9	728	316	3.2	31.4	19.4
Health and beauty aids	5.6	691	219	4.5	26.9	20.5
Automobile	5.2	641	279	2.8	34.9	28.7
Hardware	4.8	592	184	2.4	41.9	32.1
Toys	4.1	506	202	3.1	36.5	28.4
Sporting goods	3.8	469	187	2.0	36.9	26.9
Photo camera	3.3	407	603	3.2	24.5	16.6
Domestics	3.2	395	126	2.5	43.4	35.3
Personal care	2.9	358	421	3.3	30.4	20.0
Stationery	2.1	259	140	3.5	46.7	40.1
Paint	1.8	222	175	2.4	43.9	35.2
Electric housewares	1.7	210	238	3.4	33.2	21.4
Jewelry	1.4	166	290	1.8	49.9	37.7
Glassware	0.7	80	129	4.0	40.7	34.9

Source: *Standard & Poor's Industrial Survey,* July 4, 1985, p. 120.

suppliers in a difficult position. At times, chain retailers would take merchandise on a consignment basis, paying for it only if sold, thus shifting the risk to the supplier. Payment to the suppliers was, at times, delayed by retailers in order to enhance cash flow and obtain free short-term financing.

Sears and K mart were good examples of firms making sizeable use of private label merchandise. Often their private label products were made by a brand name manufacturer to similar or the exact same specifications as the brand label. The manufacture of private label products could than be contracted out to other manufacturers, giving a great deal of leverage to the retailer and reducing the bargaining power of suppliers.

In spite of such treatment by chain retailers, many suppliers were willing to take the risk and abuse. In return, they hoped to get enormous volume and nationwide distribution which high volume retailers could provide. In response to this one-sided relationship, a number of general merchandise manufacturers had broadened their product lines. By producing a wide variety of items, a supplier could reduce dependence on a single product and increase its bargaining power with the retailer.

BUYERS—THE NEW CONSUMERS

Several important demographic shifts were affecting retailers during the mid 1980s. Population shifts from the cities to the suburbs were reducing the sales volume of urban stores while helping suburban stores. Population shifts from older industrialized areas of the Northeast to the Sun Belt states had similar effects. The baby-boom teenagers of the 1960s were approaching middle age. Better educated than their parents, their perception of value, attitude towards quality merchandise, and response to promotional techniques were changing the way retailers did business.

Price still remained a key consideration, but quality and brand image had increased in importance. Many consumers were willing to trade dollars for time, as was proven by the demand for fast-food, microwave ovens, and other time-saving products and services.

While the number of households was growing rapidly, the population growth was slowing. This caused changes in the type of merchandise demanded, the way to market it effectively, and the price/quality trade-off. Health-related products, prescriptions, and leisure products were in greater demand reflecting the needs of older customers. At the same time, the market for baby food, toys, and children's clothing had declined.

Women were working in greater numbers than ever before. This contributed to the rise in discretionary income, and increased the demand for products needed by working women, such as clothes and cosmetics. A K mart survey showed that the percentage of K mart customers with household incomes from $25,000 to $40,000 had increased from 23.3 percent in 1980 to 28.1 percent in 1984.[5] Some 18.9 percent of K mart's customers in 1984 came from households with incomes greater than $40,000 as compared to 8.3 percent in 1980. A profile of who shops at a K mart, broken down by income, occupation, education, sex, and age is shown in Exhibit 9.

With more women working, men were doing retail shopping more than ever before. Men tended to be less value conscious and more likely to trust the advertising of national brands. The trend was clearly towards a more mature, affluent customer with a preference for value, quality, and fashion in merchandise.

K MART AND THE FUTURE

Sales at the average K mart store were good, but there was tremendous room for improvement. Overall, K mart's per store sales were

---

[5] K mart Corporation, *1984 Annual Report,* p. 3.

EXHIBIT 9 Demographics of K mart Shoppers

	% of K mart Shoppers
Occupation:	
Professional	12.5%
Technical	5.5
Manager	13.4
Clerical	4.5
Salesworker	6.4
Craftsman	11.7
Operative/kindred worker	9.8
Service worker	4.7
Laborer	3.1
Retired	20.7
Income:	
Over $20,000	38.7
Under $20,000	60.6
Education:	
High school or less	52.2
Some college or more	46.5
Sex:	
Male	46.6
Female	53.4
Age:	
Under 25	12.8
25–34	24.1
35–44	19.6
45–54	12.7
55–64	14.5
65+	15.3

Source: *Chain Store Age,* December 1984, p. 54.

about one third that of Sears stores. K mart's appliances and housewares departments were strong areas; however, its clothing and other soft goods, which took up almost half of the typical K mart store, had low appeal to many customers. Clearly, K mart needed to address its clothing dilemma, perhaps by reducing store space allocated for it or by improving the clothing being offered. Overall, K mart needed to decide which product lines and departments should be emphasized. Exhibit 10 provides a breakdown of total retail trade by major product areas.

Since the appointment of Bernard M. Fauber as chief executive officer in 1980, K mart had made a number of substantial changes. By the end of 1985, the store renovation program had been going for some

EXHIBIT 10 Total Retail Trade (in millions of dollars)

	1984	*% Charge 1983–84*	*10-Year Growth Rate*
Retail trade total	$1,297,015	+10.5%	+ 9.0%
Durable goods stores total	464,287	+17.1	+ 9.6
Nondurable goods stores total	832,728	+ 7.1	+ 8.8
General merchandise group	153,642	+10.2	+ 7.9
General merchandise stores	144,575	+10.6	+ 8.4
Department stores	129,284	+10.9	+ 8.6
Variety stores	9,067	+ 5.1	+ 1.8
Apparel group	66,891	+10.8	+ 8.8
Men's and boy's wear stores	8,432	+ 5.9	+ 3.1
Women's apparel accessary stores	27,899	+13.9	+ 9.3
Family & other apparel stores	17,567	+13.8	+11.1
Shoe stores	10,339	+ 5.6	+ 9.9
Furniture & appliance group	63,581	+16.3	+ 8.9
GAF total	325,938	+11.7	—
Automotive group	277,008	+19.0	+ 9.5
Gasoline service stations	100,997	+ 2.2	+10.2
Lumber, building material hardware	59,304	+15.2	+ 9.7
Eating and drinking places	124,109	+ 8.2	+10.8
Food group	269,959	+ 5.9	+ 8.3
Drug and proprietary, stores	44,165	+10.3	+ 9.2
Liquor stores	19,494	+ 2.5	+ 6.3

Source: *Standard & Poor's Industrial Survey,* July 4, 1985, p. 111.

time, and the move toward higher quality national brand merchandise was well underway. Still, as 1986 began, there were a number of important issues still facing K mart. Would the repositioning program succeed in attracting more affluent customers to buy its higher priced name-brand merchandise? What additional steps could be taken to upgrade K mart's stores? Would the new image result in a substantial loss of lower income customers which had historically been the backbone of its business? Might K mart customers be confused by the move as happened to Sears in the 1970s? How could K mart improve the performance of its clothing and soft goods? If it did, could fashion-seeking customers really be convinced that K mart was a trendy place to shop? These and other questions came to mind as CEO Fauber looked ahead to the remainder of the 1980s and into the 1990s.

Case Group E

Pricing Strategy

Case 21

Delta Airlines*

Margaret L. Friedman
University of Wisconsin–Whitewater

Nowhere has the flexibility and importance of the price variable been more boldly illustrated than in the airline industry since its deregulation in late 1978. In this free-market environment, when one carrier initiates a fare change (typically a fare decrease) other airlines follow suit, usually in a matter of a few hours using sophisticated computer technology. A typical day in the tariff department at Delta Airlines requires comparison of Delta's more than 70,000 fares against the industry's 5,000 price changes of the past 24-hour period. Since deregulation, Delta's tariff department has grown from 27 employees to approximately 150.

Prior to deregulation, the U.S. government dictated all aspects of

* This case was prepared by Margaret L. Friedman, Assistant Professor, School of Business, University of Wisconsin-Whitewater. Based on "Fare Bargains on Planes Spur Odd Routing," *The Wall Street Journal,* December 8, 1982; "Fare Wars: Have the Big Airlines Learned to Win?", *Fortune,* October 29, 1984, pp. 24-28; "Learning How to Fly," *Barron's,* November 19, 1984, pp. 8-9 and 30-38.

airline route and fare structures. Under regulation, competitors filed comparable fare increase requests with the Civil Aeronautics Board on a regular basis in order to recover the rising costs of labor, fuel, and debt. All requests were restricted to increases no higher than 5 percent above the "standard industry fare level" or 5 percent below that level, and all such requests were granted. In addition, the federal government put a 12.5 percent ceiling on allowable rate of return in the industry. In this controlled macroenvironment, price was not an important factor in competitive success. Individual members of the industry acted in concert with one another in the spirit of a fraternity. The major carriers attempted to differentiate themselves on the basis of product attributes such as the thickness of the steak served on their flights, the friendliness of their flight attendants, and overall image.

When the industry was deregulated, price suddenly became the single most important factor in competitive strategy. On almost a moment's notice carriers could raise fares by 30 percent or decrease them by 100 percent from standard levels. In other words, the airlines were allowed to give their service away and some did just that. For example, Midway Airlines offered round-trip tickets at the one-way price plus a penny. Jet America offered 405 passengers a one-way fare between Long Beach, California, and Chicago for $4.05. Texas International Airlines promoted free service to four cities for the first 100 passengers who came to them wearing Santa Claus costumes.

On the other hand, it should be noted that while the discount fares attracted a lot of attention, the average price of a ticket rose 71 percent between 1978 and 1982 to $106.34 (the consumer price index rose 43 percent during the same period), because fares increased on less traveled routes. For example, it cost $.29 a seat per mile to travel between Peoria, Illinois, and Wichita, Kansas, versus $.06 a seat per mile between Chicago and San Francisco.

The post-deregulation era in the airlines industry has been marked by other serious problems. These include a massive strike among air traffic controllers, a recessionary glut of airplane seats, and a tripling of fuel prices from 1979 to 1981. Most established carriers enthusiastically turned to price (1) to stimulate demand for their service which was in oversupply, (2) to smooth demand in an environment where supply and demand change drastically from day to day, from city to city, and from flight to flight, and (3) to compete against the lower prices offered by new, "no frills" carriers which sprang up almost overnight, especially on high volume routes. The results for the industry were large operating losses ($680 million in 1982) and several bankruptcies.

The new discount carriers had a pricing advantage over established airlines because of their lower labor costs. For example, PEOPLExpress avoided labor unions and persuaded employees to accept lower wages in return for a mandatory but generous stock-ownership plan.

Management also instituted a unique method to increase labor productivity called *cross-utilization,* whereby a pilot, when not flying, might do accounting or personnel work or a flight attendant might help out at the ticket counter. Also, customer services, such as food ($.50 for a cup of coffee) and baggage handling ($3.00 for each bag checked), are charged separately so that the price of the ticket is "honest," that is, reflective only of the cost of travel. This approach resulted in some dramatic differences in costs. For example, six years after deregulation Delta Airlines' expenses were approximately $.08 a seat per mile while PEOPLExpress' expenses were $.053 a seat per mile.

Delta Airlines had historically been considered the industry's best-managed company. However, in 1982 a market survey revealed that few travelers called Delta as their first choice when making travel plans because Delta had acquired a reputation for being high-priced in the new deregulated environment. Based on this survey, Delta introduced a promotion offering to match any competitor's fare on any of its more than 5,000 routes. While Delta was successful in attracting passengers, the number of them paying full fare dropped to 8 percent of all seats sold, creating Delta's first annual deficit in 47 years of business. Delta's pricing decisions, like those of other carriers in the industry, became increasingly complex. Prices varied on the same route according to time of day, day of the week, season of the year, advance purchase requirements, length of stay, class of service, connections, and stopovers. In one informal survey it was reported that eight different Delta agents quoted seven different fares for the exact same travel itinerary.

Delta's computer technology was critical in helping to make pricing decisions, particularly with respect to determining how many discount seats to make available. Sophisticated programs analyzed historical travel patterns on flights and compared them to present bookings on future flights. On the basis of such seat analyses, the number of discount seats available on a flight was in a constant state of flux. Consequently, a passenger who was told on one occasion that no low fare seats were available would suddenly find them available if he/she called back in a day or two. At one point it was reported that 50 Delta reservation agents worked full time at computer terminals monitoring minute-by-minute booking patterns. Their primary task was to divide up the number of discount and full-fare seats on future flights in order to maximize revenue per flight.

Discussion Questions

1. What are some of the distinguishing characteristics of a service such as air transportation that are particularly relevant to pricing strategy?

2. How did pricing methods change over time from the period during regulation, to immediately after deregulation, to six years after deregulation?
3. What should Delta Airlines do to compete successfully against the low-cost entrants in the market?
4. What do you think the long-run effect of deregulation will be on ticket prices? Consider this question from the perspective of the established carriers and from the perspective of the newer low-cost carriers.

Case 22

Young Attitudes—Pricing a New Product Line*

Jon M. Hawes
University of Akron

Young Attitudes is a large, well-known clothing store chain with more than 400 retail outlets located throughout the United States and Canada. Appealing to the teenage and young adult consumer, the success enjoyed by Young Attitudes is based largely on the firm's ability to market fashionable merchandise at reasonable and competitive prices. While Young Attitudes stocks a limited selection of national manufacturer's brands (e.g., Levi's and Haggar) to enhance its store image and to generate consumer traffic, the vast majority of each outlet's merchandise consists of the firm's own private retailer brands. To ensure a reliable source of supply for their private labels, Young Attitudes purchased the Fashion-Plus Clothing Company (FPCC) in 1982. At the time of the takeover, FPCC was a well-established national manufacturer of high quality, fashionable apparel. FPCC's product mix consisted of a wide line of both men's and women's wearing apparel.

The recent increase in the popularity and acceptance of fleece wearing apparel by many diverse consumer groups throughout all market areas of the country prompted Ralph West, the General Merchandise Manager for Young Attitudes, to investigate the possibility of adding a new line of men's shirts. Preliminary results of that investigation led Ralph to conclude that such a line would appeal to the consumer group the firm identified as "the comfort-seekers"—a consumer market segment wanting stylish, leisure clothing of good quality. While quality is a concern for these people, cost is also an important consideration in the selection of clothing apparel. As far as Ralph is concerned, the addition of a new line of men's fleece shirts makes good merchandising sense. However, it will be up to the production people at Fashion-Plus

---

* This case was prepared by Jon M. Hawes, Professor of Marketing, Department of Marketing, University of Akron.

to determine whether the new line is feasible given the price, cost, and profit constraints under which they must produce the product.

While Fashion-Plus is a wholly-owned subsidiary of Young Attitudes, FPCC's management is responsible for making all production decisions.

Presently under consideration is Ralph's request for the new line of fleece shirts. To determine the feasibility of new product lines, Bill Morris (Manager for New Product Development) must collect the necessary information to make a cost and break-even analysis, to project expected profits, and to recommend a suggested retail price as well as a manufacturer's price (the price that Fashion-Plus should charge Young Attitudes). Having spent the last two weeks collecting data, Bill feels he now has the necessary information to make the required evaluations of the new western shirt project. Before proceeding with his analysis, Bill reviews the following information he has collected:

1. Several competitors have recently introduced similar lines of men's fleece shirts. Market research indicates that these lines are selling at a brisk pace at competitive retail stores for the following prices:

Retail Selling Prices	*Number of Times Observed*
$ 14.00	2
$ 15.00	7
$ 16.00	5
$ 17.00	3

2. Young Attitudes will apply a 40 percent initial markup on the retail selling price of shirts.
3. Production costs for the new shirt are estimated to be:

Cloth	$2.20 per shirt
Buttons	.05 per shirt
Thread	.05 per shirt
Direct labor	20 minutes per shirt
Shipping weight	2 pounds per packaged shirt

4. Basic marketing costs for introducing the new line of shirts are estimated to be $300,000 the first year if a penetration pricing policy is used or $340,000 if a skimming pricing policy is employed.
5. Being a large company, FPCC has 15 production facilities strategically located throughout the United States. Last year, the average round trip distance from FPCC production facilities to Young Attitudes outlets was 225 miles. Current plans are to produce the new line of shirts at each of FPCC's production facilities.

6. An examination of FPCC's annual report reveals the following information:

Managerial salaries	$1,500,000
Rent and utilities expense	1,200,000
Transportation costs (1,250,000 miles)	750,000
Depreciation on plant and equipment	1,300,000
Other overhead	2,000,000
Direct labor costs (2,000,000 hours)	8,000,000
Total company sales	45,000,000
Average order size	1,000 pounds

7. The Midwest Market Research Corporation was hired to develop a sales forecast for the new line of western shirts. Their research findings estimate that if a skimming pricing policy were used, Young Attitudes could expect to sell approximately 110,000 to 130,000 shirts. Under a penetration-type pricing policy, Midwest estimates a unit sales volume of approximately 130,000 to 150,000 shirts.

The Problem

Assume that Bill Morris was unexpectedly called out of town and he has asked you to prepare the analysis and written report on the feasibility of the project and then to make a recommendation for the pricing strategy he should use. At a minimum, your analysis should include a cost analysis (variable cost per shirt, fixed cost allocation for the line, and total cost per shirt), a break-even analysis in units and dollars, a determination of the manufacturer's price and suggested retail price, and a statement as to expected profit the company can derive from the new line.

Case 23

Rockwood Manor*

William R. Wynd
Eastern Washington University

Dan Chapman, administrator for Rockwood Manor retirement facility, sat in his Spokane, Washington, office contemplating a recommendation to his board of directors on how Rockwood could meet the apparent demand for housing to accommodate the active elderly in Spokane County. He knew the board would ask several important questions: What is the size of the market for retirement facilities? What kind of housing facilities do active elderly want? And how should those facilities be priced?

Dan had observed the increase in elderly both nationally and locally. Many of the newly retired were healthy, active people who looked forward to a physically active lifestyle. Although they did not wish to move into a dormitory-style facility, they did want to get out from under the burdens of maintaining a home. They wanted to be free to move about as they pleased, yet have a private secure place they could call home.

In his tenure at Rockwood, Mr. Chapman had also observed that seniors were concerned about financial matters. Some wanted to build an estate for their children while others felt they should spend their hard earned money on themselves. The current pricing schedule for rooms and health care at the manor accommodated both these two viewpoints. He was not sure how pricing would be handled in a different housing/service configuration.

NATIONAL TRENDS

The nation's population of the elderly is on the rise. According to *U.S. News and World Report,* "One of every five Americans is 55 years or older, and that figure will climb to one in every three and one-half over

* This case was prepared by William R. Wynd, Professor of Marketing, Eastern Washington University. Used by permission.

the next 40 years."[1] This increase is attributed to several factors. One is a decline in the death rate of 2 percent annually since 1970, due largely to improved public health care measures. A declining birth rate over the last decade has also contributed to a higher proportion of elderly in the population. Projections indicate that by the year 1990, 30 million people will be over age 65, accounting for 28 percent of the U.S. population.

Older Americans are increasingly well off financially when they reach retirement. Women currently account for an estimated 49 percent of the work force, and, with the increased number of women working, the income from a second pension is by far one of the most important factors in the maintenance of an upward trend in income among the elderly.

Business Week recently reported a study speculating that spending by the elderly since the mid-70s may have been extensive enough to depress the national personal saving rate.[2] Those elderly currently 65 and older make up about 16 percent of all adults, but they received more than half of all interest income and close to one third of all capital gains reported to the IRS in 1982. Furthermore, while the average family held $18,695 in liquid assets in 1983, families headed by persons 65–74 averaged $30,666.

With an average age of 74, the nation's elderly can expect at least 10 more years of life. Common sense would indicate a tendency to spend their discretionary income. Most are in reasonably good health (though they hate to climb stairs), their spouse is still living, and they have the time to enjoy a wide variety of leisure activities.

Indeed, the elderly are apparently spending more of their money on housing and transportation. The Department of Labor publishes three budgets for a retired couple made up of hypothetical lines of goods and services that were specified in the mid 1960s to portray three relative levels of living: lower, intermediate, and higher. The categories include food, housing, transportation, clothing, personal care, medical care, and other family consumption. In 1981 the percentage spent on housing, transportation, and clothing increased as income increased.

Although a growing elderly population constitutes a potential market for a wide variety of goods and services, the segment represented by active, affluent seniors is being increasingly cultivated by a wide variety of providers. A. T. Sutherland, advertising manager for *Modern Maturity,* indicates that the maturity market (50+) accounts for 25

---

[1] Mary Gallean et al., "Life Begins at 55," *U. S. News and World Report,* September 1, 1980, pp. 51–60.

[2] "Are the Elderly the Key to the Savings Puzzle?" *Business Week,* December 31, 1984, p. 17.

percent of all consumer expenditures—purchasing 3 percent of all domestic cars, 30 percent of all food consumed at home, 25 percent of all cosmetics and bath products, 25 percent of all alcoholic beverages, 41 percent of all toaster ovens and food processors, 37 percent of all slenderizing treatments and health spa memberships, and 31 percent of all automobile tires.[3]

Contrary to the belief that many senior citizens are inclined to migrate to the sunbelt regions, evidence shows that many seniors prefer to live in the home they have lived in for years. Change becomes less appealing as time passes. Hence, many elderly wish to remain in familiar surroundings for as long as they can. According to the U.S. Department of Housing and Urban Development, 70 percent of the population 65 and over live in their own homes, 5–7 percent live in retirement homes, 18–20 percent live in apartments or government subsidized housing, and 5 percent live in institutions.[4]

Those elderly who opt to sell their homes have a wide variety of new concepts available to them, including condominium retirement settings, mobile home courts, and group homes as well as the traditional retirement center facilities. If they move to a new geographic location they are often drawn toward the less populous urban centers where the cost of living is usually more reasonable.

THE SETTING

Spokane, Washington, is one of the nation's most beautiful cities and has many attractions as a retirement community. Located in northeastern Washington state, Spokane was the site of the 1974 World's Fair. Conservative and rural in nature, the region is among the nation's most fertile wheat-producing areas. Most of the urban population is employed in wholesale and retail trade, financial services, and health care servicing a number of sparsely populated counties in northeastern Washington and northern Idaho. Most Spokanites reaching retirement age stay in Spokane. Taxes, costs of maintaining a household, availability of doctors and sophisticated medical facilities, and low crime rate are among the attractions.

According to the 1970 census, 44,440 of the 287,487 total county population were aged 60 or over. The 1980 census counted 54,436 of the 341,058 total county population as aged 60 or over. The number of

[3] "Misdirected Advertising Prevents Marketers from Taking Bite from 'Golden Apple' of Maturity Market," *Maturity News*, October 26, 1984, p. 19.

[4] U.S. Department of Housing and Urban Development, Office of Policy Development and Research, *Characteristics of the Elderly*, Washington, D.C.: Government Printing Office, February 1979, pp. 1–73.

EXHIBIT 1 1980 Census and Population Projections for Spokane County for 1985 and 1990

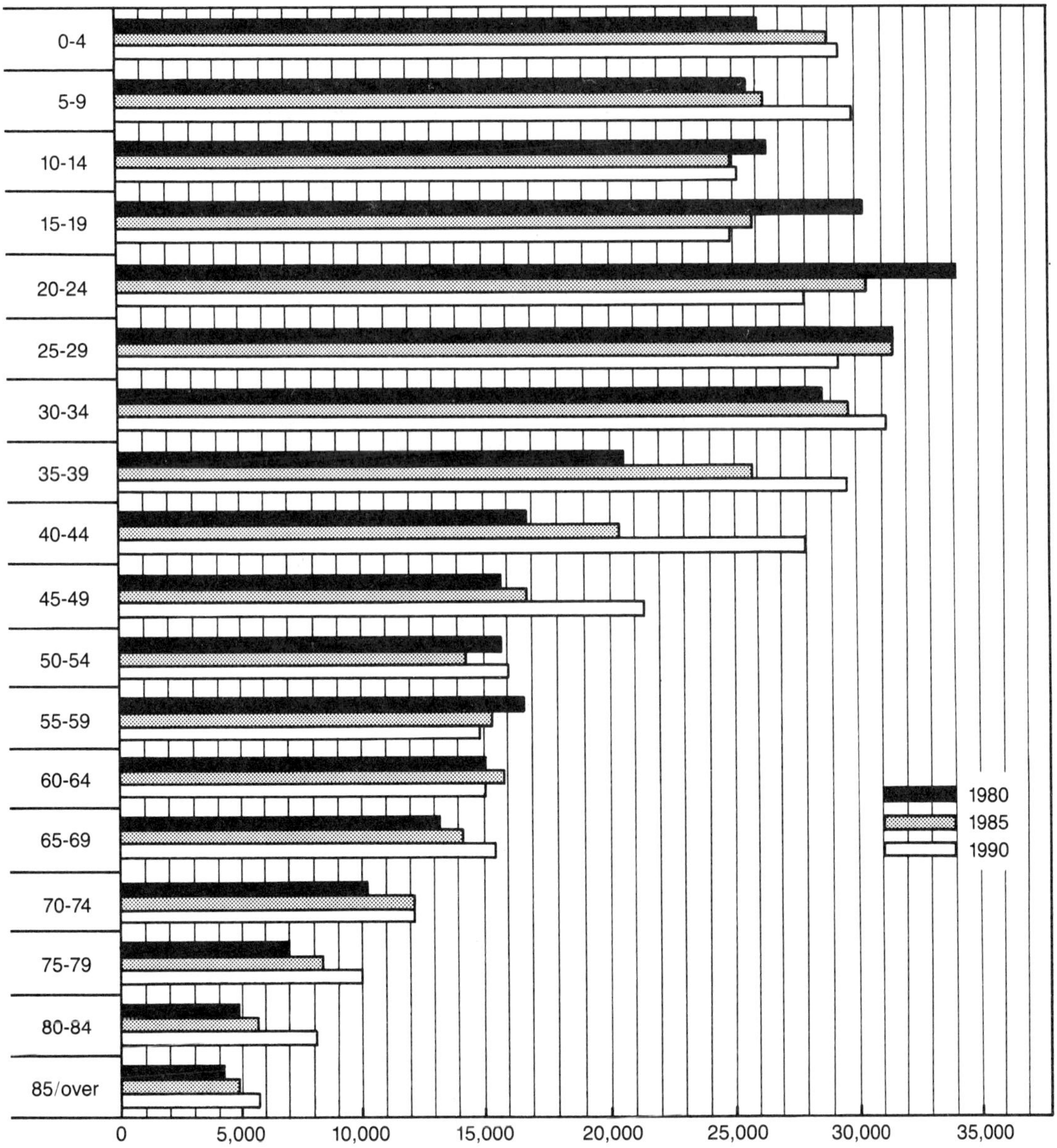

Source: Population, Enrollment, and Economic Studies Division, Office of Financial Management (November 1982).

persons 60 or over increased by 9,996 in the 10 years between the censuses. Exhibit 1 is a bar chart showing the 1980 population in Spokane County with projections for 1985 and 1990. The population by age group and sex is shown in Exhibit 2.

EXHIBIT 2 1990 Population Projection for Spokane County

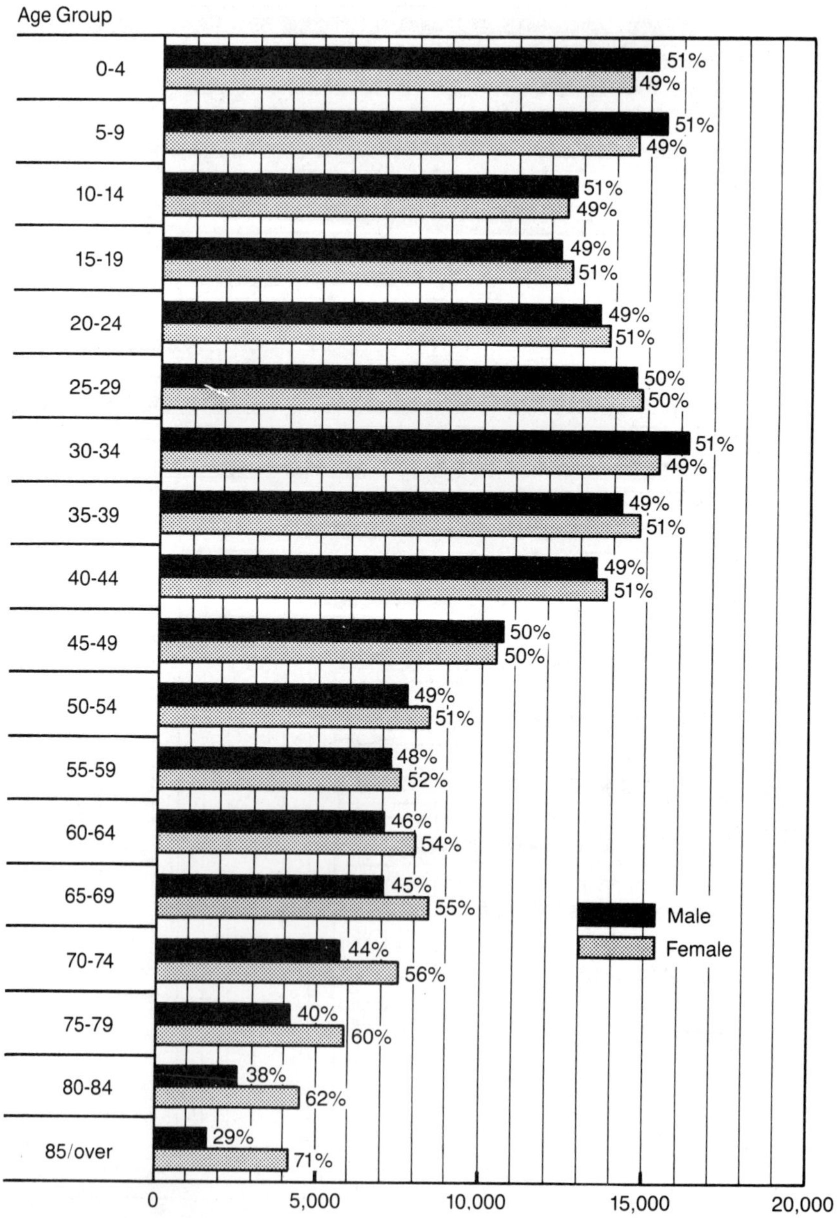

Source: Population, Enrollment, and Economic Studies Division, Office of Financial Management (November 1982).

ROCKWOOD MANOR

Rockwood Manor is a residential health facility that offers a full spectrum of services to meet the housing, nutrition, health, social, and spiritual needs of older persons. It is operated by a nonprofit corporation related to the United Methodist Church but receives no financial assistance from the church or any other organization. Residents purchase the privilege of living in a unit of their choice. Prices are based upon the charge for a standard living unit of 300 square feet. Living units may be purchased for cash or under terms of a time payment contract. A minimum down payment is required for a living unit under terms of the contract. The balance, plus interest on the declining balance, is amortized for a term of 84 months. In addition, residents pay a monthly services fee.

Residents of Rockwood Manor must be independently ambulatory and able to care for themselves at the time of admission. There is a per diem charge for infirmary care beginning with the 11th day of confinement during any one month. The amount of this per diem charge is equal to the audited cost of a day's care in the infirmary. If a resident becomes a permanent patient in the infirmary, and his living unit is paid for in full, he may then surrender his living unit to the corporation, in which case he will then receive the infirmary care for the current monthly services fee of a standard living unit.

Rooms are also available for those residents who are not bed patients but who need assistance in the activities of daily living such as bathing and dressing. These rooms are attended by a special corps of aides under the supervision of the Director of Nursing Services. A per diem charge is made for this intermediate health care.

A resident may cancel his contract by giving 60 days notice in writing, except during illness. If the living unit has been paid for in full, the "unearned balance"[5] is refunded upon the resale of the unit. If the unit has been purchased under terms of a time payment contract, no refund is made. A time payment contract terminates with death.

Rockwood Manor enjoys a reputation of being one of the finest retirement homes in the region. Its physical plant is clean, neat, and well maintained. Its personnel are pleasant, helpful, and professional.

---

[5] Unearned balance is calculated by dividing the amount paid by the tenant by the number of months the tenant is expected to live as shown by actuarial tables in use by major life insurance companies. The quotient is multiplied by the number of months the tenant occupied his/her unit. This amount is kept by Rockwood, the remainder (unearned balance) is returned to the tenant.

The location is an exclusive residential area and relatively high fees project an "elite" image.

Rockwood owns enough land to develop a variety of housing configurations catering to the active elderly. Another high rise, condominiums, duplex units or cottages were all possibilities. Construction costs per square foot were greatest for cottages, least for a high rise apartment.

THE MARKET

An increasing elderly population represents a diverse market for a wide variety of retirement centers. Traditional retirement centers have almost always been operated by not-for-profit organizations, usually church affiliated. These centers normally sign a contract with the resident for lifetime care and promise that no one will be asked to leave due to financial problems.

According to a survey by the national accounting and consulting firm of Laventhol and Horvath, the future of the nation's life care/continuing care retirement industry is rapidly changing as entrepreneurs enter the expanding market.[6] These newer facilities, though still in the minority, offer a variety of possibilities. Some still offer the life care contract, but with totally or partially refundable entry fees. Others concentrate on renting units. They have no entry or endowment fees, and health care is usually provided strictly on a pay-as-needed basis.

Increasing costs and a growing market have brought together investors and not-for-profit organizers. An increasingly common partnership occurs when an investor group finances the development in return for the tax advantages. When these are exhausted, the not-for-profit organization purchases the development for fair market value.

Since 1975, marketing for the typical life-care center development usually precedes contruction by a full year. Most developments presell half their units and achieve 66 percent occupancy within 6 months after completion and 95 percent within 18 months.

The results of a recent survey of the capacity of establishments listed in the Yellow Pages of the Spokane County Telephone Book under the heading "Retirement and Life Care Communities and Homes" is summarized in Exhibit 3.

Nearly half the retirement apartments and beds available in Spokane County are subsidized (beyond Medicare or Medicaid) by

---

[6] Aaron M. Rose, "Entrepreneurs Reshaping Lifecare," *Modern Healthcare,* July 1984, pp. 148–53.

EXHIBIT 3 Capacity of Retirement and Life Care Facilities in Spokane County, 1985

	Apartments	*Beds*	*Total*	*Percent of Total*
Subsidized	832	551	1,383	44
Private	1,031	711	1,742	56
	1,863	1,262	3,125	100

Federal or State Government. Occupancy of both apartments and beds is nearly 100 percent.

Competition in the current Spokane market to serve relatively high income retirees comes from two other not-for-profit organizations and one recently constructed for-profit condominium apartment complex with minimum health care. The retirement complex most similar to Rockwood Manor just announced a duplex/multifamily addition designed for the active elderly. Their existing and planned units are either apartments, condominiums, or duplex units. Although the existing facilities were full and often enjoyed a waiting list, what additional capacity would do to occupancy rates was a matter of conjecture. An estimated 250 new units would be added by the latest development.

PRICING/COST CONSIDERATIONS

Life care communities have an obligation to provide housing and health care for the life of their residents. This obligation can be separated into two financial cost components: housing and services. Costs in the housing component consist of debt service, maintenance, and periodic renovation. (See Exhibit 4.) Costs for monthly services cover such items as food service, laundry, recreation, and utilities. But the largest single portion of the cost of services is health care.

Dan Chapman knew that setting a fee to fund the real estate portion of the obligation would be fairly straightforward. The fee would reflect the value of discounted cash flows for debt service, maintenance, and renovation. Establishing a monthly fee for service, however, posed a problem because the aging of the community affects the cost of health care. A young community would be relatively more healthy than a "maturing" group. As the average age of the community increases so does the largest single component of monthly service. Dan wanted to treat the residents fairly and at the same time keep the monthly service fee consistent with the "market" he was trying to reach. With

EXHIBIT 4 Construction and Garage Costs Single Family Detached*

	House	*Garage*	*Total Cash Costs*	*Total Value with Land*
1,250 sq. ft.	$68,750	$10,368	$107,249	$112,249
1,000 sq. ft.	55,000	7,776	86,155	91,155
750 sq. ft.	41,250	5,184	65,060	70,060

* Construction costs for condominium units would average 12 percent less, including garages.

this in mind he saw three possible pricing methodologies aimed at the new group of active elderly.[7]

Pay as You Go

Under this methodology fees would be set annually on the basis of next year's anticipated expenses and the revenue short fall or surplus of the current period. Fees would be low to start because the group would be young and healthy. As they matured health care costs and fees would increase. Although new entrants would moderate the aging of the community, the vagaries of inflation would insure inequity.

Open Group

This methodology dictates that discounted cash flows be anticipated for a relatively long period, say 20 years. Young entrants replace those deceased, thus moderating health care costs. Overall fees set by this methodology are likely to be higher than pay as you go when the communities are young but lower as they mature. Insuring equity is difficult but not impossible.

Closed Group

In the closed group method, cash flows are anticipated for the actuarial life of residents in a cohort group (typically a group of new residents). This method differs from the open-group method because it centers on

[7] Howard E. Winklevoss and Alwyn V. Powell, *Continuing Care Retirement Communities: An Empirical, Financial, and Legal Analysis* (Homewood, Ill.: Richard D. Irwin, 1984).

a specific cohort and requires that fees be self-supporting without the benefit of new entrants. Fees are the highest when set by this pricing methodology but by definition they are most equitable to all residents.

Dan wasn't sure which pricing methodology to recommend in setting monthly service fees. He knew that any fee below what residents in the Manor were paying would likely anger them. On the other hand any fee above that would have to be justified to potential new residents.

Case 24

S.C. Johnson and Son, Limited (R)*

Carolyn Vose
University of Western Ontario

Four months ago, in November, George Styan had been appointed division manager of Innochem, at S.C. Johnson and Son, Limited[1] (SCJ), a Canadian subsidiary of S.C. Johnson & Son, Inc. Innochem's sole product line consisted of industrial cleaning chemicals for use by business, institutions, and government. George was concerned by the division's poor market share, particularly in Montreal and Toronto. Together, these two cities represented approximately 35 percent of Canadian demand for industrial cleaning chemicals, but less than 10 percent of Innochem sales. It appeared that SCJ distributors could not match the aggressive discounting practiced by direct-selling manufacturers in Metropolitan markets.

Recently, George had received a rebate proposal from his staff designed to increase the distributor's ability to cut end user prices by "sharing" part of the total margin with SCJ when competitive conditions demanded discounts of 30 percent or more off the list price to end users. George had to decide if the rebate plan was the best way to penetrate price-sensitive markets. Moreover, he wondered about the plan's ultimate impact on divisional profit performance. George either had to develop an implementation plan for the rebate plan or draft an alternative proposal to unveil at the Distributors' Annual Spring Convention, three weeks away.

---

[1] Popularly known as Canadian Johnson Wax.

THE CANADIAN MARKET FOR INDUSTRIAL CLEANING CHEMICALS

Last year, the Canadian market for industrial cleaning chemicals was approximately $100 million at end user prices. Growth was stable at an overall rate of approximately 3 percent per year.

"Industrial cleaning chemicals" included all chemical products designed to clean, disinfect, sanitize, or protect industrial, commercial, and institutional buildings and equipment. The label was broadly applied to general purpose cleaners, floor maintenance products (strippers, sealers, finishes, and detergents), carpet cleaners and deodorizers, disinfectants, air fresheners, and a host of specialty chemicals such as insecticides, pesticides, drain cleaners, oven cleansers, and sweeping compounds.

Industrial cleaning chemicals were distinct from equivalent consumer products typically sold through grocery stores. Heavy-duty industrial products were packaged in larger containers and bulk and marketed directly by the cleaning chemical manufacturers or sold through distributors to a variety of end users. Exhibit 1 includes market segmentation by primary end user categories, including janitorial service contractors and the in-house maintenance departments of government, institutions, and companies.

BUILDING MAINTENANCE CONTRACTORS

In Canada, maintenance contractors purchased 17 percent of the industrial cleaning chemicals sold during 1980 (end user price). The segment was growing at approximately 10–15 percent a year, chiefly at the expense of other end user categories. *Canadian Business* reported, "Contract cleaners have made sweeping inroads into the traditional preserve of in-house janitorial staffs, selling themselves on the strength of cost efficiency."[2] Maintenance contract billings reached an estimated $1 billion last year.

Frequently, demand for building maintenance services was highly price sensitive, and since barriers to entry were low (small capitalization, simple technology), competition squeezed contractor gross margins below 6 percent (before tax). Variable cost control was a matter of survival, and only products bringing compensatory labour savings could command a premium price in this segment of the cleaning chemical market.

---

[2] "Contract Cleaners Want to Whisk Away Ring-Around-the-Office," *Canadian Business,* 1981, p. 22.

EXHIBIT 1 Segmentation of the Canadian Market for Industrial Cleaning Chemicals

By End User Category

End User	*Percent Total*
Retail outlets	25%
Contractors	17
Hospitals	15
Industrial and office	13
Schools, colleges	8
Hotels, motels	6
Nursing homes	5
Recreation	3
Government	3
Fast food	2
Full-service restaurants	2
All others	1
Total	100% = $95 million

By Product Category

Product	*Percent Total*
Floor care products	40%
General purpose cleaners	16
Disinfectants	12
Carpet care products	8
Odor control products	5
Glass cleaners	4
All others	15
Total	100% = $95 million

A handful of contract cleaners did specialize in higher margin services to prestige office complexes, luxury apartments, art museums, and other "quality-conscious" customers. However, even contractors serving this select clientele did not necessarily buy premium cleaning supplies.

IN-HOUSE MAINTENANCE DEPARTMENTS

Government

Last year, cleaning chemical sales to various government offices (federal, provincial, and local) approached $2 million. Typically, a government body solicited bids from appropriate sources by formally advertising for quotations for given quantities of particular cleaning chemicals. Although bid requests often names specific brands, suppliers were permitted to offer "equivalent substitutes." Separate competitions were held for each item and normally covered 12 months' supply with provision for delivery "as required." Contracts were frequently awarded solely on the basis of price.

Institutions

Like government bodies, most institutions were price sensitive owing to restrictive budgets and limited ability to "pass on" expenses to users. Educational institutions and hospitals were the largest consumers of cleaning chemicals in this segment. School boards used an open-bid system patterned on the government model. Heavy sales time requirements and demands for frequent delivery of small shipments to as many as 100 locations were characteristic.

Colleges and universities tended to be operated somewhat differently. Dan Stalport, one of the purchasing agents responsible for maintenance supplies at The University of Western Ontario, offered the following comments:

> Sales reps come to UWO year 'round. If one of us (in the buying group) talks to a salesman who seems to have something—say, a labour-saving feature—we get a sample and test it. Testing can take up to a year. Floor covering, for example, has to be exposed to seasonal changes in weather and traffic.
>
> If we're having problems with a particular item, we'll compare the performance and price of three or four competitors. There are usually plenty of products that do the job. Basically, we want value—acceptable performance at the lowest available price.

Hospitals accounted for 15 percent of cleaning chemical sales. Procurement policies at University Hospital (UH), a medium-sized (450-bed) facility in London, Ontario, were typical. UH distinguished between "critical" and "non-critical" products. Critical cleaning chemicals (i.e., those significantly affecting patient health, such as phenolic germicide) could be bought only on approval of the staff microbiologist, who tested the "kill factor." This measure of effectiveness was regularly retested, and any downgrading of product performance could void a supplier's contract. In contrast, noncritical supplies, such as general purpose cleaners, floor finishes, and the like, were the exclusive province of Bob Chandler, purchasing agent attached to the Housekeeping Department. Bob explained that performance of noncritical cleaning chemicals was informally judged and monitored by the housekeeping staff:

> Just last year, for example, the cleaners found the floor polish was streaking badly. We (the Housekeeping Department) tested and compared five or six brands—all in the ballpark price-wise—and chose the best.

Business

The corporate segment was highly diverse, embracing both service and manufacturing industries. Large volume users tended to be price sensitive—particularly when profits were low. Often, however, cleaning products represented such a small percentage of the total operating budget that the cost of searching for the lowest cost supplier would be expected to exceed any realizable saving. Under such conditions, the typical industrial customer sought efficiencies in the purchasing process itself, for example, by dealing with the supplier offering the broadest mix of janitorial products (chemicals, paper supplies, equipment, etc.). Guy Breton, purchasing agent for Securitech, a Montreal-based security systems manufacturer, commented on the time economies of "one-stop shopping":

> With cleaning chemicals, it simply isn't worth the trouble to shop around and stage elaborate product performance tests. I buy all our chemicals, brushes, dusters, toweling—the works—from one or two suppliers . . . buying reputable brands from familiar suppliers saves hassles—back orders are rare, and Maintenance seldom complains.

DISTRIBUTION CHANNELS FOR INDUSTRIAL CLEANING CHEMICALS

The Canadian market for industrial cleaning chemicals was supplied through three main channels, each characterized by a distinctive set of strengths and weaknesses:

a. Distributor sales of national brands.
b. Distributor sales of private label products.
c. Direct sale by manufacturers.

Direct sellers held a 61 percent share of the Canadian market for industrial cleaning chemicals, while the distributors of national brands and private label products held shares of 25 percent and 14 percent, respectively. Relative market shares varied geographically, however. In Montreal and Toronto, for example, the direct marketers' share rose to 70 percent and private labelers' to 18 percent reducing the national brand share to 12 percent. The pattern, shown in Exhibit 2, reflected an interplay of two areas of channel differentiation, namely, discount capability at the end user level and the cost of serving distant, geographically dispersed customers.

Distributor Sales of National Brand Cleaning Chemicals

National brand manufacturers, such as S.C. Johnson and Son, Airkem, and National Labs, produces a relatively limited range of "high-

EXHIBIT 2 Effect of Geography on Market Share of Different Distribution Channels

Supplier Type	*Share Nationwide*	*Share in Montreal and Toronto*
Direct marketers	61%*	70%
Private label distributors	14	18
National brands distributors	25†	12

* Dustbane	17%	†SCJ	8%
G. H. Wood	31	N/L	4
All others	13	Airkem	3
Total	61%	All others	10
		Total	25%

quality" janitorial products, including many special purpose formulations of narrow market interest. Incomplete product range, combined with shortage of manpower and limited warehousing, made direct distribution unfeasible in most cases. Normally, a national brand company would negotiate with middlemen who handled a broad array of complementary products (equipment, tools, and supplies) by different manufacturers. "Bundling" of goods brought the distributors cost efficiencies in selling, warehousing, and delivery by spreading fixed costs over a large sales volume. Distributors were, therefore, better able to absorb the costs of after-hour emergency service, frequent routine sales and service calls to many potential buyers, and shipments of small quantities of cleaning chemicals to multiple destinations. As a rule, the greater the geographic dispersion of customers, and the smaller the average order, the greater the relative economies of distributor marketing.

Comparatively high gross margins (approximately 50 percent of wholesale price) enabled national brand manufacturers to offer distributors strong marketing support and sales training along with liberal terms of payment and freight plus low minimum order requirements. Distributors readily agreed to handle national brand chemicals, and in metropolitan markets, each brand was sold through several distributors. By the same token, most distributors carried several directly competitive product lines. George suspected that some distributor salesmen only used national brands to "lead" with and tended to offer private label whenever a customer proved price sensitive, or a competitor handled the same national brand(s). Using an industry rule of thumb, George estimated that most distributors needed at least 20 percent gross margin on retail sales to cover sales commission of 10 percent, plus delivery and inventory expenses.

Distributor Sales of Private Label Cleaning Chemicals

Direct-selling manufacturers were dominating urban markets by aggressively discounting end user prices—sometimes below the wholesale price national brand manufacturers charged their distributors. To compete against the direct seller, increasing numbers of distributors were adding low-cost private label cleaning chemicals to their product lines. Private labeling also helped differentiate a particular distributor from others carrying the same national brand(s).

Sizable minimum order requirements restricted the private label strategy to only the largest distributors. Private label manufacturers produced to order, formulating to meet low prices specified by distributors. The relatively narrow margins (30–35 percent wholesale price) associated with private label manufacturers characteristically provided to distributors. Private label producers pared their expenses further still by requiring distributors to bear the cost of inventory and accept rigid terms of payment as well as delivery (net 30 days, FOB plant).

In addition to absorbing these selling expenses normally assumed by the manufacturer, distributors paid salesmen higher commission on private label sales (15 percent of resale) than on national brands (10 percent of resale). However, the incremental administration and selling expenses associated with private label business were more than offset by the differential savings on private label wholesale goods. By pricing private label chemicals at competitive parity with national brands, the distributor could enjoy approximately a 50 percent gross margin at resale list, while preserving considerable resale discount capability.

Private label products were seldom sold outside the metropolitan areas where most were manufactured. First, the high costs of moving bulky, low-value freight diminished the relative cost advantage of private label chemicals. Second, generally speaking, it was only in metro areas where distributors dealt in volumes great enough to satisfy the private labeler's minimum order requirement. Finally, outside the city, distributors were less likely to be in direct local competition with others handling the same national brand, reducing value of the private label as a source of supplier differentiation.

For some very large distributors, backward integration into chemical production was a logical extension of the private labeling strategy. Recently, several distributors had become direct marketers through acquisition of captive manufacturers.

Direct Sale by Manufacturers of Industrial Cleaning Chemicals

Manufacturers dealing directly with the end user increased their gross margins to 60–70 percent of retail list price. Greater margins increased their ability to discount end user price—a distinct advantage in the price-competitive urban marketplace. Overall, direct marketers averaged a gross margin of 50 percent.

Many manufacturers of industrial cleaning chemicals attempted some direct selling, but relatively few relied on this channel exclusively. Satisfactory adoption of a full-time direct-selling strategy required the manufacturer to match distributor's sales and delivery capabilities without sacrificing overall profitability. These conflicting demands had been resolved successfully by two types of company: large-scale powder chemical manufacturers and full-line janitorial products manufacturers.

Large-Scale Powder Chemical Manufacturers. Economies of large-scale production plus experience in the capital-intensive manufacture of powder chemicals enabled a few established firms, such as Diversey-Wyandotte, to dominate the market for powder warewash and vehicle cleansers. Selling through distributors offered these producers few advantages. Direct-selling expense was almost entirely commission (i.e., variable). Moreover, powder concentrates were characterized by comparatively high value-to-bulk ratios, and so could absorb delivery costs even where demand was geographically dispersed. Thus, any marginal benefits from using middlemen were more than offset by the higher margins (and associated discount capability) possible through direct distribution. Among these chemical firms, competition was not limited to price. The provision of dispensing and metering equipment was important, as was 24-hour servicing.

Full-line janitorial products manufacturers. These manufacturers offered a complete range of maintenance products, including paper supplies, janitorial chemicals, tools, and mechanical equipment. Although high margins greatly enhanced retail price flexibility, overall profitability depended on securing a balance of high- and low-margin business, as well as controlling selling and distribution expenses. This was accomplished in several ways, including:

Centering on market areas of concentrated demand to minimize costs of warehousing, sales travel, and the like.

Increasing average order size, either by adding product lines which could be sold to existing customers, or by seeking new large-volume customers.

Tying sales commission to profitability to motivate sales personnel to sell volume, without unnecessary discounting of end user price.

Direct marketers of maintenance products varied in scale from established nationwide companies to hundreds of regional operators. The two largest direct marketers, G. H. Wood and Dustbane, together supplied almost a third of Canadian demand for industrial cleaning chemicals.

S.C. JOHNSON AND SON, LIMITED

S.C. Johnson and Son, Limited (SCJ), was one of 42 foreign subsidiaries owned by the U.S.-based multinational, S.C. Johnson & Son, Inc. It was ranked globally as one of the largest privately held companies. SCJ contributed substantially to worldwide sales and profits and was based in Brantford, Ontario, close to the Canadian urban markets of Hamilton, Kitchener, Toronto, London, and Niagara Falls. About 300 people worked at the head office and plant, while another 100 were employed in field sales.

Innochem Division

Innochem (Innovative Chemicals for Professional Use) was a special division established to serve corporate, institutional, and government customers of SCJ. The division manufactured an extensive line of industrial cleaning chemicals, including general purpose cleansers, waxes, polishes, and disinfectants, plus a number of specialty products of limited application, as shown in Exhibit 3. Last year, Innochem sold $4.5 million of industrial cleaning chemicals through distributors and $0.2 million direct to end users. Financial statements for Innochem are shown in Exhibit 4.

INNOCHEM MARKETING STRATEGY

Divisional strategy hinged on reliable product performance, product innovation, active promotion, and mixed channel distribution. Steve Remen, market development manager, maintained that "Customers know our products are of excellent quality. They know that the products will always perform as expected."

At SCJ, performance requirements were detailed and tolerances precisely defined. The Department of Quality Control routinely inspected and tested raw materials, work in process, packaging, and finished goods. At any phase during the manufacturing cycle, Quality Control was empowered to halt the process and quarantine suspect product or materials. SCJ maintained that nothing left the plant "without approval from Quality Control."

EXHIBIT 3 Innochem Product Line

Johnson Wax is a systems innovator. Frequently, a new product leads to a whole new system of doing things—a Johnson system of "matched" products formulated to work together. This makes the most of your time, your effort, and your expense. Call today and see how these Johnson systems can give you maximum results at a minimum cost.

For all floors except unsealed wood and unsealed cork

Stripper: **Step-Off**—powerful, fast action
Finish: **Pronto**—fast-drying, good gloss, minimum maintenance
Spray-buff solution: **The Shiner Liquid Spray Cleaner or The Shiner Aerosol Spray Finish**
Maintainer: **Forward**—cleans, disinfects, deodorizes, sanitizes

For all floors except unsealed wood and unsealed cork

Stripper: **Step-Off**—powerful, fast stripper
Finish: **Carefree**—tough, beauty, durable, minimum maintenance
Maintainer: **Forward**—cleans, disinfects, deodorizes, sanitizes

For all floors except unsealed wood and unsealed cork

Stripper: **Step-Off**—for selective stripping
Sealer: **Over & Under-Plus**—undercoater-sealer
Finish: **Scrubbable Step-Ahead**—brilliant, scrubbable
Maintainer: **Forward**—cleans, disinfects, sanitizes, deodorizes,

For all floors except unsealed wood and cork

Stripper: **Step-Off**—powerful, fast stripper
Finish: **Easy Street**—high solids, high gloss, spray buffs to a "wet look" appearance
Maintainer: **Forward**—cleans, disinfects, deodorizes
Expose—phenolic cleaner disinfectant

For all floors except unsealed wood and unsealed cork

Stripper: **Step-Off**—for selective stripping
Sealer: **Over & Under-Plus**—undercoater-sealer
Finishes: **Traffic Grade**—heavy-duty floor wax
Waxtral—extra tough, high solids
Maintainer: **Forward**—cleans, disinfects, sanitizes, deodorizes

For all floors except asphalt, mastic and rubber tile. Use sealer and wax finishes on wood, cork, and cured concrete; sealer-finish on terrazzo, marble, clay, and ceramic tile; wax finish only on vinyl, linoleum, and magnesite.

Sealer: **Johnson Gym Finish**—sealer and top-coater, cleans as it waxes
Wax finishes: **Traffic Wax Paste**—heavy-duty buffing wax
Beautiflor Traffic Wax—liquid buffing wax
Maintainers: **Forward**—cleans, disinfects, sanitizes, deodorizes
Conq-r Dust—mop treatment
Stripper: **Step-Off**—stripper for sealer and finish
Sealer: **Secure**—fast-bonding, smooth, long-lasting
Finish: **Traffic Grade**—heavy-duty floor wax
Maintainer: **Forward or Big Bare**
Sealer-finish: **Johnson Gym Finish**—seal and top-coater
Maintainer: **Conq-r-Dust**—mop treatment

General cleaning:
Break-Up—cleans soap and body scum fast
Forward—cleans, disinfects, sanitizes, deodorizes
Bon Ami—instant cleaner, pressurized or pump, disinfects

Toilet-urinals:
Go-Getter—"Working Foam" cleaner

Glass:
Bon Ami—spray-on foam or liquid cleaner

EXHIBIT 3 *(concluded)*

Disinfectant spray:
- **End-Bac II**—controls bacteria, odors

Air freshener:
- **Glade**—dewy-fresh fragrances

Spot cleaning:
- **Johnson's Pledge**—cleans, waxes, polishes
- **Johnson's Lemon Pledge**—refreshing scent
- **Bon Ami Stainless Steel Cleaner**—cleans, polishes, protects

All-purpose cleaners:
- **Forward**—cleans, disinfects, sanitizes, deodorizes
- **Break-Up**—degreaser for animal and vegetable fats
- **Big Bare**—heavy-duty industrial cleaner

Carpets:
- **Rugbee Powder & Liquid Extraction Cleaner**
- **Rugbee Soil Release Concentrate**—for pre-spraying and bonnet buffing
- **Rugbee Shampoo**—for power shampoo machines
- **Rugbee Spotter**—spot remover

Furniture:
- **Johnson's Pledge**—cleans, waxes, polishes
- **Johnson's Lemon Pledge**—refreshing scent
- **Shine-Up Liquid**—general purpose cleaning

Disinfectant spray air freshener:
- **End-Bac II**—controls bacteria, odors
- **Glade**—dewy-fresh fragrances

Glass:
- **Bon Ami**—spray-on foam or liquid cleaner

Cleaning:
- **Break-Up**—special degreaser designed to remove animal and vegetable fats

Equipment:
- **Break-Up Foamer**—special generator designed to dispense Break-Up cleaner

General cleaning:
- **Forward**—fast-working germicidal cleaner for floors, walls, all washable surfaces
- **Expose**—phenolic disinfectant cleaner

Sanitizing:
- **J80 Sanitizer**—liquid for total environmental control of bacteria; no rinse necessary if used as directed

Disinfectant spray:
- **End-Brac II Spray**—controls bacteria, odors

Flying insects:
- **Bolt Liquid Airborne** or **Pressurized Airborne,** P3610 through E10 dispenser

Crawling insects:
- **Bolt Liquid Residual** or **Pressurized Residual,** P3610 through E10 dispenser
- **Bolt Roach Bait**

Rodents:
- **Bolt Rodenticide**—for effective control of rats and mice, use with Bolt Bait Box

"Keeping the new product shelf well stocked" was central to divisional strategy, as the name Innochem implies. Products launched over the past three years represented 33 percent of divisional gross sales, 40 percent of gross profits, and 100 percent of growth.

Mixed Distribution Strategy

Innochem used a mixed distribution system in an attempt to broaden market coverage. Eighty-seven percent of divisional sales were handled by a force of 200 distributor salesmen and were serviced from 50 distributor warehouses representing 35 distributors. The indirect channel was particularly effective outside Ontario and Quebec. In part, the tendency for SCJ market penetration to increase with distances from Montreal and Toronto reflected Canadian demographics

EXHIBIT 4

S. C. JOHNSON AND SON, LIMITED
Profit Statement of the Division
(in $ thousands)

Gross sales:	$4,682
Returns	46
Allowances	1
Cash discounts	18
Net sales	4,617
Cost of sales	2,314
Gross profit:	2,303
Advertising	75
Promotions	144
Deals	—
External marketing services	2
Sales freight	292
Other distribution expenses	176
Service fees	184
Total direct expenses	873
Sales force	592
Marketing administration	147
Provision for bad debts	—
Research and development	30
Financial	68
Information resource management	47
Administration management	56
Total functional expenses	940
Total operating expenses	1,813
Operating profit	490

and the general economics of distribution. Outside the two production centres, demand was dispersed and delivery distances long.

Distributor salesmen were virtually all paid a straight commission on sales, and were responsible for selling a wide variety of products in addition to S.C. Johnson's. Several of the distributors had sales levels much higher than Innochem.

For Innochem, the impact of geography was compounded by a significant freight cost advantage: piggybacking industrial cleaning chemicals with SCJ consumer goods. In Ontario, for example, the cost of SCJ to a distributor was 30 percent above private label, while the differential in British Columbia was only 8 percent. On lower value products, the "freight effect" was even more pronounced.

SCJ had neither the salesmen nor the delivery capabilities to reach large-volume end users who demanded heavy selling effort or frequent shipments of small quantities. Furthermore, it was unlikely that SCJ could develop the necessary selling and distribution strength economically, given the narrowness of the division's range of janitorial products (i.e., industrial cleaning chemicals only).

THE REBATE PLAN

The key strategic problem facing Innochem was how best to challenge the direct marketer (and private label distributor) for large-volume, price-sensitive customers with heavy service requirements, particularly in markets where SCJ had no freight advantage. In this connection George had observed:

> Our gravest weakness is our inability to manage the total margin between the manufactured cost and consumer price in a way that is equitable and sufficiently profitable to support the investment and expenses of both the distributors and ourselves.
>
> Our prime competition across Canada is from direct-selling national and regional manufacturers. These companies control both the manufacturing and distribution gross margins. Under our pricing system, the distributor's margin at end user list on sales is 43 percent. Our margin (the manufacturing margin) is 50 percent on sales. When these margins are combined, as in the case of direct-selling manufacturers, the margin becomes 70 percent at list. This long margin provides significant price flexibility in a price-competitive marketplace. We must find a way to profitably attack the direct marketer's 61 percent market share.

The rebate plan George was now evaluating had been devised to meet the competition head-on. "Profitable partnership" between Innochem and the distributors was the underlying philosophy of the plan. Rebates offered a means to "share fairly the margins available between factory cost and consumer price." Whenever competitive conditions required a distributor to discount the resale list price by 30 percent or more, SCJ would give a certain percentage of the wholesale price back to the distributor. In other words, SCJ would sacrifice part of its margin to help offset a heavy end-user discount. Rebate percentages would vary with the rate of discount, following a set schedule. Different schedules were to be established for each product type and size. Exhibits 5, 6, and 7 outline the effect of rebates on both the unit gross margins of SCJ and individual distributors for a specific product example.

The rebate plan was designed to be applicable to new, "incremental" business only, not to existing accounts of the distributor. Distributors would be required to seek SCJ approval for end-user discounts of over

EXHIBIT 5 Distributors' Rebate Pricing Schedule: An Example Using Pronto Floor Wax

Code: 04055
Product description: Pronto Fast-Dry Finish
Size: 209-Litre
Pack: 1

EFF. DATE: 03-31-81
Resale Price List 71 613.750
Distributor Price List 74 349.837
Percent Markup on Cost with Carload and Rebate

	Quote	Rebate		2%		3%		4%		5%	
Discount Percent[1]	*(federal sales tax included)*[2]	*Percent*[3]	*Dealers*[4]	*Net*[5]	*Markup Percent*[6]	*Net*	*Markup Percent*	*Net*	*Markup Percent*	*Net*	*Markup Percent*
30.0	429.63	8.0	27.99	314.85	36	311.35	38	307.86	40	304.36	41
35.0	398.94	12.0	41.98	300.86	33	297.36	34	293.86	36	290.36	27
40.0	368.25	17.0	59.47	283.37	30	279.87	32	276.37	33	272.87	35
41.0	362.11	17.5	61.22	281.62	29	278.12	30	274.62	32	271.12	34
42.0	355.98	18.0	62.97	279.87	27	276.37	29	272.87	30	269.37	32
43.0	349.84	18.5	64.72	278.12	26	274.62	27	271.12	29	267.63	31
44.0	343.70	19.0	66.47	276.37	24	272.87	26	269.37	28	265.88	29
45.0	337.56	20.0	69.97	272.87	24	269.37	25	265.88	27	262.38	29
46.0	331.43	20.5	71.72	271.12	22	267.63	24	264.13	25	260.63	27
47.0	325.29	21.0	73.47	269.37	21	265.88	22	262.38	24	258.88	26
48.0	319.15	21.5	75.21	267.63	19	264.13	21	260.63	22	257.13	24
49.0	313.01	22.0	76.96	265.88	18	262.38	19	258.88	21	255.38	23
50.0	306.88	23.0	80.46	262.38	17	258.88	19	255.38	20	251.88	22
51.0	300.74	24.0	83.96	258.88	16	255.38	18	251.88	19	248.38	21
52.0	294.60	25.0	87.46	255.38	15	251.88	17	248.38	19	244.89	20
53.0	288.46	26.0	90.96	251.88	15	248.38	16	244.89	18	241.39	19
54.0	282.33	28.0	97.95	244.89	15	241.39	17	237.89	19	234.39	20
55.0	276.19	30.0	104.95	237.89	16	234.39	18	230.89	20	227.39	21

1 Discount extended to end user on resale list price.
2 Resale price at given discount level (includes federal sales tax).
3 Percentage of distributor's price ($613.75) rebated by SCJ.
4 Actual dollar amount of rebate by SCJ.
5 Actual net cost to distributor after deduction of rebate and "carload" (quantity) discount.
6 Effective rate of distributor markup.

EXHIBIT 6 Effect of Rebate Plan on Manufacturer and Distributor Margins: The Example of One 209-Litre Pack of Pronto Floor Finish Retailed at 40 Percent below Resale List Price

I. Under present arrangements	
Base price to distributor	$349.84
Price to distributor, assuming 2 percent carload discount*	342.84
SCJ cost	174.92
∴ SCJ margin	$167.92
Resale list price	613.75
Resale list price minus 40 percent discount	368.25
Distributor price, assuming 2 percent carload discount	342.84
∴ Distributor's margin	$ 25.41
II. Under rebate plan	
Rebate to distributor giving 40 percent discount off resale price amounted to 17 percent distributor's base price	$ 59.47
SCJ margin (minus rebate)	108.45
Distributor margin (plus rebate)	84.88
III. Competitive prices	
For this example, George estimated that a distributor could buy a private brand "comparable" product for approximately $244.	

* A form of quantity discount, which, in this case, drops the price the distributor pays to SCJ from $349.84 to $342.84.

30 percent or more of resale list. The maximum allowable end-user discount would rarely exceed 50 percent. To request rebate payments, distributors would send SCJ a copy of the resale invoice along with a written claim. The rebate would then be paid within 60 days. Currently, Innochem sales were sold by distributors at an average discount of 10 percent off list.

Proponents of the plan maintained that the resulting resale price flexibility would not only enhance Innochem competitiveness among end users but would also diminish distributor attraction to private label.

As he studied the plan, George questioned whether all the implications were fully understood and wondered what other strategies, if any, might increase urban market penetration. Any plan he devised would have to be sold to distributors as well as to corporate management. George had only three weeks to develop an appropriate action plan.

EXHIBIT 7 Effect of End User Discount Level on Manufacturer and Distributor Margins under Proposed Rebate Plan: The Example of One 209-Litre Pack of Pronto Fast-Dry Finish*

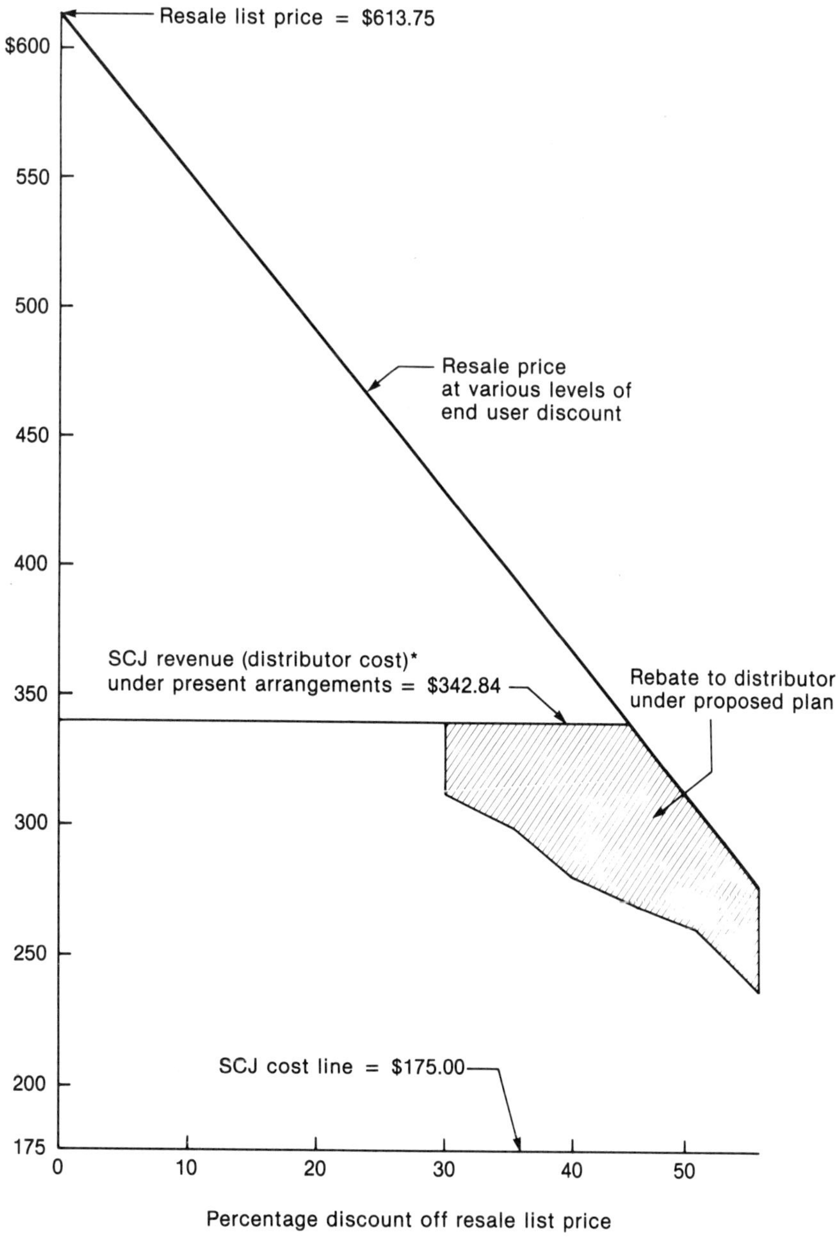

* Assuming 2 percent quantity ("carload") discount off price to distributor.

Case 25

*Island Shores**

Cynthia J. Frey
Boston College

In February 1982, Tom Smith, vice president and project manager of Enterprise Developers, Inc., was contemplating marketing alternatives available to the firm and the associated risks inherent in real estate development during such turbulent economic times. As Mr. Smith sat in his St. Petersburg, Florida, office trying to organize his thoughts and the market information at his disposal in some meaningful fashion, he was well aware that should the firm act on his recommendation, tens of millions of dollars would be at stake. Within the firm Smith was known for his good insights and solid judgment. While his previous decisions had successful outcomes, there was no guarantee that he was immune from mistakes and in this business mistakes were costly. Corporate expectations to meet a target return on investment of 18 percent, added to the pressure that the selected project be more than marginally successful. The final plan to be submitted to the board of directors would have to include consideration of the designated target market, site selection, and architectural design requirements as well as price and promotional strategy.

COMPANY BACKGROUND

The history of Enterprise Developers was characterized by risk taking and an unusually high rate of success. The firm was founded by three businessmen from New York who had grown up in one of the worst boroughs in the city. They had banded together in the late 1950s to renovate and refurbish a neighborhood tenement building. After buying the burned-out shell from the city for $1,000 they rebuilt it themselves with sweat equity into a model example of low-income housing worth several hundred thousand dollars. The group invested the profits from the sale of this building into other pieces of real estate. Middle-

* This case was written by Cynthia J. Frey, Assistant Professor of Marketing, Boston College, and Maria Sannella as a basis for class discussion rather than to illustrate either effective or ineffective handling of an administrative situation.

income housing, apartment buildings, and townhouses followed. With each renovation success the profits were reinvested in more property. The group was always alert to a new opportunity.

Encouraged by a friend and the possibility of more lucrative ventures, the trio moved to Miami in 1969. The next five years were spent developing rental units in the central city area. Close to the major business district, these mid-rise style buildings provided convenient access to the city for office workers. The skills that Enterprise acquired in New York City developing high density, urban living units were equally successful in Miami.

During this time period extensive condominum development was occurring along Florida's east coast, particularly in the Fort Lauderdale area. Two of the primary groups of buyers were retirees desiring low maintenance home ownership in a warm climate, and investment buyers who might spend three or four weeks a year in their unit and rent the remaining weeks to Florida vacationers looking for an alternative to high-price, crowded hotel accommodations. While this was a time of extraordinary growth for east coast condominium building, with units being sold before construction was even started, little of this development was occurring on the west side of the state.

In an attempt to take advantage of the condominium boom in the early 1970s, Enterprise investigated possible sites throughout the Florida peninsula but found most of the areas best suited to resort or retirement communities vastly overpriced or unavailable. One alternative which caught the trio's interest was a so-called spoil spot in Boca Ciega Bay, 350 miles from Miami between St. Petersburg and Clearwater. From dredging operations by the Army Corps of Engineers, a 320-acre island had been formed. Two bridges connected the island with the northernmost portions of the city of St. Petersburg 25 minutes away by car. The island was comprised of coarse bottom sand from the Bay. Vegetation was sparse and uncultivated giving the area a decidedly remote and desolate atmosphere.

The 320-acre island was offered for sale by a prominent insurance company. Although friends and business associates advised against the acquisition of the parcel for the planned high amenity community, Enterprise purchased the site for $18 million. While clarification of zoning ordinances was the first concern for the developers, taming the wilderness to support human creature comforts would be a time-consuming task.

ST. PETERSBURG AREA

St. Petersburg is known for its mild temperatures and beautiful year-round weather. According to the local paper, the *St. Petersburg Independent,* 361 days of sunshine per year are guaranteed. On days when the sun does not appear by 3 P.M., the newspaper distributes the afternoon edition free of charge. Since 1910, only 30 editions have been given away. The record for consecutive days with sunshine is 546.

St. Petersburg, the fourth largest city in Florida, is located on the southern tip of the Pinellas Peninsula. This point of land takes its name from the Spanish Punta Pinales or Point of the Pine Trees. Tampa Bay is on the east and to the south; the Gulf of Mexico on the west. St. Petersburg Beach, on Long Key, is one of the Holiday Isles, a ribbon of keys separated from the mainland and St. Petersburg by Boca Ciega Bay. (See Exhibit 1.)

Although the Spanish explorer Narvaez landed on the peninsula in 1528 and marched to Tampa Bay, John C. Williams of Detroit is credited as the city's founder. Williams acquired 1,700 acres of wilderness land in 1876 which later became the nucleus of downtown St. Petersburg. Williams's intention was to establish a resort community to take advantage of the fine weather. However, his remote location had no transportation connection with other Florida population centers. As a result, he agreed to a partnership with Russian exile Piotr Alexeitch Dementieff (a.k.a. Peter Demens) contingent on Demens's completion of a railroad trunk line into the area.

The Orange Belt Line from Lake Monroe near Sanford, Florida, was completed in 1888 when Williams's little community had a population of 30. As the story goes, Williams and Demens flipped a coin to decide who would name the new town. Demens won and elected to name the town St. Petersburg after his birthplace. Williams's resort hotel, completed around 1890, was fittingly named The Detroit.

As early as 1885 the American Medical Association praised the climate and healthful surroundings as ideal. With its accessibility improved by the Orange Belt Line, the population had climbed to 300 by 1892 when the town was incorporated. Many of the early settlers were British who had emigrated to the Bahamas and Key West. In an effort to expand the resort reputation of St. Petersburg, the Chamber of Commerce established its first promotional budget of $150 in 1902. In 1907 a special tax was levied on year-round residents to support tourist promotion.

Today, thousands of people arrive daily at the Tampa International Airport which also serves St. Petersburg and Clearwater. Considered one of the most modern and efficient airports in the world, Tampa International has shuttle trains from the main terminal to the gates, an assortment of restaurants and boutiques, and a hotel with a revolving penthouse. Fifteen major air carriers fly into the airport, many with international routes to Central and South America and Europe.

St. Petersburg is also known as the Boating Capital of the United States. With boating activity supported by the Municipal Marina downtown and the St. Petersburg Yacht Club, St. Petersburg is home

EXHIBIT 1

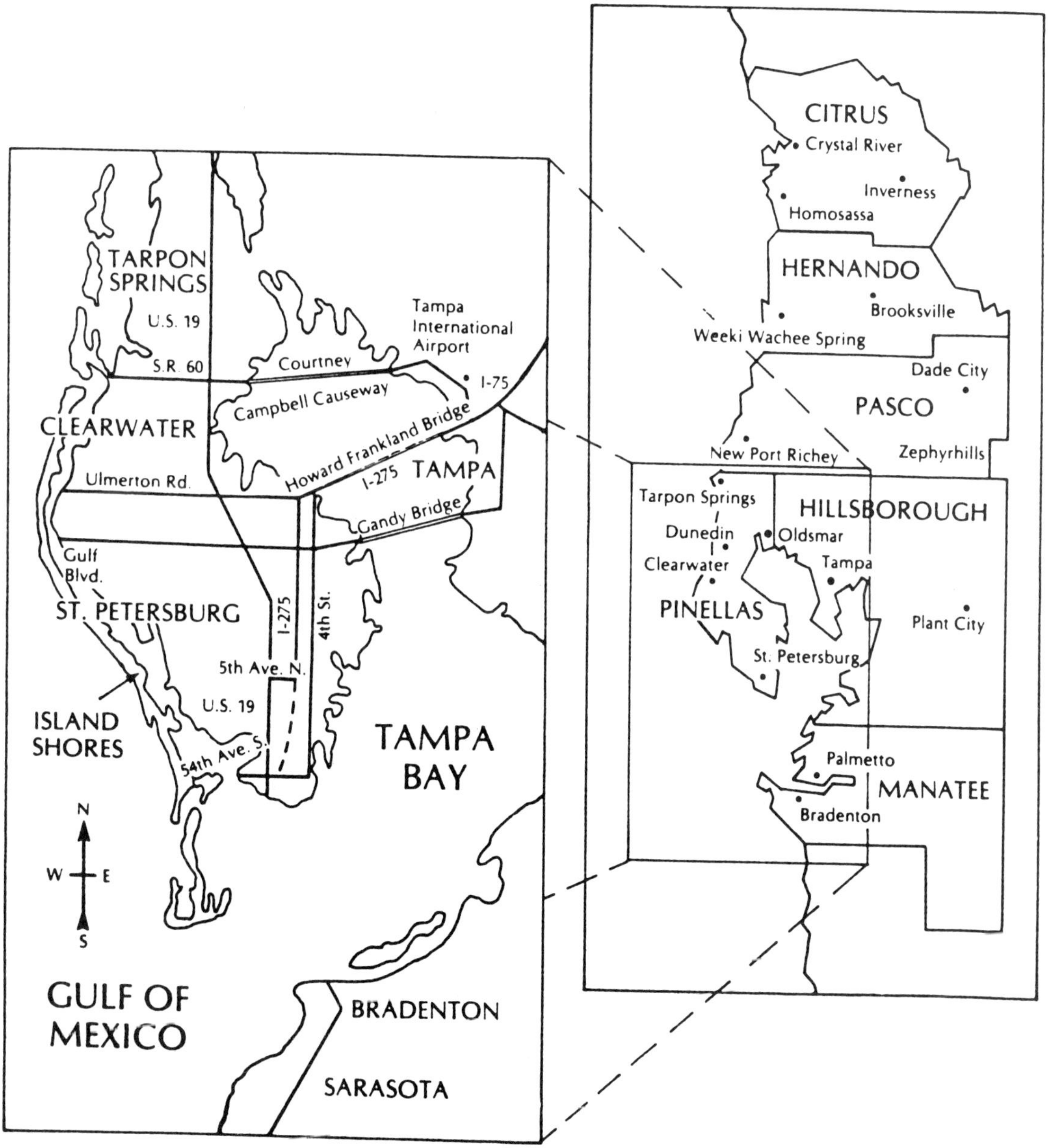
TARPON
SPRINGS
U.S. 19
S.R. 60
Courtney
Tampa
International
Airport
I-75
Campbell Causeway
CLEARWATER
Howard Frankland Bridge
I-275
TAMPA
Ulmerton Rd.
Gandy Bridge
Gulf
Blvd.
ST. PETERSBURG
I-275
4th St.
5th Ave. N.
U.S. 19
ISLAND
SHORES
54th Ave. S.
TAMPA
BAY
N
W
E
S
GULF OF
MEXICO
BRADENTON
SARASOTA
CITRUS
Crystal River
Inverness
Homosassa
HERNANDO
Brooksville
Weeki Wachee Spring
Dade City
PASCO
New Port Richey
Zephyrhills
Tarpon Springs
HILLSBOROUGH
Dunedin
Oldsmar
Clearwater
Tampa
PINELLAS
Plant City
St. Petersburg
Palmetto
MANATEE
Bradenton

EXHIBIT 2 Population and Population Characteristics Change, 1970 to 1979

	Metro Area		
	April 1, 1979 Population	*Percent of Total*	*Percent Change Since 1970*
Total population	1,521,799	100.0%	+39.8%
0–14 years	285,296	18.8	+14.7
15–24 years	217,866	14.3	+43.3
25–44 years	323,700	21.3	+51.2
45–64 years	338,423	22.2	+38.4
65 and over	356,514	23.4	+55.6
18 and over	1,165,496	76.6	+47.9
Median age	40.9 years	—	+2.5 years
White	1,385,288	91.0%	+42.5%
Nonwhite	136,511	9.0	+17.2
Male	716,075	47.1%	+39.1%
Female	805,724	52.9	+40.4

	Pinellas			*Pasco*			*Hillsborough*		
	April 1, 1979 Population	*Percent of Total*	*Percent Change Since 1970*	*April 1, 1979 Population*	*Percent of Total*	*Percent Change Since 1970*	*April 1, 1979 Population*	*Percent of Total*	*Percent Change Since 1970*
Total population	725,457	100.0%	+38.9%	161,873	100.0%	+113.1%	634,469	100.0%	+ 29.4%
0–14 years	112,546	15.5	+14.8	25,662	15.9	+ 93.7	147,088	23.2	+ 7.0
15–24 years	82,771	11.4	+40.1	17,515	10.8	+111.6	117,580	18.5	+ 38.8
25–44 years	129,227	17.8	+49.0	23,962	14.8	+122.1	170,511	26.9	+ 46.3
45–64 years	171,011	23.6	+37.3	39,528	24.4	+101.5	127,884	20.2	+ 27.4
65 and over	229,902	31.7	+49.4	55,206	34.1	+129.8	71,406	11.2	+ 39.5
18 and over	584,955	80.6	+45.5	130,413	80.6	+117.6	450,128	70.9	+ 38.1
Median age	49.5 years	—	+1.4 years	52.0 years	—	−1.4 years	31.2 years	—	+2.7 years
White	671,331	92.5%	+40.4%	157,783	97.5%	+119.4%	556,174	87.7%	+ 31.8
Nonwhite	54,126	7.5	+22.2	4,090	2.5	+ 1.5	78,295	12.3	+ 14.9
Male	334,017	46.0%	+38.9%	77,599	47.9%	+110.7%	304,459	48.0%	+ 28.1
Female	391,440	54.0	+38.8	84,274	52.1	+115.4%	330,010	52.0	+ 30.6

	Manatee			*Citrus*			*Hernando*		
	April 1, 1979 Population	*Percent of Total*	*Percent Change Since 1970*	*April 1, 1979 Population*	*Percent of Total*	*Percent Change Since 1970*	*April 1, 1979 Population*	*Percent of Total*	*Percent Change Since 1970*
Total population	141,188	100.0%	+45.4%	42,397	100.0%	+120.9%	38,182	100.0%	+124.5%
0–14 years	23,837	16.9	+27.2	7,155	16.9	+ 85.1	7,399	19.4	+ 73.8
15–24 years	15,049	10.6	+37.1	3,717	8.8	+ 81.7	4,166	10.9	+ 93.8
25–44 years	24,504	17.4	+58.1	6,215	14.6	+113.4	7,104	18.6	+120.7
45–64 years	33,874	24.0	+50.1	11,909	28.1	+121.4	10,268	26.9	+161.9
65 and over	43,924	31.1	+49.8	13,401	31.6	+168.4	9,245	24.2	+167.4
18 and over	112,346	80.0	+51.3	33,869	79.9	+134.5	29,253	76.6	+144.9
Median age	49.2 years	—	+.5 years	51.9 years	—	+2.8 years	45.8 years	—	+7.6 years
White	128,068	90.7%	+50.1%	40,622	95.8%	+134.3%	35,833	93.8%	+146.1%
Nonwhite	13,120	9.3	+11.5	1,775	4.2	− 4.4	2,349	6.2	− 3.9
Male	66,700	47.2%	+46.7%	20,397	48.1%	+119.9%	18,833	49.3%	+125.7%
Female	74,488	52.8	+44.2	22,000	51.9	+121.8%	19,349	50.7	+123.5

Source: University of Florida, Bureau of Economic and Business Research, "Age, Race, and Sex Components of Florida Population—1979," and 1970 Census. Prepared by Research Department, *St. Petersburg Times* and *Evening Independent,* May 1980.

base to some of the most important sailboat and power boat races in the Gulf. The Swift Hurricane Classic, Isla de Mujeres Race, and the Southern Ocean Racing Conference championships represent the highlights of the season.

Fishing is also a favorite pastime in St. Petersburg where people can be seen lining the bridges fishing late into the night. Golf courses are widely available as are tennis courts.

While St. Petersburg has become a preferred retirement community for many, the city has tried to promote business development in the area to balance the population demographics. Since 1970, construction of new plants and plant expansions has totaled 1,196 and 19,005 new jobs have been created. Changes in population demographics in St. Petersburg and the surrounding counties between 1970 and 1979 are presented in Exhibit 2.

A survey of newcomers to the St. Petersburg area conducted by Suncoast Opinion Surveys in 1980 reveals some further information. This group of newcomers is considered to represent approximately 19 percent of the adult population in Pinellas County. Survey results are presented in Exhibit 3.

EXHIBIT 3 Demographic Profile of Pinellas Residents

		By Length of Residency		
	Total Pinellas Adults	*Newcomers (2 years or less)*	*Midterm Residents (3–10 years)*	*Long-Term Residents (over 10 years)*
Total population	100%	19%	35%	46%
Sex				
Male	45%	46%	51%	40%
Female	55	54	49	60
Age				
18–24 years	10%	25%	7%	6%
25–34 years	17	20	22	13
35–49 years	21	24	18	22
50–64 years	22	19	23	22
65–74 years	18	10	22	18
75 years and over	12	2	8	19
Median adult age (years)	51.4	38.1	52.0	56.1
Where born:*				
Pinellas County	8%	1%	1%	16%
Other Florida	5	7	4	5
Northeast	32	31	37	29
Midwest	31	35	31	29
South	15	17	14	14
West	3	3	4	2
Outside United States	6	6	9	5

EXHIBIT 3 *(continued)*

	Total Pinellas Adults	By Length of Residency: Newcomers (2 years or less)	Midterm Residents (3–10 years)	Long-Term Residents (over 10 years)
Education				
Grammar school	4%	1%	4%	6%
Some high school	11	6	12	12
High school graduate	34	28	32	37
Technical, business school graduate	7	8	8	7
Some college	21	24	21	20
College graduate	23	33	23	18
Employment status				
Employed full time	43%	56%	46%	35%
Employed part time	7	5	7	7
Temporarily out of work	3	6	1	3
Retired	32	19	35	34
Housewife	11	11	7	15
Disabled	2	1	3	3
Other	2	2	1	3
Women				
Employed outside home	40%	49%	41%	36%
Not employed outside home	60	51	59	64
Household income				
Under $10,000	23%	21%	18%	28%
$10,000–$15,000	18	24	16	17
$15,000–$20,000	19	12	23	19
Over $20,000	40	43	43	36
Median	$17,400	$17,100	$18,500	$16,300
Own/rent residence				
Own, with mortgage	47%	37%	52%	47%
Own, no mortgage	33	19	32	40
Rent	19	42	15	13
Other	1	2	1	†
Type of residence				
Single family	69%	53%	68%	77%
Apartment	11	19	10	7
Condominium	9	11	10	7
Mobile home	9	11	10	7
Other	2	6	2	2
Household size				
1 person	21%	14%	16%	26%
2 persons	41	45	48	35
3 persons	13	15	9	14
4 persons	15	15	15	16

EXHIBIT 3 *(continued)*

	Total Pinellas Adults	By Length of Residency		
		Newcomers (2 years or less)	*Midterm Residents (3–10 years)*	*Long-Term Residents (over 10 years)*
5 or more persons	10	11	12	9
Average	2.5	2.6	2.6	2.5
Children present in household				
No children present	69%	68%	69%	69%
Child(ren) present	31	32	31	31
Race				
White	96%	97%	98%	94%
Nonwhite	4	3	2	6
Household income sources				
Wages/salaries only	40%	53%	39%	36%
Wage/salary and other regular sources‡	25	21	26	26
Other regular sources only	34	26	34	37
No income sources	1	—	1	1
Number of wage earners in household				
None	35%	26%	35%	39%
One wage earner	31	30	33	30
Two wage earners	26	36	19	27
Three wage earners	6	6	11	2
Four or more	2	2	2	2
Average	1.1	1.3	1.1	1.0
Residence				
North of Ulmerton Road	43%	55%	44%	37%
South of Ulmerton Road	57	45	56	63
Daily newspapers read regularly				
St. Petersburg Times	83%	83%	82%	84%
Evening Independent	22	15	18	27
Clearwater Sun	23	23	28	20
Tampa Tribune	3	6	4	2
Other	3	4	2	3
None	4	3	3	5
Daily newspapers read yesterday				
St. Petersburg Times	67%	59%	68%	69%
Evening Independent	16	11	8	23
Clearwater Sun	18	18	21	15
Tampa Tribune	2	3	2	2
Other	1	1	—	2
None	15	21	13	14
Sunday newspaper read last Sunday				
St. Petersburg Times	74%	72%	70%	78%
Clearwater Sun	17	16	19	15
Tampa Tribune	1	2	2	—

EXHIBIT 3 *(concluded)*

	Total Pinellas Adults	By Length of Residency: Newcomers (2 years or less)	Midterm Residents (3–10 years)	Long-Term Residents (over 10 years)
Broadcast media				
Watched television yesterday:				
6:00–8:59 A.M.	8%	7%	6%	8%
9:00–10:59 A.M.	10	7	10	11
Noon–5:59 P.M.	34	37	27	35
6:00–8:59 P.M.	67	66	70	65
9:00–10:59 P.M.	61	63	63	59
11:00 P.M. or later	30	26	30	31
Don't know when watched	1	—	2	1
Did not watch TV yesterday	11%	13%	8%	13%
Subscriber to cable TV	11	11	14	9
Not cable TV subscriber	89	89	86	91
Listened to radio yesterday:				
6:00–8:59 A.M.	34%	39%	38%	30%
9:00–11:59 A.M.	28	28	29	26
Noon–5:59 P.M.	32	27	37	31
6:00–8:59 P.M.	15	13	14	16
9:00–10:59 P.M.	9	2	11	10
11:00 P.M. or later	7	2	10	8
Don't know when listened	2	2	1	3
Did not listen to radio yesterday	37	38	34	40
Checking account	90%	92%	91%	88%
Savings account	89%	82%	92%	90%
At bank	74	76	77	71
At savings and loan	43	34	38	51
At credit union	26	21	30	24
MasterCard or Visa	55%	56%	59%	52%
MasterCard	36	39	41	31
Visa	46	48	46	45
Other credit cards:				
American Express	10%	18%	13%	6%
Diners Club	3	4	4	2
Carte Blanche	2	2	3	2
Passport	18	11	22	18
Base	(501)	(93)	(175)	(233)

* *Northeast* includes Connecticut, Maine, Massachusetts, New Hampshire, New Jersey, New York, Pennsylvania, Rhode Island, and Vermont.

Midwest includes Illinois, Indiana, Iowa, Kansas, Michigan, Minnesota, Missouri, Nebraska, North Dakota, Ohio, South Dakota, and Wisconsin.

South includes Alabama, Arkansas, Delaware, Washington, D.C., Georgia, Kentucky, Louisiana, Maryland, Mississippi, North Carolina, Oklahoma, South Carolina, Tennessee, Texas, Virginia, and West Virginia.

West includes Alaska, Arizona, California, Colorado, Hawaii, Idaho, Montana, Nevada, New Mexico, Oregon, Utah, Washington, and Wyoming.

† Less than one half of 1 percent.

‡ Other regular sources = Other than wages and salaries; includes social security, dividends, interest, alimony, child support, disability, pension, welfare, or other benefits.

BACKGROUND ON ISLAND SHORES

Management at Enterprise was convinced that careful planning and gradual development would be critical to the success of the Island Shores project given their previous experience. In order to appeal to both retiree and second-home vacationers, Island Shores had to represent a distinct combination of benefits. While many of the Florida condominium complexes were just places to hang one's hat and residents were dependent on the Ft. Lauderdale or Miami communities for things to do and places to go, the location of Island Shores required that many of these entertainment and recreation options be available on the island. Enterprise's plan called for development of the following amenities: angling, beaches, golf, jogging and bicycle paths, open areas, clubhouse and restaurant, sailing, shopping, sunbathing, swimming pools, tennis and racquetball courts, and water skiing. In order to attract buyers in the early stages of development at least some of these planned benefits had to be apparent, so the golf course and clubhouse went into construction immediately.

The plan for the island called for high density residential units to be built on the water's edge and a golf course in the center. Since the golf course was considered a major drawing feature, the problems associated with growing grass where none had grown before had to be faced immediately. In 1974 work on the golf course began at the same time as condominium construction. After several false starts and experimentation with many varieties of grass, ground-covers, and shrubs, reasonably well-manicured greens appeared three years later. It became painfully clear that landscaping a "spoil spot" would take perseverance, patience, and a great deal of money. Costs associated with construction of the golf course alone totaled a million dollars.

Michele Perez, an award-winning architect from California, was responsible for designing the residential structures in harmony with the island environment. Due to the priority given the 18-hole golf course in the 320-acre parcel and the desire to maximize picturesque views from each condo unit, the residential development plan called for high density construction along the water's edge. The land utilization goal of 14 condominiums per acre was met by Perez's plan for positioning units diagonally to the water rather than lining them up parallel to the beach frontage in traditional fashion. These clusters form miniature neighborhoods while maximizing ocean views. For each cluster a swimming pool and sunbathing deck was constructed which acts as a social gathering spot and provides a recreational area with a relatively large amount of privacy. The large "community pool" concept was considered by Enterprise to be unappealing to many potential residents who were expected to value easy access to the pool's ambience more than its Olympic proportions. Resident parking was designed underneath the buildings to minimize the asphalt perspective so typical of high density living environments.

Four-story and 12-story high-rise units, 2-story townhouses, and free-standing condominium villas were constructed. The units in greatest demand between 1975 and 1980 were villas. Many of them sold before construction was even begun. Two-bedroom units in the mid- and high-rise buildings were also very popular. One-bedroom high-rise units and townhouses were still available although on a limited basis. The primary construction materials were stucco and wood which blended with the Spanish architectural influence throughout the St. Petersburg area. As each building was completed, landscaping was carefully undertaken. The landscape architects working for Enterprise were sent to Disney World in Orlando to study plantings. Using similar shrubs which could adapt to conditions at Island Shores, sculptured shrubs and ever-blooming varieties of plants created a garden atmosphere. In 1981 alone, the cost of landscaping approached $1.5 million not counting individual building phases.

In 1975 the condominiums on Island Shores ranged in price from $42,000 to $50,000. The average market value of these units for resale in 1982 was $108,034. Smith's records showed that in December 1981, 70 units had been sold for a total of $7,562,389. Overall, new sales in 1980 were $32 million and sales in 1981 were $34 million. Prices for units still under construction in the Colony Beach portion of the project as of 1982 are shown in Exhibit 4.

Prices vary for the models depending on what floor they are on in the building and their relative exposure. Each unit has its own balcony, carpeting, a full set of appliances, and assigned parking. Two bedroom-two bath models had been the most in demand with different square

EXHIBIT 4

Colony Beach (6 story)

Model	*Size*	*Price*
Madrid	1 bedroom—1½ bath	$70,000–$ 92,900
Sevilla	2 bedroom—2 bath	$90,900–$125,000
Villa	2 bedroom—2 bath	$86,900–$107,000

Colony Beach (12 story)

Model	*Size*	*Price*
Barcelona	2 bedroom—2 bath	$133,000–$162,000
Sevilla	2 bedroom—2 bath	$135,000–$166,000
Villa	2 bedroom—2 bath	$110,000–$117,000

footage and floor plans distinguishing Sevilla, Villa, and Barcelona models. Recent prices at Island Shores for villas had been in the range of $79,000 to $112,000, mid-rise units from $70,000 to $150,000, and high-rise units $95,000 to $166,000. Smith was concerned that as costs escalated the project was being priced out of the reach of most people in the market for vacation homes. While the number of one-bedroom units could be increased, in the future they did not appear to be the most desirable. He wondered if square footage in the two bedroom-two bath models could be reduced further or if the target market should be narrowed to primary home buyers rather than including vacation home buyers. This would have implications for the physical design of the units and the required storage space. The Colony Beach area with a planned 1,200 units was not scheduled for completion until 1988. Based on previous experience, it was currently estimated that the 340 units, as yet unsold, would be fully occupied by the end of 1984.

COMPETITION

Smith knew from friends in the business and his own observations that competitors' sales had declined in recent months. While he felt Island Shores was more desirable than similar high-rise condominium units located on the Intracoastal Waterway or the Mandalay Channel, he had collected pricing information hoping it would help him develop his marketing plan. In general, unit square footage ranges from 950 to 1,450 and the selling price from $77 to $115 per square foot. Exhibit 5 presents data for projects comparable to the units in Colony Beach.

It was clear that the development firms behind the competition were aggressive and unlikely to give market share to Island Shores without a battle. Smith didn't know for sure how they would respond to the recent market downturn, but he suspected it would be through strengthened promotional efforts. It was likely that the promotion budget for the Colony Beach community would have to be increased just to keep pace with the competition and maintain the build-out schedule for 1984–85.

BUYER PROFILES

In 1975 the average age of Island Shores condominium buyers was 58. More recently, the average age had decreased to approximately 52 with many buyers in their late 40s. Smith was unsure how to interpret this trend. During the early stages of development, many retirees and investment buyers came from Illinois, Ohio, and Michigan. As economic conditions in these areas worsened, fewer and fewer newcomers

EXHIBIT 5 Competitive Prices

Marina Walk

Model	*Description*	*Price Range*	*Units/ Building*
J	2 bedroom—2 bath	$125,000-$150,000	20
K	2 bedroom—den—2 bath	$140,000-$165,000	20
L	2 bedroom—2 bath	$112,500-$142,000	20
M	1 bedroom—1½ bath	$ 90,000-$110,000	20
NE	2 bedroom—2 bath	$155,000-$185,000	20
NW	2 bedroom—2 bath	$167,500-$202,500	20

Sailfish Key

Model	*Description*	*Price Range*	*Units Building*
Sunfish	1 bedroom—1 bath	$ 97,900-$ 99,900	6
Yacht	1 bedroom—1½ bath	$110,000-$126,400	10
Corsair	2 bedroom—2 bath	$136,500-$149,500	12
Brigantine	2 bedroom—2 bath	$167,000-$175,000	6
Galleon	2 bedroom—2 bath*	$171,000-$179,500	10
Frigate	2 bedroom—2 bath—den	$215,000	2
Clipper	3 bedroom—2½ bath	$270,000	2

* Corner.

seemed to come from the Midwest. To Smith's surprise, an increasing number of European and South Americans were coming to Island Shores over any number of other condominium areas. It seemed that there were growing numbers of buyers from West Germany, France, Venezuela, Argentina, and Mexico. Each nationality tended to cluster together at Island Shores and to maintain close social ties. Whether this pattern would present problems in the long run for the total community was unclear.

A growing concern voiced by condominium residents was the issue of security. The small groupings of units actually facilitated security since neighbors knew each other's comings and goings and watched out for one another. The problem seemed to be caused by transients. When investment buyers rented their condominiums long distance they could exercise very little control over their tenants. Similarly, management at Island Shores had scant information about renters and no power to intervene unless explicit rules and regulations were being violated. Compared to other condominium developments in the St. Petersburg area the relative crime rate at Island Shores was very low. St. Petersburg itself had little crime compared to other major cities like Miami. Smith began to wonder whether the residents' perceptions of security were more at issue than the occasional burglary. Since one of the objectives of the management was to create an atmosphere of stability in a relaxing environment, any tensions caused by real or imagined security problems would have to be resolved.

Smith wondered if there was some way to encourage more permanent residents and fewer speculative investors to minimize the transient issue. If security personnel were increased it was not clear whether the result would be to alarm or calm the residents and potential buyers. As it had turned out so far, some of the individuals sampling life at Island Shores by renting from absentee owners eventually purchased units on the island although the number of such individuals was small.

MARKETING DECISIONS

Before Smith could recommend a marketing program he needed to establish the basic target market and whether or not to continue building at Island Shores. Secondary data showed that more people leave New York for the South every year than any other state. If this market was to be reached, however, there would be a lengthy process of registering Enterprise with New York state authorities in order to promote land sales to New York residents. Smith estimated this process would take about a year. Enterprise was already registered in Michigan, Illinois, Indiana, Ohio, and Pennsylvania.

Another possible market was comprised of people already in the St. Petersburg area. Considering the escalation of land values in recent years, many individuals could sell their existing property for twice its purchase price. In this event the extensive amenity package at Island Shores, offering both quality golf and boating, might prove very attractive. Promotional efforts would certainly be reduced in reaching this market segment, Smith thought.

The international market seemed to be one of growing importance. If this market was actively pursued, the cost and methods of reaching buyers were difficult to determine. The long-run potential of this market was unclear. Smith became even more unsure as he thought about international currency fluctuations and the recent devaluation of the peso.

Expanding on the plan for development at Island Shores was by far the easiest plan of action to adopt in the short run but Smith wondered if perhaps a lower amenity package with a golf course but no ocean access might not recapture the midwest market. He knew of projects such as The Westside near Tampa Airport which concentrated on patio homes, both attached and detached, with prices from $45,000 to $70,000. The patio home concept was relatively new. There was no yard to speak of with the house, just the fenced patio. In some parts of the country they were known as zero-lot homes. They offered single-family housing with very low maintenance which might prove appealing to retirees and young families. Patio homes had gained acceptance as starter homes for young couples and there seemed to be encouragement to expand the target market.

A parcel of 200 acres just east of Bradenton in Manatee County was available for purchase which might prove suitable. With the lower yield per acre of about 6 units compared to 14 units per acre at Island Shores, Smith felt there would be a potential 350–380 units with the remaining land used for a golf course. While the price of the parcel was open to negotiation, the asking figure was $6 million. Smith had 10 days to pick up a 90-day option on this property. This would mean a commitment of $5,000.

If building was continued immediately at Island Shores, the mix of high-rise, mid-rise, and villas needed to be considered as did the two-bedroom and one-bedroom proportion. If prices were to be reduced, something would have to change. Existing plans called for development of the Ocean Watch portion of the project which was a mid-rise building series with 50 two- and three-bedroom condominum units from $175,000 to $260,000. This was a 1982 estimate, but completion was not scheduled until 1985 when prices would certainly be higher. The current plan called for surface preparation of the area beginning in 1983. If the market became highly price sensitive a potential option was to sell the units under a time-sharing arrangement. Smith knew that existing owners in Colony Beach had voiced objection to such a proposal earlier, but then again, Ocean Watch was a different situation. The target market for this type of vacation home would be a totally new one for Enterprise.

Smith realized that forecasting the demand for seasonal vacation homes versus year-round retirement homes was a critical issue that would strongly influence project location and physical design decisions. Until the best target market was identified, little in the way of price or promotional decisions could be resolved. The person interested in a $200,000 condominium would not likely be the same individual considering a $60,000 patio home.

Since the attributes and amenities of the projects would be very different, the promotional messages would also be very different. Smith was responsible for developing the overall marketing strategy for his projects and would make decisions on promotional strategy as well. A local advertising agency would handle the details of implementation such as art, collateral materials, production, and media buying.

Smith felt strongly that when the real estate market picked up, the Tampa–St. Petersburg area would be among the first to lead the upturn. It was difficult to determine, however, which segments of the market represented the best opportunities for Enterprise. As Smith tried to evaluate the different opportunities facing him, he knew that it was going to be a long weekend. Next Wednesday's board meeting would come all too soon.

Case Group F

Selected Issues in Marketing Management

Case 26

Tylenol*

Margaret L. Friedman
University of Wisconsin–Whitewater

Pain relievers are a lucrative, $1.2-billion-a-year industry. Until recently, there were no chemical or medicinal differences among brands of nonaspirin pain relievers, and so aggressive marketing was the key to gain market share. For example, in a recent year $130 million was spent on advertising for pain relievers. Johnson & Johnson, producer of Tylenol analgesic, developed very successful marketing strategies and obtained the largest share of the pain reliever market, 37 percent,

* This case was prepared by Margaret L. Friedman, Assistant Professor, School of Business, University of Wisconsin-Whitewater. Used by permission. Based on "Tylenol, the Painkiller, Gives Rivals Headache in Stores and in Court," *The Wall Street Journal,* September 2, 1982; "A Death Blow for Tylenol?", *Business Week,* October 18, 1982, p. 151; "The Fight to Save Tylenol," *Fortune,* November 29, 1982, pp. 44–49; "Rivals Go After Tylenol's Market, But Gains May Be Only Temporary," *The Wall Street Journal,* December 2, 1982, pp. 25ff.

in a matter of a few years. Then a tragedy threatened their strong position.

In 1959 Johnson & Johnson acquired McNeil Laboratories which had introduced the Tylenol brand in 1955 in the form of an elixir for children as an alternative to aspirin and its irritating side effects. Traditionally, Tylenol was sold "ethically," through physicians and pharmacists and not directly to end-use consumers. Specifically, it was sold only as a prescription drug until 1960, and then as a nonprescription drug advertised only to doctors and pharmacists, who, in turn, recommended it to patients.

In 1975 Bristol-Meyers introduced Datril, a nonaspirin pain reliever, and successfully marketed it directly to end users. Datril's success forced Johnson & Johnson to expand its marketing effort to end users. The company cut prices, formed a sales force, and spent $8 million on advertising in which Tylenol was represented as an alternative to aspirin. Tylenol's solid reputation among pharmacists and physicians gave it a definite competitive advantage with end-use consumers as it was perceived to be a safe product endorsed by health professionals. In fact, two of every three Tylenol customers started using the product because it was recommended by their doctors.

In 1976 Extra-Strength Tylenol was introduced and was the first product to contain 500 milligrams of painkiller per tablet. Market research had indicated that many consumers believed that Tylenol was too gentle to be effective. Extra-Strength Tylenol was advertised as the most "potent pain reliever available without a prescription." Tylenol's market share rose from 4 percent to 25 percent in 1979, due largely to the extra-strength version of the brand. In 1982 Tylenol had 37 percent market share as shown in Exhibit 1.

Competitors frantically tried to defend their brands against Tylenol. Excedrin, Anacin, and Bayer each introduced extra-strength versions of their brands, with little success. Datril turned out to be a noncontender in the fight for market share because of failure to build a favorable reputation among physicians and pharmacists. Tylenol seemed unbeatable. The product became the largest selling health and beauty aid, breaking the 18-year dominance of Procter & Gamble's Crest toothpaste.

Tylenol employed very aggressive competitive tactics in order to dominate the industry. For example, court litigation was a very important competitive strategy, since Johnson & Johnson took several competitors to court with claims of infringement on Tylenol's trademark and name. Tylenol found that through the use of litigation, competitors could be barred from active competition for up to two years. After that time the competition was in a weakened market position and seldom recovered. This strategy was especially effective against Anacin. Tylenol sued Anacin four times, once for trademark infringe-

EXHIBIT 1 Market Shares: Pain Reliever Industry

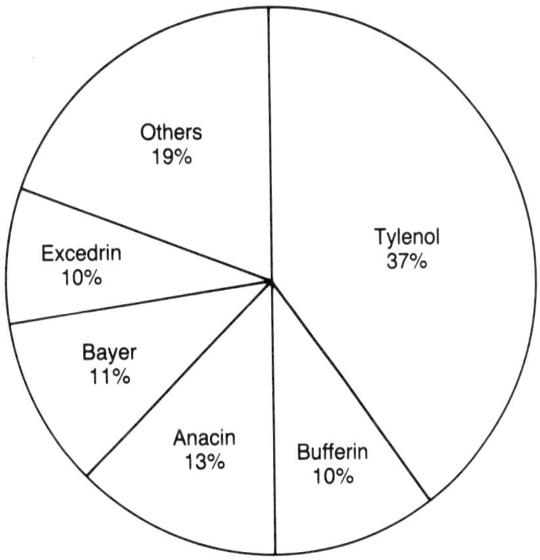

ment and three times for false advertising, and won each suit. One marketing expert went so far as to credit Johnson & Johnson with inventing the fifth "P" of marketing—plaintiff.

In the early fall of 1982 eight Chicago-area consumers of Extra-Strength Tylenol died tragically. These consumers had taken Tylenol capsules that had been tampered with and laced with cyanide. The coupling of the Tylenol name with the eight deaths caused Tylenol's market share to drop from 37 percent to 7 percent overnight.

Research indicated that many consumers had misconceptions about the poisoning incidents. For example, many consumers were not aware that (1) the company was absolved of all responsibility by the investigating authorities, (2) Tylenol's production process conformed to all safety standards, (3) only Tylenol capsules were involved, not tablets, and (4) the tragic deaths were confined to the Chicago area.

Tylenol's competitors benefited greatly from the tragedy. Anacin won about 25 percent of Tylenol's lost business, mainly by aggressively advertising Anacin-3, and Bufferin and Bayer each took 20 percent of Tylenol's business. Most experts predicted that the Tylenol brand would never recover. The situation was described as a consumer goods marketer's darkest nightmare.

Very soon after the crisis, Johnson & Johnson made a strategic decision to attempt to save the brand that had been so successful and profitable. The company had built up a reservoir of consumer trust and loyalty which management felt would play a key role in the Tylenol brand's recovery. The company had always tried to live up to the credo set for it in 1940s by its leader, General Robert Wood Johnson: "We believe our first responsibility is to the doctors, nurses, and patients, to mothers and all others who use our products and services. In meeting their needs, everything we do must be of high quality."[1] Company management interpreted the crisis as a monumental challenge to live up to this credo against overwhelming odds.

Discussion Questions

1. What tactics should Johnson & Johnson use to rebuild consumer trust in Tylenol?
2. What lessons are there for marketers of drug products in Tylenol's response to the crisis which resulted in the recovery of 90 percent of the lost market share in less than one year?
3. Should Johnson & Johnson have abandoned Tylenol and marketed a new brand?

---

[1] *The Wall Street Journal,* October 8, 1982.

Case 27

Denver Art Museum*

Patricia Stocker
University of Maryland

The Denver Art Museum, the major visual arts institution for the Rocky Mountain region, was founded as an artists' club in 1893. It had no collection and no permanent building. By 1932 it became the official art institution for Denver, but until 1971 the collection was divided among various locations, including an old mansion and a remodeled automobile showroom.

In 1971 the Denver Art Museum's spectacular six-story building was opened. The striking silver-gray structure, designed by Gio Ponti of Milan and James Sudler of Denver, was located near downtown in the city's Civic Center. The opening of that new building marked a significant boost to the visual arts of the area. According to Thomas N. Maytham, who became museum director in 1974, "In the new building, we had a doubled budget, a new board of trustees, quadrupled attendance, and a challenging question: How can we best use this building?"

The answer continued to change, but by most measures the museum had been very successful. The permanent collection numbered 35,000 objects valued at more than $70 million. The major areas in the collection were European Art, American Art, New World (including Pre-Columbian Art), Oriental Art, Native Arts (including American Indian Art), and Contemporary Art. The largest single area in the museum's collection was American Indian Art, which numbered more than 13,000 objects and was among the finest assemblages of its type in the world. It had been described as the finest collection of American Indian works in any art museum.

About twenty special circulating exhibitions were also shown at the museum each year. These were usually borrowed from other museums or from private collections. The exhibitions ranged in scope from the well-known Armand Hammer collection of European and American masterpieces and "Masterpieces of French Art" to "Art of the Muppets" and "Secret Splendors of the Chinese Court," a costume collection. (See

* This case was prepared by Professor Patricia Stocker of the University of Maryland. Used by permission.

EXHIBIT 1 Attendance at Selected Temporary Exhibitions (six-week showings)

Armand Hammer Collection	152,106
Masterpieces of French Art	56,836
The Art of the Muppets	115,531
Heritage of American Art	22,583
Frederick Remington: The Late Years	35,000
Silver in American Life	30,000

Exhibit 1). The museum had not been on the tour for such "blockbuster" exhibitions as King Tut or Picasso.

The museum also had a number of educational programs including lectures, tours, films, seminars, dance, mime, music, and other performing arts. These programs were generally planned around the circulating exhibitions or the museum's permanent collection and were designed to increase the visitors' appreciation of the visual arts they were seeing.

BACKGROUND INFORMATION

Although the Denver Art Museum was not strictly a government agency, its assets were held by a Colorado nonprofit educational corporation for the benefit of the public. It served as the official arts agency for the city and county of Denver. (The city and the county were one entity.) The museum was managed by an elected, unpaid board of trustees including civic leaders in the community and those who had special skills needed by the museum, such as lawyers, advertising agency executives, professional artists, business managers, and others.

Attendance averaged between 500,000 and 60,000 a year (See Exhibit 2), which put it ahead of the Boston, Houston, and Philadelphia art museums. Perhaps more significantly, the museum boasted the highest attendance on a per capita basis of any major art museum in the country. Of the visitors to the Denver Art Museum, about 28 percent came from out of state, another 40 percent came from Colorado but outside of Denver, and the remaining 32 percent from the city and county of Denver. Included in these attendance figures were visits from students as part of gallery tours led by museum guides. The largest community in the Rocky Mountain region, Denver had a population of 500,000, but the population of the metropolitan area was 1,650,000.

The museum was open 40 hours per week, including one evening. It was closed on Mondays. There were 105 employees, about half on the

EXHIBIT 2 Total Yearly Denver Art Museum Attendance

1972	674,299
1973	527,311
1974	555,058
1975	524,193
1976	527,859
1977	530,000
1978	608,178*
1979	466,361
1980	598,648
1981	500,000†

* The popular Armand Hammer Collection was included this year.
† Preliminary figure.

security force and the other half in curatorial and administrative positions.

The Denver Art Museum had traditionally been free to the public. However, admission fees had been charged for major circulating exhibitions. Over the past three years, the museum had collected an average of $160,000 per year in fees for these special exhibitions.

There were about 15,000 museum members, the majority of these family memberships at $30 per family per year. The greatest impetus to membership had been the major exhibitions for which admission fees were charged, because members had been admitted free. Among other membership benefits were 10 percent discounts at the museum on purchases of $5 or more, a monthly newsletter about museum activities, and previews of the 9 or 10 major traveling exhibitions per year. At each preview showing, light refreshments were served free of charge and there was a cash bar. At a few previews an arts celebrity, patron, or collector appeared. A recent example was Baron Thyssen von Bornemiza when a portion of his collection was exhibited.

The museum had been more marketing-oriented than most other art museums, with marketing considerations in terms of exhibitions, educational programs, fund raising, and acquisitions of art objects for the permanent collection. The museum had traditionally been supported financially by local, state, and federal allocations, gifts from private foundations, and museum memberships. The trend had been toward a greater percentage of the budget each year being raised from private sources. To succeed in this change, the museum had instituted a number of innovative funding ideas, such as the successful museum associates program, for which membership was limited to those individuals who contributed at least $1,250 each year in unrestricted funds for museum support. This was in contrast to restricted funds contributed by individuals and others for specific purposes, such as the support of special exhibitions or the purchase of a specific piece of art for the museum's permanent collection. In its solicitation of funds from private foundations, companies, and individuals for those restricted uses, the museum had been successful by demonstrating its relationship to the quality of life in Denver and by including recognition to the donors, such as associating a special exhibition with the sponsoring organization in the publicity about that exhibition.

The museum also had received substantial support from the federal government. In 1981, the museum received about $200,000 from federal sources, including the National Endowment for the Arts, the National Endowment for the Humanities, and the Institute for Museum Services. Much of this support had come as matching grants. Matching grants required the museum to raise $3 for each $1 of the grant. Walter Rosenberry, chairman of the museum's board of trustees, explained that these challenge grants had had a "tremendously stimulating effect" on private contributions.

The museum budget for 1981 was $3.8 million. The city provided about 24 percent of that amount, with state appropriations making up another 10 percent of the total. However, that situation began to change dramatically in 1982.

THE FUNDING CRUNCH

A combination of government cuts, inflation, and changes in tax deductions for private contributions were forcing changes in the museum's funding picture. The total allocation from the state of Colorado and the city and county of Denver was reduced by $320,000, about 25 percent, in 1982. At the same time, federal funds were slated for a 50 percent cut. This meant that the $200,000 received by the museum in 1981 would be reduced to $100,000 for 1982. Museum director Maytham noted that the halving of funds from the National Endowments for the Arts and Humanities could cut back funds for purchase of art works and for traveling exhibitions.

The museum generated about $2.4 million of its operating budget of $3.8 million in 1981 from gifts, grants, memberships, and admission fees at special exhibitions. Changes in federal tax laws for charitable contributions were also expected to reduce revenues for the museum. With the announced budget cuts for 1982, Maytham expected the Denver Art Museum to receive $420,000 less than in 1981. With 10 percent added to the budget for inflation, 1982 expenses were expected to be $380,000 higher than in 1981. This left an $800,000 gap between revenue and expenses.

BRIDGING THE GAP

Museum employees and trustees responded to the cuts by increasing their solicitation of individual, corporate, and foundation gifts. Also planned were cutbacks in the number of traveling exhibitions, with more emphasis on the museum's own permanent collection. Fewer exhibits were to be sent around the state from Denver and fewer exhibitions of international collections would be brought to Denver.

Management planned to expand the museum's retail shop to increase sales and to close a small gallery called the Discovery Gallery used for specialized shows. Maytham estimated that $30,000 a year would be saved on packing, shipping, insurance, staff time, fees to lending institutions, and other costs associated with exhibitions in that small gallery. The space would be given to the shop for expansion.

On a long-range basis, the museum would attempt to establish a substantial endowment through foundation and individual gifts, which would allow the museum more flexibility in meeting inflation and other unpredictable contingencies.

However, the most noticeable action taken by the museum was the institution of an admission fee. For about a decade, the museum had vigorously opposed such a fee, although the city administration and others had proposed the charge as a way to avoid increasing city and state aid to the museum.

Museum officials had debated not only the imposition of a fee but also what form of admission charge would be most effective in terms of generating the greatest revenue with the smallest drop in attendance. Maytham suggested as an alternative to mandatory entrance fees, a "recommended contribution" along with a sign, "Pay what you wish, but you must pay something." This flexible type of admission fee was pioneered by New York's Metropolitan Museum of Art, where it had been used with success since 1971. The Metropolitan had signs suggesting certain donations. Several months after the flexible fee was introduced by the Metropolitan Museum, the Art Institute of Chicago adopted the system, which it continues to use today.

The Denver Art Museum trustees decided to adopt this "recommended" admission fee. Maytham explained that the museum expected to net approximately $340,000 with the new fee. "While we regret that we must institute the fee," he said, "we hope the flexible system will encourage people to come to the museum regardless of their financial means."

"Our two major goals connected with inauguration of the fee are an increase in critically needed revenue and retention of our healthy attendance goals," he continued. Recommended contributions at the Denver Art Museum were $2 for adults and $1 for senior citizens and students. Museum members and children under 12 would be admitted free. There would not be separate charges for special traveling exhibitions, which had previously brought in about $160,000 each year.

Costs of implementing the fee collection were $60,000, which included such items as cash registers and turnstiles, according to Steven Schmidt, the museum's public relations director. He noted that the museum expected to generate a 26 percent increase in memberships in 1982, from about 15,000 to 19,000, in view of the free admission given to museum members.

Schmidt noted that the Denver Art Museum decision relied heavily on the experience at the Metropolitan Museum and Chicago's Art Institute and that the differences in the Denver museum and its audience might make the flexible fee more or less successful. For this reason, he suggested that the imposition of the fee be closely evaluated, and if the flexible fee was not successful, a fixed fee would be considered.

A fixed fee had been avoided by museum officials because of other museums' experiences in instituting such fees. "With a fixed fee, we'd expect a drop in attendance of 20 to 30 percent at first," Schmidt explained, "with rebuilding after that." He noted that education and advance notification might offset some of the drop in attendance.

The drop associated with a fixed fee was of particular concern in terms of the museum's efforts to attract lower-income visitors. It saw its mission as education, and museum officials worried that attendance might become restricted to middle and upper economic classes.

Case 28

The Deep South Civic Center*

Jeffrey D. Schaffer
University of New Orleans

Lafayette, Louisiana, is a city of approximately 90,000 people located in the Arcadian section of Louisiana. Arcadiana comprises most of the southwestern section of Louisiana ranging from Baton Rouge on the east to Lake Charles on the west. Most of the area is rural and populated sparsely by people of French Canadian descent. There are, however, a number of cities and towns ranging from approximately 250,000 people in Baton Rouge to small cities like Thibodaux and New Iberia with populations of 50,000 and 80,000, respectively.

The economy of the area is based on sugarcane, cotton, and rice farming; the fishing and seafood industries; and oil exploration. Some of the finest shrimp, oysters, and crabs come from the waters along the coast of Louisiana. Also many oil companies engage in exploration and production activities along the Louisiana coast and offshore in the Gulf of Mexico.

HISTORY OF THE DEEP SOUTH CIVIC CENTER

When Conceived

In the late 1950s Lafayette's only public gathering facility, the Lafayette Municipal Auditorium, caught fire and burned to the ground. At that time Lafayette was a sleepy town experiencing increasing decay in its downtown area. Some slum areas had developed and the general quality of life in the city suffered from a lack of cultural activity.

The burning of the old auditorium sparked some of the city fathers to begin thinking about what was happening to their downtown area.

* This case was prepared by Dr. Jeffrey D. Schaffer, University of New Orleans. Used by permission.

The Reasons for a New Civic Center

Shortly after the fire, discussions began in the Lafayette City Council regarding the future of downtown and of Lafayette. Lafayette was headquarters for many of the oil companies' field operations in Louisiana. As a result, a substantial portion of the population were executives of oil companies and their families. The oil industry had experienced substantial growth in Louisiana and new oil leases were being sold by the government on a regular basis. Other cities and towns in Arcadiana had begun to compete for the new field offices that were being developed as a result of the oil industry's growth.

The city fathers recognized that in order to continue to attract the interest of the oil companies to locate their offices in Lafayette, they would have to do something about the decaying environment and lack of cultural and entertainment activities in the city. In addition, there was little in the way of suitable meeting space for civic groups that were made up of the executives, bankers, merchants, and other professionals in Lafayette. These groups, such as Kiwanis and Rotary, had been growing in membership.

Discussion also centered around what appeared to be a growing trend in convention and trade show activities throughout the South. The city fathers felt that the central location of Lafayette, between New Orleans and Houston, would provide opportunities for regional and statewide conventions and trade shows. They hoped this would help promote the overall economy of the city and bring economic benefits to the retail businesses, motels, and restaurants. They discussed the need for facilities that could be used for social events such as weddings and banquets, as well as the need for a sports arena for the local high school basketball games, gymnastics events, and the like.

The Development Process

During the next two years much discussion took place regarding the development of a new civic center that could be designed to fulfill the needs of the community and help to reverse the decline of the downtown area. The area adjacent to the site of the old auditorium had become a full-fledged slum.

The City Council finally decided to take action and design the proposed civic center. To keep the project "within the community" a decision was made to call upon all five of the architectural firms in Lafayette.

The five firms created a consortium and undertook to design a new civic center for Lafayette. The site to be used was that of the old auditorium plus the slum area adjacent to it. If feasible, the city intended to condemn the buildings in the slum area and thereby be in a position to purchase and utilize the land.

Design of the Deep South Civic Center

Working together under a project director chosen from among the five architectural firms and utilizing specialized consultants such as acoustical consultants, theater consultants, and food service consultants from New York and other cities, the architects designed a three-segmented structure comprising an auditorium, an exhibit hall, and an arena. They presented their designs to the City Council nine months after the initial assignment.

Cost of the New Facility

Shortly after the design was completed the City Council passed a proposition accepting the design that the architects had prepared and authorizing a cost estimate to be made for both construction of the civic center and the purchase of the additional land necessary for the site. By late 1963 the costing process was complete and the total amount necessary to develop the facility and purchase the land was $14,800,000.

Financing the Civic Center

After much debate it was decided that the city would finance the development of the new civic center by issuing general revenue bonds for $7,800,000 at 7 percent interest for 15 years and finance the remainder from the city treasury (a surplus of $10 million existed at that time) to be repaid by increasing the utility tax on its citizens.

The proposal was put to a vote in early 1964 and defeated soundly. At that time only property owners were permitted to vote on matters concerning city financing. In 1965 a new ordinance was passed permitting all citizens of the city to vote on all matters and in 1966 a second proposal to build the Deep South Civic Center was put up for a vote. This time it was easily passed and preparations for the condemnation and purchase of the necessary land were begun immediately.

Building the Facility

Construction began in 1968 with a great citywide celebration at the ground-breaking ceremony. Finally, after three years of construction, the new civic center was opened in March 1971.

THE IMAGE OF THE DEEP SOUTH CIVIC CENTER

Early Years

There was considerable excitement and enthusiasm when the new civic center opened in 1971. Great things were expected. However, within two years it became evident that the civic center was in financial trouble. Where operating revenues were expected to cover all operating costs, substantial losses were being incurred. These losses had to be made up from city revenues. The civic center soon became known as the "white elephant" and with help from the local newspaper, public criticism grew.

The initial manager was soon fired, and his replacement, a local Chamber of Commerce executive, continued to experience criticism and growing financial losses.

Current Management

In 1977 George Smith was hired to manage the Deep South Civic Center. George had been in the amusement management business for the past 15 years. His most recent position was manager of the Baton Rouge Municipal Auditorium, a facility of about 8,000 seats. He was quite familiar with the city of Lafayette. Over the years he had watched the development of the Deep South Civic Center, had observed the local criticism grow, and was aware of the financial problems of the facilities.

George felt that to be successful in his new position he had to improve the image of the civic center in the community. He felt that to change local feeling about the civic center he needed to give lots of attention to the local community. He felt that his efforts and that of his staff must be directed toward pleasing the memberships of local organizations and especially the press. He proceeded to set up VIP tours for local people and went out of his way to roll out the red carpet whenever a member of the press came to visit. George and his staff spent a major portion of their time entertaining local dignitaries and trying to find ways to please the local press.

George was also well aware of the civic center's history of substantial financial loss. He had seen from past experience how the Baton Rouge City Council had zeroed in on the annual operating statements of the Baton Rouge Municipal Auditorium and were highly critical of any increase in operating losses. George knew that he had to find a way to achieve operating results better than his predecessors'. Cultural events, conventions, and trade shows were all part of the potential market; unfortunately, they usually paid only minimum fixed

EXHIBIT 1 Comparison of Civic Center Revenue Potential (coliseum only)

	Daily Revenue Potential
Regular fixed rate (convention, trade show, etc.)	$ 1,200
Concert revenue potential (11,000 seats—12% of gross):	
Ticket Price—$4.00	$ 5,300
Ticket Price—$5.00	$ 6,600
Ticket Price—$8.00	$10,600
Ticket Price—$10.00	$13,200

rentals. Thus, while they added much in the way of economic and cultural benefit to the city, they were not profitable to the civic center.

The big money was in concerts, especially those that could attract large numbers of people. The usual arrangement for these types of shows (mostly rock, country, and gospel concerts) was one in which the auditorium shared in the gross receipts. Usually 12 percent of the gross take went to the auditorium in the form of rent plus an additional 3 percent as a "box office" advance for selling tickets. With 11,000 seats in the coliseum, a healthy amount of revenue could be generated for a good concert.

It cost no more to set up the space for a concert than it did for a convention or trade show. In fact, it was generally easier because one had to deal only with the concert's manager, who usually was well organized and knew the ropes, as opposed to a multitude of exhibitors for conventions and trade shows. Exhibit 1 shows a comparison of the fixed-rate structure with the potential rates for various levels of concert ticket prices.

MANAGEMENT HIERARCHY

The Commission

The Deep South Civic Center, owned and operated by the city of Lafayette, is organized as a department within the city. The primary difference from other city departments is that, by City Council ordinance, a seven-member civic center commission was established. This commission is to act as an independent body and set policy for the civic center in the areas of advertising, promotions, rates, ticket sales, parking, concessions, and catering contracts. The commission is composed of private citizens of the city of Lafayette. The City Council also has seven members.

Each member of the commission is appointed by the entire City Council; candidates can be recommended by one or more council members, or any citizen can petition the council to be considered for membership.

One member of the City Council sits on the commission as a liaison to the council. This person has no voting rights on the commission. The commission serves at the pleasure of the council, and appointments to the commission are for a one-year period.

Structure within the City

The city of Lafayette is operated through the office of the city manager, the chief operating officer of the city, who is appointed by and reports directly to the City Council. The City Council is composed of six council members elected at large and the mayor. The mayor is primarily a figurehead who serves as a council member and has the same voting power as other council members.

The director of administration and public safety reports to the city manager and is responsible for the Deep South Civic Center. The manager of the Deep South Civic Center reports to the director of administration and public safety and is in turn responsible for the day-to-day operation of the civic center (Exhibit 2).

Responsibility of the Civic Center Manager

The responsibilities of the manager of the civic center include all activities related to the booking and handling of events, sales, administration of the operation, maintenance of the facility, preparation of all operating and capital budgets, and staffing. However, the civic center manager is not directly responsible for food service or concessions. This aspect of the operation is handled through a private operator under contract with the civic center commission. The contract is negotiated and set by the civic center commission. The civic center manager must coordinate with this contractor for the food service and concession needs of the activities booked into the civic center.

The Operating Organization for the Deep South Civic Center

The internal structure of the Deep South Civic Center is composed of 18 full-time people. The organization consists of the civic center manager, the assistant civic center manager, a box office supervisor, four

EXHIBIT 2 Organization of the City of Lafayette Relative to the Civic Center

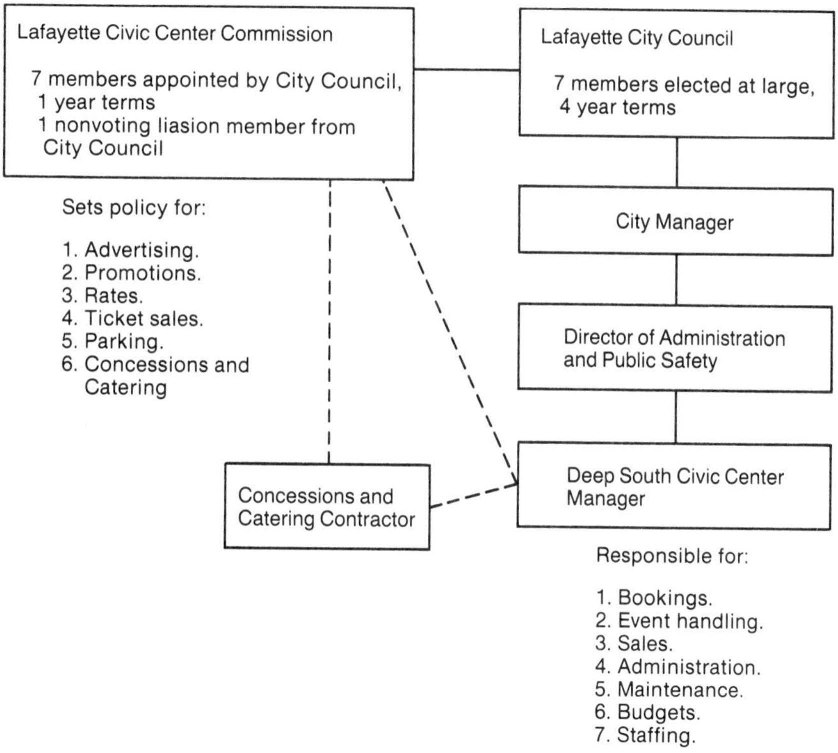

box office attendants, a parking lot supervisor, two secretaries, a promotions coordinator, and operations superintendent, four lead men, and two laborers (Exhibit 3).

Many other people are needed when events are set up and taken down. These additional part-time employees are drawn when needed from the city of Lafayette's centralized labor pool. They consist of janitors, electricians, engineers, plumbers, carpenters, and general laborers. The civic center is charged for the time of these additional employees based upon rates established by the city Finance Department. These rates include all city overhead and benefits plus an administrative cost factor. The civic center management has no control over the rates charged by the city for temporary labor. The rates charged are substantially higher than that which would have to be paid for comparable part-time help hired directly (Exhibit 4).

EXHIBIT 3 Deep South Center Management Organization

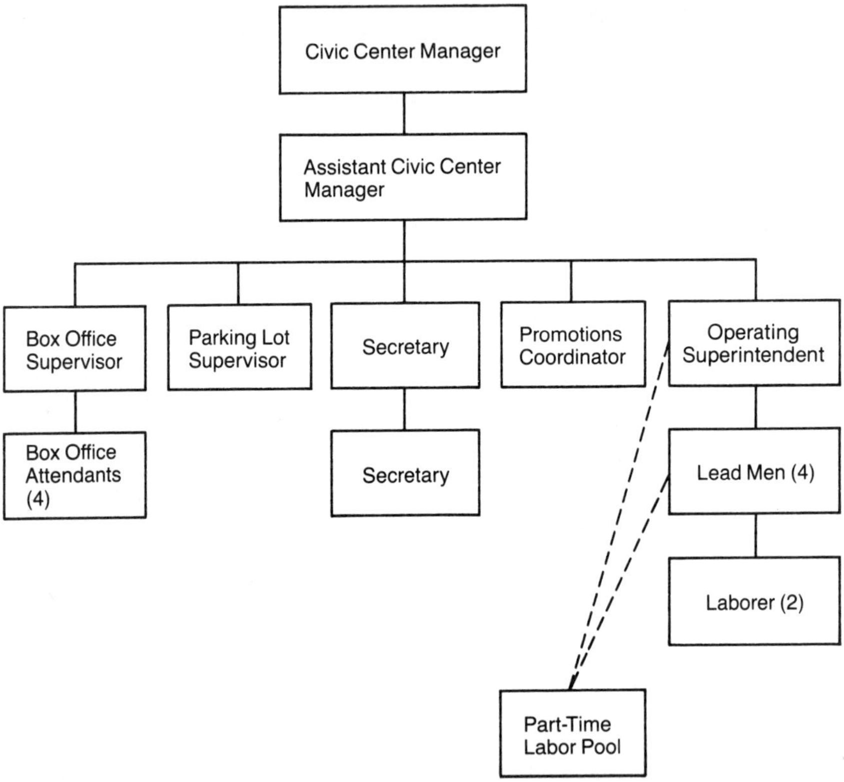

EXHIBIT 4 Deep South Civic Center City Labor Pool versus Market Wage Rates

Jobs	*City Labor Pool Rate*	*Market Rate**
Janitorial/laborer	$ 8.72/hr.	$ 3.35/hr.
Building maintenance services (electrician, plumber, etc.)	$10.84/hr.	$5.50–7.50/hr.
Grounds maintenance	$10.85/hr.	$ 3.35/hr.

* In most instances unskilled minimum wage people are all that would be required. In addition, fringe benefits would be because of the part-time nature of the jobs.

The Promotions Coordinator

The position of promotions coordinator was approved as an addition to staff about 10 months ago to generate more business for the civic center. According to George Smith, however, little actual sales development has been done yet. Most of the promotion coordinator's time has been spent dealing with local activities and publishing the calendar of events. George Smith said the primary reason for not engaging in more direct selling is that they don't have the four to five additional slide presentations they need as a selling tool. Their one slide presentation, entitled "Booking a Concert," has been shown frequently at local civic club meetings and at city high school presentations.

The Operating Superintendent

The operating superintendent and his four lead men handle the setting up and taking down of booked events. The operating superintendent's responsibility is to decide on the number of extra employees needed and to arrange for them through the city labor pool. The superintendent knows from experience how many and what kinds of people are needed for a particular event.

MARKETING AND SALES

Uses of the Deep South Civic Center

According to George Smith each area of the civic center is used somewhat differently, but there is substantial overlap in some types of use. The breakdown in Exhibit 5 provided by George Smith shows the uses to which the various areas can be put.

Key Markets

"The big money is in booking concerts in our coliseum," according to George Smith. "If we want to maintain a bottom line that won't cause the City Council to get into an uproar, we've got to make sure we book enough concerts during the year to generate the revenue we need . . . . Conventions bring a lot of people to the city, but all we get is the fixed daily rate. With the labor rates we have to pay, it costs us

EXHIBIT 5 Key Markets for Deep South Civic Center

Coliseum	*Exhibit Hall*	*Auditorium (primarily an entertainment facility)*
Ice shows	Trade shows—most frequent use	Broadway road shows
Circuses	Banquets	Symphonies
Rodeos	Dinners	Ballets
Concerts	Dances	Opera
Basketball	State testing	Individual artist presentations (concerts)
Hockey	Bar exam	Beauty pageants
Wrestling	CPA exam	Religious meetings
Boxing	Citywide tests	Corporate meetings
Trade shows	Weddings	
Antiques	Proms	
Cars	Council meetings	
Boats	Corporate meetings	
Homes		
Conventions		
Political rallies		
Association meetings		
Religious meetings		
Banquets		

more than we take in. The same is true for operas and symphonies because they get the fixed civic rate.

"Our plan is to try to keep everyone happy. We have to book some conventions and cultural events as well as cater to local civic groups. But we can't let them get in the way of our concert business." Therefore, Smith conceded, "we try not to commit our facilities to these activities too far in advance because you never know when a concert promoter will call. Yet it's obvious that our greatest source of revenue is the concert business, although I can't say exactly how much it is. We don't keep those kinds of records. . . . We are interested in how many days we have the civic center in use. That's what the city council wants to see . . . that the facility is being used as many days as possible."

Exhibit 6 summarizes the occupancy and attendance records kept monthly. A listing of events held each month and a breakdown of attendance by area of civic center facility is kept. The amount of ticket sales for each event is also recorded, but sales reflected in these reports do not reflect civic center net revenue; they represent gross ticket sales.

EXHIBIT 6 Deep South Civic Center Summary of Occupancy and Attendance

	Coliseum				*Auditorium*				*Exhibit Hall*				*Total Complex*			
			Occupancy				*Occupancy*				*Occupancy*				*Occupancy*	
Month/Year	*Attendance*	*Ticket Sales*	*(days)*	*(%)*	*Attendance*	*Ticket Sales*	*(days)*	*(%)*	*Attendance*	*Ticket Sales*	*(days)*	*(%)*	*Attendance*	*Ticket Sales*	*(days)*	*(%)*
July 1980	6,667	$ 45,518	3	10	10,142	$16,122	10	32	3,548	$ 2,459	8	26	20,357	$ 64,098	18	58
August 1980	11,110	63,093	4	13	4,867	8,415	6	19	6,549	4,862	15	48	22,526	76,370	19	61
September 1980	15,458	104,505	7	23	5,550	0	2	7	4,971	1,898	15	50	25,979	106,403	18	60
October 1980	38,910	166,913	17	55	18,037	27,769	11	35	2,328	0	16	52	59,275	194,682	25	81
November 1980	30,648	169,472	10	33	9,334	30,446	14	47	12,162	11,943	19	63	52,144	211,861	24	80
December 1980	18,528	102,180	14	45	10,646	28,269	8	26	5,697	246	15	48	34,871	130,695	23	74
January 1981	40,812	154,290	N/A	N/A	3,434	2,320	N/A	N/A	3,147	5,893	N/A	N/A	47,393	162,503	N/A	N/A
February 1981	8,886	30,808	N/A	N/A	5,525	12,424	N/A	N/A	4,737	0	N/A	N/A	19,148	43,232	N/A	N/A
March 1981	44,351	246,765	N/A	N/A	14,594	42,245	N/A	N/A	4,588	0	N/A	N/A	63,533	289,010	N/A	N/A

Advertising

Because the Deep South Civic Center, according to George Smith, is in the amusement business, most of the advertising is placed in magazines that are the "Bibles" of the industry. About $3,000 per year goes toward advertising. The budget is reached by adding the cost of placing ads in the periodicals. The periodicals usually are:

Talent & Booking Magazine

Meetings & Conventions

Trade Show & Concert Guide (annual issue)

Bill Board Magazine

Special ads are placed in magazines when they make an editorial comment about the city or region. For example, last year *Successful Meetings Magazine* ran an article about Arcadiana, and the Deep South Civic Center took an ad in that issue.

Sales Promotions

"Most of our business comes because we are here," said George Smith. "Our sales promotion is on a day-to-day basis. . . . The city doesn't have enough hotel rooms for us to go after the big conventions and our airport is served by only one carrier.

"In addition our meeting rooms are not adequate for most convention groups. We need smaller rooms and more flexibility to be able to satisfy the conventions and meetings that do come.

"What I think we need is a community room for about 400 people or fewer. This room should be flexible so that it can be broken down into smaller rooms. We also need more exhibit space and parking is at a premium. When we have concerts and conventions that draw heavily, we don't have enough room for all the cars, and we have to make arrangements with one of the hotels in the area to use its lot for our overflow. The problem is, we've got nowhere to expand. There is no more land available around our site."

Smith added, "To really make the Deep South Civic Center complete, we want to have an on-site restaurant and a small community theater of about 400 seats. That way, everything will be under one roof. People could have dinner and then see a show without going outside."

Competition

"We really have to work hard to compete with other civic centers and auditoriums in cities throughout southwestern Louisiana. We're all vying for the same concerts, conventions, and trade shows. People in the area who attend these concerts will gladly drive 100 miles or more to see a show.

"We are careful to treat the concert promoters right so they will remember us when they have another show."

BUDGETS AND FINANCIAL REPORTS

Accounting

All accounting for the civic center is done centrally by the city Finance Department. The civic center is required to follow the budgetary and planning process as prescribed by city management.

Monthly Operating Statement

Exhibit 7 is the operating statement of the Deep South Civic Center covering the nine months ending March 1981. A financial statement in this format is prepared monthly, on a cumulative basis, by the city finance department.

Budget

"When I'm not entertaining someone from the local community or a newspaper representative, I'm working on our budgets." That's the way George Smith described the budgetary process used at the Deep South Civic Center. The actual information required to complete the budget amounted to over 200 pages. The following is a list of the major summary forms and reports included in the budget report.

1. A statement of objectives and activities.
2. Personnel recap.
3. Budget worksheet A.
4. Detail of budget request.
5. Reason and justification of basic budget request.
6. Computerized form #2A.
7. Equipment request forms.
8. Revenue estimate form.
9. Budget request form.
10. Revenue estimate income generated.
11. Detailed description of each budgetary account.
12. Budget recap.
13. Supplemental budget request recap.

EXHIBIT 7

City of Lafayette, Louisiana
Civic Center Fund
Comparative Income Statement
For the 9 Months Ended March 13

	1981	*1980*
Operating revenue		
Rentals	$ 186,249	$ 205,068
Event expenses	57,693	62,383
Advertising	2,600	2,140
Admissions tax	48,840	61,657
Commissions	50,290	52,944
Event profit—city-sponsored	6,775	70
Parking fee	48,938	—
Total operating revenue	401,385	384,262
Less operating expenses before depreciation		
Administrative		
Personal services	249,385	218,350
Utilities and communications	190,768	194,965
Administrative expenses	340,139	565,658
Promotional expenses		
Personal services	38,392	32,623
Services and charges	1,591	5,305
Total operating expenses before depreciation	820,275	1,016,901
Operating (loss) before depreciation	(418,890)	(632,639)
Less depreciation	243,178	238,942
Operating (loss)	(662,068)	(871,581)
Nonoperating income		
Supplement from general fund	240,000	375,000
Miscellaneous	4,649	9,181
Interest on investments	849	3,428
Total nonoperating income	245,498	387,609
Net (loss)	$(416,570)	$ (483,972)

14. Supplemental budget request cover.
15. Improvements, maintenance, and capital budget cost request and budget estimates.
16. Equipment request recap.
17. Reason and justification of supplemental budget requests.
18. Justification for additional personnel requests.

19. 5 percent decrease budget.
20. 5 percent decrease account summary.

LOOKING AHEAD

After reviewing all these facts, Smith wondered what specific steps he should now take to ensure the viability and success of the center. There was much to be done, and things had to begin happening.

Case 29

The Arthritis Foundation*

P. A. Papke III
Jon M. Hawes
both of the University of Akron

In January of 1986, June Gold was assigned the task of developing a plan to promote the services offered by the Akron branch of the Arthritis Foundation. As Regional Director of this branch, Ms. Gold is particularly interested in developing a plan that will ensure the achievement of the following objectives:

1. Increase public awareness of the Arthritis Foundation within the eight counties served by the Akron branch.
2. Increase the awareness, among those affected by the disease, of the patient services offered by the Akron branch of the Arthritis Foundation.

ORGANIZATION OF THE ARTHRITIS FOUNDATION

The Northeastern Ohio Chapter

The Northeastern Ohio chapter of the Arthritis Foundation is located in Cleveland and serves 22 counties, with branch offices located in Akron and Amherst. The organization of the chapter is similar to that of the national organization. The chapter has a group of senior officers and a chapter Board of Trustees which holds the legal liability for the operation of the chapter. Each branch has an Advisory Board which makes recommendations to the chapter Board of Trustees.

The chapter also has Executive, Budget and Finance, Public Education and Information, Financial Development, and Governmental Affairs committees. There is also a Medical Advisory Board which is supported by the branches.

* This case was prepared by P. A. Papke III under the direction of Jon M. Hawes, Professor of Marketing, Department of Marketing, University of Akron. Used by permission.

The staff for the chapter consists of an Executive Director for the Northeastern Ohio chapter (Ms. G. G. Fine), a Director of Administration who handles the budget and financial interface with the national organization, and an Assistant Director of Development who is responsible for chapter-wide special events and other events that the Cleveland office sponsors. The chapter also has a Program Director for chapter-wide patient programs, a Public Education person for public programs, and two individuals who handle mailings, maintain donor files and records, and perform other office duties.

The Northeastern Ohio chapter staff has remained relatively stable over the last several years due to low turnover. This is somewhat unusual in nonprofit organizations.

The Akron Branch

The Akron branch serves 8 of the 22 counties which make up the geographical areas of the Northeastern Ohio chapter. These counties are Carroll, Holmes, Medina, Portage, Stark, Summit, Tuscarawas, and Wayne.

The staff consists of the Akron Regional Director (Ms. June Gold), a Program Director, a Financial Development Director, a secretary, and volunteers. Unlike the Northeastern Ohio chapter, the Akron branch has recently had considerable turnover. Ms. Jan Pagnard, Program Director, left the organization, and two new individuals were hired to perform these duties. Also, the job of the Financial Development Director has recently been upgraded from part time to full time.

The backbone of the organization is volunteers, as is the case in many other nonprofit organizations. The Akron branch has approximately 400 volunteers who contribute their time during the year. These people are involved in mailings, phone work, and any number of other duties as well as soliciting donations. The volunteer structure operates most effectively for short-term projects. If properly utilized, the volunteers can perform many of the duties which the branch needs to have completed.

PRODUCTS AND SERVICES OF THE AKRON BRANCH

The Arthritis Foundation is a nonprofit health association which provides a number of services to its customers who can be segregated into three groups: (1) patients or families of those with arthritis, (2) the general public, and (3) the professional community. Each group represents a different market and, therefore, the services provided to each

EXHIBIT 1 Arthritis Foundation Services

Market	*Services Offered*
Patients	Self-help course Support groups Warm water exercise Telephone consultation Patient education Land exercises (to begin next summer)
Public	Speakers bureau Newsletter Public forums Health fairs Media contacts Literature
Professional	Educational programs for physicians and other allied health professionals Educational programs for aquatic instructors, patient educators, and other volunteers

are different. Exhibit 1 lists the services provided to each of the three markets.

Patient Market

Each of the patient services involves interaction between the Akron branch of the Arthritis Foundation and those affected by the disease. The following discussion will define each of these services and explain the marketing utilized for each. The use of these patient services is detailed in Exhibit 2.

Self-Help Courses. The purpose of this course is to provide people who have arthritis and those who care about them with the knowledge and skills needed to take a more active part in arthritis care. The classes meet for 2½ hours once a week over a six-week period. Each course enrolls 7 to 20 people and is offered in the spring and in the fall. Most of the courses are taught during the day and the goal is to have a course taught in each county twice a year. The price is $15 per person which includes a book and handouts. Based upon financial need, however, the tuition may be waived.

This course is promoted at public forums and by news releases published in the newspaper. Also, literature is supplied to local rheumatologists for placement in their offices. This promotion is similar in each county.

EXHIBIT 2 Patient Service Statistics

Services	*1983*	*1984*	*1985*
Self-help courses	21	70	135
Support groups	205	366	921
Warm water exercise	468	1,374	1,344
Telephone consultation	653	728	1,640
Patient education	1,230	790	3,312

As can be seen from Exhibit 2, the Patient Self-Help Course enrollment has increased from 70 people in 1984 to 135 people in 1985. The trend shows a general increase in participation over the last three years.

Support Group Programs. The Arthritis Foundation would like the people completing the Self-Help Course to join a support group which is a monthly informational meeting with group discussion and support. The goal is to provide an environment where people can learn to cope with arthritis and receive practical help in dealing with the day-to-day problems that the disease presents. The support groups are typically held at hospitals or other institutional locations.

A typical program lasts about 2½ hours and consists of a presentation followed by a question and answer period. Topic subjects include medication, nutrition, pain, and home care. The topic selection is made by the Arthritis Foundation with input from the support group facilitators in that county. The meeting dates, times, and locations are selected for an entire year in advance and a schedule is published for distribution prior to the first meeting of the year.

Seven of the eight counties have support group programs. Wayne and Holmes Counties have the largest attendance, and Summit has the smallest program. If attendance is used as a measure of how successful a program is, then the most successful topics involve medication and presentations made by doctors. The ages of those who attend these programs range from the 20s to the 80s and varies depending upon the topic. The programs are held at night or on Sunday and there is no charge. Exhibit 2 shows the increasing attendance figures for the past three years, including an increase of over 250 percent in 1985.

The promotion of these programs includes the following tactics. The primary method is through press releases to the newspapers. It is important to note that in the smaller community newspapers, such as the *Dover Repository,* the announcements get favorable locations and are published in a timely manner. However, in the *Akron Beacon Journal* the placement is at times poor, and the timing of publication presents problems. The other means of promotion used are: public service announcements, word of mouth, and literature sent to health agencies, YMCA's, hospitals, and senior citizen groups. The Wooster County group also posts flyers to solicit participants.

Warm Water Exercise. The Arthritis Aquatic Program (AAP) or Warm Water Exercise is another patient service which is offered. This program is a nonclinical, recreational water exercise program developed as a combined effort of the YMCA and the Arthritis Foundation. This program is a 6- to 10-week exercise session with two to three sessions per week, each lasting 30 to 45 minutes. The exercises are a series of gentle movements in a warm-water pool (83-to-88 degrees).

There are pool locations in seven of the Akron branch's eight counties. Holmes County is the only county that does not offer this service. From 20 to 35 people take the course at any one time with the ages ranging from 30 to 80 years. The number and age of the participants varies from location to location depending upon pool size, time of day, and time of year.

This program requires approval from the patient's doctor and over half of the people attending these programs have been referred by their physicians. The cost for attending the program varies depending upon the policy of the pool. Attendance is free at the Akron Jewish Center, while the Tallmadge YWCA charges $15 for a YWCA membership ($8 for senior citizens) and $1 per visit. Most of the classes are offered during the day.

At this time both the Jewish Center and the Tallmadge YWCA are closed to additional participants because of the limits on the class size. Exhibit 2 shows that the participation in this program has remained level at about 1,370 individuals for the past two years. This may be the maximum that the existing pool programs can handle.

This program appears to be the most successful in terms of participant reaction. Once an individual starts these classes, he/she usually does not want to stop, which accounts for the closed classes. The promotion for this program is through the public forums, support group discussions, promotions by the pool facility, doctor referrals, and word of mouth.

Telephone Consultation. Another patient service offered is Telephone Consultation and Referral. The referral service provides information on sources of help from a medical and social standpoint, as well as information about programs offered by the Arthritis Foundation. Telephone consultation, to some degree, can be considered a measure of awareness in the area.

Patient Education. This program involves handling requests from patients for printed information available from the Arthritis Foundation. Press releases are sent to the newspapers on a monthly basis soliciting contacts with the Arthritis Foundation. An example of this was a published press release in the *Akron Beacon Journal* in 1985 which offered a pamphlet titled "Planning Your Will." The response to requests for this pamphlet would be considered a Patient Education Service.

Public Market

Seven different services are provided to the public by the Arthritis Foundation. These services or programs involve some type of interaction between the Arthritis Foundation and the general public. The following discussion will define each of these services and explain the promotion utilized. Exhibit 3 shows the usage of these public services.

Speakers Bureau. The Arthritis Foundation Speakers Bureau is a group of about 20 volunteers who speak to any community group wanting up-to-date information on arthritis. The speakers may be health care professionals who deal with arthritis, people who have arthritis, or others who have an interest in the disease.

Promotion for this service is provided by announcements at the public forums, through a Speakers Bureau brochure issued by the Arthritis Foundation and sent to potentially interested groups, word of mouth, and through the newspaper. The groups requesting the service then use some type of promotion to inform their members of the topic to be covered by the speaker. The Speakers Bureau is offered in all eight counties and the requests for this service increased for the years 1983 to 1985.

Newsletter. The newsletter is published each quarter by the local chapter and sent to the Arthritis Foundation members. It contains arthritis news at both the local and national levels, research findings, fund raising activities, promotional information on other services, and other information on various arthritis-related subjects.

EXHIBIT 3 Public Service Statistics

Services	*1983*	*1984*	*1985*
Speakers bureau	1,625	1,580	1,879
Newsletter circulation	13,794	6,033	5,913
Public forums	310	1,045	1,762
Health fairs	2,775	2,285	6,420
Media contacts	997	2,383	2,062
Literature	2,162	13,286	13,262

It is important to note that the newsletter is sent only to members of the Arthritis Foundation. The price of a membership is $15 per year, which entitles the member to receive the newsletter and other informational mailings. Exhibit 3 shows the statistics for the subscription of the newsletter over the last three years. There was a substantial drop in subscribers from 1983 to 1984, and a steady decline over the last two years. This decline is due to a purge from the files of people who are no longer members. The membership price rose from $10 to $15 in 1984.

Public Forums. The Arthritis Foundation public forums involve panel discussions conducted by rheumatologists, orthopedic specialists, physical therapists, occupational therapists, dieticians, pharmacists, and other health care professionals. Each forum involves two or three individuals in these professions. Each provides a 20-minute speech and then fields questions from the audience. The forum typically lasts about two hours and a wide range of topics have been discussed over the years.

Each of the public forums is cosponsored by a hospital and the Arthritis Foundation. The hospital is responsible for the promotion of the event, facilities for the forum, refreshments, and other logistic details. The Arthritis Foundation is responsible for obtaining the speakers. Medina and Wayne are the only counties in the Akron branch that have not offered public forums. The promotion for this event, while handled by the hospital or cosponsoring organization, consists of word of mouth, brochures posted on bulletin boards, brochures mailed to individuals, and public service announcements in local papers.

The number of people attending the Arthritis Foundation public forum increased from 310 in 1983 to 1,762 in 1985. During this same time, the number of events increased from five in 1983 and in 1984, to eight in 1985.

Health Fairs. These include United Way-sponsored events, county fairs, hospital fairs, and other events of this type. The Arthritis Foundation provides a booth or display for these events which provides literature on the Foundation itself and the services it offers, as well as information about specific arthritis subjects.

Health fair attendance has increased during the past three years. Health fairs were held in Medina, Portage, Summit, and Wayne Counties during 1985.

Media Contacts. This service consists of public service announcements and other information provided to newspapers, magazines, television, radio, and other media. This information is supplied to these groups by the local branch on a continuing basis throughout the year. It involves the promotion of the arthritis programs of the local branch and the national office. The goal is to increase the awareness of the public on common forms of arthritis and to motivate people in the community who may have arthritis to get information and help.

Literature. This service involves distributing information in the form of brochures to individuals who have requested it. The subjects included in this information range from topics on specific forms of arthritis and services provided by the Arthritis Foundation to the arthritis research being done. This program is not promoted in any way other than the placement of literature at health fairs. The amount of literature provided has increased over the last three years from 2,162 brochures in 1983 to 13,262 brochures during 1985.

Professional Market

The professional market includes health and human service professionals and students interested in arthritis and others who might support the efforts of the Arthritis Foundation. Exhibit 4 contains a list of some of the professions included in this sector. Two types of educational services are offered to this market.

Educational Services for Physicians and Health Professionals. The Akron branch of the Arthritis Foundation and the Northeast Ohio Arthritis Health Professions Association (NEOAHPA) offer a number of educational programs for health care professionals. These include

EXHIBIT 4 Professional Market

Administrators	Counselors
Health educators	Evaluation researchers
Hand therapists	Health service researchers
Lawyers	Laboratory technologists
Medical technologists	Medical librarians
Nurses	Nutritionists
Occupational therapists	Orthotists
Patients	Pharmacists
Physical therapists	Physicians
Podiatrists	Physician assistants
Rehabilitation counselors	Psycholgists
Sociologists	Social workers
Therapy assistants	Potential volunteers

continuing medical education programs and short-term comprehensive training programs. The branch and NEOAHPA develop standard curricula and support materials for in-service training programs and develop and maintain a communication network between rheumatologists and other medical professionals.

Information about these programs is disseminated throughout the medical and health care community through target mailings based upon the topic of a specific program.

Ninety-one doctors, five registered nurses, and one physical therapist were involved in this program in Summit County during 1986. These figures constitute a decrease from previous years, and represent only a small percentage of the potential professional market within the eight counties. This program is also very important from an awareness standpoint. Doctors and others in the professional market are important links between patients and the Arthritis Foundation. They often serve as gatekeepers of information about the Arthritis Foundation.

Educational Services for Aquatic Instructors and Patient Educators. These programs are offered by the Arthritis Foundation to train speakers, educators, instructors, and other volunteers. This training helps develop qualified individuals for the programs, classes, and services which the branch offers. During 1985, for example, 23 people were trained to become aquatic instructors.

Questions

1. To what extent has the Akron branch been successful over the past three years in increasing its service to arthritis patients and the general public?
2. Develop a promotional plan that will enable the Akron branch to achieve the two objectives identified early in the case. Remember that promotional expenditures are examined *very* closely in the nonprofit sector.

Case 30

Rogers, Nagel, Langhart (RNL PC), Architects and Planners*

H. Michael Hayes
University of Colorado–Denver

It was August 1984. John B. Rogers, one of the founders and a principal stockholder in RNL, had just completed the University of Colorado's Executive MBA program. Throughout the program John had tried to relate the concepts and principles covered in his courses to the problems of managing a large architectural practice. In particular, he was concerned about the marketing efforts of his firm. As he put it, "Marketing is still a new, and sometimes distasteful, word to most architects. Nevertheless, the firms that survive and prosper in the future are going to be those which learn how to market as effectively as they design. At RNL we are still struggling with what it means to be a marketing organization, but we feel it's a critical question that must be answered if we're going to meet our projections of roughly doubling by 1989, and we're giving it lots of attention."

RNL

In 1984, with sales (design fees) of approximately $3,300,000, RNL was one of the largest local architectural firms in Denver and the Rocky Mountain region. The firm evolved from the individual practices of John B. Rogers, Jerome K. Nagel, and Victor D. Langhart. All started their architectural careers in Denver in the 1950s. The partnership of

* This case was prepared by H. Michael Hayes, Professor of Marketing and Strategic Management, University of Colorado at Denver, as the basis for class discussion rather than to illustrate either effective or ineffective handling of an administrative situation.

Rogers, Nagel, Langhart was formed from the three individual proprietorships in 1966, and became a professional corporation in 1970.

In 1984 the firm provided professional design services to commercial, corporate, and governmental clients, not only in Denver but throughout Colorado and, increasingly, throughout the western United States. In addition to basic architectural design services, three subsidiaries had recently been formed:

Interplan, which provides pre-architectural services, programming, planning, budgeting, scheduling, and cost projections, utilized in corporate budgeting and governmental bond issues.

Denver Enterprises, formed to hold equity interests in selected projects designed by RNL and to take risk by furnishing design services early in a project and by participating in the capital requirements of a project.

Space Management Systems, Inc. (SMS), which provides larger corporations with the necessary services (heavily computer system supported) to facilitate control of their facilities with respect to space, furnishings, equipment, and the cost of change.

In 1984, the firm had 72 employees. John Rogers served as chairman, and Vic Langhart served as president. Nagel had retired in 1976. (See Exhibit 1 for an organization chart.) Development of broad-based management had been a priority since 1975. The firm had seven vice presidents. Two of these vice presidents, Phil Goedert and Rich von Luhrte, served on the Board of Directors, together with Rogers and Langhart.

Growth was financed through retained earnings. In addition, a plan to provide for more employee ownership, principally through profit sharing (ESOP in 1984), was initiated in 1973. Rogers and Langhart held 56 percent of RNL stock, and 66 percent was held by the four board members. The Colorado National Bank Profit Sharing Trust held 12 percent in its name. The remaining 22 percent was controlled by 23 other employees, either personally or through their individual profit sharing accounts. It was a goal of the firm to eventually vest stock ownership throughout the firm, in the interest of longevity and continuity.

The firm's principal assets were its human resources. Rogers and Langhart, however, had significant ownership in a limited partnership, which owned a 20,000-square-foot building in a prestigious location in downtown Denver. In 1984, RNL occupied 15,000 square feet. Use of the remaining 5,000 square feet could accommodate up to 30 percent growth in personnel. Through utilization of automation and computers, RNL felt it could double its 1984 volume of work without acquiring additional space.

EXHIBIT 1 Corporate Organization

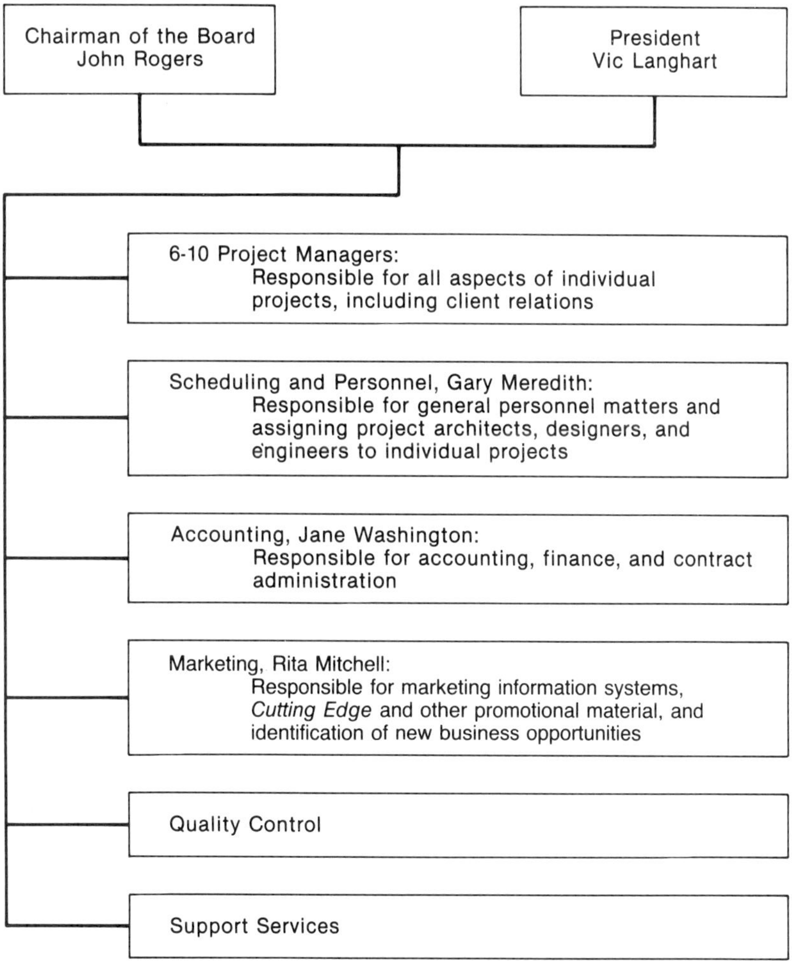

Note: RNL does not have a formal organization chart, as such. This exhibit was developed by the case writer to portray the general nature of work assignments and reporting relationships in the firm. As a general rule, project managers report to either John Rogers or Vic Langhart. Most administrative staff functions report to Vic Langhart. At the operational level, Interplan and SMS projects are handled similarly to RNL projects.

ARCHITECTURAL SERVICES

Architecture: the profession of designing buildings, open areas, communities, and other artificial constructions and environments, usually with some regard to aesthetic effect. The professional services of an architect

> often include design or selection of furnishings and decorations, supervision of construction work, and the examination, restoration, or remodeling of existing buildings.
>
> *Random House Dictionary*

Demand for architectural services is closely tied to population growth and to the level of construction activity. The population in the Denver metropolitan area grew from 929,000 in 1960 to 1,620,000 in 1980, and it is estimated to grow to 1,958,000 by 1990. Denver's annual population change of 3.4 percent in the decade 1970–80 ranked 10th for major American cities (Dallas and Phoenix ranked 1 and 2). The projected population growth for the Denver metropolitan area from 1978 to 1983 ranked third in the nation, and Colorado was predicted to be one of the 10 fastest-growing states during the 1980s.

Commercial construction permits grew from 340 in 1970 with an estimated value of $70,818,000, to 1,235 in 1980 with an estimated value of $400,294,000. This growth was not steady, however. Year-to-year changes in dollar value of commercial construction varied from 0.2 percent to 91.6 percent, and the number of permits dropped from a high of 2,245 in 1978 to 1,235 in 1980. Similar patterns of growth and variation characterized industrial construction.

Translating construction growth into estimates of demand for architectural services is difficult. One rule of thumb holds that each additional person added to the population base requires 1,000 square feet of homes, schools, churches, offices, hospitals, manufacturing facilities, retail and shopping facilities, and transportation facilities. In the Denver metro area alone, this could mean 338 million square feet. At $50 average per square foot, total construction expenditure over the decade could reach $16.9 billion, involving as much as $845 million in design fees during the 1980s.

The past and projected growth in demand for architectural services was accompanied by a significant growth in the number of architects in Colorado. From 1979 to 1982, the number of state registrations of individual architects grew from 1,400 to 3,381, an increase of 141.5 percent. Over 100 architectural firms competed actively in the Denver market. (Over 500 architects are listed in the Yellow Pages of the Denver metro area phone directory.) In recent years, a number of national firms (e.g., Skidmore, Owens and Merrill) opened offices in Denver. Other major firms came to Colorado to do one job and then returned to their home offices (e.g., Yamasaki for the Colorado National Bank Office Tower, TAC for Mansville World Headquarters). Of the 26 major firms working on 38 selected jobs in Denver in 1983, 16, or 61.5 percent, were Denver based. Of the other 10, which have headquarters offices elsewhere, all but 2 had offices in Denver.

Major categories of customers for architectural services include:

Industrial.

Commercial.
- Owner.
- Developer.

Government.
- Federal.
- State.
- Municipal.

Residential (note: RNL did not compete in this market).

Within these categories, however, not all architectural work is available to independent firms, and not all architectural work on a project is awarded to one architect. A recent Denver survey, for example, indicated that of 49 commercial jobs under construction with a known architect, 11 were handled by an "inside" architect. Of the remaining 38 jobs, 20 included shell and space design whereas 18 involved space design only. In the 18 space designs, only 50 percent were actually done by architects.

The rapid growth in the construction market in Denver came to an abrupt halt in February 1982. Triggered by the broad realization that the oil boom was over, or had at least slowed significantly, project after project was put on hold. Construction of office space literally came to a halt. Of particular concern to RNL, which had just completed negotiations for a $1 million contract with Exxon, was the Exxon announcement of the closure of its Colorado Oil Shale activities at Parachute, Colorado.

It was against the backdrop of these changes that RNL felt the pressing need to review its marketing activities.

MARKETING OF ARCHITECTURAL SERVICES

The basis of competing for architectural work has changed dramatically over the past several decades. As John Rogers recalled:

> At the beginning of my practice in 1956, you could establish an office, put a sign on your door, print calling cards, and have a "news" announcement with your picture in the *Daily Journal* that you had established a new practice of architecture. Beyond that, it was appropriate to suggest to friends and acquaintances that I was in business now and I hoped that they might recommend me to someone they knew. The Code of Ethics of the American Institute of Architects, like many other professions at the time,

> prohibited any kind of aggressive marketing or sales effort as practiced in recent times.
>
> In fact, after convincing one School Board member (an artist) in Jefferson County that design was important, and then being awarded a commission to design an elementary school, which led to another and another, it was not surprising to read in the *Daily Journal* that the School Board had met the previous evening and had elected me to design a new junior high school, one that I hadn't even known about. I called and said, "Thank you." Marketing expense was zero with the exception of an occasional lunch or courtesy call here and there.
>
> Today, the situation is vastly different. We have to compete for most jobs, against both local firms and, increasingly, large national firms. Clients are becoming more sophisticated regarding the purchase of architectural services [see Exhibit 2 for a brief description of buyer behavior]. Promotion, of some kind, and concepts such as segmentation have become a way of life.

During the 1960s, development of an architectural practice was a slow process, characterized by heavy reliance on word of mouth regarding professional experience and expertise. Overt communication about an architect's qualifications was limited to brochures. Personal acquaintances played a significant role in the development of new clients. Personal relations between principals and clients were an important part of continuing and new relations. This method of practice development tended to favor local firms, whose reputation could be checked out on a personal basis, and small firms, whose principals could provide personal management and design of client projects.

As Denver grew, the market changed. The advantage of being a successful, local architect and knowing the local business community diminished. Newcomers to Denver tended to rely on relationships with architects in other cities. For local architects there wasn't time to rely on traditional communication networks to establish relationships with these newcomers. The size of projects grew, requiring growth in the size of architectural staffs. Personal attention to every client by principals was no longer possible.

Concomitantly, there was a growing change in the attitude toward the marketing of professional services. New entrants in the fields of medicine and law, as well as architecture, were becoming impatient with the slowness of traditional methods of practice development. A Supreme Court decision significantly reduced the restrictions that state bar associations could impose on lawyers with respect to their pricing and advertising practices. In a similar vein, the American Institute of Architects signed a consent decree with the Justice Department, which prohibited the organization from publishing fee schedules for architectural services.

Perhaps of most significance for architects, however, was the start of the so-called proposal age. Investigations in Maryland and Kansas, among other states, had revealed improper involvement of architects

EXHIBIT 2 Buyer Behavior

Purchase of architectural services is both complex and varied. Subject to many qualifications, however, there seems to be a number of steps that most buying situations have in common.

Development of a list of potential architects.

Identification of those architects from whom proposals will be solicited for a specific job (usually called the short list).

Invitations to submit proposals.

Evaluation of proposals and screening of final candidates.

Selection of a finalist, based on proposal evaluation, or invitations to finalists to make oral presentations to an evaluation group.

From a marketing standpoint, the focus of interest is the process of getting on the short list and the process by which the final selection is made.

The Short List

Prospective clients find out about architects in a variety of ways. Those who are frequent users of architectural services will generally keep a file of architects, sometimes classified as to type or practice. Additions to the file can come from mailed brochures, personal calls, advertisements, press releases, or, in fact, almost any form of communication. When a specific requirement develops, the file is reviewed for apparent fit. With many variations, a short list is developed and proposals are solicited.

Those who use architects infrequently tend to rely on various businesses of social networks to develop what is in essence their short list. In either case, a previously used architect is almost always on the short list, provided the past experience was satisfactory.

As the largest single customer for architectural services, agencies of the federal government follow a well-defined series of steps, including advertisements in the *Commerce Business Daily* and mail solicitation of local firms.

The Selection Process

The selection process is significantly influenced by the nature and scope of the work and its importance to the firm. Architect selection on major buildings is usually made at the highest level in the organization: by a principal or the president in a private organization or by various forms of boards in not-for-profit organizations such as churches. In some instances, the principal, president, or board are actively involved in all phases of the process. In others, the management of the process is delegated to others who develop recommendations to the decision makers. On smaller jobs, and those of an ongoing nature (e.g., space management), the decision is usually at lower levels and may involve a plant engineer or facilities manager of some kind.

Regardless of the level at which the selection process is made there seem to be two well-defined patterns to the process. The first, and predominant one, evaluates the firms on the short list, taking into prime consideration nonprice factors such as reputation, performance on previous jobs, and current work-

EXHIBIT 2 *(concluded)*

load. Based on this evaluation, one firm is selected and a final agreement is then negotiated as to the scope of the work, the nature of the working relationship, the project team, and specific details as to price. The second, and of limited but growing use, pattern attempts to specify the requirements so completely that a firm price can accompany the proposal. In some instances, the price and the proposal are submitted separately. Evaluation of the proposals includes a dollar differential, and these dollar differentials are applied to the price quotation to determine the low evaluated bidder.

Regardless of the process, there appear to be three main criteria on which firms are evaluated:

1. *The ability of the firm to perform the particular assignment.* For standard work this assessment is relatively easy and relies on the nature of past work, size of the organization, current backlogs, and so forth. For more creative work the assessment becomes more difficult. Much importance is put on past work, but the proposal starts to take on additional importance. Sketches, drawings, and, sometimes, extensive models may be requested with the proposal. In some instances, there may actually be a design competition. Much of this evaluation is, perforce, of a subjective nature.
2. *The comfort level with the project team that will be assigned to do the work.* For any but the most standard work there is recognition that there will be constant interaction between representatives of the client's organization and members of the architectural firm. Almost without exception, therefore, some kind of evaluation is made of the project team, or at least its leaders, in terms of the client's comfort level with the personalities involved.
3. *Finally, the matter of cost.* While direct price competition is not a factor in most transactions, the cost of architectural services is always a concern. This has two components. First, there is concern with the total cost of the project, over which the architect has great control. Second, there is growing concern with the size of the architect's fee, per se.

At least some assessment of the reputation of the architect with respect to controlling project costs is made in determining the short list. Once final selection is made, there is likely to be much discussion and negotiation as to the method of calculating the fee. The traditional method of simply charging a percentage of the construction price seems to be on the wane. Increasingly, clients for architectural services are attempting to establish a fixed fee for a well-defined project. The nature of architectural work, however, is such that changes are a fact of life and that many projects cannot be sufficiently defined in the initial stages to allow precise estimation of the design costs. Some basis for modifying a basic fee must, therefore, be established. Typically this is on some kind of direct cost basis plus an overhead adder. Direct costs for various classes of staff and overhead rates obviously become matters for negotiation. In the case of the federal government, the right is reserved to audit an architect's books to determine the appropriateness of charges for changes.

and engineers with state officials. Financial kickbacks were proven on many state projects. Formal proposals, it was felt, would eliminate or reduce the likelihood of contract awards made on the basis of cronyism or kickbacks. Starting in the government sector, the requirement for proposals spread rapidly to all major clients. In 1984, for example, even a small church could receive as many as 20 detailed proposals on a modestly sized assignment.

MARKETING AT RNL

In 1984, RNL was engaged in a number of marketing activities. In addition to proposal preparation, major activities included:

- Professional involvement in the business community by principals, which provides contacts with potential clients. This included memberships in a wide variety of organizations such as the Downtown Denver Board, Chamber of Commerce, and Denver Art Museum.
- Participation in, and appearances at, conferences, both professional and business oriented.
- Daily review of *Commerce Business Daily* (a federal publication of all construction projects) along with other news services that indicate developing projects.
- Maintenance of past client contacts. (RNL found this difficult but assigned the activity to its project managers.)
- Development of relationships with potential clients, usually by giving a tour through the office plus lunch.
- VIP gourmet catered lunches for six invited guests, held once a month in the office. These involved a tour of the office and lively conversation, with some attempt at subsequent follow-up.
- Participation in appropriate local, regional, or national exhibits of architectural projects.
- Occasional publicity for a project or for a client.
- The *Cutting Edge*.[1]
- An assortment of brochures and information on finished projects.
- Special arrangements with architectural firms in other locations to provide the basis for a variety of desirable joint ventures.

---

[1] The *Cutting Edge* is an RNL publication designed to inform clients and prospects about new developments in architecture and planning and about significant RNL accomplishments (see Exhibit 3 for an example of an article on a typical issue).

EXHIBIT 3

The Cutting Edge

Planning for Parking

The recent boom in downtown Denver office building has resulted in tremendous increases in population density in Denver's core, bringing corresponding increases in the number of vehicles and their related problems as well.

Auto storage, or parking, is one of the major resulting problems. Most building zoning requires parking sufficient to serve the building's needs. Even building sites not requiring parking are now providing parking space to remain competitive in the marketplace.

RNL's design for this above-grade parking structure at 1700 Grant aided in facilitating lease of the office building.

Parking solutions can range from a simple asphalt lot to a large multi-floor parking structure; the decision is based on many factors including site access, required number of spaces, land costs, budget and user convenience.

For many suburban sites, where land costs are sufficiently low to allow on-grade parking, design entails mainly the problems of circulation and landscaping. Circulation includes issues of easy site access and optimal efficient use of the site. Landscaping, including landforming, can visually screen automobiles and break up ugly seas of asphalt common to poorly designed developments.

At the opposite end of the parking spectrum are downtown sites where high land costs necessitate careful integration of parking into the building concept. This is often accomplished by building parking underground, below the main structure. Parking design, in this case, becomes a problem of integrating the circulation and the structure of the building above. While building underground eliminates the need for acceptable outer appearance, the costs of excavation, mechanical ventilation, fire sprinklering and waterproofing make this one of the most expensive parking solutions.

Between on-grade parking and the underground structure is the above-grade detached or semi-detached parking structure. This solution is very common in areas of moderate land cost where convenience is the overriding factor.

Site conditions do much to generate the design of an above-grade parking structure, but where possible the following features should ideally be included:

1. Parking is in double loaded corridors, i.e. cars park on both sides of the circulation corridor to provide the most efficient ratio of parking to circulation area;

2. Parking at 90 degrees to circulation corridors rather than at angles, once again the most efficient use of space;

3. Access to different garage levels provided by ramping the parking floors, efficiently combining vertical circulation and parking;

4. A precast prestressed concrete structure (this structure economically provides long spans needed to eliminate columns which would interfere with parking circulation and the fireproof concrete members have a low maintenance surface that can be left exposed).

5. Classification as an "open parking garage" under the building code, meaning that the structure has openings in the walls of the building providing natural ventilation and eliminating the need for expensive mechanical ventilation of exhaust fumes;

6. A building exterior in a precast concrete finish, allowing the designer to combine structure and exterior skin into one low cost element.

RNL recently completed work on the $20,000,000 1700 Grant Office Building for Wickliff & Company. The inclusion of a 415 car parking garage in the 1700 Grant project provided one of the amenities necessary for successful leasing in a very depressed leasing market.

A Publication of RNL/Interplan • by Richard T. Anderson • Vol. II No. 1 • 1576 Sherman Street Denver, Co. 80203 (303) 832-5599

RNL participated in a number of market segments, which it identified in Exhibit 4, together with its view of the required approach.

Net fee income and allocation of marketing expenses by major segments is given in Exhibit 5. The general feeling at RNL was that there is a lapse of 6 to 18 months between the marketing effort itself and tangible results such as fee income.

Salient aspects of budgeted marketing expense for 1985, by segment, were:

1. *Government.* Heavy emphasis on increased trips to Omaha (a key Corps of Engineers location), Washington, and other out-of-state (as well as in-state) locations plus considerable emphasis on participation in municipal conferences.
2. *Private.* Personal contact at local, state, and regional levels with corporations, banks, developers, and contractors plus local promotion through Chamber of Commerce, clubs, VIP lunches, *Cutting Edge,* promotion materials, and initiation of an advertising and public relations effort.
3. *Semiprivate.* Increased level of personal contact and promotional effort.
4. *Interiors.* Major allocation of salary and expenses of a new full-time

EXHIBIT 4

Segment	*Approach*
Government	
City and county governments	Personal selling, political involvement.
School districts	Personal selling (professional educational knowledge required).
State government	Political involvement, written responses to RFPs (requests for proposals, from clients), personal selling.
Federal government	Personal selling, very detailed RFP response, no price competition in the proposal stage.
Private sector	Personal selling, social acquaintances, referrals, *Cutting Edge,* preliminary studies, price competition.
Semiprivate sector (includes utilities)	Personal selling, *Cutting Edge,* referrals, continuing relationships, some price competition.

EXHIBIT 5

	1982		*1983*		*1984 (estimated)*		*1985 (estimated)*	
	Net Fee	*Marketing Expense*	*Net Fee*	*Marketing Expense*	*Net Fee*	*Marketing Expense*	*Net Fee*	*Marketing Expense*
Government	$ 800	$104	$1,220	$101	$1,012	$150	$1,200	$140
Private	1,376	162	1,261	140	1,200	195	1,616	220
Semiprivate	88	11	118	24	100	25	140	30
Interiors	828	40	670	30	918	100	1,235	110
Urban design	95	20	31	10	170	30	220	40
Total	$3,187	$337	$3,300	$305	$3,400	$500	$4,411	$540

Note: All amounts are in $000s.

marketing person to improve direct sales locally plus other promotional support.

5. *Urban design.* Some early success indicates that land developers and urban renewal authorities are the most likely clients. Planned marketing expense is primarily for personal contact.

Additional marketing efforts being given serious consideration included:

A more structured marketing organization with more specific assignments.

Increased visibility for the firm through general media and trade journals; paid or other (e.g., public relations).

Appearances on special programs and offering special seminars.

Use of more sophisticated selling tools such as video tapes and automated slide presentations.

Increased training in client relations/selling for project managers and other staff.

Hiring a professionally trained marketing manager.

Determining how the national firms market (i.e., copy the competition).

Expansion of debriefing conferences with successful and unsuccessful clients.

Use of a focus group to develop effective sales points for RNL.

Training a marketing MBA in architecture versus training an architect in marketing.

RNL CLIENTS

RNL described its clients as:

1. Having a long history of growing expectations with respect to detail, completeness, counseling, and cost control.
2. Mandating the minimization of construction problems, including changes, overruns, and delays.
3. Having an increased concern for peer approval at the completion of a project.
4. Having an increased desire to understand and be a part of the design process.

Extensive interviews of clients by independent market researchers showed very favorable impressions about RNL. Terms used to describe the firm included:

Best and largest architectural service in Denver.

Innovative yet practical.

Designs large projects for "who's who in Denver."

Long-term resident of the business community.

Lots of expertise.

Designs artistic yet functional buildings.

RNL's use of computer-aided design systems was seen as a definite competitive edge. Others mentioned RNL's extra services, such as interior systems, as a plus, although only 35 percent of those interviewed were aware that RNL offered this service. In general, most clients felt that RNL had a competitive edge with regard to timeliness, productivity, and cost consciousness.

Two major ways that new clients heard about RNL were identified. One was the contact RNL made on its own initiative when it heard of a possible project. The other was through personal references. All those interviewed felt advertising played a minor role, and, in fact, several indicated they had questions about an architectural firm that advertises.

Clients who selected RNL identified the following as playing a role in their decision:

Tours of RNL's facilities.

Monthly receipt of *Cutting Edge.*

Low-key selling style.

RNL's ability to focus on their needs.

Thoroughness in researching customer needs and overall proposal preparation and presentation.

RNL's overall reputation in the community.

Belief that RNL would produce good, solid (not flashy) results.

Clients who did not select RNL identified the following reasons for their decision:

RNL had less experience and specialization in their particular industry.

Decided to stay with the architectural firm used previously.

Decided to go with a firm that has more national status.

Other presentations had more "pizazz."

Overall, clients' perceptions of RNL were very positive. There was less than complete understanding of the scope of RNL services, but its current approach to clients received good marks.

MARKETING ISSUES AT RNL: SOME VIEWS OF MIDDLE MANAGEMENT

Richard von Luhrte joined RNL in 1979, following extensive experience with other firms in Chicago and Denver. In 1984, he led the firm's urban design effort on major projects, served as a project manager, and participated actively in marketing. He came to RNL because the firm "fits my image." He preferred larger firms that have extensive and complementary skills. He commented on marketing as follows:

> RNL has a lot going for it. We have a higher overhead rate, but with most clients you can sell our competence and turn this into an advantage. I think RNL is perceived as a quality firm, but customers are also concerned that we will gold-plate a job. I'd like to be able to go gold-plate or inexpensive as the circumstances dictate. But it's hard to convince a customer that we can do this.
>
> For many of our clients continuity is important and we need to convey that there will be continuity beyond the founders. RNL has done well as a provider of "all things for all people," and our diversification helps us ride through periods of economic downturn. On the other hand, we lose some jobs because we're not specialized. For instance, we haven't done well in the downtown developer market. We're starting to do more, but if we had targeted the shopping center business we could have had seven or eight jobs by now. One way to operate would be to jump on a trend and ride it until the downturn and then move into something else.
>
> There's always the conflict between specialization and fun. We try to stay diversified, but we ought to be anticipating the next boom. At the same time, there's always the problem of overhead. In this business you can't carry very much, particularly in slow times.

I like the marketing part of the work, but there's a limit on how much of it I can, or should, do. Plus, I think it's important to try to match our people with our clients in terms of age and interests, which means we need to have lots of people involved in the marketing effort.

Oral presentations are an important part of marketing, and we make a lot of them. You have to make them interesting, and there has to be a sense of trying for the "close." On the other hand, I think that the presentation is not what wins the job, although a poor presentation can lose it for you. It's important that the presentation conveys a sense of enthusiasm and that we really want the job.

As comptroller, Jane Washington was involved extensively in the firm's discussions about its marketing efforts. As she described the situation:

There is little question in my mind that the people at the top are committed to developing a marketing orientation at RNL. But our objectives still aren't clear. For instance, we still haven't decided what would be a good mix of architecture, interiors, and planning. Interiors is a stepchild to some. On the other hand, it is a very profitable part of our business. But it's not easy to develop a nice neat set of objectives for a firm like this. Two years ago we had a seminar to develop a mission statement, but we still don't have one. This isn't a criticism. Rather, it's an indication of the difficulty of getting agreement on objectives in a firm of creative professionals.

One problem is that our approach to marketing has been reactive rather than proactive. Our biggest marketing expenditure is proposal preparation, and we have tended to respond to RFPs as they come in, without screening them for fit with targeted segments. From a budget standpoint we have not really allocated marketing dollars to particular people or segments, except in a pro forma kind of way. As a result, no one person is responsible for what is a very large total expenditure.

Another problem is that we don't have precise information about our marketing expenditures or the profitability of individual jobs. It would be impractical to track expenditures on the 500–1,000 proposals we make a year, but we could set up a system that tracks marketing expenditures in, say, 10 segments. This would at least let individuals see what kind of money we're spending for marketing, and where. We also could change from the present system, which basically measures performance in terms of variation from dollar budget, to one that reports on the profitability of individual jobs. I've done some studies on the profitability of our major product lines, but those don't tie to any one individual's performance.

Rita Mitchell, who has an MS in library science and information systems, joined RNL in 1981. Originally her assignment focused on organizing marketing records and various marketing information resources. In her new role as new business development coordinator she had a broader set of responsibilities. According to Rita;

We definitely need some policies about marketing, and these ought to spell out a marketing process. In my present job, I think I can help the board synthesize market information and so help to develop a marketing plan.

Colorado. He was instrumental in developing new services at RNL, including Interplan and SMS, Inc., and was heavily involved in training of the next level of management. In 1984, he supervised day-to-day operations and also served as president of Interplan and SMS, Inc. Looking to the future, Vic observed:

Our toughest issue is dealing with the rate of change in the profession today. It's probably fair to say there are too many architects today. But this is a profession of highly idealistic people, many of whom feel their contribution to a better world is more important than dollars of income and so will stay in the field at "starvation wages." We wrestle with the question of "profession or business?" but competition is now a fact of life for us. The oil boom of the 1970s in Denver triggered an inrush of national firms. Many have stayed on, and we now have a situation where one of the largest national firms is competing for a small job in Durango. We're also starting to see more direct price competition. Digital Equipment recently prequalified eight firms, selected five to submit proposals that demonstrated understanding of the assignment, and asked for a separate envelope containing the price.

Our tradition at RNL has been one of quality. I think we're the "Mercedes" of the business, and in the long haul an RNL customer will be better off economically. A lot of things contribute to this—our Interplan concept, for instance—but the key differentiation factor is our on-site-planning approach.

In 1966–68, we were almost 100 percent in education. Then I heard that they were closing some maternity wards, and we decided to diversify. Today we have a good list of products, ranging from commercial buildings to labs and vehicle maintenance facilities. In most areas, the only people who can beat us are the superspecialists, and even then there's a question. Our diversification has kept our minds free to come up with creative approaches. At Beaver Creek, for example, I think we came up with a better approach to condominium design than the specialists. Plus, we can call in special expertise, if it's necessary.

Over the past several years we've had a number of offers to merge into national, or other, firms. We decided, however, to become employee owned. Our basic notion was that RNL should be an organization that provides its employees a long-time career opportunity. This is not easy in an industry that is characterized by high turnover. Less than 10 percent of architectural firms have figured out how to do it. But we're now at 35 percent employee ownership.

I'm personally enthusiastic about Interplan. It has tremendous potential to impact our customers. In Seattle, for instance, a bank came to us for a simple expansion. Our Interplan approach, however, led to a totally different set of concepts.

We've had some discussion about expansion. Colorado Springs is a possibility, for instance. But there would be problems of keeping RNL concepts and our culture. We work hard to develop and disseminate an RNL culture. For example, we have lots of meetings, although John and I sometimes disagree about how much time should be spent in meetings. A third of our business comes from interiors, and there is as much difference between interior designers and architects as there is between architects and mechanical engineers.

In somewhat similar vein, John Rogers commented:

In the 1960s, RNL was primarily in the business of designing schools. We were really experts in that market. But then the boom in school construction came to an end, and we moved into other areas. First into banks and commercial buildings. We got started with Mountain Bell, an important relationship for us that continues today. We did assignments for mining companies and laboratories. In the late 1960s, no one knew how to use computers to manage office space problems, and we moved in that direction, which led to the formation of Interplan. We moved into local and state design work. One of our showcase assignments is the Colorado State Judicial/Heritage Center.

In the 1980s, we started to move into federal and military work, and this now represents a significant portion of our business.

We have done some developer work, but this is a tough market. It has a strong "bottom line orientation," and developers want sharp focus and expertise.

As we grow larger we find it difficult to maintain a close client relationship. The client wants to know who will work on the assignment, but some of our staff members are not good at the people side of the business.

Currently we're still doing lots of "one of a kind" work. Our assignment for the expansion of the *Rocky Mountain News* building, our design of a condominium lodge at Beaver Creek, and our design of a developer building at the Denver Tech Center are all in this category. A common theme, however, is our "on-site" design process. This is a process by which we make sure that the client is involved in the design from the start and that we are really tuned in to his requirements. I see this as one of our real competitive advantages. But I'm still concerned that we may be trying to spread ourselves too thin. Plus, there's no question that there is an increased tendency to specialization: "shopping center architects," for example.

We need to become better marketers, but we have to make sure that we don't lose sight of what has made us the leading architectural firm in Denver: service and client orientation.

Case 31

Babcock Swine, Inc.*

Lester Neidell
Floy Schrage
both of the University of Tulsa

M. James McPeak, president of Babcock Swine, Inc., sat at his desk reviewing the international sales figures for 1983, 1984, and the first quarter of 1985. Ever since the American farming community had fallen on hard economic times, Babcock had focused more of its energies on the international markets. To date, these markets had proven to be very profitable. However, Mr. McPeak questioned what role they would have in the future. Among the multitude of challenges facing the international marketer, Jim finds the most difficult problem to be the identification of potential customers. Babcock needs clients that are setting up new breeding operations that are both large-scale and "high-tech." Small farmers lack the capital for such an endeavor. The new corporate farmer is typically from the business community, but in each new country in which Jim wished to market his breeding stock the identification of such an adventuresome businessman was extremely difficult.

HISTORY OF THE COMPANY

In the early 1940s Monroe Babcock founded a farm genetics research company in Rochester, Minnesota. This company specialized in poultry genetics exclusively until 1969 when Mr. Babcock expanded into the area of swine genetics. A. H. Robins bought the entire Babcock opera-

* This case was prepared by Floy Schrage, MBA 1985, under the supervision of Professor Lester A. Neidell, both of the University of Tulsa as the basis for class discussion rather than to illustrate either effective or ineffective handling of an administrative situation. Certain data have been disguised.

tion in 1977. Two years later legislation was introduced in the Minnesota legislature that would have prevented corporations from operating in the agricultural industry. Though the bill was an attempt to protect the small farmer, Babcock's management lobbied with the legislators for exclusion, stressing their role as suppliers, not competitors, to the farmers. When the bill reached the floor there was no such exclusion for breeders.

This legislation, as well as the volatility of the commodity market, convinced A. H. Robins to divest itself of its agricultural division. In 1980, James McPeak and two partners purchased the swine portion of the business, Babcock Swine, Inc. Robins sold the poultry division to I.S.A., a French company, in 1981.

Mr. McPeak found a new location for Babcock's research farm outside LaCrosse, Wisconsin, and the center of the operation was moved. In the meantime, the Minnesota bill remained buried in committee. Babcock Swine is still a Minnesota corporation with its offices in Rochester.

Background of James McPeak

Mr. McPeak, born a Canadian but now a U.S. citizen, graduated from the University of Saskatchewan College of Agriculture in 1967 with a major in poultry science and an emphasis on nutrition and genetics. From 1968 to 1969 he worked as a swine service manager for Tripp-Way Swine Breeding Company. In 1970, he took a job as general manager of a food manufacturing plant for Burns Foods, Ltd. He became Vice President in charge of production for Babcock in 1972 and by 1977 had become Vice President-General Manager.

BREEDING PHILOSOPHIES

Hybrid breeders, by working with a number of lines of breeding stock, develop animals that emphasize different traits. Throughout its operation, Babcock's philosophy has focused on a superior economic animal. One competitor, Dekalb, breeds for carcass quality, while Pig Improvement Company (PIC) indexes its stock by leanness. Most hybrid breeders use four basic stock lines. Seagers, a British company, once developed seven lines of breeding stock, but subsequently returned to four lines when it realized that the three extra lines were not contributing to genetic superiority.

Unlike the hybrid breeders, the purebred breeders are restricted to only one line of genetic input. They stress consistency within the particular breed. Many purebred breeders exist in the United States.

Two of the largest, Monsanto and Purina, sell most of their stock in the Midwest to small- and medium-size farm operations that do not have the capital or the knowledge to take advantage of the high technology of genetic selection. Both companies do well in the market segment that cannot or does not utilize the more recent genetic developments.

The Babcock Research Center

Babcock's research and development farm near LaCrosse, Wisconsin, was recently expanded to produce 23,000 animals per year. It is located in an isolated area to eliminate the chances of disease being introduced from neighboring swine farmers. Advanced genetics doesn't mean much without a rigorous program to maximize the health of the animal. All employees who enter the center are required to remove their street clothing, "shower-in," and change into special clothing used only in the facility. The special uniforms are then washed on the premises to eliminate the possibility of bringing disease into the farm. To further avoid contamination, Babcock uses only its own vehicles and personnel to deliver boars and gilts.[1] The use of contract haulers who travel all over the country delivering other livestock is felt to be a major cause of the spread of hog diseases.

Considered by a major university swine extension veterinarian to have perhaps the highest health quality of any major swine breeder in the United States, Babcock's research and development farm had been federally inspected and designated as a U.S. Export Quarantine Station for over 10 years. This quarantine status is awarded to only those herds with no symptoms of disease. No competitor had been able to achieve this differential advantage until recent months when PIC also became an export station. This status allows Babcock and PIC to ship its animals direct, avoiding possible contamination caused by confinement with other animals in larger export stations.

The research center is open to prospective and current clients. In fact, no breeding stock has ever been sold without the customer visiting the research farm first. Jim McPeak feels that it is important for his clients to understand the technical nature of the breeding process and the care that goes into selecting the genetic traits. Customers are encouraged to bring their own veterinarians to perform any testing that is felt necessary to confirm the quality and health of the animals, including a slaughter test. The farm has its own resident veterinarian, Dr. Lux, on the premises at all times except when he is providing on-site services for both domestic and international customers.

---

[1] Boars are male swine; gilts are young female swine.

Dr. Schneider is the chief resident geneticist for the facility. It is his job to select replacement stock. The original farm had been stocked through the Caesarian method to acquire the healthiest possible animals for the breeding herd. This herd was then totally closed and no other animals have ever been brought on the farm. However, constant improvements are possible within the closed herd.

Breeding stock is selected only for genetic traits that can be measured in monetary value for the commercial producer. It takes nearly 2½ times as much feed to put on a pound of fat as it does a pound of lean meat, so Babcock breeds for leanness. The commercial producer wants fast-growing, high-yielding pigs with excellent carcass and feed conversion characteristics. Large litter size and the ability to withstand the stress of concrete floors and tight farrowing crates[2] are also important if the swine producer is to get the most pounds of pork out of his/her facility.

No purebred can maximize the economic impact of all these characteristics. It is the geneticist's responsibility to provide a balance of the genetic inputs. Babcock breeds its animals for leanness, growth rate, carcass quality, feed conversion, litter size, and durability. Concentration on any one of the variables would mean a sacrifice in another. As previously noted, one competitor focused on leanness. This resulted in a high-quality lean animal that had a very slow growth rate. Likewise, concentration on growth rate would have produced a hog that grew rapidly but had poor carcass quality due to excess fat. The leanest animals are also the slowest-growing animals. Balancing these two desirable characteristics means constant testing to make sure one is not becoming more dominant in each subsequent generation.

Based on the performance testing, each animal is computer indexed according to its rating on the desirable characteristics. The index number indicates whether the boar or gilt ranks high enough on transmittable economic traits to be used as a breeder or should be sent to market. The index selects only superior breeding stock, ensuring genetic performance that will be repeated in their progeny. The index is flexible enough to meet specific customer needs. In Taiwan, for example, a long animal is desired. The index does not rate animals on length, but because the herd is large enough, those hogs with extra length and a high index can be selected. The customer will have to sacrifice a little on quality, but when the market has different needs the formula for selection can be adjusted to fit the situation.

To ensure that the customer receives high performance tested animals, Babcock never sells, for breeding purposes, over one-third of the

---

[2] A farrowing crate is an enclosure where the sow or gilt is kept during birthing and the weaning process.

animals produced. The boars in the herd are replaced every six months and sows are replaced annually to ensure continuous genetic improvement. As long as the advanced genetic technology is concentrating on the improvement of productivity through feed conversion, there is no reason to retain high-indexed animals. The next generation will always be better than the last. This philosophy is what separates Babcock and other technologically advanced companies from the purebred breeders.

The Babcock Breeding Stock

Babcock has four distinct breeding lines arbitrarily named C, F, M, and K. Computer-indexed maternal grandparent boars are mated to computer-indexed maternal grandparent gilts on the customers' farms to produce replacement parent gilts that have been selected for reproductive traits. The computer-indexed paternal M and K lines are genetically selected for excellent carcass, growth rate, and feed conversion traits. These two lines produce the Babcock meat-line parent boar. By using Babcock parent gilts (C × F) mated to Babcock's meat-line boar (M × K), the producer is able to achieve a terminal-cross market hog that has the highest amount of pork for the fewest investment dollars. It takes generations to develop lines that can maximize the genetic potential. Babcock does not sell its grandparent boars to its clients. If a client were to try to breed within his or her own herd using parent boars, the customer would diminish the economic impact of the M and K lines.

Purebred breeders are restricted because they must try to achieve all desirable characteristics within one line. Hybrid breeders like Babcock can use different hybrid lines for specific purposes. Babcock's market hog combines genes from all four separate genetic lines of breeding stock (C, F, M, and K), resulting in 100 percent heterosis.[3] These 100 percent heterosis market hogs have an increased growth rate and are 17 days faster to market than hogs without heterosis. Babcock's feed conversion rate, including boar and sow feed, has been under 3:1 in large commercial herds while the average in the United States is 5:1. Over 23 pigs are marketed per sow per year and the carcasses yield consistently over 76 percent, which is at least 3 percent higher than the commercial average.

Because each new generation is expected to out-perform the last, internal parent stock at the research farm is replaced frequently.

---

[3] This term denotes an extraordinary capacity for growth often shown by crossbred animals or plants.

Boars only mate about 10 times and sows have only two litters before heading to market.

Breeding

The females in a commercial herd are replaced internally but the boar semen must be furnished by Babcock to prevent inbreeding and ensure the proper genetic inputs. All foreign customers except Japan and the Philippines are currently using frozen semen. When semen is needed, Babcock checks its best boars for conception rate. A boar is then sent to International Boar Semen Inc.[4], where the semen is readied for shipment and the boar then slaughtered. Since better breeders would follow the current stock, little or no inventory is kept. Often the boar is only used to fill one order.

As the client has to pay the shipping costs, it is beneficial to buy the breeding stock in frozen semen form. For example, shipping costs for live animals to Japan have ranged from $250–$300 per animal while the cost for shipping enough semen for an entire herd is only $385. As Jim McPeak explains it, "We don't care what the container looks like. Our objective is to reduce the cost for our customers."

CUSTOMER SERVICES

Once the initial herd is established, the commercial producer pays a yearly genetic input fee of up to $250,000. Pricing varies depending on the size of the herd and the amount of servicing that is needed. The fee includes the frozen semen or live boars that are necessary to continue the lines. However, most of the cost covers the multiple services that Babcock offers its customers. Below is a list of these services.

1. Management training in the United States for key personnel for new herds being established (with minimum qualifying orders).
2. Technological newsletters.
3. On-site veterinarian services.
4. Computerized feeding systems that evaluate the nutrient requirements for each customer individually, taking into account fluctuations in the prices of various grains and protein supplements.
5. Free delivery in the United States.
6. Computer software management programs to manage the herd and to index the performance of both boars and sows on the basis of

---

[4] This is a service company in Eldora, Iowa, that maintains none of its own breeding stock.

heritability traits. This eliminates subjectivity in the producers' selection of replacement gilts.
7. Genetically correct breeding stock.
8. Market surveys.
9. Continued research to improve the Babcock breeding lines.
10. Cash flow analysis and feasibility studies.
11. Preparation of all international and domestic health papers.

INTERNATIONAL MARKETS

In gross sales Babcock's domestic operations overshadow the international portion of the business, but that includes market hogs, where the profit margin is low. In net sales the percentage of business done internationally each year varies greatly. A large portion of the variation is explained by the United States hog market. The decline of the American farming community over the past three years is creating a focus on more international expansion. As of 1985, Babcock has customers in many locations around the world but is actively seeking new markets. Because of the technological sophistication of its product and services, the customers it is seeking are, by necessity, large corporate farmers.

Jim McPeak feels that it is very worthwhile to operate internationally but admits that such endeavors are not without their problems due to political, economic and communication difficulties.

He tends to all the international business himself, including initial contacts, follow-up sales and services, entertaining of foreign guests, and even writing his own contracts. These contracts cover both the establishment of the initial herd and the continuing service contract for genetic input fees.

The Far East

Korea. One large breeding herd had been established in Korea. The frozen semen that was sent there originally was not impregnating the sows. For over two years Babcock tried to locate the source of the problem. A veterinarian from the United States and technicians from Taiwan were sent to investigate and make sure all procedures were being properly followed. As a last effort, Mary Pavelko, of International Boar Semen, was sent to Korea. If she could not solve the problem, all future shipments would have to involve the transfer of live boars. Though the correct storage of frozen semen had been carefully explained many times, Mary discovered that one nitrogen tank in which the semen was stored was below required levels. When the nitrogen level is too low, the semen is killed. Korean management had a policy of using all the nitrogen in a tank, but when the pressure fell as the tank was depleted an insufficient level of nitrogen was maintained. Once this situation was corrected operations went well. The contractual arrangements with the Koreans for continuing genetic input and management services proved satisfactory to both parties and still existed in March of 1985.

Taiwan. In 1974 two herds of about 1,100 animals each were set up in Taiwan. By 1985, three herds of Babcock stock were in existence with all operations functioning profitably. Babcock is presently receiving $250,000 a year as a genetic input fee for supplying those operations with frozen semen and management services. The operations had not always been so smooth. The semen was originally sent in to Taiwan in pellet form. The pellet was then dissolved in distilled water. As in Korea, the semen was not functioning properly. When it was discovered that the water, though distilled, had more minerals than tap water in the United States, an alternate form of the product had to be developed. Today 15 percent of the market animals in Taiwan carry Babcock genetics even though no live animals have been sent there since 1976 when the Taiwan government made importation of hybrid animals illegal. Jim feels that the ban on hybrids was imposed after one of his competitors sold poor quality hybrid stock in Taiwan.

Hong Kong. Hong Kong also proved to be a difficult market to establish. Shortly after shipping the original breeding stock to Hong Kong, hog cholera and foot-and-mouth disease claimed half of the herd. Babcock explained why and how to take precautionary measures against disease with special emphasis on the need for all workers to "shower-in." Replacement stock was sent from Taiwan, but the diseases returned. When Jim McPeak went to Hong Kong he discovered that the only new precautionary measure that had been instituted was a small foot bath that workers were required to walk through. The Hong Kong farm still has recurring disease problems that fall far below Babcock's standards. Despite this, the relationship is continuing and amiable since, by Hong Kong standards, the farm is almost disease-free.

Japan. Japan is a successful market for Babcock. As a joint venture proposal, McPeak originally offered a contract with lower initial investment, but higher fees. Two Japanese investors refused this offer, paid $750,000 each for the original breeding stock, and agreed to fixed annual $55,000 genetic input fees. Each March the Japanese customers sent their orders for replacement boars along with irrevocable confirmed letters of credit to cover fees and shipping.

The Japanese market fits well with Babcock's differential advan-

EXHIBIT 1 Japan's Pig-Meat Production and Imports, 1980–1984

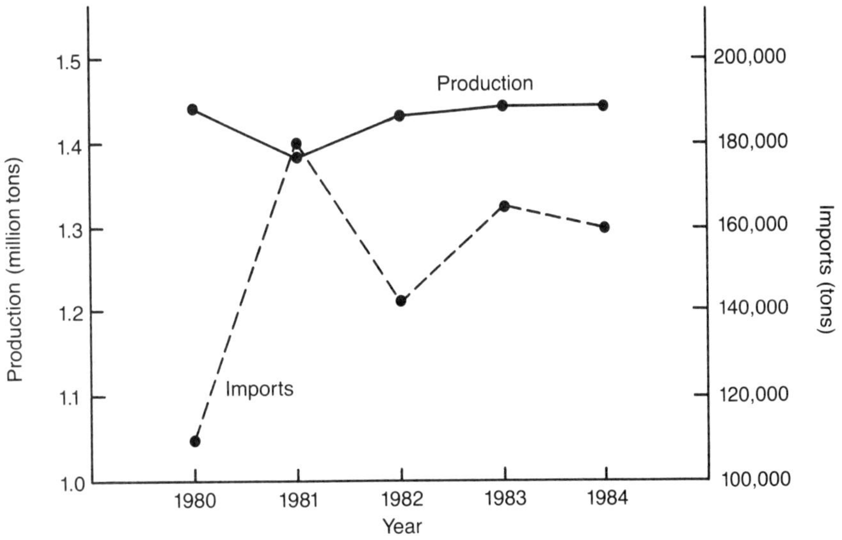

Source: Pig International, February 1985.

tages. Japan's current demand for pork far exceeds production capacity, with deficiencies being filled mostly by Canada and the European Common Market. The economic implications of excess demand has caused a shift toward the use of hybrid animals, high-tech operations, and larger breeding herds. (See Exhibits 1–5.)

Japan was not without drawbacks. The Japanese prefer to deal with large companies. As a small company, Babcock had to spend money up front to portray a successful, reputable image. In addition, the Japanese markets are protected by several trade barriers. First, it is illegal to ship frozen semen into Japan so the buyer has to pay for the high shipping costs of transporting live boars. Also, every animal entering the country has to be quarantined both in the country of origin and in Japan. The quarantine fee in Japan is $400 per animal. By the time the Japanese client receives the boars, each animal has incurred costs of more than $700 for shipping and quarantine. The health papers issued in the United States are only good for 30 days, but the quarantine period is also 30 days and must start on the day the papers are issued. The animals must be shipped on the 30th day or repeat the process. Timing becomes especially critical since the air freight charters that transport the animals are prepaid and nonrefundable.

In light of all of these obstacles and the advanced technology of the

EXHIBIT 2 Number of Japanese Pig Farms and Average Size, 1965–1984

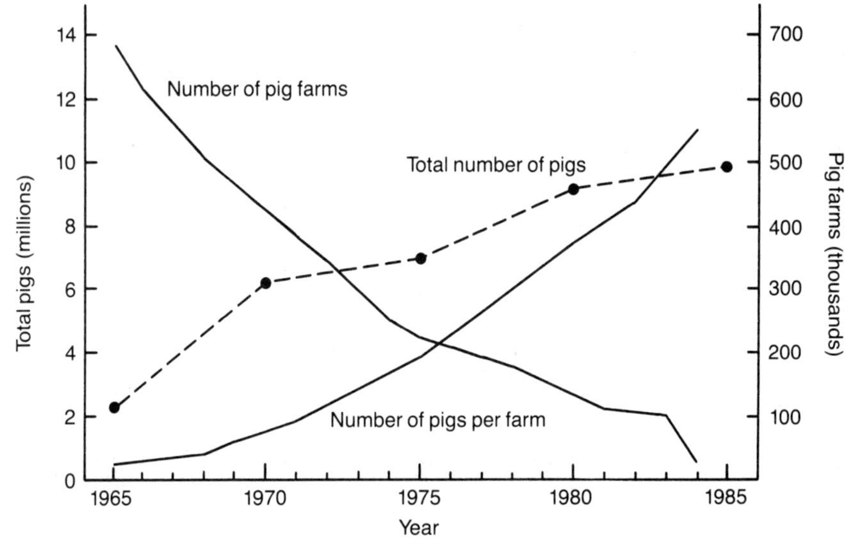

Source: Pig International, February 1985.

Japanese, Mr. McPeak expected to receive word that the Japanese firms had developed their own hybrid lines from the Babcock stock and would be replicating the business themselves. He was pleased to find the 1985 order in the mail on March 21 but would make no predictions about the possibility of the contract being honored in 1986. In June

EXHIBIT 3 Japanese Wholesale Price Index (1980 = 1.0)

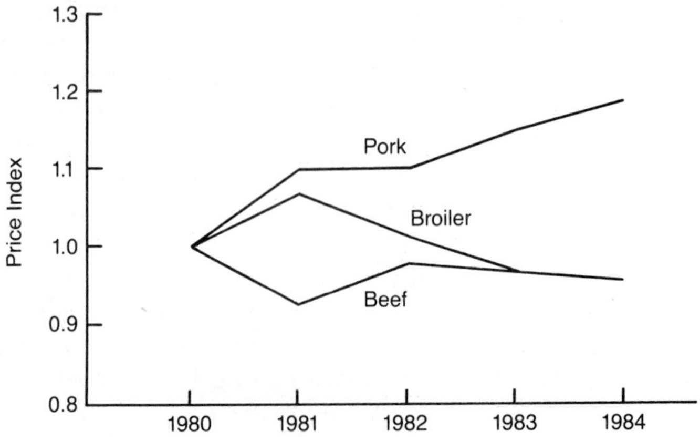

Source: Pig International, February 1985.

EXHIBIT 4 Meat Consumption in Japan, 1984

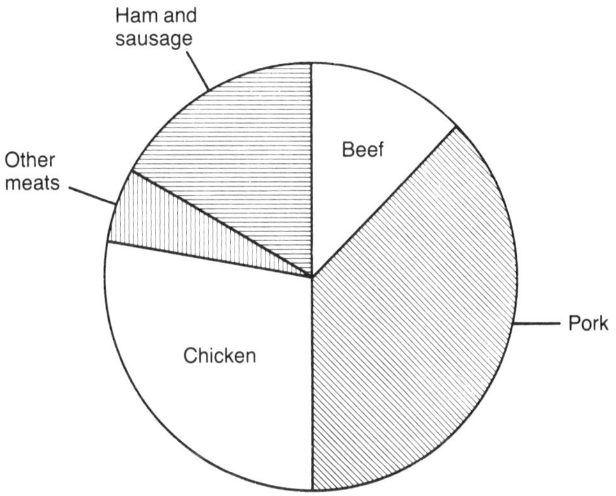

Source: Pig International, February 1985.

1985, he planned to visit the Japanese customers to further cement the relationship and to observe a new construction site.

China. Babcock has no current dealings in China, but a prospective client would be arriving the following week. Mr. McPeak felt very well prepared for this meeting. He had tried to enter that market earlier, but with disappointing results. The previous client had asked Babcock to arrange a package deal to include *all* set-up costs including the physical facilities. McPeak presented him with a plan that was similar to the facility successfully operating in Taiwan and one that he had determined to best meet the needs of the Chinese. This proposal was one-third the price charged by the competitor that received the contract. What Jim had not understood at the time was that the Chinese customer wanted the latest technology, necessary or not.

The Chinese businessman wanted air conditioning and full ventilation which Babcock's bid did not include. Though the extras weren't needed, the Chinese client wanted them and was willing to pay for them. Jim McPeak reflected on the situation. "In the United States we tend to look for the most economical way of doing business. When dealing internationally one should always list the alternatives, not just the correct solution, and let the customer make the choice. I'll never lose a package deal again because of one item."

Philippines. On March 20, 1985, Cholla Cebrero, General Manager of Luz Farms Inc., arrived from the Philippines. Cebrero was especially

EXHIBIT 5 Japan's Importation of Breeding Pigs by Type

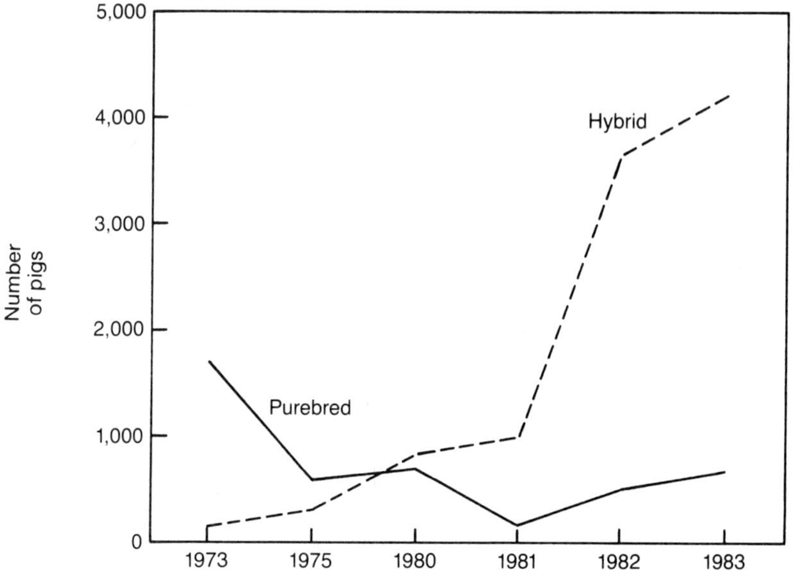

The specific figures for the period January 1981–November 1983 of imported hybrid breeding pigs, including both grandparent and parent-generation animals, were:

Babcock stock	3,395 imports
PIC Camborough	2,961 "
DeKalb	938 "
Euribrid Hypor	899 "
Four others	53 "

Source: Pig International, February 1985.

important to Babcock because the operation in the Philippines represented Babcock's first joint venture in a foreign country. In 1981, when the farm was developed, Babcock sold Cebrero the breeding stock at one-sixth its retail value in return for a share of the profits: the same terms the Japanese had turned down.

Cebrero was driven to the research farm in LaCrosse where he inspected the animals that were to be shipped to him in April, learned of new developments in farrowing equipment, and was shown how to use the computer programs for indexing his animals. Each of his animals went through a bleeding test that would have to be repeated at the time of exportation. This was not normally done, but Cebrero was particularly concerned with diseases that plagued the Philippines and Babcock wanted Cebrero to be confident of the quality of the animals. Due to the special contract, it was only now, four years after the initial sale, that Babcock would start to experience a return on its Philippine investment.

Mr. McPeak said, "I always treat other people like I would like to be treated. A bonded relationship is more important than any contract. When international people are in this country to do business with Babcock, I usually entertain them in my home." That night Cebrero ate a lavish dinner at the McPeak home and was treated as a friend as well as a business associate.

On March 21 Cebrero covered every aspect of the operation on which he had questions. Mr. McPeak was anticipating the payment that was to represent Babcock's share of the Philippine profits as well as the annual genetic input fee of $100,000. Cebrero would also be paying for supplies and an additional 125 boars and sows that he needed to expand his herd. With only three hours remaining before his flight time, Cebrero informed Jim McPeak that he could pay only a small portion of the amount that was due under their contractual agreement. The Philippine peso had taken a terrible beating, while Philippine hog prices had also dropped precipitously since the 1981 contract was signed. It was impossible for Cebrero to obtain U.S. dollars.

Western Hemisphere

Costa Rica. Babcock's involvement in Costa Rica had none of the usual problems associated with start-up operations. Everything went according to plan. But once the herd was well established and the firm seemed aware of all the operational details that were necessary for success, the Costa Ricans informed Babcock that they were confident they could continue the genetic lines themselves without Babcock boars. The contract was broken and relations severed. Babcock had lost the opportunity to capitalize on the operations in all subsequent years.

Dominican Republic. Jim McPeak had just returned from the Dominican Republic on March 18, 1985. He had been finalizing the details of a venture that looked very promising. Babcock would maintain 49 percent ownership and oversee the entire operation. Most of the output would be sold to Puerto Rico, which is currently dominated by Canadian frozen pork products. Babcock could sell fresh Dominican Republic pork for less than the Canadian competition. The hog market in the Dominican Republic was characterized by excessive price variation. The operating plan for this venture was geared to utilize the market swings. In a low market, local hogs would be purchased and processed for Puerto Rico as a means of increasing profit. When the market was high, only their own Babcock hogs would be butchered.

EXHIBIT 6 Value of Swine Sold: 1982, 1978 (in 000s)

	1982	*1978*
United States	$9,867,741	$8,071,766
States		
1. Iowa	2,550,488	2,061,298
2. Illinois	1,057,028	875,527
3. Minnesota	800,688	576,748
4. Indiana	787,389	593,164
5. Nebraska	709,743	538,294
6. Missouri	594,949	556,157
7. North Carolina	389,617	284,800
8. Ohio	370,674	295,459
9. Kansas	316,882	297,439
10. South Dakota	312,623	259,124
11. Wisconsin	258,039	213,308
12. Georgia	225,806	213,974
13. Michigan	182,764	124,746
14. Pennsylvania	165,306	105,092
Counties		
Sioux County, Iowa	75,776	53,625
Lancaster County, Pennsylvania	68,835	37,199
Delaware County, Iowa	66,327	49,638
Washington County, Iowa	62,568	49,163
Plymouth County, Iowa	60,306	46,992
Henry County, Illinois	58,872	48,747
Carroll County, Indiana	50,273	30,229
Kossuth County, Iowa	49,465	40,094
Mahaska County, Iowa	48,316	37,993
Dubuque County, Iowa	45,429	35,386

Source: Bureau of the Census.

Western Europe

Babcock has never attempted to sell in Europe because Europe has more than a dozen excellent domestic hybrid breeding companies.

THE UNITED STATES MARKET

The small American family hog producer is not as technologically advanced as Babcock's foreign customers. Most of these farmers are still raising purebreds. Purebred animals are judged on appearance, not on economic traits. This standard is perpetuated by county fairs, purebred breeders, and the government. U.S. Government Testing

Stations choose "super boars" each year based on showroom performance. Babcock purchases some of the boar semen each year for testing purposes. Only once in 10 years had any of the "super boars" performed comparably to Babcock's own stock in producing high-yield progeny. The individual farmer also typically selects his/her own "super boar." This boar, as well as high-yield sows, is kept for a long time because the new generation is expected to perform similar to the last. The emphasis is on uniformity within the herd.

Conversely, the American farmer has learned to use technological advances in fertilizing and poultry genetics. Poultry once was judged by showroom quality but no such judging exists today. Poultry breeding has evolved into a highly technical business that emphasizes only economic output. Today over 90 percent of all poultry production in the United States is accounted for by five large corporations.

The American farmer has fallen on hard times. The average income per farm fell from $12,700 in 1981 to only $6,800 in 1983.[5] The U.S. Government was planning drastic cuts in farm price supports that Agriculture Secretary John R. Block conceded would mean larger farms and fewer farmers.[6] Harold Dodd, president of the Illinois Farmer's Union, predicted that the farm subsidy cuts would drive 20 percent of American farmers out of business.[7] Other statistics concerning the American farmer are contained in the Appendix (Exhibits A1–A6).

Domestic customers for Babcock are mostly eastern, high-tech farmers. In the Hutterite colonies of Lancaster County, Pennsylvania (see Exhibit 6), as well as those in North and South Dakota, Babcock has a 70 percent market share. This success is due to the emphasis the Hutterites place on technology and to the large scale of their operations.

Because the American farm picture looked so bleak and had been slow to evolve toward hybrids, Babcock was concentrating more of its efforts on the foreign markets than it had in the past.

PROBLEMS

Jim McPeak speaks very freely about the problems he has encountered. He identified the following as the areas that cause the most difficulty.

---

[5] *U.S.A. Statistics in Brief 1985,* U.S. Department of Commerce, Bureau of the Census.

[6] *Business Week,* January 14, 1985, "Playing with Fire: Reagan Takes on the American Farmer."

[7] *Business Week,* January 14, 1985, "Why Many Farmers Could be Looking for a Job in Town."

1. The swine industry has extreme highs and lows in activity. It is a business that is changing rapidly, thus creating difficulties in maintaining market share.
2. Babcock's customers need to be large-scale operations that understand the economic advantages of high-tech genetic breeding. This eliminates the bulk of the domestic small farm population.
3. Political, economic, and communication barriers are unique in each international market.
4. International contracts can be broken with little recourse for the American company.
5. Some producers fail to understand the importance of continuing superior genetic input.
6. The most difficult problem facing Mr. McPeak is the identification of potential customers. Babcock advertises in local and international trade publications but all his customers have come through his own aggressive personal selling efforts, contacted either directly or through foreign agents. Finding possible new customers is a monumental task when your market is the world.

Appendix

EXHIBIT A1 U.S. Hog Farms—Number of Farms with Hogs

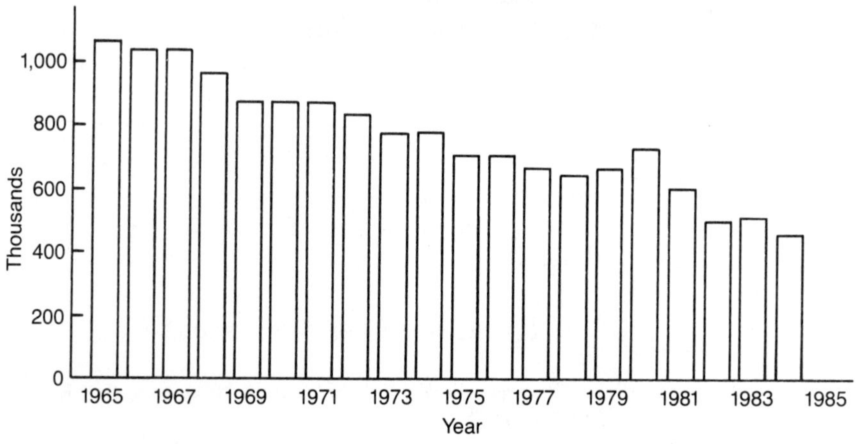

Source: Hog Farm Management 22, no. 6 (June 1985).

I do a lot of market research based on secondary data. For instance, we have access to Dialog and a number of other online databases, using our PC. Based on this research, and our own in-house competence, I think I can do some good market anticipation. The problem is what to do with this kind of information. If we move too fast, based on signals about a new market, there is obviously the risk of being wrong. On the other hand, if we wait until the signals are unmistakably clear, they will be clear to everyone else, and we will lose the opportunity to establish a preeminent position.

With respect to individual RFPs, our decision on which job to quote is still highly subjective. We try to estimate our chances of getting the job, and we talk about its fit with our other work, but we don't have much hard data or policy to guide us. We don't, for instance, have a good sense of other RFPs that are in the pipeline and how the mix of the jobs we're quoting and the resulting work fits with our present work in progress. The Marketing Committee [consisting of John Rogers, Vic Langhart, Phil Goedert, Rich Von Luhrte, Dick Shiffer, Rita Mitchell, and, occasionally, Bob Johnson] brings lots of experience and personal knowledge to bear on this, but it's not a precise process.

We have a number of sources of information about new construction projects: the *Commerce Business Daily* [a federal government publication], the *Daily Journal* [which reports on local government construction], the Western Press Clipping Bureau, Colorado trade journals, and so forth. Monitoring these is a major activity, and then we have the problem of deciding which projects fit RNL.

Bob Johnson, a project manager and member of the Marketing Committee, commented:

The way the system works now we have four board members and 12 project managers, most of whom can pursue new business. They bring these opportunities before the Marketing Committee, but it doesn't really have the clout to say no. As a result, people can really go off on their own. I'd like to see the committee flex its muscles a little more on what jobs we go after. But there's a problem with committing to just a few market segments. Right now we're involved in something like 30 segments. If we're wrong on one it's not a big deal. But if we were committed to just a few then a mistake could have really serious consequences.

For many of us, however, the major problem is managing the transfer of ownership and control to a broader set of individuals. Currently the prospective owners don't really have a forum for what they'd like the company to be. My personal preference would be to go after corporate headquarters, high-tech firms, speculative office buildings, and high-quality interiors. But there probably isn't agreement on this.

MARKETING ISSUES: THE VIEWS OF THE FOUNDERS

Vic Langhart started his practice of architecture in 1954 and has taught design in the Architecture Department of the University of

EXHIBIT A2 Sales of Farm Products—Number of Farms Selling Specified Commodities and Value of Sales, 1978 and 1982

Commodity	*Farms Selling Commodity*				*Value of Sales*			
	Number (1,000)		*Percent distribution*		*Amount ($ millions)*		*Percent distribution*	
Livestock, poultry, and their products	1569	1517	69.5	67.7	58,870	69,644	55.0	52.8
Poultry and poultry products	122	114	5.4	5.1	8,463	9,797	7.9	7.4
Dairy products	217	200	9.6	8.9	11,229	16,320	10.5	12.4
Cattle and calves	1320	1279	58.5	57.1	29,611	31,635	27.7	24.0
Hogs and pigs	424	315	18.8	14.1	8,072	9,868	7.5	7.5
Sheep, lambs and wool	89	99	3.9	4.4	645	608	.6	.5
Other livestock and livestock products	109	122	4.8	5.4	851	1,415	.8	1.1

Source: U.S. Bureau of the Census, 1982 Census of Agriculture, vol. 1.

EXHIBIT A3 Farm Debt Outstanding, 1970 to 1984 (in billions of dollars, except percentages)

Lender	*1970*	*1974*	*1975*	*1976*	*1977*	*1978*	*1979*	*1980*	*1981*	*1982*	*1983*	*1984 prel.*
Farm debt, total	53.0	73.3	81.6	91.5	103.9	122.7	140.8	165.8	182.0	201.7	216.3	214.7
Annual percent change	7.6	8.4	11.3	12.1	13.6	18.1	14.8	17.8	9.8	10.8	7.3	0.9
Farm debt/asset ratio (percent)	16.6	15.3	16.2	15.9	15.6	16.7	16.1	16.5	16.7	18.6	20.7	20.8

Amounts as of January 1. Minus sign (−) indicates decrease.

Source: U.S. Dept. of Agriculture, Economic Service, Economic Indicators of the Farm Sector: Income and Balance Sheet Statistics, annual. See also *Historical Statistics, Colonial Times to 1970,* Series K 361–367 and K 376–380.

EXHIBIT A4 Characteristics of Corporate Farms, by Type, 1982

Item	Unit	All Corporations	Family Held Corporation			Other Corporations		
			Total	*1–10 Stockholders*	*11 or More Stockholders*	*Total*	*1–10 Stockholders*	*11 or More Stockholders*
Farms	Number	59,792	52,652	50,842	1,810	7,140	5,997	1,143
Percent distribution	Percent	100.0	88.1	85.0	3.0	11.9	10.0	1.9
and in farms	Mil.acres	127.3	112.9	100.7	12.2	14.5	8.5	6.0
Average per farm	Acres	2,129	2,143	1,980	6,737	2,024	1,413	5,231
Value of—								
Land and buildings*	Bil.dol.	89.9	76.1	70.1	6.0	13.8	7.7	6.1
Average per farm*	$1,000	1,520	1,455	1,389	3,221	2,028	1,363	5,185
Farm products sold	Bil.dol.	31.5	22.9	20.7	2.3	8.6	5.5	3.1
Average per farm	$1,000	527	435	406	1,244	1,201	911	2,723

* Based on a sample of farms.

Source: U.S. Bureau of the Census, 1982 Census of Agriculture, vol. 1.

EXHIBIT A5 Indicators of Financial Stress in Agriculture, 1979 to 1983, and by Farm Region 1983 (in percent)

					1983					
Financial Stress Indication	*1979*	*1980*	*1981*	*1982*	*Total*	*North-east*[1]	*Corn Belt*[2]	*South*[3]	*Plains*[4]	*West*[5]
Average delinquency rate[6,7]	2.9	(NA)	(NA)	3.9	3.7	3.5	3.5	4.3	3.5	4.5
Farm borrowers who had bank financing discontinued	3.8	4.5	2.9	3.3	2.9	2.7	2.5	4.4	3.0	3.3
Farm borrowers loaned up to practical limits[7,8]	29	27	(NA)	32	28	27	26	40	27	32
Farmers in bank lending area who went out of business	(NA)	2.1	(NA)	2.2	2.3	2.0	2.2	3.1	2.4	2.3
Farmers in bank lending area who went through bankruptcy	(NA)	(NA)	(NA)	.8	1.1	1.0	1.0	1.9	.9	1.2

Note: For years ending in June, except as noted. Based on a survey of approximately 1,000 bankers which reflects their perception of farm financial conditions in their lending areas.
NA Not available.
[1] ME, NH, VT, MA, RI, CT, NY, NJ, PA, DE, MD, DC, MI, WI, and MN.
[2] OH, IN, IL, IA, and MO.
[3] VA, WV, NC, SC, GA, FL, KY, TN, AL, MS, AR, and LA, CA, AK, and HI.
[4] ND, SD, NE, KS, OK, and TX.
[5] MT, ID, WY, CO, NM, AZ, UT, NV, WA, OR [NV, WA, OR, CA, AK, HI]
[6] Percentage of dollar farm loan volume 30 days or more delinquent.
[7] As of June of year shown.
[8] Farm customers who have reached their maximum debt load.

Source: American Bankers Association, Washington, DC, *Agricultural Banker,* November 1983, and prior issues.

EXHIBIT A6 Farms—Number, Acreage, and Value, by Type of Organization, 1978 and 1982

						Percent Distribution			
Item	*Unit*	*Total**	*Individual or Family*	*Partner-ship*	*Corpo-ration*	*Total**	*Individual or Family*	*Partner-ship*	*Corpo-ration*
All Farms									
Number of farms: 1978	1,000	2,255	1,966	233	50	100.0	87.2	10.3	2.2
1982	1,000	2,239	1,946	223	60	100.0	86.9	10.0	2.7
Land in farms: 1978	Mil.acres	959	673	158	120	100.0	70.2	16.5	12.5
1982	Mil.acres	932	642	152	127	100.0	68.9	16.3	13.6
Value of land and buildings: 1978	Bil.dol.	623	(NA)	(NA)	(NA)	100.0	(NA)	(NA)	(NA)
1982	Bil.dol.	763	547	119	90	100.0	71.7	15.6	11.8
Value of farm products sold: 1978	Mil.dol.	106,829	(NA)	(NA)	(NA)	100.0	(NA)	(NA)	(NA)
1982	Mil.dol.	131,590	77,907	21,520	31,480	100.0	59.2	16.4	23.9
Farms With Sales of $10,000 and Over									
Number of farms: 1978	1,000	1,180	976	155	45	100.0	82.7	13.1	3.8
1982	1,000	1,143	934	152	52	100.0	81.7	13.3	4.5
Land in farms: 1978	Mil.acres	829	557	147	118	100.0	67.2	17.7	14.2
1982	Mil.acres	811	536	141	124	100.0	66.1	17.4	15.3

* Represents institutional farms, experimental and research farms, Indian reservations, etc.

Source: U.S. Bureau of the Census.

Section 5

Strategic Marketing Cases

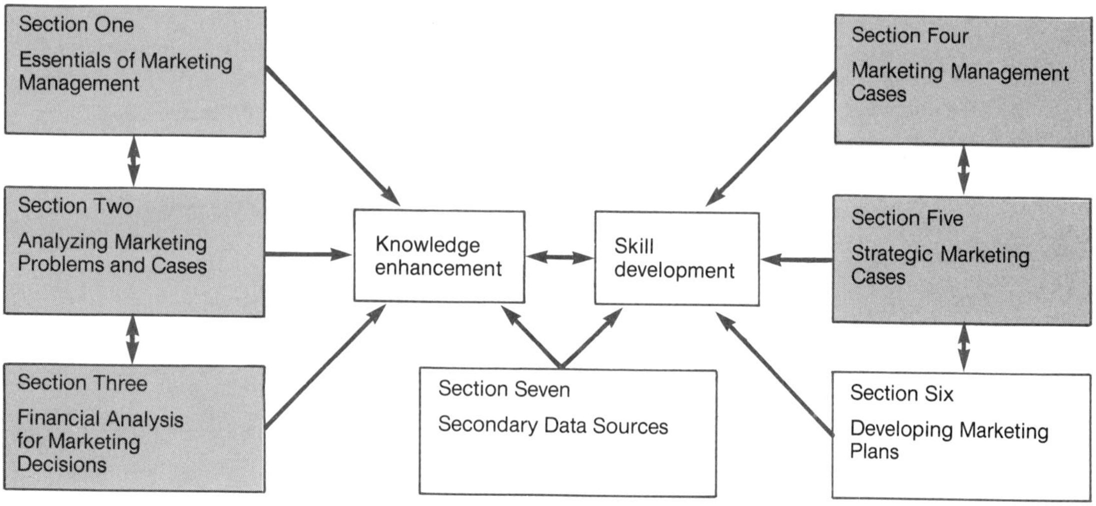

Marketing Management: Knowledge and Skills

NOTE TO THE STUDENT

The primary emphasis of the 11 cases in this section is on the role of marketing in the development of successful business or organizational strategies. While marketing is critical in these cases, successful analysis and strategy formulation will often involve other areas in the organization as well.

Keep in mind that the knowledge and skills you've developed in the analysis of the cases in the previous section will provide a useful foundation for analyzing the cases in this section. However, these cases are intended to broaden your knowledge of marketing and your skills at analyzing a variety of strategic problems.

Case 1

Maytag Company*

Lester Neidell
University of Tulsa

The Maytag Company of Newton, Iowa, has maintained an enviable position in the home-laundry market. Despite increased competition, and a price premium charged to consumers of roughly $100 per unit, it has continued to capture a "traditional" 15 percent share of the washing machine market, and has enjoyed profit margins roughly twice that of competitors. Operating results for the period 1974–1981 are given in Exhibit 1. The largest competitive share growth in laundry equipment has gone to Whirlpool, who, buoyed by the surge of its private-label sales to Sears and by Frigidaire's abandonment of the market, now sells approximately 45 percent of all home-laundry equipment in the United States.

Maytag Company backs its premium policy with a product consistently evaluated as superior in quality. The famous lonely Maytag repairman hammers home the theme that the purchase price premium buys lower service costs. But the quality gap appears to be lessening. Arnold Consdorf, editor of the trade journal *Appliance Manufacturer,* noted, "The quality gap that existed 5 or 10 years ago doesn't exist anymore. Model for model, I really don't see much difference as far as premium quality goes." A retailer notes, "The critical thing is that the rationale to run out and buy a Maytag has declined."

Maytag values highly its retail dealer relationships. A feature of the company's 1979 Annual Report was this assessment:

> Among Maytag's more than 10,000 independent retailers are most of the leading merchandisers in North America. While the wide geographic dispersion of so many dealers provides Maytag with outstanding service coverage, it is the mass merchandisers who generate much of the volume that keeps us growing. . . .

 Sources: "The Problems of Being Premium," *Forbes* (May 29, 1978), pp. 56–57; "A Duel of Giants in the Dishwasher Market," *Business Week* (October 9, 1978), pp. 137–38; Lawrence Ingrassia, "Staid Maytag Puts in Money on Stoves But May Need to Invest Expertise, Too," *The Wall Street Journal* (July 23, 1980), p. 27; "The New Maytag Recipe for Going Into Kitchens," *Business Week* (May 24, 1982), pp. 48–49; and Maytag Company Annual Reports.

EXHIBIT 1 Financial Summary for Maytag Company, 1974–1981 (in $millions)

	1974	*1975*	*1976*	*1977*	*1978*	*1979*	*1980*	*1981*
Net sales	229	238	275	299	325	369	349	409
Net income	21.1	25.9	33.1	34.5	36.7	45.3	35.6	37.4

> Historically, Maytag . . . sought dealer coverage in each community and thus had product availability, along with service, throughout the United States and Canada. [C]hanging . . . competition [required] developing quality volume accounts in major markets.
>
> Because selling quality appliances requires well-trained salespersons and outstanding parts and service availability . . . Maytag has stopped short of attempting to market its products through self-service "shopping cart" outlets. Nor do we have dealer arrangements with any chains across the board nationally, requiring instead that dealer selection be made in each market by those responsible for generating our market share in that locality.

A natural expansion of Maytag's home-laundry emphasis has been the commercial laundromat business. This business was pioneered in the 1930s when coin meters were attached to Maytag wringer-type washers. Rapid growth of coin-operated laundries occurred in the United States during the late 1950s and early 1960s. Increased competition and soaring energy costs of the 1970s cut deeply into laundromat profits. In 1975 Maytag introduced new energy-efficient machines and a "Home Style" store concept that has rejuvenated this business. More than 1,000 Home Style stores are currently in operation in the United States.

Until recently, Maytag's other major product effort has been dishwashers. Here the leading competitor is Design & Manufacturing, Inc., (D & M), whose "bread and butter" are private-label dishwashers for Sears, other retailers, and other appliance manufacturers. D & M's market share is approximately 45 percent. Other major dishwasher competitors include General Electric and Hobart Corporation's KitchenAid brand, each with approximately 19 percent shares. Maytag, who has been making dishwashers since 1966, has generally obtained annual shares in the 4–6 percent range. The "premium" price-quality segment is dominated by KitchenAid, and despite Maytag's efforts, little recognition of the Maytag name is apparent in the dishwasher business. Maytag's president, Daniel Krumm, admitted in 1978, "We might as well be selling the Jones dishwasher." A revamped 1979 product line provided an increase in sales but it is too soon to tell if the share increase is permanent.

Other product lines include food waste disposers and cooking appliances. Maytag's entry into cooking is being achieved by acquisition. In 1981 the Hardwick Stove Company was purchased for $28 million. Early 1982 saw the introduction of Maytag microwave ovens, produced by the Hardwick subsidiary. In April 1982, Maytag reached agreement with United Technologies to acquire its Jenn-Air subsidiary for an estimated $75 million. Jenn-Air is a producer of indoor barbeque grills and other innovative cooking and kitchen ventilation equipment.

President Krumm, explaining the recent Maytag thrust into kitchen appliances, noted, "Cooking equipment is a mature market, but it is an exciting one because product innovation is changing the traditional way people cook and broadening sales opportunities."

Maytag expects a profitable future:

> High inflation has not been especially detrimental to our sales, as consumers seem to buy better-quality goods during inflationary periods. Rising energy costs will play an especially important part in future sales for both home and commercial appliances. The energy-saving Maytag washers and dryers will have potentially large markets as both households and self-service laundries replace the millions of appliances purchased in the 1960s. Home kitchens and laundries will be upgraded, compensating for the slump in new housing construction. The changing composition of the American family, with more women working and subsequent increase in family incomes, will produce a growing demand for labor- and time-saving appliances.

Case 2

TSR Hobbies, Inc.—"Dungeons and Dragons"*

Margaret L. Friedman
University of Wisconsin–Whitewater

TSR (Tactical Studies Rules) Hobbies, Inc., had grown rapidly since its start in 1973 to sales of $27 million in fiscal 1983. TSR's star product responsible for this rapid growth was "Dungeons and Dragons," a unique fantasy/adventure game. The game was unique because it happened largely in the minds of its players. Its emphasis on cooperation among players and dependence upon their imaginative powers set it apart from traditional board games.

OVERVIEW

Company History

TSR Hobbies, Inc., was founded by E. Gary Gygax in a small Wisconsin resort town. Gygax never graduated from high school, but pursued his passion for fantasy in the forms of war games and science fiction books. When Gygax lost his job as an insurance underwriter in 1970, he started developing fantasy games almost full-time, while supporting his family with a shoe repair business in his basement. In 1973 Gygax pursuaded a boyhood friend and fellow war game enthusiast, Donald Kaye, to borrow $1,000 against his life insurance and TSR Hobbies, Inc., was founded.

The two gamers published a popular set of war games rules for lead miniatures called "Cavaliers and Roundheads." In January of 1974 another inveterate gamer friend, Brian Blume, invested $2,000 in the

* This case was prepared by Margaret L. Friedman, Assistant Professor, School of Business, University of Wisconsin-Whitewater.

EXHIBIT 1 TSR Hobbies Sales

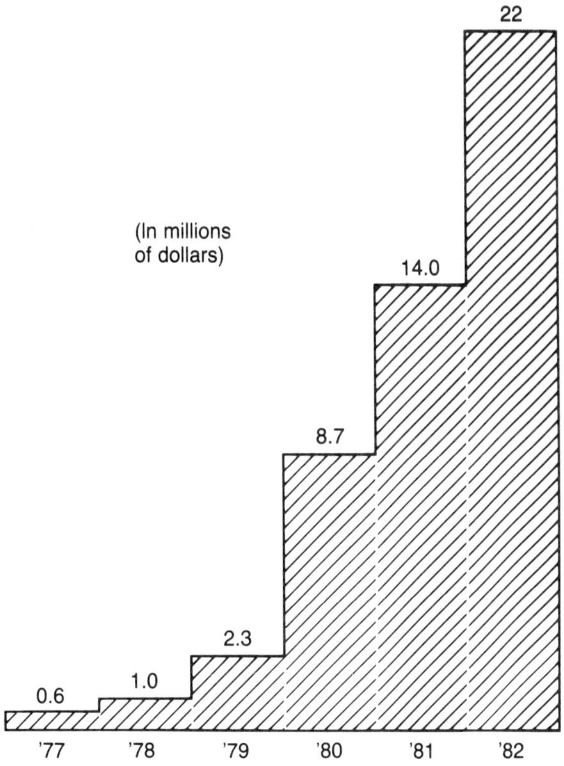

Adapted from *The Wall Street Journal,* January 7, 1983.

company, and the three partners printed the first set of rules for "Dungeons and Dragons." The game was assembled in the Gygax home and was sold through an established network of professional gamers. In 1974, 1,000 sets of the "Dungeons and Dragons" game were sold. Eight years later it was selling at the rate of 750,000 per year. The sales history for the product is shown in Exhibit 1.

The rapid growth of TSR was not necessarily a reflection of keen and experienced management skill. The three top officers in the company all lacked formal management training, but felt they could remedy this deficiency by taking management courses and seminars. Although TSR wanted to attract older, experienced toy and game managers to their ranks, most of their recruits came from outside the toy/game/hobby industry.

Between 1977 and 1982 the TSR work force grew from 12 to more than 250 employees. Gygax's original partner, Donald Kaye, died of a heart attack in 1975, and so the partnership was assumed by Gygax and brothers Brian and Kevin Blume. Gygax was president of TSR, Kevin was chief executive, and Brian was executive vice president. All company decisions were directed through Kevin Blume, from major decisions down to authorization for a $12 desk calendar for a secretary. There was some personnel turnover and evidence of employee dissatisfaction due to nepotism in the company's hiring policies. It was reported that between 10 and 20 of Brian Blume's relatives were on the company's payroll.

The "Dungeons and Dragons" Game

"Dungeons and Dragons" represented a significant innovation in the game and hobby industry. A basic set for a "Dungeons and Dragons" game consisted of a lengthy instruction book, dice, and a wax pencil, all of which sold for $12.

The game begins when each player generates a mythical character with a roll of the dice. The personality profile for each character is determined according to rigorous guidelines given in the instruction booklet. For example, there is a Dungeon Master role in each game. It is the Dungeon Master who develops a map of the dungeon layout as there is no game board. Each character has particular spells and powers which are critical in negotiating the game's adventure. The goal is to navigate through a treacherous dungeon, arrive at a particular destination, and depart alive with the treasure. The combination of mythical characters and adventure is why "Dungeons and Dragons" is called a role-playing/fantasy/adventure game. No two "Dungeons and Dragons" games are alike since the way the game unfolds depends upon the players' imaginations.

To survive, players must work together, rather than against one another, winding their way through a dangerous path to the treasure. Players are confronted with conquest after conquest involving ghouls, monsters, dragons, and other obstacles to finding the treasure and escaping with it. The instruction booklet describes the various powers and spells available to the different characters and general rules for behaving in the dungeon. The crayon is used to keep track of pathways taken and used-up spells. The game can last from two hours to weeks on end—it is all up to the imaginative powers of the players.

MARKETING STRATEGY

TSR's goal was to double sales every year. The strategy used to achieve this goal was based heavily on target market expansion, product line expansion, expansion of promotional activities, and more intensive distribution.

Expansion of Target Market

When "Dungeons and Dragons" was first introduced, it was targeted solely to experienced gamers. The first edition of the game came in a plain brown bag and the rules were so complex that only experienced gamers could decipher them. Word of the game spread to college campuses with the help of publicity involving a Michigan State University student who was rumored to be lost in the steam tunnels under the campus while playing a "live" "Dungeons and Dragons" game. This potentially negative publicity for "Dungeons and Dragons" turned into an advantage for the company since it created word-of-mouth advertising and interest among college students.

As the product matured, the median age of new buyers dropped from college age to the 10–14-year-old bracket. Typically, these consumers were boys described as introverted, intelligent, nonathletic, and very imaginative. The game provided an outlet for such boys to join in a group activity and helped bring them out of their shells. In fact, educators noted that "Dungeons and Dragons" welds a group of players into an ongoing joint project that teaches participation, assertiveness, and cooperation.

To further increase sales of the product, TSR targeted the product to new consumer groups. For example, at one point, women made up only 12 percent of the total number of purchasers. TSR conducted consumer research and found that women felt the game was created as a release for "macho" fantasies. Many women also stated that the lengthy instruction manual (63 pages) would take too long to read and be wasteful of their time. In response to such perceptions, TSR (1) publicized the fact that the game is not cutthroat and competitive, (2) reduced the length of the instruction manual, and (3) created a game which can be played in a limited amount of time. TSR also targeted downward to the younger children's market with a product that transferred the "Dungeons and Dragons" theme to a more conventional board game called "Dungeons!"

Expansion of Product Lines

Initially, the basic "Dungeons and Dragons" set was marketed as a hobby, rather than as a game. A hobby involves a starter toy which is enhanced with a myriad of add-ons. For example, a miniature train is considered a hobby since the engine and track form the basis for building an entire railroad system, including special cars, track, scenery, stations, and so on over time. Similarly, for each $12 basic "Dungeons and Dragons" set sold, retailers could expect an additional $150 in satellite or captive product purchases in the form of modules that provide supplemental adventures of varying complexity. There were at least 50 such satellite products on the market.

Since TSR management recognized that their short product line was vulnerable to competition from such toy and game giants as Mattell, Parker Brothers, Milton Bradley, and Ideal, several other new products were introduced to extend the line. Most of these new introductions followed the role-playing, fantasy theme. For example, since each fantasy world in a "Dungeons and Dragons" game has its own set of characters and monsters, a line of miniature lead figurines of these creatures was introduced. These included miniature dragons, wizards, and dwarves. Although these figures are not necessary to play the game, it was hoped that a market of figurine collectors would develop.

TSR also marketed a number of other role-playing games, including "Top Secret," a spy adventure game; "Boot Hill," a western adventure game; "Gamma World," a futuristic game; and "Star Frontiers," a science fiction game, all of which were quite successful. Somewhat less successful have been TSR's other board game entrants, "Snit's Revenge," "The Awful Green Things from Outer Space," "Escape from New York," and "Dungeons!" These more conventional board games were intended to change the company's image from that of a producer of complex, esoteric games to a producer of a broader range of game products.

TSR also added new lines to their product mix. For example, they produced a feature-length film using a "Dungeons and Dragons" theme, as well as a successful Saturday morning cartoon program for children and an hour-long pilot for a radio-theater program.

TSR's other ventures included purchase of Amazing magazine, the oldest science fiction magazine on the market (since 1926), and publishing *Dragon* magazine which we began in 1976 and obtained a circulation of over 70,000 copies per issue. The Dragon Publishing division of TSR also produced calendars and anthologies of fiction, nonfiction, and humor. TSR's most popular publications included *Endless Quest* books. Young readers determine the plot of these stories by making choices for the main character. Depending on the choices made, the reader is directed to different pages in the book. Therefore, each book contains a number of different adventure stories. TSR also developed a line of books called *Heart Quest,* which are romance novels for teenagers in this same create-your-own-plot format. TSR had performed consulting services for a failing needlework company owned by a friend of Gygax. To further its diversification efforts TSR acquired this company briefly, realizing soon, however, that it was a poor investment.

TSR found licensing to be a profitable form of product line expansion. Arrangements were made to permit 14 companies to market products that displayed the TSR and "Dungeons and Dragons" name. For example, Mattel, Inc., was sold a license for an electronic version of "Dungeons and Dragons," and St. Regis Paper Company was sold a license for a line of notebooks and school supplies.

Expansion of Promotional Activities

In the beginning, TSR relied on word-of-mouth advertising among gamers to sell the "Dungeons and Dragons" game. As their markets expanded, TSR employed other promotional methods, including television commercials and four-color magazine ads. TSR's ad budget in 1981 was $1,194,879 which was divided as follows: 13 percent on trade magazines, 28 percent on consumer magazines, and 59 percent on spot television. During the Christmas season of 1982, $1 million was spent on a television campaign for the "Dungeons!" board game.

The company's logo and accompanying slogan were updated in 1982. Formerly, the logo showed a wizard next to the letters TSR and the slogan "The Game Wizards." The updated logo included a stylized version of the letters "TSR" and the slogan "Products of the Imagination." This updated logo and slogan were designed to convey an image with broader market appeal.

TSR sponsored an annual gamers convention which attracted dozens of manufacturers and thousands of attendees to Kenosha, Wisconsin. This became the largest role-playing convention is the world which included four days of movies, demonstrations, tournaments, seminars, and manufacturers' exhibits. The company also sponsored the Role Playing Game Association. This association offered newsletters and informational services and was responsible for calculating international scoring points to rate players in official tournaments. It also provided a gift catalog of premiums available only to RPGA members.

In the beginning, the printing and artwork needed for the "Dungeons and Dragons" instruction booklet were contracted with suppliers outside of TSR. The company has since engaged in backward vertical integration into the manufacturing process by hiring a staff of artists and purchasing its own printing facility.

Expansion of Distribution Channels

Retail distribution was originally concentrated in hobby stores, but expanded rapidly into department stores and bookstores, although some mass market retailers such as Sears, Penneys, and K mart were reluctant to stock all of the satellite products generated by the basic

"Dungeons and Dragons" set. This evolution from exclusive distribution through hobby stores to intensive distribution followed naturally from the concomitant expansion of target markets and product lines.

Over time TSR employed as many as 15 manufacturers' representatives who marketed the product through independent wholesalers in nine territories. One problem with this distribution system was that the company did not have close contact with its wholesalers, and hence, were not able to offer much merchandising assistance.

TSR opened its own retail hobby shop for a brief period. However, this outlet attracted a lot of mail order business, creating channel conflict among other retail hobby outlets, and the shop was closed in 1984.

EXPANSION PROBLEMS

TSR obviously grew quickly and expanded in many different directions which caused several problems. For example, TSR announced it would hire over 100 new employees and 50 new hires were actually made in June of 1983. However, by April of 1984, over 230 employees were laid off. The rapid loss of personnel resulted in coordination problems. For example, two different products were packaged in boxes with identical graphics on the covers. The layoffs also created morale problems.

In an effort to "tighten the reigns," Kevin Blume eliminated half of the company's 12 divisions to streamline accounting, reporting, and general decision making. TSR was then divided into four separate companies: TSR Inc. for publishing games and books, TSR Ventures Inc. for supervising trademark licensing, TSR Worldwide Ltd. for managing international sales, and Dungeons and Dragons Entertainment Corporation for producing cartoons. Each company functioned independently of the others, with its own stock and board of directors. Still, the three partners sat on all four boards in order to maintain tight control over the company.

TSR's full-fledged entry into the mass market also drained their cash reserves, creating cash flow problems for the company. Business practices in the mass market were different than what TSR was accustomed to in the specialized hobby market. For example, it is common to cater to mass retailers by allowing six months payment whereas 30 days or less is more usual for small hobby shops. Also, demand is relatively smooth in the hobby market unlike the mass market which experiences a Christmas buying rush. Thus, TSR was not prepared for the retail Christmas buying rush and many items ordered were out-of-stock.

TSR also faced an image problem in the mass market, illustrated in the positioning map shown in Exhibit 2. The early success of "Dungeons and Dragons" depended largely upon its image as a mysterious

EXHIBIT 2 Positioning Map

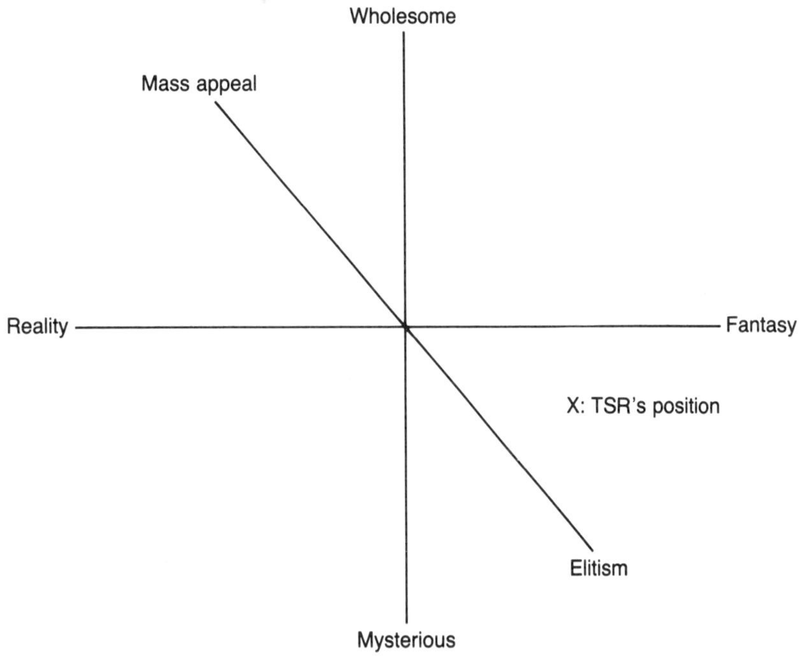

hobby that was not for just anyone, but only for an elite few. Because of this image, many consumers in the mass market were convinced that the "Dungeons and Dragons" game was "bad for the mind" because it involved hours and hours of make-believe. Dr. Joyce Brothers was engaged to endorse the product and to legitimize its role-playing format. In supporting the product she pointed to research results illustrating that children who played "Dungeons and Dragons" developed better reading skills, math skills, and basic logic and problem-solving skills.

TSR faced formidable competition in the mass market. Large companies such as Milton Bradley, Mattel, and Parker Brothers spent more on advertising each year than TSR earned in profits. However, TSR's fantasy/role-playing concept was unique. Only Mattel's "He Man" and "Masters of the Universe" could be remotely compared to TSR's product concept. While the other traditional toy and game giants had no comparable fantasy/role-playing games, they dominated the northwest quadrant of the map in Exhibit 2, the market TSR wanted to enter. Though TSR was a market leader in fantasy/role-playing games in the hobby market, it remained to be seen whether this type of product could gain a respectable share of the mass market.

Case 3

Caterpillar Tractor Company*

Donald W. Eckrich
Ithaca College

INTRODUCTION

In January 1984, Caterpillar Tractor Co. Chairman Lee L. Morgan was actively involved in corporate-wide planning efforts. These efforts were directed at reestablishing Caterpillar's tradition of profitability and world leadership in the heavy equipment and machinery industry. Looking to the coming year, he reported:

> 1984 should be a markedly better year. The 1983 loss of $345 million reflected the deep recession in most of the world's economies. Current indicators suggest . . . strong sales increases for our kinds of products. Sales should be significantly higher in 1984, and we expect to be profitable.

By year end, it was anticipated, specific plans detailed actions on new business opportunities would be completed and long-term sales and profit strategies would be identified, effective through 1995.

HISTORY

Headquartered in Peoria, Illinois, and currently the largest multinational company which designs, manufactures, and markets construction equipment, machinery, engines, and parts, Caterpillar's roots date back to the late 19th century and the evolution of mechanized agricultural equipment. In February 1889, Daniel Best introduced the first

* This case was prepared by Donald W. Eckrich, Associate Professor and Chairman, Department of Marketing, Ithaca College, as the basis for class discussion rather than to illustrate either effective or ineffective handling of administrative situations and problems. A special thanks for their invaluable assistance throughout the preparation of this case is due Charles F. Maier and Barbara A. Wright.

steam-powered harvester, replacing the 40-horse-drawn combine with an eight-man, 11-ton, self-propelled tractor using eight-foot wheels. Shortly thereafter, Benjamin Holt began field testing the first crawler-type equipment, built simply by replacing the wheels on existing equipment with new "track" structures—pairs of treads comprised of wooden slats linked loosely together.

Driven by increasing demand in agriculture, road building, military equipment, and industrial construction, the two companies prospered. The introduction of the internal combustion engine provided yet another boost for the evolving heavy equipment industry.

In 1925, the Holt and Best Companies merged to form Caterpillar Tractor Co., thereby setting the stage for several decades of dramatic and systematic growth through technological leadership and new applications in the emerging equipment and machinery industry. Agricultural applications quickly gave way to forestry opportunities, which in turn gave way to oil field and highway operations.

In 1931, the first Caterpillar Diesel Tractor was introduced. This product initiated an incredible six-year sales growth spurt from $13 million to $63 million and launched the track-type tractor into prominence as the single largest user of diesel power.

Caterpillar's growing reputation for industry leadership and technological superiority was further strengthened during World War II by U.S. government defense contracts. These contracts included demand for both existing equipment (e.g., bulldozers and graders) and special government requests for revolutionary and sophisticated equipment such as air-cooled diesel engines for advanced military operations.

Throughout the postwar years, the Korean conflict, and into the 1970s, Caterpillar generally concentrated on the development of large, industrial-sized machines and engines. In 1944, Caterpillar announced its plans to build a line of matched earthmoving equipment, and quickly found a receptive and profitable market. Later, in 1951, the Trackson Company of Milwaukee was purchased to produce hoists, pipe layers, and hydraulically operated tractor shovels for Caterpillar crawlers. In 1965, Towmotor Corporation was acquired, continuing the expansion into heavy equipment with forklift trucks and straddle carriers for a wide range of materials handling in industrial, shipping, warehousing, and other markets. Thus, by the early 1970s, Caterpillar had achieved at least foothold positions in a variety of heavy equipment product lines, with the objective of achieving industry leadership in each of the new areas.

In 1977, Caterpillar unveiled the single-largest, most technologically advanced tractor in the world—the D-10. Foremost among its advantages were (1) an elevated drive sprocket and (2) modular-designed major components. The elevation of the drive sprocket removed it from high-wear and shock-load areas, reduced overall stress on the under-carriage, and produced a smoother ride. The modular design of major components not only permitted faster and more efficient servicing, but also provided the opportunity to pretest components before final assembly. Modular designs thereby reduced repair and overall downtime in some cases by as much as 80 percent. Perhaps most significant regarding the D–10 and its modular-designed components was the extent to which they reflected the intense product quality and service orientations adhered to throughout Cat's history. It had long been assumed by management that industrial users' needs would best be served through the progress of technology, largely irrespective of the effects on pricing.

Only four years later, in 1981, several more years of research and development were capped off with the introduction of a 16-cylinder, 1,600 horsepower, 1200 kilowatt engine—also stressing modular design and repair convenience. In early 1982, a new D8L crawler tractor was introduced, the third in a series of crawler tractors to employ the elevated sprocket. Finally, several other technological advances previously introduced on smaller, track-type loaders were extended to larger models, thereby permitting the relocation of the engine to the rear and correspondingly, improving balance, operator visibility, and serviceability.

Thus, over several decades, Caterpillar Tractor Co. managed to establish a pace-setting position in the heavy equipment industry by focusing directly on state-of-the-art technology and continuous product redesign. Specifically, concern for increased *user productivity* through greater equipment capacities, enhanced reliability, and quicker serviceability contributed most heavily to Cat's success and superior image. Maintenance of this leadership position across numerous product lines has also translated into the industry's highest prices.

MANUFACTURING AND WAREHOUSING

Caterpillar manufactures products in two principal categories: (1) machines and parts (M&Ps), which includes track-type machinery like bulldozers, tractors, rippers, and track-loaders, as well as several wheel-type machines such as motor graders, loaders, off-highway trucks, and tractor-scrapers; and (2) engines, used to power a variety of equipment for highway, marine, petroleum, agricultural, industrial, and electric power generation applications, ranging from diesel to natural gas and turbines. The category of M&Ps, it should be noted, includes all related parts and equipment for all of the machines. Exhibits 1, 2, 3, and 4 present sales, profit, and other financial data for the years 1979 to 1983.

EXHIBIT 1 Consolidated Sales and Profit Data

	1983	*1982*	*1981*	*1980*	*1979*
Sales	$5,424	$6,469	$9,154	$8,598	$7,613
Profit (loss) for year-consolidated	$ (345)	$ (180)	$ 579	$ 565	$ 492
Profit (loss) per share of common stock	$(3.74)	$(2.04)	$ 6.64	$ 6.53	$ 5.69
Return on average common stock equity	(10.1)%	(4.9)%	15.9%	17.4%	16.9%
Dividends paid per share of common stock	$ 1.50	$ 2.40	$ 2.40	$2,325	$ 2.10
Current ratio at year-end	2.15 to 1	2.87 to 1	1.50 to 1	1.71 to 1	1.88 to 1
Total assets at year-end	$6,968	$7,201	$7,285	$6,098	$5,403
Long-term debt due after one year at year-end	$1,894	$2,389	$ 961	$ 932	$ 952
Capital expenditures for land, buildings, machinery, and equipment	$ 324	$ 534	$ 836	$ 749	$ 676
Depreciation and amortization	$ 506	$ 505	$ 448	$ 370	$ 312

Source: Caterpillar Tractor Company Annual Report, 1983.

EXHIBIT 2 Total Sales by Category (billions)

	1983	*1982*	*1981*	*1980*	*1979*
Inside the United States					
Machines and parts	$2.08	$1.84	$2.62	$2.84	N/A
Engines and parts	.85	.96	1.35	.85	N/A
Total inside	$2.93	$2.80	$3.97	$3.69	$3.51
Outside the United States					
Machines and parts	$2.08	$2.92	$4.48	$4.36	N/A
Engines and parts	.41	.75	.70	.55	N/A
Total outside	$2.49	$3.67	$5.28	$4.91	$4.10
By country (millions)					
Africa/Mid East	$ 680	$1,062	$1,886	$1,282	$ 960
Europe	771	927	993	1,267	1,153
Asia/Pacific	515	800	927	922	764
Latin America	266	637	903	879	716
Canada	262	239	472	563	505
Combined totals	$5.42	$6.47	$9.15	$8.60	$7.60

EXHIBIT 3 Research and Engineering Costs (in millions)

	1983	*1982*	*1981*	*1980*	*1979*	*1978*
New product development and major project improvements	n.a.*	$230	$227	$200	$191	$160
Other—general	n.a.*	$146	$136	$126	$ 92	$ 96
Total	$340	$376	$363	$326	$283	$256
Percent of sales	6.3%	5.8%	3.9%	3.8%	3.7%	3.6%

* n.a. = not available

Manufacturing and warehousing activities take place worldwide through 22 plants in the United States and several wholly or partly owned subsidiaries located in Australia, Belgium, Brazil, Canada, France, Japan, India, Indonesia, Mexico, and the United Kingdom. Each international location has been carefully selected to provide significant cost advantages by reducing global transportation costs, eliminating duty applicable to U.S.-built machinery, and by capitalizing on the manufacturing cost advantage derived from lower foreign wage levels. Such trends, it should be noted, have not been without some repercussions. The United Automobile Workers, for instance, representing over 80 percent of Cat's stateside hourly employees, is ever alert to this threat to their jobs and has become vitally concerned and quite vocal regarding possible extensions of foreign plants.

In addition, major warehouses and emergency parts depots are strategically located throughout the world. As a result, these combined facilities form a worldwide organizational network which attempts to maximize Caterpillar's flexibility and customer responsiveness. All parts manufactured by any one plant are completely interchangeable

EXHIBIT 4 Heavy Equipment and Machinery Manufacturer Earnings (in millions)

	1983	*1982*	*1981*	*1980*	*1979*
Caterpillar Tractor Co.	($ 345)	($ 180)	$ 579	$ 565	$ 492
International Harvester*	($ 539)	($1,738)	($ 393)	($ 397)	$ 369
Deere*	($.052)	($ .039)	$.250	$.228	$.310
Allis-Chalmers	($ 133)	($ 207)	($ 28)	$ 47	$ 81
Clark Equipment	($.012)	($ .155)	$.029	$.051	$.106

* Fiscal year ends October 31—latest year's figures are estimates. Losses indicated in ( ).

Source (in part): Harlan S. Byrne, "For Heavy Equipment Makers, Recovery To Be Delayed Another Year," *The Wall Street Journal,* November 3, 1982.

with the same parts manufactured by any other plant. Thus, replacement parts are generally available on extremely short notice wherever Caterpillar machines are deployed throughout the world. In short, all dealers and customers recognize Cat's parts and distribution as one of the two or three major advantages of owning Cat equipment. Heavy equipment purchasers widely acknowledge that no other firm in the industry can touch Cat in this category.

DEALERS

Recognized as the strongest in the industry, Caterpillar's dealer network handles all sales and service worldwide, with the exception of direct sales to the U.S. government, the Soviet Union, and the People's Republic of China which are handled by a subsidiary division of Cat known as CIPI (Caterpillar Industrial Products, Inc.). Comprised of 213 independent dealers (84 in the United States), Caterpillar dealers represent an enterprise almost as large as the company. They operate 1,050 sales, parts, and service outlets in more than 140 countries, employ about 75,000 people, and have a combined net worth of approximately $3.1 billion. A typical dealership sells and services Caterpillar equipment exclusively, represents an average net worth of approximately $12 million, and is likely in a second or third generation of affiliation. Industry estimates place the capitalization of Caterpillar's dealer network at 10 times that of any competitor.

With Caterpillar's sales and service activities outside the direct control of Caterpillar executives, increasing efforts have been directed at improving service to dealers and informing users of the advantages of Caterpillar products. In 1978, a computerized dealer terminal system was completed which linked dealers and Caterpillar facilities to the European parts distribution department in Belgium. Essentially it provided direct computer access for ordering and locating parts for dealers in Europe, Africa, and the Middle East. In 1979, more than 3,000 consumers and dealer personnel attended Caterpillar-sponsored seminars, 47,000 visitors viewed Caterpillar products and manufacturing operations, and representatives from 26 countries attended a week-long International Agricultural Seminar.

Comparable levels of seminar and visitation activity can be noted throughout the past few years, further promoting selective demand to both engine and equipment users. In one instance, 400 representatives of energy-related mining operations attended a seminar held at a West Virginia coal mine which not only highlighted the use of Cat machines, but perhaps more importantly, the dealers' capabilities to support special needs of mine operators. In another instance, in order to demonstrate dealer commitment to servicing the on-highway truck industry, Cat cosponsored the National Fuel Economy Challenge, a competition open to owners of new trucks equipped with Caterpillar 3406 and 3408 Economy Engines. Results confirmed impressive fuel economy statistics for Caterpillar engines and provided hands-on exposure to dealer support facilities.

In what was called "target marketing" by Cat executives, the predominant dealer support theme during the past few years has begun to focus dealer efforts on special end-user groups. U.S. dealers brought over 1,000 owners of competitive equipment to Peoria to learn about Cat equipment, its advantages and capabilities, as well as to actually operate Cat equipment. In another program, "Build Your Future," small machine owners, unfamiliar with the differential advantages of Caterpillar equipment and dealer support capabilities, were instructed on various general business topics and specific Caterpillar operations capabilities including equipment maintenance. Factory tours and machine demonstrations were also provided.

In 1983, the continuing efforts to improve service to users and dealers achieved a milestone with a major restructuring of the company's marketing organizations in the United States and Far East. The changes generally consisted of moving from a centralized, functional organization to a geographically dispersed, marketing-oriented team structure. As a result, the new structure recognizes the growing diversity of competition and product applications and the need for more individually tailored programs. It is more responsive to dealer needs and opportunities, shortens the lines of communication, and speeds up vital decision-making processes. As a result, Caterpillar's dealer organization has become widely regarded and consistently mentioned by customers as a prime reason for purchasing Cat equipment and represents Cat's single largest advantage over all competitors, both in the United States and internationally.

RESEARCH AND ENGINEERING

Improving quality and technological leadership have long been key ingredients of Caterpillar's long-term growth strategy. In a 1983 statement to stockholders, Chairman Morgan asserted, "We will not allow our product leadership to be diminished." Expenditures for research and engineering (R&E) have consistently ranked number one in the industry, and have permitted Caterpillar to develop state-of-the-art products, manufacturing processors, and apparatus. In 1982, for example, expenditures for R&E reached a record $376 million (data on other recent research and engineering expenditures appear in Exhibit 3). As a result, Caterpillar's product leadership is not only widely recognized, but manufacturing facilities, as well, are considered the most modern and best equipped in the industry.

A carryover of this commitment to product leadership is the general practice of passing along specific product advances as soon as reliably feasible rather than accumulating several modifications and incorporating them all simultaneously in periodic model changes. Not only would the latter fail to permit the entire line to be completely up-to-date at all times, but it would also fail to insure maximum sales opportunities for existing, but aging, products. As an example of the success of this market penetration strategy, a simple addition of rubber grousers on tractors used primarily for log skidding created 200 immediate new machine sales for other agricultural users.

COMPETITION

As a result of decades of domination of the heavy equipment and construction industry, Caterpillar has an estimated 45–50 percent share for earthmoving machinery in the U.S. market and roughly 30–35 percent of the market worldwide. Mr. Morgan readily admits the toughest competition facing Caterpillar is from Komatsu Ltd., of Tokyo, which has rapidly grown to second place in worldwide sales. In addition, considerable domestic competitive pressures come from J. I. Case, Inc., and Deere & Company, considered No. 2 and No. 3 respectively.

In 1981, the president of Komatsu Ltd. stated a goal of achieving 20 percent of the U.S. market within five years; the company has succeeded in boosting market share from approximately 2 percent in 1974 to 15 percent in 1983. Komatsu is gaining sales basically in selected markets such as specialty bulldozers (i.e., including amphibians and remote-controlled units especially for underground use), and in equipment larger than Caterpillar's largest. Number one in terms of the latter is Komatsu's 1,000 Hp. tractor bulldozer, which far surpasses Cat's biggest, the D–10 with only 700 Hp. In these specialty areas, Komatsu does particularly well. Projections are that Komatsu Ltd., as a result of aggressiveness, adaptability, and a number of complex economic factors, will continue to encroach into the U.S. market largely at the expense (or demise) of many smaller competitors. As one industry analyst put it, "When elephants fight, the grass dies."

Nevertheless, despite claims of durability and efficiency which rival Caterpillar, Komatsu probably will not match the current sales of Cat in the United States. With approximately 60 part-time dealerships in America (i.e., those who sell Komatsu and other manufacturer's equipment simultaneously), and several competitive handicaps in the United States, such as ocean freight costs and narrow product lines. Komatsu cannot compete head-to-head with Cat. Thus the company initially adopted a strategy of allying itself, through joint-venture subsidiaries, with International Harvester (IH) and Bucyrus-Erie (B-

E) to manufacture wheeled vehicles and excavators. In 1980, Komatsu bought out B-E with financial assistance provided directly by Japan's Fair Trade Commission and, in 1982, IH's share of the joint venture was also purchased. Thus, domestic entrance for Komatsu has been achieved through limited and well-conceived flanking attacks providing American-based manufacturing facilities and distribution links.

The U.S. presence of Komatsu, however, is considered by industry analysts more a matter of competitive visibility than an operational threat to Caterpillar's leadership position. The most direct threats to Caterpillar's domestic markets are J. I. Case and John Deere & Co. J. I. Case has an estimated 35 percent share of the earthmoving equipment market and John Deere has an estimated 30 percent share of the farm-machinery market.

However, each of these organizations, as well as several others (Allis-Chalmers, Clark Equipment, Harnischfeger Corp., IH, and Massey-Ferguson), has been undergoing considerable upheaval as a result of the early 1980s worldwide recession (see Exhibit 4 for performance data from selected competitors). As one analyst put it:

> Producers of construction, farm, and other heavy equipment have been in varying degrees of recession . . . and had expected recovery to start by now. Instead, widespread weakness is showing up, and companies are awash in red ink.
>
> Executives and analysts have been surprised by the depths and breadth of the slump. In past recessions, declines in some markets have been at least partly offset by strengths in others. Not so today. Practically all major markets are weak. For instance, the collapse of the oil and gas drilling boom and the financial problems of many countries weren't anticipated. And the farm depression has been deeper and more prolonged than machinery makers expected.[1]

Thus, although Caterpillar has probably fared better than the other firms, the most significant domestic problem for Caterpillar is the delay in the recovery of the market.

Internationally, and despite the worldwide slump, Komatsu Ltd. is Caterpillar's single-largest and growing competitor with 15 percent share of the *world market* (second only to Caterpillar), and 60 percent of the Japanese market. Cat accounts for roughly 50 percent of the world market but only 30 percent of the Japanese market (Caterpillar Mitsubishi).

Typical of many Japanese manufacturing firms, Komatsu's competitive thrust focuses directly on a long-term strategy to equal or exceed Caterpillar's position. Considering Cat vulnerable to superior

---

[1] Harlan S. Byrne, "For Heavy Equipment Makers, Recovery To Be Delayed Another Year," *The Wall Street Journal*, November 3, 1982.

managerial efficiency and operating flexibility, Komatsu's broad marketing strategy has emphasized expanding market share, largely on the basis of lower prices and efforts to match Caterpillar's follow-up service and parts capabilities. The slogan "Maru-C," is widely acknowledged as one of Komatsu's greatest challenges—to "engulf Caterpillar." Komatsu offers customers prices up to 15 percent below Caterpillar and endeavors to accommodate every conceivable special heavy equipment need through continual *adaptation* of existing products. In one instance, special equipment was developed exclusively for the particular needs of Australian coal miners. In another instance, an electric-powered bulldozer was developed for a small number of contractors whose special needs required them to operate equipment within legal noise limits.

Determined to produce the world's best earthmoving equipment, Komatsu executives lay claim to offering superior equipment in terms of power, durability, and lower fuel consumption.[2] Indeed, considerable evidence is available to support such claims, and industrial customers have responded to Komatsu's discount pricing and manufacturing flexibility. In terms of follow-up support, Komatsu maintains a crew of salespeople (engineers), ready to fly anywhere in the world to solve Komatsu equipment problems. Within the United States, Komatsu maintains five regional centers to directly support dealer efforts.

OTHER PROBLEMS

The suddenness of Caterpillar's 1982 $180 million loss, the first in 50 years, found President Robert E. Gilmore and Chairman Lee Morgan stunned and hopeful of a quick return to profitability. In a 1983 joint address to stockholders they reported:

> We hope that the worldwide economic malaise is coming to an end, and that people will soon be able to return to more normal lives.
>
> The economy will recover, and the world will need capital goods of the kinds made by Caterpillar. Roads will be built . . . ore and coal will be mined . . . fields will be cleared and dams constructed . . . oil and gas will be produced. These and other applications for our products are essential to a growing world population.
>
> Our concern isn't whether demand will revive and grow. It will.

However, by early 1984 Caterpillar's troubles were beginning to prove far more pervasive and devastating than first thought.

---

[2] Bernard Krisher, "Komatsu on the Track of Cat," *Fortune,* April 20, 1981, pp. 164–74.

In retrospect, several contributing factors began emerging as much as five years earlier, and not without Caterpillar's awareness. For instance, as the only manufacturer of pipelayers in the United States, Caterpillar was particularly hard hit by President Carter's 1979 "high tech" export control measures against the Soviet Union. Caterpillar was on the verge of a multimillion (perhaps billion) dollar contract with the Soviet Union for 2,000 heavy tractors at approximately $500,000 each and hundreds of pipelayers at $250,000 each. However, the export control measures ended this opportunity and the sale went to Komatsu.

Later in 1979, additional clouds surfaced. As a result of ever increasing oil prices, worldwide economic growth abruptly halted. Adding to the U.S. problems, the growing and unprecedented international trade deficits of the 1970s prompted ever higher interest rates and greater uncertainty regarding the future of the international trading system, and contributed significantly to inflation. The Consumer Price Index in 1979 was up 13 percent and Chairman Morgan noted, "inflation has become deeply embedded," and "solutions will neither be simple nor quick."

By 1981, effects of the world's economic recession began to appear at Caterpillar as physical sales volume declined "moderately"—as the company called it. Slowdowns in world markets, considered the most significant long-term growth opportunities for heavy construction equipment manufacturers, were particularly difficult to manage insofar as the U.S. competitive posture was slumping in general. Unlike the embargo against the Soviet Union, some developing world markets were being diminished by a variety of anti-U.S. export/import restrictions issued by developing countries themselves. Loss of accessibility to such markets, restricted information flows, and the growing trend in foreign government subsidies were leaving Caterpillar in a hopeful, but retrospective, position, as noted in a joint letter to stockholders by Chairman Morgan and President Gilmore:

> We have a competitive edge. . . . Outside authorities frequently confirm that ours is the preferred product.
>
> Our very substantial capital investment and research and engineering programs . . . should help us maintain a technological lead. . . .
>
> Toward that end, we seek the renewed commitment of Caterpillar people everywhere.

Unfortunately, throughout 1982, conditions continued to deteriorate. After the first quarter of operations, management began imposing numerous temporary plant shutdowns and indefinite layoffs. Domestic interest rates were sufficiently high to cause most U.S. capital spending to be abandoned. Worldwide, the previous decade of accelerated oil explorations and refinement had resulted in overproduction such that oil prices also began to slump, which further resulted in reduced energy development and construction. Facing the unprecedented reduction in practically all markets simultaneously, Caterpillar experienced a 29 percent sales decline, and reported the first loss in common stock prices in 50 years. Common stock prices plunged from $55–$60 per share in 1981 to $35 per share in 1982.

On October 1, 1982, the United Auto Workers Union struck (20,400 members or roughly 80 percent of Cat's active, U.S. hourly employees), seeking an extension of the existing contract. For almost 30 years, the UAW labor contract had established a pattern which provided workers with automatic, annual, 3 percent wage increases. Management now resisted these increases because the increase in labor costs would make it even more difficult to compete. Recent data, for instance, placed Cat's per capita U.S. labor costs at roughly twice those of Japanese firms.

Throughout 1983, even well after the labor settlement, ripple effects of the dispute continued to emerge. Inventory shortages of both parts and equipment resulted in lost sales, lost good will, and a considerable strain on efforts to return to profitability. These efforts included reductions in expenditures for perhaps Cat's most sacred budget item—research and engineering—as well as the second annual cut in the capital expenditures budget—from $836 million in 1981, down to $324 million in 1983. These cost-cutting efforts resulted in layoffs and plant-closings leaving employment figures at the end of 1983 markedly reduced from previous years. Hourly employees, reduced in 1982 by 21,501, dropped another 624 in 1983, while the number of salaried employees was cut 3,077 and 2,585 in these two years.

The combination of a deteriorating worldwide economic climate and postsettlement reconstruction efforts required management to assume an adaptive posture while long-term solutions were worked out. Perhaps most noteworthy in this regard is the Cost Reduction Program (CRP), aimed at positioning Cat's 1986 cost levels more than 20 percent below those of 1981 (in constant dollars adjusted for volume). These cost reductions were intended to be *permanent* and included plant closings, new applications of computer and scientific technology, inventory reduction programs, and faster deliveries from suppliers. At the end of 1983 considerable efforts were being directed at achieving a scaled-down, more efficient organization.

The achievement of a long-term, strategic growth perspective has captured management's attention. Beginning in late 1982, management initiated efforts to focus planning specifically on future opportunities in diesel, natural gas, and turbine engines, and to review the basic role of the lift truck in Cat's product mix. In 1983, Caterpillar management held a Business Strategy Conference which developed specific objectives along with a timetable for activities through 1995.

The plan involves what are designed to be the most productive means of "establishing, confirming, or modifying current strategies for . . . existing business; developing, evaluating, recommending, and selecting for implementation 'new' strategic growth opportunities; and developing corporate goals consistent with the findings and decisions produced by the conference."

Based on this planning, U.S. dealers recently launched a marketing program targetted at non-Caterpillar owners. Recognizing the strategic growth opportunities associated with market development, this program, called PLUS 3, provided a means for end users of competitors' equipment to gauge the superiority of Cat *dealers* in after-sales parts support and service. Specifically, the program guaranteed a 48-hour repair turnaround or the customer would be given a machine to use from the dealer's rental fleet, and a 48-hour parts delivery or the customer would receive the part free! It also included one of the most extensive power train warranties in the industry—36 months or 5,000 hours, whichever came first. Results of PLUS 3 were quite favorable, most notably among small- and medium-sized machine owners.

As a result of additional analyses regarding the role of the lift truck to Caterpillar, at least one U.S. plant was closed and management began labor negotiations with two non-U.S. production facilities. Indications were quite strong that more and more production throughout the product mix will be moved overseas in the future (e.g., lift trucks to Korea). Identifying future growth opportunities and detailing appropriate marketing strategies for the next decade were seen as becoming more critical as no significant upturn had been experienced through mid-1984, and the future seemed to be even more unstable and uncertain.

Case 4

Hershey Foods*

Richard T. Hise
Texas A & M University

Milton S. Hershey, the founder of the giant chocolate manufacturing firm bearing his name, did not find the road to success an easy one. He tried a number of business ventures before eventually succeeding in the chocolate business. In his early teens, he found that he was not cut out to be an apprentice typesetter, but did enjoy his four-year stint as an apprentice candy maker for Joseph H. Royer, a Lancaster, Pennsylvania, confectioner.

At the age of 19, Hershey decided to go into the candy business for himself. His venture in Philadelphia failed, as did efforts with his father in Denver and Chicago. Another solo attempt in New York also failed.

Back in his native Lancaster, Hershey began to manufacture caramels, an operation with which he was experienced, and the caramel business expanded rapidly. In 1900, he sold his company for $1 million, an unheard of price in those days, and used the proceeds to begin construction of a chocolate processing plant in Derry Township, about 15 miles east of Harrisburg.

Within 10 years, the company prospered so much that Hershey and his wife were accumulating so much money they could not possibly spend it all. In 1909, Mrs. Hershey suggested they build a home for unfortunate boys. Hershey eagerly agreed, feeling that, although his own childhood had not been all he had wished it to be, he could try to provide security and love for others. Thus, 486 of the initial 1,000-acre construction tract were set aside for the Hershey Industrial School.

In subsequent years, other community projects were built by the Hershey Company. The Community Building, containing two theaters, a dining room and cafeteria, a gymnasium, swimming pool, bowling alley, fencing and boxing room, and photographic room was

---

* This case was written as a basis for class discussion rather than to illustrate either effective or ineffective marketing management. Reprinted with permission from Richard T. Hise and Stephen W. McDaniel, *Cases in Marketing Strategy,* Columbus, Ohio: Charles E. Merrill Publishing Co., 1984.

finished in 1933. The Hershey Hotel was also completed in 1933. The 7,200-seat Hershey Sports Arena was constructed in 1936, and the Hershey Stadium was finished in 1939. Later, Hershey's Chocolate World, which contains a free ride through a simulated chocolate manufacturing operation, Hershey Park, a theme park, the Hershey Museum of American Life, and the Hershey Gardens were constructed by Hershey.

In the 1920s, Milton Hershey decided to reorganize the company. The Hershey Chocolate Company was dissolved, and three separate companies were organized. The Hershey Chocolate Corporation controlled all of the chocolate properties; the Hershey Corporation was responsible for the Cuban sugar interests; the Hershey Estates was established to conduct the various businesses and municipal services in the town of Hershey.

The Hershey Trust Company administers the funds of the Milton Hershey School. As trustee for this school, it owns or controls the other three companies because Milton Hershey provided the trust with a sizable block of shares of common stock. In 1981, the Hershey Trust Company owned about 51 percent of the company's common stock.

The Hershey Chocolate Corporation continued to prosper. During World War II, the army commissioned Hershey to develop a chocolate bar for troops in the field; the result was the "Field Ration D," and the company was soon producing 500,000 bars a day.

Milton S. Hershey died on October 13, 1945. For 15 years after his death, the Hershey Chocolate Corporation continued to emphasize its chocolate products. Since 1960, however, the company has pursued a strategy of becoming a multiproduct corporation. The name of the Hershey Chocolate Corporation was changed to the Hershey Foods Corporation, its current name. In 1961, the company's sales were $185 million, compared to over $1.4 billion in 1981.

MAJOR PRODUCT GROUPS

In 1982, Hershey had three major product groups. These included the chocolate and confectionery group, restaurant operations (Friendly Ice Cream Corporation), and the other food products and services group: San Giorgia-Skinner (pasta) and Cory Food Services, Inc. The chocolate and confectionery group has grown through both internal means and acquisitions, while the other two groups have grown primarily through acquisitions. Exhibits 1 and 2 show overall company performance between 1971 and 1981. Exhibit 3 shows performance figures for the various product groups between 1979 and 1981.

Chocolate and Confectionery Group

The company produces a broad line of chocolate and confectionery products. The major product lines in the chocolate and confectionery group are bar goods, bagged items, baking ingredients, chocolate drink mixes, and dessert toppings. Hershey uses a variety of packages, such as boxes, trays, and bags for bar products. Sizes include standard, large, and giant bars, and about 30 brand names are used. The most important of these are Hershey's Almond Bars, Hershey's Chips, Hershey's Cocoa, Hershey's Kisses, Hershey's Milk Chocolate Bar, Hershey's Miniatures, Hershey's Syrup, Kit Kat, Mr. Goodbar, Reese's Peanut Butter Cup, Reese's Pieces, Rolo, and Whatchamacallit.

While most of the company's chocolate and confectionery items have been developed internally, some were acquired or made available through licensing agreements. The Reese's products were added to Hershey's product lines through acquisition of the H.B. Reese Candy Company of Hershey, Pennsylvania, in 1963. H.B. Reese, a former Hershey employee, began operations in 1923. Since one of the major ingredients in the Reese's line is peanut butter, Hershey executives believe that these items reduce to some extent the firm's dependency on the cacao bean, the chief raw ingredient in chocolate. Y&S Candies, Inc., a licorice manufacturer with facilities in Lancaster, Pennsylvania; Moline, Illinois; Farmington, New Mexico; and Montreal, Canada, was acquired in 1977 to serve the same purpose.

A licensing agreement with Rountree Mackintosh Limited of England gives Hershey the right to manufacture and market the Kit Kat and Rolo brands. The agreement with the English firm also allows Hershey to import, manufacture, and market After Eight, a thin dinner mint. This product was being test marketed in 1981.

Hershey has three other licensing arrangements. One is with AB Marabou of Sundbyberg, Sweden, the leading Scandinavian chocolate and confectionery company. Several AB Marabou products have been imported and marketed since 1978. Hershey owns 50 percent of Nacional de Dulces, S.A. de C.V., a manufacturer and marketer of chocolate and confectionery products in Mexico. The other licensing arrangement gives Hershey the right to import and sell various high quality licorice products of the Geo. Bassett & Co. of England. In 1981, Hershey executives did not consider any of these agreements to be large moneymarkets.

Exhibit 4 delineates the company's most important chocolate and confectionery products, and when they were developed. While Hershey has had a number of successful new products, there have also been several disappointments. Chocolate-covered raisins were introduced in

EXHIBIT 1 Five-Year Financial Summary, 1971–1975 (all figures in thousands—except market price and per share statistics)

	1975	*1974*	*1973*	*1972*	*1971*
Summary of earnings:					
Continuing operations					
Net sales	$ 556,328	$491,995	$ 415,944	$ 392,004	$379,229
Cost of goods sold	368,992	357,830	294,174	255,162	247,784
Operating expenses	105,102	81,792	88,318	91,595	86,439
Interest expense (net)	1,259	2,190	4,848	3,246	2,610
Income taxes	41,682	25,812	13,929	20,679	21,947
Income from continuing operations	39,293	24,371	14,675	21,322	20,449
Losses from discontinued operations	(1,433)	(2,277)	(369)	(680)	44
Loss related to disposal of discontinued operations	(4,898)	—	—	—	—
Net income	32,962	22,094	14,306	20,642	20,493
Net income per share of common stock					
Continuing operations	3.02	1.87	1.13	1.63	1.55
Discontinued operations					
Losses from operations	(.11)	(.17)	(.03)	(.05)	—
Loss related to disposal	(.38)	—	—	—	—
Net income	2.53	1.70	1.10	1.58	1.55
Dividends per common share	.85	.80	1.10	1.10	1.10
Dividends per preferred share	.60	.60	.60	.60	.60
Average number of common shares and equivalents outstanding during the year	13,024	13,024	13,024	13,064	13,212
Percent of net income to sales*	7.1%	5.0%	3.5%	5.4%	5.4%

Financial statistics:					
Capital expenditures	$ 10,203	$ 10,887	$ 17,564	$ 25,137	$ 22,602
Depreciation*	7,541	7,912	7,010	5,622	5,597
Advertising*	9,325	1,744	9,565	13,954	10,506
Current assets	151,217	124,172	97,106	108,667	102,965
Current liabilities	52,494	57,579	23,456	29,789	44,486
Working capital	98,723	66,593	73,650	78,878	58,479
Current ratio	2.9:1	2.2:1	4.1:1	3.6:1	2.3:1
Long-term debt	$ 29,856	$ 31,730	$ 51,470	$ 51,364	$ 26,533
Debt-to-equity percent	15%	18%	32%	32%	17%
Stockholders' equity	$ 195,847	$173,173	$ 160,777	$ 159,714	$156,280
Stockholders' data:					
Outstanding common shares at year-end	13,024	11,824	11,824	11,824	11,977
Market price of common stock—					
At year-end	$ 18⅝	$ 9¾	$ 12⅝	$ 23⅞	$ 28
Range during year	$10⅛–20⅞	$ 8½–15	$12½–24¾	$21⅛–28¾	$26–31⅜
Number of common stockholders	19,279	19,362	19,095	17,980	18,346
Employees' data:					
Payrolls	$ 74,329	$ 72,936	$ 74,464	$ 67,700	$ 62,189
Number of employees—year-end	7,150	7,200	8,500	8,530	9,140

* Restated to reflect continuing operations only.

EXHIBIT 2 Six-Year Financial Summary, 1976–1981 (all figures in thousands except market price and per share statistics)

	1981	*1980*	*1979*	*1978*	*1977*	*1976*
Summary of earnings:						
Continuing operations						
Net sales	$1,451,151	$1,335,289	$1,161,295	$ 767,880	$ 671,227	$ 601,960
Cost of sales	1,015,767	971,714	855,252	560,137	489,802	417,673
Operating expenses	267,930	224,615	184,186	128,520	110,554	94,683
Interest expense	15,291	16,197	19,424	2,620	2,422	2,240
Interest (income)	(2,779)	(2,097)	(1,660)	(5,303)	(2,931)	(1,883)
Income taxes	74,580	62,805	50,589	40,450	35,349	45,562
Income from continuing operations	80,362	62,055	53,504	41,456	36,031	43,685
Income from discontinued operations	—	—	—	—	—	1,112
Gain related to disposal of discontinued operations	—	—	—	—	5,300	—
Net income	$ 80,362	$ 62,055	$ 53,504	$ 41,456	$ 41,331	$ 44,797
Income per common share						
Continuing operations	$ 5.61	4.38	3.78	3.02	2.62	3.18
Discontinued operations	—	—	—	—	—	.08
Gain related to disposal	—	—	—	—	.39	—
Net income	5.61	4.38	3.78	3.02	3.01	3.26
Cash dividends per common share	$ 1.75	$ 1.50	$ 1.35	$ 1.225	$ 1.14	$ 1.03
Average number of common shares and equivalents outstanding during the year	14,322	14,160	14,153	13,742	13,722	13,720
Percent of income from continuing operations to sales	5.5%	4.6%	4.6%	5.4%	5.4%	7.3%

Financial statistics:						
Capital additions	$ 91,673	$ 59,029	$ 56,437	$ 37,425	$ 27,535	$ 20,722
Depreciation	27,565	24,896	20,515	8,850	7,995	7,539
Advertising	56,516	42,684	32,063	21,847	17,637	13,330
Current assets	287,030	221,367	170,250	216,659	221,202	169,872
Current liabilities	117,255	111,660	103,826	74,415	83,149	47,309
Working capital	169,775	109,707	66,424	142,244	138,053	122,563
Current ratio	2.4:1	2.0:1	1.6:1	2.9:1	2.7:1	3.6:1
Long-term debt and lease obligations	$ 158,182	$ 158,758	$ 143,700	$ 35,540	$ 29,440	$ 29,440
Debt-to-equity percent	34%	44%	45%	13%	11%	13%
Stockholders' equity	$ 469,664	$ 361,550	$ 320,730	$ 284,389	$ 259,668	$ 233,529
Total assets	$ 806,800	$ 684,472	$ 607,199	$ 422,004	$ 396,153	$ 331,870
Return on average stockholders' equity	19.3%	18.2%	17.7%	15.2%	16.8%	20.5%
Aftertax return on average invested capital	13.9%	12.8%	14.3%	13.0%	14.2%	17.1%
Stockholders' data:						
Outstanding common shares at year-end	15,669	14,160	14,159	13,745	13,730	13,720
Market price of common stock						
At year-end	$ 36	$ 23½	$ 24⅝	$ 20⅝	$ 19⅞	$ 22⅜
Range during year	$ 41–23⅛	$ 26–20	$ 26½–17⅜	$ 23½–18½	$ 22⅜–16⅝	$ 27½–18½
Number of common stockholders at year-end	16,817	17,774	18,417	18,735	19,694	20,421
Employees' data:						
Payrolls	$ 273,097	$ 253,297	$ 227,987	$ 112,135	$ 99,322	$ 88,848
Number of full-time employees at year-end	12,450	12,430	11,700	8,100	7,660	7,670

EXHIBIT 3 Product Group Information for the Years Ended December 31 (in thousands)

	1981	*1980*	*1979*
Net sales:			
Chocolate and confectionery	$1,015,106	$ 929,885	$ 822,813
Restaurant operations	302,908	274,297	224,072
Other food products and services	133,137	131,107	114,410
Total net sales	$1,451,151	$1,335,289	$1,161,295
Operating income:			
Chocolate and confectionery	$ 142,658	$ 118,435	$ 99,880
Restaurant operations	29,309	25,567	23,322
Other food products and services	7,250	5,148*	6,397
Total operating income	179,217	149,150	129,599
General corporate expenses	(11,763)	(10,190)	(7,742)
Interest expense (net)	(12,512)	(14,100)	(17,764)
Income before taxes	154,942	124,860	104,093
Less: income taxes	74,580	62,805	50,589
Net income	$ 80,362	$ 62,055	$ 53,504
Identifiable assets:			
Chocolate and confectionery	$ 445,815	$ 333,232	$ 297,296
Restaurant operations	223,265	219,196	207,125
Other food products and services	63,446	62,553	63,886
Corporate	74,274	69,491	38,892
Total identifiable assets	$ 806,800	$ 684,472	$ 607,199
Depreciation:			
Chocolate and confectionery	$ 9,554	$ 8,469	$ 7,389
Restaurant operations	14,379	13,015	10,283
Other food products and services	2,675	2,671	2,185
Corporate	957	741	658
Total depreciation	$ 27,565	$ 24,896	$ 20,515
Capital additions:			
Chocolate and confectionery	$ 57,504†	$ 27,061†	$ 29,472
Restaurant operations	22,098	24,468	20,965
Other food products and services	5,525	6,141	2,233
Corporate	6,546	1,359	3,767
Total capital additions	$ 91,673	$ 59,029	$ 56,437

* After a writeoff of deferred location costs of Cory Food Services in the amount of $1.4 million.

† Includes $37.8 million in 1981 and $6.5 million in 1980 for a new manufacturing facility currently being constructed.

EXHIBIT 4 Development of Hershey Products

1894	The Hershey Bar and Almond Bar
	Hershey's Cocoa, Hershey's Baking Chocolate
1907	Hershey's Kisses
1923	Reese's Peanut Butter Cups
	Y&S Nibs
1925	Mr. Goodbar
1926	Hershey's Syrup
1928	Y&S Twizzlers
1938	Krackel
1939	Hershey's Miniatures
1940	Hershey's Hot Chocolate (now Hot Cocoa Mix)
1941	Dainties (now Semi-Sweet Chocolate Chips)
1952	Chocolate Fudge Topping
1956	Instant Cocoa Mix (Hershey's instant)
1970	Kit Kat
1971	Special Dark
1976	Reese's Crunchy
1977	Reese's Peanut Butter Flavored Chips
	Golden Almond
1978	Reese's Pieces, Giant Kiss
1979	Whatchamacallit

Source: Company document.

1975 and withdrawn the same year. The Rally Bar, a chocolate, caramel, and peanut candy bar, was removed from the market; one of its problems was that, in the initial formula, the peanuts became soggy on the retailers' shelves. The original formula was modified, but the product did not measure up to sales expectations. Exhibit 5 shows the importance of new and current products for the Chocolate and Confectionery Division from 1963 to 1977.

Restaurant Operations

This division was acquired in January 1979. The Friendly Ice Cream Corporation consists of about 626 restaurants (1982) in 16 states, primarily in the Northeast and Midwest. Exhibit 6 shows the number of restaurants in each state. The division's headquarters and major plant are in Wilbraham, Massachusetts, another plant is in Troy, Ohio. Both plants manufacture the ice cream, syrups, and toppings used by the restaurants, and their capacities are considered sufficient for the current number of resturants, as well as for some future expansion. The Wilbraham plant processes the meat required by the restaurants; it is shipped frozen to the individual restaurant units. Some

EXHIBIT 5 Sales of New and Present Chocolate and Confectionery Products, 1963–1977

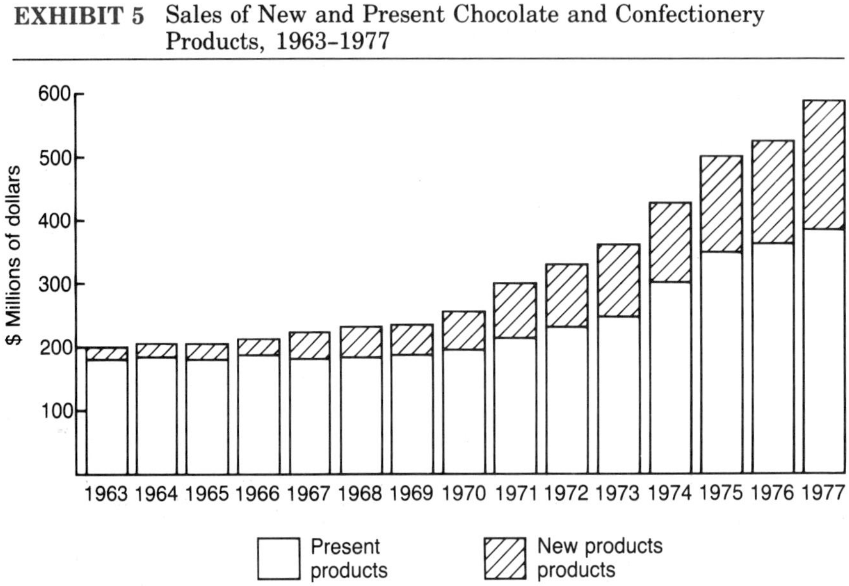

Source: The Wall Street Transcript, November 13, 1978, by permission.

items (milk, cream, baked goods, eggs, and produce) are purchased by the restaurants from local sources which are designated by Friendly's central purchasing department.

Friendly Restaurants serve high quality food at moderate prices, specializing in sandwiches, platters, and ice cream products. All units are owned outright by Friendly; there are no franchise agreements.

There are three major types of Friendly Restaurants. The *traditional* Friendly ice cream and sandwich shop offers a limited menu, featuring ice cream, hamburgers, breakfast items, platters, salad, french fries, beverages, and soup and sandwiches. Customers are served in booths or counters, or by take-out service. (The average seating capacity is 60.) There were 213 traditional operations in 1981. The 351 *modified* shop units offer most of the items available in the traditional shop, but serve a wider variety of full meals and platters. Unlike in the traditional shop, food is prepared out of the customer's sight. The modified units offer take-out service, but have a greater proportion of booth seats than the traditional restaurants. (Seating capacity averages 70 seats.) They also have more personalized service and a more pleasant dining atmosphere. The 50 *family* restaurants have the broadest menu, serving seafood, chicken, and other dinners, along with more varied breakfasts and platter meals. Desserts other than ice cream are available, and some units serve beer and wine. Seating is primarily

EXHIBIT 6 Location of Friendly Restaurants

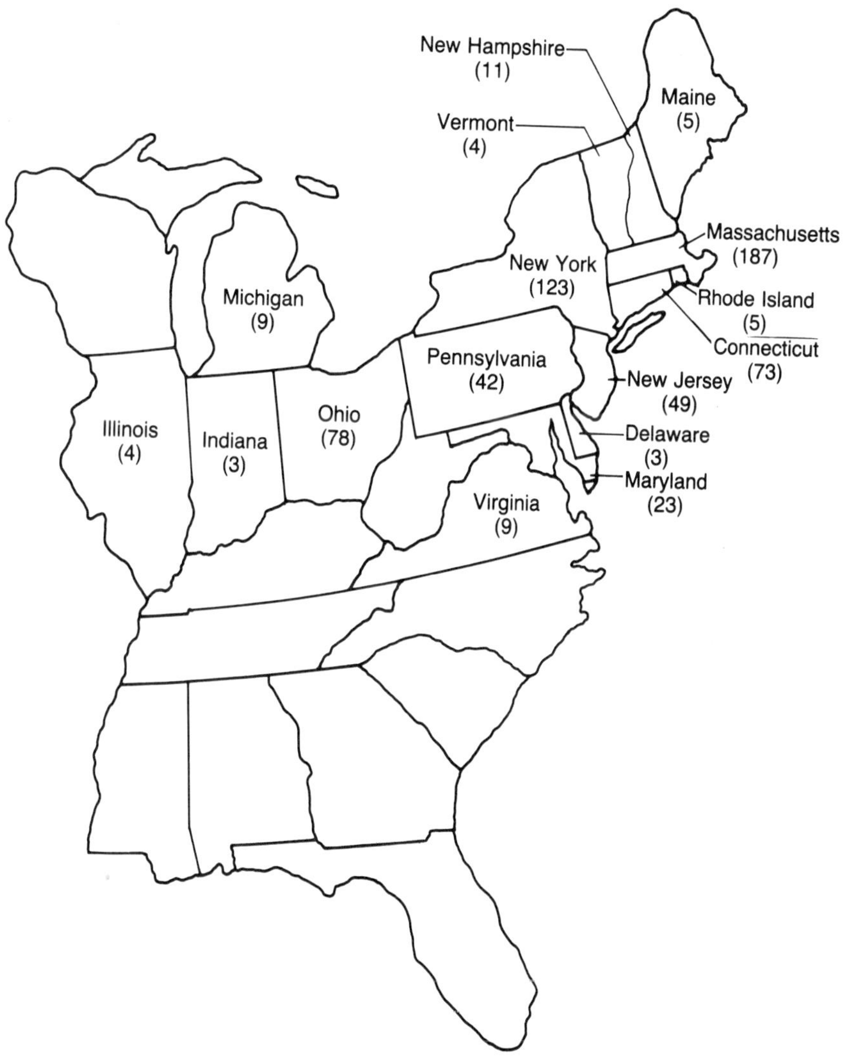

booths and tables, and the floors are usually carpeted. (Seating capacity is from 90 to 120.)

Menus and portions in each type of restaurant are standardized, but prices may vary, generally according to geographical location. Most of the units sell prepackaged ice cream for home consumption. Friendly restaurants feature a colonial decor, and free parking is available.

The Friendly Corporation has followed a policy of refurbishing its restaurants and opening newer ones. The remodeling policy involves converting traditional units into modified units; as of January 1, 1981, 351 units had been modified. Other units have been modernized. In 1980, 20 additional units, 14 of which are Family restaurants, were opened; 11 units were closed in 1980. All units use modern construction methods. Almost 400 Friendly units have opened since 1970.

As of January 1, 1981, 419 of the Friendly units were free-standing, while the rest were located in shopping centers. Seventy percent of the free-standing sites are owned by Friendly; the other 30 percent are leased, as are all the shopping center sites. Friendly's executives believe that the great majority of its customers are residents of the immediate area surrounding the restaurant. Virtually all units are in suburban areas.

Other Food Products and Services

Pasta. Four acquisitions comprise Hershey's pasta group. San Giorgio Macaroni, Inc., was acquired in 1966, with major markets in Philadelphia, Washington, D.C., Pittsburgh, and New York. Its primary plant is in Lebanon, Pennsylvania, about 20 miles from Hershey. San Giorgio produces 65 varieties of pasta and noodle products. Delmonico Foods, Inc., of Louisville, Kentucky was also acquired in 1966, and was merged with San Giorgio in 1975. Its manufacturing facility is in Louisville, and the company's products are distributed chiefly in Kentucky, Ohio, and parts of West Virginia. The Procino-Rossi Corporation was acquired in 1978. Its brands (P & R brands) are distributed chiefly in upstate New York. The largest pasta acquisition is the Skinner Macaroni Co. of Omaha, Nebraska. Purchased in 1979, it distributes its products to 20 states in the West, Southwest, and South. In 1980, Hershey merged all four pasta companies into one organization, called San Giorgio-Skinner Company.

San Giorgio-Skinner Company produces and sells a great variety of pasta items, including small shells, jumbo shells, large shells, manicotti, lasagna, rippled edge lasagna, macaroni, large elbow macaroni, shell macaroni, spaghetti, long spaghetti, thin spaghetti, curly spaghetti, mostaccioli, egg noodles, extra wide egg noodles, rigatoni, alphabets, linguine, perciatelli, fettucini, soupettes, cut ziti, and spaghetti sauce.

Cory Food Services. Cory Food Services, Inc., founded by Harvey Cory in 1933, was acquired in 1967. Cory developed a vacuum glass brewer with a glass filter that brewed a delicious coffee. In 1964, Cory introduced its coffee service to the business community in the United States and Canada. Cory's corporate headquarters is in Chicago, and the company has 51 branch offices in the United States. These branch offices are grouped into five regional offices: Arlington Heights, Illinois; Long Island, New York; Rockville, Maryland; Glendale, California; and Dallas, Texas. Six branch offices in Canada are serviced by the regional office in Toronto.

As a complement to its coffee business, Cory introduced leased water treatment units, compact refrigerator units, and microwave ovens suitable for offices. The latter two were expanded into more areas in 1981. Growth in these new ventures was good in 1981 and further expansion was anticipated in 1982.

STRATEGIC PLANNING

Hershey began to emphasize strategic planning in the late 1970s. William E. C. Dearden, Hershey's chief executive officer, stated that strategic planning was his number one priority. In 1978, Mr. Dearden established the position of vice president of corporate development, which reports directly to him.

Hershey's strategic plan for accomplishing its basic corporate objectives has centered on its efforts to diversify. In the company's 1980 annual report, Chairman of the Board Harold S. Mohler, Chief Executive Officer William E. C. Dearden, and the company's President and Chief Operating Officer, Richard A. Zimmerman, stated, "In keeping with our strategic plan, we shall continue our drive to become a major, diversified, international food and food-related company." This strategic plan is also reflected in the Statement of Corporate Philosophy developed by the same executives (see Exhibit 7). The statement also includes the company's basic objectives: "We are in business to make a reasonable profit, and to enhance the value of our shareholders' investment."

The company, however, faces strong competition. In the early 1970s, Hershey lost its lead in market share for candy bars to Mars, the privately owned, Hackettstown, New Jersey, company which markets such well known brands as Milky Way, Snickers, Three Musketeers, and m&m's. At one time, Mars had a 40 percent share of the candy bar market, compared to Hershey's 23 percent. By 1979, Mars had slipped to 36 percent of candy bar sales, while Hershey increased to 27 percent. Hershey executives maintained that in 1979 it was ahead of Mars in total candy sales.[1]

Another impediment is the slide in candy consumption. In 1978, Americans consumed an annual average of about 15 pounds of candy.

---

[1] "Hershey Steps Out," *Forbes,* March 17, 1980, p. 64.

EXHIBIT 7

Hershey Foods Corporation
Hershey, Pennsylvania 17033

STATEMENT OF CORPORATE PHILOSOPHY

We are in business to make a reasonable profit and to enhance the value of our shareholders' investment. We recognize that, to achieve this objective, we must use our resources efficiently, and we must provide for the proper balance between the fundamental obligations that we have to our shareholders, employees, customers, consumers, suppliers and society in general.

We will continue to pursue a policy of profitable growth by maintaining the excellence of our current businesses while concurrently utilizing our financial resources and the expertise and ingenuity of our people to ~~further~~ diversify into other food and food-related businesses, and/or such other businesses which offer significant opportunity for growth.

In seeking to balance our desire for profitable growth with the obligations which we have to the other various interests, we recognize that:

— All employees should be treated fairly and with dignity. They should be provided with good working conditions and competitive wages, and should be rewarded according to performance. To the fullest extent possible, in line with good business practices, promotions should be made from within the Corporation.

— Our Affirmative Action Program is a sincere commitment. Each of us has an obligation to follow it both in the spirit and letter of the law.

— We should be results oriented, and all employees should be given the opportunity to express individual initiative and judgment. Responsibility and authority, however, must be appropriately delegated.

— To successfully conduct the business of the Corporation, it is necessary that each employee strive to improve the communications relating to his or her area of responsibility.

— Our individual and company relationships should be conducted on the basis of the highest standards of conduct and ethics, and it is important that we recognize that the success of our business depends upon the character and integrity of people working in a spirit of constructive cooperation.

— We need to provide to our customers and consumers products of consistent excellent quality at competitive prices that will insure an adequate return on investment.

— We have an inherent responsibility to be a good neighbor and to support community projects, and all employees are encouraged to take an active part in improving the quality of community life.

— We have a responsibility to conduct our operations within the regulatory guidelines and in a manner that does not adversely affect our environment.

It is imperative that we create a climate throughout our entire organization which causes these philosophies to become a way of life.

Adopted: July 26, 1976
Affirmed: April 11, 1980

Chairman of the Board

Vice Chairman and
Chief Executive Officer

President and
Chief Operating Officer

Source: Company Document.

A decade earlier, the figure was about 20 pounds. The highest per capita annual candy consumption was in the 1940s, and the 1978 figure was the lowest since 1935.[2] Competition is also stiff in the pasta division. In 1979, its San Giorgio, Delmonico, Procino-Rossi, and Skinner brands had a 10.2 percent market share. This was well under the 18 percent shares of the industry leader, C. F. Mueller Co., a subsidiary of Foremost-McKesson, Inc.[3] To implement its strategic plan, Hershey has developed the corporate organization presented in Exhibit 8. Gary W. McQuaid is the vice president of marketing for the chocolate and confectionery group, John D. Burke is Friendly's vice president of marketing, and Clifford K. Larsen serves in this capacity for San Giorgio-Skinner.[4]

RESEARCH AND DEVELOPMENT

In 1979, Hershey's 114,000 square foot technical center was completed at a cost of $7.4 million. Management believes this facility and its staff will give it one of the best research and development capabilities in the industry. Included in the facility are offices, laboratories, a library, test kitchen, auditorium, animal testing facilities, and a pilot plant. A year before completion of the technical center, a major reorganization of the company's R&D effort was announced, and a new vice president of science and technology was named. This office, consisting of four groups, is responsible for heading up the company's entire R&D effort.

The *research group's* efforts have focused on three areas: vegetable fat chemistry, chocolate flavor research, and raw materials, such as peanuts and almonds. There are three subgroups in the research group. The analytical research group emphasizes chocolate analysis, and has received international acclaim for its efforts; it has compiled one of the world's largest data banks on the nutritional content of chocolate and cocoa. Microbiological research focuses on cocoa bean microbiology. This group's importance has increased as the company has purchased more chocolate liquor and less raw cocoa. The nutrition group engages in basic nutrition research projects, on subjects like tooth decay, acne, chocolate allergies, and nutrition, and it works closely with the technical committee of the Chocolate Manufacturers Association.

The *product and process development group* continually monitors consumer trends and behavioral patterns to define product oppor-

---

[2] "Indulge, Indulge! Enjoy, Enjoy!" *Forbes,* October 15, 1979, p. 45.

[3] "Hershey Steps Out."

[4] *Advertising Age,* September 9, 1982, p. 106.

EXHIBIT 8 Hershey's Corporate Organization*

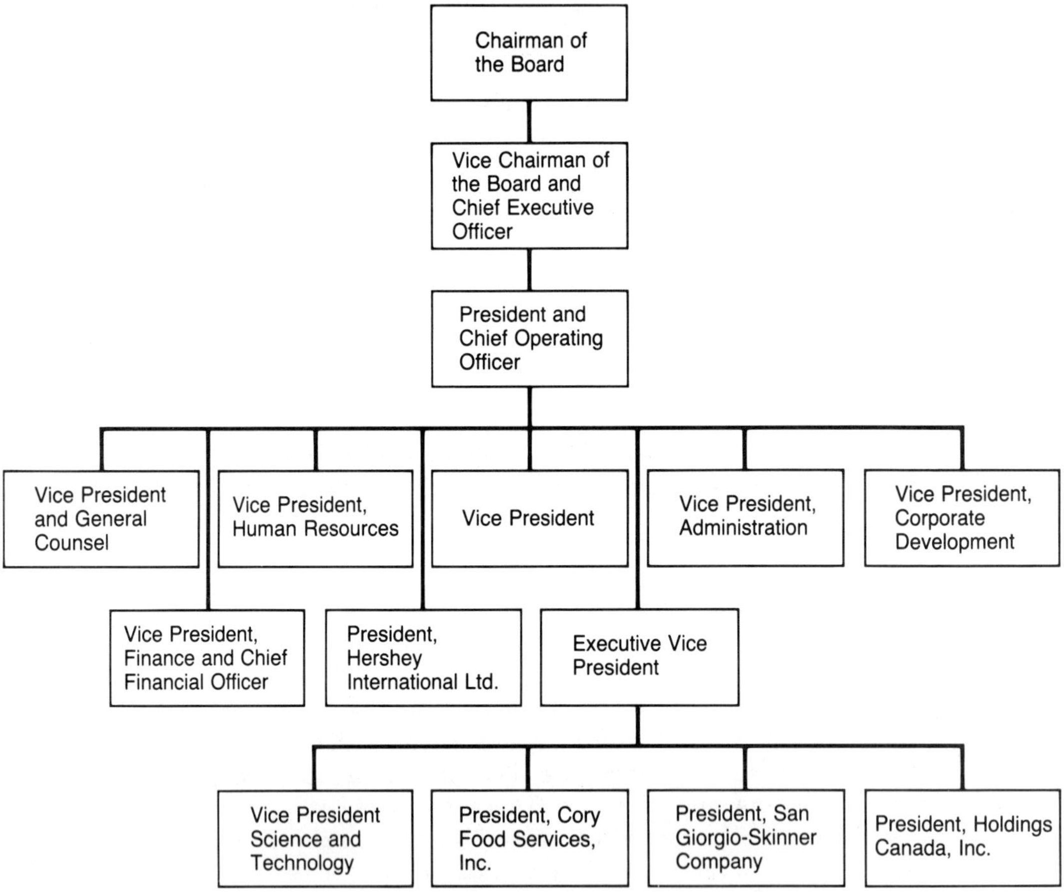

* Case writer's perception of reporting relationships.

tunities. San Giorgio's Light 'n Fluffy Noodles and the Whatchamacallit candy bar were developed in response to consumers' demand for "lightness."

The *engineering group* is mainly responsible for assisting capital programs, and it also provides some engineering skills for moving new products into production.

The *equipment design and developing group* provides support for producing new products and improving existing manufacturing systems. This group designs special equipment not generally available and integrates purchased equipment into the production line. In addition, it is responsible for designing special methods and devices unique to Hershey's products and conditions.

One of the major reasons for Hershey's purchase of Marabou in Sweden was to exchange technological information, with special emphasis on new confectionery products. An interest in Chadler Industrial de Bahia of Brazil was purchased for the same reason. Hershey was interested in Chadler's conversion processes which make chocolate liquor, cocoa butter, and cocoa powder from cacao beans. Hershey has also acquired interests in several cocoa growing ventures in Costa Rica, the Dominican Republic, and Belize, to try to increase yields from cacao bean production. Hershey is committed to continued support of the American Cocoa Research institute, which works to improve the volume and quality of cacao bean production in the western hemisphere.

The company's R&D efforts have paid important dividends. Whatchamacallit and Reese's Pieces are two successful products which were developed by the company, and their success has encouraged further research. A significant technological breakthrough was the development of a peanut butter-flavored ingredient which reduces dependence on high-priced cacao beans.

Future corporate research and development is expected to continue to work toward creating new ingredients that are readily available domestically and will reduce the dependency on imported commodities. Two major emphases have been testing alternate fat products for cocoa butter and experimenting with new high-fructose corn syrup, which could be used as a sucrose alternate in certain kinds of products.

INTERNATIONAL OPERATIONS

In recent years, Hershey has increased its overseas marketing efforts. As of 1981, the company believes that "overall sales and earnings from international operations remain modest in comparison with the corporation's total performance." However, the company is pleased with its expansion in international sales.

Hershey's major foreign market is Canada. Although some sales growth occurred in Canada in 1980, company executives considered these results well below expectations. As in the United States, higher operating costs forced the company to raise prices to 35 cents for the standard size candy bar.

During 1979 and 1980, several new products were successfully introduced in Canada. Brown Cow proved to be an immediate success, and became one of the company's leading brands in Canada. Brown Cow is a chocolate syrup milk modifier in a plastic dispenser bottle. Top Scotch, a butterscotch sundae topping, was introduced in 1979. Three other products entered the Canadian market in 1970: Special Crisp, the Canadian version of Whatchamacallit; Reese's Crunchy Peanut Butter Cups; and a boxed version of Y&S All Sorts (licorice). 1980 saw the introduction of Reese's Pieces and two clear plastic bag packages of Y&S All Sorts.

Hershey has a number of supply points for cacao beans. The major ones are La Guaria, Venezuela; Guayaquil, Ecuador; Ilheus, Brazil; Abidjan, Ivory Coast; Accra, Ghana; Lagos, Nigeria; and Douala, Cameroon.

Hershey has a policy of joint ventures in entering foreign markets. This strategy allows the company to work with well-established partners with considerable knowledge of local market conditions. Hershey entered a joint venture in 1979 with the Fujiya Confectioning Company, Ltd. of Tokyo. This Japanese firm has been in existence since 1910, and is a leader in chocolate and confectionery products, snack foods, beverages, ice cream, and bakery products in that country; it also has important restaurant operations. The joint venture agreement enables Hershey's products to be imported, manufactured, and sold in Japan, and company executives believe that this arrangement has already resulted in increased Japanese sales. Another joint venture arrangement in Mexico with Nacional de Dulces, S.A. has resulted in increased sales and earnings in that country. The company expects demand for its products to increase, and a new Mexican manufacturing facility is under construction. Two joint ventures exist in Brazil: one with Chadler Industrial de Bahia S.A. involves sales of chocolate and confectionery products. A new joint venture with S.A. Industrias Reunidas F. Matarazzo is concerned with pasta sales. Early indications were that the pasta joint venture was successful. However, the continued devaluation of the cruzeiro has adversely affected the firm's Brazilian operations.

In Sweden, AB Marabou acquired Göteborgs Kex, that country's leading cookie and cracker manufacturer. These additional sales contributed to Hershey's revenues; Hershey has a 20 percent interest in AB Marabou. In the Philippines, Hershey began in 1980 to furnish technical manufacturing assistance and cocoa growing advice to the Philippine Coca Corporation.

In 1981, Hershey formed a new subsidiary company, Hershey International Ltd. This company is responsible for Hershey's international operations outside Canada, especially those in Mexico, Brazil, the Philippines, Sweden, and Japan. Company executives believed this "consolidation will further strengthen the overall monitoring, control, and reporting of international operations." Richard M. Marcks, vice president, international, was named president of the new subsidiary company and his old position was abolished.

DISTRIBUTION

The company believes that its distribution system is critical in maintaining sales growth and providing service to its distributors. Hershey attempts to anticipate distributors' optimum stock levels and provide them with reasonable delivery times. To achieve these objectives, Hershey uses 35 field warehouses throughout the United States, Puerto Rico, and Canada. Hershey uses public carriers, contract carriers, and some private trucks to move its products from manufacturing plants to field warehouses, and then to customers. For example, a fleet of company-owned refrigerated trucks transports food and supplies from the two Friendly production sites to the individual restaurants. Some shipments go directly from manufacturing plants to customers. Hershey's executives believe that the distribution system has been very helpful in successfully introducing new products nationally.

Hershey has five major manufacturing plants in the United States and Canada for chocolate and confectionery products with an additional manufacturing site under construction. Four of the present plants (two in Hershey, one in Oakdale, California, and one in Smith Falls, Ontario) produce primarily chocolate products. The Lancaster, Pennsylvania, plant produces licorice products. A future manufacturing plant in Stuart's Draft, Virginia, will produce chocolate items.

Hershey's chocolate and confectionery products are sold mainly to wholesale, chain, and independent grocers, candy and tobacco stores, syndicated and department stores, vending and concessions, drug stores, and convenience stores. Exhibit 9 shows the percentage of sales of each of these distribution outlets. Exhibit 10 shows the geographical sales pattern for chocolate and confectionery products. Over 375 sales representatives throughout the United States and Canada service over 20,000 direct sales customers. Company executives estimate that over 1 million retail outlets are served in 20,000 cities and towns, and that no single customer accounts for more than 4 percent of the total sales of chocolate and confectionery items. The company's sales representatives are specialized according to the product sold. One type is responsible for candy bars, packaged items, and grocery products. The other handles specialty products, food service, and industrial products.

Hershey's pasta products are sold to supermarket chains, cooperatives, independent wholesalers, and wholesaler-sponsored volunteers. Four brand names are marketed (San Giorgio, Skinner, Delmonico, and P&R), but some private label merchandise is also marketed.

EXHIBIT 9 Percentage of Chocolate and Confectionery Sales by Type of Distribution Outlet

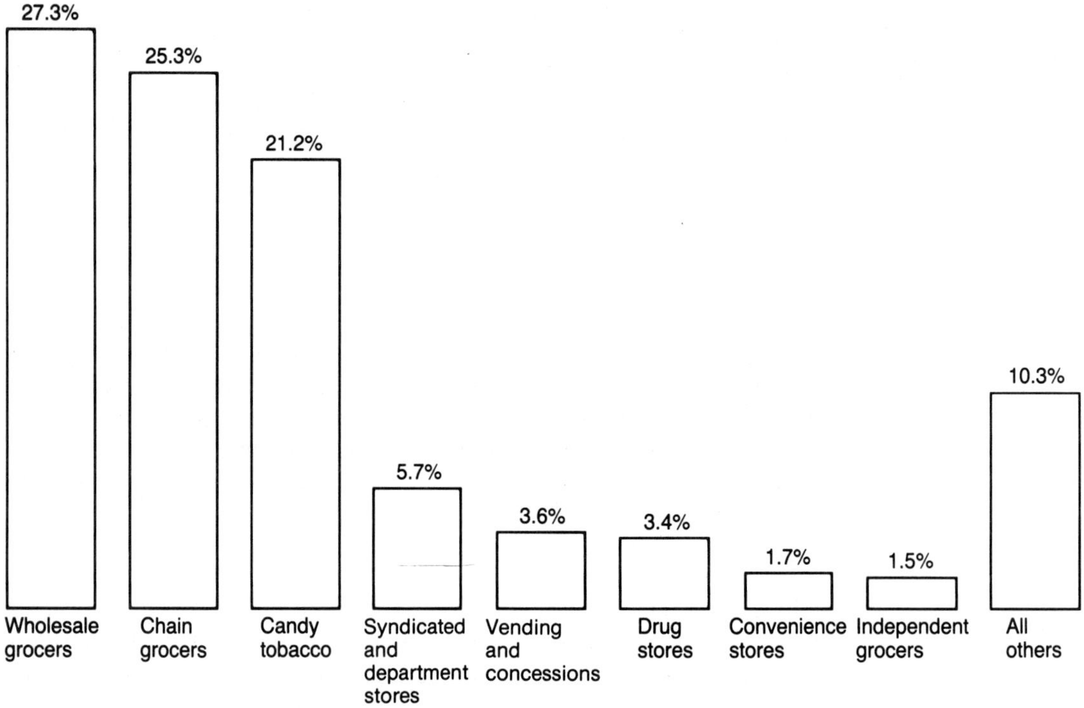

Source: The Wall Street Transcript, November 13, 1978, by permission.

ADVERTISING

For its first 66 years, Hershey did not advertise. The company relied on the quality of its products and its extensive channels of distribution system to gain acceptance in the marketplace. Milton Hershey said,

EXHIBIT 10 Geographical Sales

Region	*Percentage of Sales*	*Percentage of U.S. Population*
North	31.9%	27.6%
South	24.2	27.4
Midwest	25.9	27.9
West	18.0	17.1
Total U.S.	100.0%	100.0%

Source: The Wall Street Transcript, November 13, 1978, by permission.

"Give them quality. That's the best kind of advertising in the world." However, Hershey did use various forms of sales promotion, such as the plant tour, to promote sales. The plant tour, seen by almost 10 million people, was replaced by Hershey's Chocolate World in 1973.

In 1968, over 20 years after the death of its founder, Hershey announced plans to initiate a consumer advertising program for its confectionery and grocery products. On July 19, 1970, the program was launched with a full page ad for Hershey's Syrup, which appeared in 114 newspaper supplements. National radio and television advertising appeared in September.

Hershey decided to advertise for several reasons. There was increased competition in the confectionery industry—increased competition which often involved heavy advertising. There was the need to better acquaint people under 25 with Hershey products. In 1970, these people accounted for half of the U.S. population. As Hershey developed new products, executives believed that advertising would promote mass distribution, which would, in turn, spur mass production.

Exhibit 11 shows advertising expenditures from 1971 through 1981. Hershey's $43 million of advertising in 1980 moved it into the top 100 of U.S. advertisers, and its 1981 expenditures ranked it 86th. Mars, Inc. spent $78.4 million on advertising in 1981, good for the 69th spot. Exhibit 12 shows 1981 advertising expenditures for Hershey's major brands. Sales promotion efforts are directed to consumers by such point-of-purchase materials as shelf-takers and case cards, and by coupon and premium offers.

The company has had to defend its advertising from attacks on two fronts: some of the advertising is directed toward children, and some of its products may promote tooth decay. Hershey estimates that about 30 percent of its advertising is directed to children. The Federal Trade

EXHIBIT 11 Annual Advertising

Year	*Amount*
1971	$10,506,000
1972	13,954,000
1973	9,565,000
1974	1,744,000
1975	9,499,000
1976	13,330,000
1977	17,637,000
1978	21,847,000
1979	32,063,000
1980	42,684,000
1981	56,516,000

Source: Company Annual Reports.

EXHIBIT 12 Most Heavily Advertised Products in 1981

Product	*Advertising Expenditure*
Hershey's Candy Bars	$7.0 million
Reese's Candies	4.6 million
Hershey's Chocolate Kisses	3.7 million
Whatchamacallit	3.7 million
Hershey's Chocolate Syrup	3.1 million
Reese's Pieces	2.9 million
Chocolate Chips	2.3 million
Rolo Candy	1.6 million
Hershey's Candies	1.4 million

Source: Reprinted with permission from the September 9, 1982, issue of *Advertising Age.* Copyright 1982 by Crain Communications, Inc.

Commission on May 28, 1980, began considering a trade regulation which would adversely affect the advertising of many of the company's products. At that time, however, Congress narrowed the FTC's authority to adopt such a trade rule. As of January 1, 1981, company executives were not sure whether the FTC would continue its efforts to regulate advertising to children. In most cases, it would take several years to adopt such a trade rule. Hershey executives announced they were opposed to "any attempt to limit its rights to advertise truthfully its products to any audience." Hershey has developed material about the controversy surrounding tooth decay and nutrition. An example of these materials is presented in Exhibit 13. Exhibit 14 shows the nutritional value per serving of various foods.

PRICING

Pricing is a particularly important element of the marketing mix for Hershey, and it is difficult for a number of reasons. Hershey's chocolate and confectionery products depend on raw materials. The suppliers of these raw materials are usually in foreign countries and their supplies are frequently curtailed because of bad weather or other factors.

Cacao beans are the major raw materials for the Chocolate and Confectionery Division; two thirds of the world's supply is grown in West Africa, chiefly in Ghana. Prices fluctuated widely in the 1970s because of weather conditions, consuming countries' demands, sales policies of the producing countries, speculative influences, worldwide inflation, and currency movements. Hershey attempts to minimize the effects of bean price fluctuations through forward purchasing of large quantities of cacao beans, cocoa butter, and chocolate liquor. Cocoa

EXHIBIT 13 Example of a Hershey's Advertisement

Good Nutrition Makes Good Sense

Everyone agrees that good nutrition makes good sense. But what is good nutrition? Nowadays many people are readily willing to answer this question, but many of their answers are contradictory.

While we do not advertise our chocolate products as especially nutritious foods, they do have nutritional value and do contribute to the overall diet since they are composed of such food ingredients as milk, various nuts, chocolate and sugar.

Nearly all Hershey's Chocolate and Confectionery Division products have nutrition information printed on their labels. This practice was begun voluntarily in 1973, and to date we are the only manufacturer in the chocolate and confectionery industry to provide this consumer service. Our effort to convey this information is one clear indication of Hershey's concern for good nutrition and our respect for the consumer's right to know.

Good nutrition comes from a balanced diet; one that provides the right amounts and the right kinds of proteins, vitamins, minerals, fats and carbohydrates. The chart on the next page provides an interesting basis of comparison between Hershey Foods' products and other snack items commonly cited as "more nutritious."

Chocolate and confectionery products and other sugar containing snacks have been coming under attack recently. They are accused of being "empty calorie" or so-called "junk" foods.

We all have substantial caloric needs. At Hershey Foods we believe obtaining the right amount of calories is especially important for active, growing children. Calories come from nutrients; namely carbohydrates, fats and proteins. Our products supply these nutrients and do contribute to good nutrition.

Throughout the world, carbohydrates are the largest single component of the diet. In the United States, about half of all calories (i.e., energy) are provided by carbohydrates commonly referred to as sugars and starches. As far as the body is concerned, all carbohydrates must be reduced to simple sugars before they can be used. Once sugars and starches reach the stomach, their dietary origin is lost. It makes no difference whether they come from fruits, vegetables, milk, honey, or Hershey Bars—before entering the blood stream, they are all alike.

Sugar is currently bearing the brunt of the attack from a variety of sources. Since sugar is a significant component of many Hershey Foods' chocolate and confectionery products, we are naturally concerned about these attacks and the types of evidence used to support them.

At present sugar is not linked in substantive research to the variety of health problems usually mentioned in this context. As for dental caries, a complex issue, there is evidence that sugar, both naturally occurring and added, plays a role. On the other hand, a number of studies in dental literature show that chocolate, especially milk chocolate, does not cause an increase in dental caries.

Researchers report that milk chocolate has a high content of protein, calcium, phosphate and other minerals, all of which have exhibited positive effects on tooth enamel. In addition due to its natural fat (cocoa butter) content, milk chocolate clears the mouth quickly in comparison to some other foods. These factors are thought to be responsible for making milk chocolate less likely to cause dental caries than certain other foods.

The American public is being inundated with numerous attacks on sugar and the role it plays in the diet. Many assertions are

EXHIBIT 13 *(concluded)*

made on a partial understanding of the facts or without substantiating research.

Unfortunately the crusade against sugar containing products is well underway despite a lack of adequate, factual support. Federal, state, and local governmental bodies have entered the fray, and considerable media interest has been generated. We fear that great misunderstanding will be created before the issue is resolved, although as a company and an industry, we are trying to raise the information level on all fronts.

One aspect of this very complex situation is the role the Federal Trade Commission has been asked to play regarding the advertisement of products containing sugar. At the present time, the FTC is considering various means of limiting our industry's ability to advertise its products.

Hershey Foods has and will continue to oppose any attempt to limit its right to advertise. We believe we have the right to advertise to all of our audiences and we do not think our advertising has been out of balance. In 1978, less than one third of all our advertising impressions will be received by children.

Hershey Foods has always been concerned about the content of its advertising as well as the type of programs it supports. We have helped in the development of voluntary codes through the Children's Review Unit of the National Advertising Board, and our ads are constantly reviewed by child psychologists and public affairs specialists to make sure they are not misleading and cannot be misunderstood.

Our standard bar line, which accounts for the majority of advertising expenditures, represents an inexpensive group of products. We feel that children can be appropriately informed about them, especially in light of their nutritional value and the parental approval they have received for generations in the United States. We believe we have the right to remind consumers of our products and to inform new consumers about products their parents have used, enjoyed, and approved.

Perhaps the most paradoxical aspect of this issue is the fact that chocolate and confectionery consumption in the United States is not excessive, representing only about one percent of total food intake. What's more, consumption of these foods has not increased in the last 40 years. Since mass media advertising did not really come into being until the 1950s, it is evident that television advertising has not contributed to increased consumption of chocolate and confectionery products. As far as our industry is concerned, however, advertising has simply fostered competition.

The so-called "junk" food issue in all its complexity will continue to be an important challenge to Hershey Foods Corporation. We shall stand firmly in our position that Hershey's products are mixtures of ingredients which inherently have nutritional value. Hershey has manufactured chocolate and confectionary products of the highest quality for over 80 years. We are very proud of these products and the role they play in the lives of people throughout the world.

future contracts are purchased and sold, and the company holds memberships in the London Cocoa Terminal Market Association and the Coffee, Sugar, and Cocoa Exchange, Inc., in New York. Crop forecasts, chiefly in West Africa and Brazil, are also made.

EXHIBIT 14 Nutritional Value per Serving of Various Foods‡

	A *Milk Chocolate*	*B* *Mr. Goodbar*	*C* *Reese Cup*	*D* *Ice Cream*	*E* *Saltine Crackers*	*F* *Graham Crackers*	*G* *Cheese/Peanut Butter Crackers*	*H* *Apple*	*I* *Dried Dates*
Serving size	*1.05 oz*	*1.3 oz*	*1.2 oz*	*8 fl oz (1 cup)*	*1 oz*	*1 oz*	*1.5 oz*	*3¼ in. diam.*	*1.4 oz*
Calories	160	210	190	260	120	110	210	120	120
Protein (grams)	2	5	4	6	2	2	6	0	1
Carbohydrate (grams)	17	18	18	28	20	20	24	30	29
Fat (grams)	10	13	11	14	3	2	10	1	0
Vitamin A*	*	*	*	*	*	*	*	2	*
Vitamin C†	*	*	*	*	*	*	*	10	*
Thiamine†	*	2	*	2	*	*	*	2	2
Riboflavin†	4	4	2	15	*	4	2	2	2
Niacin†	*	8	8	*	*	2	8	*	4
Calcium†	6	4	2	20	*	*	2	*	2
Iron†	2	2	2	*	2	2	2	2	6

* Contained less than 2 percent of the U.S. RDA of these nutrients.
† Vitamin and mineral levels are expressed as a percentage of the U.S. RDA.
‡ Information for foods other than Hershey products derived from U.S.D.A. Handbook No. 456 *Nutritive Value of American Foods.* Items A, B, & C, according to at least one state's legislators' list, would be included in a "low-nutritious" category. Items D through I are identified on that list as nutritious food.

Source: Company Document.

Despite these efforts, the prices of cacao beans skyrocketed in the 1970s. The following is the average price of cacao beans for October 1 through September 30, the normal crop year:

Year	*Cents per Pound*
1969–70	32.5
1970–71	26.3
1971–72	26.3
1972–73	44.5
1973–74	62.7
1974–75	57.3
1975–76	72.1
1976–77	150.1
1977–78	141.1
1978–79	156.4
1979–80	138.8

Source: Company Document.

The other major ingredient is sugar. Like cacao beans, many factors affect the price of sugar, including quantities available, demand by consumers, speculation, currency movements, and the International Sugar Agreement. Another price determinant is the price support provided domestic sugar by the Agriculture Adjustment Act of 1978. The average price per pound of refined sugar, as reported by the U.S. Department of Agriculture, FOB Northeast, has been steadily increasing:

1977	17.3 cents
1978	20.8 cents
1979	23.2 cents
1980	41.0 cents
1981	36.1 cents

Three other raw materials are important. The company is the largest domestic user of almonds, using only almonds grown in California. The price of almonds doubled in 1979 due to a poor California crop in 1978, and have remained high despite a good 1979 California crop. Marginal crops in the rest of the world kept prices high. In 1980, the peanut crop in the United States was poor, causing significant price increases. The supply of peanuts is expected to be low in 1981, but Hershey did not expect any problem obtaining enough for production. The price of milk has also increased greatly in recent years; both milk and peanut prices are affected by various Federal Marketing Orders and by U.S. Department of Agriculture subsidy programs.

More expensive cacao beans, sugar, almonds, peanuts, and milk have forced Hershey to raise prices. The sizes of various products have also been modified. Below are the price/size adjustments for Hershey's Standard Milk Chocolate Bar since 1949:

Common Retail Price: 5 Cents	
1949	1 oz.
March 1954	7/8 oz.
June 1955	1 oz.
January 1958	7/8 oz.
August 1960	1 oz.
September 1963	7/8 oz.
September 1965	1 oz.
September 1966	7/8 oz.
May 1968	3/4 oz.
Discontinued	11-24-69
Common Retail Price: 10 Cents	
November 1969	1½ ozs.
March 1970	1⅜ ozs.
January 1973	1.26 ozs.
Discontinued	1-1-74
Common Retail Price: 15 Cents	
January 1974	1.4 ozs.
May 1974	1.2 ozs.
September 1974	1.05 ozs.
January 1976	1.2 oz.
Discontinued	12-31-76
Common Retail Price: 20 Cents	
December 1976	1.35 ozs.
April 1977	1.2 ozs.
July 1977	1.05 ozs.
Discontinued	12-1-78
Common Retail Price: 25 Cents	
December 1978	1.2 ozs.
March 1980	1.05 ozs.

Source: Company Documents.

Friendly Restaurants use many raw materials. Rising prices of items such as beef, cream, condensed milk, whole milk, and sugar and corn syrup in the late 70s forced Friendly to raise menu prices. Pasta is made from durum wheat flour grown almost exclusively in North Dakota. Poor weather conditions in 1980 sharply reduced the quality of the durum wheat crop, resulting in a 60 percent increase in price. Hershey was forced to raise prices twice in 1980. Coffee prices declined in 1980 from 1979 levels, down from historic highs earlier in the decade, and the Cory Division was able to reduce its prices during 1980.

Hershey uses price concessions to induce its distributors to carry its products. The company hopes that the distributor will feature the item because the price reductions provide them with a higher-than-normal profit.

TOWARD THE FUTURE

As Hershey Foods Corporation moved into 1982, company executives decided to thoroughly review past performance and strategy, and use these assessments to chart the future direction of the firm. Several aspects of the company's operations were chosen for appraisal:

1. Have the company's diversification efforts been effective in accomplishing its objectives? What should Hershey's future diversification strategy be?
2. How effective has Hershey's advertising been? How much emphasis should the company place on advertising in the future?
3. How effective has the company's distribution strategy been? What changes would be appropriate in the future?
4. Has Hershey been able to reduce the risks which appear to be inherent in the kinds of products it sells? What can be done to reduce these risks?
5. How viable is the company's corporate organization? What are its strengths and weaknesses? What modifications are needed?

Case 5

Comshare, Inc. (A)—Strategic Actions in the Computer Services Industry

Donald W. Scotton
Allan D. Waren
Bernard C. Reimann
all of Cleveland State University

Comshare, Inc. was a computer service firm that began operations in 1966. It was a "high tech" company offering time-sharing services to industry, government, and other nonprofit organizations. These services included network access to computers owned and operated by Comshare. Users were able to communicate with the Comshare computers, located at Ann Arbor, Michigan, via sophisticated communication networks of telephone lines. The system was designed to provide very rapid, apparently instantaneous, response to most simple requests. It appeared to the user that he had access to his own computer. All of the usual data processing and accounting functions could be performed on data stored at the computer center. Users could access their data from any of their plant locations for use in dealing with organizational problems.

During the period from 1966 until 1982, many advances occurred in the use of time-sharing and in the services offered by Comshare. These included the addition of sophisticated data bases, better methods for

This research and written case information was presented at a Case Research Symposium and evaluated by the Case Research Association's Editorial Board. This case was prepared as a basis for class discussion by Professors Donald W. Scotton, Allan D. Waren, and Bernard C. Reimann of Cleveland State University. They are professors of Marketing, Computer and Information Science, and Management, respectively. Distributed by the Case Research Association.

retrieving information, and the development of modeling methods for solving business and financial problems. Comshare was a leader in the industry in developing concepts and products to make possible this advanced technology for problem solving.

The latest and most significant of these developments was System W, an advanced Decision Support System (DSS) software product, which Comshare introduced late in 1982. This software made it possible for executives to enter or retrieve data from either mainframe or personal computers, build models to simulate their businesses, make forecasts, do statistical analyses, test assumptions or alternative "scenarios," and even display their results in customized reports or graphs. While a substantial number of competitive products existed, Comshare executives considered System W to be a technological breakthrough in that it greatly facilitated modeling in multiple dimensions. Most of the competitive products were either limited to two-dimensional "spreadsheets," or required extremely complex programming to achieve multidimensional modeling and analysis.

Comshare had recently signed a marketing arrangement with IBM concerning System W. IBM was interested in making highly sophisticated software available to its customers to complement its offerings of mainframe and personal computers. The arrangement included the agreement for IBM salespeople to recommend that users and prospects interested in DSS software consider System W. When feasible and desirable, IBM representatives could make joint sales calls with Comshare salespeople.

Shortly after this arrangement was made, Comshare executives were reflecting upon this action and its implications. Richard L. Crandall, president of Comshare, indicated:

> We will utilize our complete organization to make this arrangement successful; and we will modify and adapt System W to the changing needs of users. We are no longer only a computer-based time-sharing corporation. An important part of our future lies in the development of Decision Support Systems that permit business executives to make better decisions through the interactive use of mainframe and personal computers.

THE INDUSTRY

Product Evolution

Initially computers were developed primarily for scientific computing. Their ability to store and manipulate any information was recognized and led to more and more business-oriented applications. Information could be stored, processed, and returned to users in manageable and meaningful reports and graphs. The rapid acceptance of computers led to the development of improved computers and ancillary equipment, such as terminals for entering data and calling it out, printers and plotters to provide "hard copy" output, and supporting networks and hardware to transmit and receive information. A vital complement to the hardware configuration was the appropriate software (program) to tell computers how to process the information.

An early trend toward specialization in the computing industry occurred in the mid 1960s, at which time it was recognized that not every firm or branch operation needed its own large mainframe computer. Rather, access through a communications network to a remote computer could meet user needs more economically, with little or no capital investment. Specialists developed the time-sharing concept whereby many different firms, as well as the many branches of each firm, could share a common computer in such a fashion that it appeared to each individual user as though he had sole access to the machine. Initial reception of this approach was best among the scientific and engineering community, and these groups were initially seen as the natural market for time-sharing.

Concurrent with this phase was the development of communication networks that utilized telephone lines and supporting hardware to transmit and receive data.

By the late 1960s, it was recognized that it was the business needs of private firms, nonprofit groups, and government that comprised the most significant market for computer services. There was a growing requirement for better ways to record, store, retrieve, and manipulate information about organization functions such as accounting, finance, production, personnel, marketing, and research. Therein lay the challenge for developers of software packages: To provide the means to perform these functions with the aid of computers. Software specialist firms emerged to supplement the efforts of the large hardware developers such as IBM and Digital Equipment Corporation.

Since hardware manufacturers tended to focus their efforts on systems software, a profitable and growing niche became available in the area of applications software. As a result, a variety of "software houses" emerged to provide high quality applications software with an emphasis on "user friendliness," or ease of use, as well as on efficiency. Typical applications included material requirements planning, accounting and financial reporting, and data base management.

Another important factor contributed to the accelerating growth of this specialized software market in the 1970s. This was the inability of the data processing function, in most firms, to keep up with the burgeoning demand for its services. The resulting backlog of data processing projects led to an urgent need for highly sophisticated software which would be so easy to use that nonprogrammers, such as financial or marketing executives and their staffs, could develop their own, custom-made applications.

At the same time, the increasing competitiveness and uncertainty of the business environment were creating a growing interest in strategic planning. This in turn led to a strong need for information systems to help top executives and strategic planners make decisions. One answer to this need was DSS (Decision Support System) applications software. This highly sophisticated software made possible the bringing together of relevant information from both internal and external data bases, and the use of complex models to simulate and analyze strategic alternatives before they were implemented.

The Market

There were less than 2,000 international computer software and service firms as reported in the 1982 Comshare Annual Report. Comshare, Inc., was one of the largest of these firms, involved in the marketing of DSS software, which included data management, financial modeling, forecasting, analysis, reporting, and graphics. These DSS products were used by time-sharing customers via a worldwide computer network, as well as by customers who licensed the products for use on their mainframe computers and/or microcomputers.

The market for corporate and financial planning DSS software and processing services was reported as follows in the 1983 Comshare Annual Report:

1981 sales	$549 million
1982 sales	729 million
1987 forecast	3.1 billion

The report also indicated that 1981 industry sales of all types of software totaled $4.2 billion. Richard L. Crandall, president of Comshare, reported in an interview for this case that 17 percent, or $714 million, came from data management and financial software sales, the two main predecessors of DSS. He indicated also that "in 1975 barely one-half billion dollars of industry sales were in software." *Business Week,* in its February 27, 1984, issue, published a special report on "Software: the New Driving Force." In it they forecast that software sales in the United States would "keep on growing by a dizzying 32 percent a year, topping $30 billion in 1988."

Competition

Kevin O. N. Kalkhoven, group vice president, estimated that the 1983 DSS industry leaders, their products, and sales were as follows:

Execucom	IFPS	$ 20 million
Management Decision Systems	Express	7–8 million
Comshare	System W	7–8 million
EPS, Inc.	FCS/EPS	6–7 million

It should be noted that, prior to the introduction of System W, Comshare had been a vendor of FCS/EPS on its time-sharing service. It still supported those time-sharing customers who were not willing to switch to System W.

There were more than 60 other competitors, at least 20 of whom had entered the business in the last two or three years. Two software products were identified as being particularly significant to Comshare. These were IFPS, a product originally developed for financial risk analysis, and Express, which was originally developed for marketing research functions. Both products had subsequently been enhanced and were being marketed as full function DSS systems. Comshare viewed IFPS as being particularly easy to use but lacking integrated functionality in areas such as data management, whereas Express was seen as a very hard to use product which was functionally well integrated and quite powerful.

In order to compete effectively in this market, Comshare felt it was essential to develop a product which was easier to use than IFPS and had more capabilities and was better integrated than Express. Thus System W was designed to take advantage of this opportunity for product positioning relative to the industry leaders.

Another potential threat that Comshare management had noticed was that a number of other firms were waking up to the huge potential of the market. These firms were redoubling their efforts both to improving their products and in marketing them. Several firms had decided to "unbundle" their prices for total systems in order to be more competitive. Thus a customer interested only in modeling, for example, could buy a "starter" system for as little as $10,000. If other capabilities such as forecasting or graphics were desired, each of these additional modules could be purchased separately for $5,000–$15,000 each. Another aspect of product pricing was the increasing willingness of some vendors to discount the prices of their software, especially for multiple purchases.

Life Cycle

Time-sharing sales were of continuing importance to Comshare. A recent issue of Data Communications revealed that time-sharing expenditures in the United States were $3.1 billion in 1982 and $3.8

billion in 1983. Projected expenditures in 1984 were $4.2 billion. The bulk of Comshare's revenue continued to be realized from time-sharing services.

Mr. Kalkhoven made the following comments about the time-sharing portion of the industry:

> In the mid and late 1960s there were 800 time-sharing companies and now there are less than 100. There are 600 microcomputer manufacturers today and they will follow the same pattern as time-sharing. There will be very few in the future. I have been involved in this industry (high computer technology) since 1970. It has undergone an interesting life cycle pattern.

He proceeded to draw the following diagram on a blackboard:

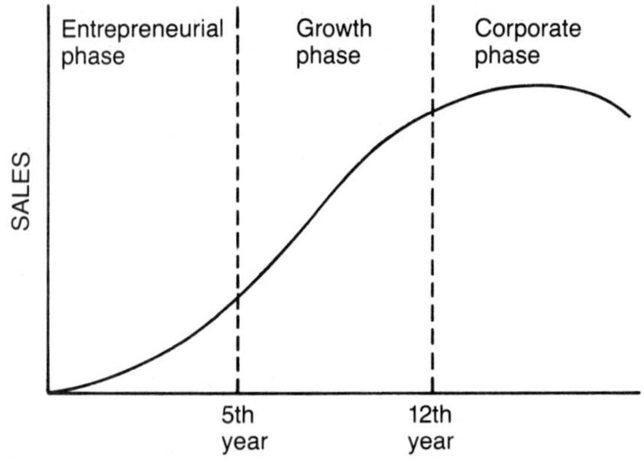

Then he described the three phases in the life cycle of a high technology computer-oriented firm as follows:

1. *Entrepreneurial Phase.* Normally the computer high tech firm remains in this phase for about five years. It takes from three to five years to realize a profit. There is a fast change in products; and a heavy capital investment is required. Management is largely drawn from technological people who are involved in the innovation of the products and concepts, for example, from engineering. A large number of firms fail and drop out because they run out of capital and cannot meet the rapidly changing technology.

2. *Growth Phase.* This period extends from about year 6 through 12. Market leaders evolve. The number of competitors is reduced dramatically. For example, in the time-sharing portion of the computer field, the number of firms was reduced from approximately 800 to 100. During this growth period, technical and management stabilities emerge. The firms begin to develop corporate missions and policies; they establish planning and marketing management approaches to guide their destinies.

However, signs of what will happen later also emerge. These include a technological slow down where profit is realized on existing technology rather than on new product developments. As an example, Comshare enjoyed profits and the fruits of a number of innovations associated with time-sharing networks. The need for significant capital becomes urgent in this phase. Furthermore, the economic climate is likely to suffer a recession at some point over this period of years. By the latter 1970s time-sharing technology had passed its period of rapid development, and the onset of a recession confronted young management with new and unanticipated conditions.

3. *Corporate Phase.* During the Corporate Phase the strategic management and marketing process, initiated in the Growth Phase, is implemented fully. Marketing opportunities are identified more specifically. Strategic and tactical planning reach maturity. Operational programs and controls are developed as the bases for achieving objectives. At this stage the firm must pick a product and go . . . you must pay for its development and introduction with the cash cows. The initial mission, technology, and products may change. For many members of the industry the Corporate Phase is just emerging. They must decide whether they will be hardware manufacturers, specialists in mainframes and/or microcomputers, time-sharing providers, systems consultants, limited software developers and purveyors, or decision support systems businesses.

COMSHARE BACKGROUND

Antecedents

The firm was founded in 1966 at Ann Arbor, Michigan. The founding president was Robert F. Guise, an independent consultant. He was joined in this venture by Richard L. Crandall, at that time a graduate student at the University of Michigan, and by four other persons.

Mr. Crandall studied computer applications under Professor Westervelt and taught computer courses at the university. In 1965, he learned about some exciting developments at Berkeley involving the design of a time-sharing operating system. He joined a group with members from Tymshare and from the University of California at Berkeley to work on this project. Crandall said:

> This was a stimulating group with which to work. We completed the operating system development and then I returned to Ann Arbor in 1966 to rejoin Comshare. (He returned as Research Director.)

Time-sharing was the first service to follow Comshare's consulting activities. Their first network consisted of direct dial access from customers to the Comshare computer. Crandall was involved in the technical aspects of developing time-sharing and the facilitating network hardware. In 1967 he became vice president of research and development and also assumed operating responsibilities, including marketing. Mr. Crandall continued his remarks:

> We went public in 1968 and took in over $5 million. It was used within one

year to open offices around the country. By January 1970 we had \$3–\$4 million sales volume but were losing so much money that there was concern about the employees and the future of the firm. At the time of our March 1970 board meeting, I was chief operating officer and serious discussions took place as to the survival of the company. In August 1970 I was given the presidency. We were \$6 million in debt and losing \$3 million a year.

Acquisitions and Divestitures

Comshare reacted to its changing environment through a variety of strategies. First there was a series of acquisitions and divestitures as indicated in Exhibit 1. These were carried out in the desire to gain new, related products, market entry, and knowledge about technical products and their adaptation to the markets.

Opportunities and complexities occurred with some acquisitions. Mr. Crandall commented:

> Computer Research Company was acquired in 1980 to learn about their use of IBM equipment and software. They were essentially a vendor of raw computer time and we did not understand the myriad of implications and options, including such items as pricing and IBM operating systems. Initially there was a culture shock between the two firms. Integration was difficult and eventually was achieved by absorbing the entire operation into the main business of the parent, Comshare. We finally learned the IBM environment, from the executive office through to the salespeople. In the meantime, Computer Research Company has been completely integrated.

T. Wallace Wrathall, group vice president, finance and administration discussed some of the acquisitions and divestitures as follows:

> The 1978 acquisition of Valuation Systems Corporation gave us their software for computing the current values of assets based on replacement costs. These financial systems products fit into the Comshare family of products and thus made the merger attractive. The corporation was eventually merged into Comshare. Currently these specific financial reports are no longer required by the Securities and Exchange Commission. However, the merger was successful.
>
> Trust Management Systems, Inc., was bought to tie into our human resources (personnel) product lines. Later it was evaluated as belonging to the bank market rather than in the domain of human resources, and it was sold.
>
> We were in the tax processing business and had purchased Systematic Computer Services to add to our line of services for CPA firms and their needs. To provide national coverage for our income-tax processing services we then acquired Digitax in 1979. These firms were then sold in 1981. They were not profitable and, to offset this trend, more product development effort would have been required.

EXHIBIT 1 Chronological Activities—Comshare, Inc.

1965	Start up and time-sharing operating system development.
1966	Incorporation as a Michigan company.
1968	Public offering of stock (traded over the counter). Start up of Canadian affiliate (Comshare, Ltd.).
1970	Start up of European operations as Canadian subsidiary (Comshare International, BV)
1974	Purchase of 30 percent interest in Comshare International, BV. License agreement to provide services in Japan (Japan Information Service, Ltd.).
1977	Acquisition of Systematic Computer Systems Inc. (individual income tax processing services).
1978	Acquisition of Valuation Systems Corporation (consultants in current measure systems). Acquisition of Trust Management Systems Inc. (Bank Trust Department services). Acquisition of 100 percent Comshare International BV.
1979	Acquisition of Digitax, Inc. (individual and fiduciary tax-return processing services). Stock split (three for two).
1980	Acquisition of Computer Research Company (supplier of large-scale IBM computer processing services). Expansion into France with a wholly-owned subsidiary (after receiving French government permission). Start up of Hardware Systems Division (to provide services to users of large-scale Xerox computer systems). Secondary public offering of shares (net $10.1 million).
1981	Sale of individual income tax processing services (including those of Systematic Computer Systems and Digitax). Acquisition of Advance Management Strategies Inc. (microcomputer software now sold as COMSHARE Target Software). Increase in ownership of Comshare Ltd. (now owns 37.3 percent of Canadian affiliate).
1982	New product release: Planner Calc and Target Financial Modeling (microcomputer based DSS products). Sale of the fiduciary income-tax processing services.
1983	New flagship product release: System W (DSS system for large-scale IBM computers). Sale of Trust Management Systems (accounting software for bank trust departments). Sale of Trilog Associates (balance of bank trust department services).
1984	Consummation of marketing agreement with IBM.

Source: Comshare, Inc., Annual Reports.

Mr. Crandall commented that the acquisitions of the Canadian, British, and European affiliates had been highly beneficial in extending markets, integrating operations, and furthering innovation and product development. As shown in Exhibit 1 this effort has extended from 1968 forward.

STRATEGY LEADING TO SYSTEM W

Comshare had been a planning-oriented company since the early 70s. In 1972 they first formulated a long range strategic plan. This plan enumerated corporate goals in broad terms and specified detailed objectives that were as quantified as possible. Strategies were developed to meet these objectives and thus the corporate goals. In general terms these goals were (*a*) to be a profitable growth company and (*b*) to be the best firm in their market segment.

As a direct result of this planning process, Comshare changed its emphasis from general purpose time-sharing sales to providing more specialized, business problem-solving assistance. This was achieved by (1) making appropriate software tools available on their time-sharing network and (2) utilizing their customer support representatives to help customers solve business problems using these software tools. As Kevin Kalkhoven stated, "It was no longer appropriate to be everything to everyone."

In 1979 Comshare undertook a major review of their current plans and strategies. Mr. Kalkhoven further commented:

> We saw three important things in 1979: (1) we had not changed—we were still primarily a time-sharing company, (2) we had not anticipated the rapid changes in hardware costs and performance, and (3) we had not anticipated the market place being dominated by the demand for microcomputers and software. Moreover, Comshare was experiencing the effects of the recession and the accompanying reduced revenues. Although we were one of the market leaders, we were in a period of technological stagnation.

Richard L. Crandall, reflecting on the results of this review, said "We were satisfied that the corporate goals spelled out in 1972 were still valid; however, the environment had changed and we needed to reassess it and its impact on our strategies."

Environmental Review

Comshare management reviewed the environment and company position in terms of strengths, weaknesses, opportunities, and threats, and they observed the following:

ʼas well developed and represented on the interna-
ket. Its international sales force provided a strong
advantage.
existed to solve business problems. Experienced peo-
rked on these problems in the sale of time-sharing

ition was established in time-sharing.
ap in inquiry and analysis software had been identi-
omshare had the research and development ca-
esolve it.
d a good cash flow and cash position. It could operate
ven position for several years.

ad no identifiable image in software.
ng organization did not have selling skills in soft-

recession and lack of a software product prevented
om taking immediate market action.

firms and products became more prevalent for in-
ter use, the demand for time-sharing services di-

reduced prices to compete for market share.
f personal computers caused both computers and
ecome available to users at lower costs.

increased demand for productivity software. Cer-
were available for data management applications.
re "first round" relatively unsophisticated finan-
packages. There was a need for a more functional
ve a variety of problems for a broader group of

vare was relatively difficult to use and not as inte-
nctional as it could be. Thus, Comshare had a
unity for a more functional and easier to operate

eview led to a number of conclusions that were
velopment of new strategies to achieve corporate
rved that:

1. Its value and importance to the customer was based on the skills of the Comshare employees and on the capabilities of the software it provided.
2. Time-sharing was only a delivery mechanism for providing access to software, which was used to solve business problems.
3. Software could also be delivered to the customer by selling mainframe software for use on customers' computers.
4. Personal computers were potentially important software delivery vehicles.

As a result of further analysis, Comshare decided that Decision Support Software was its primary product and should be delivered to customers in as many ways as possible. Time-sharing, as a delivery mechanism, remained an important aspect of the business; however, future development emphasis would be on DSS software.

To provide a finer focus for these efforts, Comshare determined that its best approach lay in the development and marketing of DSS software specifically designed for IBM computers. Thus the decision was made to develop a comprehensive, easy-to-use decision support system optimized to run on IBM systems.

The developmental work was carried out in the European Headquarters in London and resulted in a software product named Wizard. Presently this DSS is marketed in Europe under the name of Wizard and in the United States as System W. Comshare had planned to use the name Wizard in the United States. However, they discovered that a small software vendor had obtained an earlier trademark of Wizard for his product. To avoid infringement, Comshare was forced to change the name, at considerable expense, because sales brochures and other documentation had been printed bearing the designation Wizard.

Complementary Marketing Arrangement with IBM

A letter was received from IBM in September 1982 in which an invitation was extended to approximately 100 computer firms to attend an IBM-hosted conference. The purpose of the conference was to consider strategy for dealing with end users of computers and related services. The emphasis was on application software rather than data management and operating system software. Mr. Crandall attended the conference and noted that most representatives of attending firms did not seem to take the new IBM direction seriously.

However, he felt that IBM was very serious in its desire to have outsiders provide application software, while IBM concentrated on further developing its hardware—both mainframe and personal computers. This was a central part of IBM's new "Information Center" strategy, conceived to meet the pent-up demand among executives to use computers to satisfy their needs for relevant information. This concept required the development of "user friendly" software which would allow nonprogrammer executive users to develop their own decision support systems. Since IBM did not itself have any strong offerings in this type of DSS software, Crandall envisioned a desire on the part of IBM to work closely with a firm capable of developing and marketing superior DSS software.

Discussion continued between IBM and Comshare, and in early January 1984 a two-year complementary marketing arrangement was reached. As indicated in the January 9, 1984, issue of *Computerworld*, IBM would recommend System W for use in Information Centers using IBM 4300 computers. IBM and Comshare sales representatives would refer prospects to each other. In addition, provision was made for joint sales calls of IBM and Comshare personnel to prospective users of DSS. The potential advantage to IBM was the prospect of increased hardware sales resulting from the availability of Comshare's DSS software. Finally, Comshare would continue its responsibility to users to install System W and conduct training programs.

FINANCIAL CONSIDERATIONS

Comshare was founded much as other entrepreneurial firms. Capital contributions by the six founders and the Weyerhauser family provided the impetus for the firm's start. There was a public offering of the firm's stock in 1968 and it was followed by a secondary offering in 1980 which netted $10 million. Exhibits 2 and 3 contain income and balance sheet data from 1978 through fiscal year 1983. These data reveal revenue increases until 1981, at which time recessionary influences were evident.

T. Wallace Wrathall, group vice president, finance and administration, commented:

> There are notable differences in the financial management of Comshare versus industry at large. Some of these include:
>
> 1. We have no inventory—only software tapes with low unit production cost. (This does not include the cost of research and development.)
> 2. There is a short life cycle of plant and products because of the rapidly changing technology.
> 3. Investment decisions have a short life cycle. So we need a high rate of return.
> 4. Research and development expenditures are high compared to other industries.
> 5. Capital requirements are declining and are relatively low compared to the remainder of industry.
> 6. Operating, selling, and development costs are largely people costs and will go up more rapidly than industry averages.

EXHIBIT 2 Comshare's Six-Year Trend Selected Financial Information*

	Year Ending June 30					
	1983	*1982*	*1981*	*1980*	*1979*	*1978*
Revenue	$76,337	$78,453	$79,837	$68,579	$46,049	$23,404
Income from operations	$ 2,453	$ 1,406	$ 8,163	$10,672	$ 8,292	$ 3,791
Interest expense	$ 1,039	$ 1,240	$ 1,291	$ 1,486	$ 752	$ 450
Interest income	$ 1,052	$ 1,278	$ 370	$ 156	$ 116	$ 70
Income before taxes	$ 2,458	$ 1,591	$ 7,535	$ 9,146	$ 7,711	$ 3,943
Income from continuing operations	$ 1,331	$ 829	$ 4,374	$ 5,346	$ 4,383	$ 2,682
Per share	$ .31	$ .18	$ 1.03	$ 1.41	$ 1.31	$ 1.00
Average number of shares outstanding (thousands)	$ 4,340	$ 4,542	$ 4,251	$ 3,791	$ 3,334	$ 2,675
Research and development	$ 6,135	$ 6,109	$ 5,916	$ 4,539	$ 3,289	$ 1,857
As a percentage of revenue	8.0%	7.8%	7.4%	6.6%	7.1%	7.9%
Working capital	$ 9,378	$12,350	$12,244	$ 5,584	$ 3,208	$ 1,107
Capital expenditures	$ 6,377	$ 8,684	$10,516	$13,685	$11,277	$ 3,081
Total assets	$59,381	$66,842	$70,919	$62,581	$47,275	$21,663
Long-term debt	$ 2,067	$ 9,960	$ 8,485	$14,415	$ 9,553	$ 3,825
Shareholders' equity	$38,192	$37,745	$40,735	$27,736	$22,086	$12,537
Number of employees at year-end	1,084	1,164	1,215	1,282	1,100	538

* Dollar amounts in thousands of dollars except per share data.
In fiscal 1982, the company, in compliance with Statement No. 52 of the Financial Accounting Standards Board, changed its method of accounting for foreign currency translation adjustments. Financial data for periods prior to fiscal 1982 have not been restated for this change in accounting principle.
Information regarding Results of Operations excludes discontinued operations.
The average number of shares outstanding and income-per-share data have been adjusted to reflect a three-for-two stock split in July 1979.

Source: Comshare, Inc., 1983 Annual Report.

Mr. Wrathall reflected on other aspects that affect the firm:

1. Accounting rules can cause us to buy rather than make . . . the manner in which we are required to report research and development costs is all important.
2. One third of our sales are in markets outside of the United States. Because of the declining value of the British pound sterling, transferred earning and investments are reduced. Continued decline in the value of the pound could result in a real loss.
3. System W was developed in the United Kingdom (under the name of Wizard) and sold to Comshare in the United States. This developmental policy can result in the parent firm paying less for R and D because of favorable exchange rates and possibly more favorable tax rates.

Mr. Kalkhoven spoke on the necessity for a combination of product and financial policy to finance the marketing of System W and other new products. He alluded to the Boston Consulting Group's explanation of classifying products according to their growth and market share rates. Those products that no longer have a high growth rate but have retained a favorable market share can be marketed successfully for revenues to support the introduction and market development of new products under the so-called Cash Cow Strategy. The executives of Comshare had its time-sharing product line as a Cash Cow that would be useful in supporting the introduction of System W, its development, and the development of other DSS products as well. Moreover, Comshare's substantial time-sharing customer base gave it an easily accessible and somewhat captive market for System W and related products.

MANAGEMENT CONSIDERATIONS

Early in 1984, the top management group consisted of the following relatively young, but highly qualified executives:

Richard L. Crandall, 41, became president and chief executive officer in 1970. He was one of the original six founders of the firm in 1966. In 1978 he had served as president of the Association of the Data Processing Service Organizations. He was also a frequent speaker and author of numerous articles related to issues pertinent to the computer industry.

Kevin O. N. Kalkhoven, 39, was group vice president in charge of marketing product development and sales. He had been with the company since 1971. Prior to that he worked for IBM as an analytical services manager, and in sales management for SIA, Ltd. in the U.K. He lectured frequently on the subject of decision support systems to such groups as the American Marketing Association and the Planning Executives Institute.

T. Wallace Wrathall, 47, group vice president of finance and administration, had joined Comshare in 1975. Prior to that he had 17 years of broad experience in finance and accounting. His previous employer, Varian Associates, was also in the computer high technology business and also had extensive foreign operations. Other employers included Del Monte Corporation, Optical Coating Laboratory, and Eldorado Electrodata.

Ian G. McNaught-Davis, 54, became group vice president in 1978 and managed the European Operations. He was also a director of Comshare Limited. Mr. Davis was the founding chief executive of Comshare Limited (U.K.) in 1970. He was employed earlier for nine years with General Electric Information Systems. His last position with G.E. was Director of Marketing. He has been the moderator of

EXHIBIT 3

COMSHA, INC.
Consolidated Balance Sheet
As of June 30, 1983 and 1982

	1983	*1982*
Assets		
Current assets:		
Cash	$ 3,407,500	$ 3,059,300
Temporary investments, at cost	4,413,800	7,507,000
Accounts receivable, less allowance for doubtful accounts of $570,700 in 1983 and $550,400 in 1982	13,221,900	13,301,000
Prepaid expenses	2,154,200	2,512,900
Total current assets	23,197,400	26,380,200
Property and equipment, at cost:		
Land	964,400	999,200
Computers and other equipment	42,983,700	42,408,200
Building and leasehold improvements	6,221,800	6,152,000
Property and equipment under construction	2,518,800	3,530,700
	52,688,700	53,090,100
Less accumulated depreciation	26,605,200	23,694,200
Property and equipment, net	26,083,500	29,395,900
Other assets:		
Investment in affiliate	1,905,700	2,020,500
Goodwill, net of accumulated amortization of $766,200 in 1983 and $567,300 in 1982	6,242,800	6,486,300
Purchased software, net of accumulated amortization of $1,101,600 in 1983 and $496,000 in 1982	1,521,100	1,948,600
Deposits and other	430,600	610,700
Total other assets	10,100,200	11,066,100
Total assets	$59,381,100	$66,842,200

approximately 20 one-hour television programs for the British Broadcasting Corporation concerning computers and their uses. Also, he lectured throughout the United Kingdom and Europe at universities and professional conferences.

These men exercised management and intellectual leadership throughout the organization. They were innovative in the development of solutions to everyday business problems and issues. During the early years the overriding concern was bringing together people who were innovative, self-reliant, and results oriented. In this way computer services and software could be developed by a group of imaginative and dedicated people.

EXHIBIT 3 (*concluded*)

	1983	*1982*
Liabilities and Shareholders' Equity		
Current liabilities:		
Current portion of long-term debt	$ 345,200	$ 1,039,000
Notes payable	1,857,700	1,151,700
Accounts payable	3,709,600	3,437,200
Accrued liabilities		
Payroll	2,722,600	2,391,600
Taxes, other than income taxes	992,400	1,162,400
Discontinued operations	98,500	1,720,500
Other	3,186,100	2,601,300
Total accrued liabilities	6,999,600	7,875,800
Accrued income taxes	907,500	526,300
Total current liabilities	13,819,600	14,030,000
Long-term debt	2,067,300	9,959,900
Deferred income taxes	5,302,500	5,086,900
Deferred credits	—	20,900
Shareholders' equity:		
Common stock, $1.00 par value; authorized 10,000,000 shares; outstanding 4,281,414 shares in 1983 and 4,599,604 shares in 1982	4,281,400	4,599,600
Capital contributed in excess of par	24,368,400	25,871,200
Retained earnings	12,624,200	10,415,200
Currency translation adjustments	(3,082,300)	(2,377,200)
	38,191,700	38,508,800
Less treasury stock, at cost (119,000 shares in 1982)	—	764,300
Total shareholders' equity	38,191,700	37,744,500
Total liabilities and shareholders' equity	$59,381,100	$66,842,200

Source: Comshare, Inc., 1983 Annual Report.

Richard Crandall was a leader and model for personnel involved in this activity. He became involved at the age of 18. He was president at the age of 26. He indicated that this was a young man's sphere of activity populated by those who shared common levels of intelligence, curiosity, innovativeness, and the pleasure of working diligently to achieve results to be enjoyed psychologically and materially. At the present time the average ages of Comshare employees were:

Nonmanagers	26 years
Managers	32 years
Executives	38 years

Kevin Kalkhoven pointed out that successful persons at Comshare were socially adept, got on well with others, and had excellent senses of humor. They had a natural curiosity about management practices. This led them to study and adapt business management approaches to planning, programming, operating, and controlling the firm's activities.

Mr. Crandall summarized the management philosophy and direction of Comshare as follows:

> The future of our business is in knowledge-based software, and we must organize and operate properly to maintain success. We are a marketing-oriented company. Our Research and Development effort is directed to meeting market needs in creative ways. New technology can spur innovation and creativity. We must attract talented people to Comshare who can work successfully in our environment. Top management provides the key to innovation and the strategic management and marketing process. The approach and philosophy must permeate from the top of the organization.

Case 6

Comshare, Inc. (B)—Strategic Marketing of System W

Donald W. Scotton
Allan D. Waren
Bernard C. Reimann
all of Cleveland State University

A visitor to the attractively decorated corporate offices of Comshare, Inc., in Ann Arbor, Michigan, could not help but observe the air of excitement and anticipation. The firm had just announced its complementary marketing arrangement with IBM for the new decision support system (DSS) software product, System W. The firm was also finalizing a significant update to System W. Kevin Kalkhoven, group vice president, added to this enthusiasm when he stated, "With this latest release, System W will be easier to use than any of the competing products."

Comshare, Inc., was a computer service firm that was founded in 1966 to offer time-sharing services to industry, government, and other nonprofit organizations. These services made it possible for users to communicate with Comshare's computers in Ann Arbor via communication networks of telephone lines. The system was designed to provide instantaneous response, giving the user the impression of having his own computer. All of the usual data processing and accounting functions could be performed "long distance" on data stored at the computer center.

Since it started in business, Comshare had introduced many im-

---

This research and written case information was presented at a Case Research Symposium and evaluated by the Case Research Association's Editorial Board. This case was prepared as a basis for class discussion by Professors Donald W. Scotton, Allan D. Waren, and Bernard C. Reimann of Cleveland State University. They are professors of Marketing, Computer and Information Science, and Management, respectively. Distributed by the Case Research Association.

provements to its time-sharing services. These included the addition of sophisticated data bases, better methods for retrieving and displaying information, and the development of powerful and versatile modeling methods to help solve business and financial problems.

The latest and most significant of these developments was System W, an advanced Decision Support System (DSS) software product, which Comshare introduced late in 1982. This software made it possible for executives to enter or retrieve data from other mainframe or personal computers, build models to simulate their businesses, make forecasts, do statistical analyses, test assumptions or alternative scenarios, and even display their results in customized reports or graphs. While a substantial number of competitive products existed, Comshare executives considered System W to be a technological breakthrough in that it greatly facilitated modeling in multiple dimensions. Most of the competitive products were either limited to two-dimensional spreadsheets, or required extremely complex programming to achieve multidimensional modeling and analysis.

INDUSTRY TRENDS

Most computer hardware manufacturers, including IBM, focused their software efforts on systems software. Therefore, a potentially profitable and growing market segment became available for applications software. A rapidly growing number of "software houses" emerged to fill the need for high quality applications software with an emphasis on ease of use and efficiency. Typical applications included material requirements planning, accounting and financial reporting, and data base management.

Another factor which contributed to the rapid growth of this specialized software market was the inability of the data processing function, in most firms, to keep up with the burgeoning demand for its services. The resulting backlog of data processing projects led to an urgent need for highly sophisticated software which would be so easy to use that nonprogrammers, such as financial or marketing executives and their staffs, could develop their own custom-made applications.

At the same time, the increasing competitiveness and uncertainty of the business environment were creating a growing interest in strategic planning. This in turn led to a strong need for information systems to help top executives and strategic planners make decisions. One answer to this need was DSS (Decision Support System) applications software. This type of software made possible the bringing together of relevant information from both internal and external data bases, and the use of complex models to simulate and analyze strategic alternatives before they were implemented.

There were fewer than 2,000 international computer software and service firms as reported in the 1982 Comshare Annual Report. Comshare, Inc., was one of the largest of these firms involved in the marketing of DSS software, which included data management, financial modeling, forecasting, analysis, reporting, and graphics. These DSS products were used by time-sharing customers via a worldwide computer network, as well as by customers who licensed the products for use on their mainframe computers and/or microcomputers.

The market for such DSS software and processing services, as reported in the 1983 Comshare Annual Report, was:

1981 sales	$549 million
1982 sales	729 million
1987 forecast	3.1 billion

The report also indicated that 1981 industry sales of all types of software, totaled $4.2 billion. Richard L. Crandall, president of Comshare, reported in an interview for this case that 17 percent, or $714 million, came from data management and financial software sales, the two main predecessors of DSS. He indicated also that "in 1975 barely one-half billion dollars of industry sales were in software." *Business Week,* in its February 27, 1984, issue, published a special report on "Software: The New Driving Force." This issue contained a forecast that software sales in the United States would "keep growing by a dizzying 32 percent a year, topping $30 billion in 1988."

DEVELOPMENT OF SYSTEM W

Corporate Goals and Planning

Comshare management developed their first long-range strategic plan in 1972. This plan contained the general goals for the firm, which were: (*a*) to be a profitable, high-technology, growth company and (*b*) to be the best firm in their chosen market segments. As a result of this planning process, the Comshare mission was redefined. Instead of considering its primary business to be the sales of general purpose time-sharing, management now viewed its main function as one of marketing business problem-solving assistance to its customers. Initial steps taken to implement this new focus included (1) making software tools available on their time-sharing network and (2) utilizing their support representatives to assist customers in solving business problems with these software tools.

Environmental Review

A major review of plans and strategies was undertaken in 1979. President Crandall reflecting on this review, commented, "We were satisfied that the corporate goals spelled out in 1972 were still valid; however, the environment had changed and we needed to reassess it and its impact on our strategies."

The environmental review and assessment of company position revealed strengths, weaknesses, opportunities, and threats. Comshare was established in the international market and had a competitive sales force. There was sufficient talent in the organization to solve business problems. Market position was established in time-sharing. Comshare had the research and development capability to resolve the identified product gap in inquiry and analysis software. Finally the cash flow and cash position were sufficient to operate at a breakeven point for several years.

Weaknesses included: (1) Comshare had no identifiable image in software, (2) the marketing organization lacked selling skills in software, (3) immediate market action could not be taken because of the recession and lack of a software product.

Several threats were present. The increasing presence of software firms and products for in-house computer use reduced the demand for time-sharing services. Software firms reduced prices to gain market shares. The advent of personal computers caused both computers and software to become available at lower costs.

Two major opportunities were identified as follows. (1) There existed increased demand for productivity software to augment the "first round" data management applications and financial modeling packages. More functional products were needed to solve a variety of problems. (2) A more functional and easier to use DSS was needed.

Product Focus and Development

Analysis of the environmental review caused Comshare to select Decision Support Software as its primary product that was to be delivered in as many ways as possible.

Comshare management also recognized the growing importance of distributed DSS, including both microcomputers, or PCs, and mainframes. However, PCs were not suited to be the only hardware in a total DSS. They did not have the capacity for storing and processing sufficient data for large-scale problems. The market segment to which Comshare was addressing System W included management decison makers who could use the system most efficiently, if it were easily accessible from their offices. A combination of personal and mainframe computers was needed for input and interface of data for management decision making. System W was developed to facilitate problem solving within these parameters.

IBM had not concentrated on DSS software. Rather, it exercised leadership in developing and producing mainframe and personal computers. Comshare elected to develop and market DSS software specifically designed for IBM computers. The product was to be a comprehensive, easy-to-use decision support system optimized to run on IBM systems.

Complementary Marketing Arrangement with IBM

A letter was received from IBM in September 1982 in which an invitation was extended to approximately 100 computer firms to attend an IBM-hosted conference. The purpose of the conference was to consider strategy for dealing with end users of computers and related services. The emphasis was on applications software rather than data management and operating systems software. Mr. Crandall attended the conference and noted that most representatives of attending firms did not seem to take the new IBM direction seriously.

However, he felt that IBM was very serious in its desire to have outsiders provide applications software, while IBM concentrated on further developing its hardware—both mainframe and personal computers. This was a central part of IBM's new "Information Center" strategy, conceived to meet the pent-up demand among executives to use computers to satisfy their needs for relevant and timely information. This concept required the development of "user friendly" software which would allow nonprogrammer executive users to develop their own decision support systems. Since IBM did not have any strong offerings in this type of DSS software, Crandall envisioned a desire for IBM to work closely with a firm capable of developing and marketing superior DSS software.

Discussion continued between IBM and Comshare, and in early January 1984, a two-year complementary marketing arrangement was reached. As indicated in the January 9, 1984, issue of *Computerworld,* IBM would recommend System W for use in Information Centers using IBM 4300 computers. IBM and Comshare sales representatives would refer prospects to each other. In addition, provision was made for joint sales calls of IBM and Comshare personnel to prospective users of DSS. The objective of IBM was to sell more hardware by making available the expertise and DSS software of Comshare to prospective customers on the theory that more hardware would be used, if the customer problem was met properly. Finally, Comshare would continue its responsibility to users to install System W and conduct training programs.

COMPETITION

Kevin Kalkhoven estimated that the 1983 DSS industry leaders, their products, and sales (software exclusive of processing services) were:

Execucom	IFPS	$ 20 million
Management Decision Systems	Express	7–8 million
Comshare	System W	7–8 million
EPS, Inc.	FCS/EPS	6–7 million

Prior to the introduction of System W, Comshare had been a vendor of FCS/EPS on its time-sharing service. Comshare, however, still supported those time-sharing customers who were not willing to switch from FCS/EPS to System W.

There were more than 60 other competitors, at least 20 of whom had entered the business in the last two or three years. Two software products were identified as being particularly significant to Comshare. These were IFPS, a product originally developed for financial research functions, and Express, originally developed for marketing research. Both products had subsequently been enhanced and were being marketed as full function DSS systems. Comshare viewed IFPS as being particularly easy to use but lacking integrated functionality in areas such as data management, whereas Express was seen as a very hard to use product which was functionally well-integrated and quite powerful. Execucom had just announced a data management option for IFPS, which was intended to compensate for its weakness in this area.

In order to compete effectively in this market, Comshare felt it was essential to develop a product which was easier to use than IFPS and had more capabilities and was better integrated than Express. Thus System W was designed to take advantage of this opportunity for product positioning relative to the industry leaders.

Kevin Kalkhoven was confident that the most recent release of System W (including DATMAN) was much easier to use than any competing product. He pointed out that: "James Martin, an expert on applications software, has just completed his most recent comparative evaluation of financial planning software products. He ranked System W second only to Visicalc in user friendliness, ahead of IFPS and even Lotus 1-2-3." Visicalc was a limited spreadsheet program for personal computers and not considered as a competitor in the DSS software area.

Comshare management noticed that a number of other firms were waking up to the huge potential of the market. These firms were redoubling their efforts both in improving their products and in marketing them. Several firms had decided to "unbundle" their prices for total systems in order to be more competitive. Thus a customer interested only in modeling, for example, could buy a starter system for as little as $10,000. If other capabilities, such as forecasting or graphics were desired, each of these additional modules could be purchased separately for $5,000–15,000 each. Another aspect of product pricing was the increasing willingness of some vendors to discount the prices of their software, especially for multiple purchases.

Another trend in competition concerned the way in which vendors handled the consulting portion of their DSS software business. Some, such as Management Decision Systems (Express Software) and Chase Interactive Data Corporation (Xsim Software), focused on selling a package of DSS software combined with their management consulting expertise. The consulting services were designed to help the users customize the products for their individual decision support requirements. As a result, the vendors' focus was less on the "user friendliness" of their products than on developing a staff of highly effective and personable consultants and technical specialists. These consultants and specialists were important adjuncts to the vendors' personal selling efforts to large corporations.

At the other end of the spectrum, as Mr. Crandall described it, "Firms like Integrated Planning (Stratagem) and GemNet (Fame) chose the strategy of developing and selling DSS products that allegedly required minimal consulting or technical support after the sale." They emphasized product development to make their software so "friendly" and flexible that nonprogrammers, such as financial or marketing executives, could use the software to create their own DSS with minimal outside assistance. Integrated Planning used the services of professional DSS consulting firms, such as Real Decisions Corporation, to assist customers in adapting Stratagem to their needs.

The degree of centralization of selling and technical support was another area in which strategies varied among competitors. Some of the newer and smaller vendors were highly centralized in these functions, due primarily to resource constraints. However, some of the larger firms that could afford to decentralize had concentrated their sales and technical support organizations in a central location. MDS, producers of Express Software, housed all of its consultants and technical support personnel at the headquarters in Waltham, Massachusetts. A toll-free 800 number "hot line" was available to users with problems. This hot line was staffed about 12 hours each working day by rotating shifts of experienced technical people. MDS believed that this allowed better use of their high-quality, specialized technical personnel. They felt that a decentralization strategy using local offices would spread these resources too thinly and result in a reduction of the quality of their customer services. However, a number of firms, such as Boeing Computer Services, Chase IDS, and Comshare chose the decentralized option of serving their users personally from a large number of geographically dispersed offices.

Another contrast in product-market strategies concerned the firms' focus on hardware compatibility. Some, such as Execucom, with its IFPS software, prided themselves on the fact that their software would run on almost every popular brand of hardware and type of operating system, i.e., DEC, HP, IBM, Prime, etc. Even some of the smaller vendors chose this strategy of making their software compatible with as many different types of hardware as possible. GemNet, for example, was in the process of developing Fame (its DSS software) simultaneously for three different operating systems.

Although the degree of competition had increased considerably by 1984, there were signs that rivalry could become more intense in the future. It was still relatively easy for a new firm to enter the DSS industry. Little start-up capital was needed. A few intelligent and hardworking programmers could produce a new DSS software product within a year or two. A number of the most aggressive and successful new firms were founded by former employees of the older and more established firms. For example, Integrated Planning, the developer of Strategem, was founded by several former employees of Automated Data Processing who had become dissatisfied with that company's supposed lack of effort to improve its products, TSAM and FML, to meet changing customer needs. Similarly, GemNet, developer of Fame software, was started by former members of Chase Interactive Data Corporation's technical staff. Software firms had become attractive acquisition targets for hardware manufacturers and others who were eager to share in the software boom. Acquisitions were of interest also to other software producers as a means to expand their product lines. For example, GemNet had recently received an acquisition offer from Citibank. The new ownership of GemNet would provide increased capitalization and staffing to permit the organization to realize its potential. In so doing it would be regarded as a competitive threat to other members of the industry.

There was also a trend for hardware manufacturers to become more interested in the highly profitable field of applications software. IBM and others seemed to be satisfied with cooperative ventures with software suppliers. However, firms such as Hewlett-Packard were making every effort to produce their own software.

One result of these competitive activities was a downward pressure on prices of applications software and some price discounting was observed in the DSS software industry as well. However, the potential benefits of the "right" software to users could outweigh the initial cost. The "wrong" product could cost several times as much as the acquisition cost in terms of extra implementation problems.

Another competitive threat arose through the actions of time-sharing firms such as Automated Data Processing and Data Resources

International, a subsidiary of McGraw-Hill. These firms had developed software for use by their time-sharing customers. At the present time, they were exploring the possibility of selling and/or licensing these DSS products to other users who owned mainframe and personal computers. Data Resources International, for example, announced that it would release its DSS product, EPS, for sale in the Fall of 1984.

MARKETING MIX STRATEGIES

Guiding Strategy

Richard L. Crandall said that "when we decided to develop a DSS software package, it was clear that we would be the new kid on the block as far as software sales were concerned. To be successful it was necessary to carve out a specific niche and to be easily distinguished from our competitors." The firm's strategic plan provided guidance in achieving these objectives.

The plan called for Comshare to develop the best possible DSS software product and furthermore to develop it specifically for IBM computer systems. In order to have the best DSS software it had to be more functional than the rest of the competition as well as being easier to use. In order to best fit with IBM systems, it was necessary to take advantage of as many of the IBM hardware and software features as possible.

Product

Analysis of the competitive considerations and threats mentioned above caused Comshare to:

1. Concentrate on developing decision support systems and software compatible with IBM computers.
2. Offer consulting and adaptation services for users of IBM machines and Comshare software.
3. Adopt the augmented product concept of locating facilities and personnel close to users. Thus face-to-face consulting could occur rather than obtaining impersonal information received from calling an 800 telephone number.

Pricing

It was observed that purchases of more than $100,000 usually required a series of approvals associated with major capital expenditures. Thus, the executive or group electing to purchase a DSS package must receive higher approval, which could be time consuming. This practice appeared to have imposed an average industry price ceiling of $75,000 for DSS packages.

Comshare conducted research with the use of video-taped focus groups to obtain customer and prospect reaction to System W. A number of considerations were examined such as price and acceptance of the product as to quality, concept, performance, and competition. Current environmental forces were examined and the following price strategies were selected for the introduction of System W in January 1983:

1. Competitive pricing would be utilized. For example, a scaled down version of System W would be sold for $50,000 to meet Execucom's price on its IFPS product.
2. Elements of target pricing would be employed so that profits would be realized within two years. This was consistent with the dynamics of product innovation and rapid changes in the competing firms.
3. System packages would be priced from $75,000 to less than $100,000.
4. The average price per package would be $80,000 as compared to the industry average of $75,000.
5. The policy of charging for consulting to adapt System W to specific user requirements would be continued.
6. Maintenance charges would be set at an annual rate of 15 percent of the purchase price. This would include program updates and related support services.

Promotion

System W was available in time-sharing applications before the end of 1982. However, the marketing plan called for the development of the "in-house" market. This segment was comprised of organizations owning and operating mainframe computers. In addition, some were using personal computers or were likely to own personal computers in the near future. The firm implemented its program of in-house sales and supporting advertising as of January 13, 1983.

Promotion of the product was carried out in several ways. First, new stories and product information were made available to the media through the public relations activities of the firm. System W reports appeared in *Computerworld, The Wall Street Journal,* and other computer and financial journals.

Colleges and universities were viewed as influencers. Comshare executives made themselves available for lectures and consultation about DSS and System W with universities and professional groups. Several universities were given System W packages for use by students. Another group of influencers was identified as business executives who might have use for System W in their positions and to recommend it to others. This group was approached through conferences and "in-house tests."

Comshare's time-sharing customers provided another valuable avenue for product promotion. During the development of System W it was tested by 100 time-sharing customers. This test served to familiarize these potential users with the product. An additional purpose served by these customer trials was the testing of product modifications and adaptations to the specific user groups. Conferences were held with these time-sharing users to obtain their approvals of the product modifications, as well as their recommendations for use by others.

An advertising program was planned for the Spring of 1984 under the theme of "Safe Harbor." The relationship of Comshare and IBM under the marketing agreement provided the basis to inform potential users that purchasers would be in a safe harbor through the use of IBM in-house mainframes and personal computers with System W. Schedules were developed for advertising to appear in selected business journals. The advertising was to be selective and addressed to financial, marketing, and other senior executives. Not all senior executives would be contacted through the media. The conferences with senior executives mentioned above were viewed as one way to obtain coverage not presently affordable in the media coverage considered. It was recognized that the mass market of knowledgeable workers would be contacted presently through media advertising. Influencers were to be relied upon until sufficient revenues supported additional advertising.

Kevin Kalkhoven commented as follows about changing advertising requirements, "We used very limited advertising before System W since the time-sharing market does not require much advertising. However, the multitude of potential users for DSS software makes it necessary to communicate about System W through advertising."

Personal Selling

Comshare executives felt that improvements were needed in sales strategy and performance. Although some experience had been gained in the sale of software, it was believed that the sales organization did not really understand the best way to sell System W. Mr. Kalkhoven believed that the firm was very good in many other aspects of marketing such as promotion, publicity, and time-sharing sales, but that concerted effort was needed in the DSS software personal selling program.

Before System W was introduced, Comshare had initiated a five-year strategic plan for sales activity. That plan was applied to the major product lines, and System W was to be integrated fully. A one-year tactical plan was initiated under the five-year strategic plan for each product line. Every six months the yearly plan was updated to "roll over" the plan for the following 12 months. The directors of the product lines developed sales support action plans to include:

1. *Product and Market Development.* Plans for moving products through the markets were made and included things such as identification of users' and prospects' needs and adaptation to them; way of identifying needs and presenting solutions; sales and revenue plans; and management control of activities. Provisions were made for updating plans as the market and customer needs changed.
2. *Marketing Materials.* Brochures, advertising reprints, and training manuals for salesmen and customers were developed.
3. *Consultants and Technical Support.* Consultants trained in adaptation of products to customer needs were made available to work with salesmen in meeting customer needs.
4. *Training.* Comshare developed an innovative computer-aided instruction system called the "Commander Learning Station." This combined the Apple IIe microcomputer and a videotape in such a way that potential users could learn System W in self-paced, interactive learning modules. Two versions were offered; a two-day "novice" program, and a half-day refresher program for infrequent, but experienced users.

   Because time-sharing would continue to be the most significant portion of revenue for some time, salesmen would be involved in selling both time-sharing and System W. So salespeople were trained to work with and be supported by technical and local branch representatives in the sale and service of timesharing.

   Additional training was initiated to deal with Comshare time-sharing customers who were using FCS/EPS software originally recommended by Comshare salesmen. Comshare had offered support services for this software and felt obligated to continue to do this. However, they would not be able to support new releases of FCS/EPS. Salesmen were trained to explain this situation and also to persuade customers to switch to System W. In addition, Comshare salesmen were informed of the possibility that clients might (1) seek a time-sharing service which supported new versions of FCS/EPS or (2) decide to purchase the FCS/EPS software outright for in-house use.

Distribution

Distribution of goods was of less importance in the time-sharing and software industry than others. Time-sharing operated through communication networks. Some hardware was required for adapting terminals to telephone lines. However, these were installed on a one-time basis and repetitive shipments of equipment were not required. Inventories were minimal and required little capital investment and management control.

This situation could change in the future. Richard L. Crandall said that it was possible that the vendors of decision support software might consider a new channel of distribution whereby software for microcomputers, personal computers, and mainframe computers would be sold through computer stores. Comshare was examining this possibility and considering the impact of such changes in distribution. For example, a marketing segmentation plan was considered in which Comshare salesmen would call on certain classes of customers and the remainder would be serviced by the computer stores. Another possibility was that other vendors could sell System W to market areas not covered by Comshare.

PRESENT AND FUTURE

Comshare's management viewed this firm as a planning-oriented organization that had evolved in a high technology industry. Product innovation was the lifeblood of this company. However, strategic planning based on needs of the market place was equally important in directing the thrust of innovation and delivery products to significant markets.

System W was developed and offered under the aegis of strategic planning. Mr. Crandall identified Comshare as a marketing-oriented firm that translated corporate planning into strategic marketing action. Recognition of the changing environment caused the firm to meet changing needs in the market through delivery of System W. At the time of the marketing arrangement with IBM, Comshare was developing an enhancement to System W. It became available to users five months later as a fully integrated data management system named "DATMAN." This software made it possible for users to have access to total data management capability fully integrated with System W in terms of modeling, statistical analysis, reporting, etc.

Most competing products required users to utilize an additional data management software package (for example, ADABAS or INFO) which was difficult to interface with the DSS software. Therefore, Comshare's new product, DATMAN, was a major breakthrough. It provided a truly "user friendly" decision support system which would give the user full access to all data on its own or other computers (e.g., COMPUSTAT).

This rapidly changing market mandated the need to look constantly into the future. Mr. Crandall said, "System W and DATMAN are state-of-the-art today. I will leave you to conjecture on our next moves."

Case 7

The American Express Company*

James R. Lang
University of Kentucky

By the middle of 1981, the finance-related and insurance industries were in periods of rapid change and turmoil. Each industry was facing problems resulting from general economic conditions and intensified competition. The basis for competition was changing as companies departed traditional and historic roles, new and powerful entrants threatened, and technological innovation was obvious everywhere. As an active participant in these industries, American Express was also experiencing a year of transition and challenge. James D. Robinson III, chief executive officer, offered his view of the future:

> By 1990, you'll have a stockbroker in California, a banker in New York, an insurance agency in Maryland, and a realtor jetting between Chicago and Boston. All your purchases will be on the American Express Card, of course. And within the decade you'll have the option of banking by mail or by cable television.[1]

The challenge for American Express is to chart a course to this vision.

CREDIT CARD INDUSTRY

The first credit cards in the United States were issued in the 1920s by oil companies as a means of promoting brand loyalty and providing a billing convenience for traveling customers. Use of cards was expanded slightly during the 1930s when department stores issued cards to their charge account customers and major oil companies developed reciprocal billing arrangements. This relatively limited use of cards was

---

* This case was written by James R. Lang, Associate Professor and Chaiman of the Department of Management, University of Kentucky.

[1] Thomas O'Donnell, "The Tube, The Card, The Ticker, and Jim Robinson," *Forbes*, May 25, 1981.

abruptly changed in the early 1950s when the credit card industry was born with the formation of Diners Club. Diners Club began in February 1950 with 22 restaurants and 200 cardholders. After a first year loss of $158,730, Diners Club earned a $61,222 profit in its second year and then continually expanded the scope of its operations during the 1950s. American Express entered the industry in 1958 and took over industry leadership in 1959 by acquiring two smaller competitors. Carte Blanche became industry competitive in 1959 when Hilton Hotels added establishments outside of the Hilton chain to its credit card system.

Banks entered the industry in the late 1950s when the first bank credit card was issued by Franklin National Bank. Through the 1960s the bank cards grew by offering cards to a wider segment of the population and by allowing use for goods and services beyond travel and entertainment.

By 1980 there were over 600 million credit cards in circulation in the United States and it was estimated that there would be 1 billion cards worldwide by 1985. Americans are by far the greatest users of credit cards, holding about 82 percent of all cards. As of 1978 American consumers held an average of 5.2 cards and business persons an average of 11.3 cards each. Of the 1979 total installment borrowing of $300 billion in the United States, about $100 billion was through credit cards.

In spite of their early entry in the industry, travel and entertainment (T&E) cards have not maintained a significant share in terms of number of cards in circulation. In 1980 T&E accounted for one half of the cards in existence, with Sears Roebuck & Co. the single largest issuer. In 1978 Sears alone had 47 million cards in circulation. The proportion of retailers' cards has been on the decline, however, as smaller retailers are being absorbed by conglomerates which tend to favor the use of bank credit cards. In 1979 there were about 115 million bank cards in circulation and that number is expected to increase to 255 million by 1985. Oil companies maintained about 22 percent of the cards outstanding in 1980 and all other types (airlines, etc.) had about 3 percent.

Bank Cards

In 1980 banks held about 22 percent of the number of cards outstanding, but were by far the most aggressive segment of the industry. Traditionally, the bank cards have been differentiated by the fact that they extend a line of credit to the cardholder, whereas the T&E cards demand payment on request each month. Young families, families with children, and families headed by those without a college degree are most likely to use the credit features of cards, while others use the cards primarily to facilitate transactions. In the mid to late 1970s the use of the credit feature grew rapidly. In 1978 for instance, there was $23 billion of credit outstanding on bank cards, which was a 33 percent increase over the previous year. By the late 1970s, interest charges provided 70 percent of the bank's credit card earnings, which was far greater than the percentages received from merchant discounts (about 2 percent of the amount purchased) and fees. Recently, however, the costs of financing receivables have increased markedly and many banks have begun to charge annual fees of $10 to $15 or transactions fees to offset these costs. Transaction fees are typically 12 cents per transaction. In 1980 about one half of all bank card holders paid either annual or transaction fees. In 1979 there were practically none. In other moves to combat higher financing costs, some banks have been moving their operations to states which allow higher than the standard 18 percent interest rate.

In spite of these changes to improve position, most banks lost money on their credit card operations in late 1979 and 1980. More and more customers were paying off their accounts within the interest-free grace period. In 1980 the banks seemed to suffer no significant drop-off of business because of the institution of fees, but the proportion of billings incurring no interest approached 50 percent. This pay-off phenomenon has led many banks to conclude that they are not selling credit so much as convenience or "transfer of value." This conclusion has led the banks to consider offering other transfer of value instruments such as debit cards[2] and travelers' checks as potential services. For instance, bank cards have teamed up with Western Union's emergency money order service to allow callers to wire up to $300 to any of 8,100 offices in the United States and to have the amount charged to their credit cards. It is generally felt that if consumers should continue to decrease their amounts of credit card debt, the competition will intensify and bank cards will move more aggressively into travelers' checks and other segments of the travel and entertainment segment. In fact, surveys already show that more consumers are using bank cards than are using T&E cards for restaurant checks and hotel bills. As of 1978, Visa and MasterCard claimed 2.5 million outlets accepting cards; Diners Club, 400,000; American Express, 350,000; and Carte Blanche, 250,000.

The two strongest competitors among bank cards are Visa and MasterCard. While Visa has recently overtaken MasterCard as the leader in worldwide volume and number of holders, MasterCard still retains

[2] Debit cards operate similarly to credit cards except that when the bank is notified of a sale, it immediately deducts the amount from an account balance that the consumer maintains with the bank, much in the same manner as with a checking account.

an edge in the United States. Both provide debit cards and are venturing into the travelers' check business.

Visa changed its name from BankAmericard in 1977 in order to shed its national identity with its political connotations and to project more of a worldwide image. The number of Visa cardholders increased dramatically during the late 1970s with over 70 million by 1979. The volume of Visa transactions also has increased rapidly (91 percent in 1977–1979 period), primarily from retail stores and restaurants.

Visa presents increasingly formidable competition in the credit card industry displaying corporate agility that fostered innovations such as the debit card (800,000 accounts in 1980), the single, trendy name, and strong initiatives in foreign markets. Although Visa's management sees travelers' checks as a regression into paper processing (which runs counter to their electronic processing strength), they have aggressively entered the travelers' check market. Depending upon cooperation with Barclay's (presently fourth largest issuer of travelers' checks), Visa's business has been growing at a 15 percent annual rate. In 1980 Visa has 8 percent of the U.S. market and was expecting a 40 percent share by 1985. As of 1980 about 90 percent of the checks processed were, in fact, Barclay's. The largest bank to build Visa travelers' checks sales from scratch is First National Bank of Chicago. As of 1980 that bank had sold $50 million in checks. Visa's plan for the travelers' check business is to allow participating banks to place their own names on the checks. Visa hopes this approach will lure banks who have been selling American Express checks.

MasterCard, with its 65 million worldwide cardholders in 1979, has been fighting the Visa challenge with larger advertising outlays (40 percent increase in 1979), a name change from Master Charge to MasterCard, debit cards, and a delayed venture into travelers' checks. The travelers' check delay was caused by a legal roadblock set up by Citibank, a member of the MasterCard system, who already held 12 percent of the world travelers' check market. Along with Visa, the MasterCard system is large enough and integrated enough to provide economies of scale advantages in authorization and interchange procedures.

Travel and Entertainment Cards

In 1978 it was estimated that $385 billion was spent on domestic and international travel and that by 1988 the amount spent will be $755 billion. American Express is by far the largest T&E card company with 11.9 million cardholders in 1980. The American Express card is held by more than half of the country's families who earn more than $25,000 annually. They engage in heavy advertising campaigns and frequently cosponsor ads with hotels and restaurants that accept their card.

Diners Club intensified their marketing efforts in the late 1970s with large increases in marketing budgets. In 1979 Diners Club claimed 2.5 million cardholders, with about 60 percent of the holders residing outside of the United States. Carte Blanche, with 800,000 holders in 1979, serves the affluent, has snob appeal, and turned down 75 percent of its 40,000 monthly applicants in 1978. Acquired from AVCO by Citicorp in 1979, Carte Blanche was generally thought to be in need of new marketing emphasis in order to survive.

In contrast to bank cards, which credit merchants' accounts on the same day an invoice is received, T&E cards generally cause the merchants to wait several days for payments. T&E cards also charge a higher discount to the merchants, typically 3.5 to 4 percent of the price of purchase. American Express, for instance, offers retailers the option of being paid in from 1 to 30 days after receipt, with the discount rate correspondingly lower as the period is extended.

Travelers' Checks

Closely related to the T&E credit card segment is the travelers' check industry. Started in 1891 by American Express, which maintains 60 percent of the market, the major competitors are Bank of America, Citibank, Barclays, and Thomas Cook. In 1978, 735 million travelers' checks were sold at a value of $25 billion. The five major U.S. and British issuers earned an estimated total of $239 million. In the five-year period 1974–1979, the industry sales grew 120 percent and by 1979 worldwide sales had reached $30 billion.

Most income on travelers' checks is made not on the nominal fee charged (usually 1 percent of face value), but on the "float." That is, on checks which are purchased and paid for, but not yet cashed. The average float period for travelers' checks is about two months. The companies can then invest this cash for two months until the checks are cashed. American Express, for instance, had about $2.3 billion in travelers' check float in 1979. Thus, industry experts indicate that it is unlikely that a company can be profitable in travelers' checks with an annual volume of less than $2 billion.

PROPERTY CASUALTY INSURANCE INDUSTRY

In contrast to the concentration of the credit card industry, the property/casualty (P-C) insurance industry has a large number of competitors with 200 companies that have written over $40 million in premiums in 1980. Many, but not all, of the leading P-C companies are also leaders in life insurance (see Exhibit 1). Even within the P-C segment, not all companies offer full lines of P-C insurance services. The importance of the various insurance lines in the P-C segment is shown in Exhibit 2.

A historical characteristic of the insurance business is the underwriting cycle. The cycle affects profitability of insurance companies through the relationship between premium pricing and claims costs. At the peak of the cycle competition is intense and prices are forced to a low level. When claims begin to come in at a level higher than provided for in the reserves, losses occur. At this point there is a shakedown of sorts, with some companies dropping from the competition in their less profitable segments and the remaining companies raising their premiums.

The overall industry growth rate has slowed from 10.7 percent in 1980. This slowing of premium growth rate is indicative of another trough in the underwriting cycle and stiff price competition. In 1980 the top 100 companies averaged an underwriting loss of 3.53 percent of earned premiums (after dividends to policy holders). This loss totaled $2.8 billion for the industry. The forecasts for 1981 indicate that it could be even more competitive with worse results than 1980. Most insurance companies have been able to offset underwriting losses with investment income. *Best's* reported, however, that 5 of the top 100 firms were not, in fact, able to offset underwriting losses in 1980. Some industry experts predicted that this pressure, following the 1973–75 trough by only five years, may force weaker firms into insolvency.

The use of investment income to offset underwriting losses has kept the industry profitable, exhibiting a strong capital surplus in spite of the downturn in the cycle (see Exhibit 3). The increasing dependence of companies on investment income is shown dramatically in Exhibit 4 and may have permanently changed the nature of the insurance business. Some analysts feel that the ability to depend on investment income will delay the normal shakeout of unprofitable lines and companies and will prolong the present trough much longer than usual.

Given the prospect of extended competitive pricing, attention to cost reduction may be one of the keys to survival. The current trends in the industry are summarized in *Best's* as follows:

1. As product and service distinctiveness becomes more difficult to maintain, insurance is taking on the aspects of a commodity game where low-cost producers are winners.
2. Competitive pricing is assuming growth importance.
   - Competition from major new entrants is forcing insurers to offer a competitive price.
   - Independent agencies are undergoing structural changes that are increasing price competition.

EXHIBIT 1 Leading Property/Casualty Companies and Groups (1980 net premiums in thousands)

	Rank	*Total P-C Company Premiums*	*Life Insurance Premiums*	*Total Premium Volume*	*Rank*	*Percent Increase 1 Year*	*Percent Increase 5-Year Compound*
State Farm	1	8,011,787	551,365	8,563,152	3	10.83	19.10
Allstate	2	5,270,426	240,300	5,515,454	6	9.89	12.27
Aetna Life & Casualty	3	4,558,426	3,939,761	10,284,080	1	3.72	16.05
Travelers	4	2,888,253	2,526,244	7,128,640	4	9.05	5.64
Liberty Mutual	5	2,867,423	39,677	2,911,727	10	4.29	18.47
Continental Insurance	6	2,822,595	44,886	2,883,049	11	6.25	7.61
Hartford Fire	7	2,661,964	301,050	3,217,105	9	4.73	9.83
Farmers Insurance	8	2,552,756	133,413	2,719,557	13	7.32	20.69
INA	9	2,550,211	458,050	3,349,209	8	6.08	9.20
Fireman's Fund	10	2,350,283	75,354	2,525,217	17	2.43	12.94
U.S. Fidelity & Guaranty	11	2,043,653	48,008	2,093,985	20	2.63	16.40
Nationwide	12	1,951,339	574,703	2,590,320	15	10.95	18.21
Kemper	13	1,689,683	363,964	2,053,740	21	5.48	12.55
Home Insurance	14	1,689,386	45,964	1,814,049	22	4.04	14.26
Crum and Forester	15	1,620,970	—	1,620,970	25	2.38	13.07
St. Paul	16	1,520,073	96,832	1,682,636	23	9.00	14.18
CNA	17	1,418,916	413,262	2,469,170	18	8.61	16.20
American International	18	1,374,564	203,950	1,632,035	24	10.34	24.82
Chubb	19	1,142,373	88,380	1,281,117	27	6.21	9.31
Commercial Union	20	1,115,897	20,939	1,137,437	28	15.19	8.58
Prudential of America	21	1,023,892	5,847,490	9,681,087	2	11.82	28.79
Connecticut General	22	1,011,796	629,059	2,872,063	12	−1.76	10.88
Royal Insurance	23	957,059	8,890	956,949	35	3.27	7.55
American Financial	24	898,823	177,897	1,079,999	29	9.64	4.82
Reliance	25	875,799	107,299	1,036,609	30	−3.67	10.48

Source: Adapted from *Best's Review: Property/Casualty Insurance Edition,* June 1981.

EXHIBIT 2 Property/Casualty Insurance Industry (premium distribution by line)

	Total Premiums*	Percent of Total	Gain in Premiums*	Loss Ratio†			
				1980	1979	1978	1977
Fire	2,887,770	3.0	−19,425	56.1	51.6	47.5	51.0
Allied Lines	1,673,619	1.7	44,043	69.1	67.9	57.1	46.6
Farmowners Multi-Peril	594,335	0.6	60,316	76.5	61.4	60.3	61.0
Homeowners Multi-Peril	10,012,854	10.4	982,901	67.1	61.5	53.5	53.1
Commercial Multi-Peril	7,663,589	7.9	320,269	55.4	52.9	44.4	42.9
Earthquake	53,558	0.1	11,934	5.0	1.8	1.9	.9
Ocean Marine	1,015,670	1.1	74,631	87.9	82.5	66.1	60.8
Inland Marine	2,744,061	2.8	383,791	68.9	58.1	51.6	49.1
Group A&H	1,853,362	1.9	143,767	80.8	76.4	77.5	78.2
All Other A&H	655,389	0.7	1,704	64.2	62.5	62.4	60.2
Worker's Compensation	15,743,510	16.3	1,411,445	70.4	75.3	77.9	74.1
Total Miscellaneous Liability:	9,408,956	9.7	−148,140	60.9	55.4	50.6	40.4
Medical Malpractice	1,491,403	1.5	85,412	82.6	75.3	60.6	41.8
Other Liability	7,917,553	8.2	−233,552	57.1	51.6	48.7	40.1
Private Passenger Auto Liability:	18,564,090	19.2	1,188,824	67.6	66.4	64.7	63.4
No Fault	2,170,962	2.2	116,823	78.3	74.0	76.7	78.3
Other Liability	16,393,128	17.0	1,072,001	66.2	65.4	63.1	61.5
Commercial Auto Liability:	4,936,684	5.1	136,871	69.0	66.4	61.7	57.9
No-Fault	154,251	0.2	−9,769	71.1	62.7	60.3	64.9
Other Liability	4,782,433	4.9	146,640	68.9	66.5	61.7	57.7
Private Passenger Auto Physical Damage	13,188,141	13.6	1,161,405	64.9	68.7	65.2	61.6
Commercial Auto Physical Damage	2,726,160	2.8	112,358	59.4	59.6	55.4	53.2
Aircraft	389,376	0.4	71,892	82.3	78.6	101.0	63.3
Fidelity	399,686	0.4	18,517	48.1	44.8	55.2	56.0
Surety	1,000,732	1.0	98,180	46.1	33.2	43.5	36.3
Glass	31,666	0.0	−972	54.1	50.6	47.8	46.6
Burglary & Theft	125,653	0.1	−1,831	37.3	36.6	25.8	26.4
Boiler & Machinery	377,519	0.4	8,908	49.4	40.4	31.9	31.7
Credit	79,229	0.1	8,840	56.7	35.1	37.9	38.7
Miscellaneous	584,253	0.6	−54,299	54.3	85.2	46.7	46.2
Totals	96,709,863	100.0	6,015,930	65.5	64.3	60.8	57.7

* Dollars in thousands.

† Loss ratio $= \frac{\text{Losses incurred}}{\text{Premiums earned} - \text{Dividends}}$

Source: Adapted from *Best's Review: Property/Casualty Insurance Edition,* July 1981.

EXHIBIT 3 Summary of Five-Year Industry Results ($ billions)

Year	*Premiums Written*	*Rate of Increase (percent)*	*Pretax Underwriting Profits**	*Capital Gains*	*Surplus*
1976	$ 60.4	21.9%	$ −2.2	$ 2.0	$24.6
1977	72.4	19.8	1.1	−0.8	29.3
1978	81.6	12.8	1.3	0.5	35.2
1979	90.1	10.3	−1.3	2.3	42.8
1980	96.3	6.9	−3.4	4.8	52.3
Total	400.8	14.3	−4.5		

* After dividends.

Source: Best's Review: Property/Casualty Insurance Edition, September 1981.

- Customers are becoming more price conscious as insurance costs rise.

3. As competition increases among all types of insurers, companies are seeking new revenue avenues such as a fee-based administration, loss control, and claim services.
4. Since price increases and premium growth are not keeping up with inflation, primarily because of competition, companies with uncompetitive expense ratios[3] may pay a substantial penalty for their inefficiency.[4]

Among the suggestions provided for increasing expense ratios are the following:

1. Programs to increase productivity.
2. Investment in automated systems.
3. Delegation of expense management responsibilities to branches.
4. Building expense accountability into the reward systems.

AMERICAN EXPRESS COMPANY

American Express was founded in 1850 and boasts of 114 years of uninterrupted profitability. The chairman of the board and chief executive officer is James D. Robinson III, who succeeded Harold L. Clark in 1977. In the 17 years of Clark's tenure, American Express revenues

---

[3] $\text{Expense ratio} = \frac{\text{Operating costs}}{\text{Premiums earned}}$

[4] William F. Kinder, "A Look at the Leaders: Has the Game Changed?" *Best's Review: Property/Casualty Insurance Edition 82* (September, 1981), p. 132.

EXHIBIT 4 Underwriting and Investment Income Growth Trends

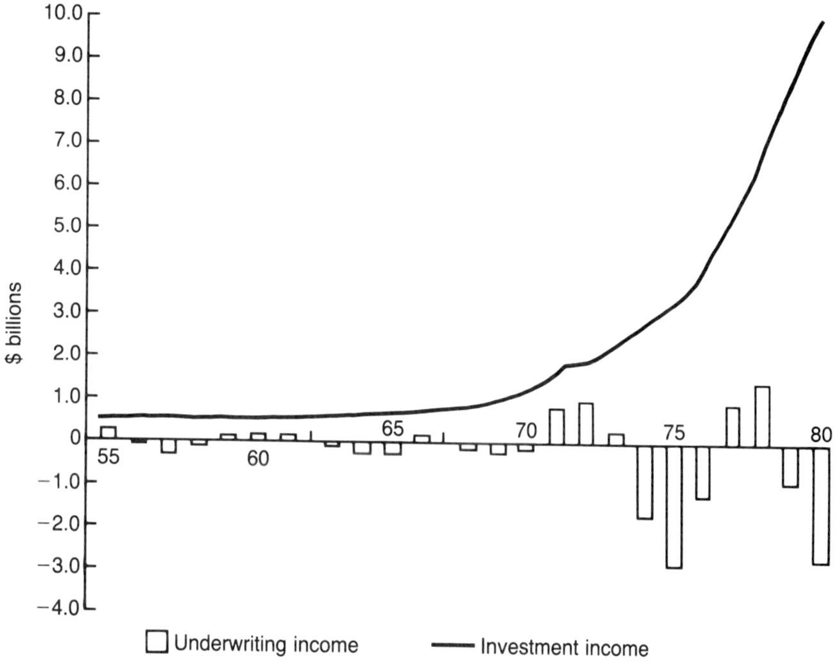

Source: Best's Review: Property/Casualty Insurance Edition, September 1981.

grew from $77 million to $3.4 billion in 1977. Clark ran the company with a very personal style of management that minimized bureaucratic controls and allowed a great deal of latitude to the division heads. He also recognized the importance of good relationships with banks to the success of American Express's business and used these contacts to build the business. When he left the company, four of the six largest banks were represented on the American Express Board of Directors.

Robinson, who has been at American Express since 1970, has indicated that, "Our prime objective is to provide, directly with banks, the widest variety of consumer financial services available from any single source." The transition from Clark to Robinson was orderly and gradual with Clark maintaining active company involvement for some time after the official transfer of duties in 1977. Although Clark and Robinson are both conservative in financial matters, differences in their management styles have become apparent. American Express has evolved into a more highly structured organization. Along with Roger Morely (who succeeded him as president), Robinson implemented a rigorous system of planning and control, which included not only annual plans, but also divisional level monthly forecasts. Morely was replaced as president in 1979 by Alva Way, formerly the chief financial officer at General Electric. Among the qualities in Way that were found attractive by Robinson were his abilities in strategic planning, data processing, and communications. Observers feel that all of this organizational emphasis has paid off in the form of significant improvements in the coordination among the divisions within the last few years.

A major part of American Express' growth has been through acquisition. In 1968 American Express acquired Fireman's Fund Insurance, the nation's ninth largest property-liability insurer. In 1972 the company bought 25 percent interest in Donaldson, Lufkin and Jenrett, but sold the interest in 1975 at a $23 million loss. Within Robinson's first three years, American Express attempted to make four acquisitions: Walt Disney Productions, Book of the Month Club, Philadelphia Life Insurance, and McGraw-Hill. The company's recent acquisitions are listed in Exhibit 5, the most significant and most recent being the merger with Shearson Loeb Rhoades.

As of early 1981, American Express was organized into four major business areas: Travel Services Group, Warner Amex Cable Services, International Banking Services, and Insurance Services. The company had assets of $19.7 billion, 44,000 employees, 1,000 travel offices, and 77 international banking and investment offices. Total revenues for 1980 were $5.5 billion with a net income of $376 million. In 1980, dividends were increased from 45 to 50 cents per share, the sixth increase in five years. The consolidated financial statements are shown in Exhibit 6 and contributions of the various segments are summarized in Exhibit 7. The scope of the company's international operations is shown in Exhibit 8.

EXHIBIT 5

Acquisition	*Date*
American Express Direct Response	April 1979
Warner Amex Cable Communications (joint venture)	December 1979
First Data Resources	January 1980
Southern Guaranty Insurance Company	September 1980
Food and Wine magazine	September 1980
Mitchell Beazley Ltd.	November 1980
WATS Marketing of America	December 1980
Interstate Group of Insurance Companies	December 1980
New England Bank Card Association	March 1981
Shearson Loeb Rhoades	Awaiting approval

Source: Moody's Bank and Finance Manual.

Travel Services Group

The Travel Services Group includes the card division, travelers' cheque division, travel division, communications division, and the financial institutions services division. Revenues for the group increased 34 percent from 1979 to $1.7 billion in 1980 and net income rose 17 percent to $177 million, which is 47 percent of the company's total earnings.

The card division provides corporate and personal credit card ser-

EXHIBIT 6

AMERICAN EXPRESS COMPANY
Consolidated Income Statement
(in $ million)

	1980	*1979*	*1978*	*1977*	*1976*
Revenues:					
Commissions and fees	$ 1,522	$ 1,130	$ 912	$ 738	$ 643
Interest and dividends	1,264	1,007	759	580	496
Property-liability and life insurance premiums	2,589	2,450	2,341	2,080	1,771
Other	129	80	64	48	48
Total revenues	5,504	4,667	4,076	3,446	2,948
Expenses:					
Provisions for losses:					
Insurance	1,545	1,482	1,393	1,255	1,142
Banking, credit, financial paper, other	214	161	127	108	100
Salaries and employee benefits	833	685	578	472	421
Interest	870	572	368	249	208
Commissions and brokerage	403	371	355	311	275
Occupancy and equipment	247	187	141	125	105
Advertising and promotion	187	140	127	84	66
Taxes other than income taxes	145	133	120	101	85
Telephone, telegraph, postage	117	93	83	74	63
Financial paper, forms, and other printed matter	82	65	51	45	35
Claims adjustment service	78	102	116	130	90
Other	362	285	234	188	162
Total expenses	5,083	4,276	3,693	3,142	2,752
Pretax income	421	391	383	304	196
Income tax provision	45	46	69	52	17
Net operating income	376	345	314	252	179
Gains on sale of investment securities	—	—	—	10	15
Net income	376	345	314	262	194
Net income per share	$ 5.27	$ 4.83	$ 4.39	$ 3.65	$ 2.70

EXHIBIT 6 ***(continued)***

AMERICAN EXPRESS COMPANY
Consolidated Income Statement
(in $ million)

	1980	*1979*	*1978*	*1977*	*1976*
Assets					
Cash	$ 1,069	$ 1,051	$ 844	$ 674	$ 542
Time deposits	1,084	976	891	858	821
Investment securities (cost):					
U.S. government	750	519	435	459	429
State and municipal	4,070	4,104	3,808	3,167	2,458
Other bonds and obligations	1,200	1,044	735	720	710
Preferred stocks	$ 57	$ 52	$ 48	$ 48	$ 43
Total*	6,077	5,719	5,026	4,388	3,640
Investment securities (lower of cost or market):					
Preferred stocks	67	83	99	111	95
Common stocks	99	83	72	66	56
Total†	166	166	171	177	151
Investment securities (market):					
Preferred stocks	63	57	50	49	45
Common stocks	$ 783	$ 652	$ 563	$ 507	$ 506
Total‡	846	709	613	556	551
Accounts receivable and accrued interest, less reserves: 1980, $287; 1979, $213; 1978, $171; 1977, $146; 1976, $125	4,887	3,597	2,705	2,164	1,754
Loans and discounts, less reserves: 1980, $89; 1979, $82; 1978, $75; 1977, $60; 1976, $52	3,690	3,369	3,320	2,571	2,073
Land, buildings and equipment (cost), less depreciation	448	347	285	263	239
Prepaid policy acquisition expenses	271	244	206	153	130
Other assets	1,171	930	637	542	467
Total assets	$19,709	$17,108	$14,698	$12,346	$10,368

vices to 11.9 million card holders. The familiar "green card" is marketed not as a credit card implying a line of credit, but as a convenience device. As such, payment in full is required on demand, with the exception of certain tour plans and airplane tickets that can be financed over an extended period. There are approximately 6.5 million personal green card holders who pay an annual fee of $35. About 1.5

EXHIBIT 6 (*concluded*)

	1980	*1979*	*1978*	*1977*	*1976*
Liabilities					
Customers deposits and credits held by subsidiaries	$ 5,087	$ 4,749	$ 4,192	$ 3,755	$ 3,024
Travelers cheques outstanding	2,542	2,343	2,105	1,859	1,716
Money orders and drafts outstanding	212	289	324	175	140
Accounts payable	1,020	889	785	593	471
Reserves for:					
Property-liability losses and expenses	2,589	2,364	2,057	1,723	1,363
Unearned premiums	1,008	974	875	792	673
Life and disability policies	259	227	184	147	130
Short-term debt	2,302	1,595	1,117	776	555
Long-term debt	1,099	689	479	330	304
Deferred income taxes	161	135	108	117	117
Other	$ 1,244	$ 996	$ 852	$ 711	$ 621
Total liabilities	17,523	15,250	13,078	10,978	9,114
Preferred stock	24	25	27	28	30
Common stock (100,000,000 shares authorized, 60 cents par values; 71,274,306 outstanding in 1980)	43	43	43	43	43
Capital surplus	208	204	202	200	201
Net unrealized security gains	208	115	87	78	116
Retained earnings	1,703	1,471	1,261	1,019	864
Total common shareholders' equity	2,162	1,833	1,593	1,340	1,224
	$19,709	$17,108	$14,698	$12,346	$10,368

* Market: 1980, $4,612; 1979, $5,070; 1978, $4,686; 1977, $4,396; 1976, $3,612.
† Cost: 1980, $191; 1979, $192; 1978, $188; 1977, $188; 1976, $167.
‡ Cost: 1980, $531; 1979, $523; 1978, $471; 1977, $433; 1976, $370.

Source: *Annual Reports.*

million customers hold the "gold cards" at an annual fee of $50. In addition to the charge features, the gold card allows members to finance purchases and to obtain cash through a line of credit that American Express has established with 1,800 participating banks.

The American Express cards are issued in 23 currencies and are honored by 438,000 establishments worldwide. The company has been attempting to build the number of establishments and added about 50,000 new establishments during 1980. Expanding beyond the traditional emphasis on food, lodging, and travel is a new emphasis on recruiting prestigious retail and department stores that are likely to provide a high average purchase value.

EXHIBIT 7 American Express Company, Industry Segments 1980 (in $ millions)

	Travel Related Services	*International Banking Services*	*Insurance Services*	*Other and Corporate*	*Adjustments and Eliminations*	*Consolidated*
Revenues	$1,661	$ 930	$2,914	$ 35	$ (36)	$ 5,504
Pretax income before general corporate	236	67	215	16	—	534
General corporate expenses	—	—	—	(113)	—	(113)
Pretax income	236	67	215	(97)	—	421
Net income	177	41	210	(52)	—	376
Assets	$6,877	$6,926	$5,846	$469	$(409)	$19,709

Insurance services comprised of:

	Commercial Lines	*Personal Lines*	*Investment Income*	*Total*	*Other*	*Total Insurance Services*
Revenues	$1,788	$626	$282	$2,696	$218	$2,914
Pretax income	$ (37)	$ (39)	$277	$ 201	$ 14	$ 215

Source: *Annual Report.*

EXHIBIT 8 American Express Company, Geographic Operations (in $ millions)

	United States	*Europe*	*Asia/ Pacific*	*All Other*	*Adjustments and Eliminations*	*Consolidated*
Revenues	$ 3,953	$ 700	$ 281	$ 604	$ (34)	$ 5,504
Pretax before general corporate expenses	435	21	15	63	—	534
General corporate expenses	(113)	—	—	—	—	(113)
Pretax income	322	21	15	63	—	421
Assets	11,718	3,704	1,774	2,603	(528)	19,271
Corporate assets						438
Total assets						$19,709

Source: *Annual Report.*

A major cost of the card business is the financing of card receivables. American Express sells its receivables to Credco, a wholly owned subsidiary. Credco then finances them through commercial paper, equity capital, lines of credit, and long-term debt. In 1980 Credco purchased $19.2 billion of receivables, up from $14.6 billion in 1979. The weighted average interest cost of all Credco financing rose from 8.48 percent in 1978 to 15.7 percent during the first two months of 1980. These increased financing costs have led American Express to tighten its collection policies by reducing the grace period and increasing the finance charge.

American Express cards have achieved a high degree of market penetration in the United States. It is estimated that about 50 percent of the families with incomes greater than $25,000 have the card, as do 64 percent of those with incomes greater than $50,000, and 71 percent with incomes over $75,000. Growth rates in membership have averaged 11 percent over the last three years. A major contribution to the growth rate has come from countries outside of the United States, where the growth rates have been on the order of 25 percent. The number of cardholders outside of the United States was 2.7 million in 1980.

The charge card volume has increased at annual rates of 26 percent (1978), 29 percent (1979), and 32 percent (1980). This positive trend in the face of government controls on credit spending during the period has reinforced management's view that the card is used by consumers as a convenience rather than a credit device. Customers also seem to be attracted to the country club style of itemizing the bills (a feature not provided by bank cards), the absence of charge limits, check cashing privileges, and the snob appeal of the card.

American Express travelers' checks are sold through 105,000 outlets worldwide, including banks, travel agents, credit unions, etc. Although check buyers are charged a fee of 1 percent of the check's face value, the issuing banks retain about two thirds of that fee. The primary source of travelers' check revenues for American Express is from the "float," or cash, the company controls from checks that have not yet been cashed. This float is invested by American Express in tax-free securities and has provided a significant amount of the company's total revenues in 1980. The average period that the checks are outstanding is two months. An advertising campaign begun in 1979, featuring actor Karl Malden, appealed to consumers to hold unused checks for emergencies—an attempt to extend the float period. The dollar value of the travelers' checks outstanding at year end has increased from $1.72 billion to 1976 to $2.5 billion in 1980.

Increasing competitive pressure is being felt in the travelers' check industry and the growth rate of American Express checks has been slowing over the last three years. Many banks, which sell the majority of the checks, are now selling their own checks under Visa or MasterCard trademarks. American Express also now owns 34 percent of Sociéte Francais du Chèque de Voyage, which began issuing French franc travelers' checks in 1980. American Express has converted all of its French franc business to the new checks.

The travel division offers retail and wholesale (tours) travel services worldwide through 1,000 offices in 126 countries. Services include trip planning, reservations, ticketing, and other incidental services. Revenues for the division are earned through commissions from carriers, hotels, and through fees from customers for incidental services.

American Express reported major changes in the travel division in 1980 including a restructuring of the organization to decentralize along geographic lines. It is anticipated that this move will provide greater flexibility to respond to localized customer needs and opportunities. The company also has been redesigning its tour packages to achieve greater consumer affordability and to eliminate low-revenue programs. A major automation step was taken in 1980 with the implementation of a computerized Travel Information Processing System (TRIPS). TRIPS eventually will become an integrated worldwide information and reservation system.

The financial performance of the travel division has varied over the years, with weak years during the period 1973–1976. A stronger revenues showing was reported for 1977, although it is not clear whether the division was profitable. In 1979 and 1980 the division reported losses, this in spite of increased revenues during 1980. The company explained that part of the problem in 1980 has been due to slackened demand for tours, lower margins on discount ticket purchasing, and the costs of restructuring the division.

The communications division was formed in January 1980 and has responsibility for American Express Publishing Corporation, Merchandise Sales, American Express Direct Response (ADR), and

Mitchell Beazley Limited, a London-based international publishing house.

The division has recently taken over publishing of *Food and Wine* magazine and has published *Travel and Leisure* magazine (circulation 925,000) since 1970. A growing emphasis in the division is in direct mail marketing through Merchandise Sales (revenues increased by 70 percent in 1980), supported by the computer services of ADR. ADR also supplies direct mail marketing services to outside businesses and to other American Express divisions.

The financial institutions services division was formed in 1980 to consolidate operations relating to the financial community. Within the division is First Data Resources, Inc., a recently acquired provider of data and telephone marketing services to financial institutions and merchandisers. Also included are the Money Order Division and Payment Systems, Inc., which provides information and research in payment systems and electronic funds transfer.

Warner Amex Cable Services

In 1979 American Express paid $175 million for one half interest in Warner Cable Company, which was owned by Warner Communications. The joint venture includes the subsidiaries, Warner Amex Cable Communications, Inc., and Warner Amex Satellite Entertainment Company. American Express sees the cable systems as the technical hardware link for the financial supermarket of the future which they expect to build around the television screen.

Warner Cable Company owns and operates 141 cable television systems with 736,000 subscribers in 27 states. Among the most recent awards are major franchises in Pittsburgh, Dallas, Cincinnati, and in areas surrounding St. Louis, Boston, Chicago and Akron. These awards provide the potential for entering 1.1 million households.

Most Warner Amex systems have 12 to 30 channels: however, new systems will provide many more channels. The company has a head start on its competition in two-way cable systems with a system called Qube. Warner Amex spent $20 million to develop the Qube system and it is presently operating in Columbus and in Cincinnati. Although the talkback feature of Qube is used primarily for entertainment purposes such as voting on boxing matches, answering viewer polls, and calling plays for football games, the two-way link is critical for potential home selling, burgler alarm, and financial transaction uses. The Qube system is now offering a retrieval service for business analysis and money management information. A 24-hour security system has recently been added to the Columbus system and is now servicing 2,500 households and businesses.

Warner Amex Satellite Entertainment Company (WASEC) operates five satellite transponders which receive television signals and transmit them over the entire country. The entertainment company offers two major services: "The Movie Channel" and "Nickelodeon." "The Movie Channel" offers 24-hour feature films, while "Nickelodeon" provides varied programming for children and young adults. The company is planning a joint venture with ABC Video Enterprises, Inc., called the Alpha Repertory Television Service which will provide programming devoted to the performing and visual arts. Firm plans also have been made to offer "The Music Channel," which will provide continuous popular music with complementary visual material.

Although a significant amount of risk exists in the cable video industry in that franchises must be awarded by local governments. Warner Amex has proven to be an effective competitor. In 1980 Warner Amex won 1.1 million of the 1.6 million households up for bids in the United States. The company anticipates a need for significant financing to support future expansion efforts. In 1980 they received a $250 million line of credit from a group of banks, but additional capital will be needed in 1981 from external sources, and from the parent companies, where appropriate.

Insurance Services

Fireman's Fund Insurance was founded in 1863 and was acquired by American Express in 1968. Fireman's Fund provides a broad range of insurance services including commercial and personal property liability insurance and life insurance and annuities. Policies are sold in the United States through 11,000 independent agents and brokers. The company also operates overseas through AFIA World Wide insurance, a consortium of United States insurance companies. The Fireman's Fund commercial insurance lines include property, general liability, multiple peril, and worker's compensation, while the personal lines include homeowners' and automobile insurance. Life insurance is offered through Fireman's Fund American Life Insurance Company (FFAL), which sells a full portfolio of life insurance products including ordinary and term life insurance, annuities, group term life insurance, and group accident and health insurance. FFAL also underwrites the supplemental life insurance offered to American Express cardholders.

Fireman's Fund was caught in the insurance underwriting cycle in 1974 when earnings dropped by 17 percent. Even at this amount, the drop was softened since the company called upon $9 million from a "catastrophe reserve" built up during more profitable years. This practice of banking earnings has since been ordered abolished for the entire industry by the Financial Accounting Standards Board, since it was considered to be misleading to investors.

Following the 1974 experience, American Express decided to institute policies to avoid the cycle. They vowed to price more aggressively when premium rates are rising and not to write unprofitable policies by cutting prices when competition stiffens.

Feeling the competitive pressures of the most recent trough in the underwriting cycle, the growth rate in premiums written has been declining as the company has attempted to concentrate on more profitable business in underwriting and investment. In 1980 $2.4 billion in premiums were written, which is a 2.5 percent increase. The increase in 1979 was 4.5 percent and in 1978 the increase was 9.1 percent.

Fireman's Fund gross revenues for 1980 were $2.9 billion, which is a 7.2 percent increase over 1979. A significant contribution to the increase in revenues has been from specialized products in rural markets, commercial group packages, and reinsurance. The company has suffered underwriting losses for the past three years due to higher claims costs which were not offset by premiums revenues. The underwriting losses were $76 million in 1980, $53 million (1979), and $13 million (1978). According to *Best,* Fireman's Fund ranked 53rd in the industry in underwriting performance with a loss ratio of 58:1. These losses were offset by investment income, which increased by 21 percent in 1980. Fireman's Fund is attempting to remedy the losses through rate increases, increased deductibles, and obtaining shorter terms so that premiums can be adjusted more frequently.

The underwriting expense ratio has been increasing over the last three years, from 30.8 percent in 1978 to 33.3 percent in 1980. This increase has been attributed to slower premium growth and long-term development spending. The company has been increasing the number of branch offices, automating its network of offices, and has been developing a program of standardization of field office procedures.

International Banking Services

American Express International Banking Company (AEIBC) accounts for 17 percent of American Express's total revenues, 35 percent of the company's total assets, and 11 percent of the net income. AEIBC operates 83 offices in 34 countries, providing commercial banking services, investment banking, wholesale banking, equipment finance, and financial advisory services. It also offers consumer banking service in certain locations, including contracted services on overseas U.S. military bases. The bank does not provide services in the United States except as incidental to its foreign operations. AEIBC is also an active dealer in foreign exchange markets; these activities contributed $35 million in revenues in 1980.

Income from interest increased 21 percent to $197 million in 1980, while commissions fees revenues increased 14 percent to $100 million in 1980. The latter increase reflects an emphasis on the expansion of nonasset related sources of revenues. In 1980 operating costs rose 19 percent, primarily as a result of inflation and automation of the banking network.

THE SHEARSON MERGER

In April 1981 American Express and Shearson Loeb Rhoades, Inc., announced that they had reached agreement on a merger. The terms were 1.3 American Express shares for each Shearson share. At the time of the merger Shearson brought into American Express 11,000 employees and $8 billion in assets, mostly in money market funds. The company reported $653 million in revenues in 1980 and had an estimated 500,000 customers.

The level of revenues in 1980 put Shearson in the number two position in the brokerage industry and is largely the product of eight acquisitions in the 10 years since Shearson went public. Shearson's acquisitions were usually of "old line" brokerage houses that were having financial difficulty. To make the acquisitions work, Shearson cut out levels of management, consolidated and automated the "back office" operations into a strong network, and added new services. The consolidated financial statements for the company are shown in Exhibit 9.

Under the terms of the merger Sanford I. (Sandy) Weill will remain in charge of Shearson and will head American Express' executive committee, while Robinson will become chairman of the merged entity. After the transaction Weill will personally own an estimated 0.6 percent of American Express's stock. Weill has built a reputation of competence along with his building of Shearson and has demonstrated a willingness and an ability for making fast decisions.

The merger is seen by many as giving strong impetus to a trend in the financial industry where many of the leading brokerage companies are looking for capital inputs to remain competitive on a national scale. The competitive surge appears to be aimed at providing consolidated "one-stop" financial services. Several securities dealers who have survived a tight decade and are showing profitable years now appear attractive to the larger insurance and other financial firms.

The trend in these acquisitions may have been triggered by Merrill Lynch, Pierce, Fenner & Smith Inc., which is the industry's number one brokerage house and has considerable capital ($1 billion) strength of its own. In 1977 Merrill Lynch broke with tradition and created a cash management account that allows customers to access cash in the account and money funds as well as providing a line of credit. All of this can be accomplished through special VISA cards or through Merrill Lynch checks. This move proved attractive to customers and was difficult for the smaller companies to match.

In March 1981 Prudential Insurance merged with Bache Group Inc. Through the merger it is expected that Prudential can provide not only the financial stability to remain competitive and to ride out the fiscal variability that is a problem in the brokerage business, but also to provide marketing and promotional support as well as new services to the Bache customers.

The American Express-Shearson merger announcement has caused considerable concern for banks, who see a new kind of financial institution that can offer a broad range of services that banks are not allowed to sell. Banks are presently prohibited from selling securities by the Glass-Steagall Act of 1933. Their reaction has been in several direc-

EXHIBIT 9

SHEARSON LOEB RHOADES, INC.
Consolidated Income Statement
(in thousands)

	*1980**	*1979**	*1978**
Revenues:			
Commissions	$ 327,497	$ 188,744	$ 136,732
Principal transactions	82,038	17,427	16,299
Interest	128,961	56,293	36,674
Investment banking	57,203	23,900	23,339
Mortgage banking	28,455	6,008	—
Other	28,312	11,658	8,181
Total revenues	652,466	304,030	221,225
Expenses:			
Employee compensation	310,065	152,802	113,078
Floor broker commissions	26,703	16,785	12,658
Interest	57,407	21,178	18,037
Other operating expenses	142,653	73,180	57,591
Total expenses	536,828	263,945	201,364
Income before distribution	115,638	40,085	19,861
Distribution to profits participation	10,669	—	—
Pretax income	104,969	40,085	19,861
Income taxes	49,162	20,010	9,857
Net income	55,805	20,075	10,004
Net income per share	$6.99	$3.78	$2.11
Dividends per share	$ .40	$ .34	$ .27

EXHIBIT 9 **(*concluded*)**

SHEARSON LOEB RHOADES, INC.
Consolidated Balance Sheet
(in thousands)

	*1980**	*1979**	*1978**
Assets			
Cash	$ 52,768	$ 15,372	$ 7,110
Segregated cash and treasury bills	316,739	167,085	123,226
Securities and deposit	52,514	9,853	13,963
Receivables from customers	966,759	547,677	485,588
Receivables from brokers	461,126	135,360	88,676
Mortgages and construction loans	69,481	92,146	—
Other receivables	17,651	7,164	7,176
Spot commodities owned	—	—	254
Securities owned (market)	248,769	127,586	122,960
Secured demand notes	716	7,394	7,394
Exchange membership	5,175	2,883	2,874
Investments in affiliates	3,203	—	—
Securities purchased	1,849	9,630	184,927
Purchased mortgage contracts	6,778	7,197	—
Deferred income taxes	5,610	—	—
Office equipment, etc.	22,011	12,197	8,286
Excess acquisition cost	14,559	4,647	4,245
Differed expenses and other assets	21,983	8,358	3,433
Total assets	$2,267,691	$1,154,549	$1,060,114
Liabilities			
Bank loans	$ 212,668	$ 154,377	$ 149,393
Payables to brokers	557,752	154,743	109,556
Payables to customers	607,497	292,992	196,189
Accrued liabilities, etc.	341,465	255,874	168,355
Securities sold†	166,260	127,683	115,583
Repurchased securities sold	43,517	1,966	211,565
Deferred income tax	—	662	749
Term notes	26,503	17,826	7,513
Subordinate debt	137,671	61,233	32,994
Secured demand obligation	—	7,394	7,394
Contributions of profit participation agreement	30,113	—	—
Preferred stock	175	1,482	2,026
Common stock	661	527	487
Paid in capital	50,665	29,639	26,259
Retained earnings	96,295	51,713	33,546
Reacquired stock	(3,561)	(3,562)	(1,496)
Total liabilities	$2,267,691	$1,154,549	$1,060,114

* Year ended June 30th.
† Securities sold, but not yet purchased.

Source: *Annual Reports,* Moody's Bank and Finance Manual.

tions. Larger banks have been lobbying to have the government restrictions on themselves lifted so that they can enter the competitive field, but others have been attempting to block formation of such strong competition. The Independent Bankers Association has written to the Justice Department asking that the American Express-Shearson merger be delayed pending investigation of the deal's "potential anticompetitive effects." The strength of the overall opposition to the merger is difficult to assess without the support of the larger banks. But given the present political trends toward less government involvement, it is unlikely that the merger will be disapproved.

Case 8

Coke Tries to Counter the Pepsi Challenge*

Dhruv Grewal
Virginia Polytechnic Institute and State University

INTRODUCTION

The Coca-Cola Company was ranked as the 46th largest industrial corporation on the basis of sales in 1984. With 36.4 percent of the domestic soft drink sales volume, Coca-Cola was still ahead of its nearest rival, Pepsi Company Inc., which had 25.6 percent of the domestic sales volume. Still, Coca-Cola needed to address several issues to ensure its leadership and growth in the soft drink industry. One issue was how best to deal with increased competition in a maturing soft drink industry. Another more specific issue was what to do about Pepsi which was gaining on Coke in recent years. These and other factors meant more intense competition within the soft drink industry.

HISTORY

Coca-Cola, perhaps the world's most renowned trademarked product, was created by Dr. Pemberton in 1886 by stirring various ingredients into a brass pot. His partner and bookkeeper, Frank Robinson, named the product Coca-Cola, something he felt would be easily remembered by customers. The product was first sold at drug store fountains for 5 cents a glass and sales averaged 13 glasses per day during 1886.

---

* This case was written by Dhruv Grewal (Ph. D. student in Marketing at Virginia Polytechnic Institute and State University) under the direction of Larry D. Alexander (Associate Professor of Strategic Management), Department of Management, The R.B. Pamplin College of Business, Virginia Polytechnic Institute and State University, Blacksburg, Virginia 24061.

During that first year, Dr. Pemberton earned $50.00; however, he spent $73.96 on advertising alone.

Later in 1889, Joseph Whitehead and Benjamin Thomas secured the exclusive rights from the company to bottle and sell Coca-Cola throughout the United States, except for six New England states, Texas, and Mississippi. This contract started the unique relationship that the Coca-Cola Company enjoyed with its largely independent bottlers. By 1894, Joseph Biedenharn started bottling the Coca-Cola product at his own facilities.

The Coca-Cola Company (which replaced the 1892 firm which was incorporated in Georgia) was incorporated in Delaware in 1919. Still, the company's headquarters remained in Atlanta, Georgia. Clearly, several of the most vital assets of the Coca-Cola Company were its trademarks. "Coca-Cola" was registered with the U.S. Patent and Trademark Office in 1893, and the shortened "Coke" was similarly registered much later in 1945. In addition, its unique contoured bottle was registered as a trademark in 1960.

The Coca-Cola Company was best known for manufacturing and distributing soft drink syrups and flavoring concentrates. While the company also operated a separate food division which produced and marketed citrus and other fruit juices, coffee, and plastic products, the focus of this case is on its soft drink division. Some of its products in this category included Hi-C fruit drinks, various Minute Maid juices, and Five-Alive beverages. The Coca-Cola Company significantly diversified its operations when it acquired Columbia Pictures in 1982. That acquired firm was engaged in the production and distribution of motion pictures and television shows. Other entertainment-related activities that Columbia participated in included the publication and distribution of sheet music and song books.

THE PEPSI CHALLENGE

In 1975, Pepsi started its "Pepsi Challenge", aimed directly at Coca-Cola through its various comparative ads. By 1983, Pepsi was targeting the teenage population, claiming it to be the "Choice of a New Generation." Popular music and television personalities endorsed Pepsi products in the advertisements. Pepsi even agreed to partially finance the Jackson Brothers' Victory Tour of 30 cities if they would appear in two Pepsi commercials. Pepsi's name would also be on all the tickets and promotions of the tour and several radio and print advertisements that featured the Jacksons. Other celebrities who signed contracts to endorse Pepsi products in recent years include singer Lionel Richie, television actor Don Johnson, rock musician Glen Frey, actor Michael J. Fox, and comedian Billy Crystal. Clearly, the Pepsi challenge had strengthened the number two soft-drink manufacturer which captured 33% of the food-store market by 1985.

Pepsi made other changes in its strategy to more effectively compete against Coca-Cola. Pepsi began to acquire some of its largest bottlers. By acquiring its third largest bottler, MEI Bottling Corporation in Minnesota, Pepsi was able to cover 33 franchise markets. Pepsi-Cola also acquired the Allegheny Bottling Company, another major bottler, which served an area stretching from south-central Pennsylvania to the coastal area of Virginia. The financial statements of PepsiCo Inc. are presented in Exhibit 1.

Pepsi's challenge to Coke's supremacy has been felt the most in recent years. During 1983 alone, Coca-Cola lost both its Burger King and Wendy's accounts to Pepsi. A major aspect of the Pepsi challenge was its comparative advertising in which Pepsi claimed its products were superior to Coke. Later in 1985, Pepsi reaped benefits when arch rival Coke first discontinued old Coke and later reintroduced it. So happy was Pepsi management that it gave its employees the day off when old Coke was discontinued, since they felt it confirmed that Pepsi was superior. Exhibit 2 shows that PepsiCo had the dominant share of the caffeine free market. It also shows that coke had increased its position in the diet soft drink market with its newly introduced diet Coke, the most popular diet drink.

Clearly, Coke and Pepsi were locked into a competitive battle for the number one position in the industry. For years, Coke's profit margins had declined while Pepsi's market share increased. To improve its profit margin, Coke replaced weak bottlers, bought Columbia Pictures, and introduced diet Coke, caffeine-free Coke, and Cherry Coke. These moves increased Coke's profit margin by 20 percent and doubled Coke's stock price. Still, Pepsi was outperforming Coke in the grocery stores with ads targeted for the teenage market. Meanwhile, Coke had been concentrating on the baby boomer market, people born after World War II (between 1946 and 1962). By the 1980s, the baby boomers were aging, which caused the teenage population to increase.

PepsiCo's attempt to acquire Seven-Up from Philip Morris in 1985 might make the Pepsi challenge an even greater threat. Philip Morris had already agreed to sell Seven-Up to PepsiCo for $380 million. All that remained for PepsiCo was to obtain approval from the Antitrust Division of the Department of Justice. If the Seven-Up acquisition is approved, PepsiCo's share of the lemon-lime soft drink would rise to 60 percent. With Seven-Up's addition, PepsiCo would have two additional soft drinks which accounted for 13 percent of the total industry sales. While Seven-Up suffered losses in past years, PepsiCo believed that its pending acquisition complemented PepsiCo's operations and would help increase its share of the soft drink market to 35 percent, only a few percentage points behind Coke.

EXHIBIT 1

PEPSI-CO INC. AND SUBSIDIARIES
Consolidated Statement of Income and Retained Earnings
Years ended December 29, 1984, December 31, 1983, and December 25, 1982
(in thousands except per share amounts)

		1984 (52 weeks)	1983 (53 weeks)	1982 (52 weeks)
Revenues	Net Sales	**$7,698,678**	$7,165,586	$6,810,929
Costs and Expenses	Cost of sales	**3,149,940**	3,007,398	2,949,160
	Marketing, administrative and other expenses	**3,853,540**	3,629,509	3,233,050
	Interest expense	**206,956**	176,759	165,270
	Interest income	**(86,131)**	(53,650)	(49,325)
		7,124,305	6,760,016	6,298,155
Income from Continuing Operations before Unusual Charges and Income Taxes		**574,373**	405,570	512,774
Unusual Charges	Provision for restructuring	**220,000**	—	—
	Reduction in net assets of foreign bottling operations (without tax benefit)	**—**	—	79,400
Income from Continuing Operations before Income Taxes		**354,373**	405,570	433,374
	Provision for United States and foreign income taxes	**147,701**	134,233	220,947
Income from Continuing Operations		**206,672**	271,337	212,427
Discontinued Operations	Income from discontinued operations (net of income taxes of $14,915, $6,728 and $5,846 in 1984, 1983 and 1982, respectively)	**20,875**	12,774	11,861
	Loss on disposal (net of $500 tax benefit)	**(15,000)**	—	—
		5,875	12,774	11,861
Net Income		**212,547**	284,111	224,288
	Retained earnings at beginning of year	**1,622,550**	1,489,797	1,412,636
	Cash dividends (per share 1984–$1.665; 1983–$1.62; 1982–$1.58)	**(156,185)**	(151,358)	(147,127)
	Retained earnings at end of year	**$1,678,912**	$1,622,550	$1,489,797
Net Income per Share	Continuing operations	**$ 2.19**	$ 2.88	$ 2.27
	Discontinued operations	**.06**	.13	.13
	Net income	**$ 2.25**	$ 3.01	$ 2.40

EXHIBIT 1 (*continued*)

PEPSI-CO INC. AND SUBSIDIARIES
Consolidated Balance Sheet
(in thousands)

	Year Ended December 29 1984	*Year Ended December 31 1983*
Assets		
Current assets		
Cash	**$ 28,139**	$ 24,434
Marketable securities	**784,684**	529,326
Notes and accounts receivable, less allowance 1984–$31,966; 1983–$33,738	**640,081**	647,329
Inventories	**451,781**	375,606
Prepaid expenses, taxes and other current assets	**242,181**	159,247
Net assets of the transportation segment held for disposal	**143,210**	149,504
	2,290,076	1,885,446
Long-term receivables and investments		
Long-term receivables and other investments	**178,647**	161,283
Investment in tax leases	**73,236**	77,941
	251,883	239,224
Property, plant and equipment		
Land	**$ 218,231**	$ 190,942
Buildings	**819,990**	732,999
Machinery and equipment	**1,988,112**	1,891,046
Capital leases	**191,924**	190,842
Bottles and cases, net of customers' deposits, 1984–$11,678; 1983–$32,777	**23,785**	56,550
	3,242,042	3,062,379
Less accumulated depreciation and amortization	**1,079,029**	1,019,000
	2,163,013	2,043,379
Goodwill	**163,904**	235,768
Other assets	**81,358**	88,919
Total assets	**$4,950,234**	$4,492,736

COCA-COLA'S FUNCTIONAL AREA STRATEGIES

Marketing/Sales

The major markets for Coke products are vending machines, restaurant sales, and grocery and convenience stores. In 1985, The Coca-Cola Company produced many soft drinks. They included the following:

Classic Coke, New Coke, caffeine-free Coke, diet Coke, caffeine-free diet Coke, Cherry Coke, TAB, caffeine-free TAB, Sprite, diet-Sprite, Fresca,

EXHIBIT 1 ***(concluded)***

	1984	*1983*
Liabilities and Shareholders Equity		
Current liabilities		
Notes payable (including current installments on long-term debt and capital lease obligations)	**$ 284,280**	$ 276,062
Accounts payable	**505,843**	406,339
United States and foreign income taxes	**114,372**	80,329
Other accrued taxes	**64,338**	66,144
Other current liabilities	**656,499**	521,704
	1,625,332	1,350,578
Long-term debt	**541,076**	668,294
Deferred income taxes	**621,300**	387,000
Capital lease obligations	**145,218**	147,519
Other liabilities and deferred credits	**163,932**	145,187
Shareholders' equity		
Capital stock par value 5¢ per share authorized 135,000,000 shares issued 1984–95,164,331 shares; 1983–94,986,557 shares	**$ 4,758**	$ 4,749
Capital in excess of par value	**251,915**	245,030
Retained earnings	**1,678,912**	1,622,550
Cumulative translation adjustment	**(49,426)**	(40,976)
Less cost of repurchased shares 1984–1,256,768; 1983–1,425,915	**(32,783)**	(37,195)
	1,853,376	1,794,158
Total liabilities and shareholders' equity	**$4,950,234**	$4,492,736

Source: Pepsico, Inc. 1984 Annual Report, pp. 41–43.

Mr. PiBB, sugar-free Mr. PiBB, Mello-Yello, Fanta, diet-Fanta, Hi-C soft drinks, Ramblin' Root Beer, sugar-free Ramblin' Root Beer, and Santiba.

The firm's product pricing structure worked in the following manner. Coca-Cola USA, which was a division of The Coca-Cola Company, manufacturered the beverage syrups and concentrates. They were sold by Coca-Cola USA to bottlers at an established price. The bottlers, in turn, charged a wholesale price to the retailers in their territories, who then sold at a retail price to the ultimate consumers. In recent years, Coke has increased its price discounting in order to increase its market share in the food store segment.

Coca-Cola had always emphasized a strong role for advertising to sell its soft drinks. In its various advertising campaigns in recent years, Coca-Cola utilized such major themes as "Things go better with Coke", "Coke is it," "The one you grow up with," and others to sell its products. Its ad campaigns seemed to be in line with the tempo of life for the period. Before an advertising campaign was approved, months of work were spent on thorough market research. The campaign was

EXHIBIT 2

A. Diet Soft Drink Consumption—Market Share (percent)

	1980	*1981*	*1982*	*1983*	*1984*
Coca-Cola	28.5%	28.8%	30.2%	40.9%	43.5%
PepsiCo	23.7	24.3	23.2	22.0	21.4
Seven-Up	8.5	8.4	8.7	8.0	7.6
Dr. Pepper	9.2	11.7	10.8	7.2	6.0
Royal Crown Cola	5.4	4.4	3.9	2.6	2.8
R. J. Reynolds	3.1	3.6	3.2	3.2	2.3
Sugar Free A & W	2.4	2.4	2.4	2.0	1.5
Dad's	0.9	0.8	0.8	0.6	0.5
Others	18.2	17.6	17.5	15.0	14.3
Percentage of total market	12.8	13.8	14.6	17.3	19.2

B. Caffeine-Free Consumption—Market Share (percent)

	1983	*1984*
PepsiCo	43.8%	40.5%
Coca-Cola	20.5	28.6
Dr. Pepper	5.5	4.9
Seven-Up	7.7	6.2
Royal Crown Cola	19.8	14.8
Others	2.7	5.0
Percentage of total market	5.6	5.9

Source: Adapted from *Beverage Industry*, March 1985, p. 68.

then pretested in one or several target markets and, if the results proved favorable, a final approval was given for it to be undertaken on a full scale effort.

To increase consumer awareness, Coke refined its popular "Coke is it" general advertising campaign in 1984. In its place, it introduced a number of commercials targeted at specific consumer groups. Different commercials were aimed at the young and the old and showed Coke as "the one you grow up with." Music video commercials were aimed at the young and comedian/actor Bill Cosby was used to emphasize the fact that coke was not as sweet as its competitors' products. This campaign was successful since it increased unit sales and market shares in food stores, vending machines, and all other segments. One 1986 advertisement featured William Perry, the huge football star of the Superbowl Champion Chicago Bears, drinking a whole case of the New Coke.

In April of 1985, the company announced the reformulation of the world's best-selling soft drink, Coke. It was a sweeter cola drink, hopefully more appealing to the teen market. Coke had spent four years doing market research before introducing the newly formulated Coke. Taste tests all pointed to New Coke as being more desirable. Once the new Coke was introduced, however, the company soon discovered just how loyal the old Coke customers were. The New Coke was losing ground to old Coke and more importantly to Pepsi. After the new Coke had been on the market for only two months, Coca-Cola president Donald Keough announced that old Coke would be reintroduced as Coca-Cola Classic, but the new Coke would remain Coca-Cola.

The blunder of reformulating Coke had caused several problems. Bottlers had to deal with double inventory and increased production scheduling problems. Coke also faced the problem of limited shelf space from retailers. Many of the retailers did not have space for all of Coke's different products. Fast food restaurants, which provided a large percentage of Coke's income, likewise lacked enough room for all of Coke's products. As a result, restaurant owners and retailers let consumer preferences decide what to carry. Still, the market share for Coke products increased since the new Coke and Coca-Cola Classic provided consumers with more choices.

The company's fountain sales continued to grow strongly in the 1980s. Overall, fountain sales represented 33 percent of total U.S. volume. The firm's aggressive marketing of Sprite resulted in McDonald's authorizing its use in all of its 6,500 restaurants. In 1985, Coca-Cola USA managed to obtain the Baskin-Robbins contract to supply Ramblin' Root Beer for its root beer floats. Baskin-Robbins, with over 3,000 stores in the U.S. and 17 foreign countries, represented over 1 million gallons of soft drink sales annually. Under this agreement, Coke, diet Coke, Sprite, and Ramblin' Root Beer would all be available to Baskin-Robbins' customers.

Manufacturing Operations

Coca-Cola USA manufacturered the beverage syrups and concentrates which were sold to more than 1,500 bottlers in over 155 countries. These bottlers were generally independent businesses who invested their own capital to purchase the necessary land, buildings, machinery and equipment, trucks, bottles, and cases. These bottlers packaged, distributed, and marketed the products throughout their respective territories. In addition to syrups and concentrates, Coca-Cola USA provided management guidance in such areas as quality control, marketing, advertising, engineering, financing, and personnel to help bottlers maintain product quality and be profitable.

Soft drink syrups and concentrates were manufacturered by the company and sold to bottlers and fountain wholesalers. The syrups were a mixture of sweeteners, water, and flavoring concentrate. Bottlers or canning operators combined the syrups with carbonated water, packaged the soft drinks in cans, bottles, and plastic containers, and then sold them to retailers. Fountain retailers purchased the syrups from fountain wholesalers and sold the product in cups and glasses. Major sweeteners that Coca-Cola used included sugar, high fructose corn syrup (HFCS-55), saccharin, and aspartame.

The company's operations were broken down into geographical subdivisions, which were each headed up by an area manager. To ensure smooth operations, the company had developed a strong and committed bottling network. In 1984, Coca-Cola sold 68 percent of its soft drink syrup and concentrate to approximately 500 U.S. bottlers. The remaining 32 percent was sold to approximately 4,000 fountain wholesalers, who sold the product to restaurants. The company continued to use multiple sweeteners in its products. It had an agreement from G. D. Searle & Co. to supply aspartame for its diet/low caloric drinks.

In 1979, Coca-Cola initiated a program to strengthen its bottling network which had high turnover. Company projections estimated that about 50 percent of its franchise ownerships would change hands during a five-year period. The company devoted a great deal of time and money to facilitate transfers or financial restructures of its bottlers. The company invested over $100 million in 1983 alone to strengthen its bottling operations to support the company's ambitious future growth goals.

Finance/Accounting

The consolidated statement of income for the Coca-Cola Company is shown in Exhibit 3 for 1982 through 1984. Its net operating revenues for 1984 were $7,363,993,000 and its net income after taxes was $628,818,000. Historically, its net operating revenues had increased from $2,425 billion in 1974 to over $7 billion in 1984. Furthermore, its net income increased from $204 million to over $600 million during that same period.

The Coca-Cola Company had recently deemphasized stock financing in favor of long-term debt. For example, in 1984 alone, the company bought back over $6 million shares of common stock, which resulted in higher earnings per share. In turn, the company started utilizing more low cost debt to finance its investment programs. In total, the company more than doubled its total debt in 1984 alone. The firm's consolidated balance sheets (including its majority owned subsidiaries) are shown in Exhibit 4.

EXHIBIT 3

THE COCA-COLA COMPANY
Consolidated Statement of Income
(in thousands except per share data)

	Year Ended December 31		
	1984	*1983*	*1982*
Net operating revenues	$7,363,993	$6,828,992	$6,021,135
Costs and services	3,992,923	3,772,741	3,310,847
Gross profit	3,371,070	3,056,251	2,710,288
Selling, administrative and general expenses	2,313,562	2,063,626	1,830,527
Operating income	1,057,508	992,625	879,761
Interest income	128,837	82,912	106,172
Interest expense	123,750	72,667	74,560
Other income (deductions) –net	5,438	(2,528)	6,679
Income from continuing operations before income taxes	1,068,033	1,000,332	918,052
Income taxes	439,215	442,072	415,076
Income from continuing operations	628,818	558,260	502,976
Income from discontinued operations (net of applicable income taxes of $414 in 1983 and $4,683 in 1982)	—	527	9,256
Net income	$ 628,818	$ 558,787	$ 512,232
Per share:			
Continuing operations	$4.76	$4.10	$3.88
Discontinued operations	—	—	.07
Net income	$4.76	$4.10	$3.95
Average shares outstanding	132,210	136,222	129,793

Source: The Coca-Cola Company, Annual Report 1984.

In the last five years, sales have exhibited a 10.7 percent growth rate, while net income has reflected a 12.4 percent growth rate. In 1984, selling, general, and administrative expenses totaled over $2 billion. Of this amount, approximately $5 million in salaries were paid to officers. The highest salaries were paid to Roberto C. Goizueta, the chief executive officer and chairman of the board, and Donald R. Keough, president and chief operating officer. These two officers earned approximately $1.7 million and $1.2 million in salaries, respectively.

EXHIBIT 4

THE COCA-COLA COMPANY
Consolidated Balance Sheet
(in thousands except per share data)

	Year Ended December 31	
	1984	*1983*
Assets		
Current assets		
Cash	$ 307,564	$ 319,385
Marketable securities, at cost (approximate market)	474,575	292,084
Trade accounts receivable, less allowance of $20,670 in 1984 and $20,169 in 1983	872,332	779,729
Inventories and unamortized costs	740,063	744,107
Prepaid expenses and other assets	241,326	195,009
Total current assets	2,635,860	2,330,314
Investments, film costs and other assets		
Investments (principally investments in affiliates)	334,220	241,780
Unamortized film costs	341,662	252,612
Long-term receivables and other assets	408,324	240,880
	1,084,206	735,272
Property, plant and equipment		
Land	130,883	128,642
Buildings and improvements	645,150	618,586
Machinery and equipment	1,518,264	1,412,697
Containers	337,993	341,597
	2,632,290	2,501,522
Less allowance for depreciation	1,009,715	940,716
	1,622,575	1,560,806
Goodwill and other intangible assets	615,428	601,430
Total assets	$5,958,069	$5,227,822

Innovation Research and Development

To maintain its number one position, Coke constantly introduced new products. In recent years this included New Coke, Cherry Coke, diet Coke, caffeine-free diet Coke, caffeine-free TAB, and others. As Brian Dyson, Coca-Cola's USA president, said to assembled bottlers, "If there's a better product we'll make it . . . if there's a better way we'll

EXHIBIT 4 ***(concluded)***

	Year Ended December 31	
	1984	1983
Liabilities and Shareholders Equity		
Current		
Loans and notes payable	$ 502,216	$ 85,913
Current maturities of long-term debt	120,300	20,783
Accounts payable and accrued expenses	1,020,807	910,951
Participations and other entertainment obligations	192,537	154,213
Accrued taxes—including income taxes	186,942	219,240
Total current liabilities	2,022,802	1,391,100
Participation and other entertainment obligations	175,234	226,129
Long-term debt	740,001	513,202
Deferred income taxes	241,966	176,635
Shareholders' equity		
Common stock, no par value— Authorized: 180,000,000 shares in 1984 and 1983; Issued: 137,263,936 shares in 1984 and 136,653,676 shares in 1983	69,009	68,704
Capital Surplus	532,186	500,031
Reinvested earnings	2,758,895	2,494,215
Foreign currency translation adjustment	(234,811)	(130,640)
Total shareholders' equity	3,125,279	2,932,310
Less treasury stock, at cost (6,438,873 shares in 1984; 300,588 shares in 1983)	347,213	11,554
	2,778,066	2,920,756
Total liabilities and shareholders' equity	$5,958,069	$5,227,822

Source: The Coca-Cola Company, Annual Report 1984.

find it."[1] In addition to new product development, the company also tried to improve the taste of existing products, like TAB, by using a blend of Saccharin and Aspartame to sweeten them.

Coke had recently introduced many new drinks. It had come out with new diet-Fanta flavors such as orange, ginger ale, strawberry, grape, root beer, and cherry. All its Fanta products were caffeine free.

[1] Anonymous. "Coke Foresees New Products, Innovation," *Beverage Industry,* July 1984, p. 1.

Its new introduction, Cherry Coke, might result in the emergence of a new soft drink segment. Coke emphasized that its Cherry Coke was not aimed at the Dr. Pepper market and that the product had its own light, smooth, and satisfying taste with a slight taste of cherry. Rather, this product was targeted at consumers in the 12 to 29 age group. Other introductions included new Minute Maid Orange soda, which contained 10 percent fruit juice, and a reformulation of Fresca by adding 1 percent grapefuit juice. These drinks were targeted at the growing health conscious and juice drinking segments. Fresca was being targeted at the over 25 age group, and was being positioned as an alternative to other soft drinks and wine coolers.

Coca-Cola had developed a number of new distributing, vending, and packaging systems over the years. For example, in 1983, the company developed a compact, integrated, and self-contained beverage dispenser (BTS 150) which utilized patented syrup packages. This dispenser was designed for the large untapped office market. During 1985, it was working on the final stages of a futuristic computerized vending machine, which featured a video display screen, voice simulator, and coupon dispenser. When completed, this machine would offer a wide range of Coca-Cola soft drinks for varying container sizes and prices.

Coke always had stressed consumer convenience and had continuously introduced new ways of packaging its product. Examples would include the two-liter bottles, six packs in plastic bottles, among others. In 1985, Coke was test marketing a 12-ounce plastic can, which was made up of uncoated plastic (PET) and had an aluminum end.

Human Resources Personnel

Overall, The Coca-Cola Company and its subsidiaries employed more than 40,500 people. Of this, 18,200 persons worked within the United States. The company contributed to various pension plans covering the majority of its employees in the United States, and certain foreign employees. Pension expenses incurred in 1984 for its present and retired employees were estimated to be about $36 million. The company also provided health care plans and life insurance benefits to most of its U.S. employees. It even provided health care benefits to most domestic employees who had retired after five or more years of service.

The company introduced a new and more attractive thrift plan for its employees in 1984. SODA, which stood for "Savings On Deferred Accounts," allowed employees to contribute up to 10 percent of their salaries while the company matched the first 3 percent of their salaries. Internal Revenue Service rulings permitted employees to contribute pre-tax dollars and this money could accumulate tax-free until the employee reached 59.5 years. Furthermore, employees could withdraw money from the plan at any time without penalty. They just had to declare the withdrawn money in the present year as additional income.

Management

The Coca-Cola Company was headed by Roberto Goizueta, who was both the chairman of the board and chief executive officer. Directly under him was Donald Keough, president and chief operating officer. These two top management officials had established (1) growth in annual earnings per share and (2) increased return on equity as the company's two main goals. The firm's various aggressive financial policies helped to support these goals by letting it exploit high return opportunities.

Under Goizueta's leadership, Coca-Cola's management had followed an aggressive pricing policy combined with new product development to win back market share. It found that this new approach was necessary to respond to changing market conditions and increased competition. The company had changed from being a sleeping giant to an aggressive risk taker.

Goizueta established a guideline that each business segment must satisfy the 20 percent corporate rate of return on investment. In accord with this guideline, the company sold its Wine Spectrum division which could not achieve this ROI level. According to Sergio Zyman, senior vice president of marketing, Coke had experienced a cultural revolution since Goizueta took over as chairman. As Zyman noted, "Before, if you were aggressive, you were out" while today "if you're not aggressive, you're out."[2]

Coca-Cola management began taking a much tougher stance and had started to face competition in a head-on manner. Coca-Cola, which had never put its famous trademark on any other product, used it for the first time on its new product, diet Coke. Goizueta said this was done because "We didn't have the Coca-Cola trademark on the fastest growing segment [diet-drink market] of the soft drink business."[3] Diet Coke benefited from this brand identification, which made it not only the largest selling diet soft drink, but also the third largest selling soft drink product.

---

[2] Thomas E. Ricks, "Coca-Cola's Tough New Ads Take Aim at the Competition," *The Wall Street Journal,* July 26, 1984, p. 29.

[3] Eric Morgenthaler, "Diet Coke Is a Big Success in Early Going, Spurring a Gush of Optimism at Coca-Cola," *The Wall Street Journal,* December 22, 1982, pp. 17.

International Operations

In its international operations, Coca-Cola Company's key objective was growth. To attract consumers to drink more of its products, Coke was making its products more readily available and increasing the product variety. The particular types of drinks that the company was targeting for international sales were low-calorie (in some developed countries such as Japan), lemon lime, and others.

To increase consumption internationally, Coca-Cola was trying to increase use of its products through vending machines and fountain outlets. The company had also increased the popularity of its products by offering larger package sizes, emphasizing their convenience and economy. The large amount of capital required by bottlers had prevented vending machines from becoming a major factor in penetrating international markets. Japan was one exception where vending machine sales were a large percentage, some 44 percent, of total company sales. Equipment investment was also a major factor in developing more fountain sales. Recent investments in equipment combined with effective merchandising and advertising had led to substantial gains in this area.

One key factor that contributed to international growth was a strong bottler network. In 1984, the company spent $100 million reconstructing its bottler system. Bottling facilities in Japan and Australia were sold to local operators while bottling facilities in South England, which included London, were purchased. The company changed the management at these facilities and participated in ownership changes at other facilities. These changes were made to ensure commitment to its goals for international growth.

In the low calorie segment, diet Coke had the most growth potential. Diet Coke's sales averaged 8 percent of Coca-Cola sales in international markets. Particular markets where diet Coke has been popular included Ireland, Australia, South Africa, and Japan. In these markets, diet Coke sales were greater in volume than those of the primary brand of the company's largest competitor. In Japan, diet Coke captured 68 percent of the low calorie carbonated soft drink segment.

Sprite was Coca-Cola's entry in the lemon-lime segment. The company had started marketing this product aggressively, focusing on Argentina, the Philippines, and Mexico. Mexico was the company's second largest market by volume and through this aggressive marketing the company was able to increase Sprite sales volumes there by 71 percent.

Coca-Cola sales were approximately 69 percent of the Company's international volume. Coca-Cola was first made available in the Soviet Union in 1985, reaching a potential market of 275 million people.

Sudan, Congo, and the German Democratic Republic were other possibilities for new markets.

THE SOFT DRINK INDUSTRY

The commercial sale of soda water first began in the United States in about 1806 by Benjamin Silliman. Initially, carbonated drinks were considered to have medicinal values. The industry made great progress with the introduction of the cork bottle cap which enabled carbonated soda to remain inside the bottle. Later, the painter's foot operated machine allowed syruping, filling, and capping to be done simultaneously.

More recently, the soft drink industry had become a highly competitive one. Major competitors included The Coca-Cola Company, Pepsi Cola Company, 7-Up, Dr. Pepper Company, and Royal Crown Cola. Competitors in the industry included a wide variety of international, national, regional, and private label producers.

The soft drink industry was influenced by the general economic outlook. Domestic sales increased as the U.S. economy experienced a growing economy in 1984 and 1985. Similarly, sales remained flat during the 1981-83 recession. Soft drink sales were clearly related to per capita income. Still, the per capita consumption of soft drinks of 19.1 gallons in 1964 increased to 41.5 gallons in 1983 as shown in Exhibit 5. Soft drink industry sales were also subjected to seasonal fluctuations due to weather conditions, with higher sales coming in the warmer, summer months and lower sales during colder, winter months.

The U.S. population had started to become very health conscious. As this trend continued, combined with the aging of the American population, the consumption of beer, wine, and spirits decreased, while the consumption of soft drinks increased. This trend had been further accelerated by the raising of legal drinking ages in several states and the growing public sentiment against drunken driving.

Advertising played a major role in the soft drink industry. Soft drink manufacturers spent $367,300,000 collectively on advertising in 1984. Top media expenditures for regular soft drinks of major brands are shown in Exhibit 6. The selection of which media to use depended on a number of factors, including the product, its popularity, the age group it was being targeted at, and whether it was a new or old product, among others. The amount spent on television promotions had increased in 1984 over the prior year. in 1984, spot advertisements increased 9 percent for regular drinks and 5 percent for diet drinks, whereas network advertisements increased 18.7 percent for regular

EXHIBIT 5 U.S. Liquid Consumption Trends (gallons per capita)

	1964	*1965*	*1966*	*1967*	*1968*	*1969*	*1970*	*1971*	*1972*	*1973*	*1974*	*1975*	*1976*	*1977*	*1978*	*1979*	*1980*	*1981*	*1982*	*1983*	*1984E*
Soft drinks	19.1	20.3	22.3	23.5	24.8	25.9	27.0	28.6	30.1	31.5	31.4	31.0	33.7	35.9	37.1	38.1	38.8	39.5	40.1	41.5	43.2
Coffee*	38.8	37.8	37.4	37.0	37.0	36.2	35.7	35.3	35.2	35.1	33.8	33.0	29.4	28.0	27.0	29.2	28.7	28.5	27.8	27.0	27.3
Beer	15.9	15.9	16.5	16.8	17.3	17.8	18.5	19.2	19.7	20.5	21.3	21.6	21.8	22.5	23.1	23.8	24.5	24.7	24.4	24.3	24.0
Milk†	25.9	26.0	25.9	25.3	25.6	25.3	23.1	23.0	23.1	22.7	22.0	22.1	21.9	21.5	21.3	21.0	20.7	20.4	20.0	20.9	21.1
Juices	3.5	3.8	4.0	4.8	4.7	4.8	5.2	5.7	6.0	5.2	6.1	6.8	6.8	6.8	6.5	6.7	6.9	6.7	6.8	7.7	6.1
Tea*	6.3	6.3	6.3	6.4	6.6	6.6	6.5	6.7	6.8	7.2	7.3	7.3	7.4	7.7	7.7	7.6	7.3	7.5	7.5	7.2	7.3
Powdered drinks	—	—	—	—	—	—	—	—	—	—	—	4.8	5.5	5.9	6.1	6.0	6.0	6.0	6.0	6.5	6.3
Wine	1.0	1.0	1.0	1.0	1.1	1.2	1.3	1.5	1.6	1.7	1.7	1.7	1.7	1.8	2.1	2.2	2.3	2.3	2.3	2.4	2.5
Bottled water	—	—	—	—	—	—	—	1.1	—	—	—	1.2	1.2	1.3	1.4	1.5	1.6	1.9	2.2	2.7	3.0
Distilled spirits	1.4	1.5	1.6	1.6	1.7	1.8	1.8	1.9	1.9	1.9	2.0	2.0	2.0	2.0	2.0	2.0	2.0	2.0	1.9	1.8	1.8
Subtotal	111.9	112.6	115.0	116.4	118.8	119.6	119.1	123.0	124.4	125.8	125.6	131.5	131.4	133.4	134.3	138.1	138.8	139.5	139.0	142.0	144.6
Inputed water consumptions‡	70.6	69.9	67.5	66.1	63.7	62.9	63.4	59.5	58.1	56.7	56.9	51.0	51.1	49.1	48.2	44.4	43.7	43.0	43.5	40.5	37.9
Total	182.5	182.5	182.5	182.5	182.5	182.5	182.5	182.5	182.5	182.5	182.5	182.5	182.5	182.5	182.5	182.5	182.5	182.5	182.5	182.5	182.5

* Coffee and Tea data are based on a three-year moving average to counterbalance swings, hereby portraying consumption more realistically. Tea numbers have been restated to reflect this.

‡ Includes all others.

† Certain milk figures have been changed based on revisions to USDA data.

Sources: USDA,DSI,MABO,ABWA, Laidlaw Ansbacher Research Estimates 1985; and "Soft Drinks, Juices, Bottled Water Pace Gains," *Beverage Industry*, February, 1985, p. 38. Copyright John C. Maxwell, *Beverage Industry*, February, 1985.

EXHIBIT 6 Top Media Expenditures of Regular Soft Drink Brands (in thousands)

Product	*4-Media Total*	*Magazines*	*Network Television*	*Spot Television*	*Outdoor*
Coca-Cola	$48,298.3	$252.9	$24,764.9	$20,647.4	$2,633.1
Pepsi-Cola	33,013.5	—	9,028.6	22,845.1	1,139.8
Sprite	23,161.7	72.4	15,399.6	7,669.5	20.0
7UP	22,759.8	95.0	13,317.0	8,926.1	431.8
Canada Dry	9,004.9	—	4,534.9	4,510.0	—
Dr. Pepper	8,321.7	—	2,433.5	5,685.8	202.4
Mountain Dew	7,772.9	—	558.3	7,191.7	22.9
Sunkist	4,438.1	—	138.9	4,292.9	6.3
A&W	4,348.7	—	2,273.3	2,075.4	—
Royal Crown	4,103.0	—	—	4,099.9	3.1

Source: Leading National Advertisers Broadcast Advertiser's Report. Copyright *Beverage Industry*, July 1985.

drinks and 125.5 percent for diet drinks. Radio spot commercials were highly effective at targeting certain audiences such as teenagers and younger people who were devoted radio music listeners. The use of billboard advertising, on the other hand, had been decreasing in recent years.

Segmentation

The soft drink industry was segmented into six categories on the basis of drink types. The six categories included cola drinks, lemon lime drinks, pepper drinks, orange drinks, root beer drinks, and all other soft drinks. Among these groups, the cola category had always been the dominant segment. Its staggering 62.6 percent market share in 1981 increased to 63.2 percent in 1984. The market shares for cola and lemon lime had remained fairly steady, whereas the pepper type drinks had increased. The orange and root beer categories, however, had decreased from 1971 to 1984.

There were certain newly emerging segments. Squirt Company introduced Diet-Squirt Plus in 1985, which became the first company to use 100 percent NutraSweet in its diet drinks. This use was considered to be partially responsible for the tremendous increase in consumption of diet drinks. Diet-Squirt Plus contained 50 percent of the recommended daily dosage of Vitamin C and 10 percent of the daily dosage of five important B complex vitamins. In coming years, this new drink could possibly establish a new vitamin-fortified soft drink segment. Other emerging segments may be the diet chocolate soda segment, the cherry coke segment, and the carbonated juice segment.

A more basic way of segmenting the soft drink industry was into full calorie regular drinks and diet drinks. Back in 1980, diet drinks constituted only 12.8 percent of the market. Their sales rose, however, to 17.3 percent in 1983 and to 19.2 percent of the market by 1984. Their sales were further stimulated in 1984 by the introduction of NutraSweet and the increase in sales of diet Coke. Thus, diet drinks were the newest and fastest growing segment in the soft drink industry.

Threats

One potential problem facing the soft drink industry was the Federal Trade Commission's complaint that the industry's exclusive territorial franchise agreements with their bottlers unnecessarily restricted competition. This complaint was still under review in mid 1985.

On another issue, there had been constant concern about whether the artificial sweeteners used in soft drinks caused cancer. This concern had been directed especially toward saccharin. The other widely used noncaloric sweetener, aspartame, had an alleged inability to remain stable at high temperatures. This problem was causing some health concerns even though it received Food and Drug Administration approval in 1981.

The entrance of The Procter & Gamble Co. (P&G) as a small, yet potentially powerful competitor in the soft-drink industry was still another threat to Coke. P&G, with 1984 sales of approximately $13 billion, acquired Orange Crush for $55 million. P&G was also trying to buy the Lexington-based Coca-Cola Bottling Mideast Inc. to learn more about how to bottle and distribute soft drinks. Coca-Cola had filed a restraining order to try to prevent this acquisition by its leading competitor. According to Brian Dyson, president of Coca-Cola USA, "The record indicates that they [P&G] have not entered the soft-drink industry in a casual way."[4] Senior Vice President Allen McCusker was even more vocal about the subject and said, "They [P&G] could be our biggest competitor."[5] There were speculations that since P&G did not possess a cola product, it might try to acquire Royal Crown Cola. This would provide them with a strong, well-established bottler network. Another possibility was that P&G might sell its product directly to the supermarkets without even going through bottlers. If successful, this change could have a major impact on the soft drink industry.

The growing sense of awareness against littering posed another

---

[4] "Is P&G Thirsty for Some of Coke's Know-How?" *Business Week,* May 30, 1983, p. 62.

[5] Ibid.

potential threat to Coke and the industry. Several states had passed antilitter laws. Various studies had found that disposable packages constituted a major portion of the litter. As a result, some states had passed, or were considering, laws against nonreturnable containers.

A final threat was the aging of the American population. The American population was growing older largely due to the fact that the population birth rate was slowing down and medical facilities were improving for Americans of all ages. These trends had resulted in a reduction of the number of youths who were the major consumers of regular soft drink products.

Substitutes

Soft drinks compete for the consumer dollar spent on all beverages. Major drinks and beverages consumed by the American population were soft drinks, water, coffee, beer, milk, fruit juice, tea, wine, distilled spirits, and others. Soft drinks had experienced tremendous growth from a paltry 9.4 percent in 1960 to 25.5 percent of the beverage consumption in 1984. The overall consumption of beverages had increased from 35 billion gallons in 1960 to 45 billion gallons in 1984. The beverage industry expected sales of beverages such as light beer, wine coolers, speciality coffees and teas, decaffeinated and flavored teas, rum, diet and caffeine-free soft drinks, and fruit juices to increase tremendously. The products that were increasing in popularity were the ones that catered to the largely health conscious public. Out of the 483 million gallons of increased consumption of soft drinks, 465 million gallons were for diet drinks. Alcoholic beverage sales had declined largely due to increased public opinion against alcohol abuse, drunk driving, and increased drinking age laws.

Suppliers

A major material cost incurred by the soft drink industry was the sweetener. The major types of sweeteners used were sugar, high fructose corn syrup (HFCS-55), saccharin, and aspartame. The increased consciousness among many consumers to be slim had resulted in the growing popularity of diet drinks utilizing noncaloric sweeteners. The two major noncaloric sweeteners being used were saccharin and aspartame. Aspartame was a low caloric sweetening agent produced in the United States and many foreign countries. Sales of NutraSweet, the trade name for aspartame, had risen from $12 million in 1981 to $110 million in the first half of 1983 alone. Even though aspartame has received FDA approval, there were certain unanswered questions regarding its safety.

FDA proposed a ban against saccharin in 1977, but a Congressional moratorium was applied to give further time for testing and researching whether the product was carcinogenic or not. The moratorium was again extended in April of 1985. Thus far, this proposed ban had not seemed to have had an effect on the sales of saccharin.

Sugar was another raw material utilized in manufacturing soft drinks. It was purchased from numerous domestic and international sources and was subject to vast price fluctuations. A large number of major soft drink manufacturers, like the Coca-Cola Company, had been authorized to utilize 100 percent high fructose corn syrup (HFCS-55) in their products.

Sugar was the major sweetener used by the soft drink industry to sweeten their products. Quotas on sugar imports resulted in artificially high prices for domestic sugar. This quota had caused soft drink manufacturers to switch from sugar to high fructose corn syrup (HFCS-55). With the increase in the consumption of diet drinks, it had resulted in the increased use of noncaloric sweeteners. By 1985, there were some other noncaloric sweeteners, such Acesulfame K and left-handed sugars, which were awaiting FDA approval.

Another major material cost of the soft drink industry was packaging. The major types of materials used in packaging soft drinks were plastic containers, aluminum cans, glass bottles, and aseptic paper packages. Greatest growth had been experienced by plastic containers, aluminum cans, and aseptic paper packages whereas glass containers application had steadily decreased.

Buyers

In the soft drink industry, the buyers of the syrups and concentrates were bottlers and fountain wholesalers. Bottlers were the ones who subsequently manufactured the finished product, packaged it, and then sold it to retailers. Still, retailers were the primary customers of the bottlers and wholesalers, not the consumers. To ensure successful sales, the bottlers and wholesalers had to cultivate a positive relationship with their retailers.

Bottlers had broadened the use of various retail outlets to sell their soft drinks in recent years. In 1974, 53 percent of their soft drinks were sold through food stores, whereas in 1984 they sold 46.2 percent. This shift was a result of the increased competition in the soft drink industry, especially between Coke and Pepsi, which resulted in numerous products being introduced in the markets. This had further resulted in reduced shelf space being available in the supermarkets and food stores to any one soft drink manufacturer. All the bottlers were fighting to increase their sales by various methods, such as increased price discounting, promotions, and maintaining full shelves of their product to consumers in stores. To increase product availability, bottlers had resorted to increased distribution through other retail outlets besides food stores. Other retail outlets included convenience stores and general merchandising stores, as well as vending machines.

Expressing market share as a percentage of soft drink sales through retail establishments, convenience stores increased their market share from 17.4 percent in 1974 to 19.6 percent in 1984, whereas food stores decreased their market share from 53 percent in 1974 to 42.6 percent in 1984. An increasingly important success factor was to get the product to the consumers, wherever they wanted it. As the number of two-wage-earner families increased, it resulted in more frequent shopping for just a few items. This trend had resulted in increased soft drink sales through convenience stores and vending machines, where a customer could make a purchase very quickly.

Vending sales clearly were on the increase. Furthermore, this was a very profitable segment since it did not include any promotional price discounting. In part, due to the new attractive machines that changed dollar bills, had video displays and voice simulators, the sales through vending machines increased 20-25 percent. The soft drink manufacturers had even developed mini vending machines that dispensed three products for the largely untapped office market.

NEW PRODUCTS/MARKET OPPORTUNITIES

Coca-Cola had introduced new products such as diet drinks, caffeine-free drinks, and juice soda drinks aimed at the health and diet conscious market. In anticipation of this new market, Coke had introduced diet Coke, diet-Sprite, diet-Fanta, caffeine-free Coca-Cola, caffeine-free diet Coke, caffeine-free TAB, sugar-free Mr. PiBB, sugar-free Ramblin' Root Beer, Minute Maid Orange Soda, and new improved Fresca.

Other product opportunities that Coca-Cola could take advantage of were the multivitamin juices and multivitamin soda segments. This might follow the lead of the successful introduction of Diet-Squirt Plus. Coke had already started to take advantage of the growing carbonated juice drink market by introducing Minute Maid Orange Soda and new improved Fresca. The juice market in schools and health care institutions might prove to be a good opportunity for market development. This market could be served through mini juice-vending machines which had recently been developed. In addition, these mini vending machines could be used to serve the growing office market.

Another product opportunity might be apple flavored sodas, which were gaining tremendous popularity in Australia, Ireland, and most of Europe.

Another fast growing segment is the diet-Chocolate Fudge Soda. If this segment captured a portion of the soft drink market, it may be an area in which Coke could introduce a product.

The international markets might provide tremendous opportunities for increasing soft drink sales. Coca-Cola products had been doing extremely well internationally. Their international soft drink sales volume increased by 4 percent alone in 1984. To further increase international sales, the company was focusing on product availability and product variety. In 1985, Coca-Cola Company products will be available for the first time in Russia, Sudan, Congo, and the German Democratic Republic.

Other important domestic segments might be the Black and Hispanic markets. The Black population in the United States represented $140 billion in purchasing power and the U.S. Hispanics represent $50–$70 billion in purchasing power. Some marketing efforts in the 1980s were not spending all of their advertising dollars on campaigns designed to reach certain segments of the population in the most cost effective manner. Television advertising utilizing certain sitcoms, sport events, and other shows to reach certain targeted audiences had increased. Outdoor advertising was being utilized to reach a particular segment of the population without other segments even being aware of it. This outdoor advertising was being increasingly used by beverage marketers to reach the Black and Hispanic markets.

In considering any product/market opportunity, The Coca-Cola Company should examine the existing soft drink firms, their product offerings, and market shares. Exhibit 7 does just this by providing market

EXHIBIT 7 Consumption of Soft Drinks by Company

	Market Share				
	1980	*1981*	*1982*	*1983*	*1984*
Coca-Cola Co.					
Coca-Cola	24.3%	24.2%	23.9%	22.5%	21.8%
Diet Coke	—	—	0.3	3.2	5.1
Sprite	2.9	2.9	2.8	2.8	3.3
Tab	3.2	3.6	3.8	2.7	1.6
Fanta	1.7	1.5	1.3	1.1	1.6
Caffeine-Free diet Coke	—	—	—	0.5	1.0
Mello Yello	0.8	0.9	0.8	0.6	0.9
Caffeine-Free Coke	—	—	—	0.5	0.6
Diet Sprite	—	—	0.4	0.3	0.5
Mr. Pibb	0.7	0.6	0.5	0.4	0.3
Caffeine-Free Tab	—	—	—	0.2	0.2
Fresca	0.4	0.4	0.3	0.2	0.1
Others	0.4	0.4	0.4	0.4	0.4
Total	34.4	34.5	34.5	35.3	36.4

EXHIBIT 7 *(concluded)*

	Market Share				
	1980	*1981*	*1982*	*1983*	*1984*
Pepsico, Inc.					
Pepsi-Cola	17.9%	18.3%	18.1%	16.9%	17.0%
Mountain Dew	2.9	3.0	2.8	2.7	2.7
Diet Pepsi	2.6	2.9	2.9	2.4	2.9
Pepsi Free	—	—	—	1.5	1.4
Sugar Free Pepsi Free	—	—	0.3	1.0	1.0
Pepsi Light	0.4	0.5	0.5	0.4	0.2
Teem	0.3	0.2	0.2	0.2	0.1
Others	0.3	0.2	0.2	0.2	0.3
Total	24.4	25.1	25.0	25.3	25.6
Seven-Up Co.					
7Up	5.4	5.0	5.2	5.4	5.2
Diet 7Up	1.1	1.2	1.3	1.3	1.4
Like	—	—	0.3	0.4	0.3
Sugar-Free Like	—	—	—	0.1	0.1
Dixie Cola	0.2	0.1	0.1	0.1	—
Howdy Flavors	—	—	—	—	—
Total	6.7	6.3	6.9	7.3	7.0
Dr Pepper					
Dr Pepper	5.5	5.4	5.1	4.9	5.1
Sugar Free Dr Pepper	1.2	1.3	1.3	1.1	1.0
Sugar Free Pepper Free	—	—	—	0.2	0.1
Pepper Free	—	—	—	0.2	0.1
Welch's	0.5	0.5	0.5	0.5	0.4
Total	7.2	7.2	6.9	6.9	6.8
R. J. Reynolds' Canada Dry Corp.					
Ginger Ale	1.0	1.1	1.1	1.2	1.2
Club Soda/Seltzer	0.5	0.5	0.6	0.6	0.6
Tonic, Bitter Lemon	0.4	0.5	0.5	0.5	0.4
Barrelhead	0.3	0.2	0.2	0.2	0.1
Wink	0.2	0.1	0.1	—	—
Others	0.5	0.4	0.3	0.3	0.3
Total	2.9	2.8	2.8	2.8	2.6
Sunkist					
Sunkist	1.3	1.5	1.6	1.5	1.5
Diet Sunkist	—	0.1	0.3	0.3	0.2
Total	1.3	1.6	1.9	1.8	1.7

Source: Adapted from *Beverage Industry*, March 1985, pp. 17–8.

shares for each soft drink offered by the various manufacturers from 1980 through 1984. By studying these statistics and trends, hopefully, it will provide support for whatever new products Coke might introduce.

COCA-COLA'S FUTURE

The Coca-Cola Company, the original inventor of cola drinks, obviously looked forward to a bright future. It had been facing more vigorous competition within the soft drink industry as a whole in recent years. Still, it was the number one soft drink manufacturer in the world. On the other hand, the gains achieved by Pepsi-Cola in recent years were substantial. Just what Coca-Cola would do to counter this growing competitive challenge in coming years remained to be seen as 1985 came to an end.

Case 9

Campbell Soup Company*

Arthur A. Thompson
Sharon Henson
Both of the University of Alabama

In mid-1985, five years after he had been appointed president and chief executive officer of Campbell Soup Company, Gordon McGovern decided it was time to review the key strategic theme he had initiated—new product development. Shortly after he became Campbell's CEO, McGovern reorganized the company into autonomous business units to foster entrepreneurial attitudes; his ultimate objective was to transform Campbell from a conservative manufacturing company into a consumer-driven, new product-oriented company. As a result of McGovern's push, Campbell had introduced 334 new products in the past five years—more than any other company in the food processing industry.

During the 1970s Campbell's earnings had increased at an annual rate just under 9 percent—a dull performance compared to the 12 percent average growth for the food industry as a whole. With prior management's eyes fixed mainly on production aspects, gradual shifts in consumer buying habits caused Campbell's unit volume growth to flatten. McGovern's five-year campaign for renewed growth via new product introduction had produced good results so far. By year-end 1984 sales were up 31 percent—to $3.7 billion—and earnings had risen by 47 percent—to $191 million. But now it appeared that Campbell's brand managers may have become so involved in new product development that they had neglected the old stand-by products, as well as not meeting cost control and profit margin targets. Campbell's growth in operating earnings for fiscal year 1985 fell far short of McGovern's 15 percent target rate. Failure to control costs and meet earnings targets threatened to leave Campbell without the internal cash flows to fund its new-product strategy. Exhibit 1 offers a summary of Campbell Soup's recent financial performance.

---

* Prepared by graduate researcher, Sharon Henson, under the supervision of Professor Arthur A. Thompson, The University of Alabama.

EXHIBIT 1 Financial Summary, Campbell Soup Company, 1979–1985 (in thousands of dollars)

	1979	*1980*	*1981*	*1982*	*1983*	*1984*	*1985*
Total sales (includes interdivisional)	n.a.	$2,566,100	$2,865,600	$2,995,800	$3,359,300	$3,744,600	$4,060,800
Net sales (excludes interdivisional)	$2,248,692	2,560,569	2,797,663	2,955,649	3,292,433	3,657,440	3,988,705
Cost of products sold	1,719,134	1,976,754	2,172,806	2,214,214	2,444,213	2,700,751	2,950,204
Marketing and sales expenses	181,229	213,703	256,726	305,700	367,053	428,062	478,341
Administrative and research expenses	94,716	102,445	93,462	136,933	135,855	169,614	194,319
Operating earnings	253,613	276,869	280,355	309,283	349,116	378,316	389,488
Interest—net	1,169	10,135	30,302	21,939	39,307	26,611	32,117
Earnings before taxes	252,444	257,532	244,367	276,863	306,005	332,402	333,724
Taxes on earnings	119,700	122,950	114,650	127,250	141,000	141,200	135,800
Net earnings, after taxes	119,817	134,582	129,717	149,613	165,005	191,202	197,824
Percent of sales	5.3%	5.3%	4.6%	5.1%	5.0%	5.2%	5.0%
Percent of stockholders' equity	13.8%	14.6%	13.2%	14.6%	15.0%	15.9%	15.0%
Per share of common stock	1.80	2.04	2.00	2.32	2.56	2.96	3.06
Dividends declared per share	.86	.93	1.02	1.05	1.09	1.14	1.22
Average shares outstanding	66,720	65,946	64,824	64,495	64,467	64,514	64,572
Salaries, wages, pensions, etc.	$ 543,984	$ 609,979	$ 680,946	$ 700,940	$ 755,073	$ 889,450	$ 950,143
Current assets	680,955	861,845	845,343	921,501	932,099	1,063,330	1,152,761
Working capital	362,187	405,628	368,246	434,627	478,899	541,515	579,490
Plant assets—gross	1,134,571	1,248,735	1,368,663	1,472,693	1,607,634	1,744,866	1,856,122
Accumulated depeciation	520,603	560,730	613,643	657,315	718,478	774,004	828,662
Plant assets purchased and acquired	159,603	155,796	155,275	175,928	178,773	201,864	222,321
Total assets	1,325,823	1,627,565	1,722,876	1,865,519	1,991,526	2,210,115	2,437,525
Long-term debt	36,298	137,879	150,587	236,160	267,465	283,034	297,146
Stockholders' equity	900,017	958,443	1,000,510	1,055,762	1,149,404	1,259,908	1,382,487
Depreciation	60,360	67,958	75,118	83,813	93,189	101,417	119,044

Source: Annual reports of Cambell Soup Company.

THE FOOD PROCESSING INDUSTRY

In the early 19th century small incomes and low urban population greatly limited the demand for packaged food. In 1859 one industry—grain mills—accounted for over three fifths of the total U.S. food processing. Several industries were in their infancy: evaporated milk, canning, candy, natural extracts, and coffee roasting. From 1860 to 1900 the industry entered a period of development and growth that made food processing the leading manufacturing industry in the United States. The driving forces behind this growth were increased urbanization, cheaper rail transport, and the advent of refrigeration and tin can manufacturing.

At the beginning of the 20th century the food processing industry was highly fragmented; the thousands of local and regional firms were too small to capture scale economies in mass production and distribution as was occurring in other industries. During the 1920s, industry consolidation via acquisition and merger began; the process was evolutionary not revolutionary and continued on into the 1960s and 1970s. Companies such as Del Monte and Kraft, whose names have since become household words, were established, as were the first two multiline food companies—General Foods and Standard Brands (later part of Nabisco Brands). With consolidation came greater production cost efficiency and national market coverages. Following World War II the bigger food companies made moves toward more product differentiation and increased emphasis on advertising. Some became multinational in scope, establishing subsidiaries in many other countries. Starting in the 1960s and continuing into the 1980s the industry went through more consolidation; this time the emphasis was on brand diversification and product line expansion. Acquisition-minded companies shopped for smaller companies with products having strong brand recognition and brand loyalty.

Then in the 1980s giants began acquiring other giants. In 1984 Nestle acquired Carnation for $3 billion. In 1985 R. J. Reynolds purchased Nabisco Brands for $4.9 billion (and then changed its corporate name to RJR Nabisco), and Philip Morris acquired General Foods Corporation for $5.7 billion—the biggest nonoil deal in U.S. industry. In 1985 the U.S. food processing industry had sales over $100 billion and combined net profits of over $4 billion. Exhibit 2 shows data for leading companies in the industry in 1985.

COMPANY BACKGROUND

Campbell Soup Company was one of the world's leading manufacturers and marketers of branded consumer food products. In 1985 the com-

EXHIBIT 2 The Top 15 Companies in the Food Processing Industry, 1985 (millions of dollars)

Company		*Sales*	*Profits*	*Assets*	*Return on Common Equity*	*Example Brands*
1. RJR Nabisco	1985	$ 16,595	$2,163	$16,930	20.3%	Nabisco, Del Monte
	1984	12,974	1,619	9,272	22.1	
2. Dart & Kraft	1985	9,942	466	5,502	17.0	Velveeta, Parkay,
	1984	9,759	456	5,285	16.5	Miracle Whip
3. Beatrice	1985	12,595	479	10,379	21.8	Swiss Miss, Wesson,
	1984	9,327	433	4,464	20.4	Tropicana
4. Kellogg	1985	2,930.1	281.1	1,726.1	48.0	Mrs. Smith's, Eggo,
	1984	2,602.4	250.5	1,667.1	27.0	Rice Krispies
5. H. J. Heinz	1985	4,047.9	266	2,473.8	22.6	Star-Kist Tuna,
	1984	3,953.8	237.5	2,343	21.0	Heinz Ketchup
6. Ralston Purina	1985	5,863.9	256.4	2,637.3	26.7	Hostess Twinkies,
	1984	4,980.1	242.7	2,004.2	23.1	Meow Mix
7. Campbell Soup	1985	3,988.7	197.8	2,437.5	15.0	Prego, Le Menu,
	1984	3,657.4	191.2	2,210.1	15.9	Vlasic pickles
8. General Mills	1985	4,285.2	(72.9)	2,662.6	(6.5)	Cheerios, Betty
	1984	5,600.8	233.4	2,858.1	19.0	Crocker
9. Sara Lee	1985	8,117	206	3,216	20.5	Popsicle, Bryan,
	1984	7,000	188	2,822	19.4	Rudy's Farm
10. CPC International	1985	4,209.9	142.0	3,016.6	10.5	Mazola, Skippy,
	1984	4,373.3	193.4	2,683.4	14.7	Hellmann's
11. Borden	1985	4,716.2	193.8	2,932.2	14.3	Wyler's, Bama,
	1984	4,568	182.1	2,767.1	13.7	Cracker Jack
12. Pillsbury	1985	4,670.6	191.8	2,778.5	17.3	Green Giant,
	1984	4,172.3	169.8	2,608.3	17.0	Häagen-Dazs
13. Archer Daniels	1985	4,738.8	163.9	2,967.1	10.8	LaRosa,
	1984	4,907	117.7	2,592.7	NA	Fleischmann's
14. Quaker Oats	1985	3,520.1	156.6	2,662.6	20.3	Gatorade, Van-
	1984	3,334.1	138.7	1,806.8	19.8	Camp's
15. Hershey Foods	1985	1,996.2	112.2	1,197.4	16.6	Delmonico, Hershey's
	1984	1,848.5	108.7	1,122.6	17.3	Chocolate
Industry composite	1985	$101,669	$4,004	$58,294	16.5%	

NA = Not available.

Source: Ranking by market value of common stock according to *Business Week*, April 18, 1986. Financial data from annual reports.

pany had approximately 44,000 employees and 80 manufacturing plants in 12 nations, with over 1,000 products on the market. Its major products were Prego spaghetti sauces, Le Menu frozen dinners, Pepperidge Farm baked goods, Mrs. Paul's frozen foods, Franco-American canned spaghettis, Vlasic pickles, and its flagship red-and-white-label canned soups.

Founded in 1869 by Joseph Campbell, a fruit merchant, and Abram Anderson, an ice box maker, the company was originally known for its jams and jellies. In 1891 it was incorporated as the Joseph Campbell Co. in Camden, New Jersey. In 1899 John T. Dorrance, a brilliant 24-year-old with a Ph. D. from MIT, developed a process for canning soup in condensed form. He was also a master salesman who came up with the idea of attaching snappy placards to the sides of New York City streetcars as a way of promoting the company's products.

From 1900 to 1954 the company was owned entirely by the Dorrance family. It was incorporated as the Campbell Soup Company in 1922. When Dorrance died in 1930 after running the company for 16 years, he left an estate of over $115 million, the third-largest up to that time. He also left a company devoted to engineering, committed to supplying value (in recessions it would rather shave margins than lower quality or raise prices), and obsessed with secrecy. John T. Dorrance, Jr., ran the company for the next 24 years (1930–54) and few, if any, important decisions were made at Campbell without his approval. In 1954 the company went public, with the Dorrance family retaining majority control. In 1985 the Dorrance family still held about 60 percent of Campbell's stock and picked the top executives of the company. In 1984 John Dorrance III became a member of the board. The more than eight decades of family dominance contributed to what some insiders described as a conservative and paternalistic company culture at Campbell.

Over the years Campbell had diversified into a number of food and food-related businesses—Swanson frozen dinners, Pepperidge Farm bakery products, Franco-American spaghetti products, Recipe pet food, fast-food restaurant chains, Godiva chocolates, and even retail garden centers. Still, about half of the company's revenues came from the sale of its original stock-in-trade: canned soup. Throughout most of its history, the company picked its top executives from among those with a production background in the soup division—most had engineering training and good track records in furthering better manufacturing efficiency. One such person, Harold A. Shaub, a 30-year veteran of the company, was named president in 1972. An industrial engineer, Shaub placed a premium on controlling production cost while maintaining acceptable product quality. There were occasions when Shaub, during unannounced inspection tours, had shut down a complete plant that didn't measure up to the strict standards he demanded.

During his tenure Shaub began to set the stage for change at Campbell, acknowledging that "The company needed changes for the changing times."[2]* He restructured the company into divisions built around major product lines. Then in 1978, realizing that Campbell's marketing skills were too weak, he hired aggressive outsiders to revitalize the company's marketing efforts. That same year Campbell purchased Vlasic Foods, Inc., the largest producer of pickles in the United States.

Also in 1978 Campbell launched Prego spaghetti sauce products, the first major new food items introduced by Campbell in 10 years. The former Campbell policy required a new product had to show a profit within a year and the pay-out on Prego was expected to be three years. But because the policy held back new product development, Shaub changed it and set a goal of introducing two additional products each year.

In 1980 Campbell broke a 111-year-old debt-free tradition, issuing $100 million in 10-year notes. Until then the company had relied primarily on internally generated funds to meet long-term capital requirements.

Because of company tradition, everyone expected Shaub's successor to come from production. Thus it came as a surprise to Gordon McGovern, president of Connecticut-based Pepperidge Farm and a marketing man, when Shaub called him into his office and said, "I'd like you to come down here and take my place."[1] When McGovern became Campbell's president and CEO on December 1, 1980, Shaub remained on the board of directors.

McGovern was at Pepperidge Farm when the company was bought by Campbell in 1961. He was in business school when Margaret Rudkin, founder of Pepperidge Farm, spoke to his class. She told how she had built her bread company from scratch in an industry dominated by giants. McGovern was impressed. He wrote to Rudkin for a job, received it in 1956, and began his climb through the ranks. When Campbell acquired Pepperidge Farm in 1961 it had sales of $40 million. When McGovern became its president in 1968 sales had reached $60 million. When he left to become president of Campbell in 1980, Pepperidge Farms' sales had climbed to $300 million. McGovern brought some of what he considered Pepperidge's success strategy with him to Campbell: experimentation, new product development, marketing savvy, and creativity.

---

* Numbers in brackets refer to references listed at the end of this case.

MANAGEMENT UNDER McGOVERN

Every Saturday morning McGovern did his family's grocery shopping, stopping to straighten Campbell's displays and inspect those of competitors, studying packaging and reading labels, and trying to learn all he could about how and what people were eating. He encouraged his managers to do the same. Several board meetings were held in the backrooms of supermarkets so that afterward directors could roam the store aisles interviewing customers about Campbell products.

McGovern's style of management was innovative to a company known as much for its stodginess as for its red and white soup can. For decades Campbell Soup operated under strict rules for decorum. Eating, smoking, or drinking coffee was not permitted in the office. Managers had to share their offices with their secretaries, and an unwritten rule required executives to keep their suitcoats on in the office. When McGovern joined Campbell he drove to work in a yellow Volkswagen that stuck out in his parking space so much that the garagemen quietly arranged to have it painted. Finding the atmosphere at headquarters stifling, he promised a change.

He began wandering through the corridors every day, mingling easily among the employees. McGovern's voluble personality and memory for names made him popular with many employees. But not everyone was impressed by McGovern's style. Some production people were suspicious of his marketing background. Others believed that his grocery trips and hobnobbing with employees were ploys calculated to win him support and a reputation. But McGovern pressed forward with several internal changes: (1) a day care center for the children of employees (complete with Campbell Kids posters on the wall), (2) a health program including workouts in a gymnasium, and (3) an unusual new benefit program which covered adoption expenses up to $1,000 and gave time off to employees who adopted children—in the same way that women were given maternity leave. He appointed the first two women vice presidents in the company's history; one of these, a former director of the Good Housekeeping Institute, was hired to identify consumers' food preferences and needs.

McGovern decentralized Campbell management to facilitate entrepreneurial risk-taking and new product development, devising a new compensation program to reward these traits. He restructured the company into some 50 autonomous units and divided the U.S. division into eight strategic profit centers: soups, beverages, pet foods, frozen foods, fresh produce, main meals, grocery, and food service. Units were encouraged to develop new products even if another unit would actually produce the products. Thus, the Prego spaghetti sauce unit—not the frozen food group—initiated frozen Mexican dinners. And although it wasn't his job, the director of market research created

"Today's Taste," a line of refrigerated entrees and side dishes. "It's like things are in constant motion," the director said. "We are overloaded, but it's fun."[3]

The new structure encouraged managers, who had to compete for corporate funding, to be more aggressive in developing promising products. According to McGovern:

> These integral units allow the company to really get its arms around chunks of the business. The managers are answerable to the bottom line—to their investments, their hiring, their products—and it's a great motivation for performance.[4]

As part of this motivation, Campbell began annually allotting around $30 million to $40 million to support new ventures, each requiring a minimum of $10 million. This strategy was intended to encourage star performers while enabling management to weed out laggards. McGovern felt that this was much easier to determine when everyone knew where the responsibilities lay—but that it was no disgrace to fail if the effort was a good one. An employee noted that McGovern was endorsing "the right to fail," adding that "it makes the atmosphere so much more positive."[4]

Every Friday McGovern held meetings to discuss new products. The fact-finding sessions were attended by financial, marketing, engineering, and sales personnel. Typical McGovern questions included: "Would you eat something like that?" "Why not?" "Have you tried the competition's product?" "Is there a consumer niche?" The marketing research director noted that in Shaub's meetings the question was "Can we make such a product cost-effectively?"[3]

Under Shaub the chain of command was inviolable, but McGovern was not hesitant about circumventing the chain when he felt it was warranted. He criticized one manager's product to another manager, expecting word to get back to the one with the problem. Although this often motivated some to prove McGovern wrong, others were unnerved by such tactics. When he became aware of this, McGovern eased up a bit.

In the past under prior CEOs, cost-cutters got promoted; now in McGovern's more creative atmosphere, the rules weren't so well defined. As one insider put it, "There's a great deal of uncertainty. No one really knows what it takes to get ahead. But that makes us all work harder."[3]

When hiring managers, McGovern, himself a college baseball player, tended to favor people with a competitive sports background. "There's teamwork and determination, but also the idea that you know how to lose and get back up again. 'Try, try, try' is what I say. I can't stress how important that is."[4]

STRATEGY

The strategic focus was on the consumer—considered to be the key to Campbell's growth and success in the 1980s. The consumer's "hot buttons" were identified as nutrition, convenience, low sodium, price, quality, and uniqueness—and managers were urged to "press those buttons." General managers were advised to take into account the consumer's perceptions, needs, and demands regarding nutrition, safety, flavor, and convenience. Key strategies were: (1) improving operating efficiency, (2) developing new products for the modern consumer, (3) updating advertising for new and established products, and (4) high quality.

When he took over, McGovern developed a five-year plan that included four financial performance objectives: a 15 percent annual increase in earnings, a 5 percent increase in volume, a 5 percent increase in sales (plus inflation), and an 18 percent return on equity by 1986. His long-range strategy included making acquisitions every two years that would bring in $200 million in annual sales. Campbell's acquisition strategy was to look for small, fast-growing food companies strong in product areas where Campbell was not and companies on the fast track that were in rapidly growing parts of their industries. Under McGovern Campbell made a number of acquisitions:

1982

- Mrs. Paul's Kitchens, Inc., a processor and marketer of frozen prepared seafood and vegetable products, with annual sales of approximately $125 million (acquired at a cost of $55 million).
- Snow King Frozen Foods, Inc., engaged in the production and marketing of a line of uncooked frozen specialty meat products, with annual sales of $32 million.
- Juice Bowl Products, Inc., a Florida producer of fruit juices.
- Win Schuler Foods, Inc., a Michigan-based producer and distributor of specialty cheese spreads, flavored melba rounds, food service salad dressings, party dips, and sauces, with annual sales of $6.5 million.
- Costa Apple Products, Inc., a producer of apple juice retailed primarily in the Eastern United States, with annual sales of $6 million.

1983

Acquired several small domestic operations at a cost of $26 million, including:

- Annabelle's restaurant chain of 12 units in the southeastern United States.
- Triangle Manufacturing Corp., a manufacturer of physical fitness and sports medicine products.

1984

- Mendelson-Zeller Co., Inc., a California distributor of fresh produce.

1985

- Continental Foods Company S.A. and affiliated companies which produced sauces, confectioneries, and other food products in Belgium and France; the cost of the acquisition was $17 million.

Campbell was by no means alone in adding companies to its portfolio; many major mergers in the food industry were taking place (see Exhibit 3). Several factors were at work:

- Many food companies had been stung by ill-fated diversification forays outside food. In the 1960s when industry growth had slowed, it was fashionable to diversify into nonfoods. Many of the acquired companies turned out to be duds, draining earnings and soaking up too much top management attention. Now food companies were refocusing their efforts on food—the business they knew best.
- Even though the food industry was regarded as a slow-growth/low-margin business, the fact remained that stable demand, moderate capital costs, and high cash flows had boosted returns on equity to almost 20 percent for some companies. Food processors discovered that they were earning better returns on their food products than they were earning in the nonfood businesses they had earlier diversified into.

While companies such as Beatrice, the nation's largest food company, and Nestle, the world's largest, paid substantial sums to buy out large established companies with extensive brand stables, others—such as Campbell—followed the route of concentrating on internal product development and smaller, selective acquisitions to complement their existing product lines. In fact Campbell was considered the leader among the food processors who were striving to limit acquisitions in favor of heavy, in-house product development. Campbell's emphasis on new product development was not without risk. It took $10 to $15 million in advertising and couponing to launch a brand. Because of the hit-or-miss nature of new products, only about one out of eight products reaching the test market state were successful. Moreover, industry analysts predicted that the continuing introduction of new products would lead to increased competition for shelf space and for the consumer's food dollar.

MARKETING

The outsiders Shaub had hired to revitalize Campbell's marketing included a vice president for marketing who was an eight-year veteran of a New York advertising firm and a soup general manager who was a former Wharton business school professor. In addition to those hired by

EXHIBIT 3 Examples of Major Acquisitions in the Food Processing Industry, 1982–1985

Buyer	*Acquired Company*	*Year*	*Price (millions of dollars)*	*Products/Brands Acquired*
Beatrice	Esmark	1984	$2,800	Swift, Hunt-Wesson Brands
CPC	C. F. Mueller	1983	122	Makes CPC biggest U.S. pasta maker
ConAgra	Peavey	1982	NA	Jams & syrups
	ACLI Seafood	1983	NA	
	Armour Food	1983	166	Processed meats
	Imperial Foods' Country Poultry	1984	18	
Dart & Kraft	Celestial Seasonings	1984	25	Herbal teas
Esmark	Norton Simon	1983	1,100	Hunt-Wesson
General Foods	Entenmann's	1982	315	Baked goods
	Otto Roth	1983	NA	Specialty cheeses
	Monterey	1983	NA	
	Peacock Foods	1983	NA	
	Ronzoni	1984	NA	Pasta
	Oroweat	1984	60	Bread
McCormick	Patterson Jenks	1984	53	Major British spice and food distributor
Nestle	Carnation	1984	3,000	Evaporated milk, Friskies pet food
Philip Morris	General Foods	1985	5,750	Jell-O, Maxwell House
Pillsbury	Häagen-Dazs	1983	75	Ice cream
	Sedutto	1984	5	
Quaker Oats	Stokely-Van Camp	1983	238	Baked beans, canned goods
Ralston Purina	Continental Baking	1984	475	Hostess Twinkies, Wonder Bread
R. J. Reynolds	Nabisco Foods	1984	4,900	Oreo cookies, Ritz crackers,
	Canada Dry	1984	175	ginger ale, soda, tonic

NA = Not available.

Source: Data compiled from various sources.

Shaub, the rest of McGovern's marketing-oriented executive team included: a frozen foods manager (a former marketing manager with General Foods), the head of the Pepperidge Farm division, and the head of the Vlasic Foods division (both marketing men from Borden).

This team boosted Campbell's marketing budget to $428 million by 1984 (up 57 percent from 1982). Advertising spending grew from $67 million in 1980 to $179 million in 1985. Prior to McGovern, Campbell used to cut ad spending at the end of a quarter to boost earnings. Besides hurting the brands, it gave the company an unfavorable reputation among the media. In 1985 the marketing expenditures (including advertising and promotion) of some of the leading food companies were: Campbell—approximately $488 million, Quaker—$619 million, Heinz—$303 million, Pillsbury—$365 million, and Sara Lee—$594 million.

In 1982 McGovern was named *Advertising Age's* Adman of the Year for his efforts in transforming Campbell into "one of the most aggressive market-driven companies in the food industry today."[4] *Advertising Age* noted that McGovern had almost doubled the advertising budget and had replaced the company's longtime ad agency for its soups, leading to a new ad campaign that helped reverse eight years of flat or lower sales. The new campaign emphasized nutrition and fitness, as opposed to the former "mmm,mmm,good" emphasis on taste. Print ads included long copy that referred to major government research studies citing soup's nutritional values. The new slogan was: "Soup is good food." New products and advertising were aimed at shoppers who were dieting, health conscious, and usually in a hurry. In keeping with the new fitness image, the 80-year-old Campbell Kids, although still cherubic, acquired a leaner look. Campbell's marketing strategy under McGovern was based on several important market research findings and projections:

- Women now comprised 43 percent of the workforce and a level of 50 percent was projected by 1990.
- Two-income marriages represented 60 percent of all U.S. families. These would take in three out of every five dollars earned.
- Upper-income households would grow 3.5 times faster than total household formations.
- More than half of all households consisted of only one or two members.
- There were 18 million singles, and 23 percent of all households contained only one person.
- The average age of the population was advancing with the number of senior citizens totaling 25 million-plus and increasing.
- The percentage of meals eaten at home was declining.
- Nearly half of the adult meal-planners in the United States were watching their weight.
- Poultry consumption had increased 26 percent since 1973.
- Ethnic food preparation at home was increasing, with 40 percent, 21 percent, and 14 percent of households preparing Italian, Mexican, and Oriental foods, respectively, at home from scratch.

- There was growing consumer concern with food avoidance: sugar, salt, calories, chemicals, cholesterol, and additives.
- The "I am what I eat" philosophy had tied food in to lifestyles along with Nautilus machines, hot tubs, jogging, racquet ball, backpacking, cross-country skiing, and aerobic dancing.

In response to growing ethnic food demand, Campbell began marketing ethnic selections in regions where interests were highest for particular food types. For instance, it marketed spicy Ranchero Beans only in the south and southwest and planned to market newly acquired Puerto Rican foods in New York City.

The product development priorities were aimed at the themes of convenience, taste, flavor, and texture. The guidelines were:

- Prepare and market products that represent superior value to consumers and constantly strive to improve those values.
- Develop products that help build markets.
- Develop products that return a fair profit to Campbell and to customers.

In support of these guidelines, Campbell adopted several tactics:

- Use ongoing consumer research to determine eating habits by checking home menus, recipe preparation, and foods that are served together. Study meal and snack eating occasions to determine which household members participate so that volume potential can be determined for possible new products and product improvement ideas.
- Develop new products and produce them in small quantities that simulate actual plant production capabilities.
- Test new or improved products in a large enough number of households which are so distributed throughout the United States that results can be projected nationally. Once the product meets pretest standards, recommend it for market testing.
- Once packaging and labels have been considered, design and pretest introductory promotion and advertising.
- Introduce a new product into selected test markets to determine actual store sales which can be projected nationally.
- If test marketing proves successful, roll out the new product on a regional or national plan using test market data as a rationale for expansion.

A key part of the strategy was the "Campbell in the Kitchen" project, consisting of some 75 homemakers across the country. Three to five times a year Campbell asked this "focus group" to try different products and give opinions. McGovern regularly dispatched company executives to the kitchens of these homemakers to observe eating patterns and see how meals were prepared. He sent Campbell's home

EXHIBIT 4 Campbell's Leading New Products Total $600 Million in Sales for Fiscal 1985

1985 Ranking	*Year Introduced*
Le Menu Frozen Dinner	1982
Prego Spaghetti Sauce	1982
Chunky New England Clam Chowder	1984
Great Starts Breakfasts	1984
Prego Plus	1985

Source: The Wall Street Journal, August 14, 1985.

economists into some of the households to work with the cooks on a one-to-one basis.

All this was in sharp contrast to the pre-McGovern era. Campbell averaged about 18 new product entries a year through the late 1970s. Many of these were really line extensions rather than new products. Substantial numbers flopped, partly because they had often been subjected to only the most rudimentary and inexpensive tests. Sometimes the testing had consisted only of a panel of the company's advertising and business executives sipping from teaspoons.

In 1983 Campbell was the biggest new products generator in the combined food and health and beauty aids categories with a total of 42 new products. Second was Esmark, 36; followed by Lever/Lipton, 33; Nabisco Brands, 25; Beatrice and General Foods, 24 each; American Home Products, 23; Quaker Oats, 21; Borden, 19; and General Mills and Noxell, 17 each. Exhibit 4 shows Campbell's leading new products from 1982 to 1985.

PRODUCTION

McGovern summarized Campbell's philosophy on quality: "I want zero defects. If we can't produce quality, we'll get out of the business."[5] In 1984 Campbell held its first Worldwide Corporate Conference dedicated to quality. Hundreds of Campbell managers from all levels and most company locations spent three days at this conference. Campbell believed that the ultimate test of quality was consumer satisfaction and its goal was to maintain a quality-conscious organization at every employee level in every single operation.

Before McGovern took over, Campbell used to emphasize new products compatible with existing production facilities. For example, a square omelet was designed for Swanson's frozen breakfasts because it was what the machine would make. After McGovern's appointment, although low-cost production was still a strategic factor, consumer trends—and not existing machinery—were the deciding factors for new product development. Other important factors considered in the production process included:

- The growing move toward consumption of refrigerated and fresh produce in contrast to canned or frozen products.
- The emerging perception that private label and/or generic label merchandise would drive out weak national and secondary brands unless there was a clear product superiority and excellent price/value on the part of the brands supported by consumer advertising.
- The polarization of food preparation time with long preparation on weekends and special occasions, but fast preparation in between via microwaves, quick foods, and instant breakfasts.
- The cost of the package—especially metal packaging—which was outrunning the cost of the product it contained.
- Energy and distribution costs—these were big targets for efficiency with regional production, aseptic packaging, and packages designed for automatic warehouse handling and lightweight containers becoming standard.

The bulk of $154 million in capital expenditures in 1983 went into improvement of production equipment, expenditures for additional production capacity, the completion of the $100 million canned foods plant in North Carolina, and the start of a mushroom-producing facility at Dublin, Georgia. In 1984 construction began on a $9 million Le Menu production line in Sumter, South Carolina. Capital expenditures in 1985 totaled $213 million. Most of this went into improvements of production equipment, packaging technology, and expenditures for additional production capacity.

Campbell was considered a model of manufacturing efficiency. Production was fully integrated from the tomato patch to the can-making factory. Campbell was the nation's third largest can manufacturer behind American Can Company and Continental Group. Yet Campbell, which made the red and white soup can with the gold medallion an American institution, had recently concluded that food packaging was headed in the direction of snazzier and more convenient containers. McGovern compared sticking with the can to the refusal of U.S. automobile makers to change their ways in the face of the Japanese challenge:

> There's a tremendous feeling of urgency because an overseas company could come in here with innovative packaging and technology and just take us to the cleaners on basic lines we've taken for granted for years.[6]

Other soup companies—including Libby, McNeill & Libby, a Nestlé

Enterprises, Inc., unit that made Crosse & Blackwell gourmet soup—had already started experimenting with can alternatives. Campbell's testing was considered the most advanced, but a mistake could mean revamping production facilities at a cost of $100 million or more.

Researchers at the Campbell Soup Company's DNA Plant Technology Corporation were working toward the development of the "perfect tomato." They were seeking ways to grow tasty, high solids tomatoes under high-temperature conditions that would cause normal plants to droop and wither. They also hoped to crossbreed high quality domestic tomatoes with tough, hardy, wild tomatoes that could withstand cold weather. A breakthrough in this area could result in two harvests a year. Conceding that they were latecomers (Heinz began similar research several years after Campbell), Campbell researchers estimated that they were four to five years ahead of Heinz.

Campbell believed its key strengths were: (1) a worldwide system for obtaining ingredients, (2) a broad range of food products that could be used as a launching pad for further innovation, and (3) an emphasis on low-cost production.

CAMPBELL'S OPERATING DIVISIONS

Campbell Soup Company was divided into six operating units—Campbell U.S., Pepperidge Farm, Vlasic Foods, Mrs. Paul's Kitchens, Other United States, and International. Sales and profit performance by division are shown in Exhibit 5.

Campbell U.S.

In 1985 the Campbell U.S. Division was Campbell's largest operating unit, accounting for almost 62 percent of the company's total consolidated sales. Operating earnings increased 5 percent over 1984. Unit volume rose 7 percent in 1983, 9 percent in 1984, and 4 percent in 1985. The Campbell U.S. division was divided into eight profit centers: Soup, Frozen Foods, Grocery Business, Beverage Business, Food Service Business, Poultry Business, Fresh Produce Business, and Pet Foods Business. Exhibit 6 shows the brands Campbell had in this division and the major competitors each brand faced.

The soup business group alone accounted for more than 25 percent of the company's consolidated sales (as compared to around 50 percent in the 1970s). Campbell's flagship brands of soups accounted for 80 percent of the $1 billion-plus annual canned soup market; in 1985 Campbell offered grocery shoppers over 50 varieties of canned soups. Heinz was second with 10 percent of the market. Heinz had earlier

EXHIBIT 5 Sales and Earnings of Campbell Soup, by Division, 1980–1985 (millions of dollars)

	1980	*1981*	*1982*	*1983*	*1984*	*1985*
Campbell U.S.:						
Sales	$1,608	$1,678	$1,773	$1,987	$2,282	$2,500
Operating earnings	205	190	211	250	278	292
Pepperidge Farm:						
Sales	283	329	392	433	435	426
Operating earnings	29	35	41	43	35	39
Vlasic Foods:						
Sales	130	137	149	168	193	199
Operating earnings	8	10	12	13	14	16
Mrs. Paul's Kitchens:						
Sales				108	126	138
Operating earnings				10	14	11
Other United States:						
Sales	35	27	56	64	84	81
Operating earnings	1	(1)	(1)	(1)	(2)	(3)
International:						
Sales	512	694	643	599	624	716
Operating earnings	33	46	46	33	34	35

Source: Campbell's annual reports.

withdrawn from producing Heinz-label soup and shifted its production over to making soups for sale under the private labels of grocery chains; Heinz was the leading private-label segment. See Exhibit 6 for information on competitors and their brands.

Although the soup business was relatively mature (McGovern preferred to call it underworked), Campbell's most ambitious consumer research took place in this unit. McGovern planned to speed up soup sales by turning out a steady flow of new varieties in convenient packages: "Ethnic, dried, refrigerated, frozen, microwave—you name it, we're going to try it."[7]

In 1985 Campbell began an assault on the $290 million dry-soup mix market dominated by Thomas J. Lipton Inc., a unit of the Anglo-Dutch Unilever Group. This move was made because dry-soup sales in the United States were growing faster than sales of canned soup. Lipton's aggressive response to test marketing of an early Campbell dry-soup product resulted in Campbell's rushing a six-flavor line into national distribution ahead of schedule.

In 1982 McGovern caused a stir when he announced publicly that Campbell's Swanson TV-dinner line was "junk food": "It was great in 1950, but in today's world it didn't go into the microwave; it didn't represent variety or a good eating experience to my palate."[7] He

EXHIBIT 6 The Campbell U.S. Division; Products, Rival Brands, Competitors

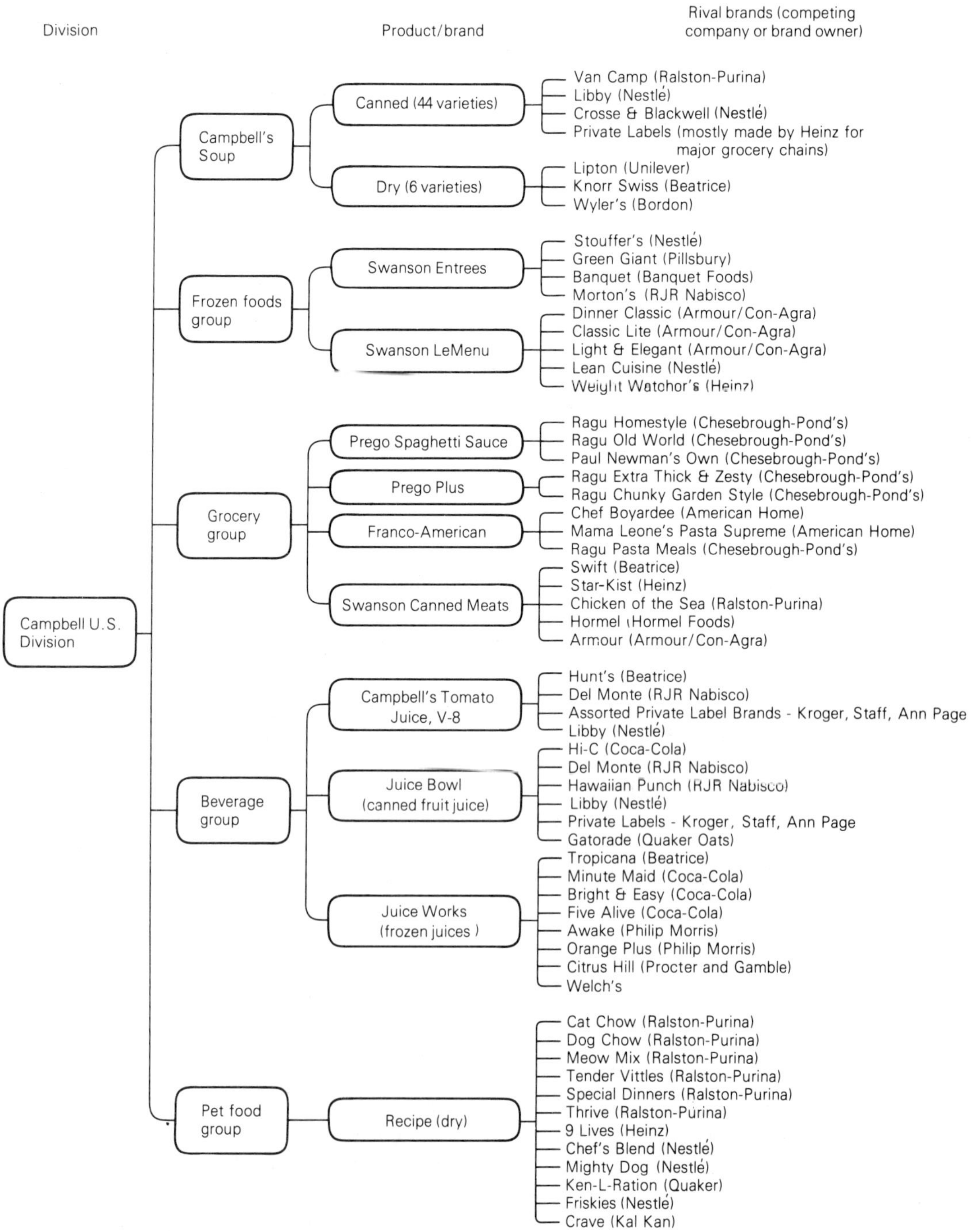
Division
Product/brand
Rival brands (competing company or brand owner)
Campbell U.S. Division
Campbell's Soup
Canned (44 varieties)
Van Camp (Ralston-Purina)
Libby (Nestlé)
Crosse & Blackwell (Nestlé)
Private Labels (mostly made by Heinz for major grocery chains)
Dry (6 varieties)
Lipton (Unilever)
Knorr Swiss (Beatrice)
Wyler's (Bordon)
Frozen foods group
Swanson Entrees
Stouffer's (Nestlé)
Green Giant (Pillsbury)
Banquet (Banquet Foods)
Morton's (RJR Nabisco)
Swanson LeMenu
Dinner Classic (Armour/Con-Agra)
Classic Lite (Armour/Con-Agra)
Light & Elegant (Armour/Con-Agra)
Lean Cuisine (Nestlé)
Weight Watcher's (Heinz)
Grocery group
Prego Spaghetti Sauce
Ragu Homestyle (Chesebrough-Pond's)
Ragu Old World (Chesebrough-Pond's)
Paul Newman's Own (Chesebrough-Pond's)
Prego Plus
Ragu Extra Thick & Zesty (Chesebrough-Pond's)
Ragu Chunky Garden Style (Chesebrough-Pond's)
Franco-American
Chef Boyardee (American Home)
Mama Leone's Pasta Supreme (American Home)
Ragu Pasta Meals (Chesebrough-Pond's)
Swanson Canned Meats
Swift (Beatrice)
Star-Kist (Heinz)
Chicken of the Sea (Ralston-Purina)
Hormel (Hormel Foods)
Armour (Armour/Con-Agra)
Beverage group
Campbell's Tomato Juice, V-8
Hunt's (Beatrice)
Del Monte (RJR Nabisco)
Assorted Private Label Brands - Kroger, Staff, Ann Page
Libby (Nestlé)
Juice Bowl (canned fruit juice)
Hi-C (Coca-Cola)
Del Monte (RJR Nabisco)
Hawaiian Punch (RJR Nabisco)
Libby (Nestlé)
Private Labels - Kroger, Staff, Ann Page
Gatorade (Quaker Oats)
Juice Works (frozen juices)
Tropicana (Beatrice)
Minute Maid (Coca-Cola)
Bright & Easy (Coca-Cola)
Five Alive (Coca-Cola)
Awake (Philip Morris)
Orange Plus (Philip Morris)
Citrus Hill (Procter and Gamble)
Welch's
Pet food group
Recipe (dry)
Cat Chow (Ralston-Purina)
Dog Chow (Ralston-Purina)
Meow Mix (Ralston-Purina)
Tender Vittles (Ralston-Purina)
Special Dinners (Ralston-Purina)
Thrive (Ralston-Purina)
9 Lives (Heinz)
Chef's Blend (Nestlé)
Mighty Dog (Nestlé)
Ken-L-Ration (Quaker)
Friskies (Nestlé)
Crave (Kal Kan)

maintained that consumers had discovered high-quality options to the TV-dinner concept. The market niche for more exotic, better quality entrees was being exploited by Nestle's Stouffer subsidiary and Pillsbury's Green Giant division (Exhibit 6).

Campbell's Frozen Foods group answered the challenge by producing its own frozen gourmet line, Le Menu. Campbell committed about $50 million in manufacturing, marketing, and trade promotion costs on the basis of encouraging marketing tests. In the five years prior to Le Menu, Swanson's sales volume had slipped 16 percent. Its biggest volume decline (23 percent) was in the area that had been its stronghold: sales of dinners and entrees. Overall industry sales in dinners and entrees grew to $2 billion during 1982. The single dish entree market had increased 58 percent since 1978 with sales being dominated by Stouffer's Lean Cuisine selections.

Le Menu—served on round heatable plates and consisting of such delicacies as chicken cordon bleu, al dente vegetables, and sophisticated wine sauces—produced 20 percent growth in the frozen meal unit with sales of $150 million during its first year of national distribution (1984). This was double Campbell's earlier projection of sales.

Under Project Fix, Swanson dinners were overhauled, putting in less salt and more meat stock in gravies and adding new desserts and sauces. The revamped line had new packaging and a redesigned logo. The Frozen Foods Business Unit reported an overall volume increase of 3 percent in 1983, 27 percent in 1984, and 2 percent in 1985. In 1985 the unit had a 52 percent increase in operating earnings as sales rose 10 percent.

Meanwhile, Pillsbury had targeted the $4 billion-a-year frozen main meal market and the rapidly expanding market in light meals and snacks as vital to its future. In 1984 Pillsbury purchased Van de Kamp's, a market leader in frozen seafood and ethnic entrees for $102 million. During 1985 Van de Kamp's became the number one seller of frozen Mexican meals. Pillsbury also sold more than one third of the 550 million frozen pizzas consumed in the United States in 1985 and made substantial investments in quality improvements and marketing support to maintain the number one position in frozen pizza.

The Grocery Business Unit's star was Prego Spaghetti Sauce that in 1984 had obtained 25 percent of the still growing spaghetti sauce market and was the number two sauce, behind Chesebrough-Pond's Ragu. (Exhibit 6 lists competing brands.) Chesebrough had recently introduced Ragu Chunky Gardenstyle sauce to try to convert cooks who still made their own sauce (about 45 percent of all spaghetti sauce users still cooked their own from scratch). The new Ragu product came in three varieties: mushrooms and onions, green peppers and mushrooms, and extra tomatoes with garlic and onions. Campbell had no plans for a similar entry because copying Ragu wouldn't be innovative. However, a Prego Plus Spaghetti Sauce line completed its first year of national distribution in 1985. To show "old-fashioned concern," all three sizes of Prego sauce came in jars with tamper-evident caps; Campbell would buy back from grocery shelves all jars that had been opened.

The Beverage Group's 1985 operating earnings were affected by a slower-than-anticipated introduction of Juice Works—a line of 100 percent natural, no-sugar-added, pure, blended fruit juices for children. This was attributed to intense competitive pressure and major technological problems. Campbell's Tomato Juice and V-8 Cocktail Vegetable Juice also reported disappointing earnings. Juice Bowl, however, showed improved earnings in 1985. Campbell's competition in this area came from Hunt's, Del Monte, and private label brands (Exhibit 6).

The Poultry Business Unit sales were up 13 percent in 1985. Operating earnings for the year were positive, compared to a loss in 1984. These results stemmed from the national rollout of frozen "finger foods"—Plump & Juicy Dipsters, Drumlets, and Cutlets—and sales of Premium Chunk White Chicken. Some of the competitors were Banquet's Chicken Drum-Snackers and Tyson's Chick'n Dippers.

Pepperidge Farm

Pepperidge Farm, Campbell's second-largest division with 12 percent of the company's consolidated sales, reported a decline in operating income and a sales gain of less than 1 percent between 1983 and 1984. In 1980 it was one of the fastest growing units; sales had risen 14 percent annually, compounded.

1984's disappointing results were largely blamed on losses incurred in the apple juice (Costa Apple Products, Inc., purchased in 1982) and "Star Wars" cookies businesses. When Pepperidge Farm introduced Star Wars cookies, McGovern called them a "travesty" because they were faddish and did not fit the brand's high-quality, upscale adult image. Plus, at $1.39 a bag, he maintained that it was a "lousy value." But he didn't veto them because, "I could be wrong."[6] As the popularity of the movies series waned, so did sales.

The frozen biscuit and bakery business unit volume was also down. New products such as Vegetables in Pastry and Deli's reportedly did not receive enough marketing support.

To remedy the division's growth decline, a number of steps were taken:

- Apple juice operations were transferred to the Campbell U.S. Division Beverage Unit.
- During the year Pepperidge divested itself of operations that no

longer fit into its strategic plan, including Lexington Gardens, Inc., a garden center chain.
- Deli's went back into research and development to improve quality.
- By the start of the 1985 fiscal year a new management team was in place and a comprehensive review of each product was being conducted in an effort to return emphasis to traditional product lines and quality standards which accounted for its success and growth in the past.

At the end of 1985, Pepperidge Farm showed an 11 percent increase in operating earnings over the previous year in spite of a 2 percent drop in sales. This was considered a result of the transfer of Pepperidge Farm beverage operations to the Campbell U.S. Beverage Group and the sale of the Lexington Gardens nursery chain. During 1985 sales in the Confectionery Business Unit increased 22 percent and seven Godiva boutiques were added. Goldfish Crackers and Puff Pastry contributed to a volume increase in the Food Service Business Unit, while some varieties of Deli's and the Snack Bar products were discontinued.

One of Pepperidge Farm's major competitors in frozen bakery products was Sara Lee, which had 40 percent of the frozen sweet goods market and an ever-increasing 33 percent share of the specialty breads category. Pepperidge Farm's fresh breads and specialty items competed against a host of local, regional, and national brands. Exhibit 7 presents more details.

Vlasic Foods

Campbell's third largest domestic division enjoyed an 11 percent increase in operating earnings in 1985. Vlasic maintained its number one position with a 31 percent share of the pickles market. Seventeen percent of Vlasic's sales were in the food service category.

In 1985 Vlasic implemented new labels which used color bands and a flavor rating scale to help consumers find their favorite tastes quickly on the supermarket shelf. Taking advantage of their marketing research, which indicated consumer desires for new and interesting flavors, Vlasic introduced "Zesty Dills" and "Bread & Butter Whole Pickle" lines in 1985. Heinz was Campbell's leading national competitor in this area (Exhibit 8), but there were a number of important regional and private label brands which competed with Heinz and Vlasic for shelf space.

Win Schuler, the Vlasic subsidiary purchased in 1982, reported flat sales in 1984 due to a general economic decline in the Michigan and upper midwest markets where its products were sold. In 1985 it was moved to Campbell's Refrigerated Foods Business Unit where there

EXHIBIT 7 The Pepperidge Farm Division: Products, Rival Brands, Competitors

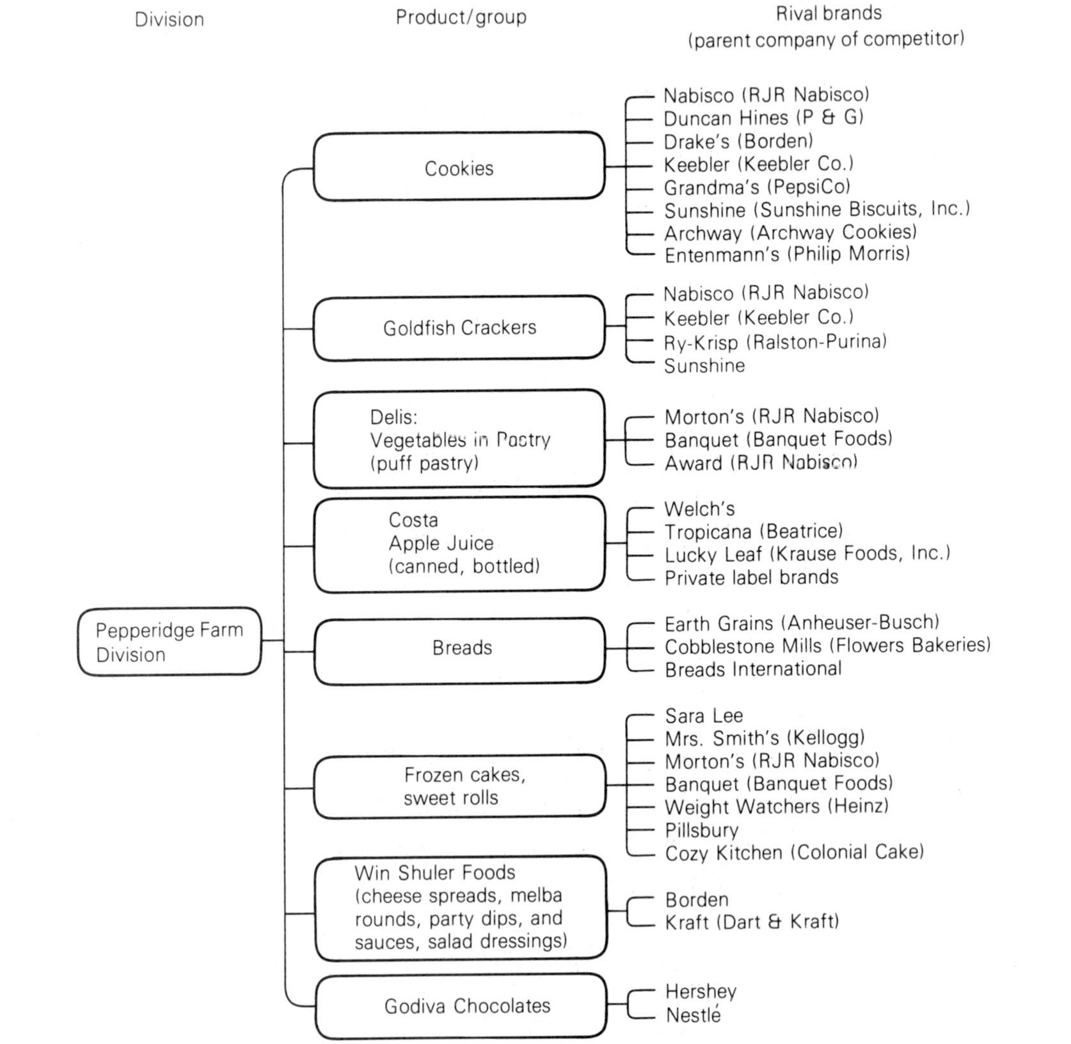

were plans to begin producing a wider range of food products under the Win Schuler brand name.

Mrs. Paul's Kitchens

Sales of this division for 1984 were up 16 percent over the previous year, operating earnings increased 36 percent, and unit volume in-

EXHIBIT 8 Vlasic Division: Products, Rival Brands, and Competitors

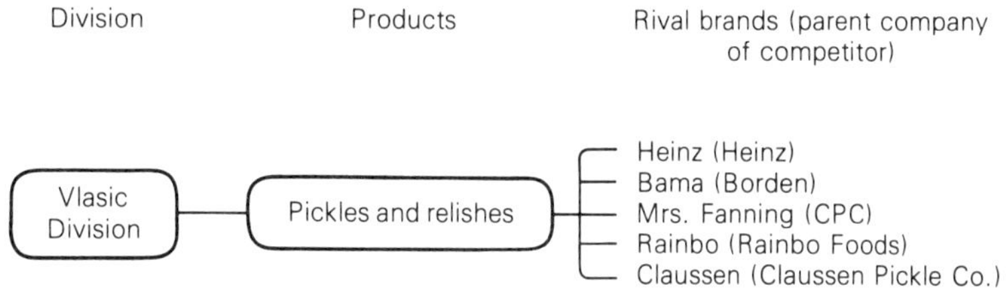

creased 9 percent. Mrs. Paul's sales represented just over 3 percent of Campbell's total business; all results exceeded goals set for the year. However, strong competitive pressure on its traditional lines was blamed for the unit's drop in operating earnings for 1985. Competing brands included Hormel and Gorton's (Exhibit 9).

When Campbell acquired Mrs. Paul's in 1982, it was rumored that Heinz and Pillsbury, among others, were considering the same acquisition. Shortly after the acquisition, Campbell responded to consumer preferences for convenience seafood products that were nutritious, low in calories, microwavable, and coated more lightly, by introducing Light & Natural Fish Fillets in 1983. Quality improvements were made to existing products, and a promising new product, Light Seafood entrees, was introduced in 1984. Market share increased about 25 percent over 1983, and Light Seafood Entrees went national in 1985. This line, which featured seven varieties of low-calorie, microwavable, seafood dishes, accounted for 11 percent of 1985's volume. However, sales of the company's established product lines of breaded frozen seafood items dipped below the 1984 level.

EXHIBIT 9 The Mrs. Paul's Kitchen Division: Products, Rival Brands, National Competitors

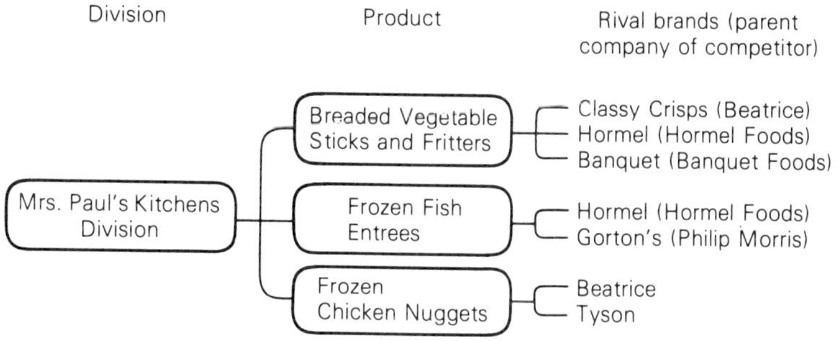

Campbell's Other U.S. Businesses

Beyond the base of Campbell's main operating groups there were several additional small businesses: Triangle Manufacturing Corp., a health and fitness products manufacturer; Campbell Hospitality, the restaurant division; and Snow King Frozen Foods, Inc., a manufacturer of frozen meat specialty products.

In 1984, the Hospitality Division, encompassing 59 Pietro's restaurants, 15 Annabelle's, and 6 H. T. McDoogal's, reported an operating loss slightly less than 1983. During the year the division added one H. T. McDoogal's, two Annabelle's, and nine Pietro's units.

In 1985 Annabelle's experienced a 14 percent increase in sales and a 43 percent rise in operating earnings. During the year Campbell announced its intention to sell four H. T. McDoogal's restaurants. Snow King reported a sales decline of 19 percent and an operating loss of almost $1 million.

Competing food companies in the restaurant business included General Mills and Pillsbury. General Mills' Red Lobster unit was the nation's largest full-service dinner-house chain. Red Lobster had 1985 sales of $827 million—an all-time high—and its operating profits also set a record. Pillsbury's Restaurants Group was comprised of Burger King and Steak & Ale Restaurants; both achieved record sales and earnings in 1985. Pillsbury opened 477 new restaurants in 1985—the most ever in a single year—bringing the total to 4,601.

Triangle, Campbell's physical fitness subsidiary, in its second full year of operation in 1985, reported that sales had more than tripled, but that increased marketing costs aimed at securing brand recognition resulted in an operating loss. Sales growth was a result of doubling the size of Triangle's distribution system. Its best known product line, "The Band" wrist and ankle weights, maintained the number two position in its category with a 14 percent market share. Triangle planned to build on its strengths by entering the exercise equipment category and by marketing its products internationally.

Campbell's International Division

Campbell's International Division provided 18 percent of the company's consolidated sales in 1984. Campbell had subsidiaries in 11 foreign countries and was planning to expand further. Total restructuring of the International Division was in progress with goals of increasing sales and earnings and building a solid base for growth.

In 1985 steps were taken toward the division's goal of contributing 25 percent of Campbell's corporate sales and earnings. A number of operations were consolidated, and new businesses were added. Other international objectives were to improve Campbell's presence in all international markets and to make Campbell into a premier international company.

RECENT EVENTS

During 1985 the market price of Campbell's stock reached a new high of $80.50 a share. In July the stock was split two for one. At year-end 1985 the market price was $51.50 and the stock price was up $4 during one December week. Analysts were puzzled by this sudden rise in market price, and there were rumors of a takeover.

Analysts observed that the company had been hurt by fierce competition in 1985, an increasing softness in many of its markets, and mistakes on new product introduction. In its *1985 Annual Report* Campbell acknowledged increased competition in the marketplace:

> The supermarket has become an arena of intense competitive activity as food companies introduce a steady stream of new consumer-oriented products and support them with massive marketing dollars in an attempt to carve out a first or second place position in the respective categories. That competitive activity is keeping the pressure on Campbell's operating results.

REFERENCES

1. *Forbes,* December 7, 1981, p. 44.
2. *The Wall Street Journal,* September 17, 1984, p. 1.
3. *The Wall Street Journal,* September 17, 1984, p. 10.
4. *Advertising Age,* January 3, 1983, p. 38.
5. *Savvy,* June 1984, p. 39.
6. *Business Week,* November 21, 1983, p. 102.
7. *Business Week,* December 24, 1984, p. 67.

Case 10

Mary Kay Cosmetics, Inc.*

Arthur A. Thompson
Robin Romblad
both of the University of Alabama

In spring 1983 Mary Kay Cosmetics Inc. (MKC), the second largest direct sales distributor of skin care products in the United States, encountered its first big slowdown in recruiting women to function as Mary Kay beauty consultants and market the Mary Kay cosmetic lines. As of April, MKC's sales force of about 195,000 beauty consultants was increasing at only a 13 percent annual rate, down from a 65 percent rate of increase in 1980. The dropoff in the percentage of new recruits jeopardized MKC's ability to sustain its reputation as a fast-growing company. MKC's strategy was predicated on getting ever larger numbers of beauty consultants to arrange "skin care classes" at the home of a hostess and her three to five guests; at the classes consultants demonstrated the Mary Kay approach to skin care, gave makeup instruction with samples from the Mary Kay Cosmetics line, and usually sold anywhere from $50 to $200 worth of Mary Kay products. MKC's historically successful efforts to build up the size of its force of beauty consultants had given the company reliable access to a growing number of "showings" annually.

Even though MKC's annual turnover rate for salespeople was lower than that of several major competitors (including Avon Products), some 120,000 Mary Kay beauty consultants had quit or been terminated in 1982, making the task of recruiting a growing sales force of consultants a major, ongoing effort at MKC. Recruiting success was seen by management as strategically important. Now recruits were encouraged to spend between $500 and $3,000 for sales kits and startup inventories; the initial orders of new recruits accounted for over one third of MKC's annual sales. The newest recruits were also instrumental in helping identify and attract others to become Mary Kay beauty consultants.

---

* Prepared by graduate researcher Robin Romblad and Professor Arthur A. Thompson, Jr., The University of Alabama. The assistance and cooperation provided by many people in the Mary Kay organization is gratefully acknowledged.

Richard Rogers, MKC's cofounder and president, promptly reacted to the recruiting slowdown by announcing five changes in the company's sales force program:

- The financial incentives offered to active beauty consultants for bringing new recruits into the Mary Kay fold were increased by as much as 50 percent.
- A new program was instituted whereby beauty consultants who (1) placed $600 a month in wholesale orders with the company for three consecutive months and (2) recruited five new consultants who together placed $3,000 in wholesale orders a month for three straight months would win the free use of a cream-colored Oldsmobile Firenza for a year (this program supplemented the existing programs whereby top performing beauty consultants could win the use of a pink Cadillac or pink Buick Regal).
- The minimum order size required of beauty consultants was increased from $400 to $600.
- The prices at which MKC wholesaled its products to consultants were raised by 4 percent.
- The requirements for attaining sales director status and heading up a sales unit were raised 25 percent; a sales director had to recruit 15 new consultants (instead of 12), and her sales unit was expected to maintain a monthly minimum of $4,000 in wholesale orders (up from $3,200).

In addition, MKC's 1984 corporate budget for recruiting was more than quadrupled and, as a special recruiting effort, the company staged a National Guest Night in September 1984 that consisted of a live closed-circuit telecast to 78 cities aired from Dallas, Texas, where MKC's corporate headquarters was located. Mary Kay sales people all over the United States were urged to invite prospective recruits and go to one of the 78 simulcast sites.

NATIONAL GUEST NIGHT IN BIRMINGHAM

Jan Currier, senior sales director for MKC in the Tuscaloosa, Alabama, area, invited two other ladies and the casewriter to drive to Birmingham in her pink Buick Regal to attend what was billed as "The Salute to the Stars." On the way, Jan explained that as well as being entertaining, the evening's event would give everyone a chance to see firsthand just how exciting and rewarding the career opportunities were with MKC; she noted with pride that Mary Kay Cosmetics was one of the companies featured in the recent book *The 100 Best Companies to Work For in America*. As the Tuscaloosa entourage neared the auditorium in Birmingham, the casewriter observed numerous pink Cadillacs and pink Buick Regals in the flow of traffic and in the parking lot. Mary Kay sales directors were stationed at each door to the lobby enthusiastically greeting each person and presenting a gift of Mary Kay cosmetics. Guests were directed to a table to register for prizes to be awarded later in the evening.

Inside the auditorium over 1,500 people awaited the beginning of the evening's program. A large theater screen was located at center stage. The lights dimmed promptly at 7 P.M. and the show began. The casewriter used her tape recorder and took extensive notes to capture what went on:

Mark Dixon: [*National Sales Administrator for the South Central Division, appears on stage in Birmingham*]: Welcome, ladies and gentlemen, to National Guest Night, Mary Kay's Salute to the Stars. Tonight, you're going to be a part of the largest teleconference ever held by a U.S. corporation.

Now please help me welcome someone all of us at Mary Kay love very dearly, National Sales Director from Houston, Texas, Lovie Quinn.

[*The crowd stands and greets Lovie with cheers and applause.*]

Lovie Quinn: [*comes out on stage in Birmingham to join Mark Dixon. Lovie is wearing this year's Mary Kay national sales director suit of red suede with black mink trim.*]: Good evening ladies and gentlemen and welcome to one of the most exciting events in the history of Mary Kay. An evening with Mary Kay as she Salutes the Stars. . . . During the evening you'll learn about career opportunities. There will be recognition of our stars. We'll see the salute to them with gifts and prizes you hear about at Mary Kay. You'll hear about . . . pink Cadillacs . . . pink Buick Regals, and Firenza Oldsmobiles.

You're going to hear about and see diamond rings and beautiful full-length mink coats. And of course we'll talk about MONEY.

If you've never attended a Mary Kay function you might very easily get the impression that we brag a lot. We like to think of it as recognition . . . But we would not be able to give this recognition of success if you, the hostesses, our special guests, did not open up your homes so we may share with you and some of your selected friends the Mary Kay skin care program. For that reason we would like to show our appreciation at this time. Will all the special guests please stand up.

[*About 40 percent of the audience stands and the remainder applaud the guests.*]

Lovie Quinn: Now I need to have all our directors line up on stage. [*Each one is dressed in a navy blue suit with either a red, green, or white blouse—the color of the blouse signifies director, senior director, or future director status*] Enthusiasm and excitement are at the root of the Mary Kay philosophy. This is why we always start a meeting like this with a song. We invite all of you to join with the directors and sing the theme song, "That Mary Kay Enthusiasm."

[*Lovie motions for the audience to stand; the choir of directors begins to clap and leads out in singing. The audience joins in quickly.*]

I've got that Mary Kay enthusiasm up in my
 head, up in my head, up in my head.
I've got that Mary Kay enthusiasm up in my
 head, up in my head to stay.

I've got that Mary Kay enthusiasm down in my
 heart, down in my heart, down in my heart.
I've got that Mary Kay enthusiasm down in my
 heart, down in my heart to stay.

I've got that Mary Kay enthusiasm down in my
 feet, down in my feet, down in my feet.
I've got that Mary Kay enthusiasm down in my
 feet, down in my feet to stay.

all over me, all over me.
all over me to stay.
I've got that Mary Kay enthusiasm up in my
 head, down in my heart, down in my feet.
I've got that Mary Kay enthusiasm all over me,
 all over me to stay.

[*The song concludes to a round of applause. The crowd is spirited.*]

Lovie Quinn: Now we'd like to recognize a group of very special consultants. These ladies have accepted a challenge from Mary Kay and have held 10 beauty shows in one week. This is something really terrific. It demonstrates the successful achievement of a goal. We have found when you want to do something for our Chairman of the Board, Mary Kay Ash . . . you don't have to give furs. The most special gift you can give to Mary Kay is your own success. . . .

[*All of those recognized are seated in the first 10 rows with their guests; seating in the front rows is a special reward for meeting the challenge. The crowd applauds*]

Lovie Quinn: It is almost time for the countdown to begin, but before it does one more special group must be recognized. These ladies are Mary Kay's Gold Medal winners. In one month they recruited *five* new consultants. [*A number of ladies stand; they beam with pride and each has been awarded a medal resembling an Olympic Gold. The audience gives them a nice round of applause.*]

Lovie Quinn [*Lovie continues to fill the crowd with excitement and anticipation.*]: The countdown is going to be in just a few moments. It will be a treat for those of you that have not met Mary Kay before. Please help me count down the final 10 seconds before the broadcast.

[*But the crowd is so excited it starts the countdown when one minute appears on the screen. As the seconds wind down, the crowd gets louder with anticipation and then gets in sync chanting: 10, 9, 8,7, 6, 5, 4, 3, 2, 1. More screams and applause.*

On the screen a Gold Mary Kay medallion appears, then the production lines at the plant are shown, and then trucks shipping the products. The audience claps as they see these on the screen. Headquarters is shown. Now a number of the Mary Kay sales directors are shown framed in stars on the screen. People clap when they recognize someone from their district. Loud applause fills the auditorium when Mary Kay Ash, MKC's chairman of the board and company cofounder, is shown in a star.

The Dallas-based part of the simulcast opens with female dancers dressed in pink and male dancers dressed in gray tuxedos. They perform the "Mary Kay Star Song" which includes a salute to various regions in the United States. The Birmingham crowd cheers when the South is highlighted.

A woman is chosen out of the audience in Dallas. Her name is Susan; the audience is told that at various intervals in the broadcast we will see her evolution into a successful Mary Kay Beauty consultant. Initially we see her get a feeling that maybe she can be a Mary Kay star. The message is that personal dreams of success can come true. Will she be successful? The answer comes back, "Yes, She Can Do It."

Mary Kay Ash is escorted on stage by her son Richard Rogers. She is elegantly dressed with accents of diamonds and feathers. The applause, the loudest so far, is genuinely enthusiastic and many in both the Dallas and Birmingham audiences are cheering loudly.]

Mary Kay Ash: Welcome everyone to our very first Salute to the Stars, National Guest Night. How exciting it is to think that right now over 100,000 people are watching this broadcast all over the United States. . . . Even though I can't see all of you, I can feel your warmth all the way to Dallas.

During the program this evening one expression you're going to hear over and over again is YOU CAN DO IT. . . . This is something we really believe in. What we have discovered is the seeds of greatness are planted in every human being. . . . Tonight we hope to inspire you, to get you to reach within yourself, to bring out some of those star qualities that I know you have. And no matter who you are and no matter where you live, I believe you can take those talents and go farther than you ever thought possible and we have a special place waiting just for you.

Now I would like to introduce someone who has a special place in my heart. Someone who has been beside me from the very beginning. Without him Mary Kay Cosmetics would not be what it is today. Please welcome your president and cofounder of our company, my son, Richard Rogers.

Richard Rogers [*Steps to the microphone, accompanied by respectful applause.*]: When we started this company over 20 years ago my mother and I never dreamed we would be standing here talking live to over 100,000 of you all across the country. . . . Tonight we've planned a memorable evening just for you. A program that conveys the spirit of Mary Kay. Going back 21 years ago, Mary Kay saw a void in the cosmetics industry. The observation she made was that others were just selling products. No one was teaching women about their skin and how to care for it. . . . This is the concept on which she based her company. So on September 13, 1963, Mary Kay Cosmetics opened its doors in Dallas, Texas.

Throughout the decade Mary Kay's concept continued to flourish. . . . By the end of the 60s Mary Kay Cosmetics had become a fully integrated manufacturer and distributor of skin care products. In 1970 the sales force had grown to 7,000 consultants in Texas and four surrounding states.

California was the first state MKC designated for expansion. When we first went there no one had ever heard of Mary Kay Cosmetics. Within three years California had more consultants selling Mary Kay Cosmetics than the state of Texas. . . . With this success, expansion continued throughout the United States. . . . By 1975 MKC had grown to 700 sales directors, 34,000 consultants, and $35 million in sales.

International expansion was initiated in 1978 by selling skin care products in Canada. In just 36 months MKC became the fourth largest Canadian cosmetic company. . . . Since that time Mary Kay has expanded to South America, Australia, and in September we opened for business in the United Kingdom.

At the end of 1983 MKC had over 195,000 consultants. Sales had reached over $600 million around the world. . . . With total commitment to excellence setting the pace, MKC is still working towards achieving the goal of being the finest teaching-oriented skin care organization in the world . . . . Mary Kay is proud to have the human resources necessary to meet this goal. At Mary Kay P&L means more than profit and loss. It also stands for People and Love. People have helped MKC reach where it is today, and they will play a big part in where it will be tomorrow.

Tonight we're proud to announce the arrival of a book that expresses the Mary Kay philosophy of Golden Rule management, a book that outlines the management style that has contributed to the success of Mary Kay Cosmetics. The new book is *Mary Kay on People Management.*

[*The crowd applauds at this announcement.*]

Mary Kay Ash [*Reappears on stage.*]: We're so excited about the new book. I am pleased to have the opportunity to talk with you about it tonight. Actually, I started to write that book over 20 years ago. I had just retired from 25 years of direct sales. I wanted to share my experiences, so I wrote down my thoughts about the companies I had worked for. What had worked and what had not. . . . After expressing my ideas I thought how wonderful it would be to put these ideas of a company designed to meet women's needs into action. That is when Mary Kay Cosmetics was born. . . . The company helps women meet the goals they set for themselves. . . . I feel this is what has contributed to the success of the organization. Everyone at MKC starts at the same place, as a consultant, and everyone has the same opportunities for success.

[*The broadcast returns to the scenario of Susan as she becomes a new Mary Kay consultant. Susan sings about the doubts people have about her joining Mary Kay. She disregards this and decides to climb to success. At the end of the scene, she projects a positive, successful image that her friends and family recognize. The audience responds favorably.*]

Dale Alexander [*National Sales Administrator for Mary Kay Cosmetics appears on stage in Dallas.*]: It is a great honor to be with you tonight and I want to add my most sincere welcome. . . . Recognition is one of the original principles on which our company is based. It's an essential ingredient in the Mary Kay formula for success. . . . I want to start out by recognizing the largest group. The group of independent businesswomen who are out there every day holding beauty shows, teaching skin care, selling our products, and sharing the Mary Kay opportunity. At this time will all of the Mary Kay beauty consultants across the nation stand to be recognized? [*In Birmingham the lights go up and the crowd applauds the consultants in the audience.*] Next we want to recognize the Star Consultants. . . . Will these ladies stand?

Many of our people are wearing small golden ladders. This is our Ladder of Success. Each ladder has a number of different jewels awarded for specific accomplishments during a calendar quarter. Star consultants earn rubies, sapphires, and diamonds to go on their ladders. The higher they climb the more dazzling their ladders become. A consultant with all diamonds is known at Mary Kay as a top Star Performer. It is like wearing a straight A report card on your lapel.

In addition to Ladders, consultants have an opportunity to earn great prizes each quarter. . . . This quarter's theme is Salute to the Stars . . . and these prizes are out of this world.

[*The scene shifts to a description of the fall 1984 sales program; it utilizes a "Star Trek" theme, and across the screen is emblazoned "Starship Mary Kay in Search of the Prize Zone." Captain Kay appears with members of her crew on Starship Mary Kay. She remarks their mission is to seek out prizes to honor those that reach for the sky. They are approaching the prize zone. The awards and prizes are flashed onto the screen.*

The Prize Zone
Bonus Prizes Available
Based on Fourth Quarter Sales

$1,800 Wholesale sales	Cubic zirconia necklace and earrings or travel set with hair dryer
$2,400 Wholesale sales	Leather briefcase with matching umbrella
$3,000 Wholesale sales	Diamond earrings with 14K gold teardrops
$3,600 Wholesale sales	Telephone answering machine
$4,200 Wholesale sales	Sapphire ring
$4,800 Wholesale sales	Electronic printer by Brother—fits in a briefcase
$6,000 Wholesale sales	Diamond pendant—nine diamonds—.5 karat on a 18K gold chain

Even though this "space" presentation of prizes is humorous, the ladies know that the rewards are real; they respond as the scene ends with a round of applause and a buzz of excitement. The scene concludes with the message, "When you reach for the sky you bring home a star."]

Mary Kay [*Returns to the stage.*]: You can climb that ladder of success at Mary Kay. It is up to you to take that very first step. . . . There are so many rewards for being a Mary Kay consultant. There are top earnings, prizes, and lots of recognition. But there is even more to a Mary Kay career and that is the fulfilment of bringing beauty into the lives of others. . . .

When a woman joins our company she knows she can do it. But not alone. She'll receive support from many people. A big sister relationship will form between a new consultant and her recruiter. . . . Whoever invited you tonight thought you were a special person. She wanted to share this evening and introduce you to our company and let you see for yourself the excitement and enthusiasm Mary Kay people have when they are together. . . . The enthusiasm of our consultants and directors is responsible for our success.

[*The vignette about Susan returns to the screen. This time she is thinking about concentrating her effort on recruiting. After five recruits she will become a team leader. A good goal to strive for, she thinks. A woman that had doubted Susan's career earlier is the first one recruited. Then four more ladies are recruited: a waitress, a teacher, a stewardess, and a nurse. All kinds of people can be Mary Kay consultants. Susan has reached her goal—she is a team leader. The crowd applauds her success.*]

Dale Alexander [*Returns to the microphone in Dallas.*]: There is the perfect goal of a Mary Kay career. And now it is time to recognize a very special group of individuals who are proof of this point. Will all the team leaders please stand and remain standing for a few moments? [*The lights go up and team leaders stand. All are wearing red jackets.*]

To qualify for a team leader each consultant must recruit five new consultants. . . . And now will you please recognize these ladies' achievements with a round of applause? [*The audience applauds.*] Now it is time to draw for the prizes. In each of the 75 locations two names will be drawn. These lucky people will both win this exquisite 14K diamond earring and pendant set. [*The crowd oohs and aahs when the jewelry is shown on the screen.*] These two winners will also be eliglble for the prize to be given by Mary Kay when the broadcast resumes.

[*The lights go up in the Birmingham auditorium. Lovie draws two tickets from a big box. When she calls out the names, the winners scream and run on stage to accept their gifts. The crowd applauds the winners.*]

Lovie Quinn [*On the stage in Birmingham*]: Please join me in counting down the final seconds left before we rejoin the broadcast.

[*Everyone stands and enthusiastically counts off "11, 10, 9, 8, 7, 6, 5, 4, 3, 2, 1." The crowd applauds and cheers.*]

Mary Kay [*Appears on the screen as the broadcast from Dallas is rejoined.*]: I wish I could be there to congratulate each winner. . . . The two lucky winners in each of the 75 cities are eligible to win the grand prize. . . . It used to be you just drew a number out of a hat. Now that is considered old-fashioned. Tonight, we'll use a computer. All I have to do is push a button and a city will be randomly selected. The local winners in that city will also win this .75 karat diamond ring. [*The crowd buzzes as a close-up of the ring is shown on the giant screen.*] Are you ready? OK. Here goes. [*Mary Kay presses a button.*] The lucky city is Philadelphia. [*The crowd applauds.*] Congratulations Philadelphia, and we will be sending each of you a ring real soon.

By the way, while we are talking about prizes. Would you happen to have a spare finger for a diamong ring? [*The crowd cheers.*] Or could you squeeze into your closet room for a full-length mink coat? [*The crowd is really excited.*] Or is there by any chance, a space in your driveway for a car? [*The crowd cheers and applauds. One member of the audience remarks how she would be glad to get rid of that old blue thing she is driving.*] Well, all you have to do is set your Mary Kay career goals high enough to achieve the recognition and rewards available just for you. . . .

I remember the first sales competition I set my goals to win. I worked so hard and all I won was a flounder light. [*The audience laughs.*] Does anyone know what you do with it? It is something you use when you put on waders and gig fish. [*The audience laughs again.*] I thought the prize was awful . . . but my manager was a fisherman and he thought it was great.

Winning that flounder light taught me a lesson. I decided if I was ever in a position to give awards they would be things women appreciate, *not* flounder lights. . . . Prizes would be things women would love to have. Absolutely no washing machines and certainly no ironing boards. [*The audience shows their approval by cheers and applause.*] At MKC you are rewarded for consistent sales and recruiting performance. . . . This past spring a new program was added. . . . We call it our VIP program. It stands for Very Important Performer. . . . This program allows a person to win a cream-colored Oldsmobile Firenza with rich brown interior. . . . A consultant is eligible for this prize only three months after joining MKC. . . .

Mary Kay Cosmetics can offer several unique career opportunities:

A 50 percent commission on everything you sell.

Earnings of a 12 percent commission on your recruit's sales.

You work your own hours.

After three months you can be eligible for a car. The car is free. MKC pays the insurance.

When you do well you get a lot of recognition. Not dumb old things like turkeys and hams. We're talking diamonds and furs.

You work up to management because of your own efforts and merit.

Other companies would think these things are part of a dream world. At Mary Kay we do live in a dream world and our dreams do come true.

[*The audience applauds loudly. The broadcast then returns to the scenario about Susan. She sets a goal to be a VIP. Through song and dance her group illustrates setting goals and receiving recognition. Step by step they climb the ladder of recognition. The audience applauds this short scene on success.*]

Dale Alexander [*Comes back to the Dallas stage.*]: We have some VIPs among us tonight. . . . Mary Kay's Very Important Performers. Will all the VIPs now stand? [*The lights go up in Birmingham; the VIPs stand and the audience applauds.*] Through her enthusiasm and hard work each VIP has worked hard to achieve this status. And to recognize her accomplishments she was awarded an Oldsmobile Firenza to show off her achievement of success. Now let's give all our VIPs a round of applause. [*The Birmingham and Dallas audiences respond with more applause.*]

Mary Kay Ash [*Comes onto the stage in Dallas and the crowd in Birmingham turns its attention to the screen.*]: With Mary Kay you can achieve success. . . . All you have to do is break down your goals into small manageable steps. . . . You are able to move on to bigger accomplishments as you gain confidence in yourself.

Let's look at some of the provisions of the Mary Kay career plan and see how it works:

Your products are purchased directly from the company.

Generous discounts are offered on large orders.

There are no territories. You can sell and recruit wherever you want.

We provide our customers the best possible way to buy cosmetics. They can try the products in their own home before they buy.

All Mary Kay products are backed by a full 100 percent money back guarantee.

Mary Kay is a good opportunity to go into business for yourself. . . . There are many benefits of running your own business. . . . You meet new people and at the same time you enjoy the support of the Mary Kay sisterhood. . . . Plus you earn financial rewards as well as prizes. . . .

Now we need to talk about the position of Mary Kay Sales Director. Directors receive income not only from shows, facials, and reorders but also from recruit commissions. . . . In addition they earn unit and recruiting bonuses from Mary Kay. . . . Some earn over $30,000 a year. And today in our company we have more women earning over $50,000 a year than any other company in America. [*The audience applauds.*] At the very top are our National Sales Directors. . . . Their average is about $150,000 a year in commissions. How about that? [*The audience applauds.*] Everyone at Mary Kay starts at the same place with the same beauty showcase. I've always said you can have anything in this world if you want it badly enough and are willing to pay the price. With that kind of attitude anyone can succeed at Mary Kay.

[*The vignette about Susan comes back onto the screen. Susan sets a goal to achieve Sales Director. She sings about how invigorating her new career is and how she now wants to be a coach, a teacher, a counselor, and a friend to others. Everyone around her recognizes how her success has positively affected her whole life. The scene ends and the audience applauds.*]

Dale Alexander [*Comes onto the screen from Dallas.*]: Those individuals that advance on to directorship lead our organization. They set the pace for their units. Will all our Sales Directors please stand? [*The sales directors stand as the lights go up in Birmingham and the audience applauds.*] Among all our directors there are some that have reached a very special level. They have earned the privilege of driving one of Mary Kay's famous pink cars. . . . One thing is guaranteed. Whenever you see one of those pink cars on the road you know there is a top achiever behind the wheel. At this time we want to honor all these ladies. [*First the Regal drivers stand and then the Cadillac drivers. The audience recognizes each group with applause.*] Finally, there is one last group we want to recognize. A group whose members have already committed to a future with Mary Kay. . . . They are our DIQs or Directors in Qualification. They are working towards meeting the goals to qualify for Directorship. . . . Will all the DIQs stand for a round of applause?

[The lights go up and the DIQs stand. They are recognized with applause from the audience. The lights fade and the scene shifts back to Dallas.]

Mary Kay: I want to congratulate these ladies. Next week I'll have the pleasure of hostessing our traditional tea for the DIQs at my home. *[The audience applauds.]* Our DIQs are a perfect example of one of the points we have tried to make this evening. . . . You can set your goals and achieve them if you want them badly enough.

I've always felt our most valuable asset is not our product but our people. . . . I wish I could tell you all the success stories of consultants at MKC. . . . We have chosen a few stories we think best represent Mary Kay consultants. The first person you'll meet is Rena.

[The audience applauds; Rena is recognized by the Mary Kay people present. The narrator of the film clip tells us that Rena has been with MKC for 17 years. She has been Queen of Unit Sales four consecutive years, an honor which was earned when the sales unit she managed exceeded $1 million in sales in one year. Her reward was four $5,000 shopping sprees at Neiman-Marcus Co. in Dallas. When she started she was living on $300 a month in government housing with her husband and three small children. One day a friend offered to buy her dinner and pay for a babysitter if she would attend a meeting. She couldn't pass up this offer so she went to the Mary Kay meeting. The meeting inspired her and she joined MKC. At the end we learn that Rena has had cancer for the last eight years, a fact that is not well known; the point is made that it has never affected her ability to succeed with Mary Kay Cosmetics. the crowd applauds her success story.

Next comes a film clip about Ruel; the audience is told that Ruel was raised in Arkansas, a daughter of a sharecropper. She joined Mary Kay in 1971. By 1976 she was a National Sales Director. A career with Mary Kay has given her confidence. She has two children in medical school and one of her sons just won a national honor, the Medal of Valor. All of this she attributes to Mary Kay. Her children saw her achieve and they knew they could too. Her career with Mary Kay has allowed her to climb up the scale from a poor sharecropper's daughter to become financially independent. Along the way she has the opportunity to meet many wonderful people. As her success story ends, the audience applauds.

The third story is about Arlene. Arlene has been a National Sales Director since 1976. She achieved this just five short years after joining MKC. She had been at home for 13 years and wanted to have her own business, set her own hours, and write her own checks. She found she could achieve these goals in a career with Mary Kay. Arlene, we are told, has been able to reach inside herself and achieve great success. Arlene testifies that one of her biggest rewards at Mary Kay has been helping other women achieve the goals they set. The audience loudly applauds the last of the success stories.]

Mary Kay: I am so proud of all these ladies. . . . It makes me feel good to be able to offer all these wonderful opportunities to so many women.

Every journey begins with just a single step. All you have to do is make up your mind that YOU can do it! Isn't it exciting. You CAN do it.

All you need to start a Mary Kay career is a beauty case. It carries everything: vanity trays, mirrors, products, and product literature.

Tonight it becomes easier. . . . If you join us as a beauty consultant tonight, we will give you your beauty showcase. [*The audience interrupts with a round of applause.*] When you submit your Beauty Consultant agreement along with your first wholesale order, you will receive the beauty case free, an $85 value.

At Mary Kay you'll make lasting friends and you'll achieve a feeling of growth. . . . Tonight we wanted to give you a feel for Mary Kay Cosmetics. We have a place for you to shine. . . . Believe in yourself and you can do anything.

[*The broadcast from Dallas concludes; the audience stands and applauds the program.*]

Lovie Quinn [*Comes onto stage in Birmingham.*]: I started at Mary Kay just to earn money for Christmas. I told Mary Kay I could only work four hours a week. Believe it or not Mary Kay welcomed me into the organization.

Things were different then. There were no manuals or guides. I was given my first cosmetics in a shoe box. Mary Kay Cosmetics has come a long way. Each consultant has her own beauty case and is trained in skin care.

Last year I earned over $112,000. This does not include my personal sales. . . . I am now driving my 13th pink Cadillac. . . . For three years I have been in the half million dollar club. The prizes for this honor include either a black mink, a white mink, or a diamond ring, all worth $10,000 each. I have all three.

Mary Kay Cosmetics offers many opportunities to women. . . . Tonight, if you join MKC, I would be honored to sign your agreement. This will let Mary Kay know you made your commitment tonight.

[*Lovie invites the new consultants to meet her up front. The audience applauds her. Many of the women eagerly go up to meet Lovie and have their agreements signed.*]

THE DIRECT SALES INDUSTRY

In 1984 Avon was the acknowledged leader among the handful of companies that chose to market cosmetics to U.S. consumers using direct sales techniques; Avon, with its door-to-door sales force of 400,000 representatives, had worldwide sales of about $2 billion. Mary Kay Cosmetics was the second leading firm (see Exhibit 1). Other well-known companies whose salespeople went either door-to-door with their products or else held "parties" in the homes of prospective customers included Amway Corp. (home cleaning products), Shaklee Corp. (vitamins and health foods), Encyclopaedia Britannica, Tupperware (plastic dishes and food containers), Consolidated Foods' Electrolux division (vacuum cleaners), and StanHome (parent of Fuller Brush). The direct sales industry also included scores of lesser known firms selling about every product imaginable—clothing, houseplants, toys, and financial services. Although Stanley Home Products invented the idea, Mary Kay and Tupperware were the best-known

EXHIBIT 1 Estimated Sales of Leading Direct Selling Cosmetic Companies, 1983

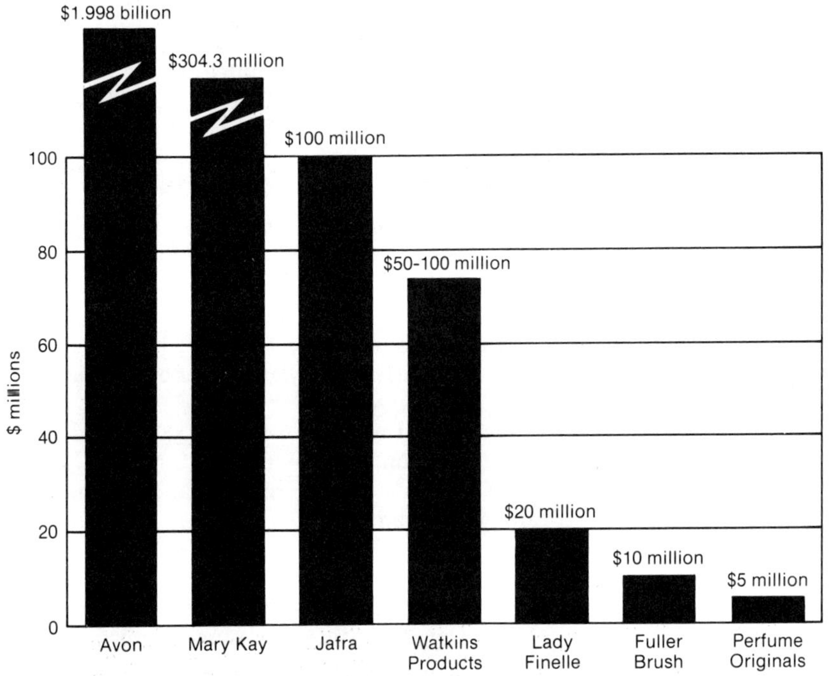

Source: "Reopening the Door to Door-to-Door Selling," *Chemical Business,* February 1984.

national companies using the "party plan" approach to direct selling.

The success enjoyed by Avon and Mary Kay was heavily dependent upon constantly replenishing and expanding their sales forces. New salespeople not only placed large initial orders for products but they also recruited new people into the organization. Revenues and revenue growth thus were a function of the number of representatives as well as the sales productivity of each salesperson. Market size was not seen as a limiting factor for growth because direct sales companies typically reached fewer than half the potential customer base.

Direct selling was grounded in capitalizing on networking relationships. Salespeople usually got their starts by selling first to relatives, friends, and neighbors, all the while looking for leads to new prospects. Direct sales specialists often believed that party plan selling was most successful among working class, ethnic, and small-town population groups where relationships were closer knit and where the social lives of women had a high carryover effect with work and high school. However, industry analysts saw several trends working against the networking approach and party plan type of direct-selling—rising divorce rates, the scattering of relatives and families across wider geographic areas, weakening ties to ethnic neighborhoods, declines in the number and strength of "the old girls" networks in many towns and neighborhoods, increased social mobility, the growing popularity of apartment and condominium living where acquaintances and relationships were most transient, and the springing up of bedroom communities and subdivisions populated by commuters and/or by families that stayed only a few years.

In the 1980s direct selling companies began to have problems recruiting and retaining salespeople, partly because of these trends but even more because of shifting employment patterns and preferences. During the two most recent recessionary periods in the United States, it was thought that the pool of potential saleswomen available for recruitment into direct sales careers would expand owing to above-normal unemployment rates. It didn't happen. As it turned out, many women became the sole family support and even greater numbers sought steady, better paying jobs in other fields. Part-time job opportunities mushroomed outside the direct-sales field as many service and retailing firms started hiring part-time permanent workers rather than full-time permanent staffs because part-time workers did not have to be paid the same extensive fringe benefits that full-time employees normally got. When the economy experienced upturns, the pool of direct sales recruits shrank even more as people sought security in the jobs offering regular hours and a salary; in 1983 all direct sales companies reported increased difficulty in getting people to accept their part-time, sales-oriented, commission-only offers of employment.

Avon and Mary Kay were both caught offguard by these unpredicted events. Staffing plans at Avon had originally called for expansion in the number of sales force representatives from 400,000 in 1983 to 650,000 by 1987; in 1984 the company revised the 1987 goal down to 500,000 representatives. Four straight years of declining earnings convinced Avon that the traditional approach of depending on increasing the number of representatives for growth was not feasible any longer.

Sarah Coventry, a home party jewelry firm, decided in 1984 that relying solely upon direct selling approaches would not only be a continuing problem but a growing problem. The company began to look for ways to supplement its direct sales methods and shortly announced a plan to begin to sell Sarah Coventry products in retail stores. Fuller Brush, a long-standing door-to-door seller, began to distribute mail-order catalogs displaying a wider line of "househelper" products.

As of 1984 virtually every company in the direct sales industry was critically evaluating the extent to which changes in the economy and in employment demographics would affect the success of direct selling. Many firms, including Avon and Mary Kay, were reviewing their incentive programs and sales organization methods. A number of industry observers as well as company officials believed some major changes would have to be made in the way the direct sales industry did business.

MARY KAY ASH

Before she reached the age of 10, Mary Kay had the responsibility of cleaning, cooking, and caring for her invalid father, while her mother worked to support the family. During these years, Mary Kay's mother encouraged her daughter to excel. Whether at school or home, Mary Kay was urged to put forth her best efforts. By the time she was a teenager, Mary Kay had become a classic overachiever, intent on getting good grades and winning school contests. Over and over again she heard her mother say "you can do it." Years later Mary Kay noted on many occasions, "The confidence my mother instilled in me has been a tremendous help."[1]

Deserted by her husband of 11 years during the Great Depression, Mary Kay found herself with the responsibility of raising and supporting three children under the age of eight. Needing a job with flexible hours, she opted to try a career in direct sales with Stanley Home Products, a home party housewares firm. One of the first goals Mary Kay set at Stanley was to win Stanley's Miss Dallas Award, a ribbon honoring the employee who recruited the most new people in one week; she won the award during her first year with Stanley. After 13 years with Stanley, Mary Kay joined World Gift, a direct sales company involved in decorative accessories; a few years later she was promoted to national training director. Her career and life were threatened in 1962 by a rare paralysis of one side of the face.

After recovery from surgery she decided to retire from World Gift; by then she had remarried and lived in a comfortable Dallas neighborhood. She got so bored with retirement she decided to write a book on her direct sales experiences. The more she wrote, the more she came to realize just how many problems women faced in the business world. Writing on a yellow legal pad at her kitchen table, Mary Kay listed everything she thought was wrong with male-run companies; on a second sheet she detailed how these wrongs could be righted, how a company could operate in ways that were responsive to the problems of working women and especially working mothers, and how women

[1] Mary Kay Ash, *Mary Kay* (New York: Harper & Row, 1981), p. 3.

could reach their top potential in the business world. Being restless with retirement, she decided to do something about what she had written on the yellow pad and began immediately to plan how she might form a direct sales company that had no sales quotas, few rules, flexible work hours, and plenty of autonomy for salespeople.

Finding a product to market was not a problem. In 1953 when she was conducting a Stanley home party at a house "on the wrong side of Dallas" she had noticed that all the ladies present had terrific-looking skin. It turned out that the hostess was a cosmetologist who was experimenting with a skin care product and all the guests were her guinea pigs. After the party everyone gathered in the hostess's kitchen to get samples of her latest batch. The product was based on a formula that the woman's father, a hide tanner, developed when he accidentally discovered that some tanning lotions he made and used regularly had caused his hands to look much younger than his face. The tanner decided to apply these solutions to his face regularly, and after a short time his facial skin began looking more youthful too. The woman had since worked with her father's discovery for 17 years, making up batches which had the chemical smell of tanning solutions, putting portions in empty jars and bottles, and selling them as a sideline; she gave out instructions for use written in longhand on notebook paper. Mary Kay offered to try some of the hostess's latest batch and, despite the fact that it was smelly and messy, soon concluded that it was so good she wouldn't use anything else. Later, she became convinced that the only reason the woman hadn't made the product a commercial success was because she lacked marketing skills.

In 1963, using $5,000 in savings as working capital, she bought the formulas and proceeded to organize a beauty products company that integrated skin care instruction into its direct sales approach. The company was named Beauty by Mary Kay; the plan was for Mary Kay to take responsibility for the sales part of the company and for her second husband to serve as chief administrator. One month before operations were to start, he dropped dead of a heart attack. Her children persuaded her to go ahead with her plans, and Mary Kay's 20-year-old son, Richard Rogers, agreed to take on the job of administration of the new company. In September 1963 they opened a small store in Dallas with one shelf of inventory and nine of Mary Kay's friends as saleswomen. Mary Kay herself had limited expectations for the company and never dreamed that its sphere of operations would extend beyond Dallas.

All of Mary Kay's life-long philosophies and experiences were incorporated into how the company operated. The importance of encouragement became deeply ingrained in what was said and done. "You Can Do It" was expanded from a technique used by her mother to a daily theme at MKC. Mary Kay's style was to "praise people to success." She put into practice again the motivating role which positive encouragement had played in her own career; recognition and awards were made a highlight of the sales incentive programs that emerged. By 1984, recognition at MKC ranged from a simple ribbon awarded for a consultant's first $100 show to a $5,000 shopping spree given to million-dollar producers.

The second important philosophy which Mary Kay stressed concerned personal priorities: "Over the years I have found that if you have your life in the proper perspective, with God first, your family second, and your career third, everything seems to work out."[2] She reiterated this belief again and again, regularly urging employees to take stock of their personal priorities and citing her own experience and belief as a positive example. She insisted on an all-out, firmwide effort to accommodate the plight of working mothers. Mary Kay particularly stressed giving beauty consultants enough control over how their selling efforts were scheduled so that problems with family matters and sick children were not incompatible with a Mary Kay career. A structure based on no sales quotas, few rules, and flexible hours was essential, Mary Kay believed, because working mothers from time to time needed the freedom to let work demands take a backseat to pressing problems at home.

Fairness and personal ethics were put in the forefront, too. The Golden Rule (treating others as you would have them treat you) was high on Mary Kay's list of management guidelines:

> I believe in the Golden Rule and try to run the company on those principles. I believe that all you send into the lives of others will come back into your own. I like to see women reaching into themselves and coming out of their shells as the beautiful person that God intended them to be. In my company women do not have to claw their way to the top. They can get ahead based on the virtue of their own ethics because there's enough for everyone.[3]

To discourage interpersonal rivalry and jealousy, all rewards and incentives were pegged to reaching plateaus of achievement; everybody who reached the target level of performance became a winner. Sales contests based on declaring first place, second place, and third place winners were avoided.

MKC INC.

The company succeeded from the start. First-year wholesale sales were $198,000; in the second year sales reached $800,000. At year-end 1983

---

[2] Ibid., p. 56.

[3] As quoted in "The Beauty of Being Mary Kay," *Marketing and Media Decisions,* December 1982, pp. 150 and 152.

wholesale revenues exceeded $320 million and MKC's staff of consultants numbered over 195,000. Major geographical expansion was initiated during the 1970s. Distribution centers were opened in California, Georgia, New Jersey, and Illinois, and the company expanded its selling efforts internationally to Canada, Argentina, Australia, and the United Kingdom.

Early on, Mary Kay and Richard decided to consult a psychologist to learn more about their personalities. Testing revealed that Mary Kay was the type who, when encountering a person bleeding all over a fine carpet, would think of the person's plight first while Richard would think first of the carpet. This solidified their decision for Mary Kay to be the company's inspirational leader and for Richard to concentrate on overseeing all the business details.

In 1968 the company name was changed to Mary Kay Cosmetics, Inc. Also, during 1968 the company went public and its stock was traded in the over-the-counter market; in 1976 MKC's stock was listed on the New York Stock Exchange. Income per common share jumped from $0.16 in 1976 to $1.22 in 1983. A 10-year financial summary is presented in Exhibit 2; Exhibits 3 and 4 provide additional company data.

Richard Rogers, president, gave two basic reasons for the success of MKC:

> We were filling a void in the industry when we began to teach skin care and makeup artistry and we're still doing that today. And second, our marketing system, through which proficient consultants achieve success by recruiting and building their own sales organization, was a stroke of genius because the by-product has been management. In other words, we didn't buy a full management team, they've been trained one by one.[4]

One of the biggest challenges MKC had to tackle during the 1970s was how to adapt its strategy and operating style in response to the influx of women into the labor force. Full- and part-time jobs interfered with attending beauty shows during normal working hours, and many working women with children at home had a hard time fitting beauty shows on weeknights and weekends into their schedules. To make the beauty show sales approach more appealing to working women, the company began to supplement its standard "try before you buy" and "on-the-spot-delivery" sales pitch themes. Consultants were trained to tout the ease with which MKC's scientifically formulated skin care system could be followed, the value of investing in good makeup and attractive appearance, the up-to-date glamor and wide selection associated with MKC's product line, the flexibility of deciding what and when to buy, and the time-saving convenience of having refills and

---

[4] Mary Kay Cosmetics, Inc., "A Company and a Way of Life," Company Literature.

EXHIBIT 2 Selected Financial Data, Mary Kay Cosmetics, Inc., 1973–1983 (in thousands except per share data)

	1973	*1974*	*1975*	*1976*	*1977*	*1978*	*1979*	*1980*	*1981*	*1982*	*1983*
Net sales	$22,199	$30,215	$34,947	$44,871	$47,856	$53,746	$91,400	$166,938	$235,296	$304,275	$323,758
Cost of sales	6,414	9,054	10,509	14,139	14,562	17,517	27,584	52,484	71,100	87,807	88,960
Selling, general, and administrative expenses	9,674	13,128	15,050	19,192	21,394	27,402	45,522	86,998	120,880	154,104	168,757
Operating income	6,111	8,033	9,388	11,540	11,900	8,827	18,304	27,456	43,316	62,364	66,041
Interest and other income, net	377	443	202	501	175	660	493	712	1,485	2,763	3,734
Interest expense	58	54	60	43	212	504	958	635	1,014	1,284	2,886
Income before income taxes	6,430	8,422	9,530	11,998	11,863	8,983	17,839	27,533	43,787	63,843	66,889
Provision for income taxes	3,035	3,973	4,480	5,854	5,711	4,110	8,207	12,398	19,632	28,471	30,235
Net income	$ 3,395	$ 4,449	$ 5,050	$ 6,144	$ 6,152	$ 4,873	$ 9,632	$ 15,135	$ 24,155	$ 35,372	$ 36,654
Net income per common share	$ .09	$ .11	$ .13	$ .16	$ .17	$ .15	$ .33	$ .52	$ .82	$ 1.18	$ 1.22
Cash dividends per share	$ .01	$ .03	$ .03	$ .05	$ .05	$ .06	$ .06	$ .09	$ .10	$ .11	$ .12
Average common shares	38,800	38,864	38,928	39,120	35,480	33,408	29,440	28,884	29,324	29,894	30,138
Total assets	$19,600	$24,743	$27,996	$34,331	$35,144	$36,305	$50,916	$ 74,431	$100,976	$152,457	$180,683
Long-term debt	$ 756	$ 87	$ 42	—	$ 5,592	$ 3,558	$ 4,000	$ 3,000	$ 2,366	$ 4,669	$ 3,915
Return on average stockholders' equity			21%	23%	24%	20%	38%	48%	48%	45%	32%
Stock prices											
Year high			2¾	2⅞	2⅝	1⅞	3⅞	8¾	18¾	28½	47⅞
Year low			1⅞	1¾	1½	1¼	1¼	3	6⅛	8⅜	13⅛

Source: Mary Kay Cosmetics, Inc., *1983 Annual Report*.

EXHIBIT 3 Growth in the Number of MKC Sales Directors and Beauty Consultants, 1973–1983

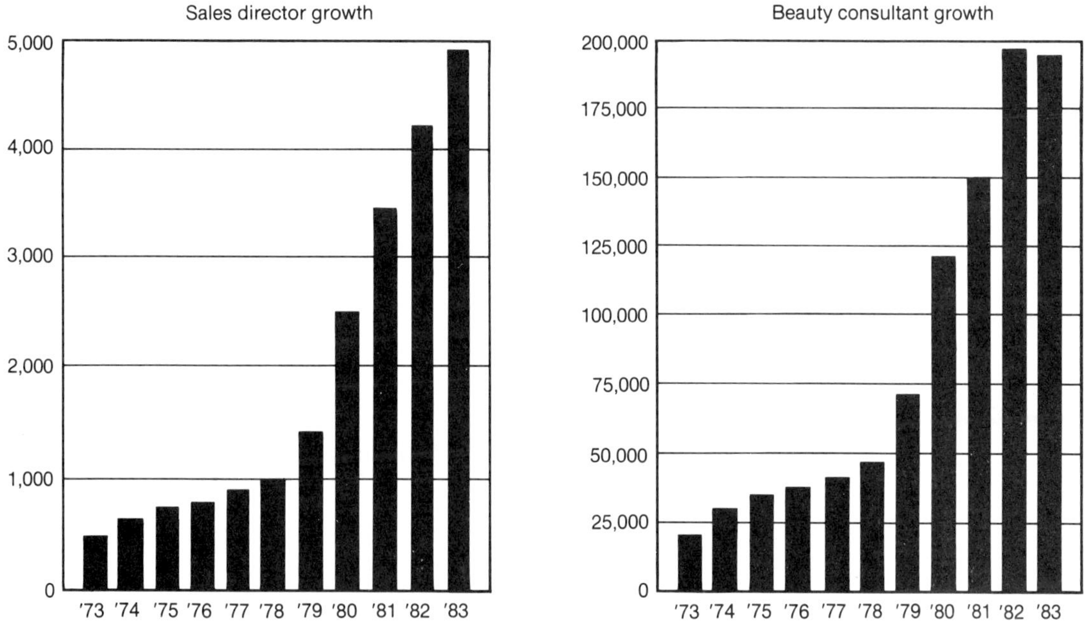

	Average Number of Consultants	*Net Sales ($000)*	*Average Annual Sales Productivity per Consultant*
1983	195,671	$323,758	$1,655
1982	173,137	304,275	1,757
1981	134,831	235,296	1,745
1980	94,983	166,938	1,758
1979	57,989	91,400	1,576

Source: 1983 Annual Report.

"specials" delivered to their door instead of having to go out shopping. Mary Kay consultants quickly picked up on the growing popularity of having beauty shows on Tuesday, Wednesday, and Thursday nights; a lesser proportion of weekday hours were used for morning and afternoon showings, and a greater proportion came to be used for seeking and delivering reorders from ongoing users.

MKC's corporate sales goal for the 80s was to reach $500 million in revenues by 1990. As of 1984 about 65 percent of total sales were made to customers at beauty shows. However, it was expected that as the size of the company's customer base grew, the percentage of orders

EXHIBIT 4 Percentage Breakdown of Product Sales at Mary Kay Cosmetics, 1979–1983

	1979	*1980*	*1981*	*1982*	*1983*
Skin care products for women	49%	52%	49%	46%	44%
Skin care products for men	1	2	1	1	1
Makeup items	26	22	26	26	30
Toiletry items for women	10	10	10	12	11
Toiletry items for men	2	2	2	2	2
Hair care	2	2	2	2	2
Accessories	10	10	10	11	10
Total	100%	100%	100%	100%	100%

Source: 1983 Annual Report.

from repeat buyers would rise well above the present 35 percent level. MKC estimated that the average client spent over $200 a year on cosmetics. The company saw its target clientele as middle-class women in the 18–34 age group primarily and in the 35–44 age group secondarily, and believed that a big percentage of its customers consisted of suburban housewives and white-collar clerical workers. The company's literature always pictured upscale women, dressed in a classy and elegant yet understated way, in either the role of a Mary Kay beauty consultant or the role of a user of Mary Kay cosmetics. As company figurehead, Mary Kay Ash personally made a point of being fashionably and expensively dressed, with perfect makeup and hairdo—a walking showcase for the company's products and a symbol of the professionally successful businesswoman (Exhibit 5).

MANUFACTURING

When Mary Kay Cosmetics commenced operations in 1963, the task of making the products was contracted out to a private Dallas-based manufacturing company. Mary Kay explained why:

> In 1963 I had no previous experience in the cosmetics industry; my forte was recruiting and training salespeople. After I acquired the formulas for the skin-care products, the first thing I did was seek out the most reputable cosmetics manufacturer I could find. Specifically I wanted a firm that not only made quality products, but observed the Food and Drug Administra-

EXHIBIT 5 Mary Kay Ash in 1983

Source: 1983 Annual Report (picture on front cover).

tion's regulatory requirements to the letter. I knew it would be a fatal mistake to attempt to cut corners. With the right people in charge, we would never have to concern ourselves with that aspect of the business.[5]

In 1969 MKC built a 300,000-square-foot manufacturing and packaging facility adjacent to corporate headquarters. Packaging, warehousing, purchasing, and research labs were all housed in this location. Also included was a printing set-up which created Mary Kay labels in English, Spanish, and French. Many of the operations were automated.

The company's scientific approach to skin care was supported by a

[5] Mary Kay Ash, *Mary Kay on People Management* (New York: Warner Books, 1984), p. 13.

staff of laboratory technicians skilled in cosmetic chemistry, dermatology, physiology, microbiology, and package engineering. Ongoing tests were conducted to refine existing items and to develop new products. Laboratory staffs were provided with the comments and reactions about the products that came in from beauty consultants and their customers; consultants were strongly encouraged to report on their experiences with items and to relay any problems that consultants had directly to the laboratory staff. About 80 percent of the R&D budget was earmarked for improving existing products.

MKC believed that it was an industry leader in researching, one, the biophysical properties of the skin (as concerning skin elasticity and moisture) and, two, skin structure and anatomical quality. Much of the research at MKC was performed in cooperation with academic institutions, particularly the University of Pennsylvania and the University of Texas Health Science Center.

PRODUCT LINE AND DISTRIBUTION POLICIES

As of 1984 the Mary Kay product line consisted of the Basic Skin Care Program for various skin types, the glamour collection, the body care products line, and a line of men's products called Mr. K. Most of the women's products were packaged in pink boxes and jars. When the company first began operations, Mary Kay personally put a lot of thought into packaging and appearance:

> Since people do leave their toiletries out, I wanted to package our cosmetics so beautifully that women would *want* to leave them out. So I was looking for a color that would make a beautiful display in all those white bathrooms. There were some shades of blue that were attractive, but the prettiest complementary color seemed to be a delicate pink. It also occurred to me that pink is considered a more feminine color. But my main reason for choosing it was that delicate pink seemed to look prettier than anything else in those white tile bathrooms. And from that I gained a *pink* reputation![6]

Mr. K, the men's line, was introduced in the 1960s in response to a number of confessions from men who used their wives' Mary Kay products. A rich chocolate brown package accented with silver was chosen for Mr. K. The men's line included a Basic Skin Care Program as well as lotions and colognes. The majority of Mr. K purchases were made by women for their husbands and boyfriends.

Consultants bought their supplies of products directly from MKC at wholesale prices and sold them at a 100 percent markup over whole-

---

[6] Ash, *Mary Kay*, pp. 150–51.

sale. To make it more feasible for consultants to keep an adequate inventory on hand, the product line at MKC was kept streamlined, about 50 products. Mary Kay consultants were encouraged to carry enough products in their personal inventories that orders could be filed on the spot at the beauty shows. As an incentive to support this practice, MKC offered special awards and prizes when consultants placed orders of $1,500 or more.

A consultant could order as many or as few of the company's products as she chose to inventory. Most consultants stockpiled those items that sold especially well with their own individual clientele, and consultants also had the freedom to offer special promotions or discounts to customers. Nearly 50 percent of sales were for the skin care products which had evolved from the hide tanner's discovery. Consultants were required to pay for all orders with cashier's checks or money orders prior to delivery. MKC dealt only on a cash basis to minimize accounts receivables problems; according to Mary Kay, "Bad debts are a major reason for failure in other direct sales companies." In 1984 the average initial order of new consultants for inventory was about $1,000 ($2,000 in retail value). Consultants who decided to get out of the business could resell their inventories to MKC at 90 percent of cost.

During the company's early years, consultants were supplied only with an inventory of items to sell; shipments arrived in plain boxes. There were no sales kits and no instruction manuals to assist in sales presentations. However, by the 1970s each new recruit received training in skin care techniques and was furnished with a number of sales aids. Later new consultants were required to buy a beauty showcase containing everything needed to conduct a beauty show (samples, pink mirrors, pink trays used to distribute the samples, and a step-by-step sales manual that included suggested dialogue. In 1984 the showcase was sold to new consultants for $85. Along with the showcase came a supply of beauty profile forms to use at showings; guests filled out the form at the beginning of the show, and from the information supplied a consultant could readily prescribe which of several product formulas was best suited for the individual's skin type.

In addition to the income earned from product sales, consultants earned bonuses or commissions on the sales made by all of the recruits they brought in. MKC paid consultants with one to four recruits a bonus commission equal to 4 percent of the wholesale orders of the recruits. A consultant with five or more recruits earned an 8 percent commission on the orders placed by recruits, or 12 percent if she also placed $600 a month in wholesale orders herself. MKC consultants who were entitled to a 12 percent commission and who had as many as 24 recruits were averaging about $950 monthly in bonuses and recruitment commissions as of 1984.

MKC'S SALES ORGANIZATION

The basic field organization unit for MKC's 195,000-person force of beauty consultants was the sales unit. Each sales unit was headed by a sales director who provided leadership and training for her group of beauty consultants. The top-performing sales directors were designated as national sales directors, a title that signified the ultimate achievement in the Mary Kay career sales ladder. A corporate staff of seven national sales administrators oversaw the activities of the sales directors in the field and their units of beauty consultants.

The sales units were not organized along strict geographical lines, and sales directors were free to recruit consultants anywhere:

> One of the first things I wanted my dream company to eliminate was assigned territories. I had worked for several direct-sales organizations in the past, and I knew how unfairly I had been treated when I had to move from Houston to St. Louis because of my husband's new job. I had been making $1,000 a month in commissions from the Houston sales unit that I had built over a period of eight years and I lost it all when I moved. I felt that it wasn't fair for someone else to inherit those Houston salespeople whom I had worked so hard to recruit and train.
>
> Because we don't have territories at Mary Kay Cosmetics, a director who lives in Chicago can be vacationing in Florida or visiting a friend in Pittsburgh and recruit someone while there. It doesn't matter where she lives in the United States; she will always draw a commission from the company on the wholesale purchases made by that recruit as long as they both remain with the company. The director in Pittsburgh will take the visiting director's new recruit under her wing and train her; the recruit will attend the Pittsburgh sales meetings and participate in the local sales contests. Although the Pittsburgh director will devote a lot of time and effort to the new recruit, the Chicago director will be paid the commissions. We call this our "adoptee" program.
>
> The Pittsburgh recruit may go on to recruit new people on her own. No matter where she lives, she becomes the nucleus for bringing in additional people for the director who brought her into the business. As long as they're both active in the company, she will receive commissions from the company on her recruit's sales activity.
>
> Today we have more than 5,000 sales directors, and most of them train and motivate people in their units who live outside their home states. Some have beauty consultants in a dozen or more states. Outsiders look at our company and say "Your adoptee program can't possibly work!" But it does work. Each director reaps the benefits from her recruits in other cities and helps other recruits in return.[7]

---

[7] Ash, *People Management*, pp. 2–3.

THE BEAUTY CONSULTANT

Nearly all of MKC's beauty consultants had their first contact with the company as a guest at a beauty show. A discussion of career opportunities with Mary Kay was a standard part of the presentation at each beauty show. As many as 10 percent of the attendees at beauty shows were serious prospects as new recruits.

All beauty consultants were self-employed and worked on a commission basis. Everyone in the entire MKC sales organization started at the consultant level. The progression of each consultant up the "ladder of success" within the MKC sales organization was tightly linked to (1) the amount of wholesale orders the consultant placed with MKC, (2) her abilities to bring in new sales recruits, and (3) the size of the wholesale orders placed by these recruits. There were five rungs on the ladder of success for consultants, with qualifications and rewards as follows:

1. *New Beauty Consultant* (member of "Perfect Start Club").
   "Perfect Start Club" qualifications:
      Study and complete Perfect Start workbook.
      Observe three beauty shows.
      Book a minimum of eight shows within two weeks of receiving beauty showcase.
   Awards and recognition:
      Receives "Perfect Start" pin.
      Earns 50 percent commission on retail sales (less any discounts given to customers on "special promotions").
      Becomes eligible for a 4 percent recruiting commission on wholesale orders placed by active personal recruits (to be considered active a consultant had to place at least a $600 minimum wholesale order during the current quarter).
      Is eligible for special prizes and bonuses given for current quarter's sales and recruiting contest.
2. *Star Consultant.*
   Qualifications:
      Must have three active recruits.
      Be an active beauty consultant (place a minimum wholesale order of $600 within the current calendar quarter).
   Awards and recognition:
      Earns a red blazer.
      Earns a star pin.

Earns "Ladder of Success" status by placing $1,800 in wholesale orders in a three-month period.

Earns 50 percent commission on personal sales at beauty shows.

Earns 4 percent personal recruiting commission on wholesale orders placed by active personal recruits.

Is eligible for special prizes and awards offered during quarterly contest.

Receives a Star of Excellence ladder pin by qualifying as a star consultant for 8 quarters (or a Double Star of Excellence pin for 16 quarters).

3. *Team Leader.*
   Qualifications:

   Must have five or more active recruits.

   Be an active beauty consultant.

   Awards and recognitions:

   Earns 50 percent commission on sales at own beauty shows.

   Earns a "Tender Loving Care" emblem for red blazer.

   Earns an 8 percent personal recruiting commission on wholesale orders of active personal recruits.

   Earns a 12 percent personal recruiting commission if (*a*) five or more active personal recruits place minimum $600 wholesale orders during the current month and (*b*) the team leader herself places a $600 wholesale order during the current month.

   Receives Team Leader pin in ladder of success program.

   Is eligible for quarterly contest prizes and bonuses.

4. *VIP (Very Important Performer).*
   Qualifications:

   Must have obtained Team Leader status.

   Must place wholesale orders of at least $600 for three consecutive months.

   Team must place wholesale orders of at least $3,000 each month for three consecutive months.

   Awards and recognition:

   Earns the use of an Oldsmobile Firenza.

   Earns 50 percent commission on sales at own beauty shows.

   Earns a 12 percent personal recruiting commission.

   Receives VIP pin in ladder of success program.

   Is eligible for quarterly contest prizes and bonuses.

5. *Future Director.*
   Qualifications:
      Must have qualified for Team Leader status.
      Must have 12 active recruits at time of application.
      Must make a commitment to Mary Kay to become a Sales Director by actually giving her letter of intent date.
   Awards and recognition:
      Earns a Future Director crest for red jacket.
      Plus all the benefits accorded Team Leaders and VIPs, as appropriate, for monthly and quarterly sales and recruiting performance.

New recruits were required to submit a signed Beauty Consultant Agreement, observe three beauty shows conducted by an experienced consultant, book a minimum of eight beauty shows, and hold at least five beauty shows within their first two weeks. Each consultant was asked to appear in attractive dress and makeup when in public and to project an image of knowledge and confidence about herself and the MKC product line. Mary Key felt the stress on personal appearance was justified: "What we are selling is beauty. A woman is not going to buy from someone who is wearing jeans and has her hair up in curlers. We want our consultants to be the type of woman others will want to emulate."[8]

Consultants spent most of their work hours scheduling and giving beauty shows. A showing took about two hours (plus about an hour for travel time), and many times the hostess and one or more of the guests turned out to be prospective recruits. New consultants were coached to start off by booking showings with friends, neighbors, and relatives and then network these into showings for friends of friends and relatives of relatives.

Consultants were instructed to follow up each beauty show by scheduling a second facial for each guest at the showing. Many times a customer would invite friends to her second facial and the result would be another beauty show. After the follow-up facial, consultants would call customers periodically to check on whether the customer was satisfied, to see if refills were needed, and to let the customer know about new products and special promotions. Under MKC's "dovetailing" plan, a consultant with an unexpected emergency at home could

---

[8] Rebecca Fannin, "The Beauty of Being Mary Kay, *Marketing & Media Decisions* 17 (December 1982), pp. 59–61.

sell her prearranged beauty show to another consultant and the two would split the commissions generated by the show.

THE SALES DIRECTOR

Consultants who had climbed to the fifth rung of the consultants' ladder of success were eligible to become sales directors and head up a sales unit. In addition to conducting her own beauty shows, a sales director's responsibilities included training new recruits, leading weekly sales meetings, and providing assistance and advice to the members of her unit. Sales directors, besides receiving the commissions on sales made at their own showings, were paid a commission on the total sales of the unit they headed and a commission on the number of new sales recruits. In June 1984 the top 100 recruiting commissions paid to sales directors ranged from approximately $660 to $1,900. It was not uncommon for sales directors to have total annual earnings in the $50,000 to $100,000 range; in 1983 the average income of the 4,500 sales directors was between $25,000 and $30,000.

There were six achievement categories for sales directors, with qualifications and awards as shown below:

1. *Director in Qualification (DIQ).*
   Qualifications:
      Must have 15 active personal recruits.
      Submits a Letter of Intent to obtain Directorship.
      Gets the Director of her sales unit to submit a letter of recommendation.
      Within three consecutive months:
         Must recruit an additional 15 consultants for a total of 30 personal active recruits.
         The unit of 30 personal active recruits must place combined wholesale orders of $4,000, $4,500, and $5,000 for months one, two, and three respectively.
   Awards and recognition:
      Earns personal sales and personal recruiting commissions (as per schedules for at least Team Leader status).
      Eligible for prizes and bonuses in quarterly contests.

2. *Sales Director.*
   Qualifications:
      Sales unit must maintain a minimum of $4,000 in wholesale orders each month for the sales director to remain as head of her unit.

Awards and recognition:

Receives commissions of 9 percent to 13 percent on unit's wholesale orders.

Receives monthly sales production bonuses:

- a $300 monthly bonus if unit places monthly wholesale orders of $3,000–$4,999.
- a $500 monthly bonus if unit places monthly wholesale orders of $5,000 and up.

Receives a monthly recruiting bonus (for personal recruits or for recruits of other consultants in the sales unit):

- $100 bonus if three to four new recruits come into unit.
- $200 bonus if five to seven new recruits come into unit.
- $300 bonus if 8 to 11 new recruits come into unit.
- $400 bonus for 12 or more recruits.

Is given a designer Director suit.

Is entitled to all commission schedules and incentives of Future Sales Directors.

3. *Regal Director.*

Qualifications:

Members of sales unit must place wholesale orders of at least $24,000 for two consecutive quarters.

Must qualify every two years.

Awards and recognition:

Earns the use of a pink Buick Regal.

Is entitled to all the commission percentages, bonuses, and other incentives of a Sales Director.

4. *Cadillac Director.*

Qualifications:

Sales unit members must place at least $36,000 in wholesale orders for two consecutive quarters.

Must qualify every two years.

Awards and recognition:

Earns the use of pink Cadillac.

Is entitled to all the commission percentages, bonuses, and other incentives of a Sales Director.

5. *Senior Sales Director.*

Qualifications:

One to four Sales Directors emerge from her unit.

Awards and recognition:

Earns a 4 percent commission on offspring Director's consultants.

Is entitled to all the commission percentages, bonuses, and other incentives of at least a Sales Director.

6. *Future National Director.*
   Qualifications:
   Five or more active Directors emerge from her unit.
   Awards and recognition:
   Is entitled to all the commission percentages, bonuses, and other incentives of a Senior Sales Director.

As of late 1983 the company had about 700 Regal Directors and about 700 Cadillac Directors; in one recent quarter 81 sales directors had met the qualifications for driving a new pink Cadillac.

THE NATIONAL SALES DIRECTOR

Top-performing sales directors became eligible for designation as a National Sales Director, the highest recognition bestowed on field sales personnel. NSDs were inspirational leaders and managers of a group of sales directors and received commissions on the total dollar sales of the group of sales units they headed. In 1984 MKC's 50 national sales directors had total sales incomes averaging over $150,000 per year. A 1985 *Fortune* article features Helen McVoy, a MKC National Sales Director since 1971, as one of the most succesful salespeople in the United States; in 1984 she earned $375,000. McVoy began her career with Mary Kay in 1965 at the age of 45. Her family was on a tight budget, having lost all of their savings in a bad mining investment. To support her plant collecting hobby, Helen started selling Mary Kay products on a part-time basis—two hours a week. Her original investment was for a beauty case; by the end of her first year she had made $17,000. From 1970 through 1984 she was the company's top volume producer.

TRAINING

Before holding a beauty show a new consultant had to observe three beauty shows, attend orientation classes conducted by a Sales Director, and complete a self-study set of MKC training materials. This training covered the fundamentals of conducting skin care shows, booking future beauty shows, recruiting new Mary Kay consultants, personal appearance, and managing a small business. Active consultants were strongly encouraged to continue to improve their sales skills and product knowledge. In addition to weekly sales meetings and frequent one-on-one contact with other consultants and sales directors, each salesperson had access to a variety of company-prepared support materials—videotapes, films, slide shows, and brochures.

In 1983 a new educational curriculum was introduced to support each phase of a Mary Kay career. A back-to-basics orientation package provided a foundation for the first stage of career development. A recruitment notebook provided dialogue of mock recruiting conversations, and sales directors were provided with an organizational kit to help them make a smooth transition from being purely a consultant to being a sales manager as well as a consultant.

Additional learning opportunities were provided in the form of special product knowledge classes, regional workshops, and annual corporate-sponsored seminars.

MOTIVATION AND INCENTIVES

New sales contests were introduced every three months. Prizes and recognition awards were always tied to achievement plateaus rather than declaring first, second, and third place winners. Top performers were spotlighted in the company's full-color monthly magazine, *Applause* (which had a circulation of several hundred thousand).

Mary Kay Ash described why MKC paid so much attention to recognition and praise:

> I believe praise is the best way for a manager to motivate people. At Mary Kay Cosmetics we think praise is so important that our entire marketing plan is based upon it.[9]
>
> Praise is an incredibly effective motivator; unfortunately, many managers are reluctant to employ it. Yet I can't help feeling that they know how much praise means, not only to others, but to themselves. . . . I believe that you should praise people whenever you can; it causes them to respond as a thirsty plant responds to water.[10]
>
> The power of positive motivation in a goal-oriented structure such as ours cannot be overstated. This is what inspires our consultants to maximize their true potentials.[11]
>
> As a manager you must recognize that everyone needs praise. But it must be given sincerely. You'll find numerous occasions for genuine praise if you'll only look for them.[12]
>
> Because we recognize the need for people to be praised, we make a concentrated effort to give as much recognition as possible. Of course with

---

[9] Ash, *People Management,* p. 21.

[10] Ibid., p. 23.

[11] Ibid., p. 26.

[12] Ibid., p. 27.

an organization as large as ours not everyone can make a speech at our Seminars, but we do attempt to have many people appear on stage, if only for a few moments. During the Directors' March, for example, hundreds of directors parade on stage before thousands of their peers. In order to appear in the Director's March a director must purchase a special designer suit. Likewise we have a Red Jacket March, in which only star recruiters, team leaders, and future directors participate. Again, a special uniform is required for participation.[13]

How important are these brief stage appearances? Frankly I think it means more for a woman to be recognized by her peers on stage than to receive an expensive present in the mail that nobody knows about! And once she gets a taste of this recognition, she wants to come back next year for more![14]

SEMINAR

MKC staged an annual "Seminar" as a salute to the company and to the salespeople who contributed to its success. The first Seminar was held on September 13, 1964 (the company's first anniversary); the banquet menu consisted of chicken, jello salad, and an anniversary cake while a three-piece band provided entertainment. By 1984 Seminar had grown into a three-day spectacular repeated four consecutive times with a budget of $4 million and attended by 24,000 beauty consultants and sales directors who paid their own way to attend the event. The setting, the Convention Center in Dallas (see Exhibit 6), was decorated in red, white, and blue in order to emphasize the theme, "Share the Spirit." The climactic highlight of Seminar was Awards Night, when the biggest prizes were awarded to the people with the biggest sales. The company went to elaborate efforts to ensure the Awards Night was charged with excitement and emotion; as one observer of the 1984 Awards Night in Dallas described it, "The atmosphere there is electric, a cross between a Las Vegas revue and a revival meeting. Hands reach up to touch Mary Kay; a pink Cadillac revolves on a mist-shrouded pedestal; a 50-piece band plays; and women sob."

Mary Kay Ash customarily made personal appearances throughout the Seminar period. In addition to Awards Night, Seminar featured sessions consisting of informational and training workshops, motivational presentations by leading sales directors, and star entertainment (Paul Anka performed in 1984, and in previous years there had

---

[13] Ibid., p. 28.

[14] Ibid., p. 26.

EXHIBIT 6 "Share the Spirit," 1984 Annual Seminar, Mary Kay Cosmetics

Source: Mary Kay Cosmetics, Inc., Interim Report, 1984.

been performances by Tennessee Ernie Ford, John Davidson, and Johnny Mathis). Over the three days Cadillacs, diamonds, mink coats, a $5,000 shopping spree at Neiman-Marcus for any director whose team sold $1 million worth of Mary Kay products, and lesser assorted prizes were awarded to the outstanding achievers of the past year. Gold-and-diamond bumblebee pins, each containing 21 diamonds and retailing for over $3,600, were presented to the Queens of Sales on Pageant Night; these pins were not only the company's ultimate badge of success, but Mary Kay felt they also had special symbolism:

> It's a beautiful pin, but that isn't the whole story. We think the bumblebee is a marvelous symbol of woman. Because, as aerodynamic engineers found a long time ago, the bumblebee cannot fly! Its wings are too weak and its body is too heavy to fly, but fortunately, the bumblebee doesn't know that, and it goes right on flying. The bee has become a symbol of women who didn't know they could fly but they DID! I think the women who own these diamond bumblebees think of them in their own personal ways. For most of us, it's

> true that we refused to believe we couldn't do it. Maybe somebody said, "It's really impossible to get this thing off the ground." But somebody else told us, "You can do it!" So we did.[15]

On the final day of seminar the Sue Z. Vickers Memorial Award—Miss Go Give—was presented. This honor was given to the individual who best demonstrated the Mary Kay spirit—a spirit described as loving, giving, and inspirational.

CORPORATE ENVIRONMENT

The company's eight-story, gold-glass corporate headquarters building in Dallas was occupied solely by Mary Kay executives. An open-door philosophy was present at MKC. Everyone from the mailroom clerk to the chairman of the board was treated with respect. The door to Mary Kay Ash's office was rarely closed. Often people touring the building peeked in her office to get a glimpse of the pink and white decor. Mary Kay and all other corporate managers took the time to talk with any employee.

First names were always used at MKC. Mary Kay herself insisted on being addressed as Mary Kay; she felt people who called her Mrs. Ash were either angry at her or didn't know her. In keeping with this informal atmosphere, offices didn't have titles on the doors, executive restrooms didn't exist, and the company cafeteria was used by the executives (there was no executive dining room).

To further enhance the informal atmosphere and enthusiasm at MKC, all sales functions were started with a group sing-along. Mary Kay offered several reasons for this policy:

> Nothing great is ever achieved without enthusiasm. . . . We have many of our own songs, and they're sung at all Mary Kay get-togethers, ranging from small weekly meetings to our annual Seminars. Our salespeople enjoy this activity, and I believe the singing creates a wonderful esprit de corps. Yet outsiders, especially men, often criticize our singing as being "strictly for women." I disagree. Singing unites people. It's like those "rah-rah-rah for our team" cheers. If someone is depressed, singing will often bring her out of it.[16]

The company sent Christmas cards, birthday cards, and anniversary cards to every single employee each year. Mary Kay personally designed the birthday cards for consultants. In addition, all the sales directors received Christmas and birthday presents from the company.

---

[15] Ash, *Mary Kay,* p. 9.

[16] Ash, *People Management,* p. 59.

THE PEOPLE MANAGEMENT PHILOSOPHY AT MKC

Mary Kay Ash had some very definite ideas about how people ought to be managed, and she willingly shared them with employees and, through her books, with the public at large. Some excerpts from her book on *People Management* reveal the approach taken at Mary Kay Cosmetics.

> People come first at Mary Kay Cosmetics—our beauty consultants, sales directors, and employees, our customers, and our suppliers. We pride ourselves as a "company known for the people it keeps." Our belief in caring for people, however, does not conflict with our need as a corporation to generate a profit. Yes, we keep our eye on the bottom line, but it's not an overriding obsession.[17]
>
> Ours is an organization with few middle management positions. In order to grow and progress, you don't move upward; you expand outward. This gives our independent sales organization a deep sense of personal worth. They know that they are not competing with one another for a spot in the company's managerial "pecking order." Therefore the contributions of each individual are of equal value. No one is fearful that his or her idea will be "stolen" by someone with more ability on the corporate ladder. And when someone—anyone—proposes a new thought, we all analyze it, improve upon it, and ultimately support it with the enthusiasm of a team.[18]
>
> Every person is special! I sincerely believe this. Each of us wants to feel good about himself or herself, but to me it is just as important to make others feel the same way. Whenever I meet someone, I try to imagine him wearing an invisible sign that says: MAKE ME FEEL IMPORTANT! I respond to this sign immediately and it works wonders.[19]
>
> At Mary Kay Cosmetics we believe in putting our beauty consultants and sales directors on a pedestal. Of all people I most identify with them because I spent many years as a salesperson. My attitude of appreciation for them permeates the company. When our salespeople visit the home office, for example, we go out of our way to give them the red-carpet treatment. Every person in the company treats them royally.[20]
>
> We go first class across the board, and although it's expensive, it's worth it because our people are made to feel important. For example, each year we take our top sales directors and their spouses on deluxe trips to Hong Kong, Bangkok, London, Paris, Geneva, and Athens to mention a few. We spare no expense, and although it costs a lot extra per person to fly the Concorde, cruise on the Love Boat, or book suites at the elegant George V in Paris, it is our way of telling them how important they are to our company.[21]
>
> My experience with people is that they generally do what you expect them

---

[17] Ibid., p. *xix*.
[18] Ibid., pp. 11–12.
[19] Ibid., p. 15.
[20] Ibid., p. 19.
[21] Ibid., p. 20.

> to do! If you expect them to perform well, they will; conversely, if you expect them to perform poorly, they'll probably oblige. I believe that average employees who try their hardest to live up to your high expectations of them will do better than above-average people with low self-esteem. Motivate your people to draw on that untapped 90 percent of their ability and their level of performance will soar![22]
>
> A good people manager will never put someone down; not only is it nonproductive—it's counterproductive. You must remember that your job is to play the role of problem solver and that by taking this approach instead of criticizing people you'll accomplish considerably more.
>
> While some managers try to forget problems they encountered early in their careers, I make a conscious effort to remember the difficulties I've had along the way. I think it's vital for a manager to empathize with the other person's problem, and the best way to have a clear understanding is to have been there yourself.[23]

Interviews with Mary Kay consultants gave credibility to the company's approach and methods. One consultant described her experience thusly:

> I had a lot of ragged edges when I started. The first time I went to a Mary Kay seminar, I signed up for classes in diction and deportment, believe me, I needed them. I didn't even have the right clothes. You can only wear dresses and skirts to beauty shows, so I sank everything I had into one nice dress. I washed it out every night in Woolite and let it drip dry in the shower.
>
> But I was determined to follow all the rules, even the ones I didn't understand—*especially* the ones I didn't understand. At times, it all seemed foolish, especially when you consider that all my clients were mill workers and didn't exactly appreciate my new grammar. But I kept telling myself to hang in there, that Mary Kay knew what was good for me.
>
> When I first started, I won a pearl and ruby ring. A man or a man's company may say I'd have been better off with the cash, but I'm not so convinced. Mary Kay is on to something there. From the moment I won that ring, I began thinking of myself as a person who deserved a better standard of living. I built a new life to go with the ring.[24]

Another consultant observed:

> The essential thing about Mary Kay is the quality of the company. When you go to Dallas, the food, the hotel, and the entertainment are all top notch. Nothing gaudy is allowed in Mary Kay.[25]

When asked if she didn't think pink Cadillacs were a tad gaudy, she

---

[22] Ibid., p. 17.

[23] Ibid., p. 6.

[24] As quoted in Kim Wright Wiley, "Cold Cream and Hard Cash," *Savvy,* June 1985, p. 39.

[25] Ibid., p. 41.

responded in a low, level tone: "When people say that, I just ask them what color car their company gave them last year."

On the morning following Awards Night 1984, a group of Florida consultants were in the hotel lobby getting ready to go to the airport for the flight home.[26] One member had by chance met Mary Kay Ash in the ladies room a bit earlier and had managed to get a maid to snap a Polaroid photograph of them together. She proudly was showing her friends the snapshot and was the only one of the group who had actually met Mary Kay. The consultant said to her friends, "She told me she was sure I'd be up there on stage with her next year. She said she'd see me there." Her sales director, in noting the scene, observed, "She's got the vision now. She really did meet her. And you've got to understand that in Mary Kaydom that's a very big deal."

THE BEAUTY SHOW

It was a few minutes past 7 P.M. on a weeknight in Tuscaloosa, Alabama. Debbie Sessoms and three of her friends (including the casewriter) were seated around the dining room table in Debbie's house. In front of each lady was a pink tray, a mirror, a pencil, and a blank personal Beauty Profile form. Jan Currier stood at the head of the table. She welcomed each of the ladies and asked them to fill out the personal Beauty Profile form in front of them.

When they were finished, Jan started her formal presentation, leading off with how MKC's products were developed by a tanner. She used a large display board to illustrate the topics she discussed. Next Jan told the group about the company and the founder, Mary Kay Ash. She showed a picture of Mary Kay and explained she was believed to be in her 70s—though no one knew for sure because Mary Kay maintained that "A woman who will tell her age will tell anything." Jerri, one of the guests, remarked that she couldn't believe how good Mary Kay looked for her age. Jan told her that Mary Kay had been using her basic skin care formulas since the 1950s.

Jan went on to talk about the growth of the sales force from nine consultants to over 195,000 in 1984. She explained how the career opportunities at MKC could be adapted to each consultant's ambitions. A consultant, she said, determined her own work hours and could choose either a full-time or part-time career. Advancement was based on sales and recruiting abilities. The possible rewards included diamonds, minks, and pink Cadillacs.

Before explaining the basic skin care program, Jan told the ladies

---

[26] Ibid.

that with the Mary Kay money-back guarantee products could be returned for any reason for a full refund. Jan distributed samples to each of the guests based on the information provided in the personal Beauty Profiles. Under Jan's guidance the ladies proceeded through the complete facial process, learning each of the five basic skin care steps advocated by Mary Kay. There was a lot of discussion about the products and how they felt on everyone's skin.

When the presentation reached the glamour segment, each guest was asked her preference of makeup colors. Jan encouraged everyone to try as many of the products and colors as they wanted. Jan helped the guests experiment with different combinations and worked with each one personally, trying to make sure that everyone would end up satisfied with her own finished appearance.

After admiring each other's new looks, three of the ladies placed orders. Jan collected their payments and filled the orders on the spot. No one had to wait for delivery.

When she finished with the orders, Jan talked with Debbie's three guests about hostessing their own shows and receiving hostess gifts. Chris agreed to book a show the next week. Debbie was then given her choice of gifts based on the evening's sales and bookings. To close the show, Jan again highlighted the benefits of a Mary Kay career—being your own boss, setting your own hours—and invited anyone interested to talk with her about these opportunities. Debbie then served some refreshments. Shortly after 9 P.M., Jan and Debbie's three guests departed.

Walking to Jan's car, the casewriter asked Jan if the evening was a success. Jan replied that it had been "a pretty good night. Sales totaled $150, I got a booking for next Wednesday. I made $75 in commissions in a little over two hours, the guests learned about skin care and have some products they are going to like, and Debbie got a nice hostess gift."

THE WEEKLY SALES MEETING

Jan Currier, senior sales director, welcomed the consultants to the weekly Monday night meeting of the members of her sales unit.[27] After calling everyone's attention to the mimeographed handout on everybody's chair (Exhibit 7), she introduced the casewriter to the

[27] Most sales directors had their sales meetings on Monday night, a practice urged upon them by Mary Kay Ash. Mary Kay saw the Monday night meeting as a good way to start the week: "If you had a bad week—you need the sales meeting. If you had a good week, the sales meeting needs you! When a consultant leaves a Monday meeting excited, she has an entire week to let excitement work for her." Ash, *Mary Kay,* p. 40.

EXHIBIT 7 Excerpt from Sales Director's Mimeographed Weekly Newsletter Distributed to Members of Sales Unit

You Are Special

Once upon a time a very competent woman went into a beautiful designer furniture store and said to the owner, "Sir, I would like to work for you. I will work hard. I will do a *Great* job for you, but I ask for the following:

1. For everything I sell I want to make a 50 percent profit.
2. I know others that I will get to sell for you too, and I want to be paid a commission on all they do, say 4 percent to 12 percent.
3. I want to work my own hours. No Sundays—just a few nights. . . . God and my family will *always* come first.
4. I will also need a car after I bring in five successful people to work for you, at no cost to me—not even insurance.
5. When I do really well, I want to receive bonuses, not little meaningless things, but things like *mink coats* and *diamonds!*

"Can you give these things to me?"

The store owner was in shock with her requests. He roared with condescending laughter. Then came his reply, "No, not one! No one could."

Only your own beautiful *Mary Kay!* You have it all right at your fingertips! Go after it! You and your family deserve it! This is your year, 1984!

Consider this story and think seriously about what you have in this wonderful opportunity!!!

You are indeed *special!* You are appreciated and loved. I'm so very proud of you. Share what you have. . . .

Jan

group and then invited everyone to stand and join in singing the Mary Kay enthusiasm song. As soon as the song was over Jan started "the Crow Period" by asking Barbara, team leader, to stand and tell about her achievement of VIP (Very Important Performer) status. Barbara told of setting and achieving the goals necessary to win the use of an Oldsmobile Firenza. Her new goal was to assist and motivate everyone on her team to do the same. Jan recognized Barbara again for being both the Queen of Sales and the Queen of Recruiting for the previous month.

Jan began the educational segment by instructing the consultants on color analysis and how it related to glamour. She continued the instruction by explaining the proper techniques of a man's facial.

Next everyone who had at least a $100 week in sales was asked to stand. Jan began the countdown "110, 120, 130 . . . 190." Barbara sat down to a round of applause for her $190 week in sales. "200, 220 . . . 270." Melissa sat down. The ladies applauded her efforts.

Mary was the only one left standing. There was anticipation of how high her sales reached as the countdown resumed. "280, 290, 300 . . . 335." Mary sat down. Everyone applauded this accomplishment of a consultant who had only been with MKC for four months and who held a 40-hour-week full-time job in addition to her Mary Kay sales efforts.

At this time Jan asked Linda and Susan to join her up front. She pinned each lady and congratulated them on joining her team. The Mary Kay pin was placed upside down on the new consultant's lapels. Jan explained this was so people would notice and ask about it. When they did, a consultant was to respond by saying; "My pin is upside down to remind me to ask you if you've had a Mary Kay facial." The pin would be turned right side up when the consultant got her first recruit. Each of the new consultants also received a pink ribbon. This marked their membership in the Jan's Beautiful People sales unit. Both Linda and Susan were given some material Jan had prepared (Exhibits 8, 9, and 10); Jan said she would go over it with them after the meeting.

Next a new competition was announced. This contest focused on

EXHIBIT 8 Example of a Sales Director's Mimeographed Handout to New Mary Kay Recruits

GETTING STARTED

Jan Currier,
Senior Sales Director

HELLO . . . AND WELCOME TO. . . .
THE BEAUTIFUL PEOPLE UNIT!!

1. You will need:
   A. Cotton balls.
   B. Swabs.
   C. Large and small zip-lock bags.
   D. Five subject spiral notebooks for note-taking.
2. This is the time to decide which merchandise order you will need. Just fill in your name and address on one of the sample orders. It's ready to go. Or change one to suit you, using the blank order. Beginning with at least $1,500 section one only. . . . makes you a ladder or success winner.
3. Be a professional consultant by ordering the "consultants kit." (1,000 gold labels, rubber stamp, name badge, 500 facial cards—style B—"Rip-off type"—for $21.95.) Send check or money order to Labeling Inc., P.O. Box 476, Lakewood, CA 90714.
4. "Buff brushes" may be ordered from Silverset Brush Co., P.O. Box 53, Greenvale, New York 11548 . . . 20 cents each ($2.00 shipping charge) style 2900 *pink* handle . . . minimum order $25. Suggest sharing an order with other Beauty Consultants where possible.

EXHIBIT 8 *(concluded)*

5. Write your mileage in your datebook today . . . for income tax purposes.
6. Memorize:
   A. Hide tanners story. (It *is* a true story.)
   B. Correct booking approach.
   C. Four Point Recruiting plan.
7. Read and read again your beauty consultants guide. *Everything* you really need to know is in the book!! Listen to your training tape over and over again. If yours hasn't arrived yet, ask to borrow your recruiter's.
8. Obtain list of Beauty Consultants and their telephone numbers in your area from your Recruiter or local Director. Call and ask to observe shows. *If you are out of town* . . . call the local Director, ask to attend her training classes and meetings, be helpful, and let her know that you support her. Always keep a positive attitude . . . especially at the sales meetings.
9. Begin booking your shows for two weeks from now. You will want to get off to a *"Perfect Start"* by *Holding* at least five shows during your beginning two weeks. Realizing that some of these may *postpone* (never "cancel") you will want to book *twice as many*. These are only practice shows. (You will have products with you should they decide to buy, of course!)

   Submit names, dates, times, and telephone numbers to your recruiter. She will call or write them, thanking them for helping you get started.

   Again, these are just "practice" shows. Simply ask your friends to "help you" get started by letting you "practice" on them. (Part of your training is to get their *honest opinions*.)

Rebook each and every basic customer for a *second* facial. . . . preferably within a week to 10 days. Then . . . "Oh, by the way, you are *entitled* to invite a few friends over to *share* your second facial, it's so much more fun and *you* win some *free!* In other words, you receive a *discount* on whatever *they* buy. In other words, THE MORE THEY BUY . . . THE *MORE YOU* RECEIVE *FREE!!"* "BUT WE CAN'T DO MORE THAN SIX. . . . IT'S NOT A PARTY. . . . IT'S A CLASS, SO WE ARE LIMITED. YOU CAN DECIDE WHAT YOU PREFER TO DO. . . . I'LL JUST GIVE YOU THIS *SUGGESTIONS FOR THE HOSTESS* (comes with your Beauty Case) AND I WILL BE CALLING YOU IN A DAY OR SO." Give her: *Beauty Book, Suggestions for the Hostess*, and *Saturday Evening Post* reprint if she looks like she would be a good recruit. *BE SURE YOUR NAME IS ON EVERYTHING!!* Send a reminder card within two days.

Vow never to miss a sales meeting. This is your continuous training . . . and it is for you. And . . . always try to bring prospective recruits as your guests. And a very, very positive attitude.

AND . . . YOU ARE OFF TO A BEAUTIFUL START!!!!

EXHIBIT 9 Example of Material Provided to New Beauty Consultants at Weekly Sales Meeting

Goal Setting is the most powerful force for human motivation
Goal + Plans + Action = Success!!!

My Goal is: ______________________________

Circle Number of Classes You Will Put On Each Week	*Class Time Plus Travel Time*	*Sales Based on each $150 Class (minutes)*	*Approximate Gross Profit per Week (before expenses)*
1	3 hours	$ 150	$ 75
2	6	300	150
3	9	450	225
4	12	600	300
5	15	750	375
6	18	900	450
7	21	1,059	525
8	24	1,200	600
9	27	1,350	675
10	30	1,500	750
11	33	1,650	825
12	36	1,800	900
13	39	1,950	975
14	42	2,100	1,050
15	45	2,250	1,125
16	48	2,400	1,200
17	51	2,550	1,275
18	54	2,700	1,350
19	57	2,850	1,425
20	60	3,000	1,500

Note: Hostess credit and hostess gift will be deducted from your gross profit. However, everything you give away is tax deductible.

Your *Attitude* and Your *Consistency* Will Determine . . .
Your Goals . . . *Your* Success!

Jan Currier
Senior Sales Director

recruiting. For each new recruit a consultant would receive one stem of Romanian crystal. So everyone could see how beautiful the rewards were, Jan showed a sample of the crystal.

A final reminder was made for attendance at the upcoming workshop on motivation. Jan sweetened the pot by providing a prize to the first one in her unit to register and pay for the seminar. Next week she would announce the winner.

The meeting was adjourned until next Monday evening.

EXHIBIT 10 Example of Material Provided to new Beauty Consultants at Weekly Sales Meeting

The Mary Kay Opportunity

		Yearly Total
3	Shows per week with $150.00 sales per show Less 15 percent hostess credit = $191.25 profit (per week) Three persons buying per show, three shows per week	$ 9,945
	468 prospective customers per year Average selling to 7 out of 10 327 new customers per year Call customers at least six times per week Average $15.00 in sales per call Yearly reorder profits will be	14,715
1	Facial per week—52 prospective customers per year Average selling to 7 of 10, 36 new customers If each buys a basic, your facial profits will be	702
36	New customers from facials Call each customer six times per year Average $15.00 in sales per call Your yearly *reorder* profit will be	1,620
Recruit one person per month	Each with at least a $1,500 initial order (wholesale) Ordering only $500.00 every month thereafter Your 4 percent—8 percent commission checks from these 12 recruits	3,490
Your yearly profits will be approximately		$30,472

This is a simple guideline designed to show you, in figures, approximately how much you can benefit from your Mary Kay career. These figures may vary a little, due to price changes. These totals are based on orders placed at our maximum discount level and do not include referrals, dovetail fees, and prizes.

Working hours per week for the above should not exceed 20 hours, if your work is well planned. Attitude and consistency are the keys to your success.

Jan Currier
Senior Sales Director

AN INTERVIEW WITH JAN CURRIER

One night shortly after attending the meeting of Jan's Beautiful People sales unit, the casewriter met with Jan to ask some questions:

Casewriter: How many are in your unit?

Jan: We're down right now. I had a small unit to start with. I only had 56. . . . A decent unit has got a hundred, 75 to 100 at least.

Casewriter: Is it the size of the town that hampers you?

Jan: No, no, it's me who hampers me. The speed of the leader is the speed of the unit. If I'm not out there doing it, then they're not going to be doing it. If I'm recruiting, they're recruiting.

Casewriter: What about your leader, is your leader not fast?

Jan: No, it's me; see when you point a finger, three come back.

Casewriter: How do you handle a situation where a consultant would like to do well but she doesn't put in the time necessary to do well?

Jan: You have to go back to that premise, that whole philosophy that you're in business for yourself but not by yourself. So if a girl comes in and says I want to make X number of dollars, then I will work with her and we will do it. I try to get them to set goals and really look at them every week and work for it. One gal comes in and wants to make $25 a week and another says "I have to support my family." There's a big difference.

Casewriter: How do you handle those that only want to make $25 a week?

Jan: If you get rid of the piddlers you wouldn't have a company. It's the piddlers that make up the company. There are only going to be one or two superstars.

Casewriter: How do you motivate the girls in your unit?

Jan: The only way you can really motivate is to call, encourage, write notes, and encourage recognition at the sales meetings and recognition in the newsletter. If they're not doing anything they usually won't come to the sales meeting, but once in a while maybe, they'll find excuses.

Casewriter: What do you do when a girl hits that stage?

Jan: Everybody has to go through that phase . . . If you're smart, you'll go to your director, read your book and go back to start where you were before—with what was working to begin with and you'll pull out of it. There are a lot of them who never pull out of it. They came in to have fun.

Casewriter: And the fun wears out.

Jan: Let's face it. This is a job. It's work, it's the best-paying hard work around, but it's work. I just finished with one gal last week who ended up saying "Well, I just thought it would be fun. I thought it was just supposed to be fun." And I said "Yes, but it's a job."

Casewriter: Can you tell before a girl starts if she'll be successful?

Jan: There's no way to predict who's going to make it, the one you think is going to be absolutely a superstar isn't. You give everybody a chance. I measure my time with their interest and I tell them that. I'll encourage them, but they are going to pretty much do what they want to do. I learned that the hard way. There is no point to laying guilt trips, no point pestering them to death, and pressure doesn't work.

Casewriter: Do you feel recognition is the best motivator?

Jan: Absolutely, recognition and appreciation. I think appreciation more than anything else. Little notes, I'm finally learning that too. Some of us are slow learners. . . . So I'll write little notes telling someone, I really appreciate your doing this, or I'm really proud of you for being a star consultant this quarter, or I'm so glad you went with us to Birmingham to the workshop.

Casewriter: Does it upset you when people don't come to the sales meetings?

Jan: I use to grieve when they wouldn't come to sales meetings. I'd ask what am I doing wrong. . . . Finally I realized that no matter how many people aren't there, the people who are there care and they are worth doing anything for. It's strange we seem to get a different batch every meeting.

Casewriter: I get the impression that you are always looking for new recruits.

Jan: Yes, I've gotten more picky. I'm looking more for directors. I'm looking for people who really want to work. I look for someone who is older, not just the 18-year-olds because they don't want to work. They want to make money but they don't want to work. . . . I'd like to build more offspring directors.

Casewriter: What kind of people do you look for?

Jan: Not everybody's right for Mary Kay. It takes somebody who genuinely cares about other people.

Casewriter: Is there a common scenario that fits most new recruits?

Jan: Mary Kay attracts a lot of insecure women who are often married to insecure men. And that woman is told over and over by Mary Kay how wonderful she is and how terrific she is and how she can do anything with God's help. She can achieve anything. And like me she is dumb enough to believe it and go along with it.

Casewriter: What do you feel is the reason for the slowdown in recruiting at Mary Kay?

Jan: The key to this drop has been partly the economy but partly a lot of people are weeding out. That's OK because the cream is going to rise to the top. I really believe that. We're going to have a stronger, much better company. I could see it at leadership (conference). The quality of people was much higher. It gets higher every year.

MKC'S FUTURE

MKC's sales in 1984 fell 14 percent to $278 million (down from $324 million in fiscal year 1983). The company's stock price, after a two for one split at about $44, tumbled from $22 in late 1983 to the $9–$12 range in 1984. Profits were down 8 percent to $33.8 million. The declines were blamed on a dropoff in recruiting and retention (owing to reduced attractiveness of part-time employment) and to the expense of starting up the European division. As of December 31, 1984, the company had about 152,000 beauty consultants and 4,500 sales directors as compared to 195,000 beauty consultants and 5,000 sales directors at year-end 1983. Average sales per consultant in 1984 was

$1,603, versus $1,655 in 1983 and a 1980–82 average of $1,753; only 60,000 of the 152,000 consultants was thought to be significantly productive. A cosmetic analysts for one Wall Street securities firm, in talking about the company's prospects, said, "Brokers loved this stock because it had such a great story. But the glory days, for the time being, are certainly over."[28]

The company's mystique was upbeat, however. Mary Kay Ash was on the UPI list of the most interviewed women in America. And when the Republicans chose Dallas for its 1984 convention, the Chamber of Commerce had to persuade Mary Kay to change the date of the 1984 Seminar which was slated for the same week in the same convention center. Positive anecdotes about Mary Kay Ash and how MKC was operated were cited in numerous books and articles.

Mary Kay Ash indicated that the company had no plans for changing the main thrust of company's sales and recruiting strategies:

> This is an excellent primary career for women, not just a way to get pin money. We see no need to alter one basic approach. It's taken us this far.[29]
>
> We have only 4 percent of the total retail cosmetics market. The way I see it 96 percent of the people in the United States are using the wrong product. There's no reason why we can't become the number one cosmetics company in the United States.[30]

---

28 As quoted in Wiley, "Cold Cream and Hard Cash," p. 40.

29 Ibid.

30 As quoted in *Business Week,* March 28, 1983, p. 130.

Case 11

MeraBank*

Michael P. Mokwa
John A. Grant
Richard E. White
all of Arizona State University

MeraBank is one of the oldest and largest financial institutions in the Southwest. Formerly First Federal Savings and Loan, MeraBank changed its name creating a new corporate identity to support and enhance its strong commitment to customer service and to facilitate new strategic thrusts. Now, MeraBank must consider the impact of its name and identity change, its expansion and repositioning strategies, and its basic services marketing challenges.

BACKGROUND

On January 1, 1986, First Federal Savings and Loan of Arizona gave banking a great new name, MeraBank (see Exhibit 1). The rich history of First Federal was a foundation and catalyst for the emergence of MeraBank.

Brief History of MeraBank

Arizona was a frontier state in 1925 when State Building and Loan opened its doors for business. State Building and Loan was a forward-thinking company, an enthusiastic group of business people determined to grow with the needs of the nation's newest state. In 1938, the company became First Federal Savings and Loan and continued to grow, becoming the state's oldest and largest thrift.

---

* This case was prepared by Michael P. Mokwa, John A. Grant, and Richard E. White of Arizona State University, in cooperation with MeraBank and the First Interstate Center for Services Marketing at Arizona State University. The case was developed as a basis for discussion rather than to illustrate either effective or ineffective management practice. The help of Robba Benjamin, Margaret B. McGuckin, and Barry Iselin of MeraBank is gratefully acknowledged.

EXHIBIT 1

First Federal
OF ARIZONA

MeraBank
A FEDERAL SAVINGS BANK

First Federal was an appropriate name for this innovative company that achieved a long list of "firsts." For example, First Federal was the first Arizona savings and loan to open a branch office. This was achieved in 1948 when a branch office was opened in Yuma. First Federal was the first savings and loan in Arizona to exceed a billion dollars in assets. It was the first savings and loan to acquire other savings and loans with the acquisitions in 1981 of American Savings in Tucson, Mohave Savings in north and northwestern parts of Arizona, and the acquisition in 1982 of Mutual Savings in El Paso, Texas. After becoming a public company in 1983, First Federal was the first Arizona savings and loan to be listed on the New York and Pacific Stock Exchanges.

In 1984 and 1985, First Federal's growth accelerated, primarily due to the injection of capital from the stock conversion. The company progressed with its mission clearly defined—to be a leading real-estate-based financial institution in the Southwest. To achieve its mission, activity centered on diversification with a real estate focus. Three companies were acquired—Realty World, a realty franchising business; First Service Title, a title and escrow service; and F.I.A. Associates, an investment consulting and advisory company. Consumer loan operations were expanded throughout eight western states. In 1985, the company changed its charter from a savings and loan association to a federal savings bank. First Federal officially became MeraBank on January 1, 1986.

In December 1986, MeraBank was acquired by Pinnacle West, formerly AZP, Incorporated. Pinnacle West is Arizona's largest corpora-

EXHIBIT 2 Pinnacle West

Line of Business	*Subsidiary*
Electric utility	Arizona Public Service Co.
Financial services	MeraBank, a Federal Savings Bank
Real estate development	Suncor Development Company
Uranium mining/sales	Malapai Resources Company
Venture capital	El Dorado Investment Company

tion. As illustrated in Exhibit 2, Pinnacle West is a diversified group of subsidiaries that include: Arizona Public Service Company, a public utility; Suncor Development Company, a real estate development company; El Dorado Investment Company, which invests through limited partnerships in private companies with significant growth potential; and Malapai Resources Company which locates and develops fuel and uranium reserves. MeraBank with its $6.3 billion in assets and banking presence could be expected to improve short-term earnings and growth potential for the diversified Pinnacle West.

MeraBank's Business Lines

Throughout all of its changes, MeraBank has positioned itself as a family-oriented financial institution, capitalizing on its real estate expertise. For over 15 years, MeraBank has set the pace in residential mortgage lending in Arizona with a market share nearly double that of its closest competitor. The company also has been a significant originator and syndicator of commercial real estate development and construction loans on a national basis. As illustrated in Exhibit 3, MeraBank's operations span eight western states. It is the 25th largest thrift in the United States, the largest thrift in Arizona, and the second largest financial institution in Arizona.

MeraBank has five major business lines: (1) retail banking; (2) consumer lending; (3) real estate lending and mortgage banking; (4) corporate banking; and (5) real estate development.

MeraBank has a well-established retail banking presence. The company offers the convenience of 78 branches including 9 in Texas. Aside from MeraBank's commitment to the Texas region, expansion is being planned for other geographic areas in the Southwest. MeraBank's core products relate to checking and savings, but utilization of electronics and the potential for cross-selling are providing new opportunities in

EXHIBIT 3 MeraBank's Areas of Operation

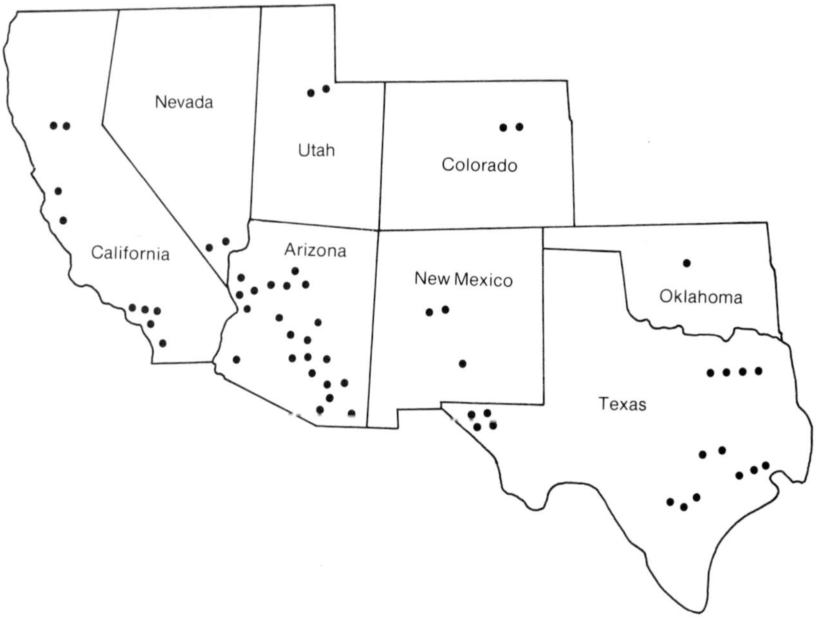

retail banking. Currently, MeraBank is a part of the largest ATM (automatic teller machine) system in the state of Arizona.

Phoenix is the largest and strongest area of operation for MeraBank's retail banking. As illustrated in Exhibit 4, MeraBank's market

EXHIBIT 4 Retail Household Penetration

	Total
Steady increases shown over time	
Third quarter 1985	231,949
Third quarter 1986	251,195
Third quarter 1987	280,663
Accounts	677,240
Deposit dollars	$2.4 billion
Market penetration	
Arizona	15%
Phoenix	17.8%
Tucson	10.7%
El Paso	12.2%

penetration is nearly 18 percent in Phoenix, which is significantly greater than in the smaller metropolitan areas of Tucson and El Paso. The Phoenix area accounts for over 45 percent of the banks business while Tucson is about 10.4 percent and El Paso is 8.8 percent. Other parts of Arizona account for 12.8 percent of the business, other areas of Texas are 4.1 percent, and other states are 18.2 percent. By reaching 15 percent of the Arizona market, MeraBank has a 7.1 percent share of the total deposit market. Exhibit 5 illustrates MeraBank's position in the total deposit market in comparison with other Arizona financial institutions. The exhibit shows each major competitor's share of the total deposit market. Valley National Bank (VNB) is the leader, followed by First Interstate Bank (FIB), the Arizona Bank (TAB), Western Savings (WS), MeraBank (MB), United Bank (UB), Pima Savings (PS), Great American Savings (GAS), Southwestern Saving (SWS), Chase Bank (CH), and CitiBank (CB).

In consumer lending, MeraBank offers customers a variety of secured and unsecured loans, including home equity lines of credit, car loans, RV loans, and boat loans. Credit cards and lines of credit are also important dimensions of the consumer lending package. Mera-

EXHIBIT 5 Consumer Banking—Total Deposit Market Share by Competitors (third quarter 1987)

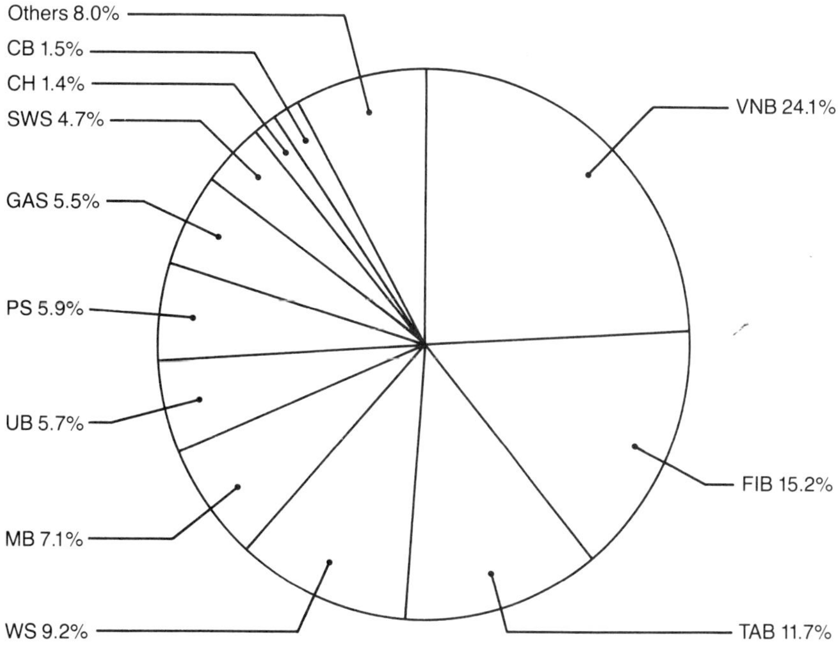

Bank views consumer lending as an expansion area and has opened new consumer lending offices called MeraFinancial Services Corporation in key expansion areas of Colorado, California, and Texas. The bank's goal in this area is to create as large a consumer loan portfolio as possible, commensurate with sound underwriting. The consumer lending group has instituted a detailed program of monthly loan reviews that will keep management well-informed on the status of the portfolio and how it is meeting underwriting standards.

A strong core of MeraBank's expertise lies in real estate financing. The mortgage lending operations originate and service more loans in Arizona than any other finance company. Exhibit 6 illustrates MeraBank's dominance in the residential mortgage market by looking at the largest of Arizona's counties. Additionally, Meracor Mortgage Corporation offices operate in Arizona, California, Colorado, Nevada, New Mexico, Texas, and Utah. They handle residential, commercial, and construction loans. A further presence of MeraBank in the real estate lending market is the marketing of its realty brokerage office franchises. Meracor Realty Corporation holds the license for a large segment of the West and Southwest having franchised more than 135 Realty World offices. Realty World brokers can offer MeraBank mort-

EXHIBIT 6 Consumer Banking—New Residential Mortgages, Maricopa County (third quarter 1987)

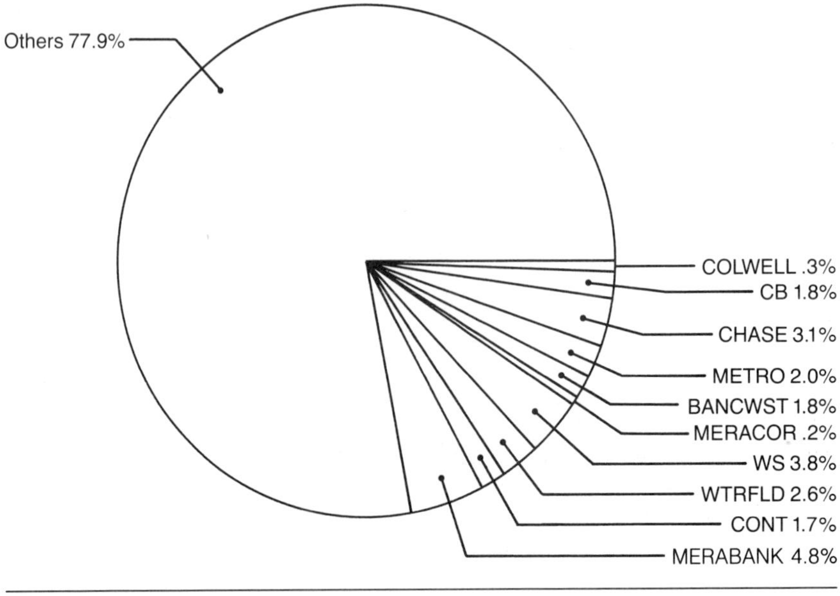

gages and services to clients, enabling the bank to reach new customers without adding its own branch office. Through ReaLoan, a computerized mortgage application system, a home buyer and broker can use a computer terminal to analyze the dozens of mortgages available through MeraBank.

In 1985, MeraBank expanded into title insurance. This service was designed to provide customers with title insurance and escrow services from national title insurance companies. Further expansion of the mortgage banking business is sought as MeraBank continues to pursue a program of nationwide lending to strengthen its position as a major force nationally in commercial and construction lending. F.I.A. Associates, the bank's real estate advisory and management company, manages over $1.5 billion in real estate properties and is viewed as a way of diversifying in the real estate business through institutional investors.

Corporate banking provides both deposit and lending services to companies throughout the Southwest. MeraBank offers corporate clients a wide variety of deposit, checking, and lending services as well as financing, secured by accounts receivable and inventory. The bank finances equipment acquisition and plant expansions as well. Cash management accounts and high yield bonds are products that were designed to meet the needs of the corporate banking customers. Corporate banking is a new area for savings institutions, and the bank is branching into this new and challenging business prudently.

MeraBank is also a significant competitor in real estate joint ventures, which includes the marketing and property management of joint venture projects. This fifth business line, real estate development, is achieved through Meracor Development Corporation, the bank's joint venture and development company. Meracor activities focus on the management of profitable, high-quality projects in Arizona, and to a lesser extent in Texas, California, Colorado, and New Mexico. Management has made a strategic decision to reduce dependence on this area and to limit the size of joint venture development in the future to assure that MeraBank retains a conservative level of leverage.

The Competitive Market Environment

Competition in financial markets is expanding and intensifying as many new institutions are entering and as traditional market and service boundaries are eroding. The basic financial market in Arizona, MeraBank's largest area of operations, can be segmented fundamentally into (1) banks and (2) savings and loans. Information about MeraBank's major competitors in each of the segments can be found in Exhibit 7. In 1985, savings and loans totaled about a 24 percent share

EXHIBIT 7 Major Competitors: Arizona Financial Market, 1986 ($ in billions)

Competitor	*Arizona Branches*	*Assets*	*Loans*	*Deposits*
Banks				
Valley National	272	$10.7	$7.3	$9.2
First Interstate	183	6.5	4.3	5.7
Arizona Bank	119	4.5	3.2	3.8
United Bank	47	2.7	1.8	2.2
MeraBank	68	6.3	5.1	4.0
Savings And Loans				
Western Savings	82	5.5	3.0	3.8
Great American	N/A*			
Southwest Savings	50	2.1	1.7	1.5
Pima Savings	28	2.6	1.8	1.3

* Arizona operations combined with parent company.

of the Arizona deposit market, while banks maintained the largest overall market share with 70 percent of the deposits.

With product deregulation, savings and loan institutions have been given freedom to expand much more into consumer banking services. This has allowed saving and loan institutions to compete directly with the banks which has resulted in a blurring of the distinction between banks and savings and loan institutions. Through mergers and acquisitions which have taken place as a result of geographical deregulation, larger national and international bank holding companies have moved into the Arizona competitive environment and made their presence known. Of the six largest banks in Arizona, four changed hands in 1986. The two largest banks that have not changed hands during this period are Valley National Bank and First Interstate Bank.

Despite increased competition and activity, total deposits in the Arizona market have begun to decline. As illustrated in Exhibit 8, Arizona's deposit base increased by $11.2 billion from 1983 through 1986, reaching a peak of $33.4 billion. However, in 1987, total deposits declined from 1986. Exhibit 9 shows that the leading financial institutions saw a stable or declining market share trend. First Interstate's market share drop from 19 percent to 15.4 percent, while Valley National and MeraBank's market shares declined 2.5 and 1.4 points respectively. Exhibit 10 shows that all competitors experienced a positive annual growth rate between 1983 and 1986. But in 1987, all but two competitors had a drop in the average deposit per branch from the first quarter of 1987 through the third quarter of 1987. This is illustrated in Exhibit 11.

EXHIBIT 8 Consumer Banking—Trend of Arizona's Total Deposits (1983–3rd quarter 1987)

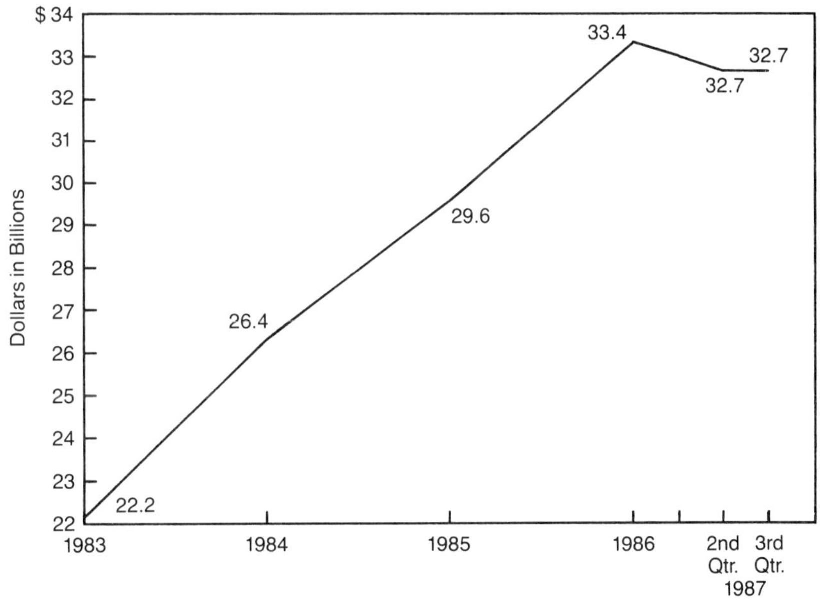

EXHIBIT 9 Consumer Banking Market Share Trend—Total Deposits (1983–3rd quarter 1987)

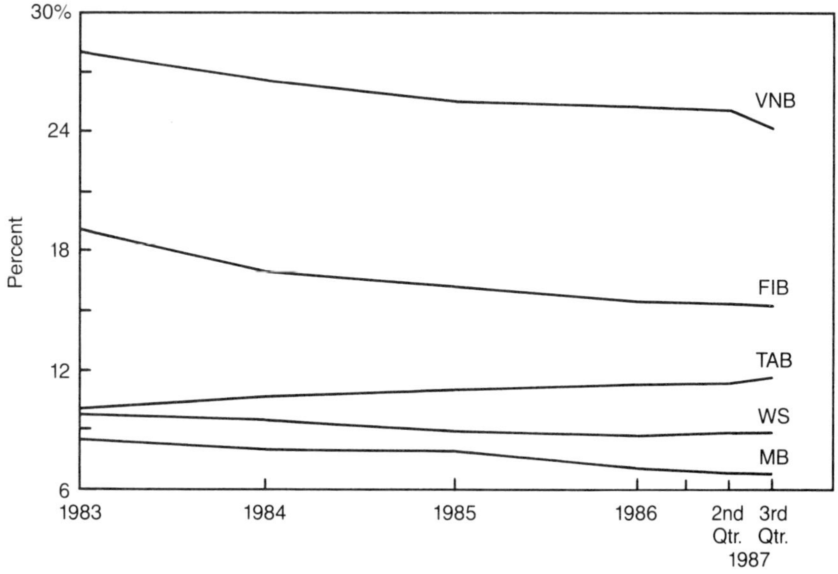

EXHIBIT 10 Growth in Total Deposits by Major Competitors—Compound Annual Growth Rate, 1983–1986

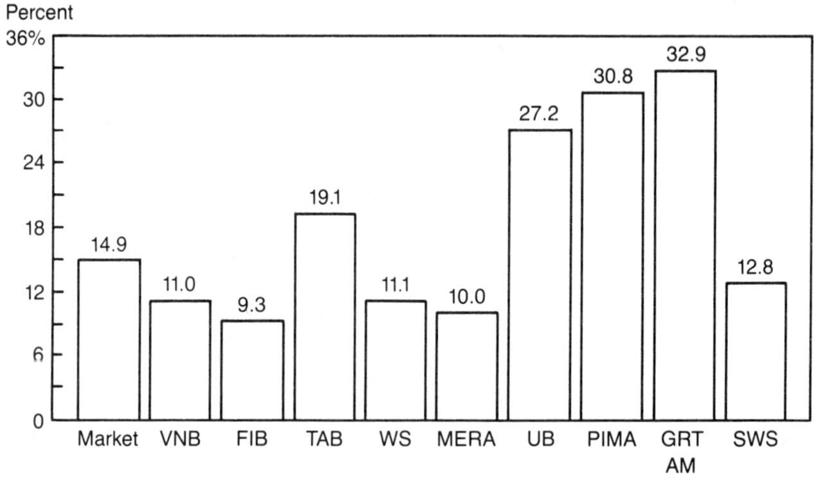

VNB—Valley National Bank
FIB—First Interstate Bank
TAB—The Arizona Bank
WS—Western Savings
MERA—MeraBank
UB—United Bank
PIMA—Pima Savings
GRT AM—Great American
SWS—Southwest Savings

Source: Deposit Institution Performance Directory.

EXHIBIT 11 Consumer Banking—Average Deposits per Branch (3rd quarter 1987)

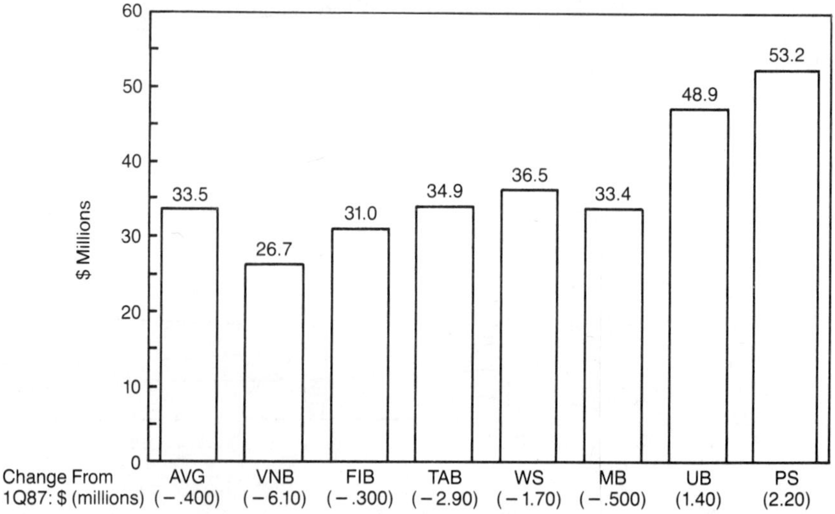

The decline in bank deposits appears to stem from consumers' desire for higher return investments. As the stock market enjoyed a record bull market period in the first three quarters of 1987, conservative banking products had a continuing decline, as seen in Exhibit 12. Certificates of deposit (CDs), which offer a guaranteed rate of return for a specified period of deposit time, declined while Money Market Accounts (MMA), which offer a varying rate of interest with no time commitment on the deposit, exhibited a dramatic increase in sales. Passbook savings (PB) and Interest-bearing checking accounts (NOW) steadily declined in 1987.

The Major Competitors

In the Arizona market, the most formidable competitor has been Valley National Bank with nearly $10 billion in assets. Valley National remains as the only bank that is headquartered in Phoenix. Valley has 277 branches in Arizona. Valley National's 24.1 percent share of the total deposit market is maintained with 25 percent of the branches. Valley National's strategy seems centered on intense penetration and physical presence, supported by regional expansion.

Valley National is also the leader in the Arizona market for electronic banking and is planning further expansion. At present, the

EXHIBIT 12 Deposit Product Mix (1983–3rd quarter 1987)

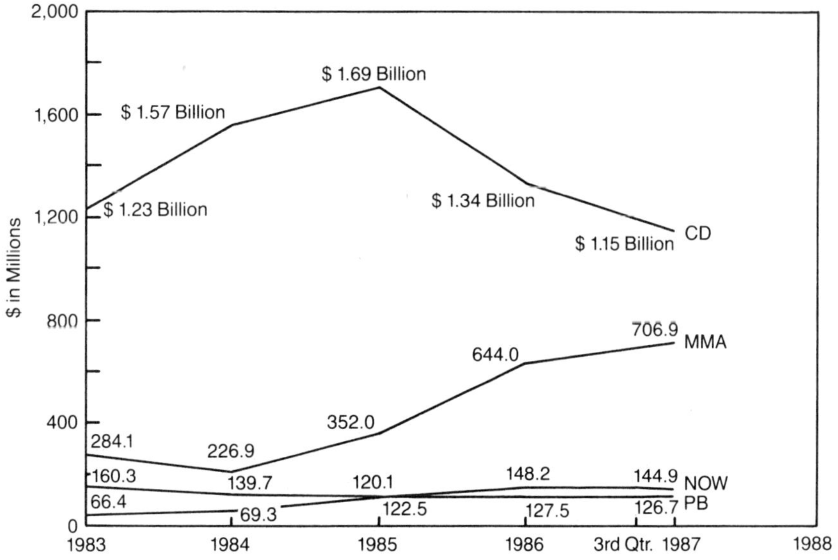

Valley National debit card is the most widely accepted in the Arizona market and can be used to make purchases at grocery stores, service stations, convenience stores, even department stores. This electronic funds transfer card has become known as a POS (point of sale). It allows a debit of the customers bank account as payment for a purchase. The POS is expected to be expanded into more retail outlets by Valley National.

In the lending end of the business, Valley National has instituted a Loan by Phone program. The bank promises answers to loans in 30 minutes. These are some of the services that Valley focuses on in its advertising to create its image as "The Leader in Your Banking Needs".

First Interstate Bank has been very close in asset size to MeraBank, but has over twice as many branch locations in Arizona. First Interstate has 15.2 percent of the deposit market share and 16.4 percent of the branches. The bank is also involved in POS capability with their debit card being accepted at all but grocery store locations First Interstate is an affiliate of First Interstate Bancorp which is the eighth largest retail banking organization in the nation. First Interstate is a relatively new name for a long standing competitor. Their advertising theme is "Serving Arizona for 110 years." First Interstate customers are the highest users of the automatic teller machines (ATMs) in Arizona, and First Interstate plans to continue to expand its ATMs, POS, and branches to stay on the leading edge in convenience banking.

The Arizona Bank is another competitor close to MeraBank in asset size with just under $5 billion. The Arizona Bank with 126 branches in Arizona was acquired in October of 1986 by Security Pacific Corporation, the sixth largest bank holding company in the United States. The bank's image is tied closely with the state it serves. To convey an Arizona image, a native American Indian is used in the bank's logo with the slogan "The Bank Arizona Turns To" and "Count on Us." The bank's plans include expansion of more branches in the Phoenix Metropolitan area and some outlying communities.

The United Bank of Arizona has been a smaller competitor with only 47 branch operations. It has maintained over $2 billion in assets. United Bank has a 5.7 percent share of the total deposits with only 3.9 percent share of the branches. United Bank was acquired by Union Bancorp in January of 1987. Union Bancorp is a holding bank in Los Angeles, a subsidiary of Standard Chartered PLC, an International Banking Network. United Bank has had the fastest percentage growth in assets, deposits, and loans of all major Arizona banks in the last five years. The bank's focus has been on responsiveness to the needs of middle market, growing businesses. This is reflected in the advertising theme "Arizona's Business Bank for Over 25 Years." Citicorp has been very interested in United Bank and would like to acquire it to enhance their presence in Arizona.

In the savings and loan segment, the largest competitor has been Western Savings with approximately $5.8 billion in assets. Headquartered in Phoenix, Western Savings has begun expansion into Tucson and Flagstaff. In their major markets, Western Savings has located branch offices in popular grocery stores. To develop their image as "The Foresight People," Western Savings plans to continue to expand products and services. The company experienced about a 2 percent drop in CDs but has seen an increasing volume of retail deposits. Western Savings is the only thrift currently involved in POS. It has only been able to have its POS card accepted by about 200 Mobil Service stations.

Great American, though substantially smaller, has been aggressively expanding in the Phoenix area following a similar location strategy to that of Western Savings. Headquartered in San Diego, the company plans continued expansion in the Phoenix area targeting high income growth markets. Great American has experienced the largest increases in the MMAs and has seen a strong increase in the volume of retail deposits in the last year. They present themselves in the image of a bank, trying to stress the name Great American "YOUR ADVANTAGE BANK."

Southwest Savings is a smaller institution with 53 branch operations. It has been an independent and closely held organization. Southwest has committed themselves to serving the growing senior citizens population in Arizona. Southwest Savings has experienced the industry trend in product performance with about a 2 percent drop in CDs, while MMAs were up sharply. However, overall total deposits have been down.

Pima Savings has operated out of Tucson where they have a 40 percent share of the total savings and loan deposits in Pima County. Pima Savings has a 5.9 percent market share of the total deposits in Arizona with only 3.7 percent of the total branches. Pima Savings has seen continued growth in total deposits and in CDs. The company is viewed in the industry as the investment rate leader. Pima is rapidly expanding branches in the Phoenix area, frequently using Safeway grocery stores as their outlets. Pima is owned by Pima Financial Corporation which is a subsidiary of Heron Financial Corporation, a U.S. holding company for one of Europe's largest privately owned companies.

To gain insight into the competitive environment, additional exhibits have been included. Exhibit 13 illustrates the net worth of the Arizona financials as a percent of their assets. The composition of loan services are expressed in terms of real estate and consumer loans for the banks in Exhibit 14, and for the saving and loan associations in Exhibit 15.

Other major competitors in the Arizona financial market began to arrive with reinstatement of interstate banking in 1986. Among the

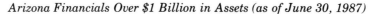

EXHIBIT 13 GAAP Net Worth as a Percent of Unconsolidated Assets

Arizona Financials Over $1 Billion in Assets (as of June 30, 1987)

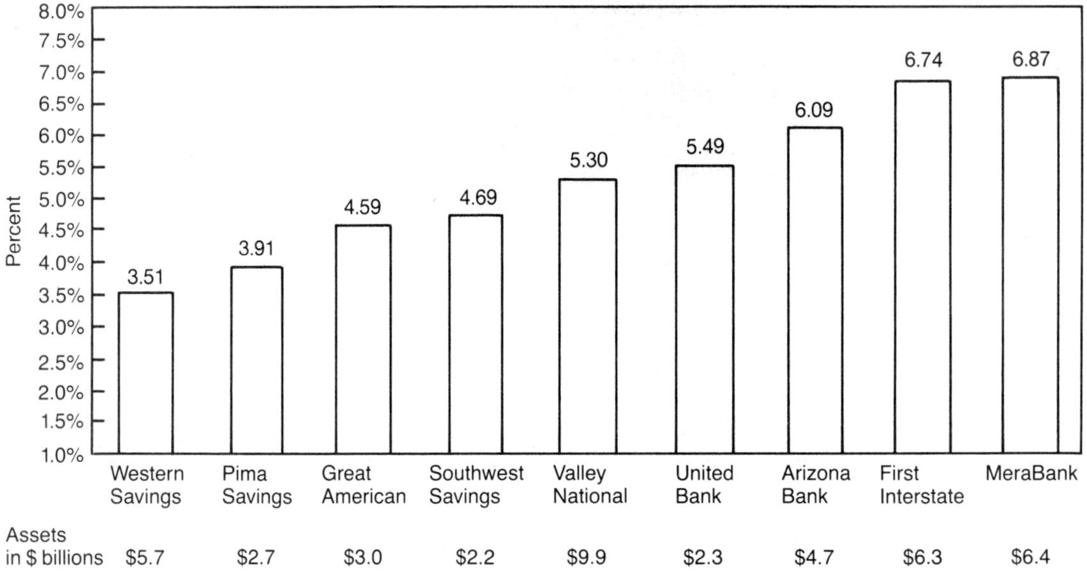

newest financial institutions are: Citibank which took over Great Western Bank & Trust of Arizona and is a subsidiary of Citicorp, the largest bank holding company in the United States; and Chase Bank of Arizona, a division of Chase, the second largest holding company in the country. Chase took over the former Continental Bank. These acquisitions should have an impact on the Arizona financial market in the near future. Interstate banking has provided the opportunity for the acquisitions of Arizona's financial institutions by out-of-state companies and could continue to be a factor in the competitive environment. Also considered as competitors in some segments of MeraBank's lines of business are insurance companies, finance companies, investment companies, money market funds, credit unions, and pension funds. Overall, many organizations are entering financial service markets.

THE NAME AND IDENTITY CHANGE

In 1985, the total population of Arizona was 3.2 million. The state had experienced a five-year increase in its total population, an increase of nearly 25 percent. Growth had been projected to continue. MeraBank's other dominant market, Texas, also had been growing. In 1985, it had

EXHIBIT 14 Major Competitors for Loan Services—Banks (September 30, 1986)

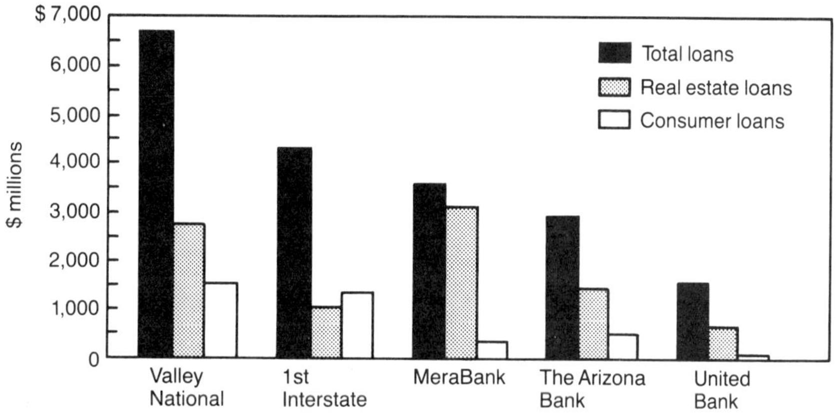

	Dollars in Millions		
	Total Loans	*Real Estate Loans*	*Consumer Loans*
Valley National	$6,718	$2,740	$1,538
1st Interstate	4,307	1,078	1,345
MeraBank	3,595	3,138	352
The Arizona Bank	2,942	1,466	569
United Bank	1,632	754	118

Source: Deposit Institution Performance Directory.

a much larger population than Arizona, over 15 million people. At that time, First Federal operated 12 offices located throughout Texas, in El Paso, Dallas, Austin, Houston, and Fort Worth.

Even though First Federal was well-positioned in its highly competitive markets, banking deregulation and legislative changes were opening doors to interstate banking and to charter changes for thrift institutions. New products and services would soon be available and a significant challenge confronted First Federal. Although First Federal offered a full range of products and services, most consumers perceived banks to be better—more full-service and service-oriented—than savings and loans.

First Federal perceived a name change as a necessity, but the corporate priorities in 1985 were complex. The company hoped to demonstrate superior financial performance, while making customer service its most effective marketing tool. Moreover, the company hoped to protect its current market share from the threat of new competition, while increasing retail banking coverage in Texas and expanding beyond Arizona and Texas.

EXHIBIT 15 Major Competitors for Loan Services—Savings Associations (September 30, 1986)

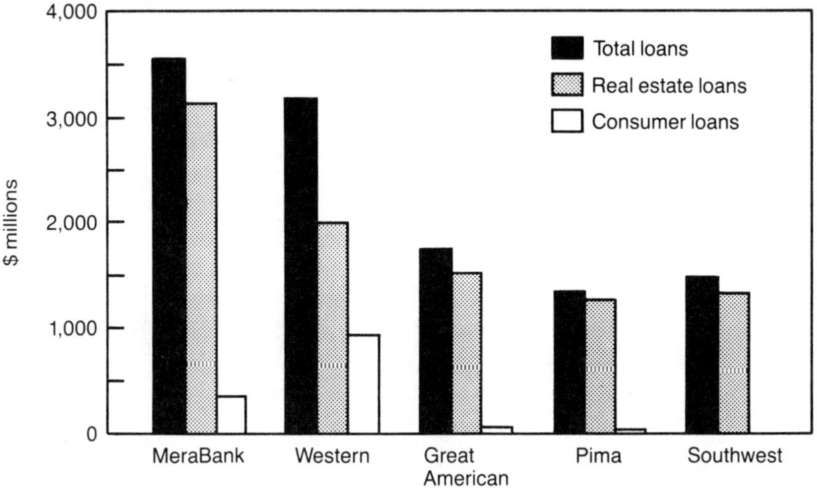

	Dollars in Millions		
	Total Loans	*Real Estate Loans*	*Consumer Loans*
MeraBank	$3,595	$3,138	$352
Western	3,180	1,978	919
Great American	1,773	1,571	90
Pima	1,345	1,286	58
Southwest	1,477	1,343	34

Source: Deposit Institution Performance Directory.

The board of directors had been considering a name change since the company went public in 1983. The name First Federal was a very common name in financial institutions. There were over 89 First Federals in Texas alone. If expansion was to be considered, the company needed a name it could grow with. Aside from expanding under one name and distinguishing itself to stockholders, the board wanted to include the word "bank" in its name and position itself as a bank in the market.

A market research company from New York was retained to help determine what the new name and bank image should be. However, the board felt the process would be easy, simply changing some signs and forms. The board decided that the First Federal logo could be maintained by simply changing the name to FEDBANK. The board dismissed the market research team, and by 1984, they were ready to make the change. In August, a new senior vice president was given the task of implementing the name change. The initial step was to check out regulations regarding the use of the word "bank" in the name of a chartered savings and loan association. However, it was discovered in the legal search that the proposed use of FED in the new name would violate law. There is a regulation banning private organizations from using a name that sounds like a federal agency. In this case, the proposed FedBank name was very similar to the federal bank known as the "FED."

The task of changing the name would have to start over. The first market research company had left with some ill feelings. So in 1985, a new consulting firm, S & O Consultants from San Francisco, was contracted for the project. S & O specialized in corporate identity. They had recently done the name change for First Interstate Bank in Arizona and were familiar with the financial institution market in the area.

The Project Objectives

Objectives were established at the beginning of the project. These objectives are outlined in Exhibit 16. The primary objective was to select a name that conveyed a positive image and new identity. The name needed to be legally available in all 50 states. It needed to fit all the business lines—everything from the title company to retail banking to real estate joint ventures. A distinctive identity was to be developed as well. The First Federal logo was very similar to other existing corporate identities and offered little value to the company as an identity. The new name needed to create excitement and set the

EXHIBIT 16 Name Objectives

The new name for First Federal of Arizona's retail bank should accomplish the following (percentages indicate weights given to each objective when evaluating names):

1. Convey an honest, hard-working, service-oriented bank. (30%)
2. Imply stature and strength. (30%)
3. Appeal to the mass-market retail banking audience. (20%)
4. Be distinctive, memorable, and easy to pronounce. (20%)
5. Be compatible with a range of financial services including retail banking, real estate development, construction lending, mortgage banking, corporate lending, etc.
6. Make no specific reference to Arizona, but may incorporate Southwestern flavor.
7. Be available and legally protectable.

tone for continued innovation and leadership. It needed to increase the employees' morale and help generate new business. However, the company did not have unlimited resources. So, a very important objective was to accomplish everything within a strict, tight budget and a short time frame.

The Process

Distinct phases were identified in the change process. First, the name itself had to be generated and selected. Second, the logo and identity surrounding the name had to be developed. Third, the identity needed to be communicated in a clear and concise way, and finally, evaluation must be undertaken.

Selecting the name was the first step. Criteria for the new name were established. These included implying stature and strength, being distinctive, memorable, and easy to pronounce. All the criteria were ranked and weighted in terms of perceived importance. The criteria of conveying a service-oriented bank and of implying stature and strength were ranked as the two most important criteria for the new name.

After a positioning statement was developed for the name itself, the process of generating the name began. Over 800 names were evaluated and critiqued. The top 20 names were further evaluated using a mathematical scoring system, and all the top 20 names were legally searched in all 50 states. The final five that were considered are evaluated in Exhibit 17.

An early favorite was Merit Savings Bank. However, this name was being used elsewhere, particularly in California. And it was associated with a brand of cigarettes. However, the name had some interesting roots. After an arduous series of executive interviews, brainstorming sessions, and stormy meetings, a consensus was reached. The name MeraBank was selected.

In phase two, the logo and identity were developed. The company desired a design that would uniquely identify them and reach across all their business lines. The logo had to be instantly recognizable, even before the name was seen. The company wanted something that would emphasize a commitment to comprehensive financial services. The logo would have to be modern, make a strong retail statement, and incorporate a taste of Southwestern imagery, but not limit the bank to Arizona.

Choices were narrowed, and focus group testing began. In Exhibit 18, the leading choices are represented. Focus group reaction favored C, a multicolored log. Group participants described the identity as "progressive," "modern," and "large". Obviously, this met the company's objectives. The colors were described as being "attractive" and "Southwestern." The vibrant yellow gold and orange-red of the sunrise with the royal purple of the mountains were well-understood Southwestern images.

Several modifications were made to the logo based on focus group work. For example, the company has had a substantial senior citizen customer base. They expressed some very strong dissatisfaction with the proposed typeface. They perceived the logo as very contemporary, but the typeface was perceived as very different and too modern. What resulted was a new and much more conservative typeface with the same multicolored contemporary logo. Perceptions were much more favorable.

Effective communication of the name and imagery were vital to establishing the identity and accomplishing performance-oriented objectives. A strategic decision was made to communicate the change from the inside-out. To accomplish this, a large task force was assembled internally to cover literally every aspect of the identity change. The name change task force began working in July of 1985. It included a project manager, 7 project leaders, and 30 employees. The task force was responsible for the signage, forms, merchant notification, employee notification and promotion, media notification and promotion, and customer notification and promotion.

To direct and guide the task force, several objectives and strategic thrusts were outlined. The first objective was to gain employee awareness and enthusiasm for the name change. Employee support was essential to communicate the name from the inside-out. A second objective of the task force was to develop a graphic plan and standards manual that clearly spelled out the proper representation and usage of the new logo. A high priority was given to the delicate task of communicating the change to primary stakeholders including board members and the stockholders. A major undertaking involved identification and revision of all forms. The effort uncovered the opportunity to reduce by 30 percent the number of forms used.

The task force also needed to develop an advertising campaign and related promotions for customer notification. A TV spot would provide only 30 seconds to communicate the new identity; a billboard would provide less time. A very complex message had to be refined to its strongest, simplest components. Also, the task force needed to develop branch employee training and information sessions including the revision of the branch operations manuals. Finally, the task force had to be prepared to handle any of the legal questions that could arise concerning the name change. Thus, one of the task force members was a staff attorney.

EXHIBIT 17 Summary of Name Choice Legal Search

	Estimated Probability of Successful Federal Registration	*Prior Federal Registration*	*Prior State Registration (if yes, how many states)*	*Prior incidence (of litigation)*	*Incidence of Common Law Usage*
Firstmark Savings Bank	5%	Yes, to Firstmark Corp, for "Consumer, Commercial and Industrial Financing"	Yes, 15 states	Yes, successfully precluded a savings and loan from use	Irrelevant
Interprise Savings Bank	50%, based upon similarity in sound to "Enterprise"	No, but Enterprise Bank *is* registered as is Enterprise Loans	No, yes for Enterprise in 2 states (including Calif. & Texas)	No	1) Enterprise S & L in Long Beach, Calif. 2) Enterprise Bancorp in San Francisco, Calif.
Landmark Savings Bank	5%	Yes, to (1) Signal, Landmark for "Residential and Commercial Construction" (2) Landmark Prime Line for "Services"	Yes, 11 registrations in Financial Services category, 10 registrations in real estate related category	Yes	Numerous examples are: Landmark National Bank (Denver) Landmark National Bank (Dallas) Landmark Thrift & Loan (San Diego) Landmark Real Estate (San Diego)

Merit Savings Bank	50%	No, but design mark registration of Merritt Commercial S & L (Maryland), Meritline (Product of Calif. First Bank of San Francisco)	No	No	Numerous, examples are: 1) Merit S & L (Los Angeles, 5 branches, $280 million Assets) 2) Merit Financial in Denver & Dallas & Houston
Pace Savings Bank	50%	No, but 3 similar word marks are registered: 1) Pace Plan (Product of Commonwealth Bank in Penna) 2) Pacecard (Product of National Bank of Commerce (W. Va.) 3) Pacesetter (Product of National Bank of Tulsa (Okla.)	Yes, as a word mark in Illinois and as initials (P.A.C.E.) in New Jersey	No	Not a common name for financial services and real estate but used by 1) Pace Mortgage in Denver 2) Pace Co. Real Estate in San Diego 3) Pace Financial Management in Dallas

EXHIBIT 18

A) MeraBank
SAVINGS BANK

B) MeraBank
SAVINGS BANK

C) MERABANK
SAVINGS BANK

The plans to generate employee awareness and enthusiasm were initiated within tight time and resource constraints. The task force knew that employee support was essential to market acceptance. The name, but not the logo, was first announced to all employees at the company's big 60th birthday celebration in September 1985. Further internal communication was initiated through a new publication called "The MeraBanker." The employee campaign even included a "mystery shopper" who went into the field asking employees questions about the name change.

A customer awareness program began in November with a teaser advertising campaign. By December, more than 1,200 stationery forms and collateral pieces had been redesigned and printed. On January 1, 1986, the new signs and the major campaign theme, "First Federal Gives Banking a Great New Name," were unveiled. Throughout the customer awareness program, the "MeraBanker" term was consistently used for name and identity related internal communication.

Extensive work was done with the press. Hundreds of press releases were sent out. Early releases included a question and answer piece that did not include the full identity. Later in the program, the logo, the name, and the advertising campaign were released to the press.

MeraBank wanted its identity to be comprehensive and wanted to maintain the integrity and power of the identity. So for the first time in the company's history, a graphic standards manual was developed to state how and for what purposes the logo could be used. This was necessary to determine proper use for advertising, promotions, and brochures, as well as use on checks, credit cards, debit cards, ATM cards, all banking forms, and annual reports. MeraBank even changed its hot-air balloon.

Results of the Name Change

The impact of the name change was very positive. Employees were enthusiastic about the change and scored extremely well on the mystery shopper quizzes. Over 96 percent of all employees answered questions about the new name correctly. The extensive amount of employee involvement in the name change stimulated a renewed sense of pride in the company. Moreover, the name change was the catalyst generating a new orientation: employees and management perceived themselves as a bank.

Market studies were undertaken to determine consumer response. Consumers were positive about the new name. Over two thirds recalled the new name, their primary source being television advertising. 55 percent of consumers could identify the new name as MeraBank, and very few people perceived the name change as negative. Overall, postname change advertising was perceived as more meaningful than previous advertising. In fact, advertising recall doubled and achieved a significant breakthrough in terms of consumer scoring. This can be seen in Exhibit 19.

The new advertising was very successful in promoting the new MeraBank image. When surveys were conducted after the name change, people began to list MeraBank in the bank category and not with the savings and loan institutions. The ad campaign also helped to promote the trial of Merabank. Of those surveyed who were likely to try MeraBank, most were impressed with the name change advertising and rated it as being very meaningful to them. Those who were willing to try MeraBank described the company as "progressive" and having a "high level of customer service."

In Exhibit 20, there is a comparison of performance figures. A year after the name change, MeraBank's assets were up 20 percent, and its advertising recall was up almost 100 percent. MeraBank's retail banking and mortgage lending market share had dropped slightly. This was planned through new pricing strategies which were undertaken to reduce the overall cost of funds. MeraBank, now positioned as a bank, lowered interest rates, getting these more in line with bank competitors versus savings and loan competitors.

EXHIBIT 19 Advertising Recall—Arizona

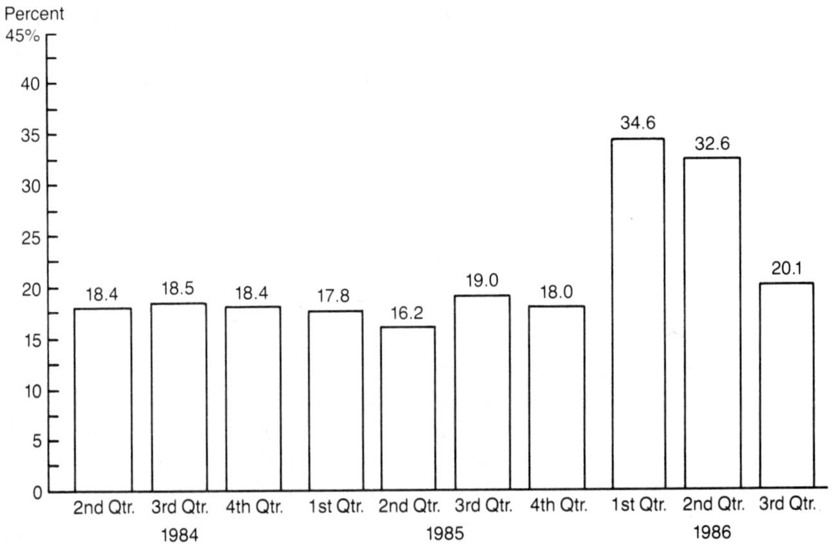

THE NEW MERABANK

MeraBank began thinking of itself as a bank after the name change. Customers, employees, and the financial market began to refer to MeraBank as a bank, not as a thrift. However, changing the charter and creating new advertising campaigns were just the beginning. A complete repositioning in the market would be necessary to educate, attract, and serve "bank" customers. Changes in products, advertising, service, and facilities would be needed to complete the identity metamorphosis.

EXHIBIT 20 Year-End Comparison

	December 1985	*December 1986*	*3rd Quarter 1987*
Assets	$5.2 billion	$6.3 billion	$6.4 billion
Retail banking market share	9.1%	8.5%	8.1%
Mortgage lending market share	6.6%*	6.4%*	5.4%
Advertising awareness	18.0%*	33.0%*	20.1%*

* Phoenix and Tucson metro combined.

Several strategic changes occurred in conjunction with the name change. Advertising positioned MeraBank directly against the banks. Management dropped interest rates on savings deposits to bring them in line with bank rates. In the six months following the name change, the six month CD rate dropped 1.1 percent. Through December 1987, the overall interest expense had been reduced by over $20 million as a result of this strategy. Interest rates and fees on credit cards were increased to be aligned with the pricing policies of banks. Customer service did not appear to suffer as a result of these changes. As seen in Exhibit 4, the number of total retail households served by MeraBank increased by 9 percent the first six months after the name change. By December 1987, the number of households served was up 22 percent.

The Marketing Group

Overall, changes were initiated to build a new corporate culture emphasizing service and measuring performance against both banks and thrifts. Strategy implementation became the major responsibility of the marketing group. As a result of the successful name change, the senior vice president of marketing was promoted to executive vice president and chief administrative officer in charge of marketing, human resources, and long range planning. She recruited a new senior vice president for the marketing group.

The basic structure of the marketing organization is presented in Exhibit 21. Headed by a senior vice president, the department is organized into four major divisions. The first division, Market Planning, Research, and Development, works on analyzing and segmenting the market and on keeping an accurate account of MeraBank's position in the financial market. Marketing Services develops and manages products, promotions, advertising, and print production for the company. Corporate Communications is responsible for public relations activities, audio/visual productions, and employee communications. The fourth division, Direct Marketing, oversees direct mail campaigns, telemarketing, customer service, and training. Though the reporting structure is set clearly, the functions interface frequently, and informal relationships appear to be very cooperative.

Consumer Market Segments

The primary demographic factors related to financial product usage appear to be age and income. Financial consumers for the banking industry often are segmented using these two criteria. Segments with the strongest potential for heavy financial product usage are: mid-age

EXHIBIT 21

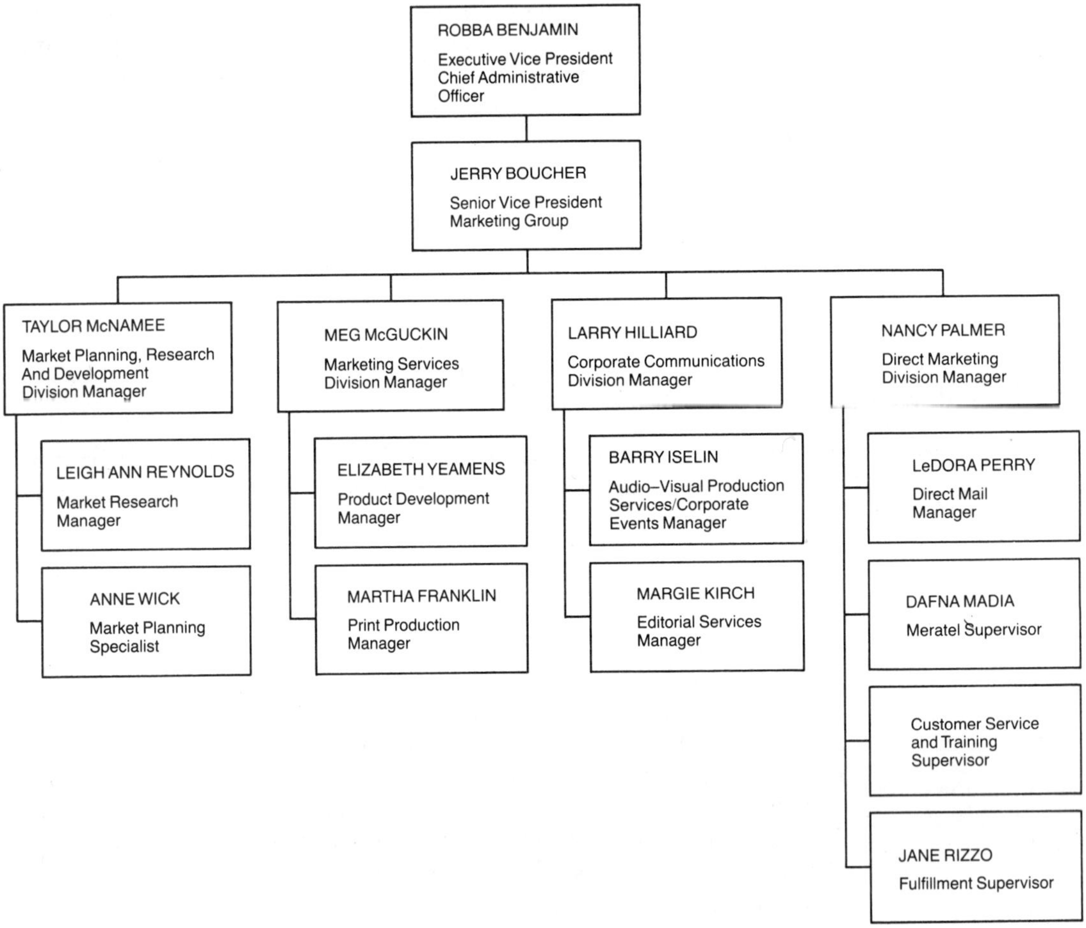

middle income; mid-age affluent; pre-retired middle income; pre-retired affluent; and retired high income groups. These segments represent 57 percent of the Phoenix metropolitan population and 47 percent of the Tucson area as seen in Exhibit 22.

Using segmentation profiles as a base, MeraBank has begun to target its distribution system as well as its products and communication efforts toward specific market segments, in particular more affluent population segments. A profile of MeraBank's customer segments appears in Exhibit 23. A major indicator of MeraBank's commitment

EXHIBIT 22 Segment Penetration

	Population
Phoenix	
Young, low income	9%
Young, middle income	21
Mid-age, middle income	17
Mid-age, affluent	16
Older, low income	6
Pre-retired, middle income	9
Pre-retired, affluent	5
Retired, higher income	10
Retired, lower income	7
Tucson	
Young, low income	16
Young, middle income	21
Mid-age, middle income	15
Mid-age, affluent	1
Older, low income	9
Pre-retired, middle income	8
Pre-retired, affluent	4
Retired, higher income	9
Retired, lower income	8

MeraBank Customer Base (percentage of households)

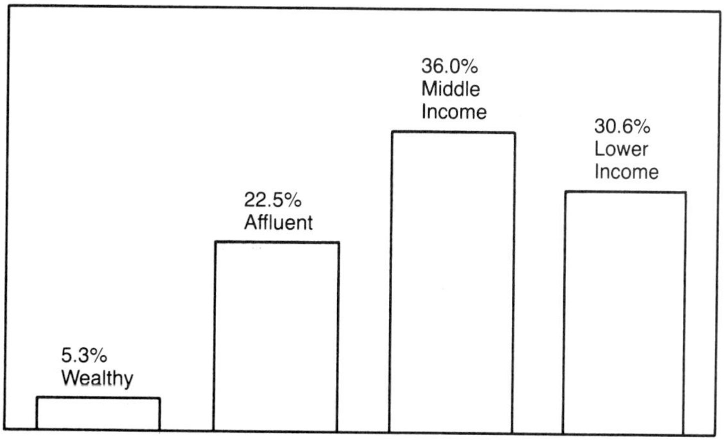

EXHIBIT 23 Market Segmentation Profiles

Communication efforts to sell specific products/packages can be directed specifically to segments by learning more about the financial styles of these groups.

Mid-Age, Middle Income These housholds will be hard to target as an entire segment, because they are widely distributed across all financial styles and thus vary greatly in their attitudes toward financial matters. Households in this segment are family oriented. Much of their financial behavior is focused on protecting their families and planning for their children's future.

Mid-Age, Affluent A large portion of this segment are "Achievers" and have the most-in-command financial style. They are likely to be receptive to marketing approaches that appeal to their self-image as successful, knowledgeable, and decisive people.

Households in this segment are value sensitive. They are receptive to distinctive product features, and are able to make price/feature trade-offs. While households in this segment are price sensitive, they are willing to pay for services that they don't have time for, especially the dual earner households. They have positive attitudes toward using electronics and are likely to own computers and other electronic/high technology products.

Pre-Retired, Middle Income Half of the households in this segment are "Belongers." Their financial style is predominantly more-safe-and-simple. Many of these households will be receptive to marketing approaches that stress traditional, conservative values and emphasize the safety of the institution. In their efforts to minimize taxes and accumulate funds for retirement, these households will require conservative, lower risk products.

Many of these households are shifting their focus away from their children to their own future retirement. Though the family is still important, these households' goals are changing as they enter a new life stage. They place a high value on the reputation of the financial institutions they use and on having trust in them.

Pre-Retired, Affluent The financial styles of the pre-retired affluent households are predominantly most-in-command and most-comfortable. They are oriented toward the present and are concerned about retaining their present lifestyles during their retirement. They are sophisticated in their approach to financial matters. These households like having access to people that they perceive as competent, but are receptive to using the telephone for financial dealings.

EXHIBIT 23 *(concluded)*

Retired, Higher Income Households in this segment are the more-safe-and-simple and prefer to keep their financial affairs uncomplicated and are generally unexperimental. Other households, called most comfortable, are sophisticated in their approach to their financial affairs. They view themselves as prosperous and financially secure. They highly value security and involvement in financial affairs. These retired households are likely to be receptive to social seminar-type events, because they have the time to attend and the interest in learning.

to reach new segments and serve new needs can be seen in their direct marketing budget, which increased 200 percent from 1985 to 1986. As a result of the repositioning effort and the move to targeting, the total households that were served increased 15 percent, to well over a quarter of a million households.

Service and Product Development

MeraBank launched two new retail banking services, since the name change. The Passport Certificate Account and the Working Capital Account. These new accounts have brought in new deposits at a time when total deposits have been declining. Many existing product lines, such as CDs, have seen a decline in sales. MeraBank has suffered a loss of about 2 percent of its CD deposits. Passbook savings accounts have also been on a decline. However, MeraBank has increased its share of interest bearing checking accounts—a conventional "bank" product, despite increases in the minimum balance of the NOW account from \$100 to \$500. Similarly, an increase in credit card fees has had only a minimal effect on the number of credit card accounts and card usage.

The Passport Certificate is targeted to the 55+ age group. The advertising campaign has used primarily newspaper. A layout of an advertisement for the product has been included as Exhibit 24. The core product is very traditional, a certificate of deposit. But, the CD is augmented with free checking as well as free and discounted travel services such as car rentals, insurance, even a 24-hour travel center is included. The account is made more tangible by giving each customer a wallet-size passport card with the account number and the package benefits included.

The Working Capital Account is targeted to the affluent, middle-aged market segment. It is patterned after a money market account. It is a liquid investment with a very high yield tied to the one year

EXHIBIT 24 Product Ad

Why the smart saver shouldn't go anywhere without a Passport.
PASSPORT
Certificate
MeraBank
MeraBank's Passport Certificate opens a new world of banking services.
ONE YEAR C.D.
7.40%
And it gives you great extras while you're saving money. Just invest $10,000 or more for six months or longer and get: ▶ Travel savings up to 60%. ▶ Discounts on car rentals. ▶ Lost luggage reimbursement...up to $1,250. ▶ Hotel/motel theft reimbursement. ▶ 24-hour travel center service. ▶ 5% cash rebate on airplane tickets, car rental, hotel/motel accommodations. ▶ Lost key and credit card protection. You'll get great extras, at home or away. ▶ Unlimited check writing—with no fees. And your first order of checks is free. ▶ And interest is paid on a checking balance of $500 or more. ▶ Discounts on auto, boat and R.V. loans upon qualification. ▶ VISA or MasterCard credit card at no cost for one year upon qualification. ▶ Government insured, guaranteed high-yielding investment. ▶ Strength, safety and an excellent return on your investment. And more. MeraBank's Passport Certificate. Open one now... visit your nearest MeraBank branch or call toll-free, 1-800-MERATEL. We'll be there.
MeraBank
A FEDERAL SAVINGS BANK

treasury bill. The account requires a high minimum balance of $10,000, but permits unlimited access to the money. The investor can gain a high-yield CD rate, but maintain checking privileges and access to the money. Once again, newspaper was the primary advertising medium for the product. A sample layout is found in Exhibit 25. The Working Capital Account provides its subscribers with monthly statements of the investment and the checking accounts. The account is the only product of its type in the Arizona market. In the first nine months after introduction, it generated a half billion dollars.

MeraBank has a strong commitment to customer service and convenience which goes beyond the traditional branch structure. The direct marketing division supervises the operations of Meratel which is a customer service hotline and "telephone bank." Customers can open an account, obtain information, or transact business by calling 1-800-MERATEL. This convenience to customers has been well received. Call volume increased 300 percent during the year following the name change. The effectiveness of the Meratel operation can be evaluated using Exhibit 26. To further improve the level of service performance, MeraBank has initiated direct marketing campaigns to retail customers, contacting them by mail and telephone. The intention is to expand this operation and begin a regular program of calling retail customers to enhance convenience.

MeraBank's management believes that its success is dependent on the capabilities and performance of employees. The company is recruiting and developing employees who are more sales oriented. Employees are expected to produce superior levels of performance, be customer-oriented, have high standards of integrity, and work in unison with a team spirit. To insure these service standards, a comprehensive training program has been instituted for the sales staff with an incentive compensation system for frontline personnel. The commission program has resulted in doubling the cross sales ratio at the front line. The training process has also been revised to reflect more product training and to amend a thrift vocabulary by incorporating banking terms. Periodically, the company will sponsor a contest to encourage high quality service and improve morale. Internal newsletters provide employees with communication and inspiration to maintain quality service.

Community service also is an important orientation at MeraBank. In 1987, MeraBank contributed over $1.2 million to charity, and many of its employees work in behalf of civic and charitable endeavors. Contributions are divided among worthy cultural, civic, educational, health, and social welfare programs. In one project, MeraBank teamed with Realty World brokers to create a "Dream House." This project benefits victims of cerebral palsy. Strong community spirit is perceived to be a direct expression of MeraBank's service philosophy and culture.

EXHIBIT 25 Product Ad

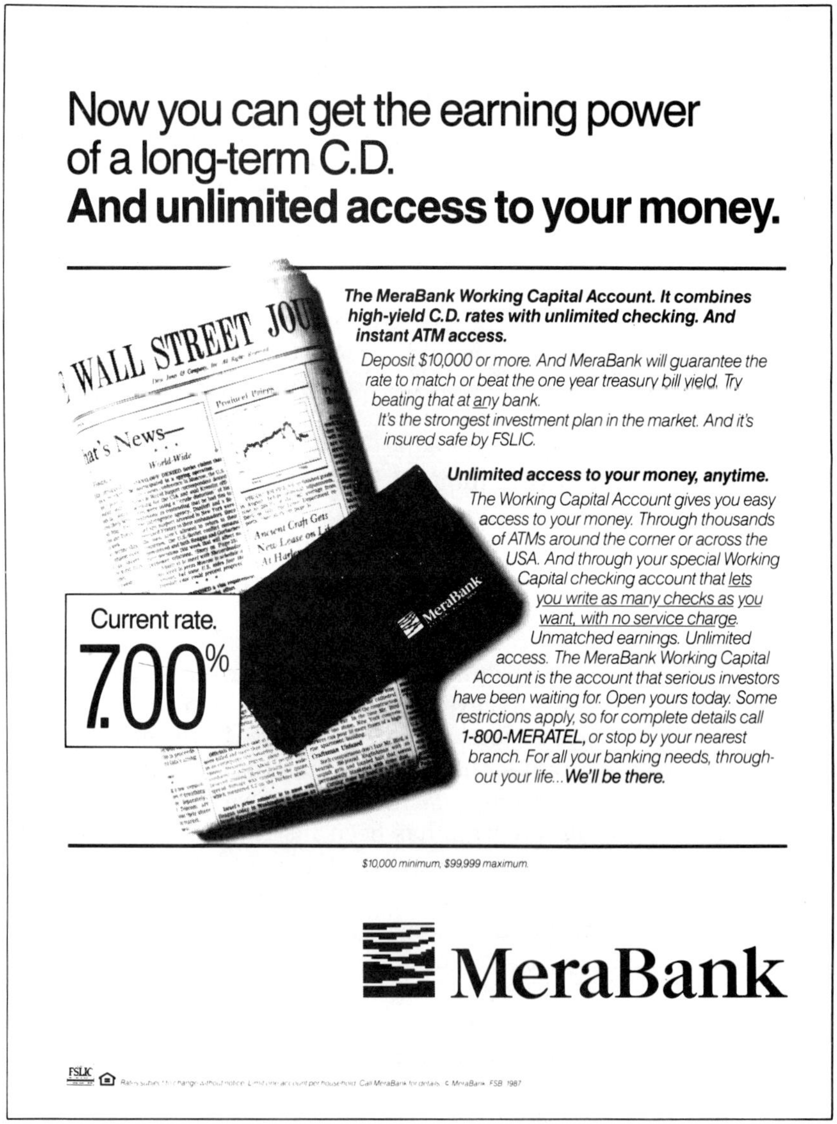
Now you can get the earning power
of a long-term C.D.
And unlimited access to your money.
WALL STREET JOU
Current rate.
7.00%
The MeraBank Working Capital Account. It combines high-yield C.D. rates with unlimited checking. And instant ATM access.
Deposit $10,000 or more. And MeraBank will guarantee the rate to match or beat the one year treasury bill yield. Try beating that at any bank.
It's the strongest investment plan in the market. And it's insured safe by FSLIC.
Unlimited access to your money, anytime.
The Working Capital Account gives you easy access to your money. Through thousands of ATMs around the corner or across the USA. And through your special Working Capital checking account that lets you write as many checks as you want, with no service charge.
Unmatched earnings. Unlimited access. The MeraBank Working Capital Account is the account that serious investors have been waiting for. Open yours today. Some restrictions apply, so for complete details call 1-800-MERATEL, or stop by your nearest branch. For all your banking needs, throughout your life... We'll be there.
$10,000 minimum, $99,999 maximum.
MeraBank
FSLIC
Call MeraBank for details. © MeraBank FSB 1987

EXHIBIT 26 Meratel

	Deposit Acquisition	*Number of Calls*
1984	$37,600,000	7,831
1985	58,014,800	22,319
1986	51,435,700	75,222
1987	80,234,630	266,000

Advertising and Promotion

Advertising and promotional strategy play a key role in positioning MeraBank. Following the name change, advertising objectives emphasized creating awareness and educating the public to the new identity. These objectives have evolved to emphasize increasing both deposits and branch traffic. The initial name change campaign required an increase in promotional expenditures. However, the current advertising budget is only slightly more than it was for First Federal Savings. The primary media used are television and newspaper, while radio is used to a lesser extent. TV advertising is targeted at the 35+ age customer, while newspaper ads are aimed at an older 55+ customer. Examples of newspaper advertisement are included in Exhibits 24 and 25. Direct mail and billboard campaigns are used less often, but have been effective for some products.

MeraBank television advertising has incorporated the new identity of the institution, while maintaining the First Federal campaign theme of "We'll Be There." This theme has been used since 1985, and there are no plans to change the theme for general TV ads. However, MeraBank has tried to develop more sophisticated messages and imagery in their ads. Also, they run special promotional campaigns using television as the primary media. For example, MeraBank has become involved in an advertising campaign promoting CDs and a contest linked with ABC television stations and the 1988 Winter Olympics.

This campaign capitalizes on patriotic interest in the Olympics and offers a free trip to the games in Canada as the grand prize. The winner of the contest will be announced at the half time of the 1988 Super Bowl. Additional prizes are large interest rates on CDs with MeraBank. TV, newspaper, and direct mail have been utilized in this campaign. The campaign also includes a contest for employees. Employee Olympics will be held to spur interest in the promotion and to encourage outstanding service. Employees will be able to nominate peers for sportsmanship, team spirit, and customer service. If the campaign is successful, it could be expanded to include the summer games.

Merchandising and Facility Management

Extending the emphasis placed on promotion, MeraBank has given more attention to branch merchandising. The entire point of sale "look" has been revised to reflect the new corporate identity. Signage, brochures, and point of purchase material incorporate the company logo and identity color scheme. Though thought has been given to a standardized interior appearance, there is not a uniform branch configuration. However, the newer and remodeled facilities reflect an interior design that is more open and modular in construction. Partitions are utilized to provide a flexible lobby setup. Interior decor and career apparel that would embody MeraBank's corporate identity through style and color schemes, both have been under serious consideration. The basic design and exterior of branch locations also is under review.

MeraBank has essentially three prototypes for branch facilities: (1) a large regional center; (2) an intermediate size complex; or (3) a small shopping center style. However, a pilot project is being undertaken with the Circle K convenience stores. A MeraBank branch and Circle K convenience store are sharing the same building, as illustrated in Exhibit 27. Though no direct internal connection was made between the bank and store, the two facilities share a parking lot and the same foundation. This approach is viewed as a way of saving on construction costs for new branches as well as providing added security to the customers who use the ATM machine outside of the branch, as the convenience store is always open. It is not, however, regarded as an expansion strategy into retail grocery outlets—a strategy that has been popular with competitors.

MeraBank is planning a new corporate headquarters. The new office building is being designed based on a careful study of the company's history and image. The building is to personify the new positioning thrust and corporate culture of MeraBank.

Emerging Technology

MeraBank belongs to an automatic teller machine network that provides its customers with the most extensive coverage of any financial institution in Arizona. Expansion of the ATM machines and a nationwide hookup are being planned. This could lead toward a future where most banking transactions could be done electronically at home using a computer terminal. Home banking appears to be a long-term technological goal of the banking industry.

The current trend in convenience bank merchandising is electronic fund transfers. Electronic fund transfers are used by many banks in

EXHIBIT 27 Exterior Facilities

the Phoenix area in the form of a debit card, POS. Though it looks like a credit card, it is used to facilitate payment at retail locations. Using the POS, a transaction is automatically debited to an account. While POS has been limited to market tests in most states, penetration in Arizona has been substantial.

A recent survey found the overall rate of POS acceptance to be 26 percent among financial service consumers. The response varied by age groups. Younger age brackets had higher usage ratings. While the ratings may not seem impressive, they are when compared with the early ratings of ATM acceptance. Investment in POS technology is very high. However, market penetration might generate transaction volumes that reduce transaction costs considerably. Though many of the larger financial institutions have been involved in POS, MeraBank is taking a conservative stance toward electronic technology and is waiting to see how others fare before they follow.

Profitability Perspectives

Examining the profit picture at MeraBank, it is easiest to consider loans as the assets of the bank and deposits as the liabilities. A key to profitability is the diversity of the bank's assets and liabilities. MeraBank attempts to spread its investment risks and not invest too heavily in any one particular business line. Currently, the retail banking, consumer lending, real estate lending, and mortgage banking lines of business contribute most significantly. Corporate banking contributes to a lesser extent. On a limited basis, the real estate development line is profitable.

MeraBank is very competitive in consumer loans such as auto loans, student loans, RV and boat loans. Home and mortgage loans are a particular strength. The home equity loan is the fastest growing loan in the Arizona market. Commercial loans are a smaller segment of MeraBank's loan operations. Given that commercial interest rates vary on a case-by-case basis, it is difficult to generalize profitability in this line of business.

One area of consumer loans that could be developed into a more profitable position is credit cards. Profit in this area relates to volume and use of the card. Since the name change, MeraBank has offered the first year of the card with no fee, but has added a $15 annual fee for each year after the first. The interest rate paid by the customer is 17.9 percent which is comparable to other Arizona banks. Anyone may apply for a MeraBank credit card. The program is not tied to a deposit in the bank. Changes in the credit card program have brought MeraBank in line with the pricing policies of the major banks. However, credit card customers decreased when the changes were initiated. This is not thought to be a long term setback.

On the liability side of the balance sheet, MeraBank offers several products that vary widely in their profit contribution. Certificates of deposit are the most profitable deposits. A bank can guarantee a certain return on the deposit, then pool them together and invest them at a higher rate. Passbook savings accounts would rank second in profitability potential. Low interest rate returns are the sacrifice for demand deposit accounts. Other less profitable deposit products would be IRA's followed by money market accounts. The least profitable deposit account is the interest bearing checking account which serves as a loss leader to attract customers and to "cross-sell" other more profitable accounts. Automatic teller cards and point of sale cards also are only marginally profitable and serve mainly as loss leaders.

Financial planning, sales of securities, estate planning, administering trusts and private bankers are services provided by many major banks. These services are very competitive in the Arizona market and require experienced personnel with established performance. However, MeraBank has not expanded into these areas. Though these services have been studied, MeraBank views them as marginally profitable and does not consider them as a hedge against the risk of any loan segment going soft.

Expansion

The objectives of reaching new consumers and offering convenience to all consumers drive the expansion of branch locations. Since the name change, new branches have been added in the existing service areas of Arizona and Texas. MeraBank now has 71 branches in Arizona and 7 in Texas. And further penetration of these states is being actively pursued.

Other expansion efforts seem to be evolving within the current eight state southwest region that already is served by divisions of MeraBank. The southwest imagery that is projected in the corporate identity should fit well into such states as Colorado and California. Moreover, MeraBank management believes that their identity and the imagery of their logo would be acceptable to all parts of the country in any future expansion.

FUTURE CHALLENGES

MeraBank is no longer a small building and loan. It has grown in sophistication, as its markets and competitors have. MeraBank aspires to continue its tradition of innovation and leadership. The financial services market will become more complex and turbulent. Diversification and expansion present significant opportunities, but also tough questions. MeraBank envisions establishing and sustaining a competitive advantage in terms of its customer service and service marketing strategies across its business lines and diverse geographic markets. With many different facilities, employees and markets, setting appropriate objectives while creating the best strategies and programs to service its markets will be challenging.

MeraBank envisions using its identity as a means to powerfully exhibit who they are as a company and to provide evidence of their marketing presence. MeraBank believes that their identity can differentiate them from competitors and provide a distinct position in the market to generate sales and performance. They recognize the problems of being a service provider with many intangibilities to manage and market. Their identity must be considered all the way throughout service design, development, and delivery.

Increasingly, MeraBank has begun to consider fundamental service marketing challenges, such as: making its services more tangible for its publics; controlling its service quality; developing its service culture; enhancing the productivity of its service encounters and environments; and protecting its new identity. MeraBank's new management orientation and renewed employee enthusiasm have generated a new strategic thrust and uncovered new challenges.

Section 6

Developing Marketing Plans

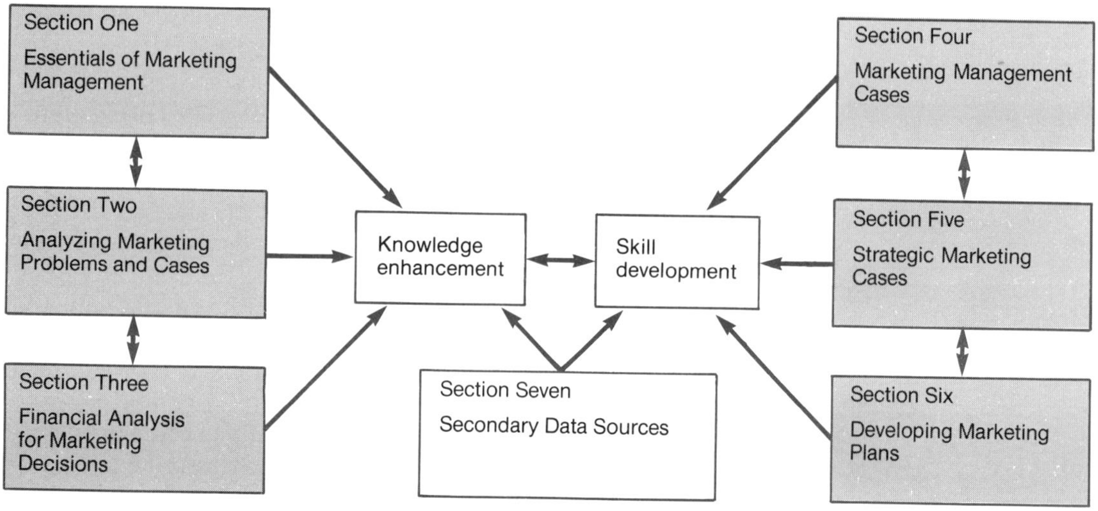

Marketing Management: Knowledge and Skills

NOTE TO THE STUDENT

This section contains an approach to developing marketing plans. It is intended to help you develop practical skills by providing a general format for structuring actual marketing plans. It also offers sources from which important marketing information can be found and explains what types of information to include in various parts of the plan.

Imagine this scenario. After receiving your bachelor's or master's degree in marketing, you are hired by a major consumer goods company. Because you've done well in school, you are confident that you have a lot of marketing knowledge and a lot to offer to the firm. You're highly motivated and are looking forward to a successful career.

After just a few days of work you are called in for a conference with the vice president of marketing. The vice president welcomes you and tells you how glad the firm is that you have joined them. The vice president also says that, since you have done so well in your marketing courses and have had such recent training, he wants you to work on a special project.

He tells you that the company has a new product, which is to be introduced in a few months. He also says, confidentially, that recent new product introductions by the company haven't been too successful. Suggesting that the recent problems are probably because the company has not been doing a very good job of developing marketing plans, the vice president tells you not to look at marketing plans for the company's other products.

Your assignment, then, is to develop a marketing plan for the proposed product in the next six weeks. The vice president explains that a good job here will lead to rapid advancement in the company. You thank the vice president for the assignment and promise that you'll do your best.

How would you feel when you returned to your desk? Surely, you'd be flattered that you had been given this opportunity and be eager to do a good job. However, how confident are you that you could develop a quality marketing plan? Would you even know where to begin?

We suspect that many of you, even those who have an excellent knowledge of marketing principles and are adept at solving marketing cases, may not yet have the skills necessary to develop a marketing plan from scratch. Thus, the purpose of this section is to offer a framework for developing marketing plans. In one sense, this section is no more than a summary of the whole text. In other words, it is an organizational framework based on the text material that can be used to direct the development of marketing plans.

Students should note that we are not presenting this framework and discussion as the only way to develop a marketing plan. While we believe this is a useful framework for logically analyzing the problems involved in developing a marketing plan, other approaches can be used just as successfully.

Often, successful firms prepare much less detailed plans, since much of the background material and current conditions are well known to everyone involved. However, our review of plans used in various firms suggests that something like this framework is not uncommon.

We would like to mention one other qualification before beginning our discussion. Students should remember that one important part of the marketing plan involves the development of a sales forecast. While we have discussed several approaches to sales forecasting in the text, we will detail only one specific approach here.

A MARKETING PLAN FRAMEWORK

Marketing plans have three basic purposes. First, they are used as a tangible record of analysis to investigate the logic involved. This is done to ensure the feasibility and internal consistency of the project and to evaluate the likely consequences of implementing the plan. Second, they are used as roadmaps or guidelines for directing appropriate actions. A marketing plan is designed to be the best available scenario and rationale for directing the firm's efforts for a particular product or brand. Third, they are used as tools to obtain funding for implementation. This funding may come from internal or external sources. For example, a brand manager may have to present a marketing plan to senior executives in a firm to get a budget request filled. This would be an internal source. Similarly, proposals for funding from investors or business loans from banks often require a marketing plan. These would be external sources.

Figure 1 presents a format for preparing marketing plans. Each of the 10 elements will be briefly discussed. We will refer to previous chapters and sections in this text and to other sources where additional information can be obtained when a marketing plan is being prepared. We also will offer additional information for focusing particular sections of the plan as well as for developing financial analysis.

FIGURE 1 A Marketing Plan Format

- Title page.
- Executive summary.
- Table of contents.
- Introduction.
- Situational analysis.
- Marketing planning.
- Implementation and control of the marketing plan.
- Summary.
- Appendix: Financial analysis.
- References.

Title Page

The *title page* should contain the following information: (1) the name of the product or brand for which the marketing plan has been prepared—for example, Marketing Plan for Little Friskies Dog Food; (2) the time period for which the plan is designed—for example, 1990–91; (3) the person(s) and position(s) of those submitting the plan—for example, submitted by Amy Lewis, brand manager; (4) the persons, group, or agency to whom the plan is being submitted—for example, submitted to Lauren Ellis, product group manager; and (5) the date of submission of the plan—for example, June 30, 1990.

While preparing the *title page* is a simple task, remember that it is the first thing readers see. Thus, a title page that is poorly laid out, is smudged, or contains misspelled words can lead to the inference that the project was developed hurriedly and with little attention to detail. As with the rest of the project, appearances are important and affect what people think about the plan.

Executive Summary

The *executive summary* is a two- to three-page summary of the contents of the report. Its purpose is to provide a quick summary of the marketing plan for executives who need to be informed about the plan but are typically not directly involved in plan approval. For instance, senior executives for firms with a broad product line may not have time to read the entire plan but need an overview to keep informed about operations.

The executive summary should include a brief introduction, the major aspects of the marketing plan, and a budget statement. This is not the place to go into detail about each and every aspect of the marketing plan. Rather, it should focus on the major market opportunity and the key elements of the marketing plan that are designed to capitalize on this opportunity.

It is also useful to state specifically how much money is required to implement the plan. In an ongoing firm, many costs can be estimated from historical data or from discussions with other executives in charge of specific functional areas. However, in many situations (such as a class project), sufficient information is not always available to give exact costs for every aspect of production, promotion, and distribution. In these cases, include a rough estimate of total marketing costs of the plan. In many ongoing firms, marketing cost elements are concentrated in the areas of promotion and marketing research, and these figures are integrated with those from other functional areas as parts of the overall business plan.

Table of Contents

The *table of contents* is a listing of everything contained in the plan and where it is located in the report. Reports that contain a variety of charts and figures may also have a *table of exhibits* listing their titles and page numbers within the report.

In addition to using the table of contents as a place to find specific information, readers may also review it to see if each section of the report is logically sequenced. For example, situational analysis logically precedes marketing planning as an activity, and this ordering makes sense in presenting the plan.

Introduction

The types of information and amount of detail reported in the *introduction* depend in part on whether the plan is being designed for a new or existing product or brand. If the product is new, the introduction should explain the product concept and the reasons why it is expected to be successful. Basically, this part of your report should make the new idea sound attractive to management or investors. In addition, it is useful to offer estimates of expected sales, costs, and return on investment.

If the marketing plan is for an existing brand in an ongoing firm, then it is common to begin the report with a brief history of the brand. The major focus here is on the brand's performance in the last three to five years. It is useful to prepare graphs of the brand's performance that show its sales, profits, and market share for previous years and to explain the reasons for any major changes. These exhibits can also be extended to include predicted changes in these variables given the new marketing plan. A brief discussion of the overall strategy followed in previous years also provides understanding of how much change is being proposed in the new marketing plan.

Also useful is to offer a precise statement of the purpose of the report as well as a "roadmap" of the report in the introduction. In other words, tell readers what this report is, how it is organized, and what will be covered in the following sections.

Situational Analysis

The *situational analysis* is not unlike the analysis discussed in Chapter 1 and Section 2 of this text. The focus remains on the most critical and relevant environmental conditions (or changes in them) that affect the success or failure of the proposed plan. While any aspect of the economic, social, political, legal, or cooperative environments might deserve considerable attention, there is seldom if ever a marketing plan in which the competitive environment does not require considerable discussion. In fact, the competitive environment may be set off as a separate section called *industry analysis.* The strengths and weaknesses of major competitors, their relative market shares, and the success of various competitive strategies are critical elements of the situation analysis.

Section 7 of the text offers some sources of information for analyzing the competitive environment, such as the *Audits and Surveys National Total-Market Index* and the *Nielson Retail Index.* In addition, trade association publications, *Fortune, Business Week,* and *The Wall Street Journal,* frequently have useful articles on competitive strategies. Firms' annual reports often provide considerable useful information.

Marketing Planning

Marketing Planning is, of course, a critical section of the report. As previously noted, it includes three major elements: marketing objectives, target market(s), and the marketing mix.

HIGHLIGHT 1
Some Questions to Consider in Competitive Analysis

Understanding an industry and the actions of competitors is critical to developing successful marketing plans. Below is a list of some questions to consider when performing competitive analysis. Thinking about these questions can aid the marketing planner in developing better marketing strategies.

1. Which firms compete in this industry and what is their financial position and marketing capability?
2. What are the relative market shares of various brands?
3. How many brands and models does each firm offer?
4. What marketing strategies have the market leaders employed?
5. Which brands have gained and which have lost market share in recent years, and what factors have led to these changes?
6. Are new competitors likely to enter the market?
7. How quickly do competitive firms react to changes in the market?
8. From which firms or brands might we be able to take market share?
9. What are the particular strengths and weaknesses of competitors in the industry?
10. How do we compare with other firms in the industry in terms of financial strength and marketing skills?

Marketing Objectives. Marketing objectives are often stated in plans in terms of the percentage of particular outcomes that are to be achieved; for example, 80 percent awareness of the brand in particular markets, increase in trial rate by 30 percent, distribution coverage of 60 percent, increase in total market share by 3 percent over the life of the plan. Similarly, there may also be objective statements in terms of sales units or dollars or increases in these. Of course, the reasons for selection of the particular objectives and rationale are important points to explain.

HIGHLIGHT 2

Stating Objectives: How to Tell a "Good" One from a "Bad" One

For the direction setting purpose of objectives to be fulfilled, objectives need to meet five specifications:

1. An objective should relate to a single, specific topic. (It should not be stated in the form of a vague abstraction or a pious platitude—"we want to be a leader in our industry" or "our objective is to be more aggressive marketers.")
2. An objective should relate to a result, not to an activity to be performed. (The objective is the result of the activity, not the performing of the activity.)
3. An objective should be measurable (stated in quantitative terms whenever feasible).
4. An objective should contain a time deadline for its achievement.
5. An objective should be challenging but achievable.

Consider the following examples:

—Poor: Our objective is to maximize profits.

Remarks: How much is "maximum"? The statement is not subject to measurement. What criterion or yardstick will management use to determine if and when actual profits are equal to maximum profits? No deadline is specified.

Better: Our total profit target in 1989 is $1 million.

—Poor: Our objective is to increase sales revenue and unit volume.

Remarks: How much? Also, because the statement relates to two topics, it may be inconsistent. Increasing unit volume may require a price cut, and if demand is price inelastic, sales revenue would fall as unit volume rises. No time frame for achievement is indicated.

Better: Our objective this calendar year is to increase sales revenues from $30 million to $35 million: we expect this to be accomplished by selling 1 million units at an average price of $35.

—Poor: Our objective in 1989 is to boost advertising expenditures by 15 percent.

Remarks: Advertising is an activity, not a result. The advertising

HIGHLIGHT 2 *(concluded)*

objective should be stated in terms of what result the extra advertising is intended to produce.

Better: Our objective is to boost our market share from 8 percent to 10 percent in 1989 with the help of a 15 percent increase in advertising expenditures.

—Poor: Our objective is to be a pioneer in research and development and to be the technological leader in the industry.

Remarks: Very sweeping and perhaps overly ambitious; implies trying to march in too many directions at once if the industry is one with a wide range of technological frontiers. More a platitude than an action commitment to a specific result.

Better: During the 1980s our objective is to continue as a leader in introducing new technologies and new devices that will allow buyers of electrically powered equipment to conserve on electric energy usage.

—Poor: Our objective is to be the most profitable company in our industry.

Remarks: Not specific enough by what measures of profit—total dollars or earnings per share or unit profit margin or return on equity investment or all of these? Also, because the objective concerns how well other companies will perform, the objective, while challenging, may not be achievable.

Better: We will strive to remain atop the industry in terms of rate of return on equity investment by earning a 25 percent after-tax return on equity investment in 1989.

Source: Arthur A. Thompson, Jr., and A. J. Strickland, *Strategic Management: Concepts and Cases*. 4th ed. (Plano, Tex.: Business Publications, 1987), pp. 22–33.

Target Markets. The *target market(s)* discussion explains the customer base and rationale or justification for it. An approach to developing appropriate target markets is contained in Chapter 5 of this text, and a useful source of secondary data for segmenting markets is the *National Purchase Diary Panel.*

This section also includes relevant discussion of changes or important issues in consumer or industrial buyer behavior; for example, what benefits consumers are seeking in this product class, what benefits does the particular brand offer, or what purchasing trends are shaping the market for this product. Discussions of consumer and industrial buyer behavior are contained in Chapters 3 and 4 of this text.

Marketing Mix. The marketing mix discussion explains in detail the selected strategy consisting of product, promotion, distribution, and price, and the rationale for it. Also, if marketing research has been done on these elements or is planned, it can be discussed in this section.

Product. The product section details a description of the product or brand, its packaging and attributes. Product life-cycle considerations should be mentioned if they affect the proposed plan.

Of critical importance in this discussion is the competitive differential advantage of the product or brand. Here it must be carefully considered whether the brand really does anything better than the competition or is purchased primarily on the basis of image. For example, many brands of toothpaste have flouride yet Crest has the largest market share primarily through promoting this attribute of its brand. Thus, does Crest do anything more than other toothpastes or is it Crest's image that accounts for sales?

Discussion of product-related issues is contained in Chapters 6 and 7, and services are discussed in Chapter 12 of this text. For discussion of marketing plans for products at the international level, see Chapter 13.

Promotion. The promotion discussion consists of a description and justification of the planned promotion mix. It is useful to explain the theme of the promotion and to include some examples of potential ads as well as the nature of the sales force if one is to be used. For mass-marketed consumer goods, promotion costs are clearly significant and need to be considered explicitly in the marketing plan.

Discussion of promotion-related issues is contained in Chapters 8 and 9 of this text. Secondary sources, such as *Standard Rate and Data, Simmons Media/Market Service, Starch Advertising Readership Service,* and the *Nielsen Television Index,* provide useful information for selecting, budgeting, and justifying media and other promotional decisions.

Distribution. The distribution discussion describes and justifies the appropriate channel or channels for the product. This includes types of middlemen and specifically who they will be. Other important issues concern the level of market coverage desired, cost, and control considerations. In many cases, the channels of distribution used by the firm, as well as competitive firms, are well established. For example, General Motors and Ford distribute their automobiles through independent dealer networks. Thus, unless there is a compelling reason to change channels, the traditional channel will often be the appropriate alternative. However, serious consideration may have to be given to methods of obtaining channel support; for example, trade deals to obtain sufficient shelf space.

Discussion of distribution-related issues is contained in Chapter 10 of this text. Useful retail distribution information can be found in the *Nielsen Retail Index* and the *Audits and Surveys National Total-Market Index.*

HIGHLIGHT 3
Some Questions to Consider in Consumer Analysis

Knowledge of consumers is paramount to developing successful marketing plans. Below is a list of questions that are useful to consider when analyzing consumers. For some of the questions, secondary sources of information or primary marketing research can be employed to aid in decision making. However, a number of them require the analyst to do some serious thinking about the relationship between brands of the product and various consumer groups to better understand the market.

1. How many people purchase and use this product?
2. How many people purchase and use each brand of the product?
3. Is there an opportunity to reach nonusers of the product with a unique marketing strategy?
4. What does the product do for consumers functionally and how does this vary by brand?
5. What does the product do for consumers in a social or psychological sense, and how does this vary by brand?
6. Where do consumers currently purchase various brands of the product?
7. How much are consumers willing to pay for specific brands, and is price a determining factor for purchase?
8. What is the market profile of the heavy user of this product, and what percentage of the total market are heavy users?
9. What media reach these consumers?
10. On average, how often is this product purchased?
11. How important is brand image for consumers of this product?
12. Why do consumers purchase particular brands?
13. How brand loyal are consumers of this product?

Price. The pricing discussion starts with a specific statement of the price of the product. Depending on what type of channel is used, manufacturer price, wholesale price, and suggested retail price need to be listed and justified. In addition, special deals or trade discounts that are to be employed must be considered in terms of their effect on the firm's selling price.

Discussion of price-related issues is contained in Chapter 11. In addition to a variety of other useful information, the *Nielsen Retail Index* provides information on wholesale and retail prices.

Marketing Research. For any aspect of marketing planning, there may be a need for marketing research. If such research is to be performed, it is important to justify it and explain its costs and benefits. Such costs should also be included in the financial analysis.

If marketing research has already been conducted as part of the marketing plan, it can be reported as needed to justify various decisions that were reached. To illustrate, if research found that two out of three consumers liked the taste of a new formula Coke, then this information would likely be included in the product portion of the report. However, the details of the research could be placed here in the marketing research section. Discussion of marketing research is contained in Chapter 2.

Implementation and Control of the Marketing Plan

This section contains a discussion and justification of how the marketing plan will be implemented and controlled. It also explains who will be in charge of monitoring and changing the plan should unanticipated events occur and how the success or failure of the plan will be mea-

HIGHLIGHT 4
Some Questions to Consider in Marketing Planning

Below is a brief list of questions to ask yourself about the marketing planning section of the report. Answering them honestly and recognizing both the strengths and weaknesses of your marketing plan should help you improve it.

1. What are the key assumptions that were made in developing the marketing plan?
2. How badly will the product's market position be hurt if these assumptions turn out to be incorrect?
3. How good is the marketing research?
4. Is the marketing plan consistent; for example, if the plan is to seek a prestige position in the market, is the product priced, promoted, and distributed to create this image?
5. Is the marketing plan feasible; for example, are the financial and other resources (such as a distribution network) available to implement it?
6. How will the marketing plan affect profits and market share, and is it consistent with corporate objectives?
7. Will implementing the marketing plan result in competitive retaliation that will end up hurting the firm?
8. Is the marketing mix designed to reach and attract new consumers or increase usage among existing users or both?
9. Will the marketing mix help to develop brand loyal consumers?
10. Will the marketing plan be successful not just in the short-run but also contribute to a profitable, long-run position?

sured. Success or failure of the plan is typically measured by a comparison of the results of implementing the plan with the stated objectives.

For a marketing plan developed within an ongoing firm, this section can be quite explicit, since procedures for implementing plans may be well established. However, for a classroom project, the key issues to be considered are (1) the persons responsible for implementing the plan, (2) a timetable for sequencing the tasks, and (3) a method of measuring and evaluating the success or failure of the plan.

Summary

This *summary* need not be much different than the executive summary stated at the beginning of the document. However, it is usually a bit longer, more detailed, and states more fully the case for financing the plan.

Appendix Financial Analysis

Financial analysis is a very important part of any marketing plan. While a complete business plan often includes extensive financial analysis, such as a complete-cost breakdown and estimated return on investment, marketing planners frequently do not have complete accounting data for computing these figures. For example, decisions concerning how much overhead is to be apportioned to the product are not usually made solely by marketing personnel. However, the marketing plan should contain at least a sales forecast and estimates of relevant marketing costs.

Sales Forecast. As noted, there are a variety of ways to develop sales forecasts. Regardless of the method, however, they all involve trying to predict the future as accurately as possible. It is, of course, necessary to justify the logic for the forecasted figures, rather than offer them with no support.

One basic approach to developing a sales forecast is outlined in Figure 2. This approach begins by estimating the total number of persons in the selected target market. This estimate comes from the market segmentation analysis and may include information from test marketing and from secondary sources, such as *Statistical Abstracts of the United States*. For example, suppose a company is marketing a

FIGURE 2 A Basic Approach to Sales Forecasting

Total number of people in target markets *(a)*		*a*
Annual number of purchases per person *(b)*	×	*b*
Total potential market *(c)*	=	*c*
Total potential market *(c)*		*c*
Percent of total market coverage *(d)*	×	*d*
Total available market *(e)*	=	*e*
Total available market *(e)*		*e*
Expected market share *(f)*	×	*f*
Sales forecast (in units) *(g)*	=	*g*
Sales forecast (in units) *(g)*		*g*
Price *(h)*	×	*h*
Sales forecast (in dollars) *(i)*	=	*i*

HIGHLIGHT 5
Some Questions to Consider in Implementation and Control

Implementation and control of a marketing plan require careful scheduling and attention to detail. While some firms have standard procedures for dealing with many of the questions raised below, thinking through each of the questions should help improve the efficiency of even these firms in this stage of the process.

1. Who is responsible for implementing and controlling the marketing plan?
2. What tasks must be performed to implement the marketing plan?
3. What are the deadlines for implementing the various tasks and how critical are specific deadlines?
4. Has sufficient time been scheduled to implement the various tasks?
5. How long will it take to get the planned market coverage?
6. How will the success or failure of the plan be determined?
7. How long will it take to get the desired results from the plan?
8. How long will the plan be in effect before changes will be made to improve it based on more current information?
9. If an ad agency or other firms are involved in implementing the plan, how much responsibility and authority will they have?
10. How frequently will the progress of the plan be monitored?

solar-powered watch that is designed not only to tell time but to take the pulse of the wearer. The product is targeted at joggers and others interested in aerobic exercise. By reviewing the literature on these activities, the marketing planner, John Murphy, finds that the average estimate of this market on a national level is 60 million persons and is growing by 4 million persons per year. Thus, John might conclude that the total number of people in the target market for next year is 64 million. If he has not further limited the product's target market and has no other information, John might use this number as a basis for starting the forecast analysis.

The second estimate John needs is the annual number of purchases per person in the product's target market. This estimate could be quite large for such products as breakfast cereal or less than one (annual purchase per person) for such products as automobiles. For watches, the estimate is likely to be much less than one since people are likely to buy a new watch only every few years. Thus John might estimate the annual number of purchases per person in the target market to be .25. Of course, as a careful marketing planner, John would probably carefully research this market to refine this estimate. In any event, multiplying these two rough numbers gives John an estimate of the *total potential market,* in this case, 64 million times .25 equals 16 million. In other words, if next year alone John's company could sell the watch to every jogger or aerobic exerciser who is buying a watch, the company could expect sales to be 16 million units.

Of course, the firm cannot expect to sell every jogger a watch for several reasons. First, it is unlikely to obtain 100 percent market coverage in the first year, if ever. Even major consumer goods companies selling convenience goods seldom reach the entire market in the first year and many never achieve even 90 percent distribution. Given the nature of the product and depending on the distribution alternative, John's company might be doing quite well to achieve 50 percent market coverage in the first year. If John's plans call for this kind of coverage, his estimate of the total available market would be 16 million times .5, which equals 8 million.

A second reason why John's plans would not call for dominating the market is that his company does not have the only product available or wanted by this target market. Many of the people who will purchase such a watch will purchase a competitive brand. He must, therefore, estimate the product's likely market share. Of all the estimates made in developing a sales forecast, this one is critical, since it is a reflection of the entire marketing plan. Important factors to consider in developing this estimate include: (1) competitive market shares and likely marketing plans; (2) competitive retaliation should the product do well; (3) differential advantage of the product, such as lower price; (4) promotion mix and budget relative to competitors; and (5) market shares obtained by similar products in the introductory year.

Overall, suppose John estimates the product's market share to be 5 percent, since other competitive products have beat his company to the market and because the company's differential advantage is only a slightly more stylish watch. In this case, the sales forecast for year one would be 8 million times .05, which equals 400,000 units. If the manufacturer's selling price was $50, then the sales forecast in dollars would be 400,000 times $50, which equals $20 million.

This approach can also be used to extend the sales forecast for any number of years. Typically, estimates of most of the figures change from year to year, depending on changes in market size, changes in distribution coverage, and changes in expected market shares. The value of this approach is that it forces an analyst to carefully consider and justify each of the estimates offered, rather than simply pulling numbers out of the air. In developing and justifying these estimates, many of the sources listed in Section 7 provide a good place to start searching for information—for example, *Selling Areas Marketing Inc.* or SAMI data.

Estimates of Marketing Costs. A complete delineation of all costs, apportionment of overhead, and other accounting tasks usually are performed by other departments within a firm. All of this information, including expected return on investment from implementing the marketing plan, is part of the overall business plan.

However, the marketing plan should at least contain estimates of major marketing costs. These include such things as advertising, salesforce training and compensation, channel development, and marketing research. Estimates may also be included for product development and package design.

For some marketing costs, reasonable estimates are available from sources such as *Standard Rate and Data.* However, some cost figures, such as marketing research, might be obtained from asking various marketing experts for the estimated price of proposed research. Other types of marketing costs might be estimated from financial statements of firms in the industry. For example, Morris's *Annual Statement Studies* offers percentage breakdowns of various income statement information by industry. These might be used to estimate the percentage of the sales forecast figure which would likely be spent in a particular cost category.

References

This section contains the sources of any secondary information that was used in developing the marketing plan. This might include company reports and memos, statements of company objectives, and articles or books used for information or support of the marketing plan.

References should be listed alphabetically using a consistent format.

One way of preparing references is to use the same approach as is used in marketing journals. For example, the format used for references in *Journal of Marketing* articles is usually acceptable.

CONCLUSION

Suppose you're now back sitting at your desk faced with the task of developing a marketing plan for a new product. Do you believe that you might have the skills to develop a marketing plan? Of course, your ability to develop a quality plan will depend on your learning experiences during your course work and the amount of practice you've had; for example, if you developed a promotion plan in your advertising course, it is likely that you could do a better job on the promotion phase of the marketing plan. Similarly, your experiences in analyzing cases should have sharpened your skills at recognizing problems and developing solutions to them. But inexperience (or experience) aside, hopefully you now feel that you understand the process of developing a marketing plan. You at least know where to start, where to seek information, how to structure the plan, and what are some of the critical issues that require analysis.

Section 7

Secondary Data Sources

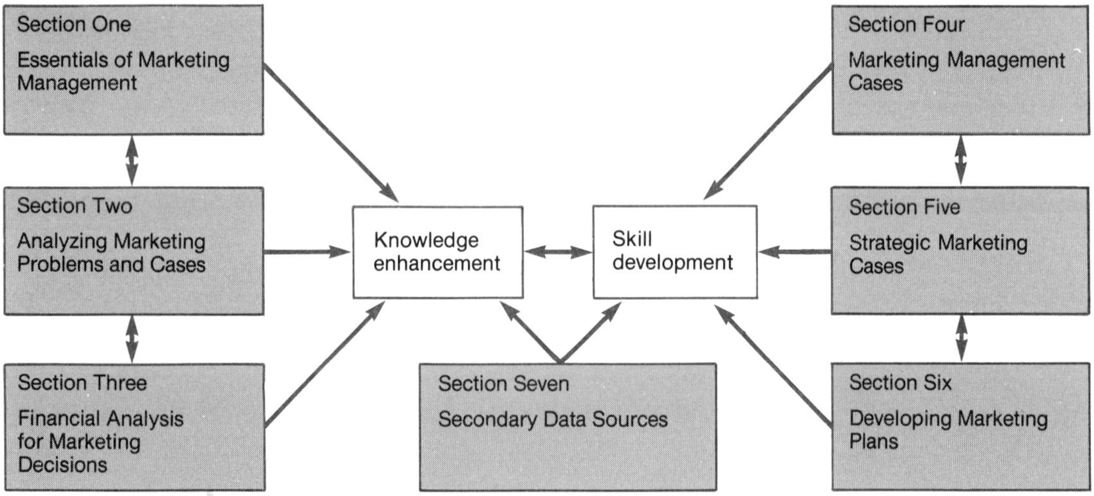

Marketing Management: Knowledge and Skills

NOTE TO THE STUDENT

This section contains a variety of information sources for enhancing your knowledge of marketing and developing your marketing and planning skills. The information is divided into the following categories:

- Selected periodicals
- General marketing information sources
- Selected marketing information services
- Selected retail trade publications
- Financial information sources
- Basic U.S. statistical sources
- General business and industry sources
- Indexes and abstracts

In analyzing and presenting cases and developing marketing plans, it is often very useful for analysts to be able to find outside data sources as a means of supporting their recommendations or conclusions. The data referred to here are from secondary sources and can be located in most business libraries. The purpose of this section is to list and briefly describe some of the key data sources that are available to analysts. The references are listed under eight specific headings: selected periodicals, general marketing information sources, selected marketing information services, selected retail trade publications, financial information sources, basic U.S. statistical sources, general business and industry sources, and indexes and abstracts.

SELECTED PERIODICALS

Advertising Age
American Demographics
Business Horizons
Business Week
California Management Review
Columbia Journal of World Business
Conference Board Record
Forbes
Fortune
Harvard Business Review
Industrial Marketing Management
Journal of the Academy of Marketing Science
Journal of Advertising
Journal of Advertising Research
Journal of Consumer Research
Journal of Experimental Psychology
Journal of Macro Marketing
Journal of Marketing
Journal of Marketing and Public Policy
Journal of Marketing Research
Journal of Personal Selling and Sales Management
Journal of Psychology
Journal of Retailing
Marketing Communications
Marketing News
Marketing Science
Michigan Business Review
Michigan State University Business Topics
Nations Business
Sales Management

GENERAL MARKETING INFORMATION SOURCES

Commercial Atlas and Marketing Guide. Skokie, Ill.: Rand-McNally & Co. Statistics on population, principal cities, business centers, trading areas, sales and manufacturing units, transportation data, and so forth.

Editor and Publisher "Market Guide." Market information for 1,500 American and Canadian cities. Data include population, household, gas meters, climate, retailing, and newspaper information.

Guide to Consumer Markets. New York: The Conference Board. This useful annual compilation of U.S. statistics on the consumer marketplace covers population, employment, income, expenditures, production, and prices.

Marketing Information Guide. Washington, D.C.: Department of Commerce. Annotations of selected current publications and reports, with basic information and statistics on marketing and distribution.

Milutinovich, J. S. "Business Facts for Decision Makers: Where To Find Them." *Business Horizons,* March-April 1985, pp. 63–80.

Population and Its Distribution: The United States Markets. J. Walter Thompson Co. New York: McGraw-Hill Book Co. A handbook of marketing facts selected from the *U.S. Census of Population* and the most recent census data on retail trade.

Sales and Marketing Management. (Formerly *Sales Management,* to October 1975.) This valuable semimonthly journal includes four useful annual statistical issues: *Survey of Buying Power* (July); *Survey of Buying Power, Part II* (October); *Survey of Industrial Purchasing Power* (April); *Survey of Selling Costs* (January). These are excellent references for buying income, buying power index, cash income, merchandise line, manufacturing line, and retail sales.

SELECTED MARKETING INFORMATION SERVICES[1]

Audits and Surveys National Total-Market Index. Contains information on various product types, including total market size, brand market shares, retail inventory, distribution coverage, and out of stock listings.

Dun & Bradstreet Market Identifiers. Relevant marketing information on over 4.3 million establishments for constructing sales prospect files, sales territories, sales territory potentials, and isolating potential new customers with particular characteristics.

National Purchase Diary Panel (NPD). Monthly purchase information based on the largest panel diary in the United States with detailed brand, frequency of purchase, characteristics of heavy buyers, and other market data.

Nielson Retail Index. Contains basic product turnover data, retail prices, store displays, promotional activity, and local advertising based on a national sample of supermarkets, drugstores, and mass merchandisers.

Nielson Television Index. Well-known index which provides estimates

[1] Excerpted from Gilbert A. Churchill, Jr., *Marketing Research,* 4th ed. (Hinsdale, Ill.: Dryden Press, 1987), pp. 188–202.

of the size and nature of the audience for individual television programs.

Selling Areas Marketing, Inc. Reports on warehouse withdrawals of various food products in each of 42 major markets covering 80 percent of national food sales.

Simmons Media/Marketing Service. Provides cross referencing of product usage and media exposure for magazine, television, newspaper, and radio based on a strict national probability sample.

Standard Rate and Data. Nine volumes on major media which include a variety of information in addition to prices for media in selected markets.

Starch Advertising Readership Service. Measures the reading of advertisements in magazines and newspapers and provides information on overall readership percentages, readers per dollar, and rank when grouped by product category.

SELECTED RETAIL TRADE PUBLICATIONS[2]

American Druggist (monthly), The Hearst Corporation, 959 Eighth Avenue, New York, N.Y. 10019.

Auto Chain Store Magazine (ACS) (monthly), Babcox Publications Inc., 11 South Forge Street, Akron, Ohio 44304.

Body Fashions & Intimate Apparel (monthly), Harcourt Brace Jovanovich Publications, 757 Third Avenue, New York, N.Y. 10017.

C. Store Business (10 times/year), Maclean Hunter Media, 1351 Washington Boulevard, Stamford, Conn. 06902.

Catalog Showroom Business (monthly), Gralla Publications, 1515 Broadway, New York, N.Y. 10036.

Catalog Showroom Merchandiser (monthly), CSM Marketing, Inc., 1020 West Jericho Turnpike, Smithtown, N.Y. 11787.

Chain Drug Review (biweekly), Racher Press, Inc., 1 Park Avenue, New York, N.Y. 10016.

Chain Store Age—Executive Edition (monthly), Lebhar-Friedman, Inc., 425 Park Avenue, New York, N.Y. 10022.

Chain Store Age—General Merchandise Edition (monthly), Lebhar-Friedman, Inc., 425 Park Avenue, New York, N.Y. 10022.

Chain Store Age—Supermarkets Edition (monthly), Lebhar-Friedman, Inc., 425 Park Avenue, New York, N.Y. 10022.

CompetitivEdge (monthly), National Home Furnishings Association, 405 Merchandise Mart, Chicago, Ill. 60654.

---

[2] This list is from William R. Davidson, Daniel J. Sweeney, and Ronald W. Stampfl, *Retailing Management*, 5th ed. (New York: John Wiley & Sons, 1984), pp. 764–66.

Consumer Electronics Monthly (monthly), CES Publishing Corporation, 135 West 50th Street, New York, N.Y. 10020.

Convenience Store Merchandiser (monthly), Associated Business Publications, Inc., 41 East 42nd Street, New York, N.Y. 10017.

Convenience Store News (monthly, with additional issues in March, April, August, and October), BMT Publications, Inc., 254 West 31st Street, New York, N.Y. 10001.

Daily News Record (daily), Fairchild Publications, 7 East 12th Street, New York, N.Y. 10003.

Decorating Retailer (monthly), National Decorating Products Association, 1050 North Lindberg Boulevard, St. Louis, Mo. 63132.

Decorative Products World (monthly, except January), 2911 Washington Avenue, St. Louis, Mo. 63103.

Direct Marketing (monthly), Hoke Communications, Inc., 224 Seventh Street, Garden City, N.Y. 11530.

Discount Merchandiser (monthly), Schwartz Publications, 2 Park Avenue, New York, N.Y. 10016.

Discount Store News (biweekly except May and December), Lebhar-Friedman, Inc., 425 Park Avenue, New York, N.Y. 10022.

Drug Store News (biweekly), Lebhar-Friedman, Inc., 425 Park Avenue, New York, N.Y. 10022.

Drug Topics (biweekly), Medical Economics Company, Inc., 680 Kinderkamack Road, Oradell, N.J. 07649.

Earnshaw's Infants, Girls, Boys Wear Review (monthly), Earnshaw Publications, Inc., 393 Seventh Avenue, New York, N.Y. 10001.

Electronics Retailer (monthly, except combined issues in January–February and June–July), Fairchild Publications, 7 East 12th Street, New York, N.Y. 10003.

Floor Covering Weekly (weekly), Hearst Business Communications, Inc., 645 Steward Avenue, Garden City, N.Y. 11530.

Food Merchandising for Nonfood Retailers (quarterly), Lebhar-Friedman, Inc., 425 Park Avenue, New York, N.Y. 10022.

Furniture/Today (biweekly), Communications/Today Ltd., 200 S. Main Street, High Point, N.C. 27261.

Garden Supply Retailer (monthly), The Miller Publishing Company, 2501 Wayzata Blvd., Minneapolis, Minn. 55440.

Giftware Business (monthly), Gralla Publications, 1515 Broadway, New York, N.Y. 10036.

Hardware Age (monthly), Chilton Company, Chilton Way, Radnor, Pa. 19089.

Hardware Merchandiser (monthly), The Irving-Cloud Publishing Company, 7300 North Cicero Avenue, Lincolnwood, Ill. 60646.

Home & Auto (semimonthly except November and December), Harcourt Brace Jovanovich Publications, 757 Third Avenue, New York, N.Y. 10017.

Home Center (monthly), Vance Publishing Corporation, 300 West Adams, Chicago, Ill. 60606.

Housewares (semimonthly plus January, July, and December issues), Harcourt Brace Jovanovich Publications, 757 Third Avenue, New York, N.Y. 10017.

Lawn & Garden Marketing (10 times annually), Intertec Publishing Corporation, 9221 Quivira Road, Overland Park, Kan. 66212.

Mart (monthly), Morgan-Grampian Publishing Co., 2 Park Avenue, New York, N.Y. 10016.

Men's Wear (semimonthly), Fairchild Publications, 7 East 12th Street, New York, N.Y. 10003.

Merchandising (monthly), Gralla Publications, 1515 Broadway, New York, N.Y. 10036.

NARDA News (monthly), NARDA, Inc., 2 North Riverside Plaza, Chicago, Ill. 60606.

Nation's Restaurants News (biweekly), Lebhar-Friedman, Inc., 425 Park Avenue, New York, N.Y. 10022.

National Jeweler (bimonthly), Gralla Publications, 1515 Broadway, New York, N.Y. 10036.

National Mall Monitor (bimonthly), National Mall Monitor, 2280 U.S. 19 North, Suite 264, Clearwater, Fla. 33575.

National Petroleum News (NPN) (monthly), Hunter Publishing Company, 950 Lee Street, Des Plaines, Ill. 60016.

Non-Foods Merchandising (monthly), Charleson Publishing Co., 124 East 40th Street, New York, N.Y. 10016.

Non-Store Marketing Report (biweekly), Maxwell Sroge Publishing Inc., Sroge Building, 731 North Cascade Avenue, Colorado Springs, Colo. 80903.

Outdoor Retailer (bimonthly), Pacifica Publishing Corporation, 31652 Second Avenue, South Laguna, Calif. 92677.

Private Label (monthly), E. W. Williams Publishing Co., 80–88th Avenue, New York, N.Y. 10011.

Professional Furniture Merchant (monthly), Vista Publications, Inc., 9600 W. Sample Road, Coral Springs, Fla. 33065.

Progressive Grocer (monthly), Maclean Hunter Media, 1351 Washington Boulevard, Stamford, Conn. 06901.

Restaurants & Institutions (semimonthly), Cahners Publishing Co., 221 Columbus Avenue, Boston, Mass. 02116.

Retail Control (monthly except April–May and June–July when bimonthly), NRMA—Financial Executives Division, 100 West 31st Street, New York, N.Y. 10001.

Retailing Home Furnishings (weekly), Fairchild Publications, 7 East 12th Street, New York, N.Y. 10003.

Shopping Center World (monthly), Communications Channels, Inc., 6255 Barfield Road, Atlanta, Ga. 30328.

Sporting Goods Business (monthly), Gralla Publications, 1515 Broadway, New York, N.Y. 10036.

Sporting Goods Dealer (monthly), The Sporting News Publishing Company, 1212 North Lindberg Boulevard, St. Louis, Mo. 63132.

Sports Retailer (monthly), National Sporting Goods Association, 1699 Wall Street, Mt. Prospect, Ill. 60056.

Stores (monthly), National Retail Merchants Association, 100 W. 31st Street, New York, N.Y. 10001.

Supermarket Business (monthly), Fieldmark Media, Inc., 25 West 43rd Street, New York, N.Y. 10036.

Supermarket News (weekly), 71 West 35th Street, Suite 1600, New York, N.Y. 10001.

Teens and Boys Magazine (monthly), 71 West 35th Street, Suite 1600, New York, N.Y. 10001.

Tire Review (monthly), Babcox Publications, 11 South Forge Street, Akron, Ohio 44304.

Toys Hobbies & Crafts (monthly except June), Harcourt Brace Jovanovich Publications, 1 East First Street, Duluth, Minn. 55802.

Video Store (monthly), Hester Communications, Inc., 1700 East Dyer Road, Suite 250, Santa Ana, Calif. 92705.

Visual Merchandising & Store Design (monthly), Signs of the Times Publishing Company, 407 Gilbert Avenue, Cincinnati, Ohio 45202.

Women's Wear Daily (daily), Fairchild Publications, 7 East 12th Street, New York, N.Y. 10003.

FINANCIAL INFORMATION SOURCES

Blue Line Investment Survey. Quarterly ratings and reports on 1,000 stocks; analysis of 60 industries and special situations analysis (monthly); supplements on new developments and editorials on conditions affecting price trends.

Commercial and Financial Chronicle. Variety of articles and new reports on business, government, and finance. Monday's issue lists new securities, dividends, and called bonds. Thursday's issuc is devoted to business articles.

Dun's Review. Dun & Bradstreet. This monthly includes very useful annual financial ratios for about 125 lines of business.

Fairchild's Financial Manual of Retail Stores. Information about officers and directors, products, subsidiaries, sales, and earnings for apparel stores, mail order firms, variety chains, and supermarkets.

Federal Reserve Bulletin. Board of Governors of the Federal Reserve System. The "Financial and Business Statistics" section of each issue of this monthly bulletin is the best single source for current U.S. banking and monetary statistics.

Financial World. Articles on business activities of interest to investors, including investment opportunities and pertinent data on firms, such as earnings and dividend records.

Moody's Bank and Finance Manual; Moody's Industrial Manual; Moody's Municipal & Government Manual; Moody's Public Utility Manual; Moody's Transportation Manual; Moody's Directors Service. Brief histories of companies and their operations, subsidiaries, officers and directors, products, and balance sheet and income statements over several years.

Moody's Bond Survey. Moody's Investors Service. Weekly data on stocks and bonds, including recommendations for purchases or sale and discussions of industry trends and developments.

Moody's Handbook of Widely Held Common Stocks. Moody's Investors Service. Weekly data on stocks and bonds, including recommendations for purchases or sale and discussions of industry trends and developments.

Security Owner's Stock Guide. Standard & Poor's Corp. Standard & Poor's rating, stock price range, and other helpful information for about 4,200 common and preferred stocks.

Security Price Index. Standard & Poor's Corp. Price indexes, bond prices, sales, yields, Dow Jones averages, etc.

Standard Corporation Records. Standard & Poor's Corp. Published in looseleaf form, offers information similar to Moody's manuals. Use of this extensive service facilitates buying securities for both the individual and the institutional investor.

BASIC U.S. STATISTICAL SOURCES

Business Service Checklist. Department of Commerce. Weekly guide to Department of Commerce publications, plus key business indicators.

Business Statistics. Department of Commerce. (Supplement to *Survey of Current Business.*) History of the statistical series appearing in the *Survey.* Also included are source references and useful explanatory notes.

Census of Agriculture. Department of Commerce. Data by states and counties on livestock, farm characteristics, values.

Census of Manufacturers. Department of Commerce. Industry statistics, area statistics, subjects reports, location of plants, industry descriptions arranged in Standard Industrial Classification, and a variety of ratios.

Census of Mineral Industries. Department of Commerce. Similar to *Census of Manufacturers.* Also includes capital expenditures and employment and payrolls.

Census of Retail Trade. Department of Commerce. Compiles data for states, SMSAs, counties, and cities with populations of 2,500 or more by kind of business. Data include number of establishments, sales, payroll, and personnel.

Census of Selected Services. Department of Commerce. Includes data on hotels, motels, beauty parlors, barber shops, and other retail service organizations.

Census of Transportation. Passenger Transportation Survey, Commodity Transportation Survey, Travel Inventory and Use Survey, Bus and Truck Carrier Survey.

Census Tract Reports. Department of Commerce, Bureau of Census. Detailed information on both population and housing subjects.

Census of Wholesale Trade. Department of Commerce. Similar to *Census of Retail Trade*—except information is for wholesale establishment.

County and City Data Book. Department of Commerce. Summary statistics for small geographical areas.

Current Business Reports. Department of Commerce. Reports monthly department store sales of selected items.

Economic Report of the President. Transmitted to the Congress, January (each year), together with the *Annual Report* of the Council of Economic Advisers. Statistical tables relating to income, employment, and production.

Handbook of Basic Economic Statistics. Economic Statistics Bureau of Washington, D.C. Current and historical statistics on industry, commerce, labor, and agriculture.

Statistical Abstract of the United States. Department of Commerce. Summary statistics in industrial, social, political, and economic fields in the United States. It is augmented by the *Cities Supplement, The County Data Book,* and *Historical Statistics of the United States*.

Statistics of Income: Corporation Income Tax Returns. Internal Revenue Service. Balance sheet and income statement statistics derived from corporate tax returns.

Statistics of Income: U.S. Business Tax Returns. Internal Revenue Service. Summarizes financial and economic data for proprietorships, partnerships, and small business corporations.

Survey of Current Business. Department of Commerce. Facts on industrial and business activity in the United States and statistical summary of national income and product accounts. A weekly supplement provides an up-to-date summary of business.

GENERAL BUSINESS AND INDUSTRY SOURCES

Aerospace Facts and Figures. Aerospace Industries Association of America.

Annual Statistical Report. American Iron and Steel Institute.

Chemical Marketing Reporter. Schnell Publishing. Includes lengthy, continuing list of "Current Prices of Chemicals and Related Materials."

Computerworld. Computerworld, Inc. December issue includes "Review and Forecast," an analysis of computer industry's past year and the outlook for the next year.

Construction Review. Department of Commerce. Current statistics on construction put in place, costs, and employment.

Distribution Worldwide. Chilton Co. Special annual issue, *Distribution Guide,* compiles information on transportation methods and wages.

Drug and Cosmetic Industry. Drug Markets, Inc. Separate publication in July, *Drug and Cosmetic Catalog,* provides list of manufacturers of drugs and cosmetics and their respective products.

Electrical World. January and February issues include two-part statistical report on expenditures, construction, and other categories by region; capacity; sales; and financial statistics for the electrical industry.

Encyclopedia of Business Information Sources. Paul Wasserman et al., eds., Gale Research Company. A detailed listing of primary subjects of interest to managerial personnel, with a record of sourcebooks, periodicals, organizations, directories, handbooks, bibliographies, and other sources of information on each topic. Two vols., nearly 17,000 entries in over 1,600 subject areas.

Forest Industries. Miller Freeman Publications, Inc. The March issue includes "Forest Industries Wood-Based Panel," a review of production and sales figures for selected wood products; extra issue in May includes a statistical review of the lumber industry.

Implement and Tractor. Intertec Publishing Corporation. January issue includes equipment specifications and operating data for farm and industrial equipment. November issue includes statistics and information on the farm industry.

Industry Surveys. Standard & Poor's Corp. Continuously revised analysis of leading industries (40 industries made up of 1,300 companies). Current analysis contains interim operating data of investment comment. Basic analysis features company ratio comparisons and balance sheet statistics.

Middle Market Directory. Dun & Bradstreet. Inventories approximately 18,000 U.S. companies with an indicated worth of $500,000 to $999,999, giving officers, products, standard industrial classification, approximate sales, and number of employees.

Million Dollar Directory. Dun & Bradstreet. Lists U.S. companies with an indicated worth of $1 million or more, giving officers and directors, products, standard industrial classification, sales, and number of employees.

Modern Brewery Age. Business Journals, Inc. February issue includes a review of sales and production figures for the brewery industry. A separate publication, *The Blue Book,* issued in May, compiles sales and consumption figures by state for the brewery industry.

National Petroleum News. McGraw-Hill, Inc. May issue includes statistics on sales and consumption of fuel oils, gasoline, and related products. Some figures are for 10 years, along with 10-year projections.

Operating Results of Department and Specialty Stores. National Retail Merchants Association.

Petroleum Facts and Figures. American Petroleum Institute.

Poor's Register of Corporations, Directors, and Executives of the United States and Canada. Standard & Poor's Corp. Divided into two sections. The first gives officers, products, sales range, and number of employees for about 30,000 corporations. The second gives brief information on executives and directors.

Quick-Frozen Foods. Harcourt Brace Jovanovich Publications. October issue includes "Frozen Food Almanac," providing statistics on the frozen food industry by product.

Statistical Sources. Paul Wasserman et al., eds. Gale Research Corp., 4th ed., 1974. A subject guide to industrial, business, social, educational, financial data, and other related topics.

The Super Market Industry Speaks. Super Market Institute.

Vending Times. February issue includes "The Buyers Guide," a special issue providing information on the vending industry; June issue includes "The Census of the Industry," a special issue containing statistics on the vending industry.

INDEXES AND ABSTRACTS

Accountants Digest. L. L. Briggs. A digest of articles appearing currently in accounting periodicals.

Accountants Index. American Institute of Certified Public Accountants. An index to books, pamphlets, and articles on accounting and finance.

Accounting Articles. Commerce Clearing House. Loose-leaf index to articles in accounting and business periodicals.

Advertising Age Editorial Index. Crain Communications, Inc. Index to articles in *Advertising Age*.

American Statistical Index. Congressional Information Service. A comprehensive two-part annual index to the statistical publications of the U.S. government.

Applied Science & Technology Index. (Formerly *Industrial Arts Index* to 1958.) H. W. Wilson Co. Reviews over 200 periodicals relevant to the applied sciences, many of which pertain to business.

Battelle Library Review. (Formerly *Battelle Technical Review* to 1962.) Battelle Memorial Institute. Annotated bibliography of books, reports, and articles on automation and automatic processes.

Bulletin of Public Affairs Information Service. Public Affairs Information Service, Inc. (Since 1915—annual index.) A selective list of the latest books, pamphlets, government publications, reports of public and private agencies, and periodicals relating to economic conditions, public administration, and international relations.

Business Education Index. McGraw-Hill Book Co. (Since 1940—annual index.) Annual author and subject index of books, articles, and theses on business education.

Business Periodicals Index. H. W. Wilson Co. A subject index to the disciplines of accounting, advertising, banking, general business, insurance, labor, management, and marketing.

Catalog of United States Census Publication. Washington, D.C.: Dept. of Commerce, Bureau of Census. Census bureau data indexes all available. Main divisions are: agriculture, business, construction, foreign trade, government, guide to locating U.S. census information.

Computer and Information Systems. (Formerly *Information Processing Journal* to 1969.) Cambridge Communications Corporation.

Cumulative Index of NICB Publications. The National Industrial Conferences Board. Annual index of NICB books, pamphlets, and articles in the area of management of personnel.

Funk and Scott Index International. Investment Index Company. Indexes articles on foreign companies and industries from over 1,000 foreign and domestic periodicals and documents.

Guide to U.S. Government Publications. McLean, Va., Documents Index. Annotated guide to publications of various U.S. government agencies.

International Abstracts in Operations Research. Operations Research Society of America.

International Journal of Abstracts of Statistical Methods in Industry. The Hague, Netherlands: International Statistical Institute.

Management Information Guides. Gale Research Company. Bibliographical references to information sources for various business subjects.

Management Review. American Management Association.

Monthly Catalog of U.S. Government Publications. U.S. Government Printing Office. Continuing list of federal government publications.

Monthly Checklist of State Publications. U.S. Library of Congress, Exchange and Gift Division. Record of state documents received by Library of Congress.

New York Times Index. New York. Very detailed index of all articles in the *Times,* arranged alphabetically with many cross-references.

Psychological Abstracts. American Psychological Association.

Public Affairs Information Service. Public Affairs Information Service, Inc. A selective subject list of books, pamphlets, and government publications covering business, banking, and economics as well as subjects in the area of public affairs.

Reader's Guide to Periodical Literature. H. W. Wilson Co. Index by author and subject to selected U.S. general and nontechnical periodicals.

Sociological Abstracts. American Sociological Association.

The Wall Street Journal Index. Dow Jones & Company, Inc. An index of all articles in *The WSJ* grouped in two sections: corporate news and general news.

Case Index

Adirondack Manor, 314–38
American Express Company, 732–55
Apple Computer Inc., 479–97
Arthritis Foundation, 598–606
Babcock Swine, Inc., 625–45

Campbell Soup Company, 781–805
Caterpillar Tractor Company, 660–72
Coca-Cola Company, 756–80
Computing Systems Ltd., 420–28
Comshare, Inc., 701–18, 719–31
Cub Foods, 463–64

Deep South Civic Center, 583–97
Delta Airlines, 523–26
Denver Art Museum, 577–82
General Foods, 409–11
Gillette Company, 386–407

Hanover-Bates Chemical Corporation, 429–35
Hershey Foods, 673–700
Island Shores (Enterprise Developers, Inc.), 556–72
K Mart Stores, 498–521

Mark-Tele, Inc., 367–85
Mary Kay Cosmetics, Inc., 806–52
Maytag Company, 649–51
Mead Corporation, 342–56
MeraBank, 853–90
MidAmerica BancSystem, Inc., 357–66

Outdoor Sporting Products, Inc., 412–19
Rockwood Manor, 530–39
Rogers, Nagel, Langhart, Architects and Planners, 607–24

S. C. Johnson & Son, Inc., 436–59, 540–55
Seven-Up Company, 339–40

TenderCare Disposable Diapers (Rocky Mountain Medical Corporation), 303–13
Texas Blueberry Growers Association, 292–302
Thompson Respiration Products, Inc., 465–78
Timex Corp., 281–83
TSR Hobbies, Inc., 652–59
Tupperware, 461–62
Tylenol, 573–76

Wyler Foods, 284–91
Young Attitudes, 527–29

Name Index

Aaker, David A., 102, 156, 203
Alexander, Dale, 811-15
Alexander, Larry D., 498, 756
Alexander, Ralph S., 153
Allaway, Arthur, 233
Allvine, Fred C., 8
Anderson, Alan, 305-6
Anderson, C., 9
Anderson, Paul F., 81, 88
Andreasen, Alan, 239
Angelmar, Reinhard, 7
Ansoff, H. Igor, 16, 129
Arens, William F., 156
Ash, Mary Kay, 810-17, 820-22, 827, 828, 830, 837-44, 852
Ash, Stephen B., 436
Assael, Henry, 75, 88
Atlas, James, 97
Avlonitis, George J., 122

Babcock, Monroe, 625
Bagozzi, Richard P., 244
Banbic, Peter J., 87
Barksdale, Hiram, 213
Bates, Albert D., 186
Beales, Howard, 59
Bearden, William O., 63, 64, 69
Belk, Russell W., 72-73
Bellenger, Danny N., 163, 175
Bello, Daniel C., 233
Benjamin, Robba, 853
Bennett, Lawrence, 304
Bennett, Peter D., 87
Berkowitz, Eric N., 203
Berlew, Kingston, 233
Berman, Barry, 80, 104, 122-25
Bernhardt, Kenneth L., 134, 177, 183, 192, 263
Berry, L. L., 207, 219
Best, Daniel, 660
Best, Roger, Jr., 75
Bettman, James R., 193
Biedenharn, Joseph, 757
Blackwell, Roger D., 75
Block, John R., 639
Bloom, Paul N., 241, 246
Blume, Brian, 654
Blume, Kevin, 654, 658
Boddewyn, J. J., 246
Bonoma, Thomas V., 105
Boone, Louis E., 84
Bosch, John, 304
Bovee, Courtland L., 156
Boyd, Harper W., Jr., 54
Boyett, Joseph E., Jr., 203
Brandt, William K., 233
Brigham, Eugene F., 273, 278
Brown, Jacqueline Johnson, 69
Brown, James R., 88
Bruzzone, Donald E., 156
Buell, Victor P., 214
Burke, John D., 685
Burt, David N., 203
Busch, Paul, 175
Buskirk, Richard H., 168
Byrne, Harlan S., 668

Cagan, Tom, 303, 305, 306
Cain, William C., 223
Calantone, Roger J., 96
Camillus, J. C., 17
Campbell, Joseph, 785
Cannon-Bonaventre, Kristina, 153
Carlson, John A., 59
Carter, Gene, 492
Carusone, Peter S., 342
Carver, Hank, 429
Cateora, Philip R., 221
Cavusgil, S. Tamer, 224
Cebrero, Cholla, 635-37
Chambers, Terry M., 81, 88
Chandler, Bob, 543
Chapman, Dan, 530
Charles, David, 358
Chase, Marilyn, 479
Chase, Marty, 499
Chonko, Lawrence B., 189, 246
Churchill, Gilbert A., Jr., 40, 42, 43, 47, 54, 64, 165, 173, 909
Clark, Harold L., 740-41
Claycamp, Henry J., 115
Coleman, Denis R., 263
Coleman, Richard P., 68
Comer, James M., 175
Coney, Kenneth A., 75
Cosmas, Stephen C., 105
Cote, Joseph A., Jr., 72
Crandall, Richard L., 702, 707-8, 715-18, 725, 727
Cravens, David W., 249, 263
Crawford, C. Merle, 129, 137
Cron, William L., 175
Crutchfield, Bryant, 342, 344, 346, 348-50
Cunningham, Harry, 500, 511
Currier, Jan, 807, 844, 846-51
Curry, David J., 203

D'Amico, Michael, 116-17, 120
Dart, Justin, 461
Daub, Steven, 314
Davis, Keith, 246
Day, George S., 30, 119
Dearden, William E., 685
Della Bitta, Albert J., 201
Deshpande, Rohit, 44
Dewar, Robert, 511
Dickson, Peter R., 100
Dixon, Mark, 808
Dodd, Harold, 639
Donnelly, James H., Jr., 8, 175, 211, 214, 219
Dorrance, John T., 785
Doyle, Peter, 105
Drucker, Peter, 11, 12, 13, 14
Dubinsky, Alan J., 163, 175
Duncan, Calvin P., 59
Dwyer, F. Robert, 187
Dyson, Brian, 774

Eckhouse, Richard H., 252, 253, 261
Eckrich, Donald W., 660
Edge, Alfred G., 263
Edwards, Mike, 386, 401, 406
El-Ansary, Adel I., 190
Engel, James F., 75, 147
Enis, Ben M., 114, 148, 245
Etzel, Michael J., 69
Evans, Joel R., 80, 104, 122-25
Evans, Richard H., 63
Ezell, Hazel F., 164, 217, 245

Fannin, Rebecca, 833
Fauber, Bernard M., 500, 511-12, 520
Fay, Charles H., 175
Feigin, Barbara, 101
Fern, Edward F., 88
Ferrell, O. C., 240
Fine, G. G., 599
Fogg, C. Davis, 199
Follet, John, 429
Ford, Gary, 203
Ford, Neil M., 165, 173
Fornell, C., 246
Foster, Brian L., 69
Fox, Karen F. A., 244
Frazier, Gary L., 189
Fredrick, William C., 246
Frey, Cynthia J., 556
Friedman, Margaret L., 523, 573, 652
Fryburger, V., 157
Futrell, Charles M., 124, 175, 187, 208

Gallean, Mary, 531
Ganesh, Gopala Krishman, 292
Gardner, David M., 62
Gaski, John F., 184, 187, 246
Gatignon, Hubert, 137

Gelb, Betsy D., 65
George, William R., 213, 219
Gerstner, Eitan, 193
Gibson, J. L., 8
Gieseke, Robert J., 59
Gillett, P. L., 47
Gillette, King C., 386, 387
Gilly, Mary C., 65
Gilmore, Robert E., 669
Glass, William, 233
Goedert, Phil, 608
Goizueta, Roberto C., 765, 769
Gold, June, 598
Goodbar, Perry, 314
Grant, John A., 853
Grant, John H., 8
Gray, Burt, 314, 318
Green, Robert, 233
Green, William C., 292
Gresham, L. G., 240
Grewal, Dhruv, 756
Greyser, Stephen A., 241
Guiltinan, Joseph P., 152, 171, 196, 214
Guise, Robert F., 707
Gupta, Ashok, K., 125
Gustafson, Karl, 367
Gygax, E. Gary, 652-54

Haas, Robert W., 83
Hagen, Mike, 420-28
Haley, Russell I., 95-96
Hamermesh, Richard G., 19
Hamman, Brad, 167
Hanna, Sherman, 70
Harrington, Diana R., 270, 278
Hartley, Robert J., 44
Hartley, Steven, W., 165
Hauser, John R., 137
Hawes, Jon M., 125, 527, 598
Hawkins, Del I., 54, 75
Hayes, H. Michael, 607
Healy, John S., 157
Heath, Robert L., 157
Henson, Sharon, 781
Hershey, Milton S., 673-74
Higgins, Victor, 465
Hinkle, Charles, 479
Hise, Richard T., 47, 673
Hitt, M. A., 11
Holak, Susan L., 246
Holt, Benjamin, 661
Hopkins, David, 137
Hornik, Jacob, 73
Houston, Franklin S., 6
Howell, Roy D., 163
Hughes, Marie Adele, 97
Hulbert, James M., 233
Hunt, Shelby D., 189, 246
Hurwitt, David, 410

Ingene, Charles A., 190
Ingram, Thomas N., 163, 175
Ingrassia, Lawrence, 649
Ireland, R. D., 11
Iselin, Barry, 853
Ivancevich, J. M., 8

Jacoby, Neil, 238
Jaworski, Bernard J., 126
Jobs, Stephen, 480, 496
John, George, 190
Johnson, Richard, 367, 368
Johnson, Robert Wood, 576

Kahle, Lynn R., 105
Kaikati, Jack G., 233
Kale, Sudhir H., 233
Kalkhoven, Kevin O. N., 704, 706-7, 710, 715, 718, 719, 724
Kanuck, Leslie, 75
Kassarjian, Harold H., 157
Kaye, Donald, 652, 653
Keegan, Warren, J., 230
Kehoe, William J., 263
Kennedy, John F., 242
Keough, Donald R., 765, 769
Kerr, Stewart, 314
Kiel, Geoffrey C., 59
Kinder, William F., 740
King, Robert L., 6
King, Ronald H., 82, 88
King, William R., 8
Kinnear, Thomas C., 54, 134, 147, 177, 183, 192, 263
Klein, H. E., 20
Klompmaker, Jay E., 386
Kniffen, Fred W., 412
Kohnken, Kent H., 199
Kosaki, Hiroshi, 233
Kotler, Philip, 9, 11, 21, 182, 194, 196, 200, 219, 238, 239, 241, 244
Krapfel, Robert E., Jr., 88
Kresge, Sebastian, 499
Krisher, Bernard, 669
Krumm, Daniel, 650, 651
Kummel, Charles M., 386

Label, Wayne A., 233
Laczniak, Gene R., 240, 246
Lamb, Charles W., Jr., 249, 263
Lambert, Zarrel V., 193, 412
Lamont, Lawrence M., 314
Lang, James R., 732
Langhart, Victor D., 607, 608, 609, 622-24
Larsen, Clifford K., 685
Lastovicka, John L., 97
Layton, Roger A., 59
Lazer, William, 233
Lehmann, Donald R., 54, 59, 61, 77
Lesser, Jack A., 97
Levitt, Theodore, 227
Levy, Sidney J., 244
Linneman, R. A., 20
Liston, Mel, 436, 441, 448, 451, 454, 459
Little, John D. C., 38
Little, John L., 498
Little, Taylor, 190
Lodge, George Cabot, 233
Lovelock, C. H., 219
Luck, David J., 245

Lusch, Robert F., 240
Lutz, Richard J., 62

McCarthy, E. Jerome, 119, 188
McCusker, Allen, 774
McDaniel, Stephen W., 673
McDonald, Hudson, 412-13, 417-18
McEnally, Martha R., 125
McGovern, Gordon, 781, 786, 787-88, 789, 792, 794-95, 797
McGuckin, Margaret B., 853
Macinnis, Deborah J., 126
McNaught-Davis, Ian G., 715-16
McPeak, M. James, 625-27, 630, 632, 635, 637
McQuaid, Gary W., 685
McVey, Phillip, 181
Maier, Charles F., 660
Marcks, Richard M., 690
Markkula, A. C., Jr., 484, 485
Maslow, A. H., 56-59
Mason, Joseph Barry, 164, 217, 245, 277
Matthews, H. Lee, 87
Mayer, Morris L., 277
Maytham, Thomas N., 577, 580, 581
Mazis, Michael B., 59
Merrill, James R., 96
Miniard, Paul W., 75
Mintzberg, H., 17
Mitchell, Andrew, 63
Mitchell, Arnold, 97
Mitchell, Rita, 621-22
Mohen, John C., 75
Mohler, Harold S., 685
Mokwa, Michael P., 367, 853
Monroe, Kent B., 193, 201, 203
Montgomery, David B., 30
Moore, R. Carl, 252, 253, 261
Moore, William L., 59, 61
Morely, Roger, 741
Morgan, Lee L., 660, 666, 667, 669, 670
Morgenthaler, Eric, 769
Moriarty, Rowland T., 80, 86
Morris, Betsy, 463
Morris, Bill, 528
Morrison, Robert, 304
Murata, Shoji, 233
Murdick, Robert G., 252, 253, 261
Murphy, Patrick E., 96, 114, 240, 246

Nagel, Jerome K., 607
Naisbitt, John, 65
Narasimhan, Chakravarthi, 137
Neidell, Lester, 625, 649
Nelson, James E., 303, 357, 465
Nelson, Richard A., 157
Nevin, John R., 187
Newman, B. M., 46
Newman, P. R., 46
Nichols, Bob, 420, 424
Norvell, Douglas G., 221
Nutt, Paul C., 12

O'Dell, William F., 263
O'Donnell, Thomas, 732

Olshavsky, Richard W., 59
Olson, Jerry C., 60, 71, 75, 99, 139, 161, 409, 463
O'Shaughnessy, John, 77
Oshauski, Frank A., 245
Ott, Leland, 101
Otte, Kenneth, 284, 286, 289-91
Oxenfeldt, Alfred R., 195

Papke, P. A., III, 598
Parasuraman, A., 175, 207, 219
Park, C. Whan, 126
Parker, Tom, 57
Patton, Wesley E., III, 82, 88
Paul, Gordon, 152, 171
Pavelko, Mary, 631
Perez, Michele, 566
Perreault, William D., Jr., 119, 188
Perry, James L., 12
Pessemier, Edgar E., 126
Peter, J. Paul, 47, 51, 60, 71, 75, 99, 139, 161, 281, 339, 409, 461, 463
Pinson, Christian, 7
Poindexter, Joseph, 50
Pollay, Richard W., 157
Ponti, Gio, 577
Powell, Alwyn V., 538
Pride, William M., 190
Puto, Christopher P., 82, 88

Quelch, John A., 153
Quinn, Lovie, 808-9, 813, 817
Raj, S. P., 125
Ramage, Brent, 292, 298, 300
Raveed, Sion, 221
Reddy, S. K., 246
Reimann, Bernard C., 701, 719
Reingen, Peter H., 69
Richers, Raimer, 233
Ricks, Thomas E., 769
Ries, Al, 99
Ring, Peter Smith, 12
Robertson, Thomas S., 75, 137
Robeson, James, 87
Robinson, James D., III, 732, 740, 741-42, 752
Rogers, John B., 607, 608, 609, 611-12, 624
Rogers, Richard, 806, 810-11, 823
Romblad, Robin, 806
Rose, Aaron M., 536
Rosenberg, L., 8
Rosenberry, Walter, 580
Ross, Bennett, 314
Rothschild, Michael L., 157, 246
Rotzell, K. R., 157
Ruppel, Andrew C., 263
Ryan, Michael J., 62
Ryans, Adrian B., 420
Ryans, J. K., Jr., 47

Salatich, William G., 401
Salop, Steven C., 59
Sandage, C. H., 157
Sannella, Maria, 556
Sarel, D., 157
Saunders, John, 105
Sawyer, Alan G., 51, 96
Schaffer, Jeffrey D., 583
Schaninger, Charles M., 69
Schewe, Charles D., 8, 19
Schiffman, Leon G., 75
Schmidt, Steven, 582
Schrage, Floy, 625
Schul, Patricia L., 190
Schultz, Don E., 284
Schumer, Fern, 50
Schwinghammer, JoAnn K. L., 292
Scott, Michael, 484
Scotton, Donald W., 701, 719
Seammon, Debra L., 203
Seeger, J. A., 19
Seidman, Stephen B., 69
Semon, Thomas T., 77
Sen, Subrata K., 137
Sewall, M. A., 157
Shansby, J. Gary, 102
Shapiro, Benson R., 105
Shaub, Harold A., 785-86
Sheffet, Mary Jane, 203
Sherrid, Pamela, 409
Sheth, Jagdish N., 81, 87, 189
Shimp, Terence A., 63
Shuptrine, F. Kelly, 245
Silliman, Benjamin, 771
Simon, Herman, 198
Sinha, P., 169
Skinner, Steven J., 175
Smart, C., 11
Smith, Chuck, 357, 358-59
Smith, David, 468
Smith, George, 586, 591-92, 594-95
Smith, Tom, 556
Sofran, Sandra, 436
Spekman, Robert E., 86
Spiro, Rosann L., 70, 161
Sprague, James, 429
Staelin, Richard, 59
Stalport, Dan, 543
Stanton, William J., 124, 168, 187, 208
Stasch, Stanley F., 54
Steinbrink, John P., 174
Steiner, Robert L., 237
Stern, Louis W., 190
Stevens, Robert E., 84
Stineman, Esther L., 479
Stocker, Patricia, 577
Strange, Larry, 292-93, 295, 300
Strickland, A. J., III, 9, 898
Sturdivant, Frederick D., 246
Styan, George, 540
Sudler, James, 588
Sujen, Harish, 161
Sujen, Mita, 161
Suneson, Paul, 463
Suprenant, Carol, 64
Sutherland, A. T., 531-32

Taylor, J. R., 54
Teel, Jesse, E., 64
Telling, Edward, 515
Tennga, Walter, 511
Thomas, Benjamin, 757
Thomas, Dan R. E., 209
Thompson, Arthur A., Jr., 9, 781, 806, 898
Thompson, T. W., 219
Thorne, Gary, 492
Traxler, Mark, 284
Trent, Robert H., 263
Trout, Jack, 99
Tull, Donald S., 54
Tupper, Earl, 461

Urban, Glen L., 137
Van Horne, James C., 277, 278
Varadarajan, P. Rajan, 126
Venkatramen, N., 17
Vertinsky, I., 11
Von Hippel, Eric, 137
Von Luhrte, Richard, 608, 620-21
Vose, Carolyn, 540
Vyas, Niren, 88

Wagner, Janet, 70
Walker, Lewis W., 11
Walker, Orville C., 165, 173
Wallace, Marc J., 175
Walton, John R., 203
Ward, Scott, 75
Wardlow, Ervin, 511
Waren, Allan D., 701, 719
Warshaw, Martin R., 147
Washington, Jane, 621
Waters, J. A., 17
Watt, James, 358, 364-65
Way, Alva, 742
Webster, Frederick E., Jr., 178, 179, 202
Weeks, William A., 96
Weill, Sanford I., 752
Weinberg, C. B., 219
Weiner, Steve, 463
Weitz, Barton A., 161
Welsh, M. Ann, 187
West, Ralph, 527
Westbrook, R. A., 246
Westfall, Ralph, 54
Weston, J. Fred, 278
White, Philip D., 186
White, Richard E., 853
White, Roderick E., 19
Whitehead, Joseph, 757
Wilemon, David, 125
Wiley, Kim Wright, 842, 852
Wilkie, William L., 75
Williams, John C., 558
Williams, Kaylene C., 161
Williamson, N. C., 233
Wilson, Brent D., 270, 278
Wind, Yoram, 91, 103, 115, 126
Winklevoss, Howard E., 538
Winters, Frederick W., 62
Witt, Robert E., 429
Woodside, Arch G., 87, 88
Woolridge, William R., 465
Wozniak, Steve, 480, 484
Wrathall, T. Wallace, 708, 713-14, 715

Wright, Barbara A., 660
Wynd, William R., 530

Young, Shirley, 101
Zaltman, Gerald, 239
Zeithaml, C. P., 9
Zeithaml, Valerie A., 105, 207, 219
Zielinski, Joan, 75
Zikmund, William, 116–17, 120
Zimmer, Thomas W., 252, 253, 261
Zimmerman, Richard A., 685
Zoltners, Andris, 169
Zyman, Sergio, 769

Subject Index

Advances in Consumer Research, 75
Advertising
  budget
    allocation of, 146-53
    determination of, 144-46
    at Gillette Co., 393
    at TSR Hobbies, 657
  campaign, 149-53
    media mix, 149-53
    media performance, 150-53
    message, 147-49
    planning, 148-49
  for Campbell Soup Co., 792
  at Comshare, 729
  for Deep South Civic Center, 594
  federal control of, 156
  at Gillette Co., 397-99
  for Hershey Foods, 692-94, 695-96
  international, 229-30
  marketing tasks of, 142-44, 146
  for MeraBank, 883, 885, 886-87
  process model for, 145
  purpose of, 140-42
  for S. C. Johnson Agree line, 439, 448-52
  in soft drink industry, 771, 773
  for TenderCare Disposable Diapers, 309, 310
  for Wyler's Unsweetened Soft Drink Mixes, 288-90
Advertising Age, 75
Alcohol and Tobacco Tax Division (Treasury Department), 156
Almanac of Business and Industrial Financial Ratios, The, 277
Annual Statement Studies, 277
Asset management ratios, 274
Audits and Surveys National Total-Market Index, 896, 899
Bank cards, 733-35
Boston Consulting Group portfolio model, 29, 31-32
Break-even analysis, 196, 197, 267-69
Business strength, 33
Business Week, 75, 896

Case analysis
  elements in, 250
  operational approach to, 259
  oral presentation of, 263
  pitfalls to avoid in, 258-61
  problem analysis in, 256-57
  problem resolution in, 257-58
  purpose of, 249
  situation analysis in, 251-56
  written report of, 261-63
Cash cows (in market share), 31
Clayton Act, 201
Commercialization
  in new product development, 134
  and Texas Blueberry Growers Association, 301-2
Competition
  for Adirondack Manor, 320-28
  for Apple Computer, 486-90
  for Campbell Soup Co., 797-99, 801-4, 805
  for Caterpillar Tractor, 667-69
  between Coke and Pepsi, 756-80
  for Comshare, 704-5, 724-27
  for Deep South Civic Center, 594-95
  for Delta Airlines, 524
  for Gillette Co., 394-95, 406
  for Hershey Foods, 685
  for Island Shores, 568
  for K mart, 513-16
  for Mark-Tele, Inc., 381-83, 385
  for Mead Corp., 346
  for MeraBank, 860-67
  for Rockwood Manor, 537
  for TenderCare Disposable Diapers, 307-8
  for Thompson Respiration Products, Inc., 466-69
  for TSR Hobbies, 659
  for Tupperware, 462
  for Wyler Foods, 285
Competitive environment, 22-23
Competitive parity, 146
Consumer behavior
  and Adirondack Manor, 328-37
  cultural influences on, 65-68
  data sources for, 75
  and evaluation of alternatives, 62
  and felt need, 56-59
  information searches in, 59-62
  and K mart, 519, 520
  and perceived risk, 62-63
  and postpurchase feelings, 63-65
  and product class, 72
  and reference groups, 69-71
  and Rogers, Nagel, Langhart, 613-14
  and S. C. Johnson Agree line, 445
  situational influences on, 72-74
  social class and, 68-69
  and Thompson Respiration Products, Inc., 475-76
  and Tylenol, 576
  and Wyler Foods, 286-87
Consumer Bill of Rights, 242
Consumer Product Safety Commission, 23
Consumerism, 240-43
Cooperative environment, 22
Correlation analysis, for sales forecasting, 168
Cost-plus pricing, 196
Credit cards, 732-36
Cultural values, 65-68
Current ratio, 273
Customer expectations method of sales forecasting, 168

Deceptive pricing, 200
Deregulation, and MidAmerica BancSystem, Inc., 365-66
Distribution channels; *see also* Marketing intermediaries
  for Apple Computers, 491-92
  for Caterpillar Tractor, 665-66
  for Comshare, 730-31
  for consumer products, 179-80
  defined, 176
  for Hershey Foods, 691-92
  for industrial products, 180, 181
  international, 228-29
  for K mart, 504-6
  management of, 185-89
  in marketing plan, 899
  for Mary Kay Cosmetics, 828-29
  for Mead Corp., 344-46
  for S. C. Johnson, 445-47, 544-48
  selection of, 180-85
  for services, 214-15
  for TenderCare Disposable Diapers, 311
  for Thompson Respiration Products, Inc., 473-74, 476-77
  for TSR Hobbies, 657-58
Diversification
  at American Express Co., 740-42
  at Campbell Soup Co., 785-86
  defined, 129
  at Hershey Foods, 674
  strategies for, 17
Dogs (in market share), 31

Economic environment, 23-24
Effectiveness-efficiency standards, 19
Effectiveness standards, 18
Efficiency standards, 19
Eight-M formula, 143
Encoding, in advertising messages, 147
Environmental Protection Agency, 23
Environmental trends, 245
Ethics in marketing, 239-40, 241
Experience curves, 29-30
Family life cycle stages, 70
Federal Communications Commission, 23, 156
Federal Trade Commission, 23, 156
Federal Trade Commission Act, 200
Financial analysis
  break-even, 196, 197, 267-69
  for Campbell Soup Company, 782

Financial analysis—*Cont.*
for Comshare, 713–14
for Deep South Civic Center, 595–97
for K mart, 506–10
in marketing plan, 902–5
net present value, 269–72
ratio, 273–77
Food and Drug Administration, 23, 156
Forbes, 75
Fortune, 75, 896
Franchises, 186

General Electric portfolio model, 32–33
Going rate pricing, 200
Grain Division of Department of Agriculture, 156
Growth functions, for sales forecasting, 168
Growth vectors (product/market matrix), 16, 129, 130
Guide to Consumer Markets, A, 75
Horizontal market, 114

Import restrictions, 222
Industrial buying behavior
behavioral influences on, 81–85
and buyer motivations, 82, 84
and buying authority, 80–81
by buying situation, 79
versus consumer behavior, 80
and joint decision making, 79
organizational influences on, 79–81
process model, 77
product influences on, 76–79
Industrial purchases; *see also* Industrial buying behavior
buying process, 85–88
information sources for, 87
Industry attractiveness, 33
International marketing; *see also* World markets
advertising in, 229–30
by American Express Co., 748
by Apple Computer, 485, 495
by Babcock Swine, 631–38
by Campbell Soup Co., 804–5
by Caterpillar Tractor, 664–65
by Coca-Cola, 770–71
cultural problems in, 222, 224, 226
distribution channels for, 228–29
versus domestic operations, 223
by Hershey Foods, 689–91
internal management problems in, 222–24
political problems in, 222
pricing for, 229
product planning in, 225, 227
research, 224–27
strategies for, 230–32
Interstate Commerce Commission, 23
Inventory turnover ratio, 274

Journal of Advertising, 75
Journal of Advertising Research, 75
Journal of Applied Psychology, 75
Journal of Consumer Marketing, 75
Journal of Consumer Research, 75
Journal of Marketing, 75
Journal of Marketing Research, 75
Jury of executive opinion method of sales forecasting, 168
Justice Department, 156
Legal environment, 24
Library of Congress, 156
Licensing
at Hershey Foods, 675
at TSR Hobbies, 657
Liquidity ratios, 273–74

Market development
defined, 129
strategies for, 16–17
Market penetration
by American Express, 743–46
for Caterpillar Tractor, 667
defined, 129
for Island Shores, 570–71
by Mary Kay Cosmetics, 821–22
by MeraBank, 858
strategies for, 16
Market segmentation
a priori, 91–92
bases for, 92–97
for Campbell Soup Company, 95
and consumer needs, 91
defined, 89
for Gillette Co., 395, 397
for K mart, 512–13
for MeraBank, 880, 881, 882–83
post hoc, 92
product positioning, 97, 99–101
relevance of, 92
for Rockwood Manor, 536–37
for S. C. Johnson, 541–44
in soft drink industry, 773–74
strategy for, 101–2
Market share
for Apple Computer, 491–92
for Gillette Co., 389–90
for Maytag Co., 649
price strategies and, 199
for S. C. Johnson Agree line, 438, 440, 444–45
soft drink market, 762
for Timex Corp., 282
for Tylenol, 574–75
Marketing; *see also* International marketing
defined, 7
ethics, 239–40, 241
of services; *see* Service marketing
social responsibility of, 237–43
Marketing Communications, 75
Marketing concept
basic elements of, 6
versus customer orientation, 5
defined, 5
generic, 244–45
versus production orientation, 5
purpose of, 5, 7
versus selling orientation, 5
societal, 238–39
Marketing decision support systems, 26
defined, 38
versus marketing information systems, 39–40
need for, 38
Marketing Information Guide, 75
Marketing information systems, 39–40; *see also* Marketing decision support systems
Marketing intermediaries; *see also* Distribution channels
costs incurred by, 177
need for, 176–77
for services, 215–17
types of, 177–79
Marketing management
defined, 20–21
at Denver Art Museum, 578–82
and organizational mission, 21–22
at Rogers, Nagel, Langhart, 620–24
situation analysis in, 22–24
strategic planning and, 8–10
Marketing-manager system, 122–23
Marketing mix; *see also* Product(s)
for Comshare, 727–31
defined, 25
in marketing plan, 898–99
strategy design, 102–4
Marketing objectives, in marketing plan, 897–98
Marketing plan
for Caterpillar Tractor, 671–72
control of, 26
elements of, 24–26, 27
financial analysis in, 902–5
format for, 893–902
for Gillette Co., 407
implementation of, 26
for Island Shores, 568–70
purpose of, 893
references in, 905–6
relation to strategic plan, 26–28
for services, 217
Marketing research
at Gillette Co., 392–94, 396–97
for Island Shores, 571
by Mark-Tele, Inc., 367–68, 384
in marketing plan, 900–901
and marketing strategy, 43
by Mead Products, 350–53
for MeraBank, 868–70
methods of, 46
by MidAmerica BancSystem, Inc., 358–61
performance of, 49–50
plan for, 45, 47–49
problems in, 51–53
process of, 44–51
purpose of, 45
reports of, 50–51
role of, 42, 44
by S. C. Johnson, 437–40
for Texas Blueberry Growers Association, 293–300, 302
for Tylenol, 573–76
for Young Attitudes, 529
Marketing strategy; *see also* Strategic planning

Marketing strategy—*Cont.*
for Campbell Soup Co., 790-94
for Caterpillar Tractor, 661-62, 666-67, 669, 671-72
for Cub Foods, 463-64
for Gillette Co., 390-92
for K mart, 501-3
for Mark-Tele, Inc., 375-78
market segmentation and, 104
marketing research influencing, 43
for MeraBank, 878-79
for MidAmerica BancSystem, Inc., 362-65
at Rogers, Nagel, Langhart, 615-18
for S. C. Johnson Agree line, 459
for S. C. Johnson Innochem division, 548-52
for TenderCare Disposable Diapers, 305-6, 308-13
for Timex Corp., 281-83
for TSR Hobbies, 654-58
Marketing success, key principles for, 8
Markup pricing, 195
Maslow's hierarchy of needs, 56-59
Middlemen; *see* Marketing intermediaries
Mission statements, 10-13
for Apple Computers, 496
for Gillette Co., 388-89
for Hershey Foods, 685, 686

Nation's Business, 75
Net present value analysis, 269-72
New product development
by Apple Computer, 480-81
by Campbell Soup Co., 792-96
by Coca-Cola, 766-68, 777-78, 780
commercialization in, 134
in computer industry, 702-4
by Comshare, 722-23
for Deep South Civic Center, 584-85
failure in, 127-28, 135-37
at Hershey Foods, 681, 689
ideas for, 131, 132-33
by Mary Kay Cosmetics, 826-28
by MeraBank, 880, 884, 886
planning for, 131-34
policy development for, 128-31
research for, 136-37
test marketing of, 134
New-product manager system, 125
Nielsen indexes, 899, 900

Office of Consumer Affairs, 23
Order generators, 164
Order takers, 164
Organizations
definition of objectives for, 14-15
marketing strategies for, 15-17
mission statements for, 10-13
strategic planning for, 10-20
Outdoor advertising, 150

Packaging, 115
Patent Office, 156
Performance standards, 18-19
Personal selling; *see also* Sales *and* Salespersons
company responsibilities in, 165
by Comshare, 729-30
importance of, 158-60
by Mary Kay Cosmetics, 817-20
process of, 160-62
versus self-service, 158
training for, 163-65
of Tupperware, 461
Political environment, 24
Portfolio models, 17-20, 29-33
Postal Service, 156
Postpurchase feelings, 63-65
Price discrimination, 200-201
Price elasticity, 193-94
Price-fixing, 200
Pricing of products
at Caterpillar Tractor, 662
and competition, 198-200
at Comshare, 727-28
cost considerations in, 195-96
decision model, 201-2
for Delta Airlines, 523-25
demand influences on, 191-94
at Denver Art Museum, 581-82
and government regulations, 200-201
by Hershey Foods, 694, 696, 698-700
international, 229
at Island Shores, 567-68
in marketing plan, 900
objectives of, 194-95
product considerations in, 196-98
for Rockwood Manor, 537-39
for S. C. Johnson, 447-48, 552-55
for TenderCare Disposable Diapers, 310, 311
for Thompson Respiration Products, Inc., 474
for Young Attitudes, 527-29
Product(s); *see also* New product development
agricultural, 111
audits of, 121-22
consumer goods, 111-14
defined, 109-11
development strategies for, 17, 129
improvements in, 122
industrial goods, 111
life cycle of, 117-21, 198
in marketing plan, 899
older, 10-point vitality test for, 124
planning for, 227
pricing of, 191-203
raw materials, 111
Product (brand) manager system, 123
Product differentiation
for Apple Computer, 492-94
by branding, 116-17, 119
at Island Shores, 566-68
for Mead Products, 342-43
by packaging, 115
Product line(s)
for Caterpillar Tractor, 661-62
defined, 114-15
full versus limited, 116-17
for Gillette Co., 390, 391, 399-406
Product line(s)—*Cont.*
for Hershey Foods, 674-75, 680-81, 684-85
for Mary Kay Cosmetics, 828
for Maytag Co., 650-51
for Mead Corp., 342-44
for MeraBank, 855-60
for Outdoor Sporting Products, Inc., 412-13
for S. C. Johnson, 443, 548-50
for Thompson Respiration Products, Inc., 470-73
for TSR Hobbies, 655-57
Young Attitudes, 527
Product management, organizing for, 122-25
Product management concept, and S. C. Johnson, 440-43
Product/market matrix, 16, 129, 130
Product mix, 114
Product-planning committee, 124-25
Product positioning, 97, 99-101; *see also* Market segmentation
by Seven-Up Company, 339-40
for TSR Hobbies, 658-59
for Tupperware, 462
Profit Impact of Marketing Strategies study, 30
Profitability ratios, 274
Project on Corporate Responsibility, 243
Promotion, 138-40; *see also* Advertising *and* Sales promotion
at Apple Computer, 482-84, 492-94
at Caterpillar Tractor, 666
at Computing Systems Ltd., 421-24
at Comshare, 728-29
at Deep South Civic Center, 591
at General Foods, 409-11
at Hanover-Bates Chemical Corp., 429-32
at Hershey Foods, 693
for Island Shores, 571-72
in marketing plan, 899
at MeraBank, 886-88
methods of, advantages and disadvantages of, 139
for S. C. Johnson Agree line, 438, 445-47, 453-58
at TSR Hobbies, 655-56
Promotional pricing, 201

Quantitative techniques, for sales forecasting, 168
Quarterly Financial Report for Manufacturing Corporations, The, 277
Questions marks (in market share), 31
Quick ratio, 273-74

Rate-of-return pricing, 196
Ratio analysis, 273-77
Return on total assets, 274
Robinson-Patman Act, 200-201

Sales
budget, 170

Sales—*Cont.*
forecasting
in marketing plan, 902-5
methods of, 167-68
responsibility for, 167
increasing, 124
profit margin on, 274
quotas, 169
territories, 168-69
Sales force(s)
for Hanover-Bates Chemical Corp., 434-35
for Mary Kay Cosmetics, 806-7, 830, 836-40
for Outdoor Sporting Products, Inc., 414-15
rating of, 159
Sales force composite method of sales forecasting, 168
Sales Management, 75
Sales managers, 165-66, 171
for Computing Systems Ltd., 425-26
for Mary Kay Cosmetics, 834-36
Sales promotion, 153-55; *see also* Personal selling *and* Promotion
for Deep South Civic Center, 594
Sales support personnel, 164
Salespersons
compensation of, 171-75
evaluation of, 171
for Outdoor Sporting Products, Inc., 416-19
profile of, 163
responsibility of, 165
training of, 163-65
Saturation point, and Texas Blueberry Growers Association, 300-301
Securities and Exchange Commission, 156
Selling Areas Marketing Inc., 905
Service marketing
by American Express, 749
by Arthritis Foundation, 599-606
by Babcock Swine, 630-31
client relationships in, 211-12
Service marketing—*Cont.*
by Delta Airlines, 524-25
difficulties in, 212-14
distribution channels, 214-18
and fluctuating demand, 210
intangibility and, 208-10, 211
intermediaries for, 215-17
by Mead Corp., 343
by MeraBank, 880, 884, 886
by MidAmerica BancSystem, Inc., 363-64
and product development, 217-18
by Rogers, Nagel, Langhart, 609-15
Sherman Antitrust Act, 200
Simmons Media/Market Service, 899
Simulation models, for sales forecasting, 168
Situation analysis, 22-24, 251-56
in market plan, 895-96
Social class and consumer behavior, 68-69
Social environment, 24
Social marketing, 239
Social Responsibilities of Business Corporations, 243
Societal concept of marketing, 238-39
Standard Industrial Classification, 252
Standard Rate and Data, 899, 905
Starch Advertising Readership Service, 899
Stars (in market share), 31
Statistical Abstracts of the United States, 902
Strategic business units, 20, 29, 31-33
Strategic planning; *see also* Marketing strategy
by Campbell Soup Co., 789-90
by Caterpillar Tractor, 668-69
by Coca-Cola, 760-71
by Comshare, 708-13, 721-23
defined, 7-8
by Hershey Foods, 685-87
and marketing management, 8-10
by Mary Kay Cosmetics, 823, 825, 852
Strategic planning—*Cont.*
by MeraBank, 870-78
and organizational mission, 10-13
and organizational objectives, 14-15
portfolio plan in, 17-20
relation to marketing plan, 26-28
strategies for, 15-17
by TSR Hobbies, 658
Strategic Planning Institute, 30

Target markets
for Apple Computer, 482-83
for Deep South Civic Center, 591-93
for Island Shores, 568-72
for Mark-Tele, Inc., 383
in marketing plan, 898
for Mead Corp., 345
selection of, 25
for Wyler's Unsweetened Soft Drink Mixes, 288
Test marketing, 134
by Hershey Foods, 681
of Mead Products, 350-53
of Wyler's Unsweetened Soft Drink Mixes, 290-91
Time series analysis, for sales forecasting, 168
Total asset utilization, 274
Travel and entertainment cards, 733, 735-36
Travelers' checks, 736

VALs psychographic segmentation, 97, 98-99
Venture team, 125
Vertical market, 114
Wall Street Journal, 896
World markets; *see also* International marketing
for Caterpillar Tractor, 669-70
for Mary Kay Cosmetics, 811